# Modern Philosophy

## An Anthology of Primary Sources

### Third Edition

# Modern Philosophy

## An Anthology of Primary Sources

### Third Edition

Edited by
**Roger Ariew**
and
**Eric Watkins**

Hackett Publishing Company, Inc.
Indianapolis/Cambridge

*For David, Daniel, Christa, and Nicholas,*
*who we hope found this anthology of use.*

For further information, please address
    Hackett Publishing Company, Inc.
    P.O. Box 44937
    Indianapolis, Indiana 46244-0937
    www.hackettpublishing.com

Cover design by E.L. Wilson
Interior design by Dan Kirklin

Cataloging-in-Publication data can be accessed via the Library of Congress Online Catalog.

ISBN-13: 978-1-62466-806-7 (cloth)
ISBN-13: 978-1-62466-805-0 (pbk.)

# CONTENTS

## 4. Locke's *Essay* and Associated Texts                                               **335**

## 5. Berkeley's *Three Dialogues, On Motion,* and Associated Texts                      **475**

## 6. Hume's Treatise, *Enquiry, Dialogues,* and Associated Texts                        **555**

## 7. Kant's *Prolegomena, Critique of Pure Reason,* and Associated Texts                **703**

# GENERAL INTRODUCTION

When G. W. Leibniz traveled to Paris in 1672, he found an intellectual environment in great turmoil. Leibniz was trained in Aristotelian (or scholastic) philosophy, which had dominated European thought ever since the thirteenth century when the majority of the Aristotelian corpus was rediscovered and translated from Greek and Arabic into Latin and then made compatible with Christian doctrine (by Thomas Aquinas and others). Until his trip to Paris, Leibniz's properly philosophical works consisted primarily of a thesis on the scholastic problem of the principle of individuation and the publication of a new edition of an obscure 16th-century philosopher who had attempted to rehabilitate a more authentic Aristotelian philosophy from the "barbarism" of the scholastics. But a philosophical revolution was taking place in mid-17th-century Paris. New scientific and philosophical doctrines had emerged from Galileo Galilei, from René Descartes and his followers, from Francis Bacon, Blaise Pascal, Thomas Hobbes, and countless others. Scholastics had fought back fiercely against the new philosophy and science; they had succeeded in getting Galileo condemned by the Catholic Church in 1633 and in putting Descartes' works on the *Index of Prohibited Books* in 1663. Still, the substantial forms and primary matter of the scholastics were giving way to a new mechanistic world of geometrical bodies, corpuscles, or atoms in motion. With this world came novel mathematical tools and scientific methods for dealing with its newly conceived entities. Old problems that seemed to have been resolved within a scholastic framework were raised again with new urgency: what can one say about necessity, contingency, and freedom in a world of atoms governed by laws of motion? The structure of the universe, whether it is finite or infinite, as well as the concepts of space and time, were up for grabs. Other basic philosophical issues were also keenly debated, including the location of the soul, its immortality, God's purpose in the creation, and his relation to the universe. With such a great intellectual upheaval came the questioning of whether humans even have knowledge at all. Leibniz, of course, became a major contributor to this intellectual movement that defined the modern world. In Paris, he read and copied Descartes' manuscripts and sought out proponents of the new philosophy, such as Antoine Arnauld and Nicholas Malebranche; his own later work was often precipitated by the correspondence he maintained with them and others such as Pierre Bayle. He traveled to London and met members of the Royal Society (Henry Oldenberg and Robert Boyle, among others, though not Isaac Newton, with whom he later corresponded). On his way back to Lower Saxony, he visited Baruch Spinoza in the Netherlands. Of course Leibniz did not have the opportunity to interact with David Hume and Immanuel Kant; Hume was born just four years prior to Leibniz's death and Kant almost a decade after that.

Yet Leibniz would have been quite interested in both of these figures' acute, albeit radically divergent reflections on these philosophical developments. For Hume's empiricist approach led to a certain kind of skepticism, while Kant's criticism of pure reason did not obviate completely the possibility of substantive knowledge of the world.

Historians of philosophy often draw a broad picture of modern European philosophy, depicting two distinct camps: rationalists (Descartes, Spinoza, and Leibniz) who emphasize reason at the expense of the senses, and empiricists (John Locke, George Berkeley, and Hume) who emphasize the senses after rejecting innate ideas. This rudimentary picture is often filled out as follows. After calling into doubt seemingly all beliefs (especially those based on the senses), Descartes, the father of modern philosophy, attempts to ground all of our knowledge on innate ideas he discovers and rationally reflects on within himself, beginning with the idea he has of himself as a thinking thing (in the *cogito*). Accordingly, reason, by coming to a clear and distinct conception of its own ideas, attempts to establish knowledge about the world with the same kind of absolute certainty, precision, and necessity attainable in mathematics. While Spinoza and Leibniz revise and even reject some of Descartes' fundamental principles, they both accept Descartes' "rationalist" approach of rejecting sensory ideas as inadequate or confused in favor of innate ideas, which alone can be adequate or clear and distinct to reason. In this way, it is often claimed, Spinoza and Leibniz carry Descartes' rationalist philosophy to its ultimate, logical conclusion.

Locke, by contrast, breaks with the rationalists' approach by rejecting innate ideas and by claiming instead that the content of all of our mental states or ideas must stem from experience, whether it be from sensation or reflection—a claim that more or less defines empiricism in this context. Locke rejects innate ideas, not only because he cannot find any ideas that enjoy universal assent, but also because he thinks that philosophers often talk about ideas without understanding clearly what meaning they have—an error encouraged by accepting innate ideas, since believing that an idea is innate precludes one from determining its true origin and thus its precise meaning. Since Locke rejects innate ideas, he views the proper task of philosophy as one of analyzing the precise meaning of the ideas we get from sensation and reflection and determining what we can come to know about the world purely on the basis of these ideas.

Just as Spinoza and Leibniz follow Descartes' rationalist assumptions to their logical conclusions, so too, it is often claimed, Berkeley and especially Hume correct the inconsistencies in Locke's position, thus drawing out the proper consequences of Locke's empiricist approach. (Often Kant is presented as the culminating figure of modern philosophy with his attempt at synthesizing the rationalist and empiricist traditions, though Kant, too, was in turn successively "corrected" by German Idealists, such as Fichte, Schelling, and Hegel.)

While there is some truth underlying this snapshot of the history of modern philosophy, one can, we think, discern a much more interesting and significant picture of the importance of these philosophies by broadening one's view beyond the issue of whether one should accept or reject reason (or innate ideas) to include an account of other domains, such as science and religion.

Consider first the fact that Descartes accepts, whereas Locke rejects the claim that matter is infinitely divisible. Descartes' claim that matter is infinitely divisible is based (at least in part) on his view that matter is simply extended substance and that because we have an innate idea of extension, we can see clearly and distinctly that it implies infinite divisibility. In short, Descartes' position on the infinite divisibility of matter would seem to be based on his doctrine of innate ideas insofar as our idea of extension is an innate idea. Since Locke rejects innate ideas, it is clear that such a justification would, in his eyes, be mistaken. However, concerns about innate ideas can be only part of the story. For even if Locke must reject Descartes' *justification* of the claim that matter is infinitely divisible, he need not immediately reject the claim itself (even if he would have to search for a new justification for it). It is clear that Locke is a corpuscularian (at least in part) because Boyle and Newton, that is, two of the most preeminent scientists of his day, presuppose corpuscularian principles in their scientific theories and Locke believes that, at least in principle, philosophy and science ought to be able to tell a single coherent story about the world. The importance of the scientific context is not, however, limited to Locke's acceptance of corpuscularianism; a similar explanation of the importance of the scientific context of the day could be developed for Locke's distinction between "primary" and "secondary" qualities as well as for his distinction between nominal and real essences.

Locke is not alone in having interests that extend beyond narrow epistemological issues. Consider also Berkeley's and Hume's attitudes toward religion. One might think that the question of the meaning of the term *God* as well as the question of God's existence would be a straightforward matter for a strict empiricist. What empirical meaning can one ascribe to the idea of a perfect being endowed with infinite attributes (such as omnipotence, omniscience, and omnibenevolence)? And what empirical evidence does one have for thinking that such a being actually exists? Hume's account of our idea of God in §1 of *An Enquiry Concerning Human Understanding* develops an interesting answer to the former question, and Philo's forcefully argued position in Hume's *Dialogues Concerning Natural Religion* famously expresses one very provocative empiricist response to the latter question (in the negative). Berkeley, by contrast, believes that even if one cannot have an idea of God, one can form a notion of God, and there is no doubt in Berkeley's mind that one can prove God's existence. In light of Hume's powerful arguments, one might suspect that Berkeley, as an Anglican priest, simply could not admit the true consequence of his own empiricist position with respect to God's existence. (Here we would have an especially clear-cut case of Hume drawing out the logical conclusion of Locke's original empiricist assumptions.) However, it is crucial to note Hume's and Berkeley's different goals and thus different versions of empiricism. Hume is interested exclusively in the laws that govern the relations that exist between ideas in our mind and refuses to speculate on what outside the mind might cause the existence of our sensations. Berkeley, by contrast, is interested primarily in refuting materialists, atheists, and skeptics and, as a part of that project, is very interested in determining what the cause of our sensations could be. Matter, as something inert, cannot be their cause and we must therefore take recourse to a mind (or spirit), which, when supplemented with further argument, turns out to be God. Thus, from a different point of view, it might seem that Berkeley's empiricism improves upon Hume's by being able to answer a question that Hume cannot, rather than Hume correcting an inconsistency in Berkeley.

The point of these two brief examples is, we hope, clear. These philosophers are important figures in the history of modern philosophy for *numerous* reasons, reasons that cannot be captured exhaustively in any simple story about a single topic, such as reason versus the senses (or innate ideas versus sensations). Their texts are complex and rich, displaying divergent interests and goals. What makes them great philosophers and their

texts significant philosophical works is the novel and sophisticated way in which they articulate their different interests and attempt to render coherent what would appear to be conflicting demands. Where we today share in their goals and interests, it is not impossible that they may help us to see more clearly truths that have been obscured over the centuries, and where we do not, it can be instructive to see how we are different and to consider how we came to be so.

It is our hope that this anthology would be able to provide a glimpse of the complex and radical movement of thought from Descartes and his contemporaries to Leibniz and his contemporaries (including Spinoza, Locke, and Berkeley), and ultimately to its culmination in Hume and Kant. For that process, we have tried, as much as possible, to provide whole texts—i.e., Descartes' *Meditations*, Leibniz's *Discourse* and *Monadology*, Berkeley's *Dialogues*, Hume's *Enquiry*, and Kant's *Prolegomena*; unfortunately, Spinoza's *Ethics* and Locke's *Essay* have had to be excerpted. We have attempted to surround these works with additional ones that would assist in understanding the primary sources—for example, selections from Hobbes' *Leviathan* and Malebranche's *Search after Truth*, or portions of Descartes' *Discourse* and the *Objections* and *Replies* to his *Meditations*. Along the way, we have tried to provide alternatives to the "main" texts—for instance, Berkeley's *Principles* and Kant's *Critique*. Of course, we have had to make many difficult choices; we hope we have supplied most, if not all the desired selections, and have not cast off too many of our readers' favorites. We believe we have provided enough materials for two semesters' worth of modern philosophy, so that we think there should be sufficient contents with which to construct a variety of single-semester courses.

Another goal of ours was to achieve some consistency among texts—especially with Kant, where we were faced with different translations of the same technical vocabulary. With Descartes, Spinoza, and Leibniz this was accomplished, we hope, by the use of the same translator for the various works of the given philosopher (Donald Cress for Descartes, Samuel Shirley for Spinoza, and Roger Ariew and Daniel Garber for Leibniz). We have also attempted to modernize and Americanize those primary texts originally written in English. We do not believe that students, who are typically given contemporary translations of foreign-language texts, must wade through 17th- or 18th-century English works just because they were originally written in English in the 17th or 18th century. We have replaced archaic words and expressions with their modern equivalents: *surface* for *superficies*, *up to now* or *previously* for *hitherto*, *admit* for *own*, *gladly* or *inclined to* for *fain*, *endow* for *endue*, etc.—not to mention what we have done to *whereunto*, *therein*, *hark*, *hath* and *doth*. Perhaps the greatest change has been our endeavor to modernize the punctuation; we have adopted an open style of punctuation. A modernization we did not undertake is the discarding of italics, that is, the use of upper-case words for emphasis, mention, etc. This early modern practice does not seem to be a significant bar to comprehension for twenty-first-century students. We also did not attempt to render historical texts into gender-neutral language. Of course, some will inevitably feel that our modernization has been too extensive, while others might have wished that we had made even greater emendations. We hope to have avoided both extremes, bearing in mind the needs of the readers for whom this anthology is intended.

We are very grateful to the authors and translators named in the footnotes at the start of each selection for permission to reproduce their materials.[1] We would also like to thank Karl Ameriks, Bill Davis, Daniel Garber, Marjorie Grene, Patricia Kitcher, Nelson Lande, Joseph Pitt, Tad Schmaltz, and Kenneth Winkler for their many helpful suggestions concerning what selections to include. Finally, we wish to thank Deborah Wilkes at Hackett Publishing Company, who suggested this project and saw it through to its completion three times over.

## Note to the Second and Third Editions

We have made numerous corrections to our anthology during the last decade. We still hope to have supplied most, if not all, our readers' desired selections, and not to have cast off too many of their favorites. For the second edition, we added a few more sources, which we think our readers will find useful. Here are the principal additions:

> Montaigne, *Apology for Raymond Sebond*, "The Senses Are Inadequate"

> Newton, *Principia*, "General Scholium," and *Optics*, "Query 31"

> Hume, *Dialogues Concerning Natural Religion*, Parts 1–5 and 9–12

> Reid, *Inquiry into the Human Mind*, Conclusion, and *Essays on the Intellectual Powers of Man*, "Of Judgment," Chapter 2, Of Common Sense

For the third edition, we have added yet more sources we think our readers will find useful, namely, selections from the corpus of traditionally under-represented philosophers. The addition and recognition of the contributions of women and minority thinkers to the canon of thinkers of the modern period is, of course, long overdue:

> Elisabeth and Descartes, *Correspondence*

> Cavendish, *Philosophical Letters*, Letters 30–42

> Conway, *The Principles of the Most Ancient and Modern Philosophy*, Chapters 8–9

> Amo, *On the Apathy of the Human Mind*, Chapter 2

> Lady Masham and Leibniz, *Correspondence*

> Lady Shepherd, *Essays on the Perception of an External Universe* and *An Essay Upon the Relation of Cause and Effect*

> Du Châtelet, *Foundations of Physics*

We are grateful to all the readers who sent in suggestions and corrections and hope that they will continue to do so.

---

1. For the primary texts from Descartes through Berkeley, with the exception of Malebranche, footnotes are always the editors'. With Hume and Kant, the age when the use of footnotes becomes common, all footnotes that the editors have inserted are in brackets.

# 1. DESCARTES' *MEDITATIONS* AND ASSOCIATED TEXTS

René Descartes was born in 1596 at La Haye, in Touraine, France. He became one of the central intellectual figures of the 17th century, making major contributions to metaphysics, natural philosophy, and mathematics. Descartes was educated at the Jesuit College of La Flèche (in Anjou) from about 1607 to about 1615; he received a Master's degree in law from Poitier in 1616. The next year he went to the Netherlands and joined the army of Prince Maurice of Nassau; at Breda he made the acquaintance of Isaac Beeckman, who introduced him to a "physico-mathematical" way of doing natural philosophy. When traveling in Germany he had a series of dreams (on 10 November 1619) about the unity of science; his first major philosophical project, the *Rules for the Direction of the Mind*, which he composed (ca. 1618–28) but did not finish, was devoted to that theme. Instead Descartes turned his thoughts to physical and astronomical topics and worked on *The World or Treatise on Light*; unfortunately he suppressed the publication of this treatise when he learned of Galileo's condemnation in 1633. His first printed work was the *Discourse on Method* (1637) to which he appended the less controversial scientific essays, *Dioptrics*, *Meteors*, and *Geometry*. A few years later he expanded Part Four of the *Discourse*

into *Meditations on First Philosophy*, which he published with sets of objections and replies (1641). In 1644, Descartes further revised his philosophy into textbook form and disseminated it with his physics as *Principles of Philosophy*. Although he spent most of his adult life in seclusion in the Netherlands, in 1649 he went to Sweden at the invitation of Queen Christina but did not last the winter, dying in Stockholm in 1650.[1]

The *Meditations* is one of the great works of philosophy, a seminal treatise for subsequent philosophers. In its compact form it raises most of the problems that they will need to address skepticism,

---

1. Descartes' philosophical works, most of his mathematical and scientific treatises, and much of his correspondence are available in English translation. References to Descartes' works are to the standard edition by Charles Adam and Paul Tannery, *Oeuvres de Descartes* (2d. ed., Paris: Vrin, 1964–74); references to this edition are abbreviated as AT volume, page. For more on Descartes' philosophy, see Margaret Wilson, *Descartes* (London: Routledge and Kegan Paul, 1978); Edwin M. Curley, *Descartes against the Skeptics* (Cambridge, Mass.: Harvard University Press, 1978); Martial Gueroult, *Descartes's Philosophy Interpreted According to the Order of Reasons*, trans. R. Ariew (Minneapolis: University of Minnesota Press, 1984–85), 2 vols.; Marjorie Grene, *Descartes* (Indianapolis: Hackett Publishing Company, 1998); John Cottingham, ed., *The*

1

the existence and nature of the self, the existence of God, the possibility of error, the nature of truth—including the truth of mathematics—the essence and existence of bodies, and so forth. The great Cartesian commentator Martial Gueroult described the *Meditations* as a diptych, a work of art in two panels. He saw the first three Meditations as the first panel, ruled by the darkness of the principle of universal deception, with a battle being fought against it by the truth of the existence of the self—a mere point of light—a narrow but piercing exception to the principle of doubt, culminating in the defeat of the principle and the victory of the exception. The second panel is then ruled by the blinding light of God's absolute veracity—that is, the principle of universal truth—and fought against by the existence of error, a narrow point of darkness and seeming exception to that principle, puncturing the light of universal veracity in the same way that the existence of the self punctured the darkness of universal deception. However, here the battle culminates with the victory of the principle, the triumph of light over darkness. Gueroult saw the Cartesian movement as unified in that its perspectives are complementary from beginning to end: to the hypothesis of the evil genius, which plays a role of segregation, elimination, and purification in the first three Meditations, corresponds the dogma of divine veracity, which is a heuristic principle, an organ of reintegration, and a rule of discipline in the last three Meditations. Thus, Gueroult thought of the *Meditations* as a single block of certainty, in which everything is so arranged that nothing can be taken away without the whole thing dissolving.

But beyond the tight composition of the *Meditations* and its closely woven fabric, one might ask about the purpose of the work, what it was intended to do. Here one can point to the integration of the

---

*Cambridge Companion to Descartes* (New York: Cambridge University Press, 1992). For the relation between Descartes' philosophy and his physics, see Daniel Garber, *Descartes's Metaphysical Physics* (Chicago: University of Chicago Press, 1992). To situate Descartes' philosophy amongst that of his contemporaries, see Roger Ariew, John Cottingham, and Tom Sorell, eds. and trans., *Cambridge Texts in Context: Descartes's Meditations* (Cambridge: Cambridge University Press, 1998).

argument of the *Meditations* into a larger framework as the foundation of the new sciences. As Descartes said to his close correspondent, Marin Mersenne, "I may tell you, between ourselves, that these six Meditations contain all the foundations of my physics. But please do not tell people, for that might make it harder for supporters of Aristotle to approve of them. I hope that readers will gradually get used to my principles, and recognize their truth, before they notice that they destroy the principles of Aristotle" (18 January 1641). The *Meditations* attempts a complete intellectual revolution: the replacement of Aristotelian philosophy with a new philosophy in order to replace Aristotelian science with a new science. For a 17th-century Aristotelian, a body is matter informed by substantial and accidental forms, and change is explained by the gain or loss of such forms: in mutation by the acquisition of a substantial form, and in what Aristotelians would call true motion (that is, augmentation and diminution, alteration, or local motion) by the successive acquisition of places or of qualitative or quantitative forms. The mechanist program consisted in doing away with qualitative forms and reducing all changes to something mathematically quantifiable: matter in motion. As Descartes said in *The World*, not only the four qualities called heat, cold, moistness, and dryness, "but also all the others (and even all the forms of inanimate bodies) can be explained without the need of supposing for that purpose anything in their matter other than the motion, size, shape, and arrangement of its parts" (*The World*, Chapter 5). Accordingly, Descartes does not need substantial forms and does not explain mutation as change of form, whether substantial or accidental. He finds no forms other than the ones he has described quantitatively. For Descartes, the only motion is local motion; hence he states, "The philosophers also suppose several motions that they think can be accomplished without any body changing place. . . . As for me, I know of none except the one which is easiest to conceive . . . , the motion by which bodies pass from one place to another" (*The World*, Chapter 7).

One can glimpse the mechanist project in the *Discourse on Method*, in which an earlier version of the *Meditations* is embedded together with a method of philosophizing and a few scientific treatises as samples of the method. Thus the context of the *Meditations* is the same as Francis Bacon's and Galileo Galilei's, except that Descartes does not champion induction, and, although he advances the corpuscularian or mechanical philosophy to the extent that he reduces physical objects to matter in motion, he makes it clear that he does not accept the reality of atoms as ultimate indivisible constituents of matter.

The *Meditations* solicited many objections, from those of Thomas Hobbes, Antoine Arnauld, and Pierre Gassendi, published with the work, to subsequent ones from G. W. Leibniz and Blaise Pascal to Baruch Spinoza, John Locke, and the rest. Indeed, it would not be an exaggeration to state that all of modern philosophy constitutes reactions to and criticisms of Descartes' *Meditations*.

# Michel de Montaigne, *Apology for Raymond Sebond* (1580–88)[1]

*Michel de Montaigne (1533–92) was a philosopher, essayist, and counselor to the Parlement, and ultimately Mayor, of Bordeaux. In 1569 he published a translation of Raymond Sebond's Natural Theology, which he had undertaken at the request of Pierre Eyquem de Montaigne, "the best father who ever was." He published the* Apology for Raymond Sebond *with the first two books of his Essays in 1580. The Apology puts forward in two major moves the thesis that the only proper attitude for a Christian is squarely based on faith, not reason. First, if it is objected to Sebond that he should not be presenting arguments in support of Christianity, it is conceded that these must always be based on the prior acceptance of revelation; if revelation comes first, reason may have a secondary, merely ancillary place. As it is, Montaigne remarks, our acceptance of religion is merely conventional; we need to turn back to living faith as the true source of our beliefs. Second, if objections are raised to Sebond's arguments themselves, this objection again supports the priority of faith, since nothing our reason produces is of much use in any case. Montaigne proceeds to undermine any claims people may make to any special knowledge, drawing in part from the tropes of Sextus Empiricus, whom he had recently been reading. Ultimately, a thoroughgoing critique of the "knowledge" gained through our senses undermines any claims we might have to any knowledge whatsoever. All our seeming knowledge arises from our five senses. But, first, how do we know there are not other senses we are lacking? Further, the senses we do have constantly deceive us. There are illusions of sense, false opinions induced by passion, dreams very like waking appearances and vice versa. Our senses, again, differ from those of animals; maybe they have access to reality that we lack. Besides, each person's sensations differ from his own in other circumstances, as well as from those of other individuals. Ultimately we face the problem of the criterion: if we try to establish some standard of judgment, that standard in turn demands another standard, and so on ad infinitum. Thus we are thrown back to sense, which guarantees nothing about its apparent objects. Only through the grace of God, in humility and obedience, can we escape our unhappy situation.[2]*

1. Translated from the French by R. Ariew and M. Grene in Michel de Montaigne, *Apology for Raymond Sebond* (Indianapolis: Hackett, 2003).

2. There are three main strata to the text of the *Essays*, and thus to the *Apology* (*Essays* II. 12). These are usually referred to as A, B, and C: the text as published before 1588, that is, from the editions of 1580 and 1582; materials Montaigne added in the edition of 1588 (indicated by < >); and those he added after

## [7. The Senses Are Inadequate]

This discussion has brought me to the consideration of the senses, in which we find the greatest foundation and proof of our ignorance. Whatever is known is doubtless known by the faculty of the knower. For since judgment comes from the activity of the person judging, it is logical that he performs this act by his own powers and his own will, not through the constraint of another, as would be the case if we knew things by the power of their essence and according to its law. But all knowledge is conveyed to us by the senses: they are our masters:

> <for by this way the paved path of belief
> Leads straightest into the heart of man and the
> temples of his mind.>[3]

Knowledge begins through them and is resolved into them. After all, we would know no more than a stone if we did not know that there is sound, smell, light, taste, measure, weight, softness, hardness, sharpness, color, smoothness, size, and depth. Here is the platform and principle of the whole structure of our knowledge. <<And, according to some, knowledge is nothing else but sensation.>> He who could push me into contradicting the senses would have me by the throat; he could not push me further back. The senses are the beginning and the end of human knowledge:

> You will find that the idea of truth is derived first
> from the senses
> And that the senses cannot be challenged . . .
> What should be thought more certain than
> sense?[4]

Let them be credited with as little as possible, they will always have to be granted this: that all our instruction is routed by their means and mediation. Cicero says that Chrysippus, when he wanted to attack the power and virtue of the senses, represented to himself so many arguments to the contrary and such vehement oppositions, that he could not satisfy himself with them. On this Carneades, who supported the opposite side, boasted that he could use the very arms and words of Chrysippus to combat him, and in this connection wrote against him: "O wretched one, your power has destroyed you!" There can be nothing more absurd in our view than to maintain that fire does not heat, that light does not illuminate, that there is no weight or solidity in iron—all of which are things conveyed to us by the senses. Nor is there belief or knowledge in man that can be compared in certainty with this.

The first consideration I have on the subject of the senses is that I doubt that man is provided with all the natural senses. I see a number of animals that live a complete and perfect life, some without sight, others without hearing. Who knows if one, two, three, or more other senses are lacking in us also? For if some sense is lacking, our reasoning cannot discover the defect. It is the privilege of the senses to be the extreme limit of our awareness; there is nothing beyond them that can help us discover them, no more than one sense can discover another,

> <Or will the ears be able to reprove the eyes,
> Or touch, the ears? Or will the taste in the
> mouth
> Refute this touch; will the nostrils disprove it
> Or the eyes prove it false?>[5]

They all establish the extreme limit of our abilities,

> For each sense has its power divided,
> Each its own force.[6]

1588 (indicated by << >>), as represented in the posthumous edition of 1595. For more on Montaigne, see Donald Frame, *Montaigne: A Biography* (New York: Harcourt, 1965); M. A. Screech, *Montaigne and Melancholy* (London: Duckworth, 1983); Richard H. Popkin, *The History of Scepticism from Savonarola to Bayle* (Oxford: Oxford University Press, 2003); and Ann Hartle, *Michel de Montaigne: Accidental Philosopher* (Cambridge: Cambridge University Press, 2003).
3. Lucretius, *De rerum natura (On the Nature of Things)*, V, 103.
4. Lucretius, *De rerum natura*, IV, 478, 482.
5. Lucretius, *De rerum natura*, IV, 487–89.
6. Lucretius, *De rerum natura*, IV, 490–91.

It is impossible to make a man blind by nature understand that he does not see, impossible to make him
want sight and regret his lack.

For this reason we should not take any confidence
from the fact that our soul is contented and satisfied
with what we have, given that it has no way of knowing its illness and its imperfection in this, if there is
one. It is impossible to say anything to that blind man
by reasoning, argument, or analogy that accommodates in his imagination any apprehension of light,
color, and vision. There is nothing further that can
make the sense evident. As to those who are born
blind, whom we find wanting to see, it is not that
they understand what they are asking for. They have
heard from us that there is something they should
say, that there is something for them to desire that we
have, <<something they can easily name, as well as
its effects and consequences;>> but still they do not
know what that is, nor do they grasp it from either
near or far.

I saw a gentleman of good family, born blind, or
at least blind from an age such that he did not know
what vision is; he understands so little what he lacks,
that he uses and employs words proper to vision as
we do, and applies them in a way that is entirely his
own and idiosyncratic. He was presented with a child
to whom he was godfather. Taking it in his arms he
said: "Oh, lord! What a lovely child! How beautiful
it looks! What a pretty face it has!" He will say like
one of us: "This room has a fine view; the weather is
good; there is bright sunshine." There is more: since
hunting, tennis, and shooting are our sports, and he
has heard this said, he takes a liking to them, and
busies himself with them, and believes he has the
same part in them that we do; he is annoyed and
pleased by them, and yet he knows about them only
through the ears. Someone calls out to him, "There's
a hare!" when he is on some plain where he can use
his spurs; and again someone says to him "There's a
hare caught," and there he is, as proud of his prize
as he has heard others say they are. He takes a tennis ball in his left hand and hits it with his racket;
he shoots with his musket at random, and is satisfied
when his people tell him he is too high or at the side.

How do we know if the human race makes a similar stupid mistake about some sense, and most of the
appearance of things is hidden from us through this
defect? How do we know if the difficulties we find
in numerous works of nature come from this? And if
numerous achievements of animals that exceed our
capacity are produced by the power of some sense
that we lack? And if by this means some of them have
a life more full and complete than ours? We grasp
the apple as it were with all our senses; we find in
it redness, smoothness, odor and sweetness; beyond
that, it may have other virtues, like drying up or
shrinking, for which we have no sense to inform us.
As to the properties we call occult in a number of
things, like the magnet's ability to attract iron, is it
not likely that there are sensitive capacities in nature
fit for judging and perceiving them, and that the lack
of such capacities produces our ignorance of the true
essence of such things? It is perhaps some particular
sense that lets cocks know the hour of morning and
of midnight, and moves them to crow, <<that teaches
chickens, before any practice or experience, to fear a
sparrow hawk and not a goose or a peacock, which
are large birds; that cautions hens against the hostile
attitude a cat has to them and tells them not to fear
a dog: to arm them against the meowing, somehow
flattering, voice, but not against the barking, harsh,
and quarrelsome voice; that teaches wasps, ants,
and rats always to choose the best cheese and the
best pear before they have tasted it,>> and which
has led the deer, <<the elephant, the snake>> to
the recognition of a certain herb able to cure them.
There is no sense that does not have a broad dominion, and that does not produce by its means infinite
items of knowledge. If we lacked the understanding
of sounds, of harmony, and of the voice, that would
bring unimaginable confusion to all the rest of our
knowledge. For, besides what is attached to the
proper activity of each sense, how many arguments,
inferences, and conclusions do we make to other
things through the comparison of one sense with another! Let an intelligent man imagine human nature
originally produced without sight, and consider how
much ignorance and trouble such a defect would
bring him, how much darkness and blindness in our

soul. From this we will see how much the privation of another such sense would bear on the knowledge of the truth, let alone of two or three, if there is such knowledge in us. We have fashioned a truth through the consultation and concurrence of our five senses; but perhaps it would need the accord of eight or ten senses and their contribution to apprehend the truth certainly and in its essence.

The sects that oppose man's knowledge do so chiefly through the uncertainty and weakness of our senses; for, since our knowledge comes to us through and by means of them, if they fail in the report they give us, if they corrupt and alter what they bring us from outside, if the light that flows into the soul is obscured in its passage, we have nothing else to hold on to. From this extreme difficulty arise all those ideas: that every subject has in itself everything we find in it; that it has nothing of what we think we find in it; and that the sun is no larger than it looks to us, as the Epicureans contend.

> <Whatever it is, is of no greater shape
> Than it seems to be, as we see it with our eyes;>[7]

that the appearances that present a body as large to a person near to it and smaller to one who is farther away are both true,

> <Nor do we conclude from this that the eyes are deceptive,
> Or charge to them the errors of the mind,>[8]

and, resolutely, that there is no deceit in the senses; that we must lie at their mercy, and seek elsewhere for reasons to excuse the diversity and contradiction we find in them—going so far as to invent any other lie and fancy (they go that far) rather than to accuse the senses. <<Timagoras swore that by pressing or turning his eye he had never seen the light of the candle doubled, and that this appearance came from the

vice of opinion, not from the instrument.>> Of all absurdities the most absurd, <<for the Epicureans,>> is to disavow the force and efficacy of the senses:

> Whatever has been seen at some time is true.
> And if reason cannot distinguish the cause
> Why those things that, seen near at hand, were square
> Are seen round at a distance, still it is better
> Through lack of argument to err in accounting
> For the causes of either shape
> Rather than to allow things clearly seen to elude your grasp,
> Attack the grounds of belief, and tear up the foundations
> On which life and existence rest.
> For not only would all reasoning collapse,
> But so, straight away, would life itself,
> Unless we choose to trust the senses,
> And avoid precipitous places
> And other things of the kind that are to be shunned.[9]

<<This desperate advice, so unphilosophical, represents nothing if not that human knowledge can maintain itself only by unreasonable, foolish, mad reasoning; but it is still better for man to put a higher value on himself by using any other remedy, however fantastic it may be, than to confess his ineluctable stupidity—a truth so disadvantageous to him! He cannot avoid the fact that the senses are the sovereign masters of his knowledge; but they are uncertain and falsifiable in all circumstances. It is there that we have to fight it out to the last, and if we lack the appropriate powers, as we do, to use at this juncture obstinacy, temerity, and impudence.>>

<In case what the Epicureans say is true, that we have no knowledge if the appearances of the senses are false, and what the Stoics say—that it is also true that the appearances of the senses are so false that they can produce no knowledge—we shall conclude,

---

7. Lucretius, *De rerum natura*, V, 577.
8. Lucretius, *De rerum natura*, IV, 380, 387.

9. Lucretius, *De rerum natura*, IV, 500–511.

at the expense of these two great dogmatic sects, that there is no knowledge.>

As to the error and uncertainty of the operation of the senses, everyone can furnish as many examples as he likes, so commonplace are the faults and deceptions they impose on us. In the echo of a valley, the sound of a trumpet coming from behind us seems to come from in front:

> *<Mountains seen far off in the waters*
> *Seem to be united in a single mass . . .*
> *The hills and plains seem to be moving toward*
>     *the stern,*
> *When it is our vessel that is driving along . . .*
> *If our horse stops in midstream,*
> *We think it is carried by a counter-current.>[10]*

If you take a musket ball under the forefinger, with the middle finger lapped around it, you have to push yourself very hard indeed, to admit that there is only one, so strongly do the senses represent them to us as two. For it is frequently seen that our senses are masters of our reasoning, and compel it to receive impressions that it knows and judges to be false. I set aside the sense of touch, which has its operations so close by, so lively and substantial, and which, through the effect of the pain that it brings to the body, so often overturns all those fine Stoic resolutions, and compels to shout at his belly the person who has with all resolution established in his soul the dogma that colic, like every other disease and pain, is an indifferent matter, having no power to lessen in any way the sovereign happiness and felicity in which the sage is housed through his virtue. There is no heart so soft that the sound of our drums and trumpets does not warm it; nor so hard that the sweetness of music does not arouse and tickle it; and no soul so harsh that it does not find itself touched with some reverence in considering that somber vastness of our churches, the diversity of ornaments and order of our ceremonies, and hear the devout sound of our organs, and the solemn and religious harmony of our voices. Even those who

enter with distrust feel some shiver in their heart and some dread that makes them question their opinion.

<As for me, I do not believe myself strong enough to listen sedately to verses of Horace or Catullus sung in a competent voice by a fair young mouth.>

<<And Zeno was right to say that the voice was the flower of beauty. Someone once wanted to make me believe that a man known to all Frenchmen had impressed me when reciting some verses he had composed, which were not the same on paper as in the air, and that my eyes were making a judgment contrary to my ears, so great a power has pronunciation to give value and style to works that are left to its sway. In this connection Philoxenus was not much to blame when, hearing someone give a bad tone to some composition of his, he started to kick and break some earthenware belonging to that person, saying, "I am breaking what is yours, as you are corrupting what is mine.">>

For what purpose did those very people who had committed themselves to dying with a certain resolution turn away their face so as not to see the blow they had asked to be given? And why cannot those who for their own health desire and order that they be cut and cauterized endure the sight of the preparations, tools, and operations of the surgeon—given that the sight has no share in the pain? Are not these good examples to verify the authority that the senses have for our reasoning? It is no use knowing that these tresses are borrowed from a page or a lackey, that this rouge came from Spain, and this whitening and polish from the ocean, it still happens that vision forces us to find the subject more loveable and more agreeable, against all reason. For in this there is nothing of its own.

> *We are won over by clothes; our judgments are*
>     *deceived*
> *By gold and jewels; the girl's least part is her own.*
> *Often you seek what you love among so many:*
> *Rich love deceives those eyes with its shield.[11]*

---

10. Lucretius, *De rerum natura*, IV, 397–98, 389–90, 420–21.

11. Ovid, *The Cure of Love*, I, 343–46.

How much the poets grant to the power of the senses, when they make Narcissus lost in the love of his shadow:

> *In all that is admired he himself is admirable;*
> *Imprudently he desires himself; and he who*
> *    praises is himself praised,*
> *And while seeking is sought; and at the same*
> *    time he both kindles and burns,*[12]

and Pygmalion's understanding so troubled by the impression of the sight of his ivory statue, which he loves and treats as if it were alive:

> *He gives kisses, and believes they are returned;*
> *He follows and holds and believes the flesh*
> *Gives way to his touching fingers*
> *And fears a bruise may come to the pressed*
> *    joints.*[13]

Put a philosopher in a cage of small bars of thin iron suspended at the top of the towers of Notre Dame de Paris, he will see for obvious reasons that it is impossible for him to fall, and yet (unless he is used to the roofer's trade) he will not be able to keep the vision of that height from frightening and astonishing him. For we have enough trouble reassuring ourselves in the galleries of our steeples if they are made with open work, even though they are built of stone. There are some who cannot even bear the thought of it. Set a plank between those two towers, of a size such as is needed for us to walk on it: there is no philosophical wisdom of such firmness as to give us the courage to walk on it as we would do if it was on the ground. I have often found in our mountains here—although I am one of those who are only moderately afraid of such things—that I could not bear the sight of that infinite depth without horror and trembling of legs and thighs, even though I was more than my length from the edge,

and could not have fallen unless I had intended to expose myself to danger. I also noticed there that, whatever the height, if there was some tree in this incline or some rock jutting out to support our view a little and divide it, this alleviates our fear and gives us assurance, as if there were something from which we could get help in falling; but we cannot face sharp and undivided precipices without turning our head away: <<"*so that we cannot look down without dizziness of both eyes and mind*,">>[14] which is an obvious deception of our sight. That fine philosopher put out his eyes to free his soul from the distractions he received from them, so that he could philosophize with greater freedom.

But on this account he would have to have his ears stopped up as well, <which Theophrastus says are the most dangerous instrument we have for receiving violent impressions to trouble and change us,> and in the end deprive himself of all the other senses, that is, of his being and his life. For they all have that power to command our reasoning and our soul. <<"*For often in some way minds are moved by the solemnity of voices and songs; often also by concern and fear*.">>[15] Physicians hold that certain dispositions are agitated to the point of fury by some sounds and instruments. I have seen people who could not bear to hear a bone gnawed under their table without losing patience; and there is hardly a man who is not disturbed by that sharp and piercing noise that files make grating on iron. In the same way some people are moved to anger and hatred at hearing someone chewing near them, or hearing someone speak who has his throat or nose blocked. Of what use was the flautist who coached Gracchus, softening, hardening, and shaping his master's voice when he was haranguing at Rome, if the movement and quality of the sound did not have the power to affect and alter the judgment of the hearers? Seriously, it's well to make such a fuss about the firmness of this fine faculty, which submits to being handled and changed by the shifts and alterations of so slight a breeze!

The same trick that the senses play on our understanding they in their turn have played on them. Our

---

12. Ovid, *Metamorphoses*, III, 424–26.
13. Ovid, *Metamorphoses*, X, 256–58.

14. Livy, *Histories*, XLVII, vi.
15. Cicero, *De divinatione*, I, xxxvii.

soul sometimes takes its own revenge: <<they lie and deceive one another as much as you like.>> What we see and hear when agitated by anger we do not see as it is:

> There appear a twin sun and two cities of Thebes.[16]

The object we love seems to us more beautiful than it is:

> <And so we see those in many ways deformed and ugly
> Dearly loved, even prospering in high favor>[17]

and uglier the one we dislike. To a man who is bored and afflicted, the light of day seems overcast and cloudy. Our senses are not only altered, but often stupefied by the passions of the soul. How many things do we see that we take no notice of if our mind is otherwise occupied?

> Even in things plain to see you can notice,
> If you are not paying attention, it is as if things
> Were cut off from you all the time, and very far away.[18]

It seems the soul retreats into itself and smiles at the powers of the senses. And so both the inside and the outside of man are full of weakness and falsehood.

<Those who have likened our life to a dream were right, perhaps more so than they thought. When we are dreaming, our soul lives, acts, exercises all its faculties, no more nor less than when it is awake, though more softly and obscurely, still not with so certain a difference as between night and bright daylight, but like night and shade: there it is asleep, here

it slumbers, more or less. There is always darkness and Cimmerian darkness.>

<<We are awake while asleep and sleeping while awake. I do not see so clearly in sleep; but as to the waking state, I never find it wholly pure and without clouds. Even sleep when it is deep sometimes puts dreams to sleep. But our waking state is never so wide awake that it purges and dissipates altogether the reveries that are waking dreams and even worse than dreams.

Since our reason and our soul receive the fancies and opinions that arise in them while we are sleeping, and authorize the actions of our dreams with the same approval they give to those of the day, why do we not wonder whether our thought, our action, is not another state of dreaming and our waking some kind of sleep?>>

If the senses are our first judges, it is not only our own senses that must be called to counsel, for in regard to this faculty animals have as much of a claim as we do, or even more. It is certain that some have more acute hearing than man, others sight, others feeling, others touch and taste. Democritus said that gods and beasts have sensitive faculties much more perfect than man. Our saliva cleans and dries our wounds; it kills the snake:

> And in these things there is a difference and disagreement
> So great that what is food to one is to the other biting poison.
> Often indeed a snake, touched by human saliva,
> Dies, and puts an end to itself by gnawing its own body.[19]

What quality do we assign to the saliva? According to us, or according to the snake? By which of the two senses shall we verify the true essence of it that we are seeking? Pliny says that in the Indies there are certain sea-hares that are poison to us and we to them, so that we kill them simply by our touch: which is truly poison, the man or the fish? Which shall we believe, the fish of the man or the man of the fish? <One quality

---

16. Virgil, *Aeneid*, IV, 470.
17. Lucretius, *De rerum natura*, IV, 1152–53.
18. Lucretius, *De rerum natura*, IV, 808–11.

---

19. Lucretius, *De rerum natura*, IV, 638–41.

of the air infects a man, but does not harm a steer; some other infects the steer, but does not harm the man. Which of the two will be the pestilent quality in truth and in nature?> Those who have jaundice see all things yellowish and paler than we do:

<Everything looks yellow to the jaundiced.>[20]

Those who have the disease that physicians call *hyposphragma*, which is a suffusion of blood under the skin, see everything red and bloody. How do we know if these humors that change in this way the operation of our vision predominate in beasts and for them are ordinary? For we see some whose eyes are yellow like our sufferers from jaundice and others who have eyes that are bloody red; it is probable that to them the color of objects looks different from what it does to us; which of the two judgments will be the true one? For it is not said that the essence of things relates to man alone. Hardness, whiteness, depth, and sharpness pertain to the needs and knowledge of animals as they do to ours; nature has given the use of them to animals as it has to us. When we press on the eye, we perceive the bodies we are looking at as longer and more extended; a number of animals have their eyes pressed down in this way: so this length is presumably the real form of this body, not the one that our eyes give it in their ordinary position. <If we squeeze the eye from below, things look double to us:

Double the lights of the lamps with their flow-
   ery flames . . .
Twofold the faces of men, and their bodies double.>[21]

If we have our ears somehow impeded, or the passage for hearing stopped, we receive the sound in an unusual fashion; animals that have their ears hairy, or have only a little hole instead of an ear, consequently do not hear what we hear, and receive the sound differently. At festivals and theaters we see that when a painted sheet of glass of a certain color is set in front of the torches, everything in that place looks to us either green or yellow or violet:

<And this is often done with yellow and red and
   steely-blue
Awnings, when they flap and flutter, stretched
   over great theaters,
Spread everywhere on masts and beams.
For there they tinge the assembly in the rows
   beneath,
And infuse the splendor of the stage, of fathers
   and mothers and gods,
And make them flutter in their colors.>[22]

It is likely that the eyes of animals, which we see are of a different color, produce for them appearances of bodies corresponding to their eyes.

To judge the action of the senses we would first have to be in agreement with the animals, and secondly among ourselves. That is what we decidedly are not; and we enter into debate all the time about the fact that we hear, see, or taste something differently from someone else, and we debate about the diversity of images the senses bring us as much as we do about anything. By the ordinary rule of nature, a child hears and sees differently from a man of thirty years, and he in turn hears and sees differently from a man in his sixties. For some the senses are more obscure and darker, for others more open and sharper. We receive things differently, according to what we are and to how they appear to us. Now, since what appears to us is so uncertain and controversial, it is no longer a miracle if we are told that we can affirm that snow looks white to us, but that to establish if it is such in its essence and in truth is more than we are able to resolve; and, with this beginning shaken, all knowledge of the world must necessarily go to rack and ruin. What about our senses themselves contradicting one another? To the sight a painting seems embossed; when handled it seems flat. Shall we say that musk, which smells good and tastes bad,

---

20. Lucretius, *De rerum natura*, IV, 330.
21. Lucretius, *De rerum natura*, IV, 451, 453.
22. Lucretius, *De rerum natura*, IV, 73–78.

is agreeable or not? There are herbs and unguents proper for one part of the body, which injure another part; honey is pleasant to the taste, unpleasant to the sight. Take those rings cut out in the form of feathers, called "endless feathers": no eye can distinguish their size, or defend itself from the illusion that they grow larger on one side and contract on the other, coming to a point, even while they are being rolled around the finger, although when you feel them they seem to you equal in size and entirely similar.

<As for those persons who, to aid their lust, in times past used magnifying glasses so that the members they were to use would please them more through that ocular enlargement: to which of their two senses did they give the prize, to vision, which represented their members as large and great as they liked, or to touch, which presented them as small and contemptible?>

Is it our senses that lend the subject these different conditions, while the subjects nevertheless have only one? That is what we see in the bread we eat; it is only bread, but our use makes of it bones, blood, flesh, hair, and nails:

> <And food, when it is distributed to all the limbs
>     and members,
> Perishes, and furnishes out of itself a new
>     nature.>[23]

The moisture sucked up by the root of a tree becomes trunk, leaf, and fruit; and the air, though itself but one, is made by the application of a trumpet into a thousand different sorts of sounds. Is it, I say, our senses that fashion these subjects into so many different qualities, or do they have them in themselves? And given this doubt, what can we determine of their true essence? Further, when the accidents of illness, of day-dreaming, or of sleep make things appear to us differently from the way they appear to the healthy, the wise, and those who are awake, is it not likely that our normal condition and our natural humors also have something to give a being to things relating to their condition, and to

accommodate them to themselves, as our disordered humors do? And is not our health just as capable of giving them their appearance as illness is? <<Why does not the temperate person have a certain form of objects relative to it, as well as the intemperate, and why will not it, too, imprint its character on them?

The sick person attributes to the wine flatness, the healthy person, flavor, the thirsty person, sheer delight.>>

Now since our condition accommodates things to itself and transforms them according to itself, we no longer know what things are in truth; for nothing comes to us except as falsified and altered by our senses. Where the compass, the square, and the rule are crooked, all the proportions derived from them, and all buildings erected by their measure are also necessarily defective and failing. The uncertainty of our senses makes uncertain all that they produce:

> Again, as in a building, if the first rule is astray
> And the square is wrong and falls out of the
>     straight lines
> And the level sags a bit anywhere,
> The whole structure will necessarily be made
>     faulty and crooked,
> All awry, bulging, leaning forward or backward,
> Out of harmony, so that some parts already
>     seem to want to fall,
> Or do fall, all betrayed by the first wrong mea-
>     surements;
> Just so must your reasoning about things be mis-
>     taken and false,
> Which all springs from false senses.[24]

For the rest, who can be fit to judge of these differences? As we say of debates about religion, that we need a judge who is not attached to one or the other side, exempt from choice or affection, which is not possible among Christians, so it is likewise in this case. For if he is old, he cannot judge of the feeling of old age, being himself a party to the debate; the same if he is young, the same if healthy, the same if ill, sleeping, and waking. It would take someone

---

23. Lucretius, *De rerum natura*, III, 702–3.

24. Lucretius, *De rerum natura*, IV, 414–21.

exempt from all these qualities so that, without pre-occupation in his judgment, he would judge of these propositions as indifferent to him; and for this reason we would need a judge who never was.

To judge appearances that we receive from subjects, we would need a judicatory instrument; to verify that instrument, we would need demonstration; to verify the demonstration, an instrument; here we are going round a circle. Since the senses cannot stop our dispute, being themselves full of uncertainty, it must be up to reason; no reason can be established without another reason: here we are regressing to infinity. Our imagination does not apply itself to foreign objects, but is formed through the mediation of the senses; and the senses do not understand a foreign object, but only their own passions; and thus what we imagine and what appears to us are not from the object, but only from the passion and suffering of the senses, which passion and which object are different things; thus he who judges by appearances judges by something other than the object. And if you say that the passions of the senses convey to the soul by resemblance the quality of the foreign objects, how can the soul and the understanding assure themselves of this resemblance, since they have in themselves no commerce with the foreign objects? Just as someone who did not know Socrates could not say that his portrait resembles him. Now if nevertheless someone wanted to judge by appearances, if by all of them, that is impossible, for they interfere with one another by their contrarieties and discrepancies, as we see by experience. Will it be the case that certain chosen appearances govern the others? That choice would have to be verified by another choice, the second by a third, and so this will never be accomplished.

## [8. Changing Man Cannot Know Changing or Unchanging Things]

Finally, there is no constant existence, neither of our being nor of that of objects. Both we and our judgment and all things mortal go on flowing and rolling endlessly. Thus nothing can be established for certain of the one or the other, both the judging and the judged being in a constant state of change and motion.

We have no communication with being, since all human nature is always in the middle between being born and dying, giving only an obscure appearance and shadow of itself, and an uncertain and weak opinion of itself.[25] And if by chance you fix your thought on wanting to grasp your being, that is no more nor less than if you wanted to take hold of water, for the more you squeeze and press what is by nature flowing everywhere, the more you lose what you wanted to seize and take hold of. Thus, since all things are subject to passing from one change to another, reason, seeking a real subsistence there, finds itself disappointed, not being able to apprehend anything subsistent and permanent, since everything is either coming into being and is not yet at all, or beginning to die before it is born. Plato said that bodies never had existence, but only birth, <<thinking that Homer had made the ocean father of the gods, and Thetis their mother, to show us that all things are in perpetual flux, motion, and variation: an opinion common to all the philosophers before his time, as he says, except only for Parmenides, who refused motion to things, attaching great value to the power of that idea.>> Pythagoras said that all matter is flowing and labile; the Stoics, that there is no present time, and that what we call present is only the joining and coupling together of the future and the past; Heraclitus, that no man has ever entered twice into the same river; <Epicharmus, that he who has long since borrowed money does not owe it now; and that he who was invited overnight to come to dinner turns out today not to be invited, given that they are no longer the same people: they have become others;> and that no mortal substance can be found twice in the same state, for, through the suddenness and quickness of change, as soon as it dissipates, so soon does it reassemble; it comes and then it goes—in such a way that what begins to be born never arrives at the perfection of being, inasmuch as birth is never completed, and never stops as being at its end, but, from the seed is always changing and being altered from one thing to another. Thus from human seed there is made in the

---

25. What follows, to the penultimate paragraph of the *Apology*, is Montaigne's paraphrase of Amyot's translation of Plutarch, *Que signifiait ce mot*: εἰ.

mother's womb a fruit without form, then a formed infant, then, leaving the womb, a sucking infant. Then it becomes a boy; next a youth, then a mature man, then a man, and finally a decrepit aged man: so that age and subsequent generation always go on destroying and spoiling what went before:

> <*For time changes the nature of the whole world*
> *One state after another must overtake all things,*
> *Nor does anything remain like itself; all things migrate,*
> *Nature alters all things and forces them to turn.*>[26]

And then we stupidly fear one kind of death, while we have already passed and are passing so many others. For not only, as Heraclitus said, is the death of fire the generation of air, and the death of air the generation of water, but we can see this even more plainly in ourselves. The flowering of the prime of life passes when old age arrives, and youth is finished in the flowering of the mature man, childhood in youth, and the first period dies in childhood, and yesterday dies in today, and today will die in tomorrow; and there is nothing that stays and is always one. For if it is thus, if we always remain the same and one, how is it that we enjoy now one thing and now another? How is it that we love and hate, praise and condemn contrary things? How do we have different affections, no longer retaining the same sentiment within the same thought? For it is not likely that we would take on different passions without changing; and what suffers change does not remain one and the same, and if it is not one and the same, then it also is not. But, as to being a complete being, that also changes being simply, constantly becoming another from another. And consequently the senses deceive us and lie to us by nature, taking what appears for what is, for lack of knowing what it is that is. But what is it, then, that truly is? What is eternal, that is, what has never been born, will never have an end; time never brings it any

change. For time is a mobile thing, which appears as in shadow, with matter always running and flowing, without ever remaining stable or permanent. Anything to which the words before and after, has been and will be, is applied shows on the face of it that it is not a thing that is. For it would be great stupidity and a very obvious falsehood to say that that thing is which is not yet in being or has already ceased to be. As to the words present, instant, now, by which it seems we chiefly support and found our awareness of time, when reason discovers it, it destroys everything on the spot, for it immediately splits and divides it into future and past, as if it wanted necessarily to see it cut in two. The same thing happens to the nature that is being measured as to the time that measures it. For there is nothing there either that remains, or that is subsistent, but all things there are are born, or being born, or dying. Thus it would be a sin to say of God, who alone is, that he was or will be. For these are terms of variation, passage, or vicissitude concerning things that cannot last or remain in being. Hence we must conclude that only God is, not in the least according to some measure of time, but according to an immutable and immobile eternity, not measured by time, nor subject to any variation, before which nothing is, nor will be afterward, nor newer or more recent, but one really real being, who with one single now fills always; and there is nothing that is truly real but him alone, without one's being able to say: He has been, or he will be without beginning and without end.

To this so religious conclusion of a pagan, I wish only to join this testimony of the same kind, as the end of this long and tedious discourse, which would afford me matter without end: "Oh, what a vile and abject thing," he says, "is man, if he does not raise himself above humanity!"[27] There you have a good word and a useful desire, but similarly absurd. For to make the hilt bigger than the hand, the armful bigger than the arm, and to hope to stride further than our legs can reach, is impossible and monstrous. Nor can man raise himself above himself and humanity, for he cannot see but with his eyes nor grasp except with his grip. He will raise himself if God extraordinarily

---

26. Lucretius, *De rerum natura*, V, 826–29.

27. Seneca, *Quaestiones Naturales*, I, Preface.

gives him his hand; he will raise himself, abandoning and renouncing his own means, and letting himself be lifted and sustained by purely celestial ones.

<<It is for our Christian faith, and not for his Stoic virtue, to aspire to that divine and miraculous metamorphosis.>>

# Francis Bacon, *New Organon*, Book I (1620)[1]

*Francis Bacon was born in London in 1561; he was a successful lawyer, politician, and essayist. Bacon entered parliament in 1584 and held various administrative political and judicial offices; he rose to Lord Chancellor, was knighted, became Lord Verulam and ultimately Viscount St. Albans. His political career ended in 1621 when he confessed to bribery. He died in London in 1626. His philosophical views, in particular* The Advancement of Learning *(1605) and* Novum Organum[2] *(1620), were enormously influential on later 17th-century thought, especially with scientific institutions such as the Royal Society. From his earliest days at Trinity College, Cambridge, Bacon was preoccupied with a philosophy and scientific method that would entail a decisive break with the past. He came to believe that the traditional process of deduction from supposedly self-evident principles had produced little new scientific knowledge; it either gave back what we already knew or else it led us astray by giving illusory support to our confusions. What was needed was a confrontation with various obstacles to knowledge, with various idols, that is, false appearances. Also needed was the systematic understanding and control of nature based on an empirical method. The axioms of Bacon's philosophy would be statements of natural causes and laws derived by induction from scientific observation and experiment.[3]*

## Aphorisms concerning the Interpretation of Nature and the Kingdom of Man

1. Man, being the servant and interpreter of Nature, can do and understand so much and so much only as he has observed in fact or in thought of the course of nature; beyond this he neither knows anything nor can do anything.

2. Neither the naked hand nor the understanding left to itself can effect much. It is by instruments and helps that the work is done, which are as much wanted for the understanding as for the hand. And as the instruments of hand either give motion or guide

---

1. From *Works*, ed. J. M. Robertson (London: Routledge, 1905), English, modified.
2. That is, *New Organon*, or new scientific method, contrasting with Aristotle's logical and methodological works, known collectively as the Organon.

3. For more about Bacon, see Antonio Perez-Ramos, *Francis Bacon's Idea of Science and the Maker's Knowledge Tradition* (Oxford: Oxford University Press, 1988) or Markku Peltonen, ed., *The Cambridge Companion to Bacon* (Cambridge: Cambridge University Press, 1996).

it, so the instruments of the mind supply either suggestions for the understanding or cautions.

3. Human knowledge and human power meet in one; for where the cause is not known, the effect cannot be produced. Nature to be commanded must be obeyed; and that which is in contemplation is as the cause is in operation as the rule. [ . . . ]

11. As the sciences we now have do not help us in finding out new works, so neither does the logic we now have help us in finding out new sciences.

12. The logic now in use serves rather to fix and give stability to the errors which have their foundation in commonly received notions than to help the search for truth. So it does more harm than good.

13. The syllogism is not applied to the first principles of science, and is applied in vain to intermediate axioms, being no match for the subtlety of nature. It commands assent therefore to the proposition, but does not take hold of the thing.

14. The syllogism consists of propositions, propositions consist of words, words are symbols of notions. Therefore, if the notions themselves (which is the root of the matter) are confused and too hastily abstracted from the facts, there can be no firmness in the superstructure. Our only hope therefore lies in a true induction.

15. There is no soundness in our notions, whether logical or physical. Substance, quality, passion, essence itself are not sound notions; much less are heavy, light, dense, rare, moist, dry, generation, corruption, attraction, repulsion, element, matter, form, and the like. But all are fantastical and ill defined.

16. Our notions of less general species, as man, dog, dove, and of the intermediate perceptions of the sense, as hot, cold, black, white, do not materially mislead us; yet even these are sometimes confused by the flux and alteration of matter and the mixing of one thing with another. All the others which men have adopted up to now are but wanderings, not being abstracted and formed from things by proper methods.

17. Nor is there less willfulness and wandering in the construction of axioms than in the formation of notions, not excepting even those very principles which are obtained by common induction, but much more in the axioms and lower propositions educed by the syllogism.

18. The discoveries which have been made in the sciences up to now are such as lie close to vulgar notions, scarcely beneath the surface. In order to penetrate into the inner and further recesses of nature, it is necessary that both notions and axioms be derived from things by a more sure and guarded way, and that a method of intellectual operation be introduced altogether better and more certain.

19. There are and can be only two ways of searching into and discovering truth. The one flies from the senses and particulars to the most general axioms, and from these principles, the truth of which it takes for settled and immovable, proceeds to judgment and to the discovery of middle axioms. And this way is now in fashion. The other derives axioms from the senses and particulars, rising by a gradual and unbroken ascent, so that it arrives at the most general axioms last of all. This is the true way, but as yet untried.

20. The understanding left to itself takes the same course (namely the former) which it takes in accordance with logical order. For the mind longs to spring up to positions of higher generality, that it may find rest there, and so after a little while wearies of experiment. But this evil is increased by logic, because of the order and solemnity of its disputations.

21. The understanding left to itself, in a sober, patient, and grave mind, especially if it is not hindered by received doctrines, tries a little that other way, which is the right one, but with little progress; for the understanding, unless directed and assisted, is a thing unequal, and quite unfit to contend with the obscurity of things.

22. Both ways set out from the senses and particulars, and rest in the lightest generalities, but the difference between them is infinite. For the one just glances at experiment and particulars in passing, the other dwells duly and orderly among them. The one, again, begins at once by establishing certain abstract and useless generalities, the other rises by gradual steps to that which is prior and better known in the order of nature.

23. There is a great difference between the idols of the human mind and the ideas of the divine, that

is to say, between certain empty dogmas, and the true signatures and marks set upon the worlds of creation as they are found in nature.

24. It cannot be that axioms established by argumentation should avail for the discovery of new works, for the subtlety of nature is greater many times over than the subtlety of argument. But axioms duly and orderly formed from particulars easily discover the way to new particulars, and thus render sciences active.

25. The axioms now in use, having been suggested by a scanty and manipular experience and a few particulars of most general occurrence, are made for the most part just large enough to fit and take these in; and therefore it is no wonder if they do not lead to new particulars. And if some opposite instance, not observed or not known before, chances to come in the way, the axiom is rescued and preserved by some frivolous distinction; whereas the truer course would be to correct the axiom itself.

26. The conclusions of human reasoning as ordinarily applied in matters of nature, I call for the sake of distinction *anticipations of nature* (as something rash or premature). That reason which is elicited from facts by a just and methodical process, I call *interpretation of nature*.

27. Anticipations are a sufficiently firm ground for consent; for even if men went mad all after the same fashion, they might agree with one another well enough.

28. For the winning of assent, indeed, anticipations are far more powerful than interpretations, because being collected from a few instances, and those for the most part of familiar occurrence, they straightway touch the understanding and fill the imagination; whereas interpretations, on the other hand, being gathered here and there from very various and widely dispersed facts, cannot suddenly strike the understanding; and therefore they must necessarily, in respect of the opinions of the time, seem harsh and out of tune, much as the mysteries of faith do.

29. In sciences founded on opinions and dogmas, the use of anticipations and logic is good; for in them the object is to command assent to the propositions, not to master the thing.

30. Though all the wits of all the ages should meet together and combine and transmit their labors, yet great progress will never be made in science by means of anticipations; for radical errors in the first concoction of the mind are not to be cured by the excellence of subsequent functions and remedies.

31. It is idle to expect any great advancement in science from the superinducing and engrafting of new things upon old. We must begin anew from the very foundations, unless we would revolve forever in a circle with mean and contemptible progress. [ . . . ]

36. One method of discovery alone remains to us, which is simply this: We must lead men to the particulars themselves, and their series and order, while men on their side must force themselves for a while to lay their notions by and begin to familiarize themselves with facts.

37. The doctrine of those who have denied certainty could be attained at all has some agreement with my way of proceeding at the first setting out, but they end in being infinitely separated and opposed. For the holders of that doctrine assert simply that nothing can be known. I also assert that not much can be known in nature by the way which is now in use. But then they go on to destroy the authority of the senses and understanding; whereas I proceed to devise and supply helps for the same.

38. The idols and false notions which are now in possession of the human understanding, and have taken deep root in there, not only so beset men's minds that truth can hardly find entrance, but even after entrance is obtained, they will again, in the very instauration of the sciences, meet and trouble us, unless men being forewarned of the danger fortify themselves as far as may be against their assaults.

39. There are four classes of idols that beset men's minds. To these for distinction's sake I have assigned names, calling the first class *idols of the tribe*; the second, *idols of the cave*; the third, *idols of the market place*; the fourth, *idols of the theater*.

40. The formation of ideas and axioms by induction is without doubt the proper remedy to be applied for the keeping off and clearing away of idols. To point them out, however, is of great use; for the doctrine of idols is to the interpretation of nature

what the doctrine of the refutation of sophisms is to common logic.

41. The idols of the tribe have their foundation in human nature itself, and in the tribe or race of men. For it is a false assertion that the sense of man is the measure of things. On the contrary, all perceptions both of the sense and of the mind are according to the measure of the individual, and not according to the measure of the universe. And the human understanding is like a false mirror, which, receiving rays irregularly, distorts and discolors the nature of things by mingling its own nature with it.

42. The idols of the cave are the idols of the individual man. For every one (besides the errors common to human nature in general) has a cave or den of his own, which refracts and discolors the light of nature, owing either to his own proper and peculiar nature; or to his education and conversation with others; or to the reading of books and the authority of those whom he esteems and admires; or to the differences of impressions, accordingly as they take place in a mind preoccupied and predisposed or in a mind indifferent and settled; or the like. So that the spirit of man (according as it is meted out to different individuals) is in fact a thing variable and full of perturbation, and governed as it were by chance. Whence it was well observed by Heraclitus that men look for sciences in their own lesser worlds, and not in the greater or common world.

43. There are also idols formed by the intercourse and association of men with each other, which I call idols of the market place, on account of the commerce and consort of men there. For it is by discourse that men associate; and words are imposed according to the apprehension of the vulgar. And therefore the ill and unfit choice of words wonderfully obstructs the understanding. Nor do the definitions or explanations, with what in some things learned men are accustomed to guard and defend themselves, by any means set the matter right. But words plainly force and overrule the understanding, and throw all into confusion, and lead men away into numberless empty controversies and idle fancies.

44. Lastly, there are idols which have immigrated into men's minds from the various dogmas of philosophies, and also from wrong laws of demonstration. These I call idols of the theater, because in my judgment all the received systems are but so many stage plays, representing worlds of their own creation after an unreal and scenic fashion. Nor is it only of the systems now in vogue or only of the ancient sects and philosophies that I speak; for many more plays of the same kind may yet be composed and in like artificial manner set forth, seeing that the most widely different errors have causes which are for the most part alike. Neither again do I mean this only of entire systems, but also of many principles and axioms in science which by tradition, credulity, and negligence have come to be received.

But of these several kinds of idols I must speak more largely and exactly, that the understanding may be duly cautioned.

45. The human understanding is of its own nature prone to suppose the existence of more order and regularity in the world than it finds. And though there may be things in nature which are singular and unmatched, yet it devises for them parallels and conjugate relatives which do not exist. Hence the fiction that all the celestial bodies move in perfect circles, spirals, and dragons being (except in name) utterly rejected. Hence too the element of fire with its own orb is brought in to make up the square with the other three which the sense perceives. Hence also the ratio of the density of the so-called elements is arbitrarily fixed at ten to one. And so on of the other dreams. And these fancies affect not only dogmas, but also simple notions.

46. The human understanding when it has once adopted an opinion (either as being the received opinion or as being agreeable to itself) draws all other things to support and agree with it. And though there is a greater number and weight of instances to be found on the other side, yet it either neglects and despises these, or else by some distinction sets aside and rejects, in order that by this great and pernicious predetermination the authority of its former conclusions may remain inviolate. And therefore it was a good answer that was made by one who, when they showed him hanging in a temple a picture of those who had paid their vows as having escaped shipwreck, and would have him

say whether he did not now acknowledge the power of the gods; "Yes," he asked again, "but where are the pictures of those who were drowned after their vows?" And such is the way of all superstition, whether in astrology, dreams, omens, divine judgments, or the like, in which men, having a delight in such vanities, notice the events where they are fulfilled, but where they fail, though this happens much more often, neglect and pass them by. But this mischief insinuates itself with much more subtlety into philosophy and the sciences, in which the first conclusion colors and brings into conformity with itself all that come after, though far sounder and better. Besides, independently of that delight and vanity which I have described, it is the peculiar and perpetual error of the human intellect to be more moved and excited by affirmatives than by negatives, whereas it ought properly to hold itself indifferently disposed towards both alike. Indeed, in the establishment of any true axiom, the negative instance is the more forcible of the two.

# Galileo Galilei, *The Assayer* (1623), "Corpuscularianism"[1]

*Galileo Galilei was born in Pisa in 1564. He studied at the University of Pisa, became lecturer in mathematics there in 1592, and then lectured at the University of Padua from 1592 to 1610. In 1610, he constructed a telescope and made observations of the moon and the satellites of Jupiter, describing his findings in* Sidereal Messenger *(1610). Due to the great popularity of that work, he moved to Florence as "Chief Philosopher and Mathematician" to the court of the Cosimo of Medici, Grand Duke of Tuscany (1610–42). In 1615, he was denounced by the Inquisition for his support of Copernican astronomy (or heliocentrism) and went to Rome to defend it, but it was condemned by the Church in 1616. Years later, in 1633, he was summoned to Rome, forced to retract his views, and placed under permanent house arrest at Arcetri (near Florence). He died there in 1642. Galileo realized that a successful defense of Copernican astronomy, as suggested by his* Sidereal Messenger *and* Letters on Sunspots *(1613) and discussed in his* Dialogues concerning the Two Chief World Systems *(1632), would require a new physics, together with an altered philosophy and theology. He sketched some aspects of the new physics in* Discourse on the Two New Sciences *(1638) and argued for a change in relations between theology and science in the* Letter to the Grand Duchess Christina on the Use of Biblical Quotations in Matters of Science *(1615); in* The Assayer *(1623), Galileo advanced corpuscularian perspectives in the methodology of science and sketched some philosophical views about causality, perception, and ontology.[2] However interesting and well-fashioned is the corpuscularian section of* The Assayer*—especially coming from so important a figure in the history of science—it should be noted that there were very many disparate sources for corpuscularian ideas in the early seventeenth century.[3]*

In accordance with the promise which I made to Your Excellency, I shall certainly state my ideas concerning the proposition "Motion is the cause of

1. Editors' title. Translated from the Italian by A. C. Danto. From *Sources in Western Civilization*, by permission of Arthur Danto and Columbia University Press.

2. English translations are available for all of Galileo's major works: *Sidereal Messenger, Letters on Sunspots, The Assayer, Two Chief World Systems*, and *Two New Sciences*. For more about Galileo, see Pietro Redondi, *Galileo Heretic* (Princeton: Princeton University Press, 1987), Richard J. Blackwell, *Galileo, Bellarmine, and the Bible* (Notre Dame: University of Notre Dame Press, 1991), or Mario Biaggioli, *Galileo Courtier* (Chicago: The University of Chicago Press, 1993).

3. Lucretius' *De rerum natura (On the Nature of Things)* was probably the most widely available source for corpuscularianism; Descartes most likely learned his corpuscularianism from Isaac Beeckman.

heat," explaining in what way it appears to me to be true. But first it will be necessary for me to say a few words concerning that which we call "heat," for I strongly suspect that the commonly held conception of the matter is very far from the truth, inasmuch as heat is generally believed to be a true accident, affection, or quality which actually resides in the material which we feel to be heated.

Now, whenever I conceive of any material or corporeal substance, I am necessarily constrained to conceive of that substance as bounded and as possessing this or that shape, as large or small in relationship to some other body, as in this or that place during this or that time, as in motion or at rest, as in contact or not in contact with some other body, as being one, many, or few—and by no stretch of imagination can I conceive of any corporeal body apart from these conditions. But I do not at all feel myself compelled to conceive of bodies as necessarily conjoined with such further conditions as being red or white, bitter or sweet, having sound or being mute, or possessing a pleasant or unpleasant fragrance. On the contrary, were they not escorted by our physical senses, perhaps neither reason nor understanding would ever, by themselves, arrive at such notions. I think, therefore, that these tastes, odors, colors, etc., so far as their objective existence is concerned, are nothing but mere names for something which resides exclusively in our sensitive body (*corpo sensitivo*), so that if the perceiving creatures were removed, all of these qualities would be annihilated and abolished from existence. But just because we have given special names to these qualities, different from the names we have given to the primary and real properties, we are tempted into believing that the former really and truly exist as well as the latter.

An example, I believe, will clearly explain my concept. Suppose I pass my hand, first over a marble statue, then over a living man. So far as the hand, considered in itself, is concerned, it will act in an identical way upon each of these objects; that is, the primary qualities of motion and contact will similarly affect the two objects, and we would use identical language to describe this in each case. But the living body, which I subject to this experiment, will feel

itself affected in various ways, depending upon the part of the body I happen to touch; for example, should it be touched on the sole of the foot or the kneecap, or under the armpit, it will feel, in addition to simple contact, a further affection to which we have given a special name: we call it "tickling." This latter affection is altogether our own, and is not at all a property of the hand itself. And it seems to me that he would be gravely in error who would assert that the hand, in addition to movement and contact, intrinsically possesses another and different faculty which we might call the "tickling faculty," as though tickling were a resident property of the hand *per se*. Again, a piece of paper or a feather, when gently rubbed over any part of our body whatsoever, will in itself act everywhere in an identical way; it will, namely, move and contact. But we, should we be touched between the eyes, on the tip of the nose, or under the nostrils, will feel an almost intolerable titillation—while if touched in other places, we will scarcely feel anything at all. Now this titillation is completely ours and not the feather's, so that if the living, sensing body were removed, nothing would remain of the titillation but an empty name. And I believe that many other qualities, such as taste, odor, color, and so on, often predicated of natural bodies, have a similar and no greater existence than this.

A solid body and, so to speak, one that is sufficiently heavy, when moved and applied against any part of my body whatsoever, will produce in me the sensation which we call "touch." Although this sense is to be found in every part of the body, it appears principally to reside in the palm of the hand, and even more so in the fingertips, with which we can feel the most minute differences of roughness, texture, and softness and hardness—differences which the other parts of the body are less capable of distinguishing. Some among these tactile sensations are more pleasing than others, depending upon the differences of configuration of tangible bodies; that is to say, in accordance with whether they are smooth or irregular, sharp or dull, flexible or rigid. And the sense of touch, being more material than the other senses and being produced by the mass of the material itself, seems to correspond to the element of earth.

Since certain material bodies are continually resolving themselves into tiny particles, some of the particles, because they are heavier than air, will descend; and some of them, because they are lighter than air, will ascend. From this, perhaps, two further senses are born, for certain of the particles penetrate two parts of our body which are effectively more sensitive than the skin, which is incapable of feeling the incursion of materials which are too fine, subtle, or flexible. The descending particles are received by the upper surface of the tongue, and penetrating, they blend with its substance and moisture. Thus our tastes are caused, pleasant or harsh in accordance with variations in the contact of diversely shaped particles, and depending upon whether they are few or many, and whether they have high or low velocity. Other particles ascend, and entering the nostrils they penetrate the various nodes (*mammilule*) which are the instruments of smell; and these particles, in like manner through contact and motion, produce savoriness or unsavoriness—again depending upon whether the particles have this or that shape, high or low velocity, and whether they are many or few. It is remarkable how providently the tongue and nasal passages are situated and disposed, the former stretched beneath to receive the ingression of descending particles, and the latter so arranged as to receive those which ascend. The arrangement whereby the sense of taste is excited in us is perhaps analogous to the way in which fluids descend through the air, and the stimulation of the sense of smell may be compared to the manner in which flames ascend in it.

There remains the element of air, which corresponds to the sense of sound. Sounds come to us indiscriminately, from above and below and from either side, since we are so constituted as to be equally disposed to every direction of the air's movement; and the ear is so situated as to accommodate itself in the highest possible degree to any position in space. Sounds, then, are produced in us and felt when (without any special quality of harmoniousness or dissonance) there is a rapid vibration of air, forming minutely small waves, which move certain cartilages of a certain drum which is in our ear. The various external ways in which this wave-motion of the air

is produced are manifold, but can in large part be reduced to the vibrating of bodies which strike the air and form the waves which spread out with great velocity. High frequencies give rise to high tones; low frequencies give rise to low tones, but I cannot believe that there exists in external bodies anything, other than their size, shape, or motion (slow or rapid), which could excite in us our tastes, sounds, and odors. And indeed I should judge that, if ears, tongues, and noses be taken away, the number, shape, and motion of bodies would remain, but not their tastes, sounds, and odors. The latter, external to the living creature, I believe to be nothing but mere names, just as (a few lines back) I asserted tickling and titillation to be, if the armpit or the sensitive skin inside the nose were removed. As to the comparison between the four senses which we have mentioned and the four elements, I believe that the sense of sight, most excellent and noble of all the senses, is like light itself. It stands to the others in the same measure of comparative excellence as the finite stands to the infinite, the gradual to the instantaneous, the divisible to the indivisible, the darkness to the light. Of this sense, and all that pertains to it, I can pretend to understand but little; yet a great deal of time would not suffice for me to set forth even this little bit that I know, or (to put it more exactly) for me to sketch it out on paper. Therefore I shall ponder it in silence.

I return to my first proposition, having now shown how some affections, often reputed to be indwelling properties of some external body, have really no existence save in us, and apart from us are mere names. I confess myself to be very much inclined to believe that heat, too, is of this sort, and that those materials which produce and make felt in us the sense of heat and to which we give the general name "fire" consist of a multitude of tiny particles of such and such a shape, and having such and such a velocity. These, when they encounter our body, penetrate it by means of their extreme subtlety; and it is their contact, felt by us in their passage through our substance, which is the affection we call "heat." It will be pleasantly warm or unpleasantly hot depending upon the number and the velocity (greater or lesser) of these pricking, penetrating particles—pleasant if by their penetration our necessary perspiring is facilitated, unpleasant if their penetrating effects too great a division and dissolution of our substance. In sum, the operation of fire, considered in itself, is nothing but movement, or the penetration of bodies by its extreme subtlety, quickly or slowly, depending upon the number and velocity of tiny corpuscles of flame (*ignicoli*) and upon the greater or lesser density of the bodies concerned. Many bodies dissolve in such a manner that the major part of them becomes transformed into further corpuscles of flame; and this dissolution continues as further dissolvable material is encountered. But that there exists in fire, apart from shape, number, movement, penetration, and contact, some further quality which we call "heat," I cannot believe. And I again judge that heat is altogether subjective, so that if the living, sensitive body is removed, what we call "heat" would be nothing but a simple word. Since it is the case that this affection is produced in us by passage of tiny corpuscles of flame through our substance and their contact with it, it is obvious that once this motion ceases, their operation upon us will be null. It is thus that we perceive that a quantity of fire, retained in the pores and pits of a piece of calcified stone, does not heat—even if we hold it in the palm of our hand—because the flame remains stationary in the stone. But should we swish the stone in water where, because of its weight, it has greater propensity for movement and where the pits of the stone open somewhat, the corpuscles of flame will escape and, encountering our hand, will penetrate it, so that we will feel heat. Since, in order for heat to be stimulated in us, the mere presence of corpuscles of flame is not by itself sufficient, and since movement is required in addition, it is with considerable reason that I declare motion to be the cause of heat.

This or that movement by which a scantling or other piece of wood is burned up or by which lead and other metals are melted will continue so long as the corpuscles of flame, moved either by their own velocity or (if this be insufficient) aided by a strong blast from a bellows, continue to penetrate the body in question; the former will resolve itself into further corpuscles of flame or into ash; the latter will liquefy and be rendered fluid like water. From a common-sense point of view, to assert that that which moves a stone, piece of iron, or a stick, is what *heats* it, seems like an extreme vanity. But the friction produced when two hard bodies are rubbed together, which either reduces them to fine flying particles or permits the corpuscles of flame contained in them to escape, can finally be analyzed as motion. And the particles, when they encounter our body and penetrate and tear through it, are felt, in their motion and contact, by the living creature, who thus feels those pleasant or unpleasant affections which we call "heat," "burning," or "scorching."

Perhaps while this pulverizing and attrition continue, and remain confined to the particles themselves, their motion will be temporary and their operation will be merely that of heating. But once we arrive at the point of ultimate and maximum dissolution into truly indivisible atoms, light itself may be created, with an instantaneous motion or (I should rather say) an instantaneous diffusion and expansion, capable—I do not know if by the atoms' subtlety, rarity, immateriality, or by different and as yet unspecifiable conditions—capable, I say, of filling vast spaces.

But I should not like, Your Excellency, inadvertently to engulf myself in an infinite ocean without the means to find my way back to port. Nor should I like, while removing one doubt, to give birth to a hundred more, as I fear might in part be the case even in this timid venture from shore. Therefore, I shall await a more opportune moment to re-embark.

# René Descartes, *Discourse on the Method for Conducting One's Reason Well and for Seeking the Truth in the Sciences* (1637)[1]

## [Author's Preface]

*If this discourse seems too long to be read at one time, it may be divided into six parts. In the first part, you will find various considerations concerning the sciences; in the second part, the chief rules of the method which the author has sought; in the third part, some of the rules of morality which he has derived from this method; in the fourth part, the arguments by which he proves the existence of God and of the human soul, which are the foundations of his metaphysics; in the fifth part, the order of the questions in physics that he has investigated, and particularly the explanation of the movement of the heart and of other difficulties that pertain to medicine, as well as the difference between our soul and that of beasts; and in the final part, what things the author believes are required in order to advance further in the investigation of nature than the author has done, and what reasons have made him write.*

## Part One

Good sense is the best distributed thing in the world, for everyone thinks himself to be so well endowed with it that even those who are the most difficult to please in everything else are not at all wont to desire more of it than they have. It is not likely that everyone is mistaken in this. Rather, it provides evidence that the power of judging well and of distinguishing the true from the false (which is, properly speaking, what people call "good sense" or "reason") is naturally equal in all men, and that the diversity of our opinions does not arise from the fact that some people are more reasonable than others, but solely from the fact that we lead our thoughts along different paths and do not take the same things into consideration. For it is not enough to have a good mind; the main thing is to apply it well. The greatest souls are capable of the greatest vices as well as of the greatest virtues. And those who proceed only very slowly can make much greater progress, provided they always follow the right path, than do those who hurry and stray from it.

For myself, I have never presumed that my mind was in any respect more perfect than that of ordinary men. In fact, I have often desired to have as quick a wit, or as keen and distinct an imagination, or as full and responsive a memory as some other people. And other than these I know of no qualities that serve in the perfecting of the mind, for as to reason or sense, inasmuch as it alone makes us men and distinguishes us from the beasts, I prefer to believe that it exists

1. Translated from the French by Donald Cress in René Descartes, *Discourse on Method* (Indianapolis/Cambridge: Hackett Publishing Company, 1980).

whole and entire in each of us, and in this to follow the opinion commonly held by the philosophers,
who say that there are differences of degree only between accidents, but not at all between forms or natures of individuals of the same species.

But I shall have no fear of saying that I think I
have been rather fortunate to have, since my youth,
found myself on certain paths that have led me to
considerations and maxims from which I have
formed a method by which, it seems to me, I have
the means to increase my knowledge by degrees and
to raise it little by little to the highest point which
the mediocrity of my mind and the short duration
of my life will be able to allow it to attain. For I have
already reaped from it such a harvest that, although
I try, in judgments I make of myself, always to lean
more on the side of diffidence than of presumption,
and although, looking with a philosopher's eye at the
various actions and enterprises of all men, there is
hardly one of them that does not seem to me vain
and useless, I cannot but take immense satisfaction
in the progress that I think I have already made in
the search for truth, and I cannot but envisage such
hopes for the future that if, among the occupations of
men purely as men, there is one that is solidly good
and important, I dare to believe that it is the one I
have chosen.

All the same, it could be that I am mistaken, and
what I take for gold and diamonds is perhaps nothing but a bit of copper and glass. I know how much
we are prone to err in what affects us, and also how
much the judgments made by our friends should be
distrusted when these judgments are in our favor. But
I will be very happy to show in this discourse what
paths I have followed and to represent my life in it as
if in a picture, so that everyone may judge it for himself; and that, learning from the common response
the opinions one will have of it, this may be a new
means of teaching myself, which I shall add to those
that I am accustomed to using.

Thus my purpose here is not to teach the method
that everyone ought to follow in order to conduct his
reason well, but merely to show how I have tried to
conduct my own. Those who take it upon themselves
to give precepts must regard themselves as more

competent than those to whom they give them; and
if they are found wanting in the least detail, they are
to blame. But putting forward this essay merely as
a story or, if you prefer, as a fable in which, among
some examples one can imitate, one will perhaps
also find many others which one will have reason not
to follow, I hope that it will be useful to some without
being harmful to anyone, and that everyone will be
grateful to me for my frankness.

I have been nourished on letters since my childhood, and because I was convinced that by means of
them one could acquire a clear and assured knowledge of everything that is useful in life, I had a tremendous desire to master them. But as soon as I had
completed this entire course of study, at the end of
which one is ordinarily received into the ranks of the
learned, I completely changed my mind. For I found
myself confounded by so many doubts and errors that
it seemed to me that I had not gained any profit from
my attempt to teach myself, except that more and
more I had discovered my ignorance. And yet I was at
one of the most renowned schools of Europe, where
I thought there must be learned men, if in fact any
such men existed anywhere on earth. There I had
learned everything the others were learning; and, not
content with the disciplines we were taught there, I
had gone through all the books I could lay my hands
on that treated those disciplines considered the most
curious and most unusual. Moreover, I knew what
judgments the others were making about me; and I
did not at all see that I was rated inferior to my fellow students, even though there already were some
among them who were destined to take the place of
our teachers. And finally our age seemed to me to
be just as flourishing and as fertile in good minds as
any of the preceding ones. This made me feel free to
judge all others by myself, and to think that there was
no doctrine in the world that was of the sort that I had
previously been led to hope for.

I did not, however, cease to hold in high regard
the academic exercises with which we occupy ourselves in the schools. I knew that the languages
learned there are necessary for the understanding
of classical texts; that the charm of fables awakens
the mind; that the memorable deeds recounted in

histories uplift it, and, if read with discretion, aid in forming one's judgment; that the reading of all good books is like a conversation with the most honorable people of past ages, who were their authors, indeed, even like a set conversation in which they reveal to us only the best of their thoughts; that oratory has incomparable power and beauty; that poetry has quite ravishing delicacy and sweetness; that mathematics has some very subtle stratagems that can serve as much to satisfy the curious as to facilitate all the arts and to lessen men's labor; that writings dealing with morals contain many lessons and many exhortations to virtue that are very useful; that theology teaches one how to reach heaven; that philosophy provides the means of speaking plausibly about all things and of making oneself admired by the less learned; that jurisprudence, medicine, and the other sciences bring honors and riches to those who cultivate them; and, finally, that it is good to have examined all these disciplines, even the most superstition-ridden and the most false of them, in order to know their true worth and to guard against being deceived by them.

But I believed I had already given enough time to languages, and also to the reading of classical texts, both to their histories and to their fables. For conversing with those of other ages is about the same thing as traveling. It is good to know something of the customs of various peoples, so as to judge our own more soundly and so as not to think that everything that is contrary to our ways is ridiculous and against reason, as those who have seen nothing have a habit of doing. But when one takes too much time traveling, one eventually becomes a stranger in one's own country; and when one is too curious about what commonly took place in past ages, one usually remains quite ignorant of what is taking place in one's own country. Moreover, fables make one imagine many events to be possible which are not so at all. And even the most accurate histories, if they neither alter nor exaggerate the significance of things in order to render them more worthy of being read, almost always at least omit the baser and less noteworthy details. Consequently, the rest do not appear as they really are, and those who govern their own conduct by means of examples drawn from these texts are liable to fall

into the extravagances of the knights of our romances and to conceive plans that are beyond their powers.

I held oratory in high regard and was enamored of poetry, but I thought both were gifts of the mind rather than fruits of study. Those who possess the strongest reasoning and who best order their thoughts in order to make them clear and intelligible can always best persuade others of what they are proposing, even if they were to speak only Low Breton[2] and had never learned rhetoric. And those who have the most pleasing rhetorical devices and who know how to express themselves with the most embellishment and sweetness would not fail to be the greatest poets, even if the art of poetry were unknown to them.

I delighted most of all in mathematics because of the certainty and the evidence of its reasonings. But I did not yet notice its true use, and, thinking that it was of service merely to the mechanical arts, I was astonished by the fact that no one had built anything more noble upon its foundations, given that they were so solid and firm. On the other hand, I compared the writings of the ancient pagans that deal with morals to very proud and very magnificent palaces that were built on nothing but sand and mud. They place virtues on a high plateau and make them appear to be valued more than anything else in the world, but they do not sufficiently instruct us about how to recognize them; and often what they call by so fine-sounding a name is nothing more than a kind of insensibility, pride, desperation, or parricide.

I revered our theology, and I desired as much as anyone else to reach heaven; but having learned as something very certain that the road to heaven is open no less to the most ignorant than to the most learned, and that the revealed truths guiding us there are beyond our understanding, I would not have dared to submit them to the frailty of my reasonings. And I thought that, in order to undertake an examination of these truths and to succeed in doing so, it would be necessary to have some extraordinary assistance from heaven and to be more than a man.

Concerning philosophy I shall say only that, seeing that it has been cultivated for many centuries by

---

2. This dialect was considered rather barbarous and hardly suitable for sophisticated literary endeavors.

the most excellent minds that have ever lived and that, nevertheless, there still is nothing in it about which there is not some dispute, and consequently nothing that is not doubtful, I was not at all so presumptuous as to hope to fare any better there than the others; and that, considering how many opinions here can be about the very same matter that are held by learned people without there ever being the possibility of more than one opinion being true, I deemed everything that was merely probable to be well nigh false.

Then, as for the other sciences, I judged that, insofar as they borrow their principles from philosophy, one could not have built anything solid upon such unstable foundations. And neither the honor nor the monetary gain they promised was sufficient to induce me to master them, for I did not perceive myself, thank God, to be in a condition that obliged me to make a career out of science in order to enhance my fortune. And although I did not make a point of rejecting glory after the manner of a Cynic, nevertheless I placed very little value on the glory that I could not hope to acquire except through false pretenses. And finally, as to the false doctrines, I thought I already knew well enough what they were worth, so as not to be liable to be deceived either by the promises of an alchemist, the predictions of an astrologer, the tricks of a magician, or the ruses or boasts of any of those who profess to know more than they do.

That is why, as soon as age permitted me to emerge from the supervision of my teachers, I completely abandoned the study of letters. And resolving to search for no knowledge other than what could be found within myself, or else in the great book of the world, I spent the rest of my youth traveling, seeing courts and armies, mingling with people of diverse temperaments and circumstances, gathering various experiences, testing myself in the encounters that fortune offered me, and everywhere engaging in such reflection upon the things that presented themselves that I was able to derive some profit from them. For it seemed to me that I could find much more truth in the reasonings that each person makes concerning matters that are important to him, and whose outcome ought to cost him dearly later on if he has judged badly, than in those reasonings engaged in by

a man of letters in his study, which touch on speculations that produce no effect and are of no other consequence to him except perhaps that, the more they are removed from common sense, the more pride he will take in them, for he will have to employ that much more wit and ingenuity in attempting to render them plausible. And I have always had an especially great desire to learn to distinguish the true from the false, in order to see my way clearly in my actions, and to go forward with confidence in this life.

It is true that, so long as I merely considered the customs of other men, I found hardly anything there about which to be confident, and that I noticed there was about as much diversity as I had previously found among the opinions of philosophers. Thus the greatest profit I derived from this was that, on seeing many things that, although they seem to us very extravagant and ridiculous, do not cease to be commonly accepted and approved among other great peoples, I learned not to believe anything too firmly of which I had been persuaded only by example and custom; and thus I little by little freed myself from many errors that can darken our natural light and render us less able to listen to reason. But after I had spent some years thus studying in the book of the world and in trying to gain some experience, I resolved one day to study within myself too and to spend all the powers of my mind in choosing the paths that I should follow. In this I had much more success, it seems to me, than had I never left either my country or my books.

## Part Two

I was then in Germany, where the occasion of the wars which are not yet over there[3] had called me; and as I was returning to the army from the coronation of the emperor, the onset of winter detained me in quarters where, finding no conversation to divert me and fortunately having no worries or passions to trouble me, I remained for an entire day shut up by myself in a stove-heated room,[4] where I was completely free

---

3. Thirty Years War (1618–48).
4. There is no need to allege that Descartes sat in or on a stove. A *poêle* is simply a room heated by an earthenware stove. Cf. E. Gilson, *Discours de la méthode: texte et commentaire* (Paris: Vrin, 1967), p. 157.

to converse with myself about my thoughts. Among them, one of the first was that it occurred to me to consider that there is often not as much perfection in works composed of many pieces and made by the hands of various master craftsmen as there is in those works on which but a single individual has worked. Thus one sees that buildings undertaken and completed by a single architect are usually more attractive and better ordered than those which many architects have tried to patch up by using old walls that had been built for other purposes. Thus those ancient cities that were once mere villages and in the course of time have become large towns are usually so poorly laid out, compared to those well-ordered places that an engineer traces out on a vacant plain as it suits his fancy, that even though, upon considering each building one by one in the former sort, one often finds as much, if not more art, than one finds in those of the latter; still, upon seeing how the buildings are arranged—here a large one, there a small one—and how they make the streets crooked and uneven, one would say that it is chance rather than the will of some men using reason that has arranged them thus. And if one considers that there have nevertheless always been officials responsible for seeing that private buildings contribute to the attractiveness of public areas, one will well understand that it is difficult to make things that are very finely crafted by laboring only on the works of others. Thus I imagined that peoples who, having once been half-savages and having been civilized only little by little, have made their laws only to the extent that the inconvenience due to crimes and quarrels forced them to do so, could not be as well ordered as those who, from the very beginning of their coming together, have followed the fundamental precepts of some prudent legislator. Likewise, it is quite certain that the state of the true religion, whose ordinances were made by God alone, must be incomparably better ordered than all the others. And, speaking of things human, I believe that if Sparta was at one time very flourishing, this was not because of the goodness of each one of its laws taken by itself, seeing that many of them were very strange and even contrary to good morals, but because, having been devised by a single individual, they all tended toward the same end. And thus I thought that book learning, at least the kind whose reasonings are merely probable and that do not have any demonstrations, having been composed and enlarged little by little from the opinions of many different persons, does not draw nearly so close to the truth as the simple reasonings that a man of good sense can naturally make about the things he encounters. And thus, too, I thought that, because we were all children before being men and because for a long time it was necessary for us to be governed by our appetites and our teachers (which were frequently in conflict with one another, and of which perhaps neither always gave us the best advice), it is nearly impossible for our judgments to be as pure or as solid as they would have been if we had had the full use of our reason from the moment of our birth and if we had always been guided by it alone.

It is true that we never see anyone pulling down all the houses in a city for the sole purpose of rebuilding them in a different style and of making the streets more attractive; but one does see very well that many people tear down their own houses in order to rebuild them, and that in some cases they are even forced to do so when their houses are in danger of collapsing and when the foundations are not very secure. This example persuaded me that it would not really be at all reasonable for a single individual to plan to reform a state by changing everything in it from the foundations up and by toppling it in order to set it up again; nor even also to reform the body of the sciences or the order established in the schools for teaching them; but that, as regards all the opinions to which I had until now given credence, I could not do better than to try to get rid of them once and for all, in order to replace them later on, either with other ones that are better, or even with the same ones once I had reconciled them to the level of reason. And I firmly believed that by this means I would succeed in conducting my life much better than if I were to build only upon old foundations and if I were to rely only on the principles of which I had allowed myself to be persuaded in my youth without ever having examined whether they were true. For although I noticed various difficulties in this undertaking, still they were not irremediable, nor were they comparable to those difficulties occurring in the reform of the least things that affect the public. These great bodies are too difficult to raise up once they have been knocked down, or even to hold up once they have been shaken; and their fall can only be very violent. Moreover, as to their imperfections, if they have any (and the mere fact of the diversity that exists among them suffices to assure one that many do have imperfections), custom has doubtless greatly mitigated them and has even prevented or imperceptibly corrected many of them, against which prudence could not provide so well. And finally, these imperfections are almost always more tolerable than changing them would be; similarly, the great roads that wind through mountains little by little become so smooth and so convenient by dint of being frequently used that it is much better to follow them than to try to take a more direct route by climbing over rocks and descending to the bottom of precipices.

That is why I could in no way approve of those troublemaking and restless personalities who, called neither by their birth nor by their fortune to manage public affairs, are forever coming up with an idea for some new reform in this matter. And if I thought there were in this writing the slightest thing by means of which one might suspect me of such folly, I would be very sorry to permit its publication. My plan has never gone beyond trying to reform my own thoughts and building upon a foundation which is completely my own. And if, my work having pleased me sufficiently, I here show you a model of it, it is not for the reason that I would wish to advise anyone to imitate it. Perhaps those with whom God has better shared his graces will have more lofty plans; but I fear that even this one here may already be too daring for many. The single resolution to rid oneself of all the opinions to which one has heretofore given credence is not an example that everyone ought to follow; and the world consists almost exclusively of two kinds of minds for whom it is not at all suitable. First, there are those who, believing themselves more capable than they are, are unable to avoid being hasty in their judgments or have enough patience to conduct all their thoughts in an orderly manner; as a result, if they have once

taken the liberty of doubting the principles they had accepted and of straying from the common path, they could never keep to the path one must take in order to go in a more straightforward direction, and they would remain lost all their lives. Second, there are those who have enough reason or modesty to judge that they are less capable of distinguishing the true from the false than certain others by whom they can be instructed; such people should content themselves more with following the opinions of these others than with looking for better ones themselves.

And as for myself, I would unquestionably have been counted among these latter persons if I had always had only one master or if I had not known at all the differences that have always existed among the opinions of the most learned. But I had learned in my college days that one cannot imagine anything so strange or so little believable that it has not been said by one of the philosophers, and since then, I had recognized in my travels that all those who have sentiments quite contrary to our own are not for that reason barbarians or savages, but that many of them use their reason as much as or more than we do. And I considered how one and the same man with the very same mind, were he brought up from infancy among the French or the Germans, would become different from what he would be had he always lived among the Chinese or the cannibals; and how, even down to the styles of our clothing, the same thing that pleased us ten years ago, and that perhaps will again please us ten years hence, now seems to us extravagant and ridiculous. Thus it is more custom and example that persuades us than any certain knowledge; and yet the majority opinion is worthless as a proof of truths that are at all difficult to discover, since it is much more likely that one man would have found them than a whole multitude of people. Hence I could not choose anyone whose opinions seemed to me preferable over those of the others, and I found myself, as it were, constrained to try to guide myself on my own.

But, like a man who walks alone and in the dark, I resolved to go so slowly and to use so much circumspection in all things that, if I advanced only very slightly, at least I would effectively keep myself from falling. Nor did I want to begin to reject totally any of the opinions that had once been able to slip into my head without having been introduced there by reason, until I had first spent sufficient time planning the work I was undertaking and seeking the true method for arriving at the knowledge of everything of which my mind would be capable.

When I was younger, I had studied, among the parts of philosophy, a little logic, and among those of mathematics, a bit of geometrical analysis and algebra—three arts or sciences that, it seemed, ought to contribute something to my plan. But in examining them, I noticed that, in the case of logic, its syllogisms and the greater part of its other lessons served more to explain to someone else the things one knows, or even, like the art of Lully,[5] to speak without judgment concerning matters about which one is ignorant, than to learn them. And although, in effect, it might well contain many very true and very good precepts, nevertheless there are so many others mixed up with them that are either harmful or superfluous, that it is almost as difficult to separate the latter precepts from the former as it is to draw a Diana or a Minerva from a block of marble that has not yet been hewn. Then, as to the analysis of the ancients and the algebra of the moderns, apart from the fact that they apply only to very abstract matters and seem to be of no use, the former is always so closely tied to the consideration of figures that it cannot exercise the understanding without greatly fatiguing the imagination; and in the case of the latter, one is so subjected to certain rules and to certain symbols, that out of it there results a confused and obscure art that encumbers the mind rather than a science that cultivates it. That is why I thought it necessary to search for some other method embracing the advantages of these three yet

free from their defects. And since the multiplicity of laws often provides excuses for vices, so that a state is much better ruled when it has but very few laws and when these are very strictly observed; likewise, in place of the large number of precepts of which logic is composed, I believed that the following four rules would be sufficient for me, provided I made a firm and constant resolution not even once to fail to observe them:

The first was never to accept anything as true that I did not plainly know to be such; that is to say, carefully to avoid hasty judgment and prejudice; and to include nothing more in my judgments than what presented itself to my mind so clearly and so distinctly that I had no occasion to call it in doubt.

The second, to divide each of the difficulties I would examine into as many parts as possible and as was required in order better to resolve them.

The third, to conduct my thoughts in an orderly fashion, by commencing with those objects that are simplest and easiest to know, in order to ascend little by little, as by degrees, to the knowledge of the most composite things, and by supposing an order even among those things that do not naturally precede one another.

And the last, everywhere to make enumerations so complete and reviews so general that I was assured of having omitted nothing.

Those long chains of utterly simple and easy reasonings that geometers commonly use to arrive at their most difficult demonstrations had given me occasion to imagine that all the things that can fall within human knowledge follow from one another in the same way, and that, provided only that one abstain from accepting any of them as true that is not true, and that one always adheres to the order one must follow in deducing the ones from the others, there cannot be any that are so remote that they are not eventually reached nor so hidden that they are not discovered. And I was not very worried about trying to find out which of them it would be necessary to begin with; for I already knew that it was with the simplest and easiest to know. And considering that, of all those who have hitherto searched for the truth in the sciences, only the mathematicians have been

---

5. Lully, that is, Ramon Lull (ca. 1235–1316), was a Catalan philosopher and Franciscan who wrote in defense of Christianity against the Moors by attempting to demonstrate the articles of faith by means of logic. Descartes seems to have encountered a Lullist in Dordrecht who could hold forth on any subject whatever for long periods of time. This encounter, more than any direct contact with the writings of Lull, seems to have colored Descartes' understanding of the "art of Lully." Cf. E. Gilson, *Discours de la méthode: texte et commentaire*, pp. 185–86.

able to find any demonstrations, that is to say, certain and evident reasonings, I did not at all doubt that it was with these same things that they had examined [that I should begin]; although I expected from them no other utility but that they would accustom my mind to nourish itself on truths and not to be content with false reasonings. But it was not my plan on that account to try to learn all those particular sciences commonly called mathematical; and seeing that, even though their objects differed, these sciences did not cease to be all in accord with one another in considering nothing but the various relations or proportions which are found in their objects, I thought it would be more worthwhile for me to examine only these proportions in general, and to suppose them to be only in subjects that would help me make the knowledge of them easier, and without at the same time in any way restricting them to those subjects, so that later I could apply them all the better to everything else to which they might pertain. Then, having noted that, in order to know these proportions, I would sometimes need to consider each of them individually, and sometimes only to keep them in mind, or to grasp many of them together, I thought that, in order better to consider them in particular, I ought to suppose them to be relations between lines, since I found nothing more simple, or nothing that I could represent more distinctly to my imagination and to my senses; but that, in order to keep them in mind or to grasp many of them together, I would have to explicate them by means of certain symbols, the briefest ones possible; and that by this means I would be borrowing all that is best in geometrical analysis and algebra, and correcting all the defects of the one by means of the other.

In fact, I dare say the strict adherence to these few precepts I had chosen gave me such facility for disentangling all the questions to which these two sciences extend, that, in the two or three months I spent examining them, having begun with the simplest and most general, and each truth that I found being a rule that later helped me to find others, not only did I arrive at a solution of many problems that I had previously judged very difficult, but also it seemed to me toward the end that, even

in those instances where I was ignorant, I could determine by what means and how far it was possible to resolve them. In this perhaps I shall not seem to you to be too vain, if you will consider that, there being but one truth with respect to each thing, whoever finds this truth knows as much about a thing as can be known; and that, for example, if a child who has been instructed in arithmetic has made an addition following its rules, he can be assured of having found everything regarding the sum he was examining that the human mind would know how to find. For ultimately, the method that teaches one to follow the true order and to enumerate exactly all the circumstances of what one is seeking contains everything that gives certainty to the rules of arithmetic.

But what pleased me most about this method was that by means of it I was assured of using my reason in everything, if not perfectly, at least as well as was in my power; and in addition that I felt that in practicing this method my mind was little by little getting into the habit of conceiving its objects more rigorously and more distinctly and that, not having restricted the method to any particular subject matter, I promised myself to apply it as usefully to the problems of the other sciences as I had to those of algebra. Not that, on this account, I would have dared at the outset to undertake an examination of all the problems that presented themselves; for that would itself have been contrary to the order prescribed by the method. But having noted that the principles of these sciences must all be derived from philosophy, in which I did not yet find any that were certain, I thought it was necessary for me first of all to try to establish some there; and that, this being the most important thing in the world, and the thing in which hasty judgment and prejudice were most feared, I should not try to accomplish that objective until I had reached a much more mature age than that of merely twenty-three, which I was then, and until I had first spent a great deal of time preparing myself for it, as much in rooting out from my mind all the wrong opinions that I had accepted before that time as in accumulating many experiences, in order for them later to be the subject matter of my reasonings, and in always practicing the method I had prescribed for myself so as to strengthen myself more and more in its use.

## Part Five

[ . . . ] I paused here in particular in order to show that, if there were such machines having the organs and the shape of a monkey or of some other animal that lacked reason, we would have no way of recognizing that they were not entirely of the same nature as these animals; whereas, if there were any such machines that bore a resemblance to our bodies and imitated our actions as far as this is practically feasible, we would always have two very certain means of recognizing that they were not at all, for that reason, true men. The first is that they could never use words or other signs, or put them together as we do in order to declare our thoughts to others. For one can well conceive of a machine being so made that it utters words, and even that it utters words appropriate to the bodily actions that will cause some change in its organs (such as if one touches it in a certain place, it asks what one wants to say to it, or, if in another place, it cries out that one is hurting it, and the like). But it could not arrange its words differently so as to respond to the sense of all that will be said in its presence, as even the dullest men can do. The second means is that, although they might perform many tasks very well or perhaps better than any of us, such machines would inevitably fail in other tasks; by this means one would discover that they were acting, not through knowledge, but only through the disposition of their organs. For while reason is a universal instrument that can be of help in all sorts of circumstances, these organs require some particular disposition for each particular action; consequently, it is for all practical purposes impossible for there to be enough different organs in a machine to make it act in all the contingencies of life in the same way as our reason makes us act.

Now by these two means one can also know the difference between men and beasts. For it is rather remarkable that there are no men so dull and so stupid (excluding not even the insane), that they are incapable of arranging various words together and of composing from them a discourse by means of which they might make their thoughts understood;

and that, on the other hand, there is no other animal at all, however perfect and pedigreed it may be, that does the like. This does not happen because they lack the organs, for one sees that magpies and parrots can utter words just as we can, and yet they cannot speak as we do, that is to say, by testifying to the fact that they are thinking about what they are saying; on the other hand, men born deaf and dumb, who are deprived just as much as, or more than, beasts of the organs that aid others in speaking, are wont to invent for themselves various signs by means of which they make themselves understood to those who, being with them on a regular basis, have the time to learn their language. And this attests not merely to the fact that the beasts have less reason than men but that they have none at all. For it is obvious it does not need much to know how to speak; and since we notice as much inequality among animals of the same species as among men, and that some are easier to train than others, it is unbelievable that a monkey or a parrot that is the most perfect of its species would not equal in this respect one of the most stupid children or at least a child with a disordered brain, if their soul were not of a nature entirely different from our own. And we should not confuse words with the natural movements that attest to the passions and can be imitated by machines as well as by animals. Nor should we think, as did some of the ancients, that beasts speak, although we do not understand their language; for if that were true, since they have many organs corresponding to our own, they could make themselves as well understood by us as they are by their fellow-creatures. It is also a very remarkable phenomenon that, although there are many animals that show more skill than we do in some of their actions, we nevertheless see that they show none at all in many other actions. Consequently, the fact that they do something better than we do does not prove that they have any intelligence; for were that the case, they would have more of it than any of us and would excel us in everything. But rather it proves that they have no intelligence at all, and that it is nature that acts in them, according to the disposition of their organs—just as we see that a clock composed exclusively of wheels and springs can count the hours and measure time more accurately than we can with all our carefulness.

After that, I described the rational soul and showed that it can in no way be derived from the potentiality of matter, as can the other things I have spoken of, but rather that it must be expressly created; and how it is not enough for it to be lodged in the human body like a pilot in his ship, unless perhaps in order to move its members, but rather that it must be more closely joined and united to the body in order to have, in addition to this, feelings and appetites similar to our own, and thus to constitute a true man. As to the rest, I elaborated here a little on the subject of the soul because it is of the greatest importance; for, after the error of those who deny the existence of God (which I think I have sufficiently refuted), there is none at all that puts weak minds at a greater distance from the straight path of virtue than to imagine that the soul of beasts is of the same nature as ours, and that, as a consequence, we have nothing to fear or to hope for after this life any more than do flies and ants. On the other hand, when one knows how different they are, one understands much better the arguments which prove that our soul is of a nature entirely independent of the body, and consequently that it is not subject to die with it. Then, since we do not see any other causes at all for its destruction, we are naturally led to judge from this that it is immortal.

# René Descartes, *Meditations on First Philosophy* (1641)[1]

## [Letter of Dedication]

*To those Most Wise and Distinguished Men, the Dean and Doctors of the Faculty of Sacred Theology of Paris*

René Descartes Sends Greetings

So right is the cause that impels me to offer this work to you that I am confident you too will find it equally right and thus take up its defense, once you have understood the plan of my undertaking; so much is this the case that I have no better means of commending it here than to state briefly what I have sought to achieve in this work.

I have always thought that two issues—namely, God and the soul—are chief among those that ought to be demonstrated with the aid of philosophy rather than theology. For although it suffices for us believers to believe by faith that the human soul does not die with the body, and that God exists, certainly no unbelievers seem capable of being persuaded of any religion or even of almost any moral virtue, until these two are first proven to them by natural reason. And since in this life greater rewards are often granted to

vices than to virtues, few would prefer what is right to what is useful, if they neither feared God nor anticipated an afterlife. Granted, it is altogether true that we must believe in God's existence because it is taught in the Holy Scriptures, and, conversely, that we must believe the Holy Scriptures because they have come from God. This is because, of course, since faith is a gift from God, the very same one who gives the grace that is necessary for believing the rest can also give the grace to believe that he exists. Nonetheless, this reasoning cannot be proposed to unbelievers because they would judge it to be circular. In fact, I have observed that not only do you and all other theologians affirm that one can prove the existence of God by natural reason, but also that one may infer from Sacred Scripture that the knowledge of him is easier to achieve than the many things we know about creatures, and is so utterly easy that those without this knowledge are blameworthy. For this is clear from *Wisdom*, Chapter 13 where it is said: "They are not to be excused, for if their capacity for knowing were so great that they could think well of this world, how is it that they did not find the Lord of it even more easily?" And in *Romans*, Chapter 1, it is said that they are "without excuse." And again in the same passage it appears we are being warned with the

---

1. Translated from the Latin by Donald Cress in René Descartes, *Meditations on First Philosophy*, 3rd ed. (Indianapolis/Cambridge: Hackett Publishing Company, 1993).

words: "What is known of God is manifest in them," that everything that can be known about God can be shown by reasons drawn exclusively from our own mind. For this reason, I did not think it unbecoming for me to inquire how this may be the case, and by what path God may be known more easily and with greater certainty than the things of this world.

And as to the soul, there are many who have regarded its nature as something into which one cannot easily inquire, and some have even gone so far as to say that human reasoning convinces them that the soul dies with the body, while it is by faith alone that they hold the contrary position. Nevertheless, because the Lateran Council held under Leo X, in Session 8, condemned such people and expressly enjoined Christian philosophers to refute their arguments and to use all their powers to demonstrate the truth, I have not hesitated to undertake this task as well.

Moreover, I know that there are many irreligious people who refuse to believe that God exists and that the human mind is distinct from the body—for no other reason than their claim that up until now no one has been able to demonstrate these two things. By no means am I in agreement with these people; on the contrary, I believe that nearly all the arguments which have been brought to bear on these questions by great men have the force of a demonstration, when they are adequately understood, and I am convinced that hardly any arguments can be given that have not already been discovered by others. Nevertheless, I judge that there is no greater task to perform in philosophy than assiduously to seek out, once and for all, the best of all these arguments and to lay them out so precisely and plainly that henceforth all will take them to be true demonstrations. And finally, I was strongly urged to do this by some people who knew that I had developed a method for solving all sorts of problems in the sciences—not a new one, mind you, since nothing is more ancient than the truth, but one they had seen me use with some success in other areas. Accordingly, I took it to be my task to attempt something on this subject.

This treatise contains all that I have been able to accomplish. Not that I have attempted to gather together in it all the various arguments that could

be brought forward as proof of the very same conclusions, for this does not seem worthwhile, except where no one proof is sufficiently certain. Rather, I have sought out the primary and chief arguments, so that I now make bold to propose these as most certain and evident demonstrations. Moreover, I will say in addition that these arguments are such that I believe there is no way open to the human mind whereby better ones could ever be found. For the urgency of the cause, as well as the glory of God, to which this entire enterprise is referred, compel me here to speak somewhat more freely on my own behalf than is my custom. But although I believe these arguments to be certain and evident, still I am not thereby convinced that they are suited to everyone's grasp. In geometry there are many arguments developed by Archimedes, Apollonius, Pappus, and others, which are taken by everyone to be evident and certain because they contain absolutely nothing which, considered by itself, is not quite easily known, and in which what follows does not square exactly with what has come before. Nevertheless, they are rather lengthy and require a particularly attentive reader; thus only a small handful of people understand them. Likewise, although the arguments I use here do, in my opinion, equal or even surpass those of geometry in certitude and obviousness, nevertheless I am fearful that many people will not be capable of adequately perceiving them, both because they too are a bit lengthy, with some of them depending on still others, and also because, first and foremost, they demand a mind that is quite free from prejudices and that can easily withdraw itself from association with the senses. Certainly there are not to be found in the world more people with an aptitude for metaphysical studies than those with an aptitude for geometry. Moreover, there is the difference that in geometry everyone is of a mind that usually nothing is put down in writing without there being a sound demonstration for it; thus the inexperienced more frequently err on the side of assenting to what is false, wanting as they do to give the appearance of understanding it, than on the side of denying what is true. But it is the reverse in philosophy: Since it is believed that there is no issue that cannot be defended from either side, few look for the truth, and many more prowl about for a reputation for profundity by arrogantly challenging whichever arguments are the best.

And therefore, regardless of the force of my arguments, because they are of a philosophical nature I do not anticipate that what I will have accomplished through them will be very worthwhile unless you assist me with your patronage. Your faculty is held in such high esteem in the minds of all, and the name of the Sorbonne has such authority that not only in matters of faith has no association, with the exception of the councils of the Church, been held in such high regard as yours, but even in human philosophy nowhere is there thought to be greater insightfulness and solidity, or greater integrity and wisdom in rendering judgments. Should you deign to show any interest in this work, I do not doubt that, first of all, its errors would be corrected by you (for I am mindful not only of my humanity but also, and most especially, of my ignorance, and thus do not claim that there are no errors in it); second, what is lacking would be added, or what is not sufficiently complete would be perfected, or what is in need of further discussion would be expanded upon more fully, either by yourselves or at least by me, after you have given me your guidance; and finally, after the arguments contained in this work proving that God exists and that the mind is distinct from the body have been brought (as I am confident they can be) to such a level of lucidity that these arguments ought to be regarded as the most precise of demonstrations, you may be of a mind to make such a declaration and publicly attest to it. Indeed, should this come to pass, I have no doubt that all the errors that have ever been entertained regarding these issues would shortly be erased from the minds of men. For the truth itself will easily cause other men of intelligence and learning to subscribe to your judgment. Your authority will cause the atheists, who more often than not are dilettantes rather than men of intelligence and learning, to put aside their spirit of contrariness, and perhaps even to defend the arguments which they will come to know are regarded as demonstrations by all who are discerning, lest they appear not to understand them. And finally, everyone else will readily give credence to so many indications of support, and there no longer will be anyone in the world who would dare call into doubt either the existence of God or the real distinction between the soul and the body. Just how great the usefulness of this thing might be, you yourselves, in virtue of your singular wisdom, are in the best position of anyone to judge; nor would it behoove me to commend the cause of God and religion at any greater length to you, who have always been the greatest pillar of the Catholic Church.

## Preface to the Reader

I have already touched briefly on the issues of God and the human mind in my *Discourse on the Method for Conducting One's Reason Well and for Seeking the Truth in the Sciences*, published in French in 1637. The intent there was not to provide a precise treatment of them, but only to offer a sample and to learn from the opinions of readers how these issues should be treated in the future. For they seemed to me to be so important that I judged they ought to be dealt with more than once. And the path I follow in order to explain them is so little trodden and so far removed from the one commonly taken that I did not think it useful to hold forth at greater length in a work written in French and designed to be read indiscriminately by everyone, lest weaker minds be in a position to think that they too ought to set out on this path.

In the *Discourse* I asked everyone who might find something in my writings worthy of refutation to do me the favor of making me aware of it. As for what I touched on regarding these issues, only two objections were worth noting, and I will respond briefly to them here before undertaking a more precise explanation of them.

The first is that, from the fact that the human mind, when turned in on itself, does not perceive itself to be anything other than a thinking thing, it does not follow that its nature or *essence* consists only in its being a thinking thing, such that the word *only* excludes everything else that also could perhaps be said to belong to the nature of the soul. To this objection I answer that in that passage I did not intend my exclusion of those things to reflect the order of the truth of the matter (I was not dealing with it then), but merely the order of my perception. Thus what I had in mind was that I was aware of absolutely nothing that I knew belonged to pertain to my essence, save that I was a thinking thing, that is, a thing having within itself the faculty of thinking. Later on, however, I will show how it follows, from the fact that I know of nothing else belonging to my essence, that nothing else really does belong to it.

The second objection is that it does not follow from the fact that I have within me an idea of a thing more perfect than me, that this idea is itself more perfect than me, and still less that what is represented by this idea exists. But I answer that there is an equivocation here in the word "idea." For "idea" can be taken either materially, for an operation of the intellect (in which case it cannot be said to be more perfect than me), or objectively, for the thing represented by means of that operation. This thing, even if it is not presumed to exist outside the intellect, can nevertheless be more perfect than me by reason of its essence. I will explain in detail in the ensuing remarks how, from the mere fact that there is within me an idea of something more perfect than me, it follows that this thing really exists.

In addition, I have seen two rather lengthy treatises, but these works, utilizing as they do arguments drawn from atheist commonplaces, focused their attack not so much on my arguments regarding these issues, as on my conclusions. Moreover, arguments of this type exercise no influence over those who understand my arguments, and the judgments of many people are so preposterous and feeble that they are more likely to be persuaded by the first opinions to come along, however false and contrary to reason they may be, than by a true and firm refutation of them which they hear subsequently. Accordingly, I have no desire to respond here to these objections, lest I first have to state what they are. I will only say in general that all the objections typically bandied about by the atheists to assail the existence of God always depend either on ascribing human emotions to God, or on arrogantly claiming for our minds such power and wisdom that we attempt to determine and grasp fully what God can and ought to do. Hence

these objections will cause us no difficulty, provided we but remember that our minds are to be regarded as finite, while God is to be regarded as incomprehensible and infinite.

But now, after having, to some degree, conducted an initial review of the judgments of men, here I begin once more to treat the same questions about God and the human mind, together with the starting points of the whole of first philosophy, but not in a way that causes me to have any expectation of widespread approval or a large readership. On the contrary, I do not advise anyone to read these things except those who have both the ability and the desire to meditate seriously with me, and to withdraw their minds from the senses as well as from all prejudices. I know all too well that such people are few and far between. As to those who do not take the time to grasp the order and linkage of my arguments, but will be eager to fuss over statements taken out of context (as is the custom for many), they will derive little benefit from reading this work. Although perhaps they might find an occasion for quibbling in several places, still they will not find it easy to raise an objection that is either compelling or worthy of response.

But because I do not promise to satisfy even the others on all counts the first time around, and because I do not arrogantly claim for myself so much that I believe myself capable of anticipating all the difficulties that will occur to someone, I will first of all narrate in the *Meditations* the very thoughts by means of which I seem to have arrived at a certain and evident knowledge of the truth, so that I may determine whether the same arguments that persuaded me can be useful in persuading others. Next, I will reply to the objections of a number of very gifted and learned gentlemen, to whom these *Meditations* were forwarded for their examination prior to their being sent to press. For their objections were so many and varied that I have dared to hope that nothing will readily occur to anyone, at least nothing of importance, which has not already been touched upon by these gentlemen. And thus I earnestly entreat the readers not to form a judgment regarding the *Meditations* until they have deigned to read all these objections and the replies I have made to them.

## Synopsis of the Following Six Meditations

In the First Meditation the reasons are given why we can doubt all things, especially material things, so long, that is, as, of course, we have no other foundations for the sciences than the ones which we have had up until now. Although the utility of so extensive a doubt is not readily apparent, nevertheless its greatest utility lies in freeing us of all prejudices, in preparing the easiest way for us to withdraw the mind from the senses, and finally, in making it impossible for us to doubt any further those things that we later discover to be true.

In the Second Meditation the mind, through the exercise of its own freedom, supposes the nonexistence of all those things about whose existence it can have even the least doubt. In so doing the mind realizes that it is impossible for it not to exist during this time. This too is of the greatest utility, since by means of it the mind easily distinguishes what things belong to it, that is, to an intellectual nature, from what things belong to the body. But because some people will perhaps expect to see proofs for the immortality of the soul in this Meditation, I think they should be put on notice here that I have attempted to write only what I have carefully demonstrated. Therefore the only order I could follow was the one typically used by geometers, which is to lay out everything on which a given proposition depends, before concluding anything about it. But the first and principal prerequisite for knowing that the soul is immortal is that we form a concept of the soul that is as lucid as possible and utterly distinct from every concept of a body. This is what has been done here. Moreover, there is the additional requirement that we know that everything that we clearly and distinctly understand is true, in exactly the manner in which we understand it; however, this could not have been proven prior to the Fourth Meditation. Moreover, we must have a distinct concept of corporeal nature, and this is formulated partly in the Second Meditation itself, and partly in the Fifth and Sixth Meditations. From all this one ought to conclude that all the things we clearly and distinctly conceive as different substances truly are substances that are really distinct from one another. (This, for example, is how mind and body are conceived.) This conclusion is arrived at in the Sixth Meditation. This same conclusion is also confirmed in this Meditation in virtue of the fact that we cannot understand a body to be anything but divisible, whereas we cannot understand the mind to be anything but indivisible. For we cannot conceive of half a mind, as we do for any body whatever, no matter how small. From this we are prompted to acknowledge that the natures of mind and body not only are different from one another, but even, in a manner of speaking, are contraries of one another. However, I have not written any further on the matter in this work, both because these considerations suffice for showing that the annihilation of the mind does not follow from the decaying of the body (and thus these considerations suffice for giving mortals hope in an afterlife), and also because the premises from which the immortality of the mind can be inferred depend upon an account of the whole of physics. First, we need to know that absolutely all substances, that is, things that must be created by God in order to exist, are by their very nature incorruptible, and can never cease to exist, unless, by the same God's denying his concurrence to them, they be reduced to nothingness. Second, we need to realize that body, taken in a general sense, is a substance and hence it too can never perish. But the human body, insofar as it differs from other bodies, is composed of merely a certain configuration of members, together with other accidents of the same sort. But the human mind is not likewise composed of any accidents, but is a pure substance. For even if all its accidents were changed, so that it understands different things, wills different things, senses different things, and so on, the mind itself does not on that score become something different. On the other hand, the human body does become something different, merely as a result of the fact that a change in the shape of some of its parts has taken place. It follows from these considerations that a body can very easily perish, whereas the mind by its nature is immortal.

In the Third Meditation I have explained at sufficient length, it seems to me, my principal argument for proving the existence of God. Nevertheless, since my intent was to draw the minds of readers as far as possible from the senses, I had no desire to draw upon comparisons based upon corporeal things. Thus many obscurities may perhaps have remained; but these, I trust, will later be entirely removed in my Replies to the Objections. One such point of contention, among others, is the following: How can the idea that is in us of a supremely perfect being have so much objective reality that it can only come from a supremely perfect cause? This is illustrated in the Replies by a comparison with a very perfect machine, the idea of which is in the mind of some craftsman. For, just as the objective ingeniousness of this idea ought to have some cause (say, the knowledge possessed by the craftsman or by someone else from whom he received this knowledge), so too, the idea of God which is in us must have God himself as its cause.

In the Fourth Meditation it is proved that all that we clearly and distinctly perceive is true, and it is also explained what constitutes the nature of falsity. These things necessarily need to be known both to confirm what has preceded as well as to help readers understand what remains. (But here one should meanwhile bear in mind that in that Meditation there is no discussion whatsoever of sin, that is, the error committed in the pursuit of good and evil, but only the error that occurs in discriminating between what is true and what is false. Nor is there an examination of those matters pertaining to the faith or to the conduct of life, but merely of speculative truths known exclusively by the means of the light of nature.)

In the Fifth Meditation, in addition to an explanation of corporeal nature in general, the existence of God is also demonstrated by means of a new proof. But again several difficulties may arise here; however, these are resolved later in my Replies to the Objections. Finally, it is shown how it is true that the certainty of even geometrical demonstrations depends upon the knowledge of God.

Finally, in the Sixth Meditation the understanding is distinguished from the imagination and the marks of this distinction are described. The mind is proved to be really distinct from the body, even though the mind is shown to be so closely joined to the body that it forms a single unit with it. All the errors commonly arising from the senses are reviewed; an account of the ways in which these errors can be avoided is provided. Finally, all the arguments on the basis of which we may infer the existence of material things are presented—not because I believed them to be very useful for proving what they prove, namely, that there really is a world, that men have bodies, and the like (things which no one of sound mind has ever seriously doubted), but rather because, through a consideration of these arguments, one realizes that they are neither so firm nor so evident as the arguments leading us to the knowledge of our mind and of God, so that, of all the things that can be known by the human mind, these latter are the most certain and the most evident. Proving this one thing was for me the goal of these Meditations. For this reason I will not review here the various issues that are also to be treated in these Meditations as the situation arises.

# Meditations on First Philosophy in Which the Existence of God and the Distinction between the Soul and the Body Are Demonstrated

## Meditation One: Concerning Those Things That Can Be Called into Doubt

Several years have now passed since I first realized how numerous were the false opinions that in my youth I had taken to be true, and thus how doubtful were all those that I had subsequently built upon them. And thus I realized that once in my life I had to raze everything to the ground and begin again from the original foundations, if I wanted to establish anything firm and lasting in the sciences. But the task seemed enormous, and I was waiting until I reached a point in my life that was so timely that no more suitable time for undertaking these plans of action would come to pass. For this reason, I procrastinated for so long that I would henceforth be at fault, were I to waste the time that remains for carrying out the project by brooding over it. Accordingly, I have today suitably freed my mind of all cares, secured for myself a period of leisurely tranquillity, and am withdrawing into solitude. At last I will apply myself earnestly and unreservedly to this general demolition of my opinions.

Yet to bring this about I will not need to show that all my opinions are false, which is perhaps something I could never accomplish. But reason now persuades me that I should withhold my assent no less carefully from opinions that are not completely certain and indubitable than I would from those that are patently false. For this reason, it will suffice for the rejection of all of these opinions, if I find in each of them some reason for doubt. Nor therefore need I survey each opinion individually, a task that would be endless. Rather, because undermining the foundations will cause whatever has been built upon them to crumble of its own accord, I will attack straightaway those principles which supported everything I once believed.

Surely whatever I had admitted until now as most true I received either from the senses or through the senses. However, I have noticed that the senses are sometimes deceptive; and it is a mark of prudence never to place our complete trust in those who have deceived us even once.

But perhaps, even though the senses do sometimes deceive us when it is a question of very small and distant things, still there are many other matters concerning which one simply cannot doubt, even though they are derived from the very same senses: for example, that I am sitting here next to the fire, wearing my winter dressing gown, that I am holding this sheet of paper in my hands, and the like. But on what grounds could one deny that these hands and this entire body are mine? Unless perhaps I were to liken myself to the insane, whose brains are impaired by such an unrelenting vapor of black bile that they steadfastly insist that they are kings when they are utter paupers, or that they are arrayed in purple robes when they are naked, or that they have heads made of clay, or that they are gourds, or that they are made of glass. But such people are mad, and I would

appear no less mad were I to take their behavior as an example for myself.

This would all be well and good, were I not a man who is accustomed to sleeping at night, and to experiencing in my dreams the very same things, or now and then even less plausible ones, as these insane people do when they are awake. How often does my evening slumber persuade me of such ordinary things as these: that I am here, clothed in my dressing gown, seated next to the fireplace—when in fact I am lying undressed in bed! But right now my eyes are certainly wide awake when I gaze upon this sheet of paper. This head which I am shaking is not heavy with sleep. I extend this hand consciously and deliberately, and I feel it. Such things would not be so distinct for someone who is asleep. As if I did not recall having been deceived on other occasions even by similar thoughts in my dreams! As I consider these matters more carefully, I see so plainly that there are no definitive signs by which to distinguish being awake from being asleep. As a result, I am becoming quite dizzy, and this dizziness nearly convinces me that I am asleep.

Let us assume then, for the sake of argument, that we are dreaming and that such particulars as these are not true: that we are opening our eyes, moving our head, and extending our hands. Perhaps we do not even have such hands, or any such body at all. Nevertheless, it surely must be admitted that the things seen during slumber are, as it were, like painted images, which could only have been produced in the likeness of true things, and that therefore at least these general things—eyes, head, hands, and the whole body—are not imaginary things, but are true and exist. For indeed when painters themselves wish to represent sirens and satyrs by means of especially bizarre forms, they surely cannot assign to them utterly new natures. Rather, they simply fuse together the members of various animals. Or if perhaps they concoct something so utterly novel that nothing like it has ever been seen before (and thus is something utterly fictitious and false), yet certainly at the very least the colors from which they fashion it ought to be true. And by the same token, although even these general things— eyes, head, hands and the like—could be imaginary, still one has to admit that at least certain other things that are even more simple and universal are true. It is from these components, as if from true colors, that all those images of things that are in our thought are fashioned, be they true or false.

This class of things appears to include corporeal nature in general, together with its extension; the shape of extended things; their quantity, that is, their size and number; as well as the place where they exist; the time through which they endure, and the like.

Thus it is not improper to conclude from this that physics, astronomy, medicine, and all the other disciplines that are dependent upon the consideration of composite things are doubtful, and that, on the other hand, arithmetic, geometry, and other such disciplines, which treat of nothing but the simplest and most general things and which are indifferent as to whether these things do or do not in fact exist, contain something certain and indubitable. For whether I am awake or asleep, two plus three make five, and a square does not have more than four sides. It does not seem possible that such obvious truths should be subject to the suspicion of being false.

Be that as it may, there is fixed in my mind a certain opinion of long standing, namely that there exists a God who is able to do anything and by whom I, such as I am, have been created. How do I know that he did not bring it about that there is no earth at all, no heavens, no extended thing, no shape, no size, no place, and yet bringing it about that all these things appear to me to exist precisely as they do now? Moreover, since I judge that others sometimes make mistakes in matters that they believe they know most perfectly, may I not, in like fashion, be deceived every time I add two and three or count the sides of a square, or perform an even simpler operation, if that can be imagined? But perhaps God has not willed that I be deceived in this way, for he is said to be supremely good. Nonetheless, if it were repugnant to his goodness to have created me such that I be deceived all the time, it would also seem foreign to that same goodness to permit me to be deceived even occasionally. But we cannot make this last assertion.

Perhaps there are some who would rather deny so powerful a God than believe that everything else is uncertain. Let us not oppose them; rather, let us grant that everything said here about God is fictitious. Now they suppose that I came to be what I am either by fate, or by chance, or by a connected chain of events, or by some other way. But because being deceived and being mistaken appear to be a certain imperfection, the less powerful they take the author of my origin to be, the more probable it will be that I am so imperfect that I am always deceived. I have nothing to say in response to these arguments. But eventually I am forced to admit that there is nothing among the things I once believed to be true which it is not permissible to doubt—and not out of frivolity or lack of forethought, but for valid and considered arguments. Thus I must be no less careful to withhold assent henceforth even from these beliefs than I would from those that are patently false, if I wish to find anything certain.

But it is not enough simply to have realized these things; I must take steps to keep myself mindful of them. For long-standing opinions keep returning, and, almost against my will, they take advantage of my credulity, as if it were bound over to them by long use and the claims of intimacy. Nor will I ever get out of the habit of assenting to them and believing in them, so long as I take them to be exactly what they are, namely, in some respects doubtful, as has just now been shown, but nevertheless highly probable, so that it is much more consonant with reason to believe them than to deny them. Hence, it seems to me I would do well to deceive myself by turning my will in completely the opposite direction and pretend for a time that these opinions are wholly false and imaginary, until finally, as if with prejudices weighing down each side equally, no bad habit should turn my judgment any further from the correct perception of things. For indeed I know that meanwhile there is no danger or error in following this procedure, and that it is impossible for me to indulge in too much distrust, since I am now concentrating only on knowledge, not on action.

Accordingly, I will suppose not a supremely good God, the source of truth, but rather an evil genius, supremely powerful and clever, who has directed his entire effort at deceiving me. I will regard the heavens, the air, the earth, colors, shapes, sounds, and all external things as nothing but the bedeviling hoaxes of my dreams, with which he lays snares for my credulity. I will regard myself as not having hands, or eyes, or flesh, or blood, or any senses, but as nevertheless falsely believing that I possess all these things. I will remain resolute and steadfast in this meditation, and even if it is not within my power to know anything true, it certainly is within my power to take care resolutely to withhold my assent to what is false, lest this deceiver, however powerful, however clever he may be, have any effect on me. But this undertaking is arduous, and a certain laziness brings me back to my customary way of living. I am not unlike a prisoner who enjoyed an imaginary freedom during his sleep, but, when he later begins to suspect that he is dreaming, fears being awakened and nonchalantly conspires with these pleasant illusions. In just the same way, I fall back of my own accord into my old opinions, and dread being awakened, lest the toilsome wakefulness which follows upon a peaceful rest must be spent thenceforward not in the light but among the inextricable shadows of the difficulties now brought forward.

## Meditation Two: Concerning the Nature of the Human Mind: That It Is Better Known Than the Body

Yesterday's meditation has thrown me into such doubts that I can no longer ignore them, yet I fail to see how they are to be resolved. It is as if I had suddenly fallen into a deep whirlpool; I am so tossed about that I can neither touch bottom with my foot, nor swim up to the top. Nevertheless I will work my way up and will once again attempt the same path I entered upon yesterday. I will accomplish this by putting aside everything that admits of the least doubt, as if I had discovered it to be completely false. I will stay on this course until I know something certain, or, if nothing else, until I at least know for certain that nothing is certain. Archimedes sought but one firm and immovable point in order to move the entire earth from one place to another. Just so, great things

are also to be hoped for if I succeed in finding just one thing, however slight, that is certain and unshaken.

Therefore I suppose that everything I see is false. I believe that none of what my deceitful memory represents ever existed. I have no senses whatever. Body, shape, extension, movement, and place are all chimeras. What then will be true? Perhaps just the single fact that nothing is certain.

But how do I know there is not something else, over and above all those things that I have just reviewed, concerning which there is not even the slightest occasion for doubt? Is there not some God, or by whatever name I might call him, who instills these very thoughts in me? But why would I think that, since I myself could perhaps be the author of these thoughts? Am I not then at least something? But I have already denied that I have any senses and any body. Still I hesitate; for what follows from this? Am I so tied to a body and to the senses that I cannot exist without them? But I have persuaded myself that there is absolutely nothing in the world: no sky, no earth, no minds, no bodies. Is it then the case that I too do not exist? But doubtless I did exist, if I persuaded myself of something. But there is some deceiver or other who is supremely powerful and supremely sly and who is always deliberately deceiving me. Then too there is no doubt that I exist, if he is deceiving me. And let him do his best at deception; he will never bring it about that I am nothing so long as I shall think that I am something. Thus, after everything has been most carefully weighed, it must finally be established that this pronouncement "I am, I exist" is necessarily true every time I utter it or conceive it in my mind.

But I do not yet understand sufficiently what I am—I, who now necessarily exist. And so from this point on, I must be careful lest I unwittingly mistake something else for myself, and thus err in that very item of knowledge that I claim to be the most certain and evident of all. Thus, I will meditate once more on what I once believed myself to be, prior to embarking upon these thoughts. For this reason, then, I will set aside whatever can be weakened even to the slightest degree by the arguments brought forward, so that eventually all that remains is precisely nothing but what is certain and unshaken.

What then did I formerly think I was? A man, of course. But what is a man? Might I not say a "rational animal"? No, because then I would have to inquire what "animal" and "rational" mean. And thus from one question I would slide into many more difficult ones. Nor do I now have enough free time that I want to waste it on subtleties of this sort. Instead, permit me here to focus on what came spontaneously and naturally into my thinking whenever I pondered what I was. Now it occurred to me first that I had a face, hands, arms, and this entire mechanism of bodily members: the very same as are discerned in a corpse, and which I referred to by the name "body." It next occurred to me that I took in food, that I walked about, and that I sensed and thought various things; these actions I used to attribute to the soul. But as to what this soul might be, I either did not think about it or else I imagined it a rarefied I-know-not-what, like a wind, or a fire, or ether, which had been infused into my coarser parts. But as to the body I was not in any doubt. On the contrary, I was under the impression that I knew its nature distinctly. Were I perhaps tempted to describe this nature such as I conceived it in my mind, I would have described it thus: By "body," I understand all that is capable of being bounded by some shape, of being enclosed in a place, and of filling up a space in such a way as to exclude any other body from it; of being perceived by touch, sight, hearing, taste, or smell; of being moved in several ways, not, of course, by itself, but by whatever else impinges upon it. For it was my view that the power of self-motion, and likewise of sensing or of thinking, in no way belonged to the nature of the body. Indeed I used rather to marvel that such faculties were to be found in certain bodies.

But now what am I, when I suppose that there is some supremely powerful and, if I may be permitted to say so, malicious deceiver who deliberately tries to fool me in any way he can? Can I not affirm that I possess at least a small measure of all those things which I have already said belong to the nature of the body? I focus my attention on them, I think about them, I review them again, but nothing comes to

mind. I am tired of repeating this to no purpose. But what about those things I ascribed to the soul? What about being nourished or moving about? Since I now do not have a body, these are surely nothing but fictions. What about sensing? Surely, this too does not take place without a body; and I seemed to have sensed in my dreams many things that I later realized I did not sense. What about thinking? Here I make my discovery: Thought exists; it alone cannot be separated from me. I am; I exist—this is certain. But for how long? For as long as I am thinking; for perhaps it could also come to pass that if I were to cease all thinking I would then utterly cease to exist. At this time I admit nothing that is not necessarily true. I am therefore precisely nothing but a thinking thing; that is, a mind, or intellect, or understanding, or reason—words of whose meanings I was previously ignorant. Yet I am a true thing and am truly existing; but what kind of thing? I have said it already: a thinking thing.

What else am I? I will set my imagination in motion. I am not that concatenation of members we call the human body. Neither am I even some subtle air infused into these members, nor a wind, nor a fire, nor a vapor, nor a breath, nor anything I devise for myself. For I have supposed these things to be nothing. The assumption still stands; yet nevertheless I am something. But is it perhaps the case that these very things which I take to be nothing, because they are unknown to me, nevertheless are in fact no different from that me that I know? This I do not know, and I will not quarrel about it now. I can make a judgment only about things that are known to me. I know that I exist; I ask now who is this "I" whom I know? Most certainly, in the strict sense the knowledge of this "I" does not depend upon things whose existence I do not yet know. Therefore, it is not dependent upon any of those things that I simulate in my imagination. But this word "simulate" warns me of my error. For I would indeed be simulating were I to "imagine" that I was something, because imagining is merely the contemplating of the shape or image of a corporeal thing. But I now know with certainty that I am and also that all these images—and, generally, everything belonging to the nature of the body—could turn out to be nothing but dreams. Once I have realized this, I would seem to be speaking no less foolishly were I to say, "I will use my imagination in order to recognize more distinctly who I am," than were I to say, "Now I surely am awake, and I see something true; but since I do not yet see it clearly enough, I will deliberately fall asleep so that my dreams might represent it to me more truly and more clearly." Thus I realize that none of what I can grasp by means of the imagination pertains to this knowledge that I have of myself. Moreover, I realize that I must be most diligent about withdrawing my mind from these things so that it can perceive its nature as distinctly as possible.

But what then am I? A thing that thinks. What is that? A thing that doubts, understands, affirms, denies, wills, refuses, and that also imagines and senses.

Indeed it is no small matter if all of these things belong to me. But why should they not belong to me? Is it not the very same "I" who now doubts almost everything, who nevertheless understands something, who affirms that this one thing is true, who denies other things, who desires to know more, who wishes not to be deceived, who imagines many things even against my will, who also notices many things which appear to come from the senses? What is there in all of this that is not every bit as true as the fact that I exist—even if I am always asleep or even if my creator makes every effort to mislead me? Which of these things is distinct from my thought? Which of them can be said to be separate from myself? For it is so obvious that it is I who doubt, I who understand, and I who will, that there is nothing by which it could be explained more clearly. But indeed it is also the same "I" who imagines; for although perhaps, as I supposed before, absolutely nothing that I imagined is true, still the very power of imagining really does exist, and constitutes a part of my thought. Finally, it is this same "I" who senses or who is cognizant of bodily things as if through the senses. For example, I now see a light, I hear a noise, I feel heat. These things are false, since I am asleep. Yet I certainly do seem to see, hear, and feel warmth. This cannot be false. Properly speaking, this is what in me is called "sensing." But this, precisely so taken, is nothing other than thinking.

From these considerations I am beginning to know a little better what I am. But it still seems (and I cannot resist believing) that corporeal things—whose images are formed by thought, and which the senses themselves examine—are much more distinctly known than this mysterious "I" which does not fall within the imagination. And yet it would be strange indeed were I to grasp the very things I consider to be doubtful, unknown, and foreign to me more distinctly than what is true, what is known—than, in short, myself. But I see what is happening: my mind loves to wander and does not yet permit itself to be restricted within the confines of truth. So be it then; let us just this once allow it completely free rein, so that, a little while later, when the time has come to pull in the reins, the mind may more readily permit itself to be controlled.

Let us consider those things which are commonly believed to be the most distinctly grasped of all: namely the bodies we touch and see. Not bodies in general, mind you, for these general perceptions are apt to be somewhat more confused, but one body in particular. Let us take, for instance, this piece of wax. It has been taken quite recently from the honeycomb; it has not yet lost all the honey flavor. It retains some of the scent of the flowers from which it was collected. Its color, shape, and size are manifest. It is hard and cold; it is easy to touch. If you rap on it with your knuckle, it will emit a sound. In short, everything is present in it that appears needed to enable a body to be known as distinctly as possible. But notice that, as I am speaking, I am bringing it close to the fire. The remaining traces of the honey flavor are disappearing; the scent is vanishing; the color is changing; the original shape is disappearing. Its size is increasing; it is becoming liquid and hot; you can hardly touch it. And now, when you rap on it, it no longer emits any sound. Does the same wax still remain? I must confess that it does; no one denies it; no one thinks otherwise. So what was there in the wax that was so distinctly grasped? Certainly none of the aspects that I reached by means of the senses. For whatever came under the senses of taste, smell, sight, touch, or hearing has now changed; and yet the wax remains.

Perhaps the wax was what I now think it is: namely that the wax itself never really was the sweetness of the honey, nor the fragrance of the flowers, nor the whiteness, nor the shape, nor the sound, but instead was a body that a short time ago manifested itself to me in these ways, and now does so in other ways. But just what precisely is this thing that I thus imagine? Let us focus our attention on this and see what remains after we have removed everything that does not belong to the wax: only that it is something extended, flexible, and mutable. But what is it to be flexible and mutable? Is it what my imagination shows it to be: namely, that this piece of wax can change from a round to a square shape, or from the latter to a triangular shape? Not at all; for I grasp that the wax is capable of innumerable changes of this sort, even though I am incapable of running through these innumerable changes by using my imagination. Therefore this insight is not achieved by the faculty of imagination. What is it to be extended? Is this thing's extension also unknown? For it becomes greater in wax that is beginning to melt, greater in boiling wax, and greater still as the heat is increased. And I would not judge correctly what the wax is if I did not believe that it takes on an even greater variety of dimensions than I could ever grasp with the imagination. It remains then for me to concede that I do not grasp what this wax is through the imagination; rather, I perceive it through the mind alone. The point I am making refers to this particular piece of wax, for the case of wax in general is clearer still. But what is this piece of wax which is perceived only by the mind? Surely, it is the same piece of wax that I see, touch, and imagine; in short it is the same piece of wax I took it to be from the very beginning. But I need to realize that the perception of the wax is neither a seeing, nor a touching, nor an imagining. Nor has it ever been, even though it previously seemed so; rather it is an inspection on the part of the mind alone. This inspection can be imperfect and confused, as it was before, or clear and distinct, as it is now, depending on how closely I pay attention to the things in which the piece of wax consists.

But meanwhile I marvel at how prone my mind is to errors. For although I am considering these things within myself silently and without words, nevertheless I seize upon words themselves and I am nearly deceived by the ways in which people commonly speak. For we say that we see the wax itself, if it is present, and not that we judge it to be present from its color or shape. Whence I might conclude straightaway that I know the wax through the vision had by the eye, and not through an inspection on the part of the mind alone. But then were I perchance to look out my window and observe men crossing the square, I would ordinarily say I see the men themselves just as I say I see the wax. But what do I see aside from hats and clothes, which could conceal automata? Yet I judge them to be men. Thus what I thought I had seen with my eyes, I actually grasped solely with the faculty of judgment, which is in my mind.

But a person who seeks to know more than the common crowd ought to be ashamed of himself for looking for doubt in common ways of speaking. Let us then go forward, inquiring on when it was that I perceived more perfectly and evidently what the piece of wax was. Was it when I first saw it and believed I knew it by the external sense, or at least by the so-called "common" sense, that is, the power of imagination? Or do I have more perfect knowledge now, when I have diligently examined both what the wax is and how it is known? Surely, it is absurd to be in doubt about this matter. For what was there in my initial perception that was distinct? What was there that any animal seemed incapable of possessing? But indeed when I distinguish the wax from its external forms, as if stripping it of its clothing, and look at the wax in its nakedness, then, even though there can be still an error in my judgment, nevertheless I cannot perceive it thus without a human mind.

But what am I to say about this mind, that is, about myself? For as yet I admit nothing else to be in me over and above the mind. What, I ask, am I who seem to perceive this wax so distinctly? Do I not know myself not only much more truly and with greater certainty, but also much more distinctly and evidently? For if I judge that the wax exists from the fact that I see it, certainly from this same fact that I see the wax it follows much more evidently that I myself exist. For it could happen that what I see is not truly wax.

It could happen that I have no eyes with which to see anything. But it is utterly impossible that, while I see or think I see (I do not now distinguish these two), I who think am not something. Likewise, if I judge that the wax exists from the fact that I touch it, the same outcome will again obtain, namely that I exist. If I judge that the wax exists from the fact that I imagine it, or for any other reason, plainly the same thing follows. But what I note regarding the wax applies to everything else that is external to me. Furthermore, if my perception of the wax seemed more distinct after it became known to me not only on account of sight or touch, but on account of many reasons, one has to admit how much more distinctly I am now known to myself. For there is not a single consideration that can aid in my perception of the wax or of any other body that fails to make even more manifest the nature of my mind. But there are still so many other things in the mind itself on the basis of which my knowledge of it can be rendered more distinct that it hardly seems worth enumerating those things which emanate to it from the body.

But lo and behold, I have returned on my own to where I wanted to be. For since I now know that even bodies are not, properly speaking, perceived by the senses or by the faculty of imagination, but by the intellect alone, and that they are not perceived through their being touched or seen, but only through their being understood, I manifestly know that nothing can be perceived more easily and more evidently than my own mind. But since the tendency to hang on to long-held beliefs cannot be put aside so quickly, I want to stop here, so that by the length of my meditation this new knowledge may be more deeply impressed upon my memory.

## Meditation Three: Concerning God, That He Exists

I will now shut my eyes, stop up my ears, and withdraw all my senses. I will also blot out from my thoughts all images of corporeal things, or rather, since the latter is hardly possible, I will regard these images as empty, false, and worthless. And as I converse with myself alone and look more deeply into myself, I will attempt to render myself gradually better known and more familiar to myself. I am a thing that thinks, that is to say, a thing that doubts, affirms, denies, understands a few things, is ignorant of many things, wills, refrains from willing, and also imagines and senses. For as I observed earlier, even though these things that I sense or imagine may perhaps be nothing at all outside me, nevertheless I am certain that these modes of thinking, which are cases of what I call sensing and imagining, insofar as they are merely modes of thinking, do exist within me.

In these few words, I have reviewed everything I truly know, or at least what so far I have noticed that I know. Now I will ponder more carefully to see whether perhaps there may be other things belonging to me that up until now I have failed to notice. I am certain that I am a thinking thing. But do I not therefore also know what is required for me to be certain of anything? Surely in this first instance of knowledge, there is nothing but a certain clear and distinct perception of what I affirm. Yet this would hardly be enough to render me certain of the truth of a thing, if it could ever happen that something that I perceived so clearly and distinctly were false. And thus I now seem able to posit as a general rule that everything I very clearly and distinctly perceive is true.

Be that as it may, I have previously admitted many things as wholly certain and evident that nevertheless I later discovered to be doubtful. What sorts of things were these? Why, the earth, the sky, the stars, and all the other things I perceived by means of the senses. But what was it about these things that I clearly perceived? Surely the fact that the ideas or thoughts of these things were hovering before my mind. But even now I do not deny that these ideas are in me. Yet there was something else I used to affirm, which, owing to my habitual tendency to believe it, I used to think was something I clearly perceived, even though I actually did not perceive it all: namely, that certain things existed outside me, things from which those ideas proceeded and which those ideas completely resembled. But on this point I was mistaken; or, rather if my judgment was a true one, it was not the result of the force of my perception.

But what about when I considered something very simple and easy in the areas of arithmetic or geometry, for example that two plus three make five, and the like? Did I not intuit them at least clearly enough so as to affirm them as true? To be sure, I did decide later on that I must doubt these things, but that was only because it occurred to me that some God could perhaps have given me a nature such that I might be deceived even about matters that seemed most evident. But whenever this preconceived opinion about the supreme power of God occurs to me, I cannot help admitting that, were he to wish it, it would be easy for him to cause me to err even in those matters that I think I intuit as clearly as possible with the eyes of the mind. On the other hand, whenever I turn my attention to those very things that I think I perceive with such great clarity, I am so completely persuaded by them that I spontaneously blurt out these words: "let him who can deceive me; so long as I think that I am something, he will never bring it about that I am nothing. Nor will he one day make it true that I never existed, for it is true now that I do exist. Nor will he even bring it about that perhaps two plus three might equal more or less than five, or similar items in which I recognize an obvious contradiction." And certainly, because I have no reason for thinking that there is a God who is a deceiver (and of course I do not yet sufficiently know whether there even is a God), the basis for doubting, depending as it does merely on the above hypothesis, is very tenuous and, so to speak, metaphysical. But in order to remove even this basis for doubt, I should at the first opportunity inquire whether there is a God, and, if there is, whether or not he can be a deceiver. For if I am ignorant of this, it appears I am never capable of being completely certain about anything else.

However, at this stage good order seems to demand that I first group all my thoughts into certain classes, and ask in which of them truth or falsity properly resides. Some of these thoughts are like images of things; to these alone does the word "idea" properly apply, as when I think of a man, or a chimera, or the sky, or an angel, or God. Again there are other thoughts that take different forms, for example, when I will, or fear, or affirm, or deny, there is always some thing that I grasp as the subject of my thought, yet I embrace in my thought something more than the likeness of that

thing. Some of these thoughts are called volitions or affects, while others are called judgments.

Now as far as ideas are concerned, if they are considered alone and in their own right, without being referred to something else, they cannot, properly speaking, be false. For whether it is a she-goat or a chimera that I am imagining, it is no less true that I imagine the one than the other. Moreover, we need not fear that there is falsity in the will itself or in the affects, for although I can choose evil things or even things that are utterly nonexistent, I cannot conclude from this that it is untrue that I do choose these things. Thus there remain only judgments in which I must take care not to be mistaken. Now the principal and most frequent error to be found in judgments consists in the fact that I judge that the ideas which are in me are similar to or in conformity with certain things outside me. Obviously, if I were to consider these ideas merely as certain modes of my thought, and were not to refer them to anything else, they could hardly give me any subject matter for error.

Among these ideas, some appear to me to be innate, some adventitious, and some produced by me. For I understand what a thing is, what truth is, what thought is, and I appear to have derived this exclusively from my very own nature. But say I am now hearing a noise, or looking at the sun, or feeling the fire; up until now I judged that these things proceeded from certain things outside me, and finally, that sirens, hippogriffs, and the like are made by me. Or perhaps I can even think of all these ideas as being adventitious, or as being innate, or as fabrications, for I have not yet clearly ascertained their true origin.

But here I must inquire particularly into those ideas that I believe to be derived from things existing outside me. Just what reason do I have for believing that these ideas resemble those things? Well, I do seem to have been so taught by nature. Moreover, I do know from experience that these ideas do not depend upon my will, nor consequently upon myself, for I often notice them even against my will. Now, for example, whether or not I will it, I feel heat. It is for this reason that I believe this feeling or idea of heat comes to me from something other than myself, namely from heat of the fire by which I am sitting.

Nothing is more obvious than the judgment that this thing is sending its likeness rather than something else into me.

I will now see whether these reasons are powerful enough. When I say here "I have been so taught by nature," all I have in mind is that I am driven by a spontaneous impulse to believe this, and not that some light of nature is showing me that it is true. These are two very different things. For whatever is shown me by this light of nature, for example, that from the fact that I doubt, it follows that I am, and the like, cannot in any way be doubtful. This is owing to the fact that there can be no other faculty that I can trust as much as this light and which could teach that these things are not true. But as far as natural impulses are concerned, in the past I have often judged myself to have been driven by them to make the poorer choice when it was a question of choosing a good; and I fail to see why I should place any greater faith in them in other matters.

Again, although these ideas do not depend upon my will, it does not follow that they necessarily proceed from things existing outside me. For just as these impulses about which I spoke just now seem to be different from my will, even though they are in me, so too perhaps there is also in me some other faculty, one not yet sufficiently known to me, which produces these ideas, just as it has always seemed up to now that ideas are formed in me without any help from external things when I am asleep.

And finally, even if these ideas did proceed from things other than myself, it does not therefore follow that they must resemble those things. Indeed it seems I have frequently noticed a vast difference in many respects. For example, I find within myself two distinct ideas of the sun. One idea is drawn, as it were, from the senses. Now it is this idea which, of all those that I take to be derived from outside me, is most in need of examination. By means of this idea the sun appears to me to be quite small. But there is another idea, one derived from astronomical reasoning, that is, it is elicited from certain notions that are innate in me, or else is fashioned by me in some other way. Through this idea the sun is shown to be several times larger than the earth. Both ideas surely cannot resemble the same sun existing outside me; and reason convinces me that the idea that seems to have emanated from the sun itself from so close is the very one that least resembles the sun.

All these points demonstrate sufficiently that up to this point it was not a well-founded judgment, but only a blind impulse that formed the basis of my belief that things existing outside me send ideas or images of themselves to me through the sense organs or by some other means.

But still another way occurs to me for inquiring whether some of the things of which there are ideas in me do exist outside me: insofar as these ideas are merely modes of thought, I see no inequality among them; they all seem to proceed from me in the same manner. But insofar as one idea represents one thing and another idea another thing, it is obvious that they do differ very greatly from one another. Unquestionably, those ideas that display substances to me are something more and, if I may say so, contain within themselves more objective reality than those which represent only modes or accidents. Again, the idea that enables me to understand a supreme deity, eternal, infinite, omniscient, omnipotent, and creator of all things other than himself, clearly has more objective reality within it than do those ideas through which finite substances are displayed.

Now it is indeed evident by the light of nature that there must be at least as much [reality] in the efficient and total cause as there is in the effect of that same cause. For whence, I ask, could an effect get its reality, if not from its cause? And how could the cause give that reality to the effect, unless it also possessed that reality? Hence it follows that something cannot come into being out of nothing, and also that what is more perfect (that is, what contains in itself more reality) cannot come into being from what is less perfect. But this is manifestly true not merely for those effects whose reality is actual or formal, but also for ideas in which only objective reality is considered. For example, not only can a stone which did not exist previously not now begin to exist unless it is produced by something in which there is, either formally or eminently, everything that is in the stone; nor heat be introduced into a subject which was not already hot unless it is done by something that is of at least as perfect an order as heat—and the same for the rest—but it is also true that there can be in me no idea of heat, or of a stone, unless it is placed in me by some cause that has at least as much reality as I conceive to be in the heat or in the stone. For although this cause conveys none of its actual or formal reality to my idea, it should not be thought for that reason that it must be less real. Rather, the very nature of an idea is such that of itself it needs no formal reality other than what it borrows from my thought, of which it is a mode. But that a particular idea contains this as opposed to that objective reality is surely owing to some cause in which there is at least as much formal reality as there is objective reality contained in the idea. For if we assume that something is found in the idea that was not in its cause, then the idea gets that something from nothing. Yet as imperfect a mode of being as this is by which a thing exists in the intellect objectively through an idea, nevertheless it is plainly not nothing; hence it cannot get its being from nothing.

Moreover, even though the reality that I am considering in my ideas is merely objective reality, I ought not on that account to suspect that there is no need for the same reality to be formally in the causes of these ideas, but that it suffices for it to be in them objectively. For just as the objective mode of being belongs to ideas by their very nature, so the formal mode of being belongs to the causes of ideas, at least to the first and preeminent ones, by their very nature. And although one idea can perhaps issue from another, nevertheless no infinite regress is permitted here; eventually some first idea must be reached whose cause is a sort of archetype that contains formally all the reality that is in the idea merely objectively. Thus it is clear to me by the light of nature that the ideas that are in me are like images that can easily fail to match the perfection of the things from which they have been drawn, but which can contain nothing greater or more perfect.

And the longer and more attentively I examine all these points, the more clearly and distinctly I know they are true. But what am I ultimately to conclude? If the objective reality of any of my ideas is found

to be so great that I am certain that the same reality was not in me, either formally or eminently, and that therefore I myself cannot be the cause of the idea, then it necessarily follows that I am not alone in the world, but that something else, which is the cause of this idea, also exists. But if no such idea is found in me, I will have no argument whatsoever to make me certain of the existence of anything other than myself, for I have conscientiously reviewed all these arguments, and so far I have been unable to find any other.

Among my ideas, in addition to the one that displays me to myself (about which there can be no difficulty at this point), are others that represent God, corporeal and inanimate things, angels, animals, and finally other men like myself.

As to the ideas that display other men, or animals, or angels, I easily understand that they could be fashioned from the ideas that I have of myself, of corporeal things, and of God—even if no men (except myself), no animals, and no angels existed in the world.

As to the ideas of corporeal things, there is nothing in them that is so great that it seems incapable of having originated from me. For if I investigate them thoroughly and examine each one individually in the way I examined the idea of wax yesterday, I notice that there are only a very few things in them that I perceive clearly and distinctly: namely, size, or extension in length, breadth, and depth; shape, which arises from the limits of this extension; position, which various things possessing shape have in relation to one another; and motion, or alteration in position. To these can be added substance, duration, and number. But as for the remaining items, such as light and colors, sounds, odors, tastes, heat and cold and other tactile qualities, I think of these only in a very confused and obscure manner, to the extent that I do not even know whether they are true or false, that is, whether the ideas I have of them are ideas of things or ideas of non-things. For although a short time ago I noted that falsity properly so called (or "formal" falsity) is to be found only in judgments, nevertheless there is another kind of falsity (called "material" falsity) which is found in ideas whenever they represent a non-thing as if it were a thing. For example, the ideas I have of heat and cold fall so far short of being clear and distinct that I cannot tell from them whether cold is merely the privation of heat or whether heat is the privation of cold, or whether both are real qualities, or whether neither is. And because ideas can only be, as it were, of things, if it is true that cold is merely the absence of heat, then an idea that represents cold to me as something real and positive will not inappropriately be called false. The same holds for other similar ideas.

Assuredly, I need not assign to these ideas an author distinct from myself. For if they were false, that is, if they were to represent non-things, I know by the light of nature that they proceed from nothing; that is, they are in me for no other reason than that something is lacking in my nature, and that my nature is not entirely perfect. If, on the other hand, these ideas are true, then because they exhibit so little reality to me that I cannot distinguish it from a non-thing, I see no reason why they cannot get their being from me.

As for what is clear and distinct in the ideas of corporeal things, it appears I could have borrowed some of these from the idea of myself: namely, substance, duration, number, and whatever else there may be of this type. For instance, I think that a stone is a substance, that is to say, a thing that is suitable for existing in itself; and likewise I think that I too am a substance. Despite the fact that I conceive myself to be a thinking thing and not an extended thing, whereas I conceive of a stone as an extended thing and not a thinking thing, and hence there is the greatest diversity between these two concepts, nevertheless they seem to agree with one another when considered under the rubric of substance. Furthermore, I perceive that I now exist and recall that I have previously existed for some time. And I have various thoughts and know how many of them there are. It is in doing these things that I acquire the ideas of duration and number, which I can then apply to other things. However, none of the other components out of which the ideas of corporeal things are fashioned (namely extension, shape, position, and motion) are contained in me formally, since I am merely a thinking thing. But since these are only certain modes of a substance, whereas I am a substance, it seems possible that they are contained in me eminently.

Thus there remains only the idea of God. I must consider whether there is anything in this idea that could not have originated from me. I understand by the name "God" a certain substance that is infinite, independent, supremely intelligent, and supremely powerful, and that created me along with everything else that exists—if anything else exists. Indeed all these are such that, the more carefully I focus my attention on them, the less possible it seems they could have arisen from myself alone. Thus, from what has been said, I must conclude that God necessarily exists.

For although the idea of substance is in me by virtue of the fact that I am a substance, that fact is not sufficient to explain my having the idea of an infinite substance, since I am finite, unless this idea proceeded from some substance which really was infinite.

Nor should I think that I do not perceive the infinite by means of a true idea, but only through a negation of the finite, just as I perceive rest and darkness by means of a negation of motion and light. On the contrary, I clearly understand that there is more reality in an infinite substance than there is in a finite one. Thus the perception of the infinite is somehow prior in me to the perception of the finite; that is, my perception of God is prior to my perception of myself. For how would I understand that I doubt and that I desire, that is, that I lack something and that I am not wholly perfect, unless there were some idea in me of a more perfect being, by comparison with which I might recognize my defects?

Nor can it be said that this idea of God is perhaps materially false and thus can originate from nothing, as I remarked just now about the ideas of heat and cold, and the like. On the contrary, because it is the most clear and distinct and because it contains more objective reality than any other idea, no idea is in and of itself truer and has less of a basis for being suspected of falsehood. I maintain that this idea of a being that is supremely perfect and infinite is true in the highest degree. For although I could perhaps pretend that such a being does not exist, nevertheless I could not pretend that the idea of such a being discloses to me nothing real, as was the case with the idea of cold which I referred to earlier. It is indeed an idea that is utterly clear and distinct; for whatever I clearly and distinctly perceive to be real and true and to involve some perfection is wholly contained in that idea. It is no objection that I do not comprehend the infinite or that there are countless other things in God that I can in no way either comprehend or perhaps even touch with my thought. For the nature of the infinite is such that it is not comprehended by a being such as I, who am finite. And it is sufficient that I understand this very point and judge that all those things that I clearly perceive and that I know to contain some perfection—and perhaps even countless other things of which I am ignorant—are in God either formally or eminently. The result is that, of all the ideas that are in me, the idea that I have of God is the most true, the most clear and distinct.

But perhaps I am something greater than I myself understand. Perhaps all these perfections that I am attributing to God are somehow in me potentially, although they do not yet assert themselves and are not yet actualized. For I now observe that my knowledge is gradually being increased, and I see nothing standing in the way of its being increased more and more to infinity. Moreover, I see no reason why, with my knowledge thus increased, I could not acquire all the remaining perfections of God. And, finally, if the potential for these perfections is in me already, I see no reason why this potential would not suffice to produce the idea of these perfections.

Yet none of these things can be the case. First, while it is true that my knowledge is gradually being increased and that there are many things in me potentially that are not yet actual, nevertheless, none of these pertains to the idea of God, in which there is nothing whatever that is potential. Indeed this gradual increase is itself a most certain proof of imperfection. Moreover, although my knowledge may always increase more and more, nevertheless I understand that this knowledge will never by this means be actually infinite, because it will never reach a point where it is incapable of greater increase. On the contrary, I judge God to be actually infinite, so that nothing can be added to his perfection. Finally, I perceive that the objective being of an idea cannot be produced by a merely potential being (which, strictly speaking, is nothing), but only by an actual or formal being.

Indeed there is nothing in all these things that is not manifest by the light of nature to one who is conscientious and attentive. But when I am less attentive, and the images of sensible things blind the mind's eye, I do not so easily recall why the idea of a being more perfect than me necessarily proceeds from a being that really is more perfect. This being the case, it is appropriate to ask further whether I myself who have this idea could exist, if such a being did not exist.

From what source, then, do I derive my existence? Why, from myself, or from my parents, or from whatever other things there are that are less perfect than God. For nothing more perfect than God, or even as perfect as God, can be thought or imagined.

But if I got my being from myself, I would not doubt, nor would I desire, nor would I lack anything at all. For I would have given myself all the perfections of which I have some idea; in so doing, I myself would be God! I must not think that the things I lack could perhaps be more difficult to acquire than the ones I have now. On the contrary, it is obvious that it would have been much more difficult for me (that is, a thing or substance that thinks) to emerge out of nothing than it would be to acquire the knowledge of many things about which I am ignorant (these items of knowledge being merely accidents of that substance). Certainly, if I got this greater thing from myself, I would not have denied myself at least those things that can be had more easily. Nor would I have denied myself any of those other things that I perceive to be contained in the idea of God, for surely none of them seem to me more difficult to bring about. But if any of them were more difficult to bring about, they would certainly also seem more difficult to me, even if the remaining ones that I possess I got from myself, since it would be on account of them that I would experience that my power is limited.

Nor am I avoiding the force of these arguments, if I suppose that perhaps I have always existed as I do now, as if it then followed that no author of my existence need be sought. For because the entire span of one's life can be divided into countless parts, each one wholly independent of the rest, it does not follow from the fact that I existed a short time ago that I must exist now, unless some cause, as it were, creates me all over again at this moment, that is to say, which preserves me. For it is obvious to one who pays close attention to the nature of time that plainly the same force and action are needed to preserve anything at each individual moment that it lasts as would be required to create that same thing anew, were it not yet in existence. Thus conservation differs from creation solely by virtue of a distinction of reason; this too is one of those things that are manifest by the light of nature.

Therefore, I must now ask myself whether I possess some power by which I can bring it about that I myself, who now exist, will also exist a little later on. For since I am nothing but a thinking thing—or at least since I am now dealing simply and precisely with that part of me which is a thinking thing—if such a power were in me, then I would certainly be aware of it. But I observe that there is no such power; and from this very fact I know most clearly that I depend upon some being other than myself.

But perhaps this being is not God, and I have been produced either by my parents or by some other causes less perfect than God. On the contrary, as I said before, it is obvious that there must be at least as much in the cause as there is in the effect. Thus, regardless of what it is that eventually is assigned as my cause, because I am a thinking thing and have within me a certain idea of God, it must be granted that what caused me is also a thinking thing and it too has an idea of all the perfections which I attribute to God. And I can again inquire of this cause whether it got its existence from itself or from another cause. For if it got its existence from itself, it is evident from what has been said that it is itself God, because, having the power of existing in and of itself, it unquestionably also has the power of actually possessing all the perfections of which it has in itself an idea—that is, all the perfections that I conceive to be in God. However, if it got its existence from another cause, I will once again inquire in similar fashion about this other cause: whether it got its existence from itself or from another cause, until finally I arrive at the ultimate cause, which will be God. For it is apparent enough that there can be no infinite regress here, especially since I am not dealing here merely with the cause

that once produced me, but also and most especially with the cause that preserves me at the present time.

Nor can one fancy that perhaps several partial causes have concurred in bringing me into being, and that I have taken the ideas of the various perfections I attribute to God from a variety of causes, so that all of these perfections are found somewhere in the universe, but not all joined together in a single being—God. On the contrary, the unity, the simplicity, that is, the inseparability of all those features that are in God is one of the chief perfections that I understand to be in him. Certainly the idea of the unity of all his perfections could not have been placed in me by any cause from which I did not also get the ideas of the other perfections; for neither could some cause have made me understand them joined together and inseparable from one another, unless it also caused me to recognize what they were.

Finally, as to my parents, even if everything that I ever believed about them were true, still it is certainly not they who preserve me; nor is it they who in any way brought me into being, insofar as I am a thinking thing. Rather, they merely placed certain dispositions in the matter which I judged to contain me, that is, a mind, which now is the only thing I take myself to be. And thus there can be no difficulty here concerning my parents. Indeed I have no choice but to conclude that the mere fact of my existing and of there being in me an idea of a most perfect being, that is, God, demonstrates most evidently that God too exists.

All that remains for me is to ask how I received this idea of God. For I did not draw it from the senses; it never came upon me unexpectedly, as is usually the case with the ideas of sensible things when these things present themselves (or seem to present themselves) to the external sense organs. Nor was it made by me, for I plainly can neither subtract anything from it nor add anything to it. Thus the only option remaining is that this idea is innate in me, just as the idea of myself is innate in me.

To be sure, it is not astonishing that in creating me, God should have endowed me with this idea, so that it would be like the mark of the craftsman impressed upon his work, although this mark need not be something distinct from the work itself. But the mere fact that God created me makes it highly plausible that I have somehow been made in his image and likeness, and that I perceive this likeness, in which the idea of God is contained by means of the same faculty by which I perceive myself. That is, when I turn the mind's eye toward myself, I understand not only ... depend ... upon ... it ... ter ... ng ... er ... ut ... y ... and ... The ... force ... the argument rests on the fact that I recognize that it would be impossible for me to exist, being of such a nature as I am (namely, having in me the idea of God), unless God did in fact exist. God, I say, that same being the idea of whom is in me: a being having all those perfections that I cannot comprehend, but can somehow touch with my thought, and a being subject to no defects whatever. From these considerations it is quite obvious that he cannot be a deceiver, for it is manifest by the light of nature that all fraud and deception depend on some defect.

But before examining this idea more closely and at the same time inquiring into other truths that can be gathered from it, at this point I want to spend some time contemplating this God, to ponder his attributes and, so far as the eye of my darkened mind can take me, to gaze upon, to admire, and to adore the beauty of this immense light. For just as we believe by faith that the greatest felicity of the next life consists solely in this contemplation of the divine majesty, so too we now experience that from the same contemplation, although it is much less perfect, the greatest pleasure of which we are capable in this life can be perceived.

## Meditation Four: Concerning the True and the False

Lately I have become accustomed to withdrawing my mind from the senses, and I have carefully taken note of the fact that very few things are truly perceived regarding corporeal things, although a great many more things are known regarding the human mind, and still many more things regarding God.

The upshot is that I now have no difficulty directing my thought away from things that can be imagined to things that can be grasped only by the understanding and are wholly separate from matter. In fact the idea I clearly have of the human mind—insofar as it is a thinking thing, not extended in length, breadth or depth, and having nothing else from the body—is far more distinct than the idea of any corporeal thing. And when I take note of the fact that I doubt, or that I am a thing that is incomplete and dependent, there comes to mind a clear and distinct idea of a being that is independent and complete, that is, an idea of God. And from the mere fact that such an idea is in me, or that I who have this idea exist, I draw the obvious conclusion that God also exists, and that my existence depends entirely upon him at each and every moment. This conclusion is so obvious that I am confident that the human mind can know nothing more evident or more certain. And now I seem to see a way by which I might progress from this contemplation of the true God, in whom, namely, are hidden all the treasures of the sciences and wisdom, to the knowledge of other things.

To begin with, I acknowledge that it is impossible for God ever to deceive me, for trickery or deception are always indicative of some imperfection. And although the ability to deceive seems to be an indication of cleverness or power, the will to deceive undoubtedly attests to maliciousness or weakness. Accordingly, deception is incompatible with God.

Next I experience that there is in me a certain faculty of judgment, which, like everything else that is in me, I undoubtedly received from God. And since he does not wish to deceive me, he assuredly has not given me the sort of faculty with which I could ever make a mistake, when I use it properly.

No doubt regarding this matter would remain, but for the fact that it seems to follow from this that I am never capable of making a mistake. For if everything that is in me I got from God, and he gave me no faculty for making mistakes, it seems I am incapable of ever erring. And thus, so long as I think exclusively about God and focus my attention exclusively on him, I discern no cause of error or falsity. But once I turn my attention back on myself, I nevertheless experience that I am subject to countless errors. As I seek a cause of these errors, I notice that passing before me is not only a real and positive idea of God (that is, of a supremely perfect being), but also, as it were, a certain negative idea of nothingness (that is, of what is at the greatest possible distance from any perfection), and that I have been so constituted as a kind of middle ground between God and nothingness, or between the supreme being and non-being. Thus insofar as I have been created by the supreme being, there is nothing in me by means of which I might be deceived or be led into error; but insofar as I participate in nothingness or non-being, that is, insofar as I am not the supreme being and lack a great many things, it is not surprising that I make mistakes. Thus I certainly understand that error as such is not something real that depends upon God, but rather is merely a defect. And thus there is no need to account for my errors by positing a faculty given to me by God for the purpose. Rather, it just so happens that I make mistakes because the faculty of judging the truth, which I got from God, is not, in my case, infinite.

Still this is not yet altogether satisfactory; for error is not a pure negation, but rather a privation or a lack of some knowledge that somehow ought to be in me. And when I attend to the nature of God, it seems impossible that he would have placed in me a faculty that is not perfect in its kind or that is lacking some perfection it ought to have. For if it is true that the more expert the craftsman, the more perfect the works he produces, what can that supreme creator of all things make that is not perfect in all respects? No doubt God could have created me such that I never erred. No doubt, again, God always wills what is best. Is it then better that I should be in error rather than not?

As I mull these things over more carefully, it occurs to me first that there is no reason to marvel at the fact that God should bring about certain things the reasons for which I do not understand. Nor is his existence therefore to be doubted because I happen to experience other things of which I fail to grasp why and how he made them. For since I know now that my nature is very weak and limited, whereas the nature of God is immense, incomprehensible, and

infinite, this is sufficient for me also to know that he can make innumerable things whose causes escape me. For this reason alone the entire class of causes which people customarily derive from a thing's "end," I judge to be utterly useless in physics. It is not without rashness that I think myself capable of inquiring into the ends of God.

It also occurs to me that whenever we ask whether the works of God are perfect, we should keep in view not simply some one creature in isolation from the rest, but the universe as a whole. For perhaps something might rightfully appear very imperfect if it were all by itself; and yet be most perfect, to the extent that it has the status of a part in the universe. And although subsequent to having decided to doubt everything, I have come to know with certainty only that I and God exist, nevertheless, after having taken note of the immense power of God, I cannot deny that many other things have been made by him, or at least could have been made by him. Thus I may have the status of a part in the universal scheme of things.

Next, as I focus more closely on myself and inquire into the nature of my errors (the only things that are indicative of some imperfection in me), I note that these errors depend on the simultaneous concurrence of two causes: the faculty of knowing that is in me and the faculty of choosing, that is, the free choice of the will, in other words, simultaneously on the intellect and will. Through the intellect alone I merely perceive ideas, about which I can render a judgment. Strictly speaking, no error is to be found in the intellect when properly viewed in this manner. For although perhaps there may exist countless things about which I have no idea, nevertheless it must not be said that, strictly speaking, I am deprived of these ideas but only that I lack them in a negative sense. This is because I cannot adduce an argument to prove that God ought to have given me a greater faculty of knowing than he did. No matter how expert a craftsman I understand him to be, still I do not for that reason believe he ought to have bestowed on each one of his works all the perfections that he can put into some. Nor, on the other hand, can I complain that the will or free choice I have received from God is insufficiently ample or perfect, since I experience that it is limited by no boundaries whatever. In fact, it seems to be especially worth noting that no other things in me are so perfect or so great but that I understand that they can be still more perfect or greater. If, for example, I consider the faculty of understanding, I immediately recognize that in my case it is very small and quite limited, and at the very same time I form an idea of another much greater faculty of understanding—in fact, an understanding which is consummately great and infinite; and from the fact that I can form an idea of this faculty, I perceive that it pertains to the nature of God. Similarly, were I to examine the faculties of memory or imagination, or any of the other faculties, I would understand that in my case each of these is without exception feeble and limited, whereas in the case of God I understand each faculty to be boundless. It is only the will or free choice that I experience to be so great in me that I cannot grasp the idea of any greater faculty. This is so much the case that the will is the chief basis for my understanding that I bear a certain image and likeness of God. For although the faculty of willing is incomparably greater in God than it is in me, both by virtue of the knowledge and power that are joined to it and that render it more resolute and efficacious and by virtue of its object inasmuch as the divine will stretches over a greater number of things, nevertheless, when viewed in itself formally and precisely, God's faculty of willing does not appear to be any greater. This is owing to the fact that willing is merely a matter of being able to do or not do the same thing, that is, of being able to affirm or deny, to pursue or to shun; or better still, the will consists solely in the fact that when something is proposed to us by our intellect either to affirm or deny, to pursue or to shun, we are moved in such a way that we sense that we are determined to it by no external force. In order to be free I need not be capable of being moved in each direction; on the contrary, the more I am inclined toward one direction—either because I clearly understand that there is in it an aspect of the good and the true, or because God has thus disposed the inner recesses of my thought—the more freely do I choose that direction. Nor indeed does divine grace or natural knowledge ever diminish one's freedom;

rather, they increase and strengthen it. However, the indifference that I experience when there is no reason moving me more in one direction than in another is the lowest grade of freedom; it is indicative not of any perfection in freedom, but rather of a defect, that is, a certain negation in knowledge. Were I always to see clearly what is true and good, I would never deliberate about what is to be judged or chosen. In that event, although I would be entirely free, I could never be indifferent.

But from these considerations I perceive that the power of willing, which I got from God, is not, taken by itself, the cause of my errors, for it is most ample as well as perfect in its kind. Nor is my power of understanding the cause of my errors. For since I got my power of understanding from God, whatever I understand I doubtless understand rightly, and it is impossible for me to be deceived in this. What then is the source of my errors? They are owing simply to the fact that, since the will extends further than the intellect, I do not contain the will within the same boundaries; rather, I also extend it to things I do not understand. Because the will is indifferent in regard to such matters, it easily turns away from the true and the good; and in this way I am deceived and I sin.

For example, during these last few days I was examining whether anything in the world exists, and I noticed that, from the very fact that I was making this examination, it obviously followed that I exist. Nevertheless, I could not help judging that what I understood so clearly was true; not that I was coerced into making this judgment because of some external force, but because a great light in my intellect gave way to a great inclination in my will, and the less indifferent I was, the more spontaneously and freely did I believe it. But now, in addition to my knowing that I exist, insofar as I am a certain thinking thing, I also observe a certain idea of corporeal nature. It happens that I am in doubt as to whether the thinking nature which is in me, or rather which I am, is something different from this corporeal nature, or whether both natures are one and the same thing. And I assume that as yet no consideration has occurred to my intellect to convince me of the one alternative rather than the other. Certainly in virtue of this very fact I am indifferent about whether to affirm or to deny either alternative, or even whether to make no judgment at all in the matter.

Moreover, this indifference extends not merely to things about which the intellect knows absolutely nothing, but extends generally to everything of which the intellect does not have a clear enough knowledge at the very time when the will is deliberating on them. For although probable guesses may pull me in one direction, the mere knowledge that they are merely guesses and not certain and indubitable proofs is all it takes to push my assent in the opposite direction. These last few days have provided me with ample experience on this point. For all the beliefs that I had once held to be most true I have supposed to be utterly false, and for the sole reason that I determined that I could somehow raise doubts about them.

But if I hold off from making a judgment when I do not perceive what is true with sufficient clarity and distinctness, it is clear that I am acting properly and am not committing an error. But if instead I were to make an assertion or a denial, then I am not using my freedom properly. Were I to select the alternative that is false, then obviously I will be in error. But were I to embrace the other alternative, it will be by sheer luck that I happen upon the truth; but I will still not be without fault, for it is manifest by the light of nature that a perception on the part of the intellect must always precede a determination on the part of the will. Inherent in this incorrect use of free will is the privation that constitutes the very essence of error: the privation, I say, present in this operation insofar as the operation proceeds from me, but not in the faculty given to me by God, nor even in its operation insofar as it depends upon him.

Indeed I have no cause for complaint on the grounds that God has not given me a greater power of understanding or a greater light of nature than he has, for it is of the essence of a finite intellect not to understand many things, and it is of the essence of a created intellect to be finite. Actually, instead of thinking that he has withheld from me or deprived me of those things that he has not given me, I ought to thank God, who never owed me anything, for what he has bestowed upon me.

Again, I have no cause for complaint on the grounds that God has given me a will that has a wider scope than my intellect. For since the will consists of merely one thing, something indivisible, as it were, it does not seem that its nature could withstand anything being removed from it. Indeed, the more ample the will is, the more I ought to thank the one who gave it to me.

Finally, I should not complain because God concurs with me in eliciting those acts of the will, that is those judgments, in which I am mistaken. For insofar as those acts depend on God, they are absolutely true and good; and in a certain sense, there is greater perfection in me in being able to elicit those acts than in not being able to do so. But privation, in which alone the defining characteristic of falsehood and wrongdoing is to be found, has no need whatever for God's concurrence, since a privation is not a thing, nor, when it is related to God as its cause, is it to be called a privation, but simply a negation. For it is surely no imperfection in God that he has given me the freedom to give or withhold my assent in those instances where he has not placed a clear and distinct perception in my intellect. But surely it is an imperfection in me that I do not use my freedom well and that I make judgments about things I do not properly understand. Nevertheless, I see that God could easily have brought it about that, while still being free and having finite knowledge, I should nonetheless never make a mistake. This result could have been achieved either by his endowing my intellect with a clear and distinct perception of everything about which I would ever deliberate, or by simply impressing the following rule so firmly upon my memory that I could never forget it: I should never judge anything that I do not clearly and distinctly understand. I readily understand that, considered as a totality, I would have been more perfect than I am now, had God made me that way. But I cannot therefore deny that it may somehow be a greater perfection in the universe as a whole that some of its parts are not immune to error, while others are, than if all of them were exactly alike. And I have no right to complain that the part God has wished me to play is not the principal and most perfect one of all.

Furthermore, even if I cannot abstain from errors in the first way mentioned above, which depends upon a clear perception of everything about which I must deliberate, nevertheless I can avoid error in the other way, which depends solely on my remembering to abstain from making judgments whenever the truth of a given matter is not apparent. For although I experience a certain infirmity in myself, namely that I am unable to keep my attention constantly focused on one and the same item of knowledge, nevertheless, by attentive and often repeated meditation, I can bring it about that I call this rule to mind whenever the situation calls for it, and thus I would acquire a certain habit of not erring.

Since herein lies the greatest and chief perfection of man, I think today's meditation, in which I investigated the cause of error and falsity, was quite profitable. Nor can this cause be anything other than the one I have described; for as often as I restrain my will when I make judgments, so that it extends only to those matters that the intellect clearly and distinctly discloses to it, it plainly cannot happen that I err. For every clear and distinct perception is surely something, and hence it cannot come from nothing. On the contrary, it must necessarily have God for its author: God, I say, that supremely perfect being to whom it is repugnant to be a deceiver. Therefore the perception is most assuredly true. Today I have learned not merely what I must avoid so as never to make a mistake, but at the same time what I must do to attain truth. For I will indeed attain it, if only I pay enough attention to all the things that I perfectly understand, and separate them off from the rest, which I apprehend more confusedly and more obscurely. I will be conscientious about this in the future.

## Meditation Five: Concerning the Essence of Material Things, and Again Concerning God, That He Exists

Several matters remain for me to examine concerning the attributes of God and myself, that is, concerning the nature of my mind. But perhaps I will take these up at some other time. For now, since I have noted what to avoid and what to do in order to attain

the truth, nothing seems more pressing than that I try to free myself from the doubts into which I fell a few days ago, and that I see whether anything certain is to be had concerning material things.

Yet, before inquiring whether any such things exist outside me, I surely ought to consider the ideas of these things, insofar as they exist in my thought, and see which ones are distinct and which ones are confused.

I do indeed distinctly imagine the quantity that philosophers commonly call "continuous," that is, the extension of this quantity, or rather of the thing quantified in length, breadth, and depth. I enumerate the various parts in it. I ascribe to these parts any sizes, shapes, positions, and local movements whatever; to these movements I ascribe any durations whatever.

Not only are these things manifestly known and transparent to me, viewed thus in a general way, but also, when I focus my attention on them, I perceive countless particulars concerning shapes, number, movement, and the like. Their truth is so open and so much in accord with my nature that, when I first discover them, it seems I am not so much learning something new as recalling something I knew beforehand. In other words, it seems as though I am noticing things for the first time that were in fact in me for a long while, although I had not previously directed a mental gaze upon them.

What I believe must be considered above all here is the fact that I find within me countless ideas of certain things, that, even if perhaps they do not exist anywhere outside me, still cannot be said to be nothing. And although, in a sense, I think them at will, nevertheless they are not something I have fabricated; rather they have their own true and immutable natures. For example, when I imagine a triangle, even if perhaps no such figure exists outside my thought anywhere in the world and never has, the triangle still has a certain determinate nature, essence, or form which is unchangeable and eternal, which I did not fabricate, and which does not depend on my mind. This is evident from the fact that various properties can be demonstrated regarding this triangle: namely, that its three angles are equal to two right angles, that its longest side is opposite its largest angle, and so on. These are properties I now clearly acknowledge, whether I want to or not, even if I previously had given them no thought whatever when I imagined the triangle. For this reason, then, they were not fabricated by me.

It is irrelevant for me to say that perhaps the idea of a triangle came to me from external things through the sense organs because of course I have on occasion seen triangle-shaped bodies. For I can think of countless other figures, concerning which there can be no suspicion of their ever having entered me through the senses, and yet I can demonstrate various properties of these figures, no less than I can those of the triangle. All these properties are patently true because I know them clearly, and thus they are something and not merely nothing. For it is obvious that whatever is true is something, and I have already demonstrated at some length that all that I know clearly is true. And even if I had not demonstrated this, certainly the nature of my mind is such that nevertheless I cannot refrain from assenting to these things, at least while I perceive them clearly. And I recall that even before now, when I used to keep my attention glued to the objects of the senses, I always took the truths I clearly recognized regarding figures, numbers, or other things pertaining to arithmetic, geometry or, in general, to pure and abstract mathematics to be the most certain of all.

But if, from the mere fact that I can bring forth from my thought the idea of something, it follows that all that I clearly and distinctly perceive to belong to that thing really does belong to it, then cannot this too be a basis for an argument proving the existence of God? Clearly the idea of God, that is, the idea of a supremely perfect being, is one I discover to be no less within me than the idea of any figure or number. And that it belongs to God's nature that he always exists is something I understand no less clearly and distinctly than is the case when I demonstrate in regard to some figure or number that something also belongs to the nature of that figure or number. Thus, even if not everything that I have meditated upon during these last few days were true, still the existence of God ought to have for me at least the same degree of certainty that truths of mathematics had until now.

However, this point is not wholly obvious at first glance, but has a certain look of a sophism about it. Since in all other matters I have become accustomed to distinguishing existence from essence, I easily convince myself that it can even be separated from God's essence, and hence that God can be thought of as not existing. But nevertheless, it is obvious to anyone who pays close attention that existence can no more be separated from God's essence than its having three angles equal to two right angles can be separated from the essence of a triangle, or than the idea of a valley can be separated from the idea of a mountain. Thus it is no less[2] contradictory to think of God (that is, a supremely perfect being) lacking existence (that is, lacking some perfection) than it is to think of a mountain without a valley.

But granted I can no more think of God as not existing than I can think of a mountain without a valley; nevertheless it surely does not follow from the fact that I think of a mountain with a valley that a mountain exists in the world. Likewise, from the fact that I think of God as existing, it does not seem to follow that God exists, for my thought imposes no necessity on things. And just as one may imagine a winged horse, without there being a horse that has wings, in the same way perhaps I can attach existence to God, even though no God exists.

But there is a sophism lurking here. From the fact that I am unable to think of a mountain without a valley, it does not follow that a mountain or a valley exists anywhere, but only that, whether they exist or not, a mountain and a valley are inseparable from one another. But from the fact that I cannot think of God except as existing, it follows that existence is inseparable from God, and that for this reason he really exists. Not that my thought brings this about or imposes any necessity on anything; but rather the necessity of the thing itself, namely of the existence of God, forces me to think this. For I am not free to think of God without existence, that is, a supremely

---

2. A literal translation of the Latin text (*non magis*) is "no more." This is obviously a misstatement on Descartes' part, since it contradicts his own clearly stated views.

perfect being without a supreme perfection, as I am to imagine a horse with or without wings.

Further, it should not be said here that even though I surely need to assent to the existence of God once I have asserted that God has all perfections and that existence is one of these perfections, nevertheless that earlier assertion need not have been made. Likewise, I need not believe that all four-sided figures can be inscribed in a circle; but given that I posit this, it would then be necessary for me to admit that a rhombus can be inscribed in a circle. Yet this is obviously false. For although it is not necessary that I should ever happen upon any thought of God, nevertheless whenever I am of a mind to think of a being that is first and supreme, and bring forth the idea of God as it were from the storehouse of my mind, I must of necessity ascribe all perfections to him, even if I do not at that time enumerate them all or take notice of each one individually. This necessity plainly suffices so that afterwards, when I realize that existence is a perfection, I rightly conclude that a first and supreme being exists. In the same way, there is no necessity for me ever to imagine a triangle, but whenever I do wish to consider a rectilinear figure having but three angles, I must ascribe to it those properties on the basis of which one rightly infers that the three angles of this figure are no greater than two right angles, even though I do not take note of this at the time. But when I inquire as to the figures that may be inscribed in a circle, there is absolutely no need whatever for my thinking that all four-sided figures are of this sort; for that matter, I cannot even fabricate such a thing, so long as I am of a mind to admit only what I clearly and distinctly understand. Consequently, there is a great difference between false assumptions of this sort and the true ideas that are inborn in me, the first and chief of which is the idea of God. For there are a great many ways in which I understand that this idea is not an invention that is dependent upon my thought, but is an image of a true and immutable nature. First, I cannot think of anything aside from God alone to whose essence existence belongs. Next, I cannot understand how there could be two or more Gods of this kind. Again, once I have asserted that one God now exists, I plainly see that it is necessary

that he has existed from eternity and will endure for eternity. Finally, I perceive many other features in God, none of which I can remove or change.

But, whatever type of argument I use, it always comes down to the fact that the only things that fully convince me are those that I clearly and distinctly perceive. And although some of these things I thus perceive are obvious to everyone, while others are discovered only by those who look more closely and inquire carefully, nevertheless, once they have been discovered, they are considered no less certain than the others. For example, in the case of a right triangle, although it is not so readily apparent that the square of the hypotenuse is equal to the sum of the squares of the other two sides as it is that the hypotenuse is opposite the largest angle, nevertheless, once the former has been ascertained, it is no less believed. However, as far as God is concerned, if I were not overwhelmed by prejudices and if the images of sensible things were not besieging my thought from all directions, I would certainly acknowledge nothing sooner or more easily than him. For what, in and of itself, is more manifest than that a supreme being exists, that is, that God, to whose essence alone existence belongs, exists?

And although I needed to pay close attention in order to perceive this, nevertheless I now am just as certain about this as I am about everything else that seems most certain. Moreover, I observe also that certitude about other things is so dependent on this, that without it nothing can ever be perfectly known.

For I am indeed of such a nature that, while I perceive something very clearly and distinctly, I cannot help believing it to be true. Nevertheless, my nature is also such that I cannot focus my mental gaze always on the same thing, so as to perceive it clearly. Often the memory of a previously made judgment may return when I am no longer attending to the arguments on account of which I made such a judgment. Thus, other arguments can be brought forward that would easily make me change my opinion, were I ignorant of God. And thus I would never have true and certain knowledge about anything, but merely fickle and changeable opinions. Thus, for example, when I consider the nature of a triangle, it appears most evident to me, steeped as I am in the principles of geometry, that its three angles are equal to two right angles. And so long as I attend to its demonstration I cannot help believing this to be true. But no sooner do I turn the mind's eye away from the demonstration, than, however much I still recall that I had observed it most clearly, nevertheless, it can easily happen that I entertain doubts about whether it is true, were I ignorant of God. For I can convince myself that I have been so constituted by nature that I might occasionally be mistaken about those things I believe I perceive most evidently, especially when I recall that I have often taken many things to be true and certain, which other arguments have subsequently led me to judge to be false.

But once I perceived that there is a God, and also understood at the same time that everything else depends on him, and that he is not a deceiver, I then concluded that everything that I clearly and distinctly perceive is necessarily true. Hence even if I no longer attend to the reasons leading me to judge this to be true, so long as I merely recall that I did clearly and distinctly observe it, no counterargument can be brought forward that might force me to doubt it. On the contrary, I have a true and certain knowledge of it. And not just of this one fact, but of everything else that I recall once having demonstrated, as in geometry, and so on. For what objections can now be raised against me? That I have been made such that I am often mistaken? But I now know that I cannot be mistaken in matters I plainly understand. That I have taken many things to be true and certain which subsequently I recognized to be false? But none of these were things I clearly and distinctly perceived. But I was ignorant of this rule for determining the truth, and I believed these things perhaps for other reasons which I later discovered were less firm. What then remains to be said? That perhaps I am dreaming, as I recently objected against myself, in other words, that everything I am now thinking of is no truer than what occurs to someone who is asleep? Be that as it may, this changes nothing; for certainly, even if I were dreaming, if anything is evident to my intellect, then it is entirely true.

And thus I see plainly that the certainty and truth of every science depends exclusively upon the knowledge of the true God, to the extent that, prior to my becoming aware of him, I was incapable of achieving perfect knowledge about anything else. But now it is possible for me to achieve full and certain knowledge about countless things, both about God and other intellectual matters, as well as about the entirety of that corporeal nature which is the object of pure mathematics.

## Meditation Six: Concerning the Existence of Material Things, and the Real Distinction between Mind and Body

It remains for me to examine whether material things exist. Indeed I now know that they can exist, at least insofar as they are the object of pure mathematics, since I clearly and distinctly perceive them. For no doubt God is capable of bringing about everything that I am capable of perceiving in this way. And I have never judged that God was incapable of something, except when it was incompatible with my perceiving it distinctly. Moreover, from the faculty of imagination, which I notice I use while dealing with material things, it seems to follow that they exist. For to anyone paying very close attention to what imagination is, it appears to be simply a certain application of the knowing faculty to a body intimately present to it, and which therefore exists.

To make this clear, I first examine the difference between imagination and pure intellection. So, for example, when I imagine a triangle, I not only understand that it is a figure bounded by three lines, but at the same time I also envisage with the mind's eye those lines as if they were present; and this is what I call "imagining." On the other hand, if I want to think about a chiliagon, I certainly understand that it is a figure consisting of a thousand sides, just as well as I understand that a triangle is a figure consisting of three sides, yet I do not imagine those thousand sides in the same way, or envisage them as if they were present. And although in that case, because of force of habit I always imagine something whenever I think about a corporeal thing, I may perchance represent to myself some figure in a confused fashion, nevertheless this figure is obviously not a chiliagon. For this figure is really no different from the figure I would represent to myself, were I thinking of a myriagon or any other figure with a large number of sides. Nor is this figure of any help in knowing the properties that differentiate a chiliagon from other polygons. But if the figure in question is a pentagon, I surely can understand its figure, just as was the case with the chiliagon, without the help of my imagination. But I can also imagine a pentagon by turning the mind's eye both to its five sides and at the same time to the area bounded by those sides. At this point I am manifestly aware that I am in need of a peculiar sort of effort on the part of the mind in order to imagine, one that I do not employ in order to understand. This new effort on the part of the mind clearly shows the difference between imagination and pure intellection.

Moreover, I consider that this power of imagining that is in me, insofar as it differs from the power of understanding, is not required for my own essence, that is, the essence of my mind. For were I to be lacking this power, I would nevertheless undoubtedly remain the same entity I am now. Thus it seems to follow that the power of imagining depends upon something distinct from me. And I readily understand that, were a body to exist to which a mind is so joined that it may apply itself in order, as it were, to look at it any time it wishes, it could happen that it is by means of this very body that I imagine corporeal things. As a result, this mode of thinking may differ from pure intellection only in the sense that the mind, when it understands, in a sense turns toward itself and looks at one of the ideas that are in it; whereas when it imagines, it turns toward the body, and intuits in the body something that conforms to an idea either understood by the mind or perceived by sense. To be sure, I easily understand that the imagination can be actualized in this way, provided a body does exist. And since I can think of no other way of explaining imagination that is equally appropriate, I make a probable conjecture from this that a body exists. But this is only a probability. And even though I may examine everything carefully, nevertheless I do not yet see how the distinct idea of corporeal nature

that I find in my imagination can enable me to develop an argument which necessarily concludes that some body exists.

But I am in the habit of imagining many other things, over and above that corporeal nature which is the object of pure mathematics, such as colors, sounds, tastes, pain, and the like, though not so distinctly. And I perceive these things better by means of the senses, from which, with the aid of the memory, they seem to have arrived at the imagination. Thus I should pay the same degree of attention to the senses, so that I might deal with them more appropriately. I must see whether I can obtain any reliable argument for the existence of corporeal things from those things that are perceived by the mode of thinking that I call "sense."

First of all, to be sure, I will review here all the things I previously believed to be true because I had perceived them by means of the senses and the causes I had for thinking this. Next I will assess the causes why I later called them into doubt. Finally, I will consider what I must now believe about these things.

So first, I sensed that I had a head, hands, feet, and other members that comprised this body which I viewed as part of me, or perhaps even as the whole of me. I sensed that this body was found among many other bodies, by which my body can be affected in various beneficial or harmful ways. I gauged what was opportune by means of a certain sensation of pleasure, and what was inopportune by a sensation of pain. In addition to pain and pleasure, I also sensed within me hunger, thirst, and other such appetites, as well as certain bodily tendencies toward mirth, sadness, anger, and other such affects. And externally, besides the extension, shapes, and motions of bodies, I also sensed their hardness, heat, and other tactile qualities. I also sensed light, colors, odors, tastes, and sounds, on the basis of whose variety I distinguished the sky, the earth, the seas, and the other bodies, one from the other. Now given the ideas of all these qualities that presented themselves to my thought, and which were all that I properly and immediately sensed, still it was surely not without reason that I thought I sensed things that were manifestly different from my thought, namely, the bodies from which these ideas proceeded. For I knew by experience that these ideas came upon me utterly without my consent, to the extent that, wish as I may, I could not sense any object unless it was present to a sense organ. Nor could I fail to sense it when it was present. And since the ideas perceived by sense were much more vivid and explicit and even, in their own way, more distinct than any of those that I deliberately and knowingly formed through meditation or that I found impressed on my memory, it seemed impossible that they came from myself. Thus the remaining alternative was that they came from other things. Since I had no knowledge of such things except from those same ideas themselves, I could not help entertaining the thought that they were similar to those ideas. Moreover, I also recalled that the use of the senses antedated the use of reason. And since I saw that the ideas that I myself fashioned were not as explicit as those that I perceived through the faculty of sense, and were for the most part composed of parts of the latter, I easily convinced myself that I had absolutely no idea in the intellect that I did not have beforehand in the sense faculty. Not without reason did I judge that this body, which by a certain special right I called "mine," belongs more to me than did any other. For I could never be separated from it in the same way I could be from other bodies. I sensed all appetites and feelings in and on behalf of it. Finally, I noticed pain and pleasurable excitement in its parts, but not in other bodies external to it. But why should a certain sadness of spirit arise from some sensation or other of pain, and why should a certain elation arise from a sensation of excitement, or why should that peculiar twitching in the stomach, which I call hunger, warn me to have something to eat, or why should dryness in the throat warn me to take something to drink, and so on? I plainly had no explanation other than that I had been taught this way by nature. For there is no affinity whatsoever, at least none I am aware of, between this twitching in the stomach and the will to have something to eat, or between the sensation of something causing pain and the thought of sadness arising from this sensation. But nature also seems to have taught me everything else as well that I judged concerning the objects of the senses, for I had

already convinced myself that this was how things were, prior to my assessing any of the arguments that might prove it.

Afterwards, however, many experiences gradually weakened any faith that I had in the senses. Towers that had seemed round from afar occasionally appeared square at close quarters. Very large statues mounted on their pedestals did not seem large to someone looking at them from ground level. And in countless other such instances I determined that judgments in matters of the external senses were in error. And not just the external senses, but the internal senses as well. For what can be more intimate than pain? But I had sometimes heard it said by people whose leg or arm had been amputated that it seemed to them that they still occasionally sensed pain in the very limb they had lost. Thus, even in my own case it did not seem to be entirely certain that some bodily member was causing me pain, even though I did sense pain in it. To these causes for doubt I recently added two quite general ones. The first was that everything I ever thought I sensed while awake I could believe I also sometimes sensed while asleep, and since I do not believe that what I seem to sense in my dreams comes to me from things external to me, I saw no reason why I should hold this belief about those things I seem to be sensing while awake. The second was that, since I was still ignorant of the author of my origin (or at least pretended to be ignorant of it), I saw nothing to prevent my having been so constituted by nature that I should be mistaken even about what seemed to me most true. As to the arguments that used to convince me of the truth of sensible things, I found no difficulty responding to them. For since I seemed driven by nature toward many things about which reason tried to dissuade me, I did not think that what I was taught by nature deserved much credence. And even though the perceptions of the senses did not depend on my will, I did not think that we must therefore conclude that they came from things distinct from me, since perhaps there is some faculty in me, as yet unknown to me, that produces these perceptions.

But now, having begun to have a better knowledge of myself and the author of my origin, I am of the opinion that I must not rashly admit everything that I seem to derive from the senses; but neither, for that matter, should I call everything into doubt.

First, I know that all the things that I clearly and distinctly understand can be made by God such as I understand them. For this reason, my ability clearly and distinctly to understand one thing without another suffices to make me certain that the one thing is different from the other, since they can be separated from each other, at least by God. The question as to the sort of power that might effect such a separation is not relevant to their being thought to be different. For this reason, from the fact that I know that I exist, and that at the same time I judge that obviously nothing else belongs to my nature or essence except that I am a thinking thing, I rightly conclude that my essence consists entirely in my being a thinking thing. And although perhaps (or rather, as I shall soon say, assuredly) I have a body that is very closely joined to me, nevertheless, because on the one hand I have a clear and distinct idea of myself, insofar as I am merely a thinking thing and not an extended thing, and because on the other hand I have a distinct idea of a body, insofar as it is merely an extended thing and not a thinking thing, it is certain that I am really distinct from my body, and can exist without it.

Moreover, I find in myself faculties for certain special modes of thinking, namely the faculties of imagining and sensing. I can clearly and distinctly understand myself in my entirety without these faculties, but not vice versa: I cannot understand them clearly and distinctly without me, that is, without a substance endowed with understanding in which they inhere, for they include an act of understanding in their formal concept. Thus I perceive them to be distinguished from me as modes from a thing. I also acknowledge that there are certain other faculties, such as those of moving from one place to another, of taking on various shapes, and so on, that, like sensing or imagining, cannot be understood apart from some substance in which they inhere, and hence without which they cannot exist. But it is clear that these faculties, if in fact they exist, must be in a corporeal or extended substance, not in a substance endowed with understanding. For some extension is contained

in a clear and distinct concept of them, though certainly not any understanding. Now there clearly is in me a passive faculty of sensing, that is, a faculty for receiving and knowing the ideas of sensible things; but I could not use it unless there also existed, either in me or in something else, a certain active faculty of producing or bringing about these ideas. But this faculty surely cannot be in me, since it clearly presupposes no act of understanding, and these ideas are produced without my cooperation and often even against my will. Therefore, the only alternative is that it is in some substance different from me, containing either formally or eminently all the reality that exists objectively in the ideas produced by that faculty, as I have just noted above. Hence this substance is either a body, that is, a corporeal nature, which contains formally all that is contained objectively in the ideas, or else it is God, or some other creature more noble than a body, which contains eminently all that is contained objectively in the ideas. But since God is not a deceiver, it is patently obvious that he does not send me these ideas either immediately by himself, or even through the mediation of some creature that contains the objective reality of these ideas not formally but only eminently. For since God has given me no faculty whatsoever for making this determination, but instead has given me a great inclination to believe that these ideas issue from corporeal things, I fail to see how God could be understood not to be a deceiver, if these ideas were to issue from a source other than corporeal things. And consequently corporeal things exist. Nevertheless, perhaps not all bodies exist exactly as I grasp them by sense, since this sensory grasp is in many cases very obscure and confused. But at least they do contain everything I clearly and distinctly understand—that is, everything, considered in a general sense, that is encompassed in the object of pure mathematics.

As far as the remaining matters are concerned, which are either merely particular (for example, that the sun is of such and such a size or shape, and so on) or less clearly understood (for example, light, sound, pain, and the like), even though these matters are very doubtful and uncertain, nevertheless the fact that God is no deceiver (and thus no falsity can be found in my opinions, unless there is also in me a faculty given me by God for the purpose of rectifying this falsity) offers me a definite hope of reaching the truth even in these matters. And surely there is no doubt that all that I am taught by nature has some truth to it; for by "nature," taken generally, I understand nothing other than God himself or the ordered network of created things which was instituted by God. By my own particular nature I understand nothing other than the combination of all the things bestowed upon me by God.

There is nothing that this nature teaches me more explicitly than that I have a body that is ill-disposed when I feel pain, that needs food and drink when I suffer hunger or thirst, and the like. Therefore, I should not doubt that there is some truth in this.

By means of these sensations of pain, hunger, thirst and so on, nature also teaches that I am present to my body not merely in the way a sailor is present in a ship, but that I am most tightly joined and, so to speak, commingled with it, so much so that I and the body constitute one single thing. For if this were not the case, then I, who am only a thinking thing, would not sense pain when the body is injured; rather, I would perceive the wound by means of the pure intellect, just as a sailor perceives by sight whether anything in his ship is broken. And when the body is in need of food or drink, I should understand this explicitly, instead of having confused sensations of hunger and thirst. For clearly these sensations of thirst, hunger, pain, and so on are nothing but certain confused modes of thinking arising from the union and, as it were, the commingling of the mind with the body.

Moreover, I am also taught by nature that various other bodies exist around my body, some of which are to be pursued, while others are to be avoided. And to be sure, from the fact that I sense a wide variety of colors, sounds, odors, tastes, levels of heat, and grades of roughness, and the like, I rightly conclude that in the bodies from which these different perceptions of the senses proceed there are differences corresponding to the different perceptions—though perhaps the latter do not resemble the former. And from the fact that some of these perceptions are pleasant while others are unpleasant, it is plainly certain that my body, or rather my whole self, insofar as I am composed of a body and a mind, can be affected by various beneficial and harmful bodies in the vicinity.

Granted, there are many other things that I seem to have been taught by nature; nevertheless it was not really nature that taught them to me but a certain habit of making reckless judgments. And thus it could easily happen that these judgments are false: for example, that any space where there is absolutely nothing happening to move my senses is empty; or that there is something in a hot body that bears an exact likeness to the idea of heat that is in me; or that in a white or green body there is the same whiteness or greenness that I sense; or that in a bitter or sweet body there is the same taste, and so on; or that stars and towers and any other distant bodies have the same size and shape that they present to my senses, and other things of this sort. But to ensure that my perceptions in this matter are sufficiently distinct, I ought to define more precisely what exactly I mean when I say that I am "taught something by nature." For I am taking "nature" here more narrowly than the combination of everything bestowed on me by God. For this combination embraces many things that belong exclusively to my mind, such as my perceiving that what has been done cannot be undone, and everything else that is known by the light of nature. That is not what I am talking about here. There are also many things that belong exclusively to the body, such as that it tends to move downward, and so on. I am not dealing with these either, but only with what God has bestowed on me insofar as I am composed of mind and body. Accordingly, it is this nature that teaches me to avoid things that produce a sensation of pain and to pursue things that produce a sensation of pleasure, and the like. But it does not appear that nature teaches us to conclude anything, besides these things, from these sense perceptions unless the intellect has first conducted its own inquiry regarding things external to us. For it seems to belong exclusively to the mind, and not to the composite of mind and body, to know the truth in these matters. Thus, although a star affects my eye no more than does the flame from a small torch, still there is no real or positive tendency in my eye toward believing that the star is no larger than the flame. Yet, ever since my youth, I have made this judgment without any reason for doing so. And although I feel heat as I draw closer to the fire, and I also feel pain upon drawing too close to it, there is not a single argument that persuades me that there is something in the fire similar to that heat, any more than to that pain. On the contrary, I am convinced only that there is something in the fire that, regardless of what it finally turns out to be, causes in us those sensations of heat or pain. And although there may be nothing in a given space that moves the senses, it does not therefore follow that there is no body in it. But I see that in these and many other instances I have been in the habit of subverting the order of nature. For admittedly I use the perceptions of the senses (which are properly given by nature only for signifying to the mind what things are useful or harmful to the composite of which it is a part, and to that extent they are clear and distinct enough), as reliable rules for immediately discerning what is the essence of bodies located outside us. Yet they signify nothing about that except quite obscurely and confusedly.

I have already examined in sufficient detail how it could happen that my judgments are false, despite the goodness of God. But a new difficulty now arises regarding those very things that nature shows me are either to be sought out or avoided, as well as the internal sensations where I seem to have detected errors, as for example, when someone is deluded by a food's pleasant taste to eat the poison hidden inside it. In this case, however, he is driven by nature only toward desiring the thing in which the pleasurable taste is found, but not toward the poison, of which he obviously is unaware. I can only conclude that this nature is not omniscient. This is not remarkable, since man is a limited thing, and thus only what is of limited perfection befits him.

But we not infrequently err even in those things to which nature impels us. Take, for example, the case of those who are ill and who desire food or drink that will soon afterwards be injurious to them. Perhaps it could be said here that they erred because their nature was corrupt. However, this does not remove our difficulty, for a sick man is no less a creature of God

than a healthy one, and thus it seems no less inconsistent that the sick man got a deception-prone nature from God. And a clock made of wheels and counterweights follows all the laws of nature no less closely when it has been badly constructed and does not tell time accurately than it does when it completely satisfies the wish of its maker. Likewise, I might regard a man's body as a kind of mechanism that is outfitted with and composed of bones, nerves, muscles, veins, blood and skin in such a way that, even if no mind existed in it, the man's body would still exhibit all the same motions that are in it now except for those motions that proceed either from a command of the will or, consequently, from the mind. I easily recognize that it would be natural for this body, were it, say, suffering from dropsy and experiencing dryness in the throat (which typically produces a thirst sensation in the mind), and also so disposed by its nerves and other parts to take something to drink, the result of which would be to exacerbate the illness. This is as natural as for a body without any such illness to be moved by the same dryness in the throat to take something to drink that is useful to it. And given the intended purpose of the clock, I could say that it deviates from its nature when it fails to tell the right time. And similarly, considering the mechanism of the human body in terms of its being equipped for the motions that typically occur in it, I may think that it too is deviating from its nature, if its throat were dry when having something to drink is not beneficial to its conservation. Nevertheless, I am well aware that this last use of "nature" differs greatly from the other. For this latter "nature" is merely a designation dependent on my thought, since it compares a man in poor health and a poorly constructed clock with the ideas of a healthy man and of a well-made clock, a designation extrinsic to the things to which it is applied. But by "nature" taken in the former sense, I understand something that is really in things, and thus is not without some truth.

When we say, then, in the case of the body suffering from dropsy, that its "nature" is corrupt, given the fact that it has a parched throat and yet does not need something to drink, "nature" obviously is merely an extrinsic designation. Nevertheless, in the case of the composite, that is, of a mind joined to such a body, it is not a mere designation, but a true error of nature that this body should be thirsty when having something to drink would be harmful to it. It therefore remains to inquire here how the goodness of God does not prevent "nature," thus considered, from being deceptive.

Now my first observation here is that there is a great difference between a mind and a body, in that a body, by its very nature, is always divisible. On the other hand, the mind is utterly indivisible. For when I consider the mind, that is, myself insofar as I am only a thinking thing, I cannot distinguish any parts within me; rather, I understand myself to be manifestly one complete thing. Although the entire mind seems to be united to the entire body, nevertheless, were a foot or an arm or any other bodily part to be amputated, I know that nothing has been taken away from the mind on that account. Nor can the faculties of willing, sensing, understanding, and so on be called "parts" of the mind, since it is one and the same mind that wills, senses, and understands. On the other hand, there is no corporeal or extended thing I can think of that I may not in my thought easily divide into parts; and in this way I understand that it is divisible. This consideration alone would suffice to teach me that the mind is wholly diverse from the body, had I not yet known it well enough in any other way.

My second observation is that my mind is not immediately affected by all the parts of the body, but only by the brain, or perhaps even by just one small part of the brain, namely, by that part where the "common" sense is said to reside. Whenever this part of the brain is disposed in the same manner, it presents the same thing to the mind, even if the other parts of the body are able meanwhile to be related in diverse ways. Countless experiments show this, none of which need be reviewed here.

My next observation is that the nature of the body is such that whenever any of its parts can be moved by another part some distance away, it can also be moved in the same manner by any of the parts that lie between them, even if this more distant part is doing nothing. For example, in the cord ABCD, if the final part D is pulled, the first part A would be moved

in exactly the same manner as it could be, if one of the intermediate parts B or C were pulled, while the end part D remained immobile. Likewise, when I feel a pain in my foot, physics teaches me that this sensation takes place by means of nerves distributed throughout the foot, like stretched cords extending from the foot all the way to the brain. When these nerves are pulled in the foot, they also pull on the inner parts of the brain to which they extend, and produce a certain motion in them. This motion has been constituted by nature so as to affect the mind with a sensation of pain, as if it occurred in the foot. But because these nerves need to pass through the shin, thigh, loins, back, and neck, to get from the foot to the brain, it can happen that even if it is not the part in the foot, but merely one of the intermediate parts that is being struck, the very same movement will occur in the brain that would occur, were the foot badly injured. The inevitable result will be that the mind feels the same pain. The same opinion should hold for any other sensation.

My final observation is that, since any given motion occurring in that part of the brain immediately affecting the mind produces but one sensation in it, I can think of no better arrangement than that it produces the one sensation that, of all the ones it is able to produce, is most especially and most often conducive to the maintenance of a healthy man. Moreover, experience shows that all the sensations bestowed on us by nature are like this. Hence there is absolutely nothing to be found in them that does not bear witness to God's power and goodness. Thus, for example, when the nerves in the foot are agitated in a violent and unusual manner, this motion of theirs extends through the marrow of the spine to the inner reaches of the brain, where it gives the mind the sign to sense something, namely, the pain as if it is occurring in the foot. This provokes the mind to do its utmost to move away from the cause of the pain, since it is seen as harmful to the foot. But the nature of man could have been so constituted by God that this same motion in the brain might have indicated something else to the mind: for example, either the motion itself as it occurs in the brain, or in the foot, or in some place in between, or something else entirely different. But

nothing else would have served so well the maintenance of the body. Similarly, when we need something to drink, a certain dryness arises in the throat that
moves the nerves in the throat, and, by means of them,
the inner parts of the brain. And this motion affects the
mind with a sensation of thirst, because in this entire
affair nothing is more useful for us to know than that
we need something to drink in order to maintain our
health; the same holds in the other cases.

From these considerations it is utterly apparent
that, notwithstanding the immense goodness of God,
the nature of man, insofar as it is composed of mind
and body, cannot help being sometimes mistaken.
For if some cause, not in the foot but in some other
part through which the nerves extend from the foot
to the brain, or perhaps even in the brain itself, were
to produce the same motion that would normally be
produced by a badly injured foot, the pain will be
felt as if it were in the foot, and the senses will naturally be deceived. For since an identical motion in
the brain can only bring about an identical sensation
in the mind, and it is more frequently the case that
this motion is wont to arise on account of a cause
that harms the foot than on account of some other
thing existing elsewhere, it is reasonable that the motion should always show pain to the mind as something belonging to the foot rather than to some other
part. And if dryness in the throat does not arise, as is
normal, from drink's contributing to bodily health,
but from a contrary cause, as happens in the case
of someone with dropsy, then it is far better that it
should deceive on that occasion than that it should
always be deceptive when the body is in good health.
The same holds for the other cases.

This consideration is most helpful, not only for
my noticing all the errors to which my nature is liable, but also for enabling me to correct or avoid
them without difficulty. To be sure, I know that all
the senses set forth what is true more frequently than
what is false regarding what concerns the welfare of
the body. Moreover, I can nearly always make use of
several of them in order to examine the same thing.
Furthermore, I can use my memory, which connects
current happenings with past ones, and my intellect, which now has examined all the causes of error. Hence I should no longer fear that those things
that are daily shown me by the senses are false. On
the contrary, the hyperbolic doubts of the last few
days ought to be rejected as ludicrous. This goes
especially for the chief reason for doubting, which
dealt with my failure to distinguish being asleep
from being awake. For I now notice that there is a
considerable difference between these two; dreams
are never joined by the memory with all the other
actions of life, as is the case with those actions that
occur when one is awake. For surely, if, while I am
awake, someone were suddenly to appear to me and
then immediately disappear, as occurs in dreams, so
that I see neither where he came from nor where he
went, it is not without reason that I would judge him
to be a ghost or a phantom conjured up in my brain,
rather than a true man. But when these things happen, and I notice distinctly where they come from,
where they are now, and when they come to me, and
when I connect my perception of them without interruption with the whole rest of my life, I am clearly
certain that these perceptions have happened to me
not while I was dreaming but while I was awake. Nor
ought I have even the least doubt regarding the truth
of these things, if, having mustered all the senses, in
addition to my memory and my intellect, in order to
examine them, nothing is passed on to me by one of
these sources that conflicts with the others. For from
the fact that God is no deceiver, it follows that I am
in no way mistaken in these matters. But because the
need to get things done does not always permit us the
leisure for such a careful inquiry, we must confess
that the life of man is apt to commit errors regarding particular things, and we must acknowledge the
infirmity of our nature.

# René Descartes, Thomas Hobbes, and Antoine Arnauld, *Objections and Replies* (1641)[1]

*Descartes had the manuscript of the* Meditations *circulated in order to solicit objections; he then published the* Meditations, *together with the* Objections *and his* Replies. *The person distributing the manuscript for Descartes was Marin Mersenne, a Minim monk who served as Descartes' link to the learned world while Descartes lived in the Netherlands.[2] Descartes initially requested a first set of objections from friends in the Netherlands. Mersenne then collected sets from Thomas Hobbes, Antoine Arnauld, and Pierre Gassendi and put together two sets out of the objections of various philosophers and theologians; a seventh set was received from the Jesuit Pierre Bourdin and published with the second edition of the* Meditations *(in 1642).[3] The* Objections *and* Replies *allow Descartes to extend some of his arguments, which were so compactly given in the* Meditations. *The Second Set of Objections contains the following remark forwarded by Mersenne (probably initiated by Jean-Baptiste Morin):[4] "It would be worthwhile if you set out the entire argument in geometrical fashion, starting from a number of definitions, postulates, and axioms. You are highly experienced in employing this method, and it would enable you to fill the mind of each reader so that he could see everything as it were at a single glance. . . ." That remark produced an extended reply from Descartes about the geometrical manner of writing, the order of demonstration, and its two divisions, analysis and synthesis. Descartes further appended a rewritten portion of the* Meditations *arranged in geometric fashion.*

*Perhaps the most intriguing function of the* Objections *and* Replies *is that they enable one to see genuine philosophical debate conducted on the spot. This is especially true for Descartes' confrontation with Hobbesian materialism in the Third Set of Objections and Replies.[5] Hobbes accepts none of Descartes'*

---

1. Translated from the Latin by Donald Cress.
2. Mersenne's main contribution to the philosophy and science of his day was his tireless promotion of scientific activity. He was educated at the Jesuit College of La Flèche (which Descartes also attended), entered the order of the Minims, and from his cell at their convent in Paris, he acted as the center of a vast correspondence network, bringing together notable philosophers, mathematicians, and scientists. He championed the new science, publishing translations (or paraphrases) of Galileo's early mechanics and his *Two New Sciences*. For more on Mersenne, see Peter Dear, *Mersenne and the Learning of the Schools* (Ithaca: Cornell University Press, 1988).
3. For more on the *Objections* and *Replies*, see Roger Ariew and Marjorie Grene, eds., *Descartes and His Contemporaries: Meditations, Objections and Replies* (Chicago: University of Chicago Press, 1995).

4. Morin was an astrologer, part of the circle around Mersenne, and author of *Quod Deus Sit (That God Exists)*, a short treatise constructed on Euclidean principles, with Definitions, Axioms, and Theorems. For more on Morin, see Daniel Garber, "J.-B. Morin and the *Second Objections*," pp. 63–82 in R. Ariew and M. Grene, eds., *Descartes and His Contemporaries*.
5. For Thomas Hobbes' biography and bibliography, see the selection from the *Leviathan* in Section 2, below.

*arguments, and the debate gets increasingly heated. Arguably, the best set of objections is the one written by Arnauld, at the time a theology doctoral candidate at the University of Paris. In the critical but sympathetic exchange one can see Arnauld's keen analytical mind working, from his criticism of Descartes' notion of material falsity, to his comments on God as positive cause of himself, to his questioning whether the* Meditations *are circular.*[6]

## Reply to the Second Set of Objections

[ . . . ] Finally, as to your suggestion that I should put forward my arguments in geometrical fashion so that the reader could perceive them, as it were, in a single intuition, it is worthwhile to indicate here how much I have already followed this suggestion and how much I think it should be followed in the future. I draw a distinction between two things in the geometrical style of writing, namely, the order and the mode [*ratio*] of the demonstration.

_____

6. Antoine Arnauld was born in Paris in 1612. He was admitted to the Paris Faculty of Theology, i.e., the Sorbonne, in 1643, and expelled from it in 1656. Throughout his life Arnauld engaged in public controversies on philosophical and theological topics. He became the leading spokesman in France for the Jansenist movement (and against the Jesuits) and one of the more outspoken defenders of Cartesian philosophy. He was forced into exile in the Netherlands in 1679 and died in Liège in 1694. Arnauld's philosophical work included the *Port-Royal Logic* (1662), written with Pierre Nicole, and *Of True and False Ideas* (1683)—both broadly Cartesian projects. Because of the latter, he was also engaged in discussion over Malebranche's theory of ideas and doctrine of grace and divine providence (for a sample of these, see the selection from Malebranche's *Search after Truth* in Section 3, below); the debate produced numerous other works and letters. Arnauld maintained an important philosophical correspondence with many of the great figures of the century, including Leibniz (see Leibniz's letters to Arnauld in Section 3, below). English translations of Arnauld's *Objections* to Descartes' *Meditations*, *Port-Royal Logic*, and *Of True and False Ideas* are available. For more on Arnauld, see Steven Nadler, *Arnauld and the Cartesian Philosophy of Ideas* (Princeton: Princeton University Press, 1989) or E. J. Kremer, ed., *The Great Arnauld and Some of His Philosophical Correspondents* (Toronto: University of Toronto Press, 1994) and *Interpreting Arnauld* (Toronto: University of Toronto Press, 1996).

Order consists simply in putting forward as first what ought to be known without any help from what comes afterward and then in arranging all the rest in such a way that they are demonstrated solely by means of what preceded them. And I certainly did try to follow this order as carefully as possible in my Meditations. And it was owing to my observance of it that I treated the distinction between the mind and the body not in the Second Meditation but at the end in the Sixth Meditation. And it also explains why I deliberately and knowingly omitted many other things, since they required an explanation of a great many more.

But the mode [*ratio*] of a demonstration is of two sorts: one that proceeds by way of analysis, the other by way of synthesis.

Analysis shows the true way by which a thing has been discovered methodically, and, as it were, "a priori," so that, were the reader willing to follow it and to pay sufficient attention to everything, he will no less perfectly understand a thing and render it his own, than had he himself discovered it. However, analysis possesses nothing with which to compel belief in a less attentive or hostile reader, for if he fails to pay attention to the least thing among those that this mode [*ratio*] proposes, the necessity of its conclusions is not apparent; and it often hardly touches at all on many things that nevertheless ought to be carefully noted, since they are obvious to anyone who is sufficiently attentive.

Synthesis, on the other hand, indeed clearly demonstrates its conclusions by an opposite way, where the investigation is conducted, as it were, "a posteriori" (although it is often the case here that this proof is more "a priori" than it is in the analytic mode). And it uses a long series of definitions, postulates, axioms, theorems, and problems, so that if something in what follows is denied, this mode may at once point out that it is contained in what went before. And thus it wrests from the reader his assent, however hostile and obstinate he may be. But this mode is not as satisfactory as the other one nor does it satisfy the minds of those who desire to learn, since it does not teach the way in which the thing was discovered.

It was this mode alone that the ancient geometers were wont to use in their writings—not that they were utterly ignorant of the other mode, but rather, as I see it, they held it in such high regard that they kept it to themselves alone as a secret.

But in my Meditations I followed analysis exclusively, which is the true and best way to teach. But as to synthesis, which is undoubtedly what you are asking me about here, even though in geometry it is most suitably placed after analysis, nevertheless it cannot be so conveniently applied to these metaphysical matters.

For there is this difference, that the first notions that are presupposed for demonstrating things geometrical are readily admitted by everyone, since they accord with the use of the senses. Thus there is no difficulty there, except in correctly deducing the consequences, which can be done by all sorts of people, even the less attentive, provided only that they remember what went before. And the minute differentiation of propositions was done for the purpose of making them easy to recite and thus can be committed to memory even by the recalcitrant.

But in these metaphysical matters, on the contrary, nothing is more an object of intense effort than causing its first notions to be clearly and distinctly perceived. For although they are by their nature no less known or even more known than those studied by geometers, nevertheless, because many of the prejudices of the senses (with which we have been accustomed since our infancy) are at odds with them, they are perfectly known only by those who are especially attentive and meditative and who withdraw their minds from corporeal things as much as possible. And if these first notions were put forward by themselves, they could easily be denied by those who are eager to engage in conflict.

This was why I wrote "meditations," rather than "disputations," as the philosophers do, or theorems and problems, as the geometers do: namely, so that by this very fact I might attest that the only dealings I would have were with those who, along with myself, did not refuse to consider the matter attentively and to meditate. For the very fact that someone girds himself to attack the truth renders him less suitable for

perceiving it, since he is withdrawing himself from considering the arguments that attest to the truth in order to find other arguments that dissuade him of the truth.

But perhaps someone will object here that a person should not seek arguments for the sake of being contentious when he knows that the truth is set before him. But so long as this is in doubt, all the arguments on both sides ought to be assessed in order to know which ones are the more firm. And it would be unfair of me to want my arguments to be admitted as true before they had been scrutinized, while at the same time not allowing the consideration of opposing arguments.

This would certainly be a just criticism, if any of those things which I desire in an attentive and non-hostile reader were such that they could withdraw him from a consideration of any other arguments in which there was the slightest hope of finding more truth than in my arguments. However, the greatest doubt is contained among the things I am proposing; moreover, there is nothing I more strongly urge than that each thing be scrutinized most diligently and that nothing is to be straightforwardly accepted except what has been so clearly and distinctly examined that we cannot but give our assent to it. On the other hand, the only matters from which I desire to divert the minds of my readers are things they have never sufficiently examined and which they derived not on the basis of a firm reason, but from the senses alone. As a consequence, I do not think anyone can believe that he will be in greater danger of error, were he to consider only those things that I propose to him, than were he to withdraw his mind from them and turn it toward other things—things that are opposed to them in some way and that spread darkness—that is, toward the prejudices of the senses.

And thus I am right in desiring especially close attention on the part of my readers; and I have chosen the one style of writing over all the others with which I thought it can most especially be procured, and from which I am convinced that readers will discern a greater profit than they would have thought, since, on the other hand, when the synthetic mode of writing is employed, people are likely to seem to themselves to have learned more than they actually did. But I also think it is fair for me straightforwardly to reject as worthless those criticisms made against me by those who have refused to meditate with me and who cling to their preformed opinions.

But I know how difficult it will be, even for those who pay close attention and earnestly search for the truth, to intuit the entire body of my Meditations and at the same time to discern its individual parts. I think both of these things ought to be done so that the full benefit may be derived from my Meditations. I shall therefore append here a few things in the synthetic style that I hope will prove somewhat helpful to my readers. Nevertheless, I wish they would take note of the fact that I did not intend to cover as much here as is found in my Meditations; otherwise I should then be more loquacious here than in the Meditations themselves; moreover, I will not explain in detail what I do include, partly out of a desire for brevity and partly to prevent anyone who thinks that my remarks here were sufficient from making a very cursory examination of the Meditations themselves, from which I am convinced that much more benefit is to be discerned.

# Arguments Proving the Existence of God and the Distinction of the Soul from the Body, Arranged in Geometrical Fashion

## Definitions

I. By the word "thought" I include everything that is in us in such a way that we are immediately aware of it. Thus all the operations of the will, understanding, imagination, and senses are thoughts. But I added "immediately" to exclude those things that follow from these operations, such as voluntary motion, which surely has thought as its principle but nevertheless is not itself a thought.

II. By the word "idea" I understand that form of any thought through the immediate perception of which I am aware of that very same thought. Thus I could not express anything in words and understand what I am saying, without this very fact making it certain that there exists in me an idea of what is being signified by those words. And thus it is not the mere images depicted in the corporeal imagination that I call "ideas." In point of fact, I in no way call these images "ideas," insofar as they are in the corporeal imagination, that is, insofar as they have been depicted in some part of the brain, but only insofar as they inform the mind itself which is turned toward that part of the brain.

III. By the "objective reality of an idea" I understand the being of the thing represented by an idea, insofar as it exists in the idea. In the same way one can speak of "objective perfection," "objective skill," and so on. For whatever we perceive to exist in the objects of our ideas exists objectively in these very ideas.

IV. The same things are said to exist "formally" in the objects of our ideas when they exist in these objects in just the way we perceive them, and to exist "eminently" in the objects of our ideas when they indeed are not in these objects in the way we perceive them, but have such an amount of perfection that they could fill the role of things existing formally.

V. Everything in which there immediately inheres, as in a subject, or through which there exists, something we perceive (that is, some property, or quality, or attribute whose real idea is in us) is called a "substance." For we have no other idea of substance itself, taken in the strict sense, except that it is a thing in which whatever we perceive or whatever is objectively in one of our ideas exists either formally or eminently, since it is evident by the light of nature that no real attribute can belong to nothing.

VI. That substance in which thought immediately resides is called "mind." However, I am speaking here of the mind rather than of the soul, since the word "soul" is equivocal, and is often used for something corporeal.

VII. That substance which is the immediate subject of local extension and of the accidents that presuppose extension, such as shape, position, movement from place to place, and so on, is called "body." Whether what we call "mind" and what we call "body" are one and the same substance or two different ones must be examined later on.

VIII. That substance which we understand to be supremely perfect and in which we conceive absolutely nothing that involves any defect or limitation upon its perfection is called "God."

IX. When we say that something is contained in the nature or concept of something, this is the same as saying that it is true of that thing or that it can be affirmed of that thing.

X. Two substances are said to be really distinct from one another when each of them can exist without the other.

## Postulates

I ask first that readers take note of how feeble are the reasons why they have up until now put their faith in their senses, and how uncertain are all the judgments that they have constructed upon them; and that they review this within themselves for so long and so often that they finally acquire the habit of no longer placing too much faith in them. For I deem this necessary for perceiving the certainty of things metaphysical.

Second, I ask that readers ponder their own mind and all its attributes. They will discover that they cannot be in doubt about these things, even though they suppose that everything they ever received from the senses is false. And I ask them not to stop pondering this point until they have acquired for themselves the habit of perceiving it clearly and of believing that it is easier to know than anything corporeal.

Third, I ask that readers weigh diligently the self-evident propositions that they find within themselves, such as that the same thing cannot be and not be at the same time, that nothingness cannot be the efficient cause of anything, and the like. And thus readers may exercise the astuteness implanted in them by nature, pure and freed from the senses, but which the objects of sense are wont to cloud and obscure as much as possible. For by this means the truth of the axioms that follow will easily be known to them.

Fourth, I ask readers to examine the ideas of those natures that contain a combination of many accidents together, such as the nature of a triangle, the nature of a square, or of some other figure; and likewise the nature of the mind, the nature of the body, and, above all, the nature of God, the supremely perfect being. And I ask them to realize that all that we perceive to be contained in them truly can be affirmed of them. For example, the equality of its three angles to two right angles is contained in the nature of a triangle, and divisibility is contained in the nature of a body, that is, of an extended thing (for we can conceive of no extended thing that is so small that we could not at least divide it in thought). Such being the case, it is true to say of every triangle that its three angles are equal to two right angles, and that every body is divisible.

Fifth, I ask the readers to dwell long and earnestly in the contemplation of the nature of the supremely perfect being; and to consider, among other things, that possible existence is indeed contained in the ideas of all other things, whereas the idea of God contains not merely possible existence, but absolutely necessary existence. For from this fact alone and without any discursive reasoning, they will know that God exists. And it will be no less self-evident to them than that the number 2 is even or that the number 3 is odd, and the like. For there are some things that are self-evident to some and understood by others only through discursive reasoning.

Sixth, I ask the readers to get into the habit of distinguishing things that are clearly known from things that are obscure, by carefully reviewing all the examples of clear and distinct perception, and likewise of obscure and confused perception, that I have recounted in my Meditations. For this is something more easily learned from examples than from rules, and I think that therein I have either explained or at least to some extent touched upon all the examples pertaining to this subject.

Seventh and finally, when readers perceive that they have never discovered any falsity in things they clearly perceived and that, on the other hand, they have never found truth in things they only obscurely grasped, except by chance, I ask them to consider that it is utterly irrational to call into doubt things that are clearly and distinctly perceived by the pure understanding merely on account of prejudices based on the senses or on account of hypotheses in which something unknown is contained. For thus they will easily admit the following axioms as true and indubitable. Nevertheless, many of these could admittedly have been much better explained and ought to have been put forward as theorems rather than as axioms, had I wanted to be more precise.

## Axioms or Common Notions

I. Nothing exists concerning which we could not ask what the cause is of its existence. For this can be asked of God himself, not that he needs any cause in order to exist, but because the very immensity of his nature is the cause or the reason why he needs no cause in order to exist.

II. The present time does not depend on the time immediately preceding it, and therefore no less a cause is required to preserve a thing than is initially required to produce it.

III. No thing, and no perfection of a thing actually existing in it, can have nothing, or a nonexisting thing, as the cause of its existence.

IV. Whatever reality or perfection there is in a thing is formally or eminently in its first and adequate cause.

V. Whence it also follows that the objective reality of our ideas requires a cause which contains this very same reality, and not merely objectively, but either formally or eminently. And we should note that the acceptance of this axiom is so necessary that on it alone depends the knowledge of all things, sensible as well as insensible. For example, how is it we know that the sky exists? Because we see it? But this vision does not touch the mind except insofar as it is an idea: an idea, I say, inhering in the mind itself, not an image depicted in the corporeal imagination. And we are able to judge on account of this idea that the sky exists only because every idea must have a really existing cause of its objective reality; and this cause we judge to be the sky itself. The same holds for the rest.

VI. There are several degrees of reality or being; for a substance has more reality than an accident or a mode; and an infinite substance has more reality than a finite substance. Thus there is also more objective reality in the idea of a substance than there is in the idea of an accident; and there is more objective reality in the idea of an infinite substance than there is in the idea of a finite substance.

VII. The will of a thing that thinks is surely borne voluntarily and freely (for this is of the essence of the will), but nonetheless infallibly, toward the good that it clearly knows; and therefore, if it should know of any perfections that it lacks, it will immediately give them to itself, if they are within its power.

VIII. Whatever can make what is greater or more difficult can also make what is less.

IX. It is greater to create or preserve a substance than to create or preserve the attributes or properties of a substance; however, it is not greater to create something than to preserve it, as has already been said.

X. Existence is contained in the idea or concept of everything, because we cannot conceive of something except as existing [*sub ratione existentiae*]. Possible or contingent existence is contained in the concept of a limited thing, whereas necessary and perfect existence is contained in the concept of a supremely perfect being.

Proposition I: The existence of God is known from the mere consideration of his nature

Demonstration: To say that something is contained in the nature or concept of a thing is the same thing as saying that it is true of that thing (Def. IX). But necessary existence is contained in the concept of God (Ax. X). Therefore it is true to say of God that necessary existence is in him, or that he exists.

And this is the syllogism I already made use of above in reply to the sixth objection;[7] and its conclusion can be self-evident to those who are free of prejudices, as was stated in Postulate V. But since it is not easy to arrive at such astuteness, we will seek the same thing in other ways.

---

7. Descartes' reply to the sixth point raised in the *Second Set of Objections* discusses the criterion of clarity and distinctness and the proof of the existence of God found in Meditation Five. This reply may be found in AT VII, 149–52.

Proposition II: The existence of God is demonstrated *a posteriori* from the mere fact that the idea of God is in us.

Demonstration: The objective reality of any of our ideas requires a cause that contains this same reality not merely objectively but either formally or eminently (Ax. V). However, we have an idea of God (Defs. II and VII), the objective reality of which is contained in us neither formally nor eminently (Ax. VI), nor could it be contained in anything other than God (Def. VIII). Therefore, this idea of God which is in us requires God as its cause, and thus God exists (Ax. III).

Proposition III: The existence of God is also demonstrated from the fact that we ourselves who have the idea of God exist.

Demonstration: Had I the power to preserve myself, so much the more would I also have the power to give myself the perfections I lack (Axs. VIII and IX); for these are merely attributes of a substance, whereas I am a substance. But I do not have the power to give myself these perfections; otherwise I would already have them (Ax. VII). Therefore, I do not have the power to preserve myself.

Next, I cannot exist without my being preserved during the time I exist, either by myself, if indeed I have this power, or by something else which has this power (Axs. I and II). But I do exist, and yet I do not have the power to preserve myself, as has already been proved. Therefore, I am being preserved by something else.

Moreover, he who preserves me has within himself either formally or eminently all that is in me (Ax. IV). However, there is in me a perception of many of the perfections I lack, and at the same time there is in me the perception of the idea of God (Defs. II and VIII). Therefore, the perception of these same perfections is also in him who preserves me.

Finally, this same being cannot have a perception of any perfections he lacks or does not have in himself, either formally or eminently (Ax. VIII), for since he has the power to preserve me, as has already been said, so much the more would he have the power to give himself those perfections were he to lack them

(Axs. VIII and IX). But he has the perception of all the perfections I lack and that I conceive to be capable of existing in God alone, as has just been proved. Therefore, he has these perfections within himself either formally or eminently, and thus he is God.

Corollary: God created the heavens and the earth and all that is in them. Moreover, he can bring about all that we clearly perceive, precisely as we perceive it.

Demonstration: All these things clearly follow from the preceding proposition. For in that proposition I proved the existence of God from the fact that there must exist someone in whom, either formally or eminently, are all the perfections of which there is some idea in us. But there is in us an idea of such great power that the one in whom this power resides, and he alone, created the heavens and the earth and can also bring about all the other things that I understand to be possible. Thus, along with the existence of God, all these things have also been proved about him.

Proposition IV: Mind and body are really distinct.

Demonstration: Whatever we clearly perceive can be brought about by God in precisely the way we perceive it (by the preceding Corollary). But we clearly perceive the mind, that is, a substance that thinks, apart from the body, that is, apart from any extended substance (Post. II); and vice versa, we clearly perceive the body apart from the mind (as everyone readily admits). Therefore, at least by the divine power, the mind can exist without the body, and the body without the mind.

Now certainly, substances that can exist one without the other are really distinct (Def. X). But the mind and the body are substances (Defs. V, VI, and VII) that can exist one without the other (as has just been proved). Therefore, the mind and the body are really distinct.

And we should note here that I used divine power as a means of separating mind and body, not because some extraordinary power is required to achieve this separation, but because I had dealt exclusively with God in what preceded, and thus I had nothing else I could use as a means. Nor is it of any importance what power it is that separates two things for us to know that they are really distinct.

# Third Set of Objections with the Author's Replies

## Against Meditation I: Concerning Those Things That Can Be Called into Doubt

Objection I: It is sufficiently obvious from what has been said in this Meditation that there is no κριτήριον [criterion] by which we may distinguish our dreams from the waking state and from true sensation; and for this reason the phantasms we have while awake and using our senses are not accidents inhering in external objects, nor do they prove that such objects do in fact exist. Therefore, if we follow our senses without any other process of reasoning, we will be justified in doubting whether anything exists. Therefore, we acknowledge the truth of this Meditation. But since Plato and other ancient philosophers have discussed this same uncertainty in sensible things, and since it is commonly observed that there is a difficulty in distinguishing waking from dreams, I would have preferred the author, so very distinguished in the realm of new speculations, not to have published these old things.

Reply: The reasons for doubting, which are accepted here as true by the philosopher, were proposed by me as merely probable; and I made use of them not to peddle them as something new, but partly to prepare the minds of readers for the consideration of matters geared to the understanding and for distinguishing them from corporeal things, goals for which these arguments seem to me wholly necessary; partly to respond to these same arguments in subsequent Meditations; and partly also to show how firm those truths are that I later propose, given the fact that they cannot be shaken by these metaphysical doubts. And thus I never sought any praise for recounting them again; but I do not think I could have omitted them any more than a medical writer could omit a description of a disease whose method of treatment he is trying to teach.

## Against Meditation II: Concerning the Nature of the Human Mind

Objection II: "I am a thing that thinks"; quite true. For from the fact that I think or have a phantasm, whether I am asleep or awake, it can be inferred that I am thinking, for "I think" means the same thing as "I am thinking." From the fact that I am thinking it follows that I am, since that which thinks is not nothing. But when he appends "that is, a mind, or soul, or understanding, or reason," a doubt arises. For it does not seem a valid argument to say, "I am thinking; therefore I am a thought" or "I am understanding; therefore I am an understanding." For in the same way I could just as well say, "I am walking; therefore I am an act of walking." Thus M. Descartes equates the thing that understands with an act of understanding, which is an act of the thing that understands. Or he at least is equating a thing that understands with the faculty of understanding, which is a power of a thing that understands. Nevertheless, all philosophers draw a distinction between a subject and its faculties and acts, that is, between a subject and its properties and essences; for a being itself is one thing and its essence is another. Therefore, it is possible for a thing that thinks to be the subject in which the mind, reason, or understanding inhere, and therefore this subject may be something corporeal. The opposite is assumed and not proved. Nevertheless, this inference is the basis for the conclusion that M. Descartes seems to want to establish.

In the same passage he says, "I know that I exist; I ask now who is this 'I' whom I know. Most certainly, in the strict sense, the knowledge of this 'I' does not depend upon things of whose existence I do not yet have knowledge."

Certainly the knowledge of the proposition "I exist" depends on the proposition "I think," as he rightly instructed us. But what is the source of the knowledge of the proposition "I think"? Certainly, from the mere fact that we cannot conceive any activity without its subject, for example, leaping without one who leaps, knowing without one who knows, or thinking apart from one who thinks.

And from this it seems to follow that a thing that thinks is something corporeal, for the subjects of all acts seem to be understood only in terms of matter [*sub ratione materiae*], as he later points out in the example of the piece of wax, which, while its color, hardness, shape, and other acts undergo change, is nevertheless understood always to be the same thing, that is, the same matter undergoing a number of changes. However, it is not to be concluded that I think by means of another thought; for although a person can think that he has been thinking (this sort of thinking being merely a case of remembering), nevertheless, it is utterly impossible to think that one thinks, or to know that one knows. For it would involve an infinite series of questions: How do you know that you know that you know that you know?

Therefore, since the knowledge of the proposition "I exist" depends on the knowledge of the proposition "I think," and the knowledge of this latter proposition depends on the fact that we cannot separate thought from the matter that thinks, it seems we should infer that a thing that thinks is material rather than immaterial.

Reply: Where I said "that is, a mind, or soul, or understanding, or reason," and so on, I did not understand by these terms merely the faculties, but the thing endowed with the faculty of thinking, and this is what everyone ordinarily has in mind with regard to the first two terms, and the second two terms are often understood in this sense. And I explained this so explicitly and in so many places that there does not seem to be any room for doubt.

Nor is there a parity here between walking and thinking, since walking is ordinarily taken to refer only to the action itself; whereas thought is sometimes taken to refer to an action, sometimes to refer to a faculty, and sometimes to refer to the thing that has the faculty.

Moreover, I am not asserting that the thing that understands and the act of understanding are identical, nor indeed that the identity of the thing that understands and the faculty of understanding are identical, if "understanding" is taken to refer to a faculty, but only when it is taken for the thing itself that understands. However, I also freely admit that I have used the most abstract terminology possible to signify the thing or substance, which I wanted to divest of all that did not belong to it, just as, contrariwise,

the philosopher uses the most concrete terminology possible (namely, "subject," "matter," and "body") to signify a thing that thinks, in order to prevent its being separated from the body.

But I am not concerned that it may seem to someone that the philosopher's way of joining several things together may be more suitable for finding the truth than mine, wherein I distinguish each single thing as much as possible. But let us put aside verbal disputes and talk about the matter at hand.

He says that it is possible for a thing that thinks to be something corporeal, but the contrary is assumed and not proved. I did not at all assume the contrary, nor did I use it in any way as a basis for my argument. Rather, I left it completely undetermined until the Sixth Meditation, where it is proved.

Then he correctly says that we cannot conceive any act without its subject, such as an act of thinking without a thing that thinks, since that which thinks is not nothing. But then he adds, without any reason at all and contrary to the usual manner of speaking and to all logic, that hence it seems to follow that a thing that thinks is something corporeal; for the subjects of all acts are surely understood from the viewpoint of their being a substance [*sub ratione substantiae*] (or even, if you please, from the viewpoint of their being matter [*sub ratione materiae*], i.e., metaphysical matter), but it does not follow from this that it must be understood from the viewpoint of their being bodies [*sub ratione corporum*].

However, logicians and people in general are wont to say that some substances are spiritual, while others are corporeal. And the only thing I proved by means of the example of the piece of wax was that color, hardness, and shape do not belong to the essence [*rationem formalem*] of the wax. For in that passage I was treating neither the essence of the mind nor that of the body.

Nor is it relevant for the philosopher to say here that one thought cannot be the subject of another thought. For who, besides him, has ever imagined that it could be? But, to explain the matter briefly, it is certainly the case that an act of thinking cannot exist without a thing that thinks, nor in general any act or accident without a substance in which it inheres.

However, since we do not immediately know this substance itself through itself, but only through its being a subject of certain acts, it is quite in keeping with the demands of reason and custom for us to call by different names those substances that we recognize to be subjects of obviously different acts or accidents, and afterwards to inquire whether these different names signify one and the same thing. But there are certain acts which we call "corporeal," such as size, shape, motion, and all the other properties that cannot be thought of apart from their being extended in space; and the substance in which they inhere we call "body." Nor is it possible to imagine that it is one substance that is the subject of shape and another substance that is the subject of movement from place to place, and so on, since all these acts have in common the one feature of being extended. In addition, there are other acts, which we call "cogitative" (such as understanding, willing, imagining, sensing, and so on), all of which have in common the one feature of thought or perception or consciousness; but the substance in which they inhere we say is "a thing that thinks," or a "mind," or any other thing we choose, provided we do not confuse it with corporeal substance, since cogitative acts have no affinity to corporeal acts, and thought, which is the feature they have in common, is utterly different in kind from extension, which is the feature [*ratio*] the others have in common. But after we have formed two distinct concepts of these two substances, it is easy, from what has been said in the Sixth Meditation, to know whether they are one and the same or different.

Objection III: "Which of these things is distinct from my thought? Which of them can be said to be separate from myself?"

Perhaps someone will answer this question thus: I myself who think am distinct from my act of thinking; and, though surely not separated from me, my act of thinking is nevertheless different from me, just as leaping is different from the one who leaps, as has been said before. But if M. Descartes were to show that he who understands and his understanding are one and the same, we shall lapse into the parlance of the schools: The understanding understands, the sight sees, the will wills, and by an exact analogy, the act of

walking or at least the faculty of walking will walk. All of this is obscure, untoward, and most unworthy of that astuteness which is typical of M. Descartes.

Reply: I do not deny that I who think am distinct from my act of thinking, as a thing is distinct from a mode. But when I ask "what then is there that is distinct from my act of thinking?" I understand this to refer to the various modes of thinking that are recounted there, and not to my substance. And when I add "what can be said to be separate from myself?" I have in mind simply that all those modes of thinking are within me. I fail to see what occasion for doubt or obscurity can be imagined here.

Objection IV: "It remains then for me to concede that I do not grasp what this piece of wax is through the imagination; rather I conceive[8] it through the mind alone."

There is a tremendous difference between imagining (that is, having some idea) and conceiving with the mind (that is, concluding by a process of reasoning that something is or exists). But M. Descartes has not explained to us the basis for their being different. Even the ancient peripatetic philosophers have taught clearly enough that a substance is not perceived by the senses, but is inferred by means of arguments.

But what are we to say now, were reasoning perhaps merely the joining together and linking of names or designations by means of the word "is"? It would follow from this that we draw no conclusions whatever by way of argument [*ratione*] about the nature of things. Rather, it is about the designations of things that we draw any conclusions, that is, whether or not we in fact join the names of things in accordance with some convention that we have arbitrarily established regarding the meanings of these terms. If this is the case, as it may well be, then reasoning will depend upon names, names upon imagination, and imagination perhaps, as I see it, upon the motions of the corporeal organs. And thus the mind will be nothing but movements in certain parts of an organic body.

Reply: I have explained here the difference between imagination and a concept of the pure mind

---

8. Hobbes here misquotes Descartes (Meditation Two; AT VII, 131). The original has "perceive" [*percipere*], whereas Hobbes has "conceive" [*concipere*].

when in the example of the piece of wax I enumerated those things in the wax that we entertain in our imagination and those that we conceive with the mind alone. But I also explained elsewhere how one and the same thing, say a pentagon, can be understood by us in one way and imagined by us in another. However, in reasoning there is a joining together not of names but of things signified by these names; and I marvel that the contrary could enter anyone's mind. For who doubts that a Frenchman and a German could come to precisely the same conclusions about the very same things, even though they conceive very different words? And does not the philosopher bring about his own undoing when he speaks of conventions [*pactis*] that we have arbitrarily established regarding the significations of words? For if he admits that something is being signified by these words, why does he not want our reasonings to be about this something which is signified rather than about mere words? And certainly by the same license with which he concludes that the mind is a motion he could also conclude that the sky is the earth, or whatever else he pleases.

## Against Meditation III: Concerning God

Objection V: "Some of these thoughts are like images of things; to these alone does the word 'idea' properly apply, as when I think of a man, or a chimera, or the sky, or an angel, or God."

When I think of a man, I recognize an idea or an image made up of shape and color, concerning which I can doubt whether or not it is the likeness of a man, and likewise, when I think of the sky. When I think of a chimera, I recognize an idea or an image, concerning which I can doubt whether or not it is the likeness of some animal that does not exist but which could exist or which may or may not have existed at some other time.

But a person who is thinking of an angel at times observes in his mind the image of a flame, at other times the image of a beautiful little boy with wings. It seems certain to me that this image bears no resemblance to an angel, and thus is not the idea of an angel. But believing that there are creatures who minister unto God, who are invisible and immaterial, we

ascribe the name "angel" to this thing that we believe in and suppose to exist. Nevertheless, the idea under which I imagine an angel is composed of the ideas of visible things.

It is the same with the sacred name "God": We have neither an image nor an idea of God. And thus we are forbidden to worship God under the form of an image, lest we seem to conceive him who is inconceivable.

It therefore seems there is no idea in us of God. But just as a person born blind who has often been brought close to a fire, and, feeling himself growing warm, recognizes that there is something that is warming him, and, on hearing that this is called "fire," concludes that fire exists, even though he does not know what shape or color it has, and has absolutely no idea or image of fire appearing before his mind; just so, a man who knows that there ought to be some cause of his images or ideas, and some other cause prior to this cause, and so on, is led finally to an end of this series, namely to the supposition of some eternal cause which, since it never began to be, cannot have a cause prior to itself, and necessarily concludes that something eternal exists. Nevertheless, he has no idea that he could call the idea of this eternal something; rather he gives a name to this thing he believes in and acknowledges, calling it "God."

Now since it is from this thesis (namely, that we have an idea of God in our soul) that M. Descartes proceeds to prove this theorem (namely, that God—that is, the supremely powerful, wise creator of the world—exists), he ought to have given a better explanation of this idea of God, and he ought thence to have deduced not only the existence of God but also the creation of the world.

Reply: Here the philosopher wants the word "idea" to be understood to refer exclusively to images that are of material things and are depicted in the corporeal imagination. Once this thesis has been posited, it is easy for him to prove that there is no proper idea either of an angel or of God. But from time to time throughout the work, and especially in this passage, I point out that I take the word "idea" to refer to whatever is immediately perceived by the mind, so that, when I will or fear something, I number those very acts of willing and fearing among my ideas, since at the same time I perceive that I will and fear. And I used this word because it was common practice for philosophers to use it to signify the forms of perception proper to the divine mind, even though we acknowledge that there is no corporeal imagination in God; moreover, I had no term available to me that was more suitable. However, I think I have given a sufficient explanation of the idea of God to take care of those wishing to pay attention to my meaning; but I could never fully satisfy those preferring to understand my words otherwise than I intend. Finally, what is added here about the creation of the world is utterly irrelevant to the question at hand.

Objection VI: "Again there are other thoughts that take different forms: for example, when I will, or fear, or affirm, or deny, there is always some thing that I grasp as the subject of my thought, yet I embrace in my thought something more than the likeness of that thing. Some of these thoughts are called volitions or affects, while others are called judgments."

When someone wills or fears, he surely has an image of the thing he fears or the action he wills; but what more it is that a person who wills or fears embraces in his thought is not explained. Although fear is indeed a thought, I fail to see how it can be anything but the thought of the thing that someone fears. For what is the fear of a charging lion if not the idea of a charging lion combined with the effect that such an idea produces in the heart, which induces in a person who is frightened that animal motion we call "flight"? Now this motion of flight is not thought. It remains therefore that there is no thought in fear except the one that consists in the likeness of the thing feared. The same thing could be said of the will.

Moreover, affirmation and negation are not found without language and designations, so that brute animals can neither affirm nor deny, not even in thought, and therefore they cannot make judgments. Nevertheless, a thought can be similar in both man and beast. For when we affirm that a man is running, the thought we have is no different from the one a dog has when it sees its master running. Therefore, the only thing affirmation or negation adds to simple thoughts is perhaps the thought that the names of

which an affirmation is composed are the names of the same thing in the one who affirms. This is not a matter of grasping in thought something more than the likeness of the thing, but merely the same likeness for a second time.

Reply: It is self-evident that seeing a lion and simultaneously fearing it is different from merely seeing it. Likewise seeing a man running is different from affirming to oneself that one sees him, an act which takes place without using language. And I find nothing here that requires an answer.

Objection VII: "All that remains for me is to ask how I received this idea of God. For I did not draw it from the senses; it never came upon me unexpectedly, as is usually the case with the ideas of sensible things when these things present themselves (or seem to present themselves) to the external sense organs. Nor was it made by me, for I plainly can neither subtract anything from it nor add anything to it. Thus the only option remaining is that this idea is innate in me, just as the idea of myself is innate in me."

If there is no idea of God (and it has not been proved that there is one), this entire inquiry falls apart. Moreover, if it is my body that is in question, then the idea of myself originates in me from sight; if it is my soul that is in question, then there is absolutely no idea of the soul. Rather, we infer by means of reasoning that there is something inside the human body that imparts to it the animal motion by which it senses and is moved. And this thing, whatever it is, we call the "soul," without having an idea of it.

Reply: If there is an idea of God (and it is obvious that there is), this entire objection falls apart. And when he adds that there is no idea of the soul, but rather that the soul is inferred by means of reasoning, this is the same thing as saying that there is no image of it depicted in the corporeal imagination, but that nevertheless there is such a thing as I have called an idea of it.

Objection VIII: "But there is another idea, one derived from astronomical reasoning; that is, it is elicited from certain notions innate in me. . . . "

It seems there is at any given moment but a single idea of the sun, regardless of whether it is looked at with the eyes or is understood by reasoning that it is many times larger than it appears. For this latter is not an idea of the sun, but an inference by way of arguments that the idea of the sun would be many times larger were it seen at much closer quarters.

But at different times there can be different ideas of the sun: for example, if it is looked at on one occasion with the naked eye and on another occasion through a telescope. But arguments drawn from astronomy do not make the idea of the sun any greater or smaller; rather, they show that an idea of the sun that is drawn from the senses is deceptive.

Reply: Here too what is said not to be an idea of the sun, and yet is described, is precisely what I call an idea.

Objection IX: "Unquestionably, those ideas that display [*exhibent*] substances to me are something more and, if I may say so, contain within themselves more objective reality than those which represent only modes or accidents. Again, the idea that enables me to understand a supreme deity, eternal, infinite, omniscient, omnipotent, and creator of all things other than himself, clearly has more objective reality in it than do those ideas through which finite substances are displayed."

I have frequently remarked above that there is no idea of God or of the soul. I now add that there is no idea of substance, for substance (given that it is matter subject to accidents and changes) is something concluded to solely by a process of reasoning; nevertheless, it is not conceived nor does it display any idea to us. If this is true, how can one say that the ideas that display substances to me are something greater and have more objective reality than those ideas that display accidents to me? Moreover, would M. Descartes please give some thought once again to what he means by "more reality"? Does reality admit of degrees? Or, if he thinks that one thing is greater than another, would he please give some thought to how this could be explained to our understanding with the same level of astuteness required in all demonstrations, and such as he himself has used on other occasions.

Reply: I have frequently noted that I call an idea that very thing which is concluded to by means of reasoning, as well as anything else that is in any way perceived. Moreover, I have sufficiently explained

how reality admits of degrees: namely, in precisely the way that a substance is a thing to a greater degree than is a mode. And if there are real qualities or incomplete substances, these are things to a greater degree than are modes, but to a lesser extent than are complete substances. And finally, if there is an infinite and independent substance, it is a thing to a greater degree than is a finite and dependent substance. But all of this is utterly self-evident.

Objection X: "Thus there remains only the idea of God. I must consider whether there is anything in this idea that could not have originated from me. I understand by the word 'God' a certain substance that is infinite, independent, supremely intelligent, and supremely powerful, and that created me along with everything else that exists—if anything else exists. Indeed all these are such that, the more carefully I focus my attention on them, the less possible it seems they could have arisen from myself alone. Thus, from what has been said above, I must conclude that God necessarily exists."

On considering the attributes of God in order thence to have an idea of God and to see whether there is anything in it that could not have proceeded from ourselves, I find, unless I am mistaken, that what we think of that corresponds to the word "God" does not originate with us, nor need it originate with anything but external objects. For by the word "God" I understand a "substance"; that is, I understand that God exists. But I understand this not through an idea but through a process of reasoning. And this substance I understand to be "infinite"; that is, it is something whose boundaries or extremities I cannot conceive or imagine without imagining still more extremities beyond these. From this it follows that what emerges as the correlate of the word "infinite" is not the idea of divine infinity, but that of my own boundaries or limits. This substance I understand to be "independent"; that is, I conceive of no cause from which God proceeds. Whence it is manifest that I have no idea corresponding to the word "independent" beyond the memory of my own ideas beginning at various times and their resulting dependencies.

Hence to say that God is "independent" is merely to say that God is among the number of those things of whose origin I form no image. In like manner, saying that God is "infinite" is tantamount to our saying that he is among the number of those things whose limits we do not conceive. And thus any idea of God is out of the question, for what sort of idea is it that has neither origin nor boundaries?

God is called "supremely understanding." I ask here: Through what idea does M. Descartes understand God's act of understanding?

God is called "supremely powerful." Again, through what idea do we understand power which is of things yet to come, that is, of things that do not exist? Certainly I understand power from the image or memory of past actions, concluding to it thus: Something did thus and so; therefore it was able to do it; and therefore, if it exists as the same thing, it will again be able to do thus and so; that is, it has the power to do something. Now these are all ideas that are capable of having arisen from external objects.

God is called "creator of all that exists." I can conjure up for myself some image of creation out of what I have observed, such as a man being born or his growing from something as small as a point to the shape and size he now possesses. No one has any other idea corresponding to the word "creator." However, to prove creation it is not enough to be able to imagine that the world was created. And thus, even if it were demonstrated that something "infinite, independent, supremely powerful, and so on" exists, it still does not follow that a creator exists, unless someone were to believe it is correct to infer from the fact that something exists which we believe to have created all other things that the world has therefore been at some time created by him.

Moreover, when he says that the idea of God and of our soul is innate in us, I would like to know if the souls of those in a deep sleep are thinking. If they are not, then during that time they have no ideas. Whence no idea is innate, for what is innate is always present.

Reply: Nothing that we ascribe to God can originate from external objects, as from an exemplar, since nothing in God bears any resemblance to things found in external, that is, corporeal things. However, if we think of something that is unlike these external objects, it obviously does not originate from them but from the cause of that diversity in our thought.

And I ask here how our philosopher deduces [his conception of] God's understanding from external things. But I easily explain the idea I have of God's understanding by saying that by the word "idea" I understand everything that is the form of some perception. For who is there that does not perceive that he understands something? And thus who is there that does not have that form or idea of an act of understanding, and, by indefinitely extending it, does not form an idea of the divine act of understanding? And the same applies to the rest of God's attributes.

But we used the idea of God which is in us to demonstrate God's existence, and such immense power is contained in this idea that we understand that, if in fact God does exist, it would be contradictory for something other than God to exist without having been created by him. And because of these considerations, it plainly follows, from the fact that his existence has been demonstrated, that it has also been demonstrated that the entire world, that is, all the things other than God that exist, has been created by him.

Finally, when we assert that some idea is innate in us, we do not have in mind that we always notice it (for in that event no idea would ever be innate), but only that we have in ourselves the power to elicit the idea.

Objection XI: "The whole force of the argument rests on the fact that I recognize that it would be impossible for me to exist, being of such a nature as I am (namely, having in me the idea of God), unless God did in fact exist. God, I say, that same being the idea of whom is in me. . . ."

Since, therefore, it has not been demonstrated that we have an idea of God, and since the Christian religion requires us to believe that God is inconceivable (that is, as I see it, that we have no idea of him), it follows that the existence of God has not been demonstrated, and much less has the creation.

Reply: When it is asserted that God is inconceivable, this is understood with respect to a concept that adequately comprehends him. But I have repeated ad nauseam how it is we have an idea of God. And nothing at all is asserted here that weakens my demonstrations.

# Fourth Set of Objections

## Concerning God

The first proof of the existence of God (the one the author spells out in the Third Meditation) has two parts. The first part is that God exists if indeed there is an idea of God in me. The second part is that I who have such an idea could be derived only from God.

Regarding the first part, there is one thing that is not proved to me, namely that when the distinguished gentleman asserted that falsity properly so-called can be found only in judgments, he nevertheless admits a bit later that ideas can be false—not formally false mind you, but materially false. This seems to me to be out of keeping with his first principles.

But I fear I should not be able to explain with enough lucidity my feelings on a matter that is decidedly obscure. An example will make it clearer. The author asserts that if cold is but the privation of heat, the idea of cold which represents it to me as if it were something positive will be materially false.

Moreover, if cold is merely a privation, then there could not be an idea of cold that represents it to me as something positive, and here the author confuses a judgment with an idea.

For what is the idea of cold? Coldness itself, insofar as it exists objectively in the understanding. But if cold is a privation it cannot exist objectively in the understanding by means of an idea whose objective existence is a positive being. Thus, if cold is but a privation, there could not be a positive idea of it, and hence there could never be an idea that is materially false.

This is confirmed by the same argument the distinguished gentleman uses to prove that the idea of an infinite cannot but be true. For although one could imagine that such a being does not exist, nevertheless one could not imagine that the idea of such a being presented nothing real to me.

We can readily say the same thing about every positive idea. For although one could imagine that cold, which I think is represented by a positive idea, is not something positive, still one cannot imagine that the positive idea presents to me nothing real and positive. This is because an idea is not said to be positive in virtue of the existence it has as a mode of thinking (for on that score all ideas would be positive), but rather in virtue of the objective existence it contains and which it presents to our mind. Therefore, though it is possible that this idea is not the idea of cold, it nevertheless cannot be a false one.

But, you may say, it is false precisely in virtue of its not being the idea of cold. Actually, it is your judgment that is false, were you to judge it to be the idea of cold. But the idea, in and of itself,[9] is most true. In like manner, the idea of God surely ought not be called false, not even materially, even though someone could transfer it to something that is not God, as idolaters have done.

Finally, what does this idea of cold, which you say is materially false, display to your mind? A privation? Then it is true. A positive being? Then it is not the idea of cold. Again, what is the cause of this positive objective being, which, in your opinion, renders this idea materially false? It is I, you say, insofar as I am derived from nothing. Therefore, the positive objective existence of some idea can be derived from nothing, a conclusion that destroys the principal foundations of the distinguished gentleman.

But let us move on to the second part of the demonstration, where he asks whether I myself who have the idea of an infinite being could be derived from something other than an infinite being, and especially whether I am derived from myself. The distinguished gentleman contends that I could not be derived from myself, in view of the fact that, were I myself to give myself existence, I would also give myself all the perfections an idea of which I observe to be within me. But the theologian replies with the astute observation that "being derived from itself" [*esse a se*] ought to be taken not in a positive sense, but in a negative sense, to the effect that it means the same thing as "not derived from another." "But," he says, "if something is derived from itself (that is to say, not from something else), how do I prove that this thing encompasses all things and that it is infinite? I do not

---

9. Reading *se* for *te* (AT VII, 207).

follow you now if you say, 'if it is derived from itself, it would have easily given itself all things.' For neither is it derived from itself as from a cause, nor did it exist prior to itself such that it would choose beforehand what it would later be."

To refute this argument, the distinguished gentleman maintains that "being derived from itself" ought to be taken in a positive rather than a negative sense, even when it applies to God, to the effect that God "stands in the same relationship to himself as an efficient cause does to its effect." This seems to me to be a harsh statement and a false one at that.

Thus, while I am partly in agreement with the distinguished gentleman, I am partly in disagreement with him. For I confess I cannot be derived from myself except in a positive fashion, but I deny that the same may be said of God. In fact, I think it a manifest contradiction that something is derived from itself positively and as it were from a cause. Thus I bring about the same result as our author, but by way of quite another route, and it goes as follows:

For me to be derived from myself, I ought to be derived from myself in a positive fashion, and as it were from a cause. Therefore, it is impossible for me to be derived from myself.

The major premise of this syllogism is proved by the gentleman's arguments that are drawn from the doctrine that, since the various parts of time can be separated from one another, the fact that I exist now does not entail my existing in the future, unless some cause, as it were, makes me over again at each individual moment.

As to the minor premise, I believe it to be so clear by the light of nature that it is largely a waste of time to try to prove it—a matter of proving the known by means of the less known. Moreover, the author seems to have recognized the truth of this since he has not made bold to disavow it publicly. Please weigh the following statement made in reply to the theologian:[10]

" . . . I did not say that it is impossible for something to be the efficient cause of itself. For although this is obviously the case when the meaning of "efficient cause" is restricted to those causes which are

temporally prior to their effects or are different from them, still it does not seem that such a restriction is appropriate in this inquiry, . . . since the light of nature does not stipulate that the nature of an efficient cause requires that it be temporally prior to its effect."

Well done, as far as the first part is concerned. But why has he left out the second part? And why has he not added that the very same light of nature does not stipulate that the essence [*ratio*] of an efficient cause requires that it be different from its effect, unless it is because the very same light of nature did not permit him to assert it?

And since every effect depends upon a cause and thus receives its existence from a cause, is it not patently clear that the same thing cannot depend on itself or receive its existence from itself?

Moreover, every cause is the cause of an effect, and every effect the effect of a cause. Thus there is a reciprocal relationship between cause and effect. But a relationship must occur between two things.

Moreover, it is absurd to conceive of something receiving existence and yet having existence prior to the time we conceive it to have received existence. But this would be the case were we to ascribe the notions of cause and effect to the very same thing in respect to itself. For what is the notion of a cause? It is the giving of existence. And what is the notion of an effect? It is the receiving of existence. But the notion of a cause is prior by nature to that of an effect.

But we cannot conceive of something as a cause [*sub ratione causae*] (as something giving existence), unless we conceive of it as having existence; for no one gives what one does not have. Therefore we would first be conceiving a thing as having existence before conceiving of it as having received it; and yet in the case of whatever receives existence, receiving existence comes before having existence.

This argument can be put differently: no one gives what he does not have; therefore, no one can give himself existence, unless he already has it. But if he already has it, why would he give it to himself?

Finally, he claims that it is manifest by the light of nature that creation differs from preservation solely by virtue of a distinction of reason. But it is manifest

---

10. Johan de Kater (Johannes Caterus), author of the *First Set of Objections*.

by the very same light of nature that nothing can create itself. Therefore, nothing can preserve itself.

But if we descend from the general thesis to the specific instance [*hypothesim*] of God, the matter will, in my judgment, be even more manifest: God cannot be derived from himself positively, but only negatively, that is, in the sense of not being derived from something else.

And first, it is manifest from the argument put forward by the distinguished gentleman to prove that if a body is derived from itself, then it ought to be derived from itself in a positive fashion. For, as he says, the parts of time do not depend on one another. Thus, the fact that this body is presumed up until the present time to have been derived from itself (that is, it has no cause) does not suffice to make it exist in the future, unless there is some power in it which, as it were, continuously "remakes" it.

But so far from this argument being relevant to the case of a supremely perfect or infinite being, the opposite result could be readily deduced, and for opposite reasons. For contained in the idea of an infinite being is the fact that its duration is also infinite; that is, it is bounded by no limits; and thus it is indivisible, permanent, and possessed of all things all at once [*tota simul*]. Temporal sequence cannot be conceived to be in this idea except erroneously and through the imperfection of our understanding.

Whence it manifestly follows that an infinite being cannot be conceived of as existing even for a moment without at the same time being conceived of as always having existed and as existing in the future for eternity (which is what the author himself teaches in another passage). Hence it is pointless to ask why it would continue to exist.

Further—as is frequently taught by St. Augustine (than whom no one after the time of the sacred authors has ever spoken more nobly and sublimely about God)—in God there is no past or future, but an eternal present. And from this it appears quite evident that it is only with absurdity that one can ask why God continues to exist, since this question obviously involves a temporal sequence of before and after, of past and future, and this ought to be excluded from the notion of an infinite being.

Moreover, God cannot be thought of as being derived from himself positively [*a se positive*], as if he had initially produced himself, for in that case he would have existed before he existed. Rather, God can be thought to be derived from himself solely in virtue of the fact that he really does preserve himself, as the author frequently states.

But preservation is no more consonant with an infinite being than is an initial production. For what, pray, is preservation, except a certain continuous remaking of something? Thus every instance of preservation presupposes an initial production; and for this reason the term "continuation," like the term "preservation," implies a certain potentiality. But an infinite being is the purest actuality, without any potentiality.

Let us conclude then that God can be conceived to be derived from himself [*esse a seipso*] in a positive fashion only by reason of the imperfection of our understanding, which conceives of God after the manner of created things. This will be established even more firmly by means of another argument.

The efficient cause of something is sought only with respect to a thing's existence, not its essence. For example, on seeing a triangle, I may seek the efficient cause that brought about the existence of this triangle, but it would be absurd for me to seek the efficient cause of the fact that the triangle has three angles equal to two right angles. Saying that an efficient cause is the reason for this is not a proper answer to someone making an inquiry; all that can be said is that it is simply the nature of a triangle to have such a property. Thus it is that mathematicians do not demonstrate by way of efficient or final causes, since they do not concern themselves with the existence of their object. But it no less belongs to the essence of an infinite being that it exists, and even, if you will, that it continues in existence, than it is of the essence of a triangle that it have three angles equal to two right angles. Therefore, just as one cannot give an answer by way of efficient causality to the person asking why a triangle has three angles equal to two right angles but must say only that such is the eternal and unchangeable nature of a triangle, just so, to the person asking why God exists or why God continues to exist, the advice should be given that no efficient cause (either inside or outside God), no "quasi-efficient" cause (for I am in disagreement about things not words) is to be sought. Rather, this alone should be claimed as the reason: that such is the nature of a supremely perfect being.

The learned gentleman states that the light of nature dictates that there exists nothing about which it is inappropriate to ask why it exists or to inquire into its efficient cause, or, if it has none, to demand to know why it does not need one. Against this my answer to the person asking why God exists is that one should not reply in terms of an efficient cause. Rather, one should say merely that it is because he is God, that is, an infinite being. And if someone were to ask for the efficient cause of God, we should answer that God needs no efficient cause. And were the inquirer once again to ask why God does not need an efficient cause, we should answer that it is because he is an infinite being, whose existence is his essence; for the only things that need an efficient cause are those in which it is appropriate to distinguish their actual existence from their essence.

Thus is overthrown all that the author adds just after the passages cited: "Thus," he says, "if I thought that nothing could in any way be related to itself the way an efficient cause is related to its effect, it is out of the question that I then conclude that something is the first cause. On the contrary, I would again ask for the cause of that which was being called the 'first cause,' and thus I would never arrive at any first cause of all things."

On the contrary, were I to think we should seek the efficient (or quasi-efficient) cause of any given thing, I would seek a cause of each individual thing that was different from that thing, since it is most evident to me that in no way can something be in the same relation to itself as an efficient cause is to its effect.

The author, in my opinion, should be put on notice so that he can consider these things attentively and diligently, since I certainly know there can scarcely be found a theologian who would not take exception to the statement that God is derived from himself in a positive fashion, and as it were from a cause.

My only remaining concern is whether the author does not commit a vicious circle, when he says that we have no other basis on which to establish that what we clearly and distinctly perceive is true, than that God exists.

But we can be certain that God exists only because we clearly and evidently perceive this fact. Therefore, before we are certain that God exists, we ought to be certain that whatever we clearly and evidently perceive is true.

I add something that had escaped me. What the distinguished gentleman affirms as certain seems to me to be false, namely, that there can be nothing in him, insofar as he is a thinking thing, of which he is unaware. For this "him, insofar as it is a thinking thing," he understands to be merely his mind, insofar as it is distinct from his body. But who does not realize that there can be a great many things in the mind, of which the mind is unaware? The mind of an infant in its mother's womb has the power to think, but it is not aware of it. I pass over countless examples similar to this one.

# Reply to the Fourth Set of Objections

## Reply to the Second Part: Concerning God

Up to this point I have attempted to refute the distinguished gentleman's arguments and to withstand his attack. From here on, as is the custom for those who struggle with those stronger than themselves, I will not place myself in direct opposition to him; rather, I will dodge his blows.

He brings up only three points in this part; and these can be readily accepted if they are taken in the sense in which he understands them. But I understood what I wrote in a different sense, which also seems to me to be true.

The first point is that certain ideas are materially false. As I understand it, these ideas are such that they present matter for error to the power of judgment.

But the gentleman, by considering these ideas taken formally, argues that no falsity is in them.

The second point is that God is derived from himself positively and as it were from a cause. Here I had in mind merely that the reason why God does not need any efficient cause in order to exist is founded on something positive, namely on the very immensity of God, than which there can be nothing more positive. The gentleman proves that God can never be produced or preserved by himself through some positive influence of an efficient cause. I too am in agreement with all of this.

The third and final point is that there can be nothing in our mind of which we are unaware. I understood this with respect to operations, whereas the gentleman, who understands this with respect to powers, denies this.

But let us carefully explain each of these one by one. When the gentleman says that if cold were merely a privation, there could not be an idea [of cold] that represents it as something positive, it is obvious that he is merely dealing with the idea taken formally. For since ideas are themselves forms of a certain sort and are not made up of any matter, whenever we consider them insofar as they represent something, we are taking them not materially but formally. But if we view them not insofar as they represent this or that thing, but merely insofar as they are operations of the understanding, then we could surely say that we are taking them materially. But in that case they would bear absolutely no relationship to the truth or falsity of their objects. Hence it seems to me that we can call these ideas materially false only in the sense I have already described: Namely, whether cold be something positive or a privation, I do not on that account have a different idea of it; rather, it remains the same in me as the one I have always had. And I say that this idea provides me with matter for error if it is true that cold is a privation and does not have as much reality as heat, because, in considering either of the ideas of heat or cold just as I received them both from the senses, I cannot observe any more reality being shown me by the one idea than by the other.

And it is obviously not the case that I have confused judgment with an idea, for I have said that

material falsity is to be found in the latter, whereas only formal falsity can exist in the former.

However, when the distinguished gentleman says that the idea of cold is coldness itself insofar as it exists objectively in the understanding, I think a distinction is in order. For it often happens in the case of obscure and confused ideas (and those of heat and cold should be numbered among them) that they are referred to something other than that of which they really are ideas. Thus, were cold merely a privation, the idea of cold would not be coldness itself as it exists objectively in the understanding, but something else which is wrongly taken for that privation: namely, a certain sensation having no existence outside the understanding.

But the same analysis does not hold in the case of the idea of God, or at least when the idea is clear and distinct, since it cannot be said to be referred to something with which it is not in conformity. But as to confused ideas of gods which are concocted by idolaters, I fail to see why they too cannot be called materially false, insofar as these ideas provide matter for their false judgments. Nevertheless, surely those ideas that offer the faculty of judgment little or no occasion for error are presumably less worthy of being called materially false than do those that offer it considerable occasion for error; however, it is easy to exemplify the fact that some ideas offer a greater occasion for error than others. For this occasion does not exist in confused ideas formed at the whim of the mind (such as the ideas of false gods) to the extent that it does in ideas that come to us confused from the senses (such as the ideas of heat and cold), if, as I said, it is in fact true that they display nothing real. But the greatest occasion of all for error is in ideas that arise from the sensitive appetite. For example, does not the idea of thirst in the man with dropsy in fact offer him matter for error when it provides him an occasion for judging that drinking something will do him good, when in fact it will do him harm?

But the distinguished gentleman asks what it is that is shown to me by this idea of cold, which I have said to be materially false. He says: if it shows a privation, then it is true; if it shows a positive being, then it is not the idea of cold. Quite true. However, the sole reason for my calling this idea materially false is that, since it is obscure and confused, I could not determine whether or not what it shows me is something positive outside my sensation. Thus I have an occasion for judging that it is something positive, although perhaps it is merely a privation.

Hence one should not ask what the cause is of this positive objective being that causes this idea to be materially false, since I am not claiming that this materially false idea is caused by some positive being, but rather that it is caused solely by the obscurity that nevertheless does have something positive as its subject, namely the sensation itself.

And surely this positive being is in me insofar as I am a true thing; but the obscurity, which alone provides me an occasion for judging that this idea of the sensation of cold represents something external to me which is called "cold," does not have a real cause, but arises solely from the fact that my nature is not perfect in every respect.

My basic principles are in no way weakened by this objection. However, since I never spent very much time reading the books of the philosophers, it might have been a cause for worry that I did not sufficiently take note of their manner of speaking when I asserted that ideas that provide the power of judgment with matter for error are materially false, had it not been for the fact that I found the word "materially" used in the same sense as my own in the first author that came into my hands: namely in Francisco Suarez's *Metaphysical Disputations*, Disp. IX, sect. 2, no. 4.

But let us move on to the most significant items about which the distinguished gentleman registers his disapproval. However, in my opinion, these things seem least deserving of disapproval: namely, in the passage where I said that it is fitting for us to think that in a sense God stands in the same relationship to himself as an efficient cause does to its effect. For in that very passage I denied what the distinguished gentleman says is a harsh saying, and a false one at that: namely, that God is the efficient cause of himself. For in asserting that "in a certain sense, God stands in the same relationship to himself as an efficient cause," I did not take the two relationships to be identical. And

in saying by way of preface that "it is wholly fitting for us to think . . . ," I meant that my sole explanation for these things is the imperfection of the human understanding. However, I asserted this throughout the rest of the passage; for right at the very beginning, where I said that there exists nothing about which it is inappropriate to inquire into its efficient cause, I added "or, if it does not have one, to demand why it does not need one." These words are a sufficient indication that I believed there exists something that needs no efficient cause. But what, besides God, can be of this sort? And a short time later I said that "in God there is such great and inexhaustible power, that he never needed the help of anything in order to exist. Moreover, God does not now need a cause in order to be preserved; thus, in a manner of speaking, God is the cause of himself." Here the expression "cause of himself" can in no way be understood to mean an efficient cause; rather, it is merely a matter of the inexhaustible power of God being the cause or the reason why he needs no cause. And since this inexhaustible power or immensity of essence is incomparably positive, I said that the cause or the reason why God does not need a cause is a positive one. This could not be said of anything finite, even if it is supremely perfect in its own kind. But if a finite thing were said to be derived from itself, this could only be understood in a negative sense, since no reason derived from its positive nature could be put forward, on the basis of which we might understand that it does not need an efficient cause.

And in like manner, in all the other passages in which I compared the formal cause or reason derived from God's essence (on account of which God does not need a cause, either in order to exist or to be preserved) with the efficient cause (without which finite things cannot come into existence), I always did this in such wise that the difference between the formal cause and the efficient cause may come to be known from my very own words. Nowhere have I said that God preserves himself by means of some positive influence, as is the case with created things preserved by him; on the contrary, I merely said that the immensity of power or essence, on account of which he needs no one to preserve him, is something positive.

And thus I can readily agree with everything the distinguished gentleman puts forward to prove that God is not the efficient cause of himself and that he preserves himself neither by means of any positive influence nor by means of a continuous reproduction of himself. This is the only thing that is achieved from his arguments. However, as I hope is the case, even he will not deny that this immensity of the power, on account of which God does not need a cause in order to exist, is in God something positive, and that nothing similarly positive can be understood in anything else on account of which it would not require an efficient cause in order to exist. This is all I meant when I said that, with the exception of God alone, nothing can be understood to be derived from itself unless this is understood in a negative sense. Nor was there any need for me to assume any more than this in order to resolve the difficulty that had been put forward.

However, since the distinguished gentleman warns me here with such seriousness that "there can scarcely be found a theologian who would not take exception to the proposition that God is derived from himself in a positive fashion, and as it were from a cause," I will explain a bit more carefully why this way of speaking seems to me to be extremely helpful and even necessary in treating this question, and also why it seems to me to be quite removed from suspicion of being likely to cause someone to take offense.

I am aware that theologians of the Latin Church do not use the word *causa* [cause] in speaking of divine matters, when they are discussing the procession of persons in the Most Holy Trinity. And whereas theologians of the Greek Church use the words αἴτιον [cause] and ἀρχὴν [principle] interchangeably, theologians of the Latin Church prefer to use only the word *principium* [principle], taking it in its most general sense, lest from their manner of speaking they provide anyone an occasion on this basis for judging the Son to be less than the Father. But where no such danger of error is possible, and the discussion concerns not God considered as triune but only as one, I fail to see why the word "cause" should be shunned to such a degree, especially when we arrive

at a point where it seems quite helpful and almost necessary to use it.

However, there can be no greater use for this term than if it aids in demonstrating the existence of God, and no greater necessity for it than if the existence of God manifestly could not be proved without it.

But I think it is obvious to everyone that a consideration of efficient causes is the primary and principal, not to say the only, means of proving the existence of God. However, we cannot pursue this proof with care unless we give our mind the freedom to inquire about the efficient causes of all things, including even God himself, for by what right would we thence exclude God before we have proved that he exists? We must therefore ask with respect to every single thing whether it is derived from itself or from something else. And the existence of God can indeed be inferred by this means, even if we do not provide an explicit account of how one is to understand that "something is derived from itself." For those who follow exclusively the lead of the light of nature immediately at this juncture form a certain concept common to both efficient and formal cause alike, i.e., what is derived from something else [*est ab alio*] is derived from it as it were from an efficient cause; but whatever is derived from itself [*est a se*] is derived as it were from a formal cause, that is, because it has an essence of such a type that it does not need an efficient cause.

For this reason I did not explain this doctrine in my *Meditations*; rather I assumed it to be self-evident.

But when those who are accustomed to judging that nothing can be the efficient cause of itself and to distinguishing carefully an efficient cause from a formal cause see the question being raised as to whether something is derived from itself, it easily happens that, while thinking that this expression refers only to an efficient cause properly so-called, they do not think the expression "derived from itself" should be understood to mean "as from a cause," but only negatively as meaning "without a cause," with the result that there arises something concerning which we must not ask why it exists. Were this rendering of the expression "derived from itself" to be accepted, there could not be an argument [*ratio*] from effects to prove the existence of God, as the author of the First Set of Objections has shown. Therefore, this rendering is in no way to be accepted.

However, to give an apt reply to this, I think it is necessary to point out that there is a middle ground between an efficient cause properly so-called and no cause at all: namely the positive essence of a thing, to which we can extend the concept of an efficient cause in the same way we are accustomed in geometry to extend the concept of an exceedingly long arc to the concept of a straight line, or the concept of a rectilinear polygon with an indefinite number of sides to the concept of a circle. And I fail to see how this can be explained any better than by saying that in this query the meaning of "efficient cause" should not be restricted to those causes which are temporally prior to their effects or are different from them. For, first, the question would be pointless, since everyone knows that the same thing cannot exist prior to itself or be different from itself. Second, we could remove one of these two conditions from its concept and yet the notion of an efficient cause would remain intact.

For the fact that an efficient cause need not be temporally prior is evident from the fact that it has the defining characteristic [*rationem*] of a cause only during the time it is producing an effect, as has been said.

But from the fact that the other condition as well cannot be set aside, one ought to infer only that it is not an efficient cause taken in the strict sense, and I grant this. However, one ought not infer that it is in no sense a positive cause which can be compared by way of analogy to an efficient cause; and this is all that is called for in my argument. For by the very same light of nature by which I perceive that I would have given myself all the perfections of which there is an idea in me (if indeed I had given myself existence), I also perceive that nothing can give itself existence in that restricted sense in which the term "efficient cause" is typically used, namely in such wise that the same thing, insofar as it gives itself existence, is different from itself, insofar as it receives existence, since being the same thing and not being the same thing (that is, being different from itself) are contradictory.

And thus, when the question arises whether something can give itself existence, one must understand this to be equivalent to asking whether the nature or essence of anything is such that it needs no efficient cause in order to exist.

And when one adds that if there were such a thing, it would give itself all the perfections of which there is some idea in it, if indeed it does not yet have them, the meaning of this is that this thing cannot fail to have in actuality all the perfections that it knows. The reason for this is that we perceive by the light of nature that a thing whose essence is so immense that it does not need an efficient cause in order to exist also does not need an efficient cause in order to possess all the perfections that it knows, and that its own proper essence gives it in an eminent fashion all that we can think an efficient cause is capable of giving to any other things.

And the words "if it does not yet have them, it will give them to itself" are helpful only in explaining the matter, since we perceive by the same light of nature that this thing cannot now have the power and the will to give itself anything new, but that its essence is such that it possesses from eternity all that we can now think it would give itself, if it did not already possess it.

Nevertheless, all these modes of speaking, which are taken from the analogy of an efficient cause, are particularly necessary in order to direct the light of nature in such wise that we pay particular attention to them. This takes place in precisely the same way in which Archimedes, by comparing the sphere and other curvilinear figures with rectilinear figures, demonstrated various properties of the sphere and other curvilinear figures that otherwise could hardly have been understood. And just as no one raises objections regarding proofs of this sort, even if during the course of them one is required to consider a sphere to be similar to a polyhedron, I likewise think I cannot be blamed here for using the analogy of an efficient cause in order to explain those things that pertain to a formal cause, that is, to the very essence of God.

And there is no possible danger of error in this matter, since that one single aspect which is a property of an efficient cause, and which cannot be extended to a formal cause, contains a manifest contradiction, and thus is incapable of being believed by anyone, namely that something is different from itself or that it simultaneously is and is not the same thing.

Moreover, one should note that we have ascribed to God the dignity inherent in being a cause in such wise that no indignity inherent in being an effect would follow thence in him. For just as theologians, in saying that the Father is the *principium* [principle] of the Son, do not on that account grant that the Son came from a principle; just so, although I have granted that God can in a certain sense be called the cause of himself, nevertheless nowhere have I in the same way called him an effect of himself. For it is customary to use the word "effect" primarily in relation to an efficient cause, and is regarded as less noble than its efficient cause, although it is often more noble than other causes.

However, when I here take the entire essence of a thing for its formal cause, I am merely following in the footsteps of Aristotle, for in his *Posterior Analytics*, Book II, Chapter 11, having passed over the material cause, he calls the αἰτίαν [cause] the τὸ τί ἦν εἶναι [the what it was to be] or, as philosophers writing in Latin traditionally render it, the *causa formalis* [formal cause], and he extends this to all the essences of all things, since at this point he is dealing not with the causes of a physical composite (any more than I am here), but more generally with the causes from which some knowledge could be sought.

But it was hardly possible for me to discuss this matter without ascribing the term "cause" to God. This can be shown from the fact that, when the distinguished gentleman attempted to do the same thing I did by a different route, he nevertheless was completely unsuccessful, at least as I see it. For after using a number of words he shows that God is not the efficient cause of himself, since the defining characteristic [*ratio*] of "efficient cause" requires it to be different from its effect. Then he shows that God is not derived from himself in a positive sense, where one understands the word "positive" to mean the positive influence of a cause. Next he shows that God does not truly preserve himself, if by "preservation" one

means the continuous production of a thing. All of this I readily grant. At length he tries to prove that God cannot be said to be the efficient cause of himself because, he says, the efficient cause of a thing is sought only with respect to the thing's existence, but not at all with respect to its essence. But existing is no less of the essence of an infinite being than having three angles equal to two right angles is of the essence of a triangle. Thus, if one is asked why God exists, one should no more answer by way of an efficient cause than one should do if asked why the three angles of a triangle are equal to two right angles. This syllogism can easily be turned against the distinguished gentleman in the following way: even if an efficient cause is not sought with respect to essence, still it can be sought with respect to existence; but in God essence and existence are not distinguished; therefore, one can seek an efficient cause of God.

But in order to reconcile these two positions, someone who seeks to know why God exists should be told that one surely ought not respond in terms of an efficient cause in the strict sense, but only in terms of the very essence or formal cause of the thing. And precisely because in God existence is not distinguished from essence, the formal cause is strikingly analogous to an efficient cause, and thus can be called a "quasi-efficient cause."

Finally, he adds that the reply to be made to someone who is seeking the efficient cause of God is that he has no need of one; and to someone quizzing us further as to why God does not need one, the reply should be that this is because God is an infinite being whose existence is his essence. For only those things that need an efficient cause are those in which actual existence can be distinguished from essence. On the basis of these considerations he says he overturns what I had said, namely that were I to think that nothing could somehow be related to itself the same way that an efficient cause is related to an effect, I would never, in inquiring into the causes of things, arrive at any first cause of all things. Nevertheless, it appears to me that my position has not been overturned nor has it been shaken or weakened. Moreover, on this depends the principal force not just of my argument but of absolutely all the arguments that can be put forward to prove the existence of God from effects. Yet virtually every theologian holds that no proof can be put forward unless it is from effects.

And thus, when he disallows the analogy of an efficient cause being ascribed to God's relationship to himself, far from making the argument for God's existence transparent, he instead prevents readers from understanding it, especially at the end where he concludes that, were he to think that an efficient or quasi-efficient cause were to be sought for anything, he would be seeking a cause of that thing which is different from it. For how would those who do not yet know God inquire into the efficient cause of other things so as in this way to arrive at a knowledge of God, unless they thought that one could seek the efficient cause of anything whatever? And finally, how would they make an end of their search for God as the first cause, if they thought that for any given thing one must look for a cause that is different from it?

The distinguished gentleman certainly appears to be doing the very same thing here that he would do, were he to follow Archimedes (who spoke of the properties that he had demonstrated of a sphere by means of an analogy with rectilinear figures) and were to say, "If I thought that a sphere could not be taken for a rectilinear or quasi-rectilinear figure having an infinite number of sides, I would attach no force to this demonstration, since strictly speaking the argument holds not for a sphere as a curvilinear figure, but merely for a sphere as a rectilinear figure having an infinite number of sides." It is, I say, as if the distinguished gentleman, while not wanting to characterize the sphere thus, and nevertheless desirous of retaining Archimedes' demonstration, were to say, "If I thought that the conclusion Archimedes drew there was supposed to be understood with respect to a rectilinear figure having an infinite number of sides, I would not admit this conclusion with respect to the sphere, since I am both certain and convinced that a sphere is in no way a rectilinear figure." Obviously, in making these remarks he would not be doing the same thing as Archimedes had done; on the contrary, he would definitely prevent himself and others from correctly understanding Archimedes' demonstration.

I have pursued these matters here at somewhat greater length than perhaps the subject required, in order to show that it is a matter of greatest importance to take care lest there be found in my writings the least thing that theologians may justly find objectionable.

Finally, as to the fact that I did not commit a vicious circle when I said that it is manifest to us that the things we clearly and distinctly perceive are true only because God exists; and that it is manifest to us that God exists only because we perceive this fact clearly, I have already given a sufficient explanation in the Reply to the Second Set of Objections, Sections 3 and 4, where I drew a distinction between what we are actually perceiving clearly and what we recall having clearly perceived sometime earlier. For first of all it is manifest to us that God exists, since we are attending to the arguments that prove this; but later on, it is enough for us to recall our having clearly perceived something in order to be certain that it is true. This would not suffice, unless we knew that God exists and does not deceive us.

Now as to the doctrine that there can be nothing in the mind, insofar as it is a thinking thing, of which it is not aware, this appears to me self-evident, because we understand that nothing is in the mind, so viewed, that is not a thought or is not dependent upon thought. For otherwise it would not belong to the mind insofar as it is a thinking thing. Nor can there exist in us any thought of which we are not aware at the very same moment it is in us. For this reason I have no doubt that the mind begins to think immediately upon its being infused into the body of an infant, and at the same time is aware of its thought, even if later on it does not recall what it was thinking of, because the images [*species*] of these thoughts do not inhere in the memory.

However, it should be noted that although we surely are always actually aware of the acts or operations of our mind, but this is not always the case with regard to faculties or powers, except potentially. In other words, when we prepare ourselves to use some faculty, if this faculty is in the mind, we are immediately and actually aware of it. And therefore we can deny that it is in the mind if we are unable to become aware of it.

# Elisabeth and Descartes, *Correspondence* (1643)[1]

*Elisabeth, Princess of Bohemia, Countess of the Palatinate (1618–1680) was the eldest daughter of Frederick of Bohemia and Elisabeth Stuart, a daughter of Charles I, king of England. After Frederick lost his throne in 1620, the family went into exile in The Hague, where they lived in relative poverty. Elisabeth, who was tutored privately by professors at Leiden University, developed an aptitude in mathematics and learned several languages, including Latin and Greek. Elisabeth's first letter to Descartes (6 May 1643, below) shows that she was familiar with Cartesian philosophy. The correspondence that ensued encompassed a multitude of interesting topics, from mathematical problems, to Machiavelli's political theory, to Seneca's Stoic ethics, to morals in general. Many of the letters concentrated on the theory of the passions and the union of body and mind. Descartes dedicated his* Principles of Philosophy *(1644) to Elisabeth. He wrote* Passions of the Soul *(1649) for her and sent her the first two parts of the treatise for her comments; the finished treatise contained a third part, responding further to Elisabeth's interests.*

## Elisabeth to Descartes, 6 May 1643

Mr. Descartes,

I learned, with much joy and regret, of your intention to see me a few days ago. I was touched equally by your charity in wanting to communicate with an ignorant and recalcitrant person, and by the misfortune that robbed me of such a profitable conversation. Mr. Pollot[2] greatly augmented this latter passion by reviewing for me the solutions you gave to the obscurities contained in Mr. Regius' physics,[3] concerning which I would have been better instructed in person, as also I would have been on a question I posed to this professor when he was in this city, about which he directed me to you to receive the required satisfaction. My embarrassment over showing you such an unruly style prevented me until now from asking you this favor by letter.

But today Mr. Pollot gave me so much assurance of your kindness toward everyone, and especially

---

1. Translated from the French by Roger Ariew.

2. Alphonse Pollot (1602–1668), a friend and correspondent of Descartes who mediated between Descartes and Princess Elisabeth.
3. Henricus Regius (1598–1679), professor of medicine at Utrecht, at the time was a follower of Descartes and supporter of his physics.

toward me, that I chased away all other considerations from my mind, except those bringing me to ask you to tell me how the soul of a man can determine the bodily spirits to make voluntary actions (the soul being only a thinking substance). For it seems that all determination of motion occurs through the impulsion of the thing moved in such a way that it is pushed by the thing that moves it, or else, by the particular qualities and shape of the surface of the latter. Contact is required by the first two conditions, and extension by the third. You exclude entirely the latter from the notion you have of the soul, and the former appears to me to be incompatible with an immaterial thing. This is why I ask you for a more specific definition of the soul than the one you give in your *Metaphysics*, that is, of its substance, separate from its action, from thought. For, although we supposed them to be inseparable (which, however, is difficult to prove for the mother's womb and great fainting spells), like the attributes of God, we can, by considering them apart, obtain a more perfect idea of them.

Knowing you are the best physician for my soul, I quite freely uncover the weaknesses of its speculations to you and hope that, in observing the Hippocratic oath, you will bring it some remedies without making them public, which I beg you to do, as I beg you to suffer these annoyances from,

Mr. Descartes,
　　　Your affectionate friend at your service,
　　　　　Elisabeth

## Descartes to Elisabeth, 21 May 1643

Madam,
The favor with which your Highness honored me in allowing me to receive her commands in writing is greater than I ever dared to hope. It comforts my failings better than what I would have hoped for with passion, which was to receive them in person, if I had been able to obtain the honor of paying homage to you and offering you my very humble services when I was last at The Hague. For I would have had too many marvels to admire at the same time; and seeing superhuman discourse issue from a body similar to

those painters give to angels, I would have been overwhelmed in the same way as those must be, I should think, who, coming from earth, are just entering into heaven. This would have rendered me less capable of replying to your Highness, who doubtless already noticed this weakness in me, when I had the honor of speaking to her before. And your mercy wished to comfort me by leaving me the traces of your thoughts on paper, where, rereading them several times, and becoming accustomed to considering them, I am truly less overcome, but even more full of admiration, observing that they not only appear ingenious at first sight, but even more judicious and solid the further they are examined.

And I can say with truth that the question your Highness proposes seems to me to be the question that can most justifiably be asked of me in view of the writings I published. For there are two things in the human soul on which all the knowledge we can have of its nature depends: one, that it thinks, the other, that, being united to a body, it can act and suffer with the body. I hardly said anything about the latter, and only tried to make the former well understood. That was because my chief aim was to prove the distinction between the soul and the body. For this purpose the former alone was of use, and the other would have been harmful. But since your Highness sees so clearly such that it is impossible to conceal anything from her, I will try to explain here the way in which I conceive of the union of the soul with the body, and how it has the power to move the body.

First, I consider that there are in us certain primitive notions, which are, as it were, originals on the pattern of which we form all our other knowledge. And there are only a very few such notions. For after the most general—of being, number, duration, etc., which apply to everything we can conceive—we have, for the body in particular, only the notion of extension, from which those of shape and motion follow. And for the soul alone, we have only the notion of thought, in which are included the perceptions of the intellect and the inclinations of the will. Finally, for the soul and the body together, we have only that of their union, on which depends the notion of the power the soul has to move the body and the body to act on the soul, causing its sensations and its passions.

I also consider that all human knowledge consists only in distinguishing these notions well, and in attributing each of them only to the things to which they belong. For when we want to explain some difficulty by means of a notion that does not belong to it, we cannot fail to be mistaken. In the same way, too, we are mistaken when we try to explain one of these notions by another. For, being primitive, each of them cannot be understood except through itself. And as the use of our senses made the notions of extension, shapes, and motion more familiar to us than the others, the chief cause of our errors consists in the fact that we ordinarily want to use these notions to explain things to which they do not belong—as when we want to use the imagination to conceive nature of the soul, or when we want to conceive ways in which the soul moves the body using the way in which one body is moved by another body.

That is why, since, in the *Meditations*, which your Highness condescended to read, I tried to give a conception of the notions belonging to the soul alone, distinguishing them from those belonging to the body alone, the first thing I have to explain subsequently is how to conceive of those things belonging to the union of the soul with the body, leaving aside those belonging to body alone or to soul alone. It seems to me that what I wrote at the end of my *Reply to the Sixth Objections* can serve this purpose. For we cannot look for these simple notions anywhere except in our soul, which by its nature contains them all in itself, but which does not always sufficiently distinguish them from one another, or does not attribute them to the objects to which they should be attributed.

Thus, I believe until now we often confused the notion of the power with which the soul acts on the body with the power by which one body acts on another; and we attributed both of them, not to the soul, since we do not yet know it, but to the various qualities of bodies, such as heaviness, heat, and others we imagined to be real, that is, having an existence distinct from that of the body, and consequently to be substances, even though we called them qualities.

And to conceive them at times we used notions in us to know the body, and at times those there to know the soul, according to whether what we attributed to them was material or immaterial. For example, in supposing that heaviness is a real quality, of which we have no other knowledge except that it has the power to move the body, in which it resides, toward the center of the earth, we have no trouble conceiving of how it moves this body, or how it is joined to it. And we do not consider at all that this is done through the real contact of one surface by another. For we experience in ourselves that we have a particular notion for conceiving of that. And I believe we misuse this notion when we apply it to heaviness—which is nothing really distinguished from body, as I hope to show in my *Physics*—but the notion given to us for conceiving of the way in which the soul moves the body.

I would be showing that I do not know well enough the incomparable mind of your Highness if I used more words to explain myself, and would be too presumptuous if I dared to think that my reply must satisfy her entirely. But I will try to avoid both, adding nothing more here, except that, if I am capable of writing or saying something that can please her, I will always count it a great honor to take up my pen, or to go to The Hague on that account, and that there is nothing in the world dearer to me than to try to obey her commands. But I cannot here find place to observe the Hippocratic oath she enjoined upon me, since she did not communicate to me anything that does not deserve to be seen and admired by all. On this subject I can only say that, prizing infinitely the letter I received from you, I will treat it as misers treat their treasures. The more they prize them, the more they hide them, and begrudging the sight of them to the rest of the world, they place their greatest happiness in looking at them. Thus I will be quite pleased to enjoy alone the good of seeing it. And my greatest ambition is to be able to say and to be truly,

Madam,
    Your Highness' Most humble and obedient servant,
        Descartes

## Elisabeth to Descartes, 10 June 1643

Mr. Descartes,

Your kindness is not only apparent in your showing me and correcting the defects in my reasoning, as I anticipated it, but also in order to make the knowledge of them less irritating to me. You attempt to console me, to the detriment of your own judgment, with false praise that would have been necessary to encourage me to work at remedying these errors if my upbringing, in a place where the ordinary way of conversing accustomed me to hearing people incapable of giving true praise, had not led me to presume I could not fail in believing the contrary of their discourses; in this way consideration of my imperfections was made so familiar to me that it no longer imparts any more emotion than necessary for achieving the desire to be rid of them.

This makes me confess, without shame, that I found in myself all the causes for error you point out in your letter, and was not yet able to banish them entirely, since the life I am constrained to lead does not leave at my disposition enough time to acquire the habit of meditating according to your rules. Sometimes I cannot neglect the interests of my house, sometimes I cannot avoid meetings and pleasantries that beat down so strongly on my feeble spirit, causing such irritation or boredom that it is rendered useless to anything else for a long time afterward. This will serve, I hope, as an excuse for my stupidity in not being able to comprehend the idea by which we must judge how the soul (non-extended and immaterial) can move the body, through that idea you once had of heaviness; nor why this power you had then falsely attributed to it under the name of a quality, to carry the body toward the center of the Earth, should instead persuade us that a body can be moved by something immaterial, than the demonstration of a contrary truth (which you promise in your *Physics*) should confirm us in our opinion of its impossibility: principally, since this idea (not being able to claim the same perfection and objective reality as that of God) could be feigned due to the ignorance of what truly moves these bodies toward the center. And since no material cause presents itself to the senses, we would attribute it to

its contrary, something immaterial that, however, I was never able to conceive except as a negation of matter, which can have no communication with it.

I admit I could more easily concede matter and extension to the soul than I could the capacity to move a body and be moved by it to an immaterial being. For if the first was achieved by being informed, it would be necessary that the spirits causing the motion were intelligent, but this is something you do not grant to anything corporeal. And although in your *Metaphysical Meditations* you show the possibility of the latter, it is however very difficult to understand that a soul, as you described it, after having acquired the faculty and habit of reasoning well, can lose all that through some vapors, and that, being able to subsist without the body and having nothing in common with it, it might still be so governed by it.

But, since you have undertaken to instruct me, I only entertain these sentiments in the manner of friends I have no intention of keeping, assuring myself you will explain just as well to me the nature of an immaterial substance and the manner of its actions and passions in the body, as all the other things you have sought to teach. I beg you also to know that you could not extend this charity to anyone who would be more sensible of the obligation she incurs to you for it, as,

Mr. Descartes,
     Your very affectionate friend,
        Elisabeth

## Descartes to Elisabeth, 28 June 1643

Madam,

I have a very great obligation to your Highness in that, after having perceived how poorly I explained myself in my previous letter, concerning the question it pleased her to propose to me, she still deigns to have the patience to hear from me on the same subject and to give me the opportunity to remark on the things I omitted. The principal ones seem to me to be that, after having distinguished three types of ideas or primitive notions that are each known in a particular way, and not through a comparison with one another—namely, the notions we have of the soul, the body, and the union of the soul and body—I should have explained the differences between these three types of notions and between the operations of the soul through which we acquire them, and elaborate on the ways of making each of them familiar and easy to us. Then, next, having said why I used the comparison with heaviness, I should have shown that, although we want to conceive the soul as material (which is properly speaking to conceive its union with the body), this does not prevent us from knowing, afterwards, that it is separable from it. This is, I believe, everything your Highness prescribed for me here.

First, then, I notice a great difference between these three sorts of notions, in that the soul is conceived only by the pure understanding; the body—that is, extension: shapes and motions—can also be known by the understanding alone, but much better by the understanding aided by the imagination; and finally, the things belonging to the union of the soul and the body are only known obscurely by the understanding alone, and also obscurely by the understanding aided by the imagination; but they are known very clearly by the senses. As a result, those who never philosophize, and who only use their senses, do not doubt that the soul moves the body and that the body acts on the soul; but they consider the one and the other as a single thing, that is, they conceive of their union, for to conceive of the union of these two things is to conceive them as a single thing. And, metaphysical thoughts, which exercise the pure understanding, serve to make the notion of the soul familiar to us; and the study of mathematics, which exercises principally the imagination in its consideration of shapes and motions, accustoms us to form quite distinct notions of bodies; and, finally, we learn to conceive the union of the soul and the body by relying only on life and ordinary conversations and abstaining from meditating on or studying things that exercise the imagination.

I am almost afraid that your Highness might think I am not speaking seriously here; but it would be contrary to the respect I owe and will never fail to render to her. And I can say, truly, that the principal rule I always observed in my studies, and

the one I believe served me best in acquiring some knowledge, was that I never spent but a few hours each day in thoughts occupying the imagination, and very few hours each year in those occupying the understanding alone, and gave all the rest of my time to relaxing the senses and resting the mind; I even count as exercising the imagination all serious conversation and everything for which attention is required. It is what made me retire to the country; for even though, in the most populated city in the world, I could have just as many hours to myself as I am now spending in study, I could not, however, use them as profitably, for my mind would be tired by the attention required by all the bothers of life. I take the liberty of writing this here to your Highness in order to show her I truly admire that, among the affairs and cares never absent from people who are both of great mind and great birth, she was able to pursue the meditations required for knowing well the distinction between the soul and the body.

But I judged it was these meditations, rather than thoughts demanding less attention, that caused your Highness to find obscurity in the notion we have of their union, since it does not seem that the human mind is capable of conceiving very distinctly, at the same time, both the distinction between the soul and body and their union. For that, one would need to conceive them as a single thing and also to conceive them as two—which is self-contradictory. And accordingly (assuming that your Highness still had very much present in her mind the reasons proving the distinction between the soul and the body and not wanting to ask her to put them aside in order to represent to herself the notion of the union each person always experiences in himself without philosophizing—namely, he is a single person, who has both a body and thought, which are of such a nature that this thought can move the body and can sense the accidents that happen to it), in my previous letter I made use of the comparison of heaviness and the other qualities we commonly imagine to be united to some bodies, as thought is united to ours. And I did not worry whether this comparison is lame, given that these qualities are not real, as we imagine them to be, because I believed your Highness was already entirely persuaded that the soul is a substance distinct from the body.

But since your Highness remarks that it is easier to attribute matter and extension to the soul than to attribute to it the capacity for moving a body and being moved by it without having matter, I ask her to attribute freely this matter and this extension to the soul; for it is nothing else than to conceive it as united to the body. And after having formed a proper conception of this, and having experienced it in herself, it will be easy for her to consider that the matter she has attributed to this thought is not thought itself, and that the extension of this matter is of a different nature than the extension of this thought, in that the former has a determinate place, such that it excludes all other extension of body, and this is not the case with the latter. And thus, your Highness will be able to return easily to the knowledge of the distinction between the soul and the body, despite having conceived their union.

Finally, I think it is very necessary to have well understood the principles of metaphysics once in one's life, because they are what give us the knowledge of God and of our soul. I also think it would be very harmful to occupy one's understanding often in meditating on them, because this would impede it from performing the functions of the imagination and the senses. The best thing for a person is to be content in keeping in memory and in belief the conclusions once derived, and then to use the rest of the time for the study of thoughts in which the understanding acts with the imagination and the senses.

The extreme devotion I have to the service of your Highness makes me hope that my frankness will not be disagreeable to her, and she would have solicited a longer discourse from me here, where I would have attempted to clarify all at once the difficulties with respect to the question posed; but some unpleasant news I have just learned from Utrecht, where the Magistrate summons me to verify what I wrote about one of their ministers (even though this is a man who very grossly slandered me, and even though what I wrote about him, in my just defense, is only too well known to the whole world), constrains me to finish here so that I may go and find a way to extricate myself, as soon as I can, from this chicanery. I am,

Madam,
　　Your Highness' Most humble and obedient servant,
　　　　Descartes

## Elisabeth to Descartes, 1 July 1643

Mr. Descartes,

I see you are not as inconvenienced by my esteem for your instruction and my desire to take advantage of it, as you are by the ingratitude of those who deprive themselves and seek to deprive humanity of it; and I would not have sent you a new product of my ignorance before I knew you to be unencumbered by those of their stubbornness, if Mr. Van Bergen had not earlier obliged me to it by his civility in agreeing to wait in this city until I gave him a reply to your letter from June 28, which makes me clearly see the three sorts of notions we have, their objects, and how to make use of them.

I also find that the senses show me that the soul moves the body, but they do not teach me (any more than the understanding and the imagination) the way in which the soul does this. And, for that, I think there are some properties of the soul unknown to us, which could perhaps overturn what your *Metaphysical Meditations* persuaded me of, with such good reasons, concerning the non-extendedness of the soul. And this doubt seems to be founded on the rule you give there, in speaking of the true and the false, and that all error arises from our forming judgments about things we do not sufficiently perceive. Although extension is not necessary for thought, not being repugnant to it, it could serve some other function of the soul no less essential to it. At least, it does not allow the contradiction of the Scholastics to stand, that the soul is both wholly in the whole body and wholly in each of its parts. I do not excuse myself for confusing the notion of the soul with that of the body for the same reason as the common people; but this does not remove the first doubt, and I will lose hope of finding certainty in anything in the world if you do not provide it for me—you who have alone prevented me from being a skeptic, that to which my first reasoning brought me here.

Although I owe you this confession out of gratitude, I would think it very imprudent if I did not know your kindness and generosity to be equal to the rest of your merits, as much by my previous experience of it as by your reputation. You could not demonstrate it in a more obliging way than by the clarifications and advice you have shared with me, which I prize more highly than the greatest treasures that could be possessed by,

    Mr. Descartes,

        Your very affectionate friend at your service,

            Elisabeth

# Baruch Spinoza, *Descartes' Principles of Philosophy* (1663), "Prolegomenon" and "Definitions"[1]

Before giving these propositions and their demonstration, it seems best to recall briefly why Descartes came to doubt all things, how he discovered the stable foundations for the sciences, and finally how he liberated himself from all his doubts. We would have put all of this in mathematical order if we had not thought that such prolixity would have impeded our understanding of these things which should be seen as clearly as though presented in a picture.

In order to proceed with his investigation with the utmost caution, Descartes was compelled

1. To lay aside all prejudices.

2. To find the foundations on which all things ought to be built.

3. To discover the cause of error.

4. To understand everything clearly and distinctly.

In order to accomplish the first three points, he doubted all things, not, however, as a skeptic who doubts merely for the sake of doubting, but in order to free his mind of all prejudices, so that he might find at length the firm and unshakable foundations of the sciences. By using this method, if any such foundations existed, they could not escape him. For the true principles of the sciences must be so clear that they need no proof, and cannot under any circumstances be doubted; every demonstration must presuppose them. These he found after a long period of doubt. And after he had once gained these principles, it was not difficult to distinguish the true from the false, or to detect the cause of error. And thus he could be on his guard lest he accept anything doubtful and false for what is certain and true.

To accomplish the last point, that is, to understand everything clearly and distinctly, his principal rule was to enumerate and examine separately all the simple ideas from which all others are composed. For when he could clearly and distinctly perceive these simple ideas, he would be able to understand with the same clarity and distinctness all others into which they entered as component parts. Having prefaced our remarks with these few words, we shall proceed with our purpose as stated above, namely, to explain why he doubted everything, how he found the true principles of the sciences, and how he extricated himself from the difficulties of his doubts.

---

1. Translated from the Latin by H. H. Britain in Benedict de Spinoza, *The Principles of Descartes's Philosophy* (La Salle, Ill.: Open Court, 1905), modified. For Spinoza's biography and bibliography, see below, Section 2.

*Concerning his universal doubt.* In the first place he calls attention to all of those things perceived through the senses, the heavens, the earth and the like, and even his own body—all the things he had until then thought to exist in nature. And he came to doubt their certainty because he had observed that his senses sometimes deceived him, and in sleep he had often persuaded himself that many things existed in which he later found he had been deceived, and finally because he had heard others affirm that they sometimes felt pain in limbs long lost. It was not without reason, therefore, that he doubted even the existence of his own body. Hence from all these reasons he was able to conclude that the senses are not the most firm foundation on which the sciences should be built (for they can be called in doubt), but certainty rests upon some principles more certain than this. To investigate further, he next considers universal things, such as corporeal nature in general, its extension, figure, quantity, etc., as well as all mathematical truth. Although these seem more certain than the objects of sense perception, nevertheless, he finds a cause for doubting them as well. Some err even in these, and besides there is an old opinion that God, who is omnipotent, and has created us with our present faculties, has perhaps so made us that we are deceived even in those things which seem most certain. These are the causes that led him to doubt all things.

*The discovery of the foundation of all science.* In order to find the true principles of the sciences, he afterward inquired whether all things which are subjects of thought could be doubted, if perhaps there was anything which he had not yet called in question. Doubting in this way he believed that if anything was found, which, for none of the reasons given above, should be doubted, this might be considered the foundation on which all knowledge rests. And although, as it now seemed, he had doubted everything (for he had called in question all that the senses give and all that is perceived by the understanding), there was something left the certainty of which had not been doubted, namely, he himself who was doubting—not, however, insofar as he consisted of head or hands or other bodily members, for he had doubted these things, but only insofar as he was doubting,

thinking, etc. Carefully examining this fact, he found that for none of the previously mentioned reasons could it be doubted, for, whether he thinks waking or sleeping, it is true that he thinks and exists; and even though he and others might fall into error, since they were in error, they must exist. Nor could he feign a creator so skillful in deceit that he could deceive him about this. For if it is supposed that he is deceived, it must also be supposed that he exists. Finally, whatever reason for doubt may be conceived, there is none which does not at the same time make one more certain of his own existence. Indeed the more reasons for doubting, the more arguments there are which convince him of his own existence. So in whatever direction he turns in order to doubt, he is forced to exclaim, "I doubt, I think; therefore I am."

This truth discovered, he finds at the same time the foundations of all the sciences as well as the measure and rule of all other truths, namely: *Whatever is as clearly and distinctly perceived as this is true.*

That there can be no other foundation of the sciences than this is more than sufficiently evident from the preceding. For we can call all the rest in doubt with no difficulty, but we cannot doubt this in any way. Concerning this principle, "I doubt, I think; therefore I am," it should be noted in the first place that it is not a syllogism in which the major premise is omitted. If it were, the premises ought to be clearer and better known than the conclusion, "therefore I am." And if this were so, "I am" would not be the first foundation of all knowledge. Moreover, it would not be a certain conclusion, for its truth depends upon universal premises which the author had called in question. Therefore "I think, therefore I am" is a single proposition equivalent to "I am thinking."

To avoid confusion in what follows (for the matter ought to be perceived clearly and distinctly), we must know what we are. For once we do understand it clearly and distinctly, we shall not confuse our essence with others. To deduce this from what precedes, our author thus continues:

He now recalled all the thoughts he formerly held, as for example, that his soul was something very fine in texture, like the wind, or fire, or air, infused throughout with the coarser particles of the body;

and that his body was better known than his soul and could be perceived more clearly and distinctly. These thoughts he now saw were clearly incompatible with what he had discovered. For he could doubt the existence of his body, but not his essence insofar as he was thinking. Moreover, he perceived these thoughts neither clearly nor distinctly, and consequently, according to the rule of his method, he was obliged to reject them as if they were false. Therefore, since he could not understand such things as pertaining to himself, so far as he was known to himself up to this point, he further inquires what there was about his essence which he could not put into doubt, and which compelled him to believe in his own existence. Such things were these: *that he had determined to be on his guard lest he be deceived; that he had desired to understand so many things; that he had doubted everything he was not able to know; that he had affirmed only one thing at a time; that he had denied all else, and even rejected it as false; that he had conceived many things though reluctantly; and finally that he had considered many things as though derived from the senses.* Since his existence was so evidently bound up with each one of these actions, and since none of them belonged to the things which he had doubted, and finally since they all can be conceived under the same attribute, it follows that these are all true and pertain to his nature. So when he said, *I think*, these modes of thought were all understood, namely, *doubting, understanding, affirming, denying, willing, not willing, imagining,* and *sensing.*

Some things must be noted here that will have importance when we come to discuss the distinction between mind and body. (1) That modes of thought may be known clearly and distinctly even though some things are still in doubt. (2) That we render a clear and distinct concept obscure and confused when we ascribe to it something concerning which we are still in doubt.

*Liberation from all doubts.* Finally, in order that he might be certain and remove all doubt from those things he had called in question, he further proceeds to inquire into the nature of the most perfect Being and whether such a Being exists. For, when he has discovered that this Being, by whose power all things

are created and conserved and to whose nature it would be repugnant to be a deceiver, exists, then that reason for doubt which is found in the fact that he was ignorant of his own cause will be removed. For he will know that the power of discerning the true from the false would not have been given to him by a God of perfect goodness and truth in order that he might be deceived. Mathematical truth, therefore, and all other of like certainty cannot be suspected. To remove the other causes for doubt, he inquires next why it is we sometimes fall into error. For when he discovered how error arose, and that we use our free will to assent even to what we perceive only confusedly, he concluded immediately that we could avoid error by withholding assent from that which is seen only confusedly.

As everyone has the power of inhibiting the will, he can easily restrain it to the limits of the understanding. And since in youth we form many prejudices from which we free ourselves only with difficulty, he enumerates and examines separately all of the simple notions and ideas of which all our thoughts are composed, so that we might be freed from our prejudices and accept nothing but what we perceive clearly and distinctly. For if he could take note of what was clear and what obscure in each, he would easily be able to distinguish the clear from the obscure and to form clear and distinct thoughts. By this means he easily found the real distinction between soul and body; what was clear and what obscure in the things derived from the senses; and finally how sleep differs from waking. When this was done, he could doubt no longer concerning the waking life, nor could he be deceived by his senses. In this way he was able to free himself from all the doubts recounted above.

Before I close this part of the discussion, it seems that some satisfaction should be given to those who object that since God's existence does not become known to us through itself, we seem unable ever to be certain of anything; for from uncertain premises (and we have said that all things are uncertain so long as we are ignorant of our origin), nothing can be concluded with certainty.

In order to remove this difficulty Descartes responded in this fashion: Although we do not yet know whether the creator of our nature has created us so that we are deceived in those things which appear most evident to us, nevertheless, we cannot doubt those things we understand clearly and distinctly either through themselves or through reasoning, as long as we attend merely to them. But we only doubt those things previously demonstrated to be true and now recalled to memory when we no longer attend closely to the reasons from which they were deduced, which perhaps are even forgotten. So although God's existence cannot come to be known through itself, but only through something else, we will be able to attain a certain knowledge of his existence, provided we attend very accurately to the premises from which the conclusion is deduced. See *Principles* I, 13; *Reply to Second Objections*, 3; and Meditation Five, at the end.

But since this reply does not satisfy everybody, I shall offer another. We saw above, when speaking of the evidence and certainty of our existence, that this was found in the fact that, consider what we will, we meet no argument for doubt which does not at the same time convince us of the certainty of our existence. This is true whether we consider our own nature, or conceive of the author of our nature as a skillful deceiver, or adduce some extraneous reason for doubt. So far we have not observed this to happen regarding any other matter. For example, considering the nature of a triangle, though we are now compelled to believe that its three angles are equal to two right angles, we are not forced to the conclusion that this is really true if perhaps we are deceived by the author of our nature. In the same way we deduce the certainty of our existence. We are not here compelled to believe that under any conditions three angles of a triangle are equal to two right angles. On the contrary we find reason for doubt, for we have no idea of God which so affects us that it is impossible for us to think that God is a deceiver. It is equally easy for one who has no true idea of God (which we now suppose ourselves not to have) to think that he is a deceiver or that he is not. So for those who have no right conception of a triangle, it is equally easy for them to think that the sum of the angles is equal to two right

angles, or that it is not. Therefore, we grant that we cannot be absolutely certain of anything except of our own existence, however closely we attend to the proof, until we have a clear concept of God which compels us to affirm (in the same way that the concept of a triangle compels us to affirm that the sum of its angles is equal to two right angles) that he is supremely veracious. But we deny that we are unable to come to any certain knowledge of anything. For, as now appears, the whole matter hinges upon this, namely, whether we can form such a concept of God that it is not as easy for us to think of him as a deceiver as to think that he is not, but which compels us to affirm that he is supremely veracious. When we have formed such an idea, all reason for doubting mathematical truth is removed. For, wherever we then direct our attention in order to doubt some one of them, we shall come upon nothing from which we must not instead infer that it is most certain—as happened concerning our existence. For example, if now having obtained this concept of God we consider the nature of a triangle, we are compelled to affirm that the sum of its three angles is equal to two right angles; or if we consider the nature of God, this too compels us to affirm that he is supremely veracious and the author and continual conserver of our nature, and therefore that he does not deceive us concerning that truth. Nor is it less impossible for us to think when we once have obtained this idea of God (which we suppose to be already found) that he is a deceiver, than when we consider the nature of a triangle to think that the sum of its angles is not equal to two right angles. As we can form such an idea of a triangle although we are not certain whether the author of our nature is not deceiving us, so also we can make the idea of God clear to ourselves and put it before our eyes, even though we still doubt whether the author of our nature deceives us in all things. And, provided only that we have such an idea of God, however it may have been obtained, it is sufficient to remove all doubt, as has just been shown.

This point having been made clear, I reply as follows to the difficulty raised: We can be certain of nothing not merely as long as we are ignorant of God's existence (for I have not yet spoken of this), but as long as we do not have a clear and a distinct idea of him. Hence if anyone should desire to oppose my conclusion, his argument should be as follows: We can be certain of nothing before we have a clear and distinct idea of God. But we cannot have a clear and a distinct idea of God as long as we do not know whether or not the author of our nature is deceiving us. Therefore, we cannot be certain of anything as long as we do not know whether or not the author of our nature is deceiving us, etc. To this I reply by conceding the major premise but denying the minor. For we have a clear and a distinct idea of a triangle although we do not know whether or not the author of our nature is deceiving us; and provided we have such an idea (as I have shown abundantly above), we will be able to doubt neither his existence, nor any mathematical truth.

Our prefatory remarks being thus completed, we proceed now to the main problem.

# Definitions

I. *Under the term* thought [cogitatio] *I include everything which is in us and of which we are immediately conscious.*

Thus all the operations of the will, the understanding, the imagination, and the senses are thoughts. I have added the term *immediately* to exclude those things that follow from thoughts; thus voluntary motion does have thought as its principle, but is not itself a thought.

II. *By the term* idea [idea] *I understand any form of thought of which I am conscious through immediate perception of that thought itself.*

I cannot express anything in words (when I understand what I say), therefore, without it being certain from this that I have in me an idea of what is signified by these words. Therefore, I do not call *idea* only the images depicted in fantasy; indeed, I do not call these images ideas at all, insofar as they are depicted in the corporeal imagination, i.e., in some portion of the brain, but only insofar as they inform the mind itself which is directed toward that portion of the brain.

III. *By the* objective reality of an idea, *I understand the entity of the thing represented by the idea, insofar as this entity is in the idea.*

In the same manner I may speak of objective perfection, or of an objective art, etc. For whatever we perceive in the objects of ideas is objectively in the ideas themselves.

IV. *These same things are said to be* formally [formaliter] *in the objects of ideas when they are in them as we perceive them. They are said to be* eminently [eminenter] *when they are not as we perceive them, but so great that they can take the place of such things.*

Note that when I say a cause contains the perfection of its own effect *eminently*, I mean that the cause contains the perfection of the effect more excellently than the effect itself. [ . . . ]

V. *Everything in which there is immediately as in a subject, or through which there exists something we perceive, that is, some property, quality, or attribute, of which we have a real idea, is called* substance.

Indeed we have no other idea of substance, taken precisely, than that it is something in which exists either formally or eminently that something we perceive, or which is objective in one of our ideas.

VI. *Substance in which thoughts immediately reside is called* mind.

I use the term *mind* [mens] rather than *soul* [animus] for the latter term is equivocal, often being used to mean a corporeal thing.

VII. *Substance, which is the immediate subject of extension, and of accidents which presuppose extension, like figure, position, and local motion, etc., is called* body [corpus].

Whether what is called mind is one and the same substance as what is called body, or whether they are different substances, will be inquired into later.

VIII. *Substance which we understand to be through itself supremely perfect and in which nothing can be conceived involving a defect or limitation of perfection is called* God.

IX. *When we say that something is contained in the nature of the thing itself or in its concept, it is the* same as to affirm that it is true of that thing, *i.e.*, that it can be truly affirmed of it.

X. *Two substances are said to be really distinct when each of them can exist without the other.* [ . . . ]

## [Part II.] Definitions

I. *Extension* is that which consists of three dimensions. We do not understand by the term the act of extending or anything else distinct from quantity.

II. By *substance* we understand that which depends only upon the concurrence of God for its existence.

III. An *atom* is a part of matter which is indivisible by nature.

IV. *Indefinite* is that whose limits, if it has any, cannot be investigated by the human mind.

V. A *vacuum* is extension without corporeal substance.

VI. We make only a distinction of reason between *space* and *extension;* that is, they are not really distinct. See *Principles* II, Article 10.

VII. That which in our thinking we understand to be divided is *divisible*, at least potentially.

VIII. *Local motion* is the transfer of one part of matter or of a body from the vicinity of other contiguous bodies considered as in a state of rest, to the vicinity of others. [ . . . ]

# G. W. Leibniz, On Descartes (from the letters to Foucher, to Elisabeth, and to Molanus) (1675–79)[1]

*As Leibniz says in the "Letter to Foucher," he first studied Descartes' philosophy seriously when he resided in Paris from 1672 to 1676. As a result, Leibniz's letters during that period contain many incisive criticisms of Descartes' various positions. Leibniz will repeat some of these (though not all of them) in his mature work, but they never seem quite as fresh as the versions from this period, dealing with many of Descartes' basic doctrines: "I think; therefore I am" is the first principle of knowledge; God is needed to guarantee truth; God's existence follows from the idea we have of him; God wills the eternal truths; we are immortal because our soul is an unextended substance, that is, a substance that cannot perish.[2]*

## Letter to Foucher (1675)

[ . . . ] The principal subject of your inquiry concerns the truths that deal with what is really outside of us. Now, in the first place, we cannot deny that the very truth of hypothetical propositions is something outside of us, something that does not depend on us. For all hypothetical propositions assert what would be or what would not be if something or its contrary were posited; and consequently, they assert that the simultaneous assumption of two things in agreement with one another is possible or impossible, necessary or indifferent, or they assert that one single thing is possible or impossible, necessary or indifferent. This possibility, impossibility, or necessity (for the necessity of something is the impossibility of its contrary) is not a chimera we create, since we do nothing more than recognize it, in spite of ourselves and in a consistent manner. Thus of all things that there actually are, the very possibility or impossibility of being is the first. Now, this possibility or this necessity forms or composes what we call the essences or natures and the truths we commonly call eternal—and we are right to call them so, for there is nothing so eternal as that which is necessary. Thus the nature of the circle with its properties is something existent and eternal. That is, there is a constant cause outside us which

1. Translated from the French by R. Ariew and D. Garber in G. W. Leibniz, *Philosophical Essays* (Indianapolis/Cambridge: Hackett Publishing Company, 1989).
2. For Leibniz's biography and bibliography, see Section 3, below. Leibniz's correspondents are Simon Foucher, a critic of Cartesian philosophy and proponent of Academic skepticism, whom Leibniz met in Paris; (possibly) Princess Elizabeth, Countess Palatine, and sister of the Duchess Sophia of Hanover—the Duke of Hanover being Leibniz's principal employer; and (possibly) Gerhardt Molanus, abbot of Loccum, near Hanover.

makes everyone who thinks carefully about the circle discover the same thing. It is not merely that their thoughts agree with each other, which could be attributed solely to the nature of the human mind, but even the phenomena or experiences confirm these eternal truths when the appearance of a circle strikes our senses. And these phenomena necessarily have some cause outside of us.

But even though the existence of necessities is the first of all truths in and of itself and in the order of nature, I agree that it is not first in the order of our knowledge. For you see, in order to prove their existence I took it for granted that we think and that we have sensations. Thus there are two absolute general truths, that is, two absolute general truths which speak of the actual existence of things: the first, that we think, and the second, that there is a great variety in our thoughts. From the former it follows that we exist, and from the latter it follows that there is something else besides us, that is, something else besides that which thinks, something which is the cause of the variety of our appearances. Now one of these two truths is just as incontestable and as independent as the other; and Descartes, having accepted only the former, failed to arrive at the perfection to which he had aspired in the course of his meditations. If he had followed precisely what I call the thread of meditating [*filum meditandi*], I believe that he would have achieved the first philosophy. But not even the world's greatest genius can force things, and we must necessarily enter through the entryways that nature has made, so that we do not stray. Moreover, one person alone cannot do everything at once, and for myself, when I think of everything Descartes has said that is beautiful and original, I am more astonished with what he has accomplished than with what he has failed to accomplish. I admit that I have not yet been able to read all his writings with all the care I had intended to bring to them, and my friends know that, as it happened, I read almost all the new philosophers before reading him. Bacon and Gassendi were the first to fall into my hands; their familiar and easy style was better adapted to a person who wants to read everything. It is true that I often glanced at Galileo and Descartes, but since I became a geometer only recently, I was soon repelled by their manner of writing, which requires deep meditation. As for myself, although I always liked to meditate, I always found it difficult to read books that cannot be understood without much meditation. For, when following one's own meditations one follows a certain natural inclination and gains profit along with pleasure; but one is enormously cramped when having to follow the meditations of others. I always liked books that contained some fine thoughts, but books that one could read without stopping, for they aroused ideas in me which I could follow at my fancy and pursue as I pleased. This also prevented me from reading geometry books with care, and I must admit that I have not yet brought myself to read Euclid in any other way than one commonly reads novels [*histoires*]. I have learned from experience that this method in general is a good one; but I have learned nevertheless that there are authors for whom one must make an exception—Plato and Aristotle among the ancient philosophers and Galileo and Descartes among ours. Yet what I know of Descartes' metaphysical and physical meditations is almost entirely derived from reading a number of books, written in a more familiar style, that report his opinions. So perhaps I have not yet understood him well. However, to the extent that I have leafed through his works myself, it seemed to me that I have glimpsed at very least what he has not accomplished and not even attempted to accomplish, that is, among other things, the analysis of all our assumptions. That is why I am inclined to applaud all those who examine the least truth to its deepest level; for I know that it is important to understand one perfectly, however small and however easy it may seem. This is the way to progress quite far and finally to establish the art of discovery which depends on a knowledge, but a most distinct and perfect knowledge of the easiest things. And for this reason I found nothing wrong in Roberval's attempt to demonstrate everything in geometry, including some axioms.[3] I admit that we

---

3. Gilles Personne de Roberval (1602–96) does attempt to demonstrate Euclid's axioms in his *Elements of Geometry*, one of Roberval's unpublished papers, which Leibniz considered publishing. See Leibniz's *New Essays on Human Understanding*, Book IV, chap. 7, sec. 1: "Of the propositions which are named maxims or axioms."

should not demand such exactness from others, but I believe that it is good to demand it from ourselves.

I return to those truths, from among those asserting that there is something outside us, which are first with respect to ourselves, namely, that we think and that there is a great variety in our thoughts. Now, this variety cannot come from that which thinks, since a single thing by itself cannot be the cause of the changes in itself. For everything would remain in the state in which it is, if there is nothing that changes it; and since it did not determine itself to have these changes rather than others, one cannot begin to attribute any variety to it without saying something which, we must admit, has no reason—which is absurd. And even if we tried to say that our thoughts had no beginning, beside the fact that we would be required to assert that each of us has existed from all eternity, we would still not escape the difficulty; for we would always have to admit that there is no reason for the particular variety which would have existed in our thoughts from all eternity, since there is nothing in us that determines us to have one kind of variety rather than another. Therefore, there is some cause outside of us for the variety of our thoughts. And since we conceive that there are subordinate causes for this variety, causes which themselves still need causes, we have established particular beings or substances certain of whose actions we recognize, that is, things from whose changes we conceive certain changes in us to follow. And we quickly proceed to construct what we call matter and body. But it is at this point that you are right to stop us a bit and renew the criticisms of the ancient Academy. For, at bottom, all our experience assures us of only two things, namely, that there is a connection among our appearances which provides us the means to predict future appearances with success, and that this connection must have a constant cause. But it does not strictly follow from all this that matter or bodies exist, but only that there is something that presents well-sequenced appearances to us. For if an invisible power took pleasure in giving us dreams that are well connected with our preceding life and in conformity among themselves, could we distinguish them from realities before having been awakened? And what prevents the course of our life from being a long well-ordered dream, a dream from which we could be wakened in a moment? And I do not see that this power would be imperfect on that account, as Descartes asserts, leaving aside the fact that it does not matter if it is imperfect. For this could be a certain subordinate power, or some genie who meddles in our affairs for some unknown reason and who has as much power over someone as had the caliph who transported a drunken man into his palace and made him taste of Mohammed's paradise when he had awakened; after this he was made drunk again and was returned to the place from which he had been taken. And when the man came to himself, he did not fail to interpret what to him appeared inconsistent with the course of his life as a vision, and spread among the people maxims and revelations that he believed he had learned in his pretended paradise—this was what the caliph wished. Now, since a reality passed for a vision, what prevents a vision from passing for a reality? It is true that the more we see some connection in what happens to us, the more we are confirmed in the opinion we have about the reality of our appearances; and it is also true that the more we examine our appearances closely, the more we find them well-sequenced, as microscopes and other aids in making experiments have shown us. This constant accord engenders great assurance, but after all, it will only be moral assurance until somebody discovers the *a priori* origin of the world we see and pursues the question as to why things are the way they appear back to the ground of essence. For having done that, he will have demonstrated that what appears to us is a reality and that it is impossible that we ever be deceived about it again. But I believe that this would nearly approach the beatific vision and that it is difficult to aspire to this in our present state. However, we would learn from this how confused the knowledge we commonly have of body and matter must be, since we believe we are certain they exist but in the end we discover that we can be mistaken. And this confirms Descartes' excellent proof of the distinction between body and soul, since we can doubt the former without being able to put the latter into question. For even if there were only appearances or dreams, we would be no less certain of the existence of that which thinks, as Descartes has said quite nicely. I add that the existence of God can be demonstrated in ways other than Descartes did, ways which, I believe, bring us farther along. For we do not need to assume a being who guarantees us against being deceived, since it is in our power to undeceive ourselves about many things, at least about the most important ones. I wish, sir, that your meditations on this have all the success you desire. But to accomplish this, it is good to proceed in order and to establish propositions; that is the way to gain ground and to make sure progress. I believe that you would oblige the public by conveying to it, from time to time, selections from the Academy and especially from Plato, for I recognize that there are things in there more beautiful and solid than commonly thought.

## Letter to Countess Elizabeth (?), On God and Formal Logic (1678?)

[ . . . ] I come, then, to metaphysics, and I can state that it is for the love of metaphysics that I have passed through all these stages. For I have recognized that metaphysics is scarcely different from the true logic, that is, from the art of invention in general; for, in fact, metaphysics is natural theology, and the same God who is the source of all goods is also the principle of all knowledge. This is because the idea of God contains within it absolute being, that is, what is simple in our thoughts, from which everything that we think draws its origin. Descartes did not go about it in this way. He gave two ways of proving the existence of God. The first is that there is an idea of God in us since, no doubt, we think about God, and we cannot think of something without having its idea.[4] Now, if we have an idea of God, and if it is true [*véritable*], that is, if it is the idea of an infinite being, and if it represents it faithfully, it could not be caused by something lesser, and consequently, God himself must be its cause. Therefore, he must exist. The other reasoning is even shorter. It is that God is a being who possesses all perfections, and consequently, he possesses existence, which is to be counted as one of

the perfections.[5] Therefore, he exists. It must be said that these reasonings are somewhat suspect, because they go too fast, and because they force themselves upon us without enlightening us. Real demonstrations, on the other hand, generally fill the mind with some solid nourishment. However, the crux of the matter is difficult to find, and I see that many able people who have formulated objections to Descartes were led astray.

Some have believed that there is no idea of God because he is not subject to imagination, assuming that idea and image are the same thing. I am not of their opinion, and I know perfectly well that there are ideas of thought, existence, and similar things, of which there are no images. For we think of something and when we notice in there what it is that allows us to recognize it, this is what constitutes the idea of the thing, insofar as it is in our soul. This is why there is also an idea of what is not material or imaginable.

Others agree that there is an idea of God, and that this idea contains all perfections, but they cannot understand how existence follows from it, either because they do not agree that existence is to be counted among the perfections, or because they do not see how a simple idea or thought can imply an existence outside us. As for me, I genuinely believe that anyone who has recognized this idea of God, and who sees that existence is a perfection, must admit that existence belongs to God. In fact, I do not question the idea of God any more than I do his existence; on the contrary, I claim to have a demonstration of it. But I do not want us to flatter ourselves and persuade ourselves that we can arrive at such a great thing with such little cost. Paralogisms are dangerous in this matter; when they occur, they reflect on us, and they strengthen the opposite side. I therefore say that we must prove with the greatest imaginable exactness that there is an idea of a completely perfect being, that is, an idea of God. It is true that the objections of those who believed that they could prove the contrary because there is no image of God are worthless, as I have just shown. But we also have to admit that the proof Descartes gives to establish the idea of God is imperfect. How, he would say, can one speak

---

4. Cf. Descartes, Meditation Three.

5. Cf. Descartes, Meditation Five.

of God without thinking of him, and how can one think of him without having an idea of him? Yes, no doubt we sometimes think about impossible things and we even construct demonstrations from them. For example, Descartes holds that squaring the circle is impossible, and yet we still think about it and draw consequences about what would happen if it were given. The motion having the greatest speed is impossible in any body whatsoever, because, for example, if we assumed it in a circle, then another circle concentric to the former circle, surrounding it and firmly attached to it, would move with a speed still greater than the former, which, consequently, would not be of the greatest degree, in contradiction to what we had assumed. In spite of all that, we think about this greatest speed, something that has no idea since it is impossible. Similarly, the greatest circle of all is an impossible thing, and the number of all possible units is no less so; we have a demonstration of this. And nevertheless, we think about all this. That is why there are surely grounds for wondering whether we should be careful about the idea of the greatest of all beings, and whether it might not contain a contradiction. For I fully understand, for example, the nature of motion and speed and what it is to be greatest, but, for all that, I do not understand whether all those notions are compatible, and whether there is a way of joining them and making them into an idea of the greatest speed of which motion is capable. Similarly, although I know what being is, and what it is to be the greatest and most perfect, nevertheless I do not yet know, for all that, whether there isn't a hidden contradiction in joining all that together, as there is, in fact, in the previously stated examples. In brief, I do not yet know, for all that, whether such a being is possible, for if it were not possible, there would be no idea of it. However, I must admit that God has a great advantage, in this respect, over all other things. For to prove that he exists, it would be sufficient to prove that he is possible, something we find nowhere else, as far as I know. Moreover, I infer from that that there is a presumption that God exists. For there is always a presumption on the side of possibility, that is, everything is held to be possible unless it is proven to be impossible. There is, therefore, a presumption that

God is possible, that is, that he exists, since in him existence follows from possibility. This is sufficient for practical matters in life, but it is not sufficient for a demonstration. I have strongly disputed this matter with several Cartesians, but I finally succeeded in this with some of the most able of them who have frankly admitted, after having understood the force of my reasons, that this possibility is still to be demonstrated. There are even some who, challenged by me to do so, have undertaken this demonstration, but they have not yet succeeded.

Since Your Highness is intelligent, you see what the state of things is and you see we can do nothing unless we prove this possibility. When I consider all this, I take pity on man's weakness, and I take care not to exclude myself from it. Descartes, who was no doubt one of the greatest men of this century, erred in so visible a manner, and many illustrious people erred with him. Nevertheless, we do not question their intelligence or their care. All of this could give some people a bad opinion of the certainty of our knowledge in general. For, one can say, with so many able men unable to avoid a trap, what can I hope for, I, who am nothing compared to them? Nevertheless, we must not lose our courage. There is a way of avoiding error, which these able men have not condescended to use; it would have been contrary to the greatness of their minds, at least in appearance, and with respect to the common people. All those who wish to appear to be great figures and who set themselves up as leaders of sects have a bit of the acrobat in them. A tightrope walker does not allow himself to be braced in order to avoid falling; if he did so, he would be sure of his act, but he would no longer appear a skillful man. I will be asked, what then is this wonderful way that can prevent us from falling? I am almost afraid to say it—it appears to be too lowly. But I am speaking to Your Highness who does not judge things by their appearance. In brief, it is to construct arguments only in proper form [*in forma*]. I seem to see only people who cry out against me and who send me back to school. But I beg them to be a little patient, for perhaps they do not understand me; arguments in proper form do not always bear the stamp of *Barbara Celarent*.[6] Any rigorous demonstration that does not omit anything necessary for the force of reasoning is of this kind, and I dare say that the account of an accountant and a calculation of analysis are arguments in proper form, since there is nothing missing in them and since the form or arrangement of the whole reasoning is the cause of their being evident. It is only the form that distinguishes an account book made according to the practice we commonly call Italian (of which Stevin has written a whole treatise) from the confused journal of someone ignorant of business. That is why I maintain that, in order to reason with evidence in all subjects, we must hold some consistent formalism [*formalité constante*]. There would be less eloquence, but more certainty. But in order to determine the formalism that would do no less in metaphysics, physics, and morals, than calculation does in mathematics, that would even give us degrees of probability when we can only reason probabilistically, I would have to relate here the thoughts I have on a new characteristic [*characteristique*], something that would take too long. Nevertheless, I will say, in brief, that this characteristic would represent our thoughts truly and distinctly, and that when a thought is composed of other simpler ones, its character would also be similarly composed. I dare not say what would follow from this for the perfection of the sciences—it would appear incredible. And yet, there is a demonstration of this. The only thing I will say here is that since that which we know is from reasoning or experience, it is certain that henceforth all reasoning in demonstrative or probable matters will demand no more skill than a calculation in algebra does; that is, one would derive from given experiments everything that can be derived, just as in algebra. But for now it is sufficient for me to note that the foundation of my characteristic is also the foundation of the demonstration of God's existence. For simple thoughts are the elements of the characteristic and simple forms are the source of things. I maintain that all simple forms are compatible among themselves. That is a proposition whose demonstration I cannot give without having to explain the fundamentals of the characteristic at length. But if that is granted, it follows that God's nature, which contains all simple forms taken absolutely, is possible. Now, we have proven above that God exists, as long as he is possible. Therefore, he exists. And that is what needed to be demonstrated.

## Letter to Molanus(?), On God and the Soul (ca. 1679)

[ . . . ] Someone might tell me that Descartes established the existence of God and the immortality of soul extremely well. But I fear that we are deceived by fine words, since Descartes' God, or perfect being, is not a God like the one we imagine or hope for, that is, a God just and wise, doing everything possible for the good of creatures. Rather, Descartes' God is something approaching the God of Spinoza, namely, the principle of things and a certain supreme power or primitive nature that puts everything into motion [*action*] and does everything that can be done. Descartes' God has neither will nor understanding, since according to Descartes he does not have the good as object of the will, nor the true as object of the understanding. Also, he does not want his God to act in accordance with some end; this is why he eliminates the search for final causes from philosophy, under the clever pretext that we are not capable of knowing God's ends.[7] On the other hand, Plato has nicely shown that if God acts in accordance with wisdom, since God is the author of things, then the true physics consists in knowing the ends and uses of things.[8] For science consists in knowing reasons, and the reasons for what was created by an understanding are the final causes or plans of the understanding that made them. These are apparent in their use and function, which is why considering the use parts

---

6. *Barbara Celarent* is a reference to the first line of some 13th-century mnemonic nonsense verses enabling students to remember the rules governing the validity of syllogisms; the full line would be "Barbara, Celarent, Darii, Ferioque prioris." Leibniz's statement, "arguments in proper form do not always bear the stamp of *Barbara Celarent*," indicates that there are valid arguments whose validity cannot be established by syllogistic means.

7. On the claim that the world is good because God created it, and not vice versa, see Descartes' *Replies to Objections VI*. On the denial of final causes, see *Principles of Philosophy*, I, 28; *Meditation Four*; and the *Replies to Objections V*.
8. See Plato, *Phaedo*, 97–98.

have is so helpful in anatomy. That is why a God like Descartes' allows us no consolation other than that of patience through strength. Descartes tells us in some places that matter passes successively through all possible forms,[9] that is, that his God created everything that can be made, and passes successively through all possible combinations, following a necessary and fated order. But for this doctrine, the necessity of matter alone would be sufficient, or rather, his God is merely this necessity or this principle of necessity acting as it can in matter. Therefore, it is impossible to believe that this God cares for intelligent creatures any more than he does for the others; each creature will be happy or unhappy depending upon how it finds itself engulfed in these great currents or vortices. Descartes has good reason to recommend, instead of felicity, patience without hope.

But one of those good people among the Cartesians, deceived by the beautiful words of his master, will tell me that Descartes has, however, quite nicely established the immortality of the soul, and consequently, a better life. When I hear such things, I am surprised by the ease with which one can deceive people merely by playing around with pleasing words, though corrupting their meaning. For as hypocrites misuse piety, heretics the Scriptures, and seditious people the word "freedom," so Descartes has misused the important words, "existence of God," and "immortality of the soul." We must therefore elucidate this mystery and show them that Descartes' immortality of soul is worth no more than his God. I believe that I will not bring pleasure to some, for people are normally unhappy to be awakened from a pleasant dream. But what should I do? Descartes wishes us to uproot false thoughts before introducing true ones.[10] We must follow his example; and I believe I would be doing the public a service if I could disabuse people of such dangerous doctrines.

I therefore assert that the immortality of soul, as established by Descartes, is useless and could not console us in any way. For let us suppose that soul is a substance and that no substance perishes; given that, the soul would not perish and, in fact, nothing would perish in nature. But just as matter, the soul will change in its way, and just as the matter that composes a man has at other times composed other plants and animals, similarly, this soul might be immortal in fact, but it might pass through a thousand changes without remembering what it once was.[11] But this immortality without memory is completely useless to morality, for it upsets all reward and punishment. What good would it do you to become the King of China under the condition that you forget what you once were? Would that not be the same as if God created a King of China at the same time as he destroyed you? That is why, in order to satisfy the hopes of humankind, we must prove that the God who governs all is wise and just, and that he will allow nothing to be without reward and without punishment; these are the great foundations of morality. But the doctrine of a God who does not act for the good, and of a soul which is immortal without any memory, serves only to deceive simple people and to undo spiritual people.

I could even show some defects in Descartes' supposed demonstration, for there is still much to be proven in order to complete it. But I believe that it would be useless to bother with this now, since these demonstrations would not be of much use for anything even if they were good demonstrations, as I have just proven. [ . . . ]

---

9. See Descartes, *Principles of Philosophy*, III, 47; and Descartes to Mersenne, 9 January 1639. These seem to be the only passages in which Descartes makes this claim. The letter was published in Leibniz's lifetime and could well have been known to him.

10. See Descartes, Meditation One.

---

11. Leibniz seems to have in mind the account of memory that Descartes gives in his *Treatise of Man*; see Descartes, *Treatise of Man*, trans. Hall (Cambridge, Mass.: Harvard University Press, 1972), pp. 87ff. There Descartes conceives of memory as brain traces which cause the soul, a mental substance distinct from the brain, to perceive representations of past events. So, when a person dies and the immortal soul separates from the mortal body, it would seem that all memory would be lost. However, it should be noted that Descartes also recognizes a kind of memory that pertains to the soul alone, a kind of memory that is not lost in death. See, for example, *The Philosophical Writings of Descartes*, Vol. III, The Correspondence, ed. J. Cottingham, R. Stoothoff, D. Murdoch, and A. Kenny (Cambridge: Cambridge University Press, 1991), pp. 146–48, 151, 216, 232–33. Leibniz does not seem to take this view into account.

# Blaise Pascal, *Pensées* (1670), "The Wager"[1]

Blaise Pascal was born in Clermont-Ferrand in 1623 and died in Paris in 1662. During his short life he worked on mathematics, physics, and religion. He devoted himself to God and the Jansenist cause after having a mystical experience on 23 November 1654. In 1658 he began the composition of an Apologia for the Christian Religion, unfinished at his death and published in its incomplete form in 1670 as the Pensées. In his lifetime Pascal was famous for the polemical Jansenist Provincial Letters (1656–57); posthumously, he is best known for the Pensées, including the notorious "Wager." In part, the Pensées can be seen as a critique of Descartes, whom Pascal called "useless and uncertain" (Pensées, nos. S118/L84 and S445/L887). Pascal's tenets place him in opposition to philosophers who offer metaphysical demonstrations of God's existence: "All those who have claimed to know God and to prove him without Jesus Christ have had only ineffective proofs. . . . Apart from him and without Scripture, without original sin, without a necessary mediator, who was promised and came, we cannot absolutely prove God, nor teach right doctrine and right morality." (Pensées, no. S221/L189). Thus, his criticism of

Descartes is not surprising; his niece reported that he "could not forgive Descartes who wanted to do without God in all of philosophy, but could not avoid having him give the first nudge to set the world in motion; after that, he had no use at all for God" (Pensées, no. L1001). In the "Wager," Pascal does not, of course, offer proofs for the existence of God, but an argument that it is rational to believe that God exists and a procedure for believing it: Behave as if he does.[2]

Infinity, nothingness.

---

Our soul is cast into the body, where it finds number, time, dimensions; it reasons about these things and calls them nature, necessity, and can believe nothing else.

---

Unity added to infinity does not increase infinity at all, any more than a foot added to an infinite length. The finite is annihilated in the presence of the infinite and becomes pure nothingness. So it is with our mind before God, with our justice before divine justice. Yet the disproportion between our

---

1. Editors' title. Translated from the French by R. Ariew in Blaise Pascal, *Pensées* (Indianapolis/Cambridge: Hackett Publishing Company, 2005).

2. For more about Pascal, see A. J. Krailsheimer, *Pascal* (Oxford: Oxford University Press, 1980).

justice and God's justice is not as great as that between unity and infinity.

———————

God's justice must be as vast as his mercy. Now, his
justice toward the damned is less vast and should be
less shocking to us than his mercy toward the chosen.

———————

We know that there is an infinite, but do not know
its nature, just as we know it to be false that numbers
are finite. It is therefore true that there is an infinite
in number, but we do not know what it is. It is false
that it is even, false that it is odd, for the addition of
a unit does not change its nature. Yet it is a number,
and every number is odd or even. (It is true that this
is understood of every finite number.)

So we may well know that there is a God without
knowing what he is.

Is there no substantial truth, seeing that there are
so many true things which are not truth itself?

———————

We know then the existence and nature of the finite, because we also are finite and have extension.

We know the existence of the infinite and do not
know its nature, because it has extension like us, but
not limits like us.

But we do not know either the existence or the
nature of God, because he has neither extension
nor limits.

———————

But by faith we know his existence. In glory we
shall know his nature.

Now, I have already shown that we can know the
existence of a thing without knowing its nature.

Let us now speak according to our natural lights.

If there is a God, he is infinitely incomprehensible, since, having neither parts nor limits, he bears no
relation to us. We are therefore incapable of knowing
either what he is or whether he is. This being so, who
will dare undertake to resolve the question? Not we,
who bear no relation to him.

Who then will blame Christians for not being
able to give rational grounds for their belief, they
who profess a religion for which they cannot give rational grounds?

They declare, in proclaiming it to the world, that
it is a folly—*stultitiam*[3]—and then you complain that
they do not prove it! If they proved it, they would
not be keeping their word. It is by lacking proofs that
they are not lacking sense. "Yes, but although this excuses those who offer their religion in this way and
removes the blame of putting it forward without rational grounds, it does not excuse those who accept
it." Let us then examine this point and say: Either
God is or he is not. But to which side shall we incline? Reason can determine nothing here. There is
an infinite chaos that separates us. At the extremity of
this infinite distance a game is being played in which
heads or tails will turn up. How will you wager? You
have no rational grounds for choosing either way or
for rejecting either alternative.

Do not, then, blame as wrong those who have
made a choice, for you know nothing of the matter!
"No, but I will blame them for having made, not this
choice, but a choice. For although the player who
chooses heads is no more at fault than the other one,
they are both in the wrong. The right thing is not to
wager at all."

Yes; but you must wager. It is not optional. You
are committed. Which will you choose, then? Let us
see. Since you must choose, let us see what is the
less profitable option. You have two things to lose,
the true and the good; and two things to stake, your
reason and your will, your knowledge and your beatitude; and your nature has two things to avoid, error and wretchedness. Since you must necessarily
choose, your reason is no more offended by choosing
one rather than the other. This settles one point. But
your beatitude? Let us weigh the gain and the loss in
calling heads that God exists. Let us assess the two
cases. If you win, you win everything; if you lose, you
lose nothing. Wager, then, without hesitation that
he exists! "This is wonderful. Yes, I must wager. But
perhaps I am wagering too much." Let us see: since
there is an equal chance of winning and losing, if
there were two lives to win for one, you could still
wager. But if there were three lives to win, you would
have to play (since you must necessarily play), and it

———————

3. Paul, I Corinthians 1:18.

would be foolish, when you are forced to play, not to risk your life to win three at a game in which there is an equal chance of losing and winning. But there is an eternity of life and happiness. This being so, if there were an infinity of chances, and only one in your favor, it would still be right to wager one life in order to win two; and, being obliged to play, you would be making the wrong choice if you refused to stake one life against three in a game in which, out of an infinity of chances, there is only one in your favor, if there were an infinite life of infinite happiness to be won. But here there is an infinite life of infinite happiness to be won, one chance of winning against a finite number of chances of losing, and what you are staking is finite. All bets are off wherever there is an infinity and wherever there is not an infinite number of chances of losing against the chance of winning. There is no time to hesitate; you must give everything. And thus, when you are forced to play, you must be renouncing reason to preserve life, instead of risking it for an infinite gain, which is as likely to happen as is a loss amounting to nothing.

It is no use saying that it is uncertain whether you will win, that it is certain you are taking a risk, and that the infinite distance between the *certainty* of what you are risking and the *uncertainty* of what you stand to gain makes the finite good you are certainly staking equal to the infinite good which is uncertain. It is not so. All players take a certain risk for an uncertain gain; and yet they take a certain finite risk for an uncertain finite gain without sinning against reason. It is not true that there is an infinite distance between the certain risk and the uncertain gain. Indeed, there is an infinity between the certainty of winning and the certainty of losing. But the uncertainty of winning is proportional to the certainty of the risk, in proportion to the chances of winning and losing. Hence, if there are as many chances on one side as on the other, you are playing for even odds, and then the certainty of what you are risking is equal to the uncertainty of what you may win—so far is it from being infinitely distant. Thus, our proposition is infinitely powerful, when the stakes are finite in a game where the chances of winning and losing are even, and the infinite is to be won.

This is conclusive and if people are capable of any truth, this is it.

"I confess it, I admit it. But, still . . . Is there no means of seeing what is in the cards?" Yes, Scripture and the rest, etc. "Yes, but my hands are tied and my mouth is shut; I am forced to wager, and am not free. I have not been released and I am made in such a way that I cannot believe. What, then, would you have me do?" That is true. But at least realize that your inability to believe comes from your passions, since reason brings you to this and yet you cannot believe. Work, then, on convincing yourself, not by adding more proofs of God's existence, but by diminishing your passions. You would like to find faith and do not know the way? You would like to be cured of unbelief and ask for the remedies? Learn from those who were bound like you, and who now wager all they have. These are people who know the way you wish to follow, and who are cured of the illness you wish to be cured of. Follow the way by which they began: They acted as if they believed, took holy water, had masses said, etc. This will make you believe naturally and mechanically.[4] "But this is what I am afraid of." And why? What do you have to lose? But to show you that this is the way, this diminishes the passions, which are your great obstacles, etc.

"Oh! This discourse moves me, charms me, etc." If this discourse pleases you and seems cogent, know that it is made by a man who has knelt, both before and after it, in prayer to that being, infinite and without parts, before whom he submits all he has, so that he might bring your being to submit all you have for your own good and for his glory, and that thus strength may be reconciled with this baseness.

## End of This Discourse

Now, what harm will come to you by taking this side? You will be faithful, honest, humble, grateful, generous, a sincere, true friend. Certainly you will not be

---

4. Pascal's word is *abêtira*—literally, will make you more like the beasts. Man is in part a beast or machine and one needs to allow that part its proper function, that is, one needs to act dispassionately or mechanically.

taken by unhealthy pleasures, by glory and by luxury, but will you not have others?

I tell you that as a result you will gain in this life, and that, at each step you take on this road, you will see such a great certainty of gain and so much nothingness in what you risk, that you will at last recognize that you have wagered for something certain and infinite, for which you have given nothing.

———————

We owe a great debt to those who point out faults. For they mortify us. They teach us that we have been despised. They do not prevent our being so in the future, for we have many other faults for which we may be despised. They prepare for us the exercise of correction and freedom from a fault.

———————

Custom is our nature. He who is accustomed to faith believes it, can no longer fear hell, and cannot believe anything else. He who is accustomed to believe that the king is terrible, etc. Who doubts, then, that our soul, being accustomed to see number, space, and motion, believes that and nothing else?

———————

Do you believe it to be impossible that God is infinite, without parts? Yes. I wish therefore to show you <an image of God and his immensity> an infinite and indivisible thing: It is a point moving everywhere with infinite speed.

For it is one in all places and completely whole in every location.

Let this effect of nature, which previously seemed impossible to you, allow you to understand that there may be others you still do not know. Do not draw the conclusion from your experiment that there remains nothing for you to learn, but rather that there remains an infinity for you to learn.

It is false that we are worthy of the love of others; it is unfair that we should want it. If we were born reasonable and indifferent, knowing ourselves and others, we would not give this inclination to our will. However, we are born with it. Therefore we are born unfair. For all tends to self; this is contrary to all order. We must tend to the general, and the tendency to self is the beginning of all disorder, in war, politics, economy, and man's particular body.

The will is therefore depraved. If the members of natural and civil communities tend toward the good of the body, the communities themselves ought to look to another more general body of which they are members. We should, therefore, tend to the general. We are, therefore, born unfair and depraved.

No religion but our own has taught that man is born in sin. No sect of philosophers has said this. Therefore none has told the truth.

No sect or religion has always existed on earth, save for the Christian religion.

The Christian religion alone makes man altogether *lovable* and *happy*. In polite society we cannot be both lovable and happy.

It is the heart that experiences God, and not reason. Here, then, is faith: God felt by the heart, not by reason.

The heart has its reasons, which reason does not know. We know this in a thousand things.

I say that the heart loves the universal being naturally and itself naturally, according to its practice. And it hardens itself against one or the other as it chooses. You have rejected the one and kept the other. Is it through reason that you love yourself?

The single knowledge contrary to common sense and human nature is the only one to have existed always among men.

# 2. SPINOZA'S *ETHICS* AND ASSOCIATED TEXTS

Baruch Spinoza was born in Amsterdam in 1632. His parents had emigrated from Portugal in 1622; they were descendants of Sephardic Jews who, like all Iberian peninsula Jews, had been forcibly converted to Catholicism many generations earlier. These "converts" who reconverted flooded the newly independent Republic of the Netherlands and created an intellectually turbulent community of individuals whose newly expressed Jewish identity was intermixed with their Catholic origins and culture. Given the heterogeneity of this community, doctrinal tensions were prevalent and excommunication from the Synagogue became a fairly common occurrence. In Amsterdam, Spinoza went to a rabbinical school, where he learned Hebrew and read the works of Jewish thinkers, such as Moses Maimonides. He also learned Latin and sought instruction in natural philosophy and in the philosophy of Descartes. In 1656 he was excommunicated from the Jewish community, and in 1660, the Jewish authorities petitioned the Amsterdam municipal government to expel him from the city, giving as their reason that he was a menace to "all piety and morals." He moved to a village south of Amsterdam and supported himself by making lenses. In 1663, he moved to a town near The Hague and ultimately resided in The Hague itself until his death in 1677. During his lifetime he published *Metaphysical Thoughts* and *Descartes' Principles of Philosophy Part I and II, Demonstrated in the Geometrical Manner* (both 1663). He also published *Theologico Political Treatise* in 1670, under the name of a fictitious publisher in Hamburg. The collection of his works published posthumously in 1677 included *Ethics, Demonstrated in Geometrical Order.*[1]

By the middle of the seventeenth century, philosophers had a number of fully developed philosophical systems available as alternatives to the previously dominant scholasticism. Among the more prominent ones were Hobbes' materialism (and empiricism) and Descartes' dualism (and innatism). Spinoza obviously had an affinity with Descartes' manner of philosophizing (though not with his method of doubt).

---

1. Spinoza's philosophical works and correspondence are available in English translation. For more on Spinoza, see Edwin Curley, *Behind the Geometrical Method* (Princeton: Princeton University Press, 1988), Yirmiyahu Yovel, *Spinoza and Other Heretics*, 2 vols. (Princeton: Princeton University Press, 1989), or Don Garrett, ed., *Cambridge Companion to Spinoza* (Cambridge: Cambridge University Press, 1996).

After all, his first publication was a geometrical exposition of the first two parts of Descartes' *Principles*.[2] Spinoza was taken with the geometrical method and its associated perspective of the whole as opposed to the usual point of view of the part (cf. Letter 32 to Oldenburg, about the worm in the blood). However, even in his representation of Descartes' *Principles*, he allowed glimpses of his disagreements with Descartes; as he said to Oldenburg (Letter 2), Descartes has gone far astray from knowledge of the first cause and origin of all things; he has failed to achieve an understanding of the true nature of the human mind; and he has never grasped the true cause of error. Spinoza's *Ethics*, then, is two steps removed from Descartes' *Principles*—Spinoza substituting his own principles and, as its subtitle indicates, exhibiting them in a geometrical presentation.

The geometrical exposition of the *Ethics* is often a source of interpretive difficulty for students of Spinoza. It is tempting to think of the work as abstract, disconnected arguments, instead of thinking about it as a paradigm of seventeenth-century thought, imbued with the concerns and aspirations of a thinker grounded in the problems of his days and writing for an audience of his peers. The geometrical apparatus also tends to make it difficult to comprehend Spinoza's philosophy itself. To conceive just a portion of those obstacles, one needs only to imagine trying to grasp Cartesian philosophy without having recourse to the *Meditations* or *Discourse*, using only the appendix to the *Second Set of Replies*, "arranged in geometrical fashion." Interestingly, it was generally agreed at the time that geometrical expositions are not best for understanding a particular philosophy. Descartes claimed that synthesis, the method of demonstration that "uses a long series of definitions, postulates, and axioms, theorems, and problems . . . is not as satisfying as the method of analysis, nor does it engage the minds of those who are eager to learn, since it does not show how the thing was discovered."[3] Spinoza agreed. He called

the geometric order cumbersome (or prolix), and sometimes set it aside "so that everyone may more easily perceive" what he thinks;[4] this remark echoes an earlier one in which he said that he would have presented Descartes' *Principles* in mathematical order if he "had not thought that such prolixity would have impeded" the understanding of such things "which should be seen as clearly as though presented in a picture."[5] So, although grateful to Spinoza for his frequent interruptions of the geometric order, and his extremely useful summations (the *scholia*), we might wish that he had provided, along with the *Ethics*, a treatise that would have revealed his doctrines according to an order of discovery.

Lacking such a treatise, one is required to construct Spinoza's steps toward the *Ethics*. Useful toward that purpose is his exposition of Descartes' *Principles*, especially his formulations of Descartes' definitions.[6] Spinoza's correspondence is also always helpful in this respect; his "Letter on the Infinite" reads more like an article for a scholarly journal than an epistle to a friendly correspondent. In any case, one way of understanding Spinoza's path of discovery is through the contrasts one can draw between his philosophy and Descartes'. Key in that enterprise is his infinitism. Spinoza's doctrine of the infinite is a radical departure from Descartes' fairly consistent finitism about everything except God, who is then termed incomprehensible, that is, beyond our mind's grasp. For Spinoza, conversely, our intellect is capable of reaching absolute knowledge, because pure understanding has the same nature in humans and God. Another key involves Spinoza's ruminations on infinite substance, and how he interprets what Descartes would have called mental and corporeal substance. The result is a metaphysics that attempts to cleave a middle ground between Descartes' dualism and Hobbes' materialism, that is, "dual aspect" theory, with the mental and corporeal realms being two of the attributes of infinite substance, and the order and

---

2. See Section 1, above.

3. See above, Section 1, Descartes, *Reply to the Second Set of Objections*.

4. *Ethics IV*, prop. 18.

5. "Prolegomenon" to *Descartes' Principles* (see above, Section 1).

6. See above, Section 1.

connection of ideas being the same as the order and connection of things. In the *Ethics*, Spinoza begins with a metaphysics of God and substance, and continues with the nature of the mind and its affects; this

leads him to discuss human bondage and ultimately human freedom—or the power of the intellect. It is

Please note: due to a printing error this section continues on the following page.

# Thomas Hobbes, *Leviathan* (1651)[1]

the end of Spinoza's journey, i.e., an intellectualist morality, that gives the work its title of *Ethics*.

*Thomas Hobbes (1588–1679) spent most of his life as tutor, secretary, and financial manager in the service of the earls of Devonshire and Newcastle. His extensive travels in Europe brought him into contact with many of the leading thinkers of the time, including Galileo, whom he visited in 1636, and Mersenne, to whose circle he belonged while in Paris in 1635, and then again when in exile in Paris from 1640 to 1651. He had met the elderly Bacon in the 1620s. Hobbes contributed the* Third Set of Objections *to Descartes'* Meditations *in 1641 and began to publish his own philosophical system,* Elements of Philosophy, *first issuing* Section Three, Concerning Government and Society (De Cive) *in 1642, then* The First Section, Concerning Body (De Corpore) *in 1655 and Section Two,* Concerning Human Nature (De Homine) *in 1658. The work for which he is best known, in which he defends his materialist philosophy and rejects Anglicanism, is* Leviathan, or the Matter, Forme, and Power of a Commonwealth Ecclesiasticall and Civill *(1651).*[2]

## The Introduction.

Nature (the art by which God has made and governs the world) is also so imitated in this by the *art* of man, as in many other things, that it can make an artificial animal. For seeing life is but a motion of limbs, the beginning of which is in some principal part within, why may we not say that all *automata* (engines that move themselves by springs and wheels as does a watch) have an artificial life? For what is the *heart*, but a *spring*; and the *nerves*, but so many *strings*; and the *joints*, but so many *wheels*, giving motion to the whole body, such as was intended by the artificer? *Art* goes yet further, imitating that rational and most

---

1. From *The English Works of Thomas Hobbes of Malmesbury*, ed. Sir William Molesworth (London, 1839–45), 11 vols., English, modified.

2. Hobbes' works are available in the original English or in translation. For more on Hobbes, see A. P. Martinich, *The Two Gods of Leviathan* (Cambridge: Cambridge University Press, 1992), Richard Tuck, *Hobbes* (Oxford: Oxford University Press, 1989), Steve Shapin and Simon Schaffer, *Leviathan and the Air-Pump* (Princeton: Princeton University Press, 1985), and Tom Sorell, ed., *Cambridge Companion to Hobbes* (Cambridge: Cambridge University Press, 1996).

excellent work of nature, *man*. For by art is created that great LEVIATHAN called a COMMONWEALTH, or STATE (in Latin CIVITAS), which is but an artificial man, though of greater stature and strength than the natural, for whose protection and defense it was intended, and in which the *sovereignty* is an artificial soul, as giving life and motion to the whole body; the *magistrates*, and other *officers* of judicature and execution, artificial *joints*; *reward* and *punishment* (by which fastened to the seat of the sovereignty every joint and member is moved to perform his duty) are the *nerves*, that do the same in the body natural; the *wealth* and *riches* of all the particular members are the *strength*; *salus populi* (the people's safety) its *business*; *counselors*, by whom all things needful for it to know are suggested unto it, are the *memory*; *equity*, and *laws*, an artificial *reason* and *will*; *concord*, *health*; *sedition*, *sickness*; and *civil war*, *death*. Lastly, the *pacts* and *covenants*, by which the parts of this body politic were at first made, set together, and united, resemble that *fiat*, or the *let us make man*, pronounced by God in the creation.

To describe the nature of this artificial man, I will consider

First, the *matter* of this, and the *artificer*—both of which is *man*.

Secondly, *how*, and by what *covenants* it is made; what are the *rights* and *just power* or *authority* of a *sovereign*; and what it is that *preserves* and *dissolves* it.

Thirdly, what is a *Christian commonwealth*.

Lastly, what is the *kingdom of darkness*.

Concerning the first, there is a saying much usurped of late, that *wisdom* is acquired, not by reading of *books*, but of *men*. Consequently to which end, those persons that for the most part can give no other proof of being wise take great delight to show what they think they have read in men, by uncharitable censures of one another behind their backs. But there is another saying not of late understood, by which they might learn truly to read one another, if they would take the pains; and that is, *nosce teipsum*, read thyself: which was not meant, as it is now used, to countenance, either the barbarous state of men in power towards their inferiors, or to encourage men of low degree to a saucy behavior towards their betters, but to teach us that for the similitude of the thoughts and passions of one man, to the thoughts and passions of another, whoever looks into himself, and considers what he does, when he does *think, opine, reason, hope, fear*, etc., and upon what grounds, he shall as a result read and know what are the thoughts and passions of all other men upon the like occasions. I say the similitude of *passions*, which are the same in all men, *desire, fear, hope*, etc., not the similitude of the objects of the passions, which are the *things desired, feared, hoped*, etc., for these the constitution individual, and particular education, do so vary, and they are so easy to be kept from our knowledge, that the characters of man's heart, blotted and confounded as they are with dissembling, lying, counterfeiting, and erroneous doctrines, are legible only to him who searches hearts. And though by men's actions we do discover their design sometimes, yet to do it without comparing them with our own, and distinguishing all circumstances by which the case may come to be altered, is to decipher without a key, and be for the most part deceived, by too much trust, or by too much diffidence, as he who reads is himself a good or evil man.

But let one man read another by his actions ever so perfectly, it serves him only with his acquaintance, which are but few. He who is to govern a whole nation must read in himself, not this or that particular man, but mankind, which though it is hard to do, harder than to learn any language or science, yet when I shall have set down my own reading orderly, and perspicuously, the pains left another, will be only to consider, if he also does not find the same in himself. For this kind of doctrine admits no other demonstration.

# Part 1. Of Man

## Chapter 1. Of *Sense*

Concerning the thoughts of man, I will consider them first *singly*, and afterwards in *train*, or dependence upon one another. *Singly*, they are every one a *representation* or *appearance* of some quality or other accident of a body without us, which is commonly called an *object*—which object works on the eyes, ears, and other parts of a man's body, and by diversity of working, produces diversity of appearances.

The origin of them all is that which we call SENSE. (For there is no conception in a man's mind, which has not at first, totally, or by parts, been begotten upon the organs of sense.) The rest are derived from that origin.

To know the natural cause of sense is not very necessary to the business now in hand; and I have elsewhere written of the same at large. Nevertheless, to fill each part of my present method, I will briefly deliver the same in this place.

The cause of sense is the external body, or object, which presses the organ proper to each sense, either immediately, as in taste and touch, or mediately, as in seeing, hearing, and smelling; this pressure, by the mediation of nerves and other strings and membranes of the body, continued inwards to the brain and heart, causes there a resistance, or counterpressure, or endeavor of the heart, to deliver itself; this endeavor, because *outward*, seems to be some matter without. And this *seeming*, or, *fancy*, is that which men call *sense*, and consists, as to the eye, in a *light*, or *color figured*; to the ear, in a *sound*; to the nostril, in an *odor*; to the tongue and palate, in a *savor*; and to the rest of the body, in *heat, cold, hardness, softness*, and such other qualities as we discern by *feeling*. All these qualities called *sensible* are in the object that causes them but so many several motions of the matter, by which it presses our organs diversely. Neither in us that are pressed are they anything else but diverse motions (for motion produces nothing but motion). But their appearance to us is fancy, the same waking as dreaming. And as pressing, rubbing, or striking the eye makes us fancy a light, and pressing

the ear produces a din, so also do the bodies we see or hear produce the same by their strong, though unobserved action. For if those colors and sounds were in the bodies, or objects that cause them, they could not be severed from them, as by glasses, and in echoes by reflection, we see they are, where we know the thing we see is in one place, the appearance in another. And though at some certain distance, the real and very object seem invested with the fancy it begets in us; yet still the object is one thing, the image or fancy is another, so that sense in all cases is nothing else but original fancy, caused (as I have said) by the pressure, that is, by the motion of external things upon our eyes, ears, and other organs ordained to it.

But the philosophy schools through all the universities of Christendom, grounded upon certain texts of *Aristotle*, teach another doctrine, and say, for the cause of *vision*, that the thing seen sends forth on every side a *visible species* (in English) a *visible show*, *apparition*, or *aspect*, or *a being seen*, the receiving of which into the eye is *seeing*. And for the cause of *hearing*, that the thing heard sends forth an *audible* species, that is, an *audible aspect*, or *audible being seen*, which entering at the ear makes *hearing*. For the cause of *understanding* also, they say the thing understood sends forth *intelligible species*, that is, an *intelligible being seen* which coming into the understanding makes us understand. I do not say this as disapproving of the use of universities; but because I am to speak hereafter of their office in a commonwealth, I must let you see on all occasions by the way what things would be amended in them, among which the frequency of insignificant speech is one.

## Chapter 2. Of *Imagination*

That when a thing lies still, unless something else stirs it, it will lie still forever is a truth that no man doubts of. But that when a thing is in motion, it will eternally be in motion, unless something else stops it, though the reason is the same (namely, that nothing can change itself), is not so easily assented to. For men measure, not only other men, but all other things, by themselves, and because they find themselves subject after motion to pain, and lassitude, think everything else grows weary of motion, and seeks repose of its own accord, little considering whether it is not some other motion in which that desire of rest they find in themselves consists. From hence it is that the schools say heavy bodies fall downwards out of an appetite to rest, and to conserve their nature in that place which is most proper for them, ascribing appetite and knowledge of what is good for their conservation (which is more than man has) to inanimate things, absurdly.

When a body is once in motion, it moves (unless something else hinders it) eternally; and whatever hinders it cannot in an instant, but in time and by degrees, quite extinguish it. And as we see in the water, though the wind ceases, the waves do not give over rolling for a long time after, so also it happens in that motion, which is made in the internal parts of a man, then, when he sees, dreams, etc. For after the object is removed or the eye shut, we still retain an image of the thing seen, though more obscure than when we see it. And this, the Latins call *imagination*, from the image made in seeing, and apply the same, though improperly, to all the other senses. But the Greeks call it *fancy*, which signifies *appearance*, and is as proper to one sense as to another. IMAGINATION therefore is nothing but *decaying sense*, and is found in men and many other living creatures, as well sleeping, as waking.

The decay of sense in men waking is not the decay of the motion made in sense, but an obscuring of it, in such manner as the light of the sun obscures the light of the stars—which stars do no less exercise their virtue, by which they are visible, in the day, than in the night. But because among many strokes which our eyes, ears, and other organs receive from external bodies, only the predominant is sensible; therefore the light of the sun being predominant, we are not affected with the action of the stars. And any object being removed from our eyes, though the impression it made in us remains, yet other objects more present succeeding and working on us, the imagination of the past is obscured and made weak, as the voice of a man is in the noise of the day. From this it follows

that the longer the time is, after the sight or sense of any object, the weaker is the imagination. For the continual change of man's body destroys in time the parts which in sense were moved, so that distance of time and of place has one and the same effect in us. For as at a great distance of place, that which we look at appears dim and without distinction of the smaller parts, and as voices grow weak and inarticulate, so also, after great distance of time, our imagination of the past is weak, and we lose (for example) many particular streets of cities we have seen, and many particular circumstances of actions. This *decaying sense*, when we would express the thing itself (I mean fancy itself), we call *imagination*, as I said before, but when we would express the *decay*, and signify that the sense is fading, old, and past, it is called *memory*. Thus, *imagination* and *memory* are but one thing which for diverse considerations have diverse names.

Much memory, or memory of many things, is called *experience*. Again, imagination being only of those things which have been formerly perceived by sense, either all at once, or by parts at several times, the former (which is the imagining the whole object, as it was presented to the sense) is *simple imagination*—as when one imagines a man, or horse, which he has seen before. The other is *compounded*—as when from the sight of a man at one time, and of a horse at another, we conceive in our mind a Centaur. So when a man compounds the image of his own person with the image of the actions of another man, as when a man imagines himself a *Hercules* or an *Alexander* (which happens often to those who are much taken with reading of romances), it is a compound imagination and properly but a fiction of the mind. There are also other imaginations that arise in men (though waking) from the great impression made in sense—as from gazing upon the sun, the impression leaves an image of the sun before our eyes a long time after, and from being long and vehemently attentive to geometrical figures, a man shall in the dark (though awake) have the images of lines and angles before his eyes—which kind of fancy has no particular name, as being a thing that does not commonly fall into men's discourse.

The imaginations of those who sleep are those we call *dreams*. And these also (as all other imaginations) have been before, either totally or by parcels in the sense. And because in sense the brain and nerves, which are the necessary organs of sense, are so benumbed in sleep, as not easily be moved by the action of external objects, there can happen in sleep no imagination, and therefore no dream, but what proceeds from the agitation of the inward parts of man's body. These inward parts, for the connection they have with the brain and other organs, when they are distempered, do keep the same in motion—by which the imaginations there formerly made appear as if a man were waking, saving that the organs of sense being now benumbed, so as there is no new object, which can master and obscure them with a more vigorous impression, a dream must necessarily be more clear, in this silence of sense, than are our waking thoughts. And hence it comes to pass that it is a hard matter, and by many thought impossible, to distinguish exactly between sense and dreaming. For my part, when I consider that in dreams, I do not often nor constantly think of the same persons, places, objects, and actions that I do waking, nor remember so long a train of coherent thoughts, dreaming, as at other times; and because waking I often observe the absurdity of dreams, but never dream of the absurdities of my waking thoughts, I am well satisfied that being awake I know I do not dream, though when I dream, I think myself awake.

And seeing dreams are caused by the distemper of some of the inward parts of the body, diverse distempers must necessarily cause different dreams. And hence it is that lying cold breeds dreams of fear and raises the thought and image of some fearful object (the motion from the brain to the inner parts, and from the inner parts to the brain being reciprocal), and that as anger causes heat in some parts of the body, when we are awake, so when we sleep the overheating of the same parts causes anger, and raises up the imagination of an enemy in the brain. In the same manner as natural kindness, when we are awake, causes desire, and desire makes heat in certain other parts of the body, so also, too much heat in those parts, while we sleep, raises an imagination

of some kindness shown in the brain. In sum, our dreams are the reverse of our waking imaginations, the motion when we are awake, beginning at one end, and when we dream, at another.

The most difficult discerning of a man's dream, from his waking thoughts, is then, when by some accident we do not observe that we have slept, which easily happens to a man full of fearful thoughts and whose conscience is much troubled, and who sleeps, without the circumstances of going to bed, or putting off his clothes, as one who nods in a chair. For he who takes pains, and industriously lays himself to sleep, in case any uncouth and exorbitant fancy come unto him, cannot easily think it other than a dream. We read of *Marcus Brutus* (one who had his life given him by *Julius Caesar*, and was also his favorite, and notwithstanding murdered him), how at *Philippi*, the night before he gave battle to *Augustus Caesar*, he saw a fearful apparition, which is commonly related by historians as a vision, but considering the circumstances, one may easily judge to have been but a short dream. For sitting in his tent, pensive and troubled with the horror of his rash act, it was not hard for him, slumbering in the cold, to dream of that which most frightened him—which fear, as by degrees it made him wake, so also it must necessarily make the apparition vanish by degrees; and having no assurance that he slept, he could have no cause to think it a dream or anything but a vision. And this is no very rare accident; for even those who are perfectly awake, if they are timorous, and superstitious, possessed with fearful tales, and alone in the dark, are subject to the like fancies, and believe they see spirits and dead men's ghosts walking in churchyards; whereas it is either their fancy only, or else the knavery of such persons, as make use of such superstitious fear to pass disguised in the night to places they would not be known to haunt.

From this ignorance of how to distinguish dreams and other strong fancies from vision and sense did arise the greatest part of the religion of the Gentiles in time past, who worshipped satyrs, fawns, nymphs, and the like, and nowadays the opinion that rude people have of fairies, ghosts, and goblins, and of the power of witches. For as for witches, I do not think that their witchcraft is any real power, but yet that they are justly punished for the false belief they have that they can do such mischief, joined with their purpose to do it if they can, their trade being nearer to a new religion than to a craft or science. And for fairies and walking ghosts, the opinion of them has I think been on purpose, either taught, or not confuted, to keep in credit the use of exorcism, of crosses, of holy water, and other such inventions of ghostly men. Nevertheless, there is no doubt but God can make unnatural apparitions. But that he does it so often as men need to fear such things more than they fear the stay or change of the course of nature, which he also can stay and change, is no point of Christian faith. But evil men under the pretext that God can do anything are so bold as to say anything when it serves their turn, though they think it untrue; it is the part of a wise man to believe them no further than right reason makes that which they say appear credible. If this superstitious fear of spirits were taken away, and with it prognostics from dreams, false prophecies, and many other things depending on it, by which crafty ambitious persons abuse the simple people, men would be much more fitted than they are for civil obedience.

And this ought to be the work of the schools; but they rather nourish such doctrine. For (not knowing what imagination, or the senses are) what they receive, they teach, some saying that imaginations arise of themselves and have no cause, others that they arise most commonly from the will, and that good thoughts are blown (inspired) into a man by God, and evil thoughts by the Devil, or that good thoughts are poured (infused) into a man by God, and evil ones by the Devil. Some say the senses receive the species of things and deliver them to the common sense, and the common sense delivers them over to the fancy, and the fancy to the memory, and the memory to the judgment, like handing of things from one to another, with many words making nothing understood.

The imagination that is raised in man (or any other creature endowed with the faculty of imagining) by words or other voluntary signs is what we generally call *understanding*, and is common to man and beast. For a dog by custom will understand the call or the rating of his master, and so will many other beasts. That understanding which is peculiar to man is the understanding not only his will, but his conceptions and thoughts, by the sequel and contexture of the names of things into affirmations, negations, and other forms of speech; and of this kind of understanding I shall speak hereafter.

## Chapter 3. Of the Consequence or *Train of Imaginations*

By *Consequence*, or TRAIN of thoughts, I understand that succession of one thought to another, which is called (to distinguish it from discourse in words) *mental discourse*.

When a man thinks on anything whatsoever, his next thought after is not altogether so casual as it seems to be. Not every thought to every thought succeeds indifferently. But as we have no imagination of which we have not formerly had sense, in whole or in parts, so we have no transition from one imagination to another of which we never had the like before in our senses. The reason of which is this: all fancies are motions within us, relics of those made in the sense, and those motions that immediately succeeded one another in the sense, continue also together after sense, inasmuch as the former coming again to take place and be predominant, the latter follows, by coherence of the matter moved, in such manner as water upon a plain table is drawn which way any one part of it is guided by the finger. But because in sense, sometimes one thing, sometimes another succeeds to one and the same thing perceived, it comes to pass in time that, in the imagining of anything, there is no certainty what we shall imagine next; only this is certain, it shall be something that succeeded the same before, at one time or another.

This train of thoughts, or mental discourse, is of two sorts. The first is *unguided, without design*, and inconstant, in which there is no passionate thought to govern and direct those that follow to itself, as the end and scope of some desire or other passion; in this case the thoughts are said to wander, and seem impertinent one to another, as in a dream. Such are commonly the thoughts of men that are not only without company, but also without care of anything, though even then their thoughts are as busy as at other times, but without harmony—as the sound which a lute out of tune would yield to any man, or in tune, to one that could not play. And yet in this wild ranging of the mind, a man may oftentimes perceive the way of it and the dependence of one thought upon another. For in a discourse of our present civil war, what could seem more impertinent than to ask (as one did) what was the value of a Roman penny? Yet the coherence was manifest enough to me. For the thought of the war introduced the thought of delivering up the king to his enemies; the thought of that brought in the thought of the delivering up of Christ; and that again the thought of the 30 pence, which was the price of that treason; and in this way easily followed that malicious question, and all this in a moment of time, for thought is quick.

The second is more constant, as being *regulated* by some desire and design. For the impression made by such things as we desire or fear is strong and permanent, or (if it ceases for a time) of quick return; so strong it is sometimes, as to hinder and break our sleep. From desire arises the thought of some means we have seen produce the like of that which we aim at; and from the thought of that, the thought of means to that mean; and so continually, until we come to some beginning within our own power. And because the end, by the greatness of the impression, comes often to mind, in case our thoughts begin to wander, they are quickly again reduced into the way; this, observed by one of the seven wise men, made him give men this precept, which is now worn out, *Respice finem*—that is to say, in all your actions, look often upon what you would have, as the thing that directs all your thoughts in the way to attain it.

The train of regulated thoughts is of two kinds: One, when of an effect imagined, we seek the causes or means that produce it; and this is common to man and beast. The other is when, imagining anything whatsoever, we seek all the possible effects that can be produced by it—that is to say, we imagine what we can do with it, when we have it. I have not at any time seen any sign of this, but in man only; for this is a curiosity hardly incident to the nature of any living creature that has no other passion but sensual, such as are hunger, thirst, lust, and anger. In sum, the discourse of the mind, when it is governed by design, is nothing but *seeking*, or the faculty of invention, which the Latins called *sagacitas* and *solertia*, a hunting out of the causes, of some effect, present or past, or of the effects of some present or past cause. Sometimes a man seeks what he has lost; and from that place and time in which he misses it, his mind runs back, from place to place, and time to time, to find where and when he had it—that is to say, to find some certain and limited time and place in which to begin a method of seeking. Again, from this his thoughts run over the same places and times, to find what action or other occasion might make him lose it. This we call *remembrance*, or calling to mind; the Latins call it *reminiscentia*, as it were a reconsideration of our former actions.

Sometimes a man knows a determinate place within the compass of which he is to seek, and then his thoughts run over all the parts of it, in the same manner as one would sweep a room to find a jewel, or as a spaniel ranges the field until he finds a scent, or as a man should run over the alphabet to start a rhyme.

Sometimes a man desires to know the event of an action, and then he thinks of some like action past, and its events one after another, supposing like events will follow like actions—as he who foresees what will become of a criminal reconsiders what he has seen follow on the like crime before, having this order of thoughts: the crime, the officer, the prison, the judge, and the gallows. This kind of thought is called *foresight*, and *prudence*, or *providence*, and sometimes *wisdom*, though such conjecture, through the difficulty of observing all circumstances, is very fallacious. But this is certain: By how much one man has more experience of things past than another, by so much also he is more prudent, and his expectations the more seldom fail him. The *present* only has a being in nature; things *past* have a being in the memory only; but things to *come* have no being at all, the *future* being but a fiction of the mind, applying the sequels of actions past to the actions that are present—which with most certainty is done by him who has most experience, but not with certainty enough.

And though it is called prudence when the event answers our expectation, yet in its own nature, it is but presumption. For the foresight of things to come, which is providence, belongs only to him by whose will they are to come. From him only, and supernaturally, proceeds prophecy. The best prophet naturally is the best guesser, and the best guesser, he who is most versed and studied in the matters he guesses at, for he has most *signs* to guess by.

A *sign* is the event antecedent of the consequent, and contrarily, the consequent of the antecedent, when the like consequences have been observed before; and the more often they have been observed, the less uncertain is the sign. And therefore he who has most experience in any kind of business has most signs by which to guess at the future time, and consequently is the most prudent, and so much more prudent than he who is new in that kind of business, as not to be equaled by any advantage of natural and extemporary wit, though perhaps many young men think the contrary.

Nevertheless it is not prudence that distinguishes man from beast. There are beasts that at a year old observe more and pursue that which is for their good more prudently than a child can do at ten.

As prudence is a *presumption* of the *future*, contracted from the *experience* of time *past*, so there is a presumption of things past taken from other things (not future but) past also. For he who has seen by what courses and degrees a flourishing state has first come into civil war and then to ruin, upon the sight of the ruins of any other state will guess the like war and the like courses have been there also. But this conjecture has the same uncertainty almost with the conjecture of the future, both being grounded only upon experience.

There is no other act of man's mind that I can remember, naturally planted in him so as to need no other thing to the exercise of it, but to be born a man, and live with the use of his five senses. Those other faculties, of which I shall speak by and by, and which seem proper to man only, are acquired and increased by study and industry, and of most men learned by instruction and discipline, and proceed all from the invention of words and speech. For besides sense,

and thoughts, and the train of thoughts, the mind of man has no other motion, though by the help of speech and method, the same faculties may be improved to such a height as to distinguish men from all other living creatures.

Whatever we imagine is *finite*. Therefore, there is no idea or conception of anything we call *infinite*. No man can have in his mind an image of infinite magnitude, nor conceive infinite swiftness, infinite time, or infinite force, or infinite power. When we say anything is infinite, we signify only that we are not able to conceive the ends and bounds of the things named, having no conception of the thing, but of our own inability. And therefore the name of God is used, not to make us conceive him (for he is *incomprehensible*, and his greatness and power are inconceivable), but that we may honor him. Also because whatever (as I said before) we conceive has been perceived first by sense, either all at once or by parts; a man can have no thought representing anything not subject to sense. No man therefore can conceive anything, but he must conceive it in some place, and endowed with some determinate magnitude, and which may be divided into parts; nor that anything is all in this place, and all in another place at the same time; nor that two, or more things can be in one and the same place at once; for none of these things ever have, or can be incident to sense, but are absurd speeches, taken upon credit (without any signification at all) from deceived philosophers, and deceived or deceiving schoolmen.

## Chapter 4. Of *Speech*

The invention of *printing*, though ingenious, compared with the invention of *letters*, is no great matter. But who was the first who found the use of letters is not known. He who first brought them into *Greece* men say was *Cadmus*, the son of *Agenor*, king of Phoenicia. A profitable invention for continuing the memory of time past and the conjunction of mankind, dispersed into so many and distant regions of the earth, and in addition difficult, as proceeding from a watchful observation of the diverse motions of the tongue, palate, lips, and other organs of speech by which to make as many differences of characters to remember them. But the most noble and profitable invention of all other was that of SPEECH, consisting of *names* or *appellations*, and their connection by which men register their thoughts, recall them when they are past, and also declare them one to another for mutual utility and conversation, without which there had been among men, neither commonwealth, nor society, nor contract, nor peace, no more than among lions, bears, and wolves. The first author of speech was *God* himself, who instructed *Adam* how to name such creatures as he presented to his sight; for the Scripture goes no further in this matter. But this was sufficient to direct him to add more names, as the experience and use of the creatures should give him occasion, and to join them in such manner by degrees as to make himself understood, and so by succession of time, so much language might be gotten as he had found use for, though not so copious as an orator or philosopher has need of. For I do not find anything in the Scripture out of which, directly or by consequence, can be gathered that *Adam* was taught the names of all figures, numbers, measures, colors, sounds, fancies, relations, much less the names of words and speech, as *general*, *special*, *affirmative*, *negative*, *interrogative*, *optative*, *infinitive*, all which are useful, and least of all, of *entity*, *intentionality*, *quiddity*, and other insignificant words of the school.

But all this language gotten and augmented by *Adam* and his posterity was again lost at the tower of *Babel*, when by the hand of God every man was stricken, for his rebellion, with an oblivion of his former language. And being as a result forced to disperse themselves into several parts of the world, it must necessarily be that the diversity of tongues that now is proceeded by degrees from them, in such manner as need (the mother of all inventions) taught them, and in tract of time grew everywhere more copious.

The general use of speech is to transfer our mental discourse into verbal, or the train of our thoughts into a train of words, and that for two commodities, of which one is the registering of the consequences of our thoughts, which being apt to slip out of our memory and put us to a new labor, may again be recalled by such words as they were marked by. So that the first use of names is to serve for *marks*, or

*notes* of remembrance. Another is when many use the same words to signify (by their connection and order) one to another, what they conceive or think of each matter, and also what they desire, fear, or have any other passion for. And for this use they are called *signs*. Special uses of speech are these: first, to register what by cogitation we find to be the cause of anything, present or past, and what we find things present or past may produce or effect—which in sum is acquiring of arts. Secondly, to show to others that knowledge which we have attained, which is to counsel and teach one another. Thirdly, to make known to others our wills and purposes that we may have the mutual help of one another. Fourthly, to please and delight ourselves and others, by playing with our words, for pleasure or ornament, innocently.

To these uses, there are also four correspondent abuses: first, when men register their thoughts wrong by the inconstancy of the signification of their words, by which they register for their conceptions that which they never conceived, and so deceive themselves. Secondly, when they use words metaphorically, that is, in a sense other than that they are ordained for, and by it deceive others. Thirdly, when by words they declare that to be their will, which is not. Fourthly, when they use them to grieve one another; for seeing nature has armed living creatures, some with teeth, some with horns, and some with hands, to grieve an enemy, it is but an abuse of speech to grieve him with the tongue, unless it is one whom we are obliged to govern; and then it is not to grieve, but to correct and amend.

The manner how speech serves to the remembrance of the consequence of causes and effects consists in the imposing of *names* and the *connection* of them.

Of names, some are *proper* and singular to only one thing, as *Peter*, *John*, *this man*, *this tree*, and some are *common* to many things, as *man*, *horse*, *tree*— every one of which though, but one name, is nevertheless the name of diverse particular things, in respect of all which together, it is called a *universal*, there being nothing in the world universal but names; for the things named are every one of them individual and singular.

One universal name is imposed on many things for their similitude in some quality or other accident; and whereas a proper name brings to mind one thing only, universals recall any one of those many.

And of names universal, some are of more, and some of less extent, the larger comprehending the less large, and some again of equal extent, comprehending each other reciprocally—as for example, the name *body* is of larger signification than the word *man*, and comprehends it, and the names *man* and *rational* are of equal extent, comprehending mutually one another. But here we must take notice that by a name is not always understood, as in grammar, only one word, but sometimes by circumlocution many words together. For all these words, *he who observes the laws of his country in his actions*, make but one name, equivalent to this one word, *just*.

By this imposition of names, some of larger, some of stricter signification, we turn the reckoning of the consequences of things imagined in the mind into a reckoning of the consequences of appellations. For example, a man who has no use of speech at all (such as is born and remains perfectly deaf and dumb), if he sets a triangle before his eyes, and by it two right angles (such as are the corners of a square figure), he may by meditation compare and find that the three angles of that triangle are equal to those two right angles that stand by it. But if another triangle is shown him, different in shape from the former, he cannot know whether the three angles of that also are equal to the same without a new labor. But he who has the use of words, when he observes that such equality was consequent, not to the length of the sides, nor to any other particular thing in his triangle, but only to this, that the sides were straight and the angles three, and that that was all for which he named it a triangle, will boldly conclude universally that such equality of angles is in all triangles whatsoever, and register his invention in these general terms, *every triangle has its three angles equal to two right angles*. And thus the consequence found in one particular comes to be registered and remembered as a universal rule, and discharges our mental reckoning of time and place, and delivers us from all labor of the mind, saving the

first, and makes that which was found true *here* and *now* be true in *all times* and *places*.

But the use of words in registering our thoughts is in nothing so evident as in numbering. A natural fool who could never learn by heart the order of numeral words, as *one*, *two*, and *three*, may observe every stroke of the clock, and nod to it, or say one, one, one, but can never know what hour it strikes. And it seems there was a time when those names of number were not in use; and men were inclined to apply their fingers of one or both hands to those things they desired to keep account of, and that as a result it proceeded that now our numeral words are but ten, in any nation, and in some but five, and then they begin again. And he who can count to ten, if he recites them out of order, will lose himself, and not know when he is done. Much less will he be able to add, and subtract, and perform all other operations of arithmetic. Thus, without words there is no possibility of reckoning of numbers, much less of magnitudes, of swiftness, of force, and other things, the reckonings of which are necessary to the being, or well-being, of mankind.

When two names are joined together into a consequence or affirmation, as thus, *a man is a living creature*, or thus, *if he is a man, he is a living creature*, if the latter name *living creature* signifies all that the former name *man* signifies, then the affirmation or consequence is *true*; otherwise *false*. For *true* and *false* are attributes of speech, not of things. And where speech is not, there is neither *truth* nor *falsehood*. *Error* there may be, as when we expect that which shall not be, or suspect what has not been; but in neither case can a man be charged with untruth.

Seeing then that *truth* consists in the right ordering of names in our affirmations, a man who seeks precise *truth* has need to remember what every name he uses stands for, and to place it accordingly, or else he will find himself entangled in words, as a bird in lime twigs, the more he struggles the more ensnared. And therefore in geometry (which is the only science that it has pleased God to bestow on mankind up to now), men begin at settling the significations of their words—which settling of significations they call *definitions*, and place them in the beginning of their reckoning.

By this it appears how necessary it is for any man who aspires to true knowledge to examine the definitions of former authors, and either to correct them, where they are negligently set down, or to make them himself. For the errors of definitions multiply themselves according as the reckoning proceeds, and lead men into absurdities, which at last they see, but cannot avoid, without reckoning anew from the beginning, in which lies the foundation of their errors. Thus it happens that they who trust to books do as they who cast up many little sums into a greater, without considering whether those little sums were rightly cast up or not, and at last finding the error visible, and not mistrusting their first grounds, do not know which way to clear themselves, but spend time in fluttering over their books—as birds that entering by the chimney, and finding themselves enclosed in a chamber, flutter at the false light of a glass window, for want of wit to consider which way they came in. Thus, in the right definition of names lies the first use of speech, which is the acquisition of science, and in wrong, or no definitions, lies the first abuse, from which proceed all false and senseless tenets, which make those men who take their instruction from the authority of books and not from their own meditation, to be as much below the condition of ignorant men as men endowed with true science are above it. For between true science and erroneous doctrines, ignorance is in the middle. Natural sense and imagination are not subject to absurdity. Nature itself cannot err; and as men abound in copiousness of language, so they become more wise or more mad than ordinary. Nor is it possible without letters for any man to become either excellently wise, or (unless his memory is hurt by disease or ill constitution of organs) excellently foolish. For words are wise men's counters—they do but reckon by them—but they are the money of fools who value them by the authority of an *Aristotle*, a *Cicero*, or a *Thomas*, or any other doctor whatsoever, if but a man.

*Subject to names* is whatever can enter into or be considered in an account, and be added one to another to make a sum, or subtracted one from another and leave a remainder. The Latins called accounts of money *rationes*, and accounting *ratiocinatio*; and

that which we call *items* in bills or books of account, they call *nomina*, that is *names*; and from this it seems to proceed that they extended the word *ratio* to the faculty of reckoning in all other things. The Greeks have but one word, *logos*, for both *speech* and *reason*—not that they thought there was no speech without reason, but no reasoning without speech and the act of reasoning they called *syllogism*, which signifies the summing up of the consequences of one saying to another. And because the same things may enter into account for diverse accidents, their names are (to show that diversity) diversely wrested and diversified. This diversity of names may be reduced to four general heads.

First, a thing may enter into account for *matter* or *body*—as *living, sensible, rational, hot, cold, moved, quiet*—with all which names the word *matter*, or *body*, is understood, all such being names of matter.

Secondly, it may enter into account, or be considered, for some accident or quality, which we conceive to be in it, as for *being moved*, for *being so long*, for *being hot*, etc.; and then, of the name of the thing itself, by a little change or wresting, we make a name for that accident, which we consider; and for *living* put into the account *life*; for *moved*, *motion*; for *hot*, *heat*; for *long*, *length*, and the like; and all such names are the names of the accidents and properties by which one matter and body is distinguished from another. These are called *abstract names*, because severed (not from matter, but) from the account of matter.

Thirdly, we bring into account the properties of our own bodies by which we make such distinction; as when anything is *seen* by us, we do not reckon the thing itself, but the *sight*, the *color*, the *idea* of it in the fancy; and when anything is *heard*, we do not reckon it, but the *hearing* or *sound* only, which is our fancy or conception of it by the ear—and such are names of fancies.

Fourthly, we bring into account, consider, and give *names* to names themselves, and to *speeches*. For *general, universal, special, equivocal* are names of names. And *affirmation, interrogation, commandment, narration, syllogism, sermon, oration*, and many other such are names of speeches. And this is all the variety of names *positive* which are put to mark something which is in nature, or may be feigned by the mind of man, as bodies that are, or may be conceived to be; or of bodies, the properties that are, or may be feigned to be; or words and speech.

There are also other names, called *negative*, which are notes to signify that a word is not the name of the thing in question—as these words *nothing, no man, infinite, unteachable, three want four,* and the like—which are nevertheless of use in reckoning, or in correcting of reckoning, and call to mind our past cogitations, though they are not names of anything, because they make us refuse to admit of names not rightly used.

All other names are but insignificant sounds, and those of two sorts. One when they are new, and yet their meaning not explained by definition—of which there have been abundance coined by schoolmen and puzzled philosophers.

Another, when men make a name of two names, whose significations are contradictory and inconsistent—as this name, an *incorporeal body*, or (which is all one) *an incorporeal substance*, and a great number more. For whenever any affirmation is false, the two names of which it is composed, put together and made one, signify nothing at all. For example, if it is a false affirmation to say a *quadrangle is round*, the word *round quadrangle* signifies nothing, but is a mere sound. So likewise, if it is false to say that virtue can be poured, or blown up and down, the words *in-poured virtue, in-blown virtue,* are as absurd and insignificant as a *round quadrangle*. And therefore you shall hardly meet with a senseless and insignificant word that is not made up of some Latin or Greek names. A Frenchman seldom hears our Savior called by the name of *parole*, but often by the name of *verbe*; yet *verbe* and *parole* differ no more, but that one is Latin, the other French.

When a man, upon the hearing of any speech, has those thoughts which the words of that speech and their connection were ordained and constituted to signify, then he is said to understand it, *understanding* being nothing else but conception caused by speech. And therefore if speech is peculiar to man (as for all I know it is), then is understanding peculiar

to him also. And therefore of absurd and false affirmations, in case they are universal, there can be no understanding; though many think they understand then, when they do but repeat the words softly, or examine them in their mind.

What kinds of speeches signify the appetites, aversions, and passions of man's mind, and of their use and abuse, I shall speak when I have spoken of the passions.

The names of such things as affect us, that is, which please and displease us, because all men are not alike affected with the same thing, nor the same man at all times, are in the common discourses of men of *inconstant* signification. For seeing all names are imposed to signify our conceptions, and all our affections are but conceptions, when we conceive the same things differently, we can hardly avoid different naming of them. For though the nature of what we conceive is the same, yet the diversity of our reception of it, in respect of different constitutions of body and prejudices of opinion, gives everything a tincture of our different passions. And therefore in reasoning a man must take heed of words, which besides the signification of what we imagine of their nature, have a signification also of the nature, disposition, and interest of the speaker—such as are the names of virtues and vices, for one man calls *wisdom* what another calls *fear*; and one *cruelty*, what another *justice*; one *prodigality*, what another *magnanimity*; and one *gravity*, what another *stupidity*, etc. And therefore such names can never be true grounds of any ratiocination. No more can metaphors, and tropes of speech; but these are less dangerous, because they profess their inconstancy, which the others do not.

## Chapter 5. Of *Reason* and *Science*

When a man *reasons*, he does nothing else but conceive a sum total from *addition* of parcels, or conceive a remainder from *subtraction* of one sum from another, which (if it is done by words) is conceiving of the consequence of the names of all the parts to the name of the whole, or from the names of the whole and one part to the name of the other part. And though in some things (as in numbers), besides *adding* and *subtracting*, men name other operations, as *multiplying* and *dividing*, yet they are the same; for multiplication is but adding together of things equal, and division, but subtracting of one thing as often as we can. These operations are not incident to numbers only, but to all manner of things that can be added together and taken one out of another. For as arithmeticians teach to add and subtract in *numbers*, so the geometers teach the same in *lines*, *figures* (solid and superficial), *angles*, *proportions*, *times*, degrees of *swiftness*, *force*, *power*, and the like. The logicians teach the same in *consequences of words*, adding together *two names* to make an *affirmation* and two *affirmations* to make a *syllogism*, and many *syllogisms* to make a *demonstration*; and from the *sum*, or *conclusion*, of a *syllogism*, they subtract one *proposition* to find the other. Writers of politics add together *contracts* to find men's *duties*, and lawyers, *laws* and *facts*, to find what is *right* and *wrong* in the actions of private men. In sum, in whatever matter there is place for *addition* and *subtraction*, there also is place for *reason*; and where these have no place, there *reason* has nothing at all to do.

Out of all this we may define (that is to say determine) what that is which is meant by this word *reason*, when we reckon it among the faculties of the mind. For REASON, in this sense, is nothing but *reckoning* (that is, adding and subtracting) of the consequences of general names agreed upon for the *marking* and *signifying* of our thoughts—I say marking them when we reckon by ourselves, and *signifying* when we demonstrate or approve our reckonings to other men.

And as in arithmetic, unpracticed men must, and professors themselves may often err and cast up false, so also in any other subject of reasoning, the ablest, most attentive, and most practiced men may deceive themselves and infer false conclusions—not but that reason itself is always right reason, as well as arithmetic is a certain and infallible art, but no one man's reason, nor the reason of any one number of men, makes the certainty, no more than an account is therefore well cast up because a great many men have unanimously approved it. And therefore, as when there is a controversy in an account, the parties must by their own accord set up for right reason

the reason of some arbitrator, or judge, to whose sentence they will both stand, or their controversy must either come to blows or be undecided, for want of a right reason constituted by nature, so is it also in all debates of whatever kind. And when men who think themselves wiser than all others clamor and demand right reason for judge, yet seek no more, but that things should be determined by no other men's reason but their own, it is as intolerable in the society of men as it is in play, after trump is turned, to use for trump on every occasion that suit which they have most in their hand. For they do nothing else, who will have every of their passions, as it comes to bear sway in them, be taken for right reason, and who in their own controversies, exposing their want of right reason by the claim they lay to it.

The use and end of reason is not the finding of the sum and truth of one, or a few consequences, remote from the first definitions and settled significations of names, but to begin at these, and proceed from one consequence to another. For there can be no certainty of the last conclusion without a certainty of all those affirmations and negations, on which it was grounded and inferred. As when a master of a family, in taking an account, casts up the sums of all the bills of expense into one sum, and not regarding how each bill is summed up by those that give them in account, nor what it is he pays for, he advantages himself no more than if he allowed the account in gross, trusting to every of the accountants' skill and honesty, so also in reasoning of all other things, he that takes up conclusions on the trust of authors, and does not fetch them from the first items in every reckoning (which are the significations of names settled by definitions), loses his labor, and does not know anything, but only believes.

When a man reckons without the use of words, which may be done in particular things (as when upon the sight of any one thing, we conjecture what was likely to have preceded, or is likely to follow upon it), if that which he thought likely to follow, does not follow, or that which he thought likely to have preceded it, has not preceded it, this is called ERROR, to which even the most prudent men are subject. But when we reason in words of general signification, and fall upon a general inference which is false, though it is commonly called *error*, it is indeed an ABSURDITY, or senseless speech. For error is but a deception in presuming that something is past, or to come, of which, though it were not past, or not to come, yet there was no impossibility discoverable. But when we make a general assertion, unless it is a true one, the possibility of it is inconceivable. And words by which we conceive nothing but the sound are those we call *absurd, insignificant*, and *nonsense*. And therefore if a man should talk to me of a *round quadrangle* or, *accidents of bread in cheese*; or *immaterial substances*; or of *a free subject*; a *free will*; or any *free*, but free from being hindered by opposition, I should not say he was in an error, but that his words were without meaning, that is to say, absurd.

I have said before (in the second chapter) that a man did excel all other animals in this faculty, that when he conceived anything whatsoever, he was apt to inquire the consequences of it, and what effects he could do with it. And now I add this other degree of the same excellence, that he can by words reduce the consequences he finds to general rules called *theorems*, or *aphorisms*—that is, he can reason, or reckon, not only in number, but in all other things, of which one may be added unto or subtracted from another.

But this privilege is allayed by another, and that is by the privilege of absurdity, to which no living creature is subject, but man only. And of men, those are of all most subject to it who profess philosophy. For it is most true that *Cicero* said of them somewhere: that there can be nothing so absurd, but may be found in the books of philosophers. And the reason is manifest. For there is not one of them who begins his ratiocination from the definitions, or explications of the names they are to use, which is a method that has been used only in geometry, whose conclusions have in this way been made indisputable.

I. The first cause of absurd conclusions I ascribe to the want of method, in that they do not begin their ratiocination from definitions, that is, from settled significations of their words, as if they could cast accounts without knowing the value of the numeral words, *one, two*, and *three*.

And whereas all bodies enter into account upon diverse considerations (which I have mentioned in the preceding chapter), these considerations being diversely named, diverse absurdities proceed from the confusion and unfit connection of their names into assertions. And therefore,

II. The second cause of absurd assertions I ascribe to the giving of names of *bodies* to *accidents*; or of *accidents* to *bodies*; as they do who say *faith is infused*, or *inspired*; when nothing can be *poured* or *breathed* into anything but body; and that *extension is body*; that *phantasms* are *spirits*, etc.

III. The third I ascribe to the giving of the names of the *accidents* of *bodies without us* to the *accidents* of our *own bodies*; as they do who say the *color is in the body*; *the sound is in the air*, etc.

IV. The fourth, to the giving of the names of *bodies* to *names*, or *speeches*; as they do who say that *there are universal things*, that *a living creature is genus* or *a general thing*, etc.

V. The fifth, to the giving of the names of *accidents* to *names* and *speeches*; as they do who say *the nature of a thing is its definition*; *a man's command is his will*, and the like.

VI. The sixth, to the use of metaphors, tropes, and other rhetorical figures, instead of proper words. For though it is lawful to say (for example) in common speech, *the way goes, or leads here, or there*; *the proverb says this or that* (whereas ways cannot go, nor proverbs speak), yet in reckoning and seeking of truth such speeches are not to be admitted.

VII. The seventh, to names that signify nothing, but are taken up and learned by rote from the schools, as *hypostatical, transubstantiate, consubstantiate, eternal-now*, and the like canting of schoolmen.

To him who can avoid these things, it is not easy to fall into any absurdity, unless it is by the length of an account, where he may perhaps forget what went before. For all men by nature reason alike, and well, when they have good principles. For who is so stupid as both to make a mistake in geometry and also to persist in it, when another detects his error to him?

By this it appears that reason is not, as sense and memory, born with us, nor gotten by experience only, as prudence is, but attained by industry, first in apt imposing of names, and secondly by getting a good and orderly method in proceeding from the elements, which are names, to assertions made by connection of one of them to another, and so to syllogisms, which are the connections of one assertion to another, until we come to a knowledge of all the consequences of names appertaining to the subject in hand; and that is what men call SCIENCE. And whereas sense and memory are but knowledge of fact, which is a thing past and irrevocable, *science* is the knowledge of consequences and dependence of one fact upon another, by which, out of what we can presently do, we know how to do something else when we will, or the like, another time, because when we see how anything comes about, upon what causes, and by what manner, when the like causes come into our power, we see how to make it produce the like effects.

Children therefore are not endowed with reason at all until they have attained the use of speech, but are called reasonable creatures, for the possibility apparent of having the use of reason in time to come. And the most part of men, though they have the use of reasoning a little way, as in numbering to some degree, yet it serves them to little use in common life, in which they govern themselves, some better, some worse, according to their differences of experience, quickness of memory, and inclinations to several ends, but specially according to good or evil fortune and the errors of one another. For as for science, or certain rules of their actions, they are so far from it that they do not know what it is. Geometry they have thought conjuring; but for other sciences, they who have not been taught the beginnings and some progress in them, that they may see how they are acquired and generated, are in this point like children who, having no thought of generation, are made believe by the women that their brothers and sisters are not born, but found in the garden.

But yet they who have no *science* are in better and nobler condition with their natural prudence than men who by misreasoning, or by trusting them who reason wrong, fall upon false and absurd general rules. For ignorance of causes and of rules does not set men so far out of their way as relying on false

rules, and taking for causes of what they aspire to, those that are not so, but rather causes of the contrary.

To conclude, the light of human minds is perspicuous words, but by exact definitions first made clearer and purged from ambiguity; *reason* is the *pace*; increase of *science*, the *way*; and the benefit of mankind, the *end*. And on the contrary, metaphors, and senseless and ambiguous words, are like *ignes fatui*, a fool's fire, and reasoning upon them is wandering among innumerable absurdities—and their end, contention and sedition, or contempt.

As much experience is *prudence*, so is much science *sapience*. For though we usually have one name of wisdom for them both, yet the Latins did always distinguish between *prudentia* and *sapientia*, ascribing the former to experience, the latter to science. But to make their difference appear more clearly, let us suppose one man endowed with an excellent natural use and dexterity in handling his arms, and another to have added to that dexterity an acquired science of where he can offend or be offended by his adversary, in every possible posture or guard; the ability of the former would be to the ability of the latter as prudence to sapience, both useful, but the latter infallible. But they who trusting only to the authority of books follow the blind blindly are like him who, trusting to the false rules of a master of fencing, ventures presumptuously upon an adversary who either kills or disgraces him.

The signs of science are some, certain and infallible, some, uncertain. Certain, when he who pretends the science of anything can teach the same, that is to say, demonstrate the truth of this perspicuously to another; uncertain, when only some particular events answer to his pretense, and upon many occasions prove so as he says they must. Signs of prudence are all uncertain, because to observe by experience and remember all circumstances that may alter the success is impossible. But in any business, of which a man does not have infallible science to proceed by, to forsake his own natural judgment and be guided by general sentences read in authors, and subject to many exceptions, is a sign of folly, and generally scorned by the name of pedantry. And even of those men themselves who in councils of the commonwealth love to show their reading of politics and history, very few do it in their domestic affairs, where their particular interest is concerned, having prudence enough for their private affairs; but in public they study more the reputation of their own wit than the success of another's business.

## Chapter 34. Of the Signification of *Spirit*, *Angel*, and *Inspiration* in the Books of Holy Scripture

Seeing the foundation of all true ratiocination is the constant signification of words, which in the doctrine following does not depend (as in natural science) on the will of the writer, nor (as in common conversation) on vulgar use, but on the sense they carry in the Scripture, it is necessary, before I proceed any further, to determine, out of the Bible, the meaning of such words, as by their ambiguity may render what I am to infer upon them, obscure, or disputable. I will begin with the words BODY and SPIRIT, which in the language of the Schools are termed *corporeal* and *incorporeal* substances.

The word *body*, in the most general meaning, signifies that which fills or occupies some certain room or imagined place, and does not depend on the imagination, but is a real part of what we call the *universe*. For the *universe*, being the aggregate of all bodies, there is no real part of it that is not also *body*, nor anything properly a *body* that is not also part of (that aggregate of all *bodies*) the *universe*. The same also, because bodies are subject to change, that is to say, to variety of appearance to the sense of living creatures is called *substance*—that is to say, *subject* to various accidents, as sometimes to be moved, sometimes to stand still—and to seem to our senses sometimes hot, sometimes cold, sometimes of one color, smell, taste, or sound, sometimes of another. And we attribute this diversity of seeming (produced by the diversity of the operation of bodies on the organs of our sense) to alterations of the bodies that operate and call them *accidents* of those bodies. And according to this meaning of the word, *substance* and *body* signify the same thing; and therefore *incorporeal substance* are words

which, when they are joined together, destroy one another, as if a man should say an *incorporeal body*.

But in the sense of common people, not all the universe is called body, but only such parts of it as they can discern by the sense of feeling to resist their force, or by the sense of their eyes to hinder them from a farther prospect. Therefore, in the common language of men, *air* and *aerial substances* are not typically to be taken for bodies, but (as often as men are sensible of their effects) are called *wind*, or *breath*, or (because the same are called in the Latin *spiritus*) *spirits*—as when they call that aerial substance, which, in the body of any living creature, gives it life and motion, *vital* and *animal spirits*. But for those idols of the brain, which represent bodies to us where they are not, as in a looking-glass, in a dream, or to a distempered brain waking, they are (as the apostle said generally of all idols) nothing— nothing at all, I say, there where they seem to be; and in the brain itself, nothing but tumult, proceeding either from the action of the objects, or from the disorderly agitation of the organs of our sense. And men, who are otherwise employed than to search into their causes, do not know of themselves what to call them, and may therefore easily be persuaded by those whose knowledge they much revere, some to call them *bodies*, and think them made of air compacted by a power supernatural, because the sight judges them corporeal, and some to call them *spirits*, because the sense of touch discerns nothing in the place where they appear to resist their fingers. So that the proper signification of *spirit* in common speech is either a subtle, fluid, and invisible body, or a ghost, or other idol or phantasm of the imagination. But for metaphorical significations, there are many; for sometimes it is taken for disposition or inclination of the mind, as when for the disposition to control the sayings of other men, we say, *a spirit of contradiction*; for *a disposition to uncleanness*, *an unclean spirit*; for *perverseness*, *an obstinate spirit*; for *sullenness*, *a dumb spirit*, and for *inclination to godliness*, *and God's service*, *the Spirit of God*—sometimes for any eminent ability, or extraordinary passion, or disease of the mind, as when *great wisdom* is called the *spirit of wisdom*; and *madmen* are said to be *possessed with a spirit*.

I do not find anywhere any other signification of *spirit*, and where none of these can satisfy the sense of that word in Scripture, the place does not fall under human understanding, and our faith in this does not consist in our opinion, but in our submission, as in all places where God is said to be a *Spirit*; or where by the *Spirit of God*, God himself is meant. For the nature of God is incomprehensible; that is to say, we understand nothing *of what he is*, but only *that he is*; and therefore the attributes we give him are not to tell one another *what he is*, nor to signify our opinion of his nature, but our desire to honor him with such names as we conceive most honorable among ourselves. [ . . . ]

The disciples of Christ, seeing him walking upon the sea (Matthew 14.26 and Mark 6.49), supposed him to be a *Spirit*, meaning by it an aerial *body* and not a phantasm; for it is said they all saw him, which cannot be understood of the delusions of the brain (which are not common to many at once, as visible bodies are, but singular, because of the differences of fancies), but of bodies only. In like manner, where he was taken for a *spirit* by the same apostles (Luke 24.3, 7). So also (Acts 12.15) when St. Peter was delivered out of prison, it would not be believed, but when the maid said he was at the door, they said it was his *angel*; by which must be meant a corporeal substance, or we must say the disciples themselves did follow the common opinion of both Jews and Gentiles that some such apparitions were not imaginary, but real, and such as did not need the fancy of man for their existence. These the Jews called *spirits* and *angels*, good or bad, as the Greeks called the same by the name of *demons*. And some such apparitions may be real, and substantial, that is to say, subtle bodies, which God can form by the same power by which he formed all things, and make use of, as of ministers, and messengers (that is to say, angels) to declare his will and execute the same when he pleases, in extraordinary and supernatural manner. But when he has so formed them, they are substances endowed with dimensions, and take up room, and can be moved from place to place, which is peculiar to bodies; and therefore are

not incorporeal ghosts, that is to say, ghosts that are in no *place*; that is to say, that are *nowhere*—that is to say, that seeming to be *somewhat* are *nothing*. But if corporeal is taken in the most vulgar manner for such substances as are perceptible by our external senses, then incorporeal substance is not an imaginary, but real thing, namely, a thin, invisible substance that has the same dimensions that are in grosser bodies.

By the name of ANGEL is signified generally a *messenger*; and most often, a *messenger of God*; and by a messenger of God is signified anything that makes known his extraordinary presence, that is to say, the extraordinary manifestation of his power, especially by a dream or vision.

Concerning the creation of *angels*, there is nothing delivered in the Scriptures. That they are spirits is often repeated, but by the name of spirit is signified both in Scripture and vulgarly, both among Jews and Gentiles, sometimes thin bodies, as the air, the wind, the spirits vital, and animal, of living creatures, and sometimes the images that arise in the fancy in dreams, and visions, which are not real substances, nor last any longer than the dream, or vision they appear in—which apparitions, though no real substances, but accidents of the brain, yet when God raises them supernaturally to signify his will, they are not improperly termed God's messengers, that is to say, his *angels*.

And as the Gentiles did vulgarly conceive the imagery of the brain for things really subsistent without them and not dependent on the fancy, and out of them framed their opinions of *demons*, good and evil, which because they seemed to subsist really they called *substances*; and because they could not feel them with their hands, *incorporeal*, so also the Jews upon the same ground, without anything in the Old Testament that constrained them to that, had generally an opinion (except the sect of the *Sadducees*) that those apparitions (which it pleased God sometimes to produce in the fancy of men, for his own service, and therefore called them his angels) were substances, not dependent on the fancy, but permanent creatures of God; of which those which they thought were good to them, they esteemed *the angels of God*, and those they thought would hurt them they called *evil angels* or evil spirits—such as was the spirit of Python, and the spirits of madmen, of lunatics, and epileptics—for they esteemed such as were troubled with such diseases, *demoniacs*.

But if we consider the places of the Old Testament where angels are mentioned, we shall find that in most of them nothing else can be understood by the word *angel* but some image raised (supernaturally) in the fancy, to signify the presence of God in the execution of some supernatural work; and therefore in the rest, where their nature is not expressed, it may be understood in the same manner. [ . . . ]

To men who understand the signification of these words, *substance* and *incorporeal*; as *incorporeal* is not taken for subtle body but for *not body*, they imply a contradiction, inasmuch as to say, an angel or spirit is (in that sense) an incorporeal substance is to say in effect there is no angel nor spirit at all. Considering therefore the signification of the word *angel* in the Old Testament, and the nature of dreams and visions that happen to men by the ordinary way of nature, I was inclined to this opinion, that angels were nothing but supernatural apparitions of the fancy raised by the special and extraordinary operation of God, by that means to make his presence and commandments known to mankind, and chiefly to his own people. But the many places of the New Testament, and our Savior's own words, and in such texts where there is no suspicion of corruption of the Scripture, have extorted from my feeble reason an acknowledgment and belief that there are also substantial and permanent angels. But to believe they are in no place, that is to say, nowhere, that is to say, nothing, as they (though indirectly) say that will have them incorporeal, cannot be evinced by Scripture.

On the signification of the word *spirit* depends that of the word INSPIRATION, which must either be taken properly, and then it is nothing but the blowing into a man some thin and subtle air or wind, in such manner as a man fills a bladder with his breath or if spirits are not corporeal, but have their existence only in the fancy, it is nothing but the blowing in of a phantasm, which is improper to say and impossible; for phantasms are not, but only seem to be somewhat. That word therefore is used in the Scripture metaphorically only, as (Gen. 2.7), where it is said that God inspired into man the breath of life, no more is meant than that God gave unto him vital motion. For we are not to think that God made first a living breath and then blew it into Adam after he was made, whether that breath were real or seeming, but only as it is (Acts 17.25) "that he gave him life and breath," that is, made him a living creature. And where it is said (2 Tim. 3.16) "all Scripture is given by inspiration from God," speaking there of the Scripture of the Old Testament, it is an easy metaphor to signify that God inclined the spirit or mind of those writers to write that which should be useful in teaching, reproving, correcting, and instructing men in the way of righteous living. But where St. Peter (2 Pet. 1.21) said that "Prophecy came not in old time by the will of man, but the holy men of God spoke as they were moved by the Holy Spirit," by the Holy Spirit is meant the voice of God in a dream or supernatural vision, which is not *inspiration*: Nor when our Savior breathing on his disciples, said "Receive the Holy Spirit," was that breath the Spirit, but a sign of the spiritual graces he gave unto them. And though it is said of many, and of our Savior himself, that he was full of the Holy *Spirit*; yet that fullness is not to be understood for *infusion* of the substance of God, but for accumulation of his gifts, such as are the gift of sanctity of life, of tongues, and the like, whether attained supernaturally or by study and industry; for in all cases they are the gifts of God. So likewise where God says (Joel 2.28) "I will pour out my Spirit upon all flesh, and your sons and your daughters shall prophesy, your old men shall dream dreams, and your young men shall see visions," we are not to understand it in the proper sense, as if his *Spirit* were like water, subject to effusion or infusion, but as if God had promised to give them prophetic dreams and visions. For the proper use of the word *infused*, in speaking of the graces of God, is an abuse of it; for those graces are virtues, not bodies to be carried hither and thither and to be poured into men as into barrels.

In the same manner, to take *inspiration* in the proper sense, or to say that good *spirits* entered into men to make them prophesy, or evil *spirits* into those that became phrenetic, lunatic, or epileptic, is not to take the word in the sense of the Scripture; for the Spirit there is taken for the power of God, working by causes to us unknown. As also (Acts 2.2) the wind that is there said to fill the house in which the apostles were assembled on the day of Pentecost is not to be understood for the Holy Spirit, which is the Deity itself, but for an external sign of God's special working on their hearts to effect in them the internal graces and holy virtues he thought requisite for the performance of their apostleship.

## Chapter 46. Of *Darkness* from *Vain Philosophy* and *Fabulous Traditions*

By PHILOSOPHY is understood *the knowledge acquired by reasoning from the manner of the generation of anything to the properties, or from the properties to some possible way of generation of the same, to the end to be able to produce, as far as matter and human force permit, such effects as human life requires.* So the geometer, from the construction of figures, finds out many properties of them, and from the properties, new ways of their construction by reasoning, to the end to be able to measure land and water, and for infinite other uses. So the astronomer, from the rising, setting, and moving of the sun and stars in diverse parts of the heavens, finds out the causes of day and night and of the different seasons of the year, by which he keeps an account of time—and the like of other sciences.

By this definition it is evident that we are not to account as any part of it that original knowledge called experience, in which consists prudence, because it is not attained by reasoning, but found as well in brute beasts as in man, and is but a memory of successions of events in times past, in which the omission of every little circumstance altering the effect frustrates the expectation of the most prudent; whereas nothing is produced by reasoning correctly, but general, eternal, and immutable truth.

Nor are we therefore to give that name to any false conclusions, for he who reasons correctly in words he understands can never conclude an error.

Nor to that which any man knows by supernatural revelation, because it is not acquired by reasoning.

Nor that which is gotten by reasoning from the authority of books, because it is not by reasoning from the cause to the effect, nor from the effect to the cause, and is not knowledge, but faith.

The faculty of reasoning being consequent to the use of speech, it was not possible but that there should have been some general truths found out by reasoning, as ancient almost as language itself. The savages of America are not without some good moral sentences; they also have a little arithmetic to add and divide in numbers not too great, but they are not therefore philosophers. For as there were plants of corn and wine in small quantity dispersed in the fields and woods before men knew their virtue or made use of them for their nourishment, or planted them apart in fields and vineyards, in which time they fed on acorns and drank water, so also there have been diverse true, general, and profitable speculations from the beginning, as being the natural plants of human reason. But they were at first but few in number. Men lived upon gross experience; there was no method, that is to say, no sowing, nor planting of knowledge by itself, apart from the weeds and common plants of error and conjecture. And the cause of it being the want of leisure from procuring the necessities of life and defending themselves against their neighbors, it was impossible, until the erecting of great commonwealths, it should be otherwise. *Leisure* is the mother of *philosophy* and *Commonwealth*, the mother of *peace* and *leisure*. Where first were great and flourishing *cities*, there was first the study of *philosophy*. The *Gymnosophists* of *India*, the *Magi* of *Persia*, and the *Priests* of *Chaldea* and *Egypt* are counted the most ancient philosophers, and those countries were the most ancient of kingdoms. *Philosophy* was not risen to the *Greeks* and other people of the west, whose *commonwealths* (no greater perhaps than *Lucca* or *Geneva*) never had peace, but when their fears of one another were equal, nor the leisure to observe anything but one another. At length, when war had united many of these *Greek* lesser cities into fewer and greater, then began seven men, of several parts of *Greece*, to get the reputation of being *wise*; some of them for *moral* and *politic* sentences, and others for the learning of the *Chaldeans* and *Egyptians*, which was *astronomy* and *geometry*. But we do not yet hear of any *schools* of *philosophy*. [ . . . ]

That which is now called a University is a joining together and an incorporation under one government of many public schools, in one and the same town or city, in which the principal schools were ordained for the three professions, that is to say, of the Roman religion, of the Roman law, and of the art of medicine. And for the study of philosophy it has no place other than as a handmaid to the Roman religion; and since the authority of Aristotle is only current there, that study is not properly philosophy (the nature of which does not depend on authors) but Aristotelity. And for geometry, until of very late times it had no place at all, as being subservient to nothing but rigid truth. And if any man by the ingenuity of his own nature had attained to any degree of perfection in it, he was commonly thought a magician, and his art diabolical.

Now to descend to the particular tenets of vain philosophy derived to the Universities and as a result into the Church, partly from Aristotle, partly from blindness of understanding, I shall first consider their principles. There is a certain *philosophia prima*, on which all other philosophy ought to depend; it consists principally in right limiting of the significations of such appellations or names as are of all others the most universal—which limitations serve to avoid ambiguity and equivocation in reasoning, and are commonly called definitions, such as are the definitions of body, time, place, matter, form, essence, subject, substance, accident, power, act, finite, infinite, quantity, quality, motion, action, passion, and diverse others, necessary to the explaining of a man's conceptions concerning the nature and generation of bodies. The explication (that is, the settling of the meaning) of these and the like terms is commonly called *metaphysics* in the Schools, as being a part of the philosophy of Aristotle which has that for a title. But it is in another sense, for there it signifies as much as *books written or placed after his natural philosophy*; but the schools take them for *books of supernatural philosophy*, for the word *metaphysics* will bear both these senses. And indeed that which is there written is for the most part so far from the possibility of being

understood, and so repugnant to natural reason, that whoever thinks there is anything to be understood by it must necessarily think it supernatural.

From these metaphysics, which are mingled with the Scripture to make school divinity, we are told there are in the world certain essences separated from bodies, which they call *abstract essences* and *substantial forms*. There is need of somewhat more than ordinary attention in this place for the interpreting of this *jargon*. Also I ask pardon of those who are not used to this kind of discourse, for applying myself to those who are. The world (I do not mean the earth only, that denominates the lovers of it *worldly men*, but the *universe*, that is, the whole mass of all things that are) is corporeal, that is to say, body, and has the dimensions of magnitude, namely, length, breadth, and depth. Also every part of body is likewise body, and has the like dimensions, and consequently every part of the universe is body; and that which is not body is not part of the universe. And because the universe is all, that which is no part of it is nothing, and consequently nowhere. Nor does it follow from this that spirits are nothing, for they have dimensions and are therefore really bodies, though that name in common speech is given to such bodies only as are visible or palpable, that is, that have some degree of opacity. But for spirits, they call them incorporeal, which is a name of more honor, and may therefore with more piety be attributed to God himself, in whom we consider not what attribute expresses best his nature, which is incomprehensible, but what best expresses our desire to honor him.

To know now upon what grounds they say there are *abstract essences* or *substantial forms*, we are to consider what those words do properly signify. The use of words is to register to ourselves and make manifest to others the thoughts and conceptions of our minds. Of which words, some are the names of the things conceived, as the names of all sorts of bodies, that work upon the senses and leave an impression in the imagination. Others are the names of the imaginations themselves, that is to say, of those ideas or mental images we have of all things we see or remember. And others again are names of names, or of different sorts of speech, as *universal, plural, singular* are the names of names, and *definition, affirmation, negation, true, false, syllogism, interrogation, promise, covenant* are the names of certain forms of speech. Others serve to show the consequence or repugnance of one name to another, as when one says *a man is a body*, he intends that the name of *body* is necessarily consequent to the name of *man*, as being but several names of the same thing, *man*, which consequence is signified by coupling them together with the word *is*. And as we use the verb *is*, so the Latins use their verb *est*, and the Greeks their *esti* through all its declinations. Whether all other nations of the world have a word that answers to it or not in their several languages, I cannot tell, but I am sure they do not have need of it. For the placing of two names in order may serve to signify their consequence, if it were the custom (for custom is it, that give words their force), as well as the words *is*, or *be*, or *are*, and the like.

And if it were so, that there was a language without any verb answerable to *est*, or *is*, or *be*; yet the men who used it would not be a jot the less capable of inferring, concluding, and of all kind of reasoning than were the Greeks and Latins. But what then would become of these terms of *entity, essence, essential, essentiality* that are derived from it, and of many more that depend on these, applied as most commonly they are? They are therefore not names of things, but signs by which we make known that we conceive the consequence of one name or attribute to another, as when we say *a man is a living body*, we do not mean that the *man* is one thing, *the living body* another, and the *is*, or *being* a third, but that the *man* and the *living body* are the same thing, because the consequence, *if he is a man, he is a living body*, is a true consequence, signified by that word *is*. Therefore, *to be a body, to walk, to be speaking, to live, to see*, and the like infinitives, also *corporeity, walking, speaking, life, sight*, and the like, that signify just the same, are the names of *nothing* — as I have elsewhere more amply expressed.

But to what purpose (some man may say) is such subtlety in a work of this nature, where I pretend to nothing but what is necessary to the doctrine of government and obedience? It is to this purpose that men may no longer suffer themselves to be abused by them, that by this doctrine of *separated essences*, built on the vain philosophy of Aristotle, would fright them from obeying the laws of their country with empty names, as men frighten birds from the corn with an empty doublet, a hat, and a crooked stick. For it is upon this ground that when a man is dead and buried, they say his soul (that is his life) can walk separated from his body and is seen by night among the graves. Upon the same ground they say that the figure, and color, and taste of a piece of bread has a being there, where they say there is no bread. And upon the same ground they say that faith, and wisdom, and other virtues are sometimes *poured* into a man, sometimes *blown* into him from heaven, as if the virtuous and their virtues could be asunder, and a great many other things that serve to lessen the dependence of subjects on the sovereign power of their country. For who will endeavor to obey the laws, if he expects obedience to be poured or blown into him? Or who will not obey a priest, who can make God, rather than his sovereign, rather than God himself? Or who that is in fear of ghosts will not bear great respect to those who can make the holy water that drives them from him? And this shall suffice for an example of the errors which are brought into the Church from the *entities* and *essences* of Aristotle, which it may be he knew to be false philosophy, but wrote it as a thing consonant to and corroborative of their religion, and fearing the fate of Socrates.

Being once fallen into this error of *separated essences*, they are as a result necessarily involved in many other absurdities that follow it. For seeing they will have these forms be real, they are obliged to assign them some place. But because they hold them incorporeal, without all dimension of quantity, and all men know that place is dimension and not to be filled but by that which is corporeal, they are driven to uphold their credit with a distinction, that they are not indeed anywhere *circumscriptive*, but *definitive* — which term, being mere words, and in this occasion insignificant, pass only in Latin, that the vanity of them may be concealed. For the circumscription of a thing is nothing else but the determination or defining of its place; and so both the terms of the distinction are the same. And in particular, of the essence of a man, which (they say) is his soul, they affirm it to be all of it in his little finger, and all of it in every other part (however small) of his body; and yet no more soul in the whole body than in any one of those parts. Can any man think that God is served with such absurdities? And yet all this is necessary to believe, to those who will believe the existence of an incorporeal soul, separated from the body.

And when they come to give account, how an incorporeal substance can be capable of pain and be tormented in the fire of hell or purgatory, they have nothing at all to answer but that it cannot be known how fire can burn souls.

Again, whereas motion is change of place, and incorporeal substances are not capable of place, they are troubled to make it seem possible how a soul can go forward, without the body, to heaven, hell, or purgatory, and how the ghosts of men (and I may add of their clothes which they appear in) can walk by night in churches, churchyards, and other places of sepulture. To which I do not know what they can answer, unless they will say they walk *definitive*, not *circumscriptive*, or *spiritually*, not *temporally*, for such egregious distinctions are equally applicable to any difficulty whatsoever.

For the meaning of *eternity*, they will not have it be an endless succession of time; for then they should not be able to render a reason how God's will and preordaining of things to come should not be before his prescience of the same, as the efficient cause before the effect or agent before the action, nor of many other of their bold opinions concerning the incomprehensible nature of God. But they will teach us that eternity is the standing still of the present time, a *nunc-stans* (as the Schools call it), which neither they nor anyone else understands, no more than they would a *hic-stans* for an infinite greatness of place.

And whereas men divide a body in their thought by numbering parts of it, and in numbering those parts number also the parts of the place it filled, it cannot be but in making many parts, we make also many places of those parts—by which there cannot be conceived in the mind of any man, more or fewer parts than there are places for. Yet they will have us believe that by the almighty power of God one body

may be at one and the same time in many places; and many bodies at one and the same time in one place, as if it were an acknowledgment of the Divine Power to say: that which is, is not; or that which has been, has not been. And these are but a small part of the incongruities they are forced to from their disputing philosophically, instead of admiring and adoring of the divine and incomprehensible nature, whose attributes cannot signify what he is, but ought to signify our desire to honor him with the best appellations we can think of. But they who venture to reason of his nature from these attributes of honor, losing their understanding in the very first attempt, fall from one inconvenience into another, without end and without number, in the same manner as when a man ignorant of the ceremonies of court, coming into the presence of a greater person than he is used to speak to, and stumbling at his entrance, to save himself from falling, lets slip his cloak; to recover his cloak, lets fall his hat; and with one disorder after another, discovers his astonishment and rusticity.

Then for *physics*, that is, the knowledge of the subordinate and secondary causes of natural events, they render none at all but empty words. If you desire to know why some kinds of bodies sink naturally downwards toward the earth and others go naturally from it, the Schools will tell you out of Aristotle that the bodies that sink downwards are *heavy*; and that this heaviness is what causes them to descend. But if you ask what they mean by heaviness, they will define it to be an endeavor to go to the center of the earth, so that the cause why things sink downward is an endeavor to be below, which is as much as to say that bodies descend or ascend because they do. Or they will tell you the center of the earth is the place of rest and conservation for heavy things; and therefore they endeavor to be there, as if stones and metals had a desire or could discern the place they would be at, as man does; or loved rest, as man does not; or that a piece of glass were less safe in the window than falling into the street.

If we would know why the same body seems greater (without adding to it) one time than another; they say: when it seems less, it is *condensed*; when greater, *rarefied*. What is that *condensed* and *rarefied*? Condensed is when there is in the very same matter less quantity than before; and rarefied, when more. As if there could be matter that had not some determined quantity, when quantity is nothing else but the determination of matter, that is to say, of body, by which we say one body is greater or lesser than another by thus or thus much. Or as if a body were made without any quantity at all, and that afterwards more or less were put into it, according as it is intended the body should be more or less dense.

For the cause of the soul of man, they say, *creatur infundendo* and *creando infunditur*—that is, it is *created by pouring it in* and *poured in by creation*.

For the cause of sense, an ubiquity of *species*, that is, of the *shows* or *apparitions* of objects, which, when they are apparitions to the eye, is *sight*; when to the ear, *hearing*; to the palate, *taste*; to the nostril, *smelling*; and to the rest of the body, *feeling*.

For the cause of the will to do any particular action, which is called *volitio*, they assign the faculty, that is to say, the capacity in general that men have to will sometimes one thing, sometimes another, which is called *voluntas*; making the *power* the cause of the *act*, as if one should assign for the cause of the good or evil acts of men, their ability to do them.

And in many occasions they put for the cause of natural events their own ignorance, but disguised in other words, as when they say, fortune is the cause of things contingent—that is, of things of which they know no cause—and as when they attribute many effects to *occult qualities*— that is, qualities not known to them and therefore also (as they think) to no one else—and to *sympathy, antipathy, antiperistasis, specifical qualities*, and other like terms, which signify neither the agent that produces them, nor the operation by which they are produced.

If such *metaphysics* and *physics* as this are not *vain philosophy*, there was never any, nor was St. Paul needed to give us warning to avoid it.

# Margaret Cavendish, *Philosophical Letters*, Letters 30–42 (1664)[1]

*Margaret Cavendish, Duchess of Newcastle (ca. 1623–73), was the youngest child of Thomas and Elizabeth Lucas. She was privately tutored; in 1642 she was sent to live with her sister in Oxford, where the royal court was residing. Margaret became a maid of honor to Queen Henrietta Maria and in 1644 accompanied her mistress into exile in Paris. There she met and became the second wife of William Cavendish, who was to become Duke of Newcastle. William Cavendish was a royalist and notable patron of science, literature, and philosophy; he was also the elder brother of Charles Cavendish, a mathematician who maintained a correspondence with the leading mathematicians and philosophers of his day, including Descartes and Hobbes. Margaret Cavendish was a prolific author, publishing poetry, works of fiction, and philosophical treatises, including* Philosophical and Physical Opinions *(1655),* Philosophical Letters *(1664),* Observations on Experimental Philosophy *(1666), and* Grounds of Natural Philosophy *(1668).* Philosophical Letters *consists of her collected letters with an imaginary correspondent, in which questions are raised about contemporary philosophers, such as Descartes.*

---

1. From Margaret Cavendish, *Philosophical Letters* (London, 1664), modernized.

## Letter 30

Madam,

I am reading now the works of that famous and most renowned author, Descartes, out of which I intend to pick out only those discourses I like best, and not to examine his opinions as they go along from the beginning to the end of his books; and in order to do this, I have chosen in the first place his discourse of motion, and do not assent to his opinion when he defines motion to be only a mode of a thing, and not the thing or body itself; for, in my opinion, there can be no abstraction made of motion from body, neither really, nor in the manner of our conception, for how can I conceive that which is not, nor cannot be in nature, that is, to conceive motion without body? Thus motion is but one thing with body, without any separation or abstraction whatsoever. Neither does it agree with my reason that one body can give or transfer motion into another body, and as much motion it gives or transfers into that body, as much it loses—as for example, in two hard bodies thrown against one another, where one, thrown with greater force, takes the other along with it, and loses as much motion as it gives it. For how can motion, being no substance, but only a mode, quit one body, and pass into another? One body may either occasion or

143

imitate another's motion, but it can neither give nor take away what belongs to its own or another body's substance, any more than matter can quit its nature from being matter; and therefore my opinion is that if motion does go out of one body into another, then substance goes too; for motion, and substance or body, as aforementioned, are all one thing, and then all bodies that receive motion from other bodies must increase in their substance and quantity, and those bodies which impart or transfer motion must decrease as much as they increase. Truly, madam, that neither motion nor figure should subsist by themselves and yet be transferrable into other bodies is very strange, and as much as to prove them to be nothing, and yet to say they are something. Similar things may be said of all others which they call accidents, such as skill, learning, knowledge, etc., saying they are not bodies, because they have no extension, but inherent in bodies or substances as in their subjects; for although the body may subsist without them, yet they being always with the body, body and they are all one thing. And so is power and body, for body cannot quit power, nor power the body, being all one thing. But to return to motion, my opinion is that all matter is partly animate, and partly inanimate, and all matter is moving and moved, and that there is no part of nature that does not have life and knowledge, for there is no part that does not have a co-mixture of animate and inanimate matter; and though the inanimate matter has no motion, nor life and knowledge of itself, as the animate has, nevertheless being both so closely joined and co-mixed as in one body, the inanimate moves as well as the animate, although not in the same manner; for the animate moves of itself, and the inanimate moves by the help of the animate, and thus the animate is moving and the inanimate moved. Not that the animate matter transfers, infuses, or communicates its own motion to the inanimate, for this is impossible, by reason it cannot part with its own nature, nor alter the nature of inanimate matter, but each retains its own nature. For the inanimate matter remains inanimate, that is, without self-motion, and the animate loses nothing of its self-motion, which otherwise it would, if it should impart or transfer its motion into the inanimate matter; but

only as I said heretofore, the inanimate works or moves with the animate, because of their close union and co-mixture. For the animate forces or causes the inanimate matter to work with her; and thus one is moving, the other moved, and consequently there is life and knowledge in all parts of nature, by reason in all parts of nature there is a co-mixture of animate and inanimate matter. And this life and knowledge is sense and reason, or sensitive and rational corporeal motions, which are all one thing with animate matter without any distinction or abstraction, and can no more quit matter, than matter can quit motion. Thus every creature being composed of this co-mixture of animate and inanimate matter, has also self-motion, that is, life and knowledge, sense and reason, so that no part needs to give or receive motion to or from another part, although it may be an occasion of such a manner of motion to another part, and cause it to move thus or thus—as for example, a watchmaker does not give the watch its motion, but he is only the occasion that the watch moves after that manner, for the motion of the watch is the watch's own motion, inherent in those parts ever since that matter was, and if the watch ceases to move after such a manner or way, that manner or way of motion is nevertheless in those parts of matter the watch is made of, and if several other figures should be made of that matter, the power of moving in the said manner or mode, would yet still remain in all those parts of matter as long as they are a body, and have motion in them. Thus one body may occasion another body to move so or so, but not give it any motion, but everybody (though occasioned by another, to move in such a way) moves by its own natural motion; for self-motion is the very nature of animate matter, and is as much in hard, as in fluid bodies, although your author denies it, saying, the nature of fluid bodies consists in the motion of those little insensible parts into which they are divided, and the nature of hard bodies, when those little particles joined closely together, do rest. For there is no rest in nature. Therefore if there were a world of gold, and a world of air, I do truly believe that the world of gold would be as much internally active, as the world of air externally. For nature's motions are not all external or perceptible by our senses, neither are they all circular, or only of one sort, but there is an infinite change and variety of motions. For I say in my philosophical opinions, as there is only one only matter, so there is only one motion, Yet I do not mean there is only one particular sort of motions, as either circular, or straight, or the like, but that the nature of motion is one and the same, simple and entire in itself, that is, it is mere motion, or nothing else but corporeal motion, and that as there are infinite divisions or parts of matter, so there are infinite changes and varieties of motions, which is the reason that I call motion infinite as well as matter. First that matter and motion are only one thing, and if matter is infinite, motion must be so too; and secondly, that motion is infinite in its changes and variations, as matter is in its parts. And thus much of motion for this time. I add no more, but rest,

Madam, your faithful friend and servant.

## Letter 31

Madam,

I observe your author in his discourse of place makes a difference between an interior and exterior place, and that according to this distinction, one body may be said to change and not to change its place at the same time, and that one body may succeed into another's place. But I am not of this opinion, for I do not believe that there is any more place than body; as for example, water being mixed with earth, the water does not take the earth's place, but as their parts intermix, so do their places, and as their parts change, so do their places, so that there is no more place than there is water and earth. The same may be said of air and water, or air and earth, that is, they did all mix together; for as their bodies join, so do their places, and as they are separated from each other, so are their places. Say a man travels a hundred miles, and so a hundred thousand paces; but yet this man has not been in a hundred thousand places, for he never had any other place but his own, he has joined and separated himself from a hundred thousand, no millions of parts, but he has left no places behind him. You will say, if he travels the same way back again, then he is said to travel through the same places. I answer, it may be the vulgar way

of expression, or the common phrase; but to speak properly, after a philosophical way, and according to the truth in nature, he cannot be said to go back again through the same places he went, because he left none behind him, or else all his way would be nothing but place after place, all the hundred miles along. Besides if place should be taken so, as to express the joining to the nearest bodies which compass him about, certainly he would never find his places again; for the air being fluid, changes or moves continually, and perchance the same parts of the air, which compassed him once, will never come near him again. But you may say if a man is hurt, or has some mischance in his body, so as to have a piece of flesh cut out, and new flesh growing there; then we say because the adjoining parts do not change, that a new piece of flesh is grown in the same place where the former flesh was, and that the place of the former flesh cut or fallen out, is the same of this new grown flesh. I answer in my opinion it is not, for the parts not being the same, the places are not, but every one has its own place. But if the wound is not filled or closed up with other new flesh, you will say that according to my opinion there is no place then at all. I say, yes, for the air or anything else may be there, as new parts joining to the other parts; nevertheless, the air, or that same body which is there, has not taken the flesh's place which was there before, but has its own; but, by reason the adjoining parts remain, man thinks the place remains there also which is no consequence. It is true a man may return to the same adjoining bodies where he was before, but then he brings his place with him again, and as his body, so his place returns also, and if a man's arm is cut off, you may say there was an arm there before, but you cannot say properly this is the place where the arm was. But to return to my first example of the mixture of water, and earth or air, suppose water is not porous, but only divisible, and has no other place but what is its own body's, and that other parts of water intermix with it by dividing and composing; I say there is no more place required than what belongs to their own parts, for if some contract, others dilate, some divide, others join, the places are the same according to the magnitude of each part or body. The same may be said of all kinds or sorts of mixtures, for one body has but one place; and so if many parts of the same nature join into one body and increase the bulk of the body, the place of that same body is accordingly; and if they are bodies of different natures which intermix and joined, each several keeps its place. And so each body and each particular part of a body has its place, for you cannot name body or part of a body, but you must also understand place to be with them, and if a point should dilate to a world, or a world contract to a point, the place would always be the same with the body. And thus I have declared my opinion of this subject, which I submit to the correction of your better judgment, and rest,

Madam, Your Ladyship's faithful friend and humble servant.

## Letter 32

Madam,

In my last letter, I hope, I have sufficiently declared my opinion, that to one body belongs but one place and that no body can leave a place behind it, but wherever body is there is also place. Now give me leave to examine this question: when a body's figure is printed on snow or any other fluid or soft matter, as air, water, and the like, whether it is the body that prints its own figure on the snow or whether it is the snow that patterns the figure of the body? My answer is that it is not the body which prints its figure on the snow, but the snow that patterns out the figure of the body; for if a seal be printed upon wax, it is true, it is the figure of the seal which is printed on the wax, but yet the seal does not give the wax the print of its own figure, but it is the wax that takes the print or pattern from the seal and patterns or copies it out in its own substance, just as the sensitive motions in the eye do pattern out the figure of an object, as I have declared previously. But you will say, perhaps, a body being printed on snow, as it leaves its print, so it also leaves its place with the print in the snow. I answer that does not follow. For the place remains still the body's place, and when the body moves out of the snow, it takes its place along with it, just like a man, whose picture is drawn by a painter, when he goes away, does not leave his place with his picture,

but his place goes with his body; and as the place of the picture is the place of the color or paint, and the place of the copy of an exterior object patterned out by the sensitive corporeal motions is the place of the sensitive organ, so the place of the print in snow, is the snow's place; or else, if the print were the body's place that is printed, and not the snow's, it might as well be said that the motion and shape of a watch were not the motion and shape of the watch, but of the hand of him that made it. And as it is with snow, so it is with air, for a man's figure is patterned out by the parts and motions of the air, wherever he moves; the difference is only that air being a fluid body does not retain the print so long, as snow or a harder body does, but when the body moves out, the print is presently dissolved. But I wonder much about, something your author denies, that there can be two bodies in one place, and yet makes two places for one body, when all is but the motions of one body. Therefore a man sailing in a ship cannot be said to keep place and to change his place; for it is not place he changes, but only the adjoining parts, as leaving some, and joining to others; and it is very improper to attribute that to place which belongs to parts and to make a change of place out of change of parts. I conclude, repeating once again that figure and place are still remaining the same with body. For example, let a stone be beat to dust and this dust be severally dispersed, no, changed into numerous figures. I say, as long as the substance of the stone remains in the power of those dispersed and changed parts and their corporeal motions, its place also continues; and as the corporeal motions change and vary, so does place, magnitude and figure, together with their parts or bodies, for they are but one thing. And so I conclude, and rest,

Madam, your faithful friend and servant.

## Letter 33

Madam,

I am absolutely of your author's opinion when he says that all bodies of this universe are of one and the same matter, really divided into many parts, and that these parts are diversely moved. But that these motions should be circular more than of any other sort, I cannot believe, although he thinks that this is the most probable way to find out the causes of natural effects; for nature is not bound to one sort of motions more than to another, and it is but in vain to endeavor to know how and by what motions God did make the world, since creation is an action of God, and God's actions are incomprehensible. Therefore his ethereal whirlpools and little particles of matter which he reduces to three sorts and calls them the three elements of the universe, their circular motions, several figures, shavings, and many the like, which you may better read, than I rehearse to you, are, to my thinking, rather fancies than rational or probable conceptions; for how can we imagine that the universe was set a moving as a top by a whip, or a wheel by the hand of a spinster, and that the vacuities were filled up with shavings? For these violent motions would rather have disturbed and disordered nature; and though nature uses variety in her motions or actions, yet these are not extravagant, nor by force or violence, but orderly, temperate, free, and easy, which causes me to believe the Earth turns about rather than the Sun; and though corporeal motions for variety make whirlwinds, yet whirlwinds are not constant. Neither can I believe that the swiftness of motion could make the matter more subtle and pure than it was by nature, for it is the purity and subtlety of the matter that causes motion and makes it swifter or slower, and not motion the subtlety and purity of matter, motion being only the action of matter. And the self-moving part of matter is the working part of nature, which is wise, and knows how to move and form every creature without instruction; and this self-motion is as much her own as the other parts of her body, matter and figure, and is one and the same with herself, as a corporeal, living, knowing, and inseparable being, and a part of herself. As for the several parts of matter, I do believe that they are not all of one and the same size, nor of one and the same figure, neither do I hold their figures to be unalterable; for if all parts in nature are corporeal, they are divisible, composable, and intermixable, and then they cannot be always of one and the same sort of figure. Besides nature would not have so much work if there were no change of figures; and since her

only action is change of motion, change of motion must needs make change of figures. And thus natural parts of matter may change from lines to points, and from points to lines, from squares to circles, and so forth, infinite ways, according to the change of motions. But though they change their figures, yet they cannot change their matter; for matter as it has been, so it remains constantly in each degree, as the rational, sensitive and inanimate, none becomes purer, none grosser than ever it was, notwithstanding the infinite changes of motions, which their figures undergo. For motion changes only the figure, not the matter itself, which continues still the same in its nature and cannot be altered without a confusion or destruction of nature. And this is the constant opinion of,

Madam, your faithful friend and humble servant.

## Letter 34

Madam,

That rarefaction is only a change of figure, according to your author's opinion, is in my reason very probable; but when he says that in rarified bodies are little intervals or pores filled up with some other subtle matter, if he means that all rarified bodies are porous, I dissent from him. For it is not necessary that all rarified bodies should be porous and all hard bodies without pores. But if there were a probability of pores, I am of the opinion that it would be more in dense and hard, than in rare and soft bodies, as for example, rarifying and dilating motions are planning, smoothing, spreading and making all parts even, which could not well be if there were holes or pores. Earth is dense and hard, and yet is porous, and flame is rare and dilating, and yet is not porous; and certainly water is not so porous as Earth. Therefore pores, in my opinion, are according to the nature or form of the figure, and not according to the rarity or thinness, and density or thickness of the substance. As for his thin and subtle matter filling up the pores of porous bodies, I assent to your author insofar as I mean that thin and thick, or rare and dense substances are joined and mixed together. As for planning, smoothing, and spreading, I do not mean so much artificial planning and spreading, as for example, when a piece of gold is beaten into a thin plate, and a board is made plain and smooth by a joiner's tool, or a napkin folded up is spread plain and even, although, when you observe these arts, you may judge somewhat of the nature of natural dilations; for a folded cloth is fuller of creases than when plain, and the beating of a thin plate is like to the motion of dilation, which is to spread out, and the form of rarifying is thinning and extending. I add only this, that I am not of your author's opinion, that rest is the cause or glue which keeps the parts of dense or hard bodies together, but it is retentive motions. And so I conclude, resting,

Madam, your faithful friend and servant.

## Letter 35

Madam,

That the mind, according to your author's opinion, is a substance really distinct from the body, and may be actually separated from it and subsist without it, if he mean the natural mind and soul of man, not the supernatural or divine, I am far from his opinion; for though the mind moves only in its own parts, and not upon, or with the parts of inanimate matter, yet it cannot be separated from these parts of matter, and subsist by itself, as being a part of one and the same matter the inanimate is of (for there is but one only matter, and one kind of matter, although of several degrees), only it is the self-moving part. But yet this cannot empower it to quit the same natural body, whose part it is. Neither can I apprehend that the mind's or soul's seat should be in the glandule or kernel of the brain, and there sit like a spider in a cobweb, to whom the least motion of the cobweb gives intelligence of a fly, which he is ready to assault, and that the brain should get intelligence by the animal spirits as his servants, which run to and fro like ants to inform it; or that the mind should, according to others' opinions, be a light, and embroidered all with ideas, like a herald's coat, and that the sensitive organs should have no knowledge in themselves, but serve only like peeping holes for the mind, or barn-doors to receive bundles of pressures, like sheaves of corn. For there being a thorough mixture of animate, rational and sensitive,

and inanimate matter, we cannot assign a certain seat or place to the rational, another to the sensitive, and another to the inanimate, but they are diffused and intermixed throughout all the body. And this is the reason that sense and knowledge cannot be bound only to the head or brain. But although they are mixed together, nevertheless they do not lose their interior natures by this mixture, nor their purity and subtlety, nor their proper motions or actions, but each moves according to its nature and substance, without confusion. The actions of the rational part in man, which is the mind or soul, are called thoughts, or thoughtful perceptions, which are numerous, and so are the sensitive perceptions; for though man, or any other animal has but five exterior sensitive organs, yet there are numerous perceptions made in these sensitive organs, and in all the body—no, every several pore of the flesh is a sensitive organ, as well as the eye, or the ear. But both sorts, as well the rational as the sensitive, are different from each other, although both do resemble another, as being both parts of animate matter, as I have mentioned before: Therefore I'll add no more, only let you know, that I constantly remain,

Madam, your faithful friend, and servant.

## Letter 36

Madam,

That all other animals, besides man, lack reason, your author endeavors to prove in his discourse of method, where his chief argument is that other animals cannot express their mind, thoughts or conceptions, either by speech or any other signs, as man can do; for, says he, it is not for lack of the organs belonging to the framing of words, as we may observe in parrots and magpies, which are apt enough to express words they are taught, but understand nothing of them. My answer is that one man expressing his mind by speech or words to another does not declare by it his excellence and supremacy above all other creatures, but for the most part more folly, for a talking man is not so wise as a contemplating man. But by reason other creatures cannot speak or discourse with each other as men, or make certain signs, by which to express themselves as dumb and deaf men do, should we conclude they have neither knowledge, sense, reason, or intelligence? Certainly this is a very weak argument; for one part of a man's body, as one hand, is not less sensible than the other, nor the heel less sensible than the heart, nor the leg less sensible than the head, but each part has its sense and reason, and so consequently its sensitive and rational knowledge; and although they cannot talk or give intelligence to each other by speech, nevertheless each has its own peculiar and particular knowledge, just as each particular man has his own particular knowledge, for one man's knowledge is not another man's knowledge. And if there is such a peculiar and particular knowledge in every several part of one animal creature, as man, well may there be such in creatures of different kinds and sorts. But this particular knowledge belonging to each creature does not prove that there is no intelligence at all between them, no more than the lack of human knowledge does prove the lack of reason; for reason is the rational part of matter and makes perception, observation, and intelligence different in every creature, and every sort of creatures, according to their proper natures, but perception, observation and intelligence do not make reason, reason being the cause and they the effects. Therefore though other creatures do not have the speech, nor mathematical rules and demonstrations, with other arts and sciences as men, yet may their perceptions and observations be as wise as men's, and they may have as much intelligence and commerce between each other, after their own manner and way, as men have after theirs. To which I leave them, and man to his conceited prerogative and excellence, resting,

Madam, your faithful friend, and servant.

## Letter 37

Madam,

Concerning sense and perception, your author's opinion is that it is made by a motion or impression from the object upon the sensitive organ, which impression, by means of the nerves, is brought to the brain, and so to the mind or soul, which only perceives in the brain. He explains it by the example of a man being blind, or walking in the dark, who by the help of his stick can perceive when he touches a stone, a tree, water, sand, and the like. He brings forward this example to make a comparison with the perception of light. For, he says, light in a shining body is nothing else but a quick and lively motion or action, which, through the air and other transparent bodies tends towards the eye in the same manner as the motion or resistance of the bodies the blind man meets with, tends through the stick towards the hand. Therefore it is no wonder that the Sun can display its rays so far in an instant, seeing that the same action by which one end of the stick is moved goes instantly also to the other end, and would do the same if the stick were as long as Heaven is distant from Earth. To this I answer first that it is not only the mind that perceives in the kernel of the brain, but that there is a double perception, rational and sensitive, and that the mind perceives by the rational, but the body and the sensitive organs by the sensitive perception. And as there is a double perception, so there is also a double knowledge, rational and sensitive, one belonging to the mind, the other to the body. For I believe that the eye, ear, nose, tongue, and all the body have knowledge as well as the mind, only the rational matter, being subtle and pure, is not encumbered with the grosser part of matter to work upon, or with it, but leaves that to the sensitive and works or moves only in its own substance, which makes a difference between thoughts, and exterior senses. Next I say that it is not the motion or reaction of the bodies the blind man meets with which makes the sensitive perception of these objects, but the sensitive corporeal motions in the hand do pattern out the figure of the stick, stone, tree, sand, and the like. And as for comparing the perception of the hand when by the help of the stick it perceives the objects with the perception of light, I confess that the sensitive perceptions do all resemble each other, because all sensitive parts of matter are of one degree, as being sensible parts, only there is a difference according to the figures of the objects presented to the senses. And there is no better proof for perception being made by the sensitive motions in the body, or sensitive organs, but that all these sensitive perceptions are alike, and resemble one another. For if they were not made in the body of the sentient, but by the impression of exterior objects, there would be so much difference between them, by reason of the diversity of objects, as they would have no resemblance at all. But for a further proof of my own opinion, did the perception proceed merely from the motion, impression and resistance of the objects, the hand could not perceive those objects, unless they touched the hand itself, as the stick does. For it is not probable that the motions of the stone, water, sand, etc., should leave their bodies and enter into the stick, and so into the hand. For motion must be either something or nothing; if something, the stick and the hand would grow bigger, and the objects touched less, or else the touching and the touched must exchange their motions, which cannot be done so suddenly, especially between solid bodies. But if motion has no body, it is nothing, and how nothing can pass or enter or move some body, I cannot conceive. It is true there is no part that can subsist singly by itself without dependence upon each other, and so parts do always join and touch each other, which I am not against; but only I say perception is not made by the exterior motions of exterior parts of objects, but by the interior motions of the parts of the body sentient. But I have discoursed on this before, and so I take my leave, resting,

Madam, your faithful friend and servant.

## Letter 38

Madam,

I cannot conceive why your author is so much for little and insensible parts out of which the elements and all other bodies are made. For though nature is divisible, yet she is also compostable; and I think there is no need to dissect every creature into such little parts to know their nature, but we can do it by another way as well. For we may dissect or divide them into ever so little parts and yet never gain the more knowledge by it. But according to these principles he describes among the rest the nature of water says that those little parts out of which water consists are in figure somewhat long, light, and slippery like little eels, which are never so closely joined and entangled, but may easily be separated.

To this I answer that I observe the nature and figure of water to be flowing, dilating, divisible, and circular; for we may see in tides, overflowings, and breaking into parts; as in rain, it will always move in a round and circular figure. And I think if its parts were long and entangled like a knot of eels, it could never be so easily contracted and condensed into snow or ice. Neither do I think that saltwater has a mixture of somewhat grosser parts, not so apt to bend. For to my observation and reason, the nature of saltwater consists in that its circle-lines are pointed, which sharp and pointed figure makes it so penetrating; yet those points may be separated from the circle-lines of water, as it is seen in the making of salt. But I am not of your author's opinion that those little points do stick so fast in flesh, as little nails, to keep it from putrefaction. For points do not always fasten; or else fire, which certainly is composed of sharp-pointed parts, would harden, and keep other bodies from dissolving, whereas on the contrary, it separates and divides them, although after several manners. But putrefaction is only a dissolving and separating of parts, after the manner of dilation. And the motion of salt is contracting as well as penetrating, for we may observe what flesh is ever dry-salted, does shrink and contract close together, I will not say, but the pointed parts of salt may fasten like nails in some sorts of bodies, but not in all they work on. And this is the reason also that seawater is of more weight than freshwater, for being composed of points, those points stick within each other, and so become more strong. But yet do they not hinder the circular dilating motion of water, for the circle-lines are within, and the points without, but only they make it more strong from being divided by other exterior bodies that swim upon it. And this is the cause that saltwater is not so easily forced or turned to vapor, as freshwater, for the points piercing into each other hold it more strongly together; but this is to be considered that the points of salt are on the outside of the watery circle, not on the inside, which causes it to be divisible from the watery circles. I will conclude when I have given the reason why water is so soon sucked up by sand, lime, and the like bodies, and say that it is the nature of all spongy, dry, and porous bodies, meeting with liquid and pliable bodies as water, do draw and suck them up, like as animal creatures being thirsty, do drink. And so I take my leave, and rest,

Madam, your faithful friend and servant.

## Letter 39

Madam,

Concerning vapor, clouds, wind, and rain, I am of your author's opinion that water is changed into vapor, and vapor into air, and that dilated vapors make wind, and condensed vapors, clouds and mists. But I am not for his little particles of which, he says, vapors are made, by the motion of a rare and subtle matter in the pores of terrestrial bodies, which I certainly should conceive to be loose atoms, did he not make them of several figures and magnitude. For, in my opinion, there are no such things in nature, which like little flies or bees do fly up into the air. And although I grant that in nature are several parts, of which some are more rare, others more dense, according to the several degrees of matter, yet they are not single, but all mixed together in one body, and the change of motions in those joined parts is the cause of all changes of figures whatever, without the assistance of any foreign parts. And thus water of itself is changed to snow, ice, or hail by its inherent figurative motions, that is, the circular dilation of water by contraction, changes into the figure of snow, ice, or hail; or by rarifying motions it turns into the figure of vapor, and this vapor again by contracting motions into the figure of hoarfrost; and when all these motions change again into the former, then the figure of ice, snow, hail, vapor, and frost, turns again into the figure of water. And this in all sense and reason is the most facile and probable way of making ice, snow, hail, etc. As for rarefaction and condensation, I will not say that they may be forced by foreign parts, but yet they are made by change and alteration of the inherent motions of their own parts, for though the motions of foreign parts may be the occasion of them, yet they are not the immediate cause or actors of this. And as for thunder, that clouds of ice and snow, the uppermost being condensed by heat, and so made heavy, should fall upon another and produce the noise of thunder, is very improbable;

for the breaking of a little small string will make a greater noise than a huge shower of snow with falling, and as for ice being hard, it may make a great noise, one part falling upon another, but then their weight would be as much as their noise, so that the clouds or roves of ice would be as soon upon our heads, if not sooner, as the noise in our ears; like as a bullet shot out of a cannon, we may feel the bullet as soon as we hear the noise. But to conclude, all condensations are not made by heat, nor all noises by pressures, for sound is more often made by division than pressure, and condensation by cold than by heat. And this is all for the present, from,

Madam, your faithful friend, and servant.

## Letter 40

Madam,

I cannot perceive the rational truth of your author's opinion concerning colors made by the agitation of little spherical bodies of an ethereal matter, transmitting the action of light; for if colors were made after this manner, there would, in my opinion, not be any fixed or lasting color, but one color would be so various, and change faster than every minute. The truth is that there would be no certain or perfect color at all: therefore it seems altogether improbable that such liquid, rare, and disunited bodies should either keep or make inherent and fixed colors. For liquid and rare bodies, whose several parts are united into one considerable bulk of body, their colors are more apt to change than the colors of those bodies that are dry, solid and dense; the reason is that rare and liquid bodies are more loose, slack, and agile, than solid and dry bodies, in so much as in every alteration of motion their colors are apt to change. And if united rare and liquid bodies be so apt to alter and change, how is it probable that those bodies, which are small and not united, should either keep or make inherent fixed colors? I will not say, but that such little bodies may range into such lines and figures, as make colors, but then they cannot last, being not united into a lasting body, that is, into a solid, substantial body, proper to make such figures as colors. But I desire you not to mistake me, Madam, for I do not mean that the substance of colors is a gross thick substance, for the substance may be as thin and rare as flame or light, or in the next degree to it; for certainly the substance of light, and the substance of colors come in their degrees very near each other. But according to the contraction of the figures, colors are paler or deeper, or more or less lasting. And as for the reason why colors will change and recharge, it is according as the figures alter or recover their forms. For colors will be as animal creatures, which sometimes are faint, pale, and sick, and yet recover. But when as a particular color is, as I may say, quite dead, then there is no recovering of it. But colors may seem altered sometimes in our eyes, and yet not be altered in themselves. For our eyes, if perfect, see things as they are presented. And for proof, if any animal should be presented in an unusual posture or shape, we could not judge of it. Also if a picture, which must be viewed sideward, should be looked upon forwards, we could not know what to make of it; so the figures of colors, if they are not placed rightly to the sight, but turned topsy-turvy as the phrase is, or upside-down, or be moved too quick, and this quick motion do make a confusion with the lines of light, we cannot possibly see the color perfectly. Also several lights or shades may make colors appear otherwise than in themselves they are, for some sorts of lights and shades may fall upon the substantial figures of colors in solid bodies, in such lines and figures, as they may overpower the natural or artificial inherent colors in solid bodies, and for a time make other colors, and many times the lines of light or of shadows will meet and sympathize so with inherent colors, and place their lines so exactly, as they will make those inherent colors more splendorous than in their own nature they are, so that light and shadows will add or diminish or alter colors very much. Likewise some sorts of colors will be altered to our sight, not by all, but only by some sorts of light, as for example, blue will seem green, and green blue by candle light, when as other colors will never appear changed, but show constantly as they are; the reason is because the lines of candle light fall in such figures upon the inherent colors, and so make them appear according to their own figures. Therefore it is only the alteration of the exterior figures of light and shadows that make colors appear otherwise, and not a change of their own natures. And hence we may rationally conclude that several lights and shadows by their spreading and dilating lines may alter the face or outside of colors, but not suddenly change them, unless the power of heat, and continuance of time, or any other cause, do help and assist them in that work of metamorphosing or transforming of colors; but if the lines of light are only, as the phrase is, skin-deep, that is, but lightly spreading and not deeply penetrating, they may soon wear out or be rubbed off. For though they hurt, yet they do not kill the natural color, but the color may recover and reassume its former vigor and luster; but time and other accidental causes will not only alter, but destroy particular colors as well as other creatures, although not all after the same manner, for some will last longer then others. And thus, Madam, there are three sorts of colors, natural, artificial, and accidental; but I have discoursed of this subject more at large in my Philosophical Opinions, to which I refer you, and rest,

Madam, your faithful friend and servant.

## Letter 41

Madam,

My answer to your author's question, Why flame ascends in a pointed figure?, is that the figure of fire consists in points, and being dilated into a flame, it ascends in lines of points slope-ways from the fired fuel; this is as if you should make two or more sticks stand upright and put the upper ends close together, but let the lower ends be asunder, in which posture they will support each other, which, if both their ends were close together, they could not do. The second question is, Why fire does not always flame?, I answer because all fuel is not flammable, some being so moist, as it does oppose the fire's dryness, and some so hard and retentive, as fire cannot so soon dissolve it. And in this contest, where one dissipates and the other retains, a third figure is produced, namely, smoke, between the heat of one and the moisture of the other. And this smoke is forced by the fire out of the fuel, and is nothing else but certain parts of fuel raised to such a degree of rarefaction. And if fire come near, it forces the smoke into flame, the smoke changing itself by its figurative motions into flame. But when smoke is above the flame, the flame cannot force the smoke to fire or enkindle itself, for the flame cannot so well encounter it; this shows, as if smoke had a swifter motion than flame, although flame is more rarified than smoke; and if moisture predominate, there is only smoke, if fire, then there is flame. But there are many figures that do not flame, until they are quite dissolved, as leather, and many other things. Neither can fire work upon all bodies alike, but according to their several natures, like as men cannot encounter several sorts of creatures after one and the same manner. For not any part in nature has an absolute power, although it has self-motion. And this is the reason that wax by fire is melted, and clay hardened. The third question is, Why some few drops of water sprinkled on fire do increase its flame? I answer by reason of their little quantity, which being over-powered by the greater quantity and force of fire, is by its self-motions converted into fire. For water being of a rare nature, and fire, for the most part, of a rarifying quality, it cannot suddenly convert itself into a more solid body than its nature is, but following its nature by force it turns into flame. The fourth question is, Why the flame of spirit of wine does consume the wine, and yet cannot burn or hurt a linen cloth? I answer the wine is the fuel that feeds the flame, and on what it feeds, it devours, and with the food, and feeder; but by reason wine is a rarer body than oil, or wood, or any other fuel, its flame is also weaker. And thus much of these questions, I rest,

Madam, your faithful friend and servant.

## Letter 42

Madam,

To conclude my discourse upon the opinions of these two famous and learned authors, which I have previously sent you in several letters, I could not choose but repeat the ground of my own opinions in this present, which I desire you to observe well, lest you mistake anything, of which I have formerly discoursed. First I am for self-moving matter, which I call the sensitive and rational matter, and the perceptive and architectonical part of nature, which is the life and knowledge of nature. Next I am of an opinion that all perception is made by corporeal, figuring self-motions, and that the perception of foreign objects is made by patterning them out, as for example, the sensitive perception of foreign objects is by making or taking copies from these objects, so as the sensitive corporeal motions in the eyes copy out the objects of sight, and the sensitive corporeal motions in the ears copy out the objects of sound. The sensitive corporeal motions in the nostrils copy out the objects of scent, the sensitive corporeal motions in the tongue and mouth copy out the objects of taste, and the sensitive corporeal motions in the flesh and skin of the body copy out the foreign objects of touch. For when you stand by the fire, it is not that the fire, or the heat of the fire enters your flesh, but that the sensitive motions copy out the objects of fire and heat. As for my book of philosophy, I must tell you that it treats more of the production and architecture of creatures than of their perceptions, and more of the causes than the effects, more in a general than peculiar way, which I thought necessary to inform you of, and so I remain,

Madam, your faithful friend and servant.

# Anne Conway, *The Principles of the Most Ancient and Modern Philosophy*, Chapters 8–9 (1692)[1]

*Lady Anne Conway (1631–19) was the daughter of Sir Heneage Finch and his second wife Elizabeth Cradock. Her early education was by private tutors and included Latin (to which she later added Greek and Hebrew). Conway made the acquaintance of Henry More (1614–87), the Cambridge Platonist and correspondent of Descartes, through the intermediary of her half-brother John Finch, who was a student at Christ's College, Cambridge, where More was a tutor. More began to instruct Conway in philosophy around 1650; the few letters that survive from this correspondence indicate that Cartesianism formed the basis of her instruction. Conway is the author of a single treatise of philosophy, published anonymously in Latin translation, in Amsterdam in 1690; it was translated back into English and published in London in 1692 as* The Principles of the Most Ancient and Modern Philosophy. *There Conway presents her philosophy as an answer to the dominant philosophies of her time: several chapters of her treatise are devoted to a refutation of Descartes' dualism; she also takes issue with Hobbes and Spinoza, whom she charges with material pantheism, or confounding God and created substance.*

---

1. From Anne Conway, *The Principles of the Most Ancient and Modern Philosophy* (London, 1692), modernized.

## Chapter 8

*§. 1. That spirit and body, as they are creatures, do not differ essentially is further proved by three other reasons: and a fourth is drawn from that intimate bond or union between body and spirit. §. 2. That would be altogether an unfit comparison, to go about to illustrate the manner how the soul moves the body by an example of God moving his creatures. §. 3. The union and sympathy of soul and body may be easily demonstrated, as also how the soul moves the body from the aforesaid principle, that spirit is body, and body spirit. §. 4. A fifth argument is taken from earth and water, which continually produces animals of diverse kinds out of putrefied or corrupted matter. §. 5. How a gross body may be changed into spirit, and become as it were the mother of spirits; where an example is laid down of our corporeal aliment, which by various transmutations in the body is changed into animal spirits, and from these into subtler and more spiritual ones. §. 6. Of the good or bad angels of men, which are properly the angels of a man, and proceed from him as branches from the root. §. 7. A sixth and last argument is drawn from certain places of scripture.*

§. 1. To prove that spirit and body do not differ essentially, but gradually, I shall deduce my fourth argument from the intimate band or union, which intercedes between bodies and spirits, by means of which the spirits have dominion over the bodies with which they are united, that they move them from one place to another, and use them as instruments in their various operations. For if spirit and body are so contrary one to another, so that a spirit is only life, or a living and sensible substance, but a body a certain mass merely dead—if a spirit is penetrable and indivisible, but a body impenetrable and divisible, which are all contrary attributes—what (I ask) is it that so joins or unites them together? Or, what are those links or chains by which they have so firm a connection, and that for so long a space of time? Moreover also, when the spirit or soul is separated from the body, so that it has no longer dominion or power over it to move it as it had before, what is the cause of this separation? If it is said that the vital agreement the soul has to the body is the cause of the said union and that the body being corrupted that vital agreement ceases, I answer we must first enquire in what this vital agreement does consist; for if they cannot tell us in what it does consist, they only trifle with empty words, which give a sound but need a signification: for certainly in that sense which they take body and spirit in, there is no agreement at all between them; for a body is always a dead thing, void of life and sense, no less when the spirit is in it than when it is gone out of it: hence there is no agreement at all between them; and if there is any agreement, that certainly will remain the same, both when the body is found and when it is corrupted. If they deny this because a spirit requires an organized body by means of which it performs its vital acts of the external senses, moves and transports the body from place to place, which organic action ceases when the body is corrupted, certainly by this the difficulty is not solved any better. For why does the spirit require such an organized body? For example, why does it require a corporeal eye so wonderfully formed and organized that I can see by it? Why does it need a corporeal light to see corporeal objects? Or, why is it requisite that the image of the object should be sent to it, through the eye, that it may see it? If the same were entirely nothing but a spirit, and no way corporeal, why does it need so many several corporeal organs, so far different from the nature of it? Furthermore, how can a spirit move its body, or any of its members, if a spirit (as they affirm) is of such a nature that no part of its body can in the least resist it, even as one body is inclined to resist another, when it is moved by it, by reason of its impenetrability? For if a spirit could so easily penetrate all bodies, as a result does it not leave the body behind it when it is moved from place to place, seeing it can so easily pass out without the least resistance? For certainly this is the cause of all motions we see in the world, where one thing moves another, namely, because both are impenetrable in the sense aforesaid: for were it not for this impenetrability one creature could not move another, because this would not oppose that, nor at all resist it. We have an example of this in the sails of a ship, by which the wind drives the ship, and that so much the more vehemently by how much the fewer holes, vents, and passages—the same finds in the sails against which it drives, when on the contrary, if instead of sails nets were expanded, through which the wind would have a freer passage, certainly by these the ship would be but little moved, although it blew with great violence; hence we see how this impenetrability causes resistance, and this makes motion. But if there were no impenetrability, as in the case of body and spirit, then there could be no resistance, and by consequence the spirit could make no motion in the body.

§. 2. And if it is objected that God is altogether incorporeal and intrinsically present in all bodies, and yet does move bodies wherever he pleases, and is the first mover of all things, and yet nothing is impenetrable to him, I answer, this motion by which God moves a body, does wonderfully differ from that manner by which the soul moves the body; for the will of God which gave being to bodies, gave them motion also, so that motion itself is of God, by whose will all motion happens. For as a creature cannot give being to itself, so neither can it move itself; for in him we live, move, and have our being, so that motion and essence come from the same cause, namely, God the creator, who remains immoveable in himself; neither is he carried from place to place, because he is equally present everywhere and gives being to creatures. But the case is far different when the soul moves the body; for the soul is not the author of motion, but only determines it to this or that particular thing. And the soul moved itself, together with the body, from place to place; and if the body is imprisoned, or held in chains, it cannot be free or deliver itself out of prison or out of chains. Therefore it would be a very unfit comparison, if one should go about to illustrate that motion the soul makes in the body by an example of God moving his creatures; so great is the difference, as if a man should go to demonstrate how a carpenter builds a ship, or an house, by an example of God creating the first matter or substance, in which certainly there is as great a disparity or disproportion; for God gave being to creatures, but a carpenter does not give being to the wood of which he builds a ship.

But no man can think, because I have said all motion of creatures is of God, that therefore he is, or can be the author or cause of sin. For although the moving power is of God, yet sin is not in the least of God, but of the creature who has abused this power and determined to some other end than it ought; so that sin is ἀταξία, or an inordinate determination of motion, or the power of moving from its due place, state, or condition unto some other, as for example a ship is moved by the wind, but governed by the mariner, that it goes to this or that place, where the mariner is not the author or cause of the wind; but the wind blowing, he makes either a good or a bad use of the same, by which he either brings the ship to the place intended, and so is commended, or else so manages her that she suffers shipwreck, for which he is blamed, and worthy of punishment.

Moreover, why is the spirit or soul so passible in corporeal pains? For if, when it is united with the body, it has nothing of corporeity, or a bodily nature, why is it grieved or wounded when the body is wounded, which is quite of a different nature? For seeing the soul can so easily penetrate the body, how can any corporeal thing hurt it? If it is said, the body only feels the pain, but not the soul; this is contrary to their own principles, because they affirm that the body has neither life nor sense. But if it is granted that the soul is of one nature and substance with the body, although it is many degrees more excellent in regard of life and spirituality, as also in swiftness of motion, and penetrability, and diverse other perfections, then all the aforesaid difficulties will vanish, and it will be easily conceived how the body and soul are united together, and how the soul moves the body, and suffers by it or with it. (What the opinion of the Hebrews is appears from a passage in *Kabbala Denudata* I, pt. 3, Diss. 8, chap. 13, pp. 171 seq.)

§. 3. For we may easily understand how one body is united with another by that true agreement that one has with another in its own nature; and so the most subtle and spiritual body may be united with a body that is very gross and thick, namely, by means of certain bodies, partaking of subtlety and grossness, according to diverse degrees, consisting between two extremes, and these middle bodies are indeed the links and chains, by which the soul, which is so subtle and spiritual, is conjoined with a body so gross. If these middle spirits cease or are absent, the union is broken or dissolved. So from the same foundation we may easily understand how the soul moves the body, namely, as one subtle body can move another gross and thick body. And seeing that body itself is a sensible life, or an intellectual substance, it is no less clearly conspicuous how one body can wound, or grieve, or gratify, or please another, because things of one or alike nature can easily affect each other. And to this argument may be reduced the like difficulties, namely, how spirits move spirits, and how some spirits strive and contend with other spirits, also concerning the unity, concord, and friendship, which good spirits reverence among themselves; for if all spirits could be intrinsically present one with another, how could they dispute or contend about place? And how can one expel or drive out another? And yet that there is such an expulsion and conflict of spirits, and especially of the good against the evil, some few who have been acquainted with their own hearts have experimentally known. If it is said, the spirit of God and Christ are intrinsically present in all things, contends with, and makes war against the devil, and his spirit, in the heart of man, I answer that this is also a very unfit similitude, namely, when God and creatures are compared in their operations. For his ways are infinitely superior to ours; yet nevertheless in this case also here remains a strong objection. For the spirits of God and Christ, when they strive against the devil, and the evil spirits in the heart of man, do unite themselves with certain good spirits, whom they have sanctified and prepared for this union, and by these, as a vehicle, or triumphant chariot, they contend against and encounter those malignant and wicked spirits. And in as much as these evil spirits contend against those good spirits in the heart of man, they contend against God and Christ. And these good spirits are the spirits of this faithful and pious man, who is become good, when as before he was evil. For God and Christ do help every pious man to prevail over the evil spirits in this conflict, but suffers the wicked and unfaithful to be captivated and overcome. For God helps none but those who fear, love, and obey him, and trust in his power, goodness, and truth. For with such he is united and the good spirits of such men are as so many swords and darts, by which those dark and unclean spirits are wounded and repulsed. But if it is demanded how the soul of man can be united with God, though it were in a state of the highest purity, because he is a mere spirit, but the soul even in its greatest purity always partakes of corporeity? I answer, it is done by Jesus Christ, who is the true and proper medium between both; for Christ and the soul may be united without a medium, by reason of that great affinity and similitude between them, which those doctors cannot demonstrate between spirit and body, who say they are of a nature so contrary one to another.

§. 4. I shall draw a fifth argument from what we observe in all visible bodies, as in earth, water, stones, wood, etc. What abundance of spirits is in all these things? For earth and water continually produce animals, as they have done from the beginning, so that a pool filled with water may produce fishes, though none were ever put there to increase or breed. And seeing that all other things do more originally proceed from earth and water, it necessarily follows that the spirits of all animals were in the water. And therefore it is said in Genesis that the spirit of God moved upon the face of the waters, namely, that from hence he might produce whatever was afterwards created.

§ 5. But if it is said, this argument does not prove that all spirits are bodies, but that all bodies have in them the spirits of all animals, so that every body has a spirit in it, and likewise a spirit and body, and although they are thus united, yet they still remain different in nature one from another, and so cannot be changed one into another, to this I answer, if every body, even the least, has in it the spirits of all animals, and other things, even as matter is said to have in it all forms, now I demand, whether a body has actually all those spirits in it or only potentially? If actually, how is it possible that so many spirits essentially distinct from body, can actually exist in their distinct essences in so small a body (even in the least that can be conceived), unless it is by intrinsic presence, which is not communicable to any creature, as is already proved; for if all kinds of spirits are in any, even the least body, how does it come to pass that such an animal is produced of this body, and not another? How does it come to pass that all kind of animals are not immediately produced out of one and the same body? Experience denies this; for we see that nature keeps her order in all her operations; thus one animal is formed of another, and one species proceeds from another, as well when it ascends to a further perfection as when it descends to a more vile state and condition. But if they say all spirits are contained in any body, not actually in their distinct essences, but only potentially as they term it, then it must be granted that the body and all those spirits are one and the same thing—that is, that a body may be turned into them, as when we say wood is potentially fire (that is, can be turned into fire) and water is potentially air (that is, may be changed into air).

Moreover, if spirits and bodies are so inseparably united that no body can be without a spirit, indeed, not without many spirits, this is certainly a great argument that they are of one original nature and substance; otherwise we could not conceive why in so various and wonderful dissolutions and separation of things they should not at length be separated one from another, as we see the subtler things may be separated from the grosser. But how is it that when a body is at length corrupted out of this corruption another species of things is generated? So out of earth and water corrupted, proceed animals. Stones if they putrefy or rot, pass into animals; so dung, or other putrefied matter, generates animals, all [of] which have spirits. But how does corruption or dissolution of body tend to a new generation, and that indeed of animals? If it is said the spirits of those animals are as it were loosed from their bonds and set at liberty by this dissolution, and that then they can form or fashion to themselves a new body, out of the aforesaid matter, by virtue of their plastic faculty, to this I reply how did the primitive body so hold it captive? Was it because it was so hard and thick? If so, it will be manifest that those spirits are nothing else but subtle bodies, because hardness and density of body could imprison them, that they could not pass out; for if a spirit could as easily penetrate the hardest body, as the softest and most fluid, it could as easily pass out of the one as the other, nor would there be need of death and corruption to a new life or generation. Therefore this kind of captivity of spirits in some kind of hard bodies, and their deliverance from this, when the bodies become soft, affords us a manifest argument that spirit and body are originally of one nature and substance, and that a body is nothing but a fixed and condensed spirit, and a spirit nothing but a subtle and volatile body.

And here is to be noted that in all hard bodies, as in stones, whether common or precious, and so also in metals, herbs, trees, and animals—indeed, in all human bodies—there do not only exist many spirits (which are as it were imprisoned in those gross bodies and united with them, and therefore cannot flow forth, or fly out into other bodies, until they have passed death or dissolution), but also many other very subtle spirits, which continually flow from them, and which by reason of their subtlety, the hardness of the body (in which they lay hid-

den) cannot detain; and these spirits are the more subtle productions, or the sutures of the grosser spirits detained in the body. For although these are detained in them, yet they are not idle in their prison, but their bodies are as it were shops for them to work out those subtler spirits, which afterwards flow out in colors, sounds, odors, tastes, and diverse other powers and virtues. As a result the gross body, and the spirits contained in them, are as it were the mother of those subtler spirits, which take the place of children; for nature still works to a further perfection of subtlety and spirituality; even as this is the most natural property of all motion and operation: for all motion wears and divides, and so renders a thing subtle and spiritual. Even thus in man's body, the meat and drink is first changed into chyle, then into blood, afterwards into spirits, which are nothing else but blood brought to perfection; and these spirits, whether good or bad, still advance to a greater subtlety or spirituality, and by those spirits which come from the blood, we see, hear, smell, taste, feel, and think, meditate, love, hate, and do all things whatsoever we do. And from this also comes the seed by which humankind is propagated. And thus especially proceeds the voice and speech of man, which is full of spirits (formed in the heart) either good or evil, as Christ has taught: that out of the plenty of the heart the mouth speaks, and that a good man out of the good treasure of his heart brings forth good things, etc. Also that which goes into a man does not defile him, but that which proceeds out of him. For in like manner as they proceed from him, so shall they again return into him.

§. 6. And these are the proper angels or ministering spirits of a man (although there are other angels also, as well good as evil, which come unto men), of which angels Christ speaks, where he speaks of those little ones who believe in him; their angels (he says) always behold the face of my heavenly father. These are the angels of those believers who become, as it were, like little infants.

§. 7. My sixth and last argument I shall deduce from certain texts of scripture, as well of the old as new testament, which do prove in plain and express words that all things have life, and do really live in some degree or measure. It is said (Acts 17.27) he gives life to all things. Again (1 Timothy 6.13) of God it is said that he quickens all things. And (Luke 20. 38) he is not called the God of the dead but of the living (which though principally meant of men, yet it is generally to be understood of all other creatures), namely, he is the God of all those things that have their regeneration and resurrection in their kind, no less than man has in his kind; for death is not the annihilation of these things, but a change from one kind and degree of life to another; for this reason also the apostle proves and illustrates the resurrection of the dead by a grain of wheat, which being fallen into the ground, dies, and rises again exceeding fruitful.

## Chapter 9

§. 1. *The philosophers (so called) of all sects have generally laid an ill foundation to their philosophy; and therefore the whole structure must needs fall. §. 2. The philosophy treated here is not Cartesian. §. 3. Nor the philosophy of Hobbes and Spinoza (falsely so feigned), but diametrically opposite to them. §. 4. That they who have attempted to refute Hobbes and Spinoza have given them too much advantage. §. 5. This philosophy is the strongest to refute Hobbes and Spinoza, but after another method. §. 6. We understand here quite another thing by body and matter than Hobbes understood, and which Hobbes and Spinoza never saw otherwise than in a dream. §. 7. Life is as really and properly an attribute of body as figure. §. 8. Figure and life are distinct but not contrary attributes of one and the same thing. §. 9. Mechanical motion and action or perfection of life distinguish things.*

§. 1. From what has been lately said and from various reasons alleged that spirit and body are originally in their first substance but one and the same thing, it evidently appears that the philosophers (so called) who have taught otherwise, whether ancient or modern, have generally erred and laid an ill foundation in the very beginning; as a result the whole house and superstructure is so feeble, and indeed so unprofitable, that the whole edifice and building must in time decay, from which absurd foundation have arisen very many gross and dangerous errors, not only in philosophy, but also in divinity (so called) to the great damage of mankind, hindrance of true piety, and contempt of God's most glorious name, as will easily appear, as well from what has been already said, as from what shall be said in this chapter.

§. 2. And no one can object that all this philosophy is no other than that of Descartes, or Hobbes under a new mask. For, first, regarding Cartesian philosophy, this says that every body is a mere dead mass, not only void of all kind of life and sense, but utterly incapable of these to all eternity; this grand error also is to be imputed to all those who affirm body and spirit to be contrary things, and inconvertible one into another, so as to deny a body all life and sense; this is quite contrary to the grounds of our philosophy. Therefore it is so far from being a Cartesian principle under a new mask that it may be truly said it is anti-Cartesian, in regard of their fundamental principles. Although it cannot be denied that Descartes taught many excellent and ingenious things concerning the mechanical part of natural operations, and how all natural motions proceed according to rules and laws mechanical, even as indeed nature herself, that is, the creature, has an excellent mechanical skill and wisdom in itself (given it from God, who is the fountain of all wisdom), by which it operates; but yet in nature and her operations they are far more than merely mechanical, and the same is not a mere organic body, like a clock, in which there is not a vital principle of motion, but a living body, having life and sense, which body is far more sublime than a mere mechanism or mechanical motion.

§. 3. But, secondly, as to what pertains to Hobbes's opinion, this is yet more contrary to this our philosophy than that of Descartes; for Descartes acknowledged God to be plainly immaterial and an incorporeal spirit. Hobbes affirms God himself to be material and corporeal, indeed nothing else but matter and body, and so confounds God and the creatures in their essences and denies that there is any essential distinction between them. These worst consequences and many more are the dictates of Hobbes's philosophy, to which may be added that of Spinoza. For this Spinoza also confounds God and creatures together, and makes but one being of both, all which are diametrically opposite to the philosophy here delivered by us.

§. 4. But the false and feeble principles of some who have undertaken to refute the philosophy of Hobbes and Spinoza, so called, have given them a greater advantage against themselves, so that they have not only in effect, not refuted them, but more exposed themselves to contempt and laughter.

Someone may object that our philosophy seems at least very like that of Hobbes, because he taught that all creatures were originally one substance, from the lowest and most ignoble, to the highest and noblest, from the smallest worm, insect, or fly, unto the most glorious angel, indeed, from the least dust or sand, unto the most excellent of all creatures, and then that every creature is material and corporeal, indeed, matter and body itself, and by consequence their most noble actions are either material and corporeal or after a certain corporeal manner. I answer that I grant all creatures are originally one substance, from the lowest to the highest, and consequently convertible or changeable, from one of their natures into another, and although Hobbes says the same, yet that is no prejudice to its truth, as neither are other parts of that philosophy where Hobbes affirms something true therefore Hobbesian or an opinion of Hobbes alone.

§. 5. Moreover, this principle is so far from defending them in their errors that nothing is so strong to refute them; for example the Hobbists argue all things are one because we see that all visible things may be changed one into another—indeed, that all visible things may be changed into invisible, as when water is made air and wood being burned (for the greatest part) is changed into a certain invisible substance, which is so subtle that it escapes all observation of our senses. Add to this that all invisible things may become visible, as when water proceeds from air, etc.

And hence he concludes nothing is so low that it cannot attain to sublimity.

But we may answer this argument that his adversaries generally deny the antecedent and on the contrary affirm that no species of things is convertible into another; and when wood is burned, many say the wood is composed of two substances, namely, matter and form, and the matter remains the same but the form of the wood is destroyed or annihilated and a new form of fire is produced in this matter. So, according to them, there is a continual annihilation of real substances and productions of new ones in this world. But this is so frivolous that many others deny that in the case of wood changed into fire and afterwards into smoke and ashes; yet they still persist in the same error in other transmutations, as when wood is changed into an animal, as we often see that of rotten wood. Indeed, living creatures are also generated in dung. Thus they deny here that the wood is changed into an animal and say that wood is nothing but matter and that matter has not life, nor a capacity to life or sense, and therefore this animal which has life and sense ought to have the same from elsewhere and must have a spirit or soul in it that is not a part of its body, neither does proceed from it, but is sent into it. But if it is demanded of them, from where is this spirit sent and who sends it, also why a spirit of this species is sent, and not of another, here they are at a standstill, and yield themselves to their adversaries.

Therefore this, our philosophy, before it is laid down more strongly conduces to the refutation of the Hobbesian and Spinozan philosophy, namely, that all kinds of creatures may be changed one into another, that the lowest may become the highest, and the highest (as considered originally in its own proper nature) may become the lowest, namely, according to that course and succession which divine wisdom has ordained, that one change may succeed another in a certain order, so that A must be first turned into B, before it can be turned into C, which must first be turned into C, before it can be changed into D, etc.

But we deny the consequence, namely, that God and creatures are one substance. For in all transmutations of creatures [there is a progression] from one species into another, as from a stone into earth, and from earth into grass, and from grass into a sheep, and from a sheep into human flesh, and from human flesh into the most servile spirits of man, and from these into his noblest spirits; but there can never be a progression or ascension made unto God, who is the most supreme of all beings, and whose nature still infinitely excels a creature placed in his highest perfection. For the nature of God is every way unchangeable, so that it does not admit of the least shadow of a change; but the nature of a creature is to be changeable.

§. 6. Secondly, if it is said, by way of objection, that according to this philosophy, every creature is material and corporeal, indeed, body and matter itself, as Hobbes teaches, now I answer that by material and corporeal, as also by matter and body, here the thing is understood far from how Hobbes understood it, and this was never discovered by Hobbes or Descartes other than in a dream: for what do they understand by matter and body? Or, what attributes do they ascribe to them? None, certainly, but these following as are extension and impenetrability, which nevertheless are but one attribute, to which also may be referred mobility and the capacity for having a figure. But, let us suppose these are distinct attributes; it certainly profits nothing, nor will ever help us to understand what that excellent substance is, which they call body and matter. For they have never proceeded beyond the husk or shell, nor ever reached the kernel. They only touch the surface, never discerning the center. They were plainly ignorant of the noblest and most excellent attributes of that substance which they call body and matter and understood nothing of them. But if it is demanded, what are those more excellent attributes? I answer these following: spirit, or life, and light, under which I comprehend a capacity of all kind of feeling, sense, and knowledge, love, joy, and fruition, and all kind of power and virtue, which the noblest creatures have or can have, so that even the vilest and most contemptible creature, indeed, dust and sand, may be capable of all those perfections, namely, through various and succeeding transmutations from the one into the other; these,

according to the natural order of things, require long periods of time for their consummation, although the absolute power of God (if it had pleased him) could have accelerated or hastened all things, and effected it in one moment. But this wisdom of God saw it to be more expedient that all things should proceed in their natural order and course; so that after this manner, that fertility or fruitfulness, which he has endowed every being with, may appear, and the creatures have time by working still to promote themselves to a greater perfection, as the instruments of divine wisdom, goodness and power, which operates in, and with them; for this in the creature has the greater joy when it possesses what it has as the fruit of its own labor.

But this capacity of the aforementioned perfections is quite a distinct attribute from life, and understanding, or knowledge—quite distinct from the former, namely, extension and figure; and so also a vital action is plainly distinct from local, or mechanical motion, although it is not nor cannot be separated from it, but still uses the same at least, as its instrument, in all its concourse with the creatures.

§. 7. I say life and figure are distinct attributes of one substance; just as one and the same body may be transmuted into all kinds of figures and as the more perfect figure comprehends that which is more imperfect, so one and the same body may be transmuted from one degree of life to another more perfect, which always comprehends in it the inferior. We have an example of figure in a triangular prism, which is the first figure of all right lined solid bodies, into which a body is convertible, and from this into a cube, which is a more perfect figure, and comprehends in it a prism. From a cube it may be turned into a more perfect figure, which comes nearer to a globe, and from this into another, which is yet nearer. And so it ascends from one figure, more imperfect, to another more perfect, to infinity. For here are no bounds, nor can it be said this body cannot be changed into a more perfect figure. But the meaning is that that body consists of plain right lines; and this is always changeable into a more perfect figure, and yet can never reach to the perfection of a globe, although it always approaches nearer to it; the case is the same in various degrees of life, which have indeed a beginning but no end, so that the creature is always capable of a further and more perfect degree of life to infinity, and yet can never attain to be equal with God. For he is still infinitely more perfect than a creature in its highest elevation or perfection, even as a globe is the most perfect of all other figures unto which none can approach.

§. 8. And thus life and figure are distinct, but no contrary attributes of one and the same substance, and figure serves the operations of life, as we see in the body of man or beast how the figure of the eye serves the sight; the figure of the ear, the hearing; the figure of the mouth, teeth, lips, and tongue, serve the speech; the figure of the hands and fingers serve to work; the figure of the feet to walk; and so the figures of all the other members have their use, and very much conduce to the vital operations, which the spirit performs in these members; indeed, the figure of the whole body is more commodious for the proper operations of human life than any other figure whatsoever is or could be made. Thus life and figure consist very well together in one body or substance, where figure is an instrument of life without which no vital operation can be performed.

§. 9. Likewise, local and mechanical motion, that is, the carrying of body from place to place, is a manner or operation distinct from action of vital operation, although they are inseparable, so that a vital action can in no way be without all local motion, because this is its instrument. So the eye cannot see unless light enters it, which is a motion, and stirs up a vital action in the eye, which is seeing; and so in all other vital operations in the whole body. But an action of life is a far nobler and more divine manner of operation than local motion. And yet both agree to one substance and consist well together; for as the eye receives the light into itself from the object which it sees from without, so also it sends the same light to the object and in this spirit and life is a vital action, uniting the object and sight together.

Therefore Hobbes, and all others who side with him, grievously err, while they teach that sense and knowledge is nothing other than a reaction of corporeal particles one upon another, where, by reaction, he means nothing other than local and mechanical motion. But indeed sense and knowledge is a thing far more noble and divine than any local or mechanical motion of any particles whatsoever; for it is the motion or action of life, which uses the other as its instrument, whose service consists in this—that is, to stir up a vital action in the subject or percipient—and can like local motion be transmitted through various bodies, although very far distant asunder, which therefore are united, and that without any new transition of body or matter. For example, a beam of wood of an exceeding great length is moved by one extreme from the North to the South, the other extreme will necessarily be moved also; and the action is transmitted through the whole beam, without any particles of matter sent hither to promote motion, from one extreme to the other, because the beam itself is sufficient to transmit the said motion. After the same manner also, a vital action can proceed together with local motion from one thing to another, and that too at a great distance, where there is an apt and fit medium to transmit it, and here we may observe a kind of divine spirituality or subtlety in every motion, and so in every action of life, which no created body or substance is capable of, namely, by intrinsic presence, which (as before is proved) agrees to no created substance, and yet agrees to every motion or action whatsoever. For motion or action is not a certain matter or substance, but only a manner of its being, and therefore is intrinsically present in the subject of which there is a mode, or manner, and can pass from body to body, at a great distance, if it finds a fit medium to transmit it. And the stronger the motion is, so much the farther it reaches. So when a stone is cast into standing waters, it causes a motion every way from the center to the circumference, forming circles still greater and greater at a great distance, by how much longer the time is, until at length it vanishes from our sight; and then without doubt, it makes yet more invisible circles for a longer space of time, which our dull senses cannot apprehend, and this motion is transmitted from the center to the circumference, not conveyed to that place by any body or substance, carrying this motion with it from the stone. And as the external light also, seeing it is an action or motion stirred up by some illuminate body, may be transmitted through glass, crystal, or any other transparent body, without any substance, body, or matter, conveyed from that illuminate body from where the said action proceeded, not that I would deny that abundance of subtle matter continually flows from all illuminate bodies, so that the whole substance of a burning candle is spent in such emanations. And this has in it that motion or action, which we call light; but this motion or action may be increased. For example by crystal, where those subtle emanations of bodies may be restrained, that they cannot pass out at least in such abundance, as may be sufficient to communicate the whole light; but seeing crystal (which does so easily transmit the light) is so hard and solid, how can it receive so many bodies, and transmit them so easily through it, when other bodies, neither so hard nor solid, do let or resist it? For wood is neither so hard nor solid as crystal, and yet crystal is transparent, but wood not. And certainly wood is more porous than crystal, because it is less solid, and consequently the light does not enter by the pores of the crystal, but through the very substance of it. And yet so as not to adhere to it, or make any inflation or increase of quantity, but by a certain intrinsic presence, because it is not a body or substance, but a mere action or motion. Now crystal is a more fit medium to receive this motion, which we call light, than wood is; and hence it is that it pervades or passes through that and not this; and as there is a great diversity of the motion and operation of bodies, so every motion requires its proper medium to transmit the same. Therefore it is manifest that motion may be transmitted through various bodies by another kind of penetration than any body or matter (however subtle it may be) is able to make—namely, by intrinsic presence. And if mere local or mechanical motion can do that, then certainly a vital action (which is a nobler kind of motion) can do the same; and if it can penetrate those bodies it passes through by intrinsic presence, then it may in one moment

be transmitted from one body to another, or rather require no time at all, I mean motion or action itself requires not the least time for its transmission, although it is impossible but that the body, in which the motion is carried from place to place, ought to have some time, either greater or lesser, according to the quality of body and vehemence of motion which carries it.

And therefore we see how every motion and action, considered in the abstract, has a wonderful subtlety or spirituality in it, beyond all created substances whatsoever, so that neither time nor place can limit the same; and yet they are nothing else but modes or manners of created substances, that is, their strength, power, and virtue, by which they are extendible into great substances, beyond what the substance itself can make. And thus we may distinguish extension into material and virtual, which two-fold extension every creature has; material extension is that which matter, body, or substance has, as considered without all motion or action; and this extension (to speak properly) is neither greater nor lesser, because it would still remain the same. A virtual extension is a motion or action which a creature has, whether immediately given from God, or immediately received from its fellow creature. That which is immediately given of God (from whom also it has its being), and which is the natural and proper effect of its essence, is in a more proper way of speaking, a proper motion of the creature, proceeding from the innermost parts of this; and therefore it may be called internal motion, as distinguished from external, which is only from another; and therefore in this respect it may be called foreign; and when the said external motion endeavors to carry a body, or any thing, to a place into which it has properly no natural inclination, then it is preternatural and violent—as when a stone is thrown up into the air, which motion being preternatural and violent, is plainly local and mechanical, and no way vital, because it does not proceed from the life of the thing so moved. But every motion, proceeding from the proper life and will of the creature, is vital; and this I call a motion of life, which is not plainly local and mechanical as the other, but has in it a life, and vital virtue, and this is the virtual extension of a creature, which is either greater or lesser, according to that kind or degree of life with which the creature is endowed, for when a creature arrives at a nobler kind and degree of life, then does it receive the greater power and virtue to move itself, and transmit its vital motions to the greatest distance.

But how motion or action may be transmitted from one body to another is with many a matter of great debate, because it is not a body or substance; and if it is only motion of body, how motion can pass properly with its own subject into another, because the very being of mode, or manner, consists in this, namely, to exist or be inherent in its own body; the answer to this objection, which seems to me best, is this, that motion is not propagated from one body to another by local motion, because motion itself is not moved, but only moves the body in which it is; for if motion could be propagated by local motion, this motion would be propagated of another, and this again of another, and so to infinity, which is absurd. Therefore the manner of the said propagation is (as it were) by real production or creation. Just as God and Christ can only create the substance of a thing, when as no creature can create or give being to any substance, not even as an instrument, so also a creature, not of itself, but in subordination to God, as his instrument may give existence to motion and vital action. And so also the motion in one creature may produce motion in another. And this is all a creature can do toward the moving itself or its fellow creatures, as being the instrument of God, by which motions a new substance is not created, but only new species of things, so that creatures may be multiplied into their kinds, while one acts upon, and moves another. And

this is the whole work of the creature, or creation, as the instrument of God. But if it moves against his will, whose instrument it is, then it sins, and is punished for it. But God (as before was said) is not the cause of sin; for when a creature sins, he abuses the power God has granted him; and so the creature is culpable, and God entirely free from every spot or blemish of this. If therefore we apply those things which have been already spoken, concerning the attributes of a body, namely, that it has not only quantity and figure, but life also, and is not only locally and mechanically but vitally moveable, and can transmit its vital action whithersoever it pleases, provided it has a medium aptly disposed, and if it has none it can extend itself by the subtle emanation of its parts, which is the fittest and most proper medium of it, to receive and transmit its vital action. As a result it will be easy to answer to all the arguments by which some endeavor to prove that a body is altogether incapable of sense and knowledge. And it may be easily demonstrated after what manner some certain body may gradually advance to that perfection, as not only to be capable of such sense and knowledge as brutes have, but of any kind of perfection whatsoever may happen in any man or angel. And so we may be able to understand the words of Christ that "God is able to raise up children to Abraham from stones" (Matthew 3.9) without flying to some strained metaphor. And if anyone should deny this omnipotence of God, namely, that God is able to raise up children to Abraham from stones, that certainly would be the greatest presumption.

# Baruch Spinoza, From the Letters to Oldenburg and to Meyer (1661–65)[1]

## To Henry Oldenburg[2] (September 1661)

Illustrious Sir,

You yourself could judge what pleasure your friendship affords me, if only your modesty would allow you to consider the estimable qualities with which you are so richly endowed. With these qualities in mind, I feel it not a little presumptuous on my part to enter into a bond of friendship with you, the more so when I reflect that between friends all things, and particularly things of the spirit, should be shared. Nevertheless, this is to be attributed to both your modesty and your kindness, rather than to me. Your modesty in so condescending and the abundant kindness that you have bestowed on me have banished any uncertainty I may have had in accepting the hand of friendship which you firmly hold out to me and deign to ask of me in return, a friendship which it shall be my earnest endeavor diligently to foster.

As for my mental endowments, such as they are, I would most willingly have you claim them for your own even if I knew that this would be to my great detriment. However, it is not my intention in this way to deny you what you ask by right of friendship, and so I shall attempt to explain my views on the subjects we spoke of, although I can scarcely believe that this will be the means of strengthening our friendship, if your kind indulgence does not intervene.

I shall therefore begin with a discussion of God, whom I define as a Being consisting of infinite attributes, each of which is infinite or supremely perfect in its own kind. Here it should be observed that by attribute I mean every thing that is conceived through itself and in itself, so that its conception does not involve the conception of anything else. For example, extension is conceived through itself and in itself, but not motion; for the latter is conceived in something else, and its conception involves extension.

That this is the true definition of God is evident from the fact that by God we understand a supremely perfect and absolutely infinite Being. The existence of such a Being is easily proved from the definition; but as this is not the place for such a proof, I shall

1. Translated from the Latin by Samuel Shirley in Baruch Spinoza, *The Ethics and Selected Letters* (Indianapolis/Cambridge: Hackett Publishing Company, 1982), letters 2, 12, and 32 (in part).
2. Henry Oldenburg (d. 1677) was a German theologian with a scientific bent. He eventually became secretary of the London Royal Society. He met Spinoza in 1661, and when he went to London, he continued to correspond with Spinoza for many years. It was through Oldenburg that Spinoza learned of Robert Boyle's work in chemistry.

pass it over. The points I need to prove here in order to satisfy your first inquiry, illustrious Sir, are as follows: first, that in the universe there cannot exist two substances without their differing entirely in essence; secondly, a substance cannot be produced, since to exist is of its essence; thirdly, every substance must be infinite, or supremely perfect in its kind.

With these points established, illustrious Sir, provided that at the same time you attend to the definition of God, you will readily perceive the direction of my thought, so that I need not be more explicit on this subject. However, in order to provide a clear, concise proof, I can think of no better expedient than to arrange them in geometrical style and to submit them to the bar of your judgment. I therefore enclose them separately herewith[3] and await your judgment.

Secondly, you ask me what errors I see in the philosophy of Descartes and Bacon. In this request, too, I shall try to oblige you, although it is not my custom to expose the errors of others. The first and most important error is this, that they have gone far astray from knowledge of the first cause and origin of all things. Secondly, they have failed to achieve understanding of the true nature of the human mind. Thirdly, they have never grasped the true cause of error. Only those who are completely destitute of all learning and scholarship can fail to see the critical importance of true knowledge of these three points.

How far astray they have wandered from true knowledge of the first cause and of the human mind can readily be gathered from the truth of the three propositions to which I have already referred. So I confine myself to pointing out the third error. Of Bacon I shall say little; he speaks very confusedly on this point, and simply makes assertions while proving hardly anything.[4] In the first place, he takes for granted that the human intellect, apart from the fallibility of the senses, is by its very nature liable to error, framing its assumptions on the analogy of its own nature, and not on the analogy of the universe, so that it is like a mirror of irregular surface receiving

rays, mingling its own nature with the nature of reality, and so forth. Secondly, he holds that the human intellect, by reason of its own nature, is prone to abstractions, and imagines that things that are in flux are stable, and so on. Thirdly, he holds that the human intellect is continually increasing and cannot come to a halt or rest. Whatever other causes he assigns can readily be reduced to the one Cartesian principle, that the human will is free and more extensive than the intellect, or, as Verulam himself more confusedly puts it (Aphorism 49), the intellect is not characterized by a dry light, but receives infusion from the will. (We should here observe that Verulam takes "intellect" for "mind," therein differing with Descartes.) This cause, then, disregarding the others as being of little importance, I shall show to be false. Indeed, they would easily have seen this for themselves, had they but given consideration to the fact that the will differs from this or that volition in the same way as whiteness differs from this or that white object, or as humanity differs from this or that human being. So to conceive the will to be the cause of this or that volition is as impossible as to conceive humanity to be the cause of Peter or Paul.

Since, then, the will is nothing more than a mental construct [*ens rationis*], it can in no way be said to be the cause of this or that volition. Particular volitions, since they need a cause in order to exist, cannot be said to be free; rather they are necessarily determined to be such as they are by their own causes. Lastly, according to Descartes, errors are themselves particular volitions, from which it necessarily follows that errors— that is, particular volitions—are not free, but are determined by external causes and in no way by the will. This is what I undertook to prove.

## To the learned and wise Ludwig Meyer,[5] Doctor in Philosophy and in Medicine, from Benedict de Spinoza (April 20, 1663)

[On the Nature of the Infinite]

---

3. See Spinoza, *Ethics*, Part I, from the beginning to Proposition 4.

4. Francis Bacon, *New Organon* I, sec. 41–51; Bacon was also Lord Verulam.

5. Ludwig Meyer, physician and philosopher, was a close friend of Spinoza. He participated in preparing Spinoza's writings for posthumous publication.

Dearest friend,

I have received two letters from you, one dated January 11 and delivered to me by our friend N. N.,[6] the other dated March 26 and sent to me by an unknown friend from Leyden. They were both very welcome, especially as I gathered from them that all is well with you and that I am often in your thoughts. My most cordial thanks are due to you for the kindness and esteem you have always shown me. At the same time I beseech you to believe that I am in no less a degree your devoted friend, and this I shall endeavor to prove whenever the occasion arises, as far as my slender abilities allow. As a first offering, I will try to answer the request made in your letters to me, in which you ask me to let you have my considered views on the question of the infinite. I am glad to oblige.

The question of the infinite has universally been found to be very difficult, indeed, insoluble, through failure to distinguish between that which must be infinite by its very nature or by virtue of its definition, and that which is unlimited not by virtue of its essence but by virtue of its cause. Then again, there is the failure to distinguish between that which is called infinite because it is unlimited, and that whose parts cannot be equated or explicated by any number, although we may know its maximum and minimum. Lastly, there is the failure to distinguish between that which we can apprehend only by intellect and not by imagination, and that which can also be apprehended by imagination. I repeat, if men had paid careful attention to these distinctions, they would never have found themselves overwhelmed by such a mountain of difficulties. They would clearly have understood what kind of infinite cannot be divided into, or possess any, parts, and what kind can be so divided without contradiction. They would also have understood what kind of infinite can be considered, without contradiction, as greater than another infinite, and what kind cannot be so conceived. This will become clear from what I am about to say. However, I shall first briefly explain these four terms: Substance, Mode, Eternity, Duration.

The points to be noted about Substance are as follow. First, existence pertains to its essence; that is, solely from its essence and definition it follows that Substance exists. This point, if my memory does not deceive me, I have proved to you in an earlier conversation without the help of any other propositions. Second, following from the first point, substance is not many; rather, there exists only one substance of the same nature. Thirdly, all Substance can be understood only as infinite.

The affections of Substance I call Modes. The definition of Modes, insofar as it is not a definition of Substance, cannot involve existence. Therefore, even when they exist, we can conceive them as not existing. It therefore follows that when we have regard only to the essence of Modes and not to the order of Nature as a whole, we cannot deduce from their present existence that they will or will not exist in the future, or that they did or did not exist in the past. Hence it is clear that we conceive the existence of Substance as of an entirely different kind from the existence of Modes. This is the source of the difference between Eternity and Duration. It is to the existence of Modes only that we can apply the term Duration; the corresponding term for the existence of Substance is Eternity, that is, the infinite enjoyment of existence or—pardon the Latin—of being [*essendi*].

What I have said makes it quite clear that when we have regard only to the essence of Modes and not to Nature's order, as is most frequently the case, we can arbitrarily limit the existence and duration of Modes (without thereby impairing to any degree our conception of them); and we can conceive this duration as greater or less, and divisible into parts. But Eternity and Substance, being conceivable only as infinite, cannot be thus treated without annulling our concept of them. So it is nonsense, bordering on insanity, to hold that extended Substance is composed of parts or bodies really distinct from one another. It is as if, by adding circle to circle and piling one on top of another, one were to attempt to construct a square or a triangle or any other figure of a completely different nature. Therefore the whole heap of arguments by which the common run of philosophers strive to prove that extended Substance

---

6. Most likely Peter Balling, another of Spinoza's close friends.

is finite collapses of its own accord. All such arguments assume that corporeal Substance is composed of parts. A parallel case is presented by those who, having convinced themselves that a line is made up of points, have devised many arguments to prove that a line is not infinitely divisible.

However, if you ask why we have such a strong natural tendency to divide extended Substance, I answer that we conceive quantity in two ways: abstractly, or superficially, as we have it in the imagination with the help of the senses; or as substance apprehended solely by means of the intellect. If we have regard to quantity as it exists in the imagination (and this is what we most frequently and readily do), it is found to be divisible, finite, composed of parts, and multiplex. But if we have regard to it as it is in the intellect and apprehend the thing as it is in itself (and this is very difficult), then it is found to be infinite, indivisible, and one alone, as I have already sufficiently proved.

Further, from the fact that we are able to limit Duration and Quantity as we please, conceiving Quantity in abstraction from Substance and ignoring the efflux of Duration from things eternal, there arise Time and Measure: Time to limit Duration, and Measure to limit Quantity in such wise that we are thereby enabled to form images of them as best we may. Again, from the fact that we separate the Affections of Substance from Substance itself, and arrange them in classes so that we can form images of them as best we may, there arises Number, whereby we limit them. Hence it can clearly be seen that Measure, Time, and Number are nothing other than modes of thinking, or rather, modes of the imagination. It is therefore not surprising that all who have attempted to understand the workings of Nature by such concepts, and without really understanding these concepts, have tied themselves into such extraordinary knots that in the end they have been unable to extricate themselves except by breaking all laws and perpetrating the grossest absurdities. For there are many things that can in no way be apprehended by the imagination but only by the intellect, such as Substance, Eternity, and the like. If anyone tries to explicate such things by notions of this kind, which are nothing more than aids to the imagination, he will meet with no more success than if he were deliberately to encourage his imagination to run mad. The Modes of Substance, too, can never be correctly understood if they are confused with such mental constructs [*entia rationis*] or aids to the imagination. For by so doing we are abstracting them from Substance and from the manner of their efflux from Eternity, and in such isolation they can never be correctly understood.

To make the matter still clearer, take the following example. If someone conceives Duration in this abstracted way and, confusing it with Time, begins dividing it into parts, he can never understand how, for instance, an hour can pass by. For in order that an hour should pass by, a half-hour must first have passed by, and then half of the remainder, and then half of what is left of the remainder; and if you go on subtracting half of the remainder to infinity, you can never reach the end of the hour. Therefore, many who are not used to distinguishing mental constructs from reality have ventured to assert that Duration is composed of moments, thus falling into the clutches of Scylla in their eagerness to avoid Charybdis. To say that Duration is made up of moments is the same as to say that Number is made up by adding noughts together.

Further, it is obvious from the above that Number, Time, and Measure, being merely aids to the imagination, cannot be infinite, for in that case Number would not be number, nor Measure measure, nor Time time. Hence one can easily see why many people, confusing these three concepts with reality because of their ignorance of the true nature of reality, have denied the actual existence of the Infinite. But let their deplorable reasoning be judged by mathematicians who, in matters that they clearly and distinctly perceive, are not to be delayed by arguments of that sort. For they not only have come upon many things inexpressible by any number, which clearly reveals the inadequacy of number to determine all things; in addition they have encountered many things that cannot be equaled by any number, and exceed any possible number. Now they do not draw the conclusion that it is because of the multitude of parts that such things exceed all number; rather, it is because the nature of the thing is such that number is inapplicable to it without manifest contradiction.

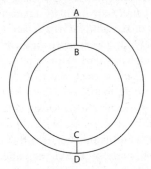

For example, all the inequalities of the space lying between the two circles ABCD in the diagram exceed any number, as do all the variations of speed of matter moving through that area. Now this conclusion is not reached because of the excessive magnitude of the intervening space; for however small a portion of it we take, the inequalities of this small portion will still be beyond any numerical expression. Nor, again, is this conclusion reached, as happens in other cases, because we do not know the maximum and minimum; in our example we know them both, the maximum being AB and the minimum CD. Our conclusion is reached because number is not applicable to the nature of the space between the two non-concentric circles. Therefore, if anyone sought to express by number all those inequalities, he would have to bring it about that a circle should not be a circle.

Similarly, to return to our main topic of discussion, if anyone were to attempt to determine all the motions of matter that have ever been, by reducing them and their duration to a certain number and time, he would be attempting to deprive corporeal Substance, which we cannot conceive as other than existing, of its Affections, and bring it about that Substance should not possess the nature which it does possess. I could here clearly demonstrate this and many other points touched on in this letter, did I not consider it unnecessary.

From all that I have said one can clearly see that certain things are infinite by their own nature and

cannot in any way be conceived as finite, while other things are infinite by virtue of the cause in which they have their being, and when the latter are conceived in abstraction, they can be divided into parts and be regarded as finite. Lastly, there are things that are called infinite, or if you prefer, indefinite, because they cannot be accurately expressed by any number, while yet being conceivable as greater or less. For it does not follow that things that cannot be accurately expressed by any number must necessarily be equal, as is evident from the given example and from many others.

To sum up, I have here briefly set before you the causes of error and of the confusions that have arisen regarding the question of the Infinite, explaining them all, unless I am mistaken, in such a way that I do not believe there is any question regarding the Infinite on which I have not touched, or which cannot be readily solved from what I have said. Therefore, I think it is pointless to detain you any longer on this matter.

However, in passing, I should like it here to be observed that in my opinion our modern Peripatetics have quite misunderstood the proof whereby scholars of old sought to prove the existence of God. According to a certain Jew named Rabbi Chasdai,[7] this proof runs as follows: "If there is granted an infinite series of causes, all things which are, are also caused. But nothing that is caused can exist necessarily by virtue of its own nature. Therefore, there is nothing in Nature to whose essence existence necessarily pertains. But this is absurd. Therefore the premise is absurd." So the force of the argument lies not in the impossibility of an actual infinite, or an infinite series of causes, but in the assumption that things which by their own nature do not necessarily exist are not determined by a thing that necessarily exists by its own nature.

I would now pass on—for I am pressed for time—to your second question, but I shall be able more conveniently to reply to the points contained there when you kindly pay me a visit. So do please try to come as soon as you can. For the time for my

_____

7. Hasdai Crescas (1340–1410), a Spanish-Jewish theologian, whose *The Light of the Lord* subjects Aristotle's physics to a "radical" critique.

departure is rapidly approaching. Enough, farewell, and keep me ever in your thoughts. Yours, etc.

## To Henry Oldenburg (November 20, 1665)

Most honorable Sir,

Please accept my most grateful thanks for the kind encouragement which you and the most honorable Master Boyle have given me in the pursuit of philosophy. As far as my poor abilities will allow, I shall continue in this way, with the assurance of your assistance and goodwill.

When you ask for my views on "how we know the way in which each part of Nature agrees with the whole, and the manner of its coherence with the other parts," I presume you are asking for the grounds of our belief that each part of Nature agrees with the whole and coheres with the other parts. As to knowing the actual manner of this coherence and the agreement of each part with the whole, I made it clear in my previous letter that this is beyond my knowledge. To know this it would be necessary to know the whole of Nature and all its parts. So I shall attempt to give the reasoning that compels me to this belief. But I would first ask you to note that I do not attribute to Nature beauty, ugliness, order, or confusion. It is only with respect to our imagination that things can be said to be beautiful, ugly, well-ordered, or confused.

By "coherence of parts" I mean simply this, that the laws or nature of one part adapts itself to the laws or nature of another part in such wise that there is the least possible opposition between them. On the question of whole and parts, I consider things as parts of a whole to the extent that their natures adapt themselves to one another so that they are in the closest possible agreement. Insofar as they are different from one another, to that extent each one forms in our mind a separate idea and is therefore considered as a whole, not a part. For example, when the motions of particles of lymph, chyle, etc. adapt themselves to one another in accordance with size and shape so as to be fully in agreement with one another and to form all together one single fluid, to that extent only are the chyle, lymph, etc. regarded as parts of the blood. But insofar as we conceive the particles of lymph as different from the particles of chyle in respect of shape and motion, to that extent we regard them each as a whole, not a part.

Now let us imagine, if you please, a tiny worm living in the blood, capable of distinguishing by sight the particles of the blood—lymph, etc.—and of intelligently observing how each particle, on colliding with another, either rebounds or communicates some degree of its motion, and so forth. That worm would be living in the blood as we are living in our part of the universe, and it would regard each individual particle as a whole, not a part, and it would have no idea as to how all the parts are modified by the overall nature of the blood and compelled to mutual adaptation as the overall nature of the blood requires, so as to agree with one another in a definite relation. For if we imagine that there are no causes external to the blood which would communicate new motions to the blood, nor any space external to the blood, nor any other bodies to which the particles of the blood could transfer their motions, it is beyond doubt that the blood will remain indefinitely in its present state and that its particles will undergo no changes other than those which can be conceived as resulting from the existing relation between the motion of the blood and that of the lymph, chyle, etc. Thus the blood would always have to be regarded as a whole, not a part. But since there are many other causes which do in fact modify the laws of the nature of the blood and are reciprocally modified by the blood, it follows that there occur in the blood other motions and other changes, resulting not solely from the reciprocal relation of its particles but from the relation between the motion of the blood on the one hand and external causes on the other. In this perspective the blood is accounted as a part, not as a whole. So much, then, for the question of whole and part.

Now all the bodies in Nature can and should be conceived in the same way as we have here conceived the blood; for all bodies are surrounded by others and are reciprocally determined to exist and to act in a fixed and determinate way, the same ratio of motion to rest being preserved in them taken all together, that is, in the universe as a whole. Hence it follows that every body, insofar as it exists as modified in a definite way, must be considered as a part of the whole universe and must agree with the whole and cohere with the other parts. Now since the nature of the universe, unlike the nature of the blood, is not limited, but is absolutely infinite, its parts are modified by the nature of this infinite potency in infinite ways and are compelled to undergo infinite variations. But I conceive that, in respect to substance, each individual part has a more intimate union with the whole. For, as I endeavored to prove in my first letter written some time ago, while I was living at Rhijnsburg,[8] since it is of the nature of substance to be infinite, it follows that each part pertains to

---

8. This is an allusion to Letter 2, this selection.

the nature of corporeal substance, and can neither be nor be conceived without it.

So you see how and why I hold that the human body is a part of Nature. As regards the human mind, I maintain that it also is a part of Nature, for I hold that in Nature there also exists an infinite power of thinking which, insofar as it is infinite, contains within itself the whole of Nature as an object of thought, and whose thoughts proceed in the same manner as does Nature, which is clearly its object of thought.

Further, I maintain that the human mind is that same power of thinking, not insofar as that power is infinite and apprehends the whole of Nature, but insofar as it is finite, apprehending the human body only. The human mind, I maintain, is in this way part of an infinite intellect. [ . . . ]

# Baruch Spinoza, *The Ethics* (1677)[1]

## Part I. Concerning God

### Definitions

1. By that which is self-caused I mean that whose essence involves existence; or that whose nature can be conceived only as existing.

2. A thing is said to be finite in its own kind [*in suo genere finita*] when it can be limited by another thing of the same nature. For example, a body is said to be finite because we can always conceive of another body greater than it. So, too, a thought is limited by another thought. But body is not limited by thought, nor thought by body.

3. By substance I mean that which is in itself and is conceived through itself; that is, that the conception of which does not require the conception of another thing from which it has to be formed.

4. By attribute I mean that which the intellect perceives of substance as constituting its essence.

5. By mode I mean the affections of substance, that is, that which is in something else and is conceived through something else.

6. By God I mean an absolutely infinite being, that is, substance consisting of infinite attributes, each of which expresses eternal and infinite essence.

*Explication*: I say "absolutely infinite," not "infinite in its kind." For if a thing is only infinite in its kind, one may deny that it has infinite attributes. But if a thing is absolutely infinite, whatever expresses essence and does not involve any negation belongs to its essence.

7. That thing is said to be free [*liber*] which exists solely from the necessity of its own nature, and is determined to action by itself alone. A thing is said to be necessary [*necessarius*] or rather, constrained [*coactus*], if it is determined by another thing to exist and to act in a definite and determinate way.

8. By eternity I mean existence itself insofar as it is conceived as necessarily following solely from the definition of an eternal thing.

*Explication*: For such existence is conceived as an eternal truth, just as is the essence of the thing, and therefore cannot be explicated through duration or time, even if duration be conceived as without beginning and end.

### Axioms

1. All things that are, are either in themselves or in something else.

---

1. Translated from the Latin by Samuel Shirley in Baruch Spinoza, *The Ethics and Selected Letters* (Indianapolis/Cambridge: Hackett Publishing Company, 1982).

2. That which cannot be conceived through another thing must be conceived through itself.

3. From a given determinate cause there necessarily follows an effect; on the other hand, if there be no determinate cause, it is impossible that an effect should follow.

4. The knowledge of an effect depends on, and involves, the knowledge of the cause.

5. Things which have nothing in common with each other cannot be understood through each other; that is, the conception of the one does not involve the conception of the other.

6. A true idea must agree with that of which it is the idea [*ideatum*].

7. If a thing can be conceived as not existing, its essence does not involve existence.

## Proposition 1. *Substance is by nature prior to its affections.*

Proof: This is evident from Defs. 3 and 5.

## Proposition 2. *Two substances having different attributes have nothing in common.*

Proof: This too is evident from Def. 3; for each substance must be in itself and be conceived through itself; that is, the conception of the one does not involve the conception of the other.

## Proposition 3. *When things have nothing in common, one cannot be the cause of the other.*

Proof: If things have nothing in common, then (Ax. 5) they cannot be understood through one another, and so (Ax. 4) one cannot be the cause of the other.

## Proposition 4. *Two or more distinct things are distinguished from one another either by the difference of the attributes of the substances or by the difference of the affections of the substances.*

Proof: All things that are, are either in themselves or in something else (Ax. l); that is (Defs. 3 and 5), nothing exists external to the intellect except substances and their affections. Therefore, there can be nothing external to the intellect through which several things can be distinguished from one another except substances or (which is the same thing) (Def. 4) the attributes and the affections of substances.

## Proposition 5. *In the universe there cannot be two or more substances of the same nature or attribute.*

Proof: If there were several such distinct substances, they would have to be distinguished from one another either by a difference of attributes or by a difference of affections (Pr. 4). If they are distinguished only by a difference of attributes, then it will be granted that there cannot be more than one substance of the same attribute. But if they are distinguished by a difference of affections, then, since substance is by nature prior to its affections (Pr. 1), disregarding therefore its affections and considering substance in itself, that is (Def. 3 and Ax. 6) considering it truly, it cannot be conceived as distinguishable from another substance. That is (Pr. 4), there cannot be several such substances but only one.

## Proposition 6. *One substance cannot be produced by another substance.*

Proof: In the universe there cannot be two substances of the same attribute (Pr. 5), that is (Pr. 2), two substances having something in common. And so (Pr. 3) one cannot be the cause of the other; that is, one cannot be produced by the other.

Corollary: Hence it follows that substance cannot be produced by anything else. For in the universe there exists nothing but substances and their affections, as is evident from Ax. 1 and Defs. 3 and 5. But, by Pr. 6, it cannot be produced by another substance. Therefore, substance cannot be produced by anything else whatsoever.

Another Proof: This can be proved even more readily by the absurdity of the contradictory. For if substance could be produced by something else, the knowledge of substance would have to depend on the knowledge of its cause (Ax. 4), and so (Def. 3) it would not be substance.

## Proposition 7. *Existence belongs to the nature of substance.*

Proof: Substance cannot be produced by anything else (Cor. Pr. 6) and is therefore self-caused [*causa sui*]; that is (Def. 1), its essence necessarily involves existence; that is, existence belongs to its nature.

## Proposition 8. *Every substance is necessarily infinite.*

Proof: There cannot be more than one substance having the same attribute (Pr. 5), and existence belongs to the nature of substance (Pr. 7). It must therefore exist either as finite or as infinite. But it cannot exist as finite, for (Def. 2) it would have to be limited by another substance of the same nature, and that substance also would have to exist (Pr. 7). And so there would exist two substances of the same attribute, which is absurd (Pr. 5). Therefore, it exists as infinite.

Scholium 1: Since in fact to be finite is in part a negation and to be infinite is the unqualified affirmation of the existence of some nature, it follows from Proposition 7 alone that every substance must be infinite.

Scholium 2: I do not doubt that for those who judge things confusedly and are not accustomed to know things through their primary causes it is difficult to grasp the proof of Proposition 7. Surely, this is because they neither distinguish between the modification of substances and substances themselves, nor do they know how things are produced. And so it comes about that they ascribe to substances a beginning which they see natural things as having; for those who do not know the true causes of things confuse everything. Without any hesitation they imagine trees as well as men talking and stones as well as men being formed from seeds; indeed, any forms whatsoever are imagined to change into any other forms. So too, those who confuse the divine nature with human nature easily ascribe to God human emotions, especially so long as they are ignorant of how the latter are produced in the mind. But if men were to attend to the nature of substance, they would not doubt at all the truth of Proposition 7; indeed, this Proposition would be an axiom to all and would be ranked among universally accepted truisms. For by substance they would understand that which is in itself and is conceived through itself; that is, that the knowledge of which does not require the knowledge of any other thing. By modifications they would understand that which is in another thing, and whose conception is formed from the thing in which they are. Therefore, in the case of nonexistent modifications we can have true ideas of them since their essence is included in something else, with the result that they can be conceived through that something else, although they do not exist in actuality externally to the intellect. However, in the case of substances, because they are conceived only through themselves, their truth external to the intellect is only in themselves. So if someone were to say that he has a clear and distinct—that is, a true—idea of substance and that he nevertheless doubts whether such a substance exists, this would surely be just the same as if he were to declare that he has a true idea but nevertheless suspects that it may be false (as is obvious to anyone who gives his mind to it). Or if anyone asserts that substance is created, he at the same time asserts that a false idea has become true, than which nothing more absurd can be conceived. So it must necessarily be admitted that the existence of substance is as much an eternal truth as is its essence.

From here we can derive in another way that there cannot be but one [substance] of the same nature, and I think it worthwhile to set out the proof here. Now to do this in an orderly fashion I ask you to note:

1. The true definition of each thing involves and expresses nothing beyond the nature of the thing defined. Hence it follows that—

2. No definition involves or expresses a fixed number of individuals, since it expresses nothing but the nature of the thing defined. For example, the definition of a triangle expresses nothing other

than simply the nature of a triangle, and not a fixed number of triangles.

3. For each individual existent thing there must necessarily be a definite cause for its existence.

4. The cause for the existence of a thing must either be contained in the very nature and definition of the existent thing (in effect, existence belongs to its nature) or must have its being independently of the thing itself.

From these premises it follows that if a fixed number of individuals exist in Nature, there must necessarily be a cause why those individuals and not more or fewer exist. If, for example, in Nature twenty men were to exist (for the sake of greater clarity I suppose that they exist simultaneously and that no others existed in Nature before them), in order to account for the existence of these twenty men, it will not be enough for us to demonstrate the cause of human nature in general; it will furthermore be necessary to demonstrate the cause why not more or fewer than twenty men exist, since (Note 3) there must necessarily be a cause for the existence of each one. But this cause (Notes 2 and 3) cannot be contained in the nature of man, since the true definition of man does not involve the number twenty. So (Note 4) the cause of the existence of these twenty men, and consequently of each one, must necessarily be external to each one, and therefore we can reach the unqualified conclusion that whenever several individuals of a kind exist, there must necessarily be an external cause for their existence. Now since existence belongs to the nature of substance (as has already been shown in this Scholium) the definition of substance must involve necessary existence, and consequently the existence of substance must be concluded solely from its definition. But the existence of several substances cannot follow from the definition of substance (as I have already shown in Notes 2 and 3). Therefore, from the definition of substance it follows necessarily that there exists only one substance of the same nature, as was proposed.

## Proposition 9. *The more reality or being a thing has, the more attributes it has.*

Proof: This is evident from Definition 4.

## Proposition 10. *Each attribute of one substance must be conceived through itself.*

Proof: For an attribute is that which intellect perceives of substance as constituting its essence (Def. 4), and so (Def. 3) it must be conceived through itself.

Scholium: From this it is clear that although two attributes be conceived as really distinct, that is, one without the help of the other, still we cannot deduce therefrom that they constitute two entities, or two different substances. For it is in the nature of substance that each of its attributes be conceived through itself, since all the attributes it possesses have always been in it simultaneously, and one could not have been produced by another; but each expresses the reality or being of substance. So it is by no means absurd to ascribe more than one attribute to one substance. Indeed, nothing in Nature is clearer than that each entity must be conceived under some attribute, and the more reality or being it has, the more are its attributes which express necessity, or eternity, and infinity. Consequently, nothing can be clearer than this, too, that an absolutely infinite entity must necessarily be defined (Def. 6) as an entity consisting of infinite attributes, each of which expresses a definite essence, eternal and infinite. Now if anyone asks by what mark can we distinguish between different substances, let him read the following Propositions, which show that in Nature there exists only one substance, absolutely infinite. So this distinguishing mark would be sought in vain.

## Proposition 11. *God, or substance consisting of infinite attributes, each of which expresses eternal and infinite essence, necessarily exists.*

Proof: If you deny this, conceive, if you can, that God does not exist. Therefore (Ax. 7), his essence does not involve existence. But this is absurd (Pr. 7). Therefore God necessarily exists.

Second Proof: For every thing a cause or reason must be assigned either for its existence or for its nonexistence. For example, if a triangle exists, there must be a reason, or cause, for its existence. If it does not exist, there must be a reason or cause which prevents it from existing, or which annuls its existence. Now this reason or cause must either be contained in the nature of the thing or be external to it. For example, the reason why a square circle does not exist is indicated by its very nature, in that it involves a contradiction. On the other hand, the reason for the existence of substance also follows from its nature alone, in that it involves existence (Pr. 7). But the reason for the existence or nonexistence of a circle or a triangle does not follow from their nature, but from the order of universal corporeal Nature. For it is from this latter that it necessarily follows that either the triangle necessarily exists at this moment or that its present existence is impossible. This is self-evident, and therefrom it follows that a thing necessarily exists if there is no reason or cause which prevents its existence. Therefore if there can be no reason or cause which prevents God from existing or which annuls his existence, we are bound to conclude that he necessarily exists. But if there were such a reason or cause, it would have to be either within God's nature or external to it; that is, it would have to be in another substance of another nature. For if it were of the same nature, by that very fact it would be granted that God exists. But a substance of another nature would have nothing in common with God (Pr. 2), and so could neither posit nor annul his existence. Since therefore there cannot be external to God's nature a reason or cause that would annul God's existence, then if indeed he does not exist, the reason or cause must necessarily be in God's nature, which would therefore involve a contradiction. But to affirm this of a Being absolutely infinite and in the highest degree perfect is absurd. Therefore neither in God nor external to God is there any cause or reason which would annul his existence. Therefore, God necessarily exists.

A Third Proof: To be able to not exist is weakness; on the other hand, to be able to exist is power, as is self-evident. So if what now necessarily exists is nothing but finite entities, then finite entities are more potent than an absolutely infinite Entity—which is absurd. Therefore either nothing exists, or an absolutely infinite Entity necessarily exists, too. But we do exist, either in ourselves or in something else which

necessarily exists (Ax. 1 and Pr. 7). Therefore, an absolutely infinite Entity—that is (Def. 6), God—necessarily exists.

Scholium: In this last proof I decided to prove God's existence *a posteriori* so that the proof may be more easily perceived, and not because God's existence does not follow *a priori* from this same basis. For since the ability to exist is power, it follows that the greater the degree of reality that belongs to the nature of a thing, the greater amount of energy it has for existence. So an absolutely infinite Entity or God will have from himself absolutely infinite power to exist, and therefore exists absolutely.

But perhaps many will not readily find this proof convincing because they are used to considering only such things as derive from external causes. Of these things they observe that those which come quickly into being—that is, which readily exist—likewise readily perish, while things which they conceive as more complex they regard as more difficult to bring into being—that is, not so ready to exist. However, to free them from these misconceptions I do not need at this point to show what measure of truth there is in the saying, "Quickly come, quickly go," neither need I raise the question whether or not everything is equally easy in respect of Nature as a whole. It is enough to note simply this, that I am not here speaking of things that come into being through external causes, but only of substances, which (Pr. 6) cannot be produced by any external cause. For whether they consist of many parts or few, things that are brought about by external causes owe whatever degree of perfection or reality they possess entirely to the power of the external cause, and so their existence has its origin solely in the perfection of the external cause, and not in their own perfection. On the other hand, whatever perfection substance possesses is due to no external cause; therefore its existence, too, must follow solely from its own nature, and is therefore nothing else but its essence. So perfection does not annul a thing's existence: on the contrary, it posits it; whereas imperfection annuls a thing's existence. So there is nothing of which we can be more certain than the existence of an absolutely infinite or perfect Entity; that is, God. For since his essence excludes all imperfection and involves absolute perfection, it thereby removes all reason for doubting his existence and affords the utmost certainty of it. This, I think, must be quite clear to all who give a modicum of attention to the matter.

## Proposition 12. *No attribute of substance can be truly conceived from which it would follow that substance can be divided.*

Proof: The parts into which substance thus conceived would be divided will either retain the nature of substance or they will not. In the first case each part will have to be infinite (Pr. 8) and self-caused (Pr. 6) and consist of a different attribute (Pr. 5); and so several substances could be formed from one substance, which is absurd (Pr. 6). Furthermore, the parts would have nothing in common with the whole (Pr. 2), and the whole could exist and be conceived without its parts (Def. 4 and Pr. 10), the absurdity of which none can doubt. But in the latter case in which the parts will not retain the nature of substance—then when the whole substance would have been divided into equal parts it would lose the nature of substance and would cease to be. This is absurd (Pr. 7).

## Proposition 13. *Absolutely infinite substance is indivisible.*

Proof: If it were divisible, the parts into which it would be divided will either retain the nature of absolutely infinite substance, or not. In the first case, there would therefore be several substances of the same nature, which is absurd (Pr. 5). In the second case, absolutely infinite substance can cease to be, which is also absurd (Pr. 11).

Corollary: From this it follows that no substance, and consequently no corporeal substance, insofar as it is substance, is divisible.

Scholium: The indivisibility of substance can be more easily understood merely from the fact that the nature of substance can be conceived only as infinite, and that a part of substance can mean only finite substance, which involves an obvious contradiction (Pr. 8).

## Proposition 14. *There can be, or be conceived, no other substance but God.*

Proof: Since God is an absolutely infinite being of whom no attribute expressing the essence of substance can be denied (Def. 6) and since he necessarily exists (Pr. 11), if there were any other substance but God, it would have to be explicated through some attribute of God, and so there would exist two substances with the same attribute, which is absurd (Pr. 5). So there can be no substance external to God, and consequently no such substance can be conceived. For if it could be conceived, it would have to be conceived necessarily as existing; but this is absurd (by the first part of this proof). Therefore, no substance can be or be conceived external to God.

Corollary 1: Hence it follows quite clearly that God is one: that is (Def. 6), in the universe there is only one substance, and this is absolutely infinite, as I have already indicated in Scholium Pr. 10.

Corollary 2: It follows that the thing extended and the thing thinking are either attributes of God or (Ax. 1) affections of the attributes of God.

## Proposition 15. *Whatever is, is in God, and nothing can be or be conceived without God.*

Proof: Apart from God no substance can be or be conceived (Pr. 14), that is (Def. 3), something which is in itself and is conceived through itself. Now modes (Def. 5) cannot be or be conceived without substance; therefore, they can be only in the divine nature and can be conceived only through the divine nature. But nothing exists except substance and modes (Ax. 1). Therefore, nothing can be or be conceived without God.

Scholium: Some imagine God in the likeness of man, consisting of mind and body, and subject to passions. But it is clear from what has already been proved how far they stray from the true knowledge of God. These I dismiss, for all who have given any consideration to the divine nature deny that God is corporeal. They find convincing proof of this in the fact that by body we understand some quantity having length, breadth, and depth, bounded by a definite shape; and nothing more absurd than this can be attributed to God, a being absolutely infinite.

At the same time, however, by other arguments which they try to prove their point, they show clearly that in their thinking corporeal or extended substance is set completely apart from the divine nature, and they assert that it is created by God. But they have no idea from what divine power it could have been created, which clearly shows that they don't know what they are saying. Now I have clearly proved—at any rate, in my judgment (Cor. Pr. 6 and Sch. 2 Pr. 8)—that no substance can be produced or created by anything else. Furthermore, in Proposition 14 we showed that apart from God no substance can be or be conceived, and hence we deduced that extended substance is one of God's infinite attributes.

However, for a fuller explanation I will refute my opponents' arguments, which all seem to come down to this. Firstly, they think that corporeal substance, insofar as it is substance, is made up of parts, and so they deny that it can be infinite, and consequently that it can pertain to God. This they illustrate with many examples, of which I will take one or two. They say that if corporeal substance is infinite, suppose it to be divided into two parts. Each of these parts will be either finite or infinite. If the former, then the infinite is made up of two finite parts, which is absurd. If the latter, then there is an infinite which is twice as great as another infinite, which is also absurd.

Again, if an infinite length is measured in feet, it will have to consist of an infinite number of feet; and if it is measured in inches, it will consist of an infinite number of inches. So one infinite number will be twelve times greater than another infinite number.

Lastly, if from one point in an infinite quantity two lines, AB and AC be drawn of fixed and determinate length, and thereafter be produced to infinity, it is clear that the distance between B and C continues to increase and finally changes from a determinate distance to an indeterminate distance.

As these absurdities follow, they think, from supposing quantity to be infinite, they conclude that corporeal substance must be finite and consequently cannot pertain to God's essence.

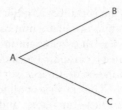

The second argument is also drawn from God's consummate perfection. Since God, they say, is a supremely perfect being, he cannot be that which is acted upon. But corporeal substance, being divisible, can be acted upon. It therefore follows that corporeal substance does not pertain to God's essence.

These are the arguments I find put forward by writers who thereby seek to prove that corporeal substance is unworthy of the divine essence and cannot pertain to it. However, the student who looks carefully into these arguments will find that I have already replied to them, since they are all founded on the same supposition that material substance is composed of parts, and this I have already shown to be absurd (Pr. 12 and Cor. Pr. 13). Again, careful reflection will show that all those alleged absurdities (if indeed they are absurdities, which is not now under discussion) from which they seek to prove that extended substance is finite do not at all follow from the supposition that quantity is infinite, but that infinite quantity is measurable and is made up of finite parts. Therefore, from the resultant absurdities no other conclusion can be reached but that infinite quantity is not measurable and cannot be made up of finite parts. And this is exactly what we have already proved (Pr. 12). So the weapon they aimed at us is in fact turned against themselves. If therefore from this "reductio ad absurdum" argument of theirs they still seek to deduce that extended substance must be finite, they are surely just like one who, having made the supposition that a circle has the properties of a square, deduces therefrom that a circle does not have a center from which all lines drawn to the circumference are equal. For corporeal substance, which can be conceived only as infinite, one, and indivisible (Prs. 8, 5, and 12) they conceive as made up of finite parts, multiplex, and divisible, so as to deduce that it is finite. In the same way others, too, having supposed that a line is composed of points, can find many arguments to prove that a line cannot be infinitely divided. Indeed, it is just as absurd to assert that corporeal substance is composed of bodies or parts as that a body is composed of surfaces, surfaces of lines, and lines of points. This must be admitted by all who know clear reason to be infallible, and particularly those who say that a vacuum cannot exist. For if corporeal substance could be so divided that its parts were distinct in reality, why could one part not be annihilated while the others remain joined together as before? And why should all the parts be so fitted together as to leave no vacuum? Surely, in the case of things which are in reality distinct from one another, one can exist without the other and remain in its original state. Since therefore there is no vacuum in Nature (of which [more] elsewhere[2]) and all its parts must so harmonize that there is no vacuum, it also follows that the parts cannot be distinct in reality; that is, corporeal substance, insofar as it is substance, cannot be divided.

If I am now asked why we have this natural inclination to divide quantity, I reply that we conceive quantity in two ways, to wit, abstractly, or superficially—in other words, as represented in the imagination— or as substance, which we do only through the intellect. If therefore we consider quantity insofar as we represent it in the imagination— and this is what we more frequently and readily do—we find it to be finite, divisible, and made up of parts. But if we consider it intellectually and conceive it insofar as it is substance—and this is very difficult—then it will be found to be infinite, one, and indivisible, as we have already sufficiently proved. This will be quite clear to those who can distinguish between the imagination and the intellect, especially if this point also is stressed, that matter is everywhere the same, and there are no distinct parts in it except insofar as we conceive matter as modified in various ways. Then its parts are distinct, not really but only modally.[3] For example, we conceive water to

be divisible and to have separate parts insofar as it is water, but not insofar as it is material substance. In this latter respect it is not capable of separation or division. Furthermore, water, qua water, comes into existence and goes out of existence; but qua substance it does not come into existence nor go out of existence [*corrumpitur*].

I consider that in the above I have also replied to the second argument, since this too is based on the supposition that matter, insofar as it is substance, is divisible and made up of parts. And even though this were not so, I do not know why matter should be unworthy of the divine nature, since (Pr. 14) there can be no substance external to God by which it can be acted upon. All things, I repeat, are in God, and all things that come to pass do so only through the laws of God's infinite nature and follow through the necessity of his essence (as I shall later show). Therefore, by no manner of reasoning can it be said that God is acted upon by anything else or that extended substance is unworthy of the divine nature, even though it be supposed divisible, as long as it is granted to be eternal and infinite.

But enough of this subject for the present.

## Proposition 16. *From the necessity of the divine nature there must follow infinite things in infinite ways [modis], (that is, everything that can come within the scope of infinite intellect).*

2. If this refers to anything in Spinoza's extant works, it must be to his early *Descartes' Principles of Philosophy*, II, 2–3.

3. In this passage Spinoza makes use of a distinction that was frequently employed by philosophers in the Middle Ages and

by Descartes as well. Indeed, it is probably the Cartesian version of the distinction that is relevant in this context. According to Descartes, a real distinction obtains between two or more substances or attributes, each one of which being clearly and distinctly conceivable without the other. Because of this clear and distinct conception of each substance, one can exist without the other. For Descartes, the mind can be clearly and distinctly conceived without the body; hence, it can exist without the latter. A modal distinction, however, is a distinction either between a mode and the substance of which it is a mode or between the various modes of a substance. There is, for example, a modal distinction between the movement of a body and the body itself; there is also a modal distinction between one movement and another movement of the same body—Descartes, *Principles of Philosophy*, I, 60–61.

Proof: This proposition should be obvious to everyone who will but consider this point, that from the given definition of any one thing the intellect infers a number of properties which necessarily follow in fact from the definition (that is, from the very essence of the thing), and the more reality the definition of the thing expresses (that is, the more reality the essence of the thing defined involves), the greater the number of its properties. Now since divine nature possesses absolutely infinite attributes (Def. 6), of which each one also expresses infinite essence in its own kind, then there must necessarily follow from the necessity of the divine nature an infinity of things in infinite ways (that is, everything that can come within the scope of the infinite intellect).

Corollary 1: Hence it follows that God is the efficient cause of all things that can come within the scope of the infinite intellect.

Corollary 2: Secondly, it follows that God is the cause through himself, not however *per accidens*.

Corollary 3: Thirdly, it follows that God is absolutely the first cause.

## Proposition 17. *God acts solely from the laws of his own nature, constrained by none.*

Proof: We have just shown that an infinity of things follow, absolutely, solely from the necessity of divine nature, or—which is the same thing—solely from the laws of that same nature (Pr. 16); and we have proved (Pr. 15) that nothing can be or be conceived without God, but that everything is in God. Therefore there can be nothing external to God by which he can be determined or constrained to act. Thus God acts solely from the laws of his own nature and is constrained by none.

Corollary 1: Hence it follows, firstly, that there is no cause, except the perfection of his nature, which either extrinsically or intrinsically moves God to act.

Corollary 2: It follows, secondly, that God alone is a free cause. For God alone exists solely from the necessity of his own nature (Pr. 11 and Cor. 1 Pr. 14) and acts solely from the necessity of his own nature (Pr. 17). So he alone is a free cause (Def. 7).

Scholium: Others take the view that God is a free cause because—so they think—he can bring it about

that those things which we have said follow from his nature—that is, which are within his power—should not come about; that is, they should not be produced by him. But this is as much as to say that God can bring it about that it should not follow from the nature of a triangle that its three angles are equal to two right angles, or that from a given cause the effect should not follow, which is absurd.

Furthermore, I shall show later on without the help of this proposition that neither intellect nor will pertain to the nature of God. I know indeed that there are many who think they can prove that intellect in the highest degree and free will belong to the nature of God; for they say they know of nothing more perfect which they may attribute to God than that which is the highest perfection in us. Again, although they conceive of God as having in actuality intellect in the highest degree, they yet do not believe he can bring about the existence of everything which in actuality he understands, for they think they would thereby be nullifying God's power. If, they say, he had created everything that is within his intellect, then he would not have been able to create anything more; and this they regard as inconsistent with God's omnipotence. So they have preferred to regard God as indifferent to everything and as creating nothing but what he has decided, by some absolute exercise of will, to create. However, I think I have shown quite clearly (Pr. 16) that from God's supreme power or infinite nature an infinity of things in infinite ways—that is, everything—has necessarily flowed or is always following from that same necessity, just as from the nature of a triangle it follows from eternity to eternity that its three angles are equal to two right angles. Therefore, God's omnipotence has from eternity been actual and will remain for eternity in the same actuality. In this way, I submit, God's omnipotence is established as being far more perfect. Indeed my opponents—let us speak frankly—seem to be denying God's omnipotence. For they are obliged to admit that God understands an infinite number of creatable things which nevertheless he can never create. If this were not so, that is, if he were to create all the things that he understands, he would exhaust his omnipotence, according to them, and render himself imperfect. Thus, to affirm God as perfect they are reduced to having to affirm at the same time that he cannot bring about everything that is within the bounds of his power. I cannot imagine anything more absurd than this, or more inconsistent with God's omnipotence.

Furthermore, I have something here to say about the intellect and will that is usually attributed to God. If intellect and will do indeed pertain to the eternal essence of God, one must understand in the case of both these attributes something very different from the meaning widely entertained. For the intellect and will that would constitute the essence of God would have to be vastly different from human intellect and will, and would have no point of agreement except the name. They could be no more alike than the celestial constellation of the Dog and the dog that barks. This I will prove as follows. If intellect does pertain to the divine nature, it cannot, like man's intellect, be posterior to (as most thinkers hold) or simultaneous with the objects of understanding, since God is prior in causality to all things (Cor. 1 Pr. 16). On the contrary, the truth and formal essence of things is what it is because it exists as such in the intellect of God as an object of thought. Therefore, God's intellect, insofar as it is conceived as constituting God's essence, is in actual fact the cause of things, in respect both of their essence and their existence. This seems to have been recognized also by those who have asserted that God's intellect, will, and power are one and the same. Since therefore God's intellect is the one and only cause of things, both of their essence and their existence, as we have shown, it must necessarily be different from them both in respect of essence and existence. For that which is caused differs from its cause precisely in what it has from its cause. For example, a man is the cause of the existence of another man, but not of the other's essence; for the essence is an eternal truth. So with regard to their essence the two men can be in full agreement, but they must differ with regard to existence; and for that reason if the existence of the one should cease, the existence of the other would not thereby cease. But if the essence of the one could be destroyed and rendered false, so too would the essence of the other. Therefore, a thing which is the

cause of the essence and existence of some effect must differ from that effect both in respect of essence and existence. But God's intellect is the cause of the essence and existence of man's intellect. Therefore, God's intellect, insofar as it is conceived as constituting the divine essence, differs from man's intellect both in respect of essence and existence, and cannot agree with it in any respect other than name—which is what I sought to prove. In the matter of will, the proof is the same, as anyone can readily see.

## Proposition 18. *God is the immanent, not the transitive, cause of all things.*

Proof: All things that are, are in God, and must be conceived through God (Pr. 15), and so (Cor. 1 Pr. 16) God is the cause of the things that are in him, which is the first point. Further, there can be no substance external to God (Pr. 14); that is (Def. 3), a thing which is in itself external to God—which is the second point. Therefore, God is the immanent, not the transitive, cause of all things.

## Proposition 19. *God [is eternal], that is, all the attributes of God are eternal.*

Proof: God is substance (Def. 6) which necessarily exists (Pr. 11); that is, (Pr. 7) a thing to whose nature it pertains to exist, or—and this is the same thing—a thing from whose definition existence follows; and so (Def. 8) God is eternal. Further, by the attributes of God must be understood that which expresses the essence of the Divine substance (Def. 4), that is, that which pertains to substance. It is this, I say, which the attributes themselves must involve. But eternity pertains to the nature of substance (as I have shown in Pr. 7). Therefore, each of the attributes must involve eternity, and so they are all eternal.

Scholium: This proposition is also perfectly clear from the manner in which I proved the existence of God (Pr. 11). From this proof, I repeat, it is obvious that God's existence is, like his essence, an eternal truth. Again, I have also proved God's eternity in another way in Proposition 19 of my *Descartes' Principles of the Philosophy*, and there is no need here to go over that ground again.

## Proposition 20. *God's existence and his essence are one and the same.*

Proof: God and all his attributes are eternal (Pr. 19); that is, each one of his attributes expresses existence (Def. 8). Therefore, the same attributes of God that explicate his eternal essence (Def. 4) at the same time explicate his eternal existence; that is, that which constitutes the essence of God at the same time constitutes his existence, and so his existence and his essence are one and the same.

Corollary 1: From this it follows, firstly, that God's existence, like his essence, is an eternal truth.

Corollary 2: It follows, secondly, that God is immutable; that is, all the attributes of God are immutable. For if they were to change in respect of existence, they would also have to change in respect of essence (Pr. 10); that is—and this is self-evident—they would have to become false instead of true, which is absurd.

## Proposition 21. *All things that follow from the absolute nature of any attribute of God must have existed always, and as infinite; that is, through the said attribute they are eternal and infinite.*

Proof: Suppose this proposition be denied and conceive, if you can, that something in some attribute of God, following from its absolute nature, is finite and has a determinate existence or duration; for example, the idea of God in Thought.[4] Now Thought, being assumed to be an attribute of God, is necessarily infinite by its own nature (Pr. 11). However, insofar as it has the idea of God, it is being supposed as finite. Now (Def. 2) it cannot be conceived as finite unless it is determined through Thought

itself. But it cannot be determined through Thought itself insofar as Thought constitutes the idea of God, for it is in that respect that Thought is supposed to be finite. Therefore, it is determined through Thought insofar as Thought does not constitute the idea of God, which Thought must nevertheless necessarily exist (Pr. 11). Therefore, there must be Thought which does not constitute the idea of God, and so the idea of God does not follow necessarily from its nature insofar as it is absolute Thought. (For it is conceived as constituting and as not constituting the idea of God.) This is contrary to our hypothesis. Therefore, if the idea of God in Thought, or anything in some attribute of God (it does not matter what is selected, since the proof is universal), follows from the necessity of the absolute nature of the attribute, it must necessarily be infinite. That was our first point.

Furthermore, that which thus follows from the necessity of the nature of some attribute cannot have a determinate existence, or duration. If this be denied, suppose that there is in some attribute of God a thing following from the necessity of the nature of the attribute, for example, the idea of God in Thought, and suppose that this thing either did not exist at some time, or will cease to exist in the future. Now since Thought is assumed as an attribute of God, it must necessarily exist, and as immutable (Pr. 11 and Cor. 2 Pr. 20). Therefore, outside the bounds of the duration of the idea of God (for this idea is supposed at some time not to have existed, or will at some point cease to exist) Thought will have to exist without the idea of God. But this is contrary to the hypothesis, for it is supposed that when Thought is granted the idea of God necessarily follows. Therefore, the idea of God in Thought, or anything that necessarily follows from the absolute nature of some attribute of God, cannot have a determinate existence, but is eternal through that same attribute. That was our second point. Note that the same holds for anything in an attribute of God which necessarily follows from the absolute nature of God.

## Proposition 22. *Whatever follows from some attribute of God, insofar as the attribute is modified by a modification that*

---

4. The term "idea of God" [*idea Dei*] is one of the more difficult phrases in Spinoza's philosophical vocabulary, and it has occasioned a variety of interpretations among Spinoza's commentators. One point is agreed upon by all: The term *does not* in this context signify a concept of God that any human may have, e.g., the Jewish-Muslim concept of God as distinct from the Christian concept. Rather, the "idea of God" represents an idea that *God* has, in particular the idea that God has of himself, or of his essence (cf. Pr. 4, II).

*exists necessarily and as infinite through that same attribute, must also exist both necessarily and as infinite.*

Proof: This proposition is proved in the same way as the preceding one.

## Proposition 23. *Every mode which exists necessarily and as infinite must have necessarily followed either from the absolute nature of some attribute of God or from some attribute modified by a modification which exists necessarily and as infinite.*

Proof: A mode is in something else through which it must be conceived (Def. 5); that is (Pr. 15), it is in God alone and can be conceived only through God. Therefore, if a mode is conceived to exist necessarily and to be infinite, both these characteristics must necessarily be inferred or perceived through some attribute of God insofar as that attribute is conceived to express infinity and necessity of existence, or (and by Def. 8 this is the same) eternity; that is (Def. 6 and Pr. 19), insofar as it is considered absolutely. Therefore, a mode which exists necessarily and as infinite must have followed from the absolute nature of some attribute of God, either directly (Pr. 21) or through the mediation of some modification which follows from the absolute nature of the attribute; that is (Pr. 22), which exists necessarily and as infinite.

## Proposition 24. *The essence of things produced by God does not involve existence.*

Proof: This is evident from Def. 1. For only that whose nature (considered in itself) involves existence is self-caused and exists solely from the necessity of its own nature.

Corollary: Hence it follows that God is the cause not only of the coming into existence of things but also of their continuing in existence, or, to use a scholastic term, God is the cause of the being of things [*essendi rerum*]. For whether things exist or do not exist, in reflecting on their essence we realize that this essence involves neither existence nor duration. So it is not their essence which can be the cause of either their existence or their duration, but only God, to whose nature alone existence pertains (Cor. 1 Pr. 14).

## Proposition 25. *God is the efficient cause not only of the existence of things but also of their essence.*

Proof: If this is denied, then God is not the cause of the essence of things, and so (Ax. 4) the essence of things can be conceived without God. But this is absurd (Pr. 15). Therefore, God is also the cause of the essence of things.

Scholium: This proposition follows more clearly from Pr. 16; for from that proposition it follows that from the given divine nature both the essence and the existence of things must be inferred. In a word, in the same sense that God is said to be self-caused he must also be said to be the cause of all things. This will be even clearer from the following Corollary.

Corollary: Particular things are nothing but affections of the attributes of God, that is, modes wherein the attributes of God find expression in a definite and determinate way. The proof is obvious from Pr. 15 and Def. 5.

## Proposition 26. *A thing which has been determined to act in a particular way has necessarily been so determined by God; and a thing which has not been determined by God cannot determine itself to act.*

Proof: That by which things are said to be determined to act in a particular way must necessarily be something positive (as is obvious). So God, from the necessity of his nature, is the efficient cause both of its essence and its existence (Prs. 25 and 16)—which was the first point. From this the second point quite clearly follows as well. For if a thing which has not been determined by God could determine itself, the first part of this proposition would be false, which, as I have shown, is absurd.

Proposition 27. A *thing which has been determined by God to act in a particular way cannot render itself undetermined.*

Proof: This proposition is evident from Axiom 3.

Proposition 28. *Every individual thing, i.e., anything whatever which is finite and has a determinate existence, cannot exist or be determined to act unless it be determined to exist and to act by another cause which is also finite and has a determinate existence, and this cause again cannot exist or be determined to act unless it be determined to exist and to act by another cause which is also finite and has a determinate existence, and so* ad infinitum.

Proof: Whatever is determined to exist and to act has been so determined by God (Pr. 26 and Cor. Pr. 24). But that which is finite and has a determinate existence cannot have been produced by the absolute nature of one of God's attributes, for whatever follows from the absolute nature of one of God's attributes is infinite and eternal (Pr. 21). It must therefore have followed from God or one of his attributes insofar as that is considered as affected by some mode; for nothing exists but substance and its modes (Ax. 1 and Defs. 3 and 5), and modes (Cor. Pr. 25) are nothing but affections of God's attributes. But neither could a finite and determined thing have followed from God or one of his attributes insofar as that is affected by a modification which is eternal and infinite (Pr. 22). Therefore, it must have followed, or been determined to exist and to act, by God or one of his attributes insofar as it was modified by a modification which is finite and has a determinate existence. That was the first point. Then again this cause or this mode (the reasoning is the same as in the first part of this proof) must also have been determined by another cause, which is also finite and has a determinate existence, and again this last (the reasoning is the same) by another, and so *ad infinitum*.

Scholium: Since some things must have been produced directly by God (those things, in fact, which necessarily follow from his absolute nature) and others through the medium of these primary things (which other things nevertheless cannot be or be conceived without God), it follows, firstly, that God is absolutely the proximate cause of things directly produced by him. I say "absolutely" [*absolute*], and not "within their own kind" [*suo genere*], as some say. For the effects of God can neither be nor be conceived without their cause (Pr. 15 and Cor. Pr. 24). It follows, secondly, that God cannot properly be said to be the remote cause of individual things, unless perchance for the purpose of distinguishing these things from things which he has produced directly, or rather, things which follow from his absolute nature. For by "remote cause" we understand a cause which is in no way conjoined with its effect. But all things that are, are in God, and depend on God in such a way that they can neither be nor be conceived without him.

Proposition 29. *Nothing in nature is contingent, but all things are from the necessity of the divine nature determined to exist and to act in a definite way.*

Proof: Whatever is, is in God (Pr. 15). But God cannot be termed a contingent thing, for (Pr. 11) he exists necessarily, not contingently. Again, the modes of the divine nature have also followed from it necessarily, not contingently (Pr. 16), and that, too, whether insofar as the divine nature is considered absolutely (Pr. 21) or insofar as it is considered as determined to act in a definite way (Pr. 27). Furthermore, God is the cause of these modes not only insofar as they simply exist (Cor. Pr. 26), but also insofar as they are considered as determined to a particular action (Pr. 26). Now if they are not determined by God (Pr. 26), it is an impossibility, not a contingency, that they should determine themselves. On the other hand (Pr. 27), if they are determined by God, it is an impossibility, not a contingency, that they should render themselves undetermined. Therefore, all things are determined from the necessity of the divine nature not only to exist but also to exist and to act in a definite way. Thus, there is no contingency.

Scholium: Before I go any further, I wish to explain at this point what we must understand by "Natura naturans" and "Natura naturata." I should perhaps say not "explain," but "remind the reader," for I consider that it is already clear from what has gone before that by "Natura naturans" we must understand that which is in itself and is conceived through itself; that is, the attributes of substance that express eternal and infinite essence; or (Cor. 1 Pr. 14 and Cor. 2 Pr. 17), God insofar as he is considered a free cause. By "Natura naturata" I understand all that follows from the necessity of God's nature, that is, from the necessity of each one of God's attributes; or all the modes of God's attributes insofar as they are considered as things which are in God and can neither be nor be conceived without God.

## Proposition 30: *The finite intellect in act or the infinite intellect in act must comprehend the attributes of God and the affections of God, and nothing else.*[5]

Proof: A true idea must agree with its object [*ideatum*] (Ax. 6); that is (as is self-evident), that which is contained in the intellect as an object of thought must necessarily exist in Nature. But in Nature (Cor. 1 Pr. 14) there is but one substance—God—and no other affections (Pr. 15) than those which are in God and that can neither be nor be conceived (Pr.

15) without God. Therefore, the finite intellect in act or the infinite intellect in act must comprehend the attributes of God and the affections of God, and nothing else.

## Proposition 31. *The intellect in act, whether it be finite or infinite, as also will, desire, love, etc., must be related to Natura naturata, not to Natura naturans.*

Proof: By intellect (as is self-evident) we do not understand absolute thought, but only a definite mode of thinking which differs from other modes such as desire, love, etc., and so (Def. 5) must be conceived through absolute thought—that is (Pr. 15 and Def. 6), an attribute of God which expresses the eternal and infinite essence of thought—in such a way that without this attribute it can neither be nor be conceived; and therefore (Sch. Pr. 29) it must be related to Natura naturata, not to Natura naturans, just like the other modes of thinking.

Scholium: The reason for my here speaking of the intellect in act is not that I grant there can be any intellect in potentiality, but that, wishing to avoid any confusion, I want to confine myself to what we perceive with the utmost clarity, to wit, the very act of understanding, than which nothing is more clearly apprehended by us. For we can understand nothing that does not lead to a more perfect cognition of the understanding.

---

5. In Propositions 30 and 31 Spinoza makes use of several terms that were widely employed in medieval psychology and metaphysics. Aristotle originally suggested that human thinking is such that we need to distinguish three phases in its development. First, there is the mere capacity for thinking, say, for doing mathematics. All humans, except those who are unfortunately diseased or mutilated, have this capacity. This kind of intellect was called by the medieval Aristotelians the material, or the potential, intellect [*intellectus in potentia*]. Second, when this capacity is exercised and brought into play, it is called the intellect in act [*intellectus in actu*], since now the intrinsic capacity for thinking possessed by all humans is "actualized." Another expression then for this aspect of intellection is the actual intellect. Finally, the medievals, influenced by Aristotle,

introduced a third character into this story to account for the stimulation, or energizing, of the potential intellect so that it actually thinks, i.e., the agent, or active, intellect [*intellectus agens*]. This latter entity was identified by some philosophers as a suprahuman, supranatural power akin to or identical with God, or by others as a distinct power in the human intellect that acts upon the mere capacity for thought, or the potential intellect. In any case, the agent, or active, intellect is *always actual*, whereas the human intellect is only *actual at times*. As Spinoza himself confesses in the Scholium to Proposition 31, he isn't really committed to this whole way of talking about thought; for he holds that intellect is always in act. If this is so, there is nothing to contrast it with, so this entire conceptual apparatus and its vocabulary become idle.

## Proposition 32. *Will cannot be called a free cause, but only a necessary cause.*

Proof: Will, like intellect, is only a definite mode of thinking, and so (Pr. 28) no single volition can exist or be determined to act unless it is determined by another cause, and this cause again by another, and so *ad infinitum*. Now if will be supposed infinite, it must also be determined to exist and to act by God, not insofar as he is absolutely infinite substance, but insofar as he possesses an attribute which expresses the infinite and eternal essence of Thought (Pr. 23). Therefore, in whatever way will is conceived, whether finite or infinite, it requires a cause by which it is determined to exist and to act; and so (Def. 7) it cannot be said to be a free cause, but only a necessary or constrained cause.

Corollary 1: Hence it follows, firstly, that God does not act from freedom of will.

Corollary 2: It follows, secondly, that will and intellect bear the same relationship to God's nature as motion-and-rest and, absolutely, as all natural phenomena that must be determined by God (Pr. 29) to exist and to act in a definite way. For will, like all the rest, stands in need of a cause by which it may be determined to exist and to act in a definite manner. And although from a given will or intellect infinite things may follow, God cannot on that account be said to act from freedom of will any more than he can be said to act from freedom of motion-and-rest because of what follows from motion-and-rest (for from this, too, infinite things follow). Therefore, will pertains to God's nature no more than do other natural phenomena. It bears the same relationship to God's nature as does motion-and-rest and everything else that we have shown to follow from the necessity of the divine nature and to be determined by that divine nature to exist and to act in a definite way.

## Proposition 33. *Things could not have been produced by God in any other way or in any other order than is the case.*

Proof: All things have necessarily followed from the nature of God (Pr. 16) and have been determined to exist and to act in a definite way from the necessity of God's nature (Pr. 29). Therefore, if things could have been of a different nature or been determined to act in a different way so that the order of Nature would have been different, then God's nature, too, could have been other than it now is, and therefore (Pr. 11) this different nature, too, would have had to exist, and consequently there would have been two or more Gods, which (Cor. 1 Pr. 14) is absurd. Therefore, things could not have been produced by God in any other way or in any other order than is the case.

Scholium 1: Since I have here shown more clearly than the midday sun that in things there is absolutely nothing by virtue of which they can be said to be "contingent," I now wish to explain briefly what we should understand by "contingent"; but I must first deal with "necessary" and "impossible." A thing is termed "necessary" either by reason of its essence or by reason of its cause. For a thing's existence necessarily follows either from its essence and definition or from a given efficient cause. Again, it is for these same reasons that a thing is termed "impossible"—that is, either because its essence or definition involves a contradiction or because there is no external cause determined to bring it into existence. But a thing is termed "contingent" for no other reason than the deficiency of our knowledge. For if we do not know whether the essence of a thing involves a contradiction, or if, knowing full well that its essence does not involve a contradiction, we still cannot make any certain judgment as to its existence because the chain of causes is hidden from us, then that thing cannot appear to us either as necessary or as impossible. So we term it either "contingent" or "possible."

Scholium 2: It clearly follows from the above that things have been brought into being by God with supreme perfection, since they have necessarily followed from a most perfect nature. Nor does this imply any imperfection in God, for it is his perfection that has constrained us to make this affirmation. Indeed, from its contrary it would clearly follow (as I have just shown) that God is not supremely perfect, because if things had been brought into being in a different way by God, we should have to attribute to God another nature different from that which consideration of a most perfect Being has made us attribute to him.

However, I doubt not that many will ridicule this view as absurd and will not give their minds to its examination, and for this reason alone, that they are in the habit of attributing to God another kind of freedom very different from that which we (Def. 7) have assigned to him, that is, an absolute will. Yet I do not doubt that if they were willing to think the matter over and carefully reflect on our chain of proofs they would in the end reject the kind of freedom which they now attribute to God not only as nonsensical but as a serious obstacle to science. It is needless for me here to repeat what was said in the Scholium to Proposition 17. Yet for their sake I shall proceed to show that, even if it were to be granted that will pertains to the essence of God, it would nevertheless follow from his perfection that things could not have been created by God in any other way or in any other order. This will readily be shown if we first consider—as they themselves grant—that on God's decree and will alone does it depend that each thing is what it is. For otherwise God would not be the cause of all things. Further, there is the fact that all God's decrees have been sanctioned by God from eternity, for otherwise he could be accused of imperfection and inconstancy. But since the eternal does not admit of "when" or "before" or "after," it follows merely from God's perfection that God can never decree otherwise nor ever could have decreed otherwise; in other words, God could not have been prior to his decrees nor can he be without them. "But," they will say, "granted the supposition that God had made a different universe, or that from eternity he had made a different decree concerning Nature and her order, no imperfection in God would follow therefrom." But if they say this, they will be granting at the same time that God can change his decrees. For if God's decrees had been different from what in fact he has decreed regarding Nature and her order—that is, if he had willed and conceived differently concerning Nature—he would necessarily have had a different intellect and a different will from that which he now has. And if it is permissible to attribute to God a different intellect and a different will without any change in his essence

and perfection, why should he not now be able to change his decrees concerning created things, and nevertheless remain equally perfect? For his intellect and will regarding created things and their order have the same relation to his essence and perfection, in whatever manner it be conceived.

Then again, all philosophers whom I have read grant that in God there is no intellect in potentiality but only intellect in act. Now since all of them also grant that his intellect and will are not distinct from his essence, it therefore follows from this, too, that if God had had a different intellect in act and a different will, his essence too would necessarily have been different. Therefore—as I deduced from the beginning—if things had been brought into being by God so as to be different from what they now are, God's intellect and will—that is (as is granted), God's essence—must have been different, which is absurd. Therefore, since things could not have been brought into being by God in any other way or order—and it follows from God's supreme perfection that this is true—surely we can have no sound reason for believing that God did not wish to create all the things that are in his intellect through that very same perfection whereby he understands them.

"But," they will say, "there is in things no perfection or imperfection; that which is in them whereby they are perfect or imperfect, and are called good or bad, depends only on the will of God. Accordingly, if God had so willed it he could have brought it about that that which is now perfection should be utmost imperfection, and vice versa." But what else is this but an open assertion that God, who necessarily understands that which he wills, can by his will bring it about that he should understand things in a way different from the way he understands them—and this, as I have just shown, is utterly absurd. So I can turn their own argument against them, as follows. All things depend on the power of God. For things to be able to be otherwise than as they are, God's will, too, would necessarily have to be different. But God's will cannot be different (as we have just shown most clearly from the consideration of God's perfection). Therefore, neither can things be different.

I admit that this view which subjects everything to some kind of indifferent will of God and asserts that everything depends on his pleasure diverges less from the truth than the view of those who hold that God does everything with the good in mind. For these people seem to posit something external to God that does not depend upon him, to which in acting God looks as if it were a model, or to which he aims, as if it were a fixed target. This is surely to subject God to fate; and no more absurd assertion can be made about God, whom we have shown to be the first and the only free cause of both the essence and the existence of things. So I need not spend any more time in refuting this absurdity.

## Proposition 34. *God's power is his very essence.*

Proof: From the sole necessity of God's essence it follows that God is self-caused (Pr. 11) and the cause of all things (Pr. 16 and Cor.). Therefore, God's power, whereby he and all things are and act, is his very essence.

## Proposition 35. *Whatever we conceive to be within God's power necessarily exists.*

Proof: Whatever is within God's power must be so comprehended in his essence (Pr. 34) that it follows necessarily from it, and thus necessarily exists.

## Proposition 36. *Nothing exists from whose nature an effect does not follow.*

Proof: Whatever exists expresses God's nature or essence in a definite and determinate way (Cor. Pr. 25); that is (Pr. 34), whatever exists expresses God's power, which is the cause of all things, in a definite and determinate way, and so (Pr. 16) some effect must follow from it.

## Appendix

I have now explained the nature and properties of God: that he necessarily exists, that he is one alone, that he is and acts solely from the necessity of his own nature, that he is the free cause of all things and how so, that all things are in God and are so dependent on him that they can neither be nor be conceived without him, and lastly, that all things have been predetermined by God, not from his free will or absolute pleasure, but from the absolute nature of God, his infinite power. Furthermore, whenever the opportunity arose I have striven to remove prejudices that might hinder the apprehension of my proofs. But since there still remain a considerable number of prejudices, which have been, and still are, an obstacle—indeed, a very great obstacle—to the acceptance of the concatenation of things in the manner which I have expounded, I have thought it proper at this point to bring these prejudices before the bar of reason.

Now all the prejudices which I intend to mention here turn on this one point, the widespread belief among men that all things in Nature are like themselves in acting with an end in view. Indeed, they hold it as certain that God himself directs everything to a fixed end; for they say that God has made everything for man's sake and has made man so that he should worship God. So this is the first point I shall consider, seeking the reason why most people are victims of this prejudice and why all are so naturally disposed to accept it. Secondly, I shall demonstrate its falsity; and lastly I shall show how it has been the source of misconceptions about good and bad, right and wrong, praise and blame, order and confusion, beauty and ugliness, and the like.

However, it is not appropriate here to demonstrate the origin of these misconceptions from the nature of the human mind. It will suffice at this point if I take as my basis what must be universally admitted, that all men are born ignorant of the causes of things, that they all have a desire to seek their own advantage, a desire of which they are conscious. From this it follows, firstly, that men believe that they are free, precisely because they are conscious of their volitions and desires; yet concerning the causes that have determined them to desire and will they do not think, not even dream about, because they are ignorant of them. Secondly, men act always with an end in view, to wit, the advantage that they seek. Hence it happens that they are always looking only for the final causes of things done, and are satisfied when they find them, having, of course, no reason for further doubt. But if they fail to discover them from some external source, they have no recourse but to turn to themselves, and to reflect on what ends would normally determine them to similar actions, and so they necessarily judge other minds by their own. Further, since they find within themselves and outside themselves a considerable number of means very convenient for the pursuit of their own advantage—as, for instance, eyes for seeing, teeth for chewing, cereals and living creatures for food, the sun for giving light, the sea for breeding fish—the result is that they look on all the things of Nature as means to their own advantage. And realizing that these were found, not produced by them, they come to believe that there is someone else who produced these means for their use. For looking on things as means, they could not believe them to be self-created, but on the analogy of the means which they are accustomed to produce for themselves, they were bound to conclude that there was some governor or governors of Nature, endowed with human freedom, who have attended to all their needs and made everything for their use. And having no information on the subject, they also had to estimate the character of these rulers by their own, and so they asserted that the gods direct everything for man's use so that they may bind men to them and be held in the highest honor by them. So it came about that every individual devised different methods of worshipping God as he thought fit in order that God should love him beyond others and direct the whole of Nature so as to serve his blind cupidity and insatiable greed. Thus it was that this misconception developed into superstition and became deep-rooted in the minds of men, and it was for this reason that every man strove most earnestly to understand and to explain the final causes of all things. But in seeking to show that Nature does nothing in vain—that is, nothing that is not to man's advantage— they seem to have shown only this, that Nature and the gods are as crazy as mankind.

Consider, I pray, what has been the upshot. Among so many of Nature's blessings they were bound to discover quite a number of disasters, such as storms, earthquakes, diseases and so forth, and they maintained that these occurred because the gods were angry at the wrongs done to them by men, or the faults committed in the course of their worship. And although daily experience cried out against this and showed by any number of examples that blessings and disasters befall the godly and the ungodly alike without discrimination, they did not on that account abandon their ingrained prejudice. For they found it easier to regard this fact as one among other mysteries they could not understand and thus maintain their innate condition of ignorance rather than to demolish in its entirety the theory they had constructed and devise a new one. Hence they made it axiomatic that the judgment of the gods is far beyond man's understanding. Indeed, it is for this reason, and this reason only, that truth might have evaded mankind forever had not Mathematics, which is concerned not with ends but only with the essences and properties of figures, revealed to men a different standard of truth. And there are other causes too—there is no need to mention them here—which could have made men aware of these widespread misconceptions and brought them to a true knowledge of things.

I have thus sufficiently dealt with my first point. There is no need to spend time in going on to show that Nature has no fixed goal and that all final causes are but figments of the human imagination. For I think that this is now quite evident, both from the basic causes from which I have traced the origin of this misconception and from Proposition 16 and the Corollaries to Proposition 32, and in addition from the whole set or proofs I have adduced to show that all things in Nature proceed from all eternal necessity and with supreme perfection. But I will make this additional point, that this doctrine of Final Causes turns Nature completely upside down, for it regards as an effect that which is in fact a cause, and vice versa. Again, it makes that which is by nature first to be last; and finally, that which is highest and most perfect is held to be the most imperfect. Omitting the first two points as self-evident, Propositions 21, 22, and 23 make it clear that that effect is most perfect which is directly produced by God, and an effect is the less perfect in proportion to the number of intermediary causes required for its production. But if the things produced directly by God were brought about to enable him to attain an end, then of necessity the last things for the sake of which the earlier things were brought about would excel all others. Again, this doctrine negates God's perfection; for if God acts with an end in view, he must necessarily be seeking something that he lacks. And although theologians and metaphysicians may draw a distinction between a purpose arising from want and an assimilative purpose,[6] they still admit that God has acted in all things for the sake of himself, and not for the sake of the things to be created. For prior to creation they are not able to point to anything but God as a purpose for God's action. Thus they have to admit that God lacked and desired those things for the procurement of which he willed to create the means—as is self-evident.

I must not fail to mention here that the advocates of this doctrine, eager to display their talent in assigning purpose to things, have introduced a new style of argument to prove their doctrine, i.e., a reduction, not to the impossible, but to ignorance, thus revealing the lack of any other argument in its favor. For example, if a stone falls from the roof on somebody's head and kills him, by this method of arguing they will prove that the stone fell in order to kill the man; for if it had not fallen for this purpose by the will of God, how could so many circumstances (and there are often many coinciding circumstances) have chanced to concur? Perhaps you will reply that the event occurred because the wind was blowing and

the man was walking that way. But they will persist in asking why the wind blew at that time and why the man was walking that way at that very time. If you again reply that the wind sprang up at that time because on the previous day the sea had begun to toss after a period of calm and that the man had been invited by a friend, they will again persist—for there is no end to questions—"But why did the sea toss, and why was the man invited for that time?" And so they will go on and on asking the causes of causes, until you take refuge in the will of God—that is, the sanctuary of ignorance. Similarly, when they consider the structure of the human body, they are astonished, and being ignorant of the causes of such skillful work they conclude that it is fashioned not by mechanical art but by divine or supernatural art, and is so arranged that no one part shall injure another.

As a result, he who seeks the true causes of miracles and is eager to understand the works of Nature as a scholar, and not just to gape at them like a fool, is universally considered an impious heretic and denounced by those to whom the common people bow down as interpreters of Nature and the gods. For these people know that the dispelling of ignorance would entail the disappearance of that astonishment, which is the one and only support for their argument and for safeguarding their authority. But I will leave this subject and proceed to the third point that I proposed to deal with.

When men become convinced that everything that is created is created on their behalf, they were bound to consider as the most important quality in every individual thing that which was most useful to them, and to regard as of the highest excellence all those things by which they were most benefited. Hence they came to form these abstract notions to explain the natures of things: Good, Bad, Order, Confusion, Hot, Cold, Beauty, Ugliness; and since they believed that they are free, the following abstract notions came into being: Praise, Blame, Right, Wrong. The latter I shall deal with later on after I have treated of human nature; at this point I shall briefly explain the former.

All that conduces to well being and to the worship of God they call Good, and the contrary, Bad.

---

6. Spinoza alludes here to a late scholastic distinction between two kinds of purposes, or goals: a purpose that satisfies some internal need or lack [*fines indigentiae*]; and a purpose that aims to share what one already has with others who lack it [*fines assimilationis*]. In the present case, this distinction implies that when God does something purposively, he acts not to fulfill a need he has, but to benefit creatures. In their commentaries on the *Ethics* both Lewis Robinson and Harry Wolfson refer to the 17th-century Dutch theologian A. Heereboord as Spinoza's source for this distinction (L. Robinson, *Kommentar zu Spinoza's Ethik* [Leipzig, 1928], pp. 234–35. H. Wolfson, *The Philosophy of Spinoza* [New York, 1969], vol. 1, p. 432). The theologians derided by Spinoza hoped to avoid by means of this distinction the suggestion that if God acts purposively, he does so because of a need on his part.

And since those who do not understand the nature of things, but only imagine things, make no affirmative judgments about things themselves and mistake their imagination for intellect,[7] they are firmly convinced that there is order in things, ignorant as they are of things and of their own nature. For when things are in such arrangement that, being presented to us through our senses, we can readily picture them and thus readily remember them, we say that they are well arranged; if the contrary, we say that they are ill arranged, or confused. And since those things we can readily picture we find pleasing compared with other things, men prefer order to confusion, as though order were something in Nature other than what is relative to our imagination. And they say that God has created all things in an orderly way, without realizing that they are thus attributing human imagination to God—unless perchance they mean that God, out of consideration for the human imagination, arranged all things in the way that men could most easily imagine. And perhaps they will find no obstacle in the fact that there are any number of things that far surpass our imagination, and a considerable number that confuse the imagination because of its weakness.

But I have devoted enough time to this. Other notions, too, are nothing but modes of imagining whereby the imagination is affected in various ways, and yet the ignorant consider them as important attributes of things because they believe—as I have

said—that all things were made on their behalf, and they call a thing's nature good or bad, healthy or rotten and corrupt, according to its effect on them. For instance, if the motion communicated to our nervous system by objects presented through our eyes is conducive to our feeling of well being, the objects which are its cause are said to be beautiful, while the objects which provoke a contrary motion are called ugly. Those things that we sense through the nose are called fragrant or fetid; through the tongue, sweet or bitter, tasty or tasteless; those that we sense by touch are called hard or soft, rough or smooth, and so on. Finally, those that we sense through our ears are said to give forth noise, sound, or harmony, the last of which has driven men to such madness that they used to believe that even God delights in harmony. There are philosophers who have convinced themselves that the motions of the heavens give rise to harmony. All this goes to show that everyone's judgment is a function of the disposition of his brain, or rather, that he mistakes for reality the way his imagination is affected. Hence it is no wonder—as we should note in passing—that we find so many controversies arising among men, resulting finally in skepticism. For although human bodies agree in many respects, there are very many differences, and so one man thinks good what another thinks bad; what to one man is well ordered, to another is confused; what to one is pleasing, to another is displeasing, and so forth. I say no more here because this is not the place to treat at length of this subject, and also because all are well acquainted with it from experience. Everybody knows those sayings: "So many heads, so many opinions," "everyone is wise in his own sight," "brains differ as much as palates," all of which show clearly that men's judgment is a function of the disposition of the brain, and they are guided by imagination rather than intellect. For if men understood things, all that I have put forward would be found, if not attractive, at any rate convincing, as Mathematics attests.

We see therefore that all the notions whereby the common people are wont to explain Nature are merely modes of imagining, and denote not the nature of any thing but only the constitution of the imagination. And because these notions have names

---

7. One of the more fundamental doctrines in Spinoza's theory of knowledge is the radical distinction between imagination and understanding, a point that will be developed in detail in Part II, Propositions 40–49. A corollary of this distinction is the important difference for Spinoza between images and ideas. The former are virtually identical with pictures, which the etymology of the word "imagine" indicates. The capacity of imagination, or better the act of imagining, is for Spinoza the ability we have to represent to ourselves things, which may or may not exist, without regard to truth. In this sense the imagination is always "free" and "spontaneous": reality doesn't tie it down. Understanding, or intellect, however, is not so "fancy free." It is concerned with reality and truth. Ideas, for Spinoza, are the products of the intellect, or understanding: They are not pictures of things but judgments about them, and hence are true or false (Part II, Proposition 43, Scholium).

as if they were the names of entities existing independently of the imagination I call them "entities of imagination" [*entia imaginationis*] rather than "entities of reason" [*entia rationis*]. So all arguments drawn from such notions against me can be easily refuted. For many are wont to argue on the following lines: If everything has followed from the necessity of God's most perfect nature, why does Nature display so many imperfections, such as rottenness to the point of putridity, nauseating ugliness, confusion, evil, sin, and so on? But, as I have just pointed out, they are easily refuted. For the perfection of things should be measured solely from their own nature and power; nor are things more or less perfect to the extent that they please or offend human senses, serve or oppose human interests. As to those who ask why God did not create men in such a way that they should be governed solely by reason, I make only this reply, that he lacked not material for creating all things from the highest to the lowest degree of perfection; or, to speak more accurately, the laws of his nature were so comprehensive as to suffice for the production of everything that can be conceived by an infinite intellect, as I proved in Proposition 16.

These are the misconceptions which I undertook to deal with at this point. Any other misconception of this kind can be corrected by everyone with a little reflection.

## Part II. Of the Nature and Origin of the Mind

I now pass on to the explication of those things that must necessarily have followed from the essence of God, the eternal and infinite Being; not indeed all of them—for we proved in Proposition 16, Part I that from his essence there must follow infinite things in infinite ways—but only those things that can lead us as it were by the hand to the knowledge of the human mind and its utmost blessedness.

### Definitions

1. By "body" I understand a mode that expresses in a definite and determinate way God's essence insofar

as he is considered as an extended thing. (See Cor. Pr. 25, I.)
2. I say that there pertains to the essence of a thing that which, when granted, the thing is necessarily posited, and by the annulling of which the thing is necessarily annulled; or that without which the thing can neither be nor be conceived, and, vice versa, that which cannot be or be conceived without the thing.
3. By idea I understand a conception of the Mind which the Mind forms because it is a thinking thing.

*Explication*: I say "conception" rather than "perception" because the term perception seems to indicate that the Mind is passive to its object whereas conception seems to express an activity of the Mind.
4. By an adequate idea I mean an idea which, insofar as it is considered in itself without relation to its object, has all the properties, that is, intrinsic characteristics, of a true idea [*ideatum*].

*Explication*: I say "intrinsic" so as to exclude the extrinsic characteristic—to wit the agreement of the idea with that of which it is an idea.
5. Duration is the indefinite continuance of existing.

*Explication*: I say "indefinite" because it can in no wise be determined through the nature of the existing thing, nor again by the thing's efficient cause which necessarily posits, but does not annul, the existence of the thing
6. By reality and perfection I mean the same thing.
7. By individual things [*res singulares*] I mean things that are finite and have a determinate existence. If several individual things concur in one act in such a way as to be all together the simultaneous cause of one effect, I consider them all, in that respect, as one individual.

### Axioms

1. The essence of man does not involve necessary existence; that is, from the order of Nature it is equally possible that a certain man exists or does not exist.
2. Man thinks.
3. Modes of thinking such as love, desire, or whatever emotions are designated by name, do not occur unless there is in the same individual the idea of the

thing loved, desired, etc. But the idea can be without any other mode of thinking.

4. We feel a certain body to be affected in many ways.

5. We do not feel or perceive any individual things except bodies and modes of thinking. [N.B.: For Postulates, see after Proposition 13.]

## Proposition 1. *Thought is an attribute of God; i.e., God is a thinking thing.*

Proof: Individual thoughts, or this and that thought, are modes expressing the nature of God in a definite and determinate way (Cor. Pr. 25, I). Therefore, there belongs to God (Def. 5, I) an attribute the conception of which is involved in all individual thoughts, and through which they are conceived. Thought, therefore, is one of God's infinite attributes, expressing the eternal and infinite essence of God (Def. 6, I); that is, God is a thinking thing.

Scholium: This Proposition is also evident from the fact that we can conceive of an infinite thinking being. For the more things a thinking being can think, the more reality or perfection we conceive it to have. Therefore, a being that can think infinite things in infinite ways is by virtue of its thinking necessarily infinite. Since therefore by merely considering Thought we conceive an infinite being, Thought is necessarily one of the infinite attributes of God (Defs. 4 and 6, I), as we set out to prove.

## Proposition 2. *Extension is an attribute of God; i.e., God is an extended thing.*

Proof: This Proposition is proved in the same way as the preceding proposition.

## Proposition 3. *In God there is necessarily the idea both of his essence and of everything that necessarily follows from his essence.*

Proof: For God can (Pr. 1, II) think infinite things in infinite ways, or (what is the same thing, by Pr. 16, I) can form the idea of his own essence and of everything that necessarily follows from it. But all

that is in God's power necessarily exists (Pr. 35, I). Therefore, such an idea necessarily exists, and only in God (Pr. 15, I).

Scholium: By God's power the common people understand free will and God's right over all things that are, which things are therefore commonly considered as contingent. They say that God has power to destroy everything and bring it to nothing. Furthermore, they frequently compare God's power with that of kings. But this doctrine we have refuted in Cors. 1 and 2, Pr. 32, I; and in Pr. 16, I, we proved that God acts by the same necessity whereby he understands himself; that is, just as it follows from the necessity of the divine Nature (as is universally agreed) that God understands himself, by that same necessity it also follows that God acts infinitely in infinite ways. Again, we showed in Pr. 34, I that God's power is nothing but God's essence in action, and so it is as impossible for us to conceive that God does not act as that God does not exist. Furthermore if one wished to pursue the matter, I could easily show here that the power that common people assign to God is not only a human power (which shows that they conceive God as a man or like a man) but also involves negation of power. But I am reluctant to hold forth so often on the same subject. I merely request the reader most earnestly to reflect again and again on what we said on this subject in Part I from Proposition 16 to the end. For nobody will rightly apprehend what I am trying to say unless he takes great care not to confuse God's power with a king's human power or right.

## Proposition 4. *The idea of God, from which infinite things follow in infinite ways, must be one, and one only.*

Proof: Infinite intellect comprehends nothing but the attributes of God and his affections (Pr. 30, I). But God is one, and one only (Cor. 1, Pr. 14, I). Therefore, the idea of God, from which infinite things follow in infinite ways, must be one, and one only.

## Proposition 5. *The formal being of ideas recognizes God as its cause only insofar as he is considered as a thinking thing, and*

*not insofar as he is explicated by any other attribute; that is, the ideas both of God's attributes and of individual things recognize as their efficient cause not the things of which they are ideas, that is, the things perceived, but God himself insofar as he is a thinking thing.*

Proof: This is evident from Pr. 3, II. For there our conclusion that God can form the idea of his own essence and of everything that necessarily follows therefrom was inferred solely from God's being a thinking thing, and not from his being the object of his own idea. Therefore, the formal being of ideas recognizes God as its cause insofar as he is a thinking thing. But there is another proof, as follows. The formal being of ideas is a mode of thinking (as is self-evident); that is (Cor. Pr. 25, I), a mode which expresses in a definite manner the nature of God insofar as he is a thinking thing, and so does not involve (Pr. 10, I) the conception of any other attribute of God. Consequently (Ax. 4, I), it is the effect of no other attribute but thought; and so the formal being of ideas recognizes God as its cause only insofar as he is considered as a thinking thing.

## Proposition 6. *The modes of any attribute have God for their cause only insofar as he is considered under that attribute, and not insofar as he is considered under any other attribute.*

Proof: Each attribute is conceived through itself independently of any other (Pr. 10, I). Therefore, the modes of any attribute involve the conception of their own attribute, and not that of any other. Therefore, they have God for their cause only insofar as he is considered under the attribute of which they are modes, and not insofar as he is considered under any other attribute (Ax. 4, I).

Corollary: Hence it follows that the formal being of things that are not modes of thinking does not follow from the nature of God by reason of his first having known them; rather, the objects of ideas

follow and are inferred from their own attributes in the same way and by the same necessity as we have shown ideas to follow from the attribute of Thought.

## Proposition 7. *The order and connection of ideas is the same as the order and connection of things.*

Proof: This is evident from Ax. 4, I; for the idea of what is caused depends on the knowledge of the cause of which it is the effect.

Corollary: Hence it follows that God's power of thinking is on par with his power of acting. That is, whatever follows formally from the infinite nature of God, all this follows from the idea of God as an object of thought in God according to the same order and connection.

Scholium: At this point, before proceeding further, we should recall to mind what I have demonstrated above—that whatever can be perceived by infinite intellect as constituting the essence of substance pertains entirely to the one sole substance. Consequently, thinking substance and extended substance are one and the same substance, comprehended now under this attribute, now under that. So, too, a mode of Extension and the idea of that mode are one and the same thing, expressed in two ways. This truth seems to have been glimpsed by some of the Hebrews, who hold that God, God's intellect, and the things understood by God are one and the same. For example, a circle existing in Nature and the idea of the existing circle—which is also in God—are one and the same thing, explicated through different attributes. And so, whether we conceive Nature under the attribute of Extension or under the attribute of Thought or under any other attribute, we find one and the same order, or one and the same connection of causes—that is, the same things following one another. When I said that God is the cause, e.g., of the idea of a circle only insofar as he is a thinking thing, and of a circle only insofar as he is an extended thing, my reason was simply this, that the formal being of the idea of a circle can be perceived only through another mode of thinking as its proximate cause, and that mode through another, and so *ad infinitum,* with the result that as long as things are considered as modes of thought, we must explicate the order of the whole of Nature, or the connection of causes, through the attribute of Thought alone; and insofar as things are considered as modes of Extension, again the order of the whole of Nature must be explicated through the attribute of Extension only. The same applies to other attributes. Therefore God, insofar as he consists of infinite attributes, is in fact the cause of things as they are in themselves. For the present, I cannot give a clearer explanation.

## Proposition 8. *The ideas of nonexisting individual things or modes must be comprehended in the infinite idea of God in the same way as the formal essences of individual things or modes are contained in the attributes of God.*

Proof: This proposition is obvious from the preceding one, but may be understood more clearly from the preceding Scholium.

    Corollary: Hence it follows that as long as individual things do not exist except insofar as they are comprehended in the attributes of God, their being as objects of thought—that is, their ideas—do not exist except insofar as the infinite idea of God exists; and when individual things are said to exist not only insofar as they are comprehended in the attributes of God but also insofar as they are said to have duration, their ideas also will involve the existence through which they are said to have duration.

    Scholium: Should anyone want an example for a clearer understanding of this matter, I can think of none at all that would adequately explicate the point with which I am here dealing, for it has no parallel. Still, I shall try to illustrate it as best I can. The nature of a circle is such that the rectangles formed from the segments of its intersecting chords are equal. Hence an infinite number of equal rectangles are contained in a circle, but none of them can be said to exist except insofar as the circle exists, nor again can the idea of any one of these rectangles be said to exist except insofar as it is comprehended in the idea of the circle. Now of this infinite number of intersecting chords let

two, E and D, exist. Now indeed their ideas also exist not only insofar as they are merely comprehended in the idea of the circle but also insofar as they involve the existence of those rectangles, with the result that they are distinguished from the other ideas of the other rectangles.

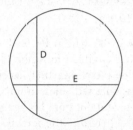

## Proposition 9. *The idea of an individual thing existing in actuality has God for its cause not insofar as he is infinite but insofar as he is considered as affected by another idea of a thing existing in actuality, of which God is the cause insofar as he is affected by a third idea, and so* ad infinitum.

Proof: The idea of an individual actually existing thing is an individual mode of thinking distinct from other modes (Cor. and Sch. Pr. 8, II), and so (Pr. 6, II) it has God as its cause only insofar as he is a thinking thing. But not (Pr. 28, I) insofar as he is a thinking thing absolutely, but insofar as he is considered as affected by another definite mode of thinking. And of this latter God is also the cause insofar as he is affected by another definite mode of thinking, and so *ad infinitum*. But the order and connection of ideas is the same as the order and connection of causes (Pr. 7, II). Therefore, an individual idea is caused by another idea; i.e., God insofar as he is considered as affected by another idea. And this last idea is caused by God, insofar as he is affected by yet another idea, and so *ad infinitum*.

    Corollary: Whatsoever happens in the individual object of any idea, knowledge of it is in God only insofar as he has the idea of that object.

    Proof: Whatsoever happens in the object of any idea, the idea of it is in God (Pr. 3, II) not insofar as he is infinite, but insofar as he is considered as affected by another idea of an individual thing (preceding Pr.). But the order and connection of ideas is the same as the order and connection of things (Pr. 7, II). Therefore, the knowledge of what happens in an individual object is in God only insofar as he has the idea of that object.

## Proposition 10. *The being of substance does not pertain to the essence of man; i.e., substance does not constitute the form [*forma*] of man.*

Proof: The being of substance involves necessary existence (Pr. 7, I). So if the being of substance pertained to the essence of man, man would necessarily be granted together with the granting of substance (Def. 2, II) and consequently man would necessarily exist, which is absurd (Ax. 1, II). Therefore . . . etc.

Scholium: This Proposition is also proved from Pr. 5, I, which states that there cannot be two substances of the same nature. Now since many men can exist, that which constitutes the form of man is not the being of substance. This Proposition is furthermore evident from the other properties of substance—that substance is by its own nature infinite, immutable, indivisible, etc., as everyone can easily see.

Corollary: Hence it follows that the essence of man is constituted by definite modifications of the attributes of God.

Proof: For the being of substance does not pertain to the essence of man (preceding Pr.), which must therefore be something that is in God, and which can neither be nor be conceived without God; i.e., an affection or mode (Cor. Pr. 25, I) which expresses the nature of God in a definite and determinate way.

Scholium: All must surely admit that nothing can be or be conceived without God. For all are agreed that God is the sole cause of all things, both of their essence and of their existence; that is, God is the cause of things not only in respect of their coming into being [*secundum fieri*], as they say, but also in respect of their being. But at the same time many assert that that without which a thing can neither be nor be conceived pertains to the essence of the thing, and so

they believe that either the nature of God pertains to the essence of created things or that created things can either be or be conceived without God; or else, more probably, they hold no consistent opinion. I think that the reason for this is their failure to observe the proper order of philosophical inquiry. For the divine nature, which they should have considered before all else—it being prior both in cognition and in Nature—they have taken to be last in the order of cognition, and the things that are called objects of sense they have taken as prior to everything. Hence it has come about that in considering natural phenomena, they have completely disregarded the divine nature. And when thereafter they turned to the contemplation of the divine nature, they could find no place in their thinking for those fictions on which they had built their natural science, since these fictions were of no avail in attaining knowledge of the divine nature. So it is little wonder that they have contradicted themselves on all sides.

But I pass over these points, for my present purpose is restricted to explaining why I have not said that that without which a thing can neither be nor be perceived pertains to the essence of the thing. My reason is that individual things can neither be nor be conceived without God, and yet God does not pertain to their essence. But I did say that that necessarily constitutes the essence of a thing which, when posited, posits the thing, and by the annulling of which the thing is annulled; i.e., that without which the thing can neither be nor be conceived, and vice versa, that which can neither be nor be conceived without the thing.

## Proposition 11. *That which constitutes the actual being of the human mind is basically nothing else but the idea of an individual actually existing thing.*

Proof: The essence of man (Cor. Pr. 10, II) is constituted by definite modes of the attributes of God, to wit (Ax. 2, II), modes of thinking. Of all these modes the idea is prior in nature (Ax. 3, II), and when the idea is granted, the other modes—modes to which the idea is prior by nature—must be in the same individual (Ax. 3, II). And so the idea is that which basically constitutes the being of the human mind. But not the idea of a nonexisting thing; for then (Cor. Pr. 8, II) the idea itself could not be said to exist. Therefore, it is the idea of an actually existing thing. But not the idea of an infinite thing, for an infinite thing (Prs. 21 and 22, I) must always necessarily exist, and this is absurd (Ax. 1, II). Therefore, that which first constitutes the actual being of the human mind is the idea of an individual actually existing thing.

Corollary: Hence it follows that the human mind is part of the infinite intellect of God; and therefore when we say that the human mind perceives this or that, we are saying nothing else but this: that God—not insofar as he is infinite but insofar as he is explicated through the nature of the human mind, that is, insofar as he constitutes the essence of the human mind—has this or that idea. And when we say that God has this or that idea not only insofar as he constitutes the essence of the human mind but also insofar as he has the idea of another thing simultaneously with the human mind, then we are saying that the human mind perceives a thing partially or inadequately.

Scholium: At this point our readers will no doubt find themselves in some difficulty and will think of many things that will give them pause. So I ask them to proceed slowly step by step with me, and to postpone judgment until they have read to the end.

## Proposition 12. *Whatever happens in the object of the idea constituting the human mind is bound to be perceived by the human mind; i.e., the idea of that thing will necessarily be in the human mind. That is to say, if the object of the idea constituting the human mind is a body, nothing can happen in that body without its being perceived by the mind.*

Proof: Whatever happens in the object of any idea, knowledge thereof is necessarily in God (Cor. Pr. 9, II) insofar as he is considered as affected by the idea of that object; that is, (Pr. 11, II) insofar as he constitutes the mind of some thing. So whatever happens in

the object of the idea constituting the human mind, knowledge thereof is necessarily in God insofar as he constitutes the nature of the human mind; that is (Cor. Pr. 11, II), knowledge of that thing is necessarily in the mind; i.e., the mind perceives it.

Scholium: This Proposition is also obvious, and is more clearly understood from Sch. Pr. 7, II, above.

## Proposition 13. *The object of the idea constituting the human mind is the body—i.e., a definite mode of extension actually existing, and nothing else.*

Proof: If the body were not the object of the human mind, the ideas of the affections of the body would not be in God (Cor. Pr. 9, II) insofar as he constitutes our mind, but insofar as he constitutes the mind of another thing; that is (Cor. Pr. 11, II), the ideas of the affections of the body would not be in our mind. But (Ax. 4, II) we do have ideas of the affections of a body. Therefore, the object of the idea constituting the human mind is a body, a body actually existing (Pr. 11, II). Again, if there were another object of the mind apart from the body, since nothing exists from which some effect does not follow (Pr. 36, I), there would necessarily have to be in our mind the idea of some effect of it (Pr. 12, II). But (Ax. 5, II) there is no such idea. Therefore, the object of our mind is an existing body, and nothing else.

Corollary: Hence it follows that man consists of mind and body, and the human body exists according as we sense it.

Scholium: From the above we understand not only that the human Mind is united to the Body but also what is to be understood by the union of Mind and Body. But nobody can understand this union adequately or distinctly unless he first gains adequate knowledge of the nature of our body. For what we have so far demonstrated is of quite general application, and applies to men no more than to other individuals, which are all animate, albeit in different degrees. For there is necessarily in God an idea of each thing whatever, of which idea God is the cause in the same way as he is the cause of the idea of the human body. And so whatever we have asserted of the idea of the human body must necessarily be asserted of the idea of each thing. Yet we cannot deny, too, that ideas differ among themselves as do their objects, and that one is more excellent and contains more reality than another, just as the object of one idea is more excellent than that of another and contains more reality. Therefore, in order to determine the difference between the human mind and others and in what way it surpasses them, we have to know the nature of its object, (as we have said) that is, the nature of the human body. Now I cannot here explain this nature, nor is it essential for the points that I intend to demonstrate. But I will make this general assertion, that in proportion as a body is more apt than other bodies to act or be acted upon simultaneously in many ways, so is its mind more apt than other minds to perceive many things simultaneously; and in proportion as the actions of one body depend on itself alone and the less that other bodies concur with it in its actions, the more apt is its mind to understand distinctly. From this can realize the superiority of one mind over others, and we can furthermore see why we have only a very confused knowledge of our body, and many other facts which I shall deduce from this basis in what follows. Therefore, I have thought it worthwhile to explicate and demonstrate these things more carefully. To this end there must be a brief preface concerning the nature of bodies.

Axiom 1: All bodies are either in motion or at rest.

Axiom 2: Each single body can move at varying speeds.

Lemma 1: Bodies are distinguished from one another in respect of motion-and-rest, quickness and slowness, and not in respect of substance.

Proof: The first part of this Lemma I take to be self-evident. As to bodies not being distinguished in respect of substance, this is evident from both Pr. 5 and Pr. 8, Part I, and still more clearly from Sch. Pr. 15, Part I.

Lemma 2: All bodies agree in certain respects.

Proof: All bodies agree in this, that they involve the conception of one and the same attribute (Def. 1, II), and also in that they may move at varying speeds, and may be absolutely in motion or absolutely at rest.

Lemma 3: A body in motion or at rest must have been determined to motion or rest by another body, which likewise has been determined to motion or rest by another body, and that body by another, and so *ad infinitum*.

Proof: Bodies are individual things (Def. 1, II) which are distinguished from one another in respect of motion-and-rest (Lemma 1), and so (Pr. 28, I) each body must have been determined to motion or rest by another individual thing, namely, another body (Pr. 6, II), which is also in motion or at rest (Ax. 1). But this body again—by the same reasoning—could not have been in motion or at rest unless it had been determined to motion or rest by another body, and this body again—by the same reasoning—by another body, and so on, *ad infinitum*.

Corollary: Hence it follows that a body in motion will continue to move until it is determined to rest by another body, and a body at rest continues to be at rest until it is determined to move by another body. This, too, is self-evident; for when I suppose, for example, that a body A is at rest and I give no consideration to other moving bodies, I can assert nothing about body A but that it is at rest. Now if it should thereafter happen that body A is in motion, this surely could not have resulted from the fact that it was at rest; for from that fact nothing else could have followed than that body A should be at rest. If on the other hand A were supposed to be in motion, as long as we consider only A, we can affirm nothing of it but that it is in motion. If it should thereafter happen that A should be at rest, this surely could not have resulted from its previous motion; for from its motion nothing else could have followed but that A was in motion. So this comes about from a thing that was not in A, namely, an external cause by which the moving body A was determined to rest.

Axiom 1: All the ways in which a body is affected by another body follow from the nature of the affected body together with the nature of the body affecting it, so that one and the same body may move in various ways in accordance with the various natures of the bodies causing its motion; and, on the other hand, different bodies may be caused to move in different ways by one and the same body.

Axiom 2: When a moving body collides with a body at rest and is unable to cause it to move, it is reflected so as to continue its motion, and the angle between the line of motion of the reflection and the plane of the body at rest with which it has collided is equal to the angle between the line of incidence of motion and the said plane.

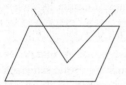

So far we have been discussing the simplest bodies, those which are distinguished from one another solely by motion-and-rest, quickness and slowness. Now let us advance to composite bodies.

Definition: When a number of bodies of the same or different magnitude form close contact with one another through the pressure of other bodies upon them, or if they are moving at the same or different rates of speed so as to preserve an unvarying relation of movement among themselves, these bodies are said to be united with one another and all together to form one body or individual thing, which is distinguished from other things through this union of bodies.

Axiom 3: The degree of difficulty with which the parts of an individual thing or composite body can be made to change their position and consequently the degree of difficulty with which the individual takes on different shapes is proportional to the extent of the surface areas along which they are in close contact. Hence bodies whose parts maintain close contact along large areas of their surfaces I term hard; those whose parts maintain contact along small surface areas I term soft; while those whose parts are in a state of motion among themselves I term liquid.

Lemma 4: If from a body, or an individual thing composed of a number of bodies, certain bodies are separated, and at the same time a like number of other bodies of the same nature take their place, the individual thing will retain its nature as before, without any change in its form [*forma*].

Proof: Bodies are not distinguished in respect of substance (Lemma 1). That which constitutes the form of the individual thing consists in a union of bodies (preceding definition). But this union, by hypothesis, is retained in spite of the continuous change of component bodies. Therefore, the individual thing will retain its own nature as before, both in respect of substance and of mode.

Lemma 5: If the parts of an individual thing become greater or smaller, but so proportionately that they all preserve the same mutual relation of motion-and-rest as before, the individual thing will likewise retain its own nature as before without any change in its form.

Proof: The reasoning is the same as in the preceding Lemma.

Lemma 6: If certain bodies composing an individual thing are made to change the existing direction of their motion, but in such a way that they can continue their motion and keep the same mutual relation as before, the individual thing will likewise preserve its own nature without any change of form.

Proof: This is evident; for, by hypothesis, the individual thing retains all that we, in defining it, asserted as constituting its form.

Lemma 7: Furthermore, the individual thing so composed retains its own nature, whether as a whole it is moving or at rest, and in whatever direction it moves, provided that each constituent part retains its own motion and continues to communicate this motion to the other parts.

Proof: This is evident from its definition, which you will find preceding Lemma 4.

Scholium: We thus see how a composite individual can be affected in many ways and yet preserve its nature. Now previously we have conceived an individual thing composed solely of bodies distinguished from one another only by motion-and-rest and speed of movement; that is, an individual thing composed of the simplest bodies. If we now conceive another individual thing composed of several individual things of different natures, we shall find that this can be affected in many other ways while still preserving its nature. For since each one of its parts is composed of several bodies, each single part can therefore (preceding Lemma), without any change in its nature, move with varying degrees of speed and consequently communicate its own motion to other parts with varying degrees of speed. Now if we go on to conceive a third kind of individual thing composed of this second kind, we shall find that it can be affected in many other ways without any change in its form. If we thus continue to infinity, we shall readily conceive the whole of Nature as one individual whose parts—that is, all the constituent bodies—vary in infinite ways without any change in the individual as a whole.

If my intention had been to write a full treatise on body, I should have had to expand my explications and demonstrations. But I have already declared a different intention, and the only reason for my dealing with this subject is that I may readily deduce therefrom what I have set out to prove.

## Postulates

1. The human body is composed of very many individual parts of different natures, each of which is extremely complex.
2. Of the individual components of the human body, some are liquid, some are soft, and some are hard.
3. The individual components of the human body, and consequently the human body itself, are affected by external bodies in a great many ways.
4. The human body needs for its preservation a great many other bodies, by which, as it were (*quasi*), it is continually regenerated.
5. When a liquid part of the human body is determined by an external body to impinge frequently on another part which is soft, it changes the surface of that part and impresses on it certain traces of the external body acting upon it.
6. The human body can move external bodies and dispose them in a great many ways.

## Proposition 14. *The human mind is capable of perceiving a great many things, and this capacity will vary in proportion to the variety of states which its body can assume.*

Proof: The human body (Posts. 3 and 6) is affected by external bodies in a great many ways and is so structured that it can affect external bodies in a great many ways. But the human mind must perceive all that happens in the human body (Pr. 12, II). Therefore, the human mind is capable of perceiving very many things, and . . . etc.

## Proposition 15. *The idea which constitutes the formal being of the human mind is not simple, but composed of very many ideas.*

Proof: The idea which constitutes the formal being of the human mind is the idea of the body (Pr. 13, II), which is composed of a great number of very composite individual parts (Postulate 1). But in God there is necessarily the idea of every individual component part (Cor. Pr. 8, II). Therefore (Pr. 7, II), the idea of the human body is composed of these many ideas of the component parts.

## Proposition 16. *The idea of any mode wherein the human body is affected by external bodies must involve the nature of the human body together with the nature of the external body.*

Proof: All the modes wherein a body is affected follow from the nature of the body affected together with the nature of the affecting body (Ax. 1 after Cor. Lemma 3). Therefore, the idea of these modes will necessarily involve the nature of both bodies (Ax. 4, I). So the idea of any mode wherein the human body is affected by an external body involves the nature of the human body and the external body.

Corollary 1: Hence it follows that the human mind perceives the nature of very many bodies along with the nature of its own body.

Corollary 2: Secondly, the ideas that we have of external bodies indicate the constitution of our own body more than the nature of external bodies. This I have explained with many examples in Appendix, Part I.

## Proposition 17. *If the human body is affected in a way* [modo] *that involves the nature of some external body, the human*

*mind will regard that same external body as actually existing, or as present to itself, until the human body undergoes a further modification which excludes the existence or presence of the said body.*

Proof: This is evident; for as long as the human body is thus affected, so long will the human mind (Pr. 12, II) regard this affection of the body that is (by the preceding Proposition), so long will it have the idea of a mode existing in actuality, an idea involving the nature of an external body; that is, an idea which does not exclude but posits the existence or presence of the nature of the external body. So the mind (Cor. 1 of the preceding proposition) will regard the external body as actually existing, or as present, until . . . etc.

Corollary: The mind is able to regard as present external bodies by which the human body has been once affected, even if they do not exist and are not present.

Proof: When external bodies so determine the fluid parts of the human body that these frequently impinge on the softer parts, they change the surfaces of these softer parts (Post. 5). Hence it comes about (Ax. 2 after Cor. Lemma 3) that the fluid parts are reflected therefrom in a manner different from what was previously the case; and thereafter, again coming into contact with the said changed surfaces in the course of their own spontaneous motion, they are reflected in the same way as when they were impelled towards those surfaces by external bodies. Consequently, in continuing this reflected motion they affect the human body in the same manner, which manner will again be the object of thought in the mind (Pr. 12, II); that is (Pr. 17, II), the mind will again regard the external body as present. This will be repeated whenever the fluid parts of the human body come into contact with those same surfaces in the course of their own spontaneous motion. Therefore, although the external bodies by which the human body has once been affected may no longer exist, the mind will regard them as present whenever this activity of the body is repeated.

Scholium: So we see how it comes about that we regard as present things which are not so, as often happens. Now it is possible that there are other causes for this fact, but it is enough for me at this point to have indicated one cause through which I can explicate the matter just as if I had demonstrated it through its true cause. Yet I do not think that I am far from the truth, since all the postulates that I have assumed contain scarcely anything inconsistent with experience; and after demonstrating that the human body exists just as we sense it (Cor. Pr. 13, II), we may not doubt experience.

In addition (preceding Cor. and Cor. 2 Pr. 16, II), this gives a clear understanding of the difference between the idea, e.g., of Peter which constitutes the essence of Peter's mind, and on the other hand the idea of Peter which is in another man, say Paul. The former directly explicates the essence of Peter's body, and does not involve existence except as long as Peter exists. The latter indicates the constitution of Paul's body rather than the nature of Peter; and so, while that constitution of Paul's body continues to be, Paul's mind will regard Peter as present to him although Peter may not be in existence. Further, to retain the usual terminology, we will assign the word "images" [*imagines*] to those affections of the human body the ideas of which set forth external bodies as if they were present to us, although they do not represent shapes. And when the mind regards bodies in this way, we shall say that it "imagines" [*imaginari*].

At this point, to begin my analysis of error, I should like you to note that the imaginations of the mind, looked at in themselves, contain no error; i.e., the mind does not err from the fact that it imagines, but only insofar as it is considered to lack the idea which excludes the existence of those things which it imagines to be present to itself. For if the mind, in imagining nonexisting things to be present to it, knew at the same time that those things did not exist in fact, it would surely impute this power of imagining not to the defect but to the strength of its own nature, especially if this faculty of imagining were to depend solely on its own nature; that is, (Def. 7, I) if this faculty of imagining were free.

## Proposition 18. *If the human body has once been affected by two or more bodies at the same time, when the mind afterwards*

*imagines one of them, it will straightway remember the others too.*

Proof: The mind imagines (preceding Cor.) any given body for the following reason, that the human body is affected and conditioned by the impressions of an external body in the same way as it was affected when certain of its parts were acted upon by the external body. But, by hypothesis, the human mind was at that time conditioned in such a way that the mind imagined two bodies at the same time. Therefore, it will now also imagine two bodies at the same time, and the mind, in imagining one of them, will straightway remember the other as well.

Scholium: Hence we clearly understand what memory is. It is simply a linking of ideas involving the nature of things outside the human body, a linking which occurs in the mind parallel to the order and linking of the affections of the human body. I say, firstly, that it is only the linking of those ideas that involve the nature of things outside the human body, not of those ideas that explicate the nature of the said things. For they are in fact (Pr. 16, II) ideas of the affections of the human body which involve the nature both of the human body and of external bodies. Secondly, my purpose in saying that this linking occurs in accordance with the order and linking of the affections of the human body is to distinguish it from the linking of ideas in accordance with the order of the intellect whereby the mind perceives things through their first causes, and which is the same in all men.

Furthermore, from this we clearly understand why the mind, from thinking of one thing, should straightway pass on to thinking of another thing which has no likeness to the first. For example, from thinking of the word "pomum" [apple] a Roman will straightway fall to thinking of the fruit, which has no likeness to that articulated sound nor anything in common with it other than that the man's body has often been affected by them both; that is, the man has often heard the word "pomum" while seeing the fruit. So everyone will pass on from one thought to another according as habit in each case has arranged the images in his body. A soldier, for example, seeing the tracks of a horse in the sand will straightway pass on from thinking of the horse to thinking of the rider, and then thinking of war, and so on. But a peasant, from thinking of a horse, will pass on to thinking of a plough, and of a field, and so on. So every person will pass on from thinking of one thing to thinking of another according as he is in the habit of joining together and linking the images of things in various ways.

## Proposition 19. *The human mind has no knowledge of the body, nor does it know it to exist, except through ideas of the affections by which the body is affected.*

Proof: The human mind is the very idea or knowledge of the human body (Pr. 13, II), and this idea is in God (Pr. 9, II) insofar as he is considered as affected by another idea of a particular thing; or, since (Post. 4) the human body needs very many other bodies by which it is continually regenerated, and the order and connection of ideas is the same (Pr. 7, II) as the order and connection of causes, this idea is in God insofar as he is considered as affected by the ideas of numerous particular things. Therefore, God has the idea of the human body, or knows the human body, insofar as he is affected by numerous other ideas, and not insofar as he constitutes the nature of the human mind; that is (Cor. Pr. 11, II), the human mind does not know the human body. But the ideas of the affections of the body are in God insofar as he does constitute the nature of human mind; i.e., the human mind perceives these affections (Pr. 12, II) and consequently perceives the human body (Pr. 16, II), and perceives it as actually existing (Pr. 17, II). Therefore, it is only to that extent that the human mind perceives the human body.

## Proposition 20. *There is also in God the idea or knowledge of the human mind, and this follows in God and is related to God in the same way as the idea or knowledge of the human body.*

Proof: Thought is an attribute of God (Pr. 1, II), and so (Pr. 3, II) the idea of both Thought and its affections—and consequently of the human mind as well—must necessarily be in God. Now this idea or knowledge of the mind does not follow in God insofar as he is infinite, but insofar as he is affected by another idea of a particular thing (Pr. 9, II). But the order and connection of ideas is the same as the order and connection of causes (Pr. 7, II). Therefore, the idea or knowledge of the mind follows in God and is related to God in the same way as the idea or knowledge of the body.

## Proposition 21. *This idea of the mind is united to the mind in the same way as the mind is united to the body.*

Proof: That the mind is united to the body we have shown from the fact that the body is the object of the mind (Prs. 12 and 13, II), and so by the same reasoning the idea of the mind must be united to its object—that is, to the mind itself—in the same way as the mind is united to the body.

Scholium: This proposition is understood far more clearly from Sch. Pr. 7, II. There we showed that the idea of the body and the body itself—that is, (Pr. 13, II) mind and body—are one and the same individual thing, conceived now under the attribute of Thought and now under the attribute of Extension. Therefore, the idea of the mind and the mind itself are one and the same thing, conceived under one and the same attribute, namely, Thought. The idea of the mind, I repeat, and the mind itself follow in God by the same necessity and from the same power of thought. For in fact the idea of the mind—that is, the idea of an idea—is nothing other than the form [*forma*] of the idea insofar as the idea is considered as a mode of thinking without relation to its object. For as soon as anyone knows something, by that very fact he knows that he knows, and at the same time he knows that he knows that he knows, and so on *ad infinitum*. But I will deal with this subject later.

## Proposition 22. *The human mind perceives not only the affections of the body but also the ideas of these affections.*

Proof: The ideas of ideas of affections follow in God and are related to God in the same way as ideas of

affections, which can be proved in the same manner as Pr. 20, II. But the ideas of affections of the body are in the human mind (Pr. 12, II); that is (Cor. Pr. 11, II), in God insofar as he constitutes the essence of the human mind. Therefore, the ideas of these ideas will be in God insofar as he has knowledge or the idea of the human mind; that is (Pr. 21, II), they will be in the human mind itself, which therefore perceives not only the affections of the body but also the ideas of these affections.

## Proposition 23. *The mind does not know itself except insofar as it perceives ideas of affections of the body.*

Proof: The idea or knowledge of the mind (Pr. 20, II) follows in God and is related to God in the same way as the idea or knowledge of the body. But since (Pr. 19, II) the human mind does not know the human body—that is, (Cor. Pr. 11, II) since the knowledge of the human body is not related to God insofar as he constitutes the nature of the human mind—therefore neither is knowledge of the mind related to God insofar as he constitutes the essence of the human mind. And so (Cor. Pr. 11, II) the human mind to that extent does not know itself. Again, the ideas of the affections by which the body is affected involve the nature of the human body (Pr. 16, II); that is, (Pr. 13, II) they are in agreement [*conveniunt*] with the nature of the mind. Therefore, the knowledge of these ideas will necessarily involve knowledge of the mind. But (preceding Pr.) the knowledge of these ideas is in the human mind. Therefore, the human mind knows itself but only to that extent.

## Proposition 24. *The human mind does not involve an adequate knowledge of the component parts of the human body.*

Proof: The component parts of the human body do not pertain to the essence of the body itself save insofar as they preserve an unvarying relation of motion with one another (Def. after Cor. Lemma 3), and not insofar as they can be considered as individual things apart from their relation to the human body. For the parts of the human body (Post. 1) are very composite individual things, whose parts can be separated from the human body (Lemma 4) without impairing in any way its nature and specific reality [*forma*], and can establish a quite different relation of motion with other bodies (Ax. 1 after Lemma 3). Therefore (Pr. 3, II), the idea or knowledge of any component part will be in God, and will be so (Pr. 9, II) insofar as he is considered as affected by another idea of a particular thing, a particular thing which is prior in Nature's order to the part itself (Pr. 7, II). Further, the same holds good of any part of an individual component part of the human body, and so of any component part of the human body there is knowledge in God insofar as he is affected by very many ideas of things, and not insofar as he has the idea only of the human body, that is (Pr. 13, II), the idea that constitutes the nature of the human mind. So (Cor. Pr. 11, II) the human mind does not involve adequate knowledge of the component parts of the human body.

## Proposition 25. *The idea of any affection of the human body does not involve an adequate knowledge of an external body.*

Proof: We have shown that the idea of an affection of the human body involves the nature of an external body insofar as the external body determines the human body in some definite way (Pr. 16, II). But insofar as the external body is an individual thing that is not related to the human body, the idea or knowledge of it is in God (Pr. 9, II) insofar as God is considered as affected by the idea of another thing which is (Pr. 7, II) prior in nature to the said external body. Therefore, an adequate knowledge of the external body is not in God insofar as he has the idea of an affection of the human body; i.e., the idea of an affection of the human body does not involve an adequate knowledge of an external body.

## Proposition 26. *The human mind does not perceive any external body as actually existing except through the ideas of affections of its own body.*

Proof: If the human body is not affected in any way by an external body, then (Pr. 7, II) neither is the idea of the human body—that is (Pr. 13, II), the human mind—affected in any way by the idea of the existence of that body; i.e., it does not in any way perceive the existence of that external body. But insofar as the human body is affected in some way by an external body, to that extent it perceives the external body (Pr. 16, II, with Cor. 1).

Corollary: Insofar as the human mind imagines [*imaginatur*] an external body, to that extent it does not have an adequate knowledge of it.

Proof: When the human mind regards external bodies through the ideas of affections of its own body, we say that it imagines [*imaginatur*] (see Sch. Pr. 17, II), and in no other way can the mind imagine external bodies as actually existing (preceding Pr.). Therefore, insofar as the mind imagines external bodies (Pr. 25, II), it does not have adequate knowledge of them.

## Proposition 27. *The idea of any affection of the human body does not involve adequate knowledge of the human body.*

Proof: Any idea whatsoever of any affection of the human body involves the nature of the human body only to the extent that the human body is considered to be affected in some definite way (Pr. 16, II). But insofar as the human body is an individual thing that can be affected in many other ways, the idea ... etc. (See Proof Pr. 25, II.)

## Proposition 28. *The ideas of the affections of the human body, insofar as they are related only to the human mind, are not clear and distinct, but confused.*

Proof: The ideas of the affections of the human body involve the nature both of external bodies and of the human body itself (Pr. 16, II), and must involve the nature not only of the human body but also of its parts. For affections are modes in which parts of the human body (Post. 3), and consequently the body as a whole, are affected. But (Prs. 24 and 25, II) an adequate knowledge of external bodies, as also of the component parts of the human body, is not in God insofar as he is considered as affected by the human mind, but insofar as he is considered as affected by other ideas. Therefore, these ideas of affections, insofar as they are related only to the human mind, are like conclusions without premises; that is, as is self-evident, confused ideas.

Scholium: The idea that constitutes the nature of the human mind is likewise shown, when considered solely in itself, not to be clear and distinct, as is also the idea of the human mind and the ideas of affections of the human body insofar as they are related only to the human mind, as everyone can easily see.

## Proposition 29. *The idea of the idea of any affection of the human body does not involve adequate knowledge of the human mind.*

Proof: The idea of an affection of the human body (Pr. 27, II) does not involve adequate knowledge of the body itself; in other words, it does not adequately express the nature of the body; that is (Pr. 13, II), it does not adequately agree [*convenit*] with the nature of the mind. So (Ax. 6, I) the idea of this idea does not adequately express the nature of the human mind; i.e., it does not involve an adequate knowledge of it.

Corollary: Hence it follows that whenever the human mind perceives things after the common order of nature, it does not have an adequate knowledge of itself, nor of its body, nor of external bodies, but only a confused and fragmentary knowledge. For the mind does not know itself save insofar as it perceives ideas of the affections of the body (Pr. 23, II). Now it does not perceive its own body (Pr. 19, II) except through ideas of affections of the body, and also it is only through these affections that it perceives external bodies (Pr. 26, II). So insofar as it has these ideas, it has adequate knowledge neither of itself (Pr. 29, II) nor of its own body (Pr. 27, II) nor of external bodies (Pr. 25, II), but only a fragmentary [*mutilatam*] and confused knowledge (Pr. 28, II and Sch.).

Scholium: I say expressly that the mind does not have an adequate knowledge, but only a confused and fragmentary knowledge, of itself, its own body, and external bodies whenever it perceives things

from the common order of nature, that is, whenever it is determined externally—namely, by the fortuitous run of circumstance—to regard this or that, and not when it is determined internally, through its regarding several things at the same time, to understand their agreement, their differences, and their opposition. For whenever it is conditioned internally in this or in another way, then it sees things clearly and distinctly, as I shall later show.

## Proposition 30. *We can have only a very inadequate knowledge of the duration of our body.*

Proof: The duration of our body does not depend on its essence (Ax. 1, II), nor again on the absolute nature of God (Pr. 21, I), but (Pr. 28, I) it is determined to exist and to act by causes which are also determined by other causes to exist and to act in a definite and determinate way, and these again by other causes, and so *ad infinitum*. Therefore, the duration of our body depends on the common order of nature and the structure of the universe. Now there is in God adequate knowledge of the structure of the universe insofar as he has ideas of all the things in the universe, and not insofar as he has only the idea of the human body (Cor. Pr. 9, II). Therefore, knowledge of the duration of our body is very inadequate in God insofar as he is considered only to constitute the nature of the human mind. That is (Cor. Pr. 11, II), this knowledge is very inadequate in the human mind.

## Proposition 31. *We can have only a very inadequate knowledge of the duration of particular things external to us.*

Proof: Each particular thing, just like the human body, must be determined by another particular thing to exist and to act in a definite and determinate way, and this latter thing again by another, and so on *ad infinitum* (Pr. 28, I). Now since we have shown in the preceding Proposition that from this common property of particular things we can have only a very inadequate knowledge of the duration of the human body, in the case of the duration of particular things we have to come to the same conclusion: that we can have only a very inadequate knowledge thereof.

Corollary: Hence it follows that all particular things are contingent and perishable. For we can have no adequate knowledge of their duration (preceding Pr.), and that is what is to be understood by contingency and perishability (Sch. 1, Pr. 33, I). For apart from this there is no other kind of contingency (Pr. 29, I).

## Proposition 32. *All ideas are true insofar as they are related to God.*

Proof: All ideas, which are in God, agree completely with the objects of which they are ideas (Cor. Pr. 7, II), and so they are all true (Ax. 6, I).

## Proposition 33. *There is nothing positive in ideas whereby they can be said to be false.*

Proof: If this be denied, conceive, if possible, a positive mode of thinking which constitutes the form [*forma*] of error or falsity. This mode of thinking cannot be in God (preceding Pr.), but neither can it be or be conceived externally to God (Pr. 15, I). Thus there can be nothing positive in ideas whereby they can be called false.

## Proposition 34. *Every idea which in us is absolute, that is, adequate and perfect, is true.*

Proof: When we say that there is in us an adequate and perfect idea, we are saying only this (Cor. Pr. 11, II), that there is adequate and perfect idea in God insofar as he constitutes the essence of our mind. Consequently, we are saying only this, that such an idea is true (Pr. 32, II).

## Proposition 35. *Falsity consists in the privation of knowledge which inadequate ideas, that is, fragmentary and confused ideas, involve.*

Proof: There is nothing positive in ideas which constitutes the form [*forma*] of falsity (Pr. 33, II). But falsity cannot consist in absolute privation (for minds, not bodies, are said to err and be deceived), nor again in absolute ignorance, for to be ignorant and to err are different. Therefore, it consists in that privation of knowledge which inadequate knowledge, that is, inadequate and confused ideas, involves.

Scholium: In Sch. Pr. 17, II I explained how error consists in the privation of knowledge, but I will give an example to enlarge on this explanation. Men are deceived in thinking themselves free, a belief that consists only in this, that they are conscious of their actions and ignorant of the causes by which they are determined. Therefore, the idea of their freedom is simply the ignorance of the cause of their actions. As to their saying that human actions depend on the will, these are mere words without any corresponding idea. For none of them knows what the will is and how it moves the body, and those who boast otherwise and make up stories of dwelling places and habitations of the soul provoke either ridicule or disgust.

As another example, when we gaze at the sun, we see it as some two hundred feet distant from us. The error does not consist in simply seeing the sun in this way but in the fact that while we do so we are not aware of the true distance and the cause of our seeing it so. For although we may later become aware that the sun is more than six hundred times the diameter of the earth distant from us, we shall nevertheless continue to see it as close at hand. For it is not our ignorance of its true distance that causes us to see the sun to be so near; it is that the affection of our body involves the essence of the sun only to the extent that the body is affected by it.

## Proposition 36. *Inadequate and confused ideas follow by the same necessity as adequate, or clear and distinct, ideas.*

Proof: All ideas are in God (Pr. 15, I), and insofar as they are related to God, they are true (Pr. 32, II) and adequate (Cor. Pr. 7, II). So there are no inadequate or confused ideas except insofar as they are related to the particular mind of someone (see Prs. 24 and 28, II). So all ideas, both adequate and inadequate, follow by the same necessity (Cor. Pr. 6, II).

**Proposition 37.** *That which is common to all things (see Lemma 2 above) and is equally in the part as in the whole does not constitute the essence of any one particular thing.*

Proof: If this is denied, conceive, if possible, that it does constitute the essence of one particular thing, B. Therefore, it can neither be nor be conceived without B (Def. 2, II). But this is contrary to our hypothesis. Therefore, it does not pertain to B's essence, nor does it constitute the essence of any other particular thing.

**Proposition 38.** *Those things that are common to all things and are equally in the part as in the whole can be conceived only adequately.*

Proof: Let A be something common to all bodies, and equally in the part of any body as in the whole. I say that A can be conceived only adequately. For its idea (Cor. Pr. 7, II) will necessarily be in God both insofar as he has the idea of the human body and insofar as he has the ideas of affections of the human body, affections which partly involve the natures of both the human body and external bodies (Prs. 16, 25, and 27, II). That is (Prs. 12 and 13, II), this idea will necessarily be adequate in God insofar as he constitutes the human mind; that is, insofar as he has the ideas which are in the human mind. Therefore, the mind (Cor. Pr. 11, II) necessarily perceives A adequately, and does so both insofar as it perceives itself and insofar as it perceives its own body or any external body; nor can A be perceived in any other way.

Corollary: Hence it follows that there are certain ideas or notions common to all men. For (by Lemma 2) all bodies agree in certain respects, which must be (preceding Pr.) conceived by all adequately, or clearly and distinctly.

**Proposition 39.** *Of that which is common and proper to the human body and to any external bodies by which the human body is customarily affected, and which is equally in the part as well as in the whole of any of these bodies, the idea also in the mind will be adequate.*

Proof: Let A be that which is common and proper to the human body and to any external bodies and which is equally in the human body as in those same external bodies, and which is finally equally in the part of any external body as in the whole. There will be in God an adequate idea of A (Cor. Pr. 7, II) both insofar as he has the idea of the human body and insofar as he has ideas of those posited external bodies. Let it now be supposed that the human body is affected by an external body through that which is common to them both, that is, A. The idea of this affection will involve the property A (Pr. 16, II), and so (Cor. Pr. 7, II) the idea of this affection, insofar as it involves the property A, will be adequate in God insofar as he is affected by the idea of the human body; that is (Pr. 13, II), insofar as he constitutes the nature of the human mind. So this idea will also be adequate in the human mind (Cor. Pr. 11, II).

Corollary: Hence it follows that the mind is more capable of perceiving more things adequately in proportion as its body has more things in common with other bodies.

**Proposition 40.** *Whatever ideas follow in the mind from ideas that are adequate in it are also adequate.*

Proof: This is evident. For when we say that an idea follows in the human mind from ideas that are adequate in it, we are saying no more than that there is in the divine intellect an idea of which God is the cause, not insofar as he is infinite nor insofar as he is affected by ideas of numerous particular things, but only insofar as he constitutes the essence of the human mind.

Scholium I: I have here set forth the causes of those notions that are called 'common,' and which are the basis of our reasoning processes. Now certain axioms or notions have other causes which it would be relevant to set forth by this method of ours; for thus we could establish which notions are useful compared with others, and which are of scarcely any value. And again, we could establish which notions are common to all, which ones are clear and distinct only to those not laboring under prejudices [*praejudiciis*] and which ones are ill-founded. Furthermore, this would clarify the origin of those notions called 'secondary'—and consequently the axioms which are based on them—as well as other related questions to which I have for some time given thought. But I have decided not to embark on these questions at this point because I have set them aside for another treatise,[8] and also to avoid wearying the reader with too lengthy a discussion of this subject. Nevertheless, to omit nothing that it is essential to know, I shall briefly deal with the question of the origin of the so-called "transcendental terms," such as "entity," "thing," "something" [*ens, res, aliquid*].

These terms originate in the following way. The human body, being limited, is capable of forming simultaneously in itself only a certain number of distinct images. (I have explained in Sch. Pr. 17, II what an image is.) If this number be exceeded, these images begin to be confused, and if the number of distinct images which the body is capable of forming simultaneously in itself be far exceeded, all the images will be utterly confused with one another. This being so, it is evident from Cor. Pr. 17 and Pr. 18, II that the human mind is able to imagine simultaneously and distinctly as many bodies as there are images that can be formed simultaneously in its body. But when the images in the body are utterly confused, the mind will also imagine all the bodies confusedly without any distinction, and will comprehend them, as it were, under one attribute, namely, that of entity, thing, etc. This conclusion can also be reached from the fact that images are not always equally vivid, and also from other causes analogous to these, which I need not here explicate. For it all comes down to this, that these terms signify ideas confused in the highest degree.

Again, from similar causes have arisen those notions called "universal," such as "man," "horse,"

"dog," etc.; that is to say, so many images are formed in the human body simultaneously (e.g., of man) that our capacity to imagine them is surpassed, not indeed completely, but to the extent that the mind is unable to imagine the unimportant differences of individuals (such as the complexion and stature of each, and their exact number) and imagines distinctly only their common characteristic insofar as the body is affected by them. For it was by this that the body was affected most repeatedly, by each single individual. The mind expresses this by the word "man," and predicates this word of an infinite number of individuals. For, as we said, it is unable to imagine the determinate number of individuals.

But it should be noted that not all men form these notions in the same way; in the case of each person the notions vary according as that thing varies whereby the body has more frequently been affected, and which the mind more readily imagines or calls to mind. For example, those who have more often regarded with admiration the stature of men will understand by the word 'man' an animal of upright stature, while those who are wont to regard a different aspect will form a different common image of man, such as that man is a laughing animal, a featherless biped, or a rational animal. Similarly, with regard to other aspects, each will form universal images according to the conditioning of his body. Therefore, it is not surprising that so many controversies have arisen among philosophers who have sought to explain natural phenomena through merely the images of these phenomena.

Scholium 2: From all that has already been said it is quite clear that we perceive many things and form universal notions:

1. From individual objects presented to us through the senses in a fragmentary [*mutilate*] and confused manner without any intellectual order (see Cor. Pr. 29, II); and therefore I call such perceptions "knowledge from casual experience."

2. From symbols. For example, from having heard or read certain words we call things to mind and we form certain ideas of them similar to those through which we imagine things (Sch. Pr. 18, II).

---

8. This is Spinoza's incomplete essay, *On the Improvement of the Understanding.*

Both these ways of regarding things I shall in future refer to as "knowledge of the first kind," "opinion" or "imagination."

3. From the fact that we have common notions and adequate ideas of the properties of things (see Cor. Pr. 38 and 39 with its Cor., and Pr. 40, II). I shall refer to this as 'reason' and "knowledge of the second kind."

Apart from these two kinds of knowledge there is, as I shall later show, a third kind of knowledge, which I shall refer to as "intuition." This kind of knowledge proceeds from an adequate idea of the formal essence of certain attributes of God to an adequate knowledge of the essence of things. I shall illustrate all these kinds of knowledge by one single example. Three numbers are given; it is required to find a fourth which is related to the third as the second to the first. Tradesmen have no hesitation in multiplying the second by the third and dividing the product by the first, either because they have not yet forgotten the rule they learnt without proof from their teachers, or because they have in fact found this correct in the case of very simple numbers, or else from the force of the proof of Proposition 19 of the Seventh Book of Euclid, to wit, the common property of proportionals. But in the case of very simple numbers, none of this is necessary. For example, in the case of the given numbers 1, 2, 3, everybody can see that the fourth proportional is 6, and all the more clearly because we infer in one single intuition the fourth number from the ratio we see the first number bears to the second.

## Proposition 41. *Knowledge of the first kind is the only cause of falsity; knowledge of the second and third kind is necessarily true.*

Proof: In the preceding Scholium we asserted that all those ideas which are inadequate and confused belong to the first kind of knowledge; and thus (Pr. 35, II) this knowledge is the only cause of falsity. Further, we asserted that to knowledge of the second and third kind there belong those ideas which are adequate. Therefore (Pr. 34, II), this knowledge is necessarily true.

## Proposition 42. *Knowledge of the second and third kind, and not knowledge of the first kind, teaches us to distinguish true from false.*

Proof: This Proposition is self-evident. For he who can distinguish the true from the false must have an adequate idea of the true and the false; that is (Sch. 2 Pr. 40, II), he must know the true and the false by the second or third kind of knowledge.

## Proposition 43. *He who has a true idea knows at the same time that he has a true idea, and cannot doubt its truth.*

Proof: A true idea in us is one which is adequate in God insofar as he is explicated through the nature of the human mind (Cor. Pr. 11, II). Let us suppose, then, that there is in God, insofar as he is explicated through the nature of the human mind, an adequate idea, A. The idea of this idea must also necessarily be in God, and is related to God in the same way as the idea A (Pr. 20, II, the proof being of general application). But by our supposition the idea A is related to God insofar as he is explicated through the nature of the human mind. Therefore, the idea of the idea A must be related to God in the same way; that is (Cor. Pr. 11, II), this adequate idea of the idea A will be in the mind which has the adequate idea A. So he who has an adequate idea, that is, he who knows a thing truly (Pr. 34, II), must at the same time have an adequate idea, that is, a true knowledge of his knowledge; that is (as is self-evident), he is bound at the same time to be certain.

Scholium: I have explained in the Scholium to Pr. 21, II what is an idea of an idea; but it should be noted that the preceding proposition is sufficiently self-evident. For nobody who has a true idea is unaware that a true idea involves absolute certainty. To have a true idea means only to know a thing perfectly, that is, to the utmost degree. Indeed, nobody can doubt this, unless he thinks that an idea is some dumb thing like a picture on a tablet, and not a mode of thinking, to wit, the very act of understanding. And who, pray, can know that he understands some thing unless he first understands it? That is, who can know that he is certain of something unless he is first certain of it? Again, what standard of truth can there be that is clearer and more certain than a true idea? Indeed, just as light makes manifest both itself and darkness, so truth is the standard both of itself and falsity.

I think I have thus given an answer to those questions which can be stated as follows: If a true idea is distinguished from a false one only inasmuch as it is said to correspond with that of which it is an idea, then a true idea has no more reality or perfection than a false one (since they are distinguished only by an extrinsic characteristic) and consequently neither is a man who has true ideas superior to one who has only false ideas. Secondly, how do we come to have false ideas? And finally, how can one know for certain that one has ideas which correspond with that of which they are ideas? I have now given an answer, I repeat, to these problems. As regards the difference between a true and a false idea, it is clear from Pr. 35, II that the former is to the latter as being to non-being. The causes of falsity I have quite clearly shown from Propositions 19 to 35 with the latter's Scholium, from which it is likewise obvious what is the difference between a man who has true ideas and one who has only false ideas. As to the last question, how can a man know that he has an idea which corresponds to that of which it is an idea, I have just shown, with abundant clarity, that this arises from the fact that he does have an idea that corresponds to that of which it is an idea; that is, truth is its own standard. Furthermore, the human mind, insofar as it perceives things truly, is part of the infinite intellect of God (Cor. Pr. 11, II), and thus it is as inevitable that the clear and distinct ideas of the mind are true as that God's ideas are true.

## Proposition 44. *It is not in the nature of reason to regard things as contingent, but as necessary*.

Proof: It is in the nature of reason to perceive things truly (Pr. 41, II), to wit, (Ax. 6, I) as they are in themselves; that is (Pr. 29, I), not as contingent, but as necessary.

Corollary I: Hence it follows that it solely results from imagination [*imaginatio*] that we regard things, both in respect of the past and of the future, as contingent.

Scholium: I shall explain briefly how this comes about. We have shown above (Pr. 17, II and Cor.) that although things may not exist, the mind nevertheless always imagines them as present unless causes arise which exclude their present existence. Further, we have shown (Pr. 18, II) that if the human body has once been affected by two external bodies at the same time, when the mind later imagines one of them, it will straightway call the other to mind as well; that is, it will regard both as present to it unless other causes arise which exclude their present existence. Furthermore, nobody doubts that time, too, is a product of the imagination, and arises from the fact that we see some bodies move more slowly than others, or more quickly, or with equal speed. Let us therefore suppose that yesterday a boy saw Peter first of all in the morning, Paul at noon, and Simon in the evening, and that today he again sees Peter in the morning. From Pr. 18, II it is clear that as soon as he sees the morning light, forthwith he will imagine the sun as traversing the same tract of sky as on the previous day, that is, he will imagine a whole day, and he will imagine Peter together with morning, Paul with midday, and Simon with evening; that is, he will imagine the existence of Paul and Simon with reference to future time. On the other hand, on seeing Simon in the evening he will refer Paul and Peter to time past by imagining them along with time past. This train of events will be the more consistent the more frequently he sees them in that order. If it should at some time occur that on another evening he sees James instead of Simon, then the following morning he will imagine along with evening now Simon, now James, but not both together. For we are supposing that he has seen only one of them in the evening, not both at the same time. Therefore, his imagination will waver, and he will imagine, along with a future evening, now one, now the other; that is, he will regard neither of them as going to be there for certain, but both of them contingently. This wavering of the imagination occurs in the same way if the imagination be of things which we regard with relation to past or present time, and consequently we shall imagine things, as related both to present and past or future time, as contingent.

Corollary 2: It is in the nature of reason to perceive things in the light of eternity [*sub quadam specie aeternitatis*].

Proof: It is in the nature of reason to regard things as necessary, not as contingent (previous Pr.). Now it perceives this necessity truly (Pr. 41, II); that is, as it is in itself (Ax. 6, I). But (Pr. 16, I) this necessity is the very necessity of God's eternal nature. Therefore, it is in the nature of reason to regard things in this light of eternity. Furthermore, the basic principles of reason are those notions (Pr. 38, II) which explicate what is common to all things, and do not explicate (Pr. 37, II) the essence of any particular thing, and therefore must be conceived without any relation to time, but in the light of eternity.

## Proposition 45. *Every idea of any body or particular thing existing in actuality necessarily involves the eternal and infinite essence of God.*

Proof: The idea of a particular thing actually existing necessarily involves both the essence and the existence of the thing (Cor. Pr. 8, II). But particular things cannot be conceived without God (Pr. 15, I). Now since they have God for their cause (Pr. 6, II) insofar as he is considered under that attribute of which the things themselves are modes, their ideas (Ax. 4, I) must necessarily involve the conception of their attribute; that is (Def. 6, I), the eternal and infinite essence of God.

Scholium: Here by existence I do not mean duration, that is, existence insofar as it is considered in the abstract as a kind of quantity. I am speaking of the very nature of existence, which is attributed to particular things because they follow in infinite numbers in infinite ways from the eternal necessity of God's nature (Pr. 16, I). I am speaking, I repeat, of the very existence of particular things insofar as they are in God. For although each particular thing is determined by another particular thing to exist in a

certain manner, the force by which each perseveres in existing follows from the eternal necessity of God's nature. (See Cor. Pr. 24, I.)

## Proposition 46. *The knowledge of the eternal and infinite essence of God which each idea involves is adequate and perfect.*

Proof: The proof of the preceding proposition is universally valid, and whether a thing be considered as a part or a whole, its idea, whether of whole or part, involves the eternal and infinite essence of God (preceding Pr.). Therefore, that which gives knowledge of the eternal and infinite essence of God is common to all things, and equally in the part as in the whole. And so this knowledge will be adequate (Pr. 38, II).

## Proposition 47. *The human mind has an adequate knowledge of the eternal and infinite essence of God.*

Proof: The human mind has ideas (Pr. 22, II) from which (Pr. 23, II) it perceives itself, its own body (Pr. 19, II), and external bodies (Cor. 1, Pr. 16 and Pr. 17, II) as actually existing, and so it has an adequate knowledge of the eternal and infinite essence of God (Prs. 45 and 46, II).

Scholium: Hence we see that God's infinite essence and his eternity are known to all. Now since all things are in God and are conceived through God, it follows that from this knowledge we can deduce a great many things so as to know them adequately and thus to form that third kind of knowledge I mentioned in Sch. 2, Pr. 40, II, of the superiority and usefulness of which we shall have occasion to speak in Part V. That men do not have as clear a knowledge of God as they do of common notions arises from the fact that they are unable to imagine God as they do bodies, and that they have connected the word "God" with the images of things which they commonly see; and this they can scarcely avoid, being affected continually by external bodies. Indeed, most errors result solely from the incorrect application of words to things. When somebody says that the lines joining the center of a circle to its circumference are unequal, he surely understands by circle, at least at that time, something different from what mathematicians understand. Likewise, when men make mistakes in arithmetic, they have different figures in mind from those on paper. So if you look only to their minds, they indeed are not mistaken; but they seem to be wrong because we think that they have in mind the figures on the page. If this were not the case, we would not think them to be wrong, just as I did not think that person to be wrong whom I recently heard shouting that his hall had flown into his neighbor's hen, for I could see clearly what he had in mind. Most controversies arise from this, that men do not correctly express what is in their mind, or they misunderstand another's mind. For, in reality, while they are hotly contradicting one another, they are either in agreement or have different things in mind, so that the apparent errors and absurdities of their opponents are not really so.

## Proposition 48. *In the mind there is no absolute, or free, will. The mind is determined to this or that volition by a cause, which is likewise determined by another cause, and this again by another, and so ad infinitum.*

Proof: The mind is a definite and determinate mode of thinking (Pr. 11, II), and thus (Cor. 2, Pr. 17, I) it cannot be the free cause of its actions: that is, it cannot possess an absolute faculty of willing and non-willing. It must be determined to will this or that (Pr. 28, I) by a cause, which likewise is determined by another cause, and this again by another, etc.

Scholium: In the same way it is proved that in the mind there is no absolute faculty of understanding, desiring, loving, etc. Hence it follows that these and similar faculties are either entirely fictitious or nothing more than metaphysical entities or universals which we are wont to form from particulars. So intellect and will bear the same relation to this or that idea, this or that volition, as stoniness to this or that stone, or man to Peter and Paul. As to the reason why men think they are free, we explained that in the Appendix to Part I.

But before proceeding further, it should here be noted that by the will I mean the faculty of affirming and denying, and not desire. I mean, I repeat, the faculty whereby the mind affirms or denies what is true or what is false, not the desire whereby the mind seeks things or shuns them. But now that we have proved that these faculties are universal notions which are not distinct from the particulars from which we form them, we must inquire whether volitions themselves are anything more than ideas of things. We must inquire, I say, whether there is in the mind any other affirmation and denial apart from that which the idea, insofar as it is an idea, involves. On this subject see the following proposition and also Def. 3, II, lest thought becomes confused with pictures. For by ideas I do not mean images such as are formed at the back of the eye—or if you like, in the middle of the brain—but conceptions of thought.

## Proposition 49. *There is in the mind no volition, that is, affirmation and negation, except that which an idea, insofar as it is an idea, involves.*

Proof: There is in the mind (preceding Pr.) no absolute faculty of willing and non-willing, but only particular volitions, namely, this or that affirmation, and this or that negation. Let us therefore conceive a particular volition, namely, a mode of thinking whereby the mind affirms that the three angles of a triangle are equal to two right angles. This affirmation involves the conception, or idea, of a triangle; that is, it cannot be conceived without the idea of a triangle. For to say that A must involve the conception of B is the same as to say that A cannot be conceived without B. Again, this affirmation (Ax. 3, II) cannot even be without the idea of a triangle. Therefore, this idea can neither be nor be conceived without the idea of a triangle. Furthermore, this idea of a triangle must involve this same affirmation, namely, that its three angles are equal to two right angles. Therefore, vice versa, this idea of a triangle can neither be nor be conceived without this affirmation, and so (Def. 2, II) this affirmation belongs to the essence of the idea of a triangle, and is nothing more than the essence itself. And what I have said of this volition (for it was arbitrarily selected) must also be said of every volition, namely, that it is nothing but an idea.

Corollary: Will and intellect are one and the same thing.

Proof: Will and intellect are nothing but the particular volitions and ideas (Pr. 48, II and Sch.). But a particular volition and idea are one and the same thing (preceding Pr.). Therefore, will and intellect are one and the same thing.

Scholium: By this means we have removed the cause to which error is commonly attributed. We have previously shown that falsity consists only in the privation that fragmentary and confused ideas involve. Therefore, a false idea, insofar as it is false, does not involve certainty. So when we say that a man acquiesces in what is false and has no doubt thereof, we are not thereby saying that he is certain, but only that he does not doubt, or that he acquiesces in what is false because there is nothing to cause his imagination to waver. On this point see Sch. Pr. 44, II. So however much we suppose a man to adhere to what is false, we shall never say that he is certain. For by certainty we mean something positive (Pr. 43, II and Sch.), not privation of doubt. But by privation of certainty we mean falsity.

But for a fuller explanation of the preceding proposition some things remain to be said. Then, again, there is the further task of replying to objections that may be raised against this doctrine of ours. Finally, to remove every shred of doubt, I have thought it worthwhile to point out certain advantages of this doctrine. I say certain advantages, for the most important of them will be better understood from what we have to say in Part V.

I begin, then, with the first point, and I urge my readers to make a careful distinction between an idea—i.e., a conception of the mind—and the images of things that we imagine. Again, it is essential to distinguish between ideas and the words we use to signify things. For since these three—images, words, and ideas—have been utterly confused by many, or else they fail to distinguish between them through lack of accuracy, or, finally, through lack of caution, our doctrine of the will, which it is essential to know

both for theory and for the wise ordering of life, has never entered their minds. For those who think that ideas consist in images formed in us from the contact of external bodies are convinced that those ideas of things whereof we can form no like image are not ideas, but mere fictions fashioned arbitrarily at will. So they look on ideas as dumb pictures on a tablet, and misled by this preconception they fail to see that an idea, insofar as it is an idea, involves affirmation or negation. Again, those who confuse words with idea, or with the affirmation which an idea involves, think that when they affirm or deny something merely by words contrary to what they feel, they are able to will contrary to what they feel. Now one can easily dispel these misconceptions if one attends to the nature of thought, which is quite removed from the concept of extension. Then one will clearly understand that an idea, being a mode of thinking, consists neither in the image of a thing nor in words. For the essence of words and images is constituted solely by corporeal motions far removed from the concept of thought. With these few words of warning, I turn to the aforementioned objections.

The first of these rests on the confident claim that the will extends more widely than the intellect, and therefore is different from it. The reason for their belief that the will extends more widely than the intellect is that they find—so they say—that they do not need a greater faculty of assent, that is, of affirming and denying, than they already possess, in order to assent to an infinite number of other things that we do not perceive, but that we do need an increased faculty of understanding. Therefore, will is distinct from intellect, the latter being finite and the former infinite.

Second, it may be objected against us that experience appears to tell us most indisputably that we are able to suspend judgment so as not to assent to things that we perceive, and this is also confirmed by the fact that nobody is said to be deceived insofar as he perceives something, but only insofar as he assents or dissents. For instance, he who imagines a winged horse does not thereby grant that there is a winged horse; that is, he is not thereby deceived unless at the same time he grants that there is a winged horse. So experience appears to tell us most indisputably that the will, that is, the faculty of assenting, is free, and different from the faculty of understanding.

Third, it may be objected that one affirmation does not seem to contain more reality than another; that is, we do not seem to need greater power in order to affirm that what is true is true than to affirm that what is false is true. On the other hand, we do perceive that one idea has more reality or perfection than another. For some ideas are more perfect than others in proportion as some objects are superior to others. This, again, is a clear indication that there is a difference between will and intellect.

Fourth, it may be objected that if man does not act from freedom of will, what would happen if he should be in a state of equilibrium like Buridan's ass? Will he perish of hunger and thirst? If I were to grant this, I would appear to be thinking of an ass or a statue, not of a man. If I deny it, then the man will be determining himself, and consequently will possess the faculty of going and doing whatever he wants.

Besides these objections there may possibly be others. But since I am not obliged to quash every objection that can be dreamed up, I shall make it my task to reply to these objections only, and as briefly as possible.

To the first objection I reply that, if by the intellect is meant clear and distinct ideas only, I grant that the will extends more widely than the intellect, but I deny that the will extends more widely than perceptions, that is, the faculty of conceiving. Nor indeed do I see why the faculty of willing should be termed infinite any more than the faculty of sensing. For just as by the same faculty of willing we can affirm an infinite number of things (but in succession, for we cannot affirm an infinite number of things simultaneously), so also we can sense or perceive an infinite number of bodies (in succession) by the same faculty of sensing. If my objectors should say that there are an infinite number of things that we cannot sense, I retort that we cannot grasp them by any amount of thought, and consequently by any amount of willing. But, they say, if God wanted to bring it about that we should perceive these too, he would have had to give us a greater faculty of perceiving, but not a greater faculty of willing than he has already given us. This

is the same as saying that if God wishes to bring it about that we should understand an infinite number of other entities, he would have to give us a greater intellect than he already has, so as to encompass these same infinite entities, but not a more universal idea of entity. For we have shown that the will is a universal entity, or the idea whereby we explicate all particular volitions; that is, that which is common to all particular volitions. So if they believe that this common or universal idea of volitions is a faculty, it is not at all surprising that they declare this faculty to extend beyond the limits of the intellect to infinity. For the term "universal" is applied equally to one, to many, and to an infinite number of individuals.

To the second objection I reply by denying that we have free power to suspend judgment. For when we say that someone suspends judgment, we are saying only that he sees that he is not adequately perceiving the thing. So suspension of judgment is really a perception, not free will. To understand this more clearly, let us conceive a boy imagining a winged horse and having no other perception. Since this imagining involves the existence of a horse (Cor. Pr. 17, II), and the boy perceives nothing to annul the existence of the horse, he will regard the horse as present and he will not be able to doubt its existence, although he is not certain of it. We experience this quite commonly in dreams, nor do I believe there is anyone who thinks that while dreaming he has free power to suspend judgment regarding the contents of his dream, and of bringing it about that he should not dream what he dreams that he sees. Nevertheless, it does happen that even in dreams we suspend judgment, to wit, when we dream that we are dreaming. Furthermore, I grant that nobody is deceived insofar as he has a perception; that is, I grant that the imaginings of the mind, considered in themselves, involve no error (see Sch. Pr. 17, II). But I deny that a man makes no affirmation insofar as he has a perception. For what else is perceiving a winged horse than affirming wings of a horse? For if the mind should perceive nothing apart from the winged horse, it would regard the horse as present to it, and would have no cause to doubt its existence nor any faculty of dissenting, unless the imagining of the winged horse were to be connected to an idea which annuls the existence of the said horse, or he perceives that the idea which he has of the winged horse is inadequate. Then he will either necessarily deny the existence of the horse or he will necessarily doubt it.

In the above I think I have also answered the third objection by my assertion that the will is a universal term predicated of all ideas and signifying only what is common to all ideas, namely, affirmation, the adequate essence of which, insofar as it is thus conceived as an abstract term, must be in every single idea, and the same in all in this respect only. But not insofar as it is considered as constituting the essence of the idea, for in that respect particular affirmations differ among themselves as much as do ideas. For example, the affirmation which the idea of a circle involves differs from the affirmation which the idea of a triangle involves as much as the idea of a circle differs from the idea of a triangle. Again, I absolutely deny that we need an equal power of thinking to affirm that what is true is true as to affirm that what is false is true. For these two affirmations, if you look to their meaning and not to the words alone, are related to one another as being to non-being. For there is nothing in ideas that constitutes the form of falsity (see Pr. 35, II with Sch. and Sch. Pr. 47, II). Therefore, it is important to note here how easily we are deceived when we confuse universals with particulars, and mental constructs [*entia rationis*] and abstract terms with the real.

As to the fourth objection, I readily grant that a man placed in such a state of equilibrium (namely, where he feels nothing else but hunger and thirst and perceives nothing but such-and-such food and drink at equal distances from him) will die of hunger and thirst. If they ask me whether such a man is not to be reckoned an ass rather than a man, I reply that I do not know, just as I do not know how one should reckon a man who hangs himself, or how one should reckon babies, fools, and madmen.

My final task is to show what practical advantages accrue from knowledge of this doctrine, and this we shall readily gather from the following points:

1. It teaches that we act only by God's will, and that we share in the divine nature, and all the more as our actions become more perfect and as we understand God more and more. Therefore, this doctrine, apart from giving us complete tranquillity of mind, has the further advantage of teaching us wherein lies our greatest happiness or blessedness, namely, in the knowledge of God alone, as a result of which we are induced only to such actions as are urged on us by love and piety. Hence we clearly understand how far astray from the true estimation of virtue are those who, failing to understand that virtue itself and the service of God are happiness itself and utmost freedom, expect God to bestow on them the highest rewards in return for their virtue and meritorious actions as if in return for the basest slavery.

2. It teaches us what attitude we should adopt regarding fortune, or the things that are not in our power, that is, the things that do not follow from our nature; namely, to expect and to endure with patience both faces of fortune. For all things follow from God's eternal decree by the same necessity as it follows from the essence of a triangle that its three angles are equal to two right angles.

3. This doctrine assists us in our social relations, in that it teaches us to hate no one, despise no one, ridicule no one, be angry with no one, envy no one. Then again, it teaches us that each should be content with what he has and should help his neighbor, not from womanish pity, or favor, or superstition, but from the guidance of reason as occasion and circumstance require. This I shall demonstrate in Part IV.

4. Finally, this doctrine is also of no small advantage to the commonwealth, in that it teaches the manner in which citizens should be governed and led; namely, not so as to be slaves, but so as to do freely what is best.

And thus I have completed the task I undertook in this Scholium, and thereby I bring to an end Part II, in which I think I have explained the nature of the human mind and its properties at sufficient length and as clearly as the difficult subject matter permits, and that from my account can be drawn many excellent lessons, most useful and necessary to know, as will partly be disclosed in what is to follow.

## Part V. Of the Power of the Intellect, or of Human Freedom

### Preface

I pass on finally to that part of the *Ethics* which concerns the method or way leading to freedom. In this part, then, I shall be dealing with the power of reason, pointing out the degree of control reason has over the emotions, and then what is freedom of mind, or blessedness, from which we shall see how much to be preferred is the life of the wise man to the life of the ignorant man. Now we are not concerned here with the manner or way in which the intellect should be perfected, nor yet with the science of tending the body so that it may correctly perform its functions. The latter is the province of medicine, the former of logic. Here then, as I have said, I shall be dealing only with the power of the mind or reason. Above all I shall be showing the degree and nature of its command over the emotions in checking and controlling them. For I have already demonstrated that we do not have absolute command over them. [ . . . ]

### Proposition 21. *The mind can exercise neither imagination nor memory save while the body endures.*

Proof: It is only while the body endures that the mind expresses the actual existence of its body and conceives the affections of the body as actual (Cor. Pr. 8, II). Consequently (Pr. 26, II), it does not conceive any body as actually existing save while its own body endures. Therefore (see Def. of Imagination in Sch. Pr. 17, II), it cannot exercise either imagination or memory save while the body endures (see Def. of Memory in Sch. P 18, II).

### Proposition 22. *Nevertheless, there is necessarily in God an idea which expresses the essence of this or that human body under a form of eternity* [sub specie aeternitatis].

Proof: God is the cause not only of the existence of this or that human body but also of its essence (Pr. 25, I), which must therefore necessarily be received through God's essence (Ax. 4, I) by a certain eternal necessity (Pr. 16, I), and this conception must necessarily be in God (Pr. 3, II).

### Proposition 23. *The human mind cannot be absolutely destroyed along with body, but something of it remains, which is eternal.*

Proof: In God there is necessarily a conception, or idea, which expresses the essence of the human body (preceding Pr.) and which therefore is necessarily something that pertains to the essence of the human mind (Pr. 13, II). But we assign to the human mind the kind of duration that can be defined by time only insofar as the mind expresses the actual existence of the body, an existence that is explicated through duration and can be defined by time. That is, we do not assign duration to the mind except while the body endures (Cor. Pr. 8, II). However, since that which is conceived by a certain eternal necessity through God's essence is nevertheless a something (preceding Pr.), this something, which pertains to the essence of mind, will necessarily be eternal.

Scholium: As we have said, this idea, which expresses the essence of the body under a form of eternity, is a definite mode of thinking which pertains to the essence of mind, and which is necessarily eternal. Yet it is impossible that we should remember that we existed before the body, since neither can there be any traces of this in the body nor can eternity be defined by time, or be in any way related to time. Nevertheless, we feel and experience that we are eternal. For the mind senses those things that it conceives by its understanding just as much as those which it has in its memory. Logical proofs are the eyes of the mind, whereby it sees and observes things. So although we have no recollection of having existed before the body, we nevertheless sense that our mind, insofar as it involves the essence of the body under a form of eternity, is eternal, and that this aspect of its existence cannot be defined by time, that is, cannot be explicated through duration. Therefore, our mind can be said to endure, and its existence to be defined by a definite period of time, only to the extent that it involves the actual existence of the body, and it is only to that extent that it has the power to determine the existence of things by time and to conceive them from the point of view of duration.

## Proposition 24. *The more we understand particular things, the more we understand God.*

Proof: This is evident from Cor. Pr. 25, I.

## Proposition 25. *The highest conatus of the mind and its highest virtue is to understand things by the third kind of knowledge.*

Proof: The third kind of knowledge proceeds from the adequate idea of certain of God's attributes to the adequate knowledge of the essence of things (see its definition in Sch. 2, Pr. 40, II), and the more we understand things in this way, the more we understand God (preceding Pr.). Therefore (Pr. 28, IV),[9] the highest virtue of the mind, that is (Def. 8, IV),[10] its power or nature, or its highest conatus (Pr. 7, III),[11] is to understand things by this third kind of knowledge.

## Proposition 26. *The more capable the mind is of understanding things by the third kind of knowledge, the more it desires to understand things by this same kind of knowledge.*

Proof: This is evident; for insofar as we conceive the mind to be capable of understanding things by the third kind of knowledge, to that extent we conceive it as determined to understand things by that same kind of knowledge. Consequently (Def. of

Emotions 1),[12] the more the mind is capable of this, the more it desires it.

## Proposition 27. *From this third kind of knowledge there arises the highest possible contentment of mind.*

Proof: The highest virtue of the mind is to know God (Pr. 28, IV),[13] that is, to understand things by the third kind of knowledge (Pr. 25, V), and this virtue is all the greater the more the mind knows things by the third kind of knowledge (Pr. 24, V). So he who knows things by this third kind of knowledge passes to the highest state of human perfection, and consequently (Def. of Emotions 2)[14] is affected by the highest pleasure, this pleasure being accompanied (Pr. 43, II) by the idea of himself and his own virtue. Therefore (Def. of Emotions 25),[15] from this kind of knowledge there arises the highest possible contentment.

## Proposition 28. *The conatus, or desire, to know things by the third kind of knowledge cannot arise from the first kind of knowledge, but from the second.*

Proof: This proposition is self-evident. For whatever we understand clearly and distinctly, we understand either through itself or through something else which is conceived through itself. That is, ideas which are clear and distinct in us or which are related to the third kind of knowledge (Sch. 2, Pr. 40, II) cannot follow from fragmentary or confused ideas which (same Sch.) are related to the first kind of knowledge, but from adequate ideas, that is (same Sch.), from the second or third kind of knowledge. Therefore (Def. of Emotions 1),[16] the desire to know things by

---

9. Pr. 28, IV: The mind's highest good is the knowledge of God, and the mind's highest virtue is to know God.
10. Def. 8, IV: By "virtue" and "power" I mean the same thing; that is (Pr. 7, III [see note 11]), virtue, insofar as it is related to man, is man's very essence, or nature, insofar as he has power by some other thing. Whatsoever thing there is, there is another more powerful by which the same thing can be destroyed.
11. Pr. 7, III: The conatus with which each thing endeavors to persist in its own being is nothing but the actual essence of the thing itself.

12. Def. of Emotions 1: Desire is the very essence of man insofar as his essence is conceived as determined to any action from a given affection of itself.
13. Pr. 28, IV: See note 9.
14. Def. of Emotions 2: Pleasure is man's transition from a state of less perfection to a state of greater perfection.
15. Def. of Emotions 25: Self-contentment is pleasure arising from a man's contemplation of himself and his power of activity.
16. Def. of Emotions 1: See note 12.

the third kind of knowledge cannot arise from the first kind of knowledge, but from the second.

## Proposition 29. *Whatever the mind understands under a form of eternity it does not understand from the fact that it conceives the present actual existence of the body, but from the fact that it conceives the essence of the body under a form of eternity.*

Proof: Insofar as the mind conceives the present existence of its body, to that extent it conceives a duration that can be determined by time, and only to that extent does it have the power to conceive things in relation to time (Pr. 21, V and Pr. 26, II). But eternity cannot be explicated through duration (Def. 8, I and its explication). Therefore, to that extent the mind does not have the power to conceive things under a form of eternity. But since it is the nature of reason to conceive things under a form of eternity (Cor. 2, Pr. 44, II), and since it belongs to the nature of mind, too, to conceive the essence of the body under a form of eternity (Pr. 23, V), and since there belongs to the essence of mind nothing but these two ways of conceiving (Pr. 13, II), it follows that this power to conceive things under a form of eternity pertains to the mind only insofar as it conceives the essence of the body under a form of eternity.

   Scholium: We conceive things as actual in two ways: either insofar as we conceive them as related to a fixed time and place, or insofar as we conceive them to be contained in God and to follow from the necessity of the divine nature. Now the things that are conceived as true or real in this second way, we conceive under a form of eternity, and their ideas involve the eternal and infinite essence of God, as we demonstrated in Pr. 45, II. See also its Scholium.

## Proposition 30. *Our mind, insofar as it knows both itself and the body under a form of eternity, necessarily has a knowledge of God, and knows that it is in God and is conceived through God.*

Proof: Eternity is the very essence of God insofar as this essence involves necessary existence (Def. 8, I). Therefore, to conceive things under a form of eternity is to conceive things insofar as they are conceived through God's essence as real entities; that is, insofar as they involve existence through God's essence. Therefore, our mind, insofar as it knows itself and the body under a form of eternity, necessarily has knowledge of God, and knows . . . etc.

## Proposition 31. *The third kind of knowledge depends on the mind as its formal cause insofar as the mind is eternal.*

Proof: The mind conceives nothing under a form of eternity except insofar as it conceives the essence of its body under a form of eternity (Pr. 29, V), that is (Prs. 21 and 23, V), except insofar as the mind is eternal. Therefore (preceding Pr.), insofar as it is eternal, it has knowledge of God, knowledge which is necessarily adequate (Pr. 46, II). Therefore, the mind, insofar as it is eternal, is capable of knowing all the things that can follow from this given knowledge of God (Pr. 40, II): that is, of knowing things by the third kind of knowledge (see its definition in Sch. 2, Pr. 40, II), of which the mind is therefore (Def. 1, III)[17] the adequate or formal cause insofar as it is eternal.

   Scholium: So the more each man is advanced in this kind of knowledge, the more clearly conscious he is of himself and of God, that is, the more perfect and blessed he is, as will become even more evident from what is to follow. But here it should be noted that although we are at this point certain that the mind is eternal insofar as it conceives things under a form of eternity, yet, to facilitate the explanation and render more readily intelligible what I intend to demonstrate, we shall consider the mind as if it were now beginning to be and were now beginning to understand things under a form of eternity, as we have been doing up to now. This we may do without any

---

17. Def. 1, III: I call that an adequate cause whose effect can be clearly and distinctly perceived through the said cause. I call that an inadequate or partial cause whose effect cannot be understood through the same cause alone.

danger of error, provided we are careful to reach no conclusion except from premises that are quite clear.

## Proposition 32. *We take pleasure in whatever we understand by the third kind of knowledge, and this is accompanied by the idea of God as cause.*

Proof: From this kind of knowledge there arises the highest possible contentment of mind (Pr. 27, V), that is (Def. of Emotions 25),[18] the highest possible pleasure, and this is accompanied by the idea of oneself, and consequently (Pr. 30, V) also by the idea of God, as cause.

Corollary: From the third kind of knowledge there necessarily arises the intellectual love of God [*amor Dei intellectualis*]. For from this kind of knowledge there arises (preceding Pr.) pleasure accompanied by the idea of God as cause, that is (Def. of Emotions 6),[19] the love of God not insofar as we imagine him as present (Pr. 29, V) but insofar as we understand God to be eternal. And this is what I call the intellectual love of God.

## Proposition 33. *The intellectual love of God which arises from the third kind of knowledge is eternal.*

Proof: The third kind of knowledge is eternal (Pr. 31, V and Ax. 3, I), and therefore (by the same Ax. 3, I) the love that arises from it is also necessarily eternal.

Scholium: Although this love towards God has had no beginning (preceding Pr.), it yet has all the perfections of love just as if it had originated in the manner we supposed in the Corollary to the preceding Proposition. There is no difference, except that the mind has possessed from eternity those perfections which we then supposed to be accruing to it, accompanied by the idea of God as eternal cause. If pleasure consists in the transition to a state of greater perfection, blessedness must surely consist in this, that the mind is endowed with perfection itself.

---

18. Def. of Emotions 25: See note 15.
19. Def. of Emotions 6: Love is pleasure accompanied by the idea of external cause.

## Proposition 34. *It is only while the body endures that the mind is subject to passive emotions.*

Proof: Imagining is the idea whereby the mind regards some thing as present (see its definition in Sch. Pr. 17, II), an idea which, however, indicates the present state of the body rather than the nature of an external thing (Cor. 2, Pr. 16, II). Therefore, an emotion (Gen. Def. of Emotions)[20] is an imagining insofar as it indicates the present state of the body. So (Pr. 21, V) it is only while the body endures that the mind is subject to passive emotions.

Corollary: Hence it follows that no love is eternal except for intellectual love [*amor intellectualis*].

Scholium: If we turn our attention to the common belief entertained by men, we shall see that they are indeed conscious of the eternity of the mind, but they confuse it with duration and assign it to imagination or to memory, which they believe to continue after death.

## Proposition 35. *God loves himself with an infinite intellectual love.*

Proof: God is absolutely infinite (Def. 6, I); that is (Def. 6, II), God's nature enjoys infinite perfection, accompanied (Pr. 3, II) by the idea of itself, that is (Pr. 11 and Def. 1, I), by the idea of its own cause; and that is what, in Cor. Pr. 32. V, we declared to be intellectual love.

## Proposition 36. *The mind's intellectual love towards God is the love of God wherewith God loves himself not insofar as he is infinite, but insofar as he can be explicated through the essence of the human mind considered under a form of eternity. That is, the mind's intellectual love towards God is part of the infinite love wherewith God loves himself.*

---

20. Gen. Def. of Emotions: The emotion called a passive experience is a confused idea whereby the mind affirms a greater or lesser force of existence of its body, or part of its body, than was previously the case, and by the occurrence of which the mind is determined to think of one thing rather than another.

Proof: This, the mind's love, must be related to the active nature of the mind (Cor. Pr. 32, V and Pr. 3, III),[21] and is therefore an activity whereby the mind regards itself, accompanied by the idea of God as cause (Pr. 32, V and Cor.); that is (Cor. Pr. 25, I and Cor. Pr. 11, II), an activity whereby God, insofar as he can be explicated through the human mind, regards himself, accompanied by the idea of himself. And therefore (preceding Pr.) this love of God is part of the infinite love wherewith God loves himself.

Corollary: Hence it follows that God, insofar as he loves himself, loves mankind, and, consequently, that the love of God towards men and the mind's intellectual love towards God are one and the same.

Scholium: From this we clearly understand in what our salvation or blessedness or freedom consists, namely, in the constant and eternal love towards God, that is, in God's love towards men. This love or blessedness is called glory in the Holy Scriptures, and rightly so. For whether this love be related to God or to the mind, it can properly be called spiritual contentment, which in reality cannot be distinguished from glory (Def. of Emotions, 25 and 30).[22] For insofar as it is related to God, it is (Pr. 35, V) pleasure (if we may still use this term) accompanied by the idea of himself, and this is also the case insofar as it is related to the mind (Pr. 27, V). Again, since the essence of our mind consists solely in knowledge, whose principle and basis is God (Pr. 15, I and Sch. Pr. 47, II), it follows that we see quite clearly how and in what way our mind, in respect of essence and existence, follows from the divine nature and is continuously dependent on God.

I have thought this worth noting here in order to show by this example the superiority of that knowledge of particular things which I have called 'intuitive' or 'of the third kind,' and its preferability to that abstract knowledge which I have called 'knowledge of the second kind.'

---

21. Pr. 3, III: The active states [*actiones*] of the mind arise only from adequate ideas; its passive states depend solely on inadequate ideas.

22. Def. of Emotions, 25: See note 15; Def. of Emotions 30: Honor is pleasure accompanied by the idea of some action of ours which we think that others praise.

For although I demonstrated in a general way in Part I that everything (and consequently the human mind, too) is dependent on God in respect of its essence and of its existence, that proof, although legitimate and exempt from any shadow of doubt, does not so strike the mind as when it is inferred from the essence of each particular thing which we assert to be dependent on God.

## Proposition 37. *There is nothing in Nature which is contrary to this intellectual love, or which can destroy it.*

This intellectual love follows necessarily from the nature of the mind insofar as that is considered as an eternal truth through God's nature (Prs. 33 and 29, V). Therefore, if there were anything that was contrary to this love, it would be contrary to truth, and consequently that which could destroy this love could cause truth to be false, which, as is self-evident, is absurd. Therefore, there is nothing in Nature . . . etc.

Scholium: The Axiom in Part IV is concerned with particular things insofar as they are considered in relation to a definite time and place, of which I think no one can be in doubt.

## Proposition 38. *The greater the number of things the mind understands by the second and third kinds of knowledge, the less subject it is to emotions that are bad, and the less it fears death.*

Proof: The essence of the mind consists in knowledge (Pr. 11, II). Therefore, the greater the number of things the mind knows by the second and third kinds of knowledge, the greater is the part of it that survives (Prs. 23 and 29, V), and consequently (preceding Pr.) the greater is that part of it that is not touched by emotions contrary to our nature; that is (Pr. 30, IV),[23] by emotions that are bad. Therefore, the greater the number of things the mind understands by the

---

23. Pr. 30, IV: No thing can be evil for us through what it possesses in common with our nature, but insofar as it is evil for us, it is contrary for us.

second and third kinds of knowledge, the greater is that part of it that remains unimpaired, and consequently the less subject it is to emotions . . . etc.

Scholium: Hence we understand that point which I touched upon in Sch. Pr. 39, IV and which I promised to explain in this part, namely that death is less hurtful in proportion as the mind's clear and distinct knowledge is greater, and consequently the more the mind loves God. Again, since (Pr. 27, V) from the third kind of knowledge there arises the highest possible contentment, hence it follows that the human mind can be of such a nature that that part of it that we have shown to perish with the body (Pr. 21, V) is of no account compared with that part of it that survives. But I shall be dealing with this at greater length in due course.

## Proposition 39. *He whose body is capable of the greatest amount of activity has a mind whose greatest part is eternal.*

Proof: He whose body is capable of the greatest amount of activity is least assailed by emotions that are evil (Pr. 38, IV),[24] that is (Pr. 30, IV),[25] by emotions that are contrary to our nature. Thus (Pr. 10, V)[26] he has the capacity to arrange and associate the affections of the body according to intellectual order and consequently to bring it about (Pr. 14, V)[27] that all the affections of the body are related to God. This will result (Pr. 15, V)[28] in his being affected with love towards God, a love (Pr. 16, V)[29] that must occupy or constitute the greatest part of the mind. Therefore (Pr. 33, V), he has a mind whose greatest part is eternal.

Scholium: Since human bodies are capable of a great many activities, there is no doubt that they can be of such a nature as to be related to minds which have great knowledge of themselves and of God, and whose greatest and principal part is eternal, with the result that they scarcely fear death. But in order that this may be more clearly understood, it should here be remarked that our lives are subject to continual variation, and as the change is for the better or worse, so we are said to be fortunate or unfortunate. For he who passes from being a baby or child into being a corpse is said to be unfortunate; while, on the other hand, to have been able to pass the whole of one's life with a healthy mind in a healthy body is regarded as a mark of good fortune. And in fact he who, like a baby or a child, has a body capable of very little activity and is most dependent on external causes, has a mind which, considered solely in itself, has practically no consciousness of itself, of God, or of things, while he whose body is capable of very considerable activity has a mind which, considered solely in itself, is highly conscious of itself and of God and of things. In this life, therefore, we mainly endeavor that the body of childhood, as far as its nature allows and is conducive thereto, should develop into a body that is capable of a great many activities and is related to a mind that is highly conscious of itself, of God, and of things, and in such a way that everything relating to its memory or imagination should be of scarcely any importance in comparison with its intellect, as I have already stated in the Scholium to the preceding Proposition.

## Proposition 40. *The more perfection a thing has, the more active and the less passive it*

---

24. Pr. 38, IV: That which so dispenses the human body that it can be affected in more ways, or which renders it capable of affecting external bodies in more ways, is advantageous to man, and proportionately more advantageous as the body is thereby rendered more capable of being affected in more ways and of affecting other bodies in more ways. On the other hand, that which renders the body less capable in these respects is harmful.
25. Pr. 30, IV: See note 23.
26. Pr. 10, V: As long as we are not assailed by emotions that are contrary to our nature, we have the power to arrange and associate the affections of the body according to the order of the intellect.
27. Pr. 14, V: The mind can bring it about that all the affections of the body—i.e., images of things—be related to the idea of God.

28. Pr. 15, V: He who clearly and distinctly understands himself and his emotions loves God, and the more so the more he understands himself and his emotions.
29. Pr. 16, V: The love towards God is bound to hold chief place in the mind.

*is. Conversely, the more active it is, the more perfect it is.*

Proof: The more perfect a thing is, the more reality it has (Def. 6, II); consequently (Pr. 3, III and Sch.),[30] the more active it is and the less passive. This proof proceeds in the same manner in inverse order, from which it follows that a thing is the more perfect as it is more active.

Corollary: Hence it follows that the part of the mind that survives, of whatever extent it may be, is more perfect than the rest. For the eternal part of the mind (Prs. 23 and 29, V) is the intellect, through which alone we are said to be active (Pr. 3, III),[31] whereas that part which we have shown to perish is the imagination (Pr. 21, V), through which alone we are said to be passive (Pr. 3, III and Gen. Def. of Emotions).[32] Therefore, the former (preceding Pr.), of whatever extent it be, is more perfect than the latter.

Scholium: This is what I had resolved to demonstrate concerning the mind insofar as it is considered without reference to the existence of the body. It is clear from this, and also from Pr. 21, I and other propositions, that our mind, insofar as it understands, is an eternal mode of thinking which is determined by another eternal mode of thinking, and this again by another, and so on *ad infinitum*, with the result that they all together constitute the eternal and infinite intellect of God.

## Proposition 41. *Even if we did not know that our mind is eternal, we should still regard as being of prime importance piety and religion and, to sum up completely, everything which in Part IV we showed to be related to courage and nobility.*

Proof: The first and only basis of virtue, that is, of the right way of life (Cor. Pr. 22 and Pr. 24, IV),[33] is

to seek one's own advantage. Now in order to determine what reason prescribes as advantageous we took no account of the mind's eternity, a topic which we did not consider until Part V. So although at that point we were unaware that the mind is eternal, we regarded as being of prime importance whatever is related to courage and nobleness. So even if now we were unaware of the mind's eternity, we should still regard the said precepts of reason as being of prime importance.

Scholium: The common belief of the multitude seems to be quite different. For the majority appear to think that they are free to the extent that they can indulge their lusts, and that they are giving up their rights to the extent that they are required to live under the commandments of the divine law. So they believe that piety and religion, in fact everything related to strength of mind, are burdens which they hope to lay aside after death, when they will receive the reward of their servitude, that is, of piety and religion. And it is not by this hope alone, but also and especially by fear of incurring dreadful punishment after death, that they are induced to live according to the commandments of the divine law as far as their feebleness and impotent spirit allows. And if men did not have this hope and this fear, and if they believed on the contrary that minds perish with bodies and that they, miserable creatures, worn out by the burden of piety, had no prospect of further existence, they would return to their own inclinations and decide to shape their lives according to their lusts, and to be ruled by fortune rather than by themselves. This seems to me no less absurd than if a man, not believing that he can sustain his body on good food forever, were to decide to glut himself on poisons and deadly fare; or, on realizing that the mind is not eternal or immortal, he preferred to be mad and to live without reason. Such attitudes are so absurd that they are scarcely worth recounting.

---

30. Pr. 3, III: See note 21.
31. Pr. 3, III: See note 21.
32. Pr. 3, III and Gen. Def. of Emotions: See notes 21 and 20.
33. Cor. Pr. 22, IV: The conatus to preserve oneself is the primary and sole basis of virtue. No other principle can be conceived as

prior to this one (by Pr. 22, IV), and no virtue can be conceived independently of it (Pr. 21, IV); Pr. 24, IV: Nobody can desire to be happy, to do well, and to live well without at the same time desiring to be, to do, and to live; that is, actually to exist.

Proposition 42. *Blessedness is not the reward of virtue, but virtue itself. We do not enjoy blessedness because we keep our lusts in check. On the contrary, it is because we enjoy blessedness that we are able to keep our lusts in check.*

Proof: Blessedness consists in love towards God (Pr. 36, V and Sch.), a love that arises from the third kind of knowledge (Cor. Pr. 32, V), and so this love (Prs. 59 and 3, III)[34] must be related to the mind insofar as the mind is active; and therefore it is virtue itself (Def. 8, IV).[35] That is the first point. Again, the more the mind enjoys this divine love or blessedness, the more it understands (Pr. 32, V); that is (Cor. Pr. 3, V),[36] the more power it has over the emotions and (Pr. 38, V) the less subject it is to emotions that are bad. So the mind's enjoyment of this divine love or blessedness gives it the power to check lusts. And since human power to keep lusts in check consists solely in the intellect, nobody enjoys blessedness because he has kept his emotions in check. On the contrary, the power to keep lusts in check arises from blessedness itself.

Scholium: I have now completed all that I intended to demonstrate concerning the power of the mind over the emotions and concerning the freedom of the mind. This makes clear how strong the wise man is and how much he surpasses the ignorant man whose motive force is only lust. The ignorant man, besides being driven hither and thither by external causes, never possessing true contentment of spirit, lives as if he were unconscious of himself, God, and things, and as soon as he ceases to be passive, he at once ceases to be at all. On the other hand, the wise man, insofar as he is considered as such, suffers scarcely any disturbance of spirit, but being conscious, by virtue of a certain eternal necessity, of himself, of God and of things, never ceases to be, but always possesses true spiritual contentment.

If the road I have pointed out as leading to this goal seems very difficult, yet it can be found. Indeed, what is so rarely discovered is bound to be hard. For if salvation were ready to hand and could be discovered without great toil, how could it be that it is almost universally neglected? All things excellent are as difficult as they are rare.

End

---

34. Pr. 59, III: Among all the emotions that are related to the mind insofar as it is active, there are none that are not related to pleasure and desire; Pr. 3, III: See note 21.

35. Def. 8, IV: See note 10.

36. Cor. Pr. 3, V: So the more an emotion is known to us, the more it is within our control, and the mind is the less passive in respect of it.

# 3. LEIBNIZ'S MONADOLOGY AND ASSOCIATED TEXTS

Gottfried Wilhelm Leibniz (1646–1716) attended the universities of Leipzig (1661–66) and Altdorf (1666–67), graduating with degrees in law and in philosophy. Invited to join the faculty at Altdorf, he chose instead to enter the service of the elector of Mainz. He was sent on diplomatic business to Paris (1672–76); there he met Antoine Arnauld and Nicolas Malebranche, among others, and accomplished the basic work on his differential and integral calculus. Leibniz returned to Germany, in 1676, in the service of the court of Hanover, and along the way he stopped in the Netherlands to meet Baruch Spinoza. In Hanover he became counselor and served in numerous roles: as mining engineer (unsuccessfully supervising the draining of the silver mines in the Harz Mountains), head librarian, adviser and diplomat, and court historian. His chosen literary form was the occasional article or essay in a learned journal. Among the important essays he wrote but did not publish are "Discourse on Metaphysics" (1686), *Dynamics* (1689–91), and "Monadology" (1714). In 1705 he finished his *New Essays on Human Understanding*, a book-length commentary on John Locke's *Essay*, but did not issue the work. He did publish several significant philosophical essays: "New System" (*Journal des Sçavants*, 1695);

"Specimen of Dynamics" (*Acta Eruditorum*, 1695); and *Theodicy* (1710). The last is a loosely structured work, consisting largely in responses to Pierre Bayle's skepticism. Leibniz maintained an extensive circle of correspondents, including Simon Foucher, Arnauld, Malebranche, and Samuel Clarke.[1]

There is nothing in Leibniz's enormous body of work that resembles, let us say, Descartes' *Meditations* or Spinoza's *Ethics*, no authoritative expression of Leibniz's philosophy in a single volume. In part, that must be due to his desire not to set himself up as head of a sect and to produce what he would disparagingly call a "learned magician's book."[2] In part,

---

1. There are a number of collections of Leibniz's philosophical essays as well as editions of the *Theodicy* and *New Essays* in English translation. For more on Leibniz, see C. D. Broad, *Leibniz: An Introduction* (Cambridge: Cambridge University Press, 1975); Stuart Brown, *Leibniz* (Minneapolis: University of Minnesota Press, 1984); Catherine Wilson, *Leibniz's Metaphysics: A Historical and Comparative Study* (Princeton: Princeton University Press, 1989); Robert Sleigh, *Leibniz and Arnauld* (New Haven: Yale University Press, 1990); Donald Rutherford, *Leibniz and the Rational Order of Nature* (Cambridge: Cambridge University Press, 1995); Nicholas Jolley, ed., *The Cambridge Companion to Leibniz* (Cambridge: Cambridge University Press, 1995).
2. See Brown, *Leibniz*, pp. 6–8.

it must also be due to his manner of philosophizing. Leibniz usually wrote essays, small treatises, and letters to learned correspondents. With the rise of intellectual journals in the second half of the seventeenth century (*Journal des Sçavants*, *Acta Eruditorum*, etc.), he had a ready means of disseminating his thought. But Leibniz's chosen form must be handled gingerly. One finds approximately the same set of typical Leibnizian theses in Leibniz's various essays (from the "Discourse on Metaphysics" and "Primary Truths" to the "New System" and ultimately to the Preface to the *New Essays* and "Monadology"). However, the formulations of the theses and the relations they have with one another vary from essay to essay; these are not always minor differences.

Take, for example, the "Discourse on Metaphysics." Leibniz intended the work as a philosophical framework within which theological disputes between Protestants and Catholics might be resolved. The structure of the "Discourse" displays this purpose. It begins with God, with an account of his perfection and the creation, as well as an application of the principle of sufficient reason, and it ends with God, with his relation to finite spirits, including humans. In between, Leibniz discusses the metaphysics required for those doctrines. Section 8 of the "Discourse" explains the notion of an individual substance so as to distinguish the actions of God from those of creatures. For that purpose, Leibniz introduces the concept-containment theory of truth: a proposition is true if and only if the concept of the predicate is contained in the concept of the subject. A consequence of this account is that "the nature of an individual substance or of a complete being is to have a notion so complete that it is sufficient to contain and to allow us to deduce from it all the predicates of the subject to which this notion is attributed." As Leibniz says in Section 9, "several notable paradoxes follow from this"; the "paradoxes," however, are metaphysical doctrines Leibniz actually holds: the identity of indiscernibles—that two substances cannot resemble each other completely and differ only in number; the indestructibility of substances—that a substance can begin only by creation and end only by annihilation; and the complete-world view of substance—that every substance is like a complete world and like a mirror of the whole universe, expressing, however confusedly, everything that happens in the universe, whether past, present, or future. As further consequences of his theory of substance, Leibniz argues against Descartes that extension cannot constitute the essence of any substance and rehabilitates substantial forms as the essence of extended substances (Sections 10–12). He distinguishes between certainty and necessity: The truth of each event, however certain, is nevertheless contingent, being based on the free will of God, whose choice always has its reasons, which incline without necessitating (Section 13, which provokes the correspondence between Leibniz and Arnauld). And he further argues a thesis of spontaneity (Sections 14–6)—that everything that happens to a substance is a consequence of its idea or of its being, and that nothing determines it, except God alone—applying the thesis to the relation between mind and body (Section 33).

By the "New System," Leibniz's concept-containment account of truth and his complete-concept theory of substance disappear. The essay begins with a consideration of the labyrinth of the continuum: the principles of a true unity cannot be found in matter alone, since everything in matter is only an aggregation of parts to infinity. A multitude can derive its reality only from true unities. This requires Leibniz to postulate formal atoms and to rehabilitate substantial forms, which, in turn, requires the indestructibility of substances: every substance that has a true unity can begin only by creation and end only by annihilation. It also requires the thesis of spontaneity: God originally created the soul (and any other real unity) in such a way that everything must arise for it from its own depths through a perfect spontaneity relative to itself, and yet with a perfect conformity relative to external things. Moreover, spontaneity entails that every substance represents the whole universe, from a certain point of view, in virtue of its own laws, as if in a world apart. Ultimately, the thesis of pre-established harmony also follows: there will be a perfect agreement among all these substances, producing the same effect that would be noticed if they communicated through the transmission of species or qualities.

The Preface to the *New Essays*[3] also contains Leibniz's characteristic set of theses, but again they are reworked. Reflecting on Locke's opinion that there is nothing in our mind which we are not actually conscious of perceiving, Leibniz develops his doctrine of *petites perceptions*: at every moment there is an infinity of perceptions in us which we do not consciously perceive. These small perceptions involve infinity; as a result, the present is filled with the future and laden with the past, everything conspires together, and the whole sequence of the universe could be read in the smallest of substances. The insensible perceptions also constitute the individual, which is individuated by the traces which these perceptions preserve of its previous states, connecting it up with his present state. That is why, according to Leibniz, death might only be a state like that of sleep. Leibniz also explains the pre-established harmony holding between the soul and the body by means of these insensible perceptions. Moreover, the thesis of the identity of indiscernibles follows as well: Because of insensible variations, two individual things cannot be perfectly alike and must always differ in something over and above number. According to Leibniz, the identity of

indiscernibles would "put an end to such doctrines as the empty tablets of the soul, a soul without thought, a substance without action, void space, atoms, and even particles in matter not actually divided, complete uniformity in a part of time, place, or matter, [ . . . ] and a thousand other fictions of philosophers which arise from their incomplete notions"—about which he disputed with Locke in the *New Essays* and subsequently debated (indirectly) with Isaac Newton in the letters to Clarke.

As is clear, the particular interpretive challenge Leibniz poses is that his characteristic doctrines change through time, depending perhaps upon the purpose of the essay, the issues he is addressing, and the audience to which he is speaking—whether he is seeking reconciliation between Catholic and Protestant churches in the "Discourse on Metaphysics," discussing Cartesian problems in learned journals such as the *Journal des Sçavants*, or commenting upon Lockean themes in the *New Essays*, or even when he is unfolding logical consequences in "Primary Truths" or explicating the foundations of his *Theodicy* in the "Monadology."

---

3. For Leibniz's Preface to the *New Essays*, see below, Part 4.

# Nicolas Malebranche, *The Search after Truth* (1674–75)[1]

*Nicolas Malebranche (1638–1715) was a philosopher and priest. He had a traditional scholastic education, including three years at the Sorbonne. He entered the Congregation of the Oratory in 1660 and was ordained in 1664. The Oratory was surely responsible for the Augustinian influence on his philosophy, but an accidental discovery in 1664 of Descartes'* Treatise on Man *provided him with his other major influence. His first and most significant work,* The Search after Truth, *was published initially in 1674–75 and subsequently printed with an increasingly long set of* Elucidations. *The work elicited critiques by Foucher and Arnauld; although he denied having a taste for polemics, Malebranche engaged in lengthy debates with these two critics, as well as others (Leibniz and the Cartesian Pierre-Sylvain Régis, for example). In* The Search after Truth, *Malebranche presents and defends the two doctrines for which he is best known, the occasionalism that denies causation between any finite substances and the claim that we see all things in God.*[2]

## Book III. Part II: The Pure Understanding. The Nature of Ideas

### Chapter 1

*I. What is understood by ideas. That they truly exist and are necessary to perceive all material objects.* I think everyone agrees that we do not perceive objects outside of us by themselves. We see the sun, the stars, and an infinity of objects outside of us; it is not likely that the soul leaves the body and, as it were, goes wandering about the heavens in order to contemplate all these objects. It does not therefore see them by themselves; the immediate object of our mind when it sees the sun, for example, is not the sun, but is something intimately united to our soul, and this is what I call an *idea*. Thus, by the word *idea*, I understand here nothing other than the immediate object, or the object closest to the mind, when it perceives

---

1. Translated from the French by Roger Ariew and Marjorie Grene.
2. For more on Malebranche, see Charles J. McCracken, *Malebranche and British Philosophy* (Oxford: Oxford University Press, 1983); Nicholas Jolley, *The Light of the Soul: Theories of Ideas in Leibniz, Malebranche, and Descartes* (Oxford: Oxford University Press, 1990); Steven Nadler, *Malebranche and Ideas* (Oxford: Oxford University Press, 1992); Tad Schmaltz, *Malebranche's Theory of the Soul: A Cartesian Interpretation* (Oxford: Oxford University Press, 1996); and Steven Nadler, ed., *Cambridge Companion to Malebranche* (Cambridge: Cambridge University Press, 1997).

something, namely, what touches and modifies the mind with the perception it has of an object.

It must be noted that for the mind to perceive an object, it is absolutely necessary for the idea of that object to be actually present to it—it is not possible to doubt this—but it is not necessary for there to be something similar to that idea outside it. For it very often happens that we perceive things which do not exist and even which have never existed; thus, we often have in the mind real ideas of things that have never existed. When, for example, a man imagines a golden mountain, it is absolutely necessary that the idea of this mountain be really present to his mind. When a madman, or someone with a high fever or who is sleeping, sees some animal as if before his eyes, it is certain that what he sees is not nothing, and that, thus, the idea of this animal really exists—but this golden mountain and this animal have never existed.

However, since men are led as if by nature to believe that only corporeal objects exist, they judge of the reality and existence of things in a completely different way than they should. For once they perceive an object, they want it to be quite certain that the object exists, even though it often happens that there is nothing outside. They want, in addition, for the object to be exactly as they see it, which never happens. But, with respect to the idea that exists necessarily and that cannot be other than as it is seen, they ordinarily judge without reflection that it is nothing—as if ideas did not have a great number of properties—as if the idea of a square, for example, were not quite different from that of a circle or of a number and did not represent completely different things—which can never happen for nothingness, since nothingness has no properties. It is therefore indubitable that ideas have a very real existence. But now let us examine what their nature is, and their essence, and let us see what in the soul can be capable of representing all things to it.

All the things the soul perceives are of two kinds: they are either in the soul or outside the soul. Those in the soul are its own thoughts, that is, all its different modifications, for by the words *thought, manner of thinking,* or *modification of the soul,* I understand generally all those things that cannot be in the soul without the soul perceiving them through the internal sensation it has of itself—such as its own sensations, imaginings, pure intellections, or simply its conceptions, even its passions and natural inclinations. Now, our soul does not need ideas in order to perceive all these things in the way it perceives them, because these things are inside the soul, or rather because they are only the soul itself in this or that fashion, just as the actual roundness and motion of a body are only that body shaped and moved in this or that fashion.

But as for things outside the soul, we can perceive them only by means of ideas, assuming that these things cannot be intimately united to the soul. There are two kinds of these, spiritual and material. As for the spiritual ones, it seems that they can be revealed to the soul without ideas and by themselves. For although experience teaches us that we cannot communicate our thoughts to one another immediately and by ourselves, but only through speech or other sensible signs to which we have attached our ideas, it might be said that God has decreed it thus only for the duration of this life, in order to prevent the disorder that would happen if people could communicate as it pleased them. But when justice and order reign and we are delivered from the captivity of our body, we shall perhaps be able to communicate through the intimate union among ourselves, as the angels seem to be able to do in heaven. Thus, it does not seem to be absolutely necessary to have ideas represent spiritual things to the soul, because it can happen that they are seen through themselves, though in a very imperfect fashion.

I shall not examine here how two minds can be united to one another and whether they can in this way reveal their thoughts to each other. I believe, however, that there is no purely intelligible substance other than God's, that nothing can be discovered with evidence except in its light, and that the union of minds cannot make them visible to each other. For although we are closely united to ourselves, we are and will be unintelligible to ourselves until we see ourselves in God, and until he presents to us the perfectly intelligible idea he has of our being contained in his being. Thus, although it seems I am here allowing that angels can by themselves make known to one another both what they are and what they are thinking—which at bottom I do not believe to be true—I warn that this is only because I do not want to argue about it, as long as you grant me what is incontestable, namely, that material things cannot be seen by themselves and without ideas.

In the seventh chapter I will explain my opinion on the way we know minds and I will show that for now we cannot know them completely by themselves, even though they might be able to be united with us. But I am speaking here primarily about material things, which certainly cannot be united to our soul in the way it is necessary for it to perceive them, because, since they are extended and the soul is not so, there is no relation between them. Moreover, our souls do not leave the body to measure the size of the heavens and, as a result, they cannot see bodies on the outside except through the ideas representing them. This is what everyone must agree with.

*II. Division of all the ways according to which objects can be seen from the outside.* We assert, therefore, that it is absolutely necessary that the ideas we have of bodies and of all the other objects we do not perceive by themselves come from these very bodies or from these objects; or else that our soul has the power of producing these ideas; or that God has produced them with it while creating it or produces them every time we think about some object; or that the soul has in itself all the perfections it sees in these bodies; or finally that it is united to a completely perfect being which contains generally all intelligible perfections, or all the ideas of created beings.

We are not able to see objects except in one of these ways. Let us examine which of these is the most likely without prejudice and without fearing the difficulty of the question. Perhaps we will resolve it clearly enough, even though we do not claim here to give incontestable demonstrations for all people, but rather very persuasive proofs for those who will at least meditate about them with serious care, for we would perhaps appear presumptuous if we were to speak otherwise.

## Chapter 2

*That material objects do not transmit species resembling them.* The most common opinion is that of the Peripatetics, who claim that external objects transmit species which resemble them, and that these species are carried by the external senses to the common sense. They call these species *impressed* because objects impress them on the external senses. These impressed species, being material and sensible, are made intelligible by the *agent* or *active intellect* and are capable of being received in the *passive intellect*. These species, thus spiritualized, are called *expressed* species, because they are expressed from the impressed species, and through them the *passive intellect* knows all material things.

We shall not pause here to explicate further these fine things and the various ways different philosophers conceive of them. For although they do not agree about the number of faculties they attribute to the interior sense and to the understanding, and there are even many of them who strongly doubt whether an *agent intellect* is needed to know sensible objects, still they almost all agree that external objects transmit species or images resembling them; and it is only on this foundation that they multiply their faculties and defend their *agent intellect*. Since this foundation has no solidity, as we will show, it is not necessary to pause further in order to overthrow everything that has been built on it.

We assert, then, that it is not likely that objects transmit images or species resembling them; and here are some reasons why. The first is derived from the impenetrability of bodies. All objects, such as the sun, the stars, and all those close to our eyes are unable to transmit species of another nature than theirs. This is why philosophers commonly say that these species are gross and material, in contrast to the expressed species, which are spiritualized. These impressed species of objects are therefore little bodies; thus, they cannot penetrate each other or all the spaces from the earth to the heavens, which must be full of them. From this it is easy to conclude that they must rub against and damage each other from every side, and that thus they cannot make objects visible.

Moreover, a great number of objects in the heavens and on earth can be seen from the same place or the same point; therefore, the species of all these objects would have to be capable of being reduced to a point.

Now since they are extended, they are impenetrable; therefore, etc.

But not only can we see a great number of very large and vast objects from the same point, there is even no point in all these great spaces of the world from which an almost infinite number of objects cannot be discovered, even objects as large as the sun, moon, and heavens. There is therefore no point in the whole world where the species of all these things cannot meet—which goes against all semblance of truth.

The second reason is taken from the change that happens in the species. It is certain that the closer an object is, the larger its species must be, since we see the object as larger. Now, we do not see what can make this species diminish or what can happen to the parts composing it when it was larger. But what is even harder to conceive of according to their view is how, if we look at this object with a telescope or a microscope, the species suddenly becomes five or six hundred times larger than it was, for still less do we see with what parts it can be so greatly increased in an instant.

The third reason is that when we look at a perfect cube, all the species of its sides are unequal, and yet we still see all its sides as equally square. And, similarly, when we consider ovals and parallelograms in a picture, which can transmit only species of the same shape, we see only circles and squares there. This clearly shows that it is not necessary for the object we are looking at to produce species similar to it in order for us to see it.

Finally, we are not able to conceive of how it can happen that a body which does not sensibly diminish can always emit species in all directions and continually fill the great spaces around it—and do this with inconceivable speed. For a hidden object can be seen at the very instant of its discovery, from several million leagues away and from all sides. And, what seems even more strange, very active bodies, such as air and some others, do not have the force to emit images resembling them—which coarser and less active bodies, such as earth, stones, and almost all hard bodies do.

But we do not wish to linger further and bring forth all the reasons opposed to this opinion, because it cannot be done, since the least mental effort yields such a great number of them that they cannot be exhausted. The reasons we have just related are enough; they were not even needed, given what we have said about this subject in Book I, where we explained the errors of the senses. But such a great number of philosophers hold this opinion that we thought it necessary to say something about it in order to make them reflect upon their thoughts.

## Chapter 3

*That the soul has no power to produce ideas. Cause of the error we make concerning this matter*. The second opinion belongs to those who believe that our souls have the power of producing the ideas of the things about which they want to think—that they are moved to produce them by the impressions objects make on the body, even though these impressions are not images resembling the objects that cause them. They claim that this is how man is made in the image of God and how he participates in God's power. Further, just as God has created all things from nothing and can annihilate them and create new ones, so can man create and annihilate ideas of all things as it pleases him. But there is good reason to distrust all these opinions that elevate man. They are normally thoughts arising from his pride and vanity, which the Father of lights did not issue.

This participation in God's power that men boast of for representing objects to themselves and for performing several other particular actions, seems to involve a certain independence, as it is generally explained. But it is also a chimerical participation, which the ignorance and vanity of men makes them imagine. Their dependence on God's power and goodness is much greater than they think, but here is not the place to explain this. Let us try only to show that men do not have the power to form ideas of the things they perceive.

No one can doubt that ideas are real beings, since they have real properties; that they differ from one another; and that they represent completely different things. Nor can we reasonably doubt that they are spiritual and very different from the bodies they represent. This seems sufficient to make us doubt whether the ideas by means of which we see bodies are not more noble than the bodies themselves. Indeed, the intelligible world must be more perfect than the material and terrestrial world, as we will see in what follows. Thus, when someone claims that men have the power to form such ideas as please them, he runs the risk of claiming that men have the power of creating beings more noble and more perfect than the world God has created. Yet we never reflect upon this, because we imagine that an idea is nothing, since it cannot be sensed, or if it is considered as a being, it is only as a meager and insignificant being, because we imagine that it is annihilated as soon as it is no longer present to the mind.

But even if it were true that ideas are only lesser and insignificant beings, they are nevertheless beings, and spiritual beings; since men do not have the power to create, it follows that they cannot produce these beings. For the production of ideas in the way it is explained is a true creation, and although they may try to palliate and soften the audacity and harshness of this view by saying that the production of ideas presupposes something existing, whereas creation presupposes nothing, still they have not resolved the difficulty.

For we ought to take heed that it is no more difficult to produce something from nothing than to produce it by supposing another thing from which it cannot be made and which can contribute nothing to its production. For example, it is no more difficult to create an angel than to produce it from a stone, because a stone is something of a totally contrary kind and cannot serve in any way toward the production of an angel. But it can contribute toward the production of bread, of gold, etc., because stone, gold, and bread are just the same extension differently configured, and all of these are material things.

It is even more difficult to produce an angel from a stone than to produce it from nothing, because to make an angel from a stone, insofar as that can be done, the stone must first be annihilated and then the angel must be created, and nothing needs to be annihilated simply to create an angel. Therefore, if the mind produces its ideas from the material impressions the brain receives from objects, it is always doing the

same thing, or something as difficult, or even more difficult, than if it created them. Since ideas are spiritual, they cannot be produced from material images, which are in the brain and have no common measure with them.

If it is said that an idea is not a substance, I would agree; but still it is a spiritual thing, and just as it is not possible to make a square out of a mind, even though a square is not a substance, it is also not possible to form a spiritual idea from a material substance, even though an idea would not be a substance.

But even if we granted to the mind of man a supreme power to annihilate and to create the ideas of things, it would still not be adequate to produce them. For just as a painter, no matter how skillful he is in his art, cannot represent an animal he has never seen and of which he has no idea (in such a way that the picture he would be required to produce could not be similar to this unknown animal), so a man cannot form the idea of an object unless he knew it beforehand, that is, unless he already has the idea of it, which does not depend on his will. But if he already has an idea of it, he knows the object, and it is useless for him to form a new idea of it. It is therefore useless to attribute to the mind of man the power to produce its ideas.

We could perhaps say that the mind has general and confused ideas it does not produce, and that those it produces are plainer and more distinct particular ideas. But this is still the same thing. For just as a painter cannot draw the portrait of a particular person in such a way that he is certain of having succeeded if he does not have a distinct idea of him (even if the person is present), so also a mind that has, for example, only the idea of being or of animal in general cannot represent a horse to itself, or form a very distinct idea of it, or be sure that the idea exactly resembles a horse if it does not already have a first idea to which it refers the second. And if it already has a first idea, it is useless to form a second, and therefore the question concerns the first idea; therefore, etc.

It is true that when we conceive of a square through pure intellection, we can still imagine it, that is to say, perceive it in us by tracing an image in the brain. But it should be noted, first, that we are neither the true nor the principal cause of that image (but it would take too long to explain this here) and second, that far from the second idea accompanying the image being more distinct and more accurate than the first idea, on the contrary, it is accurate only because it resembles the first, which serves as rule for the second. For finally we must not believe that the imagination and even the senses represent objects to us more distinctly than does the pure understanding, but only that they affect and move the mind more. For the ideas of the senses and of the imagination are distinct only through the conformity they have with the ideas of pure intellection. The image of a square that the imagination traces in the brain, for example, is only accurate and well formed through the conformity it has with the idea of a square that we conceive through pure intellection. It is this idea that rules the image. It is the mind that leads the imagination and requires it, so to speak, to consider from time to time whether the image it depicts is a figure composed of four straight and equal lines, whose angles are exactly ninety degrees—in a word, whether what one imagines is similar to what one conceives.

After what we have said, I do not think we can doubt that those who assert that the mind can itself form ideas of objects are mistaken, since they attribute to the mind the power to create, and even to create with wisdom and order, even though it does not have knowledge of what it does—for this is not conceivable. But the cause of their error is that people never fail to judge that a thing is the cause of some effect when the two are joined together, assuming that the true cause of the effect is unknown to them. This is why everyone concludes that a moving ball meeting another is the true and principal cause of the motion it communicates to the other, and that the soul's will is the true and principal cause of motion of the arm, and other such similar prejudices, because it always happens that a ball moves when it is struck by another, that our arms move almost every time we want them to, and that we do not sensibly see what other thing could be the cause of these motions.

Even when an effect does not so often follow something which is not its cause, still, there are a great number of people who believe that the thing is the cause of the effect that happens, though not everyone

falls into this error. For example: a comet appears and afterwards a prince dies; stones are exposed to the moon and they are eaten by worms; the sun is in conjunction with Mars at the birth of a child and something extraordinary happens to the child. This is enough to convince many people that the comet, the moon, and the conjunction of the sun with Mars are the causes of the effects just noted and others similar to them; and the reason why not everyone is of the same belief is that these effects are not always observed to follow these things.

But since all persons normally have ideas of things present to the mind as soon as they want them, and this happens to them many times a day, almost everyone concludes that the will accompanying the production, or rather, the presence of ideas is their true cause, because they see nothing at the time they can attribute to them as their cause, and because they imagine that ideas no longer exist once the mind no longer sees them and begin to exist again when they are represented to the mind. This is also why some people judge that external objects transmit images resembling them, as we have just pointed out in the previous chapter. Since it is not possible to see objects by themselves, but only through their ideas, they judge that the object produces the idea: once it is present, they see it; as soon as it is absent, they no longer see it; and the presence of the object almost always accompanies the idea representing it to us.

Yet if people were not so precipitous in their judgments, from the fact that the ideas of things are present to their mind as soon as they want, they would conclude only that according to the order of nature their will is generally necessary for them to have these ideas, and not that the will is the true and principal cause that makes them present to their mind, and still less that the will produces them from nothing (or in the way they explain it). Nor should they conclude that objects transmit species resembling them because the soul ordinarily perceives them only when they are present, but only that the object is ordinarily necessary for the idea to be present to the mind. Finally, they should not judge that a moving ball is the true and principal cause of the motion of the ball it finds in its path, since the former ball does not have the power to move itself. They can only judge that the collision of two balls is the occasion for the Author of all the motion of matter to execute the decree of his will, which is the universal cause of all things. This he does by communicating to the second ball part of the motion of the first—that is, to speak more clearly, by willing that the latter ball should acquire as much motion in the same direction as the former loses—for the motive force of bodies can only be the will of the one who preserves them, as we shall show elsewhere.

## Chapter 4

*That we do not see objects by means of ideas created with us. That God does not produce ideas in us at each moment we need them.* The third opinion is held by those who claim that all ideas are innate or created with us.

To recognize the implausibility of this opinion, it should be considered that there are many completely different things in the world of which we have ideas. But to mention only simple figures, it is certain that their number is infinite, and even if we attend only to one, such as the ellipse, we cannot doubt that the mind conceives of an infinite number of different kinds of them when it conceives that one of the diameters may be lengthened to infinity while the other remains always the same.

In the same way, since the height of a triangle can be increased or decreased to infinity while the base remains always the same, we conceive that there can be an infinite number of different kinds of triangles; moreover, and this is what I beg to have considered here, the mind perceives this infinite number in some way, even though we can imagine only a very few and cannot at the same time have particular and distinct ideas of many triangles of different kinds. But what should be especially noted is that the mind's general idea of this infinite number of different kinds of triangles sufficiently proves that if we do not conceive of all these different triangles by particular ideas—in short, if we do not comprehend the infinite—it is not through our lack of ideas or because the infinite is not present to us, but only through the mind's lack of capacity and scope. If a person applied himself to considering the properties of all the different kinds of triangles, and even if he should forever continue this kind of investigation, he would never lack new and particular ideas, but his mind would exhaust itself uselessly.

What I have just said about triangles can be applied to figures of five, six, a hundred, a thousand, ten thousand sides, and so on to infinity. And if the sides of a triangle can have infinite relations with one another, making an infinity of kinds of triangles, it is easy to see that figures of four, five, or a million sides can have even greater differences, since they can have a greater number of relations and combinations of their sides than simple triangles.

The mind, therefore, sees all these things; it has ideas of them. It is certain that these ideas will never be unavailable to it, even if it should spend infinite centuries considering even a single figure; and if it does not perceive these infinite figures all at once, or if it does not comprehend the infinite, it is only because its scope is quite limited. It therefore has an infinite number of ideas—I do not mean just an infinite number: it has as many infinite numbers of ideas as there are different figures, such that, since there is an infinite number of different figures, in order to know the figures alone, the mind must have an infinity of infinite numbers of ideas.

Now, I ask whether it is likely that God has created so many things along with the mind of man. It does not appear to me to be so, mainly because all this could be done in another very simple and very easy way, as we shall see shortly. For as God always acts in the simplest ways, it does not seem reasonable to explain how we know objects by assuming the creation of an infinity of beings, since this difficulty can be resolved in an easier and more natural fashion.

But even if the mind had a store of all the ideas necessary for it to see objects, nevertheless it would be impossible to explain how the soul could choose them to represent them to itself—how, for example, the soul could make itself perceive all the different objects whose size, figure, distance, and motion it discovers the instant it opens its eyes in the countryside. It could not even perceive by this means a single object, such as the sun, when it is present to the eyes of the body. For, since the image the sun impresses in the brain does not at all resemble the idea we have of it (as we have proved elsewhere) and the soul does not perceive the motion the sun produces in the back of the eyes and in the brain, it is not conceivable that it can rightly predict, among the infinite number of its ideas it would have, which one must be represented for the sun to be imagined or seen, and seen as having this or that determinate size. We cannot therefore say that the ideas of things are created with us and that this suffices for us to see the objects surrounding us.

Nor can we say that God produces at every moment as many new ideas as we perceive different things. This view is sufficiently refuted by what we have just said in this chapter. Moreover, it is necessary that at all times we actually have in us the ideas of all things, since we can at all times will to think about all things—which we could not do if we did not already perceive them confusedly, that is to say, if an infinite number of ideas were not present to our mind; for, after all, we cannot will to think about objects of which we have no idea. Moreover, it is evident that the idea or immediate object of our mind, when we think of immense spaces, or of a circle in general, or of indeterminate being, is not a created thing. For created reality can be neither infinite nor even general, such as what we perceive there. But all this will be seen more clearly in what follows.

[ . . . ]

## Chapter 6

*That we see all things in God.* In the previous chapters we have examined four different ways in which the soul might see external objects, none of which appears to us likely. There remains only the fifth way, which alone appears to conform to reason and to be most appropriate for allowing us to know the dependence that minds have on God in all their thoughts.

To understand this fifth way adequately, we must remember what we have just said in the previous chapter: It is absolutely necessary for God to have in himself the ideas of all the beings he has created, since otherwise he could not have produced them, and thus he sees all these beings by considering those perfections he contains to which they have a relation. We must know, further, that God is very closely united

to our souls through his presence, so that we can say that he is the place of minds in the same way that spaces are, in a sense, the place of bodies. Assuming these two things, it is certain that the mind can see what in God represents created beings, since the latter is very spiritual, intelligible, and present to the mind. Thus, the mind can see in God the works of God, assuming that God does indeed will to reveal to the mind what it is in him that represents them. Now, here are the reasons that seem to prove that he wills this rather than the creation of an infinite number of ideas in each mind.

Not only is it in strict conformity with reason but also it is apparent in the economy of all of nature that God never does by very difficult means what can be done by very simple and easy means. For God never does anything in vain and without reason. What shows his wisdom and his power is not his doing small things with great means—this goes against reason and indicates a limited intelligence—on the contrary, it is doing great things with very simple and easy means. Thus, it was with extension alone that he produced everything we see that is admirable in nature and even what gives life and motion to animals. Those who absolutely insist on substantial forms, faculties, and souls in animals to perform their functions (different from their blood and bodily organs) at the same time would have it that God lacks intelligence or that he cannot make all these admirable things with extension alone. They measure the power and supreme wisdom of God by the smallness of their mind. Thus, since God can reveal everything to minds simply by willing that they see what is in their midst, that is to say, what is in him which is related to and represents these things, there is no likelihood that he does it otherwise and that he produces for this as many infinities of infinite numbers of ideas as there are created minds.

But it should be carefully noted that we cannot conclude that minds see the essence of God from the fact of their seeing all things in God in this way. God's essence is his own absolute being, and minds do not see the divine substance taken absolutely but only as relative to creatures or as they are able to participate in it. What they see in God is very imperfect, and God is most perfect. They see matter shaped, divisible, and so forth, but in God there is nothing divisible or shaped, for God is all being, because he is infinite and comprises everything; but he is no particular being. However, what we see is only one or several particular beings, and we do not understand this perfect simplicity of God, which contains all beings. In addition, it might be said that we do not so much see ideas of things as we see things themselves represented by ideas; when we see a square, for example, we do not say that we see the idea of the square united to the mind but only the square outside it.

The second reason for thinking that we see beings because God wills that what is in him representing them be revealed to us—and not because we have as many ideas created with us as we can see things—is that this puts created minds in a position of complete dependence on God, the most complete possible. For, this being so, not only would we see nothing unless God wills that we see it, but we would see nothing unless God himself made us see it. [ . . . ]

For, after all, it is difficult enough to understand distinctly the dependence that our minds have on God in all their particular actions, assuming that they have everything we distinctly know to be necessary for them to act, or all the ideas of things present to their mind. And that general and confused word *concourse*, by means of which we claim to explain the dependence of creatures on God, does not awaken any distinct idea in an attentive mind; and yet it is good that people know very distinctly that they can do nothing without God.

But the strongest argument of all is the way the mind perceives all things. It is certain, and everyone knows it from experience, that when we want to think about some particular thing, we first glance over all beings and then apply ourselves to considering the object we wish to think about. Now, it is indubitable that we could not desire to see a particular object we had not already seen, though confusedly and in general. Thus, since we are able to desire to see all beings, sometimes one, sometimes another, it is certain that all beings are present to our mind; and it seems that all beings cannot be present to our mind without God—he who contains all things in the simplicity of his being— being present to it.

It even seems that the mind would not be capable of representing to itself universal ideas of genus, species, etc., had it not seen all the beings contained in one. Since every creature is a particular being, we cannot say that we see something created when, for example, we see a triangle in general. Finally, I do not think that we can account for the way the mind knows abstract and general truths, except through the presence of him who can illuminate the mind in an infinity of different ways.

Finally, the most beautiful, highest, most solid, primary proof of God's existence (or the one that makes the fewest assumptions) is the idea we have of the infinite. For it is certain that the mind perceives the infinite, though it does not comprehend it, and that it has a very distinct idea of God, which it can have only by means of its union with him, since we cannot conceive that the idea of an infinitely perfect being— the one we have of God—should be something created.

But not only does the mind have the idea of the infinite, it even has it before that of the finite. For we conceive of infinite being merely by conceiving of being, without thinking whether it is finite or infinite. But in order for us to conceive of a finite being, we must necessarily subtract something from this general notion of being, which consequently must come first. Thus, the mind perceives nothing except in the idea it has of the infinite; and as for this idea being formed from the confused assemblage of all our ideas of particular beings, as philosophers think, on the contrary, every particular idea is only a participation in the general idea of the infinite: In the same way, God does not derive his being from creatures, while every creature is only an imperfect participation in the divine being.

Here is a proof that may constitute a demonstration for those accustomed to abstract reasoning. It is certain that ideas are efficacious, since they act in the mind and illuminate it, and since they make it happy or unhappy through the pleasant or unpleasant perceptions by which they affect it. Now nothing can act in the mind immediately unless it is superior to the mind; nothing but God alone can do this. For only the Author of our being can change its modifications. Therefore, it is necessary that all our ideas are located in the efficacious substance of the divinity, which alone is intelligible or capable of illuminating us, because it alone can affect intelligences. [ . . . ]

Finally, it is not possible for God to have any other principal end for his actions than himself. This is a notion common to all people capable of some reflection; and Sacred Scripture does not allow us to doubt that God has made all things for himself. It is therefore necessary that not only our natural love—I am referring to the impulse he produces in our mind—tends toward him, but also the knowledge and light he gives the mind must allow us to know something in him, for everything coming from God can only be for God. If God made a mind and gave it the sun as an idea or as an immediate object of knowledge, it seems to me that God would be making this mind and the idea of this mind for the sun and not for himself.

God, therefore, cannot make a mind in order for it to know his works without that mind in some way being able to see God in seeing his works. Thus, it might be said that if we did not see God in some way, we would not see anything, just as if we did not love God—I mean if God did not continuously impress upon us the love of good in general—we would not love anything. For, this love being our will, we cannot love or will anything without it, since we cannot love particular goods except by determining toward these goods the motion of love God has given us for himself. Thus, in the same way that we do not love anything except through the necessary love we have for God, we do not see anything except through the natural knowledge we have of God; all the particular ideas we have of creatures are only limitations of the idea of the Creator, just as all the motions of the will toward creatures are only determinations of the motion toward the Creator. [ . . . ]

Therefore, we think that truths, even the eternal truths such as "twice two is four," are not absolute beings, much less do we think that they are God himself. For, clearly, this truth consists only in the relation of equality between twice two and four. Thus, we do not say, as does Saint Augustine, that we see God in seeing truths, but in seeing the *ideas* of these truths—for the ideas are real, whereas the equality between the ideas, which is the truth, is nothing

real. When we say, for example, that the cloth we are measuring is three ells long, the cloth and the ells are real. But the equality between the three ells and the cloth is not at all a real being; the equality is only a relation holding between the three ells and the cloth. When we say that twice two is four, the ideas of the numbers are real, but the equality between them is only a relation. Thus, according to our view, we see God when we see eternal truths, not because these truths are God but because the ideas on which these truths depend are in God; perhaps Saint Augustine also understood it that way. We also believe that we know changeable and corruptible things in God, even though Saint Augustine speaks only of immutable and incorruptible things; it is not necessary to posit some imperfection in God for this, since it is sufficient, as we have already said, that God should reveal to us what in him is related to these things.

But although I may say that we see material and sensible things in God, we must take note that I am not saying that we have sensations of them in God, but only that it is God who acts in us; for God surely knows sensible things, but he does not sense them. When we perceive something sensible, two things are found in our perception: *sensation* and pure *idea*. The sensation is a modification of our soul, and God causes it in us. He can cause this modification even though he does not have it himself, because he sees in the idea he has of our soul that it is capable of it. As for the idea united to the sensation, it is in God, and we see it because it pleases God to reveal it to us. God unites the sensation to the idea when objects are present so that we may believe them to be thus and enter into the sensations and passions we should have in relation to them.

We believe, finally, that all minds see the eternal laws, as well as other things, in God, but with some difference. They know order and the eternal truths and even the beings that God has made according to these truths or according to order, through the union these minds necessarily have with the Word, or wisdom of God, which enlightens them, as we have just explained. But it is through the impression they constantly receive from the will of God, who leads them toward him and who tries, so to speak, to render their will entirely similar to his own, that they realize that the order is a law; that is, that they know the eternal laws, such as that we must love good and shun evil, that justice must be loved more than all riches, that it is better to obey God than to command men, and an infinity of other natural laws. For the knowledge of all these laws is not different from the knowledge of this impression, which they always feel in themselves, though they do not always follow it through the free choice of their will, and which they know to be common to all minds, though it is not equally strong in all minds. [ . . . ]

## Chapter 7

In order to summarize and clarify the view I have just established about the way the mind perceives all the various objects of its knowledge, it is necessary that I distinguish in it four ways of knowing.

*I. Four ways of seeing things*. The first is to know things by themselves.

The second is to know them through their ideas, that is, as I understand it here, through something different from them.

The third is to know them through *consciousness*, or internal awareness.

The fourth is to know them through conjecture.

We know things by themselves and without ideas when they are intelligible by themselves, that is, when they can act on the mind and thereby reveal themselves to it. For the understanding is a purely passive faculty of the soul, and activity is found only in the will. Even its desires are not the true causes of ideas; they are only the occasional or natural causes of their presence, following the natural laws of the union of our soul with universal Reason, as I shall explain elsewhere. We know things through their ideas when they are not intelligible by themselves, either because they are corporeal or because they cannot affect the mind or reveal themselves to it. We know through consciousness all things not distinct from ourselves. Finally, we know through conjecture those things different from ourselves and from the ones we know in themselves or through ideas, when we think that certain things are similar to others we know.

*II. How we know God*. Only God is known through himself, for while there are other spiritual beings that seem intelligible by their nature, only he can act in the mind and reveal himself to it. Only God is seen by a direct and immediate view. Only he can illuminate the mind with his own substance. Finally, only through the union we have with him are we capable in this life of knowing what we know, as we have explained in the previous chapter; for he is the only Master, according to Saint Augustine, presiding over our mind without the intermediary of any creature.

We cannot conceive that something created can represent the infinite—that being without restriction, immense and universal being, can be perceived through an idea, that is, through a particular being, one different from universal and infinite being. But as for particular beings, it is not difficult to conceive that they can be represented by the infinite being containing them in his most efficacious and, consequently, most intelligible substance. Thus, it is necessary to say that we know God through himself, even though our knowledge of him in this life is very imperfect, and we know corporeal things through their ideas, that is, in God, since only God contains the intelligible world, in which the ideas of all things are found.

But while we can see all things in God, it does not follow that we do see them all: We see in God only the things of which we have ideas, and there are things we see without ideas, or know only through sensation.

*III. How we know bodies*. All the things in this world of which we have knowledge are either bodies or minds, properties of minds or properties of bodies. Undoubtedly, we see bodies with their properties only through their ideas, because, not being intelligible by themselves, we can see them only in that being which contains them in an intelligible way. Thus, it is in God and through their ideas that we see bodies and their properties, and for this reason, the knowledge we have of them is quite perfect—I mean that our idea of extension suffices to enable us to know all the properties of which extension is capable, and we could not wish to have a more distinct and more fruitful idea of extension, figure, and motion than the one God gives us of them.

Since the ideas of things in God contain all their properties, he who sees their ideas can also see all their properties successively; for, when we see things as they are in God, we always see them in perfect fashion, and the way we see them would be infinitely perfect if the mind seeing them were infinite. What is lacking from the knowledge we have of extension, figures, and motion is not a defect of the idea representing it, but of our mind considering it.

*IV. How we know our soul.* It is not the same for the soul: We do not at all know it through its idea; we do not at all see it in God; we know it only through *consciousness*, and because of this, the knowledge we have of it is imperfect. We know of our soul only what we sense taking place in us. If we never sensed pain, heat, light, etc., we could not know whether our soul was capable of it, because we do not know it through its idea. But if we saw in God the idea relating to our soul, we would at the same time know, or could know, all the properties of which it is capable—as we know, or can know, all the properties of which extension is capable, because we know extension through its idea.

It is true that we know enough through our consciousness, or the internal awareness we have of ourselves, that our soul is something great; but it might be that what we know of it is almost nothing compared to what it is in itself. If we knew of matter only some twenty or thirty figures by which it had been modified, we certainly would know almost nothing of it in comparison with what we can know of it through the idea representing it; therefore, to know the soul perfectly, it is not enough to know only what we know through internal awareness, since the consciousness we have of ourselves shows us perhaps only the least part of our being.

We might conclude from what we have just said that although we know the existence of our soul more distinctly than the existence of our body and those surrounding us, still we do not have as perfect a knowledge of the nature of the soul as that of the nature of bodies; this might serve to reconcile the differing views of those who say that nothing is known better than the soul and those who assert that there is nothing they know less.

This might also serve to prove that ideas representing to us things outside us are not modifications of our soul. For if the soul saw all things by considering its own modifications, it would have to know more clearly its essence or nature than that of bodies, and all the sensations or modifications of which it is capable more clearly than the figures or modifications of which bodies are capable. However, it does not at all know itself capable of such a sensation through the view it has of itself in consulting its idea, but only through experience; instead it knows that extension is capable of an infinite number of figures through the idea it has of extension. There are even certain sensations like colors and sounds which are such that most people cannot tell whether or not they are modifications of the soul, but there is no figure that everyone, through the idea he has of extension, does not recognize as the modification of a body.

What I have just said also shows us the reason why we cannot give a definition that allows us to know modifications of the soul; for since we know neither the soul nor its modifications through ideas but only through sensations, and since such sensations as, for example, pleasure, pain, heat, etc., are not attached to words, it is clear that if someone had never seen color nor felt heat, we could not make him know those sensations through any definition of them we might give him. Now, since people have their sensations only because of their bodies, which are not all disposed in the same way, it often happens that words are equivocal, that the words we use to express the modifications of our soul signify just the contrary of what we mean, and that we often make people think of bitterness, for example, when we believe we are making them think of sweetness.

While we do not have complete knowledge of our soul, what we do have of it through consciousness or internal awareness suffices to demonstrate its immortality, spirituality, freedom, and several other attributes that it is necessary for us to know; and it is apparently for this reason that God does not have us know the soul through its idea, as he has us know bodies. Granted that the knowledge that we have of our soul through consciousness is imperfect, but it is not false. In contrast, the knowledge we have of bodies through sensation or consciousness—if we can call consciousness the confused sensation we have of what happens in our body—is not only imperfect, but also false. We therefore needed an idea of bodies to correct our sensations of them, but we do not need an idea of our soul, since the consciousness we have of it does not involve us in error, and since to avoid being mistaken in our knowledge of it, it suffices that we do not confuse it with the body—which we can do through reason, since the idea we have of the body reveals to us that the modalities of which it is capable are very different from those we feel. Finally, if we had an idea of the soul as clear as the one we have of the body, that idea would have us overly consider the soul as separated from the body. It would have thus diminished the union between our soul and our body by preventing us from regarding it as dispersed through all our members—a point I shall not explain any further.

V. *How we know the souls of other men*. Of all the objects of our knowledge, only the souls of other men and pure intelligences remain; it is manifest that we know them only through conjecture. At present we do not know them either in themselves or through their ideas, and as they are different from us, it is not possible to know them through consciousness. We conjecture that the souls of other men are of the same kind as our own. We claim that they feel what we feel in ourselves, and even when these sensations have no relation to the body, we are certain we are not mistaken because we see in God certain ideas and immutable laws according to which we know with certainty that God acts uniformly in all minds. [ . . . ]

## Book VI. Part II: On Method

### Chapter 3

*The most dangerous error of the philosophy of the ancients*. Not only do philosophers say what they do not at all conceive when they explain natural effects through certain beings of which they have no particular idea, they even furnish a principle from which very false and very dangerous conclusions can be drawn directly.

For if we assume, according to their view, that there are entities distinct from matter in bodies, then, having no distinct idea of these entities, we can easily imagine that they are the true or principal causes of the effects we see happening. This is even the general opinion of ordinary philosophers: For it is principally to explain

these effects that they think there are substantial forms, real qualities, and other similar entities. Next, if we consider carefully the idea we have of cause or of power to act, we cannot doubt that this idea represents something divine. For the idea of a supreme power is the idea of a supreme divinity and the idea of a subalternate power is the idea of an inferior, but genuine, divinity, at least according to the pagans, assuming that it is the idea of a genuine power or cause. We therefore admit something divine in all the bodies around us when we admit forms, faculties, qualities, virtues, or real beings capable of producing certain effects through the force of their nature; and thus we insensibly adopt the view of the pagans because of our respect for their philosophy. It is true that faith corrects us, but perhaps it can be said that if the heart is Christian, the mind is at bottom pagan. Perhaps it will be said that substantial forms—for example, those *plastic* forms which produce animals and plants—do not know what they are doing and that, thus lacking intelligence, they have no relation to the divinities of the pagans. But who will be able to believe that what produces works manifesting a wisdom surpassing that of all the philosophers produces them without intelligence?

Furthermore, it is difficult to be persuaded that we should neither fear nor love true powers, beings that can act upon us, that can punish us with pain, or reward us with pleasure. And since love and fear are true adoration, it is also difficult to be persuaded that we should not adore them. Everything that can act upon us as a true and real cause is necessarily above us, according to Saint Augustine and according to reason; and according to the same saint and the same reason, it is an immutable law that inferior things serve superior ones. It is for these reasons that this great saint recognizes that *the body cannot act upon the soul*, and that nothing can be above the soul other than God. [ . . . ]

In order that we shall no longer be able to doubt the falsity of this unfortunate philosophy and recognize with evidence the soundness of the principles and the distinctness of the ideas we use, it is necessary to establish clearly the truths that are opposed to the errors of the ancient philosophers, and to prove in a few words that: there is only one true cause because there is only one true God; the nature or power of each thing is but the will of God; all natural causes are not at all *true* causes but only *occasional* causes; and some other truths following from these.

It is evident that bodies, large and small, do not have the power to move themselves. A mountain, a house, a rock, a grain of sand—in brief, the smallest or largest body conceivable—does not have the power to move itself. We have only two sorts of ideas, ideas of minds and ideas of bodies; and since we should say only what we conceive of, we should reason only according to these two. Thus, since the idea we have of all bodies makes us know that they cannot move themselves, it must be concluded that it is minds which move them. But when we examine the idea we have of all finite minds, we do not see any necessary connection between their will and the motion of any body whatsoever. On the contrary, we see that there is none and that there can be none. We must also conclude, if we wish to reason according to our lights, that no created mind can move any body whatsoever as a true or principal cause, just as we have said that no body could move itself.

But when we think of the idea of God, that is, of an infinitely perfect and consequently omnipotent being, we know that there is such a connection between his will and the motion of all bodies that it is impossible to conceive that he wills a body be moved and that this body not be moved. We must therefore say that only his will can move bodies if we wish to say things as we conceive of them and not as we sense them. The motive force of bodies is therefore not in the bodies that are moved, for this motive force is nothing other than the will of God. Thus, bodies have no action; and when a moving ball collides with and moves another, it communicates to it nothing of its own, for it does not itself have the force it communicates. However, a ball is the natural cause of the motion it communicates. A natural cause is therefore not a real and true but only an occasional cause, one that determines the Author of nature to act in such and such a manner in such and such a situation.

It is certain that all things are produced through the motion of bodies, visible or invisible, for experience teaches us that bodies whose parts have more motion are always those that act more and produce more change in the world. All natural forces are therefore nothing but the always efficacious will of God. God created the world because he willed it—"He spoke and it was done"—and he moves all things, and thus produces all the effects we see happening, because he also willed certain laws according to which motions are communicated upon the collision of bodies; because these laws are efficacious, they act, and bodies cannot act. There are therefore no forces, powers, or true causes in the material and sensible world; and we must not admit forms, faculties, and real qualities for producing effects that bodies do not produce and for sharing with God the force and power that are essential to him.

Not only can bodies not be the true causes of anything whatsoever, but the most noble minds are similarly powerless. They can know nothing unless God illuminates them. They can sense nothing unless God modifies them. They are capable of willing nothing if God does not move them toward good in general, that is, toward himself. I admit that they can determine toward objects other than himself the impression God gives them toward himself, but I do not know if that can be called power. If the ability to sin is a power, it will be a power that the Almighty does not have, as Saint Augustine says somewhere. If people held of themselves the power to love the good, we could say they had some power; but people can love only because God wills that they love and because his will is efficacious. People can love only because God constantly pushes them toward the good in general, that is, toward himself; for God having created them only for himself, he never preserves them without turning and pushing them toward him. It is not they who move toward the good in general, it is God who moves them. They merely follow this impression through an entirely free choice according to the law of God, or they determine it toward false goods, according to the law of the flesh, but they can determine it only through their view of the good; since they can do only what God makes them do, they can only love the good.

But if we were to assume what is true in one sense—that minds have in themselves the power to know the truth and to love the good—if their thoughts and wills produced nothing externally, we could always say that they can do nothing. Now it appears to me quite certain that the will of minds is not capable of moving the smallest body in the world; for it is evident that there is no necessary connection between the will we have to move our arm, for example, and the motion of our arm. It is true that the arm moves when we will it, and that we are thus the natural cause of the motion of our arm. But *natural* causes are not at all true causes; they are merely *occasional* causes acting only through the force and efficacy of the will of God, as I have just explained.

For how could we move our arm? To move it, we must have animal spirits, we must send them through certain nerves toward certain muscles to inflate and contract them, for that is how the arm attached to them moves; or according to some other views, we still do not know how that happens. And we see people who do not even know that they have spirits, nerves, and muscles move their arm, and move it even with more skill and ease than those who know anatomy best. Therefore, people will to move their arm, and only God is able and knows how to move it. If a person is not able to knock down a tower, at least he knows what must be done to knock it down; but no person knows what must be done to move just one of his fingers by means of animal spirits. How, then, could people move their arm? These things appear evident to me and, it seems, to all those willing to think, though they are perhaps incomprehensible to all those willing only to sense.

But not only are men not at all the true causes of the motions they produce in their body, it even seems contradictory that they could be. As I understand it, a true cause is a cause such that the mind perceives a necessary connection between it and its effect. Now the mind perceives a necessary connection only between the will of an infinitely perfect being and its effects. Therefore, only God is the true cause who truly has the power to move bodies. In addition, I say that it is inconceivable that God could communicate to people or to angels the power he has to move bodies, and that those who claim that the power we have to move our arm is a true power must admit that God can also give minds the power to create, annihilate, and

to do all possible things—in short, that he can render them omnipotent, as I shall show.

God needs no instruments to act; it suffices that he wills[3] in order for a thing to be, because it is contradictory that he should will and that what he wills should not be. Therefore, his power is his will, and to communicate his power is to communicate the efficacy of his will. But to communicate this efficacy to a person or an angel can signify nothing other than to will that, for example, when a person or angel shall will this or that body be moved, the body will actually be moved. Now in this case, I see two wills concurring when an angel moves a body—that of God and that of the angel—and in order to know which of the two is the true cause of the motion of this body, we must know which cause is efficacious. There is a necessary connection between the will of God and the thing he wills. God wills in this case that when an angel wills this or that body be moved, the body will be moved. Therefore, there is a necessary connection between the will of God and the motion of the body; and consequently God is the true cause of the motion of the body and the will of the angel is only an occasional cause.

But to show this still more clearly, let us suppose that God wills to produce the opposite of what some minds would will, as might be thought for demons or some other minds deserving of this punishment. We could not say in this case that God would communicate his power to them, since they could do nothing they wished to do. However, the wills of these minds would be the natural causes of the effects produced. Such bodies would be moved to the right only because these minds willed them to be moved to the left; and the desires of these minds would determine the will of God to act, as our will to move the parts of our bodies determines the first cause to move them. In this way, all the volitions of minds are only occasional causes.

But if after all these arguments someone still wanted to maintain that the will of an angel who moved a body would be a true and not an occasional cause, it is evident that this same angel could be the true cause of the creation and annihilation of all

---

3. Malebranche: It is clear that I am speaking here about practical volitions, or those God has when he claims to act.

things. For God could communicate his power to create and annihilate bodies to the angel, in the same way he communicates the power to move them, if he willed all things to be created and annihilated—in short, if he willed all things to happen as the angel would wish it, just as he willed bodies to be moved as the angel would will. Therefore, if someone claims that an angel and a person are truly movers because God moves bodies when they wish it, he must also say that a person and an angel can truly be creators, since God can create beings when they would will it. Perhaps he could even say that the most vile animal, or matter all alone, would effectively cause the creation of some substance, if he assumed, as do the philosophers, that God produced substantial forms when required by matter. Finally, because God resolved from all eternity to create certain things in certain times, he could also say that these times would be the causes of the creation of these beings—just as he claims that one ball colliding with another is the true cause of the motion it communicates to the latter, because God willed through his general will, which causes the order of nature, that when two bodies collide, such a communication of motion would occur.

There is therefore only a single true God and a single cause which is truly a cause, and we should not imagine that what precedes an effect is its true cause. God cannot even communicate his power to creatures, if we follow the light of reason: He cannot make true causes of them; he cannot make them gods. But even if he could, we cannot conceive of why he would. Bodies, minds, pure intelligences, all these can do nothing. It is he who makes minds, who illuminates and moves them. It is he who created heaven and earth and who regulates their motions. In the end, it is the Author of our being who executes our wills: "Once God judges, the will always obeys." He even moves our arm when we use it against his orders; for he complains through his prophet (Isa. 43.24) that we make him serve our unjust and criminal desires. [ . . . ]

## Elucidation Fifteen

*On Book VI, Part II, Chapter 3. Concerning the efficacy attributed to secondary causes.* [ . . . ] There are many reasons preventing me from attributing to *secondary* or *natural* causes a force, a power, an efficacy to produce anything whatsoever. But the principal one is that this opinion does not even appear conceivable to me. Whatever effort I make to comprehend it, I cannot find in me any idea representing to me what might be the force or power attributed to creatures. And I do not even think I am making an overly bold judgment when I assert that those who maintain that creatures have force and power in themselves advance something they do not conceive of clearly. For, in the end, if philosophers conceived clearly that secondary causes have a true force to act and produce things similar to them, then being a man as much as they are and participating like them in supreme Reason, I could apparently discover the idea representing this force to them. But whatever effort of mind I make, I can find force, efficacy, power, only in the will of the infinitely perfect being.

In addition, when I think about the different opinions of philosophers on this subject, I cannot doubt what I am proposing. For, if they saw clearly what the power of creatures is, or what is truly powerful in them, they would agree about it. When people who have no special interest preventing them from doing so cannot agree, it is a sure sign that they simply do not have a clear idea of what they are saying and do not understand each other—especially if they are disputing about subjects not overly complex or difficult to discuss, such as the question at hand, for there would be no difficulty in resolving it, if people had some clear idea of a created force or power. Here then are some of their opinions so that you might see how little they agree among themselves.

There are some philosophers[4] who assert that *secondary causes* act through their *matter*, their *shape*, and their *motion*, and these philosophers are right in a sense; others through a *substantial form*; several through *accidents* or *qualities*; and some

---

4. Malebranche: For the most extraordinary of these views, see Suarez's *Metaph.* Disp. 18. sec. 2 & 3 and others cited by him.

through matter and *form*; of these some through *form* and *accidents*, others through certain *virtues* or faculties different from the above. There are some who maintain that the substantial form produces forms and the accidental form accidents; others that forms produce other forms and accidents; and others, finally, that accidents alone are capable of producing accidents and even forms. But we should not imagine that those who say, for example, that accidents can produce forms through the virtue they have received from the form to which they are joined understand this in the same way. Some would have it that these accidents are not the same as the force or virtue of the substantial form; others that they receive in them the influence of the form and that they thus act only through its virtue; and others, finally, that they are only instrumental causes. But these last are not yet in total agreement among themselves about what we must understand by instrumental cause, nor what is the virtue that it receives from the principal cause. The philosophers do not even agree about the action by which secondary causes produce their effects. Some of them claim that *causality* must not be produced, for it is what produces; others would have them truly act through their action, but they find such great difficulty in explaining what precisely is this action, and there are so many different opinions about this, that I cannot resolve myself to relate them.

You have there a great variety of opinions, even though I have not related those of the ancient philosophers or of the ones who were born in very distant countries. But we can judge well enough that they no more entirely agree among themselves on the subject of secondary causes than those of whom I have just spoken. Avicenna, for example, does not believe that corporeal substances can produce anything other than accidents. And here is his system as related by Ruvio. He claims that God immediately produces a very perfect spiritual substance, that it produces another, less perfect, one, and this other produces a third, and so on, until the last one, which produces all corporeal substances, and corporeal substances produce the accidents. But Avicebron, unable to understand how corporeal substances that cannot penetrate each other should be capable of altering

each other, claims that only minds are capable of acting on bodies because only they can penetrate them. For since these gentlemen did not accept the void or the atoms of Democritus, and as Descartes' subtle matter was not really known to them, they did not think, in the manner of the Gassendists and the Cartesians, that there are bodies small enough to enter the pores of those that appear the hardest and most solid.

It seems to me that this diversity of opinions gives us the right to think that men often talk about things they do not know, and since the power of creatures is a fiction of the mind, of which we naturally have no idea, each one has imagined it according to his fancy.

It is true that in every century this power has been recognized as real and true by most men, but it is certain that this has been without proof—I do not say without demonstrative proof, I say without proof capable of making some impression on an attentive mind. For the confused proofs that are based only on the deceptive testimony of the senses and imagination should not be accepted by those who make use of their reason. [ . . . ]

When I see one ball strike another, my eyes tell me, or seem to tell me, that the first ball is truly the cause of the motion it impresses on the second; for the true cause that moves bodies does not appear to my eyes. But when I examine my reason, I see evidently that, since bodies cannot move themselves and their motive force is only the will of God conserving them successively in different places, they cannot communicate a power they do not have and could not even communicate if it was in their possession. For the mind will never conceive that a body, a purely passive substance, can in any way whatsoever transmit to another body the power moving it.

When I open my eyes, it appears evident to me that the sun is bursting with light, that not only is it visible by itself, but that it renders visible all the bodies around it; it covers the earth with flowers and fruits, gives life to animals, and, penetrating even into the bowels of the earth by its heat, produces stones, marble, and metals there. But when I consult Reason, I see nothing of all this; and when I consult it faithfully, I recognize clearly that my senses are seducing me, and that it is

God who does everything in all things. For, knowing that all the changes happening in bodies have no other principle than the different communications of motion taking place in visible and invisible bodies, I see that it is God who does everything, since it is his will that causes and his wisdom that regulates all these communications.

I assume that local motion is the principle of generation, corruption, alteration, and generally of all the changes occurring in bodies; this opinion is accepted well enough among the learned. But it does not matter what view is held about it. For it seems even easier to conceive that a body pushes another when it collides with the other than it is to understand that fire produces heat and light and draws from the power of matter a substance that was not previously there. And if it is necessary to recognize God alone as the true cause of the different communications of motion, so much the more must we judge that only he can create and annihilate real qualities and substantial forms. I say *create* and *annihilate*, because it seems to me at least as difficult to draw from matter a substance that was not there, or to have it return without its having been there, as it is to create or annihilate it. But I do not pause over terms; I make use of these because I know of no others that express clearly and unequivocally the changes philosophers assume are happening at every moment through the force of secondary causes.

I am somewhat troubled by reporting here the other proofs commonly given about the force and efficacy of natural causes, for they seem so weak to those who resist prejudices and prefer their reason to their senses, that it does not seem likely they could have persuaded reasonable people. However, I am reporting and replying to them because there are many philosophers who make use of them.

First Proof of the Efficacy of Secondary Causes: If secondary causes did nothing, say Suarez, Fonseca, and a few others,[5] we could not distinguish living things from those not living, for neither would have an internal principle of their actions.

5. Malebranche: Suarez, *Metaphysical Disputations*, Disputation 18, sec. 1, assert. 12; Fonseca, *Commentary on Aristotle's Metaphysics*, quest. 7, sec. 2.

Reply: I reply that men would still have the same sensible proofs which convinced them of the distinction they draw between living and non-living things. They would still see animals perform certain actions such as eating, growing, crying, running, jumping, etc., and they would observe nothing similar in stones. This alone causes ordinary philosophers to believe that beasts are alive and stones are not. For we should not imagine that they know what the life of a dog is through a clear and distinct view of the mind; it is their senses that govern their decisions on this question.

If necessary, I would prove here that the principle of the life of a dog is not very different from that of the motion of a watch. For the life of bodies, whatever they are, can consist only in the motion of their parts; and it is not difficult to judge that the same subtle matter producing in a dog the fermentation of blood and animal spirits which is the principle of its life, is no more perfect than the one giving motion to the mechanism of watches or causing the heaviness in the weights of clocks which is the principle of their life, or, to speak as others do, of their motion.

It is up to the Peripatetics to give those they call Cartesians a clear idea of what they entitle *the life of beasts, corporeal soul, body that perceives, desires, sees, senses, wills,* and then we will clearly resolve their difficulties, if they still continue to produce them.

Second Proof: We could not recognize the differences or the virtues of the elements. It could happen that fire would cool in the same way that water does; the nature of individual things would not be fixed and determinate.

Reply: I reply that, nature remaining as it is, that is, the laws of the communication of motion still remaining the same, it is contradictory that fire does not burn or separate the parts of certain bodies. Fire cannot cool like water unless it becomes water, for fire being only wood whose parts have been agitated with a violent motion by an invisible matter surrounding them, as is easy to demonstrate, it is impossible for these parts not to communicate some of their motion to the bodies with which they collide. Now, since these laws are constant, the nature of fire, its virtues, and its qualities do not change. But this nature and these virtues are only consequences of the general and efficacious will of God, who does everything in all things. As a result, it is false and useless in every way when we seek in the study of nature true causes other than the volitions of the Almighty or the general laws according to which he constantly acts.

I grant that we should not have recourse to God or to the universal cause when we seek the reason for particular effects. For it would be ridiculous to say, for example, that God dries the roads or freezes the water of rivers. We should say that the air dries the earth because it stirs and takes up the water drenching the earth, and that the air or subtle matter freezes the river in winter, because during winter it ceases to communicate enough motion to the parts making up the water to render it fluid. In a word, we must give, if we can, the natural and particular cause of the effects in question. But since the action of these causes consists only in the motive force activating them, and since this motive force is only the will of God, we should not say that in themselves they have force or power to produce some effects. And when we finally come to a general effect whose cause we seek when we reason, if we imagine any other cause of it than the general cause, we are still philosophizing badly. We must not feign a certain *nature*, a *first mobile*, a *universal soul*, or some similar *chimera* of which we have no clear and distinct idea; that would be to reason like a pagan philosopher. For example, when we ask how it happens that bodies are in motion, that agitated air communicates its motion to water, or rather that bodies push one another, we answer: since motion and its communication are a general effect on which all other effects depend, to be a philosopher (I do not say to be a Christian) it is necessary to have recourse to God, who is the universal cause, because his will is the motive force of bodies and also produces the communication of their motion. If he had willed to produce nothing new in the world, he would not have put its parts in motion. And if he wills some day to render incorruptible some of the beings he has formed—our bodies after the resurrection, for example—he

will cease to will certain communications of motion with respect to these beings.

Third Proof: It would be useless to cultivate, water, and give certain dispositions to bodies so as to prepare them for what we hope will happen to them. For God has no need to prepare the subjects on which he acts.

Reply: I reply that God can absolutely do anything that pleases him without finding dispositions in the subjects on which is he acting. But, he cannot do it without a miracle, or by natural means, that is, according to the general laws of the communication of motion he has established, and according to those by which he almost always acts. God does not multiply his volitions without reason; he always acts through the simplest ways. This is why he uses the collision of bodies to move them, not because their impact is absolutely necessary for their motion, as our senses tell us, but because very few natural laws are needed to produce all the admirable effects we see, given that impact is the occasion for the communication of motion.

It is necessary to water a plant for it to grow because, according to the laws of the communication of motion, hardly anything other than the parts of water can, by their motion and shape, slide around and climb up between the fibers of plants, carry with them some salts and other small bodies, and by congealing or attaching themselves variously to one another, take the shape necessary to nourish them. The subtle matter the sun constantly propagates can raise water in plants by agitating it, but it does not have enough motion to raise the coarse parts of earth. However, earth and even air are necessary for the growth of plants—earth to keep water at their roots and air to excite a moderate fermentation in the same water. Since the action of the sun, air, and water consists only in the motion of their parts, only God is acting, properly speaking. For, as I have just said, only he, through the efficacy of his volitions and through the infinite extent of his knowledge, can produce and regulate the infinitely infinite communications of motion occurring at each instant and conserving in the universe all the beautiful things we observe in it.

Fourth Proof: We do not struggle against ourselves; we do not resist ourselves. Bodies collide, strike, and resist each other. Therefore, God does not act in them, except through his *concourse*. If God alone produced and conserved motion in bodies, he would make them turn aside before their impact, for he knows well enough that they are impenetrable. Why push bodies to make them rebound, why make them advance to make them withdraw, why produce and conserve useless motion? Is it not an extravagant thing to say that God struggles against himself and that he destroys his works when a bull fights with a lion, when a wolf devours a sheep, and when a sheep eats the grass that God makes grow? Therefore, there are secondary causes.

Reply: Therefore, secondary causes do everything and God does nothing. For God cannot act against himself, and *concourse* is action. *To concur* with contrary actions is to give contrary *concourse*, and consequently to perform contrary actions. To concur with the actions of creatures resisting each other is to act against oneself. To concur with useless motions is to act uselessly. Now, God does nothing uselessly; he performs no contrary action at all; he does not at all struggle against himself. Therefore, he does not concur with the action of creatures, which often destroy one another and perform useless actions or motions. That is where this proof of secondary causes leads us. But here is what reason teaches us.

God does everything in all things, and nothing resists him. He does everything in all things, for his volitions produce and regulate all motions, and nothing resists him, because he does everything he wills. But here is how we must conceive this. In greater conformity with the immutable order of his attributes, having resolved to produce through the simplest ways this infinite variety of creatures we admire, he willed that bodies move in a straight line because that line is the simplest. Since bodies are impenetrable and their motions occur along opposing or intersecting lines, it is necessary that they strike each other and that, consequently, they stop moving in the same way. God foresaw this, and still he positively willed the collision or impact of bodies, not because it pleases him to struggle against

himself, but because he intended to use this impact of bodies as an occasion to establish the general law of the communication of motion, by which he foresaw that an infinity of admirable effects must be produced. For I am persuaded that these two natural laws, which are the simplest of all—namely, that all motion occurs or tends to occur in a straight line and that in impact motions are communicated in proportion to and along the line of their pressure—are sufficient, the initial motions being wisely distributed to produce the world such as we see it, that is, the heaven, stars, planets, comets, earth and water, air and fire, in a word, the elements, and all bodies not organized or living; for organized bodies depend on the initial construction of those from which they arise, and it is likely that they were formed at the creation of the world (not however such as they appear to our eyes) and that they receive with time nothing more than the growth necessary to become visible. Nevertheless, it is certain that they receive this growth only through the general laws of nature according to which all other bodies are formed; this results in their growth not always being regular and monsters being engendered. [ . . . ]

When a house crushes a right-thinking man, there occurs a greater evil than when one beast devours another, or when a body is required to rebound by the impact of the body it strikes; but God does not multiply his volitions to remedy the true or apparent disorders that are the necessary consequences of natural laws. God must neither correct nor change these laws, even though they sometimes produce monsters. He must not trouble the uniformity of his conduct and the simplicity of his ways. He must neglect insignificant things—I mean that he must not have particular volitions to produce effects that are not worth his willing them or that are unworthy of the action of the one producing them. God produces miracles only when it is required by the order he always follows—by this I understand the immutable order of justice he wills to give his attributes. And this order requires that he act in the simplest ways and that there are exceptions to his volitions only when it is absolutely necessary for his intentions, only when the simplicity and uniformity of his conduct do not as much honor his immutability and foreknowledge as miraculous conduct would honor his wisdom, justice, goodness, or other of his attributes; in short, only on certain occasions that are entirely unknown to us. Even though we are all united to the order or wisdom of God, we do not know all its rules. We see in it what we must do, but do not understand in it everything God must will, and we must not make too much effort to understand it. [ . . . ]

Sixth Proof: The main proof that the philosophers bring forth for the efficacy of secondary causes is drawn from the will and freedom of man. Man wills, he determines himself by himself, and to will and to determine oneself is to act. It is certain that man commits sin. God is no more its author than he is that of concupiscence and error. Therefore, man acts through his own efficacy.

Reply: I have explained sufficiently in several passages of the *Search after Truth* (particularly in Chapter 1 of Book I, and in Elucidation One on the same chapter) what man's will and freedom are; it is useless to repeat this. I grant that man wills and that he determines himself, but it is because God makes him will by constantly bringing him toward the good. He determines himself, but it is because God gives him all the ideas and feelings that are the motives by which he determines himself. I also grant that man alone commits sin. But I deny that in this he does something, for sin, error, and even concupiscence are nothing. They are only deficiencies. I have sufficiently explained myself on this in Elucidation One.

Man wills, but his volitions are powerless in themselves; they produce nothing. They do not at all prevent God's doing everything, because God himself produces our volitions in us through the pressure he exerts on us toward the good in general, for without this pressure we could not will anything. Man has from himself only error and sin, which are nothing.

There is a great difference between our minds and the bodies surrounding us. Our mind wills, acts, determines itself; I do not doubt this in any way. We are convinced of it by the internal awareness we have of ourselves. If we had no freedom at all, there would be no punishments or future rewards, for without freedom there are neither good nor bad actions. As a result, religion would be an illusion and a phantom. But what we do not clearly see is that bodies have the power to act; this is what appears incomprehensible, and it is also what we deny when we deny the efficacy of secondary causes.

The mind itself does not act as much as we imagine. I know that I will and that I will freely; I have no reason to doubt this any stronger than the internal awareness I have of myself. Nor do I deny the latter. But I deny that my will is the true cause of the motion of my arm, of the ideas in my mind, and of other things accompanying my volitions, for I do not see any relation between such different things. I even see very clearly that there can be no relation between the volition I have to move my arm and the agitation of the animal spirits, that is, of certain small bodies whose motion and shape I do not know; the latter choose certain nerve canals from a million others I do not know, so as to cause in me the motion I desire through an infinity of motions I do not desire. I deny that my will produces my ideas in me, for I do not even see how it could produce them, because my will, which cannot act or will without knowledge, presupposes my ideas and does not produce them. I do not even know precisely what an idea is. I do not know whether they are produced from nothing and whether they return to nothingness as soon as we stop seeing them. I am speaking according to the view of some people.

I produce my own ideas, they will say, by the faculty God has given me for thinking. I move my arm because of the *union* God has established between my mind and my body. *Faculty* and *union* are terms of logic; they are vague and indeterminate words. No particular being or mode of being can be a *faculty* or a *union*; these terms must be explained. If they say that the union of my mind with my body consists in God's willing that when I will my arm to move, animal spirits spread in the muscles making it up, so as to move it in the way I wish, I clearly understand this explanation and I accept it. But this is to say exactly what I maintain; for my will specifying God's practical will, it is evident that my arm will be moved, not by my will, which is powerless in itself, but by God's, which can never fail to have its effect.

But if they say that the union of my mind with my body consists in God's having given me the *force*[6] to move my arm, just as he has also given my body the force to make me feel pleasure and pain in order that I apply myself to this body and interest myself in its preservation, then surely they are supposing what is in question and going in a circle. They have no clear idea of this force that the soul has over the body, nor of the force that the body has over the soul; they do not know well enough what they are saying when they assert this positively. They have arrived at this view through prejudice: They believed this view from infancy as soon as they were capable of sensing; but mind, reason, and reflection have no part in it at all. This is clear enough from the things I have said in the *Search after Truth*.

But, they will say, I know through the internal awareness of my action that I truly have this force; therefore, I am not at all mistaken in believing it. I reply that when they move their arm they have an internal awareness of the actual volition by which they move it, and they are not mistaken in believing that they have this volition. In addition, they have an internal sensation of a certain effort accompanying this volition, and they must also believe that they are making this effort. Finally, I grant[7] that they have an internal sensation of the arm moving at the moment of this effort; on this assumption I also agree to what they say, that the motion of the arm

occurs at the instant we feel this effort, or that they have a *practical* volition to move it. But I deny that this effort, which is only a modification or sensation of the soul given to us to make us understand our weakness and to give us an obscure and confused sensation of our power, is by itself capable of giving motion to animal spirits or determining them. I deny that there is a relation between our thoughts and the motions of matter. I deny that the soul has the least knowledge of the animal spirits it uses to move the body it animates. Finally, even if the soul had an exact knowledge of the animal spirits and if it were capable of moving them or of determining their motion, I still deny that it could select the nerve ducts, of which it has no knowledge, in order to push the spirits into them and thus move the body with the promptness, exactness, and force we observe even in those who have the least knowledge of the structure of their body.

For, assuming even that our volitions are truly the moving force of bodies (even though this seems incomprehensible), how are we able to conceive that the soul moves its body? The arm, for example, moves only because spirits distend some of the muscles making it up. Now, in order that the motion the soul impresses on the spirits in the brain can be communicated to those in the nerves, and the latter to others in the muscles of the arm, the volitions of the soul must multiply or change in proportion to the almost infinite collisions or impacts that would occur in the small bodies making up the spirits; for bodies cannot by themselves move those they meet, as I believe I have sufficiently shown. But we cannot conceive this, if we do not allow in the soul an infinite number of volitions for the least motion of the body, because an infinite number of communications of motion necessarily takes place in order to move the body. For, finally, since the soul is a particular cause and cannot know exactly the size and agitation of an infinite number of small bodies colliding with one another when the spirits spread out in the muscles, it could neither establish a general law of the communication of motion of these spirits, nor follow it exactly if it had established it. Thus, it is evident that the soul could not move

---

6. Malebranche: I still mean a true and efficacious power.

7. Malebranche: It seems evident to me that the mind does not even know, through internal sensation or consciousness, the motion of the arm it animates. It only knows its own sensation through consciousness, for the soul is *conscious* only of its own thoughts. The sensation we have of the motion of our arm is known through internal sensation or consciousness, but it is not through consciousness that we are informed of the motion of our arm, the pain we suffer there, any more than the colors we see on objects. Or if we do not wish to agree with this, I say that internal sensation is not infallible, for error is almost always found in these sensations when they are compound. I have sufficiently proven this in Book I of *The Search after Truth*.

its arm, even if it had the power of determining the motion of the animal spirits in the brain. These things are too clear to pause any longer over them.

The same is true of the faculty we have for thinking. We know through internal awareness that we will to think about something, that we make an effort to do this, and that at the moment of our desire and effort the idea of that thing presents itself to our mind. But we do not know through internal awareness that our will or effort produces our idea. We do not see through reason that this could happen. It is through prejudice that we believe that our attention or our desires are the cause of our ideas; it is because we experience a hundred times a day that our ideas follow or accompany them. Since God and his operations contain nothing sensible and we sense nothing else preceding the presence of ideas than our desires, we think there can be no other cause of these ideas than our desires. But let us take care: We do not see in ourselves any force to produce them; reason and the internal awareness we have of ourselves tell us nothing about this. [ . . . ]

The most enlightened, and even the greatest number, of theologians, seeing on the one hand that Sacred Scripture was opposed to the efficacy of secondary causes and on the other that the impression of the senses, public opinion, and especially Aristotle's philosophy, which was esteemed by the learned, established it—for Aristotle believes that God does not involve himself in the detail of what takes place under the *concavity* of the moon, that this attention is unworthy of his greatness, and that the *nature* he supposes in all bodies suffices to produce everything occurring here below. The theologians, I say, in order to accord faith with the philosophy of the pagans, and reason with the senses, have been inclined to the view that secondary causes would do nothing unless God lent them his *concourse*. But because this immediate concourse by which God acts with secondary causes involves great difficulties, some philosophers have rejected it, claiming that in order for them to act it is enough that God should conserve them with the *virtue* he gave them in creating them. And since this opinion conforms entirely to prejudices, because God's operation in

secondary causes involves nothing sensible, it is ordinarily received by common men, and by those who have attended more to the physics and medicine of the ancients than to theology and to meditation on the truth. Most men imagine that God first created all things, that he gave them all the qualities or faculties necessary for their preservation, that, for example, he gave the first motion to matter and then left it to itself to produce by the communication of its motion this variety of forms we admire. We ordinarily suppose that bodies can move each other, and we even attribute this opinion to Descartes, contrary to what he expressly says in Articles 36 and 37 of the second part of his *Principles of Philosophy*. Since men cannot avoid the realization that creatures depend on God, they reduce this dependence as much as they can, whether through a hidden aversion for God or through stupidity and a dreadful insensitivity with respect to his operation. [ . . . ]

I hold, as I have said elsewhere, that bodies, for example, do not have the force to move themselves and that thus their motive force is but the action of God, or in order not to use a term that signifies nothing distinct, their motive force is but the will of God, always necessarily efficacious, which conserves them successively in different places. For I do not believe that God creates certain beings to make them the motive force of bodies, not only because I have no idea of this sort of being and because I do not see that they could move bodies, but also because these beings would themselves need others to move them, and so on to infinity. For only God is truly immobile and motor both at once.

This being so, when a body collides with and moves another, I can say that it acts through God's concourse, and that this concourse is not different from its own action. For a body moves the one with which it collides only by its action or its motive force, which at bottom is but God's will, which conserves this body successively in several places— the transport of a body not being its action or its motive force but the effect of its motive force. Almost all theologians say also that the action of secondary causes is not different from the action by which God concurs with them. For although they understand it in different ways, they claim that God acts in creatures through the same action as the creatures. And they are, it seems to me, obliged to speak this way, for if creatures acted through an action God did not produce in them, their action as action would be independent, it seems; now they believe, as they must, that creatures depend immediately on God, not only for their being, but also for their operation.

The same with respect to free causes, I believe that God constantly gives to the mind an impression toward the good in general, and that he even determines this impression toward particular goods by ideas or sensations he places in us, as I have explained in the first elucidation; and this is also believed by theologians, who assert that God moves and predisposes our wills. Thus, the force that sets our minds in motion is the will of God, which animates us and leads us toward the good; for God does not create beings to make them the motive force of minds for the same reasons he does not create beings to make them the motive force of bodies. Since God's volitions are efficacious by themselves, it is sufficient that he should will for them to be produced, and it is useless to multiply beings without necessity. In addition, everything real in the determinations of our motions also comes from God's action in us; this is clear from the first Elucidation. Now we act and produce nothing except through our volitions, that is, through the impression of God's will, which is our motive force. For our volitions are efficacious only insofar as they come from God, just as moving bodies impel others only insofar as they have a motive force transporting them, which motive force is but God's will that creates or conserves them successively in different places. Therefore, we act only through God's concourse, and our action considered as efficacious and capable of producing some effect is not different from that of God. [ . . . ]

# G. W. Leibniz, *Discourse on Metaphysics* (1686)[1]

*1. On divine perfection, and that God does everything in the most desirable way.* The most widely accepted and meaningful notion we have of God is expressed well enough in these words, that God is an absolutely perfect being; yet the consequences of these words are not sufficiently considered. And, to penetrate more

deeply into this matter, it is appropriate to remark that there are several entirely different perfections in nature, that God possesses all of them together, and that each of them belongs to him in the highest degree.

We must also know what a perfection is. A fairly sure test for being a perfection is that forms or natures that are not capable of a highest degree are not perfections, as for example, the nature of number or figure. For the greatest of all numbers (or even the number of all numbers), as well as the greatest of all figures, imply a contradiction, but the greatest knowledge and omnipotence do not involve any impossibility. Consequently, power and knowledge are perfections, and, insofar as they belong to God, they do not have limits.

Whence it follows that God, possessing supreme and infinite wisdom, acts in the most perfect manner, not only metaphysically, but also morally speaking, and that, with respect to ourselves, we can say that the more enlightened and informed we are about God's works, the more we will be disposed to find them excellent and in complete conformity with what we might have desired.

*2. Against those who claim that there is no goodness in God's works, or that the rules of goodness*

1. Translated from the French by R. Ariew and D. Garber in G. W. Leibniz, *Philosophical Essays* (Indianapolis/Cambridge: Hackett Publishing Company, 1989). In February 1686 Leibniz wrote a letter to the Landgrave Ernst von Hessen-Reinfels, saying: "being somewhere having nothing to do for a few days, I have lately composed a short discourse on metaphysics about which I would be very happy to have Mr. Arnauld's opinion. For questions on grace, God's concourse with creatures, the nature of miracles, the cause of sin and the origin of evil, the immortality of the soul, ideas, etc. are touched upon in a manner which seems to provide new openings capable of illuminating some very great difficulties," *Philosophische Schriften*, ed. C. I. Gerhardt (Berlin, 1875–90), II, 11. Leibniz does not appear to have sent out the full "Discourse," as it later came to be known, following Leibniz's own characterization, though he did append "summaries" of it to his letter (which the landgrave transmitted to Arnauld); the summaries are also preserved as the titles of each article of the "Discourse" (in a later version of the "Discourse" than the manuscript in Leibniz's handwriting discovered by Henri Lestienne). Arnauld replied with a letter criticizing Section 13, and the Leibniz-Arnauld correspondence began.

*and beauty are arbitrary.* Thus I am far removed from the opinion of those who maintain that there are no rules of goodness and perfection in the nature of things or in the ideas God has of them and who say that the works of God are good solely for the formal reason that God has made them.[2] For, if this were so, God, knowing that he is their author, would not have had to consider them afterwards and find them good, as is testified by the Sacred Scriptures—which seem to have used such anthropomorphic expressions only to make us understand that the excellence of God's works can be recognized by considering them in themselves, even when we do not reflect on this empty external denomination which relates them to their cause. This is all the more true, since it is by considering his works that we can discover the creator. His works must therefore carry his mark in themselves. I confess that the contrary opinion seems to me extremely dangerous and very near to the opinion of the recent innovators[3] who hold that the beauty of the universe and the goodness we attribute to the works of God are but the chimeras of those who conceive of God in terms of themselves. Thus, in saying that things are not good by virtue of any rule of goodness but solely by virtue of the will of God, it seems to me that we unknowingly destroy all of God's love and all his glory. For why praise him for what he has done if he would be equally praiseworthy in doing the exact contrary? Where will his justice and wisdom reside if there remains only a certain despotic power, if will holds the place of reason, and if, according to the definition of tyrants, justice consists in whatever pleases the most powerful? Besides, it seems that all acts of will presuppose a reason for willing and that this reason is naturally prior to the act of will. That is why I also find completely strange the expression of some other philosophers[4] who say that the eternal truths of

metaphysics and geometry and consequently also the rules of goodness, justice, and perfection are merely the effects of the will of God; instead, it seems to me, they are only the consequences of his understanding, which, assuredly, does not depend on his will, any more than does his essence.

*3. Against those who believe that God might have made things better.* Nor can I approve of the opinion of some moderns who maintain boldly that what God has made is not of the highest perfection and that he could have done much better.[5] For it seems to me that the consequences of this opinion are wholly contrary to the glory of God: As a lesser evil is relatively good, so a lesser good is relatively evil. And to act with less perfection than one could have is to act imperfectly. To show that an architect could have done better is to find fault with his work. This opinion is also contrary to the Sacred Scripture, which assures us of the goodness of God's works. For, if their view were sufficient, then since the series of imperfections descends to infinity, God's works would always have been good in comparison with those less perfect, no matter how he created them, but something is hardly praiseworthy if it can be praised only in this way. I also believe that a great many passages from Sacred Scripture and the holy fathers will be found favoring my opinion, but scarcely any will be found favoring the opinion of these moderns, an opinion which is, in my judgment, unknown to all antiquity and which is based only on the inadequate knowledge we have of the general harmony of the universe and of the hidden reasons for God's conduct. This enables us to judge audaciously that many things could have been rendered better. Besides, these moderns insist on certain dubious subtleties, for they imagine that nothing is so perfect that there is not something more perfect—this is an error.

They also believe that in this way they are able to safeguard God's freedom, as though it were not freedom of the highest sort to act in perfection following sovereign reason. For to believe that

---

2. This is Descartes' view. See, e.g., *Sixth Replies, Oeuvres*, ed. C. Adam and A. Tannery (Paris: Vrin, 1964–74), vol. VII, pp. 432, 435–36.

3. Spinoza, and by extension, Descartes. The earlier draft explicitly mentions the Spinozists alone in this regard. See Spinoza, Appendix to *Ethics*, Part I.

4. Descartes is mentioned in an earlier draft, but deleted.

---

5. See, e.g., Malebranche, *Traité de la nature et de la grace*, Pr. disc., sec. xiv. Malebranche's *Traité* seems to be one of the main targets of this essay.

God does something without having any reason for his will—overlooking the fact that this seems impossible—is an opinion that conforms little to his glory. Let us assume, for example, that God chooses between A and B and that he takes A without having any reason to prefer it to B. I say that this action of God is at the very least not praiseworthy; for all praise must be based on some reason, and by hypothesis there is none here. Instead I hold that God does nothing for which he does not deserve to be glorified.

4. *That the love of God requires our complete satisfaction and acquiescence with respect to what he has done without our being quietists[6] as a result.* The general knowledge of this great truth, that God acts always in the most perfect and desirable way possible, is, in my judgment, the foundation of the love that we owe God in all things, since he who loves seeks his satisfaction in the happiness or perfection of the object loved and in his actions. To will the same and dislike the same is true friendship. And I believe that it is difficult to love God well when we are not disposed to will what God wills, when we might have the power to change it. In fact, those who are not satisfied with what God does seem to me like dissatisfied subjects whose attitudes are not much different from those of rebels.

I hold, therefore, that, according to these principles, in order to act in accordance with the love of God, it is not sufficient to force ourselves to be patient; rather, we must truly be satisfied with everything that has come to us according to his will. I mean this acquiescence with respect to the past. As for the future, we must not be quietists and stand ridiculously with arms folded, awaiting that which God will do, according to the sophism that the ancients called *logon aergon*, the lazy reason. But we must act in accordance with what we presume to be the *will of God*, insofar as we can judge it, trying with all our might to contribute to the general good and especially to the embellishment and perfection of that which affects us or that which is near us, that

which is, so to speak, in our grasp. For, although the outcome might perhaps demonstrate that God did not wish our good will to have effect at present, it does not follow that he did not wish us to act as we have. On the contrary, since he is the best of all masters, he never demands more than the right intention, and it is for him to know the proper hour and place for letting the good designs succeed.

5. *What the rules of the perfection of divine conduct consist in, and that the simplicity of the ways is in balance with the richness of the effects.* Therefore, it is sufficient to have the confidence that God does everything for the best and that nothing can harm those who love him. But to know in detail the reasons that could have moved him to choose this order of the universe—to allow sins, to dispense his saving grace in a certain way—surpasses the power of a finite mind, especially when it has not yet attained the enjoyment of the vision of God.

However, we can make some general remarks concerning the course of providence in the governance of things. We can therefore say that one who acts perfectly is similar to an excellent geometer who can find the best constructions for a problem; or to a good architect who makes use of his location and the funds set aside for a building in the most advantageous manner, allowing nothing improper or lacking in the beauty of which it is capable; or to a good householder, who makes use of his holdings in such a way that there remains nothing uncultivated and sterile; or to a skilled machinist who produces his work in the least difficult way possible; or to a learned author who includes the greatest number of truths [*realités*] in the smallest possible volume. Now, the most perfect of all beings, those that occupy the least volume, that is, those that least interfere with one another, are minds, whose perfections consist in their virtues. That is why we mustn't doubt that the happiness of minds is the principal aim of God and that he puts this into practice to the extent that general harmony permits it. We shall say more about this below.

As for the simplicity of the ways of God, this holds properly with respect to his means, as opposed to the variety, richness, and abundance, which holds

---

6. The quietists were followers of Miguel de Molinos (ca. 1640–97), author of the *Guida spirituale* (1675), and others, who stressed passive contemplation and complete resignation to the will of God.

with respect to his ends or effects. And the one must be in balance with the other, as are the costs of a building and the size and beauty one demands of it. It is true that nothing costs God anything—even less than it costs a philosopher to build the fabric of his imaginary world out of hypotheses—since God has only to make decrees in order that a real world come into being. But in matters of wisdom, decrees or hypotheses take the place of expenditures to the extent that they are more independent of one another, because reason requires that we avoid multiplying hypotheses or principles, in somewhat the same way that the simplest system is always preferred in astronomy.

6. *God does nothing which is not orderly and it is not even possible to imagine events that are not regular*. The volitions or acts of God are commonly divided into ordinary or extraordinary. But it is good to consider that God does nothing which is not orderly. Thus, what passes for extraordinary is extraordinary only with some particular order established among creatures; for everything is in conformity with respect to the universal order. This is true to such an extent that not only does nothing completely irregular occur in the world, but we would not even be able to imagine such a thing. Thus, let us assume, for example, that someone jots down a number of points at random on a piece of paper, as do those who practice the ridiculous art of geomancy.[7] I maintain that it is possible to find a geometric line whose notion is constant and uniform, following a certain rule, such that this line passes through all the points in the same order in which the hand jotted them down.

And if someone traced a continuous line which is sometimes straight, sometimes circular, and sometimes of another nature, it is possible to find a notion, or rule, or equation common to all the points of this line, in virtue of which these very changes must occur. For example, there is no face whose contours are not part of a geometric line and cannot be traced in one stroke by a certain regular

movement. But, when a rule is extremely complex, what is in conformity with it passes for irregular.

Thus, one can say, in whatever manner God might have created the world, it would always have been regular and in accordance with a certain general order. But God has chosen the most perfect world, that is, the one which is at the same time the simplest in hypotheses and the richest in phenomena, as might be a line in geometry whose construction is easy and whose properties and effects are extremely remarkable and widespread. I use these comparisons to sketch an imperfect likeness of divine wisdom and to point out something that can at least elevate our minds to conceive in some way what cannot be sufficiently expressed. But I do not claim to explain in this way the great mystery upon which the entire universe depends.

7. *That miracles conform to the general order, even though they may be contrary to the subordinate maxims; and about what God wills or permits by a general or particular volition*. Now, since nothing can happen which is not in the order, one can say that miracles are as much within the order as are natural operations, operations which are called natural because they are in conformity with certain subordinate maxims that we call the nature of things. For one can say that this nature is only God's custom, with which he can dispense for any stronger reason than the one which moved him to make use of these maxims.

As for the general or particular volitions, depending upon how the matter is understood, we can say that God does everything following his most general will, which is in conformity with the most perfect order he has chosen, but we can also say that he has particular volitions which are exceptions to these aforementioned subordinate maxims. For the most general of God's laws, the one that rules the whole course of the universe, is without exception.

We can say also that God wills everything that is an object of his particular volition. But we must make a distinction with respect to the objects of his general volition, such as the actions of other creatures, particularly the actions of those that are reasonable, actions with which God wishes to concur. For, if the action is good in itself, we can say that God wills it and

7. Geomancy is the art of divination by means of lines or figures.

sometimes commands it, even when it does not take place. But if the action is evil in itself and becomes good only by accident, because the course of things (particularly punishment and atonement) corrects its evilness and repays the evil with interest in such a way that in the end there is more perfection in the whole sequence than if the evil had not occurred, then we must say that God permits this but does not will it, even though he concurs with it because of the laws of nature he has established and because he knows how to draw a greater good from it.

8. *To distinguish the actions of God from those of creatures we explain the notion of an individual substance.* It is rather difficult to distinguish the actions of God from those of creatures; for some believe that God does everything, while others imagine that he merely conserves the force he has given to creatures. What follows will let us see the extent to which we can say the one or the other. And since actions and passions properly belong to individual substances [*actiones sunt suppositorum*],[8] it will be necessary to explain what such an individual substance is.

It is indeed true that when several predicates are attributed to a single subject and this subject is attributed to no other, it is called an individual substance; but this is not sufficient, and such an explanation is merely nominal. We must therefore consider what it is to be attributed truly to a certain subject.

Now it is evident that all true predication has some basis in the nature of things and that, when a proposition is not an identity, that is, when the predicate is not explicitly contained in the subject, it must be contained in it virtually. That is what the philosophers call *in-esse*, when they say that the predicate is in the subject. Thus the subject term must always contain the predicate term, so that one who understands perfectly the notion of the subject would also know that the predicate belongs to it.

Since this is so, we can say that the nature of an individual substance or of a complete being is to have a notion so complete that it is sufficient to contain and to allow us to deduce from it all the predicates of the subject to which this notion is attributed. An accident, on the other hand, is a being whose notion does not include everything that can be attributed to the subject to which the notion is attributed.[9] Thus, taken in abstraction from the subject, the quality of being a king which belongs to Alexander the Great is not determinate enough to constitute an individual and does not include the other qualities of the same subject, nor does it include everything that the notion of this prince includes. On the other hand, God, seeing Alexander's individual notion or haecceity,[10] sees in it at the same time the basis and reason for all the predicates which can be said truly of him, for example, that he vanquished Darius and Porus; he even knows *a priori* (and not by experience) whether he died a natural death or whether he was poisoned, something we can know only through history. Thus when we consider carefully the connection of things, we can say that from all time in Alexander's soul there are vestiges of everything that has happened to him and marks of everything that will happen to him and even traces of everything that happens in the universe, even though God alone could recognize them all.[11]

9. *That each singular substance expresses the whole universe in its own way, and that all its events, together with all their circumstances and the whole sequence of external things, are included in its notion.* Several

---

8. Leibniz is making use of scholastic logical terminology: A *suppositum* is an individual subsistent substance; *actiones sunt suppositorum* therefore means that actions are of individual subsistent substances.

9. An earlier draft of the following passage read: "Thus the circular shape of the ring of [Gyges] [Polycrates] does not contain everything that the notion of this particular ring contains, unlike God [knowing] seeing the individual notion of this ring [seeing, for example, that it will be swallowed by a fish and yet returned to its owner]." (Words in brackets were deleted by Leibniz.)

10. The word *haecceitas* (or *hecceïté*, what we are translating as "haecceity") was coined by John Duns Scotus (ca. 1270–1308) to refer to an individual essence or "thisness"—what *haecceitas* means literally.

11. An earlier draft added: "I speak here as if it were assumed that this ring [has consciousness] [is a substance]."

notable paradoxes follow from this; among others, it follows that it is not true that two substances can resemble each other completely and differ only in number [*solo numero*],[12] and that what Saint Thomas asserts on this point about angels or intelligences (that here every individual is a lowest species)[13] is true of all substances, provided that one takes the specific difference as the geometers do with respect to their figures. It also follows that a substance can begin only by creation and end only by annihilation; that a substance is not divisible into two; that one substance cannot be constructed from two; and that thus the number of substances does not naturally increase and decrease, though they are often transformed.

Moreover, every substance is like a complete world and like a mirror of God or of the whole universe, which each one expresses in its own way, somewhat as the same city is variously represented depending upon the different positions from which it is viewed. Thus the universe is in some way multiplied as many times as there are substances, and the glory of God is likewise multiplied by as many entirely different representations of his work. It can even be said that every substance bears in some way the character of God's infinite wisdom and omnipotence and imitates him as much as it is capable. For it expresses, however confusedly, everything that happens in the universe, whether past, present, or future—this has some resemblance to an infinite perception or knowledge. And since all other substances in turn express this substance and accommodate themselves to it, one can say that it extends its power over all the others, in imitation of the creator's omnipotence.

10. *That the belief in substantial forms has some basis, but that these forms do not change anything in the phenomena and must not be used to explain particular effects.* It seems that the ancients, as well as many able men accustomed to deep meditation who have taught theology and philosophy some centuries ago (some of whom are respected for their saintliness) have had some knowledge of what we have just said; this is why they introduced and maintained the substantial forms which are so decried today. But they are not so distant from the truth nor so ridiculous as the common lot of our new philosophers imagines.

I agree that the consideration of these forms serves no purpose in the details of physics and must not be used to explain particular phenomena. That is where the Scholastics failed, as did the physicians of the past who followed their example, believing that they could account for the properties of bodies by talking about forms and qualities without taking the trouble to examine their manner of operation. It is as if we were content to say that a clock has a quality of clockness derived from its form without considering in what all of this consists; that would be sufficient for the person who buys the clock, provided that he turns over its care to another.

But this misunderstanding and misuse of forms must not cause us to reject something whose knowledge is so necessary in metaphysics that, I hold, without it one cannot properly know the first principles or elevate our minds sufficiently well to the knowledge of incorporeal natures and the wonders of God.

However, just as a geometer does not need to burden his mind with the famous labyrinth of the composition of the continuum, there is no need for any moral philosopher and even less need for a jurist or statesman to trouble himself with the great difficulties involved in reconciling free will and God's providence, since the geometer can achieve all his demonstrations and the statesman can complete all his deliberations without entering into these discussions, discussions that remain necessary and important in philosophy and theology. In the same way, a physicist can explain some experiments, at times using previous simpler experiments and at times using geometric and mechanical demonstrations, without needing[14] general considerations from another sphere. And if he uses God's concourse, or else a soul, animating force [*archée*], or something else of this nature, he is raving

---

12. An earlier draft added the following: "also, that if bodies are substances, it is not possible that their nature consists only in size, shape, and motion, but that something else is needed."

13. See Saint Thomas Aquinas, *Summa Theologiae* I, q. 50, art. 4.

14. An earlier draft continued "[forms and other] [considerations of substantial forms]."

just as much as the person who, in the course of an important practical deliberation, enters into a lofty discussion concerning the nature of destiny and the nature of our freedom. In fact, people often commit this fault without thinking when they encumber their minds with the consideration of fatalism and sometimes are even diverted from a good resolution or a necessary duty in this way.

*11. That the thoughts of the theologians and philosophers who are called Scholastics are not entirely to be disdained.* I know that I am advancing a great paradox by attempting to rehabilitate the old philosophy in some fashion and to restore the almost banished substantial forms to their former place.[15] But perhaps I will not be condemned so easily when it is known that I have long meditated upon the modern philosophy, that I have given much time to experiments in physics and demonstrations in geometry, and that I had long been persuaded about the futility of these beings, which I finally was required to embrace in spite of myself and, as it were, by force, after having myself carried out certain studies. These studies made me recognize that our moderns do not give enough credit to Saint Thomas and to the other great men of his time and that there is much more solidity than one imagines in the opinions of the Scholastic philosophers and theologians, provided that they are used appropriately and in their proper place. I am even convinced that, if some exact and thoughtful mind took the trouble to clarify and summarize their thoughts after the manner of the analytic geometers, he would find there a great treasure of extremely important and wholly demonstrative truths.

*12. That the notions involved in extension contain something imaginary and cannot constitute the substance of body.* But, to resume the thread of our discussion, I believe that anyone who will meditate about the nature of substance, as I have explained it above, will find[16] that the nature of body does not

consist merely in extension, that is, in size, shape, and motion, but that we must necessarily recognize in body something related to souls, something we commonly call substantial form, even though it makes no change in the phenomena, any more than do the souls of animals, if they have any. It is even possible to demonstrate that the notions of size, shape, and motion are not as distinct as is imagined and that they contain something imaginary and relative to our perception, as do (though to a greater extent) color, heat, and other similar qualities, qualities about which one can doubt whether they are truly found in the nature of things outside ourselves. That is why qualities of this kind cannot constitute any substance. And if there were no other principle of identity in body other than the one just mentioned, a body could not subsist for more than a moment.

Yet the souls and substantial forms of other bodies are entirely different from intelligent souls, which alone know their actions. Not only don't intelligent souls perish naturally, but they also always preserve the basis for the knowledge of what they are; this is what renders them alone susceptible to punishment and reward and makes them citizens of the republic of the universe, whose monarch is God. It also follows that all other creatures must serve them—something which we will later discuss more fully.

*13. Since the individual notion of each person includes once and for all everything that will ever happen to him, one sees in it the* a priori *proofs of the truth of each event, or, why one happened rather than another, but these truths, however certain, are nevertheless contingent, being based on the free will of God or of his creatures, whose choice always has its reasons, which incline without necessitating.* But before going further, we must attempt to resolve a great difficulty that can arise from the foundations we have set forth above. We have said that the notion of an individual substance includes once and for all everything that can ever happen to it and that, by considering this notion, one can see there everything that can truly be said of it, just as we can see in the nature of a circle all the properties that can be deduced from it. But it seems that this would eliminate the difference between contingent

---

15. A marginal note in an earlier draft: "I do this, however, only under an hypothesis, insofar as one can say that bodies are substances."

16. An earlier draft interpolates: "either that bodies are not substances in metaphysical rigor (which was, in fact, the view of the Platonists), or."

and necessary truths, that there would be no place for human freedom, and that an absolute fatalism would rule all our actions as well as all the other events of the world. To this I reply that we must distinguish between what is certain and what is necessary. Everyone grants that future contingents are certain, since God foresees them, but we do not concede that they are necessary on that account. But (someone will say) if a conclusion can be deduced infallibly from a definition or notion, it is necessary. And it is true that we are maintaining that everything that must happen to a person is already contained virtually in his nature or notion, just as the properties of a circle are contained in its definition; thus the difficulty still remains. To address it firmly, I assert that connection or following [*consécution*] is of two kinds. The one whose contrary implies a contradiction is absolutely necessary; this deduction occurs in the eternal truths, for example, the truths of geometry. The other is necessary only *ex hypothesi* and, so to speak, accidentally, but it is contingent in itself, since its contrary does not imply a contradiction. And this connection is based not purely on ideas and God's simple understanding, but on his free decrees and on the sequence of the universe.

Let us take an example. Since Julius Caesar will become perpetual dictator and master of the republic and will overthrow the freedom of the Romans, this action is contained in his notion, for we assume that it is the nature of such a perfect notion of a subject to contain everything, so that the predicate is included in the subject, *ut possit inesse subjecto*.[17] It could be said that it is not in virtue of this notion or idea that he must perform this action, since it pertains to him only because God knows everything. But someone might insist that his nature or form corresponds to this notion, and, since God has imposed this personality on him, it is henceforth necessary for him to satisfy it. I could reply by citing future contingents, since they have no reality as yet, save in God's understanding and will, and, because God gave them this form in advance, they must in the same way correspond to it.

But I much prefer to overcome difficulties rather than to excuse them by giving some other similar difficulties, and what I am about to say will illuminate the one as well as the other. It is here, then, that we must apply the distinction concerning connections, and I say that whatever happens in conformity with these predeterminations [*avances*] is certain but not necessary, and if one were to do the contrary, he would not be doing something impossible in itself, even though it would be impossible [*ex hypothesi*] for this to happen. For if someone were able to carry out the whole demonstration by virtue of which he could prove this connection between the subject, Caesar, and the predicate, his successful undertaking, he would in fact be showing that Caesar's future dictatorship is grounded in his notion or nature, that there is a reason why he crossed the Rubicon rather than stopped at it and why he won rather than lost at Pharsalus and that it was reasonable, and consequently certain, that this should happen. But this would not show that it was necessary in itself nor that the contrary implies a contradiction. It is reasonable and certain in almost the same way that God will always do the best, even though what is less perfect does not imply a contradiction.

For it will be found that the demonstration of this predicate of Caesar is not as absolute as those of numbers or of geometry, but that it supposes the sequence of things that God has freely chosen, a sequence based on God's first free decree always to do what is most perfect and on God's decree with respect to human nature, following out of the first decree, that man will always do (although freely) that which appears to be best. But every truth based on these kinds of decrees is contingent, even though it is certain; for these decrees do not change the possibility of things, and, as I have already said, even though it is certain that God always chooses the best, this does not prevent something less perfect from being and remaining possible in itself, even though it will not happen, since it is not its impossibility but its imperfection which causes it to be rejected. And nothing is necessary whose contrary is possible.

We will therefore be in a position to satisfy these sorts of difficulties, however great they may appear

---

17. The Latin is an approximate paraphrase of the preceding clause.

(and in fact they are not made any the less pressing by considering the other thinkers who have ever treated this matter), as long as we recognize that all contingent propositions have reasons to be one way rather than another or else (what comes to the same thing) that they have *a priori* proofs of their truth which render them certain and which show that the connection between subject and predicate of these propositions has its basis in the natures of both. But they do not have necessary demonstrations, since these reasons are based only on the principle of contingency or the principle of the existence of things, that is, based on what is or appears to be best from among several equally possible things. On the other hand, necessary truths are based on the principle of contradiction and on the possibility or impossibility of essences themselves, without regard to the free will of God or his creatures.

14. *God produces various substances according to the different views he has of the universe, and through God's intervention the proper nature of each substance brings it about that what happens to one corresponds with what happens to all the others, without their acting upon one another directly.* After having seen, in some way, what the nature of substances consists in, we must try to explain the dependence they have upon one another and their actions and passions. Now, first of all, it is very evident that created substances depend upon God, who preserves them and who even produces them continually by a kind of emanation, just as we produce our thoughts. For God, so to speak, turns on all sides and in all ways the general system of phenomena which he finds it good to produce in order to manifest his glory, and he views all the faces of the world in all ways possible, since there is no relation that escapes his omniscience. The result of each view of the universe, as seen from a certain position, is a substance which expresses the universe in conformity with this view, should God see fit to render his thought actual and to produce this substance. And since God's view is always true, our perceptions are always true; it is our judgments, which come from ourselves, that deceive us.

Now we said above, and it follows from what we have just said, that each substance is like a world apart, independent of all other things, except for God; thus all our phenomena, that is, all the things that can ever happen to us, are only consequences of our being. And since these phenomena maintain a certain order in conformity with our nature or, so to speak, in conformity with the world which is in us, an order which enables us to make useful observations to regulate our conduct, observations justified by the success of future phenomena, an order which thus allows us often to judge the future from the past without error, this would be sufficient to enable us to say that these phenomena are true without bothering with whether they are outside us and whether others also perceive them. Nevertheless, it is very true that the perceptions or expressions of all substances mutually correspond in such a way that each one, carefully following certain reasons or laws it has observed, coincides with others doing the same—in the same way that several people who have agreed to meet in some place at some specified time can really do this if they so desire. But although they all express the same phenomena, it does not follow that their expressions are perfectly similar; it is sufficient that they are proportional. In just the same way, several spectators believe that they are seeing the same thing and agree among themselves about it, even though each sees and speaks in accordance with his view.

And God alone (from whom all individuals emanate continually and who sees the universe not only as they see it but also entirely differently from all of them) is the cause of this correspondence of their phenomena and makes that which is particular to one of them public to all of them; otherwise, there would be no interconnection. We could therefore say in some way and properly speaking, though not in accordance with common usage, that one particular substance never acts upon another particular substance nor is acted upon by it, if we consider that what happens to each is solely a consequence of its complete idea or notion alone, since this idea already contains all its predicates or events and expresses the whole universe. In fact, nothing can happen to us except thoughts and perceptions, and all our future thoughts and perceptions are merely consequences, though contingent, of our preceding thoughts and perceptions, in such a way that, if I were capable of considering distinctly everything that happens or appears to me at this time, I could see in it everything that will ever happen or appear to me. This would never fail, and it would happen to me regardless, even if everything outside of me were destroyed, provided there remained only God and me. But since we attribute what we perceive in a certain way to other things as causes acting on us, we must consider the basis for this judgment and the element of truth there is in it.

15. *The action of one finite substance on another consists only in the increase of degree of its expression together with the diminution of the expression of the other, insofar as God requires them to accommodate themselves to one another.* But, without entering into a long discussion, in order to reconcile the language of metaphysics with practice, it is sufficient for now to remark that we ascribe to ourselves—and with reason—the phenomena that we express most perfectly and that we attribute to other substances the phenomena that each expresses best. Thus a substance, which is of infinite extension insofar as it expresses everything, becomes limited in proportion to its more or less perfect manner of expression. This, then, is how one can conceive that substances impede or limit each other, and consequently one can say that, in this sense, they act upon one another and are required, so to speak, to accommodate themselves to one another. For it can happen that a change that increases the expression of one diminishes that of another. Now, the efficacy [*vertu*] a particular substance has is to express well the glory of God, and it is by doing this that it is less limited. And whenever something exercises its efficacy or power, that is, when it acts, it improves and extends itself insofar as it acts. Therefore, when a change takes place by which several substances are affected (in fact every change affects all of them), I believe one may say that the substance which immediately passes to a greater degree of perfection or to a more perfect expression exercises its power and acts, and the substance which

passes to a lesser degree shows its weakness and *is acted upon* [*pâtit*]. I also hold that every action of a substance which has perfection involves some *pleasure*, and every passion some pain and vice versa. However, it can happen that a present advantage is destroyed by a greater evil in what follows, whence one can sin in acting, that is, in exercising one's power and finding pleasure.

16. *God's extraordinary concourse is included in that which our essence expresses, for this expression extends to everything. But this concourse surpasses the powers of our nature or of our distinct expression, which is finite and follows certain subordinate maxims.* It now only remains to explain how God can sometimes influence men and other substances by an extraordinary and miraculous concourse, since it seems that nothing extraordinary and supernatural can happen to them, given that all their events are only consequences of their nature. But we must remember what we have said above concerning miracles in the universe—that they are always in conformity with the universal law of the general order, even though they may be above the subordinate maxims. And to the extent that every person or substance is like a small world expressing the large world, we can say equally that the extraordinary action of God on this substance does not fail to be miraculous, despite the fact that it is included in the general order of the universe insofar as it is expressed by the essence or individual notion of this substance. That is why, if we include in our nature everything that it expresses, nothing is supernatural to it, for our nature extends everywhere, since an effect always expresses its cause and God is the true cause of substances. But what our nature expresses more perfectly belongs to it in a particular way, since it is in this that its power consists. But since it is limited, as I have just explained, there are many things that surpass the powers of our nature and even surpass the powers of all limited natures. Thus, to speak more clearly, I say that God's miracles and extraordinary concourse have the peculiarity that they cannot be foreseen by the reasoning of any created mind, no matter how enlightened, because the distinct comprehension of the general order

surpasses all of them. On the other hand, everything that we call natural depends on the less general maxims that creatures can understand. Thus, in order that my words may be as irreproachable as my meaning, it would be good to connect certain ways of speaking with certain thoughts. We could call that which includes everything we express our essence or idea; since this expresses our union with God himself, it has no limits and nothing surpasses it. But that which is limited in us could be called our nature or our power; and in that sense, that which surpasses the natures of all created substances is supernatural.

17. *An example of a subordinate maxim or law of nature; in which it is shown, against the Cartesians and many others, that God always conserves the same force but not the same quantity of motion.* I have already mentioned the subordinate maxims or laws of nature often enough, and it seems appropriate to give an example of one. Our new philosophers commonly make use of the famous rule that God always conserves the same quantity of motion in the world. In fact, this rule is extremely plausible, and, in the past, I held it as indubitable. But I have since recognized what is wrong with it. It is that Descartes and many other able mathematicians have believed that the quantity of motion, that is, the speed multiplied by the size of the moving body, coincides exactly with the moving force, or, to speak geometrically, that the forces are proportional to the product of the speeds and [sizes of] bodies. Now, it is extremely reasonable that the same force is always conserved in the universe. Also, when we attend to the phenomena, we see that there is no perpetual mechanical motion, because then the force of a machine, which is always diminished somewhat by friction and which must sooner or later come to an end, would restore itself, and consequently would increase by itself without any new external impulsion. We observe also that the force of a body is diminished only in proportion to the force it imparts to some bodies contiguous to it or to its own parts, insofar as they have separate motion.

Thus they believed that what can be said about force can also be said about the quantity of motion. But to show the difference between them, I assume that a body falling from a certain height acquires the force to rise up that height, if its direction carries it that way, at least, if there are no impediments. For example, a pendulum would rise again exactly to the height from which it descended, if the resistance of the air and some other small obstacles did not diminish its acquired force a little.

*I assume* also that as much force is required to elevate A, a body of one pound, to CD, a height of four fathoms, as to elevate B, a body of four pounds, to EF, a height of one fathom. All this is admitted by our new philosophers.

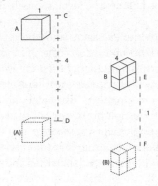

It is therefore evident that, having fallen from height CD, body A acquired exactly as much force as did body B, which fell from height EF; for since body (B) reached F and acquired the force to rise to E (by the first assumption), it has the force to carry a body of four pounds, that is, itself, to EF, the height of one fathom; similarly, since body (A) reached D and acquired the force to rise to C, it has the force to carry a body of one pound, that is, itself, to CD, a height of four fathoms. Therefore (by the second assumption), the force of these two bodies is equal.

Let us now see whether the quantity of motion is also the same in each. But here we will be surprised to find a very great difference. For Galileo demonstrated that the speed acquired by the fall CD is twice the speed acquired by the fall EF, even though the one height is four times the other. Let us therefore multiply body A, proportional to 1, with its speed, proportional to 2; the product or quantity of motion will be proportional to 2. On the other hand, let us multiply body B, proportional to 4, by its speed, proportional to 1; the product or quantity of motion will be proportional to 4. Therefore, the quantity of motion of body (A) at point D is half of the quantity of motion of body (B) at point F; yet their forces are equal. Hence, there is a great difference between quantity of motion and force—which is what needed to be proved.

Thus we see that force must be calculated from the quantity of the effect it can produce, for example, by the height to which a heavy body of a certain size and kind can be raised; this is quite different from the speed that can be imparted to it. And to give it double the speed, it must be given more than double the force.

Nothing is simpler than this proof. Descartes fell into error here only because he had too much confidence in his own thoughts, even when they were not sufficiently ripe. But I am surprised that his followers have not since then discovered this mistake; and I fear that they are beginning, little by little, to imitate some of the Peripatetics, whom they ridicule, like them gradually acquiring the habit of consulting their master's writings rather than reason and nature.[18]

18. *The distinction between force and quantity of motion is important, among other reasons, for judging that one must have recourse to metaphysical considerations distinct from extension in order to explain the phenomena of bodies*. This consideration, the distinction between force and quantity of motion, is rather important, not only in physics and mechanics, in order to find the true laws of nature and rules of motion and even to correct the several errors of practice which have slipped into the writings of some able mathematicians, but also in metaphysics, in order

to understand the principles better. For if we consider only what motion contains precisely and formally, that is, change of place, motion is not something entirely real, and when several bodies change position among themselves, it is not possible to determine, merely from a consideration of these changes, to which body we should attribute motion or rest, as I could show geometrically, if I wished to stop and do this now.

But the force or proximate cause of these changes is something more real, and there is sufficient basis to attribute it to one body more than to another. Also, it is only in this way that we can know to which body the motion belongs. Now, this force is something different from size, shape, and motion, and one can therefore judge that not everything conceived in body consists solely in extension and in its modifications, as our moderns have persuaded themselves. Thus we are once again obliged to reestablish some beings or forms they have banished. And it becomes more and more apparent that, although all the particular phenomena of nature can be explained mathematically or mechanically by those who understand them, nevertheless the general principles of corporeal nature and of mechanics itself are more metaphysical than geometrical, and belong to some indivisible forms or natures as the causes of appearances, rather than to corporeal mass or extension. This is a reflection capable of reconciling the mechanical philosophy of the moderns with the caution of some intelligent and well-intentioned persons who fear, with some reason, that we are withdrawing too far from immaterial beings, to the disadvantage of piety.

19. *The utility of final causes in physics*. Since I do not like to judge people wrongly, I do not accuse our new philosophers, who claim to banish final causes from physics.[19] But I am nevertheless obliged to confess that the consequences of this opinion appear

---

18. This section is a summary of an important paper Leibniz published in the *Acta Eruditorum* on 6 January 1686, "A Brief Demonstration of a Notable Error of Descartes," in which he argues against the conservation of quantity of motion, size times speed, a law first framed by Descartes (*Principles of Philosophy*, II, art. 36), and widely held by his followers. This essay began a long exchange in the learned journals that came to be known as the *vis viva* controversy, over the quantity, living force or *vis viva*, that Leibniz held was conserved. See "A Specimen of Dynamics," Part I.

19. The "new philosophers" Leibniz has in mind include Descartes and Spinoza, who explain everything mechanically and reject final causes. See Descartes, *Principles of Philosophy*, I, art. 28, and the Appendix to Part I of Spinoza's *Ethics*. In an earlier draft, it is impiety that Leibniz is not accusing them of, but the phrase was deleted.

dangerous to me, especially if I combine it with the one I refuted at the beginning of this discourse, which seems to go so far as to eliminate final causes altogether, as if God proposed no end or good in acting or as if the good were not the object of his will. As for myself, I hold, on the contrary, that it is here we must seek the principle of all existences and laws of nature, because God always intends the best and most perfect.

I am quite willing to admit that we are subject to deception when we wish to determine God's ends or counsels. But this is only when we try to limit them to some particular design, believing that he had only one thing in view, when instead he regards everything at the same time. For instance, it is a great mistake to believe that God made the world only for us, although it is quite true that he made it in its entirety for us and that there is nothing in the universe which does not affect us and does not also accommodate itself in accordance with his regard for us, following the principles set forth above. Thus when we see some good effect or perfection occurring or ensuing from God's works, we can say with certainty that God had proposed it. For he does nothing by chance and is not like us, who sometimes fail to do the good. That is why, far from being able to fall into error in this, as do extreme politicians who imagine too much subtlety in the designs of princes or as do commentators who look for too much erudition in their author, we cannot attribute too much reflection to this infinite wisdom, and there is no subject in which error is to be feared less, provided we limit ourselves to affirmations and avoid negative propositions that limit God's designs.

Anyone who sees the admirable structure of animals will find himself forced to recognize the wisdom of the author of things. And I advise those who have any feelings of piety and even feelings of true philosophy to keep away from the phrases of certain would-be freethinkers who say that we see because it happens that we have eyes and not that eyes were made for seeing. When one seriously holds these opinions ascribing everything to the necessity of matter or to some chance (even though both must appear ridiculous to those who understand what we have explained above), it is difficult to recognize an intelligent author of nature. For the effect must correspond to its cause; indeed, the effect is best recognized through a knowledge of

the cause. Moreover, it is unreasonable to introduce a supreme intelligence as orderer of things and then, instead of using his wisdom, use only the properties of matter to explain the phenomena. This is as if, in order to account for the conquest of an important place by a great prince, a historian were to claim that it occurred because the small particles of gunpowder, set off by the contact of a spark, escaped with sufficient speed to push a hard and heavy body against the walls of the place, while the little particles that make up the brass of the cannon were so firmly interlaced that this speed did not separate them, instead of showing how the foresight of the conqueror enabled him to choose the suitable means and times and how his power overcame all obstacles.

20. *A noteworthy passage by Socrates in Plato against the philosophers who are overly materialistic.* This reminds me of a beautiful passage by Socrates in Plato's *Phaedo*. This passage agrees marvelously with my opinions on this point and seems to be directed expressly against our overly materialistic philosophers. Thus I have been tempted to translate this account, even though it is a little long; perhaps this sample will give an incentive to some of us to share in many of the other beautiful and solid thoughts which can be found in the writings of this famous author.[20]

21. *If mechanical rules depended only on geometry without metaphysics, the phenomena would be entirely*

---

20. Leibniz's marginal note: "The passage from Plato's *Phaedo* where Socrates ridicules Anaxagoras, who introduces mind but does not make use of it, is to be inserted." Leibniz repeats the passage in "Two Sects of Naturalists":

"I heard one day (he said) someone reading in a book of Anaxagoras, in which it was said *that an intelligent being was the cause of all things and that he had disposed and arranged them.* That pleased me greatly, for I believed that if the world were the effect of an intelligence, everything would be done in the most perfect manner possible. That is why I believed that anyone who wanted to account for why things are produced or perish, or why they subsist, must look for what would be appropriate to the perfection of any given thing. And so, a man would need to consider in himself or in something else only that which would be the best or the most perfect. One who knows the most perfect could easily judge what is imperfect from this, for knowing the one amounts to knowing the other [literally: "there is only a single science for both the one and the other"].

*different*. Now, since we have always recognized God's wisdom in the detail of the mechanical structure of some particular bodies, it must also be displayed in the general economy of the world and in the constitution of the laws of nature. This is true to such an extent that one can observe the counsels of this wisdom in the laws of motion in general. For if there were nothing in bodies but extended mass and nothing in motion but change of place and if everything should and could be deduced solely from these definitions by geometrical necessity, it would follow, as I have shown elsewhere, that, upon contact, the smallest body would impart its own speed to the largest body without losing any of this speed; and we would have to accept a number of such rules which are completely contrary to the

"Considering all this, I rejoiced in having found a teacher who could teach the reasons for things—for example, whether the earth is round rather than flat, and why it was better that it be this way rather than otherwise. Moreover, I expected that when saying that the earth is at the center of the universe, or that it is not, he would explain to me why it was most appropriate for it to be this way, and I expected he would tell me as much about the sun, moon, stars, and their motions. And finally, after having shown what was most suitable for each thing in particular, he would have shown what was best in general. Filled with this hope, I quickly got hold of the books of Anaxagoras and ran through them with great haste. But I found myself far from my expectation, for I was surprised to see that he did not make use of the governing intelligence that he had first posited, that he no longer spoke of the arrangement nor of the perfection of things, and that he introduced certain ethereal matters that are hardly probable. In this he seemed like someone who, having said that Socrates does things through intelligence, and then going on to explain in particular the causes of his actions, says that he is seated here because he has a body composed of bones, flesh, and sinews, that his bones are hard, but that they are separated by intervals or junctures, that the sinews can be tightened or relaxed, and that this is why the body is flexible and finally why I am seated here. Or, if, wishing to account for this present discourse, he were to refer to the air, to the organs of voice and hearing, and the like, forgetting, however, the true causes, namely that the Athenians believed that it would be better to condemn me rather than to absolve me, and that I believed that it was better to sit here rather than to flee. For, by my faith, without this, these sinews and bones would long have been among the Boeotians and Megarians, if I hadn't thought it more just and more honorable [*honneste*] of me to suffer the penalty imposed by my native land rather than to live elsewhere as a wanderer and an exile. That is why it is

formation of a system.[21] But the decree of divine wisdom always to conserve the same total force and the same total direction has provided for this.

I even find that several effects of nature can be demonstrated doubly, that is, by considering first the efficient cause and then by considering the final cause, making use, for example, of God's decree always to produce his effect by the easiest and most determinate ways, as I have shown elsewhere in accounting for the rules of catoptrics and dioptrics;[22] I shall say more about this soon.

*22. Reconciliation of two ways of explaining things, by final causes and by efficient causes, in order to satisfy both those who explain nature mechanically and those who have recourse to incorporeal natures.* It is appropriate to make this remark in order to reconcile those who hope to explain mechanically the formation of the first tissue of an animal and the whole machinery of its parts, with those who account for this same structure using final causes. Both ways are good and both can be useful, not only for admiring the skill of the Great Worker, but also for discovering something useful in physics and in medicine. And the authors who follow these different routes should not malign each other.

For I see that those who apply themselves to explaining the beauty of the divine anatomy laugh at others who imagine that a movement of certain fluids that seems fortuitous could have produced such a beautiful variety of limbs, and call these people rash and profane. And the latter, on the other hand,

unreasonable to call these bones and sinews and their motion causes. It is true that whoever would say that I could not do all this without bones and sinew would be right. But something else is the true cause, and they constitute only a condition without which the cause could not be a cause. Those who only say, for example, that motions of bodies around the earth keep it here, where it is, forget that divine power disposes everything in the finest way, and do not understand that it is the good and the beautiful that join, form, and maintain the world."
21. See, e.g., "On the Nature of Body and the Laws of Motion" (ca. 1678–82) for the full argument.
22. The reference is to the "Unicum Opticae, Catoptricae et Dioptricae Principium, Autore G. G. L.," from the *Acta Eruditorum* (June 1682).

call the former simple and superstitious, comparing them to the ancients who regarded physicists as impious when they maintained that it is not Jupiter that thunders, but some matter present in the clouds. It would be best to join together both considerations, for if it is permitted to use a humble comparison, I recognize and praise the skill of a worker not only by showing his designs in making the parts of his machine, but also by explaining the instruments he used in making each part, especially when these instruments are simple and cleverly contrived. *And God is a skillful enough artisan* to produce a machine which is a thousand times more ingenious than that of our body, while using only some very simple fluids explicitly concocted in such a way that only the ordinary laws of nature are required to arrange them in the right way to produce so admirable an effect; but it is also true that this would not happen at all unless God were the author of nature.

However, I find that the way of efficient causes, which is in fact deeper and in some sense more immediate and *a priori*, is, on the other hand, quite difficult when one comes to details, and I believe that, for the most part, our philosophers are still far from it. But the way of final causes is easier, and is not infrequently of use in divining important and useful truths which one would be a long time in seeking by the other, more physical way; anatomy can provide significant examples of this. I also believe that Snell, who first discovered the rules of refraction, would have waited a long time before discovering them if he first had to find out how light is formed. But he apparently followed the method which the ancients used for catoptrics, which is in fact that of final causes. For, by seeking the easiest way to lead a ray from a given point to another point given by reflection on a given plane (assuming that this is nature's design), they discovered the equality of angles of incidence and angles of reflection, as can be seen in a little treatise by Heliodorus of Larissa, and elsewhere.[23]

That is what, I believe, Snell and Fermat after him (though without knowing anything about Snell) have most ingeniously applied to refraction. For when, in the same media, rays observe the same proportion between sines (which is proportional to the resistances of the media), this happens to be the easiest or, at least, the most determinate way to pass from a given point in a medium to a given point in another. And the demonstration Descartes attempted to give of this same theorem by way of efficient causes is not nearly as good. At least there is room for suspicion that he would never have found the law in this way, if he had learned nothing in Holland of Snell's discovery.[24]

23. *To return to immaterial substances, we explain how God acts on the understanding of minds and whether we always have the idea of that about which we think.* I found it appropriate to insist a bit on these considerations of final causes, incorporeal natures, and an intelligent cause with respect to bodies, in order to show their use even in physics and mathematics: on the one hand, to purge the mechanical philosophy of the impiety with which it is charged and, on the other hand, to elevate the minds of our philosophers from material considerations alone to nobler meditations. It is now appropriate to return from bodies to immaterial natures, in particular to minds, and to say something of the means God uses to enlighten them and act on them. In this matter, too, we must not doubt that there are certain laws of nature, of which I could speak more fully elsewhere. But for now it will be sufficient to touch somewhat on ideas, whether we see all things in God and how God is our light.[25]

It may be appropriate to observe that the improper use of ideas gives rise to several errors.

---

23. Heliodorus of Larissa, or Damianos, was a Greek mathematician who flourished after Ptolemy. He was probably known to Leibniz through an edition, *De opticis libri duo*, published by Erasmus Bartholinus in Paris in 1657.

24. The law of refraction was first published in the second discourse of Descartes' *Dioptrics*. Descartes does indeed attempt to derive the law from hypotheses about the nature of light. Snell discovered the same laws at roughly the same time as Descartes, and there was (and continues to be) a lively dispute about who discovered the law first, and whether Descartes actually discovered the law or learned it from Snell. Leibniz seems to favor Snell.

25. See Malebranche, *Search after Truth*, Book III, pt. 2, chap. 6.

For when we reason about something, we imagine ourselves to have the idea of that thing; and that is the foundation upon which certain ancient and new philosophers have built a certain extremely imperfect demonstration of God. For, they say, I must have an idea of God or of a perfect being since I think of him, and one cannot think without an idea. Now, the idea of this being contains all perfections, and existence is a perfection, so consequently he exists. But since we often think of impossible chimeras—for example, of the highest degree of speed, of the greatest number, of the intersection of the conchoid with its base or rule—this reasoning is insufficient. It is therefore in this sense that we can say that there are true and false ideas, depending upon whether the thing in question is possible or not. And it is only when we are certain of its possibility that we can boast of having an idea of the thing. Thus the argument above proves, at least, that God exists necessarily, if he is possible. It is indeed a prerogative of divine nature, one that surpasses all others, that divine nature needs only its possibility or essence in order actually to exist, and it is precisely this that is called *ens a se*.

24. *What is clear or obscure, distinct or confused, adequate and intuitive or suppositive*[26] *knowledge; nominal, real, causal, and essential definition.* In order to understand better the nature of ideas, we must to some extent touch on the varieties of knowledge. When I can recognize a thing from among others without being able to say what its differences or properties consist in, the knowledge is *confused*. It is in this way that we sometimes know something *clearly*, without being in any doubt whether a poem or a picture is done well or badly, simply because it has a certain something, I know not what, that satisfies or offends us. But when I can explain the marks which I have, the knowledge is called *distinct*. And such is the knowledge of an assayer, who discerns the true from the false by means of certain tests or marks which make up the definition of gold.

But distinct knowledge has degrees, for ordinarily the notions that enter into the definition would themselves need definition and are known only confusedly. But when everything that enters into a distinct definition or distinct knowledge is known distinctly, down to the primitive notions, I call this knowledge *adequate*. And when my mind understands all the primitive ingredients of a notion at once and distinctly, it has intuitive knowledge of it; this is extremely rare, since the greater part of human knowledge is only confused or *suppositive*.[27]

It is also good to distinguish nominal and real definitions. I call a definition nominal when one can still doubt whether the notion defined is possible, as, for example, if I say that an endless helix is a solid line whose parts are congruent or can be superimposed on one another; anyone who does not know from elsewhere what an endless helix is could doubt whether such a line is possible, even though having such congruent parts is in fact one of the reciprocal properties of the endless helix, for other lines whose parts are congruent (which are only the circumference of a circle and the straight line) are planar; that is, they can be inscribed on a plane. This shows that any reciprocal property can serve as a nominal definition; but when the property makes known the possibility of the thing, it constitutes a real definition. As long as we have only a nominal definition, we cannot be certain of the consequences we derive, for if it concealed some contradiction or impossibility, the opposite conclusions could be derived from it. That is why truths do not depend upon names and are not arbitrary, as some new philosophers have believed.[28]

Furthermore, there are still great differences between the kinds of real definitions. For when possibility is proved only by experience, as in the definition of quicksilver, whose possibility we know because we know that there actually is such a body which is an extremely heavy but rather volatile fluid, the definition is merely real and nothing more;

---

26. Cf. "Meditations on Knowledge, Truth, and Ideas" (1684). Instead of "suppositive" Leibniz there uses the term "symbolic."

27. In the margin: "A notion intermediate between intuitive and clear is when I have been deprived of clear knowledge of all surrounding notions."
28. Leibniz probably has Hobbes in mind here.

but when the proof of the possibility is *a priori*, the definition is both real and *causal*, as when it contains the possible generation of the thing. And when a definition pushes the analysis back to the primitive notions without assuming anything requiring an *a priori* proof of its possibility, it is perfect or *essential*.

25. *In what case our knowledge is joined to the contemplation of the idea.* Now, it is evident that we have no idea of a notion when it is impossible. And in the case in which knowledge is only *suppositive*, even when we have the idea, we do not contemplate it, for such a notion is only known in the way in which we know notions involving a hidden impossibility [*occultement impossibles*]; and if a notion is possible, we do not learn its possibility in this way. For example, when I think of a thousand or of a chiliagon, I often do this without contemplating the idea—as when I say that a thousand is ten times a hundred without bothering to think of what 10 and 100 are because I suppose I know it and do not believe I need to stop now and conceive it. Thus, it could happen, as in fact it often happens, that I am mistaken with respect to a notion I suppose or believe that I understand, although in fact the notion is impossible, or at least incompatible with those to which I join it. And whether I am mistaken or not, this suppositive way of conceiving remains the same. Therefore, only in confused notions when our knowledge is clear or in distinct notions when it is intuitive do we see the entire idea in them.[29]

26. *That we have all ideas in us; and of Plato's doctrine of reminiscence.* In order properly to conceive what an idea is, we must prevent an equivocation. For some take the idea to be the form or difference of our thoughts, and thus we have an idea in the mind only insofar as we think of it; every time we think of it again, we have other ideas of the same thing, though similar to the preceding ideas. But it seems that others take the idea as an immediate object of thought or as some permanent form that remains when we are not contemplating it. And, in fact, our soul always has

in it the quality of representing to itself any nature or form whatsoever, when the occasion to think of it presents itself. And I believe that this quality of our soul, insofar as it expresses some nature, form, or essence, is properly the idea of the thing, which is in us and which is always in us, whether we think of it or not. For our soul expresses God, the universe, and all essences, as well as all existences.

This agrees with my principles, for nothing ever enters into our mind naturally from the outside; and we have a bad habit of thinking of our soul as if it received certain species as messengers and as if it has doors and windows. We have all these forms in our mind; we even have forms from all time, for the mind always expresses all its future thoughts and already thinks confusedly about everything it will ever think about distinctly. And nothing can be taught to us whose idea we do not already have in our mind, an idea which is like the matter of which that thought is formed.

This is what Plato so excellently recognized when he proposed his doctrine of reminiscence, a very solid doctrine, provided that it is taken rightly and purged of the error of preexistence and provided that we do not imagine that at some earlier time the soul must already have known and thought distinctly what it learns and thinks now. Plato also strengthened his view by way of a fine experiment, introducing a little boy, whom he leads insensibly to extremely difficult truths of geometry concerning incommensurables without teaching him anything, merely by asking appropriate questions in proper order.[30] This demonstrates that our soul knows all these things virtually and requires only attention to recognize truths, and that, consequently, it has, at very least, the ideas upon which these truths depend. One can even say that it already possesses these truths, if they are taken as relations of ideas.

27. *How our soul can be compared to empty tablets and how our notions come from the senses.* Aristotle preferred to compare our soul to tablets that are

---

29. An earlier draft continues: "However, we actually have in our mind all possible ideas, and we always think of them in a confused way."

30. This is a reference to Plato's *Meno*, 82b et seq., where, in a familiar passage, Socrates leads a young slave boy through some geometrical arguments.

still blank, where there is room for writing,[31] and he maintained that nothing is in our understanding that does not come from the senses. That agrees better with the popular notions, as is Aristotle's way, but Plato goes deeper. However, these kinds of doxologies or practicologies may be acceptable in ordinary usage, much as we see that those who follow Copernicus do not stop saying that the sun rises and sets. I even find that they can be given a good sense, a sense according to which they have nothing false in them, just as I have already noted how one can truly say that particular substances act on one another. In this same way, one can also say that we receive knowledge from the outside by way of the senses, because some external things contain or express more particularly the reasons that determine our soul to certain thoughts. But when we are concerned with the exactness of metaphysical truths, it is important to recognize the extent and independence of our soul, which goes infinitely further than is commonly thought, though in ordinary usage in life we attribute to it only what we perceive most manifestly and what belongs to us most particularly, for it serves no purpose to go any further.

However, it would be good to choose terms proper to each conception [*sens*] in order to avoid equivocation. Thus, the expressions in our soul, whether we conceive them or not, can be called ideas, but those we conceive or form can be called notions, concepts [*conceptus*]. But however we take these expressions, it is always false to say that all our notions come from the external senses, for the notions I have of myself and of my thoughts, and consequently of being, substance, action, identity, and of many others, arise from an internal experience.

28. *God alone is the immediate object of our perceptions, which exist outside of us, and he alone is our light.* Now, in rigorous metaphysical truth, there is

no external cause acting on us except God alone, and he alone communicates himself to us immediately in virtue of our continual dependence. From this it follows that there is no other external object that touches our soul and immediately excites our perception. Thus we have ideas of everything in our soul only by virtue of God's continual action on us, that is to say, because every effect expresses its cause, and thus the essence of our soul is a certain expression, imitation or image of the divine essence, thought, and will, and of all the ideas comprised in it. It can then be said that God is our immediate external object and that we see all things by him. For example, when we see the sun and the stars, it is God who has given them to us and who conserves the ideas of them in us, and it is God who determines us really to think of them by his ordinary concourse while our senses are disposed in a certain manner, according to the laws he has established. God is the sun and the light of souls, the light that lights every man that comes into this world,[32] and this is not an opinion new to our times. After Holy Scripture and the Church Fathers, who have always preferred Plato to Aristotle, I remember having previously noted that from the time of the Scholastics, several believed that God is the light of the soul and, in their way of speaking, the active intellect of the rational soul. The Averroists gave the sense of this a bad turn,[33] but others, among whom was, I believe, William of Saint Amour, and several mystical theologians, have taken it in a manner worthy of God and capable of elevating the soul to the knowledge of its good.

29. *Yet we think immediately through our own ideas and not through those of God.* However, I am not of the opinion of certain able philosophers who seem to maintain that our very ideas are in God and not at all in us.[34] In my opinion, this arises from the fact that they have not yet considered sufficiently

---

31. Aristotle, *De Anima*, Book II, chap. 4. The doctrine that nothing is in the intellect that was not first in the senses, attributed to Aristotle by the Scholastics, does not actually occur in Aristotle; perhaps it is a rendering of *Posterior Analytics*, Book II, chap. 19, or *Nicomachean Ethics*, Book VI, chap. 3, sec. 3.

32. John 1:9.
33. Averroists were Christian followers of Averroes (or Ibn Rushd, 1126–98), the great Arabic commentator on Aristotle, who held that the active intellect in each man is part of a single active intellect. The doctrine of a single world-soul was condemned as heresy.
34. Malebranche, again, is Leibniz's primary target, as above in Sec. 23.

either what we have just explained about substances or the full extent and independence of our soul, which makes it contain everything that happens to it, and makes it express God and, with him, all possible and actual beings, just as an effect expresses its cause. Also, it is inconceivable that I think through the ideas of others. The soul must actually be affected in a certain way when it thinks of something, and it must already have in itself not only the passive power of being able to be affected in this way (which is already wholly determined) but also an active power, a power by virtue of which there have always been in its nature marks of the future production of this thought and dispositions to produce it in its proper time. And all this already involves the idea included in this thought.

30. *How God inclines our soul without necessitating it; that we do not have the right to complain and that we must not ask why Judas sins but only why Judas the sinner is admitted to existence in preference to some other possible persons. On original imperfection before sin and on the degrees of grace.* There are a number of considerations with respect to the action of God on human will which are so difficult that it would be inordinately lengthy to pursue them here. Roughly speaking, however, here is what can be said. In concurring with our actions, God ordinarily does no more than follow the laws he has established, that is, he continually conserves and produces our being in such a way that thoughts come to us spontaneously or freely in the order that the notion pertaining to our individual substance contains them, a notion in which they could be foreseen from all eternity. Moreover, in virtue of his decree that the will always tend toward the apparent good, expressing or imitating his will in certain particular respects (so that this apparent good always has some truth in it), God determines our will to choose what seems better, without, however, necessitating it. For, absolutely speaking, the will is in a state of indifference, as opposed to one of necessity, and it has the power to do otherwise or even to suspend its action completely; these two alternatives are possible and remain so.

Therefore, the soul must guard itself against deceptive appearances [*les surprises des apparences*] through a firm will to reflect and neither to act nor to judge in certain circumstances except after having deliberated fully. But it is true, and it is even assured from all eternity, that a certain soul will not make use of this power in such a situation. But who is to blame? Can the soul complain about anything other than itself? All these complaints after the fact are unjust, if they would have been unjust before the fact. Now, could this soul, a little before sinning, complain about God in good faith, as if God determined it to sin? Since God's determinations in these matters cannot be foreseen, how does the soul know that it is determined to sin, unless it is actually sinning already? It is only a matter of not willing, and God could not put forth an easier and more just condition; thus judges do not seek the reasons which have disposed a man to have a bad will, but only stop to consider the extent to which this particular will is bad. But perhaps it is certain from all eternity that I shall sin? Answer this question for yourself: perhaps not; and without considering what you cannot know and what can give you no light, act according to your duty, which you do know.

But someone else will say, why is it that this man will assuredly commit this sin? The reply is easy: Otherwise, it would not be this man. For God sees from all time that there will be a certain Judas whose notion or idea (which God has) contains this free and future action. Therefore, only this question remains, why does such a Judas, the traitor, who is merely possible in God's idea, actually exist? But no reply to this question is to be expected on earth, except that, in general, one must say that, since God found it good that he should exist, despite the sin that God foresaw, it must be that this sin is paid back with interest in the universe, that God will derive a greater good from it, and that it will be found that, in sum, the sequence of things in which the existence of that sinner is included is the most perfect among all the possible sequences. But we cannot always explain the admirable economy of this choice while we are travelers in this world; it is enough to know it without understanding it. And here is the occasion to recognize the *altitudinem divitarum*, the depth and abyss of divine wisdom, without seeking a detail that involves infinite considerations.[35]

Yet one sees clearly that God is not the cause of evil. For not only did original sin take possession of the soul after the innocence of men had been lost, but even before this, there was an original imperfection or limitation connatural to all creatures, which makes them liable to sin or capable of error. Thus, the supralapsarians[36] raise no more problems than the others do. And it is to this, in my view, that we must reduce the opinion of Saint Augustine and other authors, the opinion that the root of evil is in nothingness, that is to say, in the privation or limitation of creatures, which God graciously remedies by the degree of perfection it pleases him to give. This grace of God, whether ordinary or extraordinary, has its degrees and its measures; in itself, it is always efficacious in producing a certain proportionate effect, and, further, it is always sufficient, not only to secure us from sin, but even to produce salvation, assuming that man unites himself to it by what derives from him.[37] But it is not always sufficient to overcome man's inclinations, for otherwise he would have nothing more to strive for; this is reserved solely for the absolutely efficacious grace which is always victorious, whether it is so by itself or by way of appropriate circumstances.

31. *On the motives of election, on faith foreseen, on middle knowledge, on the absolute decree and that it all reduces to the reason why God has chosen for existence such a possible person whose notion includes just such a sequence of graces and free acts; this puts an end to all difficulties at once.* Finally, God's graces are wholly pure graces, upon which creatures have no claim. However, just as it is not sufficient to appeal to God's absolute or conditional foresight into the future actions of men in order to account for his choice in the dispensation of these graces, we also must not

imagine absolute decrees that have no reasonable motive. As for God's foreknowledge of faith or good works, it is very true that he has elected only those whose faith and charity he foresaw, whom he foreknew he would endow with faith. But the same question returns, why will God give the grace of faith or of good works to some rather than to others? And as for this knowledge God has, which is the foresight not of faith and good works, but of their grounds [*matière*] and predisposition, that is, foresight of what a man would contribute to them on his side (for it is true that there are differences among men whenever there are differences in grace and that, in fact, although a man needs to be stimulated to the good and be converted, he must also act in that direction afterward), it seems to several people that one could say that God, seeing what a man would do without grace or extraordinary assistance, or at least seeing the sort of person he is, leaving grace aside, might resolve to give grace to those whose natural dispositions were better or, at least, less imperfect or less bad. But even if that were the case, one can say that these natural dispositions, insofar as they are good, are still the effect of grace, although ordinary grace, since God has favored some more than others. And since he knows that these natural advantages he gives will serve as motives for grace or extraordinary assistance, is it not true, according to this doctrine, that in the end everything is completely reduced to his mercy?

Since we do not know how much and in what way God takes account of natural dispositions in the dispensation of grace, I believe, then, that the most exact and surest thing to say, according to our principles, as I have already noted, is that among the possible beings there must be the person of Peter or John, whose notion or idea contains this entire sequence of ordinary and extraordinary graces and all the rest of these events with their circumstances, and that it pleased God to choose him for actual existence from among an infinity of equally possible persons. After this it seems that there is nothing more to ask and that all difficulties vanish.

For, with respect to this single great question, why it pleased God to choose him from among so many other possible persons, one would have to

---

35. The Latin translates: "depth of riches," a reference to Romans 11:33.

36. Calvinists who held that God's decrees of election and reprobation preceded the fall. Cf. *Theodicy* I, sec. 77–84.

37. The text also contains "by his will" as a possible ending for the sentence.

be very unreasonable not to be content with the general reasons we have given, reasons whose details lie beyond us. Thus, instead of having recourse to an absolute decree which is unreasonable, since it is without reason, or to reasons which do not solve the difficulty completely and are in need of further reasons, it would be best to say with Saint Paul, that God here followed certain great reasons of wisdom or appropriateness, unknown to mortals and based on the general order, whose aim is the greatest perfection of the universe. It is to this that the motives of the glory of God and the manifestation of his justice are reduced, as well as of his mercy and generally of his perfections and finally the immense depth of his riches, with which the soul of Saint Paul was enraptured.

32. *The utility of these principles in matters of piety and religion.* For the rest, it seems that the thoughts we have just explained, particularly the great principle of the perfection of the operations of God and the principle that the notion of a substance contains all its events with all their circumstances, far from harming, serve to confirm religion, to dispel enormous difficulties, to enflame souls with a divine love, and to elevate minds to the knowledge of incorporeal substances, much more than hypotheses we have seen until now. For one sees clearly that all other substances depend on God, in the same way as thoughts emanate from our substance, that God is all in all, and that he is intimately united with all creatures, in proportion to their perfection, that it is he alone who determines them from the outside by his influence, and, if to act is to determine immediately, it can be said in this sense, in the language of metaphysics, that God alone operates on me, and God alone can do good or evil to me; the other substances contribute only by reason of these determinations, because God, having regard for all, shares his blessings and requires them to accommodate themselves to one another. Hence God alone brings about the connection and communication among substances, and it is through him that the phenomena of any substance meet and agree with those of others and consequently, that there is reality in our perceptions. But, in practice, one ascribes

an action to particular reasons[38] in the sense that I have explained above, because it is not necessary always to mention the universal cause in particular cases.

We also see that every substance has a perfect spontaneity (which becomes freedom in intelligent substances), that everything that happens to it is a consequence of its idea or of its being, and that nothing determines it, except God alone. And that is why a person of very exalted mind, revered for her saintliness, was in the habit of saying that the soul must often think as if there were nothing but God and itself in the world.[39]

Now, nothing gives us a stronger understanding of immortality than the independence and extent of the soul in question here, which shelters it absolutely from all external things, since the soul alone makes up its whole world and is sufficient to itself with God. And it is as impossible that it should perish without annihilation, as it is that the world (of which it is a perpetual living expression) should destroy itself; hence, it is impossible that the changes in this extended mass called our body should do anything to the soul or that the dissolution of this body should destroy what is indivisible.

33. *Explanation of the union of soul and body, a matter which has been considered as inexplicable or miraculous, and on the origin of confused perceptions.* We also see the unexpected illumination of this great mystery of the union of the soul and the body, that is, how it happens that the passions and actions of the one are accompanied by the actions and passions, or by the corresponding phenomena, of the other. For there is no way to conceive that the one has any influence on the other, and it is unreasonable simply to appeal to the extraordinary operation of the universal cause in an ordinary and particular

---

38. An earlier draft had "occasional causes" rather than "particular reasons."

39. Leibniz probably had Saint Theresa in mind here. In a letter from 1696 he wrote: "In [her writings] I once found this lovely thought, that the soul should conceive of things as if there were only God and itself in the world. This even provides a considerable object to reflect upon in philosophy, which I usefully employed in one of my hypotheses," G. Grua, *Textes inédits d'après les manuscrits de la Bibliothèque provinciale de Hanovre* (Paris: PUF, 1948), p. 103.

thing. But here is the true reason: We have said that everything that happens to the soul and to each substance follows from its notion, and therefore the very idea or essence of the soul carries with it the fact that all its appearances or perceptions must arise spontaneously from its own nature and precisely in such a way that they correspond by themselves to what happens in the whole universe. But they correspond more particularly and more perfectly to what happens in the body assigned to it, because the soul expresses the state of the universe in some way and for some time, according to the relation other bodies have to its own body. This also allows us to know how our body belongs to us, without, however, being attached to our essence. And I believe that persons who can meditate will judge our principles favorably, because they will be able to see easily what the connection between the soul and the body consists in, a connection which seems inexplicable in any other way.

We also see that the perceptions of our senses, even when they are clear, must necessarily contain some confused feeling [*sentiment*], for our body receives the impression of all other bodies, since all the bodies of the universe are in sympathy, and, even though our senses are related to everything, it is impossible for our soul to attend to everything in particular; that is why our confused sensations are the result of a truly infinite variety of perceptions. This is almost like the confused murmur coming from the innumerable set of breaking waves heard by those who approach the seashore. Now, if from several perceptions (which do not come together to make one), there is none which stands out before the others and if they make impressions that are almost equally strong or equally capable of gaining the attention of the soul, the soul can only perceive them confusedly.

34. *On the difference between minds and other substances, souls or substantial forms, and that the immortality required includes memory*. Assuming[40] that

the bodies that make up an *unum per se*, as does man, are substances, that they have substantial forms, and that animals have souls, we must admit that these souls and these substantial forms cannot entirely perish, no more than atoms or the ultimate parts of matter can, on the view of other philosophers. For no substance perishes, although it can become completely different. They also express the whole universe, although more imperfectly than minds do. But the principal difference is that they do not know what they are nor what they do, and consequently, since they do not reflect on themselves, they cannot discover necessary and universal truths. It is also because they lack reflection about themselves that they have no moral qualities. As a result, though they may pass through a thousand transformations, like those we see when a caterpillar changes into a butterfly, yet from the moral or practical point of view, the result is as if they had perished; indeed, we may even say that they have perished physically, in the sense in which we say that bodies perish through their corruption. But the intelligent soul, knowing what it is—having the ability to utter the word "I," a word so full of meaning—does not merely remain and subsist metaphysically, which it does to a greater degree than the others, but also remains the same morally and constitutes the same person. For it is memory or the knowledge of this self that renders it capable of punishment or reward. Thus the immortality required in morality and religion does not consist merely in this perpetual subsistence common to all substances, for without the memory of what one has been, there would be nothing desirable about it. Suppose that some person all of a sudden becomes the king of China, but only on the condition that he forgets what he has been, as if he were born anew; practically, or as far as the effects could be perceived, wouldn't that be the same as if he were annihilated and a king of China created at the same instant in his place? That is something this individual would have no reason to desire.

35. *The excellence of minds and that God considers them preferable to other creatures. That minds express God rather than the world, but that the other substances express the world rather than God*. But so

---

40. An earlier draft began with this first sentence: "I do not attempt to determine if bodies are substances in metaphysical rigor or if they are only true phenomena like the rainbow and, consequently, if there are true substances, souls, or substantial forms which are not intelligent."

that we may judge by natural reasons that God will always preserve not only our substance, but also our person, that is, the memory and knowledge of what we are (though distinct knowledge is sometimes suspended during sleep and fainting spells), we must join morals to metaphysics, that is, we must not only consider God as the principle and cause of all substances and all beings, but also as the leader of all persons or intelligent substances and as the absolute monarch of the most perfect city or republic, which is what the universe composed of all minds together is, God himself being the most perfect of all minds and the greatest of all beings. For certainly minds are the most perfect beings[41] and best express divinity. And since the whole nature, end, virtue, and function of substance is merely to express God and the universe, as has been sufficiently explained, there is no reason to doubt that the substances which express the universe with the knowledge of what they are doing and which are capable of knowing great truths about God and the universe, express it incomparably better than do those natures, which are either brutish and incapable of knowing truths or completely destitute of sensation and knowledge. And the difference between intelligent substances and substances that have no intelligence at all is just as great as the difference between a mirror and someone who sees.

Since God himself is the greatest and wisest of all minds, it is easy to judge that the beings with whom he can, so to speak, enter into conversation, and even into a society—by communicating to them his views and will in a particular manner and in such a way that they can know and love their benefactor—must be infinitely nearer to him than all other things, which can only pass for the instruments of minds. So we see that all wise persons value a man infinitely more than any other thing, no matter how precious it is, and it seems that the greatest satisfaction that a soul, content in other ways, can have is to see itself loved by others. With respect to God, though, there is

the difference that his glory and our worship cannot add anything to his satisfaction, since knowledge of creatures is only a consequence of his supreme and perfect happiness—far from contributing to it or being its partial cause. However, what is good and reasonable in finite minds is found preeminently in him, and, just as we would praise a king who would prefer to preserve the life of a man rather than the most precious and rarest of his animals, we should not doubt that the most enlightened and most just of all monarchs is of the same opinion.

36. *God is the monarch of the most perfect republic, composed of all minds, and the happiness of this city of God is his principal purpose.* Indeed, minds are the most perfectible substances, and their perfections are peculiar in that they interfere with each other the least, or rather they aid one another the most, for only the most virtuous can be the most perfect friends. Whence it obviously follows that God, who always aims for the greatest perfection in general, will pay the greatest attention to minds and will give them the greatest perfection that universal harmony can allow, not only in general, but to each of them in particular.

One can even say that God, insofar as he is a mind, is the originator of existences; otherwise, if he lacked the will to choose the best, there would be no reason for a possible thing to exist in preference to others. Thus the quality that God has of being a mind himself takes precedence over all the other considerations he can have toward creatures; only minds are made in his image and are, as it were, of his race or like children of his household, since they alone can serve him freely and act with knowledge in imitation of the divine nature; a single mind is worth a whole world, since it does not merely express the world but it also knows it and it governs itself after the fashion of God. In this way we may say that, although all substances express the whole universe, nevertheless the other substances express the world rather than God, while minds express God rather than the world. And this nature of minds, so noble that it brings them as near to divinity as it is possible for simple creatures, has the result that God draws infinitely more glory from them

---

41. An earlier draft of this sentence began: " . . . minds are either the only substances one finds in the world, in the case in which bodies are only true phenomena, or else they are at least the most perfect . . . "

than from all other beings, or rather the other beings only furnish minds the matter for glorifying him.

That is why this moral quality God has, which makes him the lord or monarch of minds, relates to him, so to speak, personally and in a quite singular manner. It is because of this that he humanizes himself, that he is willing to allow anthropomorphism, and that he enters into society with us, as a prince with his subjects; and this consideration is so dear to him that the happy and flourishing state of his empire, which consists in the greatest possible happiness of its inhabitants, becomes the highest of his laws. For happiness is to people what perfection is to beings. And if the first principle of the existence of the physical world is the decree to give it the greatest perfection possible, the first intent of the moral world or the City of God, which is the noblest part of the universe, must be to diffuse in it the greatest possible happiness.

Therefore, we must not doubt that God has ordered everything in such a way that minds not only may live always, which is certain, but also that they may always preserve their moral quality, so that the city does not lose a single person, just as the world does not lose any substance. And consequently they will always know what they are; otherwise they would not be susceptible to reward or punishment, something, however, essential to a republic, but above all essential to the most perfect republic, in which nothing can be neglected.

Finally, since God is at the same time the most just and most good-natured of monarchs and since he demands only a good will, as long as it is sincere and serious, his subjects cannot wish for a better condition, and, to make them perfectly happy, he wants only for them to love him.

37. *Jesus Christ has revealed to men the mystery and admirable laws of the kingdom of heaven and the greatness of the supreme happiness that God prepares for those who love him.* The ancient philosophers knew very little of these important truths; Jesus Christ alone has expressed them divinely well and in a manner so clear and familiar that the coarsest of minds have grasped them. Thus his gospel has entirely changed the course of human affairs; he has brought us to know the kingdom of heaven, or that perfect republic of minds which deserves the title of City of God, whose admirable laws he has disclosed to us. He alone has made us see how much God loves us and with what exactitude he has provided for everything that concerns us; that, caring for sparrows, he will not neglect the rational beings which are infinitely more dear to him; that all the hairs on our head are numbered; that heaven and earth will perish rather than the word of God and what pertains to the economy of our salvation; that God has more regard for the least of the intelligent souls than for the whole machinery of the world; that we must not fear those who can destroy bodies but cannot harm souls, because God alone can make souls happy or unhappy; and that the souls of the just, in his hands, are safe from all the upheavals of the universe, God alone being able to act upon them; that none of our actions are forgotten; that everything is taken account of, even idle words or a spoonful of water well used; finally, that everything must result in the greatest welfare of those who are good; that the just will be like suns; and that neither our senses nor our mind has ever tasted anything approaching the happiness that God prepares for those who love him.

# G. W. Leibniz, From the Letters to Arnauld (1686–87)[1]

## Remarks on Arnauld's Letter about My Proposition That the Individual Notion of Each Person Includes Once and for All Everything That Will Ever Happen to Him [May 1686]

*I thought* (says Arnauld) *that we might infer that God was free to create or not to create Adam, but assuming that he wanted to create him, everything that has happened to humankind had to happen, or ought to happen, by a fatal necessity, or at least, I thought that, assuming he wanted to create Adam, God is no more free, with respect to all this, than he would be not to create a creature capable of thought, assuming that he wanted to create me.* I first replied that we must distinguish between absolute and hypothetical necessity. To this, Arnauld replies here

1. Translated from the French by R. Ariew and D. Garber in G. W. Leibniz, *Philosophical Essays* (Indianapolis/Cambridge: Hackett Publishing Company, 1989). Arnauld's critique of Section 13 of the "Discourse on Metaphysics" started off a correspondence with Leibniz. Leibniz summarizes adequately the debate that ensued (from February to May 1686) in the first selection we have chosen from that correspondence. Passages in double brackets below are not in the copies Arnauld received and may be either earlier thoughts or later additions. Only selected variants are noted.

that *he is speaking only of hypothetical necessity*. After this assertion, the argument takes a different turn. The terms he used, *fatal necessity*, are ordinarily understood only as applied to absolute necessity, so I was required to make this distinction, which, however, is no longer called for, inasmuch as Arnauld does not insist upon this fatal necessity, since he uses alternative phrases: by a fatal necessity or at least, etc. It would be useless to dispute about the word. But, as for the thing itself, Arnauld still finds it strange that I seem to maintain *that all human events occur necessitate ex hypothesi, given the single assumption that God wanted to create Adam*. To this I have *two replies* to make. The *first* is that my assumption is not merely that God wanted to create an Adam whose notion was vague and incomplete, but that God wanted to create a particular Adam, sufficiently determined as an individual. And according to me, this complete individual notion involves relations to the whole series of things. This should appear more reasonable, given that Arnauld grants here the interconnections among God's resolutions; that is, he grants that God, having resolved to create Adam, takes into consideration all the resolutions he has concerning the whole series of the universe; this is somewhat like a wise man who, making a decision about one part of his plan and having the whole plan in view, would decide so much the better, if his decision could settle all the parts at once.

*The other reply* is that the conclusion [*conséquence*], by virtue of which all the events follow from the hypothesis, is indeed always certain, but it is not always necessary with metaphysical necessity as is the one found in Arnauld's example: that God in resolving to create me cannot fail to create a nature capable of thought. The conclusion is often only physical and assumes God's free decrees, as do conclusions which depend on the laws of motion or which depend on the moral principle that all minds will pursue what appears best to them. It is true that, when the assumption of those decrees that yield the conclusion is added to the first assumption which had constituted the antecedent, namely, God's resolution to create Adam, to make up a single antecedent out of all these assumptions or resolutions; then, I say, it is true in that case that the conclusion follows.

Since I have already touched upon these two replies in some way in the letter I sent to the Landgrave, Arnauld brings forward replies to them that must be considered. He admits in good faith that he took my view to be that all the events of an individual can be deduced from his individual notion in the same way and with the same necessity as the properties of a sphere can be deduced from its specific notion or definition; he also supposed that I considered the notion of the individual in itself, without taking account of the way in which it exists in the divine understanding or will. *For* (he says) *it seems to me that we don't usually consider the specific notion of a sphere in relation to its representation in God's understanding, but in relation to what it is in itself, and I thought that it was the same for the individual notion of each person. But*, he adds, *now that he knows what I think about this, that is sufficient to enable him to accept it for the purpose of asking whether it overcomes all the difficulties*; he is still doubtful of this. I see that Arnauld has not remembered, or at least did not concern himself with, the view of the Cartesians, who maintain that it is through his will that God establishes the eternal truths, like those concerning the properties of the sphere. But since I am not of their opinion any more

than Arnauld is, I will only say why I think that we must philosophize differently about the notion of an individual substance than about the specific notion of the sphere. The reason is because the notion of a *species* includes only eternal or necessary truths, but the notion of an individual includes considered as possible what, in fact, is true, that is, considerations related to the existence of things and to time, and consequently it depends upon God's free decrees considered as possible; for truths of fact or existence depend upon God's decrees. Thus the notion of sphere in general is incomplete or abstract; that is, we consider in it only the essence of a sphere in general or in theory, without regard to particular circumstances, and consequently it does not in any way include what is required for the existence of a certain sphere. But the notion of the sphere Archimedes had placed on his tomb is complete and must include everything belonging to the subject of that shape. That is why, in individual or practical considerations, which are concerned with singulars, in addition to the shape of the sphere, we must consider the matter of which it is made, the place, the time, and the other circumstances, considerations which, by a continual linkage, would in the end include the whole series of the universe, if everything these notions included could be pursued. For the notion of the piece of matter of which this sphere is made involves all the changes it has undergone and will undergo one day. And according to me, each individual substance always contains traces of what has ever happened to it and marks of what will ever happen to it. But what I have just said can suffice to explain my line of thought.

Now, Arnauld states that, by taking the individual notion of a person in relation to the knowledge God had of it when he resolved to create it, what I have said about this notion is quite certain. And similarly, he even grants that the volition to create Adam was not detached from God's volition concerning what would happen to him and to his posterity. But he now asks whether the link between Adam and what happens to his posterity is dependent on or independent of God's free decrees; *that is*, as he explains, *whether God knew what would happen to*

*Adam and his posterity only as a consequence of the free decrees by which God ordained everything that will happen, or whether there is an intrinsic and necessary connection, independent of these decrees, between Adam and the events in question.* He does not doubt that I would choose the latter alternative, and in fact I could not choose the first as he explained it, but it seems to me that there is a middle ground. However, he proves that I must choose the latter, because I consider the individual notion of Adam as possible when I maintain that, among an infinity of possible notions, God has chosen the notion of an Adam such as this, and notions possible in themselves do not depend upon God's free decrees.

But here I must explain myself a little better. Therefore, I say that the connection between Adam and human events is not independent of all of God's free decrees, but also, that it does not depend upon them so completely that each event could happen or be foreseen only in virtue of a particular primitive decree made about it. I therefore think that there are only a few free primitive decrees that regulate the course of things, decrees that can be called laws of the universe, and which, joined to the free decree to create Adam, bring about the consequence. This is a bit like needing few hypotheses to explain phenomena—something I will explain more distinctly in what follows. As for the objection that possibles are independent of God's decrees, I grant it with respect to actual decrees (even though the Cartesians do not agree with this), but I hold that possible individual notions include some possible free decrees. For example, if this world were only possible, the individual notion of some body in this world, which includes certain motions as possible, would also include our laws of motion (which are free decrees of God), but also only as possible. For, since there is an infinity of possible worlds, there is also an infinity of possible laws, some proper to one world, others proper to another, and each possible individual of a world includes the laws of its world in its notion.

The same things can be said about miracles or God's extraordinary operations. These belong to the general order and conform to God's principal plans and, consequently, are included in the notion of this universe, which is a result of these plans; just as the idea of a building results from the ends or plans of the builder, so the idea or notion of this world is a result of one of God's plans considered as possible. For everything must be explained by its cause, and God's ends are the cause of the universe. Now, in my opinion, each individual substance expresses the whole universe from a certain point of view, and consequently it also expresses the miracles in question. All this must be understood of the general order, of God's plans, of the course of this universe, of individual substance, and of miracles, whether they are taken in the actual state or whether they are considered *sub ratione possibilitatis*. For another possible world will also have all this in its own way, though the plans of our world have been preferred.

It can also be seen from what I have just said about God's plans and primitive laws that this universe has a certain principal or primitive notion, a notion of which particular events are merely the result, with the exception of what is free and contingent, to which certainty does no harm, since the certainty of events is based in part upon free acts. Now, each individual substance of this universe expresses in its notion the universe into which it enters. And not only does the assumption that God has resolved to create this Adam include resolutions for all the rest, but so does the assumption that he created any other individual substance whatsoever, because it is the nature of an individual substance to have a notion so complete that everything that can be attributed to it can be deduced from it, even the whole universe, because of the interconnection of things. Nevertheless, to proceed carefully, it must be said that it is not so much because God decided to create this Adam that he decided on all the rest. Rather, both the decision he made with regard to Adam and the one he made with regard to other particular things are the result of the decision he made with regard to the whole universe and a result of the principal plans that determine its primitive notion and establish in it this general and inviolable order. Everything is in conformity with this order, even miracles, which are, no doubt, in conformity with God's principal plans, although they do not always observe the particular maxims that are called laws of nature.

I have said that all human events can be deduced not simply by assuming the creation of a vague Adam, but by assuming the creation of an Adam determined with respect to all these circumstances, chosen from among an infinity of possible Adams. This has given Arnauld the occasion to object, not without reason, that it is as difficult to conceive of several Adams, taking Adam as a particular nature, as it is to conceive of several me's. I agree, but when speaking of several Adams, I was not taking Adam as a determinate individual. I must therefore explain myself. This is what I meant. When one considers in Adam a part of his predicates, for example, that he is the first man, set in a garden of pleasure, from whose side God fashioned a woman, and similar things conceived *sub ratione generalitatis*, in a general way (that is to say, without naming Eve, Paradise, and other circumstances that fix individuality), and when one calls Adam the person to whom these predicates are attributed, all this is not sufficient to determine the individual, for there can be an infinity of Adams, that is, an infinity of possible persons, different from one another, whom this fits. Far from disagreeing with what Arnauld says against this multiplicity of the same individual, I myself used this to make it better understood that the nature of an individual must be complete and determinate. I am even quite convinced of what Saint Thomas had already taught about intelligences, which I hold to apply generally, namely, that it is not possible for there to be two individuals entirely alike, or differing only numerically.[2] Therefore, we must not conceive of a vague Adam, that is, a person to whom certain attributes of Adam belong, when we are concerned with determining whether all human events follow from positing his existence; rather, we must attribute to him a notion so complete that everything that can be attributed to him can be deduced from it. Now, there is no room for doubting that God can

form such a notion of him, or rather that he finds it already formed in the realm of possibles, that is, in his understanding.

It, therefore, also follows that he would not have been our Adam, but another Adam, had other events happened to him, for nothing prevents us from saying that he would be another. Therefore, he is another. It seems obvious to us that this block of marble brought from Genoa would have been altogether the same if it had been left there, because our senses allow us to judge only superficially. But at bottom, because of the interconnection of things, the whole universe with all its parts would be quite different and would have been different from the beginning, if the least thing in it had happened differently than it did. It does not follow from this that events are necessary, but rather that they are certain, given God's choice of this possible universe, whose notion contains this series of things. I hope that what I am going to say will enable Arnauld himself to agree with this. Let there be a straight line ABC representing a certain time. And let there be an individual substance, for example, I, enduring or subsisting during that time. Let us first take me subsisting during time AB, and then me subsisting during time BC. Then, since the assumption is that it is the same individual substance that endures throughout, or rather that it is I who subsists in time AB, being then in Paris, and that it is still I who subsists in time BC, being then in Germany, there must necessarily be a reason allowing us truly to say that we endure, that is to say that I, who was in Paris, am now in Germany. For if there were no such reason, we would have as much right to say that it is someone else. It is true that my internal experience convinces me *a posteriori* of this identity; but there must also be an *a priori* reason. Now, it is not possible to find any reason but the fact that both my attributes in the preceding time and state and my attributes in the succeeding time and state are predicates of the same subject— they are in the subject. Now, what is it to say that the predicate is in the same subject, except that the notion of the predicate is in some way included in the notion of the subject? And since, once I began existing, it was possible truly to say of me that this or

---

2. The reference is to Saint Thomas' doctrine that, with intelligences, every individual is a lowest species; cf. the "Discourse on Metaphysics," Section 9.

that would happen to me, it must be admitted that these predicates were laws included in the subject or in my complete notion, which constitutes what is called I, which is the foundation of the connection of all my different states and which God has known perfectly from all eternity. After this, I think that all doubts should disappear, for, when I say that the individual notion of Adam includes everything that will ever happen to him, I don't mean to say anything other than what all philosophers mean when they say that the predicate is included in the subject in a true proposition. It is true that the results of so evident a doctrine are paradoxical, but that is the fault of the philosophers who do not sufficiently pursue the clearest notions.

I now think that Arnauld, being as penetrating and fair-minded as he is, will no longer find my proposition so strange, even if he is not able to approve of it entirely (though I almost flatter myself that I have his approval). I agree with what he so judiciously adds about the circumspection we must use when appealing to divine knowledge [*la science divine*] in order to find out what we ought to judge concerning the notions of things. But, properly understood, what I have just said must hold, even though we should speak of God only as much as is necessary. For even if we did not say that God, when considering Adam whom he is resolving to create, sees in him everything that will happen to him, it suffices that one can always prove that there must be a complete notion of this Adam which contains them. For all the predicates of Adam either depend upon other predicates of the same Adam or they do not. Then, setting aside all of those predicates that depend upon the others, we need only gather together all the primitive predicates in order to form Adam's complete notion, a notion sufficient for deducing everything that will ever happen to him, and this is as much as we need for us to be able to explain it. It is evident that God can construct—and even actually conceive—a notion sufficient to explain all the phenomena pertaining to Adam; but it is no less evident that this notion is possible in itself. It is true that we should not enter unnecessarily into an investigation of the divine knowledge and will, because of the great difficulties

involved. Nevertheless, we can explain what we have derived from such an investigation relevant to our question without entering into the difficulties Arnauld mentions—for example, the difficulty of understanding how God's simplicity is reconcilable with what we must distinguish in it. It is also very difficult to explain perfectly how God has knowledge he might not have had, namely, the knowledge by intuition [*la science de la vision*]; for, if things that exist contingently in the future didn't exist, God would not have any intuition of them. It is true that he would have simple knowledge of them, which would become intuition when it is joined to his will, so that this difficulty is perhaps reduced to a difficulty concerning his will, namely, how God is free to will. No doubt this is beyond us, but it is not necessary to understand it in order to resolve our question.[3]

As for the way in which we conceive that God acts by choosing the best among several possibles, Arnauld is right in finding some obscurity there. He seems, nevertheless, to recognize that we are led to conceive that there is an infinity of possible first men, each connected to a long sequence of persons and events, and that God has chosen from them the one who, together with his sequence, pleased him. So this is not as strange as it had first appeared to him. It is true that Arnauld testifies that he is strongly led to think that these purely possible substances are only chimeras. I do not wish to dispute this, but I hope that, in spite of this, he will grant me what I need. I agree that there is no other reality in pure possibles than the reality they have in the divine understanding, and we see from this that Arnauld himself will be required to fall back on divine knowledge to explain them, whereas it seemed earlier that he thought that we should seek them in themselves. When I also grant what Arnauld is convinced of and what I do not deny—that we conceive no possibles except through the ideas actually found in the things God

---

3. Knowledge of simple understanding [*scientia simplicis intelligentiae*] is God's knowledge of possibles; knowledge by intuition [*scientia visionis*] is God's knowledge of actuals, which differs from the former only in God's reflexive knowledge of his own decrees. Cf. *Philosophische Schriften*, ed. C. I. Gerhardt (Berlin, 1875–90), IV 440–41, C 16–17.

has created—it does no harm to me. For when speaking of possibilities, I am satisfied that we can form true propositions about them. For example, even if there were no perfect square in the world, we would still see that it does not imply a contradiction. And if we wished absolutely to reject pure possibles, contingency would be destroyed; for, if nothing were possible except what God actually created, then what God created would be necessary, in the case he resolved to create anything.

Finally, I agree that in order to determine the notion of an individual substance it is good to consult the one I have of myself, just as one must consult the specific notion of the sphere in order to determine its properties. Yet there is a considerable difference, for my notion and the notion of every other individual substance is infinitely broader and more difficult to understand than a specific notion, like that of the sphere, which is only incomplete. It is not enough that I sense myself [*je me sente*] to be a substance that thinks; I must distinctly conceive what distinguishes me from all other minds, and I have only a confused experience of this. The result is that, though it is easy to determine that the number of feet in the diameter is not included in the notion of sphere in general, it is not so easy to judge whether the trip I intend to make is included in my notion; otherwise, it would be as easy for us to be prophets as to be geometers. I am uncertain whether I will make the trip, but I am not uncertain that, whether I go or not, I will always be me. This is a presumption that must not be confused with a distinct notion or item of knowledge. These things appear undetermined to us only because the foreshadowings or marks which are in our substance are not recognizable to us. This is a bit like those who, consulting only the senses, would ridicule someone who says that the least motion is also communicated as far as matter extends, because experience alone cannot demonstrate this; but, when the nature of motion and matter are considered, one is convinced of this. It is the same here: when someone consults the confused experience he has of his individual notion in particular, he is far from perceiving this interconnection of events; but when the general and distinct notions which enter into it are considered,

it is discovered. In fact, in considering the notion I have of every true proposition, I find that every predicate necessary or contingent, past, present, or future is included in the notion of the subject; and I ask no more of it.

Indeed, I believe that this will open up to us a way of reconciling our views. For I suspect that Arnauld did not want to grant me this proposition only because he took the connection I am maintaining to be both intrinsic and necessary, whereas I hold it to be intrinsic, but in no way necessary; for now, I have sufficiently explained that it is founded on free decrees and acts. I do not intend any connection between the subject and the predicate other than that which holds in the most contingent of truths, that is, that we can always conceive something in the subject which serves to provide a reason why this predicate or event belongs to it, or why this happened rather than not. But these reasons for contingent truths incline, rather than necessitate. Therefore, it is true that I could fail to go on this trip, but it is certain that I shall go. This predicate or event is not connected with certainty to my other predicates, conceived incompletely or *sub ratione generalitatis*; but it is connected with certainty to my complete individual notion, since I suppose that this notion was constructed explicitly so that everything that happens to me can be deduced from it. No doubt, this notion is found *a parte rei*, and it is properly the notion that belongs to me, who finds myself in different states, since this notion alone is capable of including all of them.

I have so much deference for Arnauld and such a good opinion of his judgment that I easily give up my opinions, or at least my way of expressing them as soon as I see that he finds something objectionable in them. That is why I precisely followed the difficulties he proposed, and having attempted to satisfy them in good faith, it seems to me that I am not far removed from his opinions.

The proposition at issue is of great importance and deserves to be firmly established, for from this it follows that every soul is like a world apart, independent of every other thing outside of God, that it is not only immortal and, so to speak, undisturbable, but that it holds in its substance the traces of everything that happens to it. From this also follows that in which the interaction [*commerce*] of substances consists, particularly the union of soul and body. This interaction does not occur in accordance with the ordinary hypothesis of physical influence of one substance on another, since every present state of a substance happens to it spontaneously and is only a result of its preceding state. This interaction also does not occur in accordance with the hypothesis of occasional causes, according to which God ordinarily intervenes in some way other than conserving each substance in its course, and according to which God on the occasion of something happening in the body arouses thoughts in the soul which change the course it would have taken without this intervention. It occurs in accordance with the hypothesis of concomitance, which appears demonstrative to me. That is, each substance expresses the whole series of the universe according to the point of view or relation proper to it, from which it happens that they agree perfectly; and when we say that one acts upon another, we mean that the distinct expression of the one acted upon is diminished, and that of the one acting is augmented, in conformity with the series of thoughts involved in its notion. For although every substance expresses everything, in common usage we correctly attribute to it only the most evident expressions in accordance to its relation to us.

Finally, I believe that after this, the propositions contained in the summary sent to Arnauld will appear not only more intelligible, but perhaps also more solid and more important than might have been thought at first.[4]

## To Arnauld (28 November/8 December 1686) [excerpts][5]

As I found something extraordinary in the frankness and sincerity with which you accepted some arguments I used, I cannot avoid recognizing and admiring it. I suspected that the argument taken from the general nature of propositions would make some impression on your mind; but I also confess that there are few people able to appreciate truths so abstract, and that perhaps no one else would have been able to perceive its cogency so readily.

I should like to be informed of your meditations about the possibilities of things; they can only be profound and important since they are concerned with speaking of these possibilities in a way worthy of God. But this will be at your convenience. As for the two difficulties you found in my letter, the one concerning the hypothesis of concomitance, that is, the hypothesis of the agreement of substances among themselves, and the other concerning the nature of the forms of corporeal substances, I confess that they are considerable, and if I were able to satisfy them completely, I think that I would be able to decipher the greatest secrets of nature in its entirety. But it is something to advance to a certain point.[6] As for the first, I find that you yourself have sufficiently explained the obscurity you found in my thought concerning the hypothesis of concomitance; for when the soul has a sensation of pain at the same time that the arm is injured, I think that the situation is, in fact, as you say, Sir, that the soul itself forms this pain, which is a natural result of its state or notion. I admire Saint Augustine for having apparently recognized the same thing (as you have remarked) when he said that the pain the soul has in these encounters is nothing but a sadness that accompanies the ill disposition of the body. In fact, this great man had very solid and very profound thoughts. But (it will be asked), how does the soul know this ill disposition of the body? I reply that it is not by any impression or action of bodies on the soul, but because the nature of every substance carries a general expression of the whole universe and because the nature of the soul carries, more particularly, a more distinct expression of that which is now happening with regard to its body. That is why it

---

4. Again, Arnauld seems not to have been sent the whole "Discourse" but only a summary which corresponds closely to the titles of successive sections.
5. Arnauld wrote to Leibniz on 28 September 1686, saying that he sees "no other difficulties except about the possibility of things, and about this way of conceiving God as having chosen the universe he created from an infinity of other possible universes he saw at the same time and did not wish to

create" (*Philosophische Schriften*, II, 64). Arnauld then asked Leibniz to explain himself further about the hypothesis of concomitance and about the nature of the form of corporeal substance; he formulated a series of seven queries on the latter problem. Leibniz's response takes up each query individually.
6. Horace, *Epistles*, I. 1. 32.

is natural for the soul to mark and know the accidents of its body through accidents of its own. The situation is the same for the body when it accommodates itself to the thoughts of the soul. And when I wish to raise my arm, it is exactly at the moment when everything in the body is disposed for that effect, so that the body moves by virtue of its own laws. But through the wondrous though unfailing agreement of things among themselves, it happens that these laws work together exactly at the moment that the will is so inclined, since God took this into account in advance when he formed his resolution about this series of all the things in the universe. All these things are only consequences of the notion of an individual substance, which contains all its phenomena in such a way that nothing can happen to a substance that does not come from its own depths, though in conformity to what happens to another, despite the fact that the one acts freely and the other without choice. [[And this agreement is one of the best proofs that can be given of the necessity for there to be a substance which is the supreme cause of everything.]]

I should like to be able to explain myself as clearly and decisively about the other question, concerning the substantial forms. The first difficulty you indicated, Sir, is that our soul and our body are two really distinct substances; therefore, it seems that the one is not the substantial form of the other. I reply that, in my opinion, our body in itself or the *cadaver*, setting the soul apart, can be called a substance only in an improper sense, just as in the case of a machine or a pile of stones, which are only beings by aggregation; for regular or irregular arrangement does not constitute substantial unity. Besides, the last Lateran council declares that the soul is truly the substantial form of our body.

As for the second difficulty,[7] I grant that the substantial form of the body is indivisible, and it seems to me that this is also Saint Thomas' opinion; and I further grant that every substantial form or, indeed, every substance is indestructible and even

ingenerable—which was also the opinion of Albertus Magnus and, among the ancients, the opinion of the author of the book *De diaeta*, attributed to Hippocrates.[8] Therefore, they can only come into being by an act of creation. And I am greatly inclined to believe that all reproduction among animals deprived of reason, reproduction which does not deserve a new act of creation, is only the transformation of another animal already living but sometimes imperceptible, like the changes that happen to a silkworm and other similar animals; nature is accustomed to reveal its secrets in some cases and hide them in others. Thus the souls of brutes would have all been created from the beginning of the world, in accordance with the fruitfulness in seed mentioned in Genesis. But the rational soul is created only at the time of the formation of its body, being entirely different from the other souls we know, because it is capable of reflection and it imitates the divine nature on a small scale.

Third,[9] I think that a block of marble is, perhaps, only like a pile of stones, and thus cannot pass as a single substance, but as an assemblage of many. Suppose that there were two stones, for example, the diamond of the Great Duke and that of the Great Mogul. One could impose the same collective name for the two, and one could say that they constitute a pair of diamonds, although they are far apart from one another; but one would not say that these two diamonds constitute a substance. More and less do not make a difference here. Even if they were brought nearer together and made to touch, they would not be substantially united to any greater extent. And if, after they had touched, one joined to them another body capable of preventing their separation—for example, if they had been set in the

---

7. Arnauld asked: If the substantial form of the body is divisible, "we would not gain anything with respect to the unity of body [literally: to body being a *unum per se*]" (*Philosophische Schriften*, II, 66); if it is indivisible, "it seems that body would be as indestructible as our soul" (ibid.).

8. The reference to Saint Thomas might be to *Summa Theologica* I, q. 76, art. 8, but Leibniz is probably not representing Aquinas accurately. See below, the "New System of Nature," for a different set of attributions. The reference to Albertus Magnus is too vague to be specified. On Hippocrates, see *The Regimen* I.4. While the text is part of the Hippocratic corpus, it is probably not by Hippocrates himself. See "Letter to Samuel Masson," in which Leibniz's claims about this text are modified.

9. Arnauld asked: "What happens to this substantial form [of a block of marble] when it stops being one, because someone has broken it in two?" (*Philosophische Schriften* II, 66).

same ring—all this would make only what is called an *unum per accidens*.[10] For it is as by accident that they are required to perform the same motion. Therefore, I hold that a block of marble is not a complete single substance, any more than the water in a pond together with all the fish it contains would be, even if all the water and all the fish were frozen, or any more than a flock of sheep would be, even if these sheep were tied together so that they could only walk in step and so that one could not be touched without all the others crying out. There is as much difference between a substance and such a being as there is between a man and a community, such as a people, an army, a society, or a college; these are moral beings, beings in which there is something imaginary and dependent on the fabrication [*fiction*] of our mind. A substantial unity requires a thoroughly indivisible and naturally indestructible being, since its notion includes everything that will happen to it, something which can be found neither in shape nor in motion (both of which involve something imaginary, as I could demonstrate), but which can be found in a soul or substantial form, on the model of what is called *me*. These are the only thoroughly real beings, as was recognized by the ancients, and above all, by Plato, who clearly showed that matter alone is not sufficient to form a substance. Now, the aforementioned I, or that which corresponds to it in each individual substance, can neither be made nor destroyed by the bringing together or separation of parts, which is a thing entirely external to what constitutes a substance. I cannot say precisely whether there are true corporeal substances other than those that are animated, but souls at least serve to give us some knowledge of others by analogy.

All this can contribute to clearing up the fourth difficulty.[11] For without bothering with what the Scholastics have called the form of corporeity [*formam corporeitatis*], I assign substantial forms to all corporeal substances that are more than mech-

anically united. But fifth,[12] if I am asked in particular what I say about the sun, the earthly globe, the moon, trees, and other similar bodies, and even about beasts, I cannot be absolutely certain whether they are animated, or even whether they are substances, or, indeed, whether they are simply machines or aggregates of several substances. But at least I can say that if there are no corporeal substances such as I claim, it follows that bodies would only be true phenomena, like the rainbow. For the continuum is not merely divisible to infinity, but every part of matter is actually divided into other parts as different among themselves as the two aforementioned diamonds. And since we can always go on in this way, we would never reach anything about which we could say, here is truly a being, unless we found animated machines whose soul or substantial form produced a substantial unity independent of the external union arising from contact. And if there were none, it then follows that, with the exception of man, there is nothing substantial in the visible world.

Sixth,[13] since the notion of individual substance in general, which I have given, is as clear as that of truth, the notion of corporeal substance will also be clear and, consequently, so will that of substantial form. But even if this were not so, we are required to admit many things whose knowledge is not sufficiently clear and distinct. I hold that the notion of extension is much less clear and distinct—witness the strange difficulties of the composition of the continuum. And it can indeed be said that *because of the actual subdivision of parts, there is no definite and precise shape in bodies*. As a result, *bodies would doubtless be only imaginary and apparent, if there were only matter and its modifications*. However, it is useless to mention the unity, notion, or substantial form of bodies when we are concerned with explaining the particular phenomena of nature, just as it is useless for the geometers to examine the difficulties concerning the composition

---

10. Accidental unity.
11. Arnauld asked: "Do you give to extension a general substantial form, such as certain Scholastics admitted when they called it *forma corporeitatis*, or do you want there to be as many different substantial forms as there are different bodies, and different species when these are bodies of different species?" (*Philosophische Schriften* II, 66).

12. Arnauld asked: "Where do you situate the unity we attribute to the earth, the sun, the moon . . . ?" (*Philosophische Schriften* II, 66).
13. Arnauld wrote: "Finally, it will be said that it is not worthy of a philosopher to admit entities of which we have no clear and distinct idea" (*Philosophische Schriften* II, 67).

of the continuum when they are working on resolving some problem. These things are still important and worthy of consideration in their place. All the phenomena of bodies can be explained mechanically, that is, by the corpuscular philosophy, following certain principles of mechanics posited without troubling oneself over whether there are souls or not. But in the final analysis of the principles of physics and even of mechanics, we find that these principles cannot be explained by the modifications of extension alone, and that the nature of force already requires something else.

Finally, in the seventh place[14] I remember that Cordemoy, in his treatise, *On the Distinction between Body and Soul*, thought he needed to admit atoms, or extended indivisible bodies, to save substantial unity in bodies, so as to find something fixed to constitute a simple being. But you rightly concluded that I am not of that opinion. It appears that Cordemoy recognized something of the truth, but he did not yet see what the true notion of substance consists in; but this is the key to the most important knowledge. The atom which contains only a shaped mass of infinite hardness (which I hold not to be in conformity with divine wisdom, any more than the void is) cannot contain in itself all its past and future states, and even less all those of the entire universe.

## To Arnauld (30 April 1687)

Since your letters are of considerable benefit to me and the marks of your genuine liberality, I have no right to ask for them, and consequently your reply is never too late. However agreeable and useful they may be to me, I take into consideration what you owe to the public good, and thus I suppress my wishes. Your reflections are always instructive for me and I will take the liberty to go through them in order.

I do not think that there is any difficulty in my saying that *the soul expresses more distinctly, other things being equal, that which belongs to its body*, since it expresses the whole universe in a certain sense, in particular in accordance with the relation other bodies have to its own, since it cannot express all things equally well; otherwise there would be no differences among souls. But it does not follow from this that it must perceive perfectly everything occurring in the parts of its body, since there are degrees of relation between these very parts, parts which are not all expressed equally, any more than external things are. The greater distance of external bodies is compensated for by the smallness, or some other hindrance, with respect to the internal parts— Thales saw the stars, though he did not see the ditch at his feet.

For us the nerves are more sensitive than the other parts of our bodies, and perhaps it is only through them that we perceive the others. This apparently happens because the motions of the nerves or of the fluids in them imitate the impressions better and confuse them less, and the most distinct expressions in the soul correspond to the most distinct impressions of the body. This is not because the nerves act on the soul, or the other bodies on the nerves, metaphysically speaking, but because the former represent the state of the latter through a spontaneous relation [*spontanea relatione*]. We must also take into account that too many things take place in our bodies for us to be able to perceive them all individually. What we sense is only a certain resultant to which we are habituated, and we are not able to distinguish the things that enter into the resultant because of their multitude, just as when one hears the noise of the sea from afar, one does not discern what each wave does, even though each wave has an effect on our ears. But when a striking change happens in our body, we soon notice it and notice it more clearly than external changes which are not accompanied by a notable change in our organs.

*I do not say that the soul knows the pricking before it has the sensation of pain*, except insofar as it knows or expresses confusedly all things in accordance with my previously established principles. But this expression which the soul has of the future in advance, although obscure and confused, is the true cause of what will

---

14. Arnauld wrote: "There are Cartesians who, in order to find unity in bodies, have denied that matter is divisible to infinity, and [have asserted] that one must admit indivisible atoms. But I do not think that you share their opinion" (*Philosophische Schriften* II, 67).

happen to it and of the clearer perception it will have afterwards, when the obscurity is lifted, since the future state is a result of the preceding one.

I said that God created the universe in such a way that the soul and the body, each acting according to its laws, agree in their phenomena. You judge that *this is in accord with the hypothesis of occasional causes*. If this were so, I would not be sorry, and I am always glad to find others who hold my positions. But I have only a glimpse of your reason for thinking this; you suppose that I wouldn't say that a body can move by itself, and thus, since the soul is not the real cause of the motion of the arm, and neither is the body, the cause must therefore be God. But I am of another opinion. I hold that what is real in the state called motion proceeds as much from the corporeal substance as thought and will proceed from the mind. Everything happens to each substance as a consequence of the first state God gave to it in creating it, and, extraordinary concourse apart, his ordinary concourse consists only in the conservation of the same substance, in conformity with its preceding state and the changes it brings about. Yet it is rightly said that one body pushes another, that is, that it never happens that a body begins to have a certain tendency unless another body touching it has a proportionate loss, in accordance with the unvarying laws that we observe in phenomena. And in fact, since motions are real phenomena rather than beings, a motion considered as a phenomenon is the immediate result or effect of another phenomenon in my mind, and similarly in the minds of others, but the state of a substance is not the immediate result of the state of another particular substance.

I do not dare assert that plants have no soul, life, or substantial form, for although a part of a tree planted or grafted can produce a tree of the same kind, it is possible that there is a seminal part in it that already contains a new vegetative thing, as perhaps there are already some living animals, though extremely small, in the seeds of animals, which can be transformed within a similar animal. Therefore, I don't yet dare assert that only animals are living and endowed with a substantial form. Perhaps there is an infinity of degrees in the forms of corporeal substances.

You say that those who maintain the hypothesis of occasional causes, saying that *my will is the occasional cause and God is the real cause of the motion of my arm, do not claim that God does this in time by means of a new volition he has each time I wish to raise my arm, but through the unique act of eternal will, by which he willed to do everything he foresaw it would be necessary for him to do*. To this I reply that one could say, for the same reason, that even miracles are not accomplished by a new volition of God, since they are in conformity with his general plan, and I already remarked that each volition of God involves all the others, but in a certain order of priority. In fact, if I properly understand the views of the authors of occasional causes, they introduce a miracle which is no less miraculous for being continual. For it seems to me that the notion of miracle does not consist in rarity. One might say that in this matter God acts only according to a general rule, and consequently he acts without miracle. But I do not grant that consequence, and I believe that God can make general rules for himself even with respect to miracles. For example, if God had resolved to give his grace immediately or to perform some other action of this nature every time a certain condition was satisfied, this action, though ordinary, would nevertheless still be a miracle. I admit that the authors of occasional causes might give another definition of the term, but, according to common usage, it seems that a miracle differs internally and substantively from the performance of an ordinary action, and not by the external accident of frequent repetition; properly speaking, God performs a miracle when he does something that surpasses the forces he has given to creatures and conserves in them. [[For example, if God made a body, put into circular motion by means of a sling, freely to go in a circular path when released from the sling, without it being pushed or retained by anything whatever, that would be a miracle, for according to the laws of nature, it should continue in a straight line along a tangent; and if God decided that this should always happen, he would be performing natural miracles, since this motion could not be explained by anything simpler.]] Thus, in the same way, we must say, in accordance with the received view, that if continuing the motion exceeds the force of bodies, then the continuation of the motion is a true miracle. But I believe that corporeal substance has the ability [force] to continue its changes in accordance with the laws God put into its nature and conserves there. To make myself better understood, I believe that the actions of minds change nothing at all in the nature of bodies, nor do bodies change anything in the nature of minds, and even that God changes nothing on their occasion, except when he performs a miracle. In my opinion, things are so interconnected that the mind never wills anything efficaciously except when the body is ready to accomplish it in virtue of its own laws and forces; [[but, according to the authors of occasional causes, God changes the laws of bodies on the occasion of the action of the soul, and vice versa. That is the essential difference between our opinions.]] Thus, on my view, we should not worry about how the soul can give some motion or some new determination to animal spirits, since, in fact, it never gives them any at all, insofar as there is no proportion between mind and body, and there is nothing that can determine what degree of speed a mind can give a body, nor even what degree of speed God would want to give to a body on the occasion of the action of the mind in accordance with a certain law. The same difficulty found in the hypothesis of a real influence of soul on body, and *vice versa*, is also found in the hypothesis of occasional causes, insofar as we can see no connection nor can we see a foundation for any rule. And if someone were to say, as, it seems, Descartes wishes to say, that the soul, or God on its occasion, changes only the direction or determination of a motion and not the force which is in bodies (since it does not seem probable to him that at every moment God would violate the general law of nature that the same force must persist, on the occasion of every volition minds have), I would reply that it would still be quite difficult to explain what connection there can be between the thoughts of the soul and the paths or angles of the direction of bodies. Furthermore, there is in nature yet another general law which Descartes did not perceive, a law no less important, namely, that the same sum of determination or direction must always persist. For

I find that if one were to draw any straight line, for example, from east to west through a given point, and if one were to calculate all the directions of all the bodies in the world insofar as they advance or recede in lines parallel to this line, the difference between the sum of all the easterly directions and of all the westerly directions would always be the same. This holds both for certain particular bodies, assuming that at present they have interactions only among themselves, and for the whole universe, in which the difference is always zero, since everything is perfectly balanced, and easterly and westerly directions are perfectly equal in the universe. If God does something in violation of this rule, it is a miracle.[15]

It is therefore infinitely more reasonable and more worthy of God to suppose that, from the beginning, he created the machinery of the world in such a way that, without at every moment violating the two great laws of nature, namely, those of force and direction, but rather, by following them exactly (except in the case of miracles), it happens that the springs in bodies are ready to act of themselves, as they should, at precisely the moment the soul has a suitable volition or thought; the soul, in turn, has this volition or thought only in conformity with the preceding states of the body. Thus the union of the soul with the machinery of the body and with the parts entering into it, and the action of the one on the other, consist only in this concomitance that marks the admirable wisdom of the creator far better than any other hypothesis. It cannot be denied that this hypothesis is at least possible and that God is a sufficiently great craftsman to be able to execute it; hence, we can easily judge that this hypothesis is the most probable, being the simplest, the most beautiful, and most intelligible, at once avoiding all difficulties—to say nothing of criminal actions, in which it seems more reasonable to have God concur only through the conservation of created forces.

To use a comparison I will say that this concomitance I maintain is like several different

---

15. The rule in question here is what is now called the conservation of momentum, mass times velocity, which, Leibniz claims here, holds both for the universe as a whole and for any closed system within the universe.

bands of musicians or choirs separately playing their parts, and placed in such a way that they do not see and do not even hear each other, though they nevertheless can agree perfectly, each following his own notes, so that someone hearing all of them would find a marvelous harmony there, one more surprising than if there were a connection among them. It is quite possible that someone next to one of two such choirs could judge from the one what the other was doing (particularly if we supposed that he could hear his choir without seeing it and see the other without hearing it), he would, as a result, form such a habit that, with the help of his imagination, he would no longer think of the choir where he was, but of the other, and he would mistake his own choir for an echo of the other, attributing to his own only certain interludes in which some rules of composition [*symphonie*], by which he distinguished the other, were not satisfied. Or, attributing to his own choir a certain beating of the tempo, performed on his side according to certain plans, he might think, because of the agreement on this he finds as the melody continues, that the beating of the tempo is being imitated by the others, since he doesn't know that those on the other side are also acting in accordance with their own plans, though in agreement with his.

Yet I do not disapprove at all of the assertion that minds are in some way the occasional causes, and even the real causes, of the movements of bodies. For, with respect to divine resolutions, what God foresaw and pre-established with regard to minds was the occasion for his regulating bodies from the beginning so that they might fit together in accordance with the laws and forces he will give them. And since the state of the one is an unfailing, though frequently contingent, and even free, consequence of the state of the other, we can say that God brings about that there is a real connection by virtue of this general notion of substances, which entails that substances express one another perfectly. This connection is not, however, immediate, since it is founded only upon what God has done in creating substances.

If my opinion that substance requires a true unity were founded only on a definition I had formulated in opposition to common usage, *then the dispute*

*would be only one of words.*[16] But besides the fact that most philosophers have taken the term in almost the same fashion, distinguishing between a unity in itself and an accidental unity, between substantial and accidental form, and between perfect and imperfect, natural and artificial mixtures, I take things to a much higher level, and setting aside the question of terminology, *I believe that where there are only beings by aggregation, there aren't any real beings.* For every being by aggregation presupposes beings endowed with real unity, because every being derives its reality only from the reality of those beings of which it is composed, so that it will not have any reality at all if each being of which it is composed is itself a being by aggregation, a being for which we must still seek further grounds for its reality, grounds which can never be found in this way, if we must always continue to seek for them. I agree, Sir, that there are only machines (that are often animated) in all of corporeal nature, but I do not agree *that there are only aggregates of substances*; and if there are aggregates of substances, there must also be true substances from which all the aggregates result.[17] We must, then, necessarily come down either to mathematical points, of which some authors constitute extension, or to the atoms of Epicurus and Cordemoy (which are things you reject along with me), or else we must admit that we do not find any reality in bodies; or finally, we must recognize some substances that have a true unity. I have already said in another letter that the composite made up of the diamonds of the Grand Duke and of the Great Mogul can be called a pair of diamonds, but this is only a being of reason. And when they are brought closer to one another, it would be a being of the imagination or perception, that is to say, a phenomenon. For contact, common motion, and participation in a common plan have

---

16. Arnauld had written that Leibniz's arguments "amount to saying that all bodies whose parts are mechanically united are not substances, but only machines or aggregates of many substances," and that "there is only a quibble over words here; for Saint Augustine feels no difficulties about recognizing that bodies have no true unity" (*Philosophische Schriften* II, 86).
17. The version Arnauld received concludes: " . . . of which all aggregates are made."

no effect on substantial unity. It is true that there are sometimes more, and sometimes fewer, grounds for supposing that several things constitute a single thing, in proportion to the extent to which these things are connected. But this serves only to abbreviate our thoughts and to represent the phenomena.

It also seems that what constitutes the essence of a being by aggregation is only a mode [*manière d'être*] of the things of which it is composed. For example, what constitutes the essence of an army is only a mode of the men who compose it. This mode therefore presupposes a substance whose essence is not a mode of a substance.[18] Every machine also presupposes some substance in the pieces of which it is made, and there is no plurality without true unities. To put it briefly, I hold this identical proposition, differentiated only by the emphasis, to be an axiom, namely, *that what is not truly one being is not truly one* being *either*. It has always been thought that one and being are mutually supporting. Being is one thing and beings are another; but the plural presupposes the singular, and where there is no being still less will there be several beings. What could be clearer? [[I therefore believed that I would be allowed to distinguish beings by aggregation from substances, since these beings have their unity in our mind only, a unity founded on the relations or modes [modes] of true substances. If a machine is one substance, a circle of men holding hands will also be one substance, and so will an army, and finally, so will every multitude of substances.]]

I do not say that there is nothing substantial or nothing but appearance in things that do not have a true unity, for I grant that they always have as much reality or substantiality as there is true unity in that which enters into their composition.

You object that it might be of the essence of body not to have a true unity. But it would then be of the essence of body to be a phenomenon, deprived of all reality, like an ordered dream, for phenomena themselves, like the rainbow or a pile of stones, would be completely imaginary if they were not composed of beings with a true unity.

You say that you do not see what leads me to admit these substantial forms, or rather, these corporeal substances endowed with a true unity; but that is because I conceive no reality without a true unity. On my view, the notion of singular substance involves consequences incompatible with a being by aggregation. I conceive properties in substance that cannot be explained by extension, shape, and motion, besides the fact that there is no exact and fixed shape in bodies due to the actual subdivision of the continuum to infinity, and the fact that motion involves something imaginary insofar as it is only a modification of extension and change of location, so that we cannot determine which of the changing subjects it belongs to, unless we have recourse to the force which is the cause of motion and which is in corporeal substance. I confess that we do not need to mention these substances and qualities to explain particular phenomena, but for this we also do not need to examine God's concourse, the composition of the continuum, the plenum, and a thousand other things. I confess that we can explain the particularities of nature mechanically, but that can happen only after we recognize or presuppose the very principles of mechanics, principles which can only be established *a priori* by metaphysical reasonings. And even the difficulties concerning the composition of the continuum will never be resolved as long as extension is considered as constituting the substance of the bodies, and as long as we entangle ourselves in our own chimeras.

I also think that to want to limit true unity or substance almost exclusively to man is to be as shortsighted in metaphysics as were those in physics who wanted to confine the world in a sphere. And since there are as many true substances as there are expressions of the whole universe, and as many as there are replications of divine works, it is in conformity with the greatness and beauty of the works of God for him to produce as many substances as there can be in this universe, and as many as higher considerations allow, for these substances hardly get in one another's way. By assuming mere

18. In the draft Arnauld received Leibniz wrote: "of another substance."

extension we destroy all this marvelous variety, since mass [*massa*] by itself (if it is possible to conceive it) is as far beneath a substance which is perceptive and representative of the whole universe, according to its point of view and according to the impressions (or rather the relations) its body receives mediately or immediately from all others, as a cadaver is beneath an animal, or rather, it is as far beneath a substance as a machine is beneath a man. It is also because of this that the features of the future are formed in advance, and that the features of the past are conserved forever in each thing, and that cause and effect give way to one another exactly up to the least detail of the least circumstance, even though every effect depends on an infinity of causes, and every cause has an infinity of effects; it would not be possible for this to happen if the essence of body consisted in a certain determinate shape, motion, or modification of extension. Thus, there is nothing of the kind in nature. Everything is strictly indefinite with respect to extension, and the extensions we attribute to bodies are merely phenomena and abstractions; this enables us to see how easily we fall into error when we do not reflect in this way, something so necessary for recognizing the true principles and for having a proper idea of the universe. [[And it seems to me that there is as much prejudice in refusing such a reasonable idea as there is in not recognizing the greatness of the world, the subdivision to infinity, and mechanical explanations in nature. It is as great an error to conceive of extension as a primitive notion without conceiving the true notion of substance or action as it was to be content considering substantial forms as a whole without entering into the details of the modifications of extension.]]

The multitude of souls (to which, in any case, I do not always attribute pleasure or pain) should not trouble us, any more than does the multitude of Gassendi's atoms, which are as indestructible as these souls. On the contrary, it is a perfection of nature to have many of them, a soul or animated substance being infinitely more perfect than an atom, which is without variety or subdivision, whereas every animated thing contains a world of diversity in a true unity. Now, experience favors this multitude of animated

things. We find that there is a prodigious quantity of animals in a drop of water imbued with pepper;[19] and with one blow millions of them can be killed [[neither the frogs of the Egyptians nor the quails of the Israelites, of which you spoke, Sir, approach this number.]] Now, if these animals have souls, we would have to say of their souls what we can probably say of the animals themselves, namely, that they were already alive from the creation of the world, and that they will live to its end, and that since generation is apparently only a change consisting in growth, so death will only be a change consisting in diminution, which causes this animal to reenter the recesses of a world of minute creatures where perceptions are more limited, until the order comes, perhaps calling them to return to the stage. The ancients were mistaken in introducing the transmigration of souls instead of the transformations of the same animal which always preserves the same soul; they put *metempsychoses pro metaschematismis*.[20] But minds are not subject to these revolutions [[or rather, the revolutions in bodies must serve the divine economy with respect to minds.]] God creates them when it is time and detaches them from the body [[(at least the coarse body)]] by death, since they must always keep their moral qualities and their memory, in order to be [[perpetual]] citizens of this universal, perfect republic, of which God is the monarch; this republic can never lose any of its members and its laws are superior to those of bodies. I confess that the body by itself, without the soul, has only a unity of aggregation, but that the reality inhering in it derives from the parts composing it, which retain their [[substantial]] unity [[through the countless living bodies included in them.]]

Nevertheless, although a soul can have a body made up of parts animated by other souls, the soul or form of the whole is not, as a consequence, composed of the souls or forms of its parts. It is not necessary for the two parts of an insect cut in half to remain animated, although there may be some movement in them. At very least, the soul of the whole insect will remain only on one side. And since, in the

---

19. Leeuwenhoek experimented with pepper water.
20. Change of souls in place of change of shape.

formation and growth of the insect, the soul was, from the beginning, in a certain part that was already living, after the destruction of the insect it will still remain in a certain part that is still alive, a part as small as is necessary for it to be protected from the action of someone tearing or destroying the body of that insect. Hence, we do not need to imagine, with the Jews, that there is a little bone of insurmountable hardness in which the soul takes refuge.

I agree that there are degrees of accidental unity,[21] that an ordered society has more unity than a confused mob, and that an organized body, or rather a machine, has more unity than a society; that is to say, it is more appropriate to conceive them as a single thing, because there are more relations among the constituents. But in the end, all these unities become realized only by thoughts and appearances; like colors and other phenomena, which, nevertheless, are called real. The tangibility of a heap of stones or a block of marble does not prove its substantial reality any more than the visibility of a rainbow proves its substantial reality; and since nothing is so solid that it does not have some degree of fluidity, perhaps this block of marble is only a heap of an infinite number of living bodies, or like a lake full of fish, even though these animals cannot ordinarily be distinguished by the eye except in partially decayed bodies. We can therefore say of these composites and similar things what Democritus said so well of them; namely, they depend for their being on opinion or custom.[22] And Plato held the same opinion about everything which is purely material. Our mind notices or conceives some true substances which have certain modes; these modes involve relations to other substances, so the mind takes the occasion to join them together in thought and to make one name account for all these things together. This is useful for reasoning, but we must not allow ourselves to be misled into making substances or true beings of them; this is suitable only

for those who stop at appearances, or for those who make realities out of all abstractions of the mind, and who conceive number, time, place, motion, shape, [[and sensible qualities]] as so many separate beings. Instead I hold that philosophy cannot be better reestablished and reduced to something precise, than by recognizing only substances or complete beings endowed with a true unity, together with the different states that succeed one another; everything else is only phenomena, abstractions, or relations.

No regularity will ever be found which can make a true substance out of several beings by aggregation. For example, if parts fitting together in the same plan are more suitable for composing a true substance than those touching, then all the officers of the Dutch East India Company will make up a real substance, far better than a heap of stones. But what is a common plan other than a resemblance, or an order of actions and passions that our mind notices in different things? But if we prefer the unity of contact, we will find other difficulties. Perhaps solid bodies have nothing uniting their parts except the pressure of the surrounding bodies, and have no more union in themselves and in their substance than does a pile of sand without lime.[23] Why should several rings, interlaced so as to make a chain, compose a genuine

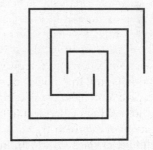

substance any more than if they had openings so that they could be separated? It may be that no part of the chain touches another, and even that none encloses another, and that, nevertheless, they are so interlaced that, unless they are approached in a certain way, they cannot be separated, as in the

---

21. Arnauld stated that "although it is true that there is true unity only in intelligent natures, all of which can say "I" [*moi*], there are nevertheless various degrees in this improper unity suitable to the body" (*Philosophische Schriften* II, 88).

22. See Diogenes Laertius, *Lives of the Eminent Philosophers*, IX 45.

---

23. I.e., shifting sands with nothing to bind them.

enclosed figure. Are we to say, in this case, that the substance composed of these things is, as it were, in abeyance and dependent on the future skill of whoever may wish to disentangle them? These are all fictions of the mind, and as long as we do not discern what a complete being, or rather a substance, really is, we will never have something at which we can stop; [[and this is the only way of establishing solid and real principles.]] In conclusion, nothing should be posited without good grounds. Therefore, those who imagine beings and substances without genuine unity are left to prove that there is more reality than what we have just said,[24] and I am waiting for a notion of substance or of being which can include all these things—after which mock suns and perhaps even dreams will someday lay claim to reality, unless very precise limits are set for this *droit de bourgeoisie*[25] that is to be granted to beings formed by aggregation.

_____

24. Writing to Arnauld, Leibniz continued: "and to show what it consists in."
25. A kind of inferior citizenship.

I have treated these matters so that you may be able to judge not only my opinions, but also, the arguments which forced me to adopt them. I submit them to your judgment, whose fairness and exactness I know. I also send something which you could have found in the *Nouvelles de la république des lettres*, to serve as a response to the Abbé Catelan.[26] I consider him an able man, given what you say of him; but what he has written against Huygens and against me makes it clear that he goes a little too fast. We will see what use he will make of this now.

I am delighted to learn of the good state of your health, and I hope for its continuation with all the zeal and all the passion which makes me what I am, etc.

P.S. I reserve for another time some other matters you have touched upon in your letter.

_____

26. The paper in question is probably the "Réplique de M. L. à M. l'Abbé D. C. . . . ," published in the *Nouvelles* in February 1687. It was part of the so-called *vis viva* controversy. See the "Discourse on Metaphysics," sec. 18.

# G. W. Leibniz, *Primary Truths* (1689)[1]

The primary truths are those which assert the same thing of itself or deny the opposite of its opposite. For example, "A is A," "A is not not-A," or "if it is true that A is B, then it is false that A is not B or that A is not-B." Also "every thing is as it is," "every thing is similar or equal to itself," "nothing is greater or less than itself," and others of this sort. Although they themselves may have their degrees of priority, nonetheless they can all be included under the name 'identities.'

Moreover, all remaining truths are reduced to primary truths with the help of definitions, that is, through the resolution of notions; in this consists *a priori* proof, proof independent of experience. As an example, I shall give this proposition from among the axioms accepted equally by mathematicians and all others alike: "the whole is greater than its part," or "the part is less than the whole," something easily demonstrated from the definition of "less" or "greater," with the addition of the primitive axiom, that is, the axiom of identity. For the *less* is that which is equal to a part of the other (the *greater*), a definition easy to understand and in agreement with the practice of the

human race, when people compare things with one another and, taking away from the greater something equal to the lesser, they find something that remains. Hence there is an argument of this sort: the part is equal to a part of the whole (it is, of course, equal to itself through the axiom of identity, that each and every thing is equal to itself), and what is equal to a part of a whole is less than the whole (from the definition of "less"). Therefore, the part is less than the whole.

Therefore, the predicate or consequent is always in the subject or antecedent, and the nature of truth in general or the connection between the terms of a statement, consists in this very thing, as Aristotle also observed. The connection and inclusion of the predicate in the subject is explicit in identities, but in all other propositions it is implicit and must be shown through the analysis of notions; *a priori* demonstration rests on this.

Moreover, this is true for every affirmative truth, universal or particular, necessary or contingent, and in both an intrinsic and extrinsic denomination. And *here* lies hidden a wonderful secret, a secret that contains the nature of contingency, that is, the essential difference between necessary and contingent truths, a secret that eliminates the

1. Translated from the Latin by R. Ariew and D. Garber in G. W. Leibniz, *Philosophical Essays* (Indianapolis/Cambridge: Hackett Publishing Company, 1989). Editors' title.

difficulty concerning the fatal necessity of even those things that are free.

Many things of great importance follow from these considerations, considerations insufficiently attended to because of their obviousness. For the received axiom that *nothing is without reason*, or *there is no effect without a cause*, directly follows from these considerations; otherwise there would be a truth which could not be proved *a priori*, that is, a truth which could not be resolved into identities, contrary to the nature of truth, which is always an explicit or implicit identity. It also follows that, when in the givens everything on the one side is the same as it is on the other side, then everything will be the same in the unknowns, that is, in the consequents. This is because no reason can be given for any difference, a reason which certainly must derive from the givens. And a corollary of this, or better, an example, is Archimedes' postulate at the beginning of the book on statics, that, given equal weights on both sides of a balance with equal arms, everything is in equilibrium.[2] And hence *there is even a reason for eternal things*. If we imagine that the world has been from eternity, and we imagine only little balls in it, then we would have to explain why there are little balls rather than cubes.

From these considerations it also follows that, *in nature, there cannot be two individual things that differ in number alone*. For it certainly must be possible to explain why they are different, and that explanation must derive from some difference they contain. And so what Saint Thomas recognized concerning separated intelligences, which, he said, never differ by number alone,[3] must also be said of other things, for never do we find two eggs or two leaves or two blades of grass in a garden that are perfectly similar. And thus, perfect similarity is found only in incomplete and abstract notions, where things are considered [*in rationes veniunt*] only in a certain respect, but not in every way, as, for example, when we consider shapes alone, and neglect the matter that has shape. And

so it is justifiable to consider two similar triangles in geometry, even though two perfectly similar material triangles are nowhere found. And although gold and other metals, also salts and many liquids might be taken to be homogeneous, this can only be admitted with regard to the senses, and it is not true that they are, in all rigor.

It also follows that *there are no purely extrinsic denominations*, denominations which have absolutely no foundation in the very thing denominated. For it is necessary that the notion of the subject denominated contain the notion of the predicate. And consequently, whenever the denomination of a thing is changed, there must be a variation in the thing itself.

The complete or perfect notion of an individual substance contains all of its predicates, past, present, and future. For certainly it is now true that a future predicate will be, and so it is contained in the notion of a thing. And thus everything that will happen to Peter or Judas, both necessary and free, is contained in the perfect individual notion of Peter or Judas, considered in the realm of possibility by withdrawing the mind from the divine decree for creating him, and is seen there by God. And from this it is obvious that God chose from an infinite number of possible individuals those he thought most in accord with the supreme and hidden ends of his wisdom. Properly speaking, he did not decide that Peter sin or that Judas be damned, but only that Peter who would sin with certainty, though not with necessity, but freely, and Judas who would suffer damnation would attain existence rather than other possible things; that is, he decreed that the possible notion become actual. And, although the future salvation of Peter is also contained in his eternal possible notion, it is, however, not without the concurrence of grace, for in the same perfect notion of that possible Peter, even the aid of divine grace to be given him is found, under the notion of possibility.

*Every individual substance contains in its perfect notion the entire universe* and everything that exists in it, past, present, and future. For there is no thing on which one cannot impose some true denomination from another thing, at very least a denomination

2. See Archimedes, *On the Equilibrium of Planes*, Book I, postulate 1, in Heath, *The Works of Archimedes* (Cambridge: Cambridge University Press, 1897 and 1912), p. 189.

3. See Saint Thomas, *Summa Theologiae* I, q. 50, art. 4.

of comparison and relation. Moreover, there is no purely extrinsic denomination. I have shown the same thing in many other ways, all in harmony with one another.

Indeed, *all individual created substances are different expressions of the same universe* and different expressions of the same universal cause, namely God. But the expressions vary in perfection, just as different representations or drawings of the same town from different points of view do.

Every individual created substance exerts physical action and passion on all the others. From a change made in one, some corresponding change follows in all the others, since the denomination[4] is changed. And this is in agreement with our experience of nature. For, in a vessel filled with a liquid (and the whole universe is just such a vessel) motion made in the middle is propagated to the edges, although it is rendered more and more insensible, the more it recedes from its origin.

Strictly speaking, one can say that *no created substance exerts a metaphysical action or influx on any other thing*. For, not to mention the fact that one cannot explain how something can pass from one thing into the substance of another, we have already shown that from the notion of each and every thing follows all of its future states. What we call causes are only concurrent requisites, in metaphysical rigor. This is also illustrated by our experience of nature. For bodies really rebound from others through the force of their own elasticity, and not through the force of other things, even if another body is required in order for the elasticity (which arises from something intrinsic to the body itself) to be able to act.

Also, *assuming the distinction between soul and body, from this we can explain their union* without the common hypothesis of an influx, which is unintelligible, and without the hypothesis of an occasional cause, which appeals to a *Deus ex machina*. For God from the beginning constituted both the soul and the body with such wisdom and such workmanship that, from the first constitution or notion of a thing, everything that happens through

itself [*per se*] in the one corresponds perfectly to everything that happens in the other, just as if something passed from one to the other. This is what I call the hypothesis of concomitance. This hypothesis is true in all substances in the whole universe but cannot be sensed in all of them, unlike the case of the soul and the body.

*There is no vacuum.* For the different parts of empty space would then be perfectly similar and mutually congruent and could not be distinguished from one another. And so they would differ in number alone, which is absurd. One can also prove that time is not a thing in the same way as we did for space.[5]

*There is no atom*, indeed, there is no body so small that it is not actually subdivided. Because of that, while it is acted upon by everything else in the whole universe and receives some effect from everything (an effect which must cause change in a body), it also preserves all past impressions and contains, before they happen, all future impressions. And if anyone were to say that that effect is contained in the motions impressed on the atom, which receives the effect as a whole without being divided, one can respond that not only must there be effects produced in an atom from all the impressions of the universe, but also, in turn, the state of the whole universe must be inferred from the atom, from the effect, the cause. But since the same motion can come about through different impressions, through no regress can one infer the impressions by means of which it [i.e., the atom] had come to its present state, from the shape and motion of an atom alone — not to mention the fact that one cannot explain why bodies of a certain smallness cannot be divided further.

From this it follows that *every particle of the universe contains a world of an infinity of creatures*. However, the continuum is not divided into points, nor is it divided in all possible ways — not into points,

---

4. Originally Leibniz wrote "extrinsic denomination."

5. The following passage was deleted here: "*There is no corporeal substance in which there is nothing but extension or size, shape, and their variations*, for in this way two substances perfectly similar to one another could exist, which would be absurd. From this it follows that there is something in corporeal substances analogous to the soul which they [i.e., the Scholastics] call form."

since points are not parts but boundaries, and not in all possible ways, since not all creatures are in a given thing, but there is only a certain progression of them *ad infinitum*, just as one who assumes a straight line and any part derived by bisection sets up divisions different from someone who trisects it.

*There is no determinate shape in actual things*, for none can be appropriate for an infinite number of impressions. And so neither a circle, nor an ellipse, nor any other line we can define exists except in the intellect, nor do lines exist before they are drawn, nor parts before they are separated off.[6]

Extension and motion, as well as bodies themselves (insofar as only motion and extension are placed in bodies) are not substances, but true phenomena, like rainbows and parhelia. For there are no shapes in things, and if we consider their extension alone, then bodies are not substances, but many substances.

Something lacking extension is required for the substance of bodies; otherwise there would be no source [*principium*] for the reality of phenomena or for true unity. There is always a plurality of bodies, and never one, and therefore, in reality, there is not even a plurality. Cordemoy proved atoms using a similar argument.[7] But since atoms are excluded, what remains is something lacking extension, analogous to the soul, which they once called form or species.

*Corporeal substance can neither arise nor perish except through creation or annihilation.* For when corporeal substance once endures, it will always endure, since there is no reason for any difference, and the dissolution of parts of a body has nothing in common with its destruction. Therefore, *animate things neither arise nor perish, but are only transformed.*

---

6. Leibniz deleted the following here: "Space, time, extension, and motion are not things, but modes of contemplating things that have a foundation."

7. See Cordemoy, *Le discernement du corps et de l'âme*, premier discours, in Cordemoy, *Oeuvres philosophiques*, ed. P. Clair and F. Girbal (Paris: PUF, 1968).

# G. W. Leibniz, A *New System of the Nature and Communication of Substances, and of the Union of the Soul and Body* (1695)[1]

A few years have already passed since I conceived this system and communicated with some learned men about it, especially with one of the greatest theologians and philosophers of our time,[2] who had learned about some of my opinions through a person of the highest nobility, and had found them extremely paradoxical. But having received my explanations, he changed his attitude in the most generous and edifying way possible; and, having approved some of my propositions, he withdrew his censure regarding the others, with which he still disagreed. Since that time I have continued my meditations, as circumstances allow, so as to give the public only well-examined opinions; I have also tried to satisfy objections raised against my essays on dynamics, which are connected with this system.[3] Finally, since some important persons have desired to see my opinions further clarified, I have risked publishing these meditations, even though they are not at all popular, nor can they be appreciated by all sorts of minds. I have decided upon this mainly to profit from the judgments of persons enlightened in these matters, since it would be too troublesome to seek out and call individually upon all those who would be disposed to give me instruction—which I shall always be glad to receive, provided that it contains the love of truth, rather than a passion for preconceived opinions.

Although I am someone who has done much work on mathematics, I have continued to meditate on philosophy since my youth, for it always seemed to me that one can establish something solid there through clear demonstrations. I had penetrated far into the territory of the Scholastics, when mathematics and the modern authors made me withdraw from it, while

---

1. Translated from the French by R. Ariew and D. Garber in G. W. Leibniz, *Philosophical Essays* (Indianapolis: Hackett Publishing Company, 1989). Leibniz published the "New System" anonymously in 1695, in the *Journal des Sçavants*. It was the first public statement of his philosophy, a particularly interesting statement because of the autobiographical or historical style adopted by Leibniz. The publication of the "New System" stimulated much discussion, with Foucher, de Beauval, Bayle, and others publishing criticisms of it, and Leibniz answering them. Leibniz's manuscript copy contains some material thought to be later additions that does not appear in the published version. These are given in the double-bracketed passages, when possible, and otherwise in the notes.

2. Leibniz indicates in his copy that he is referring to Arnauld.

3. See the "Preliminary Specimen to the Dynamics" and the "Specimen of Dynamics" in Leibniz, *Philosophical Essays*.

I was still young. I was charmed by their beautiful ways of explaining nature mechanically, and I rightly despised the method of those who use only forms or faculties, from which one can learn nothing. But since then, having attempted to examine the very principles of mechanics in order to explain the laws of nature we learn from experience, I perceived that considering *extended mass* alone was not sufficient, and that it was necessary, in addition, to make use of the notion of *force*, which is very intelligible, despite the fact that it belongs in the domain of metaphysics. It also seemed to me that although the opinion of those who transform or degrade animals into pure machines may be possible, it is improbable, and even contrary to the order of things.

In the beginning, when I had freed myself from the yoke of Aristotle, I accepted the void and atoms, for they best satisfy the imagination. But on recovering from that, after much reflection, I perceived that it is impossible to find the *principles of a true unity* in matter alone, or in what is only passive, since everything in it is only a collection or aggregation of parts to infinity. Now, a multitude can derive its reality only from *true unities*, which have some other origin and are considerably different from [[mathematical]] points [[which are only the extremities and modifications of extension,]] which all agree cannot make up the *continuum*. Therefore, in order to find these *real entities* I was forced to have recourse to a formal atom, since a material thing cannot be both material and, at the same time, perfectly indivisible, that is, endowed with a true unity.[4] Hence, it was necessary to restore, and, as it were, to rehabilitate the *substantial forms* which are in such disrepute today, but in a way that would render them intelligible, and separate the use one should make of them from the abuse that has been made of them. I found then that their nature consists in force, and that from this there follows something analogous to sensation and appetite, so that we must

conceive of them on the model of the notion we have of *souls*. But just as soul must not be used to explain the particular details of the economy of the animal's body, I judged that we must not use these forms to explain the particular problems of nature, even though they are necessary to establish the true general principles. Aristotle calls them *first entelechies*; I call them, perhaps more intelligibly, *primitive forces*, which contain not only act or the completion of possibility, but also an original *activity*.

I saw that these forms and souls must be indivisible, as our mind is; I remembered that this was Saint Thomas' view on the souls of animals.[5] But this truth revived the great difficulties about the origin and duration of souls and forms. For, since every [[*simple*]] *substance* which has a true unity can begin and end only by miracle, it follows that they can begin only by creation and end only by annihilation. Thus I was forced to recognize that, except for the souls that God wishes to create expressly, the forms constitutive of substances must have been created together with the world, and must always subsist. Moreover, certain Scholastics, like Albertus Magnus and John Bacon,[6] glimpsed a part of the truth about the origin of these forms. This should not appear extraordinary, since we ascribe to forms only duration, which the Gassendists grant their atoms.

I judged, however, that we must not indiscriminately confuse minds or rational souls [[with other forms or souls]], for they are of a higher order, and have incomparably greater perfection than the forms thrust into matter [[(which, in my view, are found everywhere)]], minds being like little gods in comparison with them, made in the image of

---

4. A later version read as follows: "Therefore, in order to find these real unities, I was forced to have recourse to a *real and animated point*, so to speak, or to an atom of substance which must include something of form or activity to make a complete being."

5. Leibniz seems to have in mind the *Summa Theologiae* I, q. 76, art. 8, in which Saint Thomas states that the souls of animals are "not able to be divided accidentally, that is, by a quantitative division." But it would not be accurate to attribute the immortality of animal souls to Saint Thomas. See, e.g., *Summa Contra Gentiles* II, chap. 82: That the souls of brute animals are not immortal.

6. Albertus Magnus, Bishop of Ratisbon, and John Bacon of Baconthorpe were, respectively, thirteenth- and fourteenth-century Scholastics. Leibniz's statement is too vague to enable one to fix a reference to precise passages of which he might be thinking.

God, and having in them some ray of the light of divinity. That is why God governs minds as a prince governs his subjects, and even as a father cares for his children, whereas he disposes of other substances as an engineer handles his machines. Thus minds have particular laws, which place them above the upheavals [revolutions] in matter, [[through the very order which God has put in them]]; and we can say that everything else is made only for them, and that these tumultuous motions themselves are adjusted for the happiness of the good and the punishment of the wicked.

However, returning to ordinary forms, or to material souls,[7] the duration that we must attribute to them, in place of the duration that had been attributed to atoms, might make us suspect that they pass from body to body—which would be *metempsychosis*—somewhat as some philosophers have believed in the transmission of motion and species. But this fancy is far removed from the nature of things. There is no such passage; this is where the transformations of Swammerdam, Malpighi, and Leeuwenhoek, the best observers of our time, have come to my aid, and have made it easier for me to admit that animals and all other organized substances have no beginning, although we think they do, and that their apparent generation is only a development, a kind of augmentation. I have also noticed that the author of the *Search after Truth*,[8] Régis, Hartsoeker, and other able persons have held opinions not far removed from this.

But the greatest question still remained: What becomes of these souls or forms at the death of the animal or at the destruction of the individual organized substance? This question is most perplexing, since it hardly seems reasonable that souls should remain uselessly in a chaos of confused matter. This made me judge that there is only one reasonable view to take—namely, the conservation not only of the soul, but also of the animal itself and its organic machine, even though the destruction of its larger parts reduces it to a smallness which escapes our senses, just as it was before its birth. Moreover, no one can specify the true time of death, which for a long time may pass

for a simple suspension of noticeable actions, and is basically never anything else in simple animals—witness the *resuscitations* of drowned flies buried under pulverized chalk, and several other similar examples which are sufficient to show that there would be many other resuscitations, and greater ones, if men were in a position to restore the machine. This may be similar to something the great Democritus discussed, complete atomist that he was, though Pliny made fun of him.[9] It is therefore natural that an animal, having always been alive and organized (as some persons of great insight are beginning to recognize), always remains so. And since there is no first birth or entirely new generation of an animal, it follows that there will not be any final extinction or complete death, in a strict metaphysical sense. Consequently, instead of the *transmigration* of souls, there is only a *transformation* of the same animal, according to whether its organs are differently enfolded and more or less developed.

However, rational souls follow much higher laws, and are exempt from anything that might make them lose the quality of being citizens of the society of minds; God has provided so well that no changes of matter can make them lose the moral qualities of their personhood. And we can say that everything tends not only toward the perfection of the universe in general, but also toward the perfection of these creatures in particular, creatures who are destined for such a degree of happiness that the universe finds itself benefited by virtue of the divine goodness that is communicated to each, to the extent that supreme wisdom can allow.

With respect to ordinary animal bodies and other corporeal substances, whose complete extinction has been accepted until now, and whose changes depend on mechanical rules rather than moral laws, I noted with pleasure that the ancient author of the book *De diaeta*, attributed to Hippocrates,[10] had glimpsed

---

7. A later version reads: "brute souls."
8. Nicolas Malebranche.

9. In Book VII, chap. 55, of his *Natural History*, Pliny mocks Democritus' theory of resuscitation, referring to "the false opinion of resuscitation, promulgated by Democritus, who himself did not come back to life."
10. See *The Regimen*, I.4: "So of all things nothing perishes and nothing comes into being that did not exist before. Things change merely by mingling and being separated."

something of the truth when he stated explicitly that animals are not born and do not die, and that things we believe to begin and perish merely appear and disappear. This was also the opinion of Parmenides and Melissus, according to Aristotle.[11] For these ancients were much more solid than people believe.

I am the most readily disposed person to do justice to the moderns, yet I find that they have carried reform too far, among other things, by confusing natural things with artificial things, because they have lacked sufficiently grand ideas of the majesty of nature. They think that the difference between natural machines and ours is only the difference between great and small. Recently this led a very able man, the author of the *Conversations on the Plurality of Worlds*,[12] to assert that when we examine nature more closely we find it less admirable than previously thought and more like the workshop of a craftsman. I believe that this conception does not give us a sufficiently just or worthy idea of nature, and that my system alone allows us to understand the true and immense distance between the least productions and mechanisms of divine wisdom and the greatest masterpieces that derive from the craft of a limited mind; this difference is not simply a difference of degree, but a difference of kind. We must then know that the machines of nature have a truly infinite number of organs, and are so well supplied and so resistant to all accidents that it is not possible to destroy them. A natural machine still remains a machine in its least parts, and moreover, it always remains the same machine that it has been, being merely transformed through the different enfolding it undergoes, sometimes extended, sometimes compressed and concentrated, as it were, when it is thought to have perished.

In addition, by means of the soul or form there is a true unity corresponding to what is called the *self* [*moy*] in us. Such a unity could not occur in the machines made by a craftsman or in a simple mass

---

11. Parmenides of Elea and his follower, Melissus of Samos, were two Presocratic philosophers (ca. 450 BC) who denied the reality of all change.
12. Bernard de Fontenelle.

of matter, however organized it may be; such a mass can only be considered as an army or a herd, or a pond full of fish, or like a watch composed of springs and wheels. Yet if there were no true *substantial unities*, there would be nothing substantial or real in the collection. That was what forced Cordemoy to abandon Descartes and to embrace the Democritean doctrine of atoms in order to find a true unity. But *atoms of matter* are contrary to reason. Furthermore, they are still composed of parts, since the invincible attachment of one part to another (if we can reasonably conceive or assume this) would not eliminate diversity of those parts. There are only *atoms of substance*, that is, real unities absolutely destitute of parts, which are the source of actions, the first absolute principles of the composition of things, and, as it were, the final elements in the analysis of substantial things. We could call them *metaphysical points*: They have *something vital*, a kind of *perception*, and *mathematical points* are the *points of view* from which they express the universe. But when corporeal substances are contracted, all their organs together constitute only a *physical point* relative to us. Thus physical points are indivisible only in appearance; mathematical points are exact, but they are merely modalities. Only metaphysical points or points of substance (constituted by forms or souls) are exact and real, and without them there would be nothing real, since without true unities there would be no multitude.

After I established these things, I thought I was entering port; but when I began to meditate about the union of soul and body, I felt as if I were thrown again into the open sea. For I could not find any way of explaining how the body makes anything happen in the soul, or vice versa, or how one substance can communicate with another created substance. Descartes had given up the game at this point, as far as we can determine from his writings. But his disciples, seeing that the common opinion is inconceivable, judged that we sense the qualities of bodies because God causes thoughts to arise in the soul on the occasion of motions of matter, and that when our soul, in turn, wishes to move the body, it is God who moves the body for it. And since the communication of motions also seemed inconceivable to them, they believed that God imparts motion to a body on the occasion of the motion of another body. That is what they call the *system of occasional causes*, which has been made very fashionable by the beautiful reflections of the author of the *Search after Truth*.

I must admit that they have penetrated the difficulty by articulating what could not possibly be the case, but their explanation of what actually happens does not appear to eliminate the difficulty. It is quite true that, speaking with metaphysical rigor, there is no real influence of one created substance on another, and that all things, with all their reality, are continually produced by the power [*vertu*] of God. But in solving problems it is not sufficient to make use of the general cause and to invoke what is called a *Deus ex machina*. For when one does that without giving any other explanation derived from the order of secondary causes, it is, properly speaking, having recourse to a miracle. In philosophy we must try to give reasons by showing how things are brought about by divine wisdom, but in conformity with the notion of the subject in question.

Therefore, since I was forced to agree that it is not possible for the soul or any other true substance to receive something from without, except by divine omnipotence, I was led, little by little, to a view that surprised me, but which seems inevitable, and which, in fact, has very great advantages and rather considerable beauty. That is, we must say that God originally created the soul (and any other real unity) in such a way that everything must arise for it from its own depths [*fonds*], through a perfect *spontaneity* relative to itself, and yet with a perfect *conformity* relative to external things. And thus, since our internal sensations (meaning those in the soul itself, and not those in the brain or in other subtile parts of the body) are merely phenomena which follow upon external beings, or better, they are true appearances and like well-ordered dreams, these internal perceptions in the soul itself must arise because of its own original constitution; that is, they must arise through the representative nature (capable of expressing external things as they relate to its organs) given to the soul from its creation, which constitutes its individual character. This is what makes every substance represent the whole universe exactly and in its own way, from a certain point of view, and makes the perceptions or expressions of external things occur in the soul at a given time, in virtue of its own laws, as if in a world apart, and as if there existed only God and itself (to make use of the manner of speaking used by a certain person of great spiritual elevation whose piety is renowned).[13] There will be a perfect agreement among all these substances, producing the same effect that would be noticed if they communicated through the transmission of species or qualities, as the common philosophers imagine they do. In addition, the organized mass, in which the point of view of the soul lies, being expressed more closely by the soul, is in turn ready to act by itself, following the laws of the corporeal machine, at the moment when the soul wills it to act, without disturbing the laws of the other—the spirits and blood then having exactly the motions that they need to respond to the passions and perceptions of the soul. It is this mutual relation, regulated in advance in each substance of the universe, which produces what we call their *communication*, and which alone brings about the *union of soul and body*. We can thus understand how the soul has its seat in the body by an immediate presence which could not be greater, since the soul is in the body as unity is in the resultant of unities, which is a multitude.

This hypothesis is entirely possible. For why should God be unable to give substance, from the beginning, a nature or an internal force that can produce in it, in an orderly way (as would happen in a *spiritual or formal* automaton, but *free* in the case in which it has a share of reason), everything that will happen to it, that is, all the appearances or expressions it will have, without the help of any created being? This is especially so since the nature of substance necessarily requires and essentially involves progress or change, without which it would not have the force to act. And since this nature that pertains to the soul is representative of the universe in

---

13. Leibniz probably has Saint Theresa in mind here. See the note to sec. 32 of the *Discourse on Metaphysics* above.

a very exact manner (though more or less distinctly), the series of representations produced by the soul will correspond naturally to the series of changes in the universe itself, just as the body, in turn, has also been accommodated to the soul for the situations in which the soul is thought to act externally. This is all the more reasonable insofar as bodies are made only for minds capable of entering into community with God and celebrating his glory. Thus, once we see the possibility of this *hypothesis of agreements*, we also see that it is the most reasonable hypothesis, and that it gives us a marvelous idea of the harmony of the universe and the perfection of the works of God.

It also has this great advantage, that instead of saying that we are free only in appearance and in a way sufficient for practical purposes, as several intelligent persons have believed,[14] we should rather say that we are determined only in appearance, and that, in rigorously metaphysical language, we have a perfect independence relative to the influence of every other creature. This also throws a marvelous light on the immortality of our soul and the always uniform conservation of our individual being, which is perfectly well regulated by its own nature and protected from all external accidents, appearances to the contrary notwithstanding. Never has any system made our eminence more evident. Since every mind is like a world apart, self-sufficient, independent of any other creature, containing infinity, and expressing the universe, it is as durable, subsistent, and absolute as the universe of creatures itself. Thus we should judge that it must always behave in the way most proper to contribute to the perfection of the society of all minds, which is their moral union in the City of God. There is also a new proof for the existence of God in our system, one which has extraordinary clarity. For the perfect agreement of so many substances which have no communication among them can only come from the common source.

Besides all the advantages that recommend this hypothesis, we can say that it is something more than a hypothesis, since it hardly seems possible to explain things in any other intelligible way, and since several serious difficulties which, until now, have troubled minds, seem to disappear by themselves when we properly understand the system. Ordinary ways of speaking are also preserved. For we can say that the substance, whose disposition accounts for change intelligibly, in the sense that we may judge that the other substances have been accommodated to this one in this regard from the beginning, according to the order of God's decree, is the substance we must consequently conceive as acting upon the others. Furthermore, the action of one substance on another is neither the emission nor the transplanting of an entity, as commonly conceived, and can reasonably be taken only in the manner just stated. It is true that we readily conceive emissions and receptions of parts in matter, by which we can reasonably explain all the phenomena of physics mechanically. But since material mass is not a substance, it is clear that action with respect to substance itself can only be as I have just described.

These considerations, however metaphysical they may seem, have yet another marvelous use in physics, in order to establish the laws of motion, as our *Dynamics* will be able to show. For we can say that in the impact of bodies, each body suffers only through its own elasticity, caused by the motion already in it. And as for absolute motion, nothing can fix it with mathematical rigor, since everything terminates in relations. This makes for the perfect equivalence of hypotheses, as in astronomy, so that no matter how many bodies we take, we may arbitrarily assign rest or a particular degree of speed to any body we choose, without being refuted by the phenomena of rectilinear, circular, or composite motion. However, it is reasonable to attribute some true motions to bodies, in accordance with the assumption that accounts for the phenomena in the most intelligible way, this denomination being in conformity with the notion of action we have just established.

---

14. Leibniz probably has Spinoza in mind here. See the Appendix to *Ethics* I.

# G. W. Leibniz, *The Principles of Philosophy, or the Monadology* (1714)[1]

1. The monad, which we shall discuss here, is nothing but a simple substance that enters into composites—simple, that is, without parts (*Theodicy*, sec. 10).

2. And there must be simple substances, since there are composites; for the composite is nothing more than a collection, or *aggregate*, of simples.

3. But where there are no parts, neither extension, nor shape, nor divisibility is possible. These monads are the true atoms of nature and, in brief, the elements of things.

4. There is also no dissolution to fear, and there is no conceivable way in which a simple substance can perish naturally.

5. For the same reason, there is no conceivable way a simple substance can begin naturally, since it cannot be formed by composition.

6. Thus, one can say that monads can only begin or end all at once—that is, they can only begin by creation and end by annihilation—whereas composites begin or end through their parts.

7. There is also no way of explaining how a monad can be altered or changed internally by some other creature, since one cannot transpose anything in it, nor can one conceive of any internal motion that can be excited, directed, augmented, or diminished within it, as can be done in composites, where there can be change among the parts. The monads have no windows through which something can enter or leave. Accidents cannot be detached, nor can they go about outside of substances, as the sensible species of the Scholastics once did. Thus, neither substance nor accident can enter a monad from without.[2]

8. However, monads must have some qualities; otherwise they would not even be beings.[3] And if simple substances did not differ at all in their qualities, there would be no way of perceiving any change in things, since what there is in a composite

---

1. Translated from the French by R. Ariew and D. Garber in G. W. Leibniz, *Philosophical Essays* (Indianapolis: Hackett Publishing Company, 1989). "Principles . . . " was probably Leibniz's title. References to the *Theodicy* are not found in the final copy, but are taken from an earlier draft. It should be stressed that the *Monadology* was not intended as an introduction to Leibniz's philosophy, but rather as a condensed statement of the main principles of his philosophy and an elucidation of some of the passages of his *Theodicy*.

2. Deleted from the first draft: "Monads are not mathematical points. For these points are only extremities, and the line cannot be composed of points."
3. Deleted from earlier drafts: "and if simple substances were nothings, the composites would reduce to nothing."

can only come from its simple ingredients; and if the monads had no qualities, they would be indiscernible from one another, since they also do not differ in quantity. As a result, assuming a plenum, in motion, each place would always receive only the equivalent of what it already had, and one state of things would be indistinguishable from another[4] (Pref. 2.b).

9. It is also necessary that each monad be different from each other. For there are never two beings in nature that are perfectly alike, two beings in which it is not possible to discover an internal difference, that is, one founded on an intrinsic denomination.

10. I also take for granted that every created being, and consequently the created monad as well, is subject to change, and even that this change is continual in each thing.

11. It follows from what we have just said that the monad's natural changes come from an *internal principle*, since no external cause can influence it internally (sec. 396, 400).

12. But, besides the principle of change, there must be *diversity* [un détail] *in that which changes*, which produces, so to speak, the specification and variety of simple substances.

13. This diversity must involve a multitude in the unity or in the simple. For, since all natural change is produced by degrees, something changes and something remains. As a result, there must be a plurality of properties [*affections*] and relations in the simple substance, although it has no parts.

14. The passing state which involves and represents a multitude in the unity or in the simple substance is nothing other than what one calls *perception*, which should be distinguished from apperception, or consciousness, as will be evident in what follows. This is where the Cartesians have failed badly, since they took no account of the perceptions that we do not apperceive. This is also what made them believe that minds alone are monads and that there are no animal souls or other entelechies. With the common people, they have confused a long stupor with death, properly speaking, which made them fall again into the scholastic prejudice of completely separated souls, and they have even confirmed unsound minds in the belief in the mortality of souls.[5]

15. The action of the internal principle which brings about the change or passage from one perception to another can be called *appetition*; it is true that the appetite cannot always completely reach the whole perception toward which it tends, but it always obtains something of it, and reaches new perceptions.

16. We ourselves experience a multitude in a simple substance when we find that the least thought we ourselves apperceive involves variety in its object. Thus, all those who recognize that the soul is a simple substance should recognize this multitude in the monad; and Mr. Bayle should not find any difficulty in this as he has done in his *Dictionary* article, "Rorarius."[6]

17. Moreover, we must confess that the *perception*, and what depends on it, *is inexplicable in terms of mechanical reasons*, that is, through shapes and motions. If we imagine that there is a machine whose structure makes it think, sense, and have perceptions, we could conceive it enlarged, keeping the same proportions, so that we could enter into it, as one enters into a mill. Assuming that, when inspecting its interior, we will only find parts that push one another, and we will never find anything to explain a perception. And so, we should seek perception in the simple substance and not in the composite or in the machine. Furthermore, this is all one can find in the simple substance—that is, perceptions and their changes. It is also in this alone that all the internal actions of simple substances can consist.

---

4. Cf. "On Nature Itself," sec. 13, in Leibniz, *Philosophical Essays*.

5. For Leibniz's critique of Descartes on the immortality of the soul, see the "Letter to Molanus," above, in the section on Descartes' *Meditations*.

6. Leibniz's *Theodicy* was, to a large extent, an attempt to answer the skeptical arguments, from Bayle's *Historical and Critical Dictionary*, regarding the impossibility of reconciling faith with reason. "Rorarius," an article of the *Dictionary*, was Bayle's occasion for a discussion of the problem of the souls of animals: Jerome Rorarius (1485–1566) wrote a treatise maintaining that men are less rational than the lower animals. In "Rorarius" Bayle criticizes Leibniz's views; see Bayle, "Rorarius," notes H and L.

18. One can call all simple substances or created monads entelechies, for they have in themselves a certain perfection [*echousi to enteles*]; they have a sufficiency [*autarkeia*] that makes them the sources of their internal actions, and, so to speak, incorporeal automata (sec. 87).

19. If we wish to call *soul* everything that has *perceptions* and *appetites* in the general sense I have just explained, then all simple substances or created monads can be called souls. But, since sensation is something more than a simple perception, I think that the general name of monad and entelechy is sufficient for simple substances which only have perceptions, and that we should only call those substances *souls* where perception is more distinct and accompanied by memory.

20. For we experience within ourselves a state in which we remember nothing and have no distinct perception; this is similar to when we faint or when we are overwhelmed by a deep, dreamless sleep. In this state the soul does not differ sensibly from a simple monad; but since this state does not last, and since the soul emerges from it, our soul is something more (sec. 64).

21. And it does not at all follow that in such a state the simple substance is without any perception. This is not possible for the previous reasons; for it cannot perish, and it also cannot subsist without some property [*affection*], which is nothing other than its perception. But when there is a great multitude of small perceptions in which nothing is distinct, we are stupefied. This is similar to when we continually spin in the same direction several times in succession, from which arises a dizziness that can make us faint and does not allow us to distinguish anything. Death can impart this state to animals for a time.

22. And since every present state of a simple substance is a natural consequence of its preceding state, the present is pregnant with the future (sec. 360).

23. Therefore, since on being awakened from a stupor, we apperceive our perceptions, it must be the case that we had some perceptions immediately before, even though we did not apperceive them; for a perception can only come naturally from another perception, as a motion can only come naturally from a motion (secs. 401–3).

24. From this we see that if, in our perceptions, we had nothing distinct or, so to speak, in relief and stronger in flavor, we would always be in a stupor. And this is the state of bare monads.

25. We also see that nature has given heightened perceptions to animals, from the care she has taken to furnish them organs that collect several rays of light or several waves of air, in order to make them more effectual by bringing them together. There is something similar to this in odor, taste, and touch, and perhaps in many other senses which are unknown to us. I will soon explain how what occurs in the soul represents what occurs in the organs.

26. Memory provides a kind of sequence in souls, which imitates reason, but which must be distinguished from it. We observe that when animals have the perception of something which strikes them, and when they previously had a similar perception of that thing, then, through a representation in their memory, they expect that which was attached to the thing in the preceding perception, and are led to have sensations similar to those they had before. For example, if we show dogs a stick, they remember the pain that it caused them and they flee (Prelim., sec. 65).

27. And the strong imagination that strikes and moves them comes from the magnitude or the multitude of the preceding perceptions. For often a strong impression produces, all at once, the effect produced by a long *habit* or by many lesser, reiterated perceptions.

28. Men act like beasts insofar as the sequence of their perceptions results from the principle of memory alone; they resemble the empirical physicians who practice without theory. We are all mere Empirics in three fourths of our actions. For example, when we expect that the day will dawn tomorrow, we act like an Empiric,[7] because until now it has always

---

7. The Empirics were a sect of physicians before Galen (ca. AD 150). In later times, the epithet "Empiric" was given to physicians who despised theoretical study and trusted tradition and their own experience.

been thus. Only the astronomer judges this by reason (Prelim., sec. 65).

29. But the knowledge of eternal and necessary truths is what distinguishes us from simple animals and furnishes us with *reason* and the sciences, by raising us to a knowledge of ourselves and of God. And that is what we call the rational soul, or *mind*, in ourselves.

30. It is also through the knowledge of necessary truths and through their abstractions that we rise to *reflective* acts, which enable us to think of that which is called "I" and enable us to consider that this or that is in us. And thus, in thinking of ourselves, we think of being, of substance, of the simple and of the composite, of the immaterial and of God himself, by conceiving that that which is limited in us is limitless in him. And these reflective acts furnish the principal objects of our reasonings (*Theod.* Preface 1.a).

31. Our reasonings are based on *two great principles*, *that of contradiction*, in virtue of which we judge that which involves a contradiction to be false, and that which is opposed or contradictory to the false to be true (sec. 44, 169).

32. And *that of sufficient reason*, by virtue of which we consider that we can find no true or existent fact, no true assertion, without there being a sufficient reason why it is thus and not otherwise, although most of the time these reasons cannot be known to us (sec. 44, 196).

33. There are also two kinds of *truths*, those of *reasoning* and those of *fact*. The truths of reasoning are necessary and their opposite is impossible; the truths of fact are contingent, and their opposite is possible. When a truth is necessary, its reason can be found by analysis, resolving it into simpler ideas and simpler truths until we reach the primitives (sec. 170, 174, 189, 280–82, 367, Abridgment, objection 3).

34. This is how the speculative *theorems* and practical *canons* of mathematicians are reduced by analysis to *definitions*, *axioms*, and *postulates*.

35. And there are, finally, *simple ideas*, whose definition cannot be given. There are also axioms and postulates, in brief, *primitive principles*, which cannot be proved and which need no proof. And

these are *identical propositions*, whose opposite contains an explicit contradiction.

36. But there must also be a *sufficient reason* in *contingent truths*, or *truths of fact*, that is, in the series of things distributed throughout the universe of creatures, where the resolution into particular reasons could proceed into unlimited detail because of the immense variety of things in nature and because of the division of bodies to infinity. There is an infinity of past and present shapes and motions that enter into the efficient cause of my present writing, and there is an infinity of small inclinations and dispositions of my soul, present and past, that enter into its final cause (sec. 36, 37, 44, 45, 49, 52, 121, 122, 337, 340, 344).

37. And since all this *detail* involves nothing but other prior or more detailed contingents, each of which needs a similar analysis in order to give its reason, we do not make progress in this way. It must be the case that the sufficient or ultimate reason is outside the sequence or *series* of this multiplicity of contingencies, however infinite it may be.

38. And that is why the ultimate reason of things must be in a necessary substance in which the diversity of changes is only eminent, as in its source. This is what we call *God* (*Theod.* sec. 7).

39. Since this substance is a sufficient reason for all this diversity, which is utterly interconnected, *there is only one God, and this God is sufficient*.

40. We can also judge that this supreme substance which is unique, universal, and necessary must be incapable of limits and must contain as much reality as is possible, insofar as there is nothing outside it which is independent of it, and insofar as it is a simple consequence of its possible existence.

41. From this it follows that God is absolutely perfect—*perfection* being nothing but the magnitude of positive reality considered as such, setting aside the limits or bounds in the things which have it. And here, where there are no limits, that is, in God, perfection is absolutely infinite (*Theod.* sec. 22; *Theod.* Preface, sec. 4.a).

42. It also follows that creatures derive their perfections from God's influence, but that they derive their imperfections from their own nature,

which is incapable of being without limits. For it is in this that they are distinguished from God (*Theod.* sec. 20, 27–31, 153, 167, 377 et seq.; sec. 30, 380, Abridgment, objection 5).[8]

43. It is also true that God is not only the source of existences, but also that of essences insofar as they are real, that is, or the source of that which is real in possibility. This is because God's understanding is the realm of eternal truths or that of the ideas on which they depend; without him there would be nothing real in possibles, and not only would nothing exist, but also nothing would be possible (*Theod.* sec. 20).

44. For if there is reality in essences or possibles, or indeed, in eternal truths, this reality must be grounded in something existent and actual, and consequently, it must be grounded in the existence of the necessary being, in whom essence involves existence, that is, in whom possible being is sufficient for actual being (sec. 184–89, 335).

45. Thus God alone (or the necessary being) has this privilege, that he must exist if he is possible. And since nothing can prevent the possibility of what is without limits, without negation, and consequently without contradiction, this by itself is sufficient for us to know the existence of God *a priori*. We have also proved this by the reality of the eternal truths. But we have also just proved it *a posteriori* since there are contingent beings, which can only have their final or sufficient reason in the necessary being, a being that has the reason of its existence in itself.

46. However, we should not imagine, as some do, that since the eternal truths depend on God, they are arbitrary and depend on his will, as Descartes appears to have held, and after him Mr. Poiret.[9] This is true only of contingent truths, whose principle is *fitness* [*convenance*] or the choice of

the *best*. But necessary truths depend solely on his understanding, and are its internal object (sec. 180, 184, 185, 335, 351, 380).

47. Thus God alone is the primitive unity or the first [*originaire*] simple substance; all created or derivative monads are products, and are generated, so to speak, by continual fulgurations of the divinity from moment to moment, limited by the receptivity of the creature, to which it is essential to be limited (sec. 382–91, 398, 395).

48. God has *power*, which is the source of everything, *knowledge*, which contains the diversity of ideas, and finally *will*, which brings about changes or products in accordance with the principle of the best (sec. 7, 149, 150). And these correspond to what, in created monads, is the subject or the basis, the perceptive faculty and the appetitive faculty. But in God these attributes are absolutely infinite or perfect, while in the created monads or in entelechies (or *perfectihabies*, as Hermolaus Barbarus translated that word)[10] they are only imitations of it, in proportion to the perfection that they have (sec. 87).

49. The creature is said to act externally insofar as it is perfect, and *to be acted upon* [*patir*] by another, insofar as it is imperfect. Thus we attribute *action* to a monad insofar as it has distinct perceptions, and *passion*, insofar as it has confused perceptions (*Theod.* sec. 32, 66, 386).

50. And one creature is more perfect than another insofar as one finds in it that which provides an *a priori* reason for what happens in the other; and this is why we say that it acts on the other.

51. But in simple substances the influence of one monad over another can only be ideal, and can only produce its effect through God's intervention, when in the ideas of God a monad reasonably asks that God take it into account in regulating the others from the beginning of things. For, since a created monad cannot have an internal physical influence upon another, this is the only way in which one can

---

8. The following appears in the second draft, but is missing in the final copy: "This *original imperfection* of creatures is noticeable in the *natural inertia* of bodies."

9. For Leibniz's critique of Descartes' concept of God, see the "Letter to Molanus," above. Pierre Poiret (1646–1719) was initially one of Descartes' followers; he published a book of reflections on God, soul, and evil, *Cogitationum rationalium de Deo, anima, et malo libri quattuor* (1677), which was attacked by Bayle.

---

10. Hermolaus Barbarus (1454–93) was an Italian scholar who attempted, through retranslations of Aristotle, to recover Aristotle's original doctrine from under the layers of scholastic interpretations. His works include popular compendia of ethics and natural philosophy, drawn from the writings of Aristotle.

depend on another (*Theod.* sec. 9, 54, 65, 66, 201, Abridgment, objection 3).

52. It is in this way that actions and passions among creatures are mutual. For God, comparing two simple substances, finds in each reasons that require him to adjust the other to it; and consequently, what is active in some respects is passive from another point of view: *active* insofar as what is known distinctly in one serves to explain what happens in another; and *passive* insofar as the reason for what happens in one is found in what is known distinctly in another (sec. 66).

53. Now, since there is an infinity of possible universes in God's ideas, and since only one of them can exist, there must be a sufficient reason for God's choice, a reason which determines him towards one thing rather than another (*Theod.* sec. 8, 10, 44, 173, 196 & seq., 225, 414–16).

54. And this reason can only be found in *fitness*, or in the degree of perfection that these worlds contain, each possible world having the right to claim existence in proportion to the perfection it contains (sec. 74, 167, 350, 201, 130, 352, 345 & seq., 354).[11]

55. And this is the cause of the existence of the best, which wisdom makes known to God, which his goodness makes him choose, and which his power makes him produce (*Theod.* sec. 8, 78, 80, 84,119, 204, 206, 208; Abridgment, objection 1, objection 8).

56. This interconnection or accommodation of all created things to each other, and each to all the others, brings it about that each simple substance has relations that express all the others, and consequently, that each simple substance is a perpetual, living mirror of the universe (sec. 130, 360).

57. Just as the same city viewed from different directions appears entirely different and, as it were, multiplied perspectively, in just the same way it happens that, because of the infinite multitude of simple substances, there are, as it were, just as many different universes, which are, nevertheless, only perspectives on a single one, corresponding to the different points of view of each monad (sec. 147).

---

11. The following appears in the second draft: "Thus there is nothing that is completely arbitrary."

58. And this is the way of obtaining as much variety as possible, but with the greatest order possible, that is, it is the way of obtaining as much perfection as possible (sec. 120, 124, 241 & seq., 214, 243, 275).

59. Moreover, this is the only hypothesis (which I dare say is demonstrated) that properly enhances God's greatness. Mr. Bayle recognized this when, in his *Dictionary* (article "Rorarius"), he set out objections to it; indeed, he was tempted to believe that I ascribed too much to God, more than is possible. But he was unable to present any reason why this universal harmony, which results in every substance expressing exactly all the others through the relations it has to them, is impossible.[12]

60. Furthermore, in what I have just discussed, we can see the *a priori* reasons why things could not be otherwise. Because God, in regulating the whole, had regard for each part, and particularly for each monad, and since the nature of the monad is representative, nothing can limit it to represent only a part of things. However, it is true that this representation is only confused as to the detail of the whole universe, and can only be distinct for a small portion of things, that is, either for those that are closest, or for those that are greatest with respect to each monad; otherwise each monad would be a divinity. Monads are limited, not as to their objects, but with respect to the modifications of their knowledge of them. Monads all go confusedly to infinity, to the whole; but they are limited and differentiated by the degrees of their distinct perceptions.

61. In this respect, composites are analogous to simples. For everything is a plenum, which makes all matter interconnected. In a plenum, every motion has some effect on distant bodies, in proportion to their distance. For each body is affected, not only by those in contact with it, and in some way feels the effects of everything that happens to them, but also, through them, it feels the effects of those in contact with the bodies with which it is itself immediately in contact. From this it follows that this communication extends to any distance whatsoever. As a result, every body is affected by everything that happens in the

---

12. See note to sec. 16, above.

universe, to such an extent that he who sees all can read in each thing what happens everywhere, and even what has happened or what will happen, by observing in the present what is remote in time as well as in space. "All things conspire [*sympnoia panta*]," said Hippocrates. But a soul can read in itself only what is distinctly represented there; it cannot unfold all its folds at once, because they go to infinity.

62. Thus, although each created monad represents the whole universe, it more distinctly represents the body which is particularly affected by it, and whose entelechy it constitutes. And just as this body expresses the whole universe through the interconnection of all matter in the plenum, the soul also represents the whole universe by representing this body, which belongs to it in a particular way (sec. 400).

63. The body belonging to a monad (which is the entelechy or soul of that body) together with an entelechy constitutes what may be called a *living being*, and together with a soul constitutes what is called an *animal*. Now, the body of a living being or an animal is always organized; for, since every monad is a mirror of the universe in its way, and since the universe is regulated in a perfect order, there must also be an order in the representing being, that is, in the perceptions of the soul, and consequently, in the body in accordance with which the universe is represented therein (sec. 403).

64. Thus each organized body of a living being is a kind of divine machine or natural automaton, which infinitely surpasses all artificial automata. For a machine constructed by man's art is not a machine in each of its parts. For example, the tooth of a brass wheel has parts or fragments which, for us, are no longer artificial things, and no longer have any marks to indicate the machine for whose use the wheel was intended. But natural machines, that is, living bodies, are still machines in their least parts, to infinity. That is the difference between nature and art, that is, between divine art and our art (sec. 134, 146, 194, 483).

65. And the author of nature has been able to practice this divine and infinitely marvelous art, because each portion of matter is not only divisible to infinity, as the ancients have recognized, but

is also actually subdivided without end, each part divided into parts having some motion of their own; otherwise, it would be impossible for each portion of matter to express the whole universe (Prelim., sec. 70, *Theodicy*, sec. 195).

66. From this we see that there is a world of creatures, of living beings, of animals, of entelechies, of souls in the least part of matter.

67. Each portion of matter can be conceived as a garden full of plants, and as a pond full of fish. But each branch of a plant, each limb of an animal, each drop of its humors, is still another such garden or pond.

68. And although the earth and air lying between the garden plants, or the water lying between the fish of the pond, are neither plant nor fish, they contain yet more of them, though of a subtleness imperceptible to us, most often.

69. Thus there is nothing fallow, sterile, or dead in the universe, no chaos and no confusion except in appearance, almost as it looks in a pond at a distance, where we might see the confused and, so to speak, teeming motion of the fish in the pond, without discerning the fish themselves (Preface 5.b, 6).

70. Thus we see that each living body has a dominant entelechy, which in the animal is the soul; but the limbs of this living body are full of other living beings, plants, animals, each of which also has its entelechy, or its dominant soul.

71. But we must not imagine, as some who have misunderstood my thought do, that each soul has a mass or portion of matter of its own, always proper to or allotted by it, and that it consequently possesses other lower living beings, forever destined to serve it. For all bodies are in a perpetual flux, like rivers, and parts enter into them and depart from them continually.

72. Thus the soul changes body only little by little and by degrees, so that it is never stripped at once of all its organs. There is often metamorphosis in animals, but there is never metempsychosis nor transmigration of souls; there are also no completely *separated souls*, nor spirits [*Génies*] without bodies. God alone is completely detached from bodies (sec. 90, 124).

73. That is why there is never total generation nor, strictly speaking, perfect death, death consisting in the separation of the soul. And what we call *generations* are developments and growths, as what we call deaths are enfoldings and diminutions.

74. Philosophers have been greatly perplexed about the origin of forms, entelechies, or souls. But today, when exact inquiries on plants, insects, and animals have shown us that organic bodies in nature are never produced from chaos or putrefaction, but always through seeds in which there is, no doubt, some *preformation*, it has been judged that, not only the organic body was already there before conception, but there was also a soul in this body; in brief, the animal itself was there, and through conception this animal was merely prepared for a great transformation, in order to become an animal of another kind. Something similar is seen outside generation, as when worms become flies, and caterpillars become butterflies (sec. 86, 89; Preface 5.b ff; sec. 90, 187, 188, 403, 86, 397).

75. Those *animals*, some of which are raised by conception to the level of the larger animals, can be called *spermatic*. But those of them that remain among those of their kind, that is, the majority, are born, multiply, and are destroyed, just like the larger animals. There are but a small number of Elect that pass onto a larger stage [*théatre*].

76. But this was only half the truth. I have, therefore, held that if the animal never begins naturally, it does not end naturally, either; and not only will there be no generation, but also no complete destruction, nor any death, strictly speaking. These *a posteriori* reasonings, derived from experience, agree perfectly with my principles deduced *a priori*, as above (sec. 90).

77. Thus one can state that not only is the soul (mirror of an indestructible universe) indestructible, but so is the animal itself, even though its mechanism often perishes in part, and casts off or puts on its organic coverings.

78. These principles have given me a way of naturally explaining the union, or rather the conformity of the soul and the organic body. The soul follows its own laws and the body also follows its own; and they agree in virtue of the harmony pre-established between all substances, since they are all representations of a single universe (Preface 6; sec. 340, 352, 353, 358).

79. Souls act according to the laws of final causes, through appetitions, ends, and means. Bodies act according to the laws of efficient causes or of motions. And these two kingdoms, that of efficient causes and that of final causes, are in harmony with each other.

80. Descartes recognized that souls cannot impart a force to bodies because there is always the same quantity of force in matter. However, he thought that the soul could change the direction of bodies. But that is because the law of nature, which also affirms the conservation of the same total direction in matter, was not known at that time. If he had known it, he would have hit upon my system of pre-established harmony (Preface; *Theod.* sec. 22, 59, 60, 61, 63, 66, 345, 346 & seq., 354, 355).

81. According to this system, bodies act as if there were no souls (though this is impossible); and souls act as if there were no bodies; and both act as if each influenced the other.

82. As for *minds* or rational souls, I find that, at bottom, what we just said holds for all living beings and animals, namely that animals and souls begin only with the world and do not end any more than the world does. However, rational animals have this peculiarity, that their little spermatic animals, as long as they only remain in this state, have only ordinary or sensitive souls. But that as soon as the Elect among them, so to speak, attain human nature by actual conception, their sensitive souls are elevated to the rank of reason and to the prerogative of minds (sec. 91, 397).

83. Among other differences which exist between ordinary souls and minds, some of which I have already noted, there are also the following: that souls, in general, are living mirrors or images of the universe of creatures, but that minds are also images of the divinity itself, or of the author of nature, capable of knowing the system of the universe, and imitating something of it through their schematic representations [*échantillons architectoniques*] of it, each mind being like a little divinity in its own realm (sec. 147).

84. That is what makes minds capable of entering into a kind of society with God, and allows him to be, in relation to them, not only what an inventor is to his machine (as God is in relation to the other creatures) but also what a prince is to his subjects, and even what a father is to his children.

85. From this it is easy to conclude that the collection of all minds must make up the city of God, that is, the most perfect possible state under the most perfect of monarchs (see 146, Abridgment, Objection 2).

86. This city of God, this truly universal monarchy, is a moral world within the natural world, and the highest and most divine of God's works. The glory of God truly consists in this city, for he would have none if his greatness and goodness were not known and admired by minds. It is also in relation to this divine city that God has goodness, properly speaking, whereas his wisdom and power are evident everywhere.

87. Since earlier we established a perfect harmony between two natural kingdoms, the one of efficient causes, the other of final causes, we ought to note here yet another harmony between the physical kingdom of nature and the moral kingdom of grace, that is, between God considered as the architect of the mechanism of the universe, and God considered as the monarch of the divine city of minds (sec. 62, 74, 118, 248, 112, 130, 247).

88. This harmony leads things to grace through the very paths of nature. For example, this globe must be destroyed and restored by natural means at such times as the governing of minds requires it, for the punishment of some and the reward of others (sec. 18 & seq., 110, 244, 245, 340).

89. It can also be said that God the architect pleases in every respect God the legislator, and, as a result, sins must carry their penalty with them by the order of nature, and even in virtue of the mechanical structure of things. Similarly, noble actions will receive their rewards through mechanical means with regard to bodies, even though this cannot, and must not, always happen immediately.

90. Finally, under this perfect government, there will be no good action that is unrewarded, no bad action that goes unpunished, and everything must result in the well being of the good, that is, of those who are not dissatisfied in this great state, those who trust in providence, after having done their duty, and who love and imitate the author of all good, as they should, finding pleasure in the consideration of his perfections according to the nature of genuinely *pure love*, which takes pleasure in the happiness of the beloved. This is what causes wise and virtuous persons to work for all that appears to be in conformity with the presumptive or antecedent divine will, and nevertheless, to content themselves with what God brings about by his secret, consequent, or decisive will, since they recognize that if we could understand the order of the universe well enough, we would find that it surpasses all the wishes of the wisest, and that it is impossible to make it better than it is.[13] This is true not only for the whole in general, but also for ourselves in particular, if we are attached, as we should be, to the author of the whole, not only as the architect and efficient cause of our being, but also as to our master and final cause; he ought to be the whole aim of our will, and he alone can make us happy (sec. 134 end, Preface 4.a.b.; *Theodicy*, sec. 278, Preface 4.b).

---

13. The distinction between God's antecedent and consequent will can be found in Thomas Aquinas, *Summa Theologiae* I, q. 19, art. 6, ad 1.

# Isaac Newton, *Principia* (1687; 2nd ed., 1713), "Scholium to Definitions" and "General Scholium," and *Optics* (1704; 2nd ed. 1718), "Query 31"[1]

*Isaac Newton (1642–1727) was the foremost mathematician and natural philosopher of the late 17th century. He attended Trinity College, Cambridge, was elected a fellow in 1667, and succeeded Isaac Barrow as Lucasian Professor of Mathematics in 1669. Newton's great work,* The Mathematical Principles of Natural Philosophy *(or* Principia*), published in 1687, was a revision and expansion of several treatises he had previously composed but did not publish. He was elected president of the Royal Society in 1703 and knighted in 1705. During his life he engaged in several bitter priority disputes about scientific and mathematical discoveries—for example, with Robert Hooke in 1686–88 over the inverse square law, and with Leibniz in 1703–15 over the calculus. His influence in the history of science is unequaled and extends well beyond science; of particular consequence are his cosmological remarks from the* Principia.[2]

## Scholium

Up to now I have defined terms that are less known and explained the sense I would have them understood in the following discourse. I do not define time, space, place, and motion, since they are well known to all. Only I must observe that the common people conceive those quantities under no other notions than from their relation to sensible objects. And from this certain prejudices arise, for the removing of which it will be convenient to distinguish the terms into absolute and relative, true and apparent, mathematical and common.

I. Absolute, true, and mathematical time, of itself, and from its own nature, flows uniformly without relation to anything external, and by another name is called *duration*. Relative, apparent, and common time is some sensible and external (whether accurate

---

1. *Principia* (that is, *Philosophiae naturalis principia mathematica*), translated from the Latin by A. Motte in *The Mathematical Principles of Natural Philosophy* . . . (London, 1729), modified. Passages added in the third edition (1726) are indicated by angle brackets in the text. *Optics* from *Opticks: or, A treatise of the reflexions, refractions, inflexions and colours of light* (2nd ed. with additions, London, 1718; 1st ed., 1704; Latin trans. by Samuel Clarke), modified. Passages added in the second edition are indicated by angle brackets in the text.

2. For more on Newton, see Richard W. Westfall, *Never at Rest* (Cambridge: Cambridge University Press, 1980), I. Bernard Cohen, *The Newtonian Revolution* (Cambridge: Cambridge University Press, 1980), or B. J. Dobbs, *The Janus Faces of Genius: The Role of Alchemy in Newton's Thought* (Cambridge: Cambridge University Press, 1991). For an account of the dispute between Newton and Leibniz on the calculus, see A. Rupert Hall, *Philosophers at War* (Cambridge: Cambridge University Press, 1980).

or varying in rate) measure of duration by the means of motion, which is commonly used instead of true time, such as an hour, a day, a month, a year.

II. Absolute space, in its own nature, without relation to anything external, always remains similar and immovable. Relative space is some movable dimension or measure of the absolute spaces, which our senses determine by its position to bodies and is commonly taken for immovable space, such as the dimension of subterraneous, aerial, or celestial space, determined by its position with respect to earth. Absolute and relative space are the same in form and magnitude, but they do not always remain numerically the same. For if the earth, for instance, moves, a space of our air, which relatively and with respect to the earth always remains the same, will at one time be one part of the absolute space into which the air passes, at another time it will be another part of the same, and so, absolutely understood, it will be continually changed.

III. Place is a part of space which a body takes up, and is absolute or relative according to the space. I say, a part of space, not the situation nor the external surface of the body. For the places of equal solids are always equal, but their surfaces, by reason of their dissimilar figures, are often unequal. Positions properly have no quantity, nor are they so much the places themselves as the properties of places. The motion of the whole is the same as the sum of the motions of the parts; that is, the translation of the whole out of its place is the same thing as the sum of the translations of the parts out of their places; and therefore the place of the whole is the same as the sum of the places of the parts, and for that reason it is internal and in the whole body.

IV. Absolute motion is the translation of a body from one absolute place into another, and relative motion the translation from one relative place into another. Thus in a ship under sail, the relative place of a body is that part of the ship the body possesses, or that part of the cavity the body fills, and which therefore moves together with the ship; and relative rest is the continuance of the body in the same part of the ship or of its cavity. But real, absolute rest is the continuance of the body in the same part of that immovable space, in which the ship itself, its cavity, and all that it contains, is moved. For that reason, if the earth is really at rest, the body which relatively rests in the ship will really and absolutely move with the same velocity which the ship has on the earth. But if the earth also moves, the true and absolute motion of the body will arise, partly from the true motion of the earth in immovable space, partly from the relative motion of the ship on the earth; and if the body moves also relatively in the ship, its true motion will arise, partly from the true motion of the earth in immovable space, and partly from the relative motions as well of the ship on the earth as of the body in the ship; and from these relative motions will arise the relative motion of the body on the earth. As if that part of the earth, where the ship is, was truly moved towards the east with a velocity of 10,010 units, while the ship itself, with a fresh gale and full sails, is carried towards the west with a velocity expressed by ten of those units, while a sailor walks in the ship towards the east, with one unit of the said velocity, then the sailor will be moved truly in immovable space towards the east with a velocity of 10,001 units, and relatively on the earth towards the west with a velocity of nine of those units.

Absolute time is distinguished from relative in astronomy by the equation or correction of the apparent time. For the natural days are truly unequal, though they are commonly considered as equal and used for a measure of time; astronomers correct this inequality that they may measure the celestial motions by a more accurate time. It may be that there is no such thing as a uniform motion by which time may be accurately measured. All motions may be accelerated and retarded, but the flowing of absolute time is not liable to any change. The duration or perseverance of the existence of things remains the same, whether the motions are swift or slow or none at all; and therefore this duration ought to be distinguished from what are only sensible measures of it, and from which we deduce it by means of the astronomical equation. The necessity of this equation for determining the times of a phenomenon is established as well from the experiments of the pendulum clock as by eclipses of the satellites of Jupiter.

As the order of the parts of time is immutable, so also is the order of the parts of space. Suppose those parts to be moved out of their places, and they will be moved (if the expression may be allowed) out of themselves. For times and spaces are, as it were, the places as well of themselves as of all other things. All things are placed in time as to order of succession, and in space as to order of situation. It is from their essence or nature that they are places, and it is absurd that the primary places of things should be movable. These are therefore the absolute places, and translations out of those places are the only absolute motions.

But because the parts of space cannot be seen or distinguished from one another by our senses, we use sensible measures of them in their stead. For from the positions and distances of things from any body considered as immovable, we define all places, and then with respect to such places, we estimate all motions, considering bodies as transferred from some of those places into others. And so, instead of absolute places and motions, we use relative ones, and that without any inconvenience in common affairs; but in philosophical disquisitions, we ought to abstract from our senses and consider things themselves, distinct from what are only sensible measures of them. For it may be that there is no body really at rest to which the places and motions of others may be referred.

But we may distinguish rest and motion, absolute and relative, one from the other by their properties, causes, and effects. It is a property of rest that bodies really at rest do rest in respect to one another. And therefore as it is possible that in the remote regions of the fixed stars, or perhaps far beyond them, there may be some body absolutely at rest, but impossible to know, from the position of bodies to one another in our regions, whether any of these do keep the same position to that remote body, it follows that absolute rest cannot be determined from the position of bodies in our regions.

It is a property of motion that the parts, which retain given positions to their wholes, do partake of the motions of those wholes. For all the parts of revolving bodies endeavor to recede from the axis of motion, and the impetus of bodies moving forwards arises from the joint impetus of all the parts. Therefore,

if surrounding bodies are moved, those that are relatively at rest within them will partake of their motion. Because of this, the true and absolute motion of a body cannot be determined by the translation of it from those which only seem to rest; for the external bodies should not only appear at rest, but be really at rest. For otherwise, all included bodies, besides their translation from near the surrounding ones, partake likewise of their true motions; and though that translation were not made, they would not be really at rest, but only seem to be so. For the surrounding bodies stand in the like relation to the surrounded as the exterior part of a whole does to the interior, or as the shell does to the kernel; but if the shell moves, the kernel will also move, as being part of the whole, without any removal from near the shell.

A property related to the preceding is that if a place is moved, whatever is placed in it moves along with it; and therefore a body which is moved from a place in motion partakes also of the motion of its place. Upon which account, all motions, from places in motion, are no other than parts of entire and absolute motions, and every entire motion is composed of the motion of the body out of its first place, and the motion of this place out of its place, and so on, until we come to some immovable place, as in the aforementioned example of the sailor. Because of this, entire and absolute motions can be no otherwise determined than by immovable places; and for that reason I did before refer those absolute motions to immovable places, but relative ones to movable places. Now no other places are immovable but those that, from infinity to infinity, do all retain the same given position one to another, and upon this account must ever remain unmoved, and do as a result constitute immovable space.

The causes by which true and relative motions are distinguished from one another are the forces impressed upon bodies to generate motion. True motion is neither generated nor altered, but by some force impressed upon the body moved; but relative motion may be generated or altered without any force impressed upon the body. For it is sufficient only to impress some force on other bodies with which the former is compared, that by their giving way, that relation in which the relative rest or motion of this other body did consist may be changed. Again, true motion always suffers some change from any force impressed upon the moving body; but relative motion does not necessarily undergo any change by such forces. For if the same forces are likewise impressed on those other bodies, with which the comparison is made, that the relative position may be preserved, then that condition will be preserved in which the relative motion consists. And therefore any relative motion may be changed when the true motion remains unaltered, and the relative may be preserved when the true suffers some change. Thus, true motion by no means consists in such relations.

The effects which distinguish absolute from relative motion are the forces of receding from the axis of circular motion. For there are no such forces in a circular motion purely relative, but in a true and absolute circular motion, they are greater or less, according to the quantity of the motion. If a vessel hung by a long cord is so often turned about that the cord is strongly twisted, then filled with water and held at rest together with the water, at once, by the sudden action of another force, it is whirled about the contrary way, and while the cord is untwisting itself, the vessel continues for some time in this motion, the surface of the water will at first be even, as before the vessel began to move; but after that the vessel, by gradually communicating its motion to the water, will make it begin to revolve sensibly and recede gradually from the middle, and ascend to the sides of the vessel, forming itself into a concave figure (as I have experienced); and the swifter the motion becomes, the higher will the water rise, until at last, performing its revolutions in the same times with the vessel, it becomes relatively at rest in it. This ascent of the water shows its endeavor to recede from the axis of its motion, and the true and absolute circular motion of the water, which is here directly contrary to the relative, becomes known and may be measured by this endeavor. At first, when the relative motion of the water in the vessel was greatest, it produced no endeavor to recede from the axis; the water showed no tendency to the circumference, nor any ascent towards the sides of the vessel, but remained of an even surface, and therefore its true circular

motion had not yet begun. But afterwards, when the relative motion of the water had decreased, its ascent towards the sides of the vessel proved its endeavor to recede from the axis; and this endeavor showed the real circular motion of the water continually increasing, until it had acquired its greatest quantity when the water rested relatively in the vessel. And therefore this endeavor does not depend upon any translation of the water in respect of the ambient bodies, nor can true circular motion be defined by such translation. There is only one real circular motion of any one revolving body corresponding to only one power of endeavoring to recede from its axis of motion as its proper and adequate effect; but relative motions in one and the same body are innumerable, according to the various relations it bears to external bodies, and like other relations are altogether destitute of any real effect, except insofar as they may perhaps partake of that unique true motion. And therefore in the system of those who suppose that our heavens revolving below the sphere of the fixed stars carry the planets along with them, the several parts of those heavens and the planets, which are indeed relatively at rest in their heavens, do yet really move. For they change their position one to another (which never happens to bodies truly at rest), and being carried together with their heavens, partake of their motions, and as parts of revolving wholes, endeavor to recede from the axis of their motions. For that reason relative quantities are not the quantities themselves, whose names they bear, but those sensible measures of them (either accurate or inaccurate), which are commonly used instead of the measured quantities themselves. And if the meaning of words is to be determined by their use, then by the names time, space, place, and motion, their sensible measures are properly to be understood; and the expression will be unusual, and purely mathematical, if the measured quantities themselves are meant. On this account, those who interpret these words for the measured quantities violate the accuracy of language, which ought to be kept precise. Nor do those who confound real quantities with their relations and sensible measure defile the purity of mathematical and philosophical truths any less.

It is indeed a matter of great difficulty to discover and effectually to distinguish the true motions of particular bodies from the apparent, because the parts of that immovable space in which those motions are performed do by no means come under the observation of our senses. Yet the thing is not altogether desperate; for we have some arguments to guide us, partly from the apparent motions, which are the differences of the true motions, partly from the forces, which are the causes and effects of the true motions. For instance, if two globes, kept at a given distance one from the other by means of a cord that connects them, were revolved about their common center of gravity, we might, from the tension of the cord, discover the endeavor of the globes to recede from the axis of their motion, and from thence we might compute the quantity of their circular motions. And then if any equal forces should be impressed at once on the alternate faces of the globes to augment or diminish their circular motions, from the increase or decrease of the tension of the cord, we might infer the increment or decrement of their motions; and hence would be found on what faces those forces ought to be impressed, that the motions of the globes might be most augmented; that is, we might discover their hindmost faces, or those which do follow in the circular motion. But the faces which follow being known, and consequently the opposite ones that precede, we should likewise know the determination of their motions. And thus we might find both the quantity and the determination of this circular motion, even in an immense vacuum, where there was nothing external or sensible with which the globes could be compared. But now, if some remote bodies that kept always a given position one to another were placed in that space, as the fixed stars do in our regions, we could not indeed determine from the relative translation of the globes among those bodies, whether the motion did belong to the globes or to the bodies. But if we observed the cord and found that its tension was that very tension which the motions of the globes required, we might conclude the motion to be in the globes and the bodies to be at rest; and then, lastly, from the translation of the globes among the bodies, we should find the determination of their

motions. But how we are to obtain the true motions from their causes, effects, and apparent differences, and the converse, shall be explained more at large in the following treatise. For to this end it was that I composed it.

## *Principia* (2nd edition, 1713), General Scholium

The hypothesis of vortices is pressed by many difficulties. In order that any planet may describe areas proportional to the time by a radius drawn to the sun, the periodic times of the parts of the vortices should observe the square of their distances from the sun; but in order that the periodic times of the planets may obtain the 3/2th power of their distances from the sun, the periodic times of the parts of the vortex ought to be as the 3/2th power of their distances. In order that the smaller vortices may maintain their lesser revolutions about Saturn, Jupiter, and other planets and float quietly and undisturbed in the greater vortex of the sun, the periodic times of the parts of the solar vortex should be equal. But the rotation of the sun and planets about their axes, which ought to correspond with the motions of their vortices, are in disagreement with all these ratios. The motions of the comets are exceedingly regular, are governed by the same laws as the motions of the planets, and cannot be accounted for by the hypothesis of vortices. For comets are carried in highly eccentric motions through all parts of the heavens, which is incompatible with the notion of a vortex.

Projectiles in our air feel only the resistance of the air. If the air is removed, as is done in Mr. Boyle's vacuum, the resistance ceases, for a bit of fine down and a piece of solid gold fall with equal velocity in this void. And the same argument must apply to the celestial spaces above the earth's atmosphere; in these spaces, where there is no air to resist their motions, all bodies will move with complete freedom, and the planets and comets will constantly revolve in orbits given in shape and position, according to the laws above explained. But although these bodies may, indeed, carry on in their orbits by the mere laws of gravity, they could by no means have attained the regular position of the orbits through these laws.

The six primary planets revolve about the sun in circles concentric with the sun, in the same direction of motion and almost in the same plane. Ten moons revolve about the earth, Jupiter, and Saturn in concentric circles in the same direction of motion and nearly in the planes of the orbits of those planets. But it is not to be conceived that mere mechanical causes could give birth to so many regular motions, since the comets range over all parts of the heavens in very eccentric orbits. In this kind of motion, the comets pass easily through the orbits of the planets and with great rapidity; and at their aphelions, where they move the slowest and delay the longest, they recede to the greatest distances from each other and hence suffer the least disturbance from their mutual attractions. This most beautiful system of the sun, planets, and comets could only proceed from the counsel and dominion of an intelligent and powerful Being. And if the fixed stars are the centers of similar other systems, since these are formed by the same counsel, they must all be subject to the dominion of One, especially since the light of the fixed stars is of the same nature as the light of the sun and light passes into all the other systems from every system <; and so that the systems of the fixed stars should not fall on each other by their gravity, he has placed those systems at immense distances from one another>.

This Being governs all things, not as the soul of the world, but as Lord over all; and because of his dominion he is usually called Lord God *Pantokrator*, or Universal Ruler. For *God* is a relative word and is relative to servants, and Deity is the dominion of God, not over his own body, as those imagine who imagine God to be the world soul, but over servants. The supreme God is a Being eternal, infinite, absolutely perfect; but a being, however perfect, without dominion cannot be said to be Lord God. For we say, "my God, your God, the God of Israel, <the God of Gods, and Lord of Lords,>" but we do not say, "my Eternal, your Eternal, the Eternal of Israel <,the Eternal of Gods"; we do not say, "my Infinite or my Perfect>." These are titles which have no relation to servants. The word *God*[3] usually signifies Lord, but not every Lord is God. It is the dominion of a

spiritual being that constitutes God—a true, supreme, or imaginary dominion makes a true, supreme, or imaginary God. From his true dominion it follows that the true God is a living, intelligent, and powerful Being, and from his other perfections, that he is supreme or most perfect. He is eternal and infinite, omnipotent and omniscient; that is, he endures from eternity to eternity and is present from infinity to infinity; he governs all things and knows all things that are or can be done. He is not eternity and infinity, but eternal and infinite; he is not duration and space, but he endures and is present. He endures forever and is present everywhere, and, by existing always and everywhere, he constitutes duration and space. Since every particle of space is always, and every indivisible moment of duration is everywhere, certainly the Maker and Lord of all things cannot be never and nowhere. <Every sentient soul is still the same indivisible person at different times and in different organs of sense and motion. Successive parts are given in duration, coexistent parts in space, but neither is given in the person of a man or his thinking principle, and much less can they be found in the thinking substance of God. Every person, insofar as he is a sentient being, is one and the same person during his whole life, in each and all of his organs of sense. God is the same God always and everywhere.> God is omnipresent not only virtually, but also substantially, for virtues cannot subsist without substance. In him[4] are all things contained and moved, yet neither affects the other. God is not affected by the motion of

---

3. Newton's marginal note: "Dr. Pocock derives the Latin word *Deus* from the Arabic *du* (in the oblique case *di*), which signifies

the Lord. And in this sense princes are called gods, Psalm 84:6 and John 10:45. And Moses is called a god to his brother Aaron and a god to Pharaoh (Exodus 4:16 and 7:1). And in the same sense the souls of dead princes were formerly called gods by the heathens, but falsely, because of their lack of dominion."
4. Newton's marginal note: "This was the opinion of the ancients, such as Pythagoras (in Cicero, *On the Nature of the Gods*, book 1), Thales, Anaxagoras, Virgil (*Georgics* 4.220 and *Aeneid* 6.721), Philo (*Allegories*, at the beginning of book 1), Aratus (*Phenomena*, at the beginning). So also the sacred writers, as Saint Paul (*Acts* 17:27–28), Saint John 14:2, Moses (*Deuteronomy* 4:39 and 10:14), David (Psalm 139:7–9), Solomon (*1 Kings* 8:27), Job 22:12–14, Jeremiah 23:23–24. Moreover, the idolaters supposed that the sun, moon, and stars, the souls of men, and other parts of the world are parts of the Supreme God, and are therefore to be worshipped, but falsely."

bodies, and bodies do not experience any resistance from God's omnipresence. It is allowed by all that the supreme God exists necessarily, and by the same necessity he exists always and everywhere. Hence also he is all similar, all eye, all ear, all brain, all arm, all power to perceive, to understand, and to act, but in a manner not at all human, in a manner not at all corporeal, in a manner entirely unknown to us. As a blind man has no idea of colors, so have we no idea of the manner by which the all-wise God perceives and understands all things. He is entirely void of all body and bodily shape, and therefore cannot be seen nor heard nor touched; nor ought he be worshipped under the image of any corporeal thing. We have ideas of his attributes, but we do not know what the real substance of anything is. We see only the shapes and colors of bodies, we hear only sounds, we touch only the external surfaces, we smell only the odors and taste the flavors; we do not know the inmost substances by our senses or by any act of reflection; much less, then, do we have any idea of the substance of God. We know him only through his most wise and excellent contrivances of things and final causes; we admire him for his perfections, but we revere and adore him on account of his dominion. <For we adore him as his servants, and a god without dominion, providence, and final causes is nothing else but fate and nature. No variation of things can arise from blind metaphysical necessity, which is certainly the same always and everywhere. All the diversity of natural things that we find suited to different times and places could only have arisen from the ideas and will of a Being existing necessarily. But, by way of allegory, God is said to see, to speak, to laugh, to love, to hate, to desire, to give, to receive, to rejoice, to be angry, to fight, to frame, to work, to build. For all our notions of God are taken from the ways of mankind by a certain similitude, which, though not perfect, has some likeness, however>. And this much concerning God, about whom a discourse from the appearances of things does certainly belong to natural philosophy.

Up to now we have explained the phenomena of the heavens and of our sea through the force of gravity but have not yet assigned the cause for this. It is certain that it must proceed from a cause that penetrates to the very centers of the sun and planets with no diminution of force, and that operates not according to the quantity of the surfaces of the particles upon which it acts (as mechanical causes usually do) but according to the quantity of the solid matter they contain, and which acts at immense distances, extended everywhere, always decreasing as the inverse square of the distances. Gravitation toward the sun is made up out of the gravitations toward the individual particles of the body, and in receding from the sun decreases precisely as the inverse square of the distances as far as the orbit of Saturn, as is evident from the aphelions of the planets being at rest, and even to the remotest aphelions of the comets, if those aphelions are also at rest. But up to now I have not been able to deduce the reason for these properties of gravity from phenomena, and I frame no hypotheses. For whatever is not deduced from the phenomena is to be called a hypothesis, and hypotheses, whether metaphysical or physical, whether of occult qualities or mechanical, have no place in experimental philosophy. In this philosophy, particular propositions are deduced from the phenomena and are rendered general by induction. The impenetrability, mobility, and impetus of bodies and the laws of motion and of gravitation were discovered in this way. And it is enough that gravity does really exist and acts according to the laws we have explained, and abundantly serves to account for all the motions of the celestial bodies and of our sea.

And now we might add something about a certain extremely subtle spirit that pervades and lies hidden in all gross bodies, by whose force and action the particles of bodies attract one another at near distances and cohere if brought into contact, and electric bodies act at greater distances, both repelling and attracting neighboring corpuscles, and light is emitted, reflected, refracted, inflected, and heats bodies, and all sensation is aroused, and the members of animals move by the will, that is, by the vibrations of this spirit, propagated through the solid filaments of the nerves from the external organs of sense to the brain, and from the brain to the muscles. But these things cannot be explained in a few words nor do we have at hand sufficient experiments by which the laws of action of this electric and elastic spirit can accurately be determined and demonstrated.

## *Optics*, Query 31

[ . . . ] And thus nature will be very conformable to herself and very simple, performing all the great motions of the heavenly bodies by the attraction of gravity that intercedes between those bodies, and almost all the small ones of their particles by some other attractive and repelling powers which intercede between the particles. The *vis inertiae* is a passive principle by which bodies persist in their motion or rest, receive motion in proportion to the force impressing it, and resist as much as they are resisted. By this principle alone there never could have been any motion in the world. Some other principle was necessary for putting bodies into motion; and now that they are in motion, some other principle is necessary for conserving the motion. For from the various composition of two motions, it is very certain that there is not always the same quantity of motion in the world. For if two globes joined by a slender rod revolve about their common center of gravity with a uniform motion, while that center moves on uniformly in a right line drawn in the plane of their circular motion, the sum of the motions of the two globes, as often as the globes are in the right line described by their common center of gravity, will be bigger than the sum of their motions, when they are in a line perpendicular to that right line. By this instance it appears that motion may be gotten or lost. But by reason of the tenacity of fluids and attrition of their parts, and the weakness of elasticity in solids, motion is much more apt to be lost than gotten, and is always upon the decay. For bodies which are either absolutely hard or so soft as to be void of elasticity will not rebound from one another. Impenetrability makes them only stop. If two equal bodies meet directly *in vacuo*, they will, by the laws of motion, stop where they meet and lose all their motion and remain in rest unless they are elastic and receive new motion from their spring. If they have so much elasticity as suffices to make them rebound with a quarter or half or three quarters of the force with which they come together, they will lose three quarters or half or a quarter of their motion. And this may be tried by letting two equal pendulums fall against one another from equal heights. If the pendulums are of lead or soft clay, they will lose all or almost all their motions; if they are of elastic bodies they will lose all but what they recover from their elasticity. If it is said that they can lose no motion but what they communicate to other bodies, the consequence is that *in vacuo* they can lose no motion, but when they meet they must go on and penetrate one another's dimensions. If three equal round vessels are filled, the one with water, the other with oil, the third with molten pitch, and the liquors are stirred about alike to give them a vortical motion, the pitch by its tenacity will lose its motion quickly, the oil being less tenacious will keep it longer, and the water being less tenacious will keep it longest but yet will lose it in a short time. From this it is easy to understand that if many contiguous vortices of molten pitch were each of them as large as those which some suppose to revolve about the sun and fixed stars, as large as the Cartesian vortices, yet these and all their parts would, by their tenacity and stiffness, communicate their motion to one another until they all rested among themselves. Vortices of oil or water or some more fluid matter might continue longer in motion, but unless the matter were void of all tenacity and attrition of parts, and communication of motion (which is not to be supposed), the motion would constantly decay. Seeing therefore the variety of motion that we find in the world is always decreasing, there is a necessity of conserving and recruiting it by active principles, such as are the cause of gravity, by which planets and comets keep their motions in their orbs and bodies acquire great motion in falling, and the cause of fermentation, by which the heart and blood of animals are kept in perpetual motion and heat, the inward parts of the earth are constantly warmed and in some places grow very hot, bodies burn and shine, mountains take fire, the caverns of the earth are blown up, and the sun continues violently hot and lucid and warms all things by his light. For we meet with very little motion in the world besides what is owing either to these active principles or to the dictates of a will. <And if it were not for these principles, the bodies of the earth, planets, comets, sun, and all things in them would grow cold and freeze and become inactive masses, and all putrefaction,

generation, vegetation, and life would cease, and the planets and comets would not remain in their orbs.>

All these things being considered, it seems probable to me that God in the beginning formed matter in solid, massy, hard, impenetrable, moveable particles of such sizes and figures and with such other properties and in such proportion to space as was most conducive to the end for which he formed them; and that these primitive particles being solids are incomparably harder than any porous bodies compounded of them, even so very hard as never to wear or break in pieces, no ordinary power being able to divide what God himself made one in the first creation. While the particles continue entire, they may compose bodies of one and the same nature and texture in all ages; but should they wear away or break in pieces, the nature of things depending on them would be changed. Water and earth, composed of old worn particles and fragments of particles, would not be of the same nature and texture now with water and earth composed of entire particles in the beginning. And therefore, that nature may be lasting, the changes of corporeal things are to be placed only in the various separations and new associations and motions of these permanent particles, since compound bodies are apt to break, not in the midst of solid particles, but where those particles are laid together and only touch in a few points.

It seems to me further that these particles have not only a *vis inertia* accompanied with such passive laws of motion as naturally result from that force but also that they are moved by certain active principles, such as is that of gravity and that which causes fermentation and the cohesion of bodies. These principles I consider not as occult qualities supposed to result from the specific forms of things, but as general laws of nature, by which the things themselves are formed, their truth appearing to us by phenomena though their causes are not yet discovered. <For these are manifest qualities, and their causes are only occult. And the Aristotelians gave the name of occult qualities not to manifest qualities but to such qualities only as they supposed to lie hidden in bodies and to be the unknown causes of manifest effects such as would be the causes of gravity and of magnetic and electric attractions and of fermentations if we should suppose that these forces or actions arose

from qualities unknown to us and incapable of being discovered and made manifest. Such occult qualities put a stop to the improvement of natural philosophy and therefore of late years have been rejected.> To tell us that every species of things is endowed with an occult specific quality by which it acts and produces manifest effects is to tell us nothing, but to derive two or three general principles of motion from phenomena and afterwards to tell us how the properties and actions of all corporeal things follow from those manifest principles would be a very great step in philosophy, though the causes of those principles were not yet discovered; and therefore I do not hesitate to propose the principles of motion above mentioned, since they are of very general extent <, and leave their causes to be found out>.

Now by the help of these principles all material things seem to have been composed of the hard and solid particles mentioned above, variously associated in the first creation by the counsel of an intelligent agent. For it became him who created them to set them in order. And if he did so, it is unphilosophical to seek for any other origin of the world or to pretend that it might arise out of a chaos by the mere laws of nature, though being once formed it may continue by those laws for many ages. For while comets move in very eccentric orbs in all manner of positions, blind fate could never make all the planets move one and the same way in concentric orbs, some inconsiderable irregularities excepted which may have arisen from the mutual actions of comets and planets upon one another and which will be apt to increase until this system needs a reformation. Such a wonderful uniformity in the planetary system must be allowed the effect of choice. And so must the uniformity in the bodies of animals, they having generally a right and a left side shaped similarly, and on either side of their bodies two legs behind and either two arms or two legs or two wings before upon their shoulders, and between their shoulders a neck running down into a backbone and a head upon it, and in the head two ears, two eyes, a nose, a mouth, and a tongue, similarly situated. Also the first contrivance of those very artificial parts of animals, the eyes, ears, brain, muscles, heart, lungs, midriff, glands, larynx, hands, wings, swimming bladders, natural spectacles, and other organs of sense and motion, and the instinct of brutes and insects can be the effect of nothing else than the wisdom and skill of a powerful ever-living agent, who, being in all places, is more able, by his will, to move the bodies within his boundless uniform sensorium and thereby to form and reform the parts of the universe than our spirit, which is, in us, the image of God is able by our will to move the parts of our own bodies. <And yet we are not to consider the world as the body of God, or the several parts of it as the parts of God. He is a uniform being, void of organs, members, or parts, and they are his creatures subordinate to him and subservient to his will; and he is no more the soul of them than the soul of man is the soul of the species of things carried through the organs of sense into the place of its sensation, where it perceives them by means of its immediate presence, without the intervention of any third thing. The organs of sense are not for enabling the soul to perceive the species of things in its sensorium but only for conveying them there; and God has no need of such organs, he being everywhere present to the things themselves.> And since space is divisible *in infinitum* and matter is not necessarily in all places, it may be also allowed that God is able to create particles of matter of several sizes and figures and in several proportions to space and perhaps of different densities and forces, and thereby to vary the laws of nature and make worlds of several sorts in several parts of the universe. At least, I see no contradiction in all this.

As in mathematics, so in natural philosophy, the investigation of difficult things by the method of analysis ought ever to precede the method of composition. This analysis consists in making experiments and observations and in drawing general conclusions from them by induction and in admitting of no objections against the conclusions but such as are taken from experiments or other certain truths. For hypotheses are not to be regarded in experimental philosophy. And although the arguing from experiments and observations by induction is no demonstration of general conclusions, yet it is the best way of arguing which the nature of things admits of, and may be looked upon as so much the stronger by how much the induction is more general. And if no exception occurs from phenomena, the conclusion may be pronounced generally. But if at any time afterwards any exception shall occur from experiments, it may then begin to be pronounced with such exceptions as occur. By this way of analysis we may proceed from compounds to ingredients and from motions to the forces producing them and in general from effects to their causes and from particular causes to more general ones, until the argument ends in the most general. This is the method of analysis; and the synthesis consists in assuming the causes discovered and established as principles, and by them explaining the phenomena proceeding from them and proving the explanations.

In the two first books of these *Optics* I proceeded by this analysis to discover and prove the original differences of the rays of light in respect of refrangibility, reflexibility, and color, and their alternate fits of easy reflection and easy transmission, and the properties of bodies, both opaque and pellucid, on which their reflections and colors depend. And these discoveries being proved may be assumed in the method of composition for explaining the phenomena arising from them; I gave an instance of this method in the end of the first book. In this third book I have only begun the analysis of what remains to be discovered about light and its effects on the frame of nature, hinting several things about it and leaving the hints to be examined and improved by the further experiments and observations of such as are inquisitive. And if natural philosophy in all its parts, by pursuing this method, shall at length be perfected, the bounds of moral philosophy will be also enlarged. For so far as we can know by natural philosophy what is the First Cause, what power he has over us, and what benefits we receive from him, so far our duty toward him as well as that toward one another will appear to us by the light of nature. And no doubt, if the worship of false gods had not blinded the heathen, their moral philosophy would have gone further than to the four cardinal virtues; and instead of teaching the transmigration of souls, and to worship the sun and moon and dead heroes, they would have taught us to worship our true Author and Benefactor, as their ancestors did under the government of Noah and his sons before they corrupted themselves.

# G. W. Leibniz, From the Letters to Clarke (1715–16)[1]

## I. Leibniz's First Paper, Being an Extract of a Letter (November 1715)

1. Natural religion itself seems to decay [in England] very much. Many will have human souls to be material; others make God himself a corporeal being.

2. Mr. Locke and his followers are uncertain, at least, whether the soul is not material and naturally perishable.

3. Sir Isaac Newton says that space is an organ which God makes use of to perceive things by. But if God stands in need of an organ to perceive things by, it will follow that they do not depend altogether on him, nor were produced by him.

4. Sir Isaac Newton and his followers also have a very odd opinion concerning the work of God. According to them, God Almighty needs to wind up his watch from time to time;[2] otherwise it would cease to move. He had not, it seems, sufficient foresight to make it a perpetual motion. No, the machine of God's making is so imperfect, according to these gentlemen, that he is obliged to clean it now and then by an extraordinary concourse, and even to mend it, as a clockmaker mends his work, who must consequently be so much the more unskillful a workman as he is more often obliged to mend his work and to set it right. According to my opinion, the same force and vigor remains always in the world and only passes from one part of matter to another agreeably to the laws of nature and the beautiful pre-established order. And I hold that when God works miracles, he

1. Translated from the French by Samuel Clarke in *A Collection of Papers which passed between the late learned Mr. Leibnitz and Dr. Clarke in the years 1715 and 1716 relating to the Principles of Natural Philosophy and Religion* (London, 1717), modified. Leibniz's first four papers are given in their entirety. Samuel Clarke was a philosopher and theologian, a friend and follower of Newton. In 1697 he translated Jacques Rohault's Cartesian physics textbook, adding to it extensive annotations that "corrected" Descartes, often by incorporating Newtonian principles. It is clear that Newton collaborated with Clarke, in his replies to Leibniz's letters, and contributed some of the arguments (there is a manuscript in Newton's hand that found its way into one of Clarke's letters). However, given that some of the arguments are to be found in Clarke's previous and contemporaneous work, one would have to conclude that much of the letters are by Clarke himself.

2. Leibniz here calls attention to a passage in Newton's *Optics*, Query 31: "For while comets move in very eccentric orbs in all manner of position, blind fate could never make all planets move one and the same way in concentric orbs, some inconsiderable irregularities excepted which may have arisen from the mutual actions of comets and planets upon one another and which will be apt to increase, until this system needs a reformation."

does not do it in order to supply the wants of nature, but those of grace. Whoever thinks otherwise must necessarily have a very mean notion of the wisdom and power of God.

## II. Leibniz's Second Letter

1. It is rightly observed in the paper delivered to the Princess of Wales, which Her Royal Highness has been pleased to communicate to me, that next to corruption of manners, the principles of the materialists do very much contribute to keep up impiety. But I believe that one has no reason to add that the mathematical principles of philosophy are opposite to those of the materialists. On the contrary, they are the same, only with this difference—that the materialists, in imitation of Democritus, Epicurus, and Hobbes, confine themselves altogether to mathematical principles and admit only bodies, whereas the Christian mathematicians admit also immaterial substances. Wherefore, not mathematical principles (according to the usual sense of that word) but *metaphysical principles* ought to be opposed to those of the materialists. Pythagoras, Plato, and Aristotle in some measure had a knowledge of these principles, but I claim to have established them demonstratively in my *Theodicy*, though I have done it in a popular manner. The great foundation of mathematics is the *principle of contradiction or identity*, that is, that a proposition cannot be true and false at the same time, and that therefore A is A and cannot be not A. This single principle is sufficient to demonstrate every part of arithmetic and geometry, that is, all mathematical principles. But in order to proceed from mathematics to natural philosophy, another principle is required, as I have observed in my *Theodicy*; I mean the *principle of sufficient reason*, namely, that nothing happens without a reason why it should be so rather than otherwise. And therefore Archimedes, being desirous to proceed from mathematics to natural philosophy, in his book *De aequilibro*, was obliged to make use of a particular case of the great principle of sufficient reason. He takes it for granted that if there is a balance in which everything is alike on both sides, and if equal weights are hung on the two ends of that balance, the whole will be at rest. That is because no

reason can be given why one side should weigh down rather than the other. Now by that single principle, namely, that there ought to be a sufficient reason why things should be so and not otherwise, one may demonstrate the being of God and all the other parts of metaphysics or natural theology and even, in some measure, those principles of natural philosophy that are independent of mathematics; I mean the dynamic principles or the principles of force.

2. The author proceeds and says that according to the *mathematical principles*, that is, according to Sir Isaac Newton's philosophy (for *mathematical principles* determine nothing in the present case), matter is the most inconsiderable part of the universe. The reason is because he admits empty space besides matter and because, according to his notions, matter fills up a very small part of space. But Democritus and Epicurus maintained the same thing; they differed from Sir Isaac Newton only as to the quantity of matter, and perhaps they believed there was more matter in the world than Sir Isaac Newton will allow; wherein I think their opinion ought to be preferred, for the more matter there is, the more God has occasion to exercise his wisdom and power. This is one reason, among others, why I maintain that there is no void at all.

3. I find, in express words in the Appendix to Sir Isaac Newton's *Optics*, that space is the sensorium of God. But the word "sensorium" has always signified the organ of sensation. He and his friends may now, if they think fit, explain themselves quite otherwise; I shall not be against it.

4. The author supposes that the presence of the soul is sufficient to make it consciously perceive what passes in the brain. But this is the very thing which Father Malebranche and all the Cartesians deny; and they rightly deny it. More is required besides bare presence to enable one thing to represent what passes in another. Some communication that may be explained, some sort of influence, or a common source [*cause*] is requisite for this purpose. Space, according to Sir Isaac Newton, is intimately present to the body contained in it and commensurate with it. Does it follow from thence that space perceives consciously what passes in a body and remembers it when that

body is gone away? Besides, the soul being indivisible, its immediate presence, which may be imagined in the body, would only be in one point. How then could it perceive consciously what happens out of that point? I claim to be the first who has shown how the soul perceives consciously what passes in the body.

5. The reason why God perceives everything consciously is not his bare presence, but also his operation. It is because he preserves things by an action which continually produces whatever is good and perfect in them. But the soul having no immediate influence over the body, nor the body over the soul, their mutual correspondence cannot be explained by their being present to each other.

6. The true and principal reason why we commend a machine is rather taken from the effects of the machine than from its cause. We don't inquire so much about the power of the artist as we do about his skill in his workmanship. And therefore, the reason alleged by the author for extolling God's machine, that he made it entirely, without borrowing any materials from outside—that reason, I say, is not sufficient. It is a mere shift the author has been forced to have recourse to, and the reason why God exceeds any other artisan is not only because he makes the whole, whereas all other artisans must have matter to work upon. This excellency in God would only be on the account of power. But God's excellency also arises from another cause, namely, wisdom, whereby his machine lasts longer and moves more regularly than those of any other artisan whatsoever. He who buys a watch does not mind whether the workman made every part of it himself, or whether he got the several parts made by others and only put them together—provided the watch goes right. And if the workman had received from God even the gift of creating the matter of the wheels, yet the buyer of the watch would not be satisfied unless the workman had also received the gift of putting them together well. In like manner, he who will be pleased with God's work cannot be so without some other reason than that which the author has here alleged.

7. Thus the skill of God must not be inferior to that of a workman; no, it must go infinitely beyond it. The bare production of everything would indeed

show the power of God, but it would not sufficiently show his wisdom. They who maintain the contrary will fall exactly into the error of the materialists and of Spinoza, from whom they profess to differ. They would, in such case, acknowledge power but not sufficient wisdom in the principle or cause of things.

8. I do not say the material world is a machine or watch that goes without God's interposition, and I have sufficiently insisted that creatures need his continual influence. But I maintain it to be a watch that goes without needing to be mended by him; otherwise we must say that God revises himself. No, God has foreseen everything. He has provided a remedy for everything beforehand. There is in his works a harmony, a beauty, already pre-established.

9. This opinion does not exclude God's providence or his government of the world; on the contrary, it makes it perfect. A true providence of God requires a perfect foresight. But then it requires, moreover, not only that he should have foreseen everything but also that he should have provided for everything beforehand with proper remedies; otherwise he must either want wisdom to foresee things or power to provide for them. He will be like the God of the Socinians who lives only from day to day, as Mr. Jurieu says. Indeed, God, according to the Socinians, does not so much as foresee inconveniences, whereas the gentlemen I am arguing with, who oblige him to mend his work, say only that he does not provide against them.[3] But this seems to me to still be a very great imperfection. According to this doctrine, God must either want power or good will.

10. I don't think I can be rightly blamed for saying that God is *intelligentia supramundana*. Will they say that he is *intelligentia mundana*, that is, the soul of the world? I hope not. However, they will do well to take care not to fall into that notion unawares.

11. The comparison of a king under whose reign everything should go on without his interposition

---

3. This is a reference to Pierre Jurieu's *Le tableau du Socinianisme* (The Hague, 1960). Socinianism was a Protestant sect, a forerunner of Unitarianism, founded by Laelius and Faustus Socinius; one of the Socinian doctrines was that God's foreknowledge was limited to what was necessary and did not apply to the possible.

is by no means to the present purpose, since God continually preserves everything and nothing can subsist without him. His kingdom therefore is not a nominal one. It is just as if one should say that a king who should originally have taken care to have his subjects so well raised, and should, by his care in providing for their subsistence, preserve them so well in their fitness for their several stations and in their good affection toward him, as that he should have no occasion ever to be amending anything among them, would be only a nominal king.

12. To conclude. If God is obliged to mend the course of nature from time to time, it must either be done supernaturally or naturally. If it is done supernaturally, we must have recourse to miracles in order to explain natural things, which is reducing a hypothesis *ad absurdum*, for everything may easily be accounted for by miracles. But if it is done naturally, then God will not be *intelligentia supramundana*; he will be comprehended under the nature of things; that is, he will be the soul of the world.

## III. Leibniz's Third Letter

1. According to the usual way of speaking, *mathematical principles* concern only pure mathematics, namely, numbers, figures, arithmetic, geometry. But *metaphysical principles* concern more general notions, such as cause and effect.

2. The author grants me this important principle, that nothing happens without a sufficient reason why it should be so rather than otherwise. But he grants it only in words and in reality denies it. This shows that he does not fully perceive the strength of it. And therefore, he makes use of an instance, which exactly falls in with one of my demonstrations against real absolute space, the idol of some modern Englishmen. I call it an idol, not in a theological sense, but in a philosophical one, as Chancellor Bacon says that there are idols of the tribe and idols of the cave.[4]

3. These gentlemen maintain, therefore, that space is a real absolute being. But this involves them in great difficulties, for it appears that such a being

must be eternal and infinite. Hence some have believed it to be God himself, or one of his attributes, his immensity. But since space consists of parts, it is not a thing which can belong to God.

4. As for my own opinion, I have said more than once that I hold space to be something merely relative, as time is, that I hold it to be an order of coexistences, as time is an order of successions. For space denotes, in terms of possibility, an order of things which exist at the same time, considered as existing together, without entering into their particular manners of existing. And when many things are seen together, one perceives this order of things among themselves.

5. I have many demonstrations to confute the fancy of those who take space to be a substance, or, at least, an absolute being. But I shall only use, at present, one demonstration, which the author here gives me occasion to insist upon. I say, then, that if space were an absolute being, something would happen for which it would be impossible that there should be a sufficient reason—which is against my axiom. And I can prove it thus. Space is something absolutely uniform, and without the things placed in it, one point of space absolutely does not differ in anything from another point of space. Now, from hence it follows (supposing space to be something in itself, besides the order of bodies among themselves) that it is impossible there should be a reason why God, preserving the same situations of bodies among themselves, should have placed them in space after one certain particular manner and not otherwise— why everything was not placed the quite contrary way, for instance, by changing east into west. But if space is nothing else but this order or relation, and is nothing at all without bodies but the possibility of placing them, then those two states, the one such as it is now, the other supposed to be the quite contrary way, would not at all differ from one another. Their difference therefore is only to be found in our chimerical supposition of the reality of space in itself. But in truth, the one would exactly be the same thing as the other, they being absolutely indiscernible, and consequently there is no room to inquire after a reason for the preference of the one to the other.

---

4. See Bacon, *New Organon*, Book I, aphorisms 38–42.

6. The case is the same with respect to time. Supposing anyone should ask why God did not create everything a year sooner, and the same person should infer from this that God has done something concerning which it is not possible that there should be a reason why he did it so and not otherwise; the answer is that his inference would be right if time was anything distinct from things existing in time. For it would be impossible that there should be any reason why things should be applied to such particular instants rather than to others, their succession continuing the same. But then the same argument proves that instants, considered without the things, are nothing at all and that they consist only in the successive order of things; this order remaining the same, one of the two states, namely, that of a supposed anticipation, would not at all differ, nor could be discerned from the other which now is.

7. It appears from what I have said that my axiom has not been well understood and that the author denies it, though he seems to grant it. It is true, says he, that there is nothing without a sufficient reason why it is, and why it is thus rather than otherwise, but he adds that this sufficient reason is often the simple or mere will of God—as when it is asked why matter was not placed otherwise in space, the same situations of bodies among themselves being preserved. But this is plainly to maintain that God wills something without any sufficient reason for his will, against the axiom or the general rule of whatever happens. This is falling back into the loose indifference which I have amply refuted and showed to be absolutely chimerical, even in creatures, and contrary to the wisdom of God, as if he could operate without acting by reason.

8. The author objects against me that, if we don't admit this simple and mere will, we take away from God the power of choosing and bring in a fatality. But quite the contrary is true. I maintain that God has the power of choosing, since I ground that power upon the reason of a choice agreeable to his wisdom. And it is not this fatality (which is only the wisest order of providence) but a blind fatality or necessity void of all wisdom and choice which we ought to avoid.

9. I had observed that by lessening the quantity of matter, the quantity of objects upon which God may exercise his goodness will be lessened. The author answers that instead of matter there are other things in the void on which God exercises his goodness. Be it so, though I don't grant it, for I hold that every created substance is attended with matter. However, let it be so. I answer that more matter was consistent with those same things, and consequently the said objects will still be lessened. The instance of a greater number of men or animals is not to the purpose, for they would fill up place in exclusion of other things.

10. It will be difficult to make me believe that sensorium does not, in its usual meaning, signify an organ of sensation. See the words of Rudolphus Goclenius in his *Dictionarium philosophicum* under *sensiterium*. "Barbarum Scholasticorum," says he, "qui interdum sunt simae Graecorum. Hi dicunt *aitheterion*. Ex quo illi fecerunt *sensiterium* pro sensorio, id est, organo sensationis."[5]

11. The mere presence of a substance, even an animated one, is not sufficient for perception. A blind man, and even someone distracted, does not see. The author must explain how the soul perceives what is outside itself.

12. God is not present to things by situation but by essence; his presence is manifest by his immediate operation. The presence of the soul is quite of another nature. To say that it is diffused all over the body is to make it extended and divisible. To say it is, the whole of it, in every part of the body is to make it divisible of itself. To fix it to a point, to diffuse it all over many points, are only abusive expressions, idols of the tribe.[6]

13. If active force should diminish in the universe by the natural laws which God has established, so that

---

5. Rudolph Goclenius, *Lexicon Philosophicum* (Frankfurt, 1613). Goclenius was a standard reference work for 17th-century school philosophers, an alphabetical compendium of standard definitions and distinctions. The passage translates: "[Sensiterium is] a barbarism due to the scholastics, who sometimes aped the Greeks. The Greeks said 'aiheterion', from which the scholastics made up 'sensiterium', in place of 'sensorium', that is, the organ of sensation."

6. See Bacon, *New Organon*, Book I, aphorism 41.

there should be need for him to give a new impression in order to restore that force, like an artisan's mending the imperfections of his machine, the disorder would not only be with respect to us but also with respect to God himself. He might have prevented it and taken better measures to avoid such an inconvenience, and therefore, indeed, he has actually done it.

14. When I said that God has provided remedies beforehand against such disorders, I did not say that God suffers disorders to happen and then finds remedies for them, but that he has found a way beforehand to prevent any disorders happening.

15. The author strives in vain to criticize my expression that God is *intelligentia supramundana*. To say that God is above the world is not denying that he is in the world.

16. I never gave any occasion to doubt but that God's conservation is an actual preservation and continuation of the beings, powers, orders, dispositions, and motions [of all things], and I think I have perhaps explained it better than many others. But, says the author, this is all I contended for. To this I answer: [I am] your humble servant for that, Sir. Our dispute consists in many other things. The question is whether God does not act in the most regular and most perfect manner; whether his machine is liable to disorder, which he is obliged to mend by extraordinary means; whether the will of God can act without reason; whether space is an absolute being; also concerning the nature of miracles; and many such things, which make a wide difference between us.

17. Theologians will not grant the author's position against me, namely, that there is no difference, with respect to God, between natural and supernatural; and it will be still less approved by most philosophers. There is an infinite difference between these two things, but it plainly appears that it has not been duly considered. The supernatural exceeds all the powers of creatures. I shall give an instance which I have often made use of with good success. If God wanted to cause a body to move free in the aether round about a certain fixed center, without any other creature acting upon it, I say it could not be done without a miracle, since it cannot be explained by the nature of bodies. For a free body naturally recedes from a curve in the tangent. And therefore, I maintain that the attraction of bodies, properly so called, is a miraculous thing, since it cannot be explained by the nature of bodies.

## IV. Leibniz's Fourth Letter

1. In absolutely indifferent things there is [no foundation for] choice,[7] and consequently no election or will, since choice must be founded on some reason or principle.

2. A mere will without any motive is a fiction, not only contrary to God's perfection, but also chimerical and contradictory, inconsistent with the definition of the will, and sufficiently confuted in my *Theodicy*.

3. It is an indifferent thing to place three bodies, equal and perfectly alike, in any order whatsoever, and consequently they will never be placed in any order by him who does nothing without wisdom. But then, he being the author of things, no such things will be produced by him at all, and consequently, there are no such things in nature.

4. There is no such thing as two individuals indiscernible from each other. An ingenious gentleman of my acquaintance, discoursing with me in the presence of Her Electoral Highness, the Princess Sophia, in the garden of Herrenhausen, thought he could find two leaves perfectly alike. The princess defied him to do it, and he ran all over the garden a long time to look for some; but it was to no purpose. Two drops of water or milk, viewed with a microscope, will appear distinguishable from each other. This is an argument against atoms, which are confuted, as well as the void, by the principles of true metaphysics.

5. Those great principles of sufficient reason and of the identity of indiscernibles change the state of metaphysics. That science becomes real and demonstrative by means of these principles, whereas before it did generally consist in empty words.

6. To suppose two things indiscernible is to suppose the same thing under two names. And therefore, the hypothesis that the universe could have

---

7. The bracketed remark is Clarke's addition.

had at first another position of time and place than that which it actually had, and yet that all the parts of the universe should have had the same situation among themselves as that which they actually had—such a supposition, I say, is an impossible fiction.

7. The same reason which shows that extramundane space is imaginary proves that all empty space is an imaginary thing, for they differ only as greater and less.

8. If space is a property or attribute, it must be the property of some substance. But of what substance will that bounded empty space be an affection or property, which the persons I am arguing with suppose to be between two bodies?

9. If infinite space is immensity, finite space will be the opposite to immensity; that is, it will be mensurability, or limited extension. Now extension must be the affection of something extended. But if that space is empty, it will be an attribute without a subject, an extension without anything extended. Wherefore, by making space a property, the author falls in with my opinion, which makes it an order of things and not anything absolute.

10. If space is an absolute reality, far from being a property or an accident opposed to substance, it will have a greater reality than substances themselves. God cannot destroy it, nor even change it in any respect. It will be not only immense in the whole but also immutable and eternal in every part. There will be an infinite number of eternal things besides God.

11. To say that infinite space has no parts is to say that it is not composed of finite spaces, and that infinite space might subsist though all finite space should be reduced to nothing. It would be as if one should say, in accordance with the Cartesian supposition of a material extended unlimited world, that such a world might subsist, though all the bodies of which it consists should be reduced to nothing.

12. The author attributes parts to space, on page 19 of the third edition of his *Defense of the Argument against Mr. Dodwell*, and makes them inseparable one from another. But on page 30 of his *Second Defense* he says they are parts improperly so called—which may be understood in a good sense.

13. To say that God can cause the whole universe to move forward in a right line or in any other line, without otherwise making any alteration in it, is another chimerical supposition. For two states indiscernible from each other are the same state, and consequently, it is a change without any change. Besides, there is neither rhyme nor reason in it. But God does nothing without reason, and it is impossible that there should be any here. Besides, it would be *agendo nihil agere*, as I have just now said, because of the indiscernibility.

14. These are idols of the tribe, mere chimeras, and superficial imaginations. All this is only grounded upon the supposition that imaginary space is real.[8]

15. It is a like fiction (that is) an impossible one, to suppose that God might have created the world some millions of years sooner. They who run into such kind of fictions can give no answer to those who would argue for the eternity of the world. For since God does nothing without reason, and no reason can be given why he did not create the world sooner, it will follow either that he has created nothing at all, or that he created the world before any assignable time, which is to say that the world is eternal. But when once it has been shown that the beginning, whenever it was, is always the same thing, the question why it was not otherwise becomes needless and insignificant.

16. If space and time were anything absolute, that is, if they were anything else besides certain orders of things, then indeed my assertion would be a contradiction. But since it is not so, the hypothesis [that space and time are anything absolute][9] is contradictory; that is, it is an impossible fiction.

17. And the case is the same as in geometry, where by the very supposition that a figure is greater than it really is, we sometimes prove that it is not greater. This indeed is a contradiction, but it lies in the hypothesis, which appears to be false for that very reason.

18. Space being uniform, there can neither be any external nor internal reason by which to distinguish its parts and to make any choice among them. For any external reason to discern between them can only be grounded upon some internal one. Otherwise

---

8. See Bacon, *New Organon*, Book I, aphorism 41.
9. The bracketed remark is Clarke's addition.

we should discern what is indiscernible or choose without discerning. A will without reason would be the chance of the Epicureans. A God who should act by such a will would be a God only in name. The cause of these errors proceeds from want of care to avoid what derogates from the divine perfections.

19. When two incompatible things are equally good, and neither in themselves, nor by their combination with other things, has the one any advantage over the other, God will produce neither of them.

20. God is never determined by external things but always by what is in himself, that is, by his knowledge, before anything exists outside himself.

21. There is no possible reason that can limit the quantity of matter, and therefore, such limitation can have no place.

22. And supposing this arbitrary limitation of the quantity of matter, something might always be added to it without derogating from the perfection of the things which do already exist, and consequently, something must always be added, in order to act according to the principle of the perfection of the divine operations.

23. And therefore, it cannot be said that the present quantity of matter is the fittest for the present constitution of things. And even supposing it is, it would follow that this present constitution of things would not be the fittest absolutely, if it hinders God from using more matter. It is therefore better to choose another constitution of things, capable of something more.

24. I should be glad to see a passage of any philosopher who takes *sensorium* in any other sense than Goclenius does.

25. If Scapula says that sensorium is the place in which the understanding resides, he means by it the organ of internal sensation. And therefore, he does not differ from Goclenius.[10]

26. *Sensorium* has always signified the organ of sensation. The pineal gland would be, according to Descartes, the *sensorium* in the above-mentioned sense of Scapula.

---

10. Johann Scapula, *Lexicon Graeco-Latinum* (Basel, 1580). Clarke had attempted to counter Goclenius with Scapula.

27. There is hardly any less appropriate expression on this subject than that which makes God have a *sensorium*. It seems to make God the soul of the world. And it will be a hard matter to put a justifiable sense upon this word, according to the use Sir Isaac Newton makes of it.

28. Though the question is about the sense put upon that word by Sir Isaac Newton, and not by Goclenius, yet I am not to blame for quoting the *Philosophical Dictionary* of that author, because the design of dictionaries is to show the use of words.

29. God perceives things in himself. Space is the place of things and not the place of God's ideas, unless we look upon space as something that makes the union between God and things in imitation of the imagined union between the soul and the body, which would still make God the soul of the world.

30. And indeed, the author is much in the wrong when he compares God's knowledge and operation with the knowledge and operation of souls. The soul knows things because God has put into it a principle representative of things without. But God knows things because he continually produces them.

31. The soul does not act upon things, according to my opinion, any otherwise than because the body adapts itself to the desires of the soul, by virtue of the harmony which God has pre-established between them.

32. But they who fancy that the soul can give a new force to the body, and that God does the same in the world to mend the imperfections of his machine, make God too much like the soul by ascribing too much to the soul and too little to God.

33. For none but God can give a new force to nature, and he does it only supernaturally. If there was need for him to do it in the natural course of things, he would have made a very imperfect work. At that rate, he would be, with respect to the world, what the soul, in the vulgar notion, is with respect to the body.

34. Those who undertake to defend the vulgar opinion concerning the soul's influence over the body by instancing God's operating on things external, still make God too much like the soul of the world. The author's affecting to find fault with the words

*intelligentia supramundana* seems also to incline that way.

35. The images with which the soul is immediately affected are within itself, but they correspond to those of the body. The presence of the soul is imperfect and can only be explained by that correspondence. But the presence of God is perfect and manifested by his operation.

36. The author wrongly supposes against me that the presence of the soul is connected with its influence over the body, for he knows I reject that influence.

37. The soul's being diffused through the brain is no less inexplicable than its being diffused through the whole body. The difference is only in more and less.

38. They who fancy that active forces decrease of themselves in the world do not well understand the principal laws of nature and the beauty of the works of God.

39. How will they be able to prove that this defect is a consequence of the dependence of things?

40. The imperfection of our machines, which is the reason why they need to be mended, proceeds from this very thing, that they do not sufficiently depend upon the workman. And therefore, the dependence of nature upon God, far from being the cause of such an imperfection, is rather the reason why there is no such imperfection in nature, because nature is so dependent upon an artist too perfect to make a work that needs to be mended. It is true that every particular machine of nature is in some measure liable to be disordered, but not the entire universe, which cannot diminish in perfection.

41. The author contends that space does not depend upon the situation of bodies. I answer: It is true, it does not depend upon such or such a situation of bodies, but it is that order which renders bodies capable of being situated, and by which they have a situation among themselves when they exist together, as time is that order with respect to their successive position. But if there were no creatures, space and time would only be in the ideas of God.

42. The author seems to acknowledge here that his notion of a miracle is not the same as that which theologians and philosophers usually have. It is therefore sufficient for my purpose that my adversaries are obliged to have recourse to what is commonly called a miracle, which one attempts to avoid in philosophy.

43. I am afraid the author, by altering the sense commonly put upon the word "miracle," will fall into an inconvenient opinion. The nature of a miracle does not at all consist in usualness or unusualness, for then monsters would be miracles.

44. There are miracles of an inferior sort which an angel can work. He can, for instance, make a man walk upon the water without sinking. But there are miracles which none but God can work, they exceeding all natural powers. Of this kind are creating and annihilating.

45. It is also a supernatural thing that bodies should attract one another at a distance without any intermediate means, and that a body should move around without receding in the tangent, though nothing hinders it from so receding. For these effects cannot be explained by the nature of things.

46. Why should it be impossible to explain the motion of animals by natural forces? Though, indeed, the beginning of animals is no less inexplicable by natural forces than the beginning of the world.

P.S. All those who maintain a vacuum are more influenced by imagination than by reason. When I was a young man, I also gave in to the notion of the void and atoms, but reason brought me into the right way. It was a pleasing imagination. Men carry their inquiries no further than those two things: They (as it were) nail down their thoughts to them; they fancy they have found out the first elements of things, a *non plus ultra*. We would have nature to go no further, and to be finite as our minds are; but this is being ignorant of the greatness and majesty of the author of things. The least corpuscle is actually subdivided *in infinitum* and contains a world of other creatures which would be wanting in the universe if that corpuscle were an atom, that is, a body of one entire piece without subdivision. In like manner, to admit the void in nature is ascribing to God a very imperfect work; it is violating the grand principle of the necessity of a sufficient reason, which many have talked of without understanding its true meaning; as I have lately shown in proving, by that principle, that space is only an order of things, as time also is, and not at all an absolute being. To omit many other arguments against the void and atoms, I shall here mention those which I ground upon God's perfection and upon the necessity of a sufficient reason. I lay it down as a principle that every perfection which God could impart to things, without derogating from their other perfections, has actually been imparted to them. Now let us fancy a space wholly empty. God could have placed some matter in it without derogating, in any respect, from all other things; therefore, he has actually placed some matter in that space; therefore, there is no space wholly empty; therefore, all is full. The same argument proves that there is no corpuscle but what is subdivided. I shall add another argument grounded upon the necessity of a sufficient reason. It is impossible there should be any principle to determine what proportion of matter there ought to be, out of all the possible degrees from a plenum to a void, or from a void to a plenum. Perhaps it will be said that the one should be equal to the other, but, because matter is more perfect than the void, reason requires that a geometrical proportion should be observed and that there should be as much more matter than void, as the former deserves to be preferred. But then, there must be no void at all, for the perfection of matter is to that of the void as something to nothing. And the case is the same with atoms: What reason can anyone assign for confining nature in the progression of subdivision? These are fictions, merely arbitrary and unworthy of true philosophy. The reasons alleged for the void are mere sophisms.

# Anton Wilhelm Amo, *On the Apathy of the Human Mind,* Chapter 2 (1734)[1]

Anton Wilhelm Amo (ca. 1703–ca. 1759) was born in what is now Ghana. He was taken to Amsterdam when very young and given to Anton Ulrich, Duke of Brunswick-Wolfenbüttel. The duke treated him as a member of his family: he was educated by private tutors and then at the Wolfenbüttel Academy and University of Helmstedt. Amo studied law at the University of Halle and wrote a thesis on the Rights of Moors in Europe (1729; the thesis is lost). He then moved to the University of Wittenberg, studying philosophy, medicine, politics, and receiving a doctorate in philosophy in 1734; his dissertation On the Apathy of the Human Mind or the Absence of Sensation and the Faculty of Sensing in the Human Mind and Their Presence in Our Organic and Living Body argued against Cartesian interactive dualism (without endorsing either Leibnizian pre-established harmony or Malebranchian occasionalism). Amo returned to the University of Halle to lecture in philosophy. He produced a second work, Treatise on the Art of Philosophizing Soberly and Accurately, in 1738 from his university lectures. In 1740 Amo took up a post in philosophy at the University of Jena, but no longer feeling welcome in Germany, he returned to Ghana circa 1747. Very little is known about the last period of his life.

With these things explained, we can finally ask what we understand by the thesis itself, that is, the apathy of the human mind. It is, of course, the absence of the faculty of sensing and sensation of immediate things in the human mind. [ . . . ]

The state of the controversy. Human beings sense material things not with the mind but through a living and organic body. These things are stated and defended against Descartes, and against his statements in *Letters* I, Letter 29, where he says: "For there are two things in the human soul on which all the knowledge we can have of its nature depends: one, that it thinks, the other, that, being united to a body, it can *act* and *suffer* with the body."[2]

---

1. Translated from the Latin by Roger Ariew, from Anton Wilhelm Amo, *Dissertatio Inauguralis de Humanae Mentis Apatheia seu Sensionis ac Facultatis Sentiendi in Mente Humana Absentia et earum in Corpore nostro Organico ac Vivo Praesentia* (Wittenberg, 1734).

2. *René Descartes to Princess Elisabeth,* 21 May 1643; Amo's emphasis. Amo's citation, "*Letters* I, Letter 29," refers to the numbering of letters in the French edition of *Lettres de M*ʳ *Descartes* by Claude Clerselier, vol. 1 (Paris, 1657), p. 90; this numbering is kept in subsequent editions, such as the Latin edition, *Epistolae,* vol. 1 (Frankfurt, 1682). Descartes' text is on p. 52 in the Frankfurt edition.

We caution and dissent against these words: we concede that the mind acts by means of the body through a mutual union. But we deny that it suffers with the body.

*Note.* To *suffer* and to *sense* are synonymous in living things; in things deprived of life, in truth, to sense is to admit changes in oneself with respect to quantity and quality coming from outside, that is, to be modified and determined from outside.

*Remark 1.* But Descartes manifestly contradicts himself, *Letters* I, Letter 99, when, examining the preceding program, he puts the nature of the soul in the faculty of thinking alone, although thinking is an action of the mind, not a passion.[3]

*Against Sennert,*[4] in his *Epitome scientiae naturalis* 8, chap. 1, on the rational soul: "and although the human soul is furnished with all of the faculties we previously attributed to the vegetative and sensitive soul, yet it has in addition two proper peculiar faculties," etc. See also Sennert 7, chap. 1, p. 562, on the sensitive soul: "For to sense is the work of the soul."

*Remark 2.* But he establishes the contrary of his own view, *ibid.* p. 563, when he writes: "to receive the sensible species is for an organ; to judge what is received is for the soul." To receive the sensible species is to sense, and this suits an organ, and consequently a body, for organs do not suit the mind but the body. Sennert himself distinguishes between sensing and judging, in that he attributes the former to the organs, and the latter to the mind.

*This also holds against Jean Le Clerc,*[5] *Physica IV*, on plants and animals, chap. 10, on the senses and motions of animals, sec. 2.

*Remark 3.* But he contradicts himself, *ibid.* §3, where he says that three things are to be distinguished: (1) the action of the objects on the organs, (2) the passion of the organ, and (3) he says, "when struck by the organ which is moved, the mind *senses* that its body was affected." For if the mind were to sense, he should have said this: "and the mind senses that it itself was affected." Now, if the mind senses that its body was affected, it senses or, better, it understands that it itself was not affected. But he confuses the act of understanding and the task of sensing: it is the same as if he said "and the mind understands its body is affected."

Likewise against: Georg Daniel Coschwitz,[6] in *Organismus et mechanismus in homine vivo obvius et stabilitus*, sec. 1, chap. 8, thesis 3, and against many others.

These agree with us: Aristotle *On Generation and Corruption* 2, chap. 9, p. 49, "it is characteristic of matter to suffer action, i.e., to be moved," etc.; Hermann Friedrich Teichmeyer,[7] in *Elementa philosophiae naturalis experimentalis*, chap. 3, on physical principles, *ibid.*, p. 18, with the words, "by sense we understand," etc.; and Johann Christoph Sturm,[8] in *Physica electiva sive hypothetica* 1, that

---

3. The "preceding program" is a reference to a 1647 broadsheet by Henricus Regius, the one-time Cartesian follower turned critic; Amo's citation, "*Letters* I, Letter 99," is to Descartes' reply (usually called *Notes against a Program*), treated as a letter in Clerselier's edition, vol. 1, pp. 435–62; Amo's paraphrase is initially to p. 435. This numbering is also maintained in the Frankfurt Latin edition, with Descartes' text being on p. 285.

4. Daniel Sennert (1572–1637) was a professor of medicine at the University of Wittenberg. He wrote on medicine and chemistry. The reference is to one of his earliest works on natural philosophy, initially published in Wittenberg in 1618 (later translated into English [London, 1661]).

5. Jean le Clerc (1657–1736) was a Protestant theologian and biblical scholar; he plays an important role in the dissemination of John Locke's works in the journal he edited (*Bibliothèque universelle*); Amo's reference is to his *Physics*, published in his collected works, *Opera philosophica* (Leipzig, 1710).

6. Georg Daniel Coschwitz (1679–1729), German physician, pharmacist, and professor of medicine at Halle University. Amo's reference is to his most cited work, published in Leipzig in 1725.

7. Hermann Friedrich Teichmeyer (1685–1746) was a German physician and botanist, a professor of experimental natural philosophy, medicine, and botany at the University of Jena. Amo's reference is to a work published in Jena in 1717.

8. Johann Christoph Sturm (1635–1703) was a German philosopher. Amo's reference is to Sturm's most noted work, published in Nuremberg in 1697. In his work Sturm criticizes Leibniz, which prompted Leibniz to reply in a famous essay "On Nature Itself" (*De ipse natura*, 1698).

is, the General Part, sec. 1, chap. 2, in the fifth Epilogue. Also in *ibid.*, p. 232 and what follows.

## The Sole Division

Thesis 1: negative.

The human mind is not affected by sensible things.

*Explanation.* The thesis means the same as if you say: the human mind is not affected by sensible things, however much they are proximately present to the body in which it is; but the mind understands the sensations arising in the body, and it applies them in its operations when they are understood. (See [Edme Didier] *Essais de physique*, chap. 8, p. 107.)

Note. In considering man logically, *mind*, an *operation of the mind, idea*, and *immediate sensation* are not to be confused. Mind and its operations are immaterial; for as a substance is, so is the property of the substance. And yet the mind is immaterial (given what we said in chap. 1, div. 1, sec. 1, etc.), so also is its property. An idea is a composite entity; for it exists when the mind makes present to itself a sensation pre-existing in the body, which is a represented sensation. (For what an immediate sensation is, see chap. I, div. 2, sec. 1, with the associated notes.) [ . . . ]

Thesis 2. The faculty of sensing is not in the mind.

*Proof.* Whatever admits the circulation of blood admits the principle of life; whatever admits the latter, admits the faculty of sensing. But the body admits the circulation of blood and the principle of life. [ . . . ]

Thesis 3. Therefore sensation and the faculty of sensing belong to the body.

*Proof.* Sense and the faculty of sensing belong either to the mind or to the body. But they do not belong to the mind, as has already been shown at length, therefore they belong to the body (see the proofs of theses 1 and 2).

*Final note.* The purpose of writing this dissertation concerned the contrary statements (see chap. 2 for these) in the formation of the question so that we can avoid confusing those things the body and the mind admit in different respects. For whatever consists in the mere operation of the mind is to be attributed to the mind alone, but whatever presupposes sensation and the faculty of sensing, and involves a material concept, is to be attributed entirely to the body.

# 4. LOCKE'S *ESSAY* AND ASSOCIATED TEXTS

John Locke (1632–1704) was a moral and political philosopher, philosopher of education, economic theorist, theological polemicist, medical doctor, and public servant. He was educated at Westminster School, 1647–52, and at Christ Church, Oxford, 1652–58 (Bachelor of Arts, 1656, and Master of Arts, 1658). He remained at Christ Church as student and tutor, spending many years studying medicine (Bachelor of Medicine, 1675). In the later 1660s he worked closely with Thomas Sydenham, a friend of Boyle, who was influenced by Descartes and Gassendi. In 1667, he moved to London to live with Anthony Ashley Cooper (later the first Earl of Shaftesbury) serving him as physician, secretary, and political adviser. In the 1670s and early 1680s, Locke worked intermittently on philosophy, but primarily assisted Shaftesbury and his circle on political matters. Shaftesbury died in exile in Holland in 1683; Locke also went into exile later that year. There he completed the *Essay Concerning Human Understanding*, begun in 1671. Locke was able to return to England in 1689, and the *Essay* was published at the end of 1690. Though not uncontroversial (especially important was a dispute with Edward Stillingfleet that began in 1697 and extended through a number of exchanges), it was an immediate success, appearing in four editions during Locke's lifetime, sometimes with significant revisions; a fifth edition, in preparation at the time of Locke's death, appeared posthumously in 1706.[1]

In his "Epistle to the Reader," which he appended to the *Essay*, Locke remarked that the *Essay* "was not meant for those who had already mastered this subject and made a thorough acquaintance with their own understandings," but for his "own information and the satisfaction of a few friends." He then related the history of the *Essay*, how he came to set about writing it: "five or six friends meeting at my chamber, and discoursing on a subject very remote from this, found themselves quickly at a standstill by the difficulties that arose on every side. After we had puzzled ourselves for a while without coming any nearer a resolution of those doubts which perplexed us, it came into my thoughts that we took a wrong course, and that before we set ourselves upon inquiries of that nature, it was necessary to examine our

---

1. For more on Locke, see R. S. Woolhouse, *Locke* (Minneapolis: University of Minnesota Press, 1983); John W. Yolton, *Thinking Matter, Materialism in Eighteenth-Century Britain* (Minneapolis: University of Minnesota Press, 1983); Michael Ayers, *Locke*, 2 vols. (London: Routledge, 1991); or Vere Chappell, ed., *The Cambridge Companion to Locke* (Cambridge: Cambridge University Press, 1994).

own abilities and see what objects our understandings were, or were not, fitted to deal with. This I proposed to the company, who all readily assented." The inquiry that Locke set out to conduct, then, was the limited one announced in his introduction: "to inquire into the origin, certainty, and extent of human knowledge, together with the grounds and degrees of belief, opinion, and assent"; Locke is thus in earnest when he says that he will "not at present meddle with the physical consideration of the mind," or trouble himself "to examine in what its essence consists." Locke's modest goals are also made explicit when, in the "Epistle to the Reader," he refers to himself as an under-laborer: "The commonwealth of learning is not at this time without master builders, whose mighty designs in advancing the sciences will leave lasting monuments to the admiration of posterity, but every one must not hope to be a Boyle or a Sydenham; and in an age that produces such masters as the great Huygens and the incomparable Mr. Newton, with some others of that strain, it is ambition enough to be employed as an under-laborer in clearing the ground a little, and removing some of the rubbish that lies in the way to knowledge." That statement, however modest it might have sounded, was surely also a reference to Descartes, who had announced that he would reform all of knowledge, sweeping it all away and starting again on new foundations.

Despite these modest pretensions, in the course of the *Essay*'s four books Locke developed an epistemology that is fundamentally distinct from that of Descartes and his other modern predecessors. While he shares Descartes' focus on ideas, he rejects Descartes' (and others') innate ideas (Book I: Of Innate Notions) in favor of experience. In particular, he claims that all of our ideas must ultimately stem from sensation and reflection (Book II: Of Ideas), where sensation includes any idea that we might get through one (or more) of our five senses and reflection is simply the act by which we turn back on our mind's own operations in thinking and willing. All complex ideas (such as those of substance, mode, and relation) are formed by combining or comparing in different ways the simple ideas gained from these two sources. The main task of Book II thus

lies in showing how all meaningful ideas can be traced back to sensation and reflection. Along the way, Locke provides very insightful discussions of a number of fascinating topics such as the distinction between primary and secondary qualities (including a causal theory of perception), personal identity, free will, and causality (or power). What cannot be traced back to sensation and reflection is meaningless and likely stems from a misuse of language—Book III (Of Words). In this context Locke introduces a distinction between real and nominal essences, claiming that due to the limited nature of our access to the real or ultimate nature of substances, we must restrict ourselves to nominal essences, that is, what is directly connected with the name of an object. (For example, the nominal essence of gold is that of a yellow metal with a particular weight as opposed to its real essence which, according to Locke, is unknown to us.) In Book IV (Of Knowledge and Opinion) Locke is finally in a position to determine what we can and cannot know, given the epistemological resources we have at our disposal. After defining knowledge as the perception of agreement or disagreement between our ideas, Locke restricts knowledge proper to intuition and demonstration, though he admits "sensitive knowledge" in a restricted way since it does go "beyond bare probability." Accordingly, we can have the following very limited kinds of knowledge: identity or diversity, relations of ideas, coexistence of our ideas, and real existence (but it must be noted that the only thing besides our ideas that we can know the real existence of is God).

## Table of Contents (Selected):[2]

_____

2. Approximately one-third of the *Essay*.

# Robert Boyle, *Of the Excellency and Grounds of the Corpuscular or Mechanical Philosophy* (1674)[1]

*Robert Boyle (1627–91) was one of the foremost experimental natural philosophers of his day. He was educated at Eton and then given private lessons in Geneva. Around 1656 he settled in Oxford and became a leading member of a circle of experimentalists who later formed the Royal Society of London (in 1660), though he turned down the presidency of the Society in 1680 because of his religious scruples against oath-taking. He debated with Hobbes over the existence of the vacuum and the nature of the "spring" of the air, and with Spinoza over the interpretation of experiments. Boyle was a prolific author; among his many works are* New Experiments Physico-Mechanicall, Touching the Spring of the Air *(1660), in which he reports the results of his experiments with an air-pump that he constructed,* The Sceptical Chymist *(1661), in which he rejects Aristotelian and Paracelsian theories of matter, and* Certain Physiological Essays *(1661), in which he announces his mechanical and corpuscularian philosophy. This philosophy, of course, is the topic of the following essay.[2]*

By embracing the corpuscular or mechanical philosophy, I am far from supposing with the Epicureans that atoms accidentally meeting in an infinite vacuum were able, of themselves, to produce a world and all its phenomena; nor do I suppose, when God had put into the whole mass of matter an invariable quantity of motion, he needed do no more to make the universe, the material parts being able by their own unguided motions to throw themselves into a regular system. The philosophy I plead for reaches only to purely corporeal things; and distinguishing between the first origin of things and the subsequent course of nature teaches that God indeed gave motion to matter, but that in the beginning he so guided the various motion of the parts of it as to contrive them into the world he designed they should compose, and established those rules of motion and that order among corporeal things which we call the laws of nature. Thus the universe being once framed

1. From *The Philosophical Works of the Honourable Robert Boyle, Abridged* . . . ed. Peter Shaw (London, 1725), 3 vols., English, modified.

2. For more on Boyle, see Peter Alexander, *Ideas, Qualities and Corpuscles: Locke and Boyle on the External World* (Cambridge: Cambridge University Press, 1985), Steve Shapin and Simon Schaffer, *Leviathan and the Air Pump* (Princeton: Princeton University Press, 1985), or Rose-Mary Sargent, *The Diffident Naturalist: Robert Boyle and the Philosophy of Experiment* (Chicago: University of Chicago Press, 1995).

by God, and the laws of motion settled and all upheld by his perpetual concourse and general providence, the same philosophy teaches that the phenomena of the world are physically produced by the mechanical properties of the parts of matter, and that they operate upon one another according to mechanical laws. It is of this kind of corpuscular philosophy that I speak.

And the first thing that recommends it is the intelligibleness or clearness of its principles and explanations. Among the Peripatetics there are many intricate disputes about matter, privation, substantial forms, their eductions, etc. And the chemists are puzzled to give such definitions and accounts of their hypostatical principles, as are consistent with one another, and to some obvious phenomena; and much more dark and intricate are their doctrines about the Archeus, Astral Beings, and other odd notions,[3] which perhaps have in part occasioned the darkness and ambiguity of their expressions, that could not be very clear when the conceptions were obscure. And if the principles of the Aristotelians and chemists are thus obscure, it is not to be expected that the explications made by the help of such principles only should be intelligible. And, indeed, many of them are so general and slight, or otherwise so unsatisfactory, that, granting their principles, it is very hard to understand or admit their applications of them to particular phenomena. And, I think, even in some of the more ingenious and subtle of the Peripatetic discourses, the authors, upon their superficial and narrow theories, have acted more like painters than philosophers, and only shown their skill in making men fancy they see castles, cities, and other structures, that appear solid, magnificent, and extensive, when the whole piece is superficial, artificially made up of colors, and comprised within a frame. But, as to the corpuscular philosophy, men do so easily understand one another's meaning when they talk of local motion, rest, magnitude, shape, order, situation, and contexture of material substances; and these principles afford such clear accounts of those

things that are rightly deduced from them alone, that even such Peripatetics or chemists, as maintain other principles, acquiesce in the explications made by these, when they can be had, and seek no further; though, perhaps, the effect is so admirable as to make it pass for that of a hidden form or an occult quality. Those very Aristotelians who believe the celestial bodies to be moved by intelligences have no recourse to any peculiar agency of theirs to account for eclipses; and we laugh at those East Indians who, to this day, go out in multitudes with some instruments to relieve the distressed luminary, whose loss of light, they fancy, proceeds from some fainting fit, out of which it must be roused. For no intelligent man, whether chemist or Peripatetic, flies to his peculiar principles after he is informed that the moon is eclipsed by the interposition of the earth between her and it, and the sun by that of the moon between him and the earth. And when we see the image of a man cast into the air by a concave spherical mirror, though most men are amazed at it, and some suspect it to be no less than an effect of witchcraft, yet he who is skilled enough in catoptrics will, without consulting Aristotle or Paracelsus or flying to hypostatical principles or substantial forms, be satisfied that the phenomenon is produced by rays of light reflected and made to converge according to optical and mathematical laws.

I next observe that there cannot be fewer principles than the two grand ones of our philosophy, matter and motion; for matter alone, unless it is moved, is wholly inactive, and, while all the parts of a body continue in one state without motion, that body will not exercise any action or suffer any alteration, though it may, perhaps, modify the action of other bodies that move against it.

Nor can we conceive any principles more primary than matter and motion; for either both of them were immediately created by God, or, if matter is eternal, motion must either be produced by some immaterial supernatural agent or it must immediately flow, by way of emanation, from the nature of the matter it appertains to.

There cannot be any physical principles more simple than matter and motion, neither of them being resoluble into any other thing.

---

3. The "chemists" referred to are followers of Paracelsus and van Helmont; hypostatical principles are essential principles or elements, and the Archeus is a vital spirit responsible for chemical and physiological reactions.

The next thing which recommends the corpuscular principles is their extensiveness. The genuine and necessary effect of the strong motion of one part of matter against another is either to drive it on in its entire bulk, or to break and divide it into particles of a determinate motion, figure, size, posture, rest, order, or texture. The two first of these, for instance, are each of them capable of numerous varieties; for the figure of a portion of matter may either be one of the five regular geometrical figures, some determinate species of solid figures, or irregular, as the grains of sand, feathers, branches, files, etc. And, as the figure, so the motion of one of these particles may be exceedingly diversified, not only by the determination to a particular part of the world but by several other things, as by the almost infinitely different degrees of celerity, by the manner of its progression, with or without rotation, etc. and more yet by the line in which it moves, as circular, elliptical, parabolic, hyperbolic, spiral, etc. For, as later geometers have shown that these curves may be compounded of several motions, that is, described by a body whose motion is mixed, and results from two or more simple motions; so, how many more curves may be made by new compositions and recompositions of motion is not easy to determine.

Now, since a single particle of matter, by virtue of only two mechanical properties that belong to it, may be diversified so many ways, what a vast number of variations may we suppose capable of being produced by the compositions and recompositions of myriads of single invisible corpuscles that may be contained and concreted in one small body, and each of them be endowed with more than two or three of the fertile universal principles above mentioned? And the aggregate of those corpuscles may be further diversified by the texture resulting from their convention into a body, which, as so made up, has its own magnitude, shape, pores, and many capacities of acting and suffering, upon account of the place it holds among other bodies, in a world constituted like ours; so that, considering the numerous diversifications that compositions and recompositions may make of a small number, those who think the mechanical principles may serve, indeed, to account for the phenomena of some particular part of natural philosophy, as statics, the theory of planetary motions, etc., but prove inapplicable to all the phenomena of things corporeal seem to imagine that by putting together the letters of the alphabet one may, indeed, make up all the words to be found in Euclid or Virgil, or in the Latin or English language, but that they can by no means supply words to all the books of a great library, much less to all the languages in the world.

There are other philosophers, who, observing the great efficacy of magnitude, situation, motion, and connection in engines, are willing to allow those mechanical principles a great share in the operations of bodies of a sensible bulk and manifest mechanism and, therefore, to be usefully employed in accounting for the effects and phenomena of such bodies, though they will not admit that these principles can be applied to the hidden transactions among the minute particles of bodies, and, therefore, think it necessary to refer these to what they call nature, substantial forms, real qualities, and the like unmechanical agents. But this is not necessary, for the mechanical properties of matter are to be found and the laws of motion take place, not only in the great masses and the middle-sized lumps, but in the smallest fragments of matter—a less portion of it being as much a body as a greater must as necessarily as the other have its determinate bulk and figure. And whoever views sand through a good microscope will easily perceive that each minute grain has its own size and shape as well as a rock or a mountain. Thus too, when we let fall a large stone and a pebble from the top of a high building, they both move conformably to the laws of acceleration in heavy descending bodies, and the rules of motion are observed, not only in cannon-bullets, but in small shot; and the one strikes down a bird according to the same laws as the other batters a wall. And though nature works with much finer materials and employs more curious contrivances than art, yet an artist, according to the quantity of the matter he employs, the exigency of the design he undertakes, and the magnitude and shape of the instruments he uses, is able to make pieces of work of the same nature or kind, of extremely different bulks where yet the like art, contrivance, and motion may be observed. Thus a smith who, with a hammer and other large instruments, can forge great bars or wedges out of masses of iron to make strong and ponderous chains to secure streets and gates may, with lesser instruments, make smaller nails, and filings, almost as minute as dust, and with yet finer tools, make links wonderfully light and slender. And therefore, to say that though in natural bodies, whose bulk is manifest and their structure visible, the mechanical principles may be usefully admitted but are not to be extended to such portions of matter whose parts and texture are invisible, is like allowing that the laws of mechanism may take place in a town clock and not in a pocket watch, or, because the terraqueous globe is a vast magnetic body, one should affirm that magnetic laws are not to be expected manifest in a small spherical piece of lodestone; yet experience shows us that, notwithstanding the immense disproportion between these two spheres, the terella[4] as well as the earth has its poles, equator, and meridians, and in several other magnetic properties resembles the terrestrial globe.

When, to solve the phenomena of nature, agents are made use of which, though they involve no contradiction in their notions, as many think substantial forms and real qualities do, yet are such that we conceive not how they operate to produce effects—such agents I mean, as the soul of the world, the universal spirit, the plastic power, etc.—the curiosity of an inquisitive person who seeks not so much to know what is the general agent that produces a phenomenon, as by what means, and after what manner it is produced, is not satisfied hereby. Sennert and other physicians tell us of diseases which proceed from incantation; but surely, it is very trivial to a sober physician who comes to visit a patient reported to be bewitched, to hear only that the strange symptoms he meets with, and would have an account of, are produced by a witch or the devil; and he will never be satisfied with so short an answer, if he can by any means reduce those extravagant symptoms to any more known and stated diseases; as epilepsies, convulsions, hysteric fits, etc. and if he cannot, he will confess his

knowledge of this distemper to come far short of what might be expected and attained in other diseases, in which he thinks himself bound to search into the morbific matter, and will not be satisfied, until he can, probably, deduce from that, and the structure of the human body, and other concurring physical causes, the phenomena of the malady. And it would be of little satisfaction to one who desires to understand the causes of the phenomena in a watch, and how it comes to point at and strike the hours to be told that a certain watchmaker so contrived it, or, to him who would know the true causes of an echo, to be answered that it is a man, a vault, or a wood, that makes it.

I come now to consider that which I observe most alienates other sects from the mechanical philosophy, namely, a supposition that it pretends to have principles so universal and mathematical that no other physical hypothesis can be tolerated by it.

This I look upon as an easy, indeed, but an important mistake, for the mechanical principles are so universal and applicable to so many purposes that they are rather fitted to take in, than to exclude any other hypothesis founded on nature. And such hypotheses, if prudently considered, will be found, as far as they have truth on their side, to be either legitimately deducible from the mechanical principles or fairly reconcilable to them. For such hypotheses will, probably, attempt to account for the phenomena of nature, either by the help of a determinate number of material ingredients, such as the *tria prima* of the chemists[5] or else by introducing some general agents, as the Platonic soul of the world and the universal spirit, asserted by some chemists, or by both these ways together.

Now, the chief thing that a philosopher should look after in explaining difficult phenomena is not so much what the agent is or does, as what changes are made in the patient to bring it to exhibit the phenomena proposed, and by what means, and after what manner those changes are effected. So that the mechanical philosopher being satisfied, one part of matter can act upon another only by virtue of local

---

4. A magnetic sphere or lodestone, described in William Gilbert's *De magnete* (1600).

5. The Paracelsian "elements" of salt, sulfur, and mercury.

motion or its effects and consequences; he considers if the proposed agent is not intelligible and physical, it can never physically explain the phenomena, and if it is intelligible and physical, it will be reducible to matter and some or other of its universal properties. And the indefinite divisibility of matter, the wonderful efficacy of motion, and the almost infinite variety of coalitions and structures that may be made of minute and insensible corpuscles being duly weighed, why may not a philosopher think it possible to make out, by their help, the mechanical possibility of any corporeal agent, however subtle, diffused, or active, that can be solidly proved to have a real existence in nature? Though the Cartesians are mechanical philosophers, yet their subtle matter which the very name declares to be a corporeal substance is, for all I know, little less diffused through the universe, or less active in it than the universal spirit of some chemists, not to say the world soul of the Platonists. But whatever is the physical agent, whether it is inanimate or living, purely corporeal or united to an intellectual substance, the above mentioned changes wrought in the body made to exhibit the phenomena may be brought about by the same or the like means, or after the same, or the like manner, as for instance, if corn is reduced to meal, the materials and shape of the millstones and their peculiar motion and adaptation will be much of the same kind; and, to be sure, the grains of corn will suffer various attritions and pulverizations in their passage to the form of meal, whether the corn is ground by a watermill, or a windmill, a horsemill, or a handmill, that is, a mill whose stones are turned by inanimate, by brute, or by rational agents. And if an angel himself should work a real change in the nature of a body, it is scarcely conceivable to men how he could do it without the assistance of local motion, since, if nothing were displaced or otherwise moved than before, it is hardly conceivable how it should be, in itself, different from what it was before.

But if the chemists or others who would deduce a complete natural philosophy from salt, sulfur, and mercury, or any determined number of ingredients of things, would well consider what they undertake, they might easily discover that the material parts of bodies can reach but to a few phenomena of nature, while these things are considered but as quiescent things; whence they would find themselves to suppose them active, and that things purely corporeal cannot but by means of local motion, and the effects that may result from it, be very variously shaped, sized, and combined parts of matter, so that the chemists must leave the greatest part of the phenomena of the universe unexplained by means of the ingredients of bodies, without taking in the mechanical and more comprehensive properties of matter, especially local motion. I willingly grant that salt, sulfur, and mercury, or some substances analogous to them, are obtainable by the action of the fire from a very great many bodies able to be dissipated here below. Nor do I deny that in explaining several phenomena of such bodies, it may be of use to a naturalist to know and consider that as sulfur, for instance, abounds in the body proposed, it may be, thence, probably argued that the qualities usually attending that principle, when predominant, may be also upon its account found in the body that so largely partakes of it. But, though chemical explications are sometimes the most obvious, yet they are not the most fundamental and satisfactory: for the chemical ingredient itself, whether sulfur or any other, must owe its nature and other qualities to the union of insensible particles in a convenient size, shape, motion, or rest, and texture, all which are but mechanical properties of convening corpuscles. And this may be illustrated by what happens in artificial fireworks. For, though in most of those sorts made either for war, or recreation, gun powder is a principal ingredient, and many of the phenomena may be derived from the greater or less proportion in which it enters the compositions, yet there may be fireworks made without gun powder, as appears by those of the ancient Greeks and Romans. And gun powder owes its aptness to fire, and to be exploded to the mechanical texture of more simple portions of matter, niter, charcoal, and sulfur. And sulfur itself, though it is mistaken for a hypostatical principle by many chemists, owes its inflammability to the union of still more simple and primary corpuscles, since chemists confess that it had an inflammable ingredient and experience shows that it very much abounds with an acid and uninflammable salt and is not destitute of a terrestrial part. It may, indeed, be here alleged that the productions of chemical analyses are simple bodies, and, upon that account, irresoluble, but that several substances, which chemists call the salts, sulfurs, or mercuries of the bodies that afford them, are not simple and homogeneous is demonstrable. Nor is their not being easily dissipable or resoluble a clear proof of their not being made up of more primitive portions of matter. For compounded bodies may be as difficulty resoluble as most of those that chemists obtain by the fire: witness common greenglass, which is far more durable and irresoluble than many of those which pass for hypostatical substances. And some enamels will, for several times, even vitrify in the forge without losing their nature or often so much as their color, yet enamel consists of salt, powder of pebbles, or sand, and calcined tin, and, if not white, usually of some tinning metal or mineral. But however indestructible the chemical principles are supposed, several of the operations ascribed to them will never be made to appear without the help of local motion; were it not for this, we can but little better solve the phenomena of many bodies by knowing what ingredients compose them than we can explain the operations of a watch by knowing of how many and of what metals, the balance, the wheels, the chain, and other parts consist, or than we can derive the operations of a windmill from barely knowing that it is made up of wood, stone, canvas, and iron. And here let me add that it would not at all overthrow the corpuscularian hypothesis, though, either by more exquisite purifications or by some other operations than the usual analysis by fire, it should appear that the material principles of mixed bodies are not the *tria prima* of the vulgar chemists, but either substances of another nature or fewer in number, or if it were true that the Helmontians had such a resolving menstruum as their master's alkahest[6] by which he affirms that he could reduce stones into salt of the same weight with the mineral, and bring both that salt and all other

_____

6. A "resolving menstruum" is a solvent, and the "alkahest" is a universal solvent.

mixed and tangible bodies into insipid water. For whatever is the number or qualities of the chemical principles, if they really exist in nature, it may very possibly be shown that they are made up of insensible corpuscles of determinate bulks and shapes, and by the various coalitions and textures of such corpuscles, many material ingredients may be composed or made to result. But though the alkahestical reductions newly mentioned should be admitted, yet the mechanical principles might well be accommodated even to them. For the solidity, taste, etc. of salt may be fairly accounted for by the stiffness, sharpness, and other mechanical properties of the minute particles of which salt consists; and if, by a further action of the alkahest, the salt or any other solid body is reduced into insipid water, this also may be explained by the same principles, supposing a further comminution of its parts and such an attrition as wears off the edges and points that enabled them to strike briskly upon the organ of taste; for as to fluidity and firmness, they principally depend upon two of our grand principles, motion and rest. And it is certain that the agitation or rest, and the looser contact or closer cohesion of the particles, is able to make the same portion of matter at one time a firm and at another a fluid body. So that, though future sagacity and industry of chemists should obtain from mixed bodies, homogeneous substances, different in number, nature, or both, from their vulgar salt, sulfur, and mercury, yet the corpuscular philosophy is so general and fertile as to be fairly reconcilable to such a discovery, and also so useful that these new material principles will, as well as the old *tria prima*, stand in need of the more universal principles of the corpuscularians, especially of local motion. And, indeed, whatever elements or ingredients men have pitched upon, yet if they do not take in the mechanical properties of matter, their principles are so deficient that I have observed both the materialists and chemists not only leave many things unexplained, to which their narrow principles will not extend, but even in the particulars they presume to give an account of, they either content themselves to assign such common and indefinite causes as are too general to be satisfactory, or if they venture to give particular causes, they assign precarious or false ones, liable to be easily disproved by circumstance or instances to which their doctrines will not agree. The chemists, however, need not be frightened from acknowledging the prerogative of the mechanical philosophy, since that may be reconcilable with the truth of their own principles, so far as they agree with the phenomena they are applied to; for these more confined hypotheses may be subordinate to those more general and fertile principles, and there can be no ingredient assigned that has a real existence in nature but may be derived either immediately or by a row of compositions from the universal matter, modified by its mechanical properties. For if with the same bricks, differently put together and ranged, several bridges, vaults, houses, and other structures may be raised merely by a various contrivance of parts of the same kind, what a great variety of ingredients may be produced by nature from the various coalitions and contextures of corpuscles that need not be supposed, like bricks, all of the same size and shape, but to have, both in the one and the other, as great a variety as could be wished for? And the primary and minute concretions that belong to these ingredients may, without opposition from the mechanical philosophy, be supposed to have their particles so minute and strongly coherent that nature of herself scarce ever tears them asunder. Thus mercury and gold may be successively made to put on a multitude of disguises, and yet so retain their nature as to be reducible to their pristine forms.

From hence it is probable if, besides rational souls, there are any immaterial substances, such as the heavenly intelligences and the substantial forms of the Aristotelians that are regularly to be numbered among natural agents, their way of working being unknown to us, they can only help to constitute and effect things, but will very little help us to conceive how things are effected, so that, by whatever principles natural things are constituted, it is by the mechanical principles that their phenomena must be clearly explained. For instance, though we grant with the Aristotelians that the planets are made of a quintessential matter and moved by angels or immaterial intelligences, yet to explain the stations, progressions and retrogradations, and other phenomena

of the planets, we must have recourse either to eccentrics, epicycles, etc. or to motions made in elliptical or other peculiar lines, and in a word to theories in which the motion, figure, situation, and other mathematical or mechanical properties are chiefly employed. But if the principles proposed are corporeal, they will then be fairly reducible or reconcilable to the mechanical principles, these being so general and fertile that, among real material things, there is none but may be derived from or reduced to them. And when the chemists shall show that mixed bodies owe their qualities to the predominance of any one of their three grand ingredients, the corpuscularians will show that the very qualities of this or that ingredient flow from its peculiar texture and the mechanical properties of the corpuscles that compose it. And to affirm that because the chemical furnaces afford a great number of uncommon productions and phenomena, that there are bodies or operations among purely corporeal things not derivable from or reconcilable to the principles of mechanical philosophy is to say, because there are many and various hymns, pavanes, threnodies, courantes, gavottes, sarabands, etc. in a music book, many of the tunes or notes have no dependence on the scale of music, or as if because excepting rhomboids, squares, pentagons, chiliagons, and numerous other polygons, one should affirm there are some rectilinear figures not reducible to triangles, or that have properties which overthrow Euclid's doctrine of triangles and polygons.

I shall only add that as mechanical principles and explanations, where they can be had, are preferred by materialists themselves for their clearness, so the sagacity and industry of modern naturalists and mathematicians, having happily applied them to several of those difficult phenomena which before were referred to occult qualities, it is probable that when this philosophy is more scrutinized and further improved, it will be found applicable to the solution of still more phenomena of nature. And it is not always necessary that he who advances an hypothesis in astronomy, chemistry, anatomy, etc. be able, *a priori*, to prove it true or demonstratively to show that the other hypothesis proposed about the same subject must be false, for as Plato said that the world is God's epistle to mankind and might have added in his own way that it was written in mathematical characters, so, in the physical explanations of the parts of the system of the world, I think there is somewhat like what happens when men conjecturally frame several keys to read a letter written in ciphers. For though one man by his sagacity finds the right key, it will be very difficult for him either to prove, otherwise than by trial, that any particular word is not such as it is guessed to be by others according to their keys, or to show *a priori* that theirs are to be rejected and his to be preferred, yet, if due trial being made, the key he proposes be found so agreeable to the characters of the letter as to enable one to understand them and make coherent sense of them, its suitableness to what it should decipher is, without either confutations or foreign positive proofs, alone sufficient to make it accepted as the right key of that cipher. Thus, in physical hypotheses, there are some that, without falling foul upon others, peaceably obtain the approbation of discerning men only by their fitness to solve the phenomena for which they were devised, without thwarting any known observation or law of nature; and therefore, if the mechanical philosophy shall continue to explain corporeal things, as it has of late, it is scarce to be doubted but that in time unprejudiced persons will think it sufficiently recommended by its being consistent with itself and applicable to so many phenomena of nature.

# John Locke, *An Essay Concerning Human Understanding* (1690)[1]

## Book I. Of Innate Notions. Chapter I. *Introduction*.

1. *An inquiry into the understanding, pleasant and useful.* Since it is the *understanding* that sets man above the rest of sensible beings and gives him all the advantage and dominion he has over them, it is certainly a subject, even for its nobleness, worth our labor to inquire into. The understanding, like the eye, while it makes us see and perceive all other things, takes no notice of itself, and it requires art and pains to set it at a distance and make it its own object. But, whatever are the difficulties that lie in the way of this inquiry, whatever it is that keeps us so much in the dark to ourselves, I am sure that all the light we can let in upon our minds, all the acquaintance we can make with our own understandings, will not only be very pleasant, but bring us great advantage in directing our thoughts in the search of other things.

2. *Design.* This, therefore, being my *purpose*—to inquire into the origin, certainty, and extent of human knowledge, together with the grounds and degrees of belief, opinion, and assent—I shall not at present meddle with the physical consideration of the mind, or trouble myself to examine in what its essence consists, or by what motions of our spirits or alterations of our bodies we come to have any sensation by our organs, or any *ideas* in our understandings, and whether those *ideas* do in their formation, any or all of them, depend on matter or not. These are speculations which, however curious and entertaining, I shall decline, as lying out of my way in the design I am now upon. It shall suffice to my present purpose to consider the discerning faculties of a man as they are employed about the objects which they have to do with. And I shall imagine I have not wholly misemployed myself in the thoughts I shall have on this occasion, if in this historical, plain method, I can give any account of the ways by which our understandings come to attain those notions of things we have, and can set down any measures of the certainty of our knowledge, or the grounds of those persuasions which are to be found among men—so various, different, and wholly contradictory—and yet asserted somewhere or other with such assurance and confidence that he who shall take a view of the opinions of mankind, observe their opposition, and at the same time consider the fondness and devotion with which they are embraced, the resolution and eagerness with which they are maintained, may perhaps have reason to suspect that either there is no such thing as truth at

---

1. From *Works* (London, 1823), 10 vols., English, modified.

all, or that mankind has no sufficient means to attain a certain knowledge of it.

3. *Method*. It is therefore worthwhile to search out the *bounds* between opinion and knowledge and examine by what measures, in things of which we have no certain knowledge, we ought to regulate our assent and moderate our persuasions. Toward that end I shall pursue this following method:

*First*, I shall inquire into the *origin* of those *ideas*, notions, or whatever else you please to call them, which a man observes and is conscious to himself he has in his mind, and the ways by which the understanding comes to be furnished with them.

*Secondly*, I shall endeavor to show what *knowledge* the understanding has by those *ideas*, and the certainty, evidence, and extent of it.

*Thirdly*, I shall make some inquiry into the nature and grounds of *faith* or *opinion*, by which I mean that assent which we give to any proposition as true, of whose truth yet we have no certain knowledge; and here we shall have occasion to examine the reasons and degrees of *assent*.

4. *Useful to know the extent of our comprehension*. If by this inquiry into the nature of the understanding, I can discover the powers thereof, *how far* they reach, to what things they are in any degree proportionate, and where they fail us, I suppose it may be of use to prevail with the busy mind of man to be more cautious in meddling with things exceeding its comprehension, to stop when it is at the utmost extent of its tether, and to sit down in a quiet ignorance of those things which, upon examination, are found to be beyond the reach of our capacities. We should not then perhaps be so eager, out of an affectation of a universal knowledge, to raise questions and perplex ourselves and others with disputes about things to which our understandings are not suited, and of which we cannot frame in our minds any clear or distinct perceptions, or about which (as it has perhaps too often happened) we do not have any notions at all. If we can find out how far the understanding can extend its view, how far it has faculties to attain certainty, and in what cases it can only judge and guess, we may learn to content ourselves with what is attainable by us in this state.

5. For, though the comprehension of our understandings comes exceedingly short of the vast extent of things, yet we shall have cause enough to magnify the bountiful author of our being for that proportion and degree of knowledge he has bestowed on us, so far above all the rest of the inhabitants of this our mansion. Men have reason to be well satisfied with what God has thought fit for them, since he has given them (as St. Peter says) *panta pros zoen kai eusebeian*, whatsoever is necessary for the conveniences of life and information of virtue, and has put within the reach of their discovery the comfortable provision for this life and the way that leads to a better. However short their knowledge may come of a universal or perfect comprehension of whatever is, it yet secures their great concerns that they have light enough to lead them to the knowledge of their maker and the sight of their own duties. Men may find matter sufficient to busy their heads and employ their hands with variety, delight, and satisfaction, if they will not boldly quarrel with their own constitution and throw away the blessings their hands are filled with, because they are not big enough to grasp everything. We shall not have much reason to complain of the narrowness of our minds, if we will only employ them about what may be of use to us; for of that they are very capable. And it will be an unpardonable, as well as childish peevishness, if we undervalue the advantages of our knowledge and neglect to improve it to the ends for which it was given us, because there are some things that are set out of the reach of it. It will be no excuse to an idle and untoward servant who would not attend his business by candlelight to plead that he does not have broad sunshine. The candle that is set up in us shines bright enough for all our purposes. The discoveries we can make with this ought to satisfy us, and we shall then use our understandings right, when we entertain all objects in that way and proportion that they are suited to our faculties, and upon those grounds they are capable of being proposed to us, and not peremptorily, or intemperately require demonstration, and demand certainty, where probability only is to be had, and which is sufficient to govern all our concerns. If we will disbelieve everything because we cannot certainly know all things,

we shall do quite as wisely as he who would not use his legs, but sit still and perish, because he had no wings to fly.

6. *Knowing the extent of our capacities will hinder us from useless curiosity, skepticism, and idleness.* When we know our own *strength*, we shall know better what to undertake with hopes of success. And when we have well surveyed the *powers* of our own minds and made some estimate what we may expect from them, we shall not be inclined either to sit still, and not set our thoughts on work at all in despair of knowing anything nor, on the other side, question everything and disclaim all knowledge, because some things are not to be understood. It is of great use to the sailor to know the length of his line, though he cannot fathom all the depths of the ocean with it. It is well he knows that it is long enough to reach the bottom at such places as are necessary to direct his voyage and caution him against running upon shoals that may ruin him. Our business here is not to know all things, but those which concern our conduct. If we can find out those measures by which a rational creature, put in that state in which man is in this world, may and ought to govern his opinions and actions depending thereon, we need not be troubled that some other things escape our knowledge.

7. *Occasion of this essay.* This was that which gave the first rise to this essay concerning the understanding. For I thought that the first step towards satisfying several inquiries, the mind of man was very apt to run into, was to take a survey of our own understandings, examine our own powers, and see to what things they were adapted. Until that was done, I suspected we began at the wrong end, and in vain sought for satisfaction in a quiet and sure possession of truths that most concerned us, while we let loose our thoughts into the vast ocean of *being*, as if all that boundless extent were the natural and undoubted possession of our understandings in which there was nothing exempt from its decisions or that escaped its comprehension. Thus men extending their inquiries beyond their capacities and letting their thoughts wander into those depths where they can find no sure footing, it is no wonder that they raise questions and multiply disputes, which, never coming to any clear resolution,

are proper only to continue and increase their doubts and to confirm them at last in perfect skepticism; whereas, were the capacities of our understandings well considered, the extent of our knowledge once discovered, and the horizon found, which sets the bounds between the enlightened and dark parts of things, between what is, and what is not comprehensible by us, men would perhaps with less scruple acquiesce in the avowed ignorance of the one and employ their thoughts and discourse with more advantage and satisfaction in the other.

8. *What* idea *stands for.* This much I thought necessary to say concerning the occasion of this inquiry into human understanding. But, before I proceed on to what I have thought on this subject, I must here in the entrance beg pardon of my reader for the frequent use of the word *idea*, which he will find in the following treatise. It being that term, which, I think, serves best to stand for whatever is the object of the understanding when a man thinks, I have used it to express whatever is meant by *phantasm, notion, species*, or whatever it is which the mind can be employed about in thinking; and I could not avoid frequently using it.

I presume it will be easily granted me that there are such *ideas* in men's minds; everyone is conscious of them in himself, and men's words and actions will satisfy him that they are in others.

Our first inquiry then shall be how they come into the mind.

## Chapter II. *No Innate Principles in the Mind, and Particularly No Innate Speculative Principles.*

1. *The way shown how we come by any knowledge, sufficient to prove it not innate.* It is an established opinion among some men that there are in the understanding certain *innate principles*; some primary notions [*koinai ennoiai*], characters, as it were, stamped upon the mind of man, which the soul receives in its very first being and brings into the world with it. It would be sufficient to convince unprejudiced readers of the falseness of this supposition, if I should only show (as I hope I shall in the

following parts of this discourse) how men, barely by the use of their natural faculties, may attain to all the knowledge they have, without the help of any innate impressions, and may arrive at certainty without any such original notions or principles. For I imagine anyone will easily grant that it would be impertinent to suppose the *ideas* of colors innate in a creature to whom God has given sight and a power to receive them by the eyes from external objects; and no less unreasonable would it be to attribute several truths to the impressions of nature and innate characters, when we may observe in ourselves faculties fit to attain as easy and certain knowledge of them as if they were originally imprinted on the mind.

But because a man is not permitted without censure to follow his own thoughts in the search of truth when they lead him ever so little out of the common road, I shall set down the reasons that made me doubt of the truth of that opinion, as an excuse for my mistake, if I am in one, which I leave to be considered by those who, with me, dispose themselves to embrace truth wherever they find it.

2. *General assent the great argument.* There is nothing more commonly taken for granted than that there are certain principles, both *speculative* and *practical* (for they speak of both), universally agreed upon by all mankind, which, therefore, they argue, must necessarily be the constant impressions which the souls of men receive in their first beings, and which they bring into the world with them, as necessarily and really as they do any of their inherent faculties.

3. *Universal consent proves nothing innate.* This argument, drawn from *universal consent*, has this misfortune in it that, if it were true in matter of fact that there were certain truths in which all mankind agreed, it would not prove them innate, if there can be any other way shown how men may come to that universal agreement in the things they do consent in, which I presume may be done.

4. What is, is, *and,* it is impossible for the same thing to be, and not to be, *not universally assented to.* But, which is worse, this argument of universal consent, which is made use of to prove innate principles, seems to me a demonstration that there are none such, because there are none to which all mankind

give a universal assent. I shall begin with the speculative, and instance in those magnified principles of demonstration, "Whatever is, is," and "It is impossible for the same thing to be and not to be," which, of all others, I think have the most allowed title to innate. These have so settled a reputation of maxims universally received that it will no doubt be thought strange if any one should seem to question it. But yet I take liberty to say that these propositions are so far from having a universal assent that there is a great part of mankind to whom they are not so much as known.

5. *Not on the mind naturally imprinted, because not known to children, idiots, etc.* For, first, it is evident that all *children* and *idiots* do not have the least apprehension or thought of them. And the lack of that is enough to destroy that universal assent which must be the necessary concomitant of all innate truths, it seeming to me near a contradiction to say that there are truths imprinted on the soul which it does not perceive or understand—imprinting, if it signifies anything, being nothing else but the making certain truths to be perceived. For to imprint anything on the mind without the mind's perceiving it seems to me hardly intelligible. If therefore children and *idiots* have souls, have minds, with those impressions upon them, they must unavoidably perceive them, and necessarily know and assent to these truths. Since they do not, it is evident that there are no such impressions. For if they are not notions naturally imprinted, how can they be innate? And if they are notions imprinted, how can they be unknown? To say a notion is imprinted on the mind, and yet at the same time to say that the mind is ignorant of it and never yet took notice of it, is to make this impression nothing. No proposition can be said to be in the mind which it never yet knew, which it was never yet conscious of. For if any one may, then, by the same reason, all propositions that are true, and the mind is capable ever of assenting to, may be said to be in the mind and to be imprinted; since, if any one can be said to be in the mind, which it never yet knew, it must be only because it is capable of knowing it; and so the mind is [capable] of all truths it ever shall know. No, thus truths may be imprinted on the mind which it never did, nor ever shall know; for a man

may live long, and die at last in ignorance of many truths which his mind was capable of knowing, and that with certainty. So that if the capacity of knowing is the natural impression contended for, all the truths a man ever comes to know will, by this account, be every one of them innate; and this great point will amount to no more, but only to a very improper way of speaking, which, while it pretends to assert the contrary, says nothing different from those who deny innate principles. For nobody, I think, ever denied that the mind was capable of knowing several truths. The capacity, they say, is innate, the knowledge acquired. But then to what end such contest for certain innate maxims? If truths can be imprinted on the understanding without being perceived, I can see no difference there can be between any truths the mind is capable of knowing in respect of their original. They must all be innate or all adventitious; in vain shall a man go about to distinguish them. He therefore who talks of innate notions in the understanding cannot (if he intends by this any distinct sort of truths) mean such truths to be in the understanding, as it never perceived, and is yet wholly ignorant of. For if these words (*to be in the understanding*) have any propriety, they signify to be understood, so that to be in the understanding and not to be understood, to be in the mind and never to be perceived, is all one, as to say anything is and is not in the mind or understanding. If therefore these two propositions, "Whatever is, is" and "It is impossible for the same thing to be and not to be," are by nature imprinted, children cannot be ignorant of them; infants, and all that have souls, must necessarily have them in their understandings, know the truth of them, and assent to it.

6. *That men know them when they come to the use of reason answered.* To avoid this, it is usually answered that all men know and assent to them, *when they come to the use of reason*, and this is enough to prove them innate. I answer,

7. Doubtful expressions, that have scarcely any signification, go for clear reasons to those who, being prepossessed, do not take the pains to examine even what they themselves say. For to apply this answer with any tolerable sense to our present purpose, it must signify one of these two things: either that as

soon as men come to the use of reason these supposed native inscriptions come to be known and observed by them; or else, that the use and exercise of men's reason assists them in the discovery of these principles, and certainly makes them known to them.

8. *If reason discovered them, that would not prove them innate.* If they mean that by the use of reason men may discover these principles, and that this is sufficient to prove them innate, their way of arguing will stand thus, namely that, whatever truths reason can certainly discover to us and make us firmly assent to, those are all naturally imprinted on the mind; since that universal assent, which is made the mark of them, amounts to no more but this—that by the use of reason we are capable to come to a certain knowledge of and assent to them, and, by this means, there will be no difference between the maxims of the mathematicians and theorems they deduce from them—all must be equally allowed innate, they being all discoveries made by the use of reason and truths that a rational creature may certainly come to know, if he applies his thoughts rightly that way.

9. *It is false that reason discovers them.* But how can these men think the *use of reason* necessary to discover principles that are supposed innate, when reason (if we may believe them) is nothing else but the faculty of deducing unknown truths from principles or propositions that are already known? That certainly can never be thought innate which we have need of reason to discover, unless, as I have said, we will have all the certain truths that reason ever teaches us to be innate. [ . . . ]

12. *The coming to the use of reason not the time we come to know these maxims.* If by knowing and assenting to them, *when we come to the use of reason*, is meant that this is the time when they come to be taken notice of by the mind, and that, as soon as children come to the use of reason they come also to know and assent to these maxims, this also is false and frivolous. *First*, it is false, because it is evident these maxims are not in the mind so early as the use of reason, and therefore the coming to the use of reason is falsely assigned as the time of their discovery. How many instances of the use of reason may we observe in children a long time before they have

any knowledge of this maxim, "That it is impossible for the same thing to be and not to be"? And a great part of illiterate people and savages pass many years, even of their rational age, without ever thinking on this and the like general propositions. I grant, men do not come to the knowledge of these general and more abstract truths, which are thought innate, until they come to the use of reason; and I add, nor then neither. This is so because, until after they come to the use of reason, those general abstract *ideas* are not framed in the mind, about which those general maxims are, which are mistaken for innate principles, but are indeed discoveries made and verities introduced and brought into the mind by the same way, and discovered by the same steps, as several other propositions, which nobody was ever so extravagant as to suppose innate. [ . . . ]

14. *If coming to the use of reason were the time of their discovery, it would not prove them innate.* But, *secondly*, were it true that the precise time of their being known and assented to were when men come to the use of reason, neither would that prove them innate. This way of arguing is as frivolous as the supposition itself is false. For, by what kind of logic will it appear that any notion is originally by nature imprinted in the mind in its first constitution, because it comes first to be observed and assented to when a faculty of the mind, which has quite a distinct province, begins to exert itself? [ . . . ]

15. *The steps by which the mind attains several truths.* The senses at first let in particular *ideas*, and furnish the yet empty cabinet, and the mind by degrees growing familiar with some of them, they are lodged in the memory, and names got to them. Afterwards the mind proceeding further abstracts them, and by degrees learns the use of general names. In this manner the mind comes to be furnished with *ideas* and language, the materials about which to exercise its discursive faculty. And the use of reason becomes daily more visible, as these materials that give it employment increase. But though the having of general *ideas* and the use of general words and reason usually grow together, yet I do not see how this any way proves them innate. The knowledge of some truths, I confess, is very early in the mind, but

in a way that shows them not to be innate. For, if we will observe, we shall find it still to be about *ideas*, not innate, but acquired—it being about those first which are imprinted by external things, with which infants have earliest to do, which make the most frequent impressions on their senses. In *ideas* thus got, the mind discovers that some agree and others differ, probably as soon as it has any use of memory, as soon as it is able to retain and perceive distinct *ideas*. But whether it is then, or not, this is certain, it does so long before it has the use of words, or comes to that which we commonly call "the use of reason." For a child knows as certainly before it can speak the difference between the *ideas* of sweet and bitter (i.e., that sweet is not bitter), as it knows afterwards (when it comes to speak) that wormwood and sugarplums are not the same thing. [ . . . ]

17. *Assenting as soon as proposed and understood does not prove them innate.* This evasion therefore of general assent when men come to the use of reason, failing as it does, and leaving no difference between those supposed innate and other truths that are afterwards acquired and learned, men have endeavored to secure a universal assent to those they call maxims, by saying they are *generally assented to as soon as proposed*, and the terms they are proposed in understood; seeing all men, even children, as soon as they hear and understand the terms, assent to these propositions, they think it is sufficient to prove them innate. For, since men never fail, after they have once understood the words, to acknowledge them for undoubted truths, they would infer that certainly these propositions were first lodged in the understanding, which, without any teaching, the mind at the very first proposal immediately closes with and assents to, and after that never doubts again.

18. *If such an assent is a mark of innate, then that one and two are equal to three, that sweetness is not bitterness, and a thousand the like, must be innate.* In answer to this I demand "whether ready assent given to a proposition, *upon first hearing* and understanding the terms, is a certain mark of an innate principle?" If it is not, such a general assent is in vain urged as a proof of them; if it is said that it is a mark of innate, they must then allow all such propositions to be

innate which are generally assented to as soon as heard, by which they will find themselves plentifully stored with innate principles. For, upon the same ground, namely, of assent at first hearing and understanding the terms, that men would have those maxims pass for innate, they must also admit several propositions about numbers to be innate; and thus, *that one and two are equal to three*, *that two and two are equal to four*, and a multitude of other like propositions in numbers that every body assents to at first hearing and understanding the terms, must have a place among these innate axioms. Nor is this the prerogative of numbers alone and propositions made about several of them, but even natural philosophy and all the other sciences afford propositions which are sure to meet with assent as soon as they are understood. *That two bodies cannot be in the same place* is a truth that nobody any more sticks at than at these maxims, that "it is impossible for the same thing to be and not to be," that "white is not black," that "a square is not a circle," "that bitterness is not sweetness." [ . . . ] But since no proposition can be innate unless the *ideas* about which it is are innate, this will be to suppose all our *ideas* of colors, sounds, tastes, figure, etc. innate, than which there cannot be anything more opposite to reason and experience. Universal and ready assent upon hearing and understanding the terms is (I grant) a mark of self-evidence; but self-evidence, depending not on innate impressions, but on something else (as we shall show afterward), belongs to several propositions which nobody was yet so extravagant as to pretend to be innate.

19. *Such less general propositions known before these universal maxims.* Nor let it be said that those more particular self-evident propositions which are assented to at first hearing as *that one and two are equal to three*, *that green is not red*, etc., are received as the consequences of those more universal propositions which are looked on as innate principles, since anyone, who will but take the pains to observe what passes in the understanding will certainly find that these, and the like less general propositions, are certainly known and firmly assented to by those who are utterly ignorant of those more general maxims; and so, being earlier in the mind than those (as they are

called) first principles, cannot owe to them the assent with which they are received at first hearing. [ . . . ]

21. *These maxims not being known sometimes until proposed does not prove them innate.* But we have not yet done with *assenting to propositions at first hearing and understanding their terms.* It is fit we first take notice that this, instead of being a mark that they are innate, is a proof of the contrary, since it supposes that several who understand and know other things are ignorant of these principles until they are proposed to them, and that one may be unacquainted with these truths, until he hears them from others. For, if they were innate, what need they be proposed in order to gaining assent, when by being in the understanding by a natural and original impression (if there were any such) they could not but be known before? [ . . . ]

22. *Implicitly known before proposing signifies that the mind is capable of understanding them, or else signifies nothing.* If it is said, "the understanding has an *implicit knowledge* of these principles, but not an *explicit*, before this first hearing," (as they must who will say, "that they are in the understanding before they are known") it will be hard to conceive what is meant by a principle imprinted on the understanding implicitly, unless it is this, that the mind is capable of understanding and assenting firmly to such propositions. And thus all mathematical demonstrations as well as first principles must be received as native impressions on the mind. [ . . . ]

## Book II. Of Ideas. Chapter I. *Of* Ideas *in General, and Their Origin.*

1. Idea *is the object of thinking.* Every man being conscious to himself that he thinks, and that which his mind is applied about while thinking being the *ideas* that are there, it is past doubt that men have in their minds several *ideas* such as are those expressed by the words *whiteness, hardness, sweetness, thinking, motion, man, elephant, army, drunkenness,* and others. It is in the first place then to be inquired how he comes by them. I know it is a received doctrine that men have native *ideas* and original characters stamped upon their minds in their very first being. This opinion I have, at large, examined already, and I suppose what I have said in the foregoing book will

be much more easily admitted when I have shown from where the understanding may get all the *ideas* it has and by what ways and degrees they may come into the mind—for which I shall appeal to everyone's own observation and experience.

2. *All* ideas *come from sensation or reflection.* Let us then suppose the mind to be, as we say, white paper, void of all characters, without any *ideas.* How does it come to be furnished? From where does it come by that vast store which the busy and boundless fancy of man has painted on it with an almost endless variety? From where does it have all the materials of reason and knowledge? To this I answer, in one word, from *experience*; our knowledge is founded in all that, and from that it ultimately derives itself. Our observation employed either about *external sensible objects or about the internal operations of our minds, perceived and reflected on by ourselves, is that which supplies our understandings with all the materials of thinking.* These two are the fountains of knowledge from which all the *ideas* we have, or can naturally have, do spring.

3. *The objects of sensation one source of* ideas. First, *our senses,* conversant about particular sensible objects, do *convey into the mind* several distinct *perceptions* of things, according to those various ways in which those objects do affect them. And thus we come by those *ideas* we have of *yellow, white, heat, cold, soft, hard, bitter, sweet,* and all those which we call sensible qualities—which when I say the senses convey into the mind, I mean, they from external objects convey into the mind what produces there those *perceptions.* This great source of most of the *ideas* we have, depending wholly upon our senses and derived by them to the understanding, I call SENSATION.

4. *The operations of our minds, the other source of them.* Secondly, the other fountain from which experience furnishes the understanding with *ideas* is the *perception of the operations of our own mind* within us, as it is employed about the *ideas* it has gotten—which operations, when the soul comes to reflect on and consider, do furnish the understanding with another set of *ideas,* which could not be had from things without. And such are *perception, thinking, doubting, believing, reasoning, knowing, willing,* and all the different actings of our own minds, which we, being conscious of and observing in ourselves, do from these receive into our understandings as distinct *ideas,* as we do from bodies affecting our senses. This source of *ideas* every man has wholly in himself; and though it is not sense, as having nothing to do with external objects, yet it is very like it, and might properly enough be called internal sense. But as I call the other *sensation,* so I call this REFLECTION, the *ideas* it affords being such only as the mind gets by reflecting on its own operations within itself. By reflection then, in the following part of this discourse, I would be understood to mean that notice which the mind takes of its own operations and the manner of them by reason of which there come to be *ideas* of these operations in the understanding. These two, I say, namely, external material things as the objects of sensation and the operations of our own minds within as the objects of reflection, are to me the only origins from which all our *ideas* take their beginnings. The term *operations* here I use in a large sense, as comprehending not barely the actions of the mind about its *ideas,* but some sort of passions arising sometimes from them, such as is the satisfaction or uneasiness arising from any thought.

5. *All our* ideas *are of the one or the other of these.* The understanding seems to me not to have the least glimmering of any *ideas* which it does not receive from one of these two. *External objects furnish the mind with the* ideas *of sensible qualities,* which are all those different perceptions they produce in us. And the *mind furnishes the understanding with* ideas *of its own operations.*

These, when we have taken a full survey of them, and their several modes, combinations, and relations, we shall find to contain all our whole stock of *ideas,* and that we have nothing in our minds which did not come in one of these two ways. Let anyone examine his own thoughts and thoroughly search into his understanding—and then let him tell me whether all the original *ideas* he has there are any other than of the objects of his *senses,* or of the operations of his mind, considered as objects of his *reflection*—and however great a mass of knowledge he imagines to be lodged there, he will, upon taking a strict view, see that he *does not have any* idea *in his mind, but what one of these two have imprinted*, though perhaps with infinite variety compounded and enlarged by the understanding, as we shall see hereafter.

6. *Observable in children*. He who attentively considers the state of a *child* at his first coming into the world will have little reason to think him stored with plenty of *ideas* that are to be the matter of his future knowledge. It is by degrees he comes to be furnished with them. And though the *ideas* of obvious and familiar qualities imprint themselves before the memory begins to keep a register of time or order, yet it is often so late before some unusual qualities come in the way that there are few men who cannot recollect the beginning of their acquaintance with them. And if it were worthwhile, no doubt a child might be so ordered as to have but a very few even of the ordinary *ideas* until he were grown up to a man. But all who are born into the world being surrounded with bodies that perpetually and diversely affect them, variety of *ideas*, whether care is taken of it or not, are imprinted on the minds of children. Light and colors are busy at hand everywhere, when the eye is but open; sounds and some tangible qualities do not fail to solicit their proper senses and force an entrance to the mind; but yet, I think, it will be granted easily that if a child were kept in a place where he never saw any other but black and white until he were a man, he would have no more *ideas* of scarlet or green than he who from his childhood never tasted an oyster or a pineapple has of those particular relishes.

7. *Men are differently furnished with these, according to the different objects they converse with.* Men then come to be furnished with fewer or more simple *ideas* from without, according as the objects they converse with afford greater or less variety, and from the operations of their minds within, according as they more or less *reflect* on them. For though he who contemplates the operations of his mind cannot but have plain and clear *ideas* of them, yet, unless he turns his thoughts that way and considers them *attentively*, he will no more have clear and distinct *ideas* of all the *operations of his mind*, and all that may be observed in there, than he will have all the particular *ideas* of any landscape or of the parts and motions of

a clock, who will not turn his eyes to it and with attention heed all the parts of it. The picture or clock may be so placed that they may come in his way every day, but yet he will have but a confused *idea* of all the parts they are made up of until he applies himself with attention to consider them each in particular.

8. Ideas *of reflection later, because they need attention*. And hence we see the reason why it is pretty late before most children get *ideas* of the operations of their own minds; and some do not have any very clear or perfect *ideas* of the greatest part of them all their lives, because, though they pass there continually, yet, like floating visions, they make not deep impressions enough to leave in their mind clear, distinct, lasting *ideas*, until the understanding turns inward upon itself, *reflects* on its own *operations*, and makes them the objects of its own contemplation. Children, when they come first into it, are surrounded with a world of new things, which, by a constant solicitation of their senses, draw the mind constantly to them, ready to take notice of new and apt to be delighted with the variety of changing objects. Thus the first years are usually employed and diverted in looking abroad. Men's business in them is to acquaint themselves with what is to be found without. And so growing up in a constant attention to outward sensation, [they] seldom make any considerable reflection on what passes within them until they come to be of riper years, and some scarcely ever at all.

9. *The soul begins to have* ideas *when it begins to perceive*. To ask *at what time a man has first any* ideas is to ask when he begins to perceive—having *ideas* and perception being the same thing. I know it is an opinion that the soul always thinks, and that it has the actual perception of *ideas* in itself constantly as long as it exists, and that actual thinking is as inseparable from the soul as actual extension is from the body—which if true, to inquire after the beginning of a man's *ideas* is the same as to inquire after the beginning of his soul. For by this account soul and its *ideas* as body and its extension will begin to exist both at the same time.

10. *The soul does not always think, for this wants proofs.* But whether the soul is supposed to exist antecedent to, or coeval with, or some time after the

first rudiments of organization or the beginnings of life in the body, I leave to be disputed by those who have better thought of that matter. I confess myself to have one of those dull souls that does not perceive itself always to contemplate *ideas*; nor can conceive it any more necessary for the *soul always to think* than for the body always to move, the perception of *ideas* being (as I conceive) to the soul what motion is to the body—not its essence, but one of its operations. And therefore, though thinking is supposed never so much the proper action of the soul, yet it is not necessary to suppose that it should be always thinking, always in action; that perhaps is the privilege of the infinite author and preserver of things who never slumbers nor sleeps, but is not competent to any finite being, at least not to the soul of man. We know certainly by experience that we sometimes think—and from there draw this infallible consequence that there is something in us that has a power to think—but whether that substance perpetually thinks or not, we can be no further assured than experience informs us. For to say that actual thinking is essential to the soul, and inseparable from it, is to beg what is in question and not to prove it by reason—which is necessary to be done, if it is not a self-evident proposition. But whether this, "that the soul always thinks," is a self-evident proposition that everybody assents to at first hearing, I appeal to mankind. It is doubted whether I thought at all last night or not; the question being about a matter of fact, it is begging it to bring, as a proof for it, an hypothesis, which is the very thing in dispute. In this way one may prove anything, and it is but supposing that all watches think while the balance beats; and it is sufficiently proved, and past doubt that my watch thought all last night. But he who would not deceive himself ought to build his hypothesis on matter of fact, and make it out by sensible experience, and not presume on matter of fact, because of his hypothesis, that is, because he supposes it to be so. This way of proving amounts to this, that I must necessarily think all last night, because another supposes I always think, though I myself cannot perceive that I always do so.

But men in love with their opinions may not only suppose what is in question, but allege wrong matter

of fact. How else could anyone make it an inference of mine that a thing is not, because we are not sensible of it in our sleep? I do not say there is no soul in a man because he is not sensible of it in his sleep. But I do say he cannot think at any time, waking or sleeping, without being sensible of it. Our being sensible of it is not necessary to anything but to our thoughts; and to them it is, and to them it always will be necessary, until we can think without being conscious of it.

11. *It is not always conscious of it.* I grant that the soul in a waking man is never without thought because it is the condition of being awake. But whether sleeping without dreaming is not an affection of the whole man, mind as well as body, may be worth a waking man's consideration, it being hard to conceive that anything should think and not be conscious of it. If the *soul* does *think in a sleeping man* without being conscious of it, I ask, whether during such thinking it has any pleasure or pain or is capable of happiness or misery? I am sure the man is not, no more than the bed or earth he lies on. For to be happy or miserable without being conscious of it seems to me utterly inconsistent and impossible. Or if it is possible that the soul can, while the body is sleeping, have its thinking, enjoyments and concerns, its pleasures or pain, apart, which the man is not conscious of nor partakes in, it is certain that *Socrates* asleep and *Socrates* awake is not the same person. But his soul when he sleeps and *Socrates* the man, consisting of body and soul when he is waking, are two persons, since waking *Socrates* has no knowledge of, or concern for that happiness or misery of his soul which it enjoys alone by itself while he sleeps, without perceiving anything of it, no more than he has for the happiness or misery of a man in the Indies, whom he does not know. For if we take wholly away all consciousness of our actions and sensations, especially of pleasure and pain, and the concern that accompanies it, it will be hard to know in what to place personal identity.

12. *If a sleeping man thinks without knowing it, the sleeping and waking man are two persons.* "The soul, during sound sleep, thinks," say these men. *While it thinks* and perceives, it is capable certainly of those of delight or trouble, as well as any other perceptions, and *it must necessarily be conscious of its*

*own perceptions*. But it has all this apart; the sleeping man, it is plain, is conscious of nothing of all this. Let us suppose then the soul of *Castor*, while he is sleeping, retired from his body—which is no impossible supposition for the men I have here to do with, who so liberally allow life without a thinking soul to all other animals. These men cannot then judge it impossible, or a contradiction, that the body should live without the soul, nor that the soul should subsist and think, or have perception, even perception of happiness or misery, without the body. Let us then, as I say, suppose the soul of *Castor* separated during his sleep from his body, to think apart. Let us suppose too, that it chooses for its scene of thinking the body of another man, e.g., *Pollux*, who is sleeping without a soul. For if *Castor's* soul can think while *Castor* is asleep, what *Castor* is never conscious of, it is no matter what place it chooses to think in. We have here then the bodies of two men with only one soul between them, which we will suppose to sleep and wake by turns; and the soul still thinking in the waking man, of which the sleeping man is never conscious, never has the least perception. I ask then, whether *Castor* and *Pollux*, thus, with only one soul between them, which thinks and perceives in one what the other is never conscious of, nor is concerned for, are not two as distinct persons as *Castor* and *Hercules* or as *Socrates* and *Plato* were? And whether one of them might not be very happy and the other very miserable? Just by the same reason they make the soul and the man two persons who make the soul think apart what the man is not conscious of. For I suppose nobody will make identity of persons to consist in the soul's being united to the very same numerical particles of matter. For if that is necessary to identity, it will be impossible, in that constant flux of the particles of our bodies, that any man should be the same person two days or two moments together.

13. *Impossible to convince those who sleep without dreaming that they think*. Thus, I think, every drowsy nod shakes their doctrine, who teach that the soul is always thinking. Those, at least, who do at any time sleep without dreaming can never be convinced that their thoughts are sometimes busy for four hours without their knowing of it, and if they are taken in

the very act, waked in the middle of that sleeping contemplation, can give no manner of account of it.

14. *That men dream without remembering it, in vain urged*. It will perhaps be said, "that the *soul* thinks even *in* the soundest *sleep, but the memory does not retain it*." That the soul in a sleeping man should be this moment busy thinking, and the next moment in a waking man not remember nor be able to recollect one jot of all those thoughts, is very hard to be conceived and would need some better proof than bare assertion to make it be believed. For who can without any more ado, but being barely told so, imagine that the greatest part of men do, during all their lives, for several hours every day, think of something, which if they were asked, even in the middle of these thoughts, they could remember nothing at all of? Most men, I think, pass a great part of their sleep without dreaming. I once knew a man who was bred a scholar and had no bad memory, who told me he had never dreamed in his life until he had that fever he was then newly recovered of, which was about the twenty-fifth or twenty-sixth year of his age. I suppose the world affords more such instances. At least everyone's acquaintance will furnish him with examples enough of such, as pass most of their nights without dreaming. [ . . . ]

19. *That a man should be busy in thinking, and yet not retain it the next moment, very improbable*. To suppose the soul to think and the man not to perceive it is, as has been said, to make two persons in one man. And if one considers well these men's way of speaking, one should be led into a suspicion that they do so. For they who tell us that the soul always thinks do never, that I remember, say that a man always thinks. Can the soul think and not the man? or a man think and not be conscious of it? This perhaps would be suspected of *jargon* in others. If they say the man always thinks but is not always conscious of it, they may as well say his body is extended without having parts. For it is altogether as intelligible to say that a body is extended without parts as that anything *thinks without being conscious of it* or perceiving that it does so. They who talk thus may, with as much reason, if it is necessary to their hypothesis, say that a man is always hungry, but that he does not always feel

it; whereas hunger consists in that very sensation, as thinking consists in being conscious that one thinks. If they say that a man is always conscious to himself of thinking, I ask how do they know it. Consciousness is the perception of what passes in a man's own mind. Can another man perceive that I am conscious of anything, when I perceive it not myself? No man's knowledge here can go beyond his experience. Wake a man out of a sound sleep and ask him what he was that moment thinking of. If he himself is conscious of nothing he then thought on, he must be a notable diviner of thoughts that can assure him that he was thinking. May he not with more reason assure him he was not asleep? This is something beyond philosophy, and it cannot be less than revelation that discovers to another thoughts in my mind when I can find none there myself; and they must necessarily have a penetrating sight who can certainly see that I think when I cannot perceive it myself and when I declare that I do not, and yet can see that dogs or elephants do not think when they give all the demonstration of it imaginable, except only telling us that they do so. This some may suspect to be a step beyond the Rosicrucians, it seeming easier to make one's self invisible to others than to make another's thoughts visible to me, which are not visible to himself. But it is but defining the soul to be "a substance that always thinks," and the business is done. If such definition is of any authority, I do not know what it can serve for, but to make many men suspect that they have no souls at all, since they find a good part of their lives pass away without thinking. For no definitions that I know, no suppositions of any sect, are of force enough to destroy constant experience; and perhaps it is the affectation of knowing beyond what we perceive that makes so much useless dispute and noise in the world.

20. No ideas *but from sensation or reflection evident, if we observe children.* I see no reason therefore to believe that the *soul thinks before the senses have furnished it with* ideas to think on; and as those are increased and retained, so it comes by exercise to improve its faculty of thinking, in the several parts of it as well as afterwards, by compounding those *ideas* and reflecting on its own operations, [and so] it increases its stock as well as facility in remembering, imagining, reasoning, and other modes of thinking. [ . . . ]

23. If it shall be demanded then *when a man begins to have any* ideas, I think the true answer is when he first has any *sensation.* For since there does not appear to be any *ideas* in the mind before the senses have conveyed any in, I conceive that *ideas* in the understanding are coeval with *sensation*—which is such an impression or motion made in some part of the body as produces some perception in the understanding. It is about these impressions made on our senses by outward objects that the mind seems first to employ itself in such operations as we call perception, remembering, consideration, reasoning, etc.

24. *The origin of all our knowledge.* In time the mind comes to reflect on its own *operations* about the *ideas* gotten by *sensation* and in this way stores itself with a new set of *ideas*, which I call *ideas* of reflection. These are the *impressions* that are made on our *senses* by outward objects that are extrinsic to the mind and its *own operations*, proceeding from powers intrinsic and proper to itself, which, when *reflected* on by itself, become also objects of its contemplation, and *are*, as I have said, *the origin of all knowledge*. Thus the first capacity of human intellect is that the mind is fitted to receive the impressions made on it either through the *senses* by outward objects or by its own operations when it *reflects* on them. This is the first step a man makes towards the discovery of anything and the groundwork on which to build all those notions which ever he shall have naturally in this world. All those sublime thoughts which tower above the clouds, and reach as high as heaven itself, take their rise and footing here. In all that great extent in which the mind wanders, in those remote speculations it may seem to be elevated with, it does not stir one jot beyond those *ideas* which *sense* or *reflection* have offered for its contemplation.

25. *In the reception of simple* ideas *the understanding is most of all passive.* In this part the *understanding* is merely *passive*; and whether or not it will have these beginnings, and as it were materials of knowledge, is not in its own power. For the objects of our senses do, many of them, obtrude their particular *ideas* upon our minds whether we will or not; and

the operations of our minds will not let us be without, at least, some obscure notions of them. No man can be wholly ignorant of what he does when he thinks. These *simple ideas*, when offered to the mind, *the understanding can* no more refuse to have, nor alter, when they are imprinted, nor blot them out and make new ones itself than a mirror can refuse, alter, or obliterate the images or *ideas* which the objects set before it do produce there. As the bodies that surround us do diversely affect our organs, the mind is forced to receive the impressions and cannot avoid the perception of those *ideas* that are annexed to them.

## Chapter II. *Of Simple* Ideas.

1. *Uncompounded appearances*. The better to understand the nature, manner, and extent of our knowledge, one thing is carefully to be observed concerning the *ideas* we have, and that is, that *some* of them are *simple*, and *some complex*.

   Though the qualities that affect our senses are, in the things themselves, so united and blended, that there is no separation, no distance between them, yet it is plain the *ideas* they produce in the mind enter by the senses simple and unmixed. For though the sight and touch often take in from the same object at the same time different *ideas*—as a man sees at once motion and color, the hand feels softness and warmth in the same piece of wax—yet the simple *ideas* thus united in the same subject are as perfectly distinct as those that come in by different senses. The coldness and hardness which a man feels in a piece of *ice* being as distinct *ideas* in the mind, as the smell and whiteness of a lily or as the taste of sugar and smell of a rose. And there is nothing can be plainer to a man than the clear and distinct perception he has of those simple *ideas*, which, being each in itself uncompounded, contains in it nothing but *one uniform appearance*, or conception in the mind, and is not distinguishable into different *ideas*.

2. *The mind can neither make nor destroy them*. These simple *ideas*, the materials of all our knowledge, are suggested and furnished to the mind only by those two ways mentioned above, namely, *sensation* and *reflection*. When the understanding is once stored with these simple *ideas*, it has the power to

repeat, compare, and unite them, even to an almost infinite variety, and so can make at pleasure new complex *ideas*. But it is not in the power of the most exalted wit or enlarged understanding, by any quickness or variety of thought, to invent or frame one new simple *idea* in the mind, not taken in by the ways before mentioned. Nor can any force of the understanding destroy those that are there. The dominion of man, in this little world of his own understanding, is much the same as it is in the great world of visible things—in which his power, however managed by art and skill, reaches no further than to compound and divide the materials that are made to his hand—but it can do nothing towards the making the least particle of new matter or destroying one atom of what is already in being. The same inability everyone will find in himself, who shall go about to fashion in his understanding any simple *idea* not received in by his senses from external objects or by reflection from the operations of his own mind about them. I would have anyone try to fancy any taste which had never affected his palate, or *frame the* idea of a scent he had never smelt. And when he can do this, I will also conclude that a blind man has *ideas* of colors, and a deaf man true distinct notions of sounds.

3. This is the reason why, though we cannot believe it impossible to God to make a creature with other organs and more ways to convey into the understanding the notice of corporeal things than those five, as they are usually counted, which he has given to man; yet I think it is *not possible* for anyone *to imagine* any other *qualities* in bodies, however constituted, by which they can be taken notice of, besides sounds, tastes, smells, visible, and tangible qualities. And had mankind been made but with four senses, the qualities then, which are the objects of the fifth sense, had been as far from our notice, imagination, and conception, as now any *belonging to a sixth, seventh, or eighth sense* can possibly be. Whether some other creatures yet, in some other parts of this vast and stupendous universe, may not have this, will be a great presumption to deny. He who will not set himself proudly at the top of all things, but will consider the immensity of this fabric and the great variety that is to be found in this little and inconsiderable part of

it which he has to do with, may be apt to think that in other mansions of it there may be other and different intelligent beings of whose faculties he has as little knowledge or apprehension, as a worm shut up in one drawer of a cabinet has of the senses or understanding of a man—such variety and excellency being suitable to the wisdom and power of the maker. I have here followed the common opinion of man's having but five senses, though, perhaps, there may be justly counted more. But either supposition serves equally to my present purpose.

## Chapter III. *Of* Ideas *of One Sense.*

1. *As colors, of seeing; sounds, of hearing.* The better to conceive the *ideas* we receive from sensation, it may not be amiss for us to consider them in reference to the different ways by which they make their approaches to our minds and make themselves perceivable by us.

*First,* then, there are some which come into our minds *by one sense* only.

*Secondly,* there are others that convey themselves into the mind *by more senses than one.*

*Thirdly,* others that are had from *reflection* only.

*Fourthly,* there are some that make themselves [a] way and are suggested to the mind *by all the ways of sensation and reflection.*

We shall consider them apart under these several heads.

*First,* there are *some* ideas *which have admittance only through one sense,* which is peculiarly adapted to receive them. Thus light and colors, as white, red, yellow, blue, with their several degrees or shades and mixtures, as green, scarlet, purple, sea-green, and the rest, come in only by the eyes; all kinds of noises, sounds, and tones, only by the ears; the several tastes and smells, by the nose and palate. And if these organs, or the nerves which are the conduits to convey them from without to their audience in the brain, the mind's presence-room (as I may so call it) are any of them so disordered as not to perform their functions, they have no postern to be admitted by, no other way to bring themselves into view and be perceived by the understanding.

The most considerable of those belonging to the touch are heat and cold and solidity. All the rest, consisting almost wholly in the sensible configuration, as smooth and rough, or else more or less firm adhesion of the parts, as hard and soft, tough and brittle, are obvious enough.

2. *Few simple* ideas *have names.* I think it will be needless to enumerate all the particular *simple ideas* belonging to each sense. Nor indeed is it possible if we would, there being a great many *more* of them belonging to most of the senses *than we have names for.* The variety of smells, which are as many almost, if not more, than species of bodies in the world, do most of them want names. Sweet and stinking commonly serve our turn for these *ideas*, which in effect is little more than to call them pleasing or displeasing, though the smell of a rose and violet, both sweet, are certainly very distinct *ideas*. Nor are the different tastes that we receive *ideas* of by our palates much better provided with names. Sweet, bitter, sour, harsh, and salt are almost all the epithets we have to denominate that numberless variety of relishes, which are to be found distinct, not only in almost every sort of creatures, but all the different parts of the same plant, fruit, or animal. The same may be said of colors and sounds. I shall, therefore, in the account of simple *ideas* I am here giving, content myself to set down only such as are most material to our present purpose, or are in themselves less apt to be taken notice of, though they are very frequently the ingredients of our complex *ideas*, among which, I think, I may well account solidity—which therefore I shall treat of in the next chapter.

## Chapter IV. *Of Solidity.*

1. *We receive this* idea *from touch.* The *idea* of *solidity* we receive by our touch. And it arises from the resistance which we find in body to the entrance of any other body into the place it possesses, until it has left it. There is no *idea* which we receive more constantly from sensation than *solidity*. Whether we move or rest, in whatever posture we are, we always feel something under us that supports us and hinders our further sinking downwards, and the bodies which we daily handle make us perceive that, while they

remain between them, they do by an insurmountable force hinder the approach of the parts of our hands that press them. That which thus hinders the approach of two bodies, when they are moved one towards another, I call *solidity*. I will not dispute whether this acceptation of the word solid is nearer to its original signification than that which mathematicians use it in. It suffices that I think the common notion of solidity will allow, if not justify, this use of it, but, if anyone thinks it better to call it *impenetrability*, he has my consent. Only I have thought the term *solidity* the more proper to express this *idea*, not only because of its vulgar use in that sense, but also because it carries something more of positive in it than *impenetrability*, which is negative and is perhaps more a consequence of *solidity* than *solidity* itself. This, of all other, seems the *idea* most intimately connected with and essential to body, so as nowhere else to be found or imagined, but only in matter. And though our senses take no notice of it but in masses of matter, of a bulk sufficient to cause a sensation in us, yet the mind, having once gotten this *idea* from such grosser sensible bodies, traces it further, and considers it, as well as figure, in the most minute particle of matter that can exist, and finds it inseparably inherent in body, wherever or however modified.

2. *Solidity fills space.* This is the *idea* which belongs to body, by which we conceive it to *fill space*. The *idea* of which filling of space is that, where we imagine any space taken up by a solid substance, we conceive it so to possess it, that it excludes all other solid substances, and will forever hinder any other two bodies that move towards one another in a straight line from coming to touch one another, unless it removes from between them in a line not parallel to that which they move in. This *idea* of it the bodies which we ordinarily handle sufficiently furnish us with.

3. *Distinct from space.* This resistance, by which it keeps other bodies out of the space which it possesses, is so great that no force, however great, can surmount it. All the bodies in the world pressing a drop of water on all sides will never be able to overcome the resistance which it will make, soft as it is, to their approaching one another, until it is removed out of their way—by which our *idea* of *solidity* is *distinguished* both *from pure space*, which is capable neither of resistance nor motion, and from the ordinary *idea* of *hardness*. [ . . . ]

4. *From hardness. Solidity* is hereby also *differenced from hardness*, in that solidity consists in repletion, and so an utter exclusion of other bodies out of the space it possesses, but hardness in a firm cohesion of the parts of matter, making up masses of a sensible bulk, so that the whole does not easily change its figure. And, indeed, hard and soft are names that we give to things only in relation to the constitutions of our own bodies—that being generally called hard by us which will put us to pain sooner than change figure by the pressure of any part of our bodies, and that on the contrary soft which changes the situation of its parts upon an easy and unpainful touch. [ . . . ]

5. *On solidity depend impulse, resistance, and protrusion.* By this *idea* of solidity is the extension of body distinguished from the extension of space, the extension of body being nothing but the cohesion or continuity of solid, separable, movable parts, and the extension of space the continuity of unsolid, inseparable, and immovable parts. *Upon the solidity of bodies* also *depend their mutual impulse, resistance, and protrusion.* Of pure space then, and solidity, there are several (among which I confess myself one) who persuade themselves they have clear and distinct *ideas*, and that they can think on space without anything in it that resists or is protruded by body. This is the *idea* of pure space, which they think they have as clear as any *idea* they can have of the extension of body. [ . . . ]

## Chapter V. *Of Simple* Ideas *by More Than One Sense.*

The *ideas* we get by more than one sense are of *space* or *extension*, *figure*, *rest*, and *motion*; for these make perceivable impressions, both on the eyes and touch, and we can receive and convey into our minds the *ideas* of the extension, figure, motion, and rest of bodies, both by seeing and feeling. But having occasion to speak more at large of these in another place, I here only enumerate them.

## Chapter VI. *Of Simple* Ideas *of Reflection.*

1. *Simple* ideas *are the operations of the mind about its other* ideas. The mind receiving the *ideas* mentioned in the foregoing chapters from without, when it turns its view inward upon itself, and observes its own actions about those *ideas* it has, takes from this other *ideas* which are as capable to be the objects of its contemplation as any of those it received from foreign things.

2. The two great and principal actions of the mind, which are most frequently considered and which are so frequent that everyone who pleases may take notice of them in himself, are these two: *perception* or *thinking*; and *volition* or *willing*. The power of thinking is called the *understanding*, and the power of volition is called the *will*, and these two powers or abilities in the mind are denominated *faculties*. Of some of the modes of these simple *ideas* of reflection, such as are *remembrance, discerning, reasoning, judging, knowledge, faith*, etc. I shall have occasion to speak hereafter.

## Chapter VII. *Of Simple* Ideas *of Both Sensation and Reflection.*

1. *Pleasure and pain.* There are other simple *ideas* which convey themselves into the mind by all the ways of sensation and reflection, namely, *pleasure* or *delight*, and its opposite, *pain* or *uneasiness*; *power*; *existence*; *unity*.

2. *The* idea *of* perception *and* idea *of* willing *we have from reflection. Delight* or *uneasiness*, one or other of them, join themselves to almost all our *ideas* both of sensation and reflection. And there is scarcely any affection of our senses from without, any retired thought of our mind within, which is not able to produce in us *pleasure* or *pain*. By *pleasure* and *pain* I would be understood to signify whatever delights or molests us, whether it arises from the thoughts of our minds or anything operating on our bodies. For whether we call it satisfaction, delight, pleasure, happiness, etc., on the one side, or uneasiness, trouble, pain, torment, anguish, misery, etc., on the other, they are still but different degrees of the same thing and belong to the *ideas* of pleasure and pain, delight

or uneasiness—which are the names I shall most commonly use for those two sorts of *ideas*. [ . . . ]

7. *Existence and unity. Existence* and *unity* are two other *ideas* that are suggested to the understanding by every object without and every *idea* within. When *ideas* are in our minds, we consider them as being actually there as well as we consider things to be actually without us which is that they exist, or have *existence*. And whatever we can consider as one thing, whether a real being or *idea*, suggests to the understanding the *idea* of *unity*.

8. *Power. Power* also is another of those simple *ideas* which we receive from *sensation and reflection*. For observing in ourselves *that we can* at pleasure move several parts of our bodies which were at rest, the effects also that natural bodies are able to produce in one another, occurring every moment to our senses, we both these ways get the *idea* of power.

9. *Succession.* Besides these there is another *idea*, which, though suggested by our senses, yet is more constantly offered to us by what passes in our minds, and that is the *idea* of *succession*. For if we look immediately into ourselves and reflect on what is observable there, we shall find our *ideas* always, while we are awake or have any thought, passing in train, one going and another coming, without intermission.

10. *Simple* ideas *the materials of all our knowledge.* These, if they are not all, are at least (as I think) the most considerable of those *simple* ideas which the mind has and out of which is made all its other knowledge. All which it receives only by the two aforementioned ways of *sensation* and *reflection*.

Nor let anyone think these too narrow bounds for the capacious mind of man to expatiate in, which takes its flight further than the stars and cannot be confined by the limits of the world, that extends its thoughts often even beyond the utmost expansion of matter, and makes excursions into that incomprehensible *inane*. I grant all this, but desire anyone to assign any *simple idea* which is not *received from* one of *those inlets* before mentioned or any *complex idea* not *made out of those simple ones*. Nor will it be so strange to think these few simple *ideas* sufficient to employ the quickest thought or largest capacity, and to furnish the materials of all that various knowledge, and more various fancies and opinions of all mankind, if we consider how many words may be made out of the various composition of twenty-four letters—or if, going one step further, we will but reflect on the variety of combinations may be made with barely one of the above mentioned *ideas*, namely, number, whose stock is inexhaustible and truly infinite. And what a large and immense field does extension alone afford the mathematicians.

## Chapter VIII. *Other Considerations Concerning Simple* Ideas.

1. *Positive* ideas *from privative causes*. Concerning the simple *ideas* of sensation, it is to be considered that whatever is so constituted in nature as to be able, by affecting our senses, to cause any perception in the mind, does thereby produce in the understanding a simple *idea*; which, whatever is the external cause of it, when it comes to be taken notice of by our discerning faculty, it is by the mind looked on and considered there to be a real *positive idea* in the understanding, as much as any other whatsoever, though perhaps the cause of it is but a privation of the subject.

2. Thus the *ideas* of heat and cold, light and darkness, white and black, motion and rest, are equally clear and *positive ideas* in the mind, though perhaps some of *the causes* which produce them are barely *privations* in subjects from which our senses derive those *ideas*. These the understanding, in its view of them, considers all as distinct positive *ideas*, without taking notice of the causes that produce them— which is an inquiry not belonging to the *idea*, as it is in the understanding, but to the nature of the things existing without us. These are two very different things and carefully to be distinguished, it being one thing to perceive and know the *idea* of white or black and quite another to examine what kind of particles they must be, and how arranged in the surfaces, to make any object appear white or black.

3. A painter or dyer who never inquired into their causes has the *ideas* of white and black, and other colors, as clearly, perfectly, and distinctly in his understanding, and perhaps more distinctly, than the philosopher who has busied himself in considering

their natures, and thinks he knows how far either of them is in its cause positive or privative; and the *idea of black* is no less *positive* in his mind than that of white, *however the cause* of that color in the external object may *be only a privation*.

4. If it were the design of my present undertaking to inquire into the natural causes and manner of perception, I should offer this as a reason *why a privative cause might*, in some cases at least, *produce a positive idea*, namely, that all sensation being produced in us only by different degrees and modes of motion in our animal spirits variously agitated by external objects, the abatement of any former motion must as necessarily produce a new sensation as the variation or increase of it, and so introduce a new *idea* which depends only on a different motion of the animal spirits in that organ.

5. But whether this is so or not, I will not here determine, but appeal to everyone's own experience whether the shadow of a man, though it consists of nothing but the absence of light (and the more the absence of light is, the more discernible is the shadow), does not, when a man looks on it, cause as clear and positive *idea* in his mind as a man himself, though covered over with clear sunshine? And the picture of a shadow is a positive thing. Indeed we have *negative names* which do not stand directly for positive *ideas*, but for their absence, such as *insipid*, *silence*, *nihil*, etc., which words denote positive *ideas*—e.g., *taste*, *sound*, *being*—with a signification of their absence.

6. And thus one may truly be said to see darkness. For supposing a hole perfectly dark from which no light is reflected, it is certain one may see the figure of it or it may be painted. Or whether the ink I write with makes any other *idea* is a question. The privative causes I have here assigned of positive *ideas* are according to the common opinion, but in truth it will be hard to determine whether there are really any *ideas* from a privative cause, until it is determined *whether rest is any more a privation than motion*.

7. Ideas *in the mind, qualities in bodies*. To discover the nature of our *ideas* the better and to discourse of them intelligibly, it will be convenient to distinguish them as they are *ideas* or perceptions in

our minds, and as they are modifications of matter in the bodies that cause such perceptions in us, so that we *may not* think (as perhaps usually is done) that they are exactly the images and *resemblances* of something inherent in the subject, most of those of sensation being in the mind no more the likeness of something existing without us than the names that stand for them are the likeness of our *ideas*, which yet upon hearing they are apt to excite in us.

8. Whatever the mind perceives in itself or is the immediate object of perception, thought, or understanding, that I call *idea*, and the power to produce any *idea* in our mind I call a *quality* of the subject in which that power is. Thus a snowball having the power to produce in us the *ideas* of *white, cold, and round*, the power to produce those *ideas* in us as they are in the snowball I call *qualities*; and as they are sensations or perceptions in our understandings I call them *ideas*; which *ideas* if I speak of sometimes as in the things themselves, I would be understood to mean those qualities in the objects which produce them in us.

9. *Primary and secondary qualities*. Qualities thus considered in bodies are, first, such as are utterly inseparable from the body in whatever state it is, such as in all the alterations and changes it suffers, all the force can be used upon it, it constantly keeps, and such as sense constantly finds in every particle of matter which has bulk enough to be perceived, and the mind finds inseparable from every particle of matter, though less than to make itself singly be perceived by our senses—e.g., take a grain of wheat, divide it into two parts, each part has still *solidity, extension, figure*, and *mobility*; divide it again, and it retains still the same qualities; and so divide it on until the parts become insensible, they must retain still each of them all those qualities. For division (which is all that a mill, or pestle, or any other body does upon another in reducing it to insensible parts) can never take away either solidity, extension, figure, or mobility from any body, but only makes two or more distinct separate masses of matter of that which was but one before. All which distinct masses reckoned as so many distinct bodies after division make a certain number. These I call *original* or *primary qualities* of body, which I think we may observe to produce simple *ideas* in us, namely, solidity, extension, figure, motion or rest, and number.

10. *Secondly*, such *qualities* which in truth are nothing in the objects themselves but powers to produce various sensations in us by their *primary qualities*—i.e., by the bulk, figure, texture, and motion of their insensible parts, as colors, sounds, tastes, etc.—these I call *secondary qualities*. To these might be added a third sort, which are allowed to be barely powers, though they are as much real qualities in the subject as those which I, to comply with the common way of speaking, call *qualities*, but for distinction, *secondary qualities*. For the power in fire to produce a new color or consistency in wax or clay, by its primary qualities, is as much a quality in fire as the power it has to produce in me a new *idea* or sensation of warmth or burning, which I did not feel before by the same primary qualities, namely, the bulk, texture, and motion of its insensible parts.

11. *How primary qualities produce their* ideas. The next thing to be considered is how *bodies* produce *ideas* in us, and that is manifestly *by impulse*, the only way which we can conceive bodies to operate in.

12. If then external objects are not united to our minds when they produce *ideas* in there, and yet we perceive *these original qualities* in such of them as singly fall under our senses, it is evident that some motion must be continued from there by our nerves, or animal spirits, by some parts of our bodies to the brains or the seat of sensation, there to *produce in our minds the particular* ideas *we have of them*. And since the extension, figure, number, and motion of bodies of an observable bigness may be perceived at a distance *by* the sight, it is evident some singly imperceptible bodies must come from them to the eyes, and thereby convey to the brain some *motion* which produces these *ideas* which we have of them in us.

13. *How secondary*. After the same manner that the *ideas* of these original qualities are produced in us, we may conceive that the *ideas of secondary qualities* are also *produced*, namely, *by the operation of insensible particles on our senses*. For it being manifest that there are bodies and good store of bodies, each of which are so small that we cannot, by any of

our senses, discover either their bulk, figure, or motion as is evident in the particles of the air and water, and others extremely smaller than those, perhaps as much smaller than the particles of air and water as the particles of air and water are smaller than peas or hailstones. Let us suppose at present that the different motions and figures, bulk and number of such particles, affecting the several organs of our senses, produce in us those different sensations which we have from the colors and smells of bodies—e.g., that a violet, by the impulse of such insensible particles of matter of peculiar figures and bulks and in different degrees and modifications of their motions, causes the *ideas* of the blue color and sweet scent of that flower to be produced in our minds—it being no more impossible to conceive that God should annex such *ideas* to such motions with which they have no similitude than that he should annex the *idea* of pain to the motion of a piece of steel dividing our flesh with which that *idea* has no resemblance.

14. What I have said concerning *colors* and *smells* may be understood also of *tastes* and *sounds, and other the like sensible qualities* which, whatever reality we by mistake attribute to them, are in truth nothing in the objects themselves but powers to produce various sensations in us, and *depend on those primary qualities*, namely, bulk, figure, texture, and motion of parts, as I have said.

15. Ideas *of primary qualities are resemblances; of secondary, not.* From which I think it easy to draw this observation that the *ideas of primary qualities* of bodies *are resemblances* of them and their patterns do really exist in the bodies themselves, but the *ideas produced* in us *by* these *secondary qualities have no resemblance* of them at all. There is nothing like our *ideas* existing in the bodies themselves. They are, in the bodies we denominate from them, only a power to produce those sensations in us. And what is sweet, blue, or warm in *idea* is but the certain bulk, figure, and motion of the insensible parts in the bodies themselves which we call so.

16. *Flame* is denominated *hot* and *light*; snow, *white* and *cold*; and *manna, white* and *sweet*, from the *ideas* they produce in us. Which qualities are commonly thought to be the same in those bodies that

those *ideas* are in us, the one the perfect resemblance of the other, as they are in a mirror, and it would by most men be judged very extravagant if one should say otherwise. And yet he who will consider that *the same fire* that, at one distance *produces* in us the sensation of *warmth*, does at a nearer approach produce in us the far different sensation of *pain*, ought to consider himself what reason he has to say that his *idea* of *warmth*, which was produced in him by the fire, is actually *in the fire*; and his *idea* of *pain*, which the same fire produced in him the same way, is *not* in the *fire*. Why are whiteness and coldness in snow, and pain not, when it produces the one and the other *idea* in us, and can do neither but by the bulk, figure, number, and motion of its solid parts?

17. The particular *bulk, number, figure, and motion of the parts of fire or snow are really in them*, whether anyone's senses perceive them or not. And therefore they may be called *real qualities*, because they really exist in those bodies. But *light, heat, whiteness* or *coldness, are no more really in them than sickness or pain is in* manna. Take away the sensation of them; let the eyes not see light, or colors, nor the ears hear sounds; let the palate not taste, nor the nose smell; and all colors, tastes, odors, and sounds as they are such particular *ideas* vanish and cease, and are reduced to their causes, i.e., bulk, figure, and motion of parts.

18. A piece of *manna* of a sensible bulk is able to produce in us the *idea* of a round or square figure and, by being removed from one place to another, the *idea* of motion. This *idea* of motion represents it as it really is in the *manna* moving. A circle or square is the same, whether in *idea* or existence, in the mind or in the *manna*; and this both *motion and figure are really in the manna*, whether we take notice of them or not. This everybody is ready to agree to. Besides, *manna*, by the bulk, figure, texture, and motion of its parts, has a power to produce the sensations of sickness and sometimes of acute pains or gripings in us. That these *ideas of sickness and pain are not in the* manna but effects of its operations on us, and are nowhere when we do not feel them, this also everyone readily agrees to. And yet men are hardly to be brought to think *that sweetness and whiteness are not*

*really in manna*; which are but the effects of the operations of *manna* by the motion, size, and figure of its particles on the eyes and palate, as the pain and sickness caused by manna are confessedly nothing but the effects of its operations on the stomach and guts, by the size, motion, and figure of its insensible parts (for by nothing else can a body operate, as has been proved). As if it could not operate on the eyes and palate, and thereby produce in the mind particular distinct *ideas* which in itself it does not have, as well as we allow it can operate on the guts and stomach, and thereby produce distinct *ideas* which in itself it does not have—these *ideas* being all effects of the operations of *manna* on several parts of our bodies by the size, figure, number, and motion of its parts. Why those produced by the eyes and palate should rather be thought to be really in the manna than those produced by the stomach and guts, or why the pain and sickness, *ideas* that are the effect of *manna*, should be thought to be nowhere when they are not felt, and yet the sweetness and whiteness, effects of the same *manna* on other parts of the body by ways equally as unknown, should be thought to exist in the *manna* when they are not seen or tasted, would need some reason to explain.

19. Let us consider the red and white colors in *porphyry*. Hinder light from striking on it, and its colors vanish; it no longer produces any such *ideas* in us. Upon the return of light, it produces these appearances on us again. Can anyone think any real alterations are made in the *porphyry* by the presence or absence of light, and that those *ideas* of whiteness and redness are really in *porphyry* in the light, when it is plain *it has no color in the dark*? It has, indeed, such a configuration of particles, both night and day, as are apt, by the rays of light rebounding from some parts of that hard stone, to produce in us the *idea* of redness and from others the *idea* of whiteness; but whiteness or redness are not in it at any time but such a texture that has the power to produce such a sensation in us.

20. Pound an almond, and the clear white *color* will be altered into a dirty one and the sweet *taste* into an oily one. What real alteration can the beating of the pestle make in any body but an alteration of the *texture* of it?

21. *Ideas* being thus distinguished and understood, we may be able to give an account how the same water, at the same time, may produce the *idea* of cold by one hand and of heat by the other, whereas it is impossible that the same water, if those *ideas* were really in it, should at the same time be both hot and cold. For if we imagine *warmth*, as it is *in our hands*, to be *nothing but a certain sort and degree of motion in the minute particles of our nerves or animal spirits*, we may understand how it is possible that the same water may, at the same time, produce the sensations of heat in one hand and cold in the other; which yet figure never does that, never producing the *idea* of a square by one hand, which has produced the *idea* of a globe by another. But if the sensation of heat and cold are nothing but the increase or diminution of the motion of the minute parts of our bodies caused by the corpuscles of any other body, it is easy to be understood that, if that motion is greater in one hand than in the other, if a body is applied to the two hands, which has in its minute particles a greater motion than in those of one of the hands, and a less than in those of the other, it will increase the motion of the one hand and lessen it in the other, and so cause the different sensations of heat and cold that depend on it.

22. I have, in what just goes before, been engaged in physical inquiries a little further than perhaps I intended. But it being necessary to make the nature of sensation a little understood and to make the *difference between the qualities in bodies and the* ideas *produced by them in the mind* to be distinctly conceived, without which it would be impossible to discourse intelligibly of them, I hope I shall be pardoned this little excursion into natural philosophy, it being necessary in our present inquiry to distinguish the *primary* and *real qualities* of bodies which are always in them (namely, solidity, extension, figure, number, and motion, or rest, and are sometimes perceived by us, namely, when the bodies they are in are big enough singly to be discerned) from those *secondary* and *imputed qualities* which are but the powers of several combinations of those primary ones, when

they operate without being distinctly discerned; by which we may also come to know what *ideas* are and what are not resemblances of something really existing in the bodies we denominate from them.

23. The *qualities* then that are in *bodies* rightly considered are of *three sorts*.

*First*, the *bulk, figure, number, situation*, and *motion, or rest* of their solid parts. Those are in them, whether we perceive them or not; and when they are of that size that we can discover them, we have by these an *idea* of the thing as it is in itself, as is plain in artificial things. These I call *primary qualities*.

*Secondly*, the *power* that is in any body *by* reason of *its* insensible *primary qualities* to operate after a peculiar manner on any of our senses and thereby *produce in us* the *different ideas* of several colors, sounds, smells, tastes, etc. These are usually called sensible qualities.

*Thirdly*, the *power* that is in any body *by* reason of the particular constitution of *its primary qualities to* make such a *change* in the *bulk, figure, texture, and motion of another body* as to make it operate on our senses differently from what it did before. Thus the sun has a power to make wax white, and fire to make lead fluid. These *are* usually called powers.

The first of these, as has been said, I think, may be properly called *real*, *original*, or *primary qualities*, because they are in the things themselves, whether they are perceived or not. And upon their different modifications it is that the secondary qualities depend.

The other two are only powers to act differently upon other things, which powers result from the different modifications of those primary qualities.

24. *Reason of our mistake in this*. But though *the two latter sorts of qualities are powers barely* and nothing but powers, relating to several other bodies and resulting from the different modifications of the original qualities, yet they are generally otherwise thought of. For the *second sort*, namely, the powers to produce several *ideas* in us by our senses, *are looked upon as real qualities in the things* thus affecting us. But *the third sort are called and esteemed barely powers*—e.g., the *idea* of heat or light which we receive by our eyes or touch from the sun are commonly thought *real qualities*, existing in the sun, and something more

than mere powers in it. But when we consider the sun, in reference to wax which it melts or blanches, we look on the whiteness and softness produced in the wax, not as qualities in the sun, but effects produced by *powers* in it. Whereas, if rightly considered, these qualities of light and warmth, which are perceptions in me when I am warmed or enlightened by the sun, are no otherwise in the sun than the changes made in the wax, when it is blanched or melted, are in the sun. They are all of them equally powers in the sun, depending on its primary qualities, by which it is able, in the one case, so to alter the bulk, figure, texture, or motion of some of the insensible parts of my eyes or hands as thereby to produce in me the *idea* of light or heat, and in the other it is able so to alter the bulk, figure, texture, or motion of the insensible parts of the wax as to make them fit to produce in me the distinct *ideas* of white and fluid.

25. The reason *why the one is ordinarily taken for real qualities and the other only for bare powers* seems to be, because the *ideas* we have of distinct colors, sounds, etc. containing nothing at all in them of bulk, figure, or motion, we are not apt to think them the effects of these primary qualities, which do not appear to our senses to operate in their production, and with which they do not have any apparent congruity or conceivable connection. Hence it is that we are so ready to imagine that those *ideas* are the resemblances of something really existing in the objects themselves, since sensation discovers nothing of bulk, figure, or motion of parts in their production, nor can reason show how bodies, by their bulk, figure, and motion, should produce in the mind the *ideas* of blue or yellow, etc. But in the other case, in the operations of bodies changing the qualities one of another, we plainly discover that the quality produced has commonly no resemblance with anything in the thing producing it, for which reason we look on it as a bare effect of power. For though receiving the *idea* of heat or light from the sun, we are apt to think it is a perception and resemblance of such a quality in the sun, yet when we see wax, or a fair face, receive change of color from the sun, we cannot imagine that to be the reception or resemblance of anything in the sun, because we do not find those

different colors in the sun itself. For our senses being able to observe a likeness or unlikeness of sensible qualities in two different external objects, we readily enough conclude the production of any sensible quality, in any subject, to be an effect of bare power and not the communication of any quality which was really in the efficient, when we find no such sensible quality in the thing that produced it. But our senses not being able to discover any unlikeness between the *idea* produced in us and the quality of the object producing it, we are apt to imagine that our *ideas* are resemblances of something in the objects and not the effects of certain powers placed in the modification of their primary qualities, with which primary qualities the *ideas* produced in us have no resemblance.

26. *Secondary qualities two-fold; first, immediately perceivable; secondly, mediately perceivable.* To conclude, besides those before mentioned *primary qualities* in bodies, namely, bulk, figure, extension, number, and motion of their solid parts, all the rest by which we take notice of bodies and distinguish them one from another are nothing else but several powers in them depending on those primary qualities, by which they are fitted, either by immediately operating on our bodies to produce several different *ideas* in us, or else by operating on other bodies so to change their primary qualities as to render them capable of producing *ideas* in us different from what before they did. The former of these, I think, may be called *secondary qualities, immediately perceivable.* The latter, *secondary qualities, mediately perceivable.*

## Chapter IX. *Of Perception.*

1. *It is the first simple* idea *of reflection. Perception*, as it is the first faculty of the mind exercised about our *ideas*; so it is the first and simplest *idea* we have from reflection, and is by some called thinking in general. Though thinking, in the propriety of the *English* tongue, signifies that sort of operation in the mind about its *ideas* in which the mind is active, where it, with some degree of voluntary attention, considers anything. For in bare naked *perception*, the mind is for the most part only passive. And what it perceives, it cannot avoid perceiving.

2. *Perception is only when the mind receives the impression. What perception is* everyone will know better by reflecting on what he does himself when he sees, hears, feels, etc., or thinks, than by any discourse of mine. Whoever reflects on what passes in his own mind cannot miss it. And if he does not reflect, all the words in the world cannot make him have any notion of it.

3. This is certain, that whatever alterations are made in the body, if they do not reach the mind, whatever impressions are made on the outward parts, if they are not taken notice of within, there is no perception. Fire may burn our bodies with no other effect than it does a billet, unless the motion is continued to the brain and there the sense of heat, or *idea* of pain, is produced in the mind—in what consists *actual perception.*

4. How often may a man observe in himself that while his mind is intently employed in the contemplation of some objects, and curiously surveying some *ideas* that are there, it takes no notice of impressions of sounding bodies made upon the organ of hearing, with the same alteration that uses to be for the producing the *idea* of sound? A sufficient impulse there may be on the organ, but, it not reaching the observation of the mind, there follows no perception. And though the motion that uses to produce the *idea* of sound be made in the ear, yet no sound is heard. Want of sensation in this case is not through any defect in the organ, or that the man's ears are less affected than at other times when he does hear; but that which uses to produce the *idea*, though conveyed in by the usual organ, not being taken notice of in the understanding and so imprinting no *idea* in the mind, there follows no sensation—*so that wherever there is sense* or *perception, there some* idea *is actually produced and present in the understanding.*

5. *Children, though they have* ideas *in the womb, have none innate.* Therefore, I do not doubt but *children*, by the exercise of their senses about objects that affect them *in the womb, receive some few ideas* before they are born, as the unavoidable effects either of the bodies that surround them or else of those wants or diseases they suffer; among which (if one may conjecture concerning things not very capable

of examination) I think the *ideas* of hunger and warmth are two, which probably are some of the first that children have, and which they scarcely ever part with again.

6. But though it is reasonable to imagine that *children* receive some *ideas* before they come into the world, yet these simple *ideas* are *far from* those *innate principles* which some contend for, and we above have rejected. These here mentioned, being the effects of sensation, are only from some affections of the body which happen to them there, and so depend on something exterior to the mind, not otherwise differing in their manner of production from other *ideas* derived from sense, but only in the precedence of time; whereas those innate principles are supposed to be quite of another nature, not coming into the mind by any accidental alterations in, or operations on the body, but, as it were, original characters impressed upon it in the very first moment of its being and constitution. [ . . . ]

8. Ideas *of sensation often changed by the judgment*. We are further to consider concerning perception that the *ideas we receive by sensation are often* in grown people *altered by the judgment* without our taking notice of it. When we set before our eyes a round globe of any uniform color — e.g., gold, alabaster, or jet — it is certain that the *idea* thereby imprinted in our mind is of a flat circle, variously shadowed, with several degrees of light and brightness coming to our eyes. But we having by use been accustomed to perceive what kind of appearance convex bodies are accustomed to make in us, what alterations are made in the reflections of light by the difference of the sensible figures of bodies, the judgment presently, by an habitual custom, alters the appearances into their causes, so that from that which is truly variety of shadow or color, collecting the figure, it makes it pass for a mark of figure and frames to itself the perception of a convex figure and a uniform color, when the *idea* we receive from this is only a plane variously colored, as is evident in painting. To which purpose I shall here insert a problem of that very ingenious and studious promoter of real knowledge, the learned and worthy Mr. *Molineaux*, which he was pleased to send me in a letter some months since; and it is

this: *Suppose a man born blind and now adult, and taught by his touch to distinguish between a cube and a sphere of the same metal and nearly of the same bigness, so as to tell, when he felt one and the other, which is the cube, which the sphere. Suppose then the cube and sphere placed on a table and the blind man be made to see. Quaere, whether by his sight, before he touched them, he could now distinguish and tell which is the globe, which the cube?* To which the acute and judicious proposer answers: No. *For though he has obtained the experience of how a globe, how a cube affects his touch, yet he has not yet obtained the experience that what affects his touch so or so must affect his sight so or so. Or that a protuberant angle in the cube that pressed his hand unequally shall appear to his eye as it does in the cube.* I agree with this thinking gentleman, whom I am proud to call my friend, in his answer to this problem, and am of opinion that the blind man at first sight would not be able with certainty to say which was the globe, which the cube, while he only saw them, though he could unerringly name them by his touch and certainly distinguish them by the difference of their figures felt. [ . . . ]

11. *Perception puts the difference between animals and inferior beings*. This faculty of *perception* seems to me to be that which *puts the distinction between the animal kingdom and the inferior parts of nature*. For however vegetables have, many of them, some degrees of motion, and, upon the different application of other bodies to them, do very briskly alter their figures and motions, and so have obtained the name of sensitive plants from a motion which has some resemblance to that which in animals follows upon sensation. Yet, I suppose, it is all bare mechanism, and no otherwise produced than the turning of a wild oat-beard by the insinuation of the particles of moisture, or the shortening of a rope by the affusion of water, all which is done without any sensation in the subject or the having or receiving any *ideas*.

12. *Perception*, I believe, is in some degree *in all sorts of animals*; though in some possibly the avenues provided by nature for the reception of sensations are so few, and the perception they are received with so obscure and dull, that it comes extremely short of the quickness and variety of sensation which is in other

animals, but yet it is sufficient for, and wisely adapted to, the state and condition of that sort of animals who are thus made. [ . . . ]

## Chapter X. *Of Retention.*

1. *Contemplation.* The next faculty of the mind by which it makes a further progress towards knowledge is that which I call *retention*, or the keeping of those simple *ideas*, which from sensation or reflection it has received. This is done two ways: first, by keeping the *idea* which is brought into it, for some time, actually in view—which is called *contemplation.*

2. *Memory.* The other way of retention is the power to revive again in our minds those *ideas* which have disappeared after imprinting, or have been as it were laid aside out of sight, and thus we do when we conceive heat or light, yellow or sweet, the object being removed. This is *memory*, which is as it were the storehouse of our *ideas*. For the narrow mind of man not being capable of having many *ideas* under view and consideration at once, it was necessary to have a repository to lay up those *ideas* which at another time it might have use of. But our *ideas* being nothing but actual perceptions in the mind, which cease to be anything when there is no perception of them, this *laying up* of our *ideas* in the repository of the memory signifies no more but this, that the mind has a power in many cases to revive perceptions which it has once had, with this additional perception annexed to them, that it has had them before. And in this sense it is that our *ideas* are said to be in our memories, when indeed they are actually nowhere, but only there is an ability in the mind when it will revive them again, and as it were paint them anew on itself, though some with more, some with less difficulty, some more lively, and others more obscurely. And thus it is by the assistance of this faculty that we are to have all those *ideas* in our understandings, which though we do not actually contemplate, yet we can bring in sight, and make appear again, and be the objects of our thoughts, without the help of those sensible qualities which first imprinted them there. [ . . . ]

## Chapter XI. *Of Discerning, and Other Operations of the Mind.*

1. *No knowledge without it.* Another faculty we may take notice of in our minds is that of *discerning* and distinguishing between the several *ideas* it has. It is not enough to have a confused perception of something in general. Unless the mind had a distinct perception of different objects and their qualities, it would be capable of very little knowledge, though the bodies that affect us were as busy about us as they are now and the mind were continually employed in thinking. On this faculty of distinguishing one thing from another depends the *evidence and certainty* of several, even very general, propositions which have passed for innate truths, because men, overlooking the true cause why those propositions find universal assent, impute it wholly to native uniform impressions, whereas it in truth *depends upon this clear discerning faculty* of the mind by which it perceives two *ideas* to be the same, or different. [ . . . ]

4. *Comparing.* The comparing them one with another in respect of extent, degrees, time, place, or any other circumstances, is another operation of the mind about its *ideas*, and is that upon which depends all that large tribe of *ideas* comprehended under *relation*; which, of how vast an extent it is, I shall have occasion to consider hereafter.

6. *Compounding.* The next operation we may observe in the mind about its *ideas* is composition, by which it puts together several of those simple ones it has received from sensation and reflection and combines them into complex ones. Under this of composition may be reckoned also that of enlarging, in which, though the composition does not so much appear as in more complex ones, yet it is nevertheless a putting several *ideas* together, though of the same kind. Thus by adding several units together we make the *idea* of a dozen, and putting together the repeated *ideas* of several perches we frame that of a furlong. [ . . . ]

8. *Naming.* When children have, by repeated sensations, got *ideas* fixed in their memories, they begin by degrees to learn the use of signs. And when they have gotten the skill to apply the organs of speech to the framing of articulate sounds, they begin to make

*use of words* to signify their *ideas* to others. These verbal signs they sometimes borrow from others and sometimes make themselves, as one may observe among the new and unusual names children often give to things in the first use of language.

9. *Abstraction*. The use of words then being to stand as outward marks of our internal *ideas* and those *ideas* being taken from particular things, if every particular *idea* that we take in should have a distinct name, names must be endless. To prevent this, the mind makes the particular *ideas* received from particular objects become general, which is done by considering them as they are in the mind such appearances, separate from all other existences, and the circumstances of real existence, as time, place, or any other concomitant *ideas*. This is called abstraction, by which *ideas* taken from particular beings become general representatives of all of the same kind, and their names general names, applicable to whatever exists conformable to such abstract *ideas*. Such precise, naked appearances in the mind, without considering how, from where, or with what others they came there, the understanding lays up (with names commonly annexed to them) as the standards to rank real existences into sorts, as they agree with these patterns, and to *denominate* them accordingly. Thus the same color being observed today in chalk or snow which the mind yesterday received from milk, it considers that appearance alone, makes it a representative of all of that kind, and having given it the name *whiteness*, by that sound it signifies the same quality wherever to be imagined or met with; and thus universals, whether *ideas* or terms, are made.

17. *Dark room*. I pretend not to teach, but to inquire, and therefore cannot but confess here again that external and internal sensation are the only passages I can find of knowledge to the understanding. These alone, as far as I can discover, are the windows by which light is let into this *dark room*. For I think the *understanding* is not much unlike a closet wholly shut from light, with only some little openings left, to let in external visible resemblances or *ideas* of things without. Would the pictures coming into such a dark room but stay there and lie so orderly as to be found upon occasion, it would very much resemble the

understanding of a man, in reference to all objects of sight and the *ideas* of them.

These are my guesses concerning the means by which the understanding comes to have and retain simple *ideas* and the modes of them with some other operations about them. I proceed now to examine some of these simple *ideas*, and their modes, a little more particularly.

## Chapter XII. *Of Complex* Ideas.

1. *Made by the mind out of simple ones*. Up to now we have considered those *ideas* in the reception of which the mind is only passive, which are those simple ones received from *sensation* and *reflection* before mentioned, of which the mind cannot make one to itself, nor have any *idea* which does not wholly consist of them. But as the mind is wholly passive in the reception of all its simple *ideas*, so it exerts several acts of its own by which, out of its simple *ideas* as the materials and foundations of the rest, the others are framed. The acts of the mind, in which it exerts its power over its simple *ideas*, are chiefly these three: 1. Combining several simple *ideas* into one compound one, and thus all complex *ideas* are made. 2. The *second* is bringing two *ideas*, whether simple or complex, together, and setting them by one another, so as to take a view of them at once without uniting them into one—by which way it gets all its *ideas* of relations. 3. The *third* is separating them from all other *ideas* that accompany them in their real existence; this is called *abstraction*. And thus all its general *ideas* are made. This shows man's power and its ways of operation to be much the same in the material and intellectual world. For the materials in both being such as he has no power over, either to make or destroy, all that man can do is either to unite them together, or to set them by one another, or wholly separate them. I shall here begin with the first of these in the consideration of complex *ideas* and come to the other two in their due places. As simple *ideas* are observed to exist in several combinations united together, so the mind has a power to consider several of them united together as one *idea*; and that not only as they are united in external objects, but as itself has joined them. Ideas thus made up of several

simple ones put together I call *complex*—such as are *beauty*, *gratitude*, *a man*, *an army*, *the universe*—which though complicated of various simple *ideas* or *complex ideas* made up of simple ones, yet are, when the mind pleases, considered each by itself as one entire thing, and signified by one name.

2. *Made voluntarily.* In this faculty of repeating and joining together its *ideas* the mind has great power in varying and multiplying the objects of its thoughts infinitely beyond what *sensation* or *reflection* furnishes it with, but all this still confined to those simple *ideas* which it received from those two sources and which are the ultimate materials of all its compositions. For simple *ideas* are all from things themselves, and of these *the mind can* have no more, nor other than what are suggested to it. It can have no other *ideas* of sensible qualities than what come from without by the senses, nor any *ideas* of other kind of operations of a thinking substance than what it finds in itself; but when it has once gotten these simple *ideas*, it is not confined barely to observation and what offers itself from without. It can, by its own power, put together those *ideas* it has and *make new complex ones* which it never received so united.

3. *Are either modes, substances, or relations.* Complex *ideas*, however compounded and decompounded, though their number is infinite and the variety endless, with which they fill and entertain the thoughts of men, yet I think they may be all reduced under these three heads: 1. *Modes*, 2. *Substances*, 3. *Relations*.

4. *Modes.* First, *modes* I call such complex *ideas* which, however compounded, do not contain in them the supposition of subsisting by themselves, but are considered as dependences on or affections of substances, such as are the *ideas* signified by the words *triangle*, *gratitude*, *murder*, etc. And if in this I use the word *mode* in somewhat a different sense from its ordinary signification, I beg pardon, it being unavoidable in discourses differing from the ordinary received notions either to make new words or to use old words in somewhat a new signification. The latter of which, in our present case, is perhaps the more tolerable of the two.

5. *Simple and mixed modes.* Of these modes, there are two sorts which deserve distinct consideration.

First, there are some which are only variations or different combinations of the same simple *idea*, without the mixture of any other—as a dozen or score, which are nothing but the *ideas* of so many distinct units added together. And these I call *simple modes*, as being contained within the bounds of one simple *idea*. Secondly, there are others compounded of simple *ideas* of several kinds put together to make one complex one—e.g., *beauty*, consisting of a certain composition of color and figure causing delight to the beholder; *theft*, which being the concealed change of the possession of anything without the consent of the proprietor contains, as is visible, a combination of several *ideas* of several kinds. And these I call *mixed modes*.

6. *Substances single or collective.* Secondly, the *ideas* of *substances* are such combinations of simple *ideas* as are taken to represent distinct particular things subsisting by themselves, in which the supposed or confused *idea* of substance, such as it is, is always the first and chief. Thus if to substance is joined the simple *idea* of a certain dull whitish color, with certain degrees of weight, hardness, ductility, and fusibility, we have the *idea* of *lead* and a combination of the *ideas* of a certain sort of figure with the powers of motion. Thought and reasoning joined to substance make the ordinary *idea* of *a man*. Now of substances also there are two sorts of *ideas*: one of single substances, as they exist separately, as of *a man* or *a sheep*; the other of several of those put together, as an army of men or *flock* of sheep—which *collective* ideas *of* several *substances* thus put together are as much each of them one single *idea* as that of a man or a unit.

7. *Relation.* Thirdly, the last sort of complex *ideas*, is that we call *relation*, which consists in the consideration and comparing one *idea* with another. Of these several kinds we shall treat in their order.

8. *The most abstruse* ideas *from the two sources*. If we will trace the progress of our minds and with attention observe how it repeats, adds together, and unites its simple *ideas* received from sensation or reflection, it will lead us further than at first perhaps we should have imagined. And, I believe, we shall find, if we warily observe the origins of our notions that even

*the most abstruse* ideas, however remote they may seem from sense or from any operations of our own minds, are yet only such as the understanding frames to itself, by repeating and joining together *ideas* that it had either from objects of sense or from its own operations about them. So that those even large *and abstract* ideas *are derived from sensation or reflection*, being no other than what the mind, by the ordinary use of its own faculties, employed about *ideas* received from objects of sense, or from the operations it observes in itself about them, may and does attain unto. This I shall endeavor to show in the *ideas* we have of *space, time,* and *infinity,* and some few others that seem the most remote from those origins.

## Chapter XIII. *Of Simple Modes and, First, of the Simple Modes of Space.*

1. *Simple modes.* Though in the foregoing part I have often mentioned simple *ideas,* which are truly the materials of all our knowledge, yet having treated of them there rather in the way that they come into the mind than as distinguished from others more compounded, it will not be perhaps amiss to take a view of some of them again under this consideration and examine those different *modifications of the same* idea—which the mind either finds in things existing or is able to make within itself without the help of any extrinsic object or any foreign suggestion.

Those *modifications of any one simple* idea (which, as has been said, *I call simple modes*) are as perfectly different and distinct *ideas* in the mind as those of the greatest distance or contrariety. For the *idea* of *two* is as distinct from that of *one* as *blueness* from *heat* or either of them from any number. And yet it is made up only of that simple *idea* of a unit repeated, and repetitions of this kind joined together make those distinct *simple modes,* of a *dozen,* a *gross,* a *million.*

2. Idea *of space.* I shall begin with the *simple idea of space.* I have showed above, chap. 4, that we get the *idea* of space both by our sight and touch; this, I think, is so evident that it would be as needless to go to prove that men perceive by their sight a distance between bodies of different colors, or between the parts of the same body, as that they see colors themselves; nor is it

less obvious that they can do so in the dark by feeling and touch.

3. *Space and extension.* This space considered barely in length between any two beings without considering anything else between them is called *distance;* if considered in length, breadth, and thickness, I think it may be called *capacity.* The term extension is usually applied to it in whatever manner considered.

4. *Immensity.* Each different distance is a different modification of space, and *each* idea *of any different distance, or space, is a simple mode of this* idea. Men for the use and by the custom of measuring settle in their minds the *ideas* of certain stated lengths, such as are an *inch, foot, yard, fathom, mile, diameter of the earth,* etc., which are so many distinct *ideas* made up only of space. When any such stated lengths or measures of space are made familiar to men's thoughts, they can in their minds repeat them as often as they will without mixing or joining to them the *idea* of body or anything else, and frame to themselves the *ideas* of long, square, or cubic *feet, yards,* or *fathoms,* here among the bodies of the universe or else beyond the utmost bounds of all bodies; and by adding these still one to another, enlarge their *ideas* of space as much as they please. The power of repeating or doubling any *idea* we have of any distance and adding it to the former as often as we will, without being ever able to come to any stop or stint, let us enlarge it as much as we will, is that which gives us the *idea* of *immensity.*

5. *Figure.* There is another modification of this *idea,* which is nothing but the relation which the parts of the termination of extension, or circumscribed space, have among themselves. This the touch discovers in sensible bodies whose extremities come within our reach, and the eye takes both from bodies and colors whose boundaries are within its view, where observing how the extremities terminate either in straight lines which meet at discernible angles, or in crooked lines in which no angles can be perceived, by considering these as they relate to one another in all parts of the extremities of any body or space, it has that *idea* we call *figure,* which affords to the mind infinite variety. [ . . . ]

11. *Extension and body not the same.* There are some who would persuade us that *body and extension are the same thing*; but I would not suspect them of changing the signification of words, given that they have so severely condemned the philosophy of others because it has been placed too much in the uncertain meaning or deceitful obscurity of doubtful or insignificant terms. If therefore they mean by *body and extension the same* that other people do—namely, by *body* something that is solid and extended, whose parts are separable and movable different ways, and by extension, only the space that lies between the extremities of those solid coherent parts, and which is possessed by them—they confound very different *ideas* one with another. For I appeal to every man's own thoughts whether the *idea* of space is not as distinct from that of solidity as it is from the *idea* of scarlet color? It is true solidity cannot exist without extension. Neither can scarlet color exist without extension. But this does not hinder but that they are distinct *ideas*. Many *ideas* require others, as necessary to their existence or conception, which yet are very distinct *ideas*. Motion can neither be, nor be conceived, without space, and yet motion is not space, nor space motion. Space can exist without it, and they are very distinct *ideas*; and so, I think, are those of space and solidity. Solidity is so inseparable an *idea* from body that upon that depends its filling of space, its contact, impulse, and communication of motion upon impulse. And if it is a reason to prove that spirit is different from body because thinking does not include the *idea* of extension in it, the same reason will be as valid, I suppose, to prove that *space is not body* because it does not include the *idea* of solidity in it—*space and solidity* being *as distinct ideas* as thinking and extension and as wholly separable in the mind one from another. *Body* then and *extension*, it is evident, are two distinct *ideas*. For,

12. *First, extension* includes no solidity, nor resistance to the motion of *body*, as body does.

13. *Secondly*, the parts of pure space are inseparable one from the other, so that the continuity cannot be separated neither really nor mentally. For I demand of anyone to remove any part of it from another with which it is continued, even so much

as in thought. To divide and separate actually is, as I think, by removing the parts one from another, to make two surfaces where before there was a continuity; and to divide mentally is to make in the mind two surfaces where before there was a continuity, and consider them as removed one from the other. This can only be done in things considered by the mind as capable of being separated—and by separation—of acquiring new distinct surfaces, which they then do not have but are capable of; but neither of these ways of separation, whether real or mental, is, as I think, compatible to pure *space*.

It is true, a man may consider so much of such a *space* as is answerable or commensurate to a foot without considering the rest—which is indeed a partial consideration, but not so much as mental separation, or division, since a man can no more mentally divide, without considering two surfaces separate one from the other, than he can actually divide, without making two surfaces disjoined one from the other. But a partial consideration is not separating. A man may consider light in the sun without its heat, or mobility in body without its extension, without thinking of their separation. One is only a partial consideration, terminating in one alone, and the other is a consideration of both as existing separately.

14. *Thirdly*, the parts of pure *space* are immovable, which follows from their inseparability, *motion* being nothing but change of distance between any two things. But this cannot be between parts that are inseparable, which therefore must necessarily be at perpetual rest one among another.

Thus the determined *idea* of simple *space* distinguishes it plainly and sufficiently from *body*, since its parts are inseparable, immovable, and without resistance to the motion of body. [ . . . ]

16. *Division of beings into bodies and spirits does not prove body and space the same.* Those who contend that *space and body* are *the same* bring this *dilemma*: either this *space* is something or nothing; if nothing is between two bodies, they must necessarily touch. If it is allowed to be something, they ask whether it is body or spirit? To which I answer by another question, who told them that there was, or could be, nothing but solid beings which could not

think, and thinking beings that were not extended?—which is all they mean by the terms *body* and *spirit*.

17. *Substance, which we do not know, no proof against space without body.* If it is demanded (as usually it is) whether this *space* void of *body* is *substance* or *accident*, I shall readily answer I do not know; nor shall be ashamed to own my ignorance, until they who ask show me a clear distinct *idea* of *substance*.

18. I endeavor as much as I can to deliver myself from those fallacies which we are apt to put upon ourselves by taking words for things. It does not help our ignorance to feign a knowledge where we have none, by making a noise with sounds, without clear and distinct significations. Names made at pleasure neither alter the nature of things nor make us understand them but as they are signs of and stand for determined *ideas*. And I desire those who lay so much stress on the sound of these two syllables, *substance*, to consider whether applying it, as they do, to the infinite incomprehensible God, to finite spirits, and to body, it is in the same sense, and whether it stands for the same *idea*, when each of those three so different beings are called *substances*. If so, whether it will follow from this that God, spirits, and body, agreeing in the same common nature of *substance*, do not differ any otherwise than in a bare different modification of that *substance*, as a tree and a pebble being in the same sense body, and agreeing in the common nature of body, differ only in a bare modification of that common matter—which will be a very harsh doctrine. If they say that they apply it to God, finite spirit, and matter, in three different significations and that it stands for one *idea* when God is said to be a *substance*; for another when the soul is called *substance*; and for a third when body is called so, if the name *substance* stands for three several distinct *ideas*, they would do well to make known those distinct *ideas*, or at least to give three distinct names to them, to prevent in so important a notion the confusion and errors that will naturally follow from the promiscuous use of so doubtful a term (which is so far from being suspected to have three distinct, that in ordinary use it has scarcely one clear distinct signification). And if they can thus make three distinct *ideas* of *substance*, what hinders why another may not make a fourth?

19. *Substance and accidents of little use in philosophy.* They who first ran into the notion of *accidents*, as a sort of real beings that needed something to inhere in, were forced to find out the word *substance* to support them. Had the poor *Indian* philosopher (who imagined that the earth also wanted something to bear it up) but thought of this word *substance*, he did not need to have been troubled to find an elephant to support it and a tortoise to support his elephant. The word *substance* would have done it effectually. And he who inquired might have taken it for as good an answer from an *Indian* philosopher that *substance*, without knowing what it is, is that which supports the earth, as we take it for a sufficient answer and good doctrine from our *European* philosophers that substance, without knowing what it is, is that which supports *accidents*—so that of *substance*, we have no *idea* of what it is, but only a confused obscure one of what it does. [ . . . ]

21. A vacuum *beyond the utmost bounds of body.* But to return to our *idea* of space. If *body* is not supposed infinite, which I think no one will affirm, I would ask whether, if God placed a man at the extremity of corporeal beings, he could not stretch his hand beyond his body? If he could, then he would put his arm where there was before *space* without *body*; and if there he spread his fingers, there would still be *space* between them without *body*. If he could not stretch out his hand, it must be because of some external hindrance (for we suppose him alive, with such a power of moving the parts of his body that he has now, which is not in itself impossible, if God so pleased to have it, or at least it is not impossible for God so to move him); and then I ask whether that which hinders his hand from moving outwards is substance or accident, something or nothing? And when they have resolved that, they will be able to resolve themselves what that is, which is or may be between two bodies at a distance, that is not body and has no solidity. In the mean time, the argument is at least as good that where nothing hinders (as beyond the utmost bounds of all bodies) a *body* put in motion may move on, as where there is nothing between, there two bodies must necessarily touch; for pure *space* between is sufficient to take away the necessity of

mutual contact, but bare *space* in the way is not sufficient to stop motion. The truth is these men must either admit that they think body infinite, though they are loath to speak it out, or else affirm that *space* is not *body*. For I would gladly meet with that thinking man who can in his thoughts set any bounds to space more than he can to duration, or by thinking hope to arrive at the end of either. And therefore, if his *idea* of eternity is infinite, so is his *idea* of immensity; they are both finite or infinite alike.

22. *The power of annihilation proves a* vacuum. Further, those who assert the impossibility of *space* existing without *matter* must not only make body infinite, but must also deny a power in God to annihilate any part of matter. No one, I suppose, will deny that God can put an end to all motion that is in matter, and fix all the bodies of the universe in a perfect quiet and rest, and continue them so long as he pleases. Whoever then will allow that God can, during such a general rest, annihilate either this book or the body of him who reads it, must necessarily admit the possibility of a *vacuum*; for it is evident that the space that was filled by the parts of the annihilated body will still remain, and be a space without body. For the surrounding bodies being in perfect rest are a wall of adamant, and in that state make it a perfect impossibility for any other body to get into that space. And indeed the necessary motion of one particle of matter into the place from which another particle of matter is removed is but a consequence from the supposition of plenitude. This will therefore need some better proof than a supposed matter of fact which experiment can never make out, our own clear and distinct *ideas* plainly satisfying us that there is no necessary connection between *space* and *solidity*, since we can conceive the one without the other. And those who dispute for or against a *vacuum* do thereby confess they have distinct *ideas* of *vacuum* and *plenum*—i.e., that they have an *idea* of extension void of solidity—though they deny its existence. Or else they dispute about nothing at all. For they who so much alter the signification of words as to call *extension body*, and consequently make the whole essence of body to be nothing but pure extension without solidity, must talk absurdly whenever they speak of *vacuum*, since

it is impossible for extension to be without extension. For *vacuum*, whether we affirm or deny its existence, signifies space without body, whose very existence no one can deny to be possible who will not make matter infinite and take from God a power to annihilate any particle of it.

23. *Motion proves a* vacuum. But not to go so far as beyond the utmost bounds of body in the universe, nor appeal to God's omnipotence to find a *vacuum*, the *motion* of bodies that are in our view and neighborhood seems to me plainly to evince it. For I desire anyone so to divide a solid body of any dimension he pleases as to make it possible for the solid parts to move up and down freely every way within the bounds of that surface, if there is not left in it a void space as big as the least part into which he has divided the said solid body. And if where the least particle of the body divided is as big as a mustard seed, a void space equal to the bulk of a mustard seed be requisite to make room for the free motion of the parts of the divided body within the bounds of its surface, where the particles of matter are 100,000,000 less than a mustard seed, there must also be a space void of solid matter as big as 100,000,000 part of a mustard seed; for if it hold in the one, it will hold in the other, and so on *in infinitum*. And let this void space be as little as it will, it destroys the hypothesis of *plenitude*. For if there can be a space void of body equal to the smallest separate particle of matter now existing in nature, it is still space without body, and makes as great a difference between space and body, as if it were *mega chasma*, a distance as wide as any in nature. And, therefore, if we do not suppose the void space necessary to motion equal to the least parcel of the divided solid matter, but to 1/10 or 1/1000 of it, the same consequence will always follow of space without matter.

24. *The* ideas *of space and body distinct*. But the question being here "whether the *idea of space* or *extension* is *the same with the idea of body*," it is not necessary to prove the real existence of a *vacuum*, but the *idea* of it, which it is plain men have when they inquire and dispute whether there is a *vacuum* or not. For if they did not have the *idea* of space without body, they could not make a question about its

existence. And if their *idea* of body did not include in it something more than the bare *idea* of space, they could have no doubt about the plenitude of the world. And it would be as absurd to demand whether there were space without body as whether there were space without space, or body without body, since these were but different names of the same *idea*.

25. *Extension being inseparable from body, proves it not the same*. It is true the *idea* of *extension* joins itself so inseparably with all visible, and most tangible qualities, that it suffers us to see no one, or feel very few external objects, without taking in impressions of extension too. This readiness of extension to make itself be taken notice of so constantly with other *ideas* has been the occasion, I guess, that some have made the whole essence of *body* to consist in extension; this is not much to be wondered at, since some have had their minds, by their eyes and touch (the busiest of all our senses), so filled with the *idea* of extension and, as it were, wholly possessed with it, that they allowed no existence to anything that did not have extension. I shall not now argue with those men who take the measure and possibility of all being only from their narrow and gross imaginations. But having here to do only with those who conclude the essence of body to be *extension* because they say they cannot imagine any sensible quality of any body without extension, I shall desire them to consider that had they reflected on their *ideas* of tastes and smells as much as on those of sight and touch—no, had they examined their *ideas* of hunger and thirst, and several other pains— they would have found that they included in them no *idea* of extension at all, which is but an affection of body, as well as the rest, discoverable by our senses, which are scarcely acute enough to look into the pure essences of things.

26. If those *ideas* which are constantly joined to all others must therefore be concluded to be the essence of those things which have constantly those *ideas* joined to them, and are inseparable from them, then unity is without doubt the essence of everything. For there is not any object of sensation or reflection which does not carry with it the *idea* of one. But the weakness of this kind of argument we have already shown sufficiently.

27. *Ideas of space and solidity distinct*. To conclude, whatever men shall think concerning the existence of a *vacuum*, this is plain to me: that we have as clear an *idea of space distinct from solidity* as we have of solidity distinct from motion, or motion from space. We do not have any two more distinct *ideas*, and we can as easily conceive space without solidity as we can conceive body or space without motion, though it is never so certain that neither body nor motion can exist without space. [ . . . ]

## Chapter XIV. *Of Duration and Its Simple Modes.*

1. *Duration is fleeting extension*. There is another sort of distance or length the *idea* of which we do not get from the permanent parts of space, but from the fleeting and perpetually perishing parts of succession. This we call *duration*, the simple modes of which are any different lengths of it of which we have distinct *ideas*, as *hours*, *days*, *years*, etc., *time* and *eternity*.

2. *Its idea from reflection on the train of our* ideas. The answer of a great man to one who asked what time was, "*Si non rogas intelligo,*" (which amounts to this: the more I set myself to think of it, the less I understand it) might perhaps persuade one that time, which reveals all other things, is itself not to be discovered. *Duration*, *time*, and *eternity*, are not without reason thought to have something very abstruse in their nature. But however remote these may seem from our comprehension, yet if we trace them right to their origins, I do not doubt but one of those sources of all our knowledge, namely, *sensation* and *reflection*, will be able to furnish us with these *ideas*, as clear and distinct as many others which are thought much less obscure, and we shall find that the *idea* of eternity itself is derived from the same common origin with the rest of our *ideas*.

3. To understand *time* and *eternity* correctly, we ought with attention consider what *idea* it is we have of *duration* and how we came by it. It is evident to anyone who will but observe what passes in his own mind that there is a train of *ideas* which constantly succeed one another in his understanding as long as he is awake. *Reflection* on these appearances of several *ideas* one after another in our minds is that

which furnishes us with the *idea* of *succession*; and the distance between any parts of that succession, or between the appearance of any two *ideas* in our minds, is what we call *duration*. For while we are thinking, or while we receive successively several *ideas* in our minds, we know that we do exist; and so we call the existence, or the continuation of the existence of ourselves or anything else commensurate to the succession of any *ideas* in our minds, the *duration* of ourselves or any such other thing coexistent with our thinking. [ . . . ]

16. Ideas, *however made, include no sense of motion*. Whether these several *ideas* in a man's mind are made by certain motions I will not here dispute. But this I am sure that they include no *idea* of motion in their appearance; and if a man did not have the *idea* of motion otherwise, I think he would have none at all. This is enough to my present purpose and sufficiently shows that the notice we take of the *ideas* of our own minds, appearing there one after another, is that which gives us the *idea* of succession and duration, without which we should have no such *ideas* at all. It is not then *motion*, but the constant train of *ideas* in our minds while we are waking that furnishes us with the idea *of duration*, of which motion does not otherwise give us any perception than as it causes in our minds a constant succession of *ideas*, as I have shown before. And we have as clear an *idea* of succession and duration by the train of other *ideas* succeeding one another in our minds, without the *idea* of any motion, as by the train of *ideas* caused by the uninterrupted sensible change of distance between two bodies, which we have from motion. And therefore we should as well have the *idea* of duration were there no sense of motion at all.

17. *Time is duration set out by measures*. Having thus gotten the *idea* of duration, the next thing natural for the mind to do is to get some *measure of* this common *duration* by which it might judge of its different lengths and consider the distinct order in which several things exist, without which a great part of our knowledge would be confused and a great part of history be rendered very useless. This consideration of duration, as set out by certain periods

and marked by certain measures or *epochs*, is that, I think, which most properly we call *time*. [ . . . ]

27. *Eternity*. By the same means therefore, and from the same origin that we come to have the *idea* of time, we have also that *idea* which we call *eternity*; namely, having gotten the *idea* of succession and duration by reflecting on the train of our own *ideas* caused in us either by the natural appearances of those *ideas* coming constantly of themselves into our waking thoughts, or else caused by external objects successively affecting our senses, and having from the revolutions of the sun gotten the *ideas* of certain lengths of duration, we can, in our thoughts, add such lengths of duration to one another as often as we please, and apply them, so added, to durations past or to come. And this we can continue to do on without bounds or limits, and proceed *in infinitum*, and apply thus the length of the annual motion of the sun to duration, supposed before the sun's, or any other motion had its being—which is no more difficult or absurd than to apply the notion I have of the moving of a shadow one hour today upon the sundial to the duration of something last night, e.g., the burning of a candle, which is now absolutely separate from all actual motion. And it is as impossible for the duration of that flame for an hour last night to coexist with any motion that now is, or forever shall be, as for any part of duration that was before the beginning of the world to coexist with the motion of the sun now. But yet this does not hinder, but that having the *idea* of the length of the motion of the shadow on a dial between the marks of two hours, I can as distinctly measure in my thoughts the duration of that candlelight last night as I can the duration of anything that does now exist. And it is no more than to think that had the sun shone then on the dial, and moved after the same rate it does now, the shadow on the dial would have passed from one hour line to another while that flame of the candle lasted. [ . . . ]

31. And thus I think it is plain that *from* those two fountains of all knowledge before mentioned, namely, *reflection and sensation, we got the ideas of duration* and the measures of it.

For, *first*, by observing what passes in our minds, how our *ideas* there in train constantly some vanish and others begin to appear, we come by the *idea* of *succession*.

*Secondly*, by observing a distance in the parts of this succession, we get the *idea* of *duration*.

*Thirdly*, by sensation observing certain appearances at certain regular and seeming equidistant periods, we get the *ideas* of certain lengths or *measures of duration* as minutes, hours, days, years, etc.

*Fourthly*, by being able to repeat those measures of time or *ideas* of stated length of duration in our minds, as often as we will, we can come to *imagine duration, where nothing does really endure or exist*; and thus we imagine tomorrow, next year, or seven years hence.

*Fifthly*, by being able to repeat *ideas* of any length of time as of a minute, a year, or an age, as often as we will in our own thoughts, and adding them one to another, without ever coming to the end of such addition any nearer than we can to the end of number, to which we can always add, we come by the *idea* of *eternity*, as the future eternal duration of our souls as well as the eternity of that infinite Being which must necessarily have always existed.

*Sixthly*, by considering any part of infinite duration as set out by periodical measures, we come by the *idea* of what we call *time* in general.

## Chapter XXI. *Of Power.*

1. *This* idea *how got*. The mind being every day informed by the senses of the alteration of those simple *ideas* it observes in things without; and taking notice how one comes to an end and ceases to be, and another begins to exist which was not before; reflecting also on what passes within itself and observing a constant change of its *ideas*, sometimes by the impression of outward objects on the senses and sometimes by the determination of its own choice; and concluding from what it has so constantly observed to have been that the like changes will for the future be made in the same things by like agents and, by the like ways, considers in one thing the possibility of having any of its simple *ideas* changed and in another the possibility of making that change; and so comes by that *idea* which we call *power*. Thus, we say: fire has a *power* to melt gold—i.e., to destroy the

consistency of its insensible parts, and consequently its hardness, and make it fluid—and gold has a *power* to be melted; that the sun has a *power* to blanch wax, and wax a *power* to be blanched by the sun, by which the yellowness is destroyed and whiteness made to exist in its room. In these and the like cases, the *power* we consider is in reference to the change of perceivable *ideas*. For we cannot observe any alteration to be made in, or operation upon anything, but by the observable change of its sensible *ideas*; nor conceive any alteration to be made, but by conceiving a change of some of its *ideas*.

2. *Power active and passive. Power*, thus considered, is two-fold, namely, as able to make or able to receive any change. The one may be called *active* and the other *passive power*. Whether matter is not wholly destitute of *active power*, as its author God is truly above all *passive power*; and whether the intermediate state of created spirits is not that alone which is capable of both *active* and *passive power*, may be worth consideration. I shall not now enter into that inquiry, my present business being not to search into the origin of power, but how we come by the *idea* of it. But since *active powers* make so great a part of our complex *ideas* of natural substances (as we shall see hereafter), and I mention them as such, according to common apprehension, yet they being not perhaps so truly *active powers* as our hasty thoughts are apt to represent them, I judge it not amiss, by this intimation, to direct our minds to the consideration of God and spirits for the clearest *idea* of *active powers*.

3. *Power includes relation*. I confess *power includes in it some kind of relation* (a relation to action or change), as indeed which of our *ideas*, of whatever kind, when attentively considered, does not? For, our *ideas* of extension, duration, and number, do they not all contain in them a secret relation of the parts? Figure and motion have something relative in them much more visibly. And sensible qualities, as colors and smells, etc., what are they but the *powers* of different bodies in relation to our perception, etc.? And if considered in the things themselves, do they not depend on the bulk, figure, texture, and motion of the parts? All which include some kind of relation in them. Our *idea* therefore of *power*, I think may well

have a place among other simple *ideas* and be considered as one of them, being one of those that make a principal ingredient in our complex *ideas* of substances, as we shall hereafter have occasion to observe.

4. *The clearest* idea *of active power had from spirit.* We are abundantly furnished with the *idea* of *passive power* by almost all sorts of sensible things. In most of them we cannot avoid observing their sensible qualities, no, their very substances, to be in a continual flux. And therefore with reason we look on them as liable still to the same change. Nor have we of *active power* (which is the more proper signification of the word *power*) fewer instances, since whatever change is observed, the mind must collect a power somewhere able to make that change as well as a possibility in the thing itself to receive it. But yet, if we will consider it attentively, bodies, by our senses, do not afford us so clear and distinct an *idea* of *active power* as we have from reflection on the operations of our minds. For all *power* relating to action, and there being but two sorts of action of which we have an *idea*, namely, thinking and motion, let us consider from where we have the clearest *ideas* of the *powers* which produce these actions. 1. Of thinking, body affords us no *idea* at all; it is only from reflection that we have that. 2. Neither have we from body any *idea* of the beginning of motion. A body at rest affords us no *idea* of any *active power* to move, and when it is set in motion itself, that motion is rather a passion than an action in it. For when the ball obeys the motion of a billiard stick, it is not any action of the ball, but bare passion. Also when by impulse it sets another ball in motion that lay in its way, it only communicates the motion it had received from another and loses in itself so much as the other received; this gives us but a very obscure *idea* of an *active power* of moving in body, while we observe it only to transfer but not produce any motion. For it is but a very obscure *idea* of *power* which does not reach the production of the action but the continuation of the passion. For so is motion in a body impelled by another, the continuation of the alteration made in it from rest to motion being little more an action than the continuation of the alteration of its figure by the same blow is an action. The *idea* of the beginning of motion we have only from reflection on what passes in ourselves, where we find by experience that barely by willing it, barely by a thought of the mind, we can move the parts of our bodies which were before at rest, so that it seems to me we have from the observation of the operation of bodies by our senses but a very imperfect obscure *idea* of *active power*, since they do not afford us any *idea* in themselves of the *power* to begin any action, either motion or thought. But if, from the impulse bodies are observed to make one upon another, anyone thinks he has a clear *idea* of *power*, it serves as well to my purpose, sensation being one of those ways by which the mind comes by its *ideas*. Only I thought it worthwhile to consider here, by the way, whether the mind does not receive its *idea* of *active power* clearer from reflection on its own operations than it does from any external sensation.

5. *Will and understanding, two powers.* This, at least, I think evident, that we find in ourselves a *power* to begin or refrain, continue or end several actions of our minds and motions of our bodies, barely by a thought or preference of the mind ordering, or as it were commanding, the doing or not doing such or such a particular action. This *power* which the mind has thus to order the consideration of any *idea* or the abstaining to consider it, or to prefer the motion of any part of the body to its rest, and *vice versa*, in any particular instance, is that which we call the *will*. The actual exercise of that power, by directing any particular action or its abstention, is that which we call *volition* or *willing*. The abstention of that action, consequent to such order or command of the mind, is called *voluntary*. And whatever action is performed without such a thought of the mind is called *involuntary*. The power of perception is that which we call the *understanding*. Perception, which we make the act of the understanding, is of three sorts: 1. The perception of *ideas* in our minds. 2. The perception of the signification of signs. 3. The perception of the connection or repugnance, agreement or disagreement, that there is between any of our *ideas*. All these are attributed to the *understanding*, or perceptive power, though it is the two latter only that use allows us to say we understand. [ . . . ]

7. *From where the* ideas *of liberty and necessity.* Everyone, I think, finds in himself a *power* to begin or refrain, continue or put an end to several actions in himself. From the consideration of the extent of this power of the mind over the actions of the man, which everyone finds in himself, arise the *ideas of liberty* and *necessity.*

8. *Liberty, what.* All the actions that we have any *idea* of reducing themselves, as has been said, to these two, namely, thinking and motion, so far as a man has power to think or not to think, to move or not to move, according to the preference or direction of his own mind, so far is a man *free.* Wherever any performance or abstention is not equally in a man's power, wherever doing or not doing will not equally follow upon the preference of his mind directing it, there he is not *free,* though perhaps the action may be voluntary. So that the *idea* of *liberty* is the *idea* of a power in any agent to do or refrain any particular action, according to the determination or thought of the mind, by which either of them is preferred to the other. Where either of them is not in the power of the agent to be produced by him according to his *volition,* there he is not at *liberty*; that agent is under *necessity.* So that *liberty* cannot be where there is no thought, no volition, no will, but there may be thought, there may be will, there may be volition, where there is no *liberty.* [ . . . ]

10. *Does not belong to volition.* Again, suppose a man is carried while fast asleep into a room where a person is he longs to see and speak with, and is there locked fast in, beyond his power to get out; he awakes and is glad to find himself in so desirable company, which he stays willingly in, i.e., prefers his stay to going away. I ask, is not this stay voluntary? I think nobody will doubt it; and yet being locked fast in, it is evident he is not at liberty not to stay, he does not have freedom to be gone. So that *liberty is not an* idea *belonging to volition,* or preferring, but to the person having the power of doing, or abstaining to do, according as the mind shall choose or direct. Our *idea* of liberty reaches as far as that power, and no further. For wherever restraint comes to check that power, or compulsion takes away that indifference of ability on

either side to act, or to refrain acting, there *liberty,* and our notion of it, presently ceases.

11. *Voluntary opposed to involuntary, not to necessary.* We have instances enough, and often more than enough, in our own bodies. A man's heart beats, and the blood circulates, which it is not in his power by any thought or volition to stop; and therefore in respect to these motions, where rest does not depend on his choice, nor would follow the determination of his mind, if it should prefer it, he is not a *free agent.* Convulsive motions agitate his legs, so that though he *wills* it ever so much, he cannot by any power of his mind stop their motion (as in that odd disease called *chorea sancti Viti*) but he is perpetually dancing; he is not at liberty in this action, but under as much necessity of moving as a stone that falls or a tennis ball struck with a racket. On the other side, a palsy or the stocks hinder his legs from obeying the determination of his mind, if it would thereby transfer his body to another place. In all these there is want of *freedom,* though the sitting still even of a paralytic, while he prefers it to a removal, is truly voluntary. *Voluntary* then *is not opposed to necessary, but to involuntary.* For a man may prefer what he can do, to what he cannot do—the state he is in, to its absence or change—though necessity has made it in itself unalterable.

12. *Liberty, what.* As it is in the motions of the body, so it is in the thoughts of our minds: where anyone is such that we have power to take it up, or lay it by, according to the preference of the mind, there we are *at liberty.* A waking man, being under the necessity of having some *ideas* constantly in his mind, is not at *liberty* to think or not to think, no more than he is at *liberty* whether his body shall touch any other or not. But whether he will remove his contemplation from one *idea* to another is many times in his choice, and then he is in respect of his *ideas* as much at *liberty* as he is in respect of bodies he rests on; he can at pleasure remove himself from one to another. But yet some *ideas* to the mind, like some motions to the body, are such as in certain circumstances it cannot avoid, nor obtain their absence by the utmost effort it can use. A man on the rack is not at liberty to lay by the *idea* of pain and divert himself with other

contemplations. And sometimes a boisterous passion hurries our thoughts, as a hurricane does our bodies, without leaving us the liberty of thinking on other things, which we would rather choose. But as soon as the mind regains the power to stop or continue, begin or refrain any of these motions of the body without, or thoughts within, according as it thinks fit to prefer either to the other, we then consider the man as a *free agent* again. [ . . . ]

14. Liberty *does not belong to the will*. If this is so (as I imagine it is), I leave it to be considered whether it may not help to put an end to that long agitated, and I think, unreasonable, because unintelligible question, namely, *whether man's will is free or not?* For if I am not mistaken, it follows from what I have said that the question itself is altogether improper; and it is as insignificant to ask whether man's *will* is free as to ask whether his sleep is swift or his virtue square, *liberty* being as little applicable to the *will* as swiftness of motion is to sleep or squareness to virtue. Everyone would laugh at the absurdity of such a question, as either of these. Because it is obvious that the modifications of motion do not belong to sleep, nor the difference of figure to virtue. And when anyone well considers it, I think he will as plainly perceive that *liberty*, which is but a power, belongs only to agents, and cannot be an attribute or modification of the *will*, which is also but a power. [ . . . ]

16. It is plain then that the *will* is nothing but one power or ability, and *freedom* another power or ability, so that to ask whether the *will has freedom* is to ask whether one power has another power, one ability another ability—a question at first sight too grossly absurd to make a dispute or need an answer. [ . . . ]

17. However, the *name faculty* which men have given to this power called the *will*, and by which they have been led into a way of talking of the will as acting, may, by an appropriation that disguises its true sense, serve a little to palliate the absurdity, yet the *will* in truth signifies nothing but a power, or ability, to prefer or choose. And when the *will*, under the name of a *faculty*, is considered as it is, barely as an ability to do something, the absurdity in saying it is free, or not free, will easily discover itself. [ . . . ]

21. *But to the agent or man*. To return then to the inquiry about liberty, I think *the question is not proper, whether the will is free, but whether a man is free*. Thus, I think,

That so far as anyone can, by the direction or choice of his mind preferring the existence of any action to the nonexistence of that action, and vice versa, make it exist or not exist, so far he is free. For if I can, by a thought directing the motion of my finger, make it move when it was at rest, or *vice versa*, it is evident that in respect of that I am free. And if I can, by a like thought of my mind, preferring one to the other, produce either words or silence, I am at liberty to speak or hold my peace. And as far as this power reaches, of acting or not acting, by the determination of his own thought preferring either, so far is a man *free*. For how can we think anyone freer than to have the power to do what he will? And so far as anyone can, by preferring any action to its not being, or rest to any action, produce that action or rest, so far can he do what he will. For such a preferring of action to its absence is the *willing* of it. And we can scarcely tell how to imagine any *being* freer than to be able to do what he *wills*. So that in respect of actions within the reach of such a power in him, a man seems as free as it is possible for freedom to make him. [ . . . ]

23. That *willing* or *volition* being an action, and freedom consisting in a power of acting or not acting, *a man in respect of willing or the act of volition, when any action in his power is once proposed to his thoughts, as presently to be done, cannot be free.* The reason of this is very manifest. For, it being unavoidable that the action depending on his *will* should exist or not exist, and its existence or not existence following perfectly the determination and preference of his will, he cannot avoid willing the existence or not existence of that action, it is absolutely necessary that he *will* the one or the other, i.e., *prefer* the one to the other, since one of them must necessarily follow; and that which does follow follows by the choice and determination of his mind, that is, by his *willing it*; for if he did not *will* it, it would not be. So that in respect of the act of *willing*, a man in such a case is not free, liberty consisting in a power to act or not to act, which, in regard of volition, a man, upon such

a proposal, does not have. For it is unavoidably necessary to prefer the doing or abstaining of an action in a man's power which is once so proposed to his thoughts. A man must necessarily *will* the one or the other of them, upon which preference or volition the action or its abstaining certainly follows and is truly voluntary. But the act of volition or preferring one of the two being that which he cannot avoid, a man in respect of that act of *willing* is under a necessity, and so cannot be free, unless necessity and freedom can consist together, and a man can be free and bound at once.

24. This then is evident that, in all proposals of present action, *a man is not at liberty to will or not to will, because he cannot refrain willing*, liberty consisting in a power to act or to refrain acting, and in that only. For a man who sits still is said yet to be at liberty, because he can walk if he wills it. But if a man sitting still does not have a power to remove himself, he is not at liberty; so likewise a man falling down a precipice, though in motion, is not at liberty, because he cannot stop that motion if he would. This being so, it is plain that a man who is walking, to whom it is proposed to give off walking, is not at liberty whether he *will* determine himself to walk, or give off walking, or not. He must necessarily prefer one or the other of them, walking or not walking; and so it is in regard of all other actions in our power so proposed, which are the far greater number. For considering the vast number of voluntary actions that succeed one another every moment that we are awake in the course of our lives, there are but few of them that are thought on or proposed to the *will*, until the time they are to be done. And in all such actions, as I have shown, the mind in respect of *willing* does not have a power to act or not to act, in which consists liberty. The mind in that case does not have a power to refrain *willing*; it cannot avoid some determination concerning them. Let the consideration be as short, the thought as quick as it will, it either leaves the man in the state he was before thinking, or changes it, continues the action, or puts an end to it—by which it is manifest that it orders and directs one, in preference to or with neglect of the other, and thereby either the continuation or change becomes unavoidably voluntary.

25. *The will determined by something without it.* Since then it is plain that in most cases a man is not at liberty whether he will or not, the next thing demanded is *whether a man is at liberty to will which of the two he pleases, motion or rest?* This question carries its absurdity so manifestly in itself that one might as a result sufficiently be convinced that liberty does not concern the will. For to ask whether a man is at liberty to will either motion or rest, speaking or silence, which he pleases, is to ask whether a man can *will* what he *wills*, or be pleased with what he is pleased with? A question which, I think, needs no answer; and they who can make a question of it must suppose one will to determine the acts of another, and another to determine that, and so on *in infinitum*.

26. To avoid these and the like absurdities, nothing can be of greater use than to establish in our minds determined *ideas* of the things under consideration. If the *ideas* of liberty and volition were well fixed in the understandings and carried along with us in our minds, as they ought, through all the questions that are raised about them, I suppose a great part of the difficulties that perplex men's thoughts and entangle their understandings would be much easier resolved, and we should perceive where the confused signification of terms or where the nature of the thing caused the obscurity.

27. First then, it is carefully to be remembered that *freedom consists in the dependence of the existence or not existence of any action, upon our volition of it, and not in the dependence of any action or its contrary, on our preference.* A man standing on a cliff is at liberty to leap twenty yards downwards into the sea, not because he has a power to do the contrary action, which is to leap twenty yards upwards, for that he cannot do. But he is therefore free because he has a power to leap or not to leap. But if a greater force than his either holds him fast, or tumbles him down, he is no longer free in that case, because the doing or abstaining of that particular action is no longer in his power. He who is a close prisoner in a room twenty feet square, being at the north side of his chamber, is at liberty to walk twenty feet southward, because he can walk or not walk

it, but is not, at the same time, at liberty to do the contrary, i.e., to walk twenty feet northward.

In this then consists freedom, namely, in our being able to act or not to act, according as we shall choose or will. [ . . . ]

30. *Will and desire must not be confounded*. But, in the way to it, it will be necessary to premise that though I have above endeavored to express the act of volition by choosing, preferring, and the like terms that signify desire as well as volition, for want of other words to mark that act of the mind whose proper name is willing or volition, yet it being a very simple act, whoever desires to understand what it is will better find it by reflecting on his own mind, and observing what it does when it wills, than by any variety of articulate sounds whatsoever. This caution of being careful not to be misled by expressions that do not enough keep up the difference between the will and several acts of the mind that are quite distinct from it, I think the more necessary, because I find the will often confounded with several of the affections, especially desire, and one put for the other—and that by men who would not willingly be thought not to have had very distinct notions of things and not to have written very clearly about them. This, I imagine, has been no small occasion of obscurity and mistake in this matter, and therefore is, as much as may be, to be avoided. For he who shall turn his thoughts inwards upon what passes in his mind when he *wills* shall see that the *will* or power of *volition* is conversant about nothing, but that particular determination of the mind, by which barely by a thought the mind endeavors to give rise, continuation, or stop, to any action which it takes to be in its power. This, well considered, plainly shows that the will is perfectly distinguished from *desire*, which in the very same action may have a quite contrary tendency from that which our *will* sets us upon. A man whom I cannot deny, may oblige me to use persuasions to another, which, at the same time I am speaking, I may wish may not prevail on him. In this case, it is plain the *will* and *desire* run counter. I will the action that tends one way, while my desire tends another, and that the direct contrary way. [ . . . ]

31. *Uneasiness determines the will*. To return then to the inquiry, *what is it that determines the will in regard to our actions?* And that, upon second thoughts, I am apt to imagine is not, as is generally supposed, the greater good in view, but some (and for the most part the most pressing) *uneasiness* a man is at present under. This is that which successively determines the *will* and sets us upon those actions we perform. This *uneasiness* we may call, as it is, *desire*, which is an uneasiness of the mind for want of some absent good. [ . . . ]

35. *The greatest positive good does not determine the will, but uneasiness*. It seems so established and settled a maxim by the general consent of all mankind that good, the greater good, determines the will that I do not at all wonder that, when I first published my thoughts on this subject, I took it for granted; and I imagine that by a great many I shall be thought more excusable for having then done so, than that now I have ventured to recede from so received an opinion. But yet, upon a stricter inquiry, I am forced to conclude that *good*, the *greater good*, though apprehended and acknowledged to be so, does not determine the *will*, until our desire, raised proportionally to it, makes us *uneasy* in the want of it. Convince a man ever so much that plenty has its advantages over poverty, make him see and admit that the handsome conveniences of life are better than nasty penury, yet as long as he is content with the latter and finds no *uneasiness* in it, he does not move—his *will* never is determined to any action that shall bring him out of it. [ . . . ]

38. *Because all who allow the joys of heaven possible do not pursue them*. Were the *will* determined by the views of good, as it appears in contemplation greater or less to the understanding, which is the state of all absent good, and that which in the received opinion the *will* is supposed to move to, and to be moved by, I do not see how it could ever get loose from the infinite eternal joys of heaven, once proposed and considered as possible. [ . . . ]

This would be the state of the mind and regular tendency of the *will* in all its determinations, were it determined by that which is considered and in view the greater good; but that it is not so is visible in experience, the infinitely greatest confessed good being often neglected, to satisfy the successive *uneasiness* of our desires pursuing trifles. [ . . . ]

41. *All desire happiness*. If it is further asked, what it is that moves *desire*? I answer, happiness, and that alone. *Happiness* and *misery* are the names of two extremes, the utmost bounds of which we do not know; it is what "eye has not seen, ear has not heard, nor has it entered into the heart of man to conceive." But of some degrees of both we have very lively impressions, made by several instances of delight and joy on the one side and torment and sorrow on the other, which, for shortness' sake, I shall comprehend under the names of pleasure and pain, there being pleasure and pain of the mind as well as the body. "With him is fullness of joy and pleasure for evermore." Or, to speak truly, they are all of the mind, though some have their rise in the mind from thought, others in the body from certain modifications of motion.

42. *Happiness, what*. *Happiness* then in its full extent is the utmost pleasure we are capable of, and *misery* the utmost pain, and the lowest degree of what can be called *happiness* is so much ease from all pain and so much present pleasure as without which anyone cannot be content. Now because pleasure and pain are produced in us by the operation of certain objects, either on our minds or our bodies, and in different degrees, therefore what has an aptness to produce pleasure in us is that we call *good*, and what is apt to produce pain in us we call *evil*, for no other reason but for its aptness to produce pleasure and pain in us, in which consists our *happiness* and *misery*. Further, though what is apt to produce any degree of pleasure is in itself good, and what is apt to produce any degree of pain is evil, yet it often happens that we do not call it so when it comes in competition with a greater of its sort, because when they come in competition, the degrees also of pleasure and pain have justly a preference, so that if we will rightly estimate what we call *good* and *evil*, we shall find it lies much in comparison. For the cause of every less degree of pain as well as every greater degree of pleasure has the nature of *good*, and vice versa.

43. *What good is desired, what not*. Though this is that which is called *good* and *evil*, and all good is the proper object of *desire* in general, yet all good, even seen and confessed to be so, does not necessarily move every particular man's *desire*, but only that part, or so much of it as is considered and taken to make a necessary part of his happiness. All other good, however great in reality or appearance, does not excite a man's *desires*, who does not look on it to make a part of that happiness with which he, in his present thoughts, can satisfy himself. Happiness, under this view, everyone constantly pursues and desires what makes any part of it. Other things acknowledged to be good, he can look upon without *desire*, pass by, and be content without. There is nobody, I think, so senseless as to deny that there is pleasure in knowledge. And for the pleasures of sense, they have too many followers to let it be questioned whether men are taken with them or not. Now let one man place his satisfaction in sensual pleasures, another in the delight of knowledge, though each of them cannot but confess there is great pleasure in what the other pursues, yet neither of them making the other's delight a part of his happiness, their *desires* are not moved, but each is satisfied without what the other enjoys, and so his will is not determined to the pursuit of it. But yet as soon as the studious man's hunger and thirst make him *uneasy*, he, whose *will* was never determined to any pursuit of good cheer, poignant sauces, delicious wine, by the pleasant taste he has found in them, is, by the uneasiness of hunger and thirst, presently determined to eating and drinking, though possibly with great indifference, what wholesome food comes in his way. And on the other side, the epicure buckles to study when shame or the desire to recommend himself to his mistress shall make him *uneasy* in the want of any sort of knowledge. Thus, however much men are in earnest and constant in pursuit of happiness, yet they may have a clear view of good, great and confessed good, without being concerned for it, or moved by it, if they think they can make up their happiness without it. Though as to pain that they are always concerned for. They can feel no *uneasiness* without being moved. And therefore being *uneasy* in the want of whatever is judged necessary to their happiness, as soon as any

good appears to make a part of their portion of happiness, they begin to *desire* it.

44. *Why the greatest good is not always desired.* This, I think, anyone may observe in himself and others that the *greater visible good* does not always raise men's *desires* in proportion to the greatness it appears and is acknowledged to have, though every little trouble moves us and sets us on work to get rid of it. The reason of which is evident from the nature of our *happiness* and *misery* itself. All present pain, whatever it be, makes a part of our present *misery*; but all absent good does not at any time make a necessary part of our present *happiness*, nor the absence of it make a part of our *misery*. [ . . . ]

47. *The power to suspend the prosecution of any desire makes way for consideration.* There being in us a great many *uneasinesses* always soliciting and ready to determine the *will*, it is natural, as I have said, that the greatest and most pressing should determine the *will* to the next action, and so it does for the most part, but not always. For the mind having in most cases, as is evident in experience, a power to *suspend* the execution and satisfaction of any of its desires, and so all, one after another, is at liberty to consider the objects of them, examine them on all sides, and weigh them with others. In this lies the liberty man has, and from the not using of it right comes all that variety of mistakes, errors, and faults which we run into in the conduct of our lives, and our endeavors after happiness, while we precipitate the determination of our *wills* and engage too soon before due *examination*. To prevent this, we have a power to *suspend* the prosecution of this or that desire, as everyone daily may experiment in himself. This seems to me the source of all liberty; in this seems to consist that which is (as I think improperly) called *free will*. For during this *suspension* of any desire, before the *will* is determined to action and the action (which follows that determination) done, we have opportunity to examine, view, and judge of the good or evil of what we are going to do, and when, upon due *examination*, we have judged, we have done our duty, all that we can or ought to do in pursuit of our happiness; and it is not a fault, but a perfection of our nature to

desire, will, and act according to the last result of a fair *examination*. [ . . . ]

52. *The reason of it.* This is the hinge on which turns the *liberty* of intellectual beings, in their constant endeavors after and a steady prosecution of true felicity that they can *suspend* this prosecution in particular cases until they have looked before them and informed themselves whether that particular thing, which is then proposed or desired, lie in the way to their main end and make a real part of that which is their greatest good. For the inclination and tendency of their nature to happiness is an obligation and motive to them, to take care not to mistake or miss it, and so necessarily puts them upon caution, deliberation, and wariness in the direction of their particular actions, which are the means to obtain it. Whatever necessity determines to the pursuit of real bliss, the same necessity with the same force establishes *suspense*, *deliberation*, and scrutiny of each successive desire, whether the satisfaction of it does not interfere with our true happiness and mislead us from it. This, as seems to me, is the great privilege of finite intellectual beings; and I desire it may be well considered whether the great inlet and exercise of all the *liberty* men have, are capable of, or can be useful to them, and that on which depends the turn of their actions, does not lie in this that they can *suspend* their desires, and stop them from determining their *wills* to any action, until they have duly and fairly *examined* the good and evil of it, insofar as the weight of the thing requires. This we are able to do, and when we have done it, we have done our duty, and all that is in our power, and indeed all that needs. For since the *will* supposes knowledge to guide its choice, all that we can do is to hold our *wills* undetermined until we have *examined* the good and evil of what we desire. What follows after that follows in a chain of consequences linked one to another, all depending on the last determination of the judgment which, whether it shall be upon a hasty and precipitate view, or upon a due and mature *examination*, is in our power, experience showing us that in most cases we are able to suspend the present satisfaction of any desire. [ . . . ]

72. Before I close this chapter, it may perhaps be to our purpose and help to give us clearer conceptions

about *power*, if we make our thoughts take a little more exact survey of *action*. I have said above that we have *ideas* but of two sorts of *action*, namely, *motion* and *thinking*. These, in truth, though called and counted *actions*, yet if nearly considered, will not be found to be always perfectly so. For, if I am not mistaken, there are instances of both kinds which, upon due consideration, will be found rather *passions* than *actions*, and consequently so far the effects barely of passive powers in those subjects which yet on their accounts are thought *agents*. For in these instances, the substance that has motion or thought receives the impression by which it is put into that *action* purely from without, and so acts merely by the capacity it has to receive such an impression from some external agent; and such a *power* is not properly an *active power*, but a mere passive capacity in the subject. Sometimes the substance or agent puts itself into *action* by its own power, and this is properly *active power*. Whatever modification a substance has by which it produces any effect that is called *action*—e.g., a solid substance by motion operates on, or alters the sensible *ideas* of another substance, and therefore this modification of motion we call action. But yet this motion in that solid substance is, when rightly considered, but a passion, if it received it only from some external agent, so that the *active power* of motion is in no substance which cannot begin motion in itself, or in another substance, when at rest. So likewise in *thinking*, a power to receive *ideas* or thoughts from the operation of any external substance is called a *power* of thinking. But this is but a *passive power* or capacity. But to be able to bring into view *ideas* out of sight at one's own choice, and to compare which of them one thinks fit, this is an *active power*. This reflection may be of some use to preserve us from mistakes about *powers* and *actions*, which grammar and the common frame of languages may be apt to lead us into, since what is signified by *verbs* that grammarians call *active* does not always signify *action*—e.g., this proposition: I see the moon, or a star, or I feel the heat of the sun, though expressed by a *verb active*, does not signify any *action* in me by which I operate on those substances, but only the reception of the *ideas* of light, roundness, and heat, in which I am not

active, but barely passive, and cannot in that position of my eyes, or body, avoid receiving them. But when I turn my eyes another way, or remove my body out of the sunbeams, I am properly active; because of my own choice, by a power within myself, I put myself into that motion. Such an *action* is the product of *active power*.

73. And thus I have, in a short draught, given a view of our *original ideas*, from which all the rest are derived, and of which they are made up, which if I would consider, as a philosopher, and examine on what causes they depend and of what they are made, I believe they all might be reduced to these very few primary and original ones, namely, *extension, solidity, mobility*, or the power of being moved, which by our senses we receive from body; *perceptivity*, or the power of perception, or thinking; *motivity*, or the power of moving. These by reflection we receive from our minds. I crave leave to make use of these two new words to avoid the danger of being mistaken in the use of those which are equivocal. To these if we add *existence, duration, number*, which belong both to the one and the other, we have, perhaps, all the original *ideas* on which the rest depend. For by these, I imagine, might be explained the nature of colors, sounds, tastes, smells, and all other *ideas* we have, if we had but faculties acute enough to perceive the severally modified extensions and motions of these minute bodies, which produce those several sensations in us. But my present purpose being only to inquire into the knowledge the mind has of things by those *ideas* and appearances which *God* has fitted it to receive from them, and how the mind comes by that knowledge, rather than into their causes, or manner of production, I shall not, contrary to the design of this essay, set myself to inquire philosophically into the peculiar constitution of bodies, and the configuration of parts, by which they have the power to produce in us the *ideas* of their sensible qualities. I shall not enter any further into that disquisition, it sufficing to my purpose to observe that gold or saffron has a power to produce in us the *idea* of yellow, and snow or milk the *idea* of white, which we can only have by our sight, without examining the texture of the parts of those bodies or the particular figures or motion of

the particles which rebound from them, to cause in us that particular sensation. Though when we go beyond the bare *ideas* in our minds, and would inquire into their causes, we cannot conceive anything else to be in any sensible object, by which it produces different *ideas* in us, but the different bulk, figure, number, texture, and motion of its insensible parts.

# Chapter XXII. *Of Mixed Modes.*

1. *Mixed modes, what.* Having treated of *simple modes* in the foregoing chapters, and given several instances of some of the most considerable of them, to show what they are, and how we come by them, we are now in the next place to consider those we call *mixed modes.* Such are the complex *ideas* we mark by the names *obligation, drunkenness,* a *lie,* etc., which consisting of several combinations of simple *ideas* of different kinds, I have called *mixed modes,* to distinguish them from the more simple modes, which consist only of simple *ideas* of the same kind. These mixed modes being also such combinations of simple *ideas* as are not looked upon to be characteristic marks of any real beings that have a steady existence, but scattered and independent *ideas* put together by the mind, are thereby distinguished from the complex *ideas* of substances.

2. *Made by the mind.* That the mind, in respect of its simple *ideas,* is wholly passive, and receives them all from the existence and operations of things, such as sensation or reflection offers them, without being able to make any one *idea,* experience shows us. But if we attentively consider these *ideas* I call *mixed modes* we are now speaking of, we shall find their origin quite different. *The mind* often *exercises an active power in making these* several *combinations.* For it being once furnished with simple *ideas,* it can put them together in several compositions, and so make a variety of complex *ideas,* without examining whether they exist so together in nature. And hence I think it is that these *ideas* are called *notions,* as if they had their origin and constant existence more in the thoughts of men than in the reality of things; and to form such *ideas,* it sufficed that the mind puts the parts of them together, and that they were consistent in the understanding, without considering whether

they had any real being. Though I do not deny but several of them might be taken from observation, and the existence of several simple *ideas* so combined as they are put together in the understanding. For the man who first framed the *idea* of *hypocrisy* might have either taken it at first from the observation of one who made show of good qualities which he did not have, or else have framed that *idea* in his mind, without having any such pattern to fashion it by. For it is evident that in the beginning of languages and societies of men, several of those complex *ideas* which were consequent to the constitutions established among them, must necessarily have been in the minds of men before they existed anywhere else. And that many names that stood for such complex *ideas* were in use, and so those *ideas* framed before the combinations they stood forever existed.

3. *Sometimes gotten by the explication of their names.* Indeed now that languages are made and abound with words standing for such combinations, *an usual way of getting these complex* ideas *is by the explication of those terms that stand for them.* For consisting of a company of simple *ideas* combined, they may by words, standing for those simple *ideas,* be represented to the mind of one who understands those words, though that complex combination of simple *ideas* was never offered to his mind by the real existence of things. Thus a man may come to have the *idea* of *sacrilege* or *murder* by enumerating to him the simple *ideas* which these words stand for, without ever seeing either of them committed.

4. *The name ties the parts of the mixed modes into one* idea. Every *mixed mode* consisting of many distinct simple *ideas,* it seems reasonable to inquire *"From where it has its unity,* and how such a precise multitude comes to make but one *idea,* since that combination does not always exist together in nature?" To which I answer, it is plain it has its unity from an act of the mind combining those several simple *ideas* together, and considering them as one complex one, consisting of those parts, and the mark of this union, or that which is looked on generally to complete it, is one name given to that combination. For it is by their names that men commonly regulate their account of their distinct species of mixed

modes, seldom allowing or considering any number of simple *ideas* to make one complex one, but such collections as there are names for. Thus, though the killing of an old man is as fit in nature to be united into one complex *idea*, as the killing a man's father, yet there being no name standing precisely for the one as there is the name of *parricide* to mark the other, it is not taken for a particular complex *idea*, nor a distinct species of actions from that of killing a young man or any other man.

5. *The cause of making mixed modes*. If we should inquire a little further to see *what* it is that *occasions men to make several combinations of simple* ideas into distinct, and, as it were, settled *modes*, and neglect others which, in the nature of things themselves, have as much an aptness to be combined and make distinct *ideas*, we shall find the reason of it to be the end of language; this being to mark, or communicate men's thoughts to one another with all the dispatch that may be, they usually make such collections of *ideas* into complex modes and affix names to them as they have frequent use of in their way of living and conversation, leaving others, which they have but seldom an occasion to mention, loose and without names to tie them together; they rather choosing to enumerate (when they have need) such *ideas* as make them up by the particular names that stand for them than to trouble their memories by multiplying of complex *ideas* with names to them, which they seldom or never have any occasion to make use of. [ . . . ]

9. *How we get the* ideas *of mixed modes*. There are therefore *three ways by which we get these complex* ideas *of mixed modes*. 1. By experience and *observation* of things themselves. Thus by seeing two men wrestle or fence, we get the *idea* of wrestling or fencing. 2. By *invention*, or voluntary putting together of several simple *ideas* in our own minds. So he who first invented printing or etching had an *idea* of it in his mind before it ever existed. 3. Which is the most usual way, by *explaining the names* of actions we never saw, or notions we cannot see; and by enumerating, and in this way, as it were, setting before our imaginations all those *ideas* which go to the making them up and are the constituent parts of them. For having by *sensation* and *reflection* stored our minds

with simple *ideas*, and by use gotten the names that stand for them, we can by those means represent to another any complex *idea* we would have him conceive, so that it has in it no simple *ideas* but what he knows and has with us the same name for. For all our complex *ideas* are ultimately resolvable into simple *ideas*, of which they are compounded and originally made up, though perhaps their immediate ingredients, as I may so say, are also complex *ideas*. Thus the *mixed mode*, which the word *lie* stands for, is made of these simple *ideas*: 1. Articulate sounds. 2. Certain *ideas* in the mind of the speaker. 3. Those words the signs of those *ideas*. 4. Those signs put together by affirmation or negation, otherwise than the *ideas* they stand for are in the mind of the speaker. I think I do not need go any further in the analysis of that complex *idea* we call a lie. What I have said is enough to show that it is made up of simple *ideas*. And it could not be but an offensive tediousness to my reader, to trouble him with a more minute enumeration of every particular simple *idea* that goes to this complex one, which, from what has been said, he cannot but be able to make out to himself. The same may be done in all our complex *ideas* whatsoever, which, however compounded and decompounded, may at last be resolved into simple *ideas*, which are all the materials of knowledge or thought we have, or can have. Nor shall we have reason to fear that the mind is as a result stinted to too scanty a number of *ideas*, if we consider what an inexhaustible stock of simple modes number and figure alone afford us. How far then *mixed modes* which admit of the various combinations of different simple *ideas*, and their infinite modes, are from being few and scanty, we may easily imagine. So that before we have done, we shall see that nobody need be afraid he shall not have scope and compass enough for his thoughts to range in, though they are, as I pretend, confined only to simple *ideas* received from sensation or reflection, and their several combinations. [ . . . ]

11. *Several words seeming to signify action, signify but the effect*. *Power* being the source from which all action proceeds, the substances in which these powers are, when they exert this power into act, are called *causes*, and the substances which then are produced,

or the simple *ideas* which are introduced into any subject by the exerting of that power, are called *effects*. The *efficacy* by which the new substance or *idea* is produced is called, in the subject exerting that power, *action*; but in the subject in which any simple *idea* is changed or produced, it is called *passion*. This efficacy however various, and the effects almost infinite, yet we can, I think, conceive it in intellectual agents to be nothing else but modes of thinking and willing; in corporeal agents, nothing else but modifications of motion. I say, I think we cannot conceive it to be any other but these two. For whatever sort of action, besides these, produces any effects, I confess myself to have no notion nor *idea* of, and so it is quite remote from my thoughts, apprehensions, and knowledge, and as much in the dark to me as five other senses, or as the *ideas* of colors to a blind man. And therefore *many words which seem to express some action* signify nothing of the action or *modus operandi* at all, *but* barely *the effect*, with some circumstances of the subject wrought on, or cause operating—e.g., creation, annihilation, contain in them no *idea* of the action or manner by which they are produced, but barely of the cause, and the thing done. And when a countryman says the cold freezes water, though the word freezing seems to import some *action*, yet truly it signifies nothing but the effect, namely that water that was before fluid has become hard and consistent, without containing any *idea* of the action by which it is done.

12. *Mixed modes, made also of other* ideas. I think I shall not need to remark here that though power and action make the greatest part of mixed modes, marked by names, and familiar in the minds and mouths of men, yet other simple *ideas* and their several combinations are *not* excluded. Much less, I think, will it be *necessary for me* to enumerate all the mixed modes, which have been settled, with names to them; that would be to make a dictionary of the greatest part of the words made use of in divinity, ethics, law, and politics, and several other sciences. All that is requisite to my present design is to show what sort of *ideas* those are which I call *mixed modes*, how the mind comes by them, and that they are compositions made

up of simple *ideas* gotten from sensation and reflection—which I suppose I have done.

## Chapter XXIII. *Of Our Complex Ideas of Substances.*

1. Ideas *of substances, how made*. The mind being, as I have declared, furnished with a great number of the simple *ideas*, conveyed in by the *senses*, as they are found in exterior things, or by *reflection* on its own operations, takes notice also that a certain number of these simple *ideas* go constantly together, which being presumed to belong to one thing, and words being suited to common apprehensions, and made use of for quick dispatch, are called, so united in one subject, by one name. This, by inadvertence, we are apt afterward to talk of, and consider as one simple *idea*, which indeed is a complication of many *ideas* together, because, as I have said, not imagining how these simple *ideas* can subsist by themselves, we accustom ourselves to suppose some *substratum* in which they do subsist and from which they do result, which therefore we call *substance*.

2. *Our* idea *of substance in general*. Thus, if anyone will examine himself concerning his *notion of pure substance in general*, he will find he has no other *idea* of it at all, but only a supposition of he knows not what support of such qualities, which are capable of producing simple *ideas* in us—which qualities are commonly called *accidents*. If anyone should be asked what is the subject in which color or weight inheres, he would have nothing to say, but the solid extended parts. And if he were demanded what is it that solidity and extension adhere in, he would not be in a much better case than the *Indian* before mentioned who, saying that the world was supported by a great elephant, was asked what the elephant rested on—to which his answer was a great tortoise. But being again pressed to know what gave support to the broad-backed tortoise, replied, something he knew not what. And thus here, as in all other cases where we use words without having clear and distinct *ideas*, we talk like children who, being questioned what such a thing is, which they do not know, readily give this satisfactory answer, that it is *something*; in truth this signifies no more, when so used either by

children or men, but that they know not what; and that the thing they pretend to know and talk of is what they have no distinct *idea* of at all, and so are perfectly ignorant of it, and in the dark. The *idea* then we have, to which we give the general name substance, being nothing but the supposed, but unknown support of those qualities we find existing, which we imagine cannot subsist, *"sine re substante,"* without something to support them, we call that support *substantia*; which, according to the true import of the word, is in plain English, *standing under* or *upholding*.

3. *Of the sorts of substances.* An obscure and relative *idea* of substance in general being thus made, we come to have the *ideas of particular sorts of substances,* by collecting such combinations of simple *ideas* as are by experience and observation of men's senses, taken notice of to exist together, and are therefore supposed to flow from the particular internal constitution or unknown essence of that substance. Thus we come to have the *ideas* of a man, horse, gold, water, etc., of which substances, whether anyone has any other clear *idea* further than of certain simple *ideas* coexistent together, I appeal to everyone's own experience. It is the ordinary qualities observable in iron, or a diamond, put together that make the true complex *idea* of those substances, which a smith or a jeweler commonly knows better than a philosopher, who, whatever substantial forms he may talk of, has no other *idea* of those substances than what is framed by a collection of those simple *ideas* which are to be found in them; only we must take notice that our complex *ideas* of substances, besides all those simple *ideas* they are made up of, have always the confused *idea* of *something* to which they belong and in which they subsist. And therefore, when we speak of any sort of substance, we say it is a *thing* having such or such qualities. As body is a *thing* that is extended, figured, and capable of motion; spirit, a *thing* capable of thinking; and so hardness, friability, and power to draw iron, we say, are qualities to be found in a lodestone. These and the like fashions of speaking intimate that the substance is supposed always *something* besides the extension, figure, solidity, motion, thinking, or other observable *ideas*, though we do not know what it is.

4. *No clear* idea *of substance in general.* Hence, when we talk or think of any particular sort of corporeal substances, as *horse, stone*, etc., though the *idea* we have of either of them is but the complication or collection of those several simple *ideas* of sensible qualities which we used to find united in the thing called *horse* or *stone*, yet because we cannot conceive how they should subsist alone, nor one in another, we suppose them existing in and supported by some common subject; *this support we denote by the name* substance, though it is certain we have no clear or distinct *idea* of that *thing* we suppose a support.

5. *As clear an* idea *of spirit as body.* The same thing happens concerning the operations of the mind, namely, thinking, reasoning, fearing, etc., which we concluding not to subsist of themselves, nor apprehending how they can belong to body or be produced by it, we are apt to think these the actions of some other *substance*, which we call *spirit*; yet by this it is evident that having no other *idea* or notion of matter but *something* in which those many sensible qualities which affect our senses do subsist, by supposing a substance in which *thinking, knowing, doubting*, and a power of moving, etc., do subsist, *we have as clear a notion of the substance of spirit, as we have of body*—the one being supposed to be (without knowing what it is) the *substratum* to those simple *ideas* we have from without, and the other supposed (with a like ignorance of what it is) to be the *substratum* to those operations we experiment in ourselves within. It is plain then that the *idea* of corporeal *substance* in matter is as remote from our conceptions and apprehensions as that of spiritual *substance* or *spirit*; and therefore from our not having any notion of the substance of spirit we can no more conclude its nonexistence than we can for the same reason deny the existence of body, it being as rational to affirm there is no body, because we have no clear and distinct *idea* of the *substance* of matter, as to say there is no spirit, because we have no clear and distinct *idea* of the *substance* of a spirit.

6. *Of the sorts of substances.* Whatever therefore is the secret, abstract nature of *substance* in general, all *the ideas we have of particular distinct sorts of substances* are nothing but several combinations of

simple *ideas*, coexisting in such, though unknown, cause of their union as makes the whole subsist of itself. It is by such combinations of simple *ideas* and nothing else that we represent particular sorts of *substances* to ourselves. Such are the *ideas* we have of their several species in our minds, and such only do we, by their specific names, signify to others, e.g., *man, horse, sun, water, iron*. Upon hearing these words, everyone who understands the language frames in his mind a combination of those several simple *ideas* which he has usually observed or fancied to exist together under that denomination; all this he supposes to rest in and be, as it were, adherent to that unknown common subject, which does not inhere in anything else. Though in the meantime it is manifest, and everyone upon inquiry into his own thoughts will find that he has no other *idea* of any *substance*, e.g., let it be *gold, horse, iron, man, vitriol, bread*, but what he has barely of those sensible qualities which he supposes to inhere, with a supposition of such a *substratum*, as gives, as it were, a support to those qualities or simple *ideas* which he has observed to exist united together. Thus the *idea* of the *sun*—what is it but an aggregate of those several simple *ideas*, bright, hot, roundish, having a constant regular motion, at a certain distance from us, and perhaps some other? As he who thinks and discourses of the *sun* has been more or less accurate in observing those sensible qualities, *ideas*, or properties, which are in that thing which he calls the sun.

7. *Powers a great part of our complex* ideas *of substances*. For he has the most perfect *idea* of any of the particular sorts of *substances* who has gathered and put together most of those simple *ideas* which do exist in it; among these are to be reckoned its active powers and passive capacities, which, though not simple *ideas*, yet in this respect for brevity's sake may conveniently enough be reckoned among them. Thus the power of drawing iron is one of the *ideas* of the complex one of that substance we call a *lodestone*; and a power to be so drawn is a part of the complex one we call *iron*—which powers pass for inherent qualities in those subjects. Because every *substance*, being as apt by the powers we observe in it to change some sensible qualities in other subjects as it is to produce in us those simple *ideas* which we receive immediately from it, does, by those new sensible qualities introduced into other subjects, discover to us those powers which do as a result mediately affect our senses as regularly as its sensible qualities do it immediately—e.g., we immediately by our senses perceive in *fire* its heat and color, which are, if rightly considered, nothing but powers in it to produce those *ideas* in us—we also by our senses perceive the color and brittleness of *charcoal*, by which we come by the knowledge of another power in fire, which it has to change the color and consistency of wood. By the former, fire immediately, by the latter, it mediately discovers to us these several powers, which therefore we look upon to be a part of the qualities of fire, and so make them a part of the complex *idea* of it. For all those powers that we take cognizance of, terminating only in the alteration of some sensible qualities in those subjects on which they operate, and so making them exhibit to us new sensible *ideas*; therefore it is that I have reckoned these powers among the simple *ideas* which make the complex ones of the sorts of *substances*, though these powers, considered in themselves, are truly complex *ideas*. And in this looser sense I crave leave to be understood, when I name any of these *potentialities among the simple ideas* which we recollect in our minds when we think *of particular substances*. For the powers that are severally in them are necessary to be considered, if we will have true distinct notions of the several sorts of substances.

8. *And why*. Nor are we to wonder that *powers make a great part of our complex* ideas *of substances*; since their secondary qualities are those which in most of them serve principally to distinguish substances one from another and commonly make a considerable part of the complex *idea* of the several sorts of them. For our senses failing us in the discovery of the bulk, texture, and figure of the minute parts of bodies, on which their real constitutions and differences depend, we are inclined to make use of their secondary qualities as the characteristic notes and marks by which to frame *ideas* of them in our minds and distinguish them one from another. All these secondary qualities, as has been shown, are nothing but bare powers. For the color and taste of *opium* are, as

well as its soporific or anodyne virtues, mere powers depending on its primary qualities, by which it is fitted to produce different operations on different parts of our bodies.

9. *Three sorts of ideas make our complex ones of substances. The* ideas *that make our complex ones of corporeal substances* are of these three sorts. *First,* the *ideas* of the primary qualities of things, which are discovered by our senses, and are in them even when we do not perceive them—such are the bulk, figure, number, situation, and motion of the parts of bodies, which are really in them, whether we take notice of them or not. *Secondly,* the sensible secondary qualities, which, depending on these, are nothing but the powers those substances have to produce several *ideas* in us by our senses; these *ideas* are not in the things themselves otherwise than as anything is in its cause. *Thirdly,* the aptness we consider in any substance to give or receive such alterations of primary qualities, as that the substance so altered should produce in us different *ideas* from what it did before; these are called active and passive powers. All these powers, as far as we have any notice or notion of them, terminate only in sensible simple *ideas.* For whatever alteration a *lodestone* has the power to make in the minute particles of iron, we should have no notion of any power it had at all to operate on iron, did not its sensible motion discover it. And I do not doubt but there are a thousand changes that bodies we daily handle have a power to cause in one another, which we never suspect, because they never appear in sensible effects.

10. *Powers make a great part of our complex* ideas *of substances.* Powers therefore justly *make a great part of our complex* ideas *of substances.* He who will examine his complex *idea* of gold will find several of its *ideas* that make it up to be only powers—as the power of being melted, but of not spending itself in the fire, of being dissolved in *aqua regia,* are *ideas* as necessary to make up our complex *idea* of gold as its color and weight, which, if duly considered, are also nothing but different powers. For to speak truly, yellowness is not actually in gold, but is a power in gold to produce that *idea* in us by our eyes, when placed in a due light; and the heat, which we cannot

leave out of our *ideas* of the sun, is no more really in the sun than the white color it introduces into wax. These are both equally powers in the sun operating, by the motion and figure of its sensible parts, so on a man, as to make him have the *idea* of heat, and so on wax, as to make it capable to produce in a man the *idea* of white.

11. *The now secondary qualities of bodies would disappear, if we could discover the primary ones of their minute parts.* Had we senses acute enough to discern the minute particles of bodies, and the real constitution on which their sensible qualities depend, I do not doubt but they would produce quite different *ideas* in us, and that which is now the yellow color of gold would then disappear, and instead of it we should see an admirable texture of parts of a certain size and figure. This microscopes plainly discover to us; for what to our naked eyes produces a certain color is, by thus augmenting the acuteness of our senses, discovered to be quite a different thing; and the thus altering, as it were, the proportion of the bulk of the minute parts of a colored object to our usual sight produces different *ideas* from what it did before. Thus sand or pounded glass, which is opaque and white to the naked eye, is pellucid in a microscope; and a hair seen this way loses its former color, and is in a great measure pellucid, with a mixture of some bright sparkling colors, such as appear from the refraction of diamonds and other pellucid bodies. Blood to the naked eye appears all red, but by a good microscope, in which its lesser parts appear, shows only some few globules of red, swimming in a pellucid liquor. And how these red globules would appear, if glasses could be found that could yet magnify them a thousand or ten thousand times more, is uncertain.

12. *Our faculties of discovery suited to our state.* The infinitely wise contriver of us, and all things about us, has fitted our senses, faculties, and organs, to the conveniences of life, and the business we have to do here. We are able, by our senses, to know and distinguish things, and to examine them so far as to apply them to our uses, and several ways to accommodate the exigencies of this life. We have insight enough into their admirable contrivances and wonderful effects to admire and magnify the wisdom,

power, and goodness of their author. Such a knowledge as this, which is suited to our present condition, we do not want faculties to attain. But it does not appear that God intended we should have a perfect, clear, and adequate knowledge of them; that perhaps is not in the comprehension of any finite being. We are furnished with faculties (dull and weak as they are) to discover enough in the creatures, to lead us to the knowledge of the Creator and the knowledge of our duty. And we are fitted well enough with abilities to provide for the conveniences of living. These are our business in this world. But were our senses altered and made much quicker and more acute, the appearance and outward scheme of things would have quite another face to us, and, I am apt to think, would be inconsistent with our being, or at least well-being, in this part of the universe which we inhabit. He who considers how little our constitution is able to bear a remove into parts of this air, not much higher than that we commonly breathe in, will have reason to be satisfied that in this globe of earth allotted for our mansion, the all-wise Architect has suited our organs, and the bodies that are to affect them, one to another. If our sense of hearing were but one thousand times quicker than it is, how would a perpetual noise distract us? And we should in the quietest retirement be less able to sleep or meditate than in the middle of a sea fight. No, if that most instructive of our senses, seeing, were in any man a thousand or a hundred thousand times more acute than it is by the best microscope, things several millions of times less than the smallest object of his sight now would then be visible to his naked eyes, and so he would come nearer to the discovery of the texture and motion of the minute parts of corporeal things, and in many of them probably get *ideas* of their internal constitutions. But then he would be in a quite different world from other people. Nothing would appear the same to him and others; the visible *ideas* of everything would be different. So that I doubt whether he and the rest of men could discourse concerning the objects of sight, or have any communication about colors, their appearances being so wholly different. And perhaps such a quickness and tenderness of sight could not endure bright sunshine, or so much as open daylight, nor take in but a very small part of any object at once, and that too only at a very near distance. And if by the help of such microscopic eyes (if I may so call them) a man could penetrate further than ordinary into the secret composition and radical texture of bodies, he would not make any great advantage by the change, if such an acute sight would not serve to conduct him to the market and exchange, if he could not see things he was to avoid, at a convenient distance, nor distinguish things he had to do with by those sensible qualities others do. [ . . . ]

14. *Complex* ideas *of substances*. But to return to the matter in hand, the *ideas* we have of substances, and the ways we come by them, I say, our *specific* ideas *of substances* are nothing else but *a collection of a certain number of simple* ideas, *considered as united in one thing*. These *ideas* of substances, though they are commonly simple apprehensions and the names of them simple terms, yet in effect are complex and compounded. Thus the *idea* which an Englishman signifies by the name *swan* is white color, long neck, red beak, black legs, and whole feet, and all these of a certain size, with a power of swimming in the water, and making a certain kind of noise. And perhaps, to a man who has long observed this kind of bird, some other properties which all terminate in sensible simple *ideas*, all united in one common subject.

15. Idea *of spiritual substances as clear as of bodily substances*. Besides the complex *ideas* we have of material sensible substances, of which I have last spoken, by the simple *ideas* we have taken from those operations of our own minds, which we experiment daily in ourselves, as thinking, understanding, willing, knowing, and power of beginning motion, etc., coexisting in some substance, we are able to frame *the complex* idea *of an immaterial spirit*. And thus, by putting together the *ideas* of thinking, perceiving, liberty, and power of moving themselves and other things, we have as clear a perception and notion of immaterial substances as we have of material. For putting together the *ideas* of thinking and willing, or the power of moving or quieting corporeal motion, joined to substance, of which we have no distinct *idea*, we have the *idea* of an immaterial spirit; and by putting together the *ideas* of coherent solid parts,

and a power of being moved, joined with substance, of which likewise we have no positive *idea*, we have the *idea* of matter. The one is as clear and distinct an *idea* as the other, the *idea* of thinking and moving a body being as clear and distinct *ideas* as the *ideas* of extension, solidity, and being moved. For our *idea* of substance is equally obscure, or none at all, in both; it is but a supposed I know not what, to support those *ideas* we call accidents. It is for want of reflection that we are apt to think that our senses show us nothing but material things. Every act of sensation, when duly considered, gives us an equal view of both parts of nature, the corporeal and spiritual. For while I know, by seeing or hearing, etc., that there is some corporeal being without me, the object of that sensation, I do more certainly know that there is some spiritual being within me that sees and hears. This, I must be convinced, cannot be the action of bare insensible matter, nor ever could be, without an immaterial thinking being.

16. *No idea of abstract substance.* By the complex *idea* of extended, figured, colored, and all other sensible qualities, which is all that we know of it, we are as far from the *idea* of the substance of body as if we knew nothing at all. *Nor* after all the acquaintance and familiarity, which we imagine we *have* with matter, and the many qualities *men* assure themselves they perceive and know in bodies, will it perhaps upon examination be found that they have any *more*, or clearer, *primary* ideas *belonging to body than they have belonging to immaterial spirit.*

17. *The cohesion of solid parts and impulse, the primary ideas of body. The primary* ideas *we have peculiar to body*, as contradistinguished to spirit, *are the cohesion of solid*, and consequently separable, *parts, and a power of communicating motion by impulse.* These, I think, are the original *ideas* proper and peculiar to body, for figure is but the consequence of finite extension.

18. *Thinking and motivity the primary* ideas *of spirit.* The *ideas* we have belonging and *peculiar to spirit are thinking and will*, or a power of putting body into motion by thought, and which is consequent to it, liberty. For as body cannot but communicate its motion by impulse to another body, which it meets with at rest, so the mind can put bodies into motion, or refrain to do so, as it pleases. The *ideas* of existence, duration, and mobility are common to them both.

19. *Spirits capable of motion.* There is no reason why it should be thought strange that I make *mobility belong to spirit.* For having no other *idea* of motion but change of distance with other beings that are considered as at rest, and finding that spirits, as well as bodies, cannot operate but where they are, and that spirits do operate at several times in several places, I cannot but attribute change of place to all finite spirits (for of the infinite spirit I do not speak here). For my soul, being a real being as well as my body, is certainly as capable of changing distance with any other body, or being, as body itself—and so is capable of motion. And if a mathematician can consider a certain distance, or a change of that distance between two points, one may certainly conceive a distance, and a change of distance between two spirits, and so conceive their motion, their approach or removal, one from another.

20. Everyone finds in himself that his soul can think, will, and operate on his body in the place where that is, but cannot operate on a body, or in a place a hundred miles distant from it. Nobody can imagine that his soul can think or move a body at *Oxford*, while he is at *London*, and cannot but know that, being united to his body, it constantly changes place all the whole journey between *Oxford* and *London*, as the coach or horse does that carries him, and I think may be said to be truly all that while in motion. Or if that will not be allowed to afford us a clear *idea* enough of its motion, its being separated from the body in death, I think, will; for to consider it as going out of the body, or leaving it, and yet to have no *idea* of its motion, seems to me impossible. [ . . . ]

22. *Idea of soul and body compared.* Let us *compare* then our complex *idea* of an immaterial spirit with our complex *idea* of body, and see whether there is any more obscurity in one than in the other, and in which most. Our *idea* of body, as I think, is an extended solid substance, capable of communicating motion by impulse. And our *idea* of soul, as an immaterial spirit, is of a substance that thinks, and has a power of exciting motion in body, by willing

or thought. These, I think, are *our complex* ideas *of soul and body, as contradistinguished*; and now let us examine which has most obscurity in it, and difficulty to be apprehended. I know that people whose thoughts are immersed in matter, and have so subjected their minds to their senses that they seldom reflect on anything beyond them, are apt to say, they cannot comprehend a thinking thing, which perhaps is true. But I affirm, when they consider it well, they can no more comprehend an extended thing.

23. *Cohesion of solid parts in body as hard to be conceived as thinking in a soul.* If anyone says he does not know what it is that thinks in him, he means he does not know what the substance is of that thinking thing. No more, say I, does he know what the substance is of that solid thing. Further, if he says he does not know how he thinks, I answer, neither does he know how he is extended, how the solid parts of body are united or cohere together to make extension. [ . . . ]

25. I allow it is usual for most people to wonder how anyone should find a difficulty in what they think they every day observe. Do we not see, will they be ready to say, the parts of bodies stick firmly together? Is there anything more common? And what doubt can there be made of it? And the like, I say, concerning *thinking* and *voluntary motion*. Do we not every moment experiment it in ourselves, and therefore can it be doubted? The matter of fact is clear, I confess; but when we would a little nearer look into it, and consider how it is done, there I think we are at a loss, both in the one and the other, and can as little understand how the parts of body cohere, as how we ourselves perceive or move. I would have anyone intelligibly explain to me how the parts of gold, or brass (that but now in fusion were as loose from one another as the particles of water or the sands of an hourglass), come in a few moments to be so united and adhere so strongly one to another that the utmost force of men's arms cannot separate them. A considering man will, I suppose, be here at a loss to satisfy his own or another man's understanding. [ . . . ]

28. *Communication of motion by impulse, or by thought, equally intelligible.* Another *idea* we have of body is the power of *communication of motion by impulse*, and of our souls the power of *exciting motion by thought*. These *ideas*, the one of body, the other of our minds, every day's experience clearly furnishes us with. But if here again we inquire how this is done, we *are equally in the dark*. For to the communication of motion by impulse, in which as much motion is lost to one body as is gotten to the other, which is the most ordinary case, we can have no other conception but of the passing of motion out of one body into another. This, I think, is as obscure and inconceivable as how our minds move or stop our bodies by thought, which we every moment find they do. The increase of motion by impulse, which is observed or believed sometimes to happen, is yet harder to be understood. We have by daily experience clear evidence of motion produced both by impulse and by thought, but the manner how hardly comes within our comprehension. We are equally at a loss in both, so that, however we consider motion and its communication, either from body or spirit, the *idea* which belongs to spirit is at least as clear as that which belongs to body. And if we consider the active power of moving, or, as I may call it, *motivity*, it is much clearer in spirit than body, since two bodies, placed by one another at rest, will never afford us the *idea* of a power in the one to move the other, but by a borrowed motion, whereas the mind, every day, affords us *ideas* of an active power of moving of bodies, and therefore it is worth our consideration, whether active power is not the proper attribute of spirits, and passive power of matter. Hence may be conjectured that created spirits are not totally separate from matter, because they are both active and passive. Pure spirit, namely, God, is only active; pure matter is only passive; those beings that are both active and passive we may judge to partake of both. [ . . . ]

30. Ideas *of body and spirit compared.* So that, in short, *the idea* we have *of spirit, compared with the idea* we have *of body*, stands thus: the substance of spirits is unknown to us, and so is the substance of body equally unknown to us. Two primary qualities or properties of body, namely, solid coherent parts and impulse, we have distinct clear *ideas* of. So likewise we know and have distinct clear *ideas* of two primary qualities or properties of spirit, namely, thinking and

a power of action, i.e. a power of beginning or stopping several thoughts or motions. We have also the *ideas* of several qualities inherent in bodies, and have the clear distinct *ideas* of them; these qualities are but the various modifications of the extension of cohering solid parts and their motion. We have likewise the *ideas* of the several modes of thinking, namely, believing, doubting, intending, fearing, hoping, all which are but the several modes of thinking. We have also the *ideas* of willing and moving the body consequent to it, and with the body itself too; for, as has been shown, spirit is capable of motion.

31. *The notion of spirit involves no more difficulty in it than that of body.* Lastly, if this notion of immaterial spirit may have, perhaps, some difficulties in it not easily to be explained, we have therefore no more reason to deny or doubt the existence of such spirits than we have to deny or doubt the existence of body, because the notion of body is encumbered with some difficulties very hard, and perhaps impossible to be explained or understood by us. For I would gladly have instanced anything in our notion of spirit more perplexed, or nearer a contradiction, than the very notion of body includes in it. The divisibility *in infinitum* of any finite extension involving us, whether we grant or deny it, in consequences impossible to be explicated or made in our apprehensions consistent—consequences that carry greater difficulty, and more apparent absurdity, than anything can follow from the notion of an immaterial knowing substance.

32. *We know nothing beyond our simple* ideas. Which we are not at all to wonder at since, we having but some few superficial *ideas* of things discovered to us only by the senses from without, or by the mind, reflecting on what it experiments in itself within, have no knowledge beyond that, much less of the internal constitution and true nature of things, being destitute of faculties to attain it. And therefore experimenting and discovering in ourselves knowledge, and the power of voluntary motion, as certainly as we experiment or discover in things without us the cohesion and separation of solid parts, which is the extension and motion of bodies, *we have as much reason to be satisfied with our notion of immaterial spirit as with our notion of body, and the existence of*

*the one as well as the other.* For, it being no more a contradiction that thinking should exist separate and independent from solidity than it is a contradiction that solidity should exist separate and independent from thinking, they being both but simple *ideas,* independent one from another; and having as clear and distinct *ideas* in us of thinking as of solidity, I do not know why we may not as well allow a thinking thing without solidity, i.e., *immaterial,* to exist, as a solid thing without thinking, i.e., *matter,* to exist— especially since it is not harder to conceive how thinking should exist without matter than how matter should think. For whenever we would proceed beyond these simple *ideas* we have from sensation and reflection, and dive further into the nature of things, we fall presently into darkness and obscurity, perplexity and difficulties, and can discover nothing further but our own blindness and ignorance. But whichever of these complex *ideas* is clearest, that of body, or immaterial spirit, this is evident that the simple *ideas* that make them up are no other than what we have received from sensation or reflection. And so is it of all our other *ideas* of substances, even of God himself.

33. Idea *of God.* For if we examine the *idea* we have of the incomprehensible supreme being, we shall find that we come by it the same way, and that the complex *ideas* we have both of God and separate spirits are made of the simple *ideas* we receive from *reflection*: e.g., having, from what we experiment in ourselves, gotten the *ideas* of existence and duration, of knowledge and power, of pleasure and happiness, and of several other qualities and powers, which it is better to have than to be without. When we would frame an *idea* the most suitable we can to the supreme being, we enlarge every one of these with our *idea* of infinity, and so putting them together make our complex *idea of God.* For that the mind has such a power of enlarging some of its *ideas,* received from sensation and reflection, has been already shown. [ . . . ]

37. *Recapitulation.* And thus we have seen *what kinds of ideas we have of substances of all kinds,* in what they consist, and how we came by them. From this, I think, it is very evident,

*First*, that all our *ideas* of the several sorts of substances are nothing but collections of simple *ideas*, with a supposition of something to which they belong, and in which they subsist, though of this supposed something we have no clear distinct *idea* at all.

*Secondly*, that all the simple *ideas*, that thus united in one common *substratum* make up our complex *ideas* of several sorts of substances, are no other but such as we have received from *sensation* or *reflection*, so that even in those which we think we are most intimately acquainted with, and that come nearest the comprehension of our most enlarged conceptions, we cannot go beyond those simple *ideas*. And even in those which seem most remote from all we have to do with, and do infinitely surpass anything we can perceive in ourselves by reflection, or discover by sensation in other things, we can attain to nothing but those simple *ideas*, which we originally received from sensation or reflection, as is evident in the complex *ideas* we have of angels and particularly of God himself.

*Thirdly*, that most of the simple *ideas* that make up our complex *ideas* of substances, when truly considered, are only powers, however we are apt to take them for positive qualities—e.g., the greatest part of the *ideas* that make our complex *idea* of *gold* are yellowness, great weight, ductility, fusibility, and solubility in *aqua regia*, etc., all united together in an unknown *substratum*. All these *ideas* are nothing else but so many relations to other substances, and are not really in the gold, considered barely in itself, though they depend on those real and primary qualities of its internal constitution, by which it has a fitness differently to operate, and be operated on by several other substances.

## Chapter XXVII. *Of Identity and Diversity*.

1. *In what identity consists*. Another occasion the mind often takes of comparing is the very being of things, when, considering anything as existing at any determined time and place, we compare it with itself existing at another time, and upon it form the *ideas* of *identity* and *diversity*. When we see anything to be in any place in any instant of time, we are sure (be it what it will) that it is that very thing, and not

another, which at that same time exists in another place, however like and indistinguishable it may be in all other respects. And in this consists *identity*, when the *ideas* it is attributed to vary not at all from what they were that moment in which we consider their former existence, and to which we compare the present. For us never finding, nor conceiving it possible, that two things of the same kind should exist in the same place at the same time, we rightly conclude that whatever exists anywhere at any time, excludes all of the same kind and is there itself alone. When therefore we demand whether anything is the same or not, it refers always to something that existed such a time in such a place, which it was certain at that instant was the same with itself, and no other. From this it follows that one thing cannot have two beginnings of existence, nor two things one beginning, it being impossible for two things of the same kind to be or exist in the same instant, in the very same place, or one and the same thing in different places. That, therefore, that had one beginning is the same thing; and that, which had a different beginning in time and place from that, is not the same, but diverse; that which has made the difficulty about this relation has been the little care and attention used in having precise notions of the things to which it is attributed.

2. *Identity of substances. Identity of modes*. We have the *ideas* but of three sorts of substances: 1. God. 2. Finite intelligences. 3. *Bodies*. First, God is without beginning, eternal, unalterable, and everywhere, and therefore concerning his identity there can be no doubt. Secondly, finite spirits having had each its determinate time and place of beginning to exist, the relation to that time and place will always determine to each of them its identity, as long as it exists. Thirdly, the same will hold of every particle of matter, to which no addition or subtraction of matter being made, it is the same. For though these three sorts of substances, as we term them, do not exclude one another out of the same place, yet we cannot conceive but that they must necessarily each of them exclude any of the same kind out of the same place. Or else the notions and names of identity and diversity would be in vain, and there could be no such distinctions of substances, or anything else one from

another. For example: could two bodies be in the same place at the same time, then those two parcels of matter must be one and the same, take them great or little. No, all bodies must be one and the same. For by the same reason that two particles of matter may be in one place, all bodies may be in one place, which, when it can be supposed, takes away the distinction of identity and diversity of one and more and renders it ridiculous. But it being a contradiction that two or more should be one, identity and diversity are relations and ways of comparing well-founded and of use to the understanding.

All other things being but modes or relations ultimately terminated in substances, the identity and diversity of each particular existence of them too will be by the same way determined. Only as to things whose existence is in succession, such as are the actions of finite beings, e.g., *motion* and *thought*, both which consist in a continued train of succession, concerning their diversity, there can be no question. Because each perishing the moment it begins, they cannot exist in different times, or in different places, as permanent beings can at different times exist in distant places; and therefore no motion or thought, considered as at different times, can be the same, each part of this having a different beginning of existence.

3. Principium individuationis. From what has been said, it is easy to discover what is so much inquired after, the *principium individuationis*; and that, it is plain, is existence itself, which determines a being of any sort to a particular time and place, incommunicable to two beings of the same kind. This, though it seems easier to conceive in simple substances or modes, yet when reflected on, is not more difficult in compound ones, if care is taken to what it is applied—e.g., let us suppose an atom, i.e., a continued body under one immutable surface, existing in a determined time and place; it is evident that, considered in any instant of its existence, it is in that instant the same with itself. For being at that instant what it is, and nothing else, it is the same, and so must continue as long as its existence is continued; for so long it will be the same, and no other. In like manner, if two or more atoms are joined together into the same mass, every one of those atoms will be

the same, by the foregoing rule. And while they exist united together, the mass, consisting of the same atoms, must be the same mass, or the same body, let the parts be ever so differently jumbled. But if one of these atoms is taken away, or one new one added, it is no longer the same mass or the same body. In the state of living creatures, their identity does not depend on a mass of the same particles, but on something else. For in them the variation of great parcels of matter does not alter the identity. An oak growing from a plant to a great tree, and then lopped, is still the same oak; and a colt grown up to a horse, sometimes fat, sometimes lean, is all the while the same horse. Though in both these cases, there may be a manifest change of the parts, so that truly they are not either of them the same masses of matter, though they are truly one of them the same oak, and the other the same horse. The reason for this is that in these two cases, a mass of matter and a living body, *identity* is not applied to the same thing.

4. *Identity of vegetables*. We must therefore consider in what an oak differs from a mass of matter, and that seems to me to be in this, that the one is only the cohesion of particles of matter any how united, the other such a disposition of them as constitutes the parts of an oak, and such an organization of those parts as is fit to receive and distribute nourishment, so as to continue and frame the wood, bark, and leaves, etc., of an oak, in which consists the vegetable life; that being then one plant which has such an organization of parts in one coherent body partaking of one common life, it continues to be the same plant as long as it partakes of the same life, though that life is communicated to new particles of matter vitally united to the living plant, in a like continued organization conformable to that sort of plants. For this organization being at any one instant in any one collection of *matter*, is in that particular concrete distinguished from all other, and is that individual life, which existing constantly from that moment both forwards and backwards, in the same continuity of insensibly succeeding parts united to the living body of the plant, it has that identity which makes the same plant, and all the parts of it, parts of the same plant, during all the time that they exist united

in that continued organization, which is fit to convey that common life to all the parts so united.

5. *Identity of animals*. The case is not so much different in *brutes*, but that anyone may hence see what makes an animal and continues it the same. Something we have like this in machines, and may serve to illustrate it. For example, what is a watch? It is plain it is nothing but a fit organization or construction of parts to a certain end, which when a sufficient force is added to it, it is capable to attain. If we would suppose this machine one continued body, all whose organized parts were repaired, increased, or diminished by a constant addition or separation of insensible parts, with one common life, we should have something very much like the body of an animal—with this difference that in an animal the fitness of the organization, and the motion in which life consists, begin together, the motion coming from within, but in machines, the force coming sensibly from without is often away when the organ is in order, and well fitted to receive it.

6. *Identity of man*. This also shows in what the identity of the same *man* consists, namely, in nothing but a participation of the same continued life, by constantly fleeting particles of matter, in succession vitally united to the same organized body. He who shall place the *identity* of man in anything else but, like that of other animals, in one fitly organized body, taken in any one instant, and from this continued under one organization of life in several successively fleeting particles of matter united to it, will find it hard to make an *embryo*, one of years, mad and sober, the same man, by any supposition that will not make it possible for *Seth, Ismael, Socrates, Pilate, St. Austin,* and *Caesar Borgia,* to be the same man. For if the *identity* of soul alone makes the same man, and there is nothing in the nature of matter why the same individual spirit may not be united to different bodies, it will be possible that those men living in distant ages, and of different tempers, may have been the same man. This way of speaking must be, from a very strange use of the word *man,* applied to an *idea,* out of which body and shape are excluded. And that way of speaking would agree yet worse with the notions of those philosophers who allow of transmigration, and

are of the opinion that the souls of men may, for their miscarriages, be thrust into the bodies of beasts, as fit habitations, with organs suited to the satisfaction of their brutal inclinations. But yet I think nobody, could he be sure that the soul of *Heliogabalus* were in one of his hogs, would yet say that hog were a *man* or *Heliogabalus.*

7. *Identity suited to the* idea. It is not therefore unity of substance that comprehends all sorts of *identity,* or will determine it in every case. But to conceive and judge of it correctly, we must consider what *idea* the word it is applied to stands for, it being one thing to be the same *substance,* another the same *man,* and a third the same *person,* if *person, man,* and *substance* are three names standing for three different *ideas;* for such as is the *idea* belonging to that name, such must be the *identity.* This, if it had been a little more carefully attended to, would possibly have prevented a great deal of that confusion which often occurs about this matter, with no small seeming difficulties, especially concerning *personal identity,* which therefore we shall in the next place a little consider.

8. *Same man*. An animal is a living organized body; and consequently the same animal, as we have observed, is the same continued life communicated to different particles of matter, as they happen successively to be united to that organized living body. And whatever is talked of other definitions, ingenuous observation puts it past doubt that the *idea* in our minds, of which the sound *man* in our mouths is the sign, is nothing else but of an animal of such a certain form. Since I think I may be confident that, whoever should see a creature of his own shape and make, though it had no more reason all its life than a *cat* or a *parrot,* would call him still a *man;* or whoever should hear a *cat* or a *parrot* discourse, reason, and philosophize would call or think it nothing but a *cat* or a *parrot* and say the one was a dull, irrational *man,* and the other a very intelligent rational *parrot.* [ . . . ] For I presume it is not the *idea* of a thinking or rational being alone that makes the *idea* of a man in most people's sense, but of a body, so and so shaped, joined to it. And if that is the *idea* of a man, the same successive body not shifted all at once must, as well

as the same immaterial spirit, go to the making of the same man.

9. *Personal identity*. This being premised, to find in what *personal identity* consists, we must consider what *person* stands for; this, I think, is a thinking intelligent being that has reason and reflection, and can consider itself as itself, the same thinking thing in different times and places, which it does only by that consciousness which is inseparable from thinking, and, as it seems to me, essential to it—it being impossible for anyone to perceive without perceiving that he does perceive. When we see, hear, smell, taste, feel, meditate, or will anything, we know that we do so. Thus it is always as to our present sensations and perceptions. And by this everyone is to himself that which he calls *self*; it not being considered in this case whether the same *self* is continued in the same or diverse substances. For since consciousness always accompanies thinking, and it is that which makes everyone to be what he calls *self*, and thereby distinguishes himself from all other thinking things, in this alone consists *personal identity*, i.e., the sameness of a rational being. And as far as this consciousness can be extended backwards to any past action or thought, so far reaches the identity of that *person*; it is the same *self* now it was then, and it is by the same *self* with this present one that now reflects on it that that action was done.

10. *Consciousness makes personal identity*. But it is further inquired whether it is the same identical substance. This few would think they had reason to doubt of, if these perceptions, with their consciousness, always remained present in the mind, by means of which the same thinking thing would be always consciously present, and, as would be thought, evidently the same to itself. But that which seems to make the difficulty is this, that this consciousness, being interrupted always by forgetfulness, there being no moment of our lives in which we have the whole train of all our past actions before our eyes in one view, but even the best memories losing the sight of one part while they are viewing another, and we sometimes, and that the greatest part of our lives, not reflecting on our past selves, being intent on our present thoughts, and in sound sleep having no thoughts

at all, or at least none with that consciousness which remarks our waking thoughts. I say, in all these cases, our consciousness being interrupted, and we losing the sight of our past *selves*, doubts are raised whether we are the same thinking thing, i.e., the same substance or not. This, however reasonable or unreasonable, does not concern *personal identity* at all, the question being what makes the same *person*, and not whether it is the same identical substance which always thinks in the same *person*; which in this case does not matter at all—different substances by the same consciousness (where they do partake in it) being united into one person, as well as different bodies by the same life are united into one animal, whose *identity* is preserved in that change of substances by the unity of one continued life. For it being the same consciousness that makes a man be himself to himself, *personal identity* depends on that only, whether it is annexed solely to one individual substance or can be continued in a succession of several substances. For as far as any intelligent being can repeat the *idea* of any past action with the same consciousness it had of it at first, and with the same consciousness it has of any present action, so far it is the same *personal self*. For it is by the consciousness it has of its present thoughts and actions that it is *self* to *itself* now, and so will be the same *self*, as far as the same consciousness can extend to actions past or to come, and would be by distance of time, or change of substance, no more two *persons* than a man is two men by wearing other clothes today than he did yesterday, with a long or a short sleep between. The same consciousness uniting those distant actions into the same *person*, whatever substances contributed to their production.

11. *Personal identity in change of substances*. That this is so, we have some kind of evidence in our very bodies, all whose particles, while vitally united to this same thinking conscious self, so that we feel when they are touched, and are affected by, and conscious of good or harm that happens to them, are a part of our*selves*; i.e., of our thinking conscious *self*. Thus the limbs of his body are to everyone a part of *himself*; he sympathizes and is concerned for them. Cut off a hand, and thereby separate it from that consciousness he had of its heat, cold, and other affections, and

it is then no longer a part of that which is *himself*, any more than the remotest part of matter. Thus we see the *substance*, of which *personal self* consisted at one time, may be varied at another, without the change of personal *identity*, there being no question about the same person, though the limbs which but now were a part of it are cut off.

12. *Whether in the change of thinking substances.* But the question is, "whether if the same substance which thinks is changed, it can be the same person, or, remaining the same, it can be different persons?"

And to this I answer: First, this can be no question at all to those who place thought in a purely material animal constitution, void of an immaterial substance. For whether their supposition is true or not, it is plain they conceive personal identity preserved in something else than identity of substance, as animal identity is preserved in identity of life, and not of substance. And therefore those who place thinking in an immaterial substance only, before they can come to deal with these men, must show why personal identity cannot be preserved in the change of immaterial substances, or variety of particular immaterial substances, as well as animal identity is preserved in the change of material substances, or variety of particular bodies. Unless they will say it is one immaterial spirit that makes the same life in brutes, as it is one immaterial spirit that makes the same person in men, which the *Cartesians* at least will not admit, for fear of making brutes thinking things too.

13. But next, as to the first part of the question, "Whether if the same thinking substance (supposing immaterial substances only to think) is changed, it can be the same person?" I answer that cannot be resolved, but by those who know what kind of substances they are that do think, and whether the consciousness of past actions can be transferred from one thinking substance to another. I grant, were the same consciousness the same individual action, it could not. But it being a present representation of a past action, why it may not be possible that that may be represented to the mind to have been which really never was, will remain to be shown. And therefore how far the consciousness of past actions is annexed to any individual agent, so that another cannot possibly have

it, will be hard for us to determine, until we know what kind of action it is that cannot be done without a reflex act of perception accompanying it, and how performed by thinking substances, who cannot think without being conscious of it. But that which we call the *same consciousness*, not being the same individual act, why one intellectual substance may not have represented to it, as done by itself, what it never did, and was perhaps done by some other agent—why, I say, such a representation may not possibly be without reality of matter of fact, as well as several representations in dreams are, which yet while dreaming we take for true, will be difficult to conclude from the nature of things. And that it never is so, will by us, until we have clearer views of the nature of thinking substances, be best resolved into the goodness of God, who as far as the happiness or misery of any of his sensible creatures is concerned in it, will not by a fatal error of theirs transfer from one to another that consciousness which draws reward or punishment with it. How far this may be an argument against those who would place thinking in a system of fleeting animal spirits, I leave to be considered. But yet to return to the question before us, it must be allowed that if the same consciousness (which, as has been shown, is quite a different thing from the same numerical figure or motion in body) can be transferred from one thinking substance to another, it will be possible that two thinking substances may make but one person. For the same consciousness being preserved, whether in the same or different substances, the personal identity is preserved.

14. As to the second part of the question, "whether the same immaterial substance remaining, there may be two distinct persons?" this question seems to me to be built on this, whether the same immaterial being, being conscious of the action of its past duration, may be wholly stripped of all the consciousness of its past existence and lose it beyond the power of ever retrieving it again, and so as it were beginning a new account from a new period, have a consciousness that cannot reach beyond this new state. All those who hold preexistence are evidently of this mind, since they allow the soul to have no remaining consciousness of what it did in that preexistent state,

either wholly separate from body, or informing any other body; and if they should not, it is plain [that] experience would be against them. Thus, personal identity reaching no further than consciousness reaches, a preexistent spirit not having continued so many ages in a state of silence must necessarily make different persons. Suppose a Christian, *Platonist*, or *Pythagorean* should, upon God's having ended all his works of creation the seventh day, think his soul has existed ever since, and should imagine it has revolved in several human bodies, as I once met with one, who was persuaded his had been the soul of *Socrates*; (how reasonably I will not dispute; this I know that in the post he filled, which was no inconsiderable one, he passed for a very rational man, and the press has shown that he did not want parts or learning) would anyone say that he, being not conscious of any of *Socrates'* actions or thoughts, could be the same person with *Socrates*? Let anyone reflect upon himself, and conclude that he has in himself an immaterial spirit, which is that which thinks in him, and in the constant change of his body keeps him the same, and is that which he calls himself. Let him also suppose it to be the same soul that was in *Nestor* or *Thersites* at the siege of *Troy* (for souls being, as far as we know anything of them, in their nature, indifferent to any parcel of matter, the supposition has no apparent absurdity in it), which it may have been, as well as it is now the soul of any other man. But he now having no consciousness of any of the actions either of *Nestor* or *Thersites*, does or can he conceive himself the same person with either of them? Can he be concerned in either of their actions, attribute them to himself, or think them his own more than the actions of any other men that ever existed? Thus, this consciousness not reaching to any of the actions of either of those men, he is no more one self with either of them than if the soul or immaterial spirit that now informs him had been created and began to exist, when it began to inform his present body, though it were ever so true that the same spirit that informed *Nestor's* or *Thersites'* body was numerically the same that now informs his. For this would no more make him the same person with *Nestor* than if some of the particles of matter that were once a part

of *Nestor* were now a part of this man—the same immaterial substance, without the same consciousness, no more making the same person by being united to any body than the same particle of matter, without consciousness united to any body, makes the same person. But let him once find himself conscious of any of the actions of *Nestor*, he then finds himself the same person with *Nestor*.

15. And thus we may be able, without any difficulty, to conceive the same person at the resurrection, though in a body not exactly in make or parts the same which he had here, the same consciousness going along with the soul that inhabits it. But yet the soul alone, in the change of bodies, would scarcely to anyone but to him who makes the soul the *man* be enough to make the same *man*. For should the soul of a prince, carrying with it the consciousness of the prince's past life, enter and inform the body of a cobbler, as soon as deserted by his own soul, everyone sees he would be the same person with the prince, accountable only for the prince's actions. But who would say it was the same man? The body too goes to the making the man, and would, I guess, to everybody determine the man in this case, in which the soul, with all its princely thoughts about it, would not make another man. But he would be the same cobbler to everyone besides himself. I know that, in the ordinary way of speaking, the same person and the same man, stand for one and the same thing. And indeed everyone will always have a liberty to speak as he pleases, and to apply what articulate sounds to what *ideas* he thinks fit, and change them as often as he pleases. But yet when we will inquire what makes the same *spirit*, *man*, or *person*, we must fix the *ideas* of *spirit*, *man*, or *person* in our minds; and having resolved with ourselves what we mean by them, it will not be hard to determine in either of them, or the like, when it is the *same*, and when not.

16. *Consciousness makes the same person.* But though the same immaterial substance or soul does not alone, wherever it is, and in whatever state, make the same man, yet it is plain consciousness, as far as ever it can be extended, should it be to ages past, unites existences and actions very remote in time into the same person, as well as it does the existences

and actions of the immediately preceding moment, so that whatever has the consciousness of present and past actions is the same person to whom they both belong. Had I the same consciousness that I saw the ark and *Noah's* flood as that I saw an overflowing of the *Thames* last winter, or as that I write now, I could no more doubt that I who write this now that saw the *Thames* overflowed last winter, and that viewed the flood at the general deluge, was the same *self*—place that *self* in what substance you please—than that I who write this am the same *myself* now while I write (whether I consist of all the same substance, material or immaterial, or no) that I was yesterday. For as to this point of being the same *self*, it does not matter whether this present *self* is made up of the same or other substances, I being as much concerned, and as justly accountable for any action that was done a thousand years since, appropriated to me now by this self-consciousness, as I am for what I did the last moment.

17. *Self depends on consciousness. Self* is that conscious thinking thing, whatever substance made up of (whether spiritual or material, simple or compounded, it matters not), which is sensible, or conscious of pleasure and pain, capable of happiness or misery, and so is concerned for it*self*, as far as that consciousness extends. Thus everyone finds that, while comprehended under that consciousness, the little finger is as much a part of him*self* as what is most so. Upon separation of this little finger, should this consciousness go along with the little finger, and leave the rest of the body, it is evident the little finger would be the *person*, the *same person*; and self then would have nothing to do with the rest of the body. As in this case it is the consciousness that goes along with the substance, when one part is separate from another, which makes the same *person* and constitutes this inseparable *self*, so it is in reference to substances remote in time; that with which the *consciousness* of this present thinking thing can join itself makes the same *person*, and is one *self* with it, and with nothing else, and so attributes to it*self* and owns all the actions of that thing as its own, as far as that consciousness reaches, and no further—as everyone who reflects will perceive.

18. *Objects of reward and punishment.* In this *personal identity* is founded all the right and justice of reward and punishment, happiness and misery being that for which everyone is concerned for *himself*, and not mattering what becomes of any substance not joined to, or affected with that consciousness. For as it is evident in the instance I gave but now, if the consciousness went along with the little finger when it was cut off, that would be the same *self* which was concerned for the whole body yesterday as making part of it*self*, whose actions then it cannot but admit as its own now. Though if the same body should still live, and immediately, from the separation of the little finger, have its own peculiar consciousness, of which the little finger knew nothing, it would not at all be concerned for it, as a part of itself, or could own any of its actions, or have any of them imputed to him.

19. This may show us in what *personal identity* consists, not in the identity of substance, but, as I have said, in the identity of *consciousness*; in which, if *Socrates* and the present mayor of *Queenborough* agree, they are the same person. If the same *Socrates* waking and sleeping do not partake of the same *consciousness*, *Socrates* waking and sleeping is not the same person. And to punish *Socrates* waking for what sleeping *Socrates* thought, and waking *Socrates* was never conscious of, would be no more of right than to punish one twin for what his twin brother did, of which he knew nothing, because their outsides were so like that they could not be distinguished; for such twins have been seen.

20. But yet possibly it will still be objected, suppose I wholly lose the memory of some parts of my life beyond a possibility of retrieving them, so that perhaps I shall never be conscious of them again, yet am I not the same person that did those actions, had those thoughts that I once was conscious of, though I have now forgot them? To which I answer that we must here take notice what the word *I* is applied to, which, in this case, is the man only. And the same man being presumed to be the same person, I is easily here supposed to stand also for the same person. But if it is possible for the same man to have distinct incommunicable consciousness at different times, it is past doubt the same man would at different times

make different persons, which, we see, is the sense of mankind in the solemnest declaration of their opinions, human laws not punishing the *mad man* for the *sober man's* actions, nor the *sober man* for what the *mad man* did, by that means making them two persons. This is somewhat explained by our way of speaking in *English*, when we say such a one *is not himself*, or is *beside himself*; in which phrases it is insinuated, as if those who now, or at least first used them, thought that *self* was changed, the *self*-same person was no longer in that man.

21. *Difference between identity of man and person.* But yet it is hard to conceive that *Socrates*, the same individual man, should be two persons. To help us a little in this, we must consider what is meant by *Socrates*, or the same individual *man*.

*First*, it must be either the same individual, immaterial, thinking substance—in short, the same numerical soul, and nothing else.

*Secondly*, or the same animal, without any regard to an immaterial soul.

*Thirdly*, or the same immaterial spirit united to the same animal.

Now take which of these suppositions you please, it is impossible to make personal identity to consist in anything but consciousness or reach any further than that does.

For by the first of them, it must be allowed possible that a man born of different women, and in distant times, may be the same man. A way of speaking, which whoever admits, must allow it possible for the same man to be two distinct persons, as any two who have lived in different ages, without the knowledge of one another's thoughts.

By the second and thirdly, *Socrates* in this life, and after it, cannot be the same man any way but by the same consciousness; and so making *human identity* to consist in the same thing in which we place *personal identity*, there will be no difficulty to allow the same man to be the same person. But then they who place *human identity* in consciousness only, and not in something else, must consider how they will make the infant *Socrates* the same man with *Socrates* after the resurrection. But whatever to some men makes a *man*, and consequently the same individual man, in

what perhaps few are agreed, personal identity can by us be placed in nothing but consciousness (which is that alone which makes what we call *self*) without involving us in great absurdities.

22. But is not a man drunk and sober the same person? Why else is he punished for the fact he commits when drunk, though he is never afterwards conscious of it? Just as much the same person as a man who walks, and does other things in his sleep, is the same person, and is answerable for any mischief he shall do in it. Human laws punish both, with a justice suitable to their way of knowledge, because in these cases, they cannot distinguish certainly what is real, what counterfeit. And so the ignorance in drunkenness or sleep is not admitted as a plea. For though punishment is annexed to personality, and personality to consciousness, and the drunkard perhaps is not conscious of what he did, yet human judicatures justly punish him, because the fact is proved against him, but want of consciousness cannot be proved for him. But in the great day in which the secrets of all hearts shall be laid open, it may be reasonable to think, no one shall be made to answer for what he knows nothing of, but shall receive his doom, his conscience accusing or excusing him.

23. *Consciousness alone makes self.* Nothing but consciousness can unite remote existences into the same person; the identity of substance will not do it, for whatever substance there is, however framed, without consciousness there is no person. And a carcass may be a person, as well as any sort of substance be so, without consciousness.

Could we suppose two distinct incommunicable consciousnesses acting [in] the same body, the one constantly by day, the other by night, and, on the other side, the same consciousness acting by intervals [in] two distinct bodies. I ask in the first case, whether the *day* and the *night man* would not be two as distinct persons as *Socrates* and *Plato*? And whether, in the second case, there would not be one person in two distinct bodies, as much as one man is the same in two distinct clothings? Nor is it at all material to say that this same, and this distinct *consciousness*, in the cases above mentioned, is owing to the same and distinct immaterial substances, bringing it with them to those bodies, which, whether true or not, alters not the case, since it is evident the *personal identity* would equally be determined by the consciousness, whether that consciousness were annexed to some individual immaterial substance or not. For granting that the thinking substance in man must be necessarily supposed immaterial, it is evident that immaterial thinking thing may sometimes part with its past consciousness, and be restored to it again, as appears in the forgetfulness men often have of their past actions. And the mind many times recovers the memory of a past consciousness, which it had lost for twenty years together. Make these intervals of memory and forgetfulness take their turns regularly by day and night, and you have two persons with the same immaterial spirit, as much as in the former instance two persons with the same body. Thus, *self* is not determined by identity or diversity of substance, which it cannot be sure of but only by identity of consciousness.

24. Indeed it may conceive the substance, of which it is now made up, to have existed formerly, united in the same conscious being. But consciousness removed that substance is no more it*self*, or makes no more a part of it than any other substance, as is evident in the instance we have already given of a limb cut off, of whose heat, or cold, or other affections, having no longer any consciousness, it is no more of a man's self than any other matter of the universe. In like manner it will be in reference to any immaterial substance, which is void of that consciousness by which I am my*self* to my*self*. If there is any part of its existence, which I cannot upon recollection join with that present consciousness by which I am now my*self*, it is in that part of its existence no more my*self* than any other immaterial being. For whatever any substance has thought or done, which I cannot recollect and by my consciousness make my own thought and action, it will no more belong to me, whether a part of me thought or did it, than if it had been thought or done by any other immaterial being anywhere existing.

25. I agree, the more probable opinion is that this consciousness is annexed to, and the affection of, one individual immaterial substance.

But let men, according to their diverse hypotheses, resolve of that as they please; this every intelligent being, sensible of happiness or misery, must grant: that there is something that is *himself* that he is concerned for, and would have happy; that this *self* has existed in a continued duration more than one instant, and therefore it is possible may exist, as it has done, months and years to come, without any certain bounds to be set to its duration; and may be the same *self*, by the same consciousness continued on for the future. And thus, by this consciousness he finds himself to be the *same self* which did such or such an action some years since, by which he comes to be happy or miserable now. In all which account of *self*, the same numerical substance is not considered as making the same *self*, but the same continued consciousness, in which several substances may have been united, and again separated from it, which, while they continued in a vital union with that in which this consciousness then resided, made a part of that same *self*. Thus any part of our bodies, vitally united to that which is conscious in us, makes a part of our*selves*. But upon separation from the vital union by which that consciousness is communicated, that which a moment since was part of our*selves*, is now no more so than a part of another man's *self* is a part of me, and it is not impossible but in a little time may become a real part of another person. And so we have the same numerical substance become a part of two different persons, and the same person preserved under the change of various substances. Could we suppose any spirit wholly stripped of all its memory or consciousness of past actions, as we find our minds always are of a great part of ours, and sometimes of them all, the union or separation of such a spiritual substance would make no variation of personal identity, any more than that of any particle of matter does. Any substance vitally united to the present thinking being is a part of that very *same self* which now is. Anything united to it by a consciousness of former actions makes also a part of the *same self*, which is the same both then and now.

26. *Person a forensic term*. Person, as I take it, is the name for this *self*. Wherever a man finds what he calls *himself*, there I think another may say is the

same *person*. It is a forensic term appropriating actions and their merit, and so belongs only to intelligent agents capable of a law, and happiness and misery. This personality extends *itself* beyond present existence to what is past, only by consciousness, by which it becomes concerned and accountable, owns and imputes to it*self* past actions, just upon the same ground and for the same reason that it does the present. All this is founded in a concern for happiness, the unavoidable concomitant of consciousness, that which is conscious of pleasure and pain, desiring that that *self* that is conscious should be happy. And therefore whatever past actions it cannot reconcile or appropriate to that present *self* by consciousness, it can be no more concerned in than if they had never been done. And to receive pleasure or pain, i.e., reward or punishment, on the account of any such action, is all one as to be made happy or miserable in its first being, without any demerit at all. For supposing a man punished now for what he had done in another life, of which he could be made to have no consciousness at all, what difference is there between that punishment and being created miserable? And therefore conformable to this the apostle tells us that at the great day, when everyone shall *"receive according to his doings, the secrets of all hearts shall be laid open."* The sentence shall be justified by the consciousness all persons shall have that they *themselves*, in whatever bodies they appear or whatever substances that consciousness adheres to, are the *same* who committed those actions, and deserve that punishment for them.

27. I am apt enough to think I have, in treating of this subject, made some suppositions that will look strange to some readers, and possibly they are so in themselves. But yet, I think, they are such as are pardonable in this ignorance we are in of the nature of that thinking thing that is in us, and which we look on as our*selves*. Did we know what it was, or how it was tied to a certain system of fleeting animal spirits; or whether it could or could not perform its operations of thinking and memory out of a body organized as ours is; and whether it has pleased God that no one such spirit shall ever be united to any but one such body, upon the right constitution of whose organs its memory should depend. We might see the absurdity

of some of those suppositions I have made. But taking, as we ordinarily now do (in the dark concerning these matters), the soul of a man for an immaterial substance, independent from matter, and indifferent alike to it all, there can from the nature of things be no absurdity at all to suppose that the same soul may, at different times, be united to different bodies, and with them make up, for that time, one man—as well as we suppose a part of a sheep's body yesterday should be a part of a man's body tomorrow, and in that union make a vital part of *Meliboeus* himself, as well as it did of his ram.

28. *The difficulty from ill use of names.* To conclude: Whatever substance begins to exist, it must, during its existence, necessarily be the same. Whatever compositions of substances begin to exist, during the union of those substances the concrete must be the same. Whatever mode begins to exist, during its existence it is the same. And so if the composition is of distinct substances and different modes, the same rule holds. By this it will appear that the difficulty or obscurity that has been about this matter rather rises from the names ill used than from any obscurity in things themselves. For whatever makes the specific *idea* to which the name is applied, if that *idea* is steadily kept to, the distinction of anything into the same and diverse will easily be conceived, and there can arise no doubt about it.

29. *Continued existence makes identity.* For supposing a rational spirit is the *idea* of a *man*, it is easy to know what is the *same man*; namely, the *same spirit*, whether separate or in a body, will be the *same man*. Supposing a rational spirit vitally united to a body of a certain conformation of parts to make a *man*, while that rational spirit, with that vital conformation of parts, though continued in a fleeting successive body, remains, it will be the same man. But if to anyone the *idea* of a *man* is but the vital union of parts in a certain shape, as long as that vital union and shape remain, in a concrete not otherwise the same, but by a continued succession of fleeting particles, it will be the same *man*. For whatever is the composition of which the complex *idea* is made, whenever existence makes it one particular thing under any denomination, the

same existence, continued, preserves it the same individual under the same denomination.

# Book III. Of Words. Chapter III.
## Of General Terms.

1. *The greatest part of words general.* All things that exist being particulars, it may perhaps be thought reasonable that words, which ought to be conformed to things, should be so too—I mean in their signification; but yet we find the quite contrary. The far *greatest part of words* that make all languages *are general terms*, which has not been the effect of neglect or chance, but of reason and necessity.

2. *For every particular thing to have a name is impossible.* First, it is impossible that every particular thing should have a distinct peculiar name. For the signification and use of words depending on that connection which the mind makes between its *ideas* and the sounds it uses as signs of them, it is necessary, in the application of names to things, that the mind should have distinct *ideas* of the things, and retain also the particular name that belongs to every one, with its peculiar appropriation to that *idea*. But it is beyond the power of human capacity to frame and retain distinct *ideas* of all the particular things we meet with: Every bird and beast men saw, every tree and plant that affected the senses, could not find a place in the most capacious understanding. If it is looked on as an instance of a prodigious memory that some generals have been able to call every soldier in their army by his proper name, we may easily find a reason why men have never attempted to give names to each sheep in their flock, or crow that flies over their heads, much less to call every leaf of plants or grain of sand that came in their way by a peculiar name.

3. *And useless. Secondly,* if it were possible, *it would yet be useless,* because it would not serve to the chief end of language. Men would in vain heap up names of particular things that would not serve them to communicate their thoughts. Men learn names, and use them in talk with others, only that they may be understood; this is then only done when, by use or consent, the sound I make by the organs of speech excites in another man's mind who hears it the *idea* I apply it to in mine when I speak it. This cannot be done by names applied to particular things, of which I alone having the *ideas* in my mind, the names of them could not be significant or intelligible to another, who was not acquainted with all those very particular things which had fallen under my notice.

4. Thirdly, but yet, granting this also feasible (which I think is not), yet *a distinct name for every particular thing would not be of any great use for the improvement of knowledge,* which, though founded in particular things, enlarges itself by general views, to which things reduced into sorts, under general names, are properly subservient. [ . . . ]

6. *How general words are made.* The next thing to be considered is *how general words come to be made.* For, since all things that exist are only particulars, how do we come by general terms, or where do we find those general natures they are supposed to stand for? Words become general by being made the signs of general *ideas;* and *ideas* become general by separating from them the circumstances of time and place, and any other *ideas* that may determine them to this or that particular existence. By this way of abstraction they are made capable of representing more individuals than one; each of these, having in it a conformity to that abstract *idea,* is (as we call it) of that sort.

7. But to deduce this a little more distinctly, it will not perhaps be amiss to trace our notions and names from their beginning, and observe by what degrees we proceed, and by what steps we enlarge our *ideas* from our first infancy. There is nothing more evident than that the *ideas* of the persons children converse with (to instance in them alone) are like the persons themselves, only particular. The *ideas* of the nurse and the mother are well framed in their minds, and, like pictures of them there, represent only those individuals. The names they first gave to them are confined to these individuals, and the names of *nurse* and *mamma* the child uses determine themselves to those persons. Afterwards, when time and a larger acquaintance have made them observe that there are a great many other things in the world that in some common agreements of shape, and several other qualities, resemble their father and mother and those persons they have been used to, they frame an *idea,*

which they find those many particulars do partake in; and to that they give, with others, the name *man* for example. And *thus they come to have a general name* and a general *idea*. They make nothing new in this, but only leave out of the complex *idea* they had of *Peter* and *James*, *Mary* and *Jane*, that which is peculiar to each, and retain only what is common to them all.

8. By the same way that they come by the general name and *idea* of *man*, they easily *advance to more general names and notions*. For, observing that several things that differ from their *idea* of *man*, and cannot therefore be comprehended under that name, have yet certain qualities in which they agree with *man*, by retaining only those qualities, and uniting them into one *idea*, they have again another and more general *idea*; to which having given a name they make a term of a more comprehensive extension; this new *idea* is made, not by any new addition, but only as before, by leaving out the shape, and some other properties signified by the name *man*, and retaining only a body, with life, sense, and spontaneous motion, comprehended under the name *animal*.

9. *General natures are nothing but abstract ideas*. That this is the way *by which men first formed general* ideas, *and general names to them*, I think, is so evident that there needs no other proof of it, but the considering of a man's self, or others, and the ordinary proceedings of their minds in knowledge. And he who thinks general natures or notions are anything else but such abstract and partial *ideas* of more complex ones, taken at first from particular existences, will, I fear, be at a loss where to find them. For let any one reflect, and then tell me in what does his *idea* of *man* differ from that of *Peter* and *Paul*, or his *idea* of *horse* from that of *Bucephalus*, but in the leaving out something that is peculiar to each individual, and retaining so much of those particular complex *ideas* of several particular existences as they are found to agree in? Of the complex *ideas* signified by the names *man* and *horse*, leaving out but those particulars in which they differ, and retaining only those in which they agree, and of those making a new distinct complex *idea*, and giving the name *animal* to it, one has a more general term that comprehends with man several other creatures. Leave out of the *idea* of *animal* sense, and

spontaneous motion, and the remaining complex *idea*, made up of the remaining simple ones of body, life, and nourishment, becomes a more general one, under the more comprehensive term *vivens*. And not to dwell longer upon this particular, so evident in itself, by the same way the mind proceeds to *body*, *substance*, and at last to *being*, *thing*, and such universal terms which stand for any of our *ideas* whatsoever. To conclude, this whole *mystery* of *genera* and *species*, which make such a noise in the schools and are with justice so little regarded out of them, is nothing else but abstract *ideas*, more or less comprehensive, with names annexed to them. In all this, it is constant and invariable that every more general term stands for such an *idea*, and is but a part of any of those contained under it.

10. *Why the* genus *is ordinarily of use in definitions*. This may show us the reason *why, in the defining of words*, which is nothing but declaring their significations, *we make use of the genus*, or next general word that comprehends it. This is not out of necessity, but only to save the labor of enumerating the several simple *ideas* which the next general word or genus stands for, or, perhaps, sometimes the shame of not being able to do it. But though defining by *genus* and *differentia* (I beg permission to use these terms of art, though originally Latin, since they most properly suit those notions they are applied to) I say, though defining by the *genus* is the shortest way, yet I think it may be doubted whether it is the best. This I am sure, it is not the only, and so not absolutely necessary. For, definition being nothing but making another understand by words what *idea* the term defined stands for, a definition is best made by enumerating those simple *ideas* that are combined in the signification of the term defined; and if, instead of such an enumeration, men have accustomed themselves to use the next general term, it has not been out of necessity, or for greater clearness, but for quickness and dispatch sake. For I think that, to one who desired to know what *idea* the word man stood for, if it should be said that man was a solid extended substance, having life, sense, spontaneous motion, and the faculty of reasoning, I do not doubt but the meaning of the term man would be as well understood, and the *idea*

it stands for be at least as clearly made known, as when it is defined to be a rational animal, which by the several definitions of *animal*, *vivens*, and *corpus*, resolves itself into those enumerated *ideas*. I have, in explaining the term *man*, followed here the ordinary definition of the schools, which, though perhaps not the most exact, yet serves well enough to my present purpose. And one may, in this instance, see what gave occasion to the rule that a definition must consist of *genus* and *differentia*; and it suffices to show us the little necessity there is of such a rule, or advantage in the strict observing of it. For definitions, as has been said, being only the explaining of one word by several others, so that the meaning or *idea* it stands for may be certainly known; languages are not always so made according to the rules of logic that every term can have its signification exactly and clearly expressed by two others. Experience sufficiently satisfies us to the contrary: Or else those who have made this rule have done ill, that they have given us so few definitions conformable to it. But of definitions more in the next chapter.

11. *General and universal are creatures of the understanding*. To return to general words, it is plain, by what has been said, that *general and universal* do not belong to the real existence of things, but are the *inventions and creatures of the understanding*, made by it for its own use, *and concern only signs*, whether words or *ideas*. Words are general, as has been said, when used for signs of general *ideas*, and so are applicable indifferently to many particular things, and *ideas* are general when they are set up as the representatives of many particular things; but universality does not belong to things themselves, which are all of them particular in their existence, even those words and *ideas* which in their signification are general. When therefore we quit particulars, the generals that rest are only creatures of our own making, their general nature being nothing but the capacity they are put into by the understanding of signifying or representing many particulars. For the signification they have is nothing but a relation that, by the mind of man, is added to them.

12. *Abstract* ideas *are the essences of the* genera *and* species. The next thing therefore to be considered is,

*what kind of signification it is that general words have*. For as it is evident that they do not signify barely one particular thing—for then they would not be general terms but proper names—so on the other side it is as evident they do not signify a plurality, for man and men would then signify the same and the distinction of numbers (as the grammarians call them) would be superfluous and useless. That then which general words signify is a sort of things, and each of them does that by being a sign of an abstract *idea* in the mind, to which *idea*, as things existing are found to agree, so they come to be ranked under that name, or, which is all one, be of that sort. In this way it is evident that the *essences of the sorts, or* (if the Latin word pleases better) *species* of things, are nothing else but these abstract *ideas*. For the having the essence of any species being that which makes anything to be of that species, and the conformity to the *idea* to which the name is annexed being that which gives a right to that name, the having the essence, and the having that conformity, must necessarily be the same thing, since to be of any species and to have a right to the name of that species is all one. As for example, to be a *man*, or of the species *man*, and to have right to the name *man*, is the same thing. Again, to be a *man*, or of the species *man*, and have the essence of a *man*, is the same thing. Now since nothing can be a *man*, or have a right to the name *man*, but what has a conformity to the abstract *idea* the name *man* stands for, nor anything be a man, or have a right to the species *man*, but what has the essence of that species, it follows that the abstract *idea* for which the name stands, and the essence of the species, is one and the same. From this it is easy to observe that the essences of the sorts of things, and consequently the sorting of things, is the workmanship of the understanding that abstracts and makes those general *ideas*.

13. *They are the workmanship of the understanding, but have their foundation in the similitude of things*. I would not here be thought to forget, much less to deny, that nature in the production of things makes several of them alike. There is nothing more obvious, especially in the races of animals, and all things propagated by seed. But yet I think we may say the *sorting* of them under names *is the workmanship of the*

*understanding, taking occasion from the similitude* it observes among them to make abstract general *ideas*, and set them up in the mind, with names annexed to them as patterns or forms (for in that sense the word form has a very proper signification) to which, as particular things existing are found to agree, so they come to be of that species, have that denomination, or are put into that *class*. For when we say, this is a man, that a horse; this justice, that cruelty; this a watch, that a jack; what else do we but rank things under different specific names, as agreeing to those abstract *ideas*, of which we have made those names the signs? And what are the essences of those species set out and marked by names, but those abstract *ideas* in the mind, which are, as it were, the bonds between particular things that exist and the names they are to be ranked under? And when general names have any connection with particular beings, these abstract *ideas* are the medium that unites them, so that the essences of species, as distinguished and denominated by us, neither are nor can be anything but these precise abstract *ideas* we have in our minds. And therefore the supposed real essences of substances, if different from our abstract *ideas*, cannot be the essences of the species we rank things into. For two species may be one, as rationally as two different essences be the essence of one species; and I demand what are the alterations which may or may not be made in a *horse* or *lead*, without making either of them to be of another species? In determining the species of things by our abstract *ideas*, this is easy to resolve; but if anyone will regulate himself here by supposed real essences, he will, I suppose, be at a loss; and he will never be able to know when anything precisely ceases to be of the species of a *horse* or *lead*. [ . . . ]

15. *Real and nominal essence*. But since the essences of things are thought by some (and not without reason) to be wholly unknown, it may not be amiss to consider the *several significations of the word essence*.

*First*, essence may be taken for the very being of anything, by which it is what it is. And thus the real internal, but generally, in substances, unknown constitution of things on which their discoverable qualities depend, may be called their *essence*. This is the proper original signification of the word, as is evident

from the formation of it, *essentia*, in its primary notation, signifying properly *being*. And in this sense it is still used, when we speak of the *essence* of particular things, without giving them any name.

*Secondly*, the learning and disputes of the schools having been much busied about *genus* and *species*, the word *essence* has almost lost its primary signification, and instead of the real constitution of things, has been almost wholly applied to the artificial constitution of *genus* and *species*. It is true there is ordinarily supposed a real constitution of the sorts of things, and it is past doubt there must be some real constitution on which any collection of simple *ideas* co-existing must depend. But it being evident that things are ranked under names into sorts or *species* only as they agree to certain abstract *ideas* to which we have annexed those names, the *essence* of each *genus*, or sort, comes to be nothing but that abstract *idea* which the general, or *sortal* (if I may have leave so to call it from *sort*, as I do *general* from *genus*) name stands for. And this we shall find to be that which the word *essence* imports in its most familiar use. These two sorts of *essences*, I suppose, may not unfitly be termed, the one the *real*, the other *nominal essence*.

16. *Constant connection between the name and nominal essence*. Between the nominal essence and the name there is so *near a connection* that the name of any sort of things cannot be attributed to any particular being but what has this *essence*, by which it answers that abstract *idea* of which that name is the sign.

17. *Supposition that species are distinguished by their real essences useless*. Concerning the real essences of corporeal substances (to mention these only) there are, if I am not mistaken, two opinions. The one is of those who, using the word *essence* for they know not what, suppose a certain number of those essences, according to which all natural things are made, and in which they do exactly every one of them partake, and so become of this or that *species*. The other and more rational opinion is of those who look on all natural things to have a real, but unknown constitution of their insensible parts, from which flow those sensible qualities which serve us to distinguish them one from another, according as we have occasion to rank them into sorts under common denominations.

The former of these opinions, which supposes these *essences* as a certain number of forms or molds, in which all natural things that exist are cast, and do equally partake, has, I imagine, very much perplexed the knowledge of natural things. The frequent productions of monsters, in all the species of animals, and of changelings, and other strange issues of human birth, carry with them difficulties, not possible to consist with this *hypothesis*, since it is as impossible that two things partaking exactly of the same real *essence* should have different properties, as that two figures partaking of the same real *essence* of a circle should have different properties. But were there no other reason against it, yet the *supposition of essences that cannot be known*, and the making of them nevertheless to be that which distinguishes the species of things, is so wholly useless and unserviceable to any part of our knowledge, that that alone were sufficient to make us lay it by, and content ourselves with such essences of the sorts or species of things as come within the reach of our knowledge. When seriously considered, this will be found, as I have said, to be nothing else but those abstract complex *ideas* to which we have annexed distinct general names.

18. *Real and nominal essence the same in simple ideas and modes, different in substances.* Essences being thus distinguished into *nominal and real*, we may further observe that, in the species of *simple* ideas *and modes,* they *are always the same*, but in *substances always quite different*. Thus a figure including a space between three lines is the real as well as nominal *essence* of a triangle, it being not only the abstract *idea* to which the general name is annexed, but the very *essentia* or being of the thing itself, that foundation from which all its properties flow, and to which they are all inseparably annexed. But it is far otherwise concerning that parcel of matter which makes the ring on my finger, in which these two essences are apparently different. For it is the real constitution of its insensible parts, on which depend all those properties of color, weight, fusibility, fixedness, etc. which are to be found in it, which constitution we know not, and so having no particular *idea* of, have no name that is the sign of it. But yet it is its color, weight, fusibility, fixedness, etc. which makes it to be *gold*, or gives it a right to that name, which is therefore its nominal *essence*. Since nothing can be called *gold* but what has a conformity of qualities to that abstract complex *idea* to which that name is annexed. But this distinction of *essences* belonging particularly to substances, we shall, when we come to consider their names, have an occasion to treat of more fully. [ . . . ]

## Chapter VI. *Of the Names of Substances.*

1. *The common names of substances stand for sorts. The common names of substances*, as well as other general terms, *stand for sorts*, which is nothing else but the being made signs of such complex *ideas*, in which several particular substances do or might agree, by virtue of which they are capable of being comprehended in one common conception, and signified by one name. I say do or might agree; for though there is but one sun existing in the world, yet the *idea* of it being abstracted so that more substances (if there were several) might each agree in it, it is as much a sort as if there were as many suns as there are stars. They do not lack their reasons who think there are, and that each fixed star would answer the *idea* the name *sun* stands for, to one who was placed in a due distance—which, by the way, may show us how much the sorts or, if you please, *genera* and *species* of things (for those Latin terms signify to me no more than the English word *sort*) depend on such collections of *ideas* as men have made, and not on the real nature of things, since it is not impossible but that, in propriety of speech, that might be a sun to one which is a star to another.

2. *The essence of each sort is the abstract idea.* The measure and boundary of each sort, or species, by which it is constituted that particular sort, and distinguished from others, are what we call its *essence*, which is nothing but that *abstract* idea *to which the name is annexed*, so that every thing contained in that *idea* is essential to that sort. This, though it is all the *essence* of natural substances that we know, or by which we distinguish them into sorts, yet I call it by a peculiar name, the *nominal essence*, to distinguish it from the real constitution of substances, upon which depends this *nominal essence* and all

the properties of that sort; this therefore, as has been said, may be called the *real essence*: e.g., the *nominal essence* of *gold* is that complex *idea* the word *gold* stands for—let it be, for instance, a body yellow, of a certain weight, malleable, fusible, and fixed. But the *real essence* is the constitution of the insensible parts of that body, on which those qualities and all the other properties of *gold* depend. How far these two are different, though they are both called *essence*, is obvious at first sight to discover.

3. *The nominal and real essence different*. For, though perhaps voluntary motion, with sense and reason, joined to a body of a certain shape, is the complex *idea* to which I, and others, annex the name *man*, and so is the *nominal essence* of the *species* so called, yet nobody will say that complex *idea* is the *real essence* and source of all those operations which are to be found in any individual of that sort. The foundation of all those qualities which are the ingredients of our complex *idea* is something quite different; and had we such a knowledge of that constitution of *man*, from which his faculties of moving, sensation, and reasoning, and other powers flow, and on which his so regular shape depends, as it is possible angels have, and it is certain his Maker has, we should have a quite other *idea* of his *essence* than what now is contained in our definition of that species, be it what it will; and our *idea* of any individual *man* would be as far different from what it is now, as is his who knows all the springs and wheels and other contrivances within of the famous clock at *Strasbourg*, from that which a gazing countryman has for it, who barely sees the motion of the hand, and hears the clock strike, and observes only some of the outward appearances.

4. *Nothing essential to individuals*. That *essence*, in the ordinary use of the word, relates to *sorts*—and that it is considered in particular beings no further than as they are ranked into *sorts*—appears from hence: that, take but away the abstract *ideas* by which we sort individuals, and rank them under common names, and then the thought of anything *essential* to any of them instantly vanishes; we have no notion of the one without the other; which plainly shows their relation. It is necessary for me to be as I am—God

and nature has made me so; but there is nothing I have that is essential to me. An accident or disease may very much alter my color, or shape; a fever or fall may take away my reason or memory, or both; and an apoplexy leave neither sense nor understanding, no, nor life. Other creatures of my shape may be made with more and better, or fewer and worse faculties than I have; and others may have reason and sense in a shape and body very different from mine. None of these are essential to the one or the other, or to any individual whatever, until the mind refers it to some sort or *species* of things; and then presently, according to the abstract *idea* of that sort, something is found *essential*. Let any one examine his own thoughts, and he will find that as soon as he supposes or speaks of *essential*, the consideration of some *species*, or the complex *idea*, signified by some general name, comes into his mind; and it is in reference to that, that this or that quality is said to be *essential*. So that if it is asked whether it is *essential* to me or any other particular corporeal being to have reason, I say no; no more than it is *essential* to this white thing I write on to have words in it. But if that particular being is to be counted of the sort *man*, and to have the name *man* given it, then reason is *essential* to it, supposing reason to be a part of the complex *idea* the name *man* stands for—as it is *essential* to this thing I write on to contain words, if I will give it the name *treatise*, and rank it under that *species*. So that *essential and not essential relate only to our abstract* ideas, *and the names annexed to them*, which amounts to no more than this, that whatever particular thing does not have in it those qualities which are contained in the abstract *idea* which any general term stands for, cannot be ranked under that *species*, nor be called by that name, since that abstract *idea* is the very *essence* of that *species*.

5. Thus, if the *idea* of *body* with some people is bare extension or space, then solidity is not *essential* to body. If others make the *idea* to which they give the name *body* to be solidity and extension, then solidity is essential to *body*. That, therefore, and *that alone* is considered as *essential, which makes a part of the complex* idea *the name of a sort stands for*, without which no particular thing can be reckoned of that

sort, nor be entitled to that name. Should there be found a parcel of matter that had all the other qualities that are in *iron*, but lacked obedience to the lodestone, and would neither be drawn by it nor receive direction from it, would any one question whether it wanted anything *essential*? It would be absurd to ask whether a thing really existing wanted anything *essential* to it. Or could it be demanded whether this made an *essential* or *specific* difference or not, since we have no other measure of *essential* or *specific* but our abstract *ideas*? And to talk of specific differences in nature, without reference to general *ideas* and names, is to talk unintelligibly. For I would ask anyone what is sufficient to make an essential difference in nature between any two particular beings, without any regard had to some abstract *idea*, which is looked upon as the essence and standard of a *species*? All such patterns and standards being quite laid aside, particular beings, considered barely in themselves, will be found to have all their qualities equally *essential*; and everything, in each individual, will be *essential* to it, or, which is more, nothing at all. For though it may be reasonable to ask whether obeying the magnet is *essential* to *iron*, yet, I think, it is very improper and insignificant to ask whether it is *essential* to the particular parcel of matter I cut my pen with, without considering it under the name *iron*, or as being of a certain *species*. And if, as has been said, our abstract *ideas*, which have names annexed to them, are the boundaries of *species*, nothing can be *essential* but what is contained in those *ideas*.

6. It is true, I have often mentioned a *real essence*, distinct in substances from those abstract *ideas* of them which I call their *nominal essence*. By this *real essence* I mean the real constitution of anything, which is the foundation of all those properties that are combined in, and are constantly found to coexist with, the *nominal essence*—that particular constitution which everything has within itself, without any relation to anything without it. But *essence*, even in this sense, *relates to a sort*, and supposes a *species*: for being that real constitution on which the properties depend, it necessarily supposes a sort of things, properties belonging only to *species*, and not to individuals; e.g., supposing the nominal essence of *gold* to be

a body of such a peculiar color and weight, with malleability and fusibility, the real essence is that constitution of the parts of matter on which these qualities and their union depend, and is also the foundation of its solubility in *aqua regia* and other properties accompanying that complex *idea*. Here are *essences* and *properties*, but all upon supposition of a sort, or general abstract *idea*, which is considered as immutable; but there is no individual parcel of matter to which any of these qualities are so annexed as to be *essential* to it, or inseparable from it. That which is *essential* belongs to it as a condition, by which it is of this or that sort; but take away the consideration of its being ranked under the name of some abstract *idea*, and then there is nothing necessary to it, nothing inseparable from it. Indeed, as to the *real essences* of substances, we only suppose their being, without precisely knowing what they are; but that which annexes them still to the *species* is the nominal essence, of which they are the supposed foundation and cause.

7. *The nominal essence bounds the species*. The next thing to be considered is, by which of those essences it is that *substances are determined into* sorts, or *species*; and that, it is evident, is *by the nominal essence*. For it is that alone that the name, which is the mark of the sort, signifies. It is impossible therefore that anything should determine the sorts of things, which we rank under general names, but that *idea* which that name is designed as a mark for, which is that, as has been shown, which we call *nominal essence*. Why do we say, this is a *horse*, that a *mule*; this is an *animal*, that an *herb*? How does any particular thing come to be of this or that sort, but because it has that nominal essence or, which is all one, agrees to that abstract *idea* that name is annexed to? And I desire anyone but to reflect on his own thoughts, when he hears or speaks any of those, or other names of substances, to know what sort of *essences* they stand for.

8. And that the *species of things to us are nothing but the ranking them under distinct names, according to the complex* ideas *in us*, and not according to precise, distinct, real essences in them, is plain from this, that we find many of the individuals that are ranked into one sort, called by one common name, and so

received as being of one *species*, have yet qualities depending on their real constitutions, as far different one from another as from others, from which they are accounted to differ *specifically*. [ . . . ]

9. *Not the real essence, which we do not know*. Nor indeed *can we* rank and *sort things*, and consequently (which is the end of sorting) denominate them *by their real essences*, because we do not know them. Our faculties carry us no further towards the knowledge and distinction of substances than a collection of those sensible *ideas* which we observe in them—which, however made with the greatest diligence and exactness we are capable of, yet is more remote from the true internal constitution from which those qualities flow than, as I said, a countryman's *idea* is from the inward contrivance of that famous clock at *Strasbourg*, of which he only sees the outward figure and motions. There is not so contemptible a plant or animal that does not confound the most enlarged understanding. Though the familiar use of things about us take off our wonder, yet it does not cure our ignorance. When we come to examine the stones we tread on, or the iron we daily handle, we presently find we do not know their make, and can give no reason of the different qualities we find in them. It is evident the internal constitution, on which their properties depend, is unknown to us. For to go no further than the grossest and most obvious we can imagine among them, what is that texture of parts, that real essence, that makes lead and antimony fusible, wood and stones not? What makes lead and iron malleable, antimony and stones not? And yet how infinitely these come short of the fine contrivances and inconceivable real essences of plants or animals, everyone knows. The workmanship of the all-wise and powerful God, in the great fabric of the universe, and every part of it, further exceeds the capacity and comprehension of the most inquisitive and intelligent man than the best contrivance of the most ingenious man does the conceptions of the most ignorant of rational creatures. Therefore, we in vain pretend to range things into sorts and dispose them into certain classes, under names, *by their real essences*, that are so far from our discovery or comprehension. [ . . . ]

12. *There are probably numberless species of spirits*. It is not impossible to conceive, nor repugnant to reason, that there may be many *species of spirits*, as much separated and diversified one from another by distinct properties of which we have no *ideas*, as the *species* of sensible things are distinguished one from another by qualities which we know and observe in them. That there should be more *species* of intelligent creatures above us than there are of sensible and material below us is probable to me from this: that in all the visible corporeal world we see no chasms or gaps. All quite down from us the descent is by easy steps, and a continued series of things, that in each remove differ very little one from the other. There are fishes that have wings and are not strangers to the airy region; and there are some birds that are inhabitants of the water whose blood is cold as fishes, and their flesh so like in taste that the scrupulous are allowed them on fish-days. There are animals so near of kin both to birds and beasts that they are in the middle between both. Amphibious animals link the terrestrial and aquatic together, seals live at land and sea, and porpoises have the warm blood and entrails of a hog, not to mention what is confidently reported of mermaids or seamen. There are some brutes that seem to have as much knowledge and reason, as some that are called men; and the animal and vegetable kingdoms are so nearly joined that, if you will take the lowest of one and the highest of the other, there will scarcely be perceived any great difference between them, and so on, until we come to the lowest and the most inorganic parts of matter, we shall find everywhere that the several *species* are linked together, and differ but in almost insensible degrees. [ . . . ]

14. *Difficulties against a certain number of real essences*. To distinguish substantial beings into *species*, according to the usual supposition that there are certain precise *essences* or *forms* of things, by which all the individuals existing are by nature distinguished into *species*, these things are necessary:

15. *First*, to be assured that nature, in the production of things, always designs them to partake of certain regulated established *essences*, which are to be the models of all things to be produced. This, in that

crude sense it is usually proposed, would need some better explication before it can fully be assented to.

16. *Secondly*, it would be necessary to know whether nature always attains that essence it designs in the production of things. The irregular and monstrous births, that in various sorts of animals have been observed, will always give us reason to doubt of one or both of these.

17. *Thirdly*, it ought to be determined whether those we call *monsters* are really a distinct *species*, according to the scholastic notion of the word *species*; since it is certain that everything that exists has its particular constitution. And yet we find that some of these monstrous productions have few or none of those qualities which are supposed to result from, and accompany the *essence* of that *species*, from which they derive their origins, and to which, by their descent, they seem to belong.

18. *Fourthly*, the *real essences* of those things which we distinguish into *species*, and as so distinguished we name, ought to be known; i.e., we ought to have *ideas* of them. But since we are ignorant in these four points, *the supposed real essences of things do not stand us in stead for the distinguishing substances into species.*

19. *Our nominal essences of substances, not perfect collections of properties.* Fifthly, the only imaginable help in this case would be that, having framed perfect complex *ideas* of the *properties* of things flowing from their different real essences, we should distinguish them into *species* by them. But neither can this be done; for, being ignorant of the real essence itself, it is impossible to know all those properties that flow from it, and are so annexed to it that, any one of them being away, we may certainly conclude that that essence is not there, and so the thing is not of that *species*. [ . . . ]

26. *Therefore very various and uncertain.* Since then it is evident that we sort and name substances by their *nominal* and not by their real *essences*, the next thing to be considered is how, and by whom, these essences come to be made. As to the latter, it is evident they *are made by the mind*, and not by nature; for were they nature's workmanship, they could not be so various and different in several men as

experience tells us they are. For if we will examine it, we shall not find the nominal essence of any one *species* of substances in all men the same—no, not of that which of all others we are the most intimately acquainted with. [ . . . ]

28. *But not so arbitrary as mixed modes.* But though these *nominal essences of substances* are made by the mind, they are *not yet made so arbitrarily as those of mixed modes*. To the making of any nominal essence, it is necessary, *first*, that the *ideas* of which it consists have such a union as to make but one *idea*, however compounded. *Secondly*, that the particular *idea* so united be exactly the same, neither more nor less. For if two abstract complex *ideas* differ either in number or sorts of their component parts, they make two different, and not one and the same essence. In the first of these, the mind, in making its complex *ideas* of substances, only follows nature, and puts none together which are not supposed to have a union in nature. Nobody joins the voice of a sheep with the shape of a horse, nor the color of lead with the weight and fixedness of gold, to be the complex *ideas* of any real substances, unless he has a mind to fill his head with chimeras and his discourse with unintelligible words. Men, observing certain qualities always joined and existing together, copied nature in this, and of *ideas* so united made their complex ones of substances. For though men may make what complex *ideas* they please, and give what names to them they will, yet if they will be understood when they speak of things really existing, they must in some degree conform their *ideas* to the things they would speak of; or else men's language will be like that of *Babel*; and every man's words, being intelligible only to himself, would no longer serve to conversation and the ordinary affairs of life, if the *ideas* they stand for are not some way answering the common appearances and agreement of substances as they really exist.

29. *Though very imperfect.* Secondly, though the mind of man, *in making* its *complex* ideas *of substances*, never puts any together that do not really or are not supposed to coexist, and so it truly borrows that union from nature, yet the number it combines *depends upon the various care, industry, or fancy of him that makes it.* Men generally content themselves

with some few sensible obvious qualities, and often, if not always, leave out others as material and as firmly united as those that they take. [ . . . ]

32. *The more general our ideas are, the more incomplete and partial they are.* If the *number of simple* ideas *that make the nominal essence* of the lowest *species*, or first sorting, of individuals *depends on the mind* of man variously collecting them, it is much more evident that they do so in the more comprehensive *classes*, which, by the masters of logic are called *genera*. These are complex *ideas* designedly imperfect; and it is visible at first sight that several of those qualities that are to be found in the things themselves are purposely left out of *generical ideas*. For, as the mind, to make general *ideas* comprehending several particulars, leaves out those of time, and place, and such other that make them incommunicable to more than one individual, so to make other yet more general *ideas*, that may comprehend different sorts, it leaves out those qualities that distinguish them, and puts into its new collection only such *ideas* as are common to several sorts. [ . . . ]

36. *Though nature makes the similitude.* This then, in short, is the case: *Nature makes many particular things which do agree* one with another in many sensible qualities, and probably too in their internal frame and constitution; but it is not this real essence that distinguishes them into *species*; it is *men* who, taking occasion from the qualities they find united in them, and in which they observe often several individuals to agree, *range them into sorts, in order to their naming,* for the convenience of comprehensive signs; under these individuals, according to their conformity to this or that abstract *idea*, come to be ranked as under ensigns: so that this is of the blue, that the red regiment; this is a man, that a drill; and in this, I think, consists the whole business of *genus* and *species*. [ . . . ]

## Book IV. Of Knowledge and Opinion. Chapter I. *Of Knowledge in General.*

1. *Our knowledge conversant about our* ideas. Since the *mind* in all its thoughts and reasonings has no other immediate object but its own *ideas*, which it alone does or can contemplate, it is evident that our knowledge is only conversant about them.

2. *Knowledge is the perception of the agreement, or disagreement, of two ideas. Knowledge* then seems to me to be nothing but *the perception of the connection and agreement, or disagreement and repugnance, of any of our ideas.* In this alone it consists. Where this perception is, there is knowledge, and where it is not, there, though we may fancy, guess, or believe, yet we always come short of knowledge. For when we know that *white is not black*, what do we else but perceive that these two *ideas* do not agree? When we possess ourselves with the utmost security of the demonstration that the *three angles of a triangle are equal to two right ones*, what do we more but perceive that equality to two right ones does necessarily agree to, and is inseparable from, the three angles of a triangle?

3. *This agreement fourfold.* But to understand a little more distinctly in what this agreement or disagreement consists, I think we may reduce it all to these four sorts.

1. *Identity* or *diversity.*

2. *Relation.*

3. *Coexistence* or *necessary connection.*

4. *Real existence.*

4. *First, of identity or diversity.* First, as to the first sort of agreement or disagreement, namely, *identity* or *diversity*. It is the first act of the mind, when it has any sentiments or *ideas* at all, to perceive its *ideas*; and so far as it perceives them, to know each what it is, and in this way also to perceive their difference, and that one is not another. This is so absolutely necessary that without it there could be no knowledge, no reasoning, no imagination, no distinct thoughts, at all. By this the mind clearly and infallibly perceives each *idea* to agree with itself, and to be what it is, and all distinct *ideas* to disagree, i.e., the one not to be the other. And this it does without pains, labor, or deduction, but at first view, by its natural power of perception and distinction. And though men of art have reduced this into those general rules, "*what is, is,*" *and* "*it is impossible for the same thing to be and*

*not to be*," for ready application in all cases in which there may be occasion to reflect on it, yet it is certain that the first exercise of this faculty is about particular *ideas*. A man infallibly knows, as soon as ever he has them in his mind that the *ideas* he calls *white* and *round*, are the very *ideas* they are, and that they are not other *ideas* which he calls *red* or *square*. Nor can any maxim or proposition in the world make him know it clearer or surer than he did before, and without any such general rule. This then is the first agreement or disagreement which the mind perceives in its *ideas*, which it always perceives at first sight. And if there ever happens to be any doubt about it, it will always be found to be about the names, and not the *ideas* themselves, whose identity and diversity will always be perceived, as soon and clearly as the *ideas* themselves are; nor can it possibly be otherwise.

5. *Secondly, relation. Secondly,* the next sort of agreement or disagreement the mind perceives in any of its *ideas* may, I think, be called *relative*, and is nothing but *the perception of the relation between any two ideas*, of whatever kind, whether substances, modes, or any other. For since all distinct *ideas* must eternally be known not to be the same, and so be universally and constantly denied one of another, there could be no room for any positive knowledge at all, if we could not perceive any relation between our *ideas*, and find out the agreement or disagreement they have one with another, in several ways the mind takes of comparing them.

6. *Thirdly, of coexistence.* Thirdly, the third sort of agreement or disagreement to be found in our *ideas*, which the perception of the mind is employed about, is *coexistence*, or *non-coexistence* in the same subject, and this belongs particularly to substances. Thus when we pronounce concerning *gold* that it is fixed, our knowledge of this truth amounts to no more but this that fixedness, or a power to remain in the fire unconsumed, is an *idea* that always accompanies, and is joined with that particular sort of yellowness, weight, fusibility, malleableness, and solubility in *aqua regia*, which make our complex *idea*, signified by the word *gold*.

7. *Fourthly, of real existence.* Fourthly, the fourth and last sort is that of *actual real existence* agreeing to any *idea*. Within these four sorts of agreement or disagreement is, I suppose, contained all the knowledge we have, or are capable of. For all the inquiries we can make concerning any of our *ideas*, all that we know or can affirm concerning any of them, is that it is, or is not, the same with some other; that it does or does not always coexist with some other *idea* in the same subject; that it has this or that relation with some other *idea*; or that it has a real existence without the mind. Thus "*blue is not yellow*" is of identity. "*Two triangles upon equal bases between two parallels are equal*" is of relation. "*Iron is susceptible of magnetic impressions*" is of coexistence. "*God is*" is of real existence. Though identity and coexistence are truly nothing but relations, yet they are such peculiar ways of agreement or disagreement of our *ideas* that they deserve well to be considered as distinct heads, and not under relation in general, since they are so different grounds of affirmation and negation, as will easily appear to anyone who will but reflect on what is said in several places of this essay. I should now proceed to examine the several degrees of our knowledge, but that it is necessary first to consider the different acceptations of the word *knowledge*.

8. *Knowledge actual or habitual.* There are several ways in which the mind is possessed of truth, each of which is called *knowledge*.

1. There is *actual knowledge*, which is the present view the mind has of the agreement or disagreement of any of its *ideas*, or of the relation they have one to another.

2. A man is said to know any proposition, which having been once laid before his thoughts, he evidently perceived the agreement or disagreement of the *ideas* of which it consists, and so lodged it in his memory that whenever that proposition comes again to be reflected on, he, without doubt or hesitation, embraces the right side, assents to, and is certain of the truth of it. This, I think, one may call *habitual knowledge*. And thus a man may be said to know all those truths which are lodged in his memory, by a foregoing clear and full perception,

of which the mind is assured past doubt as often as it has occasion to reflect on them. For our finite understandings being able to think clearly and distinctly but on one thing at once, if men had no knowledge of any more than what they actually thought on, they would all be very ignorant; and he who knew most would know but one truth, that being all he was able to think on at one time.

9. *Habitual knowledge twofold*. Of habitual knowledge there are also, vulgarly speaking, two degrees.

*First*, the one is of *such truths laid up in the memory as, whenever they occur to the mind, it actually perceives the relation between those ideas*. And this is in all those truths of which we have an *intuitive knowledge*, where the *ideas* themselves, by an immediate view, discover their agreement or disagreement one with another.

*Secondly*, the other is of *such truths of which the mind having been convinced, it retains the memory of the conviction, without the proofs*. Thus a man who remembers certainly that he once perceived the demonstration that the three angles of a triangle are equal to two right ones is certain that he knows it, because he cannot doubt the truth of it. In his adherence to a truth where the demonstration by which it was at first known is forgot—though a man may be thought rather to believe his memory than really to know, and this way of entertaining a truth seemed formerly to me like something between opinion and knowledge, a sort of assurance which exceeds bare belief, for that relies on the testimony of another—yet upon a due examination I find it does not come short of perfect certainty and is in effect true knowledge; that which is apt to mislead our first thoughts into a mistake in this matter is that the agreement or disagreement of the *ideas* in this case is not perceived, as it was at first, by an actual view of all the intermediate *ideas*, by which the agreement or disagreement of those in the proposition was at first perceived, but by other intermediate *ideas* that show the agreement or disagreement of the *ideas* contained in the proposition whose certainty we remember. For example, in this proposition that "the three angles of a triangle are equal to two right

ones," one who has seen and clearly perceived the demonstration of this truth knows it to be true, when that demonstration is gone out of his mind, so that at present it is not actually in view and possibly cannot be recollected. But he knows it in a different way from what he did before. The agreement of the two *ideas* joined in that proposition is perceived, but it is by the intervention of other *ideas* than those which at first produced that perception. He remembers, i.e., he knows (for remembrance is but the reviving of some past knowledge), that he was once certain of the truth of this proposition that the three angles of a triangle are equal to two right ones. The immutability of the same relations between the same immutable things is now the *idea* that shows him that if the three angles of a triangle were once equal to two right ones, they will always be equal to two right ones. And hence he comes to be certain that what was once true in the case is always true; what *ideas* once agreed will always agree; and consequently what he once knew to be true, he will always know to be true, as long as he can remember that he once knew it. Upon this ground it is that particular demonstrations in mathematics afford general knowledge. If then the perception that the same *ideas* will eternally have the same habitudes and relations is not a sufficient ground of knowledge, there could be no knowledge of general propositions in mathematics, for no mathematical demonstration would be any other than particular. And when a man had demonstrated any proposition concerning one triangle or circle, his knowledge would not reach beyond that particular diagram. If he would extend it further, he must renew his demonstration in another instance, before he could know it to be true in another like triangle, and so on. By these means one could never come to the knowledge of any general propositions. Nobody, I think, can deny that Mr. *Newton* certainly knows any proposition that he now at any time reads in his book to be true, though he does not have in actual view that admirable chain of intermediate *ideas* by which he at first discovered it to be true. Such a memory as that, able to retain such a train of particulars, may be well thought beyond the reach of human faculties, when the very discovery, perception, and laying together that wonderful connection of *ideas* is found to surpass most readers' *comprehension*. But yet it is evident the author himself knows the proposition to be true, remembering he once saw the connection of those *ideas*, as certainly as he knows such a man wounded another, remembering that he saw him run him through. But because the memory is not always so clear as actual perception and does in all men more or less decay in length of time, this among other differences is one which shows that *demonstrative knowledge* is much more imperfect than *intuitive*, as we shall see in the following chapter.

## Chapter II. *Of the Degrees of Our Knowledge.*

1. *Intuitive*. All our knowledge consisting, as I have said, in the view the mind has of its own *ideas*, which is the utmost light and greatest certainty we, with our faculties, and in our way of knowledge, are capable of, it may not be amiss to consider a little the degrees of its evidence. The different clearness of our knowledge seems to me to lie in the different way of perception the mind has of the agreement or disagreement of any of its *ideas*. For if we will reflect on our own ways of thinking, we shall find that sometimes the mind perceives the agreement or disagreement of two *ideas* immediately by themselves, without the intervention of any other. And this, I think, we may call *intuitive knowledge*. For in this the mind is at no pains of proving or examining, but perceives the truth, as the eye does light, only by being directed towards it. Thus the mind perceives that *white* is not *black*, that a *circle* is not a *triangle*, that *three* are more than *two*, and equal to *one* and *two*. Such kinds of truths the mind perceives at the first sight of the *ideas* together, by bare *intuition*, without the intervention of any other *idea*; and this kind of knowledge is the clearest and most certain that human frailty is capable of. This part of knowledge is irresistible, and like bright sunshine forces itself immediately to be perceived, as soon as ever the mind turns its view that way, and leaves no room for hesitation, doubt, or examination, but the mind is presently filled with the clear light of it. It is on this *intuition* that depends all the certainty and evidence of all our knowledge; this

certainty everyone finds to be so great that he cannot imagine and therefore not require a greater. For a man cannot conceive himself capable of a greater certainty than to know that any *idea* in his mind is such as he perceives it to be, and that two *ideas* in which he perceives a difference are different and not precisely the same. He who demands a greater certainty than this, demands he knows not what, and shows only that he has a mind to be a skeptic, without being able to be so. Certainty depends so wholly on this intuition that in the next degree of *knowledge*, which I call *demonstrative*, this intuition is necessary in all the connections of the intermediate *ideas*, without which we cannot attain knowledge and certainty.

2. *Demonstrative*. The next degree of knowledge is where the mind perceives the agreement or disagreement of any *ideas*, but not immediately. Though wherever the mind perceives the agreement or disagreement of any of its *ideas*, there is certain knowledge; yet it does not always happen that the mind sees that agreement or disagreement which there is between them, even where it is discoverable, and in that case remains in ignorance, and at most gets no further than a probable conjecture. The reason why the mind cannot always perceive presently the agreement or disagreement of two *ideas* is because those *ideas*, concerning whose agreement or disagreement the inquiry is made, cannot by the mind be so put together as to show it. In this case then, when the mind cannot so bring its *ideas* together, as by their immediate comparison and as it were juxtaposition or application one to another, to perceive their agreement or disagreement, it is inclined, by the intervention of other *ideas* (one or more, as it happens) to discover the agreement or disagreement which it searches; and this is that which we call *reasoning*. Thus the mind, being willing to know the agreement or disagreement in bigness between the three angles of a triangle and two right ones, cannot by an immediate view and comparing them do it, because the three angles of a triangle cannot be brought at once and be compared with any other one or two angles; and so of this the mind has no immediate, no intuitive knowledge. In this case the mind is inclined to find out some other angles to which the three angles of a

triangle have an equality, and, finding those equal to two right ones, comes to know their equality to two right ones.

3. *Depends on proofs*. Those intervening *ideas*, which serve to show the agreement of any two others, are called *proofs*; and where the agreement or disagreement is by this means plainly and clearly perceived, it is called *demonstration*, it being *shown* to the understanding, and the mind made to see that it is so. A quickness in the mind to find out these intermediate *ideas* (that shall discover the agreement or disagreement of any other) and to apply them right is, I suppose, that which is called *sagacity*.

4. *But not so easy*. This knowledge by intervening proofs, though it is certain, yet the evidence of it is *not* altogether *so clear* and bright, nor the assent so ready, *as in intuitive* knowledge. For though in *demonstration* the mind does at last perceive the agreement or disagreement of the *ideas* it considers, yet it is not without pains and attention. There must be more than one transient view to find it. A steady application and pursuit are required to this discovery. And there must be a progression by steps and degrees before the mind can in this way arrive at certainty and come to perceive the agreement or repugnance between two *ideas* that need proofs and the use of reason to show it.

5. *Not without precedent doubt*. Another difference between intuitive and demonstrative knowledge is that though in the latter all doubt is removed when, by the intervention of the intermediate *ideas*, the agreement or disagreement is perceived, yet before the demonstration there was a doubt, which in intuitive knowledge cannot happen to the mind that has its faculty of perception left to a degree capable of distinct *ideas*, no more than it can be a doubt to the eye (that can distinctly see white and black) whether this ink and this paper are all of a color. If there is sight in the eyes, it will at first glimpse, without hesitation, perceive the words printed on this paper different from the color of the paper. And so if the mind has the faculty of distinct perception, it will perceive the agreement or disagreement of those *ideas* that produce intuitive knowledge. If the eye has lost the faculty of seeing, or the mind of perceiving, we in vain inquire after the quickness of sight in one, or clearness of perception in the other.

6. *Not so clear*. It is true the perception produced by *demonstration* is also very clear, yet it is often with a great abatement of that evident luster and full assurance that always accompany that which I call *intuitive*; like a face reflected by several mirrors one to another, where as long as it retains the similitude and agreement with the object, it produces a knowledge; but it is still, in every successive reflection, with a lessening of that perfect clearness and distinctness which is in the first; until at last, after many removes, it has a great mixture of dimness, and is not at first sight so knowable, especially to weak eyes. Thus it is with knowledge made out by a long train of proof.

7. *Each step must have intuitive evidence*. Now, *in every step reason makes in demonstrative knowledge, there is an intuitive knowledge* of that agreement or disagreement it seeks with the next intermediate *idea* which it uses as a proof; for if it were not so, that yet would need a proof, since without the perception of such agreement or disagreement, there is no knowledge produced. If it is perceived by itself, it is intuitive knowledge. If it cannot be perceived by itself, there is need of some intervening *idea*, as a common measure, to show their agreement or disagreement. By this it is plain that every step in reasoning that produces knowledge has intuitive certainty, which, when the mind perceives, there is no more required but to remember it, to make the agreement or disagreement of the *ideas* concerning which we inquire visible and certain. So that to make anything a *demonstration*, it is necessary to perceive the immediate agreement of the intervening *ideas*, by which the agreement or disagreement of the two *ideas* under examination (of which the one is always the first, and the other the last in the account) is found. This intuitive perception of the agreement or disagreement of the intermediate *ideas*, in each step and progression of the *demonstration*, must also be carried exactly in the mind, and a man must be sure that no part is left out—which because in long deductions and the use of many proofs the memory does not always so readily and exactly retain; therefore it comes to pass that this is more

imperfect than intuitive knowledge, and men embrace often falsehood for demonstrations. [ . . . ]

9. *Demonstration not limited to quantity*. It has been generally taken for granted that mathematics alone is capable of demonstrative certainty; but to have such an agreement or disagreement as may intuitively be perceived, being, as I imagine, not the privilege of the *ideas* of *number*, *extension*, and *figure* alone, it may possibly be the want of due method and application in us, and not of sufficient evidence in things, that demonstration has been thought to have so little to do in other parts of knowledge, and been scarcely so much as aimed at by any but mathematicians. For whatever *ideas* we have in which the mind can perceive the immediate agreement or disagreement that is between them, there the mind is capable of intuitive knowledge; and where it can perceive the agreement or disagreement of any two *ideas* by an intuitive perception of the agreement or disagreement they have with any intermediate *ideas*, there the mind is capable of demonstration, which is not limited to *ideas* of extension, figure, number, and their modes.

10. *Why it has been so thought*. The reason why it has been generally sought for, and supposed to be only in those, I imagine, has been not only the general usefulness of those sciences, but because, in comparing their equality or excess, the modes of numbers have every the least difference very clear and perceivable; and though in extension every the least excess is not so perceptible, yet the mind has found out ways to examine and discover demonstratively the just equality of two angles, or extensions, or figures. And both these, i.e., numbers and figures, can be set down by visible and lasting marks, in which the *ideas* under consideration are perfectly determined, which for the most part they are not, where they are marked only by names and words.

11. But in other simple *ideas*, whose modes and differences are made and counted by degrees, and not quantity, we have not so nice and accurate a distinction of their differences as to perceive, or find ways to measure, their just equality, or the least differences. For those other simple *ideas*, being appearances of sensations produced in us by the size, figure, number, and motion of minute corpuscles singly insensible, their different degrees also depend upon the variation of some or of all those causes, which, since it cannot be observed by us in particles of matter of which each is too subtle to be perceived, it is impossible for us to have any exact measures of the different degrees of these simple *ideas*. [ . . . ]

13. Not knowing therefore what number of particles, nor what motion of them is fit to produce any precise degree of *whiteness*, we cannot demonstrate the certain equality of any two degrees of *whiteness*; because we have no certain standard to measure them by, nor means to distinguish every the least real difference, the only help we have being from our senses, which in this point fail us. But where the difference is so great as to produce in the mind clearly distinct *ideas* whose differences can be perfectly retained, there these *ideas* or colors, as we see in different kinds, as blue and red, are as capable of demonstration as *ideas* of number and extension. What I have here said of *whiteness* and colors, I think, holds true in all secondary qualities and their modes.

14. *Sensitive knowledge of particular existence*. These two, namely, intuition and demonstration, are the degrees of our knowledge; whatever comes short of one of these, with whatever assurance embraced, is but faith or opinion, but not knowledge, at least in all general truths. There is, indeed, another *perception* of the mind, employed about *the particular existence of finite beings* without us, which going beyond bare probability, and yet not reaching perfectly to either of the foregoing degrees of certainty, passes under the name of knowledge. There can be nothing more certain than that the *idea* we receive from an external object is in our minds; this is intuitive knowledge. But whether there is anything more than barely that *idea* in our minds, whether we can certainly infer from this the existence of anything without us, which corresponds to that *idea*, is that of which some men think there may be a question made; because men may have such *ideas* in their minds when no such thing exists, no such object affects their senses. But yet here, I think, we are provided with an evidence that puts us past doubting. For I ask anyone whether he is not invincibly conscious to himself of a different

perception when he looks on the sun by day, and thinks on it by night—when he actually tastes wormwood, or smells a rose, or only thinks on that savor or odor? We as plainly find the difference there is between any *idea* revived in our minds by our own memory and actually coming into our minds by our senses, as we do between any two distinct *ideas*. If anyone says a dream may do the same thing, and all these *ideas* may be produced in us without any external objects, he may please to dream that I make him this answer: 1. That it is no great matter, whether I remove his scruple or not; where all is but dream, reasoning and arguments are of no use, truth and knowledge nothing. 2. That I believe he will allow a very manifest difference between dreaming of being in the fire and being actually in it. But yet if he is resolved to appear so skeptical, as to maintain that what I call being actually in the fire is nothing but a dream, and that we cannot thereby certainly know that any such thing as fire actually exists without us, I answer that we certainly find that pleasure or pain follows upon the application of certain objects to us, whose existence we perceive, or dream that we perceive by our senses; this certainty is as great as our happiness or misery, beyond which we have no concern to know or to be. Thus, I think, we may add to the two former sorts of *knowledge* this also, of the existence of particular external objects, by that perception and consciousness we have of the actual entrance of *ideas* from them, and allow these *three degrees of knowledge*, namely, *intuitive, demonstrative, and sensitive*, in each of which there are different degrees and ways of evidence and certainty.

15. *Knowledge not always clear, where the* ideas *are so*. But since our knowledge is founded on and employed about our *ideas* only, will it not follow from this that it is conformable to our *ideas*; and that where our *ideas* are clear and distinct, or obscure and confused, our knowledge will be so too? To which I answer, no. For our knowledge consisting in the perception of the agreement or disagreement of any two *ideas*, its clearness or obscurity consists in the clearness or obscurity of that perception, and not in the clearness or obscurity of the *ideas* themselves—e.g., a man who has as clear *ideas* of the angles of a triangle,

and of equality to two right ones, as any mathematician in the world, may yet have but a very obscure perception of their agreement, and so have but a very obscure knowledge of it. But *ideas*, which by reason of their obscurity or otherwise, are confused, cannot produce any clear or distinct knowledge, because, as far as any *ideas* are confused, so far the mind cannot perceive clearly, whether they agree or disagree. Or to express the same thing in a way less apt to be misunderstood: he who has not determined *ideas* to the words he uses cannot make propositions of them of whose truth he can be certain.

## Chapter III. *Of the Extent of Human Knowledge*.

1. *First, no further than we have* ideas. Knowledge, as has been said, lying in the perception of the agreement or disagreement of any of our *ideas*, it follows from hence that,

*First*, we can have *knowledge* no further than we have *ideas*.

2. *Secondly, no further than we can perceive their agreement or disagreement*. *Secondly* that we can have no *knowledge* further than we can have perceptions of that agreement or disagreement, which perception being: 1. either by *intuition*, or the immediate comparing any two *ideas*; or, 2. by *reason*, examining the agreement or disagreement of two *ideas*, by the intervention of some others; or, 3. by *sensation*, perceiving the existence of particular things. Hence it also follows:

3. *Thirdly, intuitive knowledge does not extend itself to all the relations of all our* ideas. *Thirdly* that we cannot have an *intuitive knowledge* that shall extend itself to all our *ideas*, and all that we would know about them, because we cannot examine and perceive all the relations they have one to another by *juxta*position, or an immediate comparison one with another. Thus having the *ideas* of an obtuse and an acute angled triangle, both drawn from equal bases, and between parallels, I can, by intuitive knowledge, perceive the one not to be the other, but cannot that way know whether they are equal or not, because their agreement or disagreement in equality can never be perceived by an immediate comparing of them. The

difference of figure makes their parts incapable of an exact immediate application; and therefore there is need of some intervening qualities to measure them by, which is demonstration or rational knowledge.

4. *Fourthly, nor demonstrative knowledge.* Fourthly, it follows also, from what is above observed that our *rational knowledge* cannot reach to the whole extent of our *ideas*, because between two different *ideas* we would examine, we cannot always find such *mediums* as we can connect one to another with an intuitive knowledge in all the parts of the deduction; and wherever that fails, we come short of knowledge and demonstration.

5. *Fifthly, sensitive knowledge, narrower than either.* Fifthly, *sensitive knowledge* reaching no further than the existence of things actually present to our senses is yet much narrower than either of the former.

6. *Sixthly, our knowledge, therefore, narrower than our* ideas. From all which it is evident that *the extent of our knowledge* comes not only short of the reality of things, but even of the extent of our own *ideas*. Though our knowledge is limited to our *ideas* and cannot exceed them either in extent or perfection, and though these are very narrow bounds, in respect of the extent of all being, and far short of what we may justly imagine to be in some even created understandings, not tied down to the dull and narrow information, is to be received from some few and not very acute ways of perception, such as are our senses, yet it would be well with us if our knowledge were but as large as our *ideas*, and there were not many doubts and inquiries concerning the *ideas* we have, of which we are not, nor I believe ever shall be in this world resolved. Nevertheless I do not question but that human knowledge, under the present circumstances of our beings and constitutions, may be carried much further than it has been up to now, if men would sincerely and with freedom of mind employ all that industry and labor of thought in improving the means of discovering truth, which they do for the coloring or support of falsehood to maintain a system, interest, or party, they are once engaged in. But yet after all, I think I may, without injury to human perfection, be confident that our knowledge would never reach to all we might desire to know concerning those *ideas*

we have, nor be able to surmount all the difficulties and resolve all the questions that might arise concerning any of them. We have the *ideas* of a *square*, a *circle*, and *equality*, and yet, perhaps, shall never be able to find a circle equal to a square, and certainly know that it is so. We have the *ideas* of *matter* and *thinking*, but possibly shall never be able to know whether any mere material being thinks or not, it being impossible for us, by the contemplation of our own *ideas*, without revelation, to discover whether omnipotence has not given to some systems of matter fitly disposed a power to perceive and think, or else joined and fixed to matter so disposed a thinking immaterial substance—it being in respect of our notions not much more remote from our comprehension to conceive that God can, if he pleases, superadd to matter a faculty of thinking than that he should superadd to it another substance with a faculty of thinking, since we do not know in what thinking consists, nor to what sort of substances the Almighty has been pleased to give that power, which cannot be in any created being, but merely by the good pleasure and bounty of the Creator. For I see no contradiction in it that the first eternal thinking Being or omnipotent Spirit should, if he pleased, give to certain systems of created senseless matter, put together as he thinks fit, some degrees of sense, perception, and thought, though as I think I have proved, *lib. iv.* chap. 10, sec. 14, etc., it is no less than a contradiction to suppose matter (which is evidently in its own nature void of sense and thought) should be that eternal first-thinking being. What certainty of knowledge can anyone have that some perceptions, such as, e.g., pleasure and pain, should not be in some bodies themselves after a certain manner modified and moved, as well as that they should be in an immaterial substance upon the motion of the parts of body? Body, as far as we can conceive, being able only to strike and affect body, and motion, according to the utmost reach of our *ideas*, being able to produce nothing but motion; so that when we allow it to produce pleasure or pain, or the *idea* of a color or sound, we are inclined to quit our reason, go beyond our *ideas*, and attribute it wholly to the good pleasure of our Maker. For since we must allow he has annexed effects to motion, which we can no way conceive motion able to produce, what reason have we to conclude that he could not order them as well to be produced in a subject we cannot conceive capable of them, as well as in a subject we cannot conceive the motion of matter can any way operate upon? I do not say this that I would any way lessen the belief of the soul's immateriality. I am not here speaking of probability, but knowledge; and I think not only that it becomes the modesty of philosophy not to pronounce magisterially where we want that evidence that can produce knowledge, but also that it is of use to us to discern how far our knowledge does reach, for the state we are at present in, not being that of vision, we must in many things content ourselves with faith and probability; and in the present question about the immateriality of the soul if our faculties cannot arrive at demonstrative certainty, we need not think it strange. All the great ends of morality and religion are well enough secured without philosophical proofs of the soul's immateriality, since it is evident that he who made us at the beginning to subsist here, sensible intelligent beings, and for several years continued us in such a state, can and will restore us to the like state of sensibility in another world, and make us capable there to receive the retribution he has designed to men, according to their doings in this life. And therefore it is not of such mighty necessity to determine one way or the other as some over-zealous for or against the immateriality of the soul have been ready to make the world believe. Who, either on the one side, indulging too much their thoughts, immersed altogether in matter, can allow no existence to what is not material. Or who, on the other side, not finding *cogitation* within the natural powers of matter, examined over and over again by the utmost intention of mind, have the confidence to conclude that omnipotence itself cannot give perception and thought to a substance which has the modification of solidity. He who considers how hardly sensation is, in our thoughts, reconcilable to extended matter, or existence to anything that has no extension at all, will confess that he is very far from certainly knowing what his soul is. It is a point which seems to me to be put out of the reach of our knowledge. And

he who will give himself leave to consider freely, and look into the dark and intricate part of each hypothesis, will scarcely find his reason able to determine him fixedly for or against the soul's materiality. Since on whichever side he views it, either as an unextended substance or as a thinking extended matter, the difficulty to conceive either will, while either alone is in his thoughts, still drive him to the contrary side — an unfair way which some men take with themselves who, because of the inconceivableness of something they find in one, throw themselves violently into the contrary hypothesis, though altogether as unintelligible to an unbiased understanding. This serves not only to show the weakness and the scantiness of our knowledge, but the insignificant triumph of such sort of arguments, which, drawn from our own views, may satisfy us that we can find no certainty on one side of the question, but do not at all thereby help us to truth by running into the opposite opinion, which, on examination, will be found clogged with equal difficulties. For what safety, what advantage to anyone is it, for the avoiding the seeming absurdities, and to him insurmountable rubs he meets with in one opinion, to take refuge in the contrary, which is built on something altogether as inexplicable, and as far remote from his comprehension? It is past controversy that we have in us something that thinks; our very doubts about what it is confirm the certainty of its being, though we must content ourselves in the ignorance of what *kind* of being it is. And it is in vain to go about to be skeptical in this, as it is unreasonable in most other cases to be positive against the being of anything, because we cannot comprehend its nature. For I would gladly know what substance exists that does not have something in it which manifestly baffles our understandings. Other spirits who see and know the nature and inward constitution of things, how much must they exceed us in knowledge? To which if we add larger comprehension, which enables them at one glance to see the connection and agreement of very many *ideas*, and readily supplies to them the intermediate proofs, which we by single and slow steps, and long poring in the dark, hardly at last find out, and are often ready to forget one before we have hunted out another. We may guess at some part of the happiness of superior ranks of spirits, who have a quicker and more penetrating sight, as well as a larger field of knowledge. But to return to the argument in hand, our *knowledge*, I say, is not only limited to the paucity and imperfections of the *ideas* we have and which we employ it about, but even comes short of that too. But how far it reaches, let us now inquire.

7. *How far our knowledge reaches*. The affirmations or negations we make concerning the *ideas* we have may, as I have before intimated in general, be reduced to these four sorts, namely, identity, coexistence, relation, and real existence. I shall examine how far our knowledge extends in each of these.

8. *First, our knowledge of identity and diversity, as far as our* ideas. *First, as to identity and diversity*, in this way of agreement or disagreement of our *ideas*, *our intuitive knowledge is as far extended as our ideas* themselves; and there can be no *idea* in the mind which it does not presently, by an intuitive knowledge, perceive to be what it is and to be different from any other.

9. *Secondly, of coexistence, a very little way*. *Secondly, as to* the second sort, which is *the agreement or disagreement* of our *ideas in coexistence*, in this our knowledge is very short, though in this consists the greatest and most material part of our knowledge concerning substances. For our *ideas* of the species of substances being, as I have showed, nothing but certain collections of simple *ideas* united in one subject, and so coexisting together: e.g., our *idea* of *flame* is a body hot, luminous, and moving upward; of *gold*, a body heavy to a certain degree, yellow, malleable, and fusible. These, or some such complex *ideas* as these in men's minds, stand for these two names of the different substances, *flame* and *gold*. When we would know anything further concerning these, or any other sort of substances, what do we inquire, but what other qualities or power these substances have or have not? This is nothing else but to know what other simple *ideas* do or do not coexist with those that make up that complex *idea*.

10. *Because the connection between most simple* ideas *is unknown*. This, however weighty and considerable a part of human science, is yet very narrow, and scarcely any at all. The reason of which is that the simple *ideas*, of which our complex *ideas* of substances are made up, are, for the most part, such as carry with them, in their own nature, no visible necessary connection or inconsistency with any other simple *ideas*, whose coexistence with them we would inform ourselves about.

11. *Especially of secondary qualities*. The *ideas* that our complex ones of substances are made up of, and about which our knowledge concerning substances is most employed, are those of their *secondary qualities*. These depending all (as has been shown) upon the primary qualities of their minute and insensible parts, or if not upon them, upon something yet more remote from our comprehension, it is impossible we should know which have a necessary union or inconsistency one with another. For not knowing the root they spring from, not knowing what size, figure, and texture of parts they are, on which depend, and from which result, those qualities which make our complex *idea* of gold, it is impossible we should know what other qualities result from, or are incompatible with, the same constitution of the insensible parts of gold, and so consequently must always coexist with that complex *idea* we have of it, or else are *inconsistent* with it.

12. *And further, because all connection between any secondary and primary qualities is undiscoverable*. Besides this ignorance of the primary qualities of the insensible parts of bodies, on which depend all their secondary qualities, there is yet another and more incurable part of ignorance, which sets us more remote from a certain knowledge of the *coexistence* or *in-coexistence* (if I may so say) of different *ideas* in the same subject, and that is, that there is no discoverable connection between any *secondary quality and those primary qualities* which it depends on.

13. That the size, figure, and motion of one body should cause a change in the size, figure, and motion of another body is not beyond our conception. The separation of the parts of one body upon the intrusion of another and the change from rest to motion upon impulse, these and the like seem to have some *connection* one with another. And if we knew these primary qualities of bodies, we might have reason to

hope we might be able to know a great deal more of these operations of them one upon another. But our minds not being able to discover any *connection* between these primary qualities of bodies and the sensations that are produced in us by them, we can never be able to establish certain and undoubted rules of the consequence or *coexistence* of any secondary qualities, though we could discover the size, figure, or motion of those invisible parts which immediately produce them. We are so far from knowing what figure, size, or motion of parts produce a yellow color, a sweet taste, or a sharp sound that we can by no means conceive how any *size*, *figure*, or *motion* of any particles can possibly produce in us the *idea* of any *color*, *taste*, or *sound* whatsoever; there is no conceivable *connection* between the one and the other.

14. In vain therefore shall we endeavor to discover by our *ideas* (the only true way of certain and universal knowledge) what other *ideas* are to be found constantly joined with that of our complex *idea* of any substance. Since we neither know the real constitution of the minute parts on which their qualities do depend, nor, did we know them, could we discover any necessary *connection* between them and any of the *secondary qualities*; which is necessary to be done before we can certainly know their *necessary coexistence*. So that, let our complex *idea* of any species of substances be what it will, we can hardly, from the simple *ideas* contained in it, certainly determine the necessary coexistence of any other quality whatsoever. Our knowledge in all these inquiries reaches very little further than our experience. Indeed, some few of the primary qualities have a necessary dependence and visible connection one with another, as figure necessarily supposes extension. Receiving or communicating motion by impulse supposes solidity. But though these and perhaps some others of our *ideas* have, yet there are so *few* of them that have a *visible connection* one with another that we can by intuition or demonstration discover the coexistence of very few of the qualities that are to be found united in substances. And we are left only to the assistance of our senses to make known to us what qualities they contain. For of all the qualities that are *coexistent* in any subject, without this dependence and evident connection of their *ideas* one with another, we cannot know certainly any two to *coexist* any further than experience, by our senses, informs us. Thus though we see the yellow color, and upon trial find the weight, malleableness, fusibility, and fixedness that are united in a piece of gold, yet because no one of these *ideas* has any evident *dependence* or necessary connection with the other, we cannot certainly know that where any four of these are, the fifth will be there also, however highly probable it may be, because the highest probability amounts not to certainty, without which there can be no true knowledge. For this *coexistence* can be no further known than it is perceived; and it cannot be perceived but either in particular subjects, by the observation of our senses, or in general, by the necessary *connection* of the *ideas* themselves.

15. *Of repugnance to coexist, larger. As to the incompatibility or repugnance to coexistence*, we may know that any subject may have of each sort of primary qualities but one particular at once: e.g., each particular extension, figure, number of parts, motion, excludes all other of each kind. The like also is certain of all sensible *ideas* peculiar to each sense, for whatever of each kind is present in any subject excludes all others of that sort: e.g., no one subject can have two smells or two colors at the same time. To this perhaps will be said, has not an opal, or the infusion of *lignum nephriticum*, two colors at the same time? To which I answer that these bodies, to eyes differently placed, may at the same time afford different colors. But I take liberty also to say that to eyes differently placed, it is different parts of the object that reflect the particles of light. And therefore it is not the same part of the object, and so not the very same subject, which at the same time appears both yellow and azure. For it is as impossible that the very same particle of any body should at the same time differently modify or reflect the rays of light, as that it should have two different figures and textures at the same time.

16. *Of the coexistence of powers, a very little way.* But *as to the powers of substances* to change the sensible qualities of other bodies, which make a great part of our inquiries about them, and is no inconsiderable

branch of our knowledge, I doubt, as to these, whether *our knowledge reaches* much further than our experience, or whether we can come to the discovery of most of these powers, and be certain that they are in any subject, by the connection with any of those *ideas* which to us make its essence. Because the active and passive powers of bodies, and their ways of operating, consisting in a texture and motion of parts, which we cannot by any means come to discover, it is but in very few cases we can be able to perceive their dependence on, or repugnance to, any of those *ideas* which make our complex one of that sort of things. I have here instanced in the corpuscularian hypothesis as that which is thought to go furthest in an intelligible explication of those qualities of bodies; and I fear the weakness of human understanding is scarcely able to substitute another, which will afford us a fuller and clearer discovery of the necessary connection and *coexistence* of the powers which are to be observed united in several sorts of them. This at least is certain that whichever hypothesis is clearest and truest (for of that it is not my business to determine), our knowledge concerning corporeal substances will be very little advanced by any of them, until we are made to see what qualities and powers of bodies have a *necessary connection or repugnance* one with another—which in the present state of philosophy, I think, we know but to a very small degree. And I doubt whether, with those faculties we have, we shall ever be able to carry our general knowledge (I say not particular experience) in this part much further. Experience is that which in this part we must depend on. And it is to be wished that it would be more improved. We find the advantages some men's generous pains have this way brought to the stock of natural knowledge. And if others, especially the philosophers by fire, who pretend to it, had been so wary in their observations, and sincere in their reports, as those who call themselves philosophers ought to have been, our acquaintance with the bodies here about us, and our insight into their powers and operations, had been yet much greater.

17. *Of the spirits yet narrower*. If we are at a loss in respect of the powers and operations of bodies, I think it is easy to conclude, *we are much more in the dark in reference to spirits*; of which we naturally have no *ideas*, but what we draw from that of our own, by reflecting on the operations of our own souls within us, as far as they can come within our observation. But how inconsiderable a rank the spirits that inhabit our bodies hold among those various and possibly innumerable kinds of nobler beings, and how far short they come of the endowments and perfections of cherubims and seraphims, and infinite sorts of spirits above us, is what by a transient hint, in another place, I have offered to my reader's consideration.

18. *Thirdly, of other relations, it is not easy to say how far. Morality capable of demonstration*. As to the third sort of our knowledge, namely, the *agreement or disagreement of any of our* ideas *in any other relation*, this, as it is the largest field of our knowledge, so it is hard to determine how far it may extend. Because the advances that are made in this part of knowledge, depending on our sagacity in finding intermediate *ideas* that may show the *relations* and *habitudes* of ideas, whose coexistence is not considered, it is a hard matter to tell when we are at an end of such discoveries, and when reason has all the helps it is capable of, for the finding of proofs, or examining the agreement or disagreement of remote *ideas*. They who are ignorant of *algebra* cannot imagine the wonders in this kind are to be done by it. And what further improvements and helps, advantageous to other parts of knowledge, the sagacious mind of man may yet find out, it is not easy to determine. This at least I believe that the *ideas* of quantity are not those alone that are capable of demonstration and knowledge, and that other, and perhaps more useful parts of contemplation, would afford us certainty, if vices, passions, and domineering interest did not oppose or menace such endeavors.

The *idea* of a supreme being, infinite in power, goodness, and wisdom, whose workmanship we are, and on whom we depend, and the *idea* of our selves, as understanding rational creatures, being such as are clear in us, would, I suppose, if duly considered and pursued, afford such foundations of our duty and rules of action as might place *morality among the sciences capable of demonstration*; in which I do not doubt but from self-evident propositions, by necessary consequences, as incontestable as those in mathematics, the measures of right and wrong might be made out to anyone who will apply himself with the same indifference and attention to the one as he does to the other of these sciences. The *relation* of other *modes* may certainly be perceived, as well as those of number and extension. And I cannot see why they should not also be capable of demonstration, if due methods were thought on to examine or pursue their agreement or disagreement. "*Where there is no property, there is no injustice,*" is a proposition as certain as any demonstration in *Euclid.* For the *idea* of *property* being a right to anything, and the *idea* to which the name *injustice* is given being the invasion or violation of that right, it is evident that these *ideas*, being thus established, and these names annexed to them, I can as certainly know this proposition to be true as that a triangle has three angles equal to two right ones. Again, "No *government allows absolute liberty.*" The *idea* of government being the establishment of society upon certain rules or laws which require conformity to them, and the *idea* of absolute liberty being for anyone to do whatever he pleases, I am as capable of being certain of the truth of this proposition as of any in the mathematics.

19. *Two things have made moral ideas thought incapable of demonstration. Their complexity and want of sensible representations.* That which in this respect has given the advantage to the *ideas* of quantity, and made them thought more capable of certainty and demonstration is,

*First* that they can be set down and represented by sensible marks, which have a greater and nearer correspondence with them than any words or sounds whatsoever. Diagrams drawn on paper are copies of the *ideas* in the mind, and not liable to the uncertainty that words carry in their signification. An angle, circle, or square, drawn in lines, lies open to the view, and cannot be mistaken. It remains unchangeable, and may at leisure be considered and examined, and the demonstration be revised, and all the parts of it may be gone over more than once without any danger of the least change in the *ideas*. This cannot be thus done in *moral ideas*; we have no sensible marks that resemble them by which we can set them down; we have nothing but words to express

them by, which though, when written, they remain the same, yet the *ideas* they stand for may change in the same man; and it is very seldom that they are not different in different persons.

*Secondly*, another thing that makes the greater difficulty in *ethics* is that *moral ideas* are commonly more complex than those of the figures ordinarily considered in mathematics. From this these two inconveniences follow: *first*, that their names are of more uncertain signification, the precise collection of simple *ideas* they stand for not being so easily agreed on, and so the sign that is used for them in communication always, and in thinking often, does not steadily carry with it the same *idea*, upon which the same disorder, confusion, and error follow, as would if a man, going to demonstrate something of an heptagon, should, in the diagram he took to do it, leave out one of the angles, or by oversight make the figure with one angle more than the name ordinarily imported, or he intended it should, when at first he thought of his demonstration. This often happens, and is hardly avoidable in very complex moral *ideas*, where the same name being retained, one angle, i.e., one simple *idea*, is left out or put in the complex one (still called by the same name) more at one time than another. *Secondly*, from the complexity of these moral *ideas* there follows another inconvenience, namely, that the mind cannot easily retain those precise combinations so exactly and perfectly as is necessary in the examination of the habitudes and correspondences, agreements or disagreements, of several of them one with another, especially where it is to be judged of by long deductions and the intervention of several other complex *ideas*, to show the agreement or disagreement of two remote ones.

The great help against this which mathematicians find in diagrams and figures, which remain unalterable in their drafts, is very apparent, and the memory would often have great difficulty otherwise to retain them so exactly, while the mind went over the parts of them step by step, to examine their several correspondences. And though in casting up a long sum either in addition, multiplication, or division, every part is only a progression of the mind, taking a view of its own *ideas*, and considering their agreement or disagreement; and the resolution of the question is nothing but the result of the whole, made up of such particulars, of which the mind has a clear perception. Yet without setting down the several parts by marks, whose precise significations are known, and by marks that last and remain in view when the memory had let them go, it would be almost impossible to carry so many different *ideas* in the mind, without confounding or letting slip some parts of the reckoning, and thereby making all our reasonings about it useless. In which case, the ciphers or marks help not the mind at all to perceive the agreement of any two or more numbers, their equalities or proportions; that the mind has only by intuition of its own *ideas* of the numbers themselves. But the numerical characters are helps to the memory, to record and retain the several *ideas* about which the demonstration is made, by which a man may know how far his intuitive knowledge, in surveying several of the particulars, has proceeded; that so he may without confusion go on to what is yet unknown, and at last have in one view before him the result of all his perceptions and reasonings.

20. *Remedies of those difficulties*. One part of *these disadvantages* in moral *ideas*, which has made them be thought not capable of demonstration, may in a good measure be *remedied* by definitions, setting down that collection of simple *ideas*, which every term shall stand for, and then using the terms steadily and constantly for that precise collection. And what methods algebra, or something of that kind, may hereafter suggest to remove the other difficulties, it is not easy to foretell. Confident I am that if men would, in the same method and with the same indifference, search after moral as they do mathematical truths, they would find them have a stronger connection one with another, and a more necessary consequence from our clear and distinct *ideas*, and to come nearer perfect demonstration than is commonly imagined. [ . . . ]

21. *Fourthly, of real existence, we have an intuitive knowledge of our own, demonstrative of God's, sensible of some few other things*. As to the fourth sort of our knowledge, namely, *of the real actual existence of things*, we have an intuitive knowledge of our own *existence*; and a demonstrative knowledge of the *existence* of a God; of the *existence* of anything else, we have no other but a sensitive knowledge, which does not extend beyond the objects present to our senses.

22. *Our ignorance great*. Our knowledge being so narrow, as I have showed, it will perhaps give us some light into the present state of our minds, if we look a little into the dark side and take a view of *our ignorance*, which, being infinitely larger than our knowledge, may serve much to the quieting of disputes and improvement of useful knowledge. If discovering how far we have clear and distinct *ideas*, we confine our thoughts within the contemplation of those things that are within the reach of our understandings, and do not launch out into that abyss of darkness (where we do not have eyes to see, nor faculties to perceive anything) out of a presumption that nothing is beyond our comprehension, we need not go far to be satisfied of the folly of such a conceit. He who knows anything knows this in the first place that he does not need to seek long for instances of his ignorance. The meanest and most obvious things that come in our way have dark sides that the quickest sight cannot penetrate into. The clearest and most enlarged understandings of thinking men find themselves puzzled, and at a loss, in every particle of matter. We shall the less wonder to find it so, when we consider the *causes of our ignorance*, which, from what has been said, I suppose, will be found to be these three:

*First*, want of *ideas*.

*Secondly*, want of a discoverable connection between the *ideas* we have.

*Thirdly*, want of tracing and examining our *ideas*.

23. *First, one cause of it, want of* ideas, *either such as we have no conception of, or such as particularly we have not*. First, there are some things, and those not a few that we are ignorant of, for *want of ideas*.

*First*, all the simple *ideas* we have are confined (as I have shown) to those we receive from corporeal objects by sensation, and from the operations of our own minds as the objects of reflection. But how much these few and narrow inlets are disproportionate to the vast whole extent of all beings will not be hard to persuade those who are not so foolish as to think their span the measure of all things.

What other simple *ideas* it is possible the creatures in other parts of the universe may have, by the assistance of senses and faculties more, or more perfect, than we have, or different from ours, it is not for us to determine. But to say, or think there are no such, because we conceive nothing of them, is no better an argument than if a blind man should be positive in it that there was no such thing as sight and colors, because he had no manner of *idea* of any such thing, nor could by any means frame to himself any notions about seeing. [ . . . ]

24. *Because of their remoteness. Secondly*, another great cause of ignorance is the *want of* ideas *we are capable of.* As the want of *ideas* which our faculties are not able to give us shuts us wholly from those views of things, which it is reasonable to think other beings more perfect than we have, of which we know nothing, so the want of *ideas* I now speak of keeps us in ignorance of things we conceive capable of being known to us. *Bulk, figure,* and *motion* we have *ideas* of. But though we are not without *ideas* of these primary qualities of bodies in general, yet not knowing what is the particular *bulk, figure,* and *motion* of the greatest part of the bodies of the universe, we are ignorant of the several powers, efficacies, and ways of operation, by which the effects, which we daily see, are produced. These are hidden from us, in some things by being *too remote, and* in others by being too *minute.* When we consider the vast distance of the known and visible parts of the world, and the reasons we have to think that what lies within our ken is but a small part of the universe, we shall then discover a huge abyss of ignorance. What are the particular fabrics of the great masses of matter which make up the whole stupendous frame of corporeal beings, how far they are extended, what is their motion, and how continued or communicated, and what influence they have one upon another, are contemplations that, at first glimpse, our thoughts lose themselves in. If we narrow our contemplations and confine our thoughts to this little canton, I mean this system of our sun, and the grosser masses of matter that visibly move about it, what several sorts of vegetables, animals, and intellectual corporeal beings, infinitely different from those of our little spot of earth, may

there probably be in the other planets, to the knowledge of which, even of their outward figures and parts, we can no way attain, while we are confined to this earth, there being no natural means, either by sensation or reflection, to convey their certain *ideas* into our minds? They are out of the reach of those inlets of all our knowledge. And what sorts of furniture and inhabitants those mansions contain in them, we cannot so much as guess, much less have clear and distinct *ideas* of them.

25. *Because of their minuteness.* If a great, no, far the greatest part of the several ranks of *bodies* in the universe escape our notice by their remoteness, there are others that are no less concealed from us by their *minuteness.* These insensible corpuscles being the active parts of matter, and the great instruments of nature, on which depend not only all their secondary qualities, but also most of their natural operations, our want of precise distinct *ideas* of their primary qualities keeps us in an incurable ignorance of what we desire to know about them. I do not doubt but if we could discover the figure, size, texture, and motion of the minute constituent parts of any two bodies, we should know without trial several of their operations one upon another, as we do now the properties of a square or a triangle. Did we know the mechanical affections of the particles of *rhubarb, hemlock, opium,* and a *man*; as a watchmaker does those of a watch, by which it performs its operations, and of a file which by rubbing on them will alter the figure of any of the wheels, we should be able to tell beforehand that *rhubarb* will purge, *hemlock* kill, and *opium* make a man sleep, as well as a watchmaker can, that a little piece of paper laid on the balance will keep the watch from going until it is removed, or that, some small part of it being rubbed by a file, the machine would quite lose its motion, and the watch go no more. The dissolving of silver in *aqua fortis,* and gold in *aqua regia,* and not *vice versa,* would be then perhaps no more difficult to know than it is to a smith to understand why the turning of one key will open a lock, and not the turning of another. But while we are destitute of senses acute enough to discover the minute particles of bodies and to give us *ideas* of their mechanical affections, we must be content to be ignorant of their

properties and ways of operation; nor can we be assured about them any further than some few trials we make are able to reach. But whether they will succeed again another time we cannot be certain. This hinders our certain knowledge of universal truths concerning natural bodies; and our reason carries us here very little beyond particular matter of fact.

26. *Hence no science of bodies.* And therefore I am apt to doubt that, however far human industry may advance useful and *experimental* philosophy *in physical things, scientific* will still be out of our reach, because we want perfect and adequate *ideas* of those very bodies which are nearest to us, and most under our command. Those which we have ranked into classes under names, and we think ourselves best acquainted with, we have but very imperfect and incomplete *ideas* of. Distinct *ideas* of the several sorts of bodies that fall under the examination of our senses perhaps we may have. But adequate *ideas*, I suspect, we do not have of anyone among them. And though the former of these will serve us for common use and discourse, yet while we want the latter, we are not capable of *scientific knowledge*; nor shall ever be able to discover general, instructive, unquestionable truths concerning them. *Certainty* and *demonstration* are things we must not, in these matters, pretend to. By the color, figure, taste, and smell, and other sensible qualities, we have as clear and distinct *ideas* of sage and hemlock as we have of a circle and a triangle. But having no *ideas* of the particular primary qualities of the minute parts of either of these plants, nor of other bodies which we would apply them to, we cannot tell what effects they will produce; nor when we see those effects, can we so much as guess, much less know, their manner of production. [ . . . ]

28. *Secondly, want of a discoverable connection between* ideas *we have. Secondly,* what a small part of the substantial beings that are in the universe, the want of *ideas* leaves open to our knowledge, we have seen. In the next place, another cause of ignorance, of no less moment, is a want of a *discoverable connection* between those *ideas* we have. For wherever we want that, we are utterly incapable of universal and certain knowledge, and are, in the former case, left only to observation and experiment, which, how narrow and

confined it is, how far from general knowledge, we need not be told. I shall give some few instances of this cause of our ignorance, and so leave it. It is evident that the bulk, figure, and motion of several bodies about us produce in us several sensations, as of colors, sounds, tastes, smells, pleasure and pain, etc. These mechanical affections of bodies having no affinity at all with those *ideas* they produce in us (there being no conceivable connection between any impulse of any sort of body and any perception of a color or smell, which we find in our minds), we can have no distinct knowledge of such operations beyond our experience, and can reason no otherwise about them than as effects produced by the appointment of an infinitely wise agent, which perfectly surpass our comprehensions. As the *ideas* of sensible secondary qualities which we have in our minds can by us be no way deduced from bodily causes, nor any correspondence or connection be found between them and those primary qualities which (experience shows us) produce them in us, so on the other side, the operation of our minds upon our bodies is as inconceivable. How any thought should produce a motion in body is as remote from the nature of our *ideas* as how any body should produce any thought in the mind; that it is so, if experience did not convince us, the consideration of the things themselves would never be able in the least to discover to us. These, and the like, though they have a constant and regular connection, in the ordinary course of things, yet that connection being not discoverable in the *ideas* themselves, which appearing to have no necessary dependence one on another, we can attribute their connection to nothing else but the arbitrary determination of that all-wise agent who has made them to be and to operate as they do, in a way wholly above our weak understandings to conceive.

29. *Instances.* In some of our *ideas* there are certain relations, habitudes, and connections, so visibly included in the nature of the *ideas* themselves that we cannot conceive them separable from them by any power whatsoever. And in these only we are capable of certain and universal knowledge. Thus the *idea* of a right-lined triangle necessarily carries with it an equality of its angles to two right ones. Nor can

we conceive this relation, this connection of these two *ideas*, to be possibly mutable, or to depend on any arbitrary power, which of choice made it thus, or could make it otherwise. But the coherence and continuity of the parts of matter, the production of sensation in us of colors and sounds, etc., by impulse and motion—no, the original rules and communication of motion being such that we can discover no natural connection with any *ideas* we have in them—we cannot but ascribe them to the arbitrary will and good pleasure of the wise architect. I need not, I think, here mention the resurrection of the dead, the future state of this globe of earth, and such other things, which are by everyone acknowledged to depend wholly on the determination of a free agent. The things that, as far as our observation reaches, we constantly find to proceed regularly, we may conclude do act by a law set them, but yet by a law that we know not. Though causes work steadily in this, and effects constantly flow from them, yet their *connections* and *dependencies* being not discoverable in our *ideas*, we can have but an experimental knowledge of them. From all this it is easy to perceive what a darkness we are involved in, how little it is of being, and the things that are that we are capable to know. And therefore we shall do no injury to our knowledge when we modestly think with ourselves that we are so far from being able to comprehend the whole nature of the universe, and all the things contained in it, that we are not capable of a philosophical knowledge of the bodies that are about us, and make a part of us. Concerning their secondary qualities, powers, and operations, we can have no universal certainty. Several effects come every day within the notice of our senses, of which we have so far *sensitive knowledge*; but the causes, manner, and certainty of their production, for the two foregoing reasons, we must be content to be very ignorant of. In these we can go no further than particular experience informs us of matter of fact, and by analogy to guess what effects the like bodies are, upon other trials, like to produce. But as to a perfect *science* of natural bodies (not to mention spiritual beings) we are, I think, so far from being capable of any such thing that I conclude it lost labor to seek after it.

30. *Thirdly, want of tracing our* ideas. Thirdly, where we have adequate *ideas*, and where there is a certain and discoverable connection between them, yet we are often ignorant, for want of *tracing* those *ideas* which we have, or may have, and for want of finding out those intermediate *ideas*, which may show us what habitude of agreement or disagreement they have one with another. And thus many are ignorant of mathematical truths, not out of any imperfection of their faculties, or uncertainty in the things themselves, but for lack of application in acquiring, examining, and by due ways comparing those *ideas*; that which has most contributed to hinder the due *tracing* of our *ideas*, and finding out their relations, and agreements or disagreements one with another, has been, I suppose, the ill use of *words*. It is impossible that men should ever truly seek or certainly discover the agreement or disagreement of *ideas* themselves, while their thoughts flutter about or stick only in sounds of doubtful and uncertain significations. Mathematicians abstracting their thoughts from names and accustoming themselves to set before their minds the *ideas* themselves that they would consider, and not sounds instead of them, have avoided by these means a great part of that perplexity, puddering, and confusion, which has so much hindered men's progress in other parts of knowledge. For while they stick in words of undetermined and uncertain signification, they are unable to distinguish true from false, certain from probable, consistent from inconsistent, in their own opinions. This having been the fate or misfortune of a great part of men of letters, the increase brought into the stock of real knowledge has been very little, in proportion to the schools, disputes, and writings, the world has been filled with, while students being lost in the great wood of words did not know where they were, how far their discoveries were advanced, or what was wanting in their own or the general stock of knowledge. Had men, in the discoveries of the material, done as they have in those of the intellectual world, [that is,] involved all in the obscurity of uncertain and doubtful ways of talking, [then] volumes written of navigation and voyages, theories and stories of zones and tides, multiplied and disputed, no, ships built, and fleets sent out,

would never have taught us the way beyond the line, and the Antipodes would be still as much unknown as when it was declared heresy to hold there were any. But having spoken sufficiently of words and the ill or careless use that is commonly made of them, I shall not say anything more of it here.

31. *Extent in respect of universality.* Up to now we have examined the *extent* of our knowledge in respect of the several sorts of beings that are. There is another *extent of it in respect of universality*, which will also deserve to be considered; and in this regard, our knowledge follows the nature of our *ideas*. If the *ideas* are abstract, whose agreement or disagreement we perceive, our knowledge is universal. For what is known of such general *ideas* will be true of every particular thing in whom that essence, i.e., that abstract *idea* is to be found, and what is once known of such *ideas* will be perpetually and forever true, so that as to all general knowledge we must search and find it only in our minds, and it is only the examining of our own *ideas* that furnishes us with that. Truths belonging to essences of things (that is, to abstract *ideas*) are eternal and are to be found out by the contemplation only of those essences, as the existence of things is to be known only from experience. But having more to say of this in the chapters where I shall speak of general and real knowledge, this may here suffice as to the universality of our knowledge in general.

## Chapter IV. *Of the Reality of Knowledge.*

1. *Objection, knowledge placed in* ideas *may be all bare vision.* I do not doubt but my reader by this time may be apt to think that I have been all this while only building a castle in the air, and be ready to say to me, To what purpose all this stir? Knowledge, you say, is only the perception of the agreement or disagreement of our own *ideas*. But who knows what those *ideas* may be? Is there anything so extravagant as the imaginations of men's brains? Where is the head that has no *chimeras* in it? Or if there is a sober and a wise man, what difference will there be, by your rules, between his knowledge and that of the most extravagant fancy in the world? They both have their *ideas* and perceive their agreement and disagreement one with another. If there is any difference between them,

the advantage will be on the warm-headed man's side as having the more *ideas*, and the more lively. And so, by your rules, he will be the more knowing. If it is true that all knowledge lies only in the perception of the agreement or disagreement of our own *ideas*, the visions of an enthusiast and the reasonings of a sober man will be equally certain. It is no matter how things are; so a man observes but the agreement of his own imaginations and talks conformably, it is all truth, all certainty. Such castles in the air will be as strongholds of truth as the demonstrations of *Euclid*. That a harpy is not a centaur is by this way as certain knowledge, and as much a truth, as that a square is not a circle.

But *of what use is all this fine knowledge of men's own imaginations* to a man who inquires after the reality of things? It does not matter what men's fancies are, it is the knowledge of things that is only to be prized. It is this alone gives a value to our reasonings and preference to one man's knowledge over another's that it is of things as they really are, and not of dreams and fancies.

2. *Answer. Not so, where* ideas *agree with things.* To which I answer that if our knowledge of our *ideas* terminate in them, and reach no further, where there is something further intended, our most serious thoughts will be of little more use than the reveries of a crazy brain, and the truths built upon this of no more weight than the discourses of a man who sees things clearly in a dream, and with great assurance utters them. But, I hope, before I have done, to make it evident that this way of certainty, by the knowledge of our own *ideas*, goes a little further than bare imagination. And I believe it will appear that all the certainty of general truths a man has lies in nothing else.

3. It is evident the mind does not know things immediately, but only by the intervention of the *ideas* it has of them. *Our knowledge* therefore is *real*, only so far as there is a conformity between our *ideas* and the reality of things. But what shall be here the criterion? How shall the mind, when it perceives nothing but its own *ideas*, know that they agree with things themselves? This, though it seems not to want difficulty, yet, I think, there are two sorts of *ideas* that, we may be assured, agree with things.

4. *As, first, all simple* ideas *do. First,* the first are simple *ideas,* which since the mind, as has been shown, can by no means make to itself, must necessarily be the product of things operating on the mind in a natural way, and producing in there those perceptions which by the wisdom and will of our maker they are ordained and adapted to. From which it follows that *simple* ideas *are not fictions* of our fancies, but the natural and regular productions of things without us, really operating upon us, and so carry with them all the conformity which is intended, or which our state requires. For they represent to us things under those appearances which they are fitted to produce in us, by which we are enabled to distinguish the sorts of particular substances, to discern the states they are in, and so to take them for our necessities, and apply them to our uses. Thus the *idea* of whiteness, or bitterness, as it is in the mind, exactly answering that power which is in any body to produce it there, has all the real conformity it can or ought to have, with things without us. And this conformity between our simple *ideas* and the existence of things is sufficient for real knowledge.

5. *Secondly, all complex* ideas, *except of substances. Secondly, all our complex* ideas, *except those of substances,* being *archetypes* of the mind's own making, not intended to be the copies of anything, nor referred to the existence of anything, as to their origins, *cannot want any conformity necessary to real knowledge.* For that which is not designed to represent anything but itself can never be capable of a wrong representation, nor mislead us from the true apprehension of anything, by its dislikeness to it; and such, excepting those of substances, are all our complex *ideas,* which, as I have shown in another place, are combinations of *ideas* which the mind, by its free choice, puts together, without considering any connection they have in nature. And hence it is that in all these sorts the *ideas* themselves are considered as the archetypes, and things no otherwise regarded but as they are conformable to them. So that we cannot but be infallibly certain that all the knowledge we attain concerning these *ideas* is real, and reaches things themselves, because in all our thoughts, reasonings, and discourses of this kind, we intend things

no further than as they are conformable to our *ideas.* So that in these we cannot miss of a certain and undoubted reality.

6. *Hence the reality of mathematical knowledge.* I do not doubt but it will be easily granted that the *knowledge* we have of *mathematical truths* is not only certain, but *real knowledge,* and not the bare empty vision of vain insignificant *chimeras* of the brain. And yet, if we will consider, we shall find that it is only of our own *ideas.* The mathematician considers the truth and properties belonging to a rectangle or circle only as they are an *idea* in his own mind. For it is possible he never found either of them existing mathematically, i.e., precisely true, in his life. But yet the knowledge he has of any truths or properties belonging to a circle or any other mathematical figure is nevertheless true and certain, even of real things existing, because real things are no further concerned, nor intended to be meant by any such propositions, than as things really agree to those *archetypes* in his mind. Is it true of the *idea* of a *triangle* that its three angles are equal to two right ones? It is true also of a *triangle,* wherever it really exists. Whatever other figure exists, that is not exactly answerable to that *idea* of a *triangle* in his mind, is not at all concerned in that proposition. And therefore he is certain all his knowledge concerning such *ideas* is real knowledge, because intending things no further than they agree with those his *ideas,* he is sure what he knows concerning those figures, when they have barely an *ideal existence* in his mind, will hold true of them also when they have real existence in matter, his consideration being barely of those figures which are the same, wherever or however they exist.

7. *And of moral.* And hence it follows that *moral knowledge* is as *capable of real certainty* as mathematics. For certainty being but the perception of the agreement or disagreement of our *ideas;* and demonstration nothing but the perception of such agreement, by the intervention of other *ideas* or mediums, our moral *ideas,* as well as mathematical, being archetypes themselves, and so adequate and complete *ideas;* all the agreement or disagreement which we shall find in them will produce real knowledge, as well as in mathematical figures.

8. *Existence not required to make it real*. For the attaining of knowledge and certainty, it is requisite that we have determined *ideas*, and, to make our knowledge *real*, it is requisite that the *ideas* answer their *archetypes*. Nor let it be wondered that I place the certainty of our knowledge in the consideration of our *ideas*, with so little care and regard (as it may seem) to the real existence of things. Since most of those discourses, which take up the thoughts, and engage the disputes of those who pretend to make it their business to inquire after truth and certainty, will, I presume, upon examination be found to be *general propositions* and notions in which existence is not at all concerned. All the discourses of the mathematicians about the squaring of a circle, conic sections, or any other part of mathematics, *do not concern* the *existence* of any of those figures, but their demonstrations, which depend on their *ideas*, are the same, whether there is any square or circle existing in the world or not. In the same manner the truth and certainty of *moral* discourses abstract from the lives of men and the existence of those virtues in the world of which they treat. Nor are *Tully's* offices less true because there is nobody in the world who exactly practices his rules and lives up to that pattern of a virtuous man which he has given us, and which existed nowhere when he wrote, but in *idea*. If it is true in speculation, i.e., in *idea*, that *murder deserves death*, it will also be true in reality of any action that exists conformable to that *idea* of *murder*. [ . . . ]

11. Ideas *of substances have their archetypes without us*. *Thirdly*, there is another sort of *complex ideas*, which, being referred to *archetypes* without us, may differ from them, and so our knowledge about them may come short of being real. Such are our *ideas* of substances, which, consisting of a collection of simple *ideas* supposed taken from the works of nature, may yet vary from them by having more or different *ideas* united in them than are to be found united in the things themselves. From this it comes to pass that they may, and often do, fail of being exactly conformable to things themselves.

12. *So far as they agree with those so far our knowledge concerning them is real*. I say then that to have *ideas* of *substances*, which, by being conformable to

things, may afford us real knowledge, it is not enough, as in modes, to put together such *ideas* as have no inconsistency, though they did never before so exist: e.g., the *ideas* of *sacrilege* or *perjury*, etc., were as real and true *ideas* before as after the existence of any such fact. But *our ideas of substances*, being supposed copies and referred to *archetypes* without us, must still be taken from something that does or has existed; they must not consist of *ideas* put together at the pleasure of our thoughts, without any real pattern they were taken from, though we can perceive no inconsistency in such a combination. The reason of this is because we knowing not what real constitution it is of substances on which our simple *ideas* depend, and which really is the cause of the strict union of some of them one with another, and the exclusion of others, there are very few of them that we can be sure are or are not inconsistent in nature, any further than experience and sensible observation reach. In this therefore is founded the *reality* of our knowledge concerning *substances* that all our complex *ideas* of them must be such, and such only, as are made up of such simple ones as have been discovered to coexist in nature. And our *ideas* being thus true, though not, perhaps, very exact copies, are yet the subjects of *real* (as far as we have any) *knowledge* of them—which (as has been already shown) will not be found to reach very far; but so far as it does, it will still be *real knowledge*. [ . . . ]

## Chapter X. *Of Our Knowledge of the Existence of a God.*

1. *We are capable of knowing certainly that there is a God*. Though God has given us no innate *ideas* of himself, though he has stamped no original characters on our minds in which we may read his being, yet having furnished us with those faculties our minds are endowed with, he has not left himself without witness, since we have sense, perception, and reason, and cannot want a clear proof of him, as long as we carry ourselves about us. Nor can we justly complain of our ignorance in this great point, since he has so plentifully provided us with the means to discover and know him, so far as is necessary to the end of our being and the great importance of our happiness. But though this is the most obvious truth that reason

discovers, and though its evidence is (if I am not mistaken) equal to mathematical certainty, yet it requires thought and attention and the mind must apply itself to a regular deduction of it from some part of our intuitive knowledge, or else we shall be as uncertain and ignorant of this as of other propositions, which are in themselves capable of clear demonstration. To show therefore that we are capable of *knowing*, i.e., *being certain that there is a* God, and how we may come by this certainty, I think we need go no further than ourselves and that undoubted knowledge we have of our own existence.

2. *Man knows that he himself is*. I think it is beyond question that *man has a clear idea of his own being;* he knows certainly he exists, and that he is something. He who can doubt whether he is anything or not, I do not speak to, no more than I would argue with pure nothing or endeavor to convince nonentity that it were something. If anyone pretends to be so skeptical as to deny his own existence (for really to doubt of it is manifestly impossible), let him for me enjoy his beloved happiness of being nothing until hunger, or some other pain, convinces him of the contrary. This then, I think, I may take for a truth which everyone's certain knowledge assures him of beyond the liberty of doubting, namely, that he is something that actually exists.

3. *He knows also that nothing cannot produce a being, therefore something eternal*. In the next place, man knows by an intuitive certainty that bare *nothing can no more produce any real being than it can be equal to two right angles*. If a man does not know that nonentity, or the absence of all being, cannot be equal to two right angles, it is impossible he should know any demonstration in *Euclid*. If therefore we know there is some real being, and that nonentity cannot produce any real being, it is an evident demonstration that from eternity there has been something, since what was not from eternity had a beginning, and what had a beginning must be produced by something else.

4. That *eternal Being must be most powerful*. Next, it is evident that what had its being and beginning from another must also have all that which is in, and belongs to its being, from another too. All the powers

it has must be owing to and received from the same source. This eternal source then of all being must also be the source and origin of all power; and *so this eternal being must be also the most powerful*.

5. *And most knowing*. Again, a man finds in himself *perception* and *knowledge*. We have then gotten one step further, and we are certain now that there is not only some being, but some knowing intelligent being in the world.

There was a time, then, when there was no knowing being and when knowledge began to be; or else there has been also *a knowing being from eternity*. If it is said, there was a time when no being had any knowledge, when that eternal being was void of all understanding, I reply that then it was impossible there should ever have been any knowledge—it being as impossible that things wholly void of knowledge, and operating blindly, and without any perception, should produce a knowing being, as it is impossible that a triangle should make itself three angles bigger than two right ones. For it is as repugnant to the *idea* of senseless matter that it should put into itself, sense, perception, and knowledge, as it is repugnant to the *idea* of a triangle that it should put into itself greater angles than two right ones.

6. *And therefore God*. Thus from the consideration of ourselves and what we infallibly find in our own constitutions, our reason leads us to the knowledge of this certain and evident truth that *there is an eternal, most powerful, and most knowing being*, which, whether anyone will please to call *God*, it matters not. The thing is evident, and from this *idea* duly considered will easily be deduced all those other attributes, which we ought to ascribe to this eternal being. If nevertheless anyone should be found so senselessly arrogant as to suppose man alone knowing and wise, but yet the product of mere ignorance and chance, and that all the rest of the universe acted only by that blind haphazard, I shall leave with him that very rational and emphatic rebuke of *Tully*, I. ii. *De Leg.*, to be considered at his leisure. "What can be more sillily arrogant and misbecoming than for a man to think that he has a mind and understanding in him, but yet in all the universe besides there is no such thing? Or that those things which with

the utmost stretch of his reason he can scarcely comprehend should be moved and managed without any reason at all?" [ . . . ]

From what has been said, it is plain to me we have a more certain knowledge of the existence of a God than of anything our senses have not immediately discovered to us. No, I presume I may say that we more certainly know that there is a God than that there is anything else without us. When I say we *know* I mean there is such a knowledge within our reach which we cannot miss, if we will but apply our minds to that, as we do to several other inquiries.

7. *Our idea of a most perfect Being not the sole proof of a God. How far the* idea *of a most perfect being* which a man may frame in his mind does or does not prove *the existence of a* God, I will not here examine. For in the different make of men's tempers and application of their thoughts, some arguments prevail more on one, and some on another, for the confirmation of the same truth. But yet, I think, this I may say that it is an ill way of establishing this truth and silencing atheists to lay the whole stress of so important a point as this upon that sole foundation, and take some men's having that *idea* of God in their minds (for it is evident some men have none, and some worse than none, and the most very different) for the only proof of a deity. And out of an over-fondness of that darling invention dismiss, or at least endeavor to invalidate, all other arguments, and forbid us to listen to those proofs as being weak or fallacious, which our own existence and the sensible parts of the universe offer so clearly and cogently to our thoughts that I deem it impossible for a considering man to withstand them. For I judge it as certain and clear a truth as can anywhere be delivered that "*the invisible things of* God *are clearly seen from the creation of the world, being understood by the things that are made, even his eternal power and Godhead*"—though our own being furnishes us, as I have shown, with an evident and incontestable proof of a deity, and I believe nobody can avoid the cogency of it who will but as carefully attend to it as to any other demonstration of so many parts. Yet this being so fundamental a truth, and of that consequence that all religion and genuine morality depend on it, I do

not doubt but I shall be forgiven by my reader, if I go over some parts of this argument again and enlarge a little more upon them.

8. *Something from eternity.* There is no truth more evident than that *something* must be *from eternity*. I never yet heard of anyone so unreasonable, or that could suppose so manifest a contradiction, as a time in which there was perfectly nothing, this being of all absurdities the greatest, to imagine that pure nothing, the perfect negation and absence of all beings, should ever produce any real existence.

It being then unavoidable for all rational creatures to conclude that something has existed from eternity, let us next see what kind of thing that must be.

9. *Two sorts of beings, cogitative and incogitative.* There are but two sorts of beings in the world that man knows or conceives.

*First,* such as are purely material, without sense, perception, or thought, as the clippings of our beards, and parings of our nails.

*Secondly,* sensible, thinking, perceiving beings, such as we find ourselves to be, which, if you please, we will hereafter call *cogitative and incogitative beings,* which to our present purpose, if for nothing else, are perhaps better terms than material and immaterial.

10. *Incogitative being cannot produce a cogitative.* If then there must be something eternal, let us see what sort of being it must be. And to that it is very obvious to reason that it must necessarily be a *cogitative* being. For it is as impossible to conceive that ever bare incogitative matter should produce a thinking intelligent being as that nothing should of itself produce matter. Let us suppose any parcel of matter eternal, great or small, we shall find it, in itself, able to produce nothing. For example, let us suppose the matter of the next pebble we meet with eternal, closely united, and the parts firmly at rest together; if there were no other being in the world, must it not eternally remain so, a dead inactive lump? Is it possible to conceive it can add motion to itself, being purely matter, or produce anything? Matter then, by its own strength, cannot produce in itself so much as motion. The motion it has must also be from eternity, or else be produced and added to matter by some other being more powerful than

matter—matter, as is evident, not having power to produce motion in itself. But let us suppose motion eternal too; yet matter, *incogitative matter* and motion, whatever changes it might produce of figure and bulk, *could never produce thought*. Knowledge will still be as far beyond the power of motion and matter to produce as matter is beyond the power of *nothing* or *nonentity* to produce. And I appeal to everyone's own thoughts, whether he cannot as easily conceive matter produced by *nothing*, as thought to be produced by pure matter, when, before, there was no such thing as thought or an intelligent being existing? Divide matter into as minute parts as you will (which we are apt to imagine a sort of spiritualizing or making a thinking thing of it) vary the figure and motion of it as much as you please—a globe, cube, cone, prism, cylinder, etc., whose diameters are but 1,000,000th part of a gry,[2] will operate not otherwise upon other bodies of proportional bulk than those of an inch or foot diameter—and you may as rationally expect to produce sense, thought, and knowledge, by putting together, in a certain figure and motion, gross particles of matter, as by those that are the very minutest that do anywhere exist. They knock, impel, and resist one another, just as the greater do; and that is all they can do. So that if we will suppose nothing first, or eternal, *matter* can never begin to be. If we suppose bare matter, without *motion*, eternal motion can never begin to be. If we suppose only matter and motion first, or eternal, *thought* can never begin to be. For it is impossible to conceive that matter, either with or without motion, could have originally in and from itself sense, perception, and knowledge; as is evident from hence that then sense, perception, and knowledge must be a property eternally inseparable from matter and every particle of it. Not to add that though our general or specific conception of matter makes us speak of it as one thing, yet really all matter is not one individual thing, neither is there any such thing existing as one material being, or one single body that we know or can conceive. And therefore if matter were the eternal first cogitative being, there would not be one eternal infinite cogitative being, but an infinite number of eternal finite cogitative

beings, independent one of another, of limited force and distinct thoughts, which could never produce that order, harmony, and beauty which are to be found in nature. Since therefore whatever is the first eternal *being* must necessarily be cogitative, and whatever is first of all things must necessarily contain in it and actually have, at least, all the perfections that can ever after exist, nor can it ever give to another any perfection that it has not either actually in itself, or at least in a higher degree, it necessarily follows that the first eternal being cannot be matter.

11. *Therefore there has been an eternal Wisdom*. If therefore it is evident that *something* necessarily must *exist from eternity*, it is also as evident that *that something must* necessarily *be a cogitative being*. For it is as impossible that incogitative matter should produce a cogitative being, as that nothing, or the negation of all being, should produce a positive being or matter.

12. Though this discovery of the *necessary existence of an eternal mind* does sufficiently lead us into the knowledge of God, since it will hence follow that all other knowing beings that have a beginning must depend on him, and have no other ways of knowledge, or extent of power, than what he gives them; and therefore if he made those, he made also the less excellent pieces of this universe, all inanimate beings, by which his *omniscience*, *power*, and *providence* will be established and all his other attributes necessarily follow. Yet to clear up this a little further, we will see what doubts can be raised against it.

13. *Whether material or not*. First, perhaps it will be said that though it is as clear as demonstration can make it that there must be an eternal being, and that being must also be knowing, yet it does not follow but that thinking being may also be material. Let it be so; it equally still follows that there is a God. For if there is an eternal, omniscient, omnipotent being, it is certain that there is a God, whether you imagine that Being to be material or not. But in this, I suppose, lies the danger and deceit of that supposition. There being no way to avoid the demonstration that there is an eternal knowing being, men, devoted to matter, would willingly have it granted that this knowing being is material, and then, letting slide out of their minds, or the discourse, the demonstration

---

2. A "gry" is one hundredth of an inch.

by which an eternal knowing being was proved necessarily to exist, would argue all to be matter, and so deny a God, that is, an eternal cogitative being—by which means they are so far from establishing that they destroy their own hypothesis. For if there can be, in their opinion, eternal matter, without any eternal cogitative being, they manifestly separate matter and thinking, and suppose no necessary connection of the one with the other, and so establish the necessity of an eternal spirit, but not of matter, since it has been proved already that an eternal cogitative being is unavoidably to be granted. Now if thinking and matter may be separated, *the eternal existence of matter will not follow from the eternal existence of a cogitative being*, and they suppose it to no purpose.

14. *Not material, first, because every particle of matter is not cogitative.* But now let us see how they can satisfy themselves or others that this *eternal thinking being* is *material*.

*First*, I would ask them whether they imagine that all matter, *every particle of matter, thinks*? This, I suppose, they will scarcely say, since then there would be as many eternal thinking beings as there are particles of matter, and so an infinity of gods. And yet if they will not allow matter as matter, that is, every particle of matter to be cogitative as well as extended, they will have as hard a task to make out to their own reasons a cogitative being out of incogitative particles, as an extended being out of unextended parts, if I may so speak.

15. *Secondly, one particle alone of matter cannot be cogitative. Secondly*, if all matter does not think, I next ask "whether it is *only one atom that does so?*" This has as many absurdities as the other, for then this atom of matter must be alone eternal or not. If this alone is eternal, then this alone, by its powerful thought or will, made all the rest of matter. And so we have the creation of matter by a powerful thought, which is what the materialists stick at. For if they suppose one single thinking atom to have produced all the rest of matter, they cannot ascribe that preeminence to it upon any other account than that of its thinking, the only supposed difference. But allow it to be by some other way which is above our conception, it must still be creation, and these men must

give up their great maxim, "*ex nihilo nil fit*." If it is said that all the rest of matter is equally eternal as that thinking atom, it will be to say anything at pleasure, though ever so absurd, for to suppose all matter eternal, and yet one small particle in knowledge and power infinitely above all the rest, is without any the least appearance of reason to frame an hypothesis. Every particle of matter as matter is capable of all the same figures and motions of any other; and I challenge anyone, in his thoughts, to add anything else to one above another.

16. *Thirdly, a system of incogitative matter cannot be cogitative.* If then neither one peculiar atom alone can be this eternal thinking being, nor all matter as matter, i.e., every particle of matter, can be, it only remains that it is *some certain system of matter* duly put together that is this *thinking eternal being*. This is that which, I imagine, is that notion which men are most apt to have of God, who would have him a material being, as most readily suggested to them by the ordinary conceit they have of themselves and other men, which they take to be material thinking beings. But this imagination, however more natural, is no less absurd than the other. For to suppose the eternal thinking being to be nothing else but a composition of particles of matter each of which is incogitative is to ascribe all the wisdom and knowledge of that eternal being only to the *juxtaposition* of parts—than which nothing can be more absurd. For unthinking particles of matter, however put together, can have nothing thereby added to them, but a new relation of position, which it is impossible should give thought and knowledge to them.

17. *Whether in motion or at rest.* But further, this *corporeal system* either has all its parts at rest or it is a certain motion of the parts in which its thinking consists. If it is perfectly at rest, it is but one lump, and so can have no privileges above one atom.

If it is the motion of its parts on which its thinking depends, all the thoughts there must be unavoidably accidental and limited, since all the particles that by motion cause thought, being each of them in itself without any thought, cannot regulate its own motions, much less be regulated by the thought of the whole; since that thought is not the cause of motion (for then it must be antecedent to it, and so without it) but the consequence of it, by means of which freedom, power, choice, and all rational and wise thinking or acting will be quite taken away. So that such a thinking being will be no better nor wiser than pure blind matter, since to resolve all into the accidental unguided motions of blind matter, or into thought depending on unguided motions of blind matter, is the same thing—not to mention the narrowness of such thoughts and knowledge that must depend on the motion of such parts. But there needs no enumeration of any more absurdities and impossibilities in this hypothesis (however full of them it be) than that before mentioned, since let this thinking system be all, or a part of the matter of the universe, it is impossible that any one particle should either know its own, or the motion of any other particle, or the whole know the motion of every particle, and so regulate its own thoughts or motions, or indeed have any thought resulting from such motion.

18. *Matter not coeternal with an eternal Mind.* Others would have *matter* be *eternal*, notwithstanding that they allow an eternal, cogitative, immaterial being. This, though it does not take away the being of a God, yet, since it denies one and the first great piece of his workmanship, the creation, let us consider it a little. *Matter* must be allowed eternal. Why? Because you cannot conceive how it can be made out of nothing. Why do you not also think yourself eternal? You will answer perhaps because, about twenty or forty years since, you began to be. But if I ask you what is that *you*, which began then to be, you can scarcely tell me. The matter of which you are made did not begin then to be, for if it did, then it is not eternal. But it began to be put together in such a fashion and frame as makes up your body; but yet that frame of particles is not you; it does not make that thinking thing you are (for I have now to do with one who allows an eternal, immaterial thinking being, but would have unthinking matter eternal too); therefore when did that thinking thing begin to be? If it did never begin to be, then have you always been a thinking thing from eternity—the absurdity of which I need not confute, until I meet with one who is so void of understanding as to admit it. If therefore you

can allow a thinking thing to be made out of nothing (as all things that are not eternal must be), why also can you not allow it possible for a material being to be made out of nothing by an equal power, but that you have the experience of the one in view and not of the other? Though, when well considered, creation of a spirit will be found to require no less power than the creation of matter. No, possibly, if we would emancipate ourselves from vulgar notions, and raise our thoughts as far as they would reach, to a closer contemplation of things, we might be able to aim at some dim and seeming conception how matter might at first be made and begin to exist by the power of that eternal first being. But to give beginning and being to a spirit would be found a more inconceivable effect of omnipotent power. But, this being what would perhaps lead us too far from the notions on which the philosophy now in the world is built, it would not be pardonable to deviate so far from them, or to inquire, so far as grammar itself would authorize, if the common settled opinion opposes it, especially in this place where the received doctrine serves well enough to our present purpose, and leaves this past doubt that the creation or beginning of any one substance out of nothing, being once admitted, the creation of all other, but the Creator himself, may, with the same ease, be supposed.

19. But you will say is it not impossible to admit of the *making anything out of nothing*, since we cannot possibly conceive it? I answer, No. Because it is not reasonable to deny the power of an infinite being, because we cannot comprehend its operations. We do not deny other effects upon this ground, because we cannot possibly conceive the manner of their production. We cannot conceive how anything but impulse of body can move body, and yet that is not a reason sufficient to make us deny it possible, against the constant experience we have of it in ourselves, in all our voluntary motions, which are produced in us only by the free action or thought of our own minds, and are not, nor can be, the effects of the impulse or determination of the motion of blind matter in or upon our own bodies; for then it could not be in our power or choice to alter it. For example: My right hand writes, while my left hand is still. What causes

rest in one, and motion in the other? Nothing but my will, a thought of my mind; my thought only changing, the right hand rests, and the left hand moves. This is matter of fact which cannot be denied. Explain this and make it intelligible, and then the next step will be to understand creation. For the giving a new determination to the motion of the animal spirits (which some make use of to explain voluntary motion) does not clear the difficulty one jot—to alter the determination of motion, being in this case no easier nor less than to give motion itself, since the new determination given to the animal spirits must be either immediately by thought, or by some other body put in their way by thought, which was not in their way before, and so must owe its motion to thought, either of which leaves voluntary motion as unintelligible as it was before. In the meantime it is an overvaluing ourselves to reduce all to the narrow measure of our capacities, and to conclude all things impossible to be done whose manner of doing exceeds our comprehension. This is to make our comprehension infinite, or God finite, when what he can do is limited to what we can conceive of it. If you do not understand the operations of your own finite mind that thinking thing within you, do not deem it strange that you cannot comprehend the operations of that eternal infinite mind, who made and governs all things, and whom the heaven of heavens cannot contain.

## Chapter XI. *Of Our Knowledge of the Existence of Other Things.*

1. *Is to be had only by sensation.* The knowledge of our own being we have by intuition. The existence of a God reason clearly makes known to us, as has been shown.

The *knowledge of the existence* of any other thing we can have only by *sensation*. For there being no necessary connection of *real existence* with any *idea* a man has in his memory, nor of any other existence but that of God with the existence of any particular man, no particular man can know the *existence* of any other being, but only when, by actual operating upon him, it makes itself perceived by him. For the having the *idea* of anything in our mind no more proves the existence of that thing than the picture of a man evidences his being in the world, or the visions of a dream make by this means a true history.

2. *Instance*: *whiteness of this paper*. It is therefore the actual receiving of *ideas* from without that gives us notice of the *existence* of other things and makes us know that something does exist at that time without us, which causes that *idea* in us, though perhaps we neither know nor consider how it does it. For it does not take from the certainty of our senses and the *ideas* we receive by them, that we do not know the manner in which they are produced—e.g., while I write this, I have, by the paper affecting my eyes, that *idea* produced in my mind, which, whatever object causes, I call *white*; by this I know that that quality or accident (i.e., whose appearance before my eyes always causes that *idea*) does really exist and has a being without me. And of this the greatest assurance I can possibly have, and to which my faculties can attain, is the testimony of my eyes, which are the proper and sole judges of this thing, whose testimony I have reason to rely on as so certain that I can no more doubt, while I write this, that I see white and black and that something really exists that causes that sensation in me, than that I write or move my hand—which is a certainty as great as human nature is capable of, concerning the existence of anything but a man's self alone, and of God.

3. *This, though not so certain as demonstration, yet may be called knowledge, and proves the existence of things without us. The notice we have by our senses of the existing of things without* us, though it is not altogether so certain as our intuitive knowledge, or the deductions of our reason employed about the clear abstract *ideas* of our own minds, yet it is an assurance that *deserves the name of knowledge*. If we persuade ourselves that our faculties act and inform us right concerning the existence of those objects that affect them, it cannot pass for an ill grounded confidence. For I think nobody can, in earnest, be so skeptical as to be uncertain of the existence of those things which he sees and feels. At least, he who can doubt so far (whatever he may have with his own thoughts) will never have any controversy with me, since he can never be sure I say anything contrary to his own opinion. As to myself, I think God has given me assurance

enough of the existence of things without me, since by their different application I can produce in myself both pleasure and pain, which is one great concern of my present state. This is certain: The confidence that our faculties do not deceive us in this is the greatest assurance we are capable of, concerning the existence of material beings. For we cannot act [on] anything but by our faculties, nor talk of knowledge itself, but by the help of those faculties which are fitted to apprehend even what knowledge is. But besides the assurance we have from our senses themselves that they do not err in the information they give us of the existence of things without us, when they are affected by them, we are further confirmed in this assurance by other concurrent reasons.

4. *First, because we cannot have them but by the inlets of the senses. First*, it is plain those perceptions are produced in us by exterior causes affecting our senses, because *those who want the organs of any sense never can have the* ideas *belonging to that sense* produced in their minds. This is too evident to be doubted. And therefore we cannot but be assured that they come in by the organs of that sense and no other way. The organs themselves, it is plain, do not produce them, for then the eyes of a man in the dark would produce colors, and his nose smell roses in the winter. But we see nobody gets the relish of a pineapple, until he goes to the *Indies*, where it is, and tastes it.

5. *Secondly, because an idea from actual sensation and another from memory are very distinct perceptions. Secondly*, because *sometimes I find that I cannot avoid the having those* ideas *produced in my mind*. For though, when my eyes are shut, or windows fast, I can at pleasure recall to my mind the *ideas* of *light*, or the *sun*, which former sensations had lodged in my memory; so I can at pleasure lay by that *idea*, and take into my view that of the *smell* of a rose, or *taste* of sugar. But, if I turn my eyes at noon towards the sun, I cannot avoid the *ideas* which the light or sun then produces in me, so that there is a manifest difference between the *ideas* laid up in my memory (over which, if they were there only, I should have constantly the same power to dispose of them, and lay them by at pleasure), and those

which force themselves upon me and I cannot avoid having. And therefore it must necessarily be some exterior cause, and the brisk acting of some objects without me, whose efficacy I cannot resist that produces those *ideas* in my mind, whether I will or not. Besides, there is nobody who does not perceive the difference in himself between contemplating the sun, as he has the *idea* of it in his memory, and actually looking upon it; of which two, his perception is so distinct that few of his *ideas* are more distinguishable one from another. And therefore he has certain knowledge that they are not both memory, or the actions of his mind, and fancies only within him, but that actual seeing has a cause without.

6. *Thirdly, pleasure or pain, which accompanies actual sensation, does not accompany the returning of those* ideas *without the external objects. Thirdly*, add to this that *many of those* ideas *are produced in us with pain, which afterwards we remember without the least offense*. Thus the pain of heat or cold, when the *idea* of it is revived in our minds, gives us no disturbance, which, when felt, was very troublesome, and is again, when actually repeated. This is occasioned by the disorder the external object causes in our bodies when applied to it. And we remember the pains of *hunger*, *thirst*, or the *headache*, without any pain at all, which would either never disturb us, or else constantly do it, as often as we thought of it, were there nothing more but *ideas* floating in our minds and appearances entertaining our fancies, without the real existence of things affecting us from abroad. The same may be said of pleasure accompanying several actual sensations. And though mathematical demonstration does not depend upon sense, yet the examining them by diagrams gives great credit to the evidence of our sight and seems to give it a certainty approaching to that of demonstration itself. For it would be very strange that a man should allow it for an undeniable truth that two angles of a figure, which he measures by lines and angles of a diagram, should be bigger one than the other, and yet doubt of the existence of those lines and angles, which by looking on he makes use of to measure that by.

7. *Fourthly, our senses assist one another's testimony of the existence of outward things. Fourthly,*

our *senses* in many cases bear *witness* to the truth of each other's report, concerning the existence of sensible things without us. He who sees a *fire* may, if he doubts whether it is anything more than a bare fancy, feel it too, and be convinced by putting his hand in it, which certainly could never be put into such exquisite pain by a bare *idea* or phantom, unless the pain is a fancy too. This yet he cannot, when the burn is well, by raising the *idea* of it, bring upon himself again.

Thus I see, while I write this, I can change the appearance of the paper, and by designing the letters tell beforehand what new *idea* it shall exhibit the very next moment by barely drawing my pen over it. This will neither appear (let me fancy as much as I will) if my hands stand still, or though I move my pen, if my eyes are shut. Nor when those characters are once made on the paper, can I choose afterwards but see them as they are, that is, have the *ideas* of such letters as I have made. From where it is manifest that they are not barely the sport and play of my own imagination, when I find that the characters that were made at the pleasure of my own thoughts do not obey them, nor yet cease to be, whenever I shall fancy it, but continue to affect my senses constantly and regularly, according to the figures I made them. To this if we will add that the sight of those shall, from another man, draw such sounds, as I beforehand design they shall stand for, there will be little reason left to doubt that those words I write do really exist without me, when they cause a long series of regular sounds to affect my ears, which could not be the effect of my imagination, nor could my memory retain them in that order.

8. *This certainty is as great as our condition needs.* But yet, if after all this anyone will be so skeptical as to distrust his senses and affirm that all we see and hear, feel and taste, think and do, during our whole being, is but the series and deluding appearances of a long dream, of which there is no reality, and therefore will question the existence of all things or our knowledge of anything, I must desire him to consider that if all is a dream, then he does but dream that he makes the question, and so it does not much matter that a waking man should answer him. But yet, if he

pleases, he may dream that I make him this answer that *the certainty of* things existing *in rerum natura*, when we have *the testimony of our senses* for it, is not only *as great* as our frame can attain to, but *as our condition needs*. For our faculties being suited not to the full extent of being, nor to a perfect, clear, comprehensive knowledge of things free from all doubt and scruple, but to the preservation of us in whom they are, and accommodated to the use of life, they serve to our purpose well enough, if they will but give us certain notice of those things, which are convenient or inconvenient to us. For he who sees a candle burning, and has experimented the force of its flame by putting his finger in it, will little doubt that this is something existing without him, which does him harm and puts him to great pain. This is assurance enough, when no man requires greater certainty to govern his actions by, than what is as certain as his actions themselves. And if our dreamer pleases to try whether the glowing heat of a glass furnace is barely a wandering imagination in a drowsy man's fancy, by putting his hand into it, he may perhaps be wakened into a certainty greater than he could wish that it is something more than bare imagination. Thus this evidence is as great as we can desire, being as certain to us as our pleasure or pain, i.e., happiness or misery; beyond which we have no concern, either of knowing or being. Such an assurance of the existence of things without us is sufficient to direct us in the attaining the good and avoiding the evil, which is caused by them; this is the important concern we have of being made acquainted with them.

9. *But reaches no further than actual sensation.* Finally then, when our senses do actually convey into our understandings any *idea*, we cannot but be satisfied that there does something at that time really exist without us which does affect our senses, and by them give notice of itself to our apprehensive faculties, and actually produce that *idea* which we then perceive. And we cannot so far distrust their testimony as to doubt that such collections of simple *ideas* as we have observed by our senses to be united together do really exist together. But *this knowledge extends as far as the present testimony of our senses*, employed about particular objects that do then affect them, *and no*

*further*. For if I saw such a collection of simple *ideas*, as is accustomed to be called *man*, existing together one minute since, and am now alone, I cannot be certain that the same man exists now, since there is no necessary connection of his existence a minute since, with his existence now. By a thousand ways he may cease to be, since I had the testimony of my senses for his existence. And if I cannot be certain that the man I saw last today is now in being, I can less be certain that he is so, who has been longer removed from my senses, and I have not seen since yesterday, or since the last year; and much less can I be certain of the existence of men that I never saw. And therefore though it is highly probable that millions of men do now exist, yet, while I am alone writing this, I do not have that certainty of it which we strictly call knowledge, though the great likelihood of it puts me past doubt, and it is reasonable for me to do several things upon the confidence that there are men (and men also of my acquaintance, with whom I have to do) now in the world. But this is but probability, not knowledge.

10. *Folly to expect demonstration in everything*. By means of which yet we may observe how foolish and vain a thing it is for a man of a narrow knowledge, who having reason given him to judge of the different evidence and probability of things, and to be swayed accordingly—how *vain*, I say, it is *to expect demonstration* and certainty *in things not capable of it*, and refuse assent to very rational propositions, and act contrary to very plain and clear truths, because they cannot be made out so evident as to surmount every the least (I will not say reason, but) pretense of doubting. He who, in the ordinary affairs of life, would admit of nothing but direct plain demonstration would be sure of nothing in this world, but of perishing quickly. The wholesomeness of his meat or drink would not give him reason to venture on it. And I would gladly know what it is he could do upon such grounds as are capable of no doubt, no objection.

11. *Past existence is known by memory*. As when our senses are actually employed about any object, we do know that it does exist, so *by our memory* we may be assured that previously things that affected our senses have existed. And thus *we have knowledge of the past existence* of several things, of which our senses having informed us, our memories still retain the *ideas*; and of this we are past all doubt, so long as we remember well. But this knowledge also reaches no further than our senses have formerly assured us. Thus seeing water at this instant, it is an unquestionable truth to me that water does exist. And remembering that I saw it yesterday, it will also be always true, and as long as my memory retains it, always an undoubted proposition to me that water did exist the 10th of *July*, 1688, as it will also be equally true that a certain number of very fine colors did exist, which at the same time I saw upon a bubble of that water. But, being now quite out of sight both of the water and bubbles too, it is no more certainly known to me that the water does now exist than that the bubbles or colors in there do so, it being no more necessary that water should exist today, because it existed yesterday, than that the colors or bubbles exist today, because they existed yesterday, though it is exceedingly much more probable, because water has been observed to continue long in existence, but bubbles and the colors on them quickly cease to be.

12. *The existence of spirits not knowable*. What *ideas* we have of spirits and how we come by them, I have already shown. But though we have those *ideas* in our minds and know we have them there, the having the *ideas* of spirits does not make us *know* that any such things do exist without us, or *that there are any finite spirits*, or any other spiritual beings but the Eternal God. We have ground from revelation, and several other reasons, to believe with assurance that there are such creatures. But, our senses not being able to discover them, we want the means of knowing their particular existences. For we can no more know that there are finite spirits really existing, by the *idea* we have of such beings in our minds, than by the *ideas* anyone has of fairies or centaurs, he can come to know that things answering those *ideas* do really exist.

And therefore concerning the existence of finite spirits, as well as several other things, we must content ourselves with the evidence of faith; but universal certain propositions concerning this matter are beyond our reach. For however true it may be, e.g., that all the intelligent spirits that God ever created do still exist, yet it can never make a part of our certain knowledge. These and the like propositions we may assent to as highly probable, but are not, I fear, in this state capable of knowing. We are not then to put others upon demonstrating, nor ourselves upon search of universal certainty in all those matters, in which we are not capable of any other knowledge, but what our senses give us in this or that particular.

13. *Particular propositions concerning existence are knowable.* By which it appears that there are two sorts of *propositions.* 1. There is one sort of propositions *concerning* the *existence* of anything answerable to such an *idea*—as having the *idea* of an *elephant, phoenix, motion,* or an *angel,* in my mind, the first and natural inquiry is whether such a thing does anywhere exist? And this knowledge is only of *particulars.* No existence of anything without us, but only of God, can certainly be known further than our senses inform us. 2. There is another sort of *propositions* in which is expressed the agreement or disagreement of our abstract *ideas* and their dependence on one another. Such propositions may be *universal* and certain. So having the *idea* of God and myself, of fear and obedience, I cannot but be sure that God is to be feared and obeyed by me, and this proposition will be certain, concerning *man* in general, if I have made an abstract *idea* of such a species, of which I am one particular. But yet this proposition, however certain that men ought to fear and obey God does not prove to me the existence of men in the world, but will be true of all such creatures, whenever they do exist. Which *certainty* of such general propositions depends on the agreement or disagreement to be discovered in those abstract *ideas.*

14. *And general propositions concerning abstract* ideas. In the former case, our knowledge is the consequence of the existence of things producing *ideas* in our minds by our senses. In the latter, knowledge is the consequence of the *ideas* (be they what they will) that are in our minds producing there general certain propositions. Many of these are called *eternal truths* (*aeternae veritates*), and all of them indeed are so, not from being written all or any of them in the minds of all men, or that they were any of them propositions in anyone's mind, until he, having gotten the abstract *ideas*, joined or separated them by affirmation or negation. But wherever we can suppose such a creature as *man* is endowed with such faculties, and by this means furnished with such *ideas* as we have, we must conclude, he must necessarily, when he applies his thoughts to the consideration of his *ideas,* know the truth of certain propositions that will arise from the agreement or disagreement which he will perceive in his own *ideas.* Such propositions are therefore called *eternal truths,* not because they are eternal propositions actually formed, and antecedent to the understanding that at any time makes them, nor because they are imprinted on the mind from any patterns that are anywhere out of the mind and existed before. But because being once made about abstract *ideas,* so as to be true, they will, whenever they can be supposed to be made again at any time past or to come, by a mind having those *ideas,* always actually be true. For names being supposed to stand perpetually for the same *ideas,* and the same *ideas* having immutably the same habitudes one to another, propositions concerning any abstract *ideas* that are once true must necessarily be *eternal verities.*

## Chapter XV. *Of Probability.*

1. *Probability is the appearance of agreement upon fallible proofs.* As demonstration is the showing the agreement or disagreement of two *ideas* by the intervention of one or more proofs which have a constant, immutable, and visible connection one with another, so *probability* is nothing but the appearance of such an agreement or disagreement by the intervention of proofs whose connection is not constant and immutable, or at least is not perceived to be so, but is, or appears for the most part to be so, and is enough to induce the mind to *judge* the proposition to be true or false, rather than the contrary. For example, in the demonstration of it a man perceives the certain immutable connection there is of equality between the three angles of a *triangle* and those intermediate ones which are made use of to show their equality to two right ones; and so, by an intuitive knowledge of the agreement or disagreement of the intermediate *ideas* in each step of the progress, the whole series is continued with an evidence, which clearly shows

the agreement or disagreement of those three angles in equality to two right ones. And thus he has certain knowledge that it is so. But another man, who never took the pains to observe the demonstration, hearing a mathematician, a man of credit, affirm the three angles of a triangle to be equal to two right ones, *assents* to it, i.e., receives it for true. In this case the foundation of his assent is the probability of the thing, the proof being such as for the most part carries truth with it; the man on whose testimony he receives it not being accustomed to affirm anything contrary to or besides his knowledge, especially in matters of this kind. So that that which causes his assent to this proposition, that the three angles of a triangle are equal to two right ones, that which makes him take these *ideas* to agree, without knowing them to do so, is the accustomed veracity of the speaker in other cases, or his supposed veracity in this.

2. *It is to supply the want of knowledge.* Our knowledge, as has been shown, being very narrow, and we not happy enough to find certain truth in everything which we have occasion to consider, most of the propositions we think, reason, discourse, no, act upon, are such as we cannot have undoubted knowledge of their truth; yet some of them border so near upon certainty that we make no doubt at all about them, but *assent* to them as firmly, and act, according to that assent, as resolutely as if they were infallibly demonstrated, and that our knowledge of them was perfect and certain. But there being degrees in this from the very neighborhood of certainty and demonstration, quite down to improbability and unlikeness, even to the confines of impossibility, and also degrees of *assent* from full assurance and confidence, quite down to *conjecture, doubt,* and *distrust,* I shall come now (having, as I think, found out the bounds of human knowledge and certainty) in the next place to consider *the several degrees and grounds of probability, and assent or faith.*

3. *Being that which makes us presume things to be true, before we know them to be so.* Probability is likeliness to be true, the very notation of the word signifying such a proposition, for which there are arguments or proofs to make it pass or be received for true. The entertainment the mind gives this sort of propositions is called *belief, assent,* or *opinion,* which is the admitting or receiving any proposition for true, upon arguments or proofs that are found to persuade us to receive it as true, without certain knowledge that it is so. And in this lies the *difference between probability* and *certainty, faith* and *knowledge,* that in all the parts of knowledge there is intuition; each immediate *idea,* each step has its visible and certain connection; in belief, not so. That which makes me believe is something extraneous to the thing I believe, something not evidently joined on both sides to, and so not manifestly showing the agreement or disagreement of those *ideas* that are under consideration.

4. *The grounds of probability are two: conformity with our own experience or the testimony of others' experience. Probability* then, being to supply the defect of our knowledge and to guide us where that fails, is always conversant about propositions, of which we have no certainty, but only some inducements to receive them for true. The *grounds of it* are, in short, these two following:

*First,* the conformity of anything with our own knowledge, observation, and experience.

*Secondly,* the testimony of others, vouching their observation and experience. In the testimony of others, is to be considered: 1. The number. 2. The integrity. 3. The skill of the witnesses. 4. The design of the author, where it is a testimony out of a book cited. 5. The consistency of the parts, and circumstances of the relation. 6. Contrary testimonies.

5. *In this, all the arguments pro and con ought to be examined before we come to a judgment.* Probability wanting that intuitive evidence which infallibly determines the understanding and produces certain knowledge, *the mind, if it will proceed rationally, ought to examine all the grounds of probability,* and see how they make more or less *for or against* any proposition, before it assents to, or dissents from it, and upon a due balancing the whole, reject, or receive it, with a more or less firm assent, proportionally to the preponderance of the greater grounds of probability on one side or the other. For example:

If I myself see a man walk on the ice, it is past *probability*; it is knowledge. But if another tells me he saw a man in *England,* in the midst of a sharp winter, walk upon water hardened with cold, this has so great conformity with what is usually observed to happen, that I am disposed by the nature of the thing itself to assent to it, unless some manifest suspicion attend the relation of that matter of fact. But if the same thing is told to one born between the tropics, who never saw nor heard of any such thing before, there the whole probability relies on testimony; and as the relators are more in number, and of more credit, and have no interest to speak contrary to the truth, so that matter of fact is likely to find more or less belief. Though to a man whose experience has always been quite contrary, and who has never heard of anything like it, the most untainted credit of a witness will scarcely be able to find belief. As it happened to a Dutch ambassador, who entertaining the King of *Siam* with the particularities of *Holland*, which he was inquisitive after, among other things told him that the water in his country would sometimes in cold weather be so hard that men walked upon it, and that it would bear an elephant if he were there—to which the king replied, "Up to now I have believed the strange things you have told me, because I look upon you as a sober fair man, but now I am sure you lie." [ . . . ]

## Chapter XVI. *Of the Degrees of Assent.*

1. *Our assent ought to be regulated by the grounds of probability.* We have laid down the grounds of probability in the foregoing chapter; as they are the foundations on which our *assent* is built, so are they also the measure by which its several degrees are, or ought to be, *regulated*: Only we are to take notice that, whatever grounds of probability there may be, they yet operate no further on the mind which searches after truth, and endeavors to judge right, than they appear, at least, in the first judgment or search that the mind makes. I confess, in the opinions men have and firmly stick to, in the world, their assent is not always from an actual view of the reasons that at first prevailed with them, it being in many cases almost impossible, and in most very hard, even for those who have very admirable memories, to retain all the proofs which, upon a due examination, made them embrace that side of the question. It suffices that they have once with care and fairness sifted the matter as

far as they could, and that they have searched into all the particulars that they could imagine to give any light to the question, and, with the best of their skill, cast up the account upon the whole evidence; and thus, having once found on which side the probability appeared to them, after as full and exact an inquiry as they can make, they lay up the conclusion in their memories as a truth they have discovered; and for the future they remain satisfied with the testimony of their memories, that this is the opinion that, by the proofs they have once seen of it, deserves such a *degree* of their *assent* as they afford it. [ . . . ]

3. *The ill consequence of the remembrance that we once saw ground for such a degree of assent, if our former judgment were not rightly made.* I cannot but admit that men's *sticking to* their *past judgment*, and adhering firmly to conclusions formerly made, is often the cause of great obstinacy in error and mistake. But the fault is not that they rely on their memories for what they have before well judged, but because they judged before they had well examined. [ . . . ] Who almost is there who has the leisure, patience, and means to collect together all the proofs concerning most of the opinions he has, so as safely to conclude that he has a clear and full view, and that there is no more to be alleged for his better information? And yet we are forced to determine ourselves on the one side or other. The conduct of our lives and the management of our great concerns will not bear delay; for those depend, for the most part, on the determination of our judgment in points in which we are not capable of certain and demonstrative knowledge, and in which it is necessary for us to embrace the one side or the other.

4. *The right use of it is mutual charity and forbearance.* Since therefore it is unavoidable to the greatest part of men, if not all, to have several *opinions*, without certain and indubitable proofs of their truth; and it carries too great an imputation of ignorance, lightness, or folly, for men to quit and renounce their former tenets presently upon the offer of an argument, which they cannot immediately answer, and show the insufficiency of; it would, I think, become all men to maintain *peace*, and the common offices of humanity *and friendship, in the diversity of opinions,* since we

cannot reasonably expect that anyone should readily and obsequiously quit his own opinion, and embrace ours, with a blind resignation to an authority which the understanding of man does not acknowledge. [ . . . ] For where is the man who has incontestable evidence of the truth of all that he holds, or of the falsehood of all he condemns, or can say that he has examined to the bottom all his own or other men's opinions? The necessity of believing without knowledge, no, often upon very slight grounds, in this fleeting state of action and blindness we are in, should make us more busy and careful to inform ourselves than constrain others. At least those who have not thoroughly examined to the bottom all their own tenets must confess they are unfit to prescribe to others; and are unreasonable in imposing that as truth on other men's belief, which they themselves have not searched into, nor weighed the arguments of probability, on which they should receive or reject it. [ . . . ]

5. *Probability is either of matter of fact or speculation*. But to return to the grounds of assent, and the several degrees of it, we are to take notice that the propositions we receive upon inducements of *probability* are *of two sorts*: either concerning some particular existence, or, as it is usually termed, matter of fact which, falling under observation, is capable of human testimony; or else concerning things which, being beyond the discovery of our senses, are not capable of any such testimony.

6. *The concurrent experience of all other men with ours produces assurance approaching to knowledge*. Concerning the *first* of these, namely, *particular matter of fact*.

*First*, where any particular thing, consonant to the constant observation of ourselves and others in the like case, comes attested by the concurrent reports of all that mention it, we receive it as easily, and build as firmly upon it, as if it were certain knowledge; and we reason and act upon this with as little doubt, as if it were perfect demonstration. Thus, if all Englishmen who have occasion to mention it should affirm that it froze in England the last winter, or that there were swallows seen there in the summer, I think a man could almost as little doubt of it as that seven and four are eleven. The first, therefore, and *highest*

*degree of probability* is, when the general consent of all men, in all ages, as far as it can be known, concurs with a man's constant and never failing experience in like cases, to confirm the truth of any particular matter of fact attested by fair witnesses; such are all the stated constitutions and properties of bodies, and the regular proceedings of causes and effects in the ordinary course of nature. This we call an argument from the nature of things themselves. For what our own and other men's constant observation has found always to be after the same manner, that we with reason conclude to be the effect of steady and regular causes, though they do not come within the reach of our knowledge. Thus, that fire warmed a man, made lead fluid, and changed the color or consistency in wood or charcoal, that iron sunk in water, and swam in quicksilver, these and the like propositions about particular facts, being agreeable to our constant experience, as often as we have to do with these matters, and being generally spoken of (when mentioned by others) as things found constantly to be so, and therefore not so much as controverted by anybody, we are put past doubt that a relation affirming any such thing to have been, or any predication that it will happen again in the same manner, is very true. These *probabilities* rise so near to *certainty* that they govern our thoughts as absolutely, and influence all our actions as fully, as the most evident demonstration, and in what concerns us we make little or no difference between them and certain knowledge. Our belief, thus grounded, rises to *assurance*.

7. *Unquestionable testimony and experience for the most part produce confidence. Secondly, the next degree of probability* is, when I find by my own experience, and the agreement of all others that mention it, a thing to be for the most part so and that the particular instance of it is attested by many and undoubted witnesses, e.g., history giving us such an account of men in all ages, and my own experience, as far as I had an opportunity to observe, confirming it, that most men prefer their private advantage to the public; if all historians who write of *Tiberius* say that *Tiberius* did so, it is extremely probable. And in this case, our assent has a sufficient foundation to raise itself to a degree which we may call *confidence*.

8. *Fair testimony, and the nature of the thing indifferent, produces also confident belief.* *Thirdly,* in things that happen indifferently, as that a bird should fly this or that way, that it should thunder on a man's right or left hand, etc., when any particular matter of fact is vouched by the concurrent testimony of unsuspected witnesses, there our assent is also unavoidable. Thus, that there is such a city in *Italy* as *Rome*; that, about one thousand seven hundred years ago, there lived in it a man called *Julius Caesar*; that he was a general, and that he won a battle against another, called *Pompey*: This, though in the nature of the thing there is nothing for nor against it, yet being related by historians of credit, and contradicted by no one writer, a man cannot avoid believing it, and can as little doubt of it as he does of the being and actions of his own acquaintance, of which he himself is a witness.

9. *Experience and testimonies clashing, infinitely vary the degrees of probability.* Thus far the matter goes easy enough. Probability upon such grounds carries so much evidence with it, that it naturally determines the judgment, and leaves us as little liberty to believe, or disbelieve, as a demonstration does, whether we will know, or be ignorant. The difficulty is, when testimonies contradict common experience, and the reports of history and witnesses clash with the ordinary course of nature, or with one another; there it is, where diligence, attention, and exactness are required, to form a right judgment, and to proportion the *assent* to the different evidence and probability of the thing, which rises and falls, according as those two foundations of credibility, namely, common observation in like cases, and particular testimonies in that particular instance, favor or contradict it. These are liable to so great variety of contrary observations, circumstances, reports, different qualifications, tempers, designs, oversights, etc. of the reporters, that it is impossible to reduce to precise rules the various degrees in which men give their assent. This only may be said in general, that as the arguments and proofs *pro* and *con,* upon due examination, nicely weighing every particular circumstance, shall to anyone appear, upon the whole matter, in a greater or less degree to preponderate on either side; so they are

fitted to produce in the mind such different entertainments, as we call *belief, conjecture, guess, doubt, wavering, distrust, disbelief,* etc.

10. *Traditional testimonies, the further removed, the less their proof.* This is what concerns assent in matters in which testimony is made use of; concerning which, I think, it may not be amiss to take notice of a rule observed in the law of England, which is, that though the attested copy of a record be good proof, yet the copy of a copy ever so well attested, and by ever so credible witnesses, will not be admitted as a proof in judicature. This is so generally approved as reasonable, and suited to the wisdom and caution to be used in our inquiry after material truths, that I never yet heard of anyone that blamed it. This practice, if it be allowable in the decisions of right and wrong, carries this observation along with it, namely, that any testimony, the further off it is from the original truth, the less force and proof it has. The being and existence of the thing itself is what I call the original truth. A credible man vouching his knowledge of it is a good proof; but if another equally credible does witness it from his report, the testimony is weaker; and a third that attests the hearsay of a hearsay is yet less considerable. So that *in traditional truths each remove weakens the force of the proof,* and the more hands the tradition has successively passed through, the less strength and evidence does it receive from them. This I thought necessary to be taken notice of, because I find among some men the quite contrary commonly practiced, who look on opinions to gain force by growing older; and what a thousand years since would not, to a rational man contemporary with the first voucher, have appeared at all probable, is now urged as certain beyond all question, only because several have since, from him, said it one after another. Upon this ground propositions, evidently false or doubtful enough in their first beginning, come by an inverted rule of probability to pass for authentic truths; and those which found or deserved little credit from the mouths of their first authors are thought to grow venerable by age, and are urged as undeniable.

11. *Yet history is of great use.* I would not be thought here to lessen the credit and use of *history*: It is all the light we have in many cases, and we receive from

it a great part of the useful truths we have, with a convincing evidence. I think nothing more valuable than the records of antiquity; I wish we had more of them, and more uncorrupted. But this truth itself forces me to say that no *probability* can arise higher than its first origin. [ . . . ]

12. *In things which sense cannot discover, analogy is the great rule of probability*. The probabilities we have mentioned up to now are only such as concern matter of fact, and such things as are capable of observation and testimony. There remains that other sort, *concerning* which men entertain opinions with variety of assent, though the *things* are such, *that not falling under the reach of our senses, they are not capable of testimony*. Such are 1. The existence, nature, and operations of finite immaterial beings without us; as spirits, angels, devils, etc., or the existence of material beings which, either for their smallness in themselves, or remoteness from us, our senses cannot take notice of, as whether there are any plants, animals, and intelligent inhabitants in the planets, and other mansions of the vast universe. 2. Concerning the manner of operation in most parts of the works of nature, in which, though we see the sensible effects, yet their causes are unknown, and we do not perceive the ways and manner how they are produced. We see animals are generated, nourished, and move, the lodestone draws iron, and the parts of a candle, successively melting, turn into flame, and give us both light and heat. These and the like effects we see and know, but the causes that operate, and the manner they are produced in, we can only guess and probably conjecture. For these and the like, not coming within the scrutiny of human senses, cannot be examined by them, or be attested by anybody, and therefore can appear more or less probable, only as they more or less agree to truths that are established in our minds, and as they hold proportion to other parts of our knowledge and observation. Analogy in these matters is the only help we have, and it is from that alone we draw all our grounds of probability. Thus, observing that the bare rubbing of two bodies violently one upon another produces heat, and very often fire itself, we have reason to think that what we call heat and fire consists in a violent agitation of

the imperceptible minute parts of the burning matter. Observing likewise that the different refractions of pellucid bodies produce in our eyes the different appearances of several colors, and also that the different ranging and laying the superficial parts of several bodies, as of velvet, watered silk, etc. do the like, we think it probable that the color and shining of bodies are in them nothing but the different arrangement and refraction of their minute and insensible parts. Thus, finding in all parts of the creation that fall under human observation, that there is a gradual connection of one with another, without any great or discernible gaps between, in all that great variety of things we see in the world, which are so closely linked together, that, in the several ranks of beings, it is not easy to discover the bounds between them, we have reason to be persuaded that by such gentle steps things ascend upwards in degrees of perfection. It is a hard matter to say where sensible and rational begin, and where insensible and irrational end; and who is there quick-sighted enough to determine precisely which is the lowest species of living things, and which the first of those which have no life? Things, as far as we can observe, lessen and augment, as the quantity does in a regular cone, where, though there is a manifest odds between the bigness of the diameter at a remote distance, yet the difference between the upper and under, where they touch one another, is hardly discernible. The difference is exceeding great between some men and some animals; but if we will compare the understanding and abilities of some men and some brutes, we shall find so little difference that it will be hard to say that that of the man is either clearer or larger. Observing, I say, such gradual and gentle descents downwards in those parts of the creation that are beneath man, the rule of analogy may make it probable that it is so also in things above us and our observation, and that there are several ranks of intelligent beings, excelling us in several degrees of perfection, ascending upwards towards the infinite perfection of the Creator, by gentle steps and differences, that are every one at no great distance from the next to it. This sort of probability, which is the best conduct of rational experiments, and the rise of hypothesis, has also its use and influence; and a wary reasoning from analogy leads us often into the discovery of truths and useful productions, which would otherwise lie concealed.

13. *One case where contrary experience lessens not the testimony.* Though the common experience and the ordinary course of things have justly a mighty influence on the minds of men, to make them give or refuse credit to anything proposed to their belief, yet there is one case, in which the strangeness of the fact does not lessen the assent to a fair testimony given of it. For where such supernatural events are suitable to ends aimed at by him who has the power to change the course of nature, there, under such circumstances, they may be the fitter to procure belief, by how much the more they are beyond or contrary to ordinary observation. This is the proper case of *miracles*, which, well attested, do not only find credit themselves, but give it also to other truths, which need such confirmation.

14. *The bare testimony of revelation is the highest certainty.* Besides those we have mentioned up to now, there is one sort of propositions that challenge the highest degree of our assent upon bare testimony, whether the thing proposed agree or disagree with common experience, and the ordinary course of things, or not. The reason of this is, because the testimony is of such a one as cannot deceive nor be deceived, and that is of God himself. This carries with it an assurance beyond doubt, evidence beyond exception. This is called by a peculiar name, *revelation*; and our assent to it, faith, which as absolutely determines our minds, and as perfectly excludes all wavering, as our knowledge itself; and we may as well doubt of our own being, as we can whether any revelation from God is true. So that faith is a settled and sure principle of assent and assurance, and leaves no manner of room for doubt or hesitation. Only we must be sure that it be a divine revelation, and that we understand it right; else we shall expose ourselves to all the extravagance of enthusiasm, and all the error of wrong principles, if we have faith and assurance in what is not divine revelation. And therefore, in those cases, our assent can be rationally no higher than the evidence of its being a revelation, and that this is the meaning of the expressions it is delivered in. If the evidence of its being a revelation, or that this is its true sense, is only on probable proofs, our assent can reach no higher than an assurance or diffidence, arising from the more or less apparent probability of the proofs. But of faith, and the precedence it ought to have before other arguments of persuasion, I shall speak more afterward, where I treat of it as it is ordinarily placed, in contradistinction to reason, though in truth it is nothing else but an assent founded on the highest reason.

# Lady Masham and Leibniz, *Correspondence* (1704)[1]

*Damaris Cudworth, Lady Masham (1659–1708), was the daughter of Damaris and Ralph Cudworth, the leading figure of the Cambridge Platonists, whose major work,* The True Intellectual System of the Universe, *was a refutation of determinism as atheistic (in relation to the works of Descartes and in opposition to those of Hobbes). Lady Masham is particularly noted for her long, close friendship with Locke, who took up residence in her household from 1691 until his death in 1704. During this time she published her first work,* A Discourse Concerning the Love of God *(1696), and shortly after Locke's death,* Thoughts in Reference to a Vertuous or Christian Life *(1705). Her correspondence with Leibniz explored their respective views, including Cudworth's various doctrines, Leibniz's pre-established harmony, and the relationship between body and soul.*

## Lady Masham to Leibniz, 29 March 1704

Though I am not in the number of those who can confirm the advantageous idea you have of English ladies yet I have been too much conversant among learned men not to have contracted (as far as I am capable of it) a just value for them, or to have been ignorant of the rank you hold in the commonwealth of letters. This has disposed me long since to entertain with pleasure any occasion of testifying a great respect for you, and has lately suggested to me that my father's *Intellectual System* might possibly not be unacceptable to you. The esteem you express for that work pleases me very much both on this account, and also as it is a new confirmation to me of the worth of that performance.

I should be glad to have a further view into the intellectual world; and would therefore willingly have right conceptions of the system you propose. To this purpose upon the receipt of your obliging letter, I looked into the article "Rorarius" in the first edition of Mr. Bayle's *Dictionary* (not having the second edition with me) and being directed to the *Journal des Savans* 1695 by his quotation of you there, I read what is published of it there. Perhaps my not being accustomed to such abstract speculations made me not comprehend well what you say there of *forms*, upon which I think you build your hypothesis: for (as it seems to me) you sometimes call them *primitive forces*, sometimes *souls*, sometimes *forms constitutive*

---

1. Leibniz's portion of the correspondence was translated from the French by Roger Ariew; Lady Masham's portion was written in English and modernized.

*of substances*, and sometimes substances themselves; but since these are neither spirit nor matter, as a result I confess I have no clear idea of what you call *forms*.

That a man whose correspondence is so highly esteemed as yours by all the learned men of Europe should employ any of his valuable moments in the instruction of an ignorant woman is what I should not perhaps presume to importune you for, if your character was known to me only as a learned man; for those who are far advanced in learned studies and high speculations may think themselves excused from such a condescension, but I am confident you would not condemn the most ignorant lover of truth, were I not secured by my sex of a favorable distinction from the obliging civility of a man conversant in courts. I take the liberty therefore to request the favor of you that you will by some explication or definition of them help me to conceive what your *forms* are; for I cannot but desire to understand a system recommended to me not only by the eminence of its author, but particularly also as tending to enlarge our idea of the divine perfections and the beauty of his works. If you please add in short the sum of your answers to Mr. Bayle's objections in his second edition of his *Dictionary* it will be an additional obligation in giving me still further light into this matter.

I have ordered my father's *Discourse Concerning the Lord's Supper* to be sent you together with his *Intellectual System* in the same volume; the value you express for the author makes me think you will not dislike to look into anything of his and though this treatise was written when he was a young man, yet it was highly commended by our famous Selden. You will much oblige me in accepting this book as from one who is with great esteem and respect etc.

Mr. Locke whose company I am so happy as to enjoy in my family, desires me to present you his humble service.

## Leibniz to Lady Masham, beginning of May 1704

Receiving the honor of your command by a precious answer from your hand, I learned at the same time the good news that your present, of which I am infinitely honored, has happily crossed the sea. Thus I hope to enjoy it soon, something I had desired more than once, because I do believe that the book of the *Intellectual System* with what you had the kindness, Madam, to add of its illustrious author on a very important topic of theology (with which you increased my obligation) cannot be found in this country nor in neighboring countries, because of its language. And it will be all the more important for me to reread this system, since I have been thinking for some time to review my meditations on similar subjects, something that will enable me, Madam, to better satisfy your orders. However, I will now make an effort to obey you, which you will have the kindness to take rather for a mark of my gratitude rather than the effect of a self-confidence that might deserve to be blamed.

Since I am completely in favor of the principle of uniformity which I believe nature observes at the bottom of things, although it varies in manners, degrees, and perfections, the whole of my hypothesis amounts to recognizing in substances distant from our sight and observation something proportional to what is evident in those within our reach. Thus taking now for granted that there is in us a simple being endowed with action and perception, I find that nature would not be sufficiently linked, if this particle of matter that constitutes human bodies was alone endowed with what would make it infinitely different from the rest (even in physics) and completely heterogeneous compared to all other known bodies. This makes me judge that there are such active beings everywhere in matter, and that there is difference only in the manner of perception. And since our own perceptions are sometimes accompanied by *reflection*, and sometimes not, and from reflection are born *abstractions* and *universal and necessary truths*, of which we do not notice any vestiges in animals, and still less in the other bodies surrounding us, there is reason to believe that this simple being in us, called soul, is distinguished by this from those of other known bodies.

Whether these principles of action and perception are now called *forms*, *entelechies*, *souls*, *spirits*, or that these terms are distinguished according to the notions we are willing to attribute to them, the things will not be changed at all by this. I will be asked what will become of these simple beings or souls I put into animals and other creatures to the extent they are organic; I will answer that they must not be less inextinguishable than ours and that they cannot be produced or destroyed by the forces of nature.

But moreover, to keep the *analogy* as much the *future* or the *past* with the *other* bodies and what we are *currently* experiencing in our *own*, I hold not only that these souls or entelechies all have a kind of organic body with them proportionate to their perceptions, and even that they will always have and always had one, as long as they have existed; thus not only the soul, but also the animal itself (or what has analogy with the soul and animal, so as not to dispute over words) remains, and that thus generation and death can only be developments and coverings of which nature visibly show us some samples according to its custom, to help us uncover what it hides. And therefore neither iron nor fire, nor any other violence of nature, whatever ravage they make on the body of an animal, would be able to prevent the soul from keeping a certain organic body, especially as the *organism*, that is, the order and artifice, is something essential to the matter produced and arranged by sovereign wisdom, the production always having to keep the traces of its author. This also makes me judge that there are no spirits entirely separated from matter, except the first and sovereign being, and that genies, however marvelous they may be, are always accompanied by bodies worthy of them. This must also be said of souls we may call separated though only in relation to this gross body. You see, then, Madam, that all this is only to suppose that *everything is everywhere and always as it is with us and now* (the supernatural excepted) except for variations in degrees of perfections; and I allow you to judge whether there is any way to think in any case of a simpler and more intelligible hypothesis.

This same maxim *of not supposing without necessity in creatures except what responds to our experiences has also led me to my system of pre-established harmony*. For we experience that bodies act among themselves according to the mechanical laws, and

that souls produce in themselves some internal actions. And we see no means of conceiving of the action of the soul on matter, or of matter on the soul, nor anything responding to it, not being explicable by any machine whatsoever, than material variations, that is, mechanical laws giving rise to a perception; nor that perception can give rise to a change in velocity or direction in animal spirits and other bodies, however subtle or crude they may be. Thus both the inconceivability of another hypothesis and the good order of nature, which is uniform with itself (without mentioning any other consideration here) have made me judge that the soul and the body follow perfectly their law, each one its own by itself, without the bodily laws being disturbed by the actions of the soul, nor bodies finding windows to bring their influences into the souls. We will ask, then, where does this agreement of the soul with the body come from? Defenders of occasional causes want God to accommodate the soul to the body at all times, and the body to the soul. But this can only be miraculous, and is not very suitable to the philosophy which ought to explain the ordinary course of nature, for God would have to continually disturb the natural laws of bodies. That is why I thought it was infinitely more worthy of God's economy and the uniformity and constant order of his work to conclude that he first created souls and bodies so that each one following its own laws accords with the other—that which one cannot deny to be possible to him whose wisdom and power are infinite. In this I am only attributing to souls and bodies forever and everywhere what one experiences every time the experience is distinct, that is, mechanical laws in bodies, and actions internal in the soul: the whole consisting only in the present state joined to the tendency for changes, which are made in the body according to the moving forces, and in the soul according to the perceptions of good and evil.

Everything surprising in what follows is that the works of God are infinitely more beautiful and harmonious than had been thought. And one can say that the subterfuge of the Epicureans against the argument taken from the beauty of visible things (when they say that among an infinity of the productions of chance is it not marvelous that some world, like ours, has fairly succeeded) is destroyed in that the perpetual correspondence of the beings which have no influence on one another can come only from a common cause of this harmony. Mr. Bayle (who is profound) having meditated on the consequences of this hypothesis, recognizes that we have never given more eminence to what we conceive of divine perfections, and that the infinite wisdom of God, as great as it is, it is not too great to produce such a pre-established harmony, of which he seemed to doubt the possibility. But I had placed into consideration that men themselves produce automatons which act as if they were rational, and that God (who is an infinitely greater artist, or rather in whom everything is art to the greatest extent possible) has traced for him the path for having matter act the way spirits ask of him. So, after that, one should be no more astonished in that it acts with so much reason, than at the course of some rockets in fireworks, along a rope that cannot be seen, which makes it seem that it is a man who leads them. God's designs can only be grasped by the extent of the perfections discovered, and bodies being subjected to souls in advance to be accommodated in time to their voluntary actions, the soul in turn is expressive of bodies by virtue of its primordial nature, needing to represent them by its involuntary and confused perceptions; thus each is the original or the copy of the other to the extent of the perfections or imperfections it envelops.

But I almost forgot, Madam, that I have the honor of writing to you, and this reflection makes me ask forgiveness for my prolixity, where I let myself go. I should have considered that few words would suffice for your penetration and that what cannot be explained to you save by using many words will ordinarily be something unintelligible; but when we are in a process, we are not in control of the end, and I thought it was better to fail by excess. I will also be happy with all my prolixity, if I would not have omitted anything of what I should have said.

I see, Madam, that my happiness has been redoubled in that your good graces have attracted to me a new mark of the kindness of an author of a merit as recognized as that of Mr. Locke, who is so advanced in the honor of your acquaintance: I do not know if I ought to dare to beg you to indicate to him my sentiments full of esteem and my wish to merit his approbation or his teaching. I read carefully the important work he gave to the public, because it contains many things about which I have meditated as well, which incited me even to make remarks. And as it is easier to push against what a clever man has begun, it seems to me I am in a position to raise some difficulties and fulfill some desiderata. And one can judge by the plan I just gave you, Madam, in this letter, whether I have any reason to flatter myself about it. But I dare not flatter myself that I can satisfy a judgment as penetrating as yours; it will be a lot if there is something that will not displease you. Your discernment on this will enlighten mine, and increase the obligation in which I find myself, being with all the respect and all the veneration of which one is capable, etc.

## Lady Masham to Leibniz, 3 June 1704

Your great civility obliges me not the less for having presumed from your goodness upon more than I had any right to pretend to when I requested you would give yourself the pains of informing me further concerning your hypothesis. To a mind possessed in any measure with a due admiration of the works of God nothing is more grateful than by further discoveries therein of his divine Perfections, to be sensibly engaged to adore that being which reason pronounces ought to be the supreme object of our affections.

A hypothesis thought by yourself and others conducing to such an end as this, could not but excite my enquiry; and it did so the more because, in reading what you have published, it seemed to myself also you had views there which gave a very becoming idea of the wisdom of God in his works. The letter you have favored me with confirms me in this thought: but that I may be sure of having a certain and clear knowledge of your hypothesis, permit me to tell you what I conceive it to be—in hopes you will rectify my mistakes if I am in any—which is what may easily happen to one so little conversant as I am in such speculations.

You take for granted that *there is a simple being in us endowed with action and perception*. The same you say, *differing only in the manner of perception, is in matter everywhere*. That that *simple being* in us, which is called soul, is distinguished from that of beasts (and yet more from that of other bodies about us) by the power of *abstraction* and thereby framing universal ideas. All these *simple beings* you think have, will always have, and ever since they existed have had *organic bodies, proportioned to their perception*. So that not only after death does the soul remain, but even the *animal* also, since generation and death is but a displaying or concealment of these beings to, or from, our view. The same principle of uniformity in the works of nature which has led you to believe this has, you say, led you also to your system of the *pre-established harmony between substances*— that which I understand thus.

Any action of the soul upon matter, or of matter upon the soul is inconceivable: these two have their laws distinct. Bodies follow the laws of mechanism and have a tendency to change *following moving forces*. *Souls produce in themselves internal* actions and have a tendency to change according to the *perception that they have of good or ill*. Now *soul* and *body* following each their proper laws, and neither of them acting thereby upon or affecting the other, such effects are yet produced from a *pre-established harmony between these substances*, as if there was a real communication between them. So that the body acting constantly by its own laws of mechanism without receiving any variation or change therein from any action of the soul does yet always correspond to the passions and perceptions which the soul has. And the soul in like manner, though not operated upon by the motions of matter, has yet at the same time that the body acts according to its laws of mechanism, certain perceptions or modifications which do not fail to answer to this.

This is what I conceive you to say; in which (to tell you thoughts so insignificant as mine) I see nothing peculiar, which does not seem possible. I find a uniformity in it which pleases me: and the

advantages proposed from this hypothesis are very desirable. But it does not yet appear to me that this is more than a hypothesis; for as God's ways are not limited by our conceptions; the un-intelligibleness or inconceivableness by us of any way but one, does not, I think, much induce a belief of that, being the way which God has chosen to make use of. Yet such an inference as this from our ignorance, I remember Father Malebranche (or some other assertor of his hypothesis) would make in behalf of occasional causes: to which hypothesis, among other exceptions, I think there is one, which I cannot without your help see, but that yours is similarly liable to, and that is from the organization of the body, in which all that nice curiosity that is discoverable seeming useless, becomes superfluous and lost labor. To this difficulty likewise let me add that I do not conceive why *organism* should be or can be thought, as you say is, *essential to matter*.

But these enquiries or other that might it may be on further thoughts occur to me, are less pertinent for me to make, than such a one as is more fundamental, although it does not peculiarly respect your hypothesis. Forms, explained by you to signify *simple beings* you elsewhere call *atoms of substance* and *primitive forces*, the nature of which you, in another place say, you find to consist in *force*.

Force I presume cannot be the essence of any substance, but is the attribute of what you call a *form, soul* or *atom of substance*, of the essence of which I find no positive idea, and your negation of their having any dimensions, makes their existence I confess inconceivable to me; as not being able to conceive an existence of that which is nowhere. If the locality of these substances were accounted for by their being, as you say, they are always in organized bodies, then they are somewhere: but if these *atoms of substance* are somewhere then they must have some extension, which you deny of them, who, I think, also place the union of the soul with its respective body in nothing else but that correspondence or conformity whereby in virtue of a *pre-established harmony*; souls and bodies acting apart, each by their own laws, the same effects are produced as if there was a real communication between them. Though whether or not I perfectly comprehend your meaning in this part I am in doubt.

What I have here said I think enough for me to venture to trouble you with at once: and it will perhaps be more than enough to show you that you have judged by much too favorably of my apprehension. For I remember my father as well as other assertors of unextended substance to have said: *That it is an imposition of imagination upon their reason in those who cannot be convinced of the reality of substances unextended.*

So great authority as his was to me could not hinder me, if this is so, from being always under such an influence of imagination; which is what would not willingly be in any case. But wherever I have no idea of a thing—or demonstration of the truth of any proposition, the truth of which is inconceivable by me, I deny and conclude that I ought not to assent to what is asserted of either—since should I once do this, I know not where I should stop; what should be the boundaries of assent. Or why I might not believe alike one thing as well as another.

Mr. Locke presents you his humble service and desires me to tell you he takes himself to be mightily obliged to you for your great civility expressed to him; in this he finds you a master as well as in philosophy and everything else. His want of health he says now, and the little remains he counts he has of life, has put an end to his enquiries into philosophical speculations. Though if he were still in the heat of that pursuit he could not be so ignorant of you or himself as to take upon him to be the judge of what you have well considered—much less to be the instructor of a man of your known extraordinary parts and merit. He takes it for a great honor done him that you have condescended to read and consider, as you say, his *Essay* upon the understanding and that you think it worthwhile by your larger views to remove some difficulties and supply some defects that are in it. This, if he had any other end in publishing that treatise but some small service to truth and knowledge, would flatter his vanity. That it would be preserved to posterity by the touches of so great a master, by whose hand it would be redeemed from some of its own imperfections. All of Mr. Locke's

friends have at present the grief to apprehend that they shall enjoy the happiness of his friendship but a little time; the infirmity of ill lungs daily increasing upon him, in an age that is considerable.

I am much pleased Sir to have made you a present, that is both acceptable to you, and that can possibly contribute anything to your enriching the world by the effects of your meditations. If you shall think me worthy of your instruction, or at any time of any communication of your thoughts I shall always (as I ought to do) look upon it as condescension in you which will oblige me to be with the greatest acknowledgment as well as esteem, etc.

## Leibniz to Lady Masham, 30 June 1704

I see that your kindness has made my letter appear passable, even though I saw only too much when writing it, how little satisfaction it should have given to a lady whose discernment is so delicate. And, noticing it even more by your reply, where clarity and support are joined with an extraordinary depth, I am still more uncomfortable with the success of what I am writing. But the honor of your command reassures me, and will excuse me at least.

You have taken the trouble, Madam, to first represent my hypothesis in a few words, to make me judge whether you have understood it well: it is a very useful method in these kinds of discourses; and I admire the accuracy and sharpness of your expressions in such an abstract subject. They are such that I will take advantage of them another time when it comes to explaining myself to someone else.

After that you come to make reflections on these which are certainly worthy of you and deserve that I try to enter into and accommodate my notions to them. First, you give this praise to my hypothesis, that it seems possible to you, that it observes the uniformity of nature, and even that it contains things in conformity with our desires.

But you add, Madam, that it does not appear as yet that it is more than a hypothesis. And although it may be more conceivable than other hypotheses, this does not conclude that it is true, since the *ways of God* are not limited by our conceptions; and though every other way, except one, might appear unintelligible and inconceivable, this one way is not demonstrably proved.

To add my remarks, according to your orders, I would say (1) that it seems to be something considerable that a hypothesis would seem possible, when all the others do not seem to be so, and (2) that it is extremely likely that such a hypothesis is the true one. As a result we have always recognized in astronomy and physics that the most intelligible hypotheses have in the end found to be true: for example, the hypothesis of the earth's motion, to save the appearances of the stars, and that of the weight of air, to account for the suction pumps and other attractions formerly attributed to the fear of the void.

Moreover (3) since our understanding comes from God, and must be considered like a ray of this sun, we must judge that what is most consonant with our understanding (when proceeding in order and since the very nature of the understanding requires it) is consistent with divine wisdom; and judging by this method, we follow the orders God has given us. So we have always found (4) that our judgments, when given according to this natural light, so to speak, have never been belied by the facts; and the oppositions that the Skeptics have made against this, have always been taken by rational people as a game of wits.

But to better come to the point, (5) it is good to consider that the ways of God are of two kinds, some natural, others extraordinary or miraculous. Those that are *natural* are always such that a created mind could conceive them if it had the openings and the opportunities it takes for that; but the *miraculous* ones surpass all created minds. Thus the operation of the magnet is natural, being entirely mechanical or explicable, even though we are perhaps not yet in a state to explain it perfectly in detail, for lack of information; but if someone claimed that the magnet does not operate mechanically and does everything by pure attraction from afar, without means or medium, and without visible or invisible instruments, it would be something inexplicable to any created mind, however penetrating or informed it could be; and in a word, it would be something miraculous. Now the reason and the very order of divine wisdom requires that we should not resort to miracles without

necessity. It is the same here, when it comes to *the system of the union of the soul and the body*, because it is not more explicable to say that a body operates at a distance without means and instruments, than to say that completely different substances, such as the soul and the body, operate immediately on one another, the gap between natures being still greater than the one between places. Thus the communication of these two so heterogeneous substances could not be obtained except by a miracle, any more than the immediate communication of two distant bodies, and wanting to attribute it to some I do not know what influence of one on the other is to hide the miracle under words that signify nothing. The same is true of the way of occasional causes, the difference being only that a perpetual miracle is introduced by the authors of this way, not in secret as in the way of influence, but openly, whether it is admitted or not. For though this action of God, of pushing the soul on the occasion of the body, and the body on the occasion of the soul, would be continual and common, it would be no less miraculous, since it would always be something inexplicable for every created mind, however informed it might be, and an opening that God could give to it, especially since this effect would only depend on God's immediate operation, without providing any other means or explanation, and it is admitted that God would thus continually disturb the laws of the body in order to accommodate it to the soul, and vice versa; instead, what is explicable is in conformity to the natural laws of things, and must be explained only by them.

Thus (6) it seems that my hypothesis is something more than a hypothesis, being not only simply possible, but also the most in conformity with God's wisdom and the order of things. And I think it is safe to say that God always works in the most suitable manner to his perfections, of which wisdom is one of the greatest. Now it is evident that nothing is more beautiful or better directed than that suitable agreement God has established in natural things, and nothing denotes better that it is he who made them, being worthy of him to settle everything in advance, in order to have nothing to do in what follows against his rules in conformity with the nature of things.

Thus it would not be possible for them to agree so perfectly by themselves through a pre-established harmony, if they did not come from a common cause, and if this cause were infinitely powerful and far-sighted, to spread over all things with so much justice.

But what is more, (7) suppose that ordinary things should be done naturally, and not miraculously, it seems that one can say, as a result, that my *hypothesis is demonstrated*. For the other two hypotheses necessarily resort to miracles as I have just shown in no. 5. And one cannot find other hypotheses than these three altogether. For the laws of bodies and souls are disturbed, or they are preserved. If these laws are disturbed (which cannot fail to come from something external), either one of these two things must be disturbing the other, which is the *hypothesis of influence*, common in the Schools; or that it is a third that disturbs them, that is God, in the *hypothesis of occasional causes*. But in the end, if the laws of souls and bodies are conserved without being disturbed, it is the *hypothesis of pre-established harmony*, which is consequently the only natural one.

(8) This preference that must be given to the natural over the miraculous in the ordinary course of nature is something, I think, all philosophers up to now agree on (except for some near-fanatics like Fludd in his Mosaic philosophy). I say this preference is also the reason why I hold that it is not matter that thinks, but a being, simple and apart by itself, that is, independent but joined to matter. It is true that the illustrious Locke maintained in his excellent *Essay* and in his writings against the late Bishop of Worcester that God can give matter the power of thinking, because he can make everything we can conceive happen. But then matter would think only by a perpetual miracle, since there is nothing in matter in itself, that is, in extension and impenetrability, from which thought could be deduced, or upon which it could be based. We can therefore say that the *natural immortality of the soul* is demonstrated and we can maintain its destruction only by maintaining a miracle, either by attributing the power of thinking to matter, a power which is *received and maintained* miraculously—in which

case the soul could perish through the cessation of the miracle—or by wanting the thinking substance, which is distinct from the body, to be annihilated, which would also be miraculous, but a new miracle. Now I say that God, in this case of thinking matter, must not only *give* matter the capacity to think, but he must also *maintain* it continually by the same miracle, since this capacity has no basis, unless God adds a new nature to matter. But if one says that God gives matter this new nature or the radical power to think, since that power is maintained by itself, he would simply have given it a thinking soul, or else something that differs from a thinking soul only by name. And since this radical power is not properly a modification of matter (for modifications are explicable by the natures they modify and this power is not so explicable), it would be independent of matter.

After that, Madam, I come to some important difficulties that came to your mind. You noted, then, that it seems that organs are of no use, if the soul suffices. I reply that if the soul of Caesar (for example) was to be alone in nature, the author of things could have dispensed with giving him organs. But this same author wanted to make an infinity of other beings, who are all contained in one another's organs. Our body is a kind of world full of an infinity of creatures that also deserved to exist, and if our body was not organized, our microcosm or small world would not have all the perfection it must have, and the great world itself would not be so rich as it is.

(10) It is also on this foundation that I said, not absolutely, that the *organism is essential to matter*, but *to matter arranged by a sovereign wisdom*. And it is for this reason that I define the *organism*, or the natural machine, as a machine of which each part is a machine, and consequently that the subtlety of its artifice goes to infinity, nothing being small enough to be neglected, while the parts of our artificial machines are not machines. This is the essential difference between *nature* and *art*, which our moderns did not sufficiently consider.

(11) It still seems to you, Madam, that force cannot be the essence of any substance. This is no doubt because you speak of changeable forces,

such as they are commonly understood. Instead by *primitive force* I mean the principle of action whose changeable forces are only modifications.

(12) The *positive idea* of this simple substance or primitive force is completely discovered, since it must always have in it a regulated progress of perceptions, following the analogy which it must have with our souls.

(13) The question, whether it is *somewhere* or *nowhere*, is a verbal one: for its nature does not consist in extension, but it relates to the extension it represents; thus we must place the soul in the body, where is its point of view according to which it presently represents the universe. To want something more and to enclose souls in dimensions is to want to imagine souls as bodies.

(14) As for complete substances without extension, I believe with you, Madam, that there are none among the creatures, because souls or forms without bodies would be something incomplete, to the extent that, in my opinion, *the soul is never without an animal* or something analogous. And God himself is known to us only by an idea containing a relation to extension, that is, by a continual and orderly variety of things existing at the same time that he produces; also it is only by effects that we manage to know his existence. But the sovereign reason shows us afterwards that there is in him something beyond extension, and which even is its source, as well as changes in it; although this is not something imaginable of which we should not be astonished, for even mathematics furnishes us with an infinity of things that cannot be imagined, witness the *incommensurables* whose truth is however demonstrated. This is why we must not reject truths under the pretext that the imagination cannot reach them. It is not the imagination that gives the limits to assent, and Mr. Locke has shown very well that our ideas of reflection have something that goes beyond the images of the senses.

I am touched, Madam, by the poor health of this excellent person; those who resemble him cannot live too long. If he is still with you, this stay, which can only be charming, will be the best medicine he can use; and the obligation that studious people will have

to you for it (and especially me who hopes by this means to profit still more by his enlightenments on my essays) will be an addition to what the doctrines you have honored by your elaborating on them owe you. I am with respect, etc.

P.S. I just received your beautiful present, Madam, and I am already beginning to enjoy it, which renews my gratitude.

## Lady Masham to Leibniz, 8 August 1704

Whatever allowances are to be made for the language of civility to ladies differ but little from what would look like flattery to one of your own sex; yet I find a pleasure in being praised by you, which I justify to myself from a belief that when you honor me with such expressions of your good opinion, you make me the best return in your power for that well-grounded esteem I have for you, by a desire which that has created in you of finding me worthy of yours. Nor shall I ever reckon it a small matter if I have merit enough to engage those of a distinguished merit to wish that I had more. Thus, if I do flatter myself, I am by a vanity but very little moderated, or rather refined beyond that of others, pleased with the favorable things you say of me, without that cruel allay attending this satisfaction which a consciousness of not resembling the picture you have made for me must otherwise give me.

Whether I have rightly represented your system you best can tell—and I am proud of what you say on that subject—while the inferences you would draw from this to my advantage can give me only a proper acknowledgment for your wishing me so much fitter for your correspondence than I am. But however justly I may have expressed your sense so far as I endeavored to represent it, your answers to some of my enquiries makes me question whether I fully apprehended all that is included in your hypothesis. For I do not yet sufficiently see upon what you ground *organism's being essential to matter*—or indeed very well understand your meaning in these words that organism is not absolutely essential to matter but to matter *arranged by a sovereign wisdom*. What you would build upon this forms a very transcendent conception of the divine artifice—and such as I think could only occur to the thoughts of one possessed with the highest admiration of the wisdom of his maker—but if you infer the truth of this notion only from its being the most agreeable one that you can frame to that attribute of God, this singly seems to me not to be conclusive: since we can in my opinion only infer from this that whatsoever God does must be according to infinite wisdom, but are not able with our short and narrow views to determine what the operations of an infinitely wise being must be.

The *principle of action* called by you *primitive force* is you say a *substance*: of this I still do not perceive the positive idea perception being but the *action* of this substance: what you add concerning its *perceptions*, in these words, *following the analogy it must have with our soul*, makes me again believe that I do not fully understand your scheme: since I thought before that the soul this *primitive force*, or principle of action, had been the same thing. You say that *to enclose souls in dimensions is to want to imagine souls as if they were bodies*. In regard of *extension* this is true; and *extension* is to me inseparable from the notion of all substance. I am yet sensible that we ought not reject truths because they are not imaginable by us (where there is ground to admit them). But truth is but the attributing certain affections conceived to belong to the subject in question. I can by no means attribute any thing to a subject of which I have no conception at all; as I am conscious to myself I do not have of unextended substance. What you give as an instance therefore of *incommensurable lines* does not seem to me to answer the case; for here I do conceive the proposition, and have clear ideas of incommensurable lines, though I do not see the reason of their incommensurability: but of an *unextended substance* I do not have any conception from which I can affirm or deny anything concerning it.

Why you think that there *is no created substance complete without extension*: or that the soul (which you suppose a distinct substance) would without the body be an incomplete substance without extension, I do not understand: but my own belief that there is no unextended substance whatever is (as I have already said) grounded upon this, that I have no con-

ception of such a thing. I cannot yet but conceive two very different substances to be in the universe, though extension alike agrees to them both. For I clearly conceive an extension without *solidity*, and *a solid extension*: to some system of which if it should be affirmed that God did annex *thought*, I see no absurdity in this from there being nothing in *extension* and *impenetrability* or *solidity*, from this thought can *naturally*, or by a train of causes be derived; it cannot be that which I believe to be demonstrable. But that was never supposed by me; and my question in the case would be this: whether God could not as conceivably by us as create an unextended substance, and then unite it to an extended substance (in which, by the way, there is I think on your side two difficulties for one) whether God, I say, could not as conceivably by us as his doing this would be, add (if he so pleased) the *power of thinking* to that substance which has solidity. *Solidity* and *thought* being both of them but attributes of some unknown substance and I do not see why it may not be one and the same which is the common support of both of these; there appearing to me no contradiction in such existence of *thought* and *solidity* in the same substance. Neither can I apprehend it to be more inexplicable that God should give *thought* to a substance which I do not know, but of which I know some of its attributes, than to another, supposed, substance of whose very being I have no conception at all, and that any substance whatsoever should have *thought* belonging to it, or resulting from it, otherwise than as God has willed it shall have so, I cannot apprehend.

That God does in framing and ordering of all his works always make use of the most simple means I do not doubt, this appearing to me most suitable to his wisdom, but whether or not these simple means or methods are always such as not to surpass a created intelligence, I do not know: but am very apt to believe *that God's ways are past our finding out, in this sense*.

I have no sooner scribbled to you these thoughts of mine, than I fear wearying you by my dullness. I shall therefore wave taking notice of anything more that has occurred to me in considering the several parts of your letter; or making any such further inquiries as perhaps were there resolved, I might be able in some measure to clear to myself. I will however now mention to you one difficulty (as I conceive) in your hypothesis, which I do not think that I could ever extricate from it without your assistance and it is to me a very material one. Namely, how to reconcile your system to *liberty* or *free agency*: for though in regard of any compulsion from other causes, we are according thereto *free*, yet I see not how we can be so in respect of the first mover. This I omitted taking notice of in my last letter not only because I thought it too remote an inquiry for one who wanted to be enlightened concerning the very foundation you built upon: but also because I must acknowledge that I cannot make out liberty either with or without any hypothesis whatsoever. Though as being persuaded that I feel myself a *free agent* and that *freedom to act* is necessary to our being accountable for our actions, I not only conclude we are endowed with it, but am very tenacious of this: thus I should be sorry to find from any new hypothesis new difficulties in maintaining of this. I think not much that I need seek to justify to you the part which I own my inclination has in this opinion; since what you have said in print persuades me that you have the same belief with the same bias. I might else perhaps, allege (in my excuse

at least) that as I am a true English woman, I cannot but naturally have a passion for liberty in all senses in which I consider it: and I would not have so much as the philosophy of Hanover unfavorable to any kind of it.

What you write on the subject of Mr. Locke's health, he is much obliged by: and I am no less so when you recommend to me the care of one of the best friends I have in the world as a matter in which you interest yourself. If I could contribute to the prolonging of so valuable a life as his, I should think this one of the best uses I could ever make of my own. He is not only still with me, but in all probability will never have health enough to permit him the thoughts of leaving any more a place which he has made agreeable to others by having for many years chosen to spend therein a great part of his time. Rational conversation with mutual good will has the greatest charms that I know in life, and I have hitherto been very happy in respect of that enjoyment. To my felicity in which kind I think it a considerable addition to be honored with your correspondence at such a distance, and that I am allowed to assure you of my being with great esteem, etc.

# G. W. Leibniz, Preface to the *New Essays* (1703–5)[1]

Since the *Essays on the Understanding*, published by an illustrious Englishman, is one of the finest and most esteemed works of our age, I resolved to comment on it, insofar as I had given sufficient thought for some time to the same subject and to most of the matters touched upon there; I thought that this would be a good opportunity to publish something entitled *New Essays on the Understanding* and to procure a more favorable reception for my thoughts by putting them in such good company. I further thought that I might profit from someone else's work, not only to make my task easier (since, in fact, it is easier to follow the thread of a good author than to work out everything anew), but also to add something to what he has given us, which is always easier than starting from the beginning. It is true that I often hold an opinion different from his, but far from denying on that account the merit of this famous writer, I bear witness to it by showing in what and why, I differ from his view, when I deem it necessary to prevent his authority from prevailing against reason on some important points.

In fact, although the author of the *Essay* says a thousand fine things of which I approve, our systems are very different. His bears more relation to Aristotle's and mine to Plato's, although we both differ in many ways from the doctrines of these two ancients. He is more popular, while I am forced at times to be a little more esoteric and abstract, which is not an advantage to me, especially when writing in a living language. However, I believe that by making two characters speak, one of whom presents the views of the author of the *Essay*, while the other adds my observations, the parallel will be more to the liking of the reader than some dry remarks, whose reading would have to be interrupted at every moment by the necessity of having to return to the author's book in order to understand mine. Nevertheless, it would be

---

1. Translated from the French by R. Ariew and D. Garber in G. W. Leibniz, *Philosophical Essays* (Indianapolis: Hackett Publishing Company, 1989). Leibniz became acquainted with the outline of John Locke's *Essay Concerning Human Understanding* before it was actually published, through an abstract of the book, written by Locke, translated into French, and published in Le Clerc's *Bibliothèque Universelle* (1688). Leibniz read the *Essay* in English, after it was published in 1690, and sent some criticisms of it to Locke through Thomas Burnet (ca. 1635–1715) and Lady Masham (1658–1708). When, in 1700, Pierre Coste's French translation of the *Essay* was published, Leibniz was able to make a thorough study of it; he planned to publish his critique under the title *New Essays on the Understanding*. Locke died in 1704, and Leibniz abandoned his project to publish the work.

good to compare our writings from time to time, and to judge his views by his work alone, even though I have usually retained his expressions. It is true that the constraint of having to follow the thread of someone else's discourse in making my remarks has meant that I could not think of capturing the charm of which the dialogue is capable, but I hope that the content will make up for the defect in style.

Our differences are about subjects of some importance. There is the question about whether the soul in itself is completely empty like tablets upon which nothing has been written [*tabula rasa*], as Aristotle and the author of the *Essay* maintain, and whether everything inscribed on it comes solely from the senses and from experience, or whether the soul contains from the beginning the source [*principe*] of several notions and doctrines, which external objects awaken only on certain occasions, as I believe with Plato and even with the Schoolmen, and with all those who find this meaning in the passage of St. Paul (Romans 2:15) where he states that the law of God is written in our hearts. The Stoics call these principles *Prolepses*, that is, fundamental assumptions, or what is taken as agreed in advance. Mathematicians call them *common notions* [koinai ennoiai]. Modern philosophers give them other fine names, and Julius Scaliger in particular called them the seeds of eternity, and also *zopyra*, meaning living fires, or flashes of light hidden inside us but made to appear through the contact of the senses, like sparks that can be struck from a steel. And it is not unreasonable to believe that these flashes reveal something divine and eternal, something that especially appears in necessary truths. This raises another question, namely, whether all truths depend upon experience, that is, upon induction and instances, or whether some of them have another foundation. For if some occurrences can be foreseen before they have been tested, it is obvious that we contribute something of our own here. Although the senses are necessary for all our actual knowledge, they are not sufficient to give us all of it, since the senses never give us anything but instances, that is, particular or individual truths. Now all the instances confirming a general truth, however numerous they may be, are not sufficient to establish

the universal necessity of that same truth, for it does not follow that what has happened before will always happen in the same way. For example, the Greeks, Romans, and all other people of the earth have always observed that before the passage of twenty-four hours, day changes into night and night into day. But they would have been mistaken if they had believed that the same rule is observed everywhere, since the contrary was observed during a visit to Nova Zembla. And anyone who believed that this is a necessary and eternal truth, at least in our climate, would also be mistaken, since we must recognize that the earth and even the sun do not exist necessarily, and that there may be a time when this beautiful star will no longer exist, at least in its present form, and neither will its whole system. As a result it appears that necessary truths, such as we find in pure mathematics and particularly in arithmetic and geometry, must have principles whose proof does not depend on instances nor, consequently, on the testimony of the senses, although without the senses it would never occur to us to think of them. This is a distinction that should be noted carefully, and it is one Euclid understood so well that he proves by reason things that are sufficiently evident through experience and sensible images. Logic, together with metaphysics and morals, of which the one shapes natural theology and the other natural jurisprudence, are full of such truths, and consequently, their proof can only arise from internal principles, which are called innate. It is true that we must not imagine that we can read these eternal laws of reason in the soul from an open book, as the edict of the praetor can be read from his tablet without effort and scrutiny. But it is enough that they can be discovered in us by dint of attention; the senses furnish occasions for this, and the success of experiments also serves to confirm reason, a bit like empirical trials help us avoid errors of calculation in arithmetic when the reasoning is long. Also, it is in this respect that human knowledge differs from that of beasts. Beasts are purely empirical and are guided solely by instances, for, as far as we are able to judge, they never manage to form necessary propositions, whereas man is capable of demonstrative knowledge [*sciences demonstratives*]. In this, the faculty beasts have for drawing consequences is inferior to the reason humans have. The consequences beasts draw are just like those of simple empirics,[2] who claim that what has happened will happen again in a case where what strikes them is similar, without being able to determine whether the same reasons are at work. This is what makes it so easy for men to capture beasts, and so easy for simple empirics to make mistakes. Not even people made skillful by age and experience are exempt from this when they rely too much on their past experiences. This has happened to several people in civil and military affairs, since they do not take sufficiently into consideration the fact that the world changes and that men have become more skillful in finding thousands of new tricks, unlike the stags and hares of today, who have not become any more clever than those of yesterday. The consequences beasts draw are only a shadow of reasoning; that is, they are only connections of imagination, transitions from one image to another; for, when a new situation appears similar to the preceding one, they expect to find again what was previously joined to it, as though things were linked in fact, just because their images are linked in the memory. It is, indeed, true that reason ordinarily counsels us to expect that we will find in the future that which conforms to our long experience of the past; but this is not, on that account, a necessary and infallible truth, and it can fail us when we least expect it, when the reasons which have maintained it change. This is why the wisest people do not rely on it to such an extent that they do not try to probe into the reason for what happens (if that is possible), so as to judge when exceptions must be made. For only reason is capable of establishing sure rules and of providing what uncertain rules lack by formulating exceptions to them, and lastly, capable of finding connections that are certain in the compulsion [*force*] of necessary consequences. This often provides a way of foreseeing an occurrence without having to experience the sensible links between images, which the beasts are reduced to doing. Thus what justifies the internal principles of necessary truths also distinguishes humans from beasts.

Perhaps our able author will not entirely disagree with my opinion. For after having devoted his whole first book to rejecting innate illumination, understood in a certain way, he admits, however, at the beginning of the second book and in what follows, that the ideas which do not originate in sensation come from reflection. Now, reflection is nothing other than attention to what is within us, and the senses do not give us what we already bring with us. Given this, can anyone deny that there is a great deal innate in our mind, since we are innate to ourselves, so to speak, and since we have within ourselves being, unity, substance, duration, change, action, perception, pleasure, and a thousand other objects of our intellectual ideas? And since these objects are immediate and always present to our understanding (though they may not always be perceived consciously [*aperçus*] on account of our distractions and our needs), why should it be surprising that we say that these ideas, and everything that depends upon them, are innate in us? I have also used the comparison with a block of veined marble, rather than a completely uniform block of marble, or an empty tablet, that is, what the philosophers call a *tabula rasa*. For if the soul were like these empty tablets, truths would be in us as the shape of Hercules is in a block of marble, when the marble is completely indifferent to receiving this shape or another. But if the stone had veins which marked out the shape of Hercules rather than other shapes, then that block would be more determined with respect to that shape and Hercules would be as though innate in it in some sense, even though some labor would be required for these veins to be exposed and polished into clarity by the removal of everything that prevents them from appearing. This is how ideas and truths are innate in us, as natural inclinations, dispositions, habits, or potentialities [*virtualités*] are, and not as actions are, although these potentialities are always accompanied by some corresponding, though often insensible, actions.

Our able author seems to claim that there is nothing *potential* [virtuel] in us, and even nothing that we

---

2. The Empirics were a sect of physicians before Galen (ca. AD 150). In later times, the epithet "Empiric" was given to physicians who despised theoretical study and trusted tradition and their own experience.

are not always actually conscious of perceiving [*ap-percevions*]. But he cannot hold this in all strictness; otherwise his position would be too paradoxical, since, again, acquired habits and the contents of our memory are not always consciously perceived [*apperçues*] and do not even always come to our aid when needed, though often we easily recall them to mind when some trivial occasion reminds us of them, as when we need only the beginning of a song to make us remember the rest. He also limits his thesis in other places, saying that there is nothing in us that we did not at least previously perceive consciously [*apperçu*]. But no one can guarantee by reason alone how far back our past and perhaps forgotten apperceptions can go, especially in view of the Platonists' doctrine of reminiscence, which, fabulous though it is, is not at all incompatible with pure reason. Furthermore, why must it be that everything is acquired by apperceptions of external things and that nothing can be unearthed from within ourselves? Is our soul in itself so empty that, without images borrowed from the outside, it is nothing? This is not, I am convinced, a view our judicious author could approve. Where could one find some tablets which do not have a certain amount of variety in themselves? Will we ever see a perfectly homogeneous and uniform surface? Then why could we not also provide ourselves some object of thought from our own depths, when we are willing to dig there? Thus I am led to believe that, fundamentally, his view on this point is no different from mine, or rather from the common view, insofar as he recognizes two sources of our knowledge, the senses and reflection.

I do not know whether it will be as easy to reconcile him with me and with the Cartesians when he maintains that the mind does not always think, and in particular, that it is without perception during dreamless sleep, and when he objects that since bodies can be without motion, souls can just as well be without thought. But here I reply somewhat differently from what is customary. For I maintain that a substance cannot naturally be without action, and that there is never even any body without motion. Experience already supports me, and to be convinced of this, one need only consult the book of the illustrious Mr. Boyle against absolute rest.[3] But I believe that reason also supports this, and it is one of the proofs I use for refuting atoms. Moreover, there are a thousand indications that allow us to judge that at every moment there is an infinity of perceptions in us, but without apperception and without reflection—that is, changes in the soul itself, which we do not consciously perceive [*appercevons*], because these impressions are either too small or too numerous, or too homogeneous, in the sense that they have nothing sufficiently distinct in themselves; but combined with others, they do have their effect and make themselves felt in the assemblage, at least confusedly. It is in this way that custom makes us ignore the motion of a mill or of a waterfall, after we have lived nearby for some time. It is not that this motion ceases to strike our organs and that there is nothing corresponding to it in the soul, on account of the harmony of the soul and the body, but that the impressions in the soul and in the body, lacking the appeal of novelty, are not sufficiently strong to attract our attention and memory, which are applied only to more demanding objects. All attention requires memory, and when we are not alerted, so to speak, to pay heed to some of our own present perceptions, we let them pass without reflection and without even noticing them. But if someone alerts us to them right away and makes us take note, for example, of some noise we have just heard, we remember it, and we consciously perceive that we just had some sensation of it. Thus there were perceptions that we did not consciously perceive right away, the apperception in this case arising only after an interval, however brief. In order better to recognize [*juger*] these tiny perceptions [*petites perceptions*] that cannot be distinguished in a crowd, I usually make use of the example of the roar or noise of the sea that strikes us when we are at the shore. In order to hear this noise as we do, we must hear the parts that make up this whole; that is, we must hear the noise of each wave, even though each of these small noises is known only in the confused assemblage of all the others, and

3. Robert Boyle, *Discourse about the Absolute Rest in Bodies* (London, 1669).

would not be noticed if the wave making it were the only one. For we must be slightly affected by the motion of this wave, and we must have some perception of each of these noises, however small they may be; otherwise we would not have the noise of a hundred thousand waves, since a hundred thousand nothings cannot make something. Moreover, we never sleep so soundly that we do not have some weak and confused sensation, and we would never be awakened by the greatest noise in the world if we did not have some perception of its beginning, small as it might be, just as we could never break a rope by the greatest effort in the world, unless it were stretched and strained slightly by the least efforts, even though the slight extension they produce is not apparent.

These tiny perceptions are therefore more effectual than one thinks. They make up this I-know-not-what, those flavors, those images of the sensory qualities, clear in the aggregate but confused in their parts; they make up those impressions the surrounding bodies make on us, which involve the infinite, and this connection that each being has with the rest of the universe. It can even be said that as a result of these tiny perceptions, the present is filled with the future and laden with the past, that everything conspires together (*sympnoia panta*, as Hippocrates said), and that eyes as piercing as those of God could read the whole sequence of the universe in the smallest of substances.

*The things that are, the things that have been, and the things that will soon be brought in by the future.*[4]

These insensible perceptions also indicate and constitute the individual, which is individuated [*caractérise*] by the traces which these perceptions preserve of its previous states, connecting it up with his present state. They can be known by a superior mind, even when the individual himself does not sense them, that is, when he no longer has an explicit memory of them. But these perceptions even provide a way of recovering the memory, as needed, through periodic unfoldings which may occur one day. That is why death might only be a state of sleep, and might not even remain one, insofar as the perceptions merely cease to be sufficiently distinct and,

in animals, are reduced to a state of confusion which suspends apperception, but which cannot last forever; I shall not speak here of man, who ought to have great prerogatives in this matter in order to retain his personality.

It is also by means of these insensible perceptions that I explain the marvelous pre-established harmony between the soul and the body, and also between all the monads or simple substances, which takes the place of that untenable influence of the one on the others, and which, in the judgment of the author of the finest of dictionaries,[5] raises the greatness of divine perfections beyond anything ever conceived before. After this I would add little if I said that it is these tiny perceptions which determine us in many situations without our thinking of them, and which deceive the common people by giving the appearance of an *indifference of equilibrium*, as if it made no difference to us, for example, whether we turned right or left. Nor is it necessary for me to point out here, as I've done in the book itself,[6] that they cause this uneasiness, which I show to consist in something that differs from pain only as the small differs from the great, and yet which often brings about our desire and even our pleasure by giving it a kind of spice. The insensible parts of our sensible perceptions also bring about a relation between those perceptions of color, heat, and other sensible qualities, and the motions in bodies that correspond to them. But the Cartesians and our author, penetrating though he is, think of the perceptions we have of these qualities as arbitrary, that is, as if God had given them to the soul according to his good pleasure without having regard to any essential relation between perceptions and their objects, a view which surprises me and seems to me unworthy of the wisdom of the author of things, who does nothing without harmony and reason.

In short, *insensible perceptions* have as much use in philosophy of mind [*Pneumatique*] as corpuscles do in physics; and it is equally unreasonable to reject

---

4. Virgil, *Georgics* IV 393.

5. Pierre Bayle. The reference is to Bayle's discussion of Leibniz in notes H and L to the article "Rorarius" in his *Dictionary*. Bayle's point is that Leibniz's pre-established harmony puts implausibly severe demands on God's power.
6. In the *New Essays* II.23.

the one as the other under the pretext that they are beyond the reach of the senses. Nothing takes place all at once, and it is one of the greatest and best verified maxims that *nature never makes leaps*; this is what I called the *law of continuity* when I once spoke about this in the *Nouvelles de la république des lettres*,[7] and this law is of considerable use in physics. It entails that one always passes from the small to the large and back again through what lies between, both in degrees and in parts, and that a motion never arises immediately from rest nor is it reduced to rest except through a lesser motion, just as we never manage to pass through any line or length before having passed through a shorter one. But until now, those who have given the laws of motion have not observed this law, believing that a body can instantaneously receive a motion opposite to the previous motion. All this can allow us to judge that noticeable perceptions arise by degrees from ones too small to be noticed. To judge otherwise is to know little of the immense subtlety of things, which always and everywhere involves an actual infinity.

I have also noticed that because of insensible variations, two individual things cannot be perfectly alike and must always differ in something over and above number. This puts an end to the empty tablets of the soul, a soul without thought, a substance without action, void space, atoms, and even particles in matter not actually divided, complete uniformity in a part of time, place, or matter, the perfect globes of the second element that derive from the perfect original cubes, and a thousand other fictions of philosophers which arise from their incomplete notions. These are things that the nature of things does not allow, things that are allowed to pass because of our ignorance and lack of attention; they cannot be tolerated unless we limit them to being abstractions of the mind, which protests that it does not deny the things it sets aside, but only judges that they need not enter into consideration at present. If we thought in earnest that things we do not consciously perceive [*s'apperçoit*] are not in the soul or in the body, we would fail in

philosophy as in politics, by neglecting the *mikron*, imperceptible changes. But an abstraction is not an error, provided we know that what we are ignoring is really there. This is similar to what mathematicians do when they talk about the perfect lines they propose to us, uniform motions and other regular effects, although *matter* (that is, the mixture of the effects of the surrounding infinity) always provides some exception. We proceed in this way in order to distinguish various considerations and, as far as is possible, to reduce effects to their reasons, and foresee some of their consequences. For the more careful we are not to neglect any consideration we can subject to rules [*reguler*], the more closely practice corresponds to theory. But only the supreme reason, which nothing escapes, can distinctly understand the whole infinite, all the reasons, and all the consequences. With respect to infinities, we can only know them confusedly, but at least we can distinctly know that they exist; otherwise we would be very poor judges of the beauty and greatness of the universe, just as we would also be unable to develop a good physics which explains the nature of things in general, and still less a good philosophy of mind [*Pneumatique*], which includes the knowledge of God, of souls, and of simple substances in general.

This knowledge of insensible perceptions also serves to explain why and how two souls of the same species, whether human or otherwise, never leave the hands of the creator perfectly alike, and why and how each of them always has its original relation to the point of view it will have in the universe. But this already follows from what I pointed out previously about two individuals, namely that the *difference* between them is always *more than numerical*. There is another significant point on which I must differ, not only from the opinion of our author, but also from those of most of the moderns. I hold with most of the ancients that all spiritual beings [*génies*], all souls, all simple created substances, are always joined to a body, and that souls are never completely separated from bodies. I have *a priori* reasons for this, but this doctrine will be found to have the further advantage that it resolves all the philosophical difficulties about the state of souls, their perpetual conservation, their

---

7. The reference is to "A Letter of Mr. Leibniz on a General Principle Useful in Explaining the Laws of Nature . . . ," which appeared in the July 1687 issue of the *Nouvelles*.

immortality, and their operation. Since the difference between one of their states and another is never, nor has it ever been anything but the difference between the more and the less sensible, between the more and the less perfect (or the other way around), the past or future state of souls is just as explicable as their present one. The slightest reflection is sufficient to show that this is reasonable, and that a leap from one state to an infinitely different one cannot be natural. I am surprised that the schools, by needlessly abandoning nature, have been willing to readily plunge into enormous difficulties, and thus to give free thinkers [*esprits forts*] an opportunity for their apparent triumphs. The arguments of the free thinkers collapse all at once with this explanation of things, in which it is no more difficult to conceive the preservation of souls (or rather, on my view, of the animal), than it is to conceive the change from caterpillar to butterfly and the preservation of thought in sleep, to which Jesus Christ has divinely compared death.[8] Also, I have already said that no sleep can last forever; but it will have less duration or almost no duration at all in the case of rational souls, which are always destined to remain the persons [*personnage*] they were in the city of God, and consequently, to retain their memory, so that they can be better able to receive rewards and punishments. I further add that, in general, no disordering of its visible organs is capable of bringing things in the animal to the point of complete confusion, or to destroy all its organs, and to deprive the soul of the whole of its organic body and of the ineradicable remains of all its preceding traces. But the ease with which people have abandoned the ancient doctrine that angels have subtle bodies (a doctrine which has been confused with the corporality of angels), the introduction of the allegedly separated intelligences among created things (to which the intelligences that rotated Aristotle's heavens have contributed much), and finally the poorly understood opinion some have held that we cannot retain the souls of beasts without falling into metempsychosis, all these in my opinion have resulted in the neglect of the natural way of explaining the preservation of the soul. This has done great harm

---

8. John 11:11.

to natural religion, and has led many to believe that our immortality is nothing but a miraculous grace of God. Our celebrated author speaks with some doubt about this, as I will soon point out. But I wish that all who are of this opinion discussed it as wisely and as sincerely as he does. For it is to be feared that several who speak of immortality through grace merely do so in order to preserve appearances, and are at bottom not very far from those Averroists and certain pernicious Quietists who imagine an absorption and reunion of the soul with the ocean of divinity, a notion whose impossibility is clearly shown by my system alone, perhaps.

It seems, moreover, that we also disagree about matter, insofar as the author judges that the void is necessary for motion, since he believes that the small parts of matter are rigid. I admit that if matter were composed of such parts, motion in a plenum would be impossible; it would be as if a room were filled with a quantity of little pebbles without containing the least empty place. But I cannot grant this assumption, for which there seems to be no reason, even though this able author goes so far as to believe that the rigidity or the cohesion of the small parts constitutes the essence of bodies. Rather, we should conceive of space as filled with matter that was originally fluid, matter capable of any division, and indeed, actually subjected to division and subdivision to infinity, but with this difference, however, that it is unequally divisible and unequally divided in different places because of the motions there, motions which are already more or less harmonious. This brings it about that it has rigidity as well as fluidity everywhere, and that no body is hard or fluid to the ultimate degree, that is, that no atom has insuperable hardness, nor is any mass entirely indifferent to division. The order of nature, and particularly the law of continuity, also destroys both alternatives equally well.

I have also shown that *cohesion*, which is not itself an effect of impulsion or motion, would cause *traction*, properly speaking. For if there were an originally rigid body, an Epicurean atom, for example, which had a part projecting in the form of a hook (since we can imagine atoms in all sorts of shapes), this hook when pushed would pull with it the rest of the atom, that is to say, the part not pushed and not falling within the line of the impulse. However, our able author is himself opposed to those philosophical tractions, like the ones formerly attributed to the fear of the void, and he reduces them to impulses, maintaining with the moderns that one part of matter operates on another only by pushing against it from close by. I think that they are right about this, because otherwise the operation would not be intelligible at all.

I must not, however, conceal the fact that I have noticed a kind of retraction on this point on the part of our excellent author, and I cannot refrain from praising his modest sincerity about it, just as I have admired his penetrating insight on other occasions. His retraction occurs on page 408 of the reply to the second letter of the late Bishop of Worcester, printed in 1699. There, in order to justify the view he maintained against this learned prelate, namely that matter is capable of thought, he says among other things: *"It is true,"* I say *"that bodies operate by impulse and nothing else" (Essay, II, chap. 8, sec. 11). And so I thought when I writ it, and can yet conceive no other way of their operation. But I am since convinced by the judicious Mr. Newton's incomparable book, that it is too bold a presumption to limit God's power, [in this point,] by our narrow conceptions. The gravitation of matter towards matter, by ways inconceivable to me, is not only a demonstration that God can, if he pleases, put into bodies powers and ways of operation, above what can be derived from our idea of body or can be explained by what we know of matter, but also an unquestionable [and everywhere visible] instance, that he has actually done so. And therefore, in the next edition of my book I shall take care to have that passage rectified."*[9] I find in the French version of this book, which was no doubt taken from the latest editions, that sec. 11 reads thus: *It is manifest, at least insofar as we can conceive it, that it is by impulse and nothing else that bodies operate one upon another, it being impossible to conceive that a body should operate on what it does*

not touch, which is all one to imagine that it can operate where it is not.*[10]

I can only praise the modest piety of our famous author, who recognizes that God can do what goes beyond our understanding, and thus, that there may be inconceivable mysteries in the articles of faith. But I would not want us to be obliged to appeal to miracles in the ordinary course of nature, and to admit absolutely inexplicable powers and operations there. Otherwise, on the strength of what God can do, we would grant too much license to bad philosophers, allowing them those *centripetal virtues* or those *immediate attractions* at a distance, without it being possible to make them intelligible; I do not see what would prevent our Scholastics from saying that everything happens simply through faculties and from maintaining their intentional species, which go from objects to us and find a way of entering our souls. If this is acceptable,

What I said could not be will now happen.*[11]

So it seems to me that our author, judicious as he is, is here going rather too much from one extreme to the other. He raises difficulties about the operations of *souls*, when it is merely a matter of admitting what is not *sensible*, while here he grants *bodies* what is not even *intelligible*, allowing them powers and actions beyond everything which, in my opinion, a created mind could do or understand; for he grants them attraction, even at great distances, without limitation to any sphere of activity, and he does so in order to maintain a view which is no less inexplicable, namely the possibility of matter thinking in the natural order of things.*[12]

---

9. *Works* III, 467–68. The two passages in the brackets were omitted in Leibniz's French translation of Locke's text. In addition, Locke talks of "my narrow conceptions" rather than "our narrow conceptions."

10. Leibniz is referring here to Pierre Coste's translation, *Esau Philosophique Concernant l'Entendement Humain*. Published in 1700, the same year as the important 4th edition of the *Essay*, it represents an intermediate stage between the 3rd and 4th editions.

11. Ovid, *Tristia*, I.7.7.

12. In his notes for the preface, Leibniz wrote: "The philosophy of the author destroys what appears to me to be the most important thing, that the soul is imperishable, whereas on his view there must be a miracle for it to endure. This is directly opposed to the Platonic philosophy joined to that of Democritus and Aristotle, such as mine is." *Sämtliche Schriften und Briefe* (Darmstadt and Leipzig, 1923– ), VI, 6, 48.

The question he is discussing with the noted prelate who had attacked him is whether *matter can think*. Since this is an important point, and an important point for the present work as well, I cannot avoid going into it a bit, and taking account of their debate. I shall represent the substance of their dispute and take the liberty of saying what I think of it. The late Bishop of Worcester [Edward Stillingfleet], fearing (but without great cause, in my opinion) that the author's doctrine of ideas was subject to some abuses prejudicial to the Christian faith, undertook to examine some aspects of it in his *Vindication of the Doctrine of the Trinity*. He first gives this excellent writer his due, by recognizing that the writer judges that the existence of the mind is as certain as that of the body, even though as regards these substances, the one is as little known as the other. He then asks (pages 241 seqq.) how reflection could assure us of the existence of the mind if God can give matter the faculty of thinking, as our author believes (Book IV, chap. 3, [sec. 6]) since, as a consequence, the way of ideas, which should serve to discriminate what can belong to the soul or to the body, would become useless. However, it was said in Book II of the *Essay on the Understanding* (chap. 23, sec. 15, 27, 28), that the operations of the soul provide us with the idea of the mind, and that the understanding, together with the will, makes this idea as intelligible to us as the nature of body is made intelligible by solidity and impulse. Here is how our author replies to this in his First Letter (pp. 65 seqq.): [[*I think that I have proved that there is a spiritual substance in us. For*]] *we experiment in ourselves thinking. The idea of this action, or mode of thinking, is inconsistent with the idea of self-subsistence, and therefore has a necessary connection with a support or subject of inhesion: the idea of that support is what we call substance. . . . The general idea of substance being the same everywhere, the modification of thinking, or the power of thinking, joined to it, makes it a spirit, without considering what other modification it has, as whether it has the modification of solidity or not. As, on the other side, substance, that has the modification of solidity, is matter, whether it has the modification of thinking or no. And therefore, if your lordship means by a spiritual,*

*an immaterial substance, I grant I have not proved, nor upon my principles, can it be proved [ . . . ] that there is an immaterial substance in us [ . . . . ] Though I presume, what I have said about the supposition of a system of matter [ . . . ]* (Book IV, chap 10, sec. 16) *(which there demonstrates that God is immaterial) will prove it in the highest degree probable, that the thinking substance in us is immaterial. . . .* [[*Yet I have shown* (adds the author, p. 68)]] *that all the great ends of religion and morality are secured . . . by the immortality of the soul, without a necessary supposition that the soul is immaterial.*[13]

In his *Reply* to this letter, to show that our author was of another opinion when he wrote Book II of the *Essay*, the learned Bishop quotes (p. 51) the following passage (Book II, chap. 23, sec. 15), where it is said that *by the simple ideas we have taken from those operations of our own minds [ . . . ] we are able to frame the complex idea of spirit. And thus, by putting together the ideas of thinking, perceiving, liberty, and power of moving our bodies, we have as clear a [ . . . ] notion of immaterial substances as we have of material.*[14] He further cites other passages to show that the author opposed mind to body. He says (p. 54) that the end of religion and morality is better secured by proving that the soul is immortal by its very nature, that is, immaterial. He further cites this passage (p. 70), that *all the ideas we have of particular, distinct sorts of substances are nothing but several combinations of simple ideas,*[15] and that, consequently, the author believed that the idea of thinking and willing results in a substance different from that given by the idea of solidity and impulse. And he says that in sec. 17 the author remarks that the latter ideas constitute the body as opposed to the mind.

The Bishop of Worcester could have added that from the fact that the general idea of substance is in body and in mind, it does not follow that their differences are *modifications* of a single thing, as our author just said in the passage I cited from his *First*

---

13. *Works* III 33–34. Passages in double brackets are transitional phrases added by Leibniz.
14. In Locke, it was "themselves" rather than "our bodies." In later editions Leibniz added "immaterial" to spirit.
15. *Essay*, II.23.6.

*Letter*. We must distinguish between modifications and attributes. The faculties of having perception and of acting, as well as extension, and solidity, are attributes, or perpetual and principal predicates; but thought, impetuosity, shapes, and motions are modifications of these attributes. Moreover, we must distinguish between the physical (or real) genus and logical (or ideal) genus. The things of the same physical genus, or those which are *homogeneous*, are of the same matter, so to speak, and can often be changed from one into another by changing their modifications, like circles and squares. But two heterogeneous things can have a common logical genus, and then their *differences* are neither simple accidental modifications of a single subject, nor of a single metaphysical or physical matter. Thus time and space are quite heterogeneous things, and we would be wrong to imagine some common real subject I-know-not-what which had only continuous quantity in general and whose modifications resulted in time or space. Yet their common logical genus is continuous quantity. Someone might perhaps make fun of these philosophical distinctions between two genera, the one only logical and the other real, and between two matters, the one physical—that of bodies—and the other only metaphysical or general, as if someone were to say that two parts of space are of the same matter or that two hours are also of the same matter as one another. Yet these distinctions concern not only terms, but also things themselves, and seem to be particularly relevant here, where their confusion has given rise to a false conclusion. These two genera have a common notion, and the notion of real genus is common to both sets of matters, so that their genealogy would be as follows:

GENUS
- the merely *logical*, distinguished by simple *differences*
- the *real*, that is, MATTER, where differences are *modifications*
  - the merely *metaphysical*, in which there is homogeneity
  - the *physical*, in which there is a solid, homogeneous mass

I have not seen the author's *Second Letter* to the bishop; the *Reply* that the prelate makes to it hardly touches the point about the thinking of matter. But our author's *Reply* to this *Second Reply* returns to it. *God* (he says, nearly in these words, page 397) *adds the qualities and perfections that please him to the essence of matter; to some parts [he adds] simple motion, to plants vegetation, and to animals sensation. Those who agree with me so far exclaim against me as soon as I go a step further and say that God may give to matter thought, reason, and volition—as if this would destroy the essence of matter. But to prove this assertion they advance that thought or reason is not included in the essence of matter; this proves nothing since motion and life are not included in it either. They also advance that we cannot conceive that matter can think; but our conception is not the measure of God's power.*[16] After this he quotes the example of the attraction of matter (p. 99, but especially p. 408), in which he speaks of the gravitation of matter toward matter, attributed to Mr. Newton, in the words I quoted above, admitting that we can never conceive how this happens. This is, in fact, a return to occult qualities or, what is more, to inexplicable qualities. He adds (p. 401) that nothing is more apt to favor the skeptics than denying what we don't understand, and (p. 402) that we do not even conceive how the soul thinks. He holds (p. 403) that since the two substances, material and immaterial, can be conceived in their bare essence without any activity, it is up to God to give the power of thinking to the one or to the other. And he wants to take advantage of his adversary's view, which grants sensation to beasts, but does not grant them any immaterial substance. He claims that freedom, self-consciousness (p. 408), and the power of making abstractions can be given to matter, not as matter, but as enriched by divine power. Finally he reports (p. 434) the observation of a traveler as eminent and judicious as Mr. de la Loubere that the pagans of the East know of the immortality of the soul without being able to understand its immateriality.

---

16. This is a paraphrase of *Works* III 460–61.

With regard to all this I will note, before coming to the explanation of my opinion, that it is certain that matter is as little capable of producing sensation mechanically as it is of producing reason, as our author agrees. Furthermore, I note, indeed, that I recognize that we are not allowed to deny what we do not understand, though I add that we have the right to deny (at least in the order of nature) what is absolutely unintelligible and inexplicable. I also maintain that substances (material or immaterial) cannot be conceived in their bare essence without activity, and that activity is of the essence of substance in general. And finally, I maintain that the conception of creatures is not the measure of God's power, but that their conceptivity, or ability [*force*] to conceive, is the measure of nature's power; everything in conformity with the natural order can be conceived or understood by some creature.

Those who understand my system will judge that I will not be in complete agreement with either of these two excellent authors, whose dispute, however, is very instructive. But to explain myself distinctly, one must above all take into account that the modifications which can come naturally or without miracle to a single subject must come to it from the limitations or variations of a real genus or of an original nature, constant and absolute. For this is how in philosophy we distinguish the modes of an absolute being from the being itself; for example, we know that magnitude, shape, and motion are obviously limitations and variations of corporeal nature. For it is clear how a limitation of extension produces shapes, and that the change which takes place there is nothing but motion. And every time we find some quality in a subject, we ought to think that, if we understood the nature of this subject and of this quality, we would understand how this quality could result from that nature. Thus in the order of nature (setting miracles aside) God does not arbitrarily give these or those qualities indifferently to substances; he never gives them any but those which are natural to them, that is to say, those that can be derived from their nature as explicable modifications. Thus we can judge that matter does not naturally have the attraction mentioned above, and does not of itself move on a curved

path, because it is not possible to conceive how this takes place, that is to say, it is not possible to explain it mechanically, whereas that which is natural should be capable of becoming distinctly conceivable, if we were admitted into the secrets of things. This distinction between what is natural and explicable and what is inexplicable and miraculous removes all the difficulties: If we were to reject it, we would uphold something worse than occult qualities, and in doing so we would renounce philosophy and reason, and throw open refuges for ignorance and idleness through a hollow system, a system which admits not only that there are qualities we do not understand (of which there are only too many) but also that there are some qualities that the greatest mind could not understand, even if God provided him with every possible advantage, that is, qualities that would be either miraculous or without rhyme or reason. And it would indeed be without rhyme or reason that God should ordinarily perform miracles, so that this do-nothing hypothesis would equally destroy philosophy, which searches for reasons, and the divine wisdom, which provides them.

As for the question of thinking, it is certain—and our author recognizes in more than one place—that thinking cannot be an intelligible modification of matter, that is, that a sensing or thinking being is not a mechanical thing like a watch or a windmill, in the sense that we could conceive of magnitudes, shapes, and motions whose mechanical conjunction could produce something thinking, and even sensing, in a mass in which there was nothing of the kind, that would likewise cease to be if the mechanism got out of order. Thus it is not natural for matter to sense and to think, and there are only two ways in which it could do so. One of these would be for God to join to it a substance to which thought is natural, and the other would be for God to endow it with thought miraculously. In this, then, I agree entirely with the Cartesians, except that I extend the view to beasts as well, and believe that they have sensation and souls which are, properly speaking, immaterial and as imperishable as the atoms of Democritus or Gassendi. But the Cartesians, who are confused about the souls of beasts, and do not know what to do with them if they are preserved (since it did not occur to them that the animal might be preserved in a reduced form), have been forced to deny them even sensation, contrary to all appearances, and contrary to the judgment of mankind. But if someone said that God, at very least, can add this faculty of thinking to a mechanism properly prepared, I would answer that if this occurred, and if God added this faculty to matter without at the same time endowing it with a substance that was the subject in which this same faculty inhered (as I conceive it), that is, without adding an immaterial soul there, then matter would have to be raised miraculously so as to be capable of receiving a power of which it is not capable naturally, just as some Scholastics claim that God raises fire to the point of giving it the power directly to burn minds separated from matter, which would be a miracle, pure and simple. It is enough that we can maintain that matter thinks only if we attribute to it either an imperishable soul, or else a miracle, and thus, that the immortality of our souls follows from what is natural, since we could then hold that they are destroyed only by miracle, whether by exalting matter or by annihilating the soul. For we know, of course, that the power of God could make our souls mortal, even though they may be immaterial (or immortal by nature alone), since he is capable of annihilating them.

Now the truth of the immateriality of the soul is undoubtedly important. For it is infinitely more useful to religion and morality, especially in our days (when many people have scant respect for revelation by itself or for miracles), to show that souls are naturally immortal, and that it would be a miracle if they were not, than it would be to maintain that our souls must naturally die, and that it is due to a miraculous grace, based solely on God's promise, that they do not die. Moreover, we have known for a long time that those who wished to destroy natural religion, and reduce everything to revelation, as if reason taught us nothing about it, have been held suspect, and not always without reason. But our author is not of their number. He maintains a demonstration of God's existence and he attributes to the immateriality of the soul *a probability of the highest degree*, which may consequently pass for a *moral certainty*, so that I imagine that, having as much sincerity as penetration, he might quite well come to agree with the doctrine I have just expounded, a doctrine fundamental in every reasonable philosophy. For otherwise, I do not see how we can prevent ourselves from falling back into a fanatical philosophy, such as the *Mosaic philosophy* of Fludd, which saves all phenomena by attributing them immediately and miraculously to God, or into a barbaric philosophy, like that of certain philosophers and physicians of former days, who still savored of the barbarism of their own age, and who today are justly despised. They saved the appearances by explicitly fabricating suitable occult qualities or faculties, which were thought to be like little demons or spirits able to do what was required of them without any fuss, just as if pocket watches told time by some faculty of clockness without the need of wheels, or mills crushed grain by a fractive faculty without the need of anything like millstones. As for the difficulty many people have had in conceiving an immaterial substance, it soon ceases (at least in large part) when one no longer requires substances separated from matter; I hold, in fact, that such substances have never existed naturally among created things.

# 5. BERKELEY'S *THREE DIALOGUES, ON MOTION,* AND ASSOCIATED TEXTS

George Berkeley was born in Kilkenny, Ireland, in 1685, attended Kilkenny College from 1696 to 1700 and then Trinity College, Dublin, earning his B.A. in 1704 and his M.A. in 1707; he was then elected a Fellow of Trinity College. An ordained Anglican priest, he traveled first to London in 1713, where Swift presented him at Court and introduced him to Pope, Gay, Addison, and Steele, and then to France and Italy (1713–14 and again 1716–20). In 1728, after marrying Anne Foster, he sailed to Newport, Rhode Island, in hopes of founding a college in Bermuda to train the sons of mainland colonists and Native Americans in religion and the useful arts. After several years of waiting for funds that were promised but never sent, he returned to England in 1731. In 1734 he became Anglican Bishop of Cloyne (in southern Ireland) and remained there until he retired to Oxford in 1752. He died a year later. Throughout the course of his career, he worked in a wide variety of areas of natural philosophy, including optics, mathematics, and physics as well as epistemology and metaphysics. Specifically, he published *An Essay towards a New Theory of Vision* in 1709, *A Treatise concerning the Principles of Human Knowledge* in 1710, *Three Dialogues between Hylas and Philonous* in 1713, *On Motion* in 1721, *Alciphron: or the Minute Philosopher* in 1732, *The Theory of Vision, or Visual Language Vindicated and Explained* in 1733, *The Analyst* in 1734, and *Siris* in 1744.[1]

While the literary form of Berkeley's two best-known philosophical works, namely, the *Principles* and *Three Dialogues* are very different, the doctrines presented in each are virtually identical. The *Principles* begins with a straightforward statement of Berkeley's main principles (in the Introduction and in §§1–33 of Part I) and is then followed by discussions of possible objections one might make to these principles (§§34–84) and of how to understand their consequences (§§85–156), while the *Three Dialogues* takes the form of a spirited debate between Hylas, who attempts to articulate and defend a position that accepts material substance, and Philonous, who represents Berkeley's own idealistic position.

The doctrine for which Berkeley is best known is his thesis that *esse est percipi aut percipere*, that

---

1. For more on Berkeley, see Ian C. Tipton, *Berkeley: The Philosophy of Immaterialism* (London: Methuen, 1974), Robert Merrihew Adams, "Berkeley's 'Notion' of Spiritual Substance," *Archiv für Geschichte der Philosophie* 55 (1973), pp. 47–69, Kenneth Winkler, *Berkeley: An Interpretation* (Oxford: Oxford University Press, 1989), or Margaret Atherton, *Berkeley's Revolution in Vision* (Ithaca: Cornell University Press, 1990).

is, to be is to be perceived or to perceive. In other words, the only things that exist, according to Berkeley, are ideas and the minds (or immaterial spirits) that have them. Most importantly, in both works he argues at length against independently existing material substance (of the sort that Locke accepted, albeit as "something I know not what" that underlies an object's properties and that causes one's ideas of it). The general thrust of Berkeley's argument is that we can have no intelligible (i.e., non-contradictory) conception of such a substance and even if we could form such a conception, we could have no reason (or evidence) for believing that such a substance existed. Such a substance cannot be conceived, because it is contradictory to talk of conceiving of a thing that is unconceived. (Material substance must be "unconceived" insofar as, by definition, it exists independently of any mind.) Even if we could form an idea of such a substance, we have no reason to accept that such a substance exists, since all we ever directly perceive are our ideas as opposed to material substance. Plus, it is admitted by all that our perceptions could be what they are even if no material substance existed at all (e.g., if God caused us to have all the ideas we have). In fact, Berkeley claims important advantages for his theory. For example, it eliminates the problem of skepticism, since one need not worry about whether one's ideas correspond to an external reality (given that external reality is being denied). He also thinks that matter is the main support for atheism and fatalism. Accordingly, rejecting matter takes away support from doctrines that are, in his eyes, dangerous.

One can also see how Berkeley is influenced by and reacts to both Locke and Malebranche. While he seems to agree with Locke's broadly empiricist framework (according to which experience, as opposed to innate ideas, forms the basis for all ideas), he rejects Locke's distinction between primary and secondary qualities. At least part of Locke's motive for drawing the distinction was to show that the ideas we have of at least some qualities, namely secondary qualities (such as color, taste, sound, etc.), do not imply the existence of those qualities in the object on the grounds that they are not required to explain what occurs in these objects (since the primary qualities such as bulk, figure, number, and motion are supposed to suffice for such explanations). Obviously, Berkeley is sympathetic to arguments showing that our ideas of certain properties do not imply the existence of these properties in the object. However, since Berkeley rejects not just secondary qualities, but material substances altogether, he must also reject the primary qualities that are alleged to inhere in them. To this end, he develops many of Locke's arguments against secondary qualities in such a way that they apply to primary qualities as well. In effect, he shows that there is no distinction between our ideas of primary and secondary qualities and thus that a rejection of the one implies a rejection of the other. Of course, without either primary or secondary qualities, there is no content to our notion of material substances.

Given that Berkeley rejects material substances, it is clear that they cannot be invoked to explain the perceptions that minds have. So what does? What causes me to sense this book in front of me, given that the book does not exist independently of me? Berkeley's answer is God. At this point, Berkeley's position might appear to be very close to Malebranche's. Malebranche rejects all causation at the level of finite substances, insisting that God alone is a real cause. This general doctrine then implies that it is God rather than any finite substance (whether material or immaterial) who creates ideas. Malebranche famously develops his epistemology on this basis, claiming that we can have knowledge of objects only through a vision in God, that is, by participating in God's ideas. Obviously, Berkeley is sympathetic to Malebranche's idea that God rather than any material substance causes our ideas of objects (as well as to Malebranche's view of self-consciousness, according to which the mind is aware of itself immediately, i.e., not by way of ideas). His *On Motion*, in particular, can be read as developing the implications of this Malebranchean thesis for physics. However, Berkeley does not accept Malebranche's theory of the vision in God. For, according to Berkeley, "it is evident that the things I perceive are my own ideas," not God's.

The point is often made against Berkeley's idealism (e.g., by his contemporary, Samuel Johnson) that it cannot account for our common sense view of the world: If there are no material substances, no matter or material object that exists independently of me, then the stone that I see in front of me would not hurt my foot in the least, were I to kick it; after all, the stone is merely an idea. However, Berkeley argues that this objection is misplaced. Although the stone is nothing beyond the idea I have, that in no way precludes the pain that I have when I kick it. For the pain, too, is nothing more than an idea. This response follows from Berkeley's more general advice to think with the learned, but to speak with the vulgar. For Berkeley thinks that idealism does not force one to change the way one speaks, though it may force one to change what one understands by what one says; one can say that the stone exists (and that I would hurt my foot if I decided to kick it), but one should not understand this to mean that the stone exists independently of the mind.

# George Berkeley, *A Treatise Concerning the Principles of Human Knowledge* (1710)[1]

## Preface

What I make public here has, after a long and scrupulous inquiry, seemed to me evidently true and not unuseful to be known—particularly to those who are tainted with skepticism or want a demonstration of the existence and immateriality of God or the natural immortality of the soul. Whether it is so or not, I am content the reader should impartially examine, since I do not think myself any further concerned for the success of what I have written than as it is agreeable to truth. But to the end this may not suffer, I make it my request that the reader suspend his judgment until he has, at least, once read the whole through with that degree of attention and thought which the subject matter shall seem to deserve. For as there are some passages that, taken by themselves, are very liable to gross misinterpretation (nor could it be remedied), and to be charged with most absurd consequences, which, nevertheless, upon an entire perusal will appear not to follow from them; so likewise, though the whole should be read over, yet if this is done transiently, it is very probable my sense may be mistaken, but to a thinking reader, I flatter myself, it will be throughout clear and obvious. As for the characters of novelty and singularity, which some of the following notions may seem to bear, it is, I hope, needless to make any apology on that account. He must surely be either very weak or very little acquainted with the sciences, who shall reject a truth that is capable of demonstration, for no other reason but because it is newly known and contrary to the prejudices of mankind. This much I thought fit to premise in order to prevent, if possible, the hasty censures of a sort of men who are too apt to condemn an opinion before they rightly comprehend it.

## Introduction

1. Philosophy being nothing else but the study of wisdom and truth, it may with reason be expected that those who have spent most time and pains in it should enjoy a greater calm and serenity of mind, a greater clearness and evidence of knowledge, and be less disturbed with doubts and difficulties than other men. Yet so it is, we see the illiterate bulk of mankind who walk the high road of plain, common sense, and are governed by the dictates of nature, for the most part easy and undisturbed. To them nothing that is familiar appears unaccountable or difficult to comprehend. They do not complain of any want of evidence in their senses, and are out of all danger

---

1. From *The Works of George Berkeley*, ed. G. N. Wright (London, 1843), 2 vols., English, modified.

of becoming *skeptics*. But no sooner do we depart from sense and instinct to follow the light of a superior principle, to reason, meditate, and reflect on the nature of things, but a thousand scruples spring up in our minds concerning those things which before we seemed fully to comprehend. Prejudices and errors of sense do from all parts discover themselves to our view, and, endeavoring to correct these by reason, we are insensibly drawn into uncouth paradoxes, difficulties, and inconsistencies, which multiply and grow upon us as we advance in speculation, until at length, having wandered through many intricate mazes, we find ourselves just where we were, or, which is worse, sit down in a forlorn skepticism.

2. The cause of this is thought to be the obscurity of things or the natural weakness and imperfection of our understandings. It is said the faculties we have are few and those designed by nature for the support and comfort (pleasure) of life and not to penetrate into the inward essence and constitution of things. Besides, the mind of man being finite, when it treats of things which partake of infinity, it is not to be wondered at if it runs into absurdities and contradictions, out of which it is impossible it should ever extricate itself, it being of the nature of infinite not to be comprehended by that which is finite.

3. But, perhaps, we may be too partial to ourselves in placing the fault originally in our faculties and not rather in the wrong use we make of them. It is a hard thing to suppose that right deductions from true principles should ever end in consequences which cannot be maintained or made consistent. We should believe that God has dealt more bountifully with the sons of men than to give them a strong desire for that knowledge which he had placed quite out of their reach. This would not be agreeable to the accustomed indulgent methods of Providence, which, whatever appetites it may have implanted in the creatures, does usually furnish them with such means as, if rightly made use of, will not fail to satisfy them. Upon the whole I am inclined to think that the far greater part, if not all, of those difficulties which have up to now amused philosophers and blocked up the way to knowledge are entirely owing

to ourselves—that we have first raised a dust and then complain we cannot see.

4. My purpose, therefore, is to try if I can discover what those principles are which have introduced all that doubtfulness and uncertainty, those absurdities and contradictions into the several sects of philosophy, inasmuch as the wisest men have thought our ignorance incurable, conceiving it to arise from the natural dullness and limitation of our faculties. And surely it is a work well deserving our pains to make a strict inquiry concerning the first principles of *human knowledge*, to sift and examine them on all sides, especially since there may be some grounds to suspect that those obstacles and difficulties which stay and embarrass the mind in its search after truth do not spring from any darkness and intricacy in the objects or natural defect in the understanding so much as from false principles which have been insisted on and might have been avoided.

5. However difficult and discouraging this attempt may seem when I consider how many great and extraordinary men have gone before me in the same designs, yet I am not without some hopes, upon the consideration that the largest views are not always the clearest, and that he who is shortsighted will be obliged to draw the object nearer, and may, perhaps, by a close and narrow survey discern that which had escaped far better eyes.

6. In order to prepare the mind of the reader for the easier conceiving what follows it is proper to premise somewhat, by way of introduction, concerning the nature and abuse of language. But unraveling this matter leads me in some measure to anticipate my design by taking notice of what seems to have had a chief part in rendering speculation intricate and perplexed and to have occasioned innumerable errors and difficulties in almost all parts of knowledge. And that is the opinion that the mind has a power of framing *abstract ideas* or notions of things. He who is not a perfect stranger to the writings and disputes of philosophers must necessarily acknowledge that no small part of them are spent about abstract ideas. These are in a more especial manner thought to be the object of those sciences which go by the name of *logic* and *metaphysics* and of all that which passes

under the notion of the most abstracted and sublime learning, in all of which one shall scarce find any question handled in such a manner as does not suppose their existence in the mind and that it is well acquainted with them.

7. It is agreed on all hands that the qualities or modes of things never do really exist each of them apart by itself and separated from all others, but are mixed, as it were, and blended together, several in the same object. But we are told the mind, being able to consider each quality singly or abstracted from those other qualities with which it is united, does by that means frame abstract ideas to itself. For example, there is perceived by sight an object extended, colored, and moved; this mixed or compound idea the mind resolving into its simple, constituent parts, and viewing each by itself, exclusive of the rest, does frame the abstract ideas of extension, color, and motion. Not that it is possible for color or motion to exist without extension, but only that the mind can frame to itself by *abstraction* the idea of color exclusive of extension and of motion exclusive of both color and extension.

8. Again, the mind having observed that, in the particular extensions perceived by sense, there is something common and alike in all, and some other things peculiar as this or that figure or magnitude, which distinguish them one from another, it considers apart or singles out by itself that which is common, making thereof a most abstract idea of extension, which is neither line, surface, nor solid, nor has any figure or magnitude, but is an idea entirely prescinded from all these. So likewise the mind, by leaving out of the particular colors perceived by sense that which distinguishes them one from another and retaining that only which is common to all, makes an idea of color in abstract which is neither red, nor blue, nor white, nor any other determinate color. And, in like manner, by considering motion abstractly not only from the body moved, but likewise from the figure it describes and all particular directions and velocities, the abstract idea of motion is framed—which equally corresponds to all particular motions whatsoever that may be perceived by sense.

9. And as the mind frames to itself abstract ideas of qualities or modes, so it does, by the same precision or mental separation, attain abstract ideas of the more compounded beings, which include several coexistent qualities. For example, the mind, having observed that *Peter*, *James*, and *John* resemble each other in certain common agreements of shape and other qualities, leaves out of the complex or compounded idea it has of *Peter*, *James*, and any other particular man that which is peculiar to each, retaining only what is common to all, and so makes an abstract idea in which all the particulars equally partake, abstracting entirely from and cutting off all those circumstances and differences which might determine it to any particular existence. And after this manner it is said we come by the abstract idea of *man* or, if you please, humanity or human nature, in which it is true there is included color, because there is no man but has some color; but then it can be neither white, nor black, nor any particular color, because there is no one particular color in which all men partake. So likewise there is included stature, but then it is neither tall stature nor short stature, nor yet middle stature, but something abstracted from all these. And so of the rest. Moreover, there being a great variety of other creatures that partake in some parts, but not all, of the complex idea of *man*, the mind, leaving out those parts which are peculiar to men and retaining those only which are common to all the living creatures, frames the idea of *animal* which abstracts not only from all particular men, but also all birds, beasts, fishes, and insects. The constituent parts of the abstract idea of animal are body, life, sense, and spontaneous motion. By *body* is meant body without any particular shape or figure, there being no one shape or figure common to all animals without covering either of hair or feathers, or scales, etc., nor yet naked—hair, feathers, scales, and nakedness being the distinguishing properties of particular animals, and, for that reason, left out of the *abstract idea*. Upon the same account the spontaneous motion must be neither walking, nor flying, nor creeping; it is nevertheless a motion, but what that motion is, it is not easy to conceive.

10. Whether others have this wonderful faculty of *abstracting their ideas* they best can tell, for myself I find indeed I have a faculty of imagining, or representing to myself the ideas of those particular things I have perceived and of variously compounding and dividing them. I can imagine a man with two heads or the upper parts of a man joined to the body of a horse. I can consider the hand, the eye, the nose, each by itself abstracted or separated from the rest of the body. But then whatever hand or eye I imagine, it must have some particular shape and color. Likewise the idea of man that I frame to myself must be either of a white or a black or a tawny, a straight or a crooked, a tall or a short or a middle-sized man. I cannot by any effort of thought conceive the abstract idea above described. And it is equally impossible for me to form the abstract idea of motion distinct from the body moving, and which is neither swift nor slow, curvilinear nor rectilinear; and the like may be said of all other abstract general ideas whatsoever. To be plain, I admit myself able to abstract in one sense, as when I consider some particular parts or qualities separated from others with which, though they are united in some object, yet it is possible they may really exist without them. But I deny that I can abstract one from another or conceive separately those qualities which it is impossible should exist so separated or that I can frame a general notion by abstracting from particulars in the manner aforesaid—which two last are the proper meanings of *abstraction*. And there are grounds to think most men will acknowledge themselves to be in my case. The generality of men which are simple and illiterate never pretend to *abstract notions*. It is said they are difficult and not to be attained without pains and study. We may therefore reasonably conclude that if there are such, they are confined only to the learned.

11. I proceed to examine what can be alleged in defense of the doctrine of abstraction and try if I can discover what it is that inclines the men of speculation to embrace an opinion so remote from common sense as that seems to be. There has been a late deservedly esteemed philosopher who, no doubt, has given it very much countenance by seeming to think that having abstract general ideas is what puts the widest difference in point of understanding between man and beast.[2] "The having of general ideas," he says, "is that which puts a perfect distinction between man and brutes, and is an excellency which the faculties of brutes do by no means attain unto. For it is evident we observe no footsteps in them of making use of general signs for universal ideas, from which we have reason to imagine that they do not have the faculty of *abstracting* or making general ideas, since they have no use of words or any other general signs." And a little after: "Therefore, I think, we may suppose that it is in this that the species of brutes are discriminated from men, and it is that proper difference in which they are wholly separated, and which at last widens to so wide a distance. For if they have any ideas at all, and are not bare machines (as some would have them), we cannot deny them to have some reason. It seems as evident to me that they do some of them in certain instances reason as that they have sense, but it is only in particular ideas, just as they receive them from their senses. They are the best of them tied up within those narrow bounds, and have not (as I think) the faculty to enlarge them by any kind of *abstraction*." *Essay on Human Understanding* II, chap. 9, sec. 10, 11. I readily agree with this learned author that the faculties of brutes can by no means attain to *abstraction*. But then if this is made the distinguishing property of that sort of animals, I fear a great many of those that pass for men must be reckoned into their number. The reason that is here assigned why we have no grounds to think brutes have abstract general ideas is that we observe in them no use of words or any other general signs, which is built on this supposition, namely, that the making use of words implies the having general ideas. From this it follows that men who use language are able to abstract or generalize their ideas. That this is the sense and argument of the author will further appear by his answering the question he puts in another place. "Since all things that exist are only particulars, how do we come by general terms?" His answer is, "Words become general by being made the signs of general ideas." *Essay on Human Understanding* III, chap. 3, sec. 6. But to this I cannot assent, for

_____

2. Berkeley is referring to Locke.

it seems that a word becomes general by being made the sign, not of an abstract general idea, but of several particular ideas, any one of which it indifferently suggests to the mind. For example, when it is said *the change of motion is proportional to the impressed force*, or that *whatever has extension is divisible*, these propositions are to be understood of motion and extension in general, and nevertheless it will not follow that they suggest to my thoughts an idea of motion without a body moved or any determinate direction and velocity, or that I must conceive an abstract general idea of extension, which is neither line, surface, nor solid, neither great nor small, black, white, nor red, nor of any other determinate color. It is only implied that whatever motion I consider, whether it is swift or slow, perpendicular, horizontal, or oblique, or in whatever object, the axiom concerning it holds equally true. As does the other of every particular extension, it does not matter whether line, surface, or solid, whether of this or that magnitude or figure.

12. By observing how ideas become general, we may the better judge how words are made so. And here it is to be noted that I do not deny absolutely there are general ideas, but only that there are any *abstract general ideas*, for, in the passages above quoted, in which there is mention of general ideas, it is always supposed that they are formed by abstraction, after the manner set forth in sec. 8 and 9. Now, if we will annex a meaning to our words and speak only of what we can conceive, I believe we shall acknowledge that an idea, which considered in itself is particular, becomes general by being made to represent or stand for all other particular ideas of the same sort. To make this plain by an example, suppose a geometrician is demonstrating the method of cutting a line in two equal parts. He draws, for instance, a black line of an inch in length; this, which in itself is a particular line, is nevertheless with regard to its signification general, since, as it is used there, it represents all particular lines whatsoever, so that what is demonstrated of it is demonstrated of all lines or, in other words, of a line in general. And as that particular line becomes general by being made a sign, so the name *line*, which, taken absolutely is particular, by being a sign is made general. And as the former owes

its generality not to its being the sign of an abstract or general line, but of all particular right lines that may possibly exist, so the latter must be thought to derive its generality from the same cause, namely, the various particular lines which it indifferently denotes.

13. To give the reader a yet clearer view of the nature of abstract ideas and the uses they are thought necessary to, I shall add one more passage out of the *Essay on Human Understanding*, which is as follows. "*Abstract ideas* are not so obvious or easy to children or the yet unexercised mind as particular ones. If they seem so to grown men, it is only because by constant and familiar use they are made so. For when we nicely reflect upon them, we shall find that general ideas are fictions and contrivances of the mind that carry difficulty with them, and do not so easily offer themselves as we are apt to imagine. For example, does it not require some pains and skill to form the general idea of a triangle? (which is yet none of the most abstract, comprehensive, and difficult) for it must be neither oblique nor rectangle, neither equilateral, isosceles, nor scalene, but *all and none* of these at once. In effect, it is something imperfect that cannot exist, an idea in which some parts of several different and *inconsistent* ideas are put together. It is true the mind in this imperfect state has need of such ideas, and makes all the haste to them it can, for the convenience of communication and enlargement of knowledge, to both which it is naturally very much inclined. But yet one has reason to suspect such ideas are marks of our imperfection. At least this is enough to show that the most abstract and general ideas are not those that the mind is first and most easily acquainted with, nor such as its earliest knowledge is conversant about." IV, chap. 7, sec. 9. If any man has the faculty of framing in his mind such an idea of a triangle as is here described, it is in vain to pretend to dispute him out of it, nor would I go about it. All I desire is that the reader would fully and certainly inform himself whether he has such an idea or not. And this, I think, can be no hard task for anyone to perform. What is more easy than for anyone to look a little into his own thoughts and there try whether he has, or can attain to have, an idea that shall correspond with the description that is here given of the

general idea of a triangle, which is *neither oblique, nor rectangle, equilateral, isosceles, nor scalene, but all and none of these at once?*

14. Much is here said of the difficulty that abstract ideas carry with them and the pains and skill requisite to the forming them. And it is on all hands agreed that there is need of great toil and labor of the mind to emancipate our thoughts from particular objects and raise them to those sublime speculations that are conversant about abstract ideas, from all of which the natural consequence should seem to be that so difficult a thing as forming abstract ideas was not necessary for *communication*, which is so easy and familiar to all sorts of men. But, we are told, if they seem obvious and easy to grown men, *it is only because by constant and familiar use they are made so.* Now I would gladly know at what time it is men are employed in surmounting that difficulty and furnishing themselves with those necessary helps for discourse. It cannot be when they are grown up, for then it seems they are not conscious of any such pains-taking; it remains, therefore, to be the business of their childhood. And surely the great and multiplied labor of framing abstract notions will be found a hard task for that tender age. Is it not a hard thing to imagine that a couple of children cannot chatter together about their sugarplums, and rattles, and the rest of their little trinkets, until they have first tacked together countless inconsistencies and so framed in their minds *abstract general ideas* and annexed them to every common name they make use of?

15. Nor do I think them a whit more needful for the *enlargement of knowledge* than for *communication*. It is, I know, a point much insisted on, that all knowledge and demonstration are about universal notions, to which I fully agree, but then it does not appear to me that those notions are formed by *abstraction* in the manner premised; *universality*, so far as I can comprehend, not consisting in the absolute, positive nature or conception of anything, but in the relation it bears to the particulars signified or represented by it, by virtue of which it is the case that things, names, or notions, being in their own nature *particular*, are rendered *universal*. Thus, when I demonstrate any proposition concerning triangles, it is to

be supposed that I have in view the universal idea of a triangle, which ought not be understood as if I could frame an idea of a triangle which was neither equilateral, nor scalene, nor isosceles, but only that the particular triangle I consider—whether of this or that sort it does not matter—does equally stand for and represent all rectilinear triangles whatsoever, and is in that sense *universal*. All this seems very plain and not to include any difficulty in it.

16. But here it will be demanded how we can know any proposition to be true of all particular triangles, except we have first seen it demonstrated of the abstract idea of a triangle which equally agrees to all? For, because a property may be demonstrated to agree to some one particular triangle, it will not then follow that it equally belongs to any other triangle which in all respects is not the same with it. For example, having demonstrated that the three angles of an isosceles rectangular triangle are equal to two right ones, I cannot therefore conclude this affection agrees to all other triangles, which have neither a right angle nor two equal sides. It seems therefore that to be certain this proposition is universally true we must either make a particular demonstration for every particular triangle, which is impossible, or once and for all demonstrate it of the *abstract idea of a triangle*, in which all the particulars do indifferently partake and by which they are all equally represented. To which I answer that, though the idea I have in view while I make the demonstration is, for instance, that of an isosceles rectangular triangle whose sides are of a determinate length, I may nevertheless be certain it extends to all other rectilinear triangles of whatever sort or bigness—and that because neither the right angle, nor the equality, nor determinate length of the sides are at all concerned in the demonstration. It is true the diagram I have in view includes all these particulars, but then there is not the least mention made of them in the proof of the proposition. It is not said the three angles are equal to two right ones because one of them is a right angle or because the sides comprehending it are of the same length. This sufficiently shows that the right angle might have been oblique and the sides unequal, and for all that the demonstration has held good. And for this reason

it is that I conclude that to be true of any obliquangular or scalene, which I had demonstrated of a particular right-angled, isosceles triangle, and not because I demonstrated the proposition of the abstract idea of a triangle. And here it must be acknowledged that a man may consider a figure merely as triangular, without attending to the particular qualities of the angles or relations of the sides. So far he may abstract, but this will never prove that he can frame an abstract general inconsistent idea of a triangle. In like manner we may consider *Peter* insofar as he is a man or insofar as he is an animal without framing the aforementioned abstract idea either of man or of animal inasmuch as all that is perceived is not considered.

17. It would be an endless as well as a useless thing, to trace the *schoolmen*, those great masters of abstraction, through all the manifold, inextricable labyrinths of error and dispute which their doctrine of abstract natures and notions seems to have led them into. What bickerings and controversies, and what a learned dust has been raised about those matters, and what mighty advantage has been derived to mankind from this, are things at this day too clearly known to need being insisted on. And it had been well if the ill effects of that doctrine were confined to those only who make the most avowed profession of it. When men consider the great pains, industry, and parts that have, for so many ages, been laid out on the cultivation and advancement of the sciences, and that notwithstanding all this the far greater part of them remain full of darkness and uncertainty, and disputes that are likely never to have an end, and even those that are thought to be supported by the most clear and cogent demonstrations, contain in them paradoxes which are perfectly irreconcilable to the understandings of men, and that, taking all together, a small portion of them does supply any real benefit to mankind, otherwise than by being an innocent diversion and amusement—I say, the consideration of all this is apt to throw them into a despondency and perfect contempt of all study. But this may perhaps cease, upon a view of the false principles that have obtained in the world, among all of which there is none, I think, has a more wide influence over the thoughts of speculative men than this of abstract general ideas.

18. I come now to consider the *source* of this prevailing notion, and that seems to me to be language. And surely nothing of less extent than reason itself could have been the source of an opinion so universally received. The truth of this appears as from other reasons so also from the plain confession of the ablest patrons of abstract ideas, who acknowledge that they are made in order to naming—from which it is a clear consequence that if there had been no such thing as speech or universal signs, there never had been any thought of abstraction. See book III, chap. 6, sec. 39, and elsewhere, of the *Essay on Human Understanding*. Let us therefore examine the manner in which words have contributed to the origin of that mistake. First, then, it is thought that every name has, or ought to have, only one precise and settled signification, which inclines men to think there are certain *abstract, determinate ideas*, which constitute the true and only immediate signification of each general name. And that it is by the mediation of these abstract ideas that a general name comes to signify any particular thing. Whereas, in truth, there is no such thing as one precise and definite signification annexed to any general name, they all signifying indifferently a great number of particular ideas—all of which does evidently follow from what has been already said and will clearly appear to anyone by a little reflection. To this it will be objected that every name that has a definition is thereby restrained to one certain signification. For example, a *triangle* is defined to be a *plain surface comprehended by three right lines*, by which that name is limited to denote one certain idea and no other. To this I answer that in the definition it is not said whether the surface is great or small, black or white, nor whether the sides are long or short, equal or unequal, nor with what angles they are inclined to each other, in all of which there may be great variety, and consequently there is no one settled idea which limits the signification of the word *triangle*. It is one thing to keep a name constantly to the same definition and another to make it stand everywhere for the same idea—the one is necessary, the other useless and impracticable.

19. Secondly, but to give a further account how words came to produce the doctrine of abstract ideas, it must be observed that it is a received opinion that language has no other end but the communicating of our ideas and that every significant name stands for an idea. This being so, and it being in addition certain that names which yet are not thought altogether insignificant do not always mark out particular conceivable ideas, it is straightway concluded that they stand for abstract notions. That there are many names in use among speculative men which do not always suggest to others determinate particular ideas is what nobody will deny. And a little attention will discover that it is not necessary (even in the strictest reasonings) that significant names which stand for ideas should, every time they are used, excite in the understanding the ideas they are made to stand for—in reading and discoursing, names being for the most part used as letters are in *algebra*, in which, though a particular quantity is marked by each letter, yet to proceed right it is not requisite that in every step each letter suggest to your thoughts that particular quantity it was appointed to stand for.

20. Besides, the communicating of ideas marked by words is not the chief and only end of language, as is commonly supposed. There are other ends such as the raising of some passion, the exciting to or deterring from an action, the putting the mind in some particular disposition—to which the former is in many cases barely subservient, and sometimes entirely omitted, when these can be obtained without it, as I think does not infrequently happen in the familiar use of language. I entreat the reader to reflect with himself and see if it does not often happen either in hearing or reading a discourse that the passions of fear, love, hatred, admiration, disdain, and the like, arise immediately in his mind upon the perception of certain words without any ideas coming between. At first, indeed, the words might have occasioned ideas that were fit to produce those emotions; but, if I am not mistaken, it will be found that when language is once grown familiar, the hearing of the sounds or sight of the characters is often immediately attended with those passions which at first were accustomed to be produced by the intervention of ideas that are now

quite omitted. May we not, for example, be affected with the promise of a *good thing*, though we do not have an idea of what it is? Or is not being threatened with danger sufficient to excite a dread, though we do not think of any particular evil likely to befall us, nor yet frame to ourselves an idea of danger in abstract? If anyone shall join ever so little reflection of his own to what has been said, I believe it will evidently appear to him that general names are often used in the propriety of language without the speaker's designing them for marks of ideas in his own which he would have them raise in the mind of the hearer. Even proper names themselves do not seem always spoken with a design to bring into our view the ideas of those individuals that are supposed to be marked by them. For example, when a schoolman tells me "Aristotle has said it," all I conceive he means by it is to dispose me to embrace his opinion with the deference and submission which custom has annexed to that name. And this effect may be so instantly produced in the minds of those who are accustomed to resign their judgment to the authority of that philosopher, as it is impossible any idea either of his person, writings, or reputation should go before. Innumerable examples of this kind may be given, but why should I insist on those things which everyone's experience will, I do not doubt, plentifully suggest unto him?

21. We have, I think, shown the impossibility of *abstract ideas*. We have considered what has been said for them by their ablest patrons, and endeavored to show they are of no use for those ends to which they are thought necessary. And lastly, we have traced them to the source from which they flow, which appears to be language. It cannot be denied that words are of excellent use in that by their means all that stock of knowledge which has been purchased by the joint labors of inquisitive men in all ages and nations may be drawn into the view and made the possession of one single person. But at the same time it must be admitted that most parts of knowledge have been strangely perplexed and darkened by the abuse of words and general ways of speech in which they are delivered. Since, therefore, words are so apt to impose on understanding whatever ideas I consider, I shall endeavor to take them bare and naked into

my view, keeping out of my thoughts, so far as I am able, those names which long and constant use has so strictly united with them—from which I may expect to derive the following advantages:

22. First, I shall be sure to get clear of all controversies purely verbal—the springing up of which weeds in almost all the sciences has been a main hindrance to the growth of true and sound knowledge. Secondly, this seems to be a sure way to extricate myself out of that fine and subtle net of *abstract ideas* which has so miserably perplexed and entangled the minds of men; and that with this peculiar circumstance, that by how much the finer and more curious was the wit of any man, by so much the deeper was he like to be ensnared and faster held there. Thirdly, so long as I confine my thoughts to my own ideas divested of words, I do not see how I can be easily mistaken. The objects I consider I clearly and adequately know. I cannot be deceived in thinking I have an idea which I do not have. It is not possible for me to imagine that any of my own ideas are alike or unlike that are not truly so. To discern the agreements or disagreements that are between my ideas, to see what ideas are included in any compound idea and what not, there is nothing more requisite than an attentive perception of what passes in my own understanding.

23. But the attainment of all these advantages does presuppose an entire deliverance from the deception of words, which I dare hardly promise myself—so difficult a thing it is to dissolve a union so early begun and confirmed by so long a habit as that between words and ideas. This difficulty seems to have been very much increased by the doctrine of *abstraction*. For so long as men thought abstract ideas were annexed to their words, it does not seem strange that they should use words for ideas, it being found an impracticable thing to lay aside the word and retain the abstract idea in the mind, which in itself was perfectly inconceivable. This seems to me the principal cause why those men who have so emphatically recommended to others the laying aside all use of words in their meditations and contemplating their bare ideas have yet failed to perform it themselves. Of late many have been very sensible of the absurd opinions and insignificant disputes which grow out of the abuse of words. And in order to remedy these evils they advise well that we attend to the ideas signified and draw off our attention from the words which signify them. But however good this advice may be they have given others, it is plain they could not have a due regard to it themselves so long as they thought the only immediate use of words was to signify ideas and that the immediate signification of every general name was a *determinate, abstract idea*.

24. But, these being known to be mistakes, a man may with greater ease prevent his being imposed on by words. He who knows he has no other than *particular* ideas will not puzzle himself in vain to find out and conceive the *abstract* idea annexed to any name. And he who knows names do not always stand for ideas will spare himself the labor of looking for ideas where there are none to be had. It is, therefore, to be wished that everyone would use his utmost endeavors to obtain a clear view of the ideas he would consider, separating from them all that dress and encumbrance of words which so much contribute to blind the judgment and divide the attention. In vain do we extend our view into the heavens and pry into the entrails of the earth, in vain do we consult the writings of learned men and trace the dark footsteps of antiquity; we need only draw the curtain of words to behold the fairest tree of knowledge, whose fruit is excellent and within the reach of our hand.

25. Unless we take care to clear the first principles of knowledge from the embarrassment and delusion of words, we may make infinite reasonings upon them to no purpose; we may draw consequences from consequences and be never the wiser. The further we go, we shall only lose ourselves the more irrecoverably and be the deeper entangled in difficulties and mistakes. Whoever, therefore, designs to read the following sheets, I entreat him to make my words the occasion of his own thinking and endeavor to attain the same train of thoughts in reading that I had in writing them. By this means it will be easy for him to discover the truth or falsity of what I say. He will be out of all danger of being deceived by my words and I do not see how he can be led into an error by considering his own naked, undisguised ideas.

## Part I

1. It is evident to anyone who takes a survey of the objects of human knowledge that they are either ideas actually imprinted on the senses or else such as are perceived by attending to the passions and operations of the mind or, lastly, ideas formed by help of memory and imagination, either compounding, dividing, or barely representing those originally perceived in the aforesaid ways. By sight I have the ideas of light and colors with their several degrees and variations. By touch I perceive, for example, hard and soft, heat and cold, motion and resistance, and of all these more and less either as to quantity or degree. Smelling furnishes me with odors, the palate with tastes, and hearing conveys sounds to the mind in all their variety of tone and composition. And as several of these are observed to accompany each other, they come to be marked by one name, and so to be reputed as one thing. Thus, for example, a certain color, taste, smell, figure, and consistency having been observed to go together are accounted one distinct thing and signified by the name *apple*. Other collections of ideas constitute a stone, a tree, a book, and the like sensible things—which as they are pleasing or disagreeable excite the passions of love, hatred, joy, grief, and so forth.

2. But, besides all that endless variety of ideas or objects of knowledge, there is likewise something which knows or perceives them and exercises various operations as willing, imagining, remembering about them. This perceiving, active being is what I call *mind, spirit, soul,* or *myself,* by which words I do not denote any one of my ideas, but a thing entirely distinct from them, in which they exist or, which is the same thing, by which they are perceived—for the existence of an idea consists in being perceived.

3. That neither our thoughts, nor passions, nor ideas formed by the imagination exist without the mind is what everybody will allow. And (to me) it seems no less evident that the various sensations or ideas imprinted on the sense, however blended or combined together (that is, whatever objects they compose), cannot exist otherwise than in a mind perceiving them. I think an intuitive knowledge may be obtained of this by anyone who shall attend to what is meant by the term *exist* when applied to sensible things. The table I write on, I say, exists; that is, I see and feel it; and if I were out of my study I should say it existed—meaning by that that if I was in my study I might perceive it, or that some other spirit actually does perceive it. There was an odor; that is, it was smelled; there was a sound, that is to say, it was heard; a color or figure, and it was perceived by sight or touch. This is all that I can understand by these and the like expressions. For as to what is said of the absolute existence of unthinking things without any relation to their being perceived that seems perfectly unintelligible. Their *esse* is *percipi*, nor is it possible they should have any existence out of the minds or thinking things which perceive them.

4. It is indeed an opinion strangely prevailing among men that houses, mountains, rivers, and, in a word, sensible objects have an existence, natural or real, distinct from their being perceived by the understanding. But with however great an assurance and acquiescence this principle may be entertained in the world, yet whoever shall find in his heart to call it in question may, if I am not mistaken, perceive it to involve a manifest contradiction. For what are the aforementioned objects but the things we perceive by sense? And what do we perceive besides our own ideas or sensations? And is it not plainly repugnant that any one of these or any combination of them should exist unperceived?

5. If we thoroughly examine this tenet, it will, perhaps, be found at bottom to depend on the doctrine of *abstract ideas*. For can there be a nicer strain of abstraction than to distinguish the existence of sensible objects from their being perceived, so as to conceive them existing unperceived? Light and colors, heat and cold, extension and figures—in a word, the things we see and feel—what are they but so many sensations, notions, ideas, or impressions on the sense? And is it possible to separate, even in thought, any of these from perception? For my part I might as easily divide a thing from itself. I may indeed divide in my thoughts or conceive apart from each other those things which, perhaps, I never perceived by sense so divided. Thus I imagine the trunk of a human body without the limbs or conceive the smell of

a rose without thinking of the rose itself. So far I will not deny I can abstract, if that may properly be called *abstraction* which extends only to the conceiving separately such objects as it is possible may really exist or be actually perceived asunder. But my conceiving or imagining power does not extend beyond the possibility of real existence or perception. Hence, as it is impossible for me to see or feel anything without an actual sensation of that thing, so is it impossible for me to conceive in my thoughts any sensible thing or object distinct from the sensation or perception of it. In truth, the object and the sensation are the same thing and cannot therefore be abstracted from each other.

6. Some truths are so near and obvious to the mind that a man need only open his eyes to see them. Such I take this important one to be, namely, that all the choir of heaven and furniture of the earth, in a word, all those bodies which compose the mighty frame of the world, do not have any subsistence without a mind—that their being [*esse*] is to be perceived or known, that consequently so long as they are not actually perceived by me or do not exist in my mind or that of any other created spirit, they must either have no existence at all or else subsist in the mind of some eternal spirit—it being perfectly unintelligible and involving all the absurdity of abstraction to attribute to any single part of them an existence independent of a spirit. To be convinced of this, the reader need only reflect and try to separate in his own thoughts the being of a sensible thing from its being perceived.

7. From what has been said it follows there is not any other substance than *spirit*, or that which perceives. But for the fuller proof of this point, let it be considered the sensible qualities are color, figure, motion, smell, taste, and qualities of a similar kind—that is, the ideas perceived by sense. Now for an idea to exist in an unperceiving thing is a manifest contradiction, for to have an idea is all one as to perceive; that, therefore, in which color, figure, and the like qualities exist must perceive them; hence it is clear there can be no unthinking substance or *substratum* of those ideas.

8. But, you say, though the ideas themselves do not exist without the mind, yet there may be things like them of which they are copies or resemblances, which things exist without the mind in an unthinking substance. I answer, an idea can be like nothing but an idea; a color or figure can be like nothing but another color or figure. If we look but ever so little into our thoughts, we shall find it impossible for us to conceive a likeness except only between our ideas. Again, I ask whether those supposed originals or external things of which our ideas are the pictures or representations are themselves perceivable or not? If they are, then they are ideas and we have gained our point; but if you say they are not, I appeal to anyone whether it makes sense to assert a color is like something which is invisible; hard or soft, like something which is intangible; and so of the rest.

9. There are some who make a distinction between *primary* and *secondary* qualities. By the former they mean extension, figure, motion, rest, solidity or impenetrability, and number; by the latter they denote all other sensible qualities, as colors, sounds, tastes, and so forth. The ideas we have of these they acknowledge not to be the resemblances of anything existing without the mind or unperceived, but they will have our ideas of the primary qualities to be patterns or images of things which exist without the mind, in an unthinking substance which they call matter. By matter therefore we are to understand an inert, senseless substance, in which extension, figure, and motion do actually subsist. But it is evident from what we have already shown that extension, figure, and motion are only ideas existing in the mind, and that an idea can be like nothing but another idea, and that consequently neither they nor their archetypes can exist in an unperceiving substance. Hence it is plain that the very notion of what is called matter, or corporeal substance, involves a contradiction in it.[3]

---

3. Berkeley: Inasmuch as I should not think it necessary to spend more time in exposing its absurdity. But because the tenet of the existence of matter seems to have taken so deep a root in the minds of philosophers, and draws after it so many ill consequences, I choose rather to be thought prolix and tedious than omit anything that might conduce to the full discovery and extirpation of that prejudice.

10. Those who assert that figure, motion, and the rest of the primary or original qualities do exist without the mind in unthinking substances do at the same time acknowledge that colors, sounds, heat, cold, and secondary qualities of a similar kind do not—which they tell us are sensations existing in the mind alone that depend on and are occasioned by the different size, texture, and motion of the minute particles of matter. This they take for an undoubted truth which they can demonstrate beyond all exception. Now, if it is certain that those original qualities are inseparably united with the other sensible qualities and not, even in thought, capable of being abstracted from them, it plainly follows that they exist only in the mind. But I desire anyone to reflect and try whether he can, by any abstraction of thought, conceive the extension and motion of a body without all other sensible qualities. For my own part, I see evidently that it is not in my power to frame an idea of a body extended and moved, but I must in addition give it some color or other sensible quality which is acknowledged to exist only in the mind. In short, extension, figure, and motion, abstracted from all other qualities, are inconceivable. Where, therefore, the other sensible qualities are, these must be also, namely, in the mind and nowhere else.

11. Again, *great* and *small*, *swift* and *slow*, are allowed to exist nowhere without the mind, being entirely relative, and changing as the frame or position of the organs of sense varies. The extension, therefore, which exists without the mind is neither great nor small, the motion neither swift nor slow—that is, they are nothing at all. But, you say, they are extension in general and motion in general; thus we see how much the tenet of extended, movable substances existing without the mind depends on that strange doctrine of *abstract ideas*. And here I cannot but remark how nearly the vague and indeterminate description of matter or corporeal substance which the modern philosophers are run into by their own principles resembles that antiquated and so much ridiculed notion of *materia prima*, to be met with in *Aristotle* and his followers. Without extension solidity cannot be conceived; since, therefore, it has been shown that extension exists not in an unthinking substance, the same must also be true of solidity.

12. That number is entirely the creature of the mind, even though the other qualities are allowed to exist without, will be evident to whoever considers that the same thing bears a different denomination of number as the mind views it with different respects. Thus, the same extension is one, or three, or thirty six, according as the mind considers it with reference to a yard, a foot, or an inch. Number is so visibly relative and dependent on men's understanding that it is strange to think how anyone should give it an absolute existence without the mind. We say one book, one page, one line; all these are equally units, though some contain several of the others. And in each instance it is plain the unit relates to some particular combination of ideas arbitrarily put together by the mind.

13. Unity, I know, some will have to be a simple or uncompounded idea accompanying all other ideas into the mind. That I have any such idea answering the word *unity* I do not find; and if I had, I think I could not miss finding it; on the contrary, it should be the most familiar to my understanding, since it is said to accompany all other ideas and to be perceived by all the ways of sensation and reflection. To say no more, it is an *abstract idea*.

14. I shall further add that, after the same manner as modern philosophers prove certain sensible qualities to have no existence in matter, or without the mind, the same thing may be likewise proved of all other sensible qualities whatsoever. Thus, for instance, it is said that heat and cold are affections only of the mind and not at all patterns of real beings, existing in the corporeal substances which excite them, for that the same body which appears cold to one hand seems warm to another. Now, why may we not as well argue that figure and extension are not patterns or resemblances of qualities existing in matter, because to the same eye at different stations, or eyes of a different texture at the same station, they appear various and cannot, therefore, be the images of anything settled and determinate without the mind? Again, it is proved that sweetness is not really in the said thing, because, the thing remaining unaltered,

the sweetness is changed into bitter as in case of a fever or otherwise vitiated palate. Is it not as reasonable to say that motion is not without the mind, since if the succession of ideas in the mind becomes swifter, the motion, it is acknowledged, shall appear slower without any alteration in any external object?

15. In short, let anyone consider those arguments which are thought manifestly to prove that colors and tastes exist only in the mind, and he shall find they may with equal force be brought to prove the same thing of extension, figure, and motion. Though it must be confessed this method of arguing does not so much prove that there is no extension or color in an outward object as that we do not know by sense which is the true extension or color of the object. But the previous arguments plainly show it to be impossible that any color or extension at all, or other sensible quality whatsoever, should exist in an unthinking subject without the mind or, in truth, that there should be any such thing as an outward object.

16. But let us examine a little the received opinion. It is said extension is a mode or accident of matter, and that matter is the *substratum* that supports it. Now I desire that you would explain what is meant by matter's *supporting* extension; you say, I have no idea of matter and, therefore, cannot explain it. I answer, though you have no positive, yet if you have any meaning at all, you must at least have a relative idea of matter; though you do not know what it is, yet you must be supposed to know what relation it bears to accidents, and what is meant by its supporting them. It is evident *support* cannot here be taken in its usual or literal sense, as when we say that pillars support a building; in what sense therefore must it be taken?

17. If we inquire into what the most accurate philosophers declare themselves to mean by *material substance*, we shall find them acknowledge they have no other meaning annexed to those sounds but the idea of being in general together with the relative notion of its supporting accidents. The general idea of being appears to me the most abstract and incomprehensible of all others; and as for its supporting accidents, this, as we have just now observed, cannot be understood in the common sense of those words; it must, therefore, be taken in some other sense,

but what that is they do not explain. So that when I consider the two parts or branches which make the signification of the words *material substance*, I am convinced there is no distinct meaning annexed to them. But why should we trouble ourselves any further in discussing this material *substratum* or support of figure and motion and other sensible qualities? Does it not suppose they have an existence without the mind? And is not this a direct repugnance and altogether inconceivable?

18. But though it is possible that solid, figured, movable substances may exist without the mind corresponding to the ideas we have of bodies, yet how is it possible for us to know this? Either we must know it by sense or by reason. As for our senses, by them we have knowledge only of our sensations, ideas, or those things that are immediately perceived by sense, call them what you will; but they do not inform us that things exist without the mind, or unperceived, like those which are perceived. This the materialists themselves acknowledge. It remains, therefore, that if we have any knowledge at all of external things, it must be by reason, inferring their existence from what is immediately perceived by sense. But what reason can induce us to believe the existence of bodies without the mind from what we perceive, since the very patrons of matter themselves do not pretend there is any necessary connection between them and our ideas? I say it is granted on all hands (and what happens in dreams, frenzies, and the like, puts it beyond dispute) that it is possible we might be affected with all the ideas we have now, though no bodies resembling them existed without. Hence it is evident the supposition of external bodies is not necessary for the producing our ideas, since it is granted they are produced sometimes and might possibly be produced always in the same order we see them in at present without their concurrence.

19. But though we might possibly have all our sensations without them, yet perhaps it may be thought easier to conceive and explain the manner of their production by supposing external bodies in their likeness rather than otherwise; and so it might be at least probable there are such things as bodies that excite their ideas in our minds. But neither

can this be said, for though we give the materialists their external bodies, they by their own confession are never the nearer knowing how our ideas are produced, since they admit themselves unable to comprehend in what manner body can act upon spirit or how it is possible it should imprint any idea in the mind. Hence it is evident the production of ideas or sensations in our minds can be no reason why we should suppose matter or corporeal substances, since that is acknowledged to remain equally inexplicable with or without this supposition. If, therefore, it were possible for bodies to exist without the mind, yet to hold they do so must necessarily be a very precarious opinion, since it is to suppose, without any reason at all that God has created innumerable beings that are entirely useless and serve to no manner of purpose.

20. In short, if there were external bodies, it is impossible we should ever come to know it; and if there were not, we might have the very same reasons to think there were that we have now. Suppose—what no one can deny possible—an intelligence, without the help of external bodies, to be affected with the same train of sensations or ideas that you are, imprinted in the same order and with like vividness in his mind. I ask whether that intelligence does not have all the reason to believe the existence of corporeal substances, represented by his ideas and exciting them in his mind, that you can possibly have for believing the same thing? Of this there can be no question—this one consideration is enough to make any reasonable person suspect the strength of whatever arguments he may think himself to have for the existence of bodies without the mind.

21. Were it necessary to add any further proof against the existence of matter after what has been said, I could instance several of those errors and difficulties (not to mention impieties) which have sprung from that tenet. It has occasioned countless controversies and disputes in philosophy, and not a few of greater moment in religion. But I shall not enter into the detail of them in this place as well because I think arguments *a posteriori* are unnecessary for confirming what has been, if I am not mistaken, sufficiently demonstrated *a priori*, as because I shall find occasion to say something about them below.

22. I am afraid I have given cause to think me needlessly prolix in handling this subject. For to what purpose is it to dilate on that which may be demonstrated with the utmost evidence in a line or two to anyone who is capable of the least reflection? It is but looking into your own thoughts and so trying whether you can conceive it possible for a sound, or figure, or motion, or color, to exist without the mind or unperceived. This easy trial may make you see that what you contend for is a downright contradiction. Inasmuch as I am content to put the whole upon this issue, if you can but conceive it possible for one extended, movable substance, or in general, for any one idea, or anything like an idea, to exist otherwise than in a mind perceiving it, I shall readily give up the cause; and as for all that *compages*[4] of external bodies which you contend for, I shall grant you its existence, though you cannot either give me any reason why you believe it exists or assign any use to it when it is supposed to exist. I say the bare possibility of your opinion's being true shall pass for an argument that it is so.

23. But, you say, surely there is nothing easier than to imagine trees, for instance, in a park or books existing in a closet and nobody nearby to perceive them. I answer: you may so, there is no difficulty in it; but what is all this, I beseech you, more than framing in your mind certain ideas which you call *books* and *trees* and at the same time omitting to frame the idea of anyone that may perceive them? But do not you yourself perceive or think of them all the while? This, therefore, is nothing to the purpose; it only shows you have the power of imagining or forming ideas in your mind, but it does not show that you can conceive it possible that the objects of your thought may exist without the mind. To make this out, it is necessary that you conceive them existing unconceived or unthought of, which is a manifest repugnance. When we do our utmost to conceive the existence of external bodies, we are all the while only contemplating our own ideas. But the mind, taking no notice of itself, is deluded to think it can and does conceive

---

4. Wholes formed by the juncture of parts, frameworks or systems of conjoined parts, or complex structures.

bodies existing unthought of or without the mind, though at the same time they are apprehended by or exist in itself. A little attention will discover to anyone the truth and evidence of what is said here and make it unnecessary to insist on any other proofs against the existence of material substance.

24. It is very obvious, upon the least inquiry into our own thoughts, to know whether it is possible for us to understand what is meant by the *absolute existence of sensible objects in themselves or without the mind*. To me it is evident those words mark out either a direct contradiction or else nothing at all. And to convince others of this, I know no readier or fairer way than to entreat they would calmly attend to their own thoughts; and if by this attention the emptiness or repugnance of those expressions does appear, surely nothing more is requisite for their conviction. It is on this, therefore, that I insist, namely, that "the absolute existence of unthinking things" are words without a meaning or which include a contradiction. This is what I repeat and inculcate, and earnestly recommend to the attentive thoughts of the reader.

25. All our ideas, sensations, or the things which we perceive, by whatever names they may be distinguished, are visibly inactive—there is nothing of power or agency included in them. So that one idea or object of thought cannot produce or make any alteration in another. To be satisfied of the truth of this, there is nothing else requisite but a bare observation of our ideas. For since they and every part of them exist only in the mind, it follows that there is nothing in them but what is perceived. But whoever shall attend to his ideas, whether of sense or reflection, will not perceive in them any power or activity; there is, therefore, no such thing contained in them. A little attention will discover to us that the very being of an idea implies passiveness and inertness in it, inasmuch as it is impossible for an idea to do anything or, strictly speaking, to be the cause of anything; neither can it be the resemblance or pattern of any active being, as is evident from sec. 8. From this it plainly follows that extension, figure, and motion cannot be the cause of our sensations. To say, therefore, that these are the effects of powers

resulting from the configuration, number, motion, and size of corpuscles must certainly be false.

26. We perceive a continual succession of ideas; some are excited anew, others are changed or totally disappear. There is, therefore, some cause of these ideas on which they depend and which produces and changes them. That this cause cannot be any quality or idea or combination of ideas is clear from the preceding section. It must, therefore, be a substance; but it has been shown that there is no corporeal or material substance. It remains, therefore, that the cause of ideas is an incorporeal active substance or spirit.

27. A spirit is one simple, undivided, active being; as it perceives ideas it is called the *understanding*, and as it produces or otherwise operates about them it is called the *will*. Hence there can be no idea formed of a soul or spirit; for all ideas whatever, being passive and inert (see sec. 25), they cannot represent unto us, by way of image or likeness, that which acts. A little attention will make it plain to anyone that to have an idea which shall be like that active principle of motion and change of ideas is absolutely impossible. Such is the nature of *spirit*, or that which acts, that it cannot be of itself perceived but only by the effects which it produces. If any man shall doubt of the truth of what is here delivered, let him but reflect and try if he can frame the idea of any power or active being, and whether he has ideas of two principal powers marked by the names *will* and *understanding*, distinct from each other as well as from a third idea of substance or being in general, with a relative notion of its supporting or being the subject of the aforesaid powers— which is signified by the name *soul* or *spirit*. This is what some hold; but, so far as I can see, the words *will*, *soul*, *spirit* do not stand for different ideas or, in truth, for any idea at all, but for something which is very different from ideas, and which, being an agent, cannot be like or represented by any idea whatsoever—though it must be admitted at the same time that we have some notion of soul, spirit, and the operations of the mind, such as willing, loving, hating, inasmuch as we know or understand the meaning of those words.

28. I find I can excite ideas in my mind at pleasure and vary and shift the scene as often as I think fit. It is

no more than willing and straightway this or that idea arises in my fancy; and by the same power it is obliterated and makes way for another. This making and unmaking of ideas does very properly denominate the mind active. This much is certain and grounded on experience, but when we talk of unthinking agents or of exciting ideas exclusive of volition, we only amuse ourselves with words.

29. But whatever power I may have over my own thoughts, I find the ideas actually perceived by sense do not have a like dependence on my will. When in broad daylight I open my eyes, it is not in my power to choose whether I shall see or not, or to determine what particular objects shall present themselves to my view; and so likewise as to the hearing and other senses—the ideas imprinted on them are not creatures of my will. There is, therefore, some other will or spirit that produces them.

30. The ideas of sense are more strong, lively, and distinct than those of the imagination; they have likewise a steadiness, order, and coherence and are not excited at random as those which are the effects of human wills often are, but in a regular train or series, the admirable connection of which sufficiently testifies to the wisdom and benevolence of its author. Now the set rules or established methods in which the mind we depend on excites in us the ideas of sense are called the *laws of nature*; and these we learn by experience, which teaches us that such and such ideas are attended with such and such other ideas in the ordinary course of things.

31. This gives us a sort of foresight which enables us to regulate our actions for the benefit of life. And without this we should be eternally at a loss; we could not know how to do anything that might procure us the least pleasure or remove the least pain of sense. That food nourishes, sleep refreshes, and fire warms us; that to sow in the seedtime is the way to reap in the harvest; and, in general, that to obtain such or such ends, such or such means are conducive—all this we know, not by discovering any necessary connection between our ideas, but only by the observation of the settled laws of nature, without which we should be all in uncertainty and confusion and a grown man would no more know how to manage himself in the affairs of life than an infant just born.

32. And yet this consistent, uniform working which so evidently displays the goodness and wisdom of that governing Spirit whose will constitutes the laws of nature is so far from leading our thoughts to him that it rather sends them wandering after second causes. For when we perceive certain ideas of sense constantly followed by other ideas and we know this is not of our own doing, we immediately attribute power and agency to the ideas themselves and make one the cause of another, than which nothing can be more absurd and unintelligible. Thus, for example, having observed that when we perceive by sight a certain round luminous figure, we at the same time perceive by touch the idea or sensation called *heat*, we do conclude from this the sun to be the cause of heat. And in like manner perceiving the motion and collision of bodies to be attended with sound, we are inclined to think the latter an effect of the former.

33. The ideas imprinted on the senses by the author of nature are called *real things*; and those excited in the imagination, being less regular, vivid, and constant, are more properly termed *ideas*, or *images of things* which they copy and represent. But then our sensations, be they never so vivid and distinct, are nevertheless *ideas*; that is, they exist in the mind or are perceived by it as truly as the ideas of its own framing. The ideas of sense are allowed to have more reality in them, that is, to be more strong, orderly, and coherent than the creatures of the mind, but this is no argument that they exist without the mind. They are also less dependent on the spirit, or thinking substance which perceives them in that they are excited by the will of another and more powerful spirit, yet still they are *ideas*; and certainly no *idea*, whether faint or strong, can exist otherwise than in a mind perceiving it.

# George Berkeley, *Three Dialogues between Hylas and Philonous, in Opposition to Skeptics and Atheists* (1713)[1]

## The Preface

Though it seems the general opinion of the world, no less than the design of nature and providence, that the end of speculation is practice or the improvement and regulation of our lives and actions, yet those who are most addicted to speculative studies seem as generally of another mind. And, indeed, if we consider the pains that have been taken to perplex the plainest things—that distrust of the senses, those doubts and scruples, those abstractions and refinements that occur in the very entrance of the sciences—it will not seem strange that men of leisure and curiosity should lay themselves out in fruitless disquisitions without descending to the practical parts of life or informing themselves in the more necessary and important parts of knowledge.

Upon the common principles of philosophers, we are not assured of the existence of things from their being perceived. And we are taught to distinguish their real nature from that which falls under our senses. Hence arise *skepticism* and *paradoxes*. It is not enough that we see and feel, that we taste and smell a thing. Its true nature, its absolute external entity, is still concealed. For, though it is the fiction of our own brain, we have made it inaccessible to all our faculties. Sense is fallacious, reason defective. We spend our lives in doubting of those things which other men evidently know and believing those things which they laugh at and despise.

In order, therefore, to divert the busy mind of man from vain researches, it seemed necessary to inquire into the source of its perplexities and, if possible, to lay down such principles as by an easy solution of them together with their own native evidence may at once recommend themselves for genuine to the mind and rescue it from those endless pursuits it is engaged in. This, with a plain demonstration of the immediate providence of an all-seeing God and the natural immortality of the soul, should seem the readiest preparation as well as the strongest motive to the study and practice of virtue.

This design I proposed in the First Part of a Treatise concerning the *Principles of Human Knowledge*, published in the year 1710. But before I proceed to publish the Second Part,[2] I thought it requisite to treat more clearly and fully of certain principles laid

1. From *The Works of George Berkeley*, ed. G. N. Wright (London, 1843), 2 vols., English, modified.

2. A few years later, while traveling in Italy, Berkeley lost his partly written draft of the Second Part of the *Principles*. He never rewrote or finished it.

down in the First, and to place them in a new light, which is the business of the following *Dialogues*.

In this treatise, which does not presuppose in the reader any knowledge of what was contained in the former, it has been my aim to introduce the notions I advance into the mind in the most easy and familiar manner, especially because they carry with them a great opposition to the prejudices of philosophers, which have so far prevailed against the common sense and natural notions of mankind.

If the principles which I here endeavor to propagate are admitted for true, the consequences which, I think, evidently flow from them are that *atheism* and *skepticism* will be utterly destroyed, many intricate points made plain, great difficulties solved, several useless parts of science retrenched, speculation referred to practice, and men reduced from paradoxes to common sense.

And although it may perhaps seem an uneasy reflection to some that when they have taken a circuit through so many refined and unvulgar notions they should at last come to think like other men, yet I think that this return to the simple dictates of nature after having wandered through the wild mazes of philosophy is not unpleasant. It is like coming home from a long voyage—a man reflects with pleasure on the many difficulties and perplexities he has passed through, sets his heart at ease, and enjoys himself with more satisfaction for the future.

As it was my intention to convince *skeptics* and *infidels* by reason, so it has been my endeavor strictly to observe the most rigid laws of reasoning. And, to an impartial reader, I hope, it will be manifest that the sublime notion of a God and the comfortable expectation of immortality do naturally arise from a close and methodical application of thought whatever may be the result of that loose, rambling way, not altogether improperly termed *freethinking* by certain libertines in thought who can no more endure the restraints of *logic* than those of *religion* or *government*.

It will perhaps be objected to my design that so far as it tends to ease the mind of difficult and useless inquiries it can affect only a few speculative persons; but if by their speculations rightly placed, the study of morality and the law of nature were brought more

into fashion among men of parts and genius, the discouragements that draw to *skepticism* removed, the measures of right and wrong accurately defined, and the principles of natural religion reduced into regular systems, as artfully disposed and clearly connected as those of some other sciences, then there are grounds to think these effects would not only have a gradual influence in repairing the too much defaced sense of virtue in the world, but also by showing that such parts of revelation as lie within the reach of human inquiry are most agreeable to right reason, it would dispose all prudent, unprejudiced persons to a modest and wary treatment of those sacred mysteries, which are above the comprehension of our faculties.

It remains that I desire the reader to withhold his censure of these *Dialogues* until he has read them through. Otherwise, he may lay them aside in a mistake of their design or on account of difficulties or objections which he would find answered in the sequel. A treatise of this nature would require to be once read over coherently in order to comprehend its design, the proofs, solution of difficulties, and the connection and disposition of its parts. If it is thought to deserve a second reading, this, I imagine, will make the entire scheme very plain—especially if recourse is had to an Essay I wrote some years since upon *Vision*,[3] and the *Treatise Concerning the Principles of Human Knowledge*. There various notions advanced in these *Dialogues* are further pursued or placed in different lights, and other points handled which naturally tend to confirm and illustrate them.

## The First Dialogue

*Philonous.* Good morning, Hylas; I did not expect to find you up so early.

*Hylas.* It is indeed something unusual, but my thoughts were so taken up with a subject I was discoursing of last night that, finding I could not sleep, I resolved to rise and take a turn in the garden.

*Phil.* It happened well to let you see what innocent and agreeable pleasures you lose every morning. Can there be a pleasanter time of the day, or a more delightful season of the year? That purple sky, those

---

3. *An Essay towards a New Theory of Vision* (1709).

wild but sweet notes of birds, the fragrant bloom upon the trees and flowers, the gentle influence of the rising sun, these and a thousand nameless beauties of nature inspire the soul with secret transports; its faculties too being at this time fresh and lively are fit for these meditations, which the solitude of a garden and tranquillity of the morning naturally dispose us to. But I am afraid I interrupt your thoughts, for you seemed very intent on something.

*Hyl.* It is true, I was, and shall be obliged to you if you will permit me to go on in the same vein; not that I would by any means deprive myself of your company, for my thoughts always flow more easily in conversation with a friend than when I am alone, but my request is that you would allow me to impart my reflections to you.

*Phil.* With all my heart, it is what I should have requested myself, if you had not prevented me.

*Hyl.* I was considering the odd fate of those men who have in all ages, through an affectation of being distinguished from the vulgar—or some unaccountable turn of thought—pretended either to believe nothing at all or to believe the most extravagant things in the world. This, however, might be borne, if their paradoxes and skepticism did not draw after them some consequences of general disadvantage to mankind. But the mischief lies here, that when men of less leisure see them who are supposed to have spent their whole time in the pursuits of knowledge, professing an entire ignorance of all things or advancing such notions as are repugnant to plain and commonly received principles, they will be tempted to entertain suspicions concerning the most important truths, which they had up to now held sacred and unquestionable.

*Phil.* I entirely agree with you as to the ill tendency of the affected doubts of some philosophers and fantastic conceits of others. I am even so far gone of late in this way of thinking that I have discarded several of the sublime notions I had got in their schools for vulgar opinions. And I give it you on my word, since this revolt from metaphysical notions to the plain dictates of nature and common sense, I find my understanding strangely enlightened so that I can now easily comprehend a great many things which before were all mystery and riddle.

*Hyl.* I am glad to find there was nothing in the accounts I heard of you.

*Phil.* Pray, what were those?

*Hyl.* You were represented in last night's conversation as one who maintained the most extravagant opinion that ever entered into the mind of man, namely, that there is no such thing as *material substance* in the world.

*Phil.* That there is no such thing as what philosophers call *material substance*, I am seriously persuaded, but if I were made to see anything absurd or skeptical in this, I should then have the same reason to renounce this, that I imagine I have now to reject the contrary opinion.

*Hyl.* What! Can anything be more fantastic, more repugnant to common sense, or a more manifest piece of skepticism, than to believe there is no such thing as *matter*?

*Phil.* Softly, good Hylas. What if it should prove that you, who hold there is, are by virtue of that opinion a greater skeptic and maintain more paradoxes and repugnancies to common sense than I who believe no such thing?

*Hyl.* You may as soon persuade me the part is greater than the whole, as that, in order to avoid absurdity and skepticism, I should ever be obliged to give up my opinion in this point.

*Phil.* Well then, are you content to admit that opinion for true which upon examination shall appear most agreeable to common sense and remote from skepticism?

*Hyl.* With all my heart. Since you are for raising disputes about the plainest things in nature, I am content for once to hear what you have to say.

*Phil.* Pray, Hylas, what do you mean by a *skeptic*?

*Hyl.* I mean what all men mean, one that doubts of everything.

*Phil.* He then who entertains no doubt concerning some particular point, with regard to that point, cannot be thought a *skeptic*.

*Hyl.* I agree with you.

*Phil.* Whether doubting consists in embracing the affirmative or negative side of a question?

*Hyl.* In neither; for whoever understands English cannot but know that *doubting* signifies a suspense between both.

*Phil.* He then who denies any point can no more be said to doubt of it than he who affirms it with the same degree of assurance.

*Hyl.* True.

*Phil.* And, consequently, in this case his denial is no more to be esteemed *skeptical* than the other.

*Hyl.* I acknowledge it.

*Phil.* How does it come to pass then, Hylas, that you pronounce me a *skeptic*, because I deny what you affirm, namely, the existence of matter? Since, for all you can tell, I am as peremptory in my denial as you in your affirmation.

*Hyl.* Hold on, Philonous, I have been a little out in my definition, but every false step a man makes in discourse is not to be insisted on. I said, indeed, that a *skeptic* was one who doubted of everything, but I should have added: or who denies the reality and truth of things.

*Phil.* What things? Do you mean the principles and theorems of sciences? But these you know are universal intellectual notions and consequently independent of matter; the denial of this therefore does not imply denying them.

*Hyl.* I grant it. But are there no other things? What do you think of distrusting the senses, of denying the real existence of sensible things, or pretending to know nothing of them? Is not this sufficient to call a man a *skeptic*?

*Phil.* Shall we therefore examine which of us it is that denies the reality of sensible things or professes the greatest ignorance of them, since, if I take you rightly, he is to be esteemed the greatest *skeptic*?

*Hyl.* That is what I desire.

*Phil.* What do you mean by sensible things?

*Hyl.* Those things which are perceived by the senses. Can you imagine that I mean anything else?

*Phil.* Pardon me, Hylas, if I am desirous clearly to apprehend your notions, since this may much shorten our inquiry. Allow me then to ask you this further question. Are those things only perceived by the senses which are perceived immediately? Or may those things properly be said to be *sensible* which are perceived mediately or not without the intervention of others?

*Hyl.* I do not sufficiently understand you.

*Phil.* In reading a book, what I immediately perceive are the letters, but mediately, or by means of these, are suggested to my mind the notions of God, virtue, truth, etc. Now that the letters are truly sensible things, or perceived by sense, there is no doubt; but I would like to know whether you take the things suggested by them to be so too.

*Hyl.* No, certainly, it would be absurd to think *God* or *virtue* sensible things, though they may be signified and suggested to the mind by sensible marks with which they have an arbitrary connection.

*Phil.* It seems then, that by *sensible things* you mean those only which can be perceived immediately by sense.

*Hyl.* Right.

*Phil.* Does it not follow from this that though I see one part of the sky red, and another blue, and that my reason does then evidently conclude there must be some cause of that diversity of colors, yet that cause cannot be said to be a sensible thing or perceived by the sense of seeing?

*Hyl.* It does.

*Phil.* In like manner, though I hear a variety of sounds, yet I cannot be said to hear the causes of those sounds.

*Hyl.* You cannot.

*Phil.* And when by my touch I perceive a thing to be hot and heavy, I cannot say with any truth or propriety that I feel the cause of its heat or weight.

*Hyl.* To prevent any more questions of this kind, I tell you once and for all that by *sensible things* I mean those only which are perceived by sense and that in truth the senses perceive nothing which they do not perceive immediately, for they make no inferences. The deducing therefore of causes or occasions from effects and appearances, which alone are perceived by sense, entirely relates to reason.

*Phil.* This point then is agreed between us—that *sensible things are those only which are immediately perceived by sense.* You will further inform me whether we immediately perceive by sight anything besides light, and colors, and figures; or by hearing anything but sounds; by the palate, anything besides tastes; by the smell, besides odors; or by the touch, more than tangible qualities.

*Hyl.* We do not.

*Phil.* It seems, therefore, that if you take away all sensible qualities, there remains nothing sensible.

*Hyl.* I grant it.

*Phil.* Sensible things therefore are nothing else but so many sensible qualities or combinations of sensible qualities.

*Hyl.* Nothing else.

*Phil.* Heat then is a sensible thing.

*Hyl.* Certainly.

*Phil.* Does the reality of sensible things consist in being perceived? Or, is it something distinct from their being perceived and that bears no relation to the mind?

*Hyl.* To *exist* is one thing and to be *perceived* is another.

*Phil.* I speak with regard to sensible things only; and of these I ask whether by their real existence you mean a subsistence exterior to the mind and distinct from their being perceived?

*Hyl.* I mean a real absolute being, distinct from and without any relation to their being perceived.

*Phil.* Heat, therefore, if it is allowed a real being, must exist without the mind.

*Hyl.* It must.

*Phil.* Tell me, Hylas, is this real existence equally compatible to all degrees of heat which we perceive, or is there any reason why we should attribute it to some and deny it others? And if there is, pray let me know that reason.

*Hyl.* Whatever degree of heat we perceive by sense, we may be sure the same exists in the object that occasions it.

*Phil.* What! The greatest as well as the least?

*Hyl.* I tell you, the reason is plainly the same in respect of both: They are both perceived by sense; no, the greater degree of heat is more sensibly perceived and, consequently, if there is any difference, we are more certain of its real existence than we can be of the reality of a lesser degree.

*Phil.* But is not the most vehement and intense degree of heat a very great pain?

*Hyl.* No one can deny it.

*Phil.* And is any unperceiving thing capable of pain or pleasure?

*Hyl.* No, certainly.

*Phil.* Is your material substance a senseless being or a being endowed with sense and perception?

*Hyl.* It is senseless without doubt.

*Phil.* It cannot therefore be the subject of pain.

*Hyl.* By no means.

*Phil.* Nor consequently of the greatest heat perceived by sense, since you acknowledge this to be no small pain.

*Hyl.* I grant it.

*Phil.* What shall we say then of your external object; is it a material substance or not?

*Hyl.* It is a material substance with the sensible qualities inhering in it.

*Phil.* How then can a great heat exist in it, since you admit it cannot in a material substance? I desire you would clear this point.

*Hyl.* Hold on, Philonous, I fear I was wrong in yielding intense heat to be a pain. It should seem rather that pain is something distinct from heat and the consequence or effect of it.

*Phil.* Upon putting your hand near the fire, do you perceive one simple uniform sensation or two distinct sensations?

*Hyl.* But one simple sensation.

*Phil.* Is not the heat immediately perceived?

*Hyl.* It is.

*Phil.* And the pain?

*Hyl.* True.

*Phil.* Seeing therefore they are both immediately perceived at the same time and the fire affects you only with one simple or uncompounded idea, it follows that this same simple idea is both the intense heat immediately perceived and the pain, and, consequently, that the intense heat immediately perceived is nothing distinct from a particular sort of pain.

*Hyl.* It seems so.

*Phil.* Again, try in your thoughts, Hylas, if you can conceive a vehement sensation to be without pain or pleasure.

*Hyl.* I cannot.

*Phil.* Or can you frame to yourself an idea of sensible pain or pleasure in general, abstracted from every particular idea of heat, cold, tastes, smells, etc.?

*Hyl.* I do not find that I can.

*Phil.* Does it not therefore follow that sensible pain is nothing distinct from those sensations or ideas in an intense degree?

*Hyl* It is undeniable, and, to speak the truth, I begin to suspect a very great heat cannot exist but in a mind perceiving it.

*Phil.* What! Are you then in that *skeptical* state of suspense between affirming and denying?

*Hyl.* I think I may be positive in the point. A very violent and painful heat cannot exist without the mind.

*Phil.* It does not, therefore, according to you, have any real being.

*Hyl.* I admit it.

*Phil.* Is it therefore certain that there is no body in nature really hot?

*Hyl.* I have not denied there is any real heat in bodies. I only say there is no such thing as an intense real heat.

*Phil.* But did you not say before that all degrees of heat were equally real or, if there was any difference, that the greater would be more undoubtedly real than the lesser?

*Hyl.* True, but it was because I did not then consider the ground there is for distinguishing between them which I now plainly see. And it is this: Because intense heat is nothing else but a particular kind of painful sensation and pain cannot exist but in a perceiving being, it follows that no intense heat can really exist in an unperceiving corporeal substance. But this is no reason why we should deny heat in an inferior degree to exist in such a substance.

*Phil.* But how shall we be able to discern those degrees of heat which exist only in the mind, from those which exist without it?

*Hyl.* That is no difficult matter. You know the least pain cannot exist unperceived; therefore, whatever degree of heat is a pain exists only in the mind. But as for all other degrees of heat nothing obliges us to think the same of them.

*Phil.* I think you granted before that no unperceiving being was capable of pleasure any more than of pain.

*Hyl.* I did.

*Phil.* And is not warmth, or a more gentle degree of heat than what causes uneasiness, a pleasure?

*Hyl.* What then?

*Phil.* Consequently, it cannot exist without the mind in any unperceiving substance or body.

*Hyl.* So it seems.

*Phil.* Since, therefore, those degrees of heat that are not painful as well as those that are can exist only in a thinking substance, may we not conclude that external bodies are absolutely incapable of any degree of heat whatsoever?

*Hyl.* On second thought, I do not think it so evident that warmth is a pleasure as that a great degree of heat is a pain.

*Phil.* I do not pretend that warmth is as great a pleasure as heat is a pain. But if you grant it to be even a small pleasure, it serves to make good my conclusion.

*Hyl.* I could rather call it an *indolence*. It seems to be nothing more than a privation of both pain and pleasure. And that such a quality or state as this may agree to an unthinking substance, I hope you will not deny.

*Phil.* If you are resolved to maintain that warmth, or a gentle degree of heat, is no pleasure, I do not know how to convince you otherwise than by appealing to your own sense. But what do you think of cold?

*Hyl.* The same that I do of heat. An intense degree of cold is a pain, for to feel a very great cold is to perceive a great uneasiness; it cannot, therefore, exist without the mind, but a lesser degree of cold may as well as a lesser degree of heat.

*Phil.* Those bodies, therefore, upon whose application to our own we perceive a moderate degree of heat, must be concluded to have a moderate degree of heat or warmth in them; and those, upon whose application we feel a like degree of cold, must be thought to have cold in them.

*Hyl.* They must.

*Phil.* Can any doctrine be true that necessarily leads a man into an absurdity?

*Hyl.* Without doubt it cannot.

*Phil.* Is it not an absurdity to think that the same thing should be at the same time both cold and warm?

*Hyl.* It is.

*Phil.* Suppose now one of your hands hot, and the other cold, and that they are both at once put into the same vessel of water in an intermediate state; will not the water seem cold to one hand and warm to the other?

*Hyl.* It will.

*Phil.* Ought we not therefore by your principles conclude: It is really both cold and warm at the same time, that is, according to your own concession, believe an absurdity?

*Hyl.* I confess it seems so.

*Phil.* Consequently, the principles themselves are false, since you have granted that no true principle leads to an absurdity.

*Hyl.* But, after all, can anything be more absurd than to say *there is no heat in the fire*?

*Phil.* To make the point still clearer, tell me whether in two cases exactly alike we ought not make the same judgment?

*Hyl.* We ought.

*Phil.* When a pin pricks your finger, does it not rend and divide the fibers of your flesh?

*Hyl.* It does.

*Phil.* And when a coal burns your finger, does it do so any more?

*Hyl.* It does not.

*Phil.* Since, therefore, you neither judge the sensation itself occasioned by the pin, nor anything like it to be in the pin, you should not, conformably to what you have now granted, judge the sensation occasioned by the fire, or anything like it, to be in the fire.

*Hyl.* Well, since it must be so, I am content to yield this point and acknowledge that heat and cold are only sensations existing in our minds, but there still remain qualities enough to secure the reality of external things.

*Phil.* But what will you say, Hylas, if it shall appear that the case is the same with regard to all other sensible qualities and that they can no more

be supposed to exist without the mind than heat and cold?

*Hyl.* Then indeed you will have done something to the purpose, but that is what I despair of seeing proved.

*Phil.* Let us examine them in order. What think you of tastes—do they exist without the mind or not?

*Hyl.* Can any man in his senses doubt whether sugar is sweet or wormwood bitter?

*Phil.* Inform me, Hylas. Is a sweet taste a particular kind of pleasure or pleasant sensation, or is it not?

*Hyl.* It is.

*Phil.* And is not bitterness some kind of uneasiness or pain?

*Hyl.* I grant it.

*Phil.* If therefore sugar and wormwood are unthinking corporeal substances existing without the mind, how can sweetness and bitterness, that is, pleasure and pain, agree to them?

*Hyl.* Hold on, Philonous, I now see what deluded me all this time. You asked whether heat and cold, sweetness and bitterness, were not particular sorts of pleasure and pain—to which I answered simply that they were. Whereas I should have distinguished thus: Those qualities, as perceived by us, are pleasures or pains, but not as existing in the external objects. We must not, therefore, conclude absolutely that there is no heat in the fire or sweetness in the sugar, but only that heat or sweetness, as perceived by us, is not in the fire or sugar. What do you say to this?

*Phil.* I say it is nothing to the purpose. Our discourse proceeded altogether concerning sensible things, which you defined to be the things we *immediately perceive by our senses*. Therefore, whatever other qualities you speak of as distinct from these, I know nothing of them, nor do they at all belong to the point in dispute. You may indeed pretend to have discovered certain qualities which you do not perceive and assert those insensible qualities exist in fire and sugar. But what use can be made of this to your present purpose, I am at a loss to conceive. Tell me then once more—do you acknowledge that heat and cold, sweetness and bitterness (meaning those qualities which are perceived by the senses), do not exist without the mind?

*Hyl.* I see it is to no purpose to hold out, so I give up the cause as to those mentioned qualities. Though I profess it sounds odd to say that sugar is not sweet.

*Phil.* But for your further satisfaction, take this along with you: That which at other times seems sweet shall to a distempered palate appear bitter. And nothing can be plainer than that various persons perceive different tastes in the same food, since that which one man delights in, another abhors. And how could this be, if the taste was something really inherent in the food?

*Hyl.* I acknowledge I do not know how.

*Phil.* In the next place, odors are to be considered. And with regard to these, I would gladly know whether what has been said of tastes does not exactly agree to them? Are they not so many pleasing or displeasing sensations?

*Hyl.* They are.

*Phil.* Can you then conceive it possible that they should exist in an unperceiving thing?

*Hyl.* I cannot.

*Phil.* Or can you imagine that filth and garbage affect those brute animals that feed on them out of choice with the same smells which we perceive in them?

*Hyl.* By no means.

*Phil.* May we not therefore conclude of smells, as of the other aforementioned qualities, that they cannot exist in any but a perceiving substance or mind?

*Hyl.* I think so.

*Phil.* Then as to sounds, what must we think of them—are they accidents really inherent in external bodies or not?

*Hyl.* That they do not inhere in the sonorous bodies is plain from this: because a bell struck in the exhausted receiver of an air pump sends forth no sound. The air, therefore, must be thought the subject of sound.

*Phil.* What reason is there for that, Hylas?

*Hyl.* Because, when any motion is raised in the air, we perceive a greater or lesser sound in proportion to the air's motion, but without some motion in the air we never hear any sound at all.

*Phil.* And granting that we never hear a sound but when some motion is produced in the air, yet I do not see how you can infer from this that the sound itself is in the air.

*Hyl.* It is this very motion in the external air that produces in the mind the sensation of *sound*. For striking on the drum of the ear, it causes a vibration, which, being communicated to the brain by the auditory nerves, then affects the soul with the sensation called sound.

*Phil.* What! Is sound then a sensation?

*Hyl.* I tell you, as perceived by us, it is a particular sensation in the mind.

*Phil.* And can any sensation exist without the mind?

*Hyl.* No, certainly.

*Phil.* How then can sound, being a sensation, exist in the air if by the air you mean a senseless substance existing without the mind?

*Hyl.* You must distinguish, Philonous, between sound as it is perceived by us and as it is in itself, or (which is the same thing) between the sound we immediately perceive and that which exists without us. The former indeed is a particular kind of sensation, but the latter is merely a vibrational or undulatory motion in the air.

*Phil.* I thought I had already obviated that distinction by the answer I gave when you were applying it in a like case before. But, to say no more of that, are you sure then that sound is really nothing but motion?

*Hyl.* I am.

*Phil.* Whatever therefore agrees to real sound may with truth be attributed to motion.

*Hyl.* It may.

*Phil.* It is then good sense to speak of *motion*, as of a thing that is *loud*, *sweet*, *acute*, or *grave*.

*Hyl.* I see you are resolved not to understand me. Is it not evident those accidents or modes belong only to sensible sound, or *sound* in the common meaning of the word, but not to *sound* in the real and philosophic sense, which, as I just now told you, is nothing but a certain motion of the air?

*Phil.* It seems then there are two sorts of sound, the one vulgar, or that which is heard, the other philosophical and real.

*Hyl.* Even so.

*Phil.* And the latter consists in motion.

*Hyl.* I told you so before.

*Phil.* Tell me, Hylas, to which of the senses, do you think, the idea of motion belongs—to the hearing?

*Hyl.* No, certainly, but to the sight and touch.

*Phil.* It should follow then, that according to you, real sounds may possibly be *seen* or *felt*, but never *heard*.

*Hyl.* Look, Philonous, you may if you please make a jest of my opinion, but that will not alter the truth of things. I admit, indeed, the inferences you draw me into sound something odd, but common language, you know, is framed by and for the use of the vulgar. We must not therefore wonder if expressions adapted to exact philosophic notions seem uncouth and out of the way.

*Phil.* Is it come to that? I assure you, I imagine myself to have gained no small point, since you make so light of departing from common phrases and opinions, it being a main part of our inquiry to examine whose notions are widest of the common road and most repugnant to the general sense of the world. But can you think it no more than a philosophical paradox to say that *real sounds are never heard* and that the idea of them is obtained by some other sense. And is there nothing in this contrary to nature and the truth of things?

*Hyl.* To deal ingenuously, I do not like it. And after the concessions already made, I had as well grant that sounds too have no real being without the mind.

*Phil.* And I hope you will make no difficulty to acknowledge the same of colors.

*Hyl.* Pardon me, the case of colors is very different. Can anything be plainer than that we see them on the objects?

*Phil.* The objects you speak of are, I suppose, corporeal substances existing without the mind.

*Hyl.* They are.

*Phil.* And have true and real colors inhering in them?

*Hyl.* Each visible object has that color which we see in it.

*Phil.* How! Is there anything visible but what we perceive by sight?

*Hyl.* There is not.

*Phil.* And do we perceive anything by sense which we do not perceive immediately?

*Hyl.* How often must I be obliged to repeat the same thing? I tell you, we do not.

*Phil.* Have patience, good Hylas, and tell me once more whether there is anything immediately perceived by the senses except sensible qualities. I know you asserted there was not, but I would now be informed whether you still persist in the same opinion.

*Hyl.* I do.

*Phil.* Pray, is your corporeal substance either a sensible quality or made up of sensible qualities?

*Hyl.* What a question that is! Who ever thought it was?

*Phil.* My reason for asking was because in saying *each visible object has that color which we see in it*, you make visible objects be corporeal substances, which implies either that corporeal substances are sensible qualities or else that there is something besides sensible qualities perceived by sight; but as this point was formerly agreed between us and is still maintained by you, it is a clear consequence that your corporeal substance is nothing distinct from sensible qualities.

*Hyl.* You may draw as many absurd consequences as you please and endeavor to perplex the plainest things, but you shall never persuade me out of my senses. I clearly understand my own meaning.

*Phil.* I wish you would make me understand it too. But since you are unwilling to have your notion of corporeal substance examined, I shall urge that point no further. Only be pleased to let me know whether the same colors which we see exist in external bodies or some other.

*Hyl.* The very same.

*Phil.* What! Are then the beautiful red and purple we see on yonder clouds really in them? Or do you imagine they have in themselves any other form than that of a dark mist or vapor?

*Hyl.* I must admit, Philonous, those colors are not really in the clouds as they seem to be at this distance. They are only apparent colors.

*Phil.* *Apparent* call you them? How shall we distinguish these apparent colors from real?

*Hyl.* Very easily. Those are to be thought apparent which, appearing only at a distance, vanish upon a nearer approach.

*Phil.* And those, I suppose, are to be thought real which are discovered by the most near and exact survey.

*Hyl.* Right.

*Phil.* Is the nearest and most exact survey made by the help of a microscope or by the naked eye?

*Hyl.* By a microscope, doubtless.

*Phil.* But a microscope often discovers colors in an object different from those perceived by the unassisted sight. And in case we had microscopes magnifying to any assigned degree, it is certain that no object whatsoever viewed through them would appear in the same color which it exhibits to the naked eye.

*Hyl.* And what will you conclude from all this? You cannot argue that there are really and naturally no colors on objects because they may be altered or made to vanish by artificial managements.

*Phil.* I think it may evidently be concluded from your own concessions that all the colors we see with our naked eyes are only apparent as those on the clouds, since they vanish upon a more close and accurate inspection, which is afforded us by a microscope. Then as to what you say by way of prevention, I ask you whether the real and natural state of an object is better discovered by a very sharp and piercing sight or by one which is less sharp.

*Hyl.* By the former without doubt.

*Phil.* Is it not plain from *Dioptrics* that microscopes make the sight more penetrating and represent objects as they would appear to the eye, in case it were naturally endowed with a most exquisite sharpness?

*Hyl.* It is.

*Phil.* Consequently, the microscopic representation is to be thought that which best sets forth the real nature of the thing or what it is in itself. The colors therefore perceived by it are more genuine and real than those perceived otherwise.

*Hyl.* I confess there is something in what you say.

*Phil.* Besides, it is not only possible but manifest that there actually are animals whose eyes are by nature framed to perceive those things which by reason of their minuteness escape our sight. What do you think of those inconceivably small animals perceived by glasses? Must we suppose they are all stark blind? Or, in case they see, can it be imagined their sight does not have the same use in preserving their bodies from injuries which appears in that of all other animals? And if it does, is it not evident they must see particles less than their own bodies, which will present them with a far different view in each object from that which strikes our senses? Even our own eyes do not always represent objects to us after the same manner. With *jaundice*, everyone knows that all things seem yellow. Is it not therefore highly probable that those animals in whose eyes we discern a very different texture from that of ours and whose bodies abound with different humors, do not see the same colors in every object that we do? From all of which, should it not seem to follow that all colors are equally apparent and that none of those which we perceive are really inherent in any outward object?

*Hyl.* It should.

*Phil.* The point will be past all doubt if you consider that in case colors were real properties or affections inherent in external bodies, they could admit of no alteration without some change made in the very bodies themselves. But is it not evident from what has been said that upon the use of microscopes, upon a change happening in the humors of the eye, or a variation of distance, without any manner of real alteration in the thing itself, the colors of any object are either changed or totally disappear? No, all other circumstances remaining the same, change but the situation of some objects and they shall present different colors to the eye. The same thing happens upon viewing an object in various degrees of light. And what is more known than that the same bodies appear differently colored by candlelight from what they do in the open day? Add to these the experiment of a prism which, separating the heterogeneous rays of light, alters the color of any object and will cause the whitest to appear of a deep blue or red to the naked eye. And now tell me whether you are still of the opinion that every body has its true, real color inhering in it; and if you think it has, I would gladly know further from you what certain distance and position of the object, what peculiar texture and formation of the eye, what degree or kind of light is necessary for ascertaining that true color and distinguishing it from apparent ones.

*Hyl.* I admit myself entirely satisfied that they are all equally apparent and that there is no such thing as color really inhering in external bodies, but that it is altogether in the light. And what confirms me in this opinion is that, in proportion to the light, colors are still more or less vivid, and if there is no light, then there are no colors perceived. Besides, allowing there are colors on external objects, yet how is it possible for us to perceive them? For no external body affects the mind unless it acts first on our organs of sense. But the only action of bodies is motion, and motion cannot be communicated otherwise than by impulse. A distant object, therefore, cannot act on the eye, nor consequently make itself or its properties perceivable to the soul. From this it plainly follows that it is immediately some contiguous substance which, operating on the eye, occasions a perception of colors—and such is light.

*Phil.* How! Is light then a substance?

*Hyl.* I tell you, Philonous, external light is nothing but a thin fluid substance whose minute particles, being agitated with a brisk motion and in various manners reflected from the different surfaces of outward objects to the eyes, communicate different motions to the optic nerves, which being propagated to the brain, cause various impressions in it; and these are attended with the sensations of red, blue, yellow, etc.

*Phil.* It seems, then, the light does no more than shake the optic nerves.

*Hyl.* Nothing else.

*Phil.* And, consequent to each particular motion of the nerves, the mind is affected with a sensation, which is some particular color.

*Hyl.* Right.

*Phil.* And these sensations have no existence without the mind.

*Hyl.* They do not.

*Phil.* How then do you affirm that colors are in the light, since by light you understand a corporeal substance external to the mind?

*Hyl.* Light and colors, as immediately perceived by us, I grant cannot exist without the mind. But in themselves they are only the motions and configurations of certain insensible particles of matter.

*Phil.* Colors then, in the vulgar sense, or taken for the immediate objects of sight, cannot agree to any but a perceiving substance.

*Hyl.* That is what I say.

*Phil.* Well then, since you give up the point as to those sensible qualities which are alone thought colors by all mankind besides, you may hold what you please with regard to those invisible ones of the philosophers. It is not my business to dispute about them; only I would advise you to envision yourself, whether, considering the inquiry we are upon, it would be prudent for you to affirm: *The red and blue which we see are not real colors, but certain unknown motions and figures which no man ever did or can see are truly so.* Are not these shocking notions, and are not they subject to as many ridiculous inferences as those you were obliged to renounce before in the case of sounds?

*Hyl.* I frankly admit, Philonous, that it is in vain to stand out any longer. Colors, sounds, tastes, in a word, all those termed *secondary qualities*, have certainly no existence without the mind. But by this acknowledgment I must not be supposed to derogate anything from the reality of matter or external objects, seeing it is no more than several philosophers maintain who nevertheless are the furthest imaginable from denying matter. For the clearer understanding of this you must know sensible qualities are by philosophers divided into *primary* and *secondary*. The former are extension, figure, solidity, gravity, motion, and rest. And these they hold exist really in bodies. The latter are those above enumerated or, briefly, all sensible qualities besides the primary, which they assert are only so many sensations or ideas existing nowhere but in the mind. But all this, I do not doubt, you are already apprised of. For my part, I have been a long time sensible there was such an opinion current among philosophers, but was never thoroughly convinced of its truth until now.

*Phil.* You are still then of the opinion that extension and figures are inherent in external unthinking substances.

*Hyl.* I am.

*Phil.* But what if the same arguments which are brought against secondary qualities will hold proof against these also?

*Hyl.* Why then I shall be obliged to think they too exist only in the mind.

*Phil.* Is it your opinion that the very figure and extension which you perceive by sense exist in the outward object or material substance?

*Hyl.* It is.

*Phil.* Have all other animals as good grounds to think the same of the figure and extension which they see and feel?

*Hyl.* Without doubt, if they have any thought at all.

*Phil.* Answer me, Hylas. Do you think the senses were bestowed upon all animals for their preservation and well being in life? Or were they given to men alone for this end?

*Hyl.* I make no question but they have the same use in all other animals.

*Phil.* If so, is it not necessary they should be enabled by them to perceive their own limbs and those bodies which are capable of harming them?

*Hyl.* Certainly.

*Phil.* A mite therefore must be supposed to see his own foot, and things equal or even less than it, as bodies of some considerable dimension, though at the same time they appear to you scarce discernible or at best as so many visible points.

*Hyl.* I cannot deny it.

*Phil.* And to creatures less than the mite they will seem yet larger.

*Hyl.* They will.

*Phil.* To the extent that what you can hardly discern will to another extremely minute animal appear as some huge mountain.

*Hyl.* All this I grant.

*Phil.* Can one and the same thing be at the same time in itself of different dimensions?

*Hyl.* That would be absurd to imagine.

*Phil.* But from what you have laid down it follows that both the extension perceived by you and that perceived by the mite itself, as likewise all those perceived by lesser animals, are each of them the true extension of the mite's foot—that is to say, by your own principles you are led into an absurdity.

*Hyl.* There seems to be some difficulty in the point.

*Phil.* Again, have you not acknowledged that no real inherent property of any object can be changed without some change in the thing itself?

*Hyl.* I have.

*Phil.* But as we approach to or recede from an object, the visible extension varies, being at one distance ten or a hundred times greater than at another. Does it not therefore follow from this, likewise, that it is not really inherent in the object?

*Hyl.* I admit I am at a loss what to think.

*Phil.* Your judgment will soon be determined if you will venture to think as freely concerning this quality as you have done concerning the rest. Was it not admitted as a good argument that neither heat nor cold was in the water because it seemed warm to one hand and cold to the other?

*Hyl.* It was.

*Phil.* Is it not the very same reasoning to conclude there is no extension or figure in an object because to one eye it shall seem little, smooth, and round, when at the same time it appears to the other, great, uneven, and angular?

*Hyl.* The very same. But does this latter fact ever happen?

*Phil.* You may at any time make the experiment by looking with one eye bare and with the other through a microscope.

*Hyl.* I do not know how to maintain it, and yet I am loath to give up *extension*; I see so many odd consequences following upon such a concession.

*Phil.* Odd, you say? After the concessions already made, I hope you will stick at nothing for its oddness. But on the other hand should it not seem very odd if the general reasoning which includes all other sensible qualities did not also include extension? If it is allowed that no idea nor anything like an idea can exist in an unperceiving substance, then surely it follows that no figure or mode of extension, which we can either perceive or imagine or have any idea of, can be really inherent in matter—not to mention the peculiar difficulty there must be in conceiving a material substance, prior to and distinct from extension, to be the *substratum* of extension. Whatever the sensible quality is, figure, or sound, or color, it seems equally impossible it should subsist in that which does not perceive it.

*Hyl.* I give up the point for the present, reserving still a right to retract my opinion, in case I shall hereafter discover any false step in my progress to it.

*Phil.* That is a right you cannot be denied. Figures and extension being dispatched, we proceed next to *motion*. Can a real motion in any external body be at the same time both very swift and very slow?

*Hyl.* It cannot.

*Phil.* Is not the motion of a body swift in a reciprocal proportion to the time it takes up in describing any given space? Thus a body that describes a mile in an hour moves three times faster than it would in case it described only a mile in three hours.

*Hyl.* I agree with you.

*Phil.* And is not time measured by the succession of ideas in our minds?

*Hyl.* It is.

*Phil.* And is it not possible ideas should succeed one another twice as fast in your mind as they do in mine or in that of some spirit of another kind?

*Hyl.* I admit it.

*Phil.* Consequently, the same body may to another seem to perform its motion over any space in half the time that it does to you. And the same reasoning will hold as to any other proportion—that is to say, according to your principles (since the motions perceived are both really in the object) it is possible one and the same body shall be really moved the same way at once, both very swift and very slow. How is this consistent either with common sense or with what you just now granted?

*Hyl.* I have nothing to say to it.

*Phil.* Then as for *solidity*, either you do not mean any sensible quality by that word, and so it is besides our inquiry, or if you do, it must be either hardness or resistance. But both the one and the other are plainly relative to our senses, it being evident that what seems hard to one animal may appear soft to another who has greater force and firmness of limbs. Nor is it less plain that the resistance I feel is not in the body.

*Hyl.* I admit the very sensation of resistance, which is all you immediately perceive, is not in the *body*, but the cause of that sensation is.

*Phil.* But the causes of our sensations are not things immediately perceived, and, therefore, not sensible. This point I thought had been already determined.

*Hyl.* I admit it was, but you will pardon me if I seem a little embarrassed; I do not know how to quit my old notions.

*Phil.* To help you out, do but consider that if extension is once acknowledged to have no existence without the mind, the same must necessarily be granted of motion, solidity, and gravity, since they all evidently suppose extension. It is therefore superfluous to inquire particularly concerning each of them. In denying extension, you have denied them all to have any real existence.

*Hyl.* I wonder, Philonous, if what you say is true, why those philosophers who deny the secondary qualities any real existence should yet attribute it to the primary. If there is no difference between them, how can this be accounted for?

*Phil.* It is not my business to account for every opinion of the philosophers. But among other reasons which may be assigned for this, it seems probable that pleasure and pain being annexed to the former rather than the latter may be one. Heat and cold, tastes and smells, have something more vividly pleasing or disagreeable than the ideas of extension, figure, and motion affect us with. And it being too visibly absurd to hold that pain or pleasure can be in an unperceiving substance, men are more easily weaned from believing the external existence of the secondary than the primary qualities. You will be satisfied there is something in this if you recollect the difference you made between an intense and more moderate degree of heat, allowing the one a real existence, while you denied it to the other. But after all, there is no rational ground for that distinction, for surely an indifferent sensation is as truly *a sensation* as one more pleasing or painful, and consequently should not any more than they be supposed to exist in an unthinking subject.

*Hyl.* It has just come into my head, Philonous, that I have somewhere heard of a distinction between absolute and sensible extension. Now though it is acknowledged that great and small, consisting merely in the relation which other extended beings have to the parts of our own bodies, do not really inhere in the substances themselves, yet nothing obliges us to hold the same with regard to *absolute extension,* which is something abstracted from *great* and *small,* from this or that particular magnitude or figure. So likewise as to motion, *swift* and *slow* are altogether relative to the succession of ideas in our own minds. But it does not follow, because those modifications of motion do not exist without the mind, that absolute motion abstracted from them therefore does not.

*Phil.* Pray what is it that distinguishes one motion or one part of extension from another? Is it not something sensible, as some degree of swiftness or slowness, some certain magnitude or figure peculiar to each?

*Hyl.* I think so.

*Phil.* These qualities, therefore, stripped of all sensible properties, are without all specific and numerical differences, as the schools call them.

*Hyl.* They are.

*Phil.* That is to say, they are extension in general and motion in general.

*Hyl.* Let it be so.

*Phil.* But it is a universally received maxim that *everything which exists is particular.* How then can motion in general or extension in general exist in any corporeal substance?

*Hyl.* I will take time to solve your difficulty.

*Phil.* But I think the point may be speedily decided. Without doubt you can tell whether you are able to frame this or that idea. Now I am content to put our dispute on this issue. If you can frame in your thoughts a distinct abstract idea of motion or extension, divested of all those sensible modes as swift and slow, great and small, round and square, and the like, which are acknowledged to exist only in the mind, I

will then yield the point you contend for. But if you cannot, it will be unreasonable on your side to insist any longer upon what you have no notion of.

*Hyl.* To confess ingenuously, I cannot.

*Phil.* Can you even separate the ideas of extension and motion from the ideas of all those qualities which they who make the distinction term *secondary?*

*Hyl.* What! Is it not an easy matter to consider extension and motion by themselves, abstracted from all other sensible qualities? Pray how do the mathematicians treat of them?

*Phil.* I acknowledge, Hylas, it is not difficult to form general propositions and reasonings about those qualities without mentioning any other and in this sense to consider or treat of them abstractly. But how does it follow that because I can pronounce the word *motion* by itself, I can form the idea of it in my mind exclusive of body? Or because theorems may be made of extension and figures without any mention of *great* or *small,* or any other sensible mode or quality, that therefore it is possible such an abstract idea of extension without any particular size or figure, or sensible quality, should be distinctly formed and apprehended by the mind? Mathematicians treat of quantity without regarding what other sensible qualities it is attended with, as being altogether indifferent to their demonstrations. But when, laying aside the words, they contemplate the bare ideas, I believe you will find they are not the pure abstracted ideas of extension.

*Hyl.* But what do you say to *pure intellect?* May not abstracted ideas be framed by that faculty?

*Phil.* Since I cannot frame abstract ideas at all, it is plain I cannot frame them by the help of *pure intellect,* whatever faculty you understand by those words. Besides, not to inquire into the nature of pure intellect and its spiritual objects, as *virtue, reason, God,* or the like—this much seems manifest—that sensible things are only to be perceived by sense or represented by the imagination. Figures, therefore, and extension, being originally perceived by sense, do not belong to pure intellect. But for your further satisfaction, try if you can frame the idea of any figure abstracted from all particularities of size or even from other sensible qualities.

*Hyl.* Let me think a little—I do not find that I can.

*Phil.* And can you think it possible that what implies a repugnance in its conception should really exist in nature?

*Hyl.* By no means.

*Phil.* Since, therefore, it is impossible even for the mind to disunite the ideas of extension and motion from all other sensible qualities, does it not follow that where the one exists, there necessarily the other exists likewise?

*Hyl.* It should seem so.

*Phil.* Consequently, the very same arguments which you admitted as conclusive against the secondary qualities are without any further application of force against the primary too. Besides, if you will trust your senses, is it not plain all sensible qualities coexist or appear to them as being in the same place? Do they ever represent a motion, or figure, as being divested of all other visible and tangible qualities?

*Hyl.* You need say no more on this head. I am free to admit, if there is no secret error or oversight in our proceedings up to now, that all sensible qualities are alike to be denied existence without the mind. But my fear is that I have been too liberal in my former concessions or overlooked some fallacy or other. In short, I did not take time to think.

*Phil.* For that matter, Hylas, you may take what time you please in reviewing the progress of our inquiry. You are at liberty to recover any slips you might have made or offer whatever you have omitted, which makes for your first opinion.

*Hyl.* One great oversight I take to be this: that I did not sufficiently distinguish the *object* from the *sensation*. Now though this latter may not exist without the mind, yet it will not follow from this that the former cannot.

*Phil.* What object do you mean? The object of the senses?

*Hyl.* The same.

*Phil.* It is then immediately perceived?

*Hyl.* Right.

*Phil.* Make me understand the difference between what is immediately perceived and a sensation.

*Hyl.* The sensation I take to be an act of the mind perceiving, besides which there is something

perceived, and this I call the *object*. For example, there is red and yellow on that tulip. But then the act of perceiving those colors is in me only, and not in the tulip.

*Phil.* What tulip do you speak of? Is it that which you see?

*Hyl.* The same.

*Phil.* And what do you see besides color, figure, and extension?

*Hyl.* Nothing.

*Phil.* What you would say then is that the red and yellow are coexistent with the extension; is it not?

*Hyl.* That is not all. I would say they have a real existence without the mind in some unthinking substance.

*Phil.* That the colors are really in the tulip, which I see, is manifest. Neither can it be denied that this tulip may exist independent of your mind or mine; but that any immediate object of the senses, that is, any idea or combination of ideas, should exist in an unthinking substance or exterior to all minds, is in itself an evident contradiction. Nor can I imagine how this follows from what you said just now, namely, that the red and yellow were on the tulip *you saw*, since you do not pretend to see that unthinking substance.

*Hyl.* You have an artful way, Philonous, of diverting our inquiry from the subject.

*Phil.* I see you have no mind to be pressed that way. To return then to your distinction between *sensation* and *object*; if I take you right, you distinguish in every perception two things, the one an action of the mind, the other not.

*Hyl.* True.

*Phil.* And this action cannot exist in or belong to any unthinking thing, but whatever besides is implied in a perception, may.

*Hyl.* That is my meaning.

*Phil.* So that if there was a perception without any act of the mind, it was possible such a perception should exist in an unthinking substance.

*Hyl.* I grant it. But it is impossible there should be such a perception.

*Phil.* When is the mind said to be active?

*Hyl.* When it produces, puts an end to, or changes anything.

*Phil.* Can the mind produce, discontinue, or change anything but by an act of the will?

*Hyl.* It cannot.

*Phil.* The mind therefore is to be accounted active in its perceptions, insofar as volition is included in them.

*Hyl.* It is.

*Phil.* In plucking this flower I am active, because I do it by the motion of my hand, which was consequent upon my volition—so likewise in applying it to my nose. But is either of these smelling?

*Hyl.* No.

*Phil.* I act too in drawing the air through my nose, because my breathing so rather than otherwise is the effect of my volition. But neither can this be called *smelling*, for if it were, I should smell every time I breathed in that manner.

*Hyl.* True.

*Phil.* Smelling then is somewhat consequent to all this.

*Hyl.* It is.

*Phil.* But I do not find my will concerned any further. Whatever more there is, as that I perceive such a particular smell or any smell at all, this is independent of my will and I am altogether passive in this. Do you find it otherwise with you, Hylas?

*Hyl.* No, the very same.

*Phil.* Then as to seeing, is it not in your power to open your eyes or keep them shut, to turn them this or that way?

*Hyl.* Without doubt.

*Phil.* But does it in like manner depend on your will that, in looking on this flower, you perceive *white* rather than any other color? Or directing your open eyes towards that part of the heaven beyond, can you avoid seeing the sun? Or is light or darkness the effect of your volition?

*Hyl.* No, certainly.

*Phil.* You are then in these respects altogether passive.

*Hyl.* I am.

*Phil.* Tell me now, whether *seeing* consists in perceiving light and colors or in opening and turning the eyes?

*Hyl.* Without doubt, in the former.

*Phil.* Since, therefore, you are in the very perception of light and colors altogether passive, what has become of that action you were speaking of as an ingredient in every sensation? And does it not follow from your own concessions that the perception of light and colors, including no action in it, may exist in an unperceiving substance? And is this not a plain contradiction?

*Hyl.* I do not know what to think of it.

*Phil.* Besides, since you distinguish the *active* and *passive* in every perception, you must do it in that of pain. But how is it possible that pain—let it be as little active as you please—should exist in an unperceiving substance? In short, do but consider the point and then confess ingenuously whether light and colors, tastes, sounds, etc., are not all equally passions or sensations in the soul. You may indeed call them *external objects* and give them in words what subsistence you please. But examine your own thoughts and then tell me whether it is not as I say?

*Hyl.* I acknowledge, Philonous, that upon a fair observation of what passes in my mind, I can discover nothing else but that I am a thinking being, affected with variety of sensations; neither is it possible to conceive how a sensation should exist in an unperceiving substance. But then, on the other hand, when I look on sensible things in a different view, considering them as so many modes and qualities, I find it necessary to suppose a material *substratum*, without which they cannot be conceived to exist.

*Phil. Material substratum* call you it? Pray, by which of your senses did you become acquainted with that being?

*Hyl.* It is not itself sensible, its modes and qualities only being perceived by the senses.

*Phil.* I presume, then, it was by reflection and reason you obtained the idea of it.

*Hyl.* I do not pretend to any proper positive idea of it. However, I conclude it exists, because qualities cannot be conceived to exist without a support.

*Phil.* It seems then you have only a relative notion of it, or that you conceive it not otherwise than by conceiving the relation it bears to sensible qualities.

*Hyl.* Right.

*Phil.* Be pleased, therefore, to let me know in what that relation consists.

*Hyl.* Is it not sufficiently expressed in the term *substratum* or *substance*?

*Phil.* If so, the word *substratum* should import that it is spread under the sensible qualities or accidents.

*Hyl.* True.

*Phil.* And consequently under extension.

*Hyl.* I admit it.

*Phil.* It is therefore somewhat in its own nature entirely distinct from extension.

*Hyl.* I tell you extension is only a mode, and matter is something that supports modes. And is it not evident the thing supported is different from the thing supporting?

*Phil.* So that something distinct from and exclusive of extension is supposed to be the *substratum* of extension.

*Hyl.* Just so.

*Phil.* Answer me, Hylas. Can a thing be spread without extension? Or is not the idea of extension necessarily included in *spreading*?

*Hyl.* It is.

*Phil.* Whatever, therefore, you suppose spread under anything must have in itself an extension distinct from the extension of that thing under which it is spread.

*Hyl.* It must.

*Phil.* Consequently, every corporeal substance being the *substratum* of extension must have in itself another extension by which it is qualified to be a *substratum*, and so on to infinity. And I ask whether this is not absurd in itself and repugnant to what you granted just now, namely, that the *substratum* was something distinct from and exclusive of extension.

*Hyl.* Yes, but, Philonous, you take me wrong. I do not mean that matter is *spread* in a gross literal sense under extension. The word *substratum* is used only to express in general the same thing with *substance*.

*Phil.* Well then, let us examine the relation implied in the term *substance*. Is it not that it stands under accidents?

*Hyl.* The very same.

*Phil.* But that one thing may stand under or support another, must it not be extended?

*Hyl.* It must.

*Phil.* Is not therefore this supposition liable to the same absurdity with the former?

*Hyl.* You still take things in a strict literal sense; that is not fair, Philonous.

*Phil.* I am not for imposing any sense on your words; you are at liberty to explain them as you please. Only I beseech you, make me understand something by them. You tell me matter supports or stands under accidents. How? Is it as your legs support your body?

*Hyl.* No; that is the literal sense.

*Phil.* Pray let me know any sense, literal or not literal, that you understand it in. How long must I wait for an answer, Hylas?

*Hyl.* I declare I do not know what to say. I once thought I understood well enough what was meant by matter's supporting accidents. But now the more I think on it, the less can I comprehend it; in short, I find that I know nothing of it.

*Phil.* It seems then you have no idea at all, neither relative nor positive, of matter; you know neither what it is in itself nor what relation it bears to accidents.

*Hyl.* I acknowledge it.

*Phil.* And yet you asserted that you could not conceive how qualities or accidents should really exist without conceiving at the same time a material support of them.

*Hyl.* I did.

*Phil.* That is to say, when you conceive the real existence of qualities, you do in addition conceive something which you cannot conceive.

*Hyl.* It was wrong, I admit. But still I fear there is some fallacy or other. Pray what do you think of this? It has just come into my head that the ground of all our mistake lies in your treating of each quality by itself. Now, I grant that each quality cannot singly subsist without the mind. Color cannot exist without extension, neither can figure without some other sensible quality. But as the several qualities united or blended together form entire sensible things, nothing hinders why such things may not be supposed to exist without the mind.

*Phil.* Either, Hylas, you are jesting or have a very bad memory. Though indeed we went through all the qualities by name one after another, yet my arguments, or rather your concessions, nowhere tended to prove that the secondary qualities did not subsist each alone by itself, but that they were not *at all* without the mind. Indeed in treating of figure and motion, we concluded they could not exist without the mind because it was impossible even in thought to separate them from all secondary qualities so as to conceive them existing by themselves. But then this was not the only argument made use of upon that occasion. But (to pass by all that has been said up to now, and reckon it for nothing, if you will have it so) I am content to put the whole upon this issue. If you can conceive it possible for any mixture or combination of qualities or any sensible object whatever to exist without the mind, then I will grant it actually to be so.

*Hyl.* If it comes to that, the point will soon be decided. What is more easy than to conceive a tree or house existing by itself, independent of, and unperceived by any mind whatsoever? I do at this present time conceive them existing after that manner.

*Phil.* What are you saying, Hylas—can you see a thing which is at the same time unseen?

*Hyl.* No, that would be a contradiction.

*Phil.* Is it not as great a contradiction to talk of *conceiving* a thing which is *unconceived*?

*Hyl.* It is.

*Phil.* The tree or house, therefore, which you think of is conceived by you.

*Hyl.* How should it be otherwise?

*Phil.* And what is conceived is surely in the mind.

*Hyl.* Without question, that which is conceived is in the mind.

*Phil.* How then did you come to say you conceived a house or tree existing independent and out of all minds whatsoever?

*Hyl.* That was, I admit, an oversight; but stay, let me consider what led me into it. It is a pleasant mistake enough. As I was thinking of a tree in a solitary place where no one was present to see it, I thought that was to conceive a tree as existing unperceived or unthought of, not considering that I myself conceived it all the while. But now I plainly see that all I can do is to frame ideas in my own mind. I may

indeed conceive in my own thoughts the idea of a tree, or a house, or a mountain, but that is all. And this is far from proving that I can conceive them *existing out of the minds of all spirits*.

*Phil.* You acknowledge then that you cannot possibly conceive how any one corporeal sensible thing should exist otherwise than in a mind.

*Hyl.* I do.

*Phil.* And yet you will earnestly contend for the truth of that which you cannot so much as conceive.

*Hyl.* I profess I do not know what to think, but still some scruples remain with me. Is it not certain I see things at a distance? Do we not perceive the stars and moon, for example, to be a great way off? Is this not, I say, manifest to the senses?

*Phil.* Do you not in a dream too perceive those or the like objects?

*Hyl.* I do.

*Phil.* And do they not then have the same appearance of being distant?

*Hyl.* They have.

*Phil.* But you do not then conclude the apparitions in a dream to be without the mind?

*Hyl.* By no means.

*Phil.* You ought not therefore conclude that sensible objects are without the mind from their appearance or manner in which they are perceived.

*Hyl.* I acknowledge it. But does not my sense deceive me in those cases?

*Phil.* By no means. Of the idea or thing which you immediately perceive, neither sense nor reason informs you that it actually exists without the mind. By sense you only know that you are affected with such certain sensations of light and colors, etc. And these you will not say are without the mind.

*Hyl.* True, but besides all that, do you not think the sight suggests something of *outness* or *distance*?

*Phil.* Upon approaching a distant object, do the visible size and figure change perpetually or do they appear the same at all distances?

*Hyl.* They are in a continual change.

*Phil.* Sight, therefore, does not suggest or in any way inform you that the visible object you immediately perceive exists at a distance or will be perceived when you advance further onward, there being a continued series of visible objects succeeding each other during the whole time of your approach.

*Hyl.* It does not; but still I know, upon seeing an object, what object I shall perceive after having passed over a certain distance—no matter whether it be exactly the same or no—there is still something of distance suggested in the case.

*Phil.* Good Hylas, do but reflect a little on the point and then tell me whether there is any more in it than this: From the ideas you actually perceive by sight, you have by experience learned to collect what other ideas you will (according to the standing order of nature) be affected with, after such a certain succession of time and motion.

*Hyl.* Upon the whole, I take it to be nothing else.

*Phil.* Now is it not plain that if we suppose a man born blind was suddenly made to see, he could at first have no experience of what may be suggested by sight.

*Hyl.* It is.

*Phil.* He would not then, according to you, have any notion of distance annexed to the things he saw; but would take them for a new set of sensations existing only in his mind.

*Hyl.* It is undeniable.

*Phil.* But to make it still more plain: is not *distance* a line turned endwise to the eye?

*Hyl.* It is.

*Phil.* And can a line so situated be perceived by sight?

*Hyl.* It cannot.

*Phil.* Does it not therefore follow that distance is not properly and immediately perceived by sight?

*Hyl.* It should seem so.

*Phil.* Again, is it your opinion that colors are at a distance?

*Hyl.* It must be acknowledged they are only in the mind.

*Phil.* But do not colors appear to the eye as coexisting in the same place with extension and figures?

*Hyl.* They do.

*Phil.* How can you then conclude from sight that figures exist without, when you acknowledge colors do not, the sensible appearance being the very same with regard to both?

*Hyl.* I do not know what to answer.

*Phil.* But allowing that distance was truly and immediately perceived by the mind, yet it would not then follow it existed out of the mind. For whatever is immediately perceived is an idea; and can any idea exist out of the mind?

*Hyl.* To suppose that would be absurd, but inform me, Philonous, can we perceive or know nothing besides our ideas?

*Phil.* As for the rational deducing of causes from effects, that is beside our inquiry. And by the senses you can best tell whether you perceive anything which is not immediately perceived. And I ask you whether the things immediately perceived are other than your own sensations or ideas? You have indeed more than once, in the course of this conversation, declared yourself on those points; but you seem, by this last question, to have departed from what you then thought.

*Hyl.* To speak the truth, Philonous, I think there are two kinds of objects, the one perceived immediately, which are likewise called ideas, the other are real things or external objects perceived by the mediation of ideas, which are their images and representations. Now I admit ideas do not exist without the mind, but the latter sort of object does. I am sorry I did not think of this distinction sooner; it would probably have cut short your discourse.

*Phil.* Are those external objects perceived by sense or by some other faculty?

*Hyl.* They are perceived by sense.

*Phil.* How! Is there anything perceived by sense which is not immediately perceived?

*Hyl.* Yes, Philonous, in some sort there is. For example, when I look on a picture or statue of Julius Caesar, I may be said, after a manner, to perceive him (though not immediately) by my senses.

*Phil.* It seems then you will have our ideas, which alone are immediately perceived, to be pictures of external things, and that these also are perceived by sense inasmuch as they have a conformity or resemblance to our ideas.

*Hyl.* That is my meaning.

*Phil.* And in the same way that Julius Caesar, in himself invisible, is nevertheless perceived by sight;

real things, in themselves imperceptible, are perceived by sense.

*Hyl.* In the very same.

*Phil.* Tell me, Hylas, when you behold the picture of Julius Caesar, do you see with your eyes any more than some colors and figures, with a certain symmetry and composition of the whole?

*Hyl.* Nothing else.

*Phil.* And would not a man who had never known anything of Julius Caesar see as much?

*Hyl.* He would.

*Phil.* Consequently, he has his sight and the use of it in as perfect a degree as you.

*Hyl.* I agree with you.

*Phil.* From where does it come then that your thoughts are directed to the Roman emperor and his are not? This cannot proceed from the sensations or ideas of sense by you then perceived, since you acknowledge you have no advantage over him in that respect. It should seem therefore to proceed from reason and memory, should it not?

*Hyl.* It should.

*Phil.* Consequently, it will not follow from that instance that anything is perceived by sense which is not immediately perceived. Though I grant we may in one meaning be said to perceive sensible things mediately by sense, that is, when, from a frequently perceived connection, the immediate perception of ideas by one sense suggests to the mind others perhaps belonging to another sense which are accustomed to be connected with them. For instance, when I hear a coach drive along the streets, immediately I perceive only the sound; but, from the experience I have had that such a sound is connected with a coach, I am said to hear the coach. It is nevertheless evident that, in truth and strictness, nothing can be *heard* but *sound*, and the coach is not then properly perceived by sense, but suggested from experience. So likewise when we are said to see a red-hot bar of iron, the solidity and heat of the iron are not the objects of sight, but suggested to the imagination by the color and figure, which are properly perceived by that sense. In short, those things alone are actually and strictly perceived by any sense which would have been perceived in case that same sense had then

been first conferred on us. As for other things, it is plain they are only suggested to the mind by experience grounded on former perceptions. But to return to your comparison of Caesar's picture, it is plain, if you keep to that, you must hold that the real things or archetypes of our ideas are not perceived by sense, but by some internal faculty of the soul as reason or memory. I would therefore gladly know what arguments you can draw from reason for the existence of what you call *real things* or *material objects*, or whether you remember to have seen them formerly as they are in themselves, or if you have heard or read of anyone who did.

*Hyl.* I see, Philonous, you are disposed to raillery, but that will never convince me.

*Phil.* My aim is only to learn from you the way to come at the knowledge of *material beings*. Whatever we perceive is perceived either immediately or mediately, by sense, or by reason and reflection. But as you have excluded sense, pray show me what reason you have to believe their existence, or what *medium* you can possibly make use of to prove it, either to mine or your own understanding.

*Hyl.* To deal ingenuously, Philonous, now that I consider the point, I do not find I can give you any good reason for it. But this much seems pretty plain—that it is at least possible such things may really exist, and as long as there is no absurdity in supposing them, I am resolved to believe as I did, until you bring good reasons to the contrary.

*Phil.* What! Has it come to this that you only believe the existence of material objects and that your belief is founded barely on the possibility of its being true? Then you will have me bring reasons against it, though another would think it reasonable the proof should lie on him who holds the affirmative. And after all, this very point which you are now resolved to maintain without any reason is, in effect, what you have more than once during this discourse seen good reason to give up. But to pass over all this—if I understand you rightly, you say our ideas do not exist without the mind, but that they are copies, images, or representations of certain originals that do.

*Hyl.* You take me right.

*Phil.* They are then like external things.

*Hyl.* They are.

*Phil.* Have those things a stable and permanent nature independent of our senses, or are they in a perpetual change upon our producing any motions in our bodies, suspending, exerting, or altering our faculties or organs of sense.

*Hyl.* Real things, it is plain, have a fixed and real nature, which remains the same, notwithstanding any change in our senses or in the posture and motion of our bodies, which indeed may affect the ideas in our minds, but it would be absurd to think they had the same effect on things existing without the mind.

*Phil.* How then is it possible that things perpetually fleeting and variable as our ideas should be copies or images of anything fixed and constant? Or, in other words, since all sensible qualities, as size, figure, color, etc., that is, our ideas, are continually changing upon every alteration in the distance, medium, or instruments of sensation, how can any determinate material objects be properly represented or painted forth by several distinct things, each of which is so different from and unlike the rest? Or if you say it resembles some one only of our ideas, how shall we be able to distinguish the true copy from all the false ones?

*Hyl.* I profess, Philonous, I am at a loss. I do not know what to say to this.

*Phil.* But neither is this all. Which are material objects in themselves—perceptible or imperceptible?

*Hyl.* Properly and immediately nothing can be perceived but ideas. All material things, therefore, are in themselves insensible and to be perceived only by their ideas.

*Phil.* Ideas then are sensible, and their archetypes or originals insensible.

*Hyl.* Right.

*Phil.* But how can that which is sensible be like that which is insensible? Can a real thing in itself *invisible* be like a *color*; or a real thing which is not *audible* be like a *sound*? In a word, can anything be like a sensation or idea but another sensation or idea?

*Hyl.* I must admit, I think not.

*Phil.* Is it possible there should be any doubt in the point? Do you not perfectly know your own ideas?

*Hyl.* I know them perfectly, since what I do not perceive or know can be no part of my idea.

*Phil.* Consider, therefore, and examine them, and then tell me if there is anything in them which can exist without the mind or if you can conceive anything like them existing without the mind.

*Hyl.* Upon inquiry, I find it is impossible for me to conceive or understand how anything but an idea can be like an idea. And it is most evident that *no idea can exist without the mind*.

*Phil.* You are, therefore, by your principles forced to deny the reality of sensible things, since you made it to consist in an absolute existence exterior to the mind. That is to say, you are a downright *skeptic*. So I have gained my point, which was to show your principles led to skepticism.

*Hyl.* For the present I am, if not entirely convinced, at least silenced.

*Phil.* I would gladly know what more you would require in order to have a perfect conviction. Have you not had the liberty of explaining yourself all manner of ways? Were any little slips in discourse laid hold and insisted on? Or were you not allowed to retract or reinforce anything you had offered, as best served your purpose? Has not everything you could say been heard and examined with all the fairness imaginable? In a word, have you not in every point been convinced out of your own mouth? And if you can at present discover any flaw in any of your former concessions, or think of any remaining subterfuge, any new distinction, color, or comment whatsoever, why do you not produce it?

*Hyl.* A little patience, Philonous. I am at present so amazed to see myself ensnared, and as it were imprisoned in the labyrinths you have drawn me into, that on the sudden it cannot be expected I should find my way out. You must give me time to look about me and recollect myself.

*Phil.* Listen, is not this the college bell?

*Hyl.* It rings for prayers.

*Phil.* We will go in then if you please, and meet here again tomorrow morning. In the meantime you may employ your thoughts on this morning's discourse, and try if you can find any fallacy in it, or invent any new means to extricate yourself.

*Hyl.* Agreed.

## The Second Dialogue

*Hylas*. I beg your pardon, Philonous, for not meeting you sooner. All this morning my head was so filled with our late conversation that I had not leisure to think of the time of the day, or indeed of anything else.

*Philonous*. I am glad you were so intent upon it, in hopes if there were any mistakes in your concessions or fallacies in my reasonings from them, you will now discover them to me.

*Hyl*. I assure you, I have done nothing ever since I saw you but search after mistakes and fallacies—and, with that view, have minutely examined the whole series of yesterday's discourse—but all in vain, for the notions it led me into, upon review, appear still more clear and evident, and the more I consider them, the more irresistibly do they force my assent.

*Phil*. And is this not, you think, a sign that they are genuine, that they proceed from nature and are conformable to right reason? Truth and beauty are in this alike, that the strictest survey sets them both off to advantage. While the false luster of error and disguise cannot endure being reviewed or too nearly inspected.

*Hyl*. I admit there is a great deal in what you say. Nor can anyone be more entirely satisfied of the truth of those odd consequences so long as I have in view the reasonings that lead to them. But when these are out of my thoughts, there seems, on the other hand, something so satisfactory, so natural and intelligible in the modern way of explaining things that I profess I do not know how to reject it.

*Phil*. I do not know what way you mean.

*Hyl*. I mean the way of accounting for our sensations or ideas.

*Phil*. How is that?

*Hyl*. It is supposed the soul makes her residence in some part of the brain from which the nerves take their rise and are thus extended to all parts of the body, and that outward objects, by the different impressions they make on the organs of sense, communicate certain vibrational motions to the nerves, and these being filled with spirits, propagate them to the brain or seat of the soul, which, according to the various impressions or traces thereby made in the brain, is variously affected with ideas.

*Phil*. And do you call this an explication of the manner whereby we are affected with ideas?

*Hyl*. Why not, Philonous? Have you anything to object against it?

*Phil*. I would first know whether I rightly understand your hypothesis. You make certain traces in the brain to be the causes or occasions of our ideas. Pray tell me whether by the *brain* you mean any sensible thing?

*Hyl*. What else do you think I could mean?

*Phil*. Sensible things are all immediately perceivable; and those things which are immediately perceivable are ideas; and these exist only in the mind. This much you have, if I am not mistaken, long since agreed to.

*Hyl*. I do not deny it.

*Phil*. The brain therefore you speak of, being a sensible thing, exists only in the mind. Now, I would gladly know whether you think it reasonable to suppose that one idea or thing existing in the mind occasions all other ideas. And if you think so, pray how do you account for the origin of that primary idea or brain itself?

*Hyl*. I do not explain the origin of our ideas by that brain which is perceivable to sense, this being itself only a combination of sensible ideas, but by another which I imagine.

*Phil*. But are not things imagined as truly *in the mind* as things perceived?

*Hyl*. I must confess they are.

*Phil*. It comes, therefore, to the same thing, and you have been all this while accounting for ideas by certain motions or impressions in the brain, that is, by some alterations in an idea—whether sensible or imaginable, it does not matter.

*Hyl*. I begin to suspect my hypothesis.

*Phil*. Beside spirits, all that we know or conceive are our own ideas. When, therefore, you say all ideas are occasioned by impressions in the brain, do you conceive this brain or not? If you do, then you talk of ideas imprinted in an idea causing that same idea, which is absurd. If you do not conceive it, you talk unintelligibly instead of forming a reasonable hypothesis.

*Hyl*. I now clearly see it was a mere dream. There is nothing in it.

*Phil.* You need not be much concerned at it; for, after all, this way of explaining things, as you called it, could never have satisfied any reasonable man. What connection is there between a motion in the nerves and the sensations of sound or color in the mind? Or how is it possible these should be the effect of that?

*Hyl.* But I could never think it had so little in it as now it seems to have.

*Phil.* Well then, are you at length satisfied that no sensible things have a real existence, and that you are in truth a thoroughgoing *skeptic*?

*Hyl.* It is too plain to be denied.

*Phil.* Look! Are not the fields covered with a delightful greenery? Is there not something in the woods and groves, in the rivers and clear springs, that soothes, that delights, that transports the soul? At the prospect of the wide and deep ocean, or some huge mountain whose top is lost in the clouds, or of an old gloomy forest, are not our minds filled with a pleasing horror? Even in rocks and deserts, is there not an agreeable wildness? How sincere a pleasure is it to behold the natural beauties of the earth! To preserve and renew our relish for them, is not the veil of night alternately drawn over her face, and does she not change her dress with the seasons? How aptly are the elements disposed! What variety and use in the meanest production of nature! What delicacy, what beauty, what contrivance in animal and vegetable bodies? How exquisitely are all things suited as well to their particular ends as to constitute opposite parts of the whole! And while they mutually aid and support, do they not also set off and illustrate each other! Raise now your thoughts from this ball of earth to all those glorious luminaries that adorn the high arch of heaven. The motion and situation of the planets, are they not admirable for use and order. Were those (miscalled *erratic*) globes ever known to stray in their repeated journeys through the pathless void? Do they not measure areas round the sun ever proportioned to the times? So fixed, so immutable, are the laws by which the unseen Author of nature actuates the universe. How vivid and radiant is the luster of the fixed stars! How magnificent and rich that negligent profusion with which they appear to be scattered throughout the whole azure vault! Yet if you take the telescope, it brings into your sight a new host of stars that escape the naked eye. Here they seem contiguous and minute, but to a nearer view immense orbs of light at various distances, far sunk in the abyss of space. Now you must call imagination to your aid. The feeble narrow sense cannot ascertain innumerable worlds revolving round the central fires, and in those worlds the energy of an all-perfect mind displayed in endless forms. But neither sense nor imagination is big enough to comprehend the boundless extent with all its glittering furniture. Though the laboring mind exerts and strains each power to its utmost reach, there still stands out ungrasped an immeasurable surplus. Yet all the vast bodies that compose this mighty frame, however distant and remote, are by some secret mechanism, some divine art and force, linked in a mutual dependence and intercourse with each other, even with this earth, which was almost slipped from my thoughts and lost in the crowd of worlds. Is not the whole system immense, beautiful, glorious beyond expression and beyond thought? What treatment then do those philosophers deserve who would deprive these noble and delightful scenes of all reality? How should those principles be entertained that lead us to think all the visible beauty of the creation a false imaginary glare? To be plain, can you expect this skepticism of yours will not be thought extravagantly absurd by all men of sense?

*Hyl.* Other men may think as they please, but for your part you have nothing to reproach me with. My comfort is you are as much a skeptic as I am.

*Phil.* There, Hylas, I must beg leave to differ from you.

*Hyl.* What! Have you all along agreed to the premises, and do you now deny the conclusion and leave me to maintain these paradoxes which you led me into by myself? This surely is not fair.

*Phil.* I deny that I agreed with you in those notions that led to skepticism. You indeed said the reality of sensible things consisted in an *absolute existence* out of the minds of spirits or distinct from their being perceived. And, pursuant to this notion of reality, you are obliged to deny sensible things any real existence, that is, according to your own definition, you profess yourself a *skeptic*. But I neither said nor thought the reality of sensible things was to be defined after that manner. To me it is evident, for the reasons you allow of, that sensible things cannot exist otherwise than in a mind or spirit. From this I conclude, not that they have no real existence, but that, seeing they do not depend on my thought, and have an existence distinct from being perceived by me, *there must be some other mind in which they exist.* As sure, therefore, as the sensible world really exists, so sure is there an infinite, omnipresent Spirit who contains and supports it.

*Hyl.* What! This is no more than I and all Christians hold—no, and all others too who believe there is a God and that he knows and comprehends all things.

*Phil.* Yes, but here lies the difference. Men commonly believe that all things are known or perceived by God because they believe the being of a God, whereas I, on the other side, immediately and necessarily conclude the being of a God because all sensible things must be perceived by him.

*Hyl.* But so long as we all believe the same thing, what matter is it how we come by that belief?

*Phil.* But neither do we agree in the same opinion. For philosophers, though they acknowledge all corporeal beings to be perceived by God, yet they attribute to them an absolute subsistence distinct from their being perceived by any mind whatever, which I do not. Besides, is there no difference between saying *there is a God, therefore he perceives all things,* and saying *sensible things do really exist—and if they really exist, they are necessarily perceived by an infinite mind—therefore there is an infinite mind, or God?* This furnishes you with a direct and immediate demonstration, from a most evident principle, of the *being of a God.* Theologians and philosophers had proved beyond all controversy, from the beauty and usefulness of the several parts of the creation, that it was the workmanship of God. But that—setting aside all help of astronomy and natural philosophy, all contemplation of the contrivance, order, and adjustment of things—an infinite mind should be necessarily inferred from the bare existence of the sensible world is an advantage peculiar to them only who have made this easy reflection: that the sensible world is that which we perceive by our several senses; and that nothing is perceived by the senses besides ideas; and that no idea or archetype of an idea can exist otherwise than in a mind. You may now, without any laborious search into the sciences, without any subtlety of reason or tedious length of discourse, oppose and baffle the most strenuous advocate for atheism. Those miserable refuges, whether in an eternal succession of unthinking causes and effects or in a fortuitous concourse of atoms—those wild imaginations of Vanini, Hobbes, and Spinoza, in a word, the whole system of atheism—is it not entirely overthrown by this single reflection on the repugnance included in supposing the whole or any part, even the most rude and shapeless of the visible world to exist without a mind? Let anyone of those abettors of impiety but look into his own thoughts and there try if he can conceive how so much as a rock, a desert, a chaos, or confused jumble of atoms, how anything at all, either sensible or imaginable, can exist independent of a mind, and he need go no further to be convinced of his folly. Can anything be fairer than to put a dispute on such an issue and leave it to a man himself to see if he can conceive, even in thought, what he holds to be true in fact, and to allow it a real existence from a notion?

*Hyl.* It cannot be denied, there is something highly serviceable to religion in what you advance. But do you not think it looks very like a notion entertained by some eminent moderns, of *seeing all things in God?*

*Phil.* I would gladly know that opinion; pray explain it to me.

*Hyl.* They conceive that the soul, being immaterial, is incapable of being united with material things so as to perceive them in themselves, but that she perceives them by her union with the substance of God, which, being spiritual, is therefore purely intelligible or capable of being the immediate object of a spirit's thought. Besides, the divine essence contains in it perfections correspondent to each created being, and which are, for that reason, proper to exhibit or represent them to the mind.

*Phil.* I do not understand how our ideas, which are things altogether passive and inert, can be the essence or any part (or like any part) of the essence or substance of God, who is an impassive, indivisible, purely active being. Many more difficulties and objections occur at first view against this hypothesis, but I shall only add that it is liable to all the absurdities of the common hypotheses in making a created world exist otherwise than in the mind of a spirit. Besides all which, it has this peculiar to itself that it makes that material world serve to no purpose. And if it passes for a good argument against other hypotheses in the sciences that they suppose nature or the Divine Wisdom to make something in vain or do by tedious round-about methods what might have been performed in a much more easy and compendious way, what shall we think of that hypothesis which supposes the whole world made in vain?

*Hyl.* But what do you say, are not you too of the opinion that we see all things in God? If I am not mistaken, what you advance comes near it.

*Phil.* Few men think, yet all will have opinions. Hence men's opinions are superficial and confused. It is nothing strange that tenets which in themselves are ever so different should nevertheless be confounded with each other by those who do not consider them attentively. I shall not therefore be surprised if some men imagine that I run into the enthusiasm of Malebranche, though in truth I am very remote from it. He builds on the most abstract general ideas, which I entirely disclaim. He asserts an absolute external world, which I deny. He maintains that we are deceived by our senses and do not know the real natures or the true forms and figures of extended beings—to all of which I hold the direct contrary. So that, upon the whole, there are no principles more fundamentally opposite than his and mine. It must be admitted I entirely agree with what the Holy Scripture says that "in God we live, and move, and have our being" (Acts 17:28). But that we see things in his essence, after the manner above set forth, I am far from believing. Take here in brief my meaning. It is evident that the things I perceive are my own ideas and that no idea can exist unless it be in a mind. Nor is it less plain that these ideas, or things perceived by me, either themselves or their archetypes, exist independently of my mind, since I do not know myself to be their author, it being out of my power to determine at pleasure what particular ideas I shall

be affected with upon opening my eyes or ears. They must therefore exist in some other mind, whose will it is they should be exhibited to me. The things, I say, immediately perceived, are ideas or sensations, call them which you will. But how can any idea or sensation exist in, or be produced by, anything but a mind or spirit? This indeed is inconceivable, and to assert that which is inconceivable is to talk nonsense, is it not?

*Hyl.* Without doubt.

*Phil.* But, on the other hand, it is very conceivable that they should exist in and be produced by a spirit, since this is no more than I daily experience in myself—inasmuch as I perceive numberless ideas and, by an act of my will, can form a great variety of them and raise them up in my imagination, though it must be confessed, these creatures of the fancy are not altogether so distinct, so strong, vivid, and permanent, as those perceived by my senses, which latter are called *real things*. From all which I conclude *there is a mind which affects me every moment with all the sensible impressions I perceive*. And from the variety, order, and manner of these, I conclude the author of them to be *wise, powerful, and good beyond comprehension*. Mark it well: I do not say I see things by perceiving that which represents them in the intelligible substance of God. This I do not understand; but I say the things perceived by me are known by the understanding and produced by the will of an infinite Spirit. And is not all this most plain and evident? Is there any more in it than what a little observation of our own minds, and that which passes in them, not only enables us to conceive but also obliges us to acknowledge?

*Hyl.* I think I understand you very clearly and admit the proof you give of a Deity seems no less evident than it is surprising. But allowing that God is the supreme and universal cause of all things, yet may not there be still a third nature besides spirits and ideas? May we not admit a subordinate and limited cause of our ideas? In a word, may there not for all that be *matter*?

*Phil.* How often must I inculcate the same thing? You allow the things immediately perceived by sense to exist nowhere without the mind, but there is nothing perceived by sense which is not perceived immediately. Therefore, there is nothing sensible that exists without the mind. The matter, therefore, which you still insist on is something intelligible, I suppose, something that may be discovered by reason and not by sense.

*Hyl*. You are in the right.

*Phil*. Pray let me know what reasoning your belief of matter is grounded on, and what this matter is in your present sense of it.

*Hyl*. I find myself affected with various ideas of which I know I am not the cause; neither are they the cause of themselves or of one another, or capable of subsisting by themselves, as being altogether inactive, fleeting, dependent beings. They have therefore some cause distinct from me and them, of which I pretend to know no more than that it is *the cause of my ideas*. And this thing, whatever it is, I call matter.

*Phil*. Tell me, Hylas, has everyone a liberty to change the current proper signification annexed to a common name in any language? For example, suppose a traveler should tell you that in a certain country men might pass unhurt through the fire, and, upon explaining himself, you found he meant by the word *fire* that which others call *water*, or if he should assert there are trees which walk upon two legs, meaning men by the term *trees*. Would you think this reasonable?

*Hyl*. No, I should think it very absurd. Common custom is the standard of propriety in language. And for any man to affect speaking improperly is to pervert the use of speech and can never serve to a better purpose than to protract and multiply disputes where there is no difference in opinion.

*Phil*. And does not *matter*, in the common current meaning of the word, signify an extended, solid, movable, unthinking, inactive substance?

*Hyl*. It does.

*Phil*. And has it not been made evident that no such substance can possibly exist? And though it should be allowed to exist, yet how can that which is *inactive* be a *cause* or that which is *unthinking* be a *cause of thought*? You may, indeed, if you please, annex to the word *matter* a contrary meaning to what is vulgarly received, and tell me you understand by it

an unextended, thinking, active being, which is the cause of our ideas. But what else is this than to play with words and run into that very fault you just now condemned with so much reason? I do by no means find fault with your reasoning, in that you collect a cause from the *phenomena*, but I deny that the cause deducible by reason can properly be termed matter.

*Hyl*. There is indeed something in what you say. But I am afraid you do not thoroughly comprehend my meaning. I would by no means be thought to deny that God, or an infinite spirit, is the supreme cause of all things. All I contend for is that subordinate to the supreme agent there is a cause of a limited and inferior nature, which concurs in the production of our ideas, not by any act of will or spiritual efficiency, but by that kind of action which belongs to matter, namely *motion*.

*Phil*. I find you are at every turn relapsing into your old exploded conceit of a movable and consequently an extended substance existing without the mind. What! Have you already forgot you were convinced, or are you willing I should repeat what has been said on that head? In truth this is not fair dealing in you still to suppose the being of that which you have so often acknowledged to have no being. But not to insist further on what has been so largely handled, I ask whether all your ideas are not perfectly passive and inert, including nothing of action in them?

*Hyl*. They are.

*Phil*. And are sensible qualities anything else but ideas?

*Hyl*. How often have I acknowledged that they are not?

*Phil*. But is not motion a sensible quality?

*Hyl*. It is.

*Phil*. Consequently, it is no action.

*Hyl*. I agree with you. And indeed it is very plain that when I stir my finger, it remains passive, but my will which produced the motion is active.

*Phil*. Now I desire to know, in the first place, whether motion being allowed to be no action, you can conceive any action besides volition; and, in the second place, whether to say something and conceive nothing is not to talk nonsense; and, lastly, whether having considered the premises, you do not perceive that to suppose any efficient or active cause of our ideas other than *spirit* is highly absurd and unreasonable?

*Hyl.* I give up the point entirely. But though matter may not be a cause, yet what hinders its being an *instrument* subservient to the supreme agent in the production of our ideas?

*Phil.* An instrument, you say; pray what may be the figure, springs, wheels, and motions of that instrument?

*Hyl.* Those I pretend to determine nothing of, both the substance and its qualities being entirely unknown to me.

*Phil.* What? You are then of the opinion, it is made up of unknown parts, that it has unknown motions, and an unknown shape.

*Hyl.* I do not believe it has any figure or motion at all, being already convinced that no sensible qualities can exist in an unperceiving substance.

*Phil.* But what notion is it possible to frame of an instrument void of all sensible qualities, even extension itself?

*Hyl.* I do not pretend to have any notion of it.

*Phil.* And what reason do you have to think this unknown, this inconceivable somewhat does exist? Is it that you imagine God cannot act as well without it or that you find by experience the use of some such thing when you form ideas in your own mind?

*Hyl.* You are always teasing me for reasons of my belief. Pray what reasons do you have not to believe it?

*Phil.* It is to me a sufficient reason not to believe the existence of anything if I see no reason for believing it. But, not to insist on reasons for believing, you will not so much as let me know what it is you would have me believe, since you say you have no manner of notion of it. After all, let me entreat you to consider whether it is like a philosopher, or even like a man of common sense, to pretend to believe you do not know what and you do not know why.

*Hyl.* Hold on, Philonous. When I tell you matter is an *instrument*, I do not mean altogether nothing. It is true, I do not know the particular kind of instrument, but, however, I have some notion of *instrument in general*, which I apply to it.

*Phil.* But what if it should prove that there is something, even in the most general notion of *instrument*, as taken in a distinct sense from *cause*, which makes the use of it inconsistent with the divine attributes?

*Hyl.* Make that appear and I shall give up the point.

*Phil.* What do you mean by the general nature or notion of *instrument*?

*Hyl.* That which is common to all particular instruments composes the general notion.

*Phil.* Is it not common to all instruments that they are applied to the doing those things only which cannot be performed by the mere act of our wills? Thus, for instance, I never use an instrument to move my finger because it is done by a volition. But I should use one if I were to remove part of a rock or tear up a tree by the roots. Are you of the same mind? Or can you show any example where an instrument is made use of in producing an effect immediately depending on the will of the agent?

*Hyl.* I admit I cannot.

*Phil.* How, therefore, can you suppose that an all-perfect Spirit, on whose will all things have an absolute and immediate dependence, should need an instrument in his operations or, not needing it, make use of it? Thus it seems to me that you are obliged to admit the use of a lifeless inactive instrument to be incompatible with the infinite perfection of God—that is, by your own confession to give up the point.

*Hyl.* It does not readily occur what I can answer you.

*Phil.* But I think you should be ready to admit the truth when it has been fairly proved to you. We, indeed, who are beings of finite powers, are forced to make use of instruments. And the use of an instrument shows the agent to be limited by rules of another's prescription and that he cannot obtain his end, but in such a way and by such conditions. From this it seems a clear consequence that the supreme unlimited agent uses no tool or instrument at all. The will of an omnipotent Spirit is no sooner exerted than executed, without the application of means, which, if they are employed by inferior agents, it is not upon account of any real efficacy that is in them or necessary aptitude to produce any effect, but merely in compliance with the laws of nature or those conditions prescribed to them by the first cause, who is himself above all limitation or prescription whatsoever.

*Hyl.* I will no longer maintain that matter is an instrument. However, I would not be understood to give up its existence either, since, notwithstanding what has been said, it may still be an *occasion*.

*Phil.* How many shapes is your matter to take? Or how often must it be proved not to exist before you are content to part with it? But to say no more of this (though by all the laws of disputation I may justly blame you for so frequently changing the signification of the principal term) I would gladly know what you mean by affirming that matter is an occasion, having already denied it to be a cause. And when you have shown in what sense you understand *occasion*, pray, in the next place, be pleased to show me what reason induces you to believe there is such an occasion of our ideas.

*Hyl.* As to the first point: By *occasion* I mean an inactive, unthinking being, at the presence of which God excites ideas in our minds.

*Phil.* And what may be the nature of that inactive, unthinking being?

*Hyl.* I know nothing of its nature.

*Phil.* Proceed then to the second point and assign some reason why we should allow an existence to this inactive, unthinking, unknown thing.

*Hyl.* When we see ideas produced in our minds after an orderly and constant manner, it is natural to think they have some fixed and regular occasions at the presence of which they are excited.

*Phil.* You acknowledge then God alone to be the cause of our ideas and that he causes them at the presence of those occasions.

*Hyl.* That is my opinion.

*Phil.* Those things which you say are present to God, without doubt he perceives.

*Hyl.* Certainly. Otherwise they could not be to him an occasion of acting.

*Phil.* Not to insist now on your making sense of this hypothesis or answering all the puzzling questions and difficulties it is liable to: I only ask whether the order and regularity observable in the series of our ideas, or the course of nature, are not sufficiently accounted for by the wisdom and power of God, and whether it does not derogate from those attributes to suppose he is influenced, directed, or put in mind, when and how he is to act, by any unthinking substance. And, lastly, whether in case I granted all you contend for, it would make anything to your purpose, it not being easy to conceive how the external or absolute existence of an unthinking substance, distinct from its being perceived, can be inferred from my allowing that there are certain things perceived by the mind of God which are to him the occasion of producing ideas in us.

*Hyl.* I am perfectly at a loss what to think, this notion of *occasion* seeming now altogether as groundless as the rest.

*Phil.* Do you not at length perceive that in all these different meanings of *matter*, you have been only supposing you do not know what, for no manner of reason, and to no kind of use?

*Hyl.* I freely admit myself less fond of my notions since they have been so accurately examined. But still, I think I have some confused perception that there is such a thing as *matter*.

*Phil.* Either you perceive the being of matter immediately or mediately. If immediately, pray inform me by which of the senses you perceive it. If mediately, let me know by what reasoning it is inferred from those things which you perceive immediately. So much for the perception. Then for the matter itself, I ask whether it is object, *substratum*, cause, instrument, or occasion? You have already pleaded for each of these, shifting your notions and making matter to appear sometimes in one shape, then in another. And what you have offered has been disapproved and rejected by yourself. If you have anything new to advance, I would gladly hear it.

*Hyl.* I think I have already offered all I had to say on those heads. I am at a loss what more to urge.

*Phil.* And yet you are loath to part with your old prejudice. But to make you quit it more easily, I desire that, besides what has been suggested up to now, you will further consider whether, upon the supposition that matter exists, you can possibly conceive how you should be affected by it? Or, supposing it did not exist, whether it is not evident you might for all that be affected with the same ideas you now are, and consequently have the very same reasons to believe its existence that you now can have?

*Hyl.* I acknowledge it is possible we might perceive all things just as we do now, though there was no matter in the world; neither can I conceive, if there is matter, how it should produce any idea in our minds. And I do further grant you have entirely satisfied me that it is impossible there should be such a thing as matter in any of the foregoing senses. But still I cannot help supposing that there is *matter* in some sense or other. What that is I do not indeed pretend to determine.

*Phil.* I do not expect you should define exactly the nature of that unknown being. Only be pleased to tell me whether it is a substance, and if so, whether you can suppose a substance without accidents, or in case you suppose it to have accidents or qualities, I desire you will let me know what those qualities are, at least what is meant by matter's supporting them.

*Hyl.* We have already argued on those points. I have no more to say to them. But to prevent any further questions, let me tell you, I at present understand by *matter* neither substance nor accident, thinking nor extended being, neither cause, instrument, nor occasion, but something entirely unknown, distinct from all these.

*Phil.* It seems then you include in your present notion of matter nothing but the general abstract of idea of *entity*.

*Hyl.* Nothing else, save only that I superadd to this general idea the negation of all those particular things, qualities, or ideas that I perceive, imagine, or in any way apprehend.

*Phil.* Pray where do you suppose this unknown matter to exist?

*Hyl.* Oh Philonous! Now you think you have entangled me; for if I say it exists in place, then you will infer that it exists in the mind, since it is agreed that place or extension exists only in the mind, but I am not ashamed to admit my ignorance. I do not know where it exists; only I am sure it does not exist in place. There is a negative answer for you and you must expect no other to all the questions you put for the future about matter.

*Phil.* Since you will not tell me where it exists, be pleased to inform me after what manner you suppose it to exist or what you mean by its existence.

*Hyl.* It neither thinks nor acts, neither perceives, nor is perceived.

*Phil.* But what is there positive in your abstracted notion of its existence?

*Hyl.* Upon a nice observation, I do not find I have any positive notion or meaning at all. I tell you again I am not ashamed to admit my ignorance. I do not know what is meant by its *existence* or how it exists.

*Phil.* Continue, good Hylas, to act the same ingenuous part and tell me sincerely whether you can frame a distinct idea of entity in general, prescinded from and exclusive of all thinking and corporeal beings, all particular things whatsoever.

*Hyl.* Hold on, let me think a little—I profess, Philonous, I do not find that I can. At first glance I thought I had some dilute and airy notion of pure entity in abstract, but upon closer attention it has quite vanished out of sight. The more I think on it, the more am I confirmed in my prudent resolution of giving none but negative answers and not pretending to the least degree of any positive knowledge or conception of matter, its *where*, its *how*, its *entity*, or anything belonging to it.

*Phil.* When, therefore, you speak of the existence of matter, you do not have any notion in your mind.

*Hyl.* None at all.

*Phil.* Pray tell me if the case does not stand thus: at first, from a belief in material substance, you would have it that the immediate objects existed without the mind; then, that they are archetypes; then causes; next instruments; then occasions; lastly, *something in general*, which being interpreted proves *nothing*. So matter comes to nothing. What do you think, Hylas? Is not this a fair summary of your whole proceeding?

*Hyl.* Be that as it will, yet I still insist upon it that our not being able to conceive a thing is no argument against its existence.

*Phil.* That from a cause, effect, operation, sign, or other circumstance, there may reasonably be inferred the existence of a thing not immediately perceived, and that it would be absurd for any man to argue against the existence of that thing from his having no direct and positive notion of it, I freely admit. But where there is nothing of all this; where neither reason nor revelation induces us to believe the existence of a thing; where we have not even a relative notion of it; where an abstraction is made from perceiving and being perceived, from spirit and idea; lastly, where there is not so much as the most inadequate or faint idea pretended to, I will not, indeed, then conclude against the reality of any notion or existence of anything, but my inference shall be that you mean nothing at all, that you imply words to no manner of purpose, without any design or signification whatsoever. And I leave it to you to consider how mere jargon should be treated.

*Hyl.* To deal frankly with you, Philonous, your arguments seem in themselves unanswerable, but they do not have so great an effect on me as to produce that entire conviction, that hearty acquiescence which attends demonstration. I find myself still relapsing into an obscure surmise of I do not know what—*matter*.

*Phil.* But are you not sensible, Hylas, that two things must concur to take away all scruple and work a plenary assent in the mind? Let a visible object be set in never so clear a light, yet, if there is any imperfection in the sight, or if the eye is not directed towards it, it will not be distinctly seen. And though a demonstration be never so well grounded and fairly proposed, yet, if there is in addition a stain of prejudice or a wrong bias on the understanding, can it be expected on a sudden to perceive clearly and adhere firmly to the truth? No, there is need of time and pains; the attention must be awakened and detained by a frequent repetition of the same thing placed often in the same, often in different lights. I have said it already, and find I must still repeat and inculcate, that it is an unaccountable license you take in pretending to maintain you do not know what, you do not know for what reason, you do not know to what purpose. Can this be paralleled in any art or science, any sect or profession of men? Or is there anything so barefacedly groundless and unreasonable to be met with even in the lowest of common conversation? But perhaps you will still say, matter may exist, though at the same time you neither know what is meant by *matter*, nor by its *existence*. This indeed is surprising, and the more so because it is altogether voluntary, you not being led to it by any one reason; for I challenge you to show me that thing in nature which needs matter to explain or account for it.

*Hyl.* The reality of things cannot be maintained without supposing the existence of matter. And is not this, you think, a good reason why I should be earnest in its defense?

*Phil.* The reality of things! What things, sensible or intelligible?

*Hyl.* Sensible things.

*Phil.* My glove, for example?

*Hyl.* That or any other thing perceived by the senses.

*Phil.* But to fix on some particular thing, is it not a sufficient evidence to me of the existence of this *glove* that I see it, and feel it, and wear it? Or if this will not do, how is it possible I should be assured of the reality of this thing, which I actually see in this place, by supposing that some unknown thing, which I never did or can see, exists after an unknown manner, in an unknown place, or in no place at all? How can the supposed reality of that which is intangible be a proof that anything tangible really exists? Or of that which is invisible, that any visible thing, or in general of anything which is imperceptible, that a perceptible exists? Do but explain this and I shall think nothing too hard for you.

*Hyl.* Upon the whole, I am content to admit the existence of matter is highly improbable; but the direct and absolute impossibility of it does not appear to me.

*Phil.* But granting matter to be possible, yet, upon that account merely, it can have no more claim to existence than a golden mountain or a centaur.

*Hyl.* I acknowledge it, but still you do not deny it is possible; and that which is possible, for all you know, may actually exist.

*Phil.* I deny it to be possible, and have, if I am not mistaken, evidently proved from your own concessions that it is not. In the common meaning of the word *matter*, is there any more implied than an extended, solid, figured, movable substance, existing without the mind? And have not you acknowledged over and over that you have seen evident reason for denying the possibility of such a substance?

*Hyl.* True, but that is only one sense of the term *matter*.

*Phil.* But is it not the only proper genuine received sense? And if matter in such a sense is proved impossible, may it not be thought with good grounds absolutely impossible? How else could anything be proved impossible? Or indeed how could there be any proof at all one way or the other to a man who takes the liberty to unsettle and change the common signification of words?

*Hyl.* I thought philosophers might be allowed to speak more accurately than the vulgar and were not always confined to the common meaning of a term.

*Phil.* But this now mentioned is the common received sense among philosophers themselves. But not to insist on that, have you not been allowed to take matter in what sense you pleased? And have you not used this privilege in the utmost extent, sometimes entirely changing, at others leaving out or putting into the definition of it whatever for the present best served your design, contrary to all the known rules of reason and logic? And has not this shifting, unfair method of yours spun out our dispute to an unnecessary length, matter having been particularly examined and by your own confession refuted in each of those senses? And can any more be required to prove the absolute impossibility of a thing than the proving it impossible in every particular sense that either you or anyone else understands it in?

*Hyl.* But I am not so thoroughly satisfied that you have proved the impossibility of matter in the last most obscure, abstracted, and indefinite sense.

*Phil.* When is a thing shown to be impossible?

*Hyl.* When a repugnance is demonstrated between the ideas comprehended in its definition.

*Phil.* But where there are no ideas, there no repugnance can be demonstrated between ideas.

*Hyl.* I agree with you.

*Phil.* Now, in that which you call the obscure, indefinite sense of the word matter, it is plain, by your own confession, there was included no idea at all, no sense except an unknown sense, which is the same thing as none. You are not, therefore, to expect I should prove a repugnance between ideas where there are no ideas, or the impossibility of matter taken in an *unknown* sense—that is, no sense at all. My business was only to show you meant *nothing*, and this you were brought to admit. So that in all your various senses, you have been shown either to mean nothing at all or, if anything, an absurdity. And if this is not sufficient to prove the impossibility of a thing, I desire you will let me know what is.

*Hyl.* I acknowledge you have proved that matter is impossible; nor do I see what more can be said in defense of it. But, at the same time that I give up this, I suspect all my other notions. For surely none could be more seemingly evident than this once was, and yet it now seems as false and absurd as ever it did true before. But I think we have discussed the point sufficiently for the present. The remaining part of the day I would willingly spend in running over in my thoughts the several heads of this morning's conversation, and tomorrow shall be glad to meet you here again about the same time.

*Phil.* I will not fail to attend you.

## The Third Dialogue

*Philonous.* Tell me, Hylas, what are the fruits of yesterday's meditation? Has it confirmed you in the same mind you were in at parting? Or have you since seen cause to change your opinion?

*Hylas.* Truly my opinion is that all our opinions are alike vain and uncertain. What we approve today, we condemn tomorrow. We keep a stir about knowledge and spend our lives in the pursuit of it, when, alas, we know nothing all the while; nor do I think it possible for us ever to know anything in this life. Our faculties are too narrow and too few. Nature certainly never intended us for speculation.

*Phil.* What! You say we can know nothing, Hylas?

*Hyl.* There is not that single thing in the world of which we can know the real nature, or what it is in itself.

*Phil.* Will you tell me I do not really know what fire or water is?

*Hyl.* You may indeed know that fire appears hot and water fluid, but this is no more than knowing what sensations are produced in your own mind, upon the application of fire and water to your organs of sense. Their internal constitution, their true and real nature, you are utterly in the dark as to *that*.

*Phil.* Do I not know this to be a real stone that I stand on and that which I see before my eyes to be a real tree?

*Hyl. Know?* No, it is impossible you or any man alive should know it. All you know is that you have such a certain idea or appearance in your own mind. But what is this to the real tree or stone? I tell you that color, figure, and hardness, which you perceive, are not the real natures of those things or in the least like them. The same may be said of all other real things or corporeal substances which compose the world. They have, none of them, anything in themselves like those sensible qualities perceived by us. We should not, therefore, pretend to affirm or know anything of them as they are in their own nature.

*Phil.* But surely, Hylas, I can distinguish gold, for example, from iron, and how could this be, if I knew not what either truly was?

*Hyl.* Believe me, Philonous, you can only distinguish between your own ideas. That yellowness, that weight, and other sensible qualities, do you think they are really in the gold? They are only relative to the senses and have no absolute existence in nature. And in pretending to distinguish the species of real things by the appearances in your mind, you may perhaps act as wisely as he who should conclude two men were of a different species because their clothes were not of the same color.

*Phil.* It seems, then, we are altogether put off with the appearances of things, and those false ones too. The very meat I eat and the cloth I wear have nothing in them like what I see and feel.

*Hyl.* Even so.

*Phil.* But is it not strange the whole world should be thus imposed on and so foolish as to believe their senses? And yet I do not know how it is, but men eat, and drink, and sleep, and perform all the offices of life as comfortably and conveniently as if they really knew the things they are conversant about.

*Hyl.* They do so, but you know ordinary practice does not require a nicety of speculative knowledge. Hence the vulgar retain their mistakes, and for all

that make a shift to bustle through the affairs of life. But philosophers know better things.

*Phil.* You mean, they know that they *know nothing*.

*Hyl.* That is the very top and perfection of human knowledge.

*Phil.* But are you all this while in earnest, Hylas; and are you seriously persuaded that you know nothing real in the world? Suppose you are going to write, would you not call for pen, ink, and paper, like another man; and do you not know what it is you call for?

*Hyl.* How often must I tell you that I do not know the real nature of any one thing in the universe? I may, indeed, upon occasion, make use of pen, ink, and paper. But what any one of them is in its own true nature, I declare positively I do not know. And the same is true with regard to every other corporeal thing. And, what is more, we are not only ignorant of the true and real nature of things, but even of their existence. It cannot be denied that we perceive such certain appearances or ideas; but it cannot be concluded from this that bodies really exist. No, now I think on it, I must, agreeably to my former concessions, further declare that it is impossible any real corporeal thing should exist in nature.

*Phil.* You amaze me. Was anything ever more wild and extravagant than the notions you now maintain, and is it not evident you are led into all these extravagances by the belief of *material substance*? This makes you dream of those unknown natures in everything. It is this which occasions your distinguishing between the reality and sensible appearances of things. It is to this you are indebted for being ignorant of what everybody else knows perfectly well. Nor is this all: you are not only ignorant of the true nature of everything, but you do not know whether anything really exists or whether there are any true natures at all. For as much as you attribute to your material beings an absolute or external existence, in which you suppose their reality consists, and as you are forced, in the end, to acknowledge such an existence means either a direct repugnance or nothing at all, it follows that you are obliged to pull down your own hypothesis of material substance and positively to deny the real existence of any part of the universe. And so you are plunged into the deepest and most deplorable *skepticism* that ever man was. Tell me, Hylas, is it not as I say?

*Hyl.* I agree with you. *Material substance* was no more than an hypothesis, and a false and groundless one too. I will no longer spend my breath in defense of it. But whatever hypothesis you advance, or whatever scheme of things you introduce in its stead, I do not doubt it will appear every whit as false; let me but be allowed to question you upon it. That is, allow me to serve you in your own kind and I warrant it shall conduct you through as many perplexities and contradictions to the very same state of skepticism that I myself am in at present.

*Phil.* I assure you, Hylas, I do not pretend to frame any hypothesis at all. I am of a vulgar cast, simple enough to believe my senses and leave things as I find them. To be plain, it is my opinion that the real things are those very things I see and feel and perceive by my senses. These I know, and, finding they answer all the necessities and purposes of life, have no reason to be solicitous about any other unknown beings. A piece of sensible bread, for instance, would stay my stomach better than ten thousand times as much of that insensible, unintelligible, real bread you speak of. It is likewise my opinion that colors and other sensible qualities are in the objects. I cannot for my life help thinking that snow is white and fire hot. You indeed, who by *snow* and *fire* mean certain external, unperceived, unperceiving substances, are in the right to deny whiteness or heat to be affections inherent in them. But I, who understand by those words the things I see and feel, am obliged to think like other folks. And as I am no skeptic with regard to the nature of things, so neither am I as to their existence. That a thing should be really perceived by my senses and at the same time not really exist is to me a plain contradiction, since I cannot prescind or abstract, even in thought, the existence of a sensible thing from its being perceived. Wood, stones, fire, water, flesh, iron, and the like things, which I name and discourse of, are things that I know. And I should not have known them but that I perceived them by my senses; and things perceived by the senses are immediately perceived; and things immediately perceived are ideas; and ideas cannot exist without

the mind; their existence, therefore, consists in being perceived; when, therefore, they are actually perceived, there can be no doubt of their existence. Away then with all that skepticism, all those ridiculous philosophical doubts. What a jest is it for a philosopher to question the existence of sensible things until he has it proved to him from the veracity of God or to pretend our knowledge in this point falls short of intuition or demonstration! I might as well doubt of my own being as of the being of those things I actually see and feel.

*Hyl.* Not so fast, Philonous; you say you cannot conceive how sensible things should exist without the mind. Do you not?

*Phil.* I do.

*Hyl.* Supposing you were annihilated, cannot you conceive it possible that things perceivable by sense may still exist?

*Phil.* I can; but then it must be in another mind. When I deny sensible things an existence out of the mind, I do not mean my mind in particular, but all minds. Now it is plain they have an existence exterior to my mind, since I find them by experience to be independent of it. There is, therefore, some other mind in which they exist during the intervals between the times of my perceiving them, as likewise they did before my birth and would do after my supposed annihilation. And as the same is true with regard to all other finite created spirits, it necessarily follows there is an *omnipresent, eternal Mind* which knows and comprehends all things, and exhibits them to our view in such a manner and according to such rules as he himself has ordained and are by us termed the *laws of nature*.

*Hyl.* Answer me, Philonous. Are all our ideas perfectly inert beings? Or do they have any agency included in them?

*Phil.* They are altogether passive and inert.

*Hyl.* And is not God an agent, a being purely active?

*Phil.* I acknowledge it.

*Hyl.* No idea, therefore, can be like or represent the nature of God.

*Phil.* It cannot.

*Hyl.* Since, therefore, you have no idea of the mind of God, how can you conceive it possible that things should exist in his mind? Or, if you can conceive the mind of God without having an idea of it, why may I not be allowed to conceive the existence of matter, notwithstanding that I have no idea of it?

*Phil.* As to your first question, I admit I have properly no idea, either of God or any other spirit; for these, being active, cannot be represented by things perfectly inert as our ideas are. I do nevertheless know that I, who am a spirit or thinking substance, exist as certainly as I know my ideas exist. Further, I know what I mean by the terms *I* and *myself*; and I know this immediately, or intuitively, though I do not perceive it as I perceive a triangle, a color, or a sound. The mind, spirit, or soul, is that indivisible, unextended thing, which thinks, acts, and perceives. I say *indivisible*, because unextended, and *unextended*, because extended, figured, movable things are ideas; and that which perceives ideas, which thinks and wills, is plainly itself no idea, nor like an idea. Ideas are things inactive and perceived, and spirits a sort of beings altogether different from them. I do not therefore say my soul is an idea or like an idea. However, taking the word *idea* in a large sense, my soul may be said to furnish me with an idea, that is, an image or likeness of God, though indeed extremely inadequate. For all the notion I have of God is obtained by reflecting on my own soul, heightening its powers and removing its imperfections. I have, therefore, though not an inactive idea, yet in myself some sort of an active thinking image of the Deity. And though I do not perceive him by sense, yet I have a notion of him or know him by reflection and reasoning. My own mind and my own ideas I have an immediate knowledge of, and, by the help of these, do mediately apprehend the possibility of the existence of other spirits and ideas. Further, from my own being and from the dependency I find in myself and my ideas, I do by an act of reason necessarily infer the existence of a God and of all created things in the mind of God. So much for your first question. For the second, I suppose by this time you can answer it yourself. For you neither perceive matter objectively, as you do an inactive being or idea, nor know it, as you do yourself, by a reflective act—neither do you mediately apprehend it by similitude of the one or the other, nor yet collect it by reasoning from that which you know immediately—all of which makes the case of *matter* widely different from that of the *Deity*.

*Hyl.* You say your own soul supplies you with some sort of an idea or image of God. But at the same time you acknowledge you have, properly speaking, no idea of your own soul. You even affirm that spirits are a sort of beings altogether different from ideas, consequently, that no idea can be like a spirit. We have, therefore, no idea of any spirit. You admit nevertheless that there is spiritual substance, although you have no idea of it, while you deny there can be such a thing as material substance, because you have no notion or idea of it. Is this fair dealing? To act consistently, you must either admit matter or reject spirit. What do you say to this?

*Phil.* I say, in the first place, that I do not deny the existence of material substance merely because I have no notion of it, but because the notion of it is inconsistent or, in other words, because it is repugnant that there should be a notion of it. Many things, for all I know, may exist, of which neither I nor any other man has or can have any idea or notion whatsoever. But then those things must be possible; that is, nothing inconsistent must be included in their definition. I say, secondly, that, although we believe things to exist which we do not perceive, yet we may not believe that any particular thing exists without some reason for such belief, but I have no reason for believing the existence of matter. I have no immediate intuition of this; neither can I mediately from my sensations, ideas, notions, actions, or passions infer an unthinking, unperceiving, inactive substance, either by probable deduction or necessary consequence, whereas the being of myself, that is, my own soul, mind, or thinking principle, I evidently know by reflection. You will forgive me if I repeat the same things in answer to the same objections. In the very notion or definition of material substance, there is included a manifest repugnance and inconsistency. But this cannot be said of the notion of spirit. That ideas should exist in what does not perceive, or be produced by what does not act, is repugnant. But it is no repugnance to say that a perceiving thing should be the subject of ideas or an active thing the cause of them. It is granted we have neither an immediate evidence nor a demonstrative knowledge of the existence of other finite spirits, but it will not then follow that such spirits are on a foot with material substances, if to suppose the one is inconsistent and it is not inconsistent to suppose the other; if the one can be inferred by no argument, and there is a probability for the other; if we see signs and effects indicating distinct finite agents like ourselves, and see no sign or symptom whatever that leads to a rational belief of matter. I say, lastly, that I have a notion of spirit, though I do not have, strictly speaking, an idea of it. I do not perceive it as an idea or by means of an idea, but know it by reflection.

*Hyl.* Notwithstanding all you have said, it seems to me that, according to your own way of thinking, and in consequence of your own principles, it should follow that you are only a system of floating ideas without any substance to support them. Words are not to be used without a meaning. And as there is no more meaning in spiritual substance than in material substance, the one is to be exploded as well as the other.

*Phil.* How often must I repeat that I know or am conscious of my own being and that I myself am not my ideas, but something else, a thinking, active principle that perceives, knows, wills, and operates about ideas? I know that I, one and the same self, perceive both colors and sounds; that a color cannot perceive a sound nor a sound a color; that I am therefore one individual principle, distinct from color and sound, and, for the same reason, from all other sensible things and inert ideas. But I am not in like manner conscious of either the existence or essence of matter. On the contrary, I know that nothing inconsistent can exist and that the existence of matter implies an inconsistency. Further, I know what I mean when I affirm that there is a spiritual substance or support of ideas, that is, that a spirit knows and perceives ideas. But I do not know what is meant when it is said that an unperceiving substance has inherent in it and supports either ideas or the archetypes of ideas. There is, therefore, upon the whole no parity of case between spirit and matter.

*Hyl.* I admit myself satisfied in this point. But do you in earnest think the real existence of sensible things consists in their being actually perceived? If so, how does it come that all mankind distinguishes between them? Ask the first man you meet, and he shall tell you, *to be perceived* is one thing and *to exist* is another.

*Phil.* I am content, Hylas, to appeal to the common sense of the world for the truth of my notion. Ask the gardener why he thinks the cherry tree over there exists in the garden, and he shall tell you because he sees and feels it—in a word, because he perceives it by his senses. Ask him why he thinks an orange tree is not there, and he shall tell you because he does not perceive it. What he perceives by sense, that he terms a real being and says it *is*, or *exists*; but that which is not perceivable, the same, he says, has no being.

*Hyl.* Yes, Philonous, I grant the existence of a sensible thing consists in being perceivable, but not in being actually perceived.

*Phil.* And what is perceivable but an idea? And can an idea exist without being actually perceived? These are points long since agreed between us.

*Hyl.* But be your opinion never so true, yet surely you will not deny it is shocking and contrary to the common sense of men. Ask the fellow, whether tree over there has an existence out of his mind, what answer, do you think, he would make?

*Phil.* The same that I should myself, namely, that it does exist out of his mind. But then to a Christian it cannot surely be shocking to say the real tree existing without his mind is truly known and comprehended by (that is, *exists in*) the infinite mind of God. Probably he may not at first glance be aware of the direct and immediate proof there is of this, inasmuch as the very being of a tree or any other sensible thing implies a mind in which it is. But the point itself he cannot deny. The question between the materialists and me is not whether things have a real existence out of the mind of this or that person, but whether they have an absolute existence, distinct from being perceived by God and exterior to all minds. This, indeed, some heathens and philosophers have affirmed, but whoever entertains notions of the Deity suitable to the Holy Scriptures will be of another opinion.

*Hyl.* But, according to your notions, what difference is there between real things and chimeras formed by the imagination or the visions of a dream, since they are all equally in the mind?

*Phil.* The ideas formed by the imagination are faint and indistinct; they have, besides, an entire dependence on the will. But the ideas perceived by sense, that is, real things, are more vivid and clear, and, being imprinted on the mind by a spirit distinct from us, have not a like dependence on our will. There is, therefore, no danger of confounding these with the foregoing, and there is as little of confounding them with the visions of a dream, which are dim, irregular, and confused. And though they should happen to be never so lively and natural, yet, by their not being connected and of a piece with the preceding and subsequent transactions of our lives, they might easily be distinguished from realities. In short, by whatever method you distinguish *things* from *chimeras* on your own scheme, the same, it is evident, will hold also upon mine. For it must be, I presume, by some perceived difference, and I am not for depriving you of any one thing that you perceive.

*Hyl.* But still, Philonous, you hold there is nothing in the world but spirits and ideas. And this, you must necessarily acknowledge, sounds very odd.

*Phil.* I admit the word *idea*, not being commonly used for *thing*, sounds something out of the way. My reason for using it was because a necessary relation to the mind is understood to be implied by that term and it is now commonly used by philosophers to denote the immediate objects of the understanding. But however odd the proposition may sound in words, yet it includes nothing so very strange or shocking in its sense, which in effect amounts to no more than this, namely, that there are only things perceiving and things perceived; or that every unthinking being is necessarily and from the very nature of its existence perceived by some mind, if not by any finite created mind, yet certainly by the infinite mind of God, in whom "we live, and move, and have our being" (Acts 17:28). Is this as strange as to say the sensible qualities are not in the objects or that we cannot be sure

of the existence of things, or know anything of their real natures, though we both see and feel them and perceive them by all our senses?

*Hyl.* And, in consequence of this, must we not think there are no such things as physical or corporeal causes, but that a spirit is the immediate cause of all the *phenomena* in nature? Can there be anything more extravagant than this?[4]

*Phil.* Yes, it is infinitely more extravagant to say a thing which is inert operates on the mind and a thing which is unperceiving is the cause of our perceptions. Besides, that which to you, I do not know for what reason, seems so extravagant is no more than the Holy Scriptures assert in a hundred places. In them God is represented as the sole and immediate author of all those effects which some heathens and philosophers are accustomed to ascribe to nature, matter, fate, or the like unthinking principle. This is so much the constant language of Scripture that it would be needless to confirm it by citations.

*Hyl.* You are not aware, Philonous, that in making God the immediate author of all the motions in nature, you make him the author of murder, sacrilege, adultery, and the like heinous sins.

*Phil.* In answer to that I observe, first, that the imputation of guilt is the same whether a person commits an action with or without an instrument. In case, therefore, you suppose God to act by the mediation of an instrument or occasion called *matter*, you

---

4. In §51 of *A Treatise concerning the Principles of Human Knowledge*, Berkeley presents and responds to a similar objection as follows: "*Seventhly*, it will upon this be demanded whether it does not seem absurd to take away natural causes and ascribe everything to the immediate operation of spirits? We must no longer say upon these principles that fire heats or water cools, but that a spirit heats, and so forth. Would not a man be deservedly laughed at, who should talk after this manner? I answer: He would so; in such things we ought to *think with the learned and speak with the vulgar*. They who to demonstration are convinced of the truth of the Copernican system do nevertheless say the sun rises, the sun sets, or comes to the meridian: and if they affected a contrary style in common talk, it would without doubt appear very ridiculous. A little reflection on what is here said will make it manifest that the common use of language would receive no manner of alteration or disturbance from the admission of our tenets."

as truly make him the author of sin as I, who think him the immediate agent in all those operations vulgarly ascribed to nature. I further observe that sin or moral turpitude does not consist in the outward physical action or motion, but in the internal deviation of the will from the laws of reason and religion. This is plain, in that the killing an enemy in a battle, or putting a criminal legally to death, is not thought sinful, though the outward acts are the very same with that in the case of murder. Since, therefore, sin does not consist in the physical action, making God an immediate cause of all such actions is not making him the author of sin. Lastly, I have nowhere said that God is the only agent who produces all the motions in bodies. It is true I have denied there are any other agents besides spirits, but this is very consistent with allowing to thinking, rational beings, in the production of motions, the use of limited powers ultimately indeed derived from God, but immediately under the direction of their own wills, which is sufficient to entitle them to all the guilt of their actions.

*Hyl.* But denying matter, Philonous, or corporeal substance—there is the point. You can never persuade me that this is not repugnant to the universal sense of mankind. Were our dispute to be determined by most voices, I am confident you would give up the point without gathering the votes.

*Phil.* I wish both our opinions were fairly stated and submitted to the judgment of men who had plain common sense without the prejudices of a learned education. Let me be represented as one who trusts his senses, who thinks he knows the things he sees and feels and entertains no doubts of their existence, and you fairly set forth with all your doubts, your paradoxes, and your skepticism about you, and I shall willingly acquiesce in the determination of any indifferent person. That there is no substance in which ideas can exist besides spirit is evident to me. And that the objects immediately perceived are ideas is agreed on all hands. And that sensible qualities are objects immediately perceived no one can deny. It is therefore evident there can be no *substratum* of those qualities but spirit, in which they exist, not by way of mode or property, but as a thing perceived in that which perceives it. I deny, therefore, that there is any

unthinking *substratum* of the objects of sense and, in that meaning, that there is any material substance. But if by *material substance* is meant only sensible body, that which is seen and felt (and the unphilosophical part of the world, I dare say, mean no more), then I am more certain of matter's existence than you or any other philosopher pretend to be. If there is anything which makes the generality of mankind averse from the notions I espouse, it is a misapprehension that I deny the reality of sensible things, but as it is you who are guilty of that and not I, it follows that in truth their aversion is against your notions and not mine. I do therefore assert that I am as certain of my own being as that there are bodies or corporeal substances (meaning the things I perceive by my senses), and that, granting this, the bulk of mankind will take no thought about, nor think themselves at all concerned in the fate of those unknown natures and philosophical quiddities, which some men are so fond of.

*Hyl.* What do you say to this? Since, according to you, men judge of the reality of things by their senses, how can a man be mistaken in thinking the moon a plain lucid surface about a foot in diameter; or a square tower, seen at a distance, round; or an oar, with one end in the water, crooked?

*Phil.* He is not mistaken with regard to the ideas he actually perceives, but in the inferences he makes from his present perceptions. Thus, in the case of the oar, what he immediately perceives by sight is certainly crooked, and so far he is in the right. But if he then concludes that upon taking the oar out of the water he shall perceive the same crookedness, or that it would affect his touch as crooked things are accustomed to do, in that he is mistaken. In like manner, if he should conclude from what he perceives in one station, that, in case he advances toward the moon or tower, he should still be affected with the like ideas, he is mistaken. But his mistake does not lie in what he perceives immediately and at present (it being a manifest contradiction to suppose he should err in respect of that), but in the wrong judgment he makes concerning the ideas he apprehends to be connected with those immediately perceived, or concerning the ideas that, from what he perceives at present, he imagines would be perceived in other circumstances. The case is the same with regard to the Copernican system. We do not here perceive any motion of the earth, but it would be erroneous to conclude from this that, in case we were placed at as great a distance from that as we are now from the other planets, we should not then perceive its motion.

*Hyl.* I understand you and must necessarily admit you say things plausible enough, but give me leave to put you in mind of one thing. Pray, Philonous, were you not formerly as positive that matter existed as you are now that it does not?

*Phil.* I was. But here lies the difference. Before, my positiveness was founded without examination, upon prejudice; but now, after inquiry, upon evidence.

*Hyl.* After all, it seems our dispute is rather about words than things. We agree in the thing, but differ in the name. That we are affected with ideas from without is evident; and it is no less evident that there must be (I will not say archetypes, but) powers outside the mind corresponding to those ideas. And as these powers cannot subsist by themselves, there is some subject of them necessarily to be admitted, which I call *matter* and you call *spirit*. This is all the difference.

*Phil.* Pray, Hylas, is that powerful being, or subject of powers, extended?

*Hyl.* It has not extension; but it has the power to raise in you the idea of extension.

*Phil.* It is therefore itself unextended.

*Hyl.* I grant it.

*Phil.* Is it not also active?

*Hyl.* Without doubt; otherwise, how could we attribute powers to it?

*Phil.* Now let me ask you two questions: *First*, whether it is agreeable to the usage either of philosophers or others to give the name *matter* to an unextended active being? And *secondly*, whether it is not ridiculously absurd to misapply names contrary to the common use of language?

*Hyl.* Well then, let it not be called matter, since you will have it so, but some *third nature* distinct from matter and spirit. For what reason is there why you should call it spirit? Does not the notion of spirit imply that it is thinking as well as active and unextended?

*Phil.* My reason is this: Because I have a mind to have some notion or meaning in what I say, but I have no notion of any action distinct from volition, neither can I conceive volition to be anywhere but in a spirit; therefore, when I speak of an active being, I am obliged to mean a spirit. Besides, what can be plainer than that a thing which has no ideas in itself cannot impart them to me; and if it has ideas, surely it must be a spirit. To make you comprehend the point still more clearly, if it is possible, I assert as well as you that since we are affected from without, we must allow powers to be without in a being distinct from ourselves. So far we are agreed. But then we differ as to the kind of this powerful being. I will have it to be spirit, you matter or I do not know what (I may add too, you do not know what) third nature. Thus I prove it to be spirit. From the effects I see produced, I conclude there are actions; and because actions, volitions; and because there are volitions, there must be a will. Again, the things I perceive must have an existence, they or their archetypes, out of my mind, but, being ideas, neither they nor their archetypes can exist otherwise than in an understanding; there is therefore an understanding. But will and understanding constitute in the strictest sense a mind or spirit. The powerful cause, therefore, of my ideas is in strict propriety of speech a *spirit*.

*Hyl.* And now I warrant you think you have made the point very clear, little suspecting that what you advance leads directly to a contradiction. Is it not an absurdity to imagine any imperfection in God?

*Phil.* Without doubt.

*Hyl.* To suffer pain is an imperfection.

*Phil.* It is.

*Hyl.* Are we not sometimes affected with pain and uneasiness by some other being?

*Phil.* We are.

*Hyl.* And have you not said that being is a spirit, and is not that spirit God?

*Phil.* I grant it.

*Hyl.* But you have asserted that whatever ideas we perceive from without are in the mind which affects us. The ideas, therefore, of pain and uneasiness are in God; or in other words, God suffers pain—that is to say, there is an imperfection in the divine nature, which you acknowledged was absurd. So you are caught in a plain contradiction.

*Phil.* That God knows or understands all things and that he knows among other things what pain is, even every sort of painful sensation, and what it is for his creatures to suffer pain, I make no question. But that God, though he knows and sometimes causes painful sensations in us, can himself suffer pain, I positively deny. We, who are limited and dependent spirits, are liable to impressions of sense, the effects of an external agent, which, being produced against our wills, are sometimes painful and uneasy. But God, whom no external being can affect, who perceives nothing by sense as we do, whose will is absolute and independent, causing all things and liable to be thwarted or resisted by nothing, it is evident such a being as this can suffer nothing, nor be affected with any painful sensation, or indeed any sensation at all. We are chained to a body, that is to say, our perceptions are connected with corporeal motions. By the law of our nature we are affected upon every alteration in the nervous parts of our sensible body—which sensible body rightly considered is nothing but a complexion of such qualities or ideas as have no existence distinct from being perceived by a mind—so that this connection of sensations with corporeal motions means no more than a correspondence in the order of nature between two sets of ideas or things immediately perceivable. But God is a pure spirit, disengaged from all such sympathy or natural ties. No corporeal motions are attended with the sensations of pain or pleasure in his mind. To know everything knowable is certainly a perfection; but to endure, or suffer, or feel anything by sense, is an imperfection. The former, I say, agrees to God, but not the latter. God knows or has ideas, but his ideas are not conveyed to him by sense as ours are. Your not distinguishing where there is so manifest a difference makes you fancy you see an absurdity where there is none.

*Hyl.* But all this while you have not considered that the quantity of matter has been demonstrated to be proportioned to the gravity of bodies. And what can withstand demonstration?

*Phil.* Let me see how you demonstrate that point.

*Hyl.* I lay it down for a principle that the moments or quantities of motion in bodies are in a direct compounded reason of the velocities and quantities of matter contained in them. Hence, where the velocities are equal, it follows the moments are directly as the quantity of matter in each. But it is found by experience that all bodies (bating the small inequalities arising from the resistance of the air) descend with an equal velocity, the motion therefore of descending bodies, and consequently their gravity, which is the cause or principle of that motion, is proportional to the quantity of matter—which was to be demonstrated.

*Phil.* You lay it down as a self-evident principle that the quantity of motion in any body is proportional to the velocity and *matter* taken together; and this is made use of to prove a proposition from which the existence of *matter* is inferred. Pray is not this arguing in a circle?

*Hyl.* In the premise I only mean that the motion is proportional to the velocity, jointly with the extension and solidity.

*Phil.* But allowing this to be true, yet it will not then follow that gravity is proportional to *matter* in your philosophic sense of the word, except you take it for granted that unknown *substratum*, or whatever else you call it, is proportional to those sensible qualities—which to suppose is plainly begging the question. That there is magnitude and solidity, or resistance, perceived by sense, I readily grant, as likewise that gravity may be proportional to those qualities, I will not dispute. But that either these qualities as perceived by us or the powers producing them do exist in a *material substratum*; this is what I deny and you indeed affirm, but notwithstanding your demonstration have not yet proved.

*Hyl.* I shall insist no longer on that point. Do you think, however, you shall persuade me that natural philosophers have been dreaming all this while? Pray what becomes of all their hypotheses and explications of the *phenomena* which suppose the existence of matter?

*Phil.* What do you mean, Hylas, by the *phenomena*?

*Hyl.* I mean the appearances which I perceive by my senses.

*Phil.* And the appearances perceived by sense, are they not ideas?

*Hyl.* I have told you so a hundred times.

*Phil.* Therefore, to explain the *phenomena* is to show how we come to be affected with ideas, in that manner and order in which they are imprinted on our senses. Is it not?

*Hyl.* It is.

*Phil.* Now if you can prove that any philosopher has explained the production of any one idea in our minds by the help of *matter*, I shall forever acquiesce and look on all that has been said against it as nothing, but if you cannot, it is in vain to urge the explication of *phenomena*. That a being endowed with knowledge and will should produce or exhibit ideas is easily understood. But that a being which is utterly destitute of these faculties should be able to produce ideas, or in any sort to affect an intelligence, this I can never understand. This I say, though we had some positive conception of matter, though we knew its qualities and could comprehend its existence, would yet be so far from explaining things that it is itself the most inexplicable thing in the world. And yet for all this, it will not follow that philosophers have been doing nothing; for by observing and reasoning upon the connection of ideas, they discover the laws and methods of nature, which is a part of knowledge both useful and entertaining.

*Hyl.* After all, can it be supposed God would deceive all mankind? Do you imagine he would have induced the whole world to believe the being of matter if there was no such thing?

*Phil.* That every epidemic opinion arising from prejudice, or passion, or thoughtlessness, may be imputed to God, as the author of it, I believe you will not affirm. Whatever opinion we father on him, it must be either because he has discovered it to us by supernatural revelation or because it is so evident to our natural faculties, which were framed and given us by God, that it is impossible we should withhold our assent from it. But where is the revelation or where is the evidence that extorts the belief of matter? No, how does it appear that matter, taken for something distinct from what we perceive by our senses, is thought to exist by all mankind, or indeed by any except a few philosophers who do not know what they would be at? Your question supposes these points are clear; and when you have cleared them, I shall think myself obliged to give you another answer. In the meantime let it suffice that I tell you I do not suppose God has deceived mankind at all.

*Hyl.* But the novelty, Philonous, the novelty! There lies the danger. New notions should always be discountenanced; they unsettle men's minds and nobody knows where they will end.

*Phil.* Why rejecting a notion that has no foundation either in sense or in reason or in divine authority should be thought to unsettle the belief of such opinions as are grounded on all or any of these, I cannot imagine. That innovations in government and religion are dangerous and ought to be discountenanced, I freely admit. But is there the like reason why they should be discouraged in philosophy? Making anything known which was unknown before is an innovation in knowledge, and if all such innovations had been forbidden, men would [not] have made a notable progress in the arts and sciences. But it is none of my business to plead for novelties and paradoxes. That the qualities we perceive are not in the objects; that we must not believe our senses; that we know nothing of the real nature of things and can never be assured even of their existence; that real colors and sounds are nothing but certain unknown figures and motions; that motions are in themselves neither swift nor slow; that there are in bodies absolute extensions, without any particular magnitude or figure; that a thing stupid, thoughtless, and inactive operates on a spirit; that the least particle of a body contains innumerable extended parts. These are the novelties, these are the strange notions which shock the genuine uncorrupted judgment of all mankind, and, being once admitted, embarrass the mind with endless doubts and difficulties. And it is against these and the like innovations I endeavor to vindicate common sense. It is true, in doing this, I may perhaps be obliged to use some *ambages*[5] and ways of speech not common. But if my notions are once thoroughly understood, that which is most singular in them will

_____

5. Round-about ways of speech.

in effect be found to amount to no more than this: that it is absolutely impossible and a plain contradiction to suppose that any unthinking being should exist without being perceived by a mind. And if this notion is singular, it is a shame it should be so at this time of day and in a Christian country.

*Hyl.* As for the difficulties other opinions may be liable to, those are out of the question. It is your business to defend your own opinion. Can anything be plainer than that you are for changing all things into ideas? You, I say, who are not ashamed to charge me with *skepticism*. This is so plain there is no denying it.

*Phil.* You mistake me. I am not for changing things into ideas, but rather ideas into things, since those immediate objects of perception, which, according to you, are only appearances of things, I take to be the real things themselves.

*Hyl.* Things! You may pretend what you please, but it is certain you leave us nothing but the empty forms of things, the outside only which strikes the senses.

*Phil.* What you call the empty forms and outside of things seems to me the very things themselves. Nor are they empty or incomplete otherwise than upon your supposition that matter is an essential part of all corporeal things. We both, therefore, agree in this: that we perceive only sensible forms, but we differ in this: You will have them to be empty appearances; I, real beings. In short, you do not trust your senses; I do.

*Hyl.* You say you believe your senses and seem to applaud yourself that in this you agree with the vulgar. According to you, therefore, the true nature of a thing is discovered by the senses. If so, where does that disagreement come from? Why is not the same figure and other sensible qualities perceived all manner of ways? And why should we use a microscope, the better to discover the true nature of a body, if it were discoverable to the naked eye?

*Phil.* Strictly speaking, Hylas, we do not see the same object that we feel; neither is the same object perceived by the microscope which was by the naked eye. But in case every variation was thought sufficient to constitute a new kind or individual, the endless number or confusion of names would render language impracticable. Therefore, to avoid this as well as other inconveniences which are obvious upon a little thought, men combine together several ideas, apprehended by various senses, or by the same sense at different times, or in different circumstances, but observed, however, to have some connection in nature, either with respect to coexistence or succession; all which they refer to one name and consider as one thing. Hence it follows that when I examine by my other senses a thing I have seen, it is not in order to understand better the same object which I had perceived by sight, the object of one sense not being perceived by the other senses. And when I look through a microscope, it is not that I may perceive more clearly what I perceived already with my bare eyes, the object perceived by the glass being quite different from the former. But in both cases my aim is only to know what ideas are connected together; and the more a man knows of the connection of ideas, the more he is said to know of the nature of things. What, therefore, if our ideas are variable? What if our senses are not in all circumstances affected with the same appearances? It will not then follow they are not to be trusted, or that they are inconsistent either with themselves or anything else, except with your preconceived notion of (I do not know what) one single, unchanged, unperceivable, real nature, marked by each name, which prejudice seems to have taken its rise from not rightly understanding the common language of men speaking of several distinct ideas as united into one thing by the mind. And, indeed, there is cause to suspect several erroneous conceits of the philosophers are owing to the same original: while they began to build their schemes, not so much on notions as words which were framed by the vulgar merely for convenience and dispatch in the common actions of life, without any regard to speculation.

*Hyl.* I think I apprehend your meaning.

*Phil.* It is your opinion the ideas we perceive by our senses are not real things, but images or copies of them. Our knowledge, therefore, is no further real than as our ideas are the true representations of those originals. But as these supposed originals are in themselves unknown, it is impossible to know how far our ideas resemble them or whether they resemble them at all. We cannot, therefore, be sure we have any real knowledge. Further, as our ideas are perpetually varied, without any change in the supposed real things, it necessarily follows they cannot all be true copies of them, or, if some are and others are not, it is impossible to distinguish the former from the latter. And this plunges us yet deeper in uncertainty. Again, when we consider the point, we cannot conceive how any idea, or anything like an idea, should have an absolute existence out of a mind, nor consequently, according to you, how there should be any real thing in nature. The result of all this is that we are thrown into the most hopeless and abandoned *skepticism*. Now give me leave to ask you, *first*, whether your referring ideas to certain absolutely existing unperceived substances, as their originals, is not the source of all this *skepticism*? *Secondly*, whether you are informed, either by sense or reason, of the existence of those unknown originals? And in case you are not, whether it is not absurd to suppose them? *Thirdly*, whether upon inquiry, you find there is anything distinctly conceived or meant by the *absolute or external existence of unperceiving substances*? *Lastly*, whether, the premises considered, it is not the wisest way to follow nature, trust your senses, and laying aside all anxious thought about unknown natures or substances, admit with the vulgar those for real things which are perceived by the senses?

*Hyl.* For the present, I have no inclination to the answering part. I would much rather see how you can get over what follows. Pray, are not the objects perceived by the senses of one likewise perceivable to others present? If there were a hundred more here, they would all see the garden, the trees, and flowers as I see them. But they are not in the same manner affected with the ideas I frame in my imagination. Does not this make a difference between the former sort of objects and the latter?

*Phil.* I grant it does. Nor have I ever denied a difference between the objects of sense and those of imagination. But what would you infer from this? You cannot say that sensible objects exist unperceived because they are perceived by many.

*Hyl.* I admit I can make nothing of that objection, but it has led me into another. Is it not your opinion that by our senses we perceive only the ideas existing in our minds?

*Phil.* It is.

*Hyl.* But the same idea which is in my mind cannot be in yours or in any other mind. Does it not, therefore, follow from your principles that no two can see the same thing? And is not this highly absurd?

*Phil.* If the term *same* be taken in the vulgar meaning, it is certain (and not at all repugnant to the principles I maintain) that different persons may perceive the same thing, or the same thing or idea exist in different minds. Words are of arbitrary imposition; and since men are accustomed to apply the word *same* where no distinction or variety is perceived, and I do not pretend to alter their perceptions, it follows that, as men have said before, *several saw the same thing*, so they may upon like occasions, still continue to use the same phrase without any deviation either from propriety of language or the truth of things. But if the term *same* is used in the meaning of philosophers who pretend to an abstracted notion of identity, then, according to their sundry definitions of this notion (for it is not yet agreed in what that philosophic identity consists), it may or may not be possible for various persons to perceive the same thing. But whether philosophers shall think fit to call a thing the *same* or not, is, I conceive, of small importance. Let us suppose several men together, all endowed with the same faculties, and consequently affected in like sort by their senses, and who had yet never known the use of language; they would without question agree in their perceptions. Though perhaps, when they came to the use of speech, some regarding the uniformity of what was perceived might call it the *same* thing; others, especially regarding the diversity of persons who perceived, might choose the denomination of different things. But who does not see that all the dispute is about a word—namely, whether what is perceived by different persons—may yet have the term *same* applied to it? Or suppose a house whose walls or outward shell remaining unaltered, the chambers are all pulled down, and new ones built in their place, and that you should call this the *same*, and I should say it was not the *same* house—would we not for all this perfectly agree in our thoughts of the house considered in itself? And would not all the difference consist in a sound? If you should say we differ in our notions, for that you superadded to your idea of the house the simple abstracted idea of identity, whereas I did not; I would tell you I do not know what you mean by that *abstracted idea of identity*; and I should desire you to look into your own thoughts and be sure you understood yourself. — Why so silent, Hylas? Are you not yet satisfied that men may dispute about identity and diversity without any real difference in their thoughts and opinions abstracted from names? Take this further reflection with you, that whether matter be allowed to exist or not, the case is exactly the same as to the point in hand. For the materialists themselves acknowledge what we immediately perceive by our senses to be our own ideas. Your difficulty, therefore, that no two see the same thing makes equally against the materialists and me.

*Hyl.* But they suppose an external archetype to which, referring their several ideas, they may truly be said to perceive the same thing.

*Phil.* And (not to mention your having discarded those archetypes) so may you suppose an external archetype on my principles—*external*, I mean, to your own mind, though indeed it must be supposed to exist in that mind which comprehends all things; but then this serves all the ends of identity as well as if it existed out of a mind. And I am sure you yourself will not say it is less intelligible.

*Hyl.* You have indeed clearly satisfied me, either that there is no difficulty at bottom in this point or if there is, it counts equally against both opinions.

*Phil.* But that which counts equally against two contradictory opinions can be a proof against neither.

*Hyl.* I acknowledge it. But, after all, Philonous, when I consider the substance of what you advance against *skepticism*, it amounts to no more than this: We are sure that we really see, hear, feel—in a word, that we are affected with sensible impressions.

*Phil.* And how are we concerned any further? I see this *cherry*, I feel it, I taste it—and I am sure *nothing* cannot be seen or felt or tasted—it is therefore *real*. Take away the sensations of softness, moisture, redness, tartness, and you take away the *cherry*. Since it is not a being distinct from sensations, a *cherry*, I say, is nothing but a congeries of sensible impressions or ideas perceived by various senses, which ideas are united into one thing (or have one name given them) by the mind because they are observed to attend each other. Thus, when the palate is affected with such a particular taste, the sight is affected with a red color, the touch with roundness, softness, etc. Hence, when I see and feel and taste in sundry certain manners, I am sure the *cherry* exists or is real, its reality being in my opinion nothing abstracted from those sensations. But if by the word *cherry* you mean an unknown nature distinct from all those sensible qualities, and by its existence something distinct from its being perceived, then indeed I admit neither you nor I nor anyone else can be sure it exists.

*Hyl.* But what would you say, Philonous, if I should bring the very same reasons against the existence of sensible things in a mind which you have offered against their existing in a material *substratum*?

*Phil.* When I see your reasons, you shall hear what I have to say to them.

*Hyl.* Is the mind extended or unextended?

*Phil.* Unextended, without doubt.

*Hyl.* Do you say the things you perceive are in your mind?

*Phil.* They are.

*Hyl.* Again, have I not heard you speak of sensible impressions?

*Phil.* I believe you may.

*Hyl.* Explain to me now, O Philonous, how it is possible there should be room for all those trees and houses to exist in your mind. Can extended things be contained in that which is unextended? Or are we to imagine impressions made on a thing void of all solidity? You cannot say objects are in your mind as books in your study or that things are imprinted on it as the figure of a seal upon wax. In what sense, therefore, are we to understand those expressions? Explain this to me, if you can, and I shall then be able to answer all those queries you formerly put to me about my *substratum*.

*Phil.* Look you, Hylas, when I speak of objects as existing in the mind or imprinted on the senses, I would not be understood in the gross literal sense, as when bodies are said to exist in a place or a seal to make an impression upon wax. My meaning is only that the mind comprehends or perceives them and that it is affected from without or by some being distinct from itself. This is my explication of your difficulty, and how it can serve to make your tenet of an unperceiving material *substratum* intelligible, I would gladly know.

*Hyl*. No, if that be all, I confess I do not see what use can be made of it. But are you not guilty of some abuse of language in this?

*Phil*. None at all, it is no more than common custom, which you know is the rule of language, has authorized, nothing being more usual than for philosophers to speak of the immediate objects of the understanding as things existing in the mind. Nor is there anything in this, but what is conformable to the general analogy of language, most part of the mental operations being signified by words borrowed from sensible things—as is plain in the terms *comprehend*, *reflect*, *discourse*, etc., which being applied to the mind, must not be taken in their gross original sense.

*Hyl*. You have, I admit, satisfied me in this point. But there still remains one great difficulty, which I do not know how you will get over. And, indeed, it is of such importance that if you could solve all others, without being able to find a solution for this, you must never expect to make me a proselyte to your principles.

*Phil*. Let me know this mighty difficulty.

*Hyl*. The Scripture account of the creation is what appears to me utterly irreconcilable with your notions. Moses tells us of a creation, a creation of what? of ideas? No, certainly, but of things, of real things, solid corporeal substances. Bring your principles to agree with this and I shall perhaps agree with you.

*Phil*. Moses mentions the sun, moon, and stars, earth and sea, plants and animals—that all these do really exist and were in the beginning created by God, I make no question. If by *ideas* you mean fictions and fancies of the mind, then these are no ideas. If by *ideas* you mean immediate objects of the understanding, or sensible things which cannot exist unperceived, or out of a mind, then these things are ideas. But whether you do or do not call them *ideas*, it matters little. The difference is only about a name. And whether that name is retained or rejected, the sense, the truth, and reality of things continues the same. In common talk, the objects of our senses are not termed *ideas*, but *things*. Call them so still, provided you do not attribute to them any absolute external existence, and I shall never quarrel with you for a word. The creation, therefore, I allow to have been a creation of things, of *real* things. Neither is this in the least inconsistent with my principles, as is evident from what I have now said, and would have been evident to you without this, if you had not forgotten what had been so often said before. But as for solid corporeal substances, I desire you to show where Moses makes any mention of them, and if they should be mentioned by him or any other inspired writer, it would still be incumbent on you to show those words were not taken in the vulgar meaning, for things falling under our senses, but in the philosophic meaning, for matter, or an unknown quiddity, with an absolute existence. When you have proved these points, then (and not until then) may you bring the authority of Moses into our dispute.

*Hyl*. It is in vain to dispute about a point so clear. I am content to refer it to your own conscience. Are you not satisfied there is some peculiar repugnance between the Mosaic account of the creation and your notions?

*Phil*. If all possible sense which can be put on the first chapter of Genesis may be conceived as consistently with my principles as any other, then it has no peculiar repugnance with them. But there is no sense you may not as well conceive, believing as I do. Since, besides spirits, all you conceive are ideas, and the existence of these I do not deny. Neither do you pretend they exist without the mind.

*Hyl*. Pray let me see any sense you can understand it in.

*Phil*. Why I imagine that if I had been present at the creation, I should have seen things produced into being, that is, become perceptible, in the order described by the sacred historian. I ever before believed the Mosaic account of the creation and now find no alteration in my manner of believing it. When things are said to begin or end their existence, we do not mean this with regard to God, but his creatures. All objects are eternally known by God, or, which is the same thing, have an eternal existence in his mind, but when things, before imperceptible to creatures, are by a decree of God made perceptible to them, then are they said to begin a relative existence with respect to created minds. Upon reading therefore the Mosaic account of the creation, I understand that the several parts of the world became gradually perceivable to finite spirits, endowed with proper faculties, so that, whoever such were present, they were in truth perceived by them. This is the literal, obvious sense suggested to me by the words of the Holy Scripture, in which is included no mention or no thought, either of *substratum*, instrument, occasion, or absolute existence. And upon inquiry, I do not doubt it will be found that most plain, honest men, who believe the creation, never think of those things any more than I. What metaphysical sense you may understand it in, you only can tell.

*Hyl.* But, Philonous, you do not seem to be aware that you allow created things in the beginning only a relative, and, consequently, hypothetical being— that is to say, upon supposition there were men to perceive them, without which they have no actuality of absolute existence in which creation might terminate. Is it not, therefore, according to you, plainly impossible that the creation of any inanimate creatures should precede that of man? And is not this directly contrary to the Mosaic account?

*Phil.* In answer to that, I say, *first*, created beings might begin to exist in the mind of other created intelligences besides men. You will not, therefore, be able to prove any contradiction between Moses and my notions unless you first show there was no other order of finite created spirits in being before man. I say further, in case we conceive the creation as we should at this time a parcel of plants or vegetables of all sorts produced by an invisible power in a desert where nobody was present—that this way of explaining or conceiving it is consistent with my principles, since they deprive you of nothing, either sensible or imaginable; that it exactly suits with the common, natural, undebauched notions of mankind; that it manifests the dependence of all things on God, and consequently has all the good effect or influence which it is possible that important article of our faith should have in making men humble, thankful, and

resigned to their Creator. I say, moreover, that in this naked conception of things, divested of words, there will not be found any notion of what you call the *actuality of absolute existence*. You may indeed raise a dust with those terms and so lengthen our dispute to no purpose. But I entreat you calmly to look into your own thoughts and then tell me if they are not a useless and unintelligible jargon.

*Hyl.* I admit I have no very clear notion annexed to them. But what do you say to this? Do you not make the existence of sensible things consist in their being in a mind? And were not all things eternally in the mind of God? Did they not therefore exist from all eternity, according to you? And how could that which was eternal be created in time? Can anything be clearer or better connected than this?

*Phil.* And are not you too of the opinion that God knew all things from eternity?

*Hyl.* I am.

*Phil.* Consequently, they always had a being in the divine intellect.

*Hyl.* This I acknowledge.

*Phil.* By your own confession, therefore, nothing is new, or begins to be, in respect of the mind of God. So we are agreed in that point.

*Hyl.* What shall we make then of the creation?

*Phil.* May we not understand it to have been entirely in respect of finite spirits, so that things with regard to us may properly be said to begin their existence, or be created, when God decreed they should become perceptible to intelligent creatures in that order and manner which he then established and we now call the laws of nature? You may call this a *relative*, or *hypothetical existence* if you please. But so long as it supplies us with the most natural, obvious, and literal sense of the Mosaic history of the creation—so long as it answers all the religious ends of that great article—in a word, so long as you can assign no other sense or meaning in its stead, why should we reject this? Is it to comply with a ridiculous skeptical humor of making everything nonsense and unintelligible? I am sure you cannot say it is for the glory of God. For allowing it to be a thing possible and conceivable that the corporeal world should have an absolute subsistence extrinsic to the mind of God, as well as to the minds of all created spirits, yet how could this set forth either the immensity or omniscience of the Deity or the necessary and immediate dependence of all things on him? No, would it not rather seem to derogate from those attributes?

*Hyl.* Well, but as to this decree of God's for making things perceptible, what do you say, Philonous, is it not plain God did either execute that decree from all eternity or at some certain time began to will what he had not actually willed before, but only designed to will? If the former, then there could be no creation or beginning of existence in finite things. If the latter, then we must acknowledge something new to befall the Deity, which implies a sort of change; and all change argues imperfection.

*Phil.* Pray consider what you are doing. Is it not evident this objection concludes equally against a creation in any sense, no, against every other act of the Deity discoverable by the light of nature? None of which can we conceive otherwise than as performed in time and having a beginning. God is a being of transcendent and unlimited perfections; his nature, therefore, is incomprehensible to finite spirits. It is not, therefore, to be expected that any man, whether *materialist* or *immaterialist*, should have exactly just notions of the Deity, his attributes, and ways of operation. If then you would infer anything against me, your difficulty must not be drawn from the inadequateness of our conceptions of the divine nature, which is unavoidable on any scheme, but from the denial of matter, of which there is not one word directly or indirectly in what you have now objected.

*Hyl.* I must acknowledge the difficulties you are concerned to clear are such only as arise from the nonexistence of matter and are peculiar to that notion. So far you are in the right. But I cannot by any means bring myself to think there is no such peculiar repugnance between the creation and your opinion, though indeed where to fix it I do not distinctly know.

*Phil.* What would you have? Do I not acknowledge a twofold state of things, the one ectypal[6] or natural, the other archetypal and eternal? The former was created in time, the latter existed from everlasting in the mind of God. Is not this agreeable to the

common notions of theologians? Or is any more than this necessary in order to conceive the creation? But you suspect some peculiar repugnance, though you do not know where it lies. To take away all possibility of scruple in the case, do but consider this one point. Either you are not able to conceive the creation on any hypothesis whatsoever, and if so, there is no ground for dislike or complaint against my particular opinion on that score, or you are able to conceive it, and if so, why not on my principles, since nothing conceivable is taken away by that means? You have all along been allowed the full scope of sense, imagination, and reason. Whatever, therefore, you could before apprehend, either immediately or mediately by your senses, or by ratiocination from your senses, whatever you could perceive, imagine, or understand remains still with you. If, therefore, the notion you have of the creation by other principles is intelligible, you have it still upon mine; if it is not intelligible, I conceive it to be no notion at all, and so there is no loss of it. And, indeed, it seems to me very plain that the supposition of matter, that is, a thing perfectly unknown and inconceivable, cannot serve to make us conceive anything. And I hope it does not need to be proved to you that if the existence of matter does not make the creation conceivable, the creation's being without it inconceivable can be no objection against its nonexistence.

*Hyl.* I confess, Philonous, you have almost satisfied me in this point of the creation.

*Phil.* I would gladly know why you are not quite satisfied. You tell me indeed of a repugnance between the Mosaic history and immaterialism, but you do not know where it lies. Is this reasonable, Hylas? Can you expect I should solve a difficulty without knowing what it is? But to pass by all that, would not a man think you were assured there is no repugnance between the received notions of materialists and the inspired writings?

*Hyl.* And so I am.

*Phil.* Ought the historical part of Scripture to be understood in a plain, obvious sense, or in a sense which is metaphysical and out of the way?

*Hyl.* In the plain sense, doubtless.

---

6. Copied from something else.

*Phil.* When Moses speaks of herbs, earth, water, etc., as having been created by God, do you not think the sensible things, commonly signified by those words, are suggested to every unphilosophical reader?

*Hyl.* I cannot help thinking so.

*Phil.* And are not all ideas, or things perceived by sense, to be denied a real existence by the doctrine of the materialists?

*Hyl.* This I have already acknowledged.

*Phil.* The creation, therefore, according to them, was not the creation of sensible things, which have only a relative being, but of certain unknown natures, which have an absolute being in which creation might terminate.

*Hyl.* True.

*Phil.* Is it not, therefore, evident the asserters of matter destroy the plain obvious sense of Moses, with which their notions are utterly inconsistent, and instead of it obtrude on us I do not know what, something equally unintelligible to themselves and me.

*Hyl.* I cannot contradict you.

*Phil.* Moses tells us of a creation. A creation of what? Of unknown quiddities, of occasions, or *substratums*? No, certainly; but of things obvious to the senses. You must first reconcile this with your notions if you expect I should be reconciled to them.

*Hyl.* I see you can assault me with my own weapons.

*Phil.* Then as to *absolute existence*, was there ever known a more jejune notion than that? Something it is, so abstracted and unintelligible, that you have frankly owned you could not conceive it, much less explain anything by it. But allowing matter to exist and the notion of absolute existence to be as clear as light, yet was this ever known to make the creation more credible? No, has it not furnished the *atheists* and *infidels* of all ages with the most plausible argument against a creation? That a corporeal substance, which has an absolute existence without the minds of spirits, should be produced out of nothing by the mere will of a spirit has been looked upon as a thing so contrary to all reason, so impossible and absurd that not only the most celebrated among the ancients, but even various modern and Christian philosophers have thought matter coeternal with the Deity. Lay

these things together and then judge whether materialism disposes men to believe the creation of things.

*Hyl.* I admit, Philonous, I think it does not. This of the *creation* is the last objection I can think of, and I must necessarily admit it has been sufficiently answered as well as the rest. Nothing now remains to be overcome but a sort of unaccountable backwardness that I find in myself toward your notions.

*Phil.* When a man is swayed to one side of a question, he does not know why; can this, do you think, be anything else but the effect of prejudice, which never fails to attend old and rooted notions? And indeed in this respect I cannot deny the belief of matter to have very much the advantage over the contrary opinion with men of a learned education.

*Hyl.* I confess it seems to be as you say.

*Phil.* As a balance, therefore, to this weight of prejudice, let us throw into the scale the great advantages that arise from the belief of immaterialism, both in regard to religion and human learning. The being of a God and incorruptibility of the soul, those great articles of religion, are they not proved with the clearest and most immediate evidence? When I say the being of a *God*, I do not mean an obscure, general cause of things, of which we have no conception, but *God* in the strict and proper sense of the word. A being whose spirituality, omnipresence, providence, omniscience, infinite power, and goodness are as conspicuous as the existence of sensible things, of which (notwithstanding the fallacious pretenses and affected scruples of *skeptics*) there is no more reason to doubt than of our own being. Then with relation to human sciences: In natural philosophy, what intricacies, what obscurities, what contradictions, has the belief of matter led men into! To say nothing of the numberless disputes about its extent, continuity, homogeneity, gravity, divisibility, etc., do they not pretend to explain all things by bodies operating on bodies, according to the laws of motion? And yet, are they able to comprehend how any one body should move another? No, admitting there was no difficulty in reconciling the notion of an inert being with a cause or in conceiving how an accident might pass from one body to another, yet by all their strained thoughts and extravagant suppositions, have they been able to reach the mechanical production of any one animal or vegetable body? Can they account, by the laws of motion, for sounds, tastes, smells, or colors, or for the regular course of things? Have they accounted, by physical principles, for the aptitude and contrivance even of the most inconsiderable parts of the universe? But laying aside matter and corporeal causes and admitting only the efficiency of an all-perfect mind, are not all the effects of nature easy and intelligible? If the *phenomena* are nothing else but *ideas*, God is a *spirit*, but matter an unintelligent, unperceiving being. If they demonstrate an unlimited power in their cause, God is active and omnipotent, but matter an inert mass. If the order, regularity, and usefulness of them can never be sufficiently admired, God is infinitely wise and provident, but matter destitute of all contrivance and design. These surely are great advantages in *physics*. Not to mention that the apprehension of a distant Deity naturally disposes men to a negligence in their *moral* actions, which they would be more cautious of in case they thought him immediately present and acting on their minds without the interposition of matter or unthinking second causes. Then in *metaphysics:* what difficulties concerning entity in abstract, substantial forms, hylarchic principles, plastic natures, substance and accident, principle of individuation, possibility of matter's thinking, origin of ideas, the manner how two independent substances, so widely different as *spirit* and *matter*, should mutually operate on each other! What difficulties, I say, and endless disquisitions concerning these and innumerable other the like points, do we escape by supposing only spirits and ideas? Even *mathematics* itself, if we take away the absolute existence of extended things, becomes much more clear and easy, the most shocking paradoxes and intricate speculations in those sciences depending on the infinite divisibility of finite extension, which depends on that supposition. But what need is there to insist on the particular sciences? Is not that opposition to all science whatsoever, that frenzy of the ancient and modern *skeptics*, built on the same foundation? Or can you produce so much as one argument against the reality of corporeal things, or in behalf of that avowed utter ignorance of their natures which does not suppose their reality to consist in an external absolute existence? Upon this supposition indeed the objections from the change of colors in a pigeon's neck or the appearances of a broken oar in the water must be allowed to have weight. But those and the like objections vanish if we do not maintain the being of absolute external originals, but place the reality of things in ideas, fleeting indeed, and changeable, however, not changed at random, but according to the fixed order of nature. For in this consists that constancy and truth of things which secures all the concerns of life and distinguishes that which is *real* from the irregular visions of the fancy.

*Hyl.* I agree to all you have now said and must admit that nothing can incline me to embrace your opinion more than the advantages I see it is attended with. I am by nature lazy and this would be a mighty abridgment in knowledge. What doubts, what hypotheses, what labyrinths of amusement, what fields of disputation, what an ocean of false learning may be avoided by that single notion of *immaterialism*?

*Phil.* After all, is there anything further remaining to be done? You may remember you promised to embrace that opinion which upon examination should appear most agreeable to common sense and remote from *skepticism*. This, by your own confession, is that which denies matter or the absolute existence of corporeal things. Nor is this all; the same notion has been proved several ways, viewed in different lights, pursued in its consequences, and all objections against it cleared. Can there be a greater evidence of its truth? Or is it possible it should have all the marks of a true opinion and yet be false?

*Hyl.* I admit myself entirely satisfied for the present in all respects. But what security can I have that I shall still continue the same full assent to your opinion and that no unthought-of objection or difficulty will occur hereafter?

*Phil.* Pray, Hylas, do you in other cases, when a point is once evidently proved, withhold your assent on account of objections or difficulties it may be liable to? Are the difficulties that attend the doctrine of incommensurable quantities, of the angle of contact, of the asymptotes to curves, or the like, sufficient to make you hold out against mathematical demonstration? Or will you disbelieve the providence of God because there may be some particular things which you do not know how to reconcile with it? If there are difficulties attending immaterialism, there are at the same time direct and evident proofs for it. But for the existence of matter there is not one proof and far more numerous and insurmountable objections lie against it. But where are those mighty difficulties you insist on? Alas, you do not know where or what they are—something which may possibly occur later. If this is a sufficient pretense for withholding your full assent, you should never yield it to any proposition, however free from exceptions, however clearly and solidly demonstrated.

*Hyl.* You have satisfied me, Philonous.

*Phil.* But to arm you against all future objections, do but consider that what bears equally hard on two contradictory opinions can be a proof against neither. Whenever, therefore, any difficulty occurs, try if you can find a solution for it on the hypothesis of the *materialists*. Be not deceived by words, but sound your own thoughts. And in case you cannot conceive it easier by the help of *materialism*, it is plain it can be no objection against *immaterialism*. Had you proceeded all along by this rule, you would probably have spared yourself abundance of trouble in objecting, since of all your difficulties I challenge you to show one that is explained by matter, no, which is not more unintelligible with than without that supposition, and consequently makes rather *against* than *for* it. You should consider, in each particular, whether the difficulty arises from the *nonexistence of matter*. If it does not, you might as well argue from the infinite divisibility of extension against divine foreknowledge as from such a difficulty against *immaterialism*. And yet, upon recollection, I believe you will find this to have been often if not always the case. You should likewise take heed not to argue on a *petitio principii*. One is apt to say the unknown substances ought to be esteemed real things rather than the ideas in our minds; and who can tell but the unthinking external substance may concur as a cause or instrument in the production of our ideas? But is not this proceeding on a supposition that there are such external substances? And to suppose this, is it not begging the

question? But, above all things, you should beware of imposing on yourself by that vulgar sophism, which is called *ignoratio elenchi*. You talked often as if you thought I maintained the nonexistence of sensible things, whereas in truth no one can be more thoroughly assured of their existence than I am, and it is you who doubt—I should have said, positively deny it. Everything that is seen, felt, heard, or any way perceived by the senses is, on the principles I embrace, a real being, but not on yours. Remember, the matter you contend for is an unknown somewhat (if indeed it may be termed *somewhat*), which is quite stripped of all sensible qualities, and can be neither perceived by sense, nor apprehended by the mind. Remember, I say that it is not any object which is hard or soft, hot or cold, blue or white, round or square, etc. For all these things I affirm do exist. Though, indeed, I deny they have existence distinct from being perceived or that they exist out of all minds whatsoever. Think on these points; let them be attentively considered and still kept in view. Otherwise you will not comprehend the state of the question—without which your objections will always be wide of the mark and, instead of mine, may possibly be directed (as more than once they have been) against your own notions.

*Hyl.* I must necessarily admit, Philonous, nothing seems to have kept me from agreeing with you more than this same *mistaking the question*. In denying matter, at first glimpse I am tempted to imagine you deny the things we see and feel, but, upon reflection, find there is no ground for it. What do you think, therefore, of retaining the name *matter* and applying it to sensible things? This may be done without any change in your sentiments, and, believe me, it would be a means of reconciling them to some persons who may be more shocked at an innovation in words than in opinion.

*Phil.* With all my heart, retain the word *matter* and apply it to the objects of sense, if you please, provided you do not attribute to them any subsistence distinct from their being perceived. I shall never quarrel with you for an expression. *Matter* or *material substance* are terms introduced by philosophers, and, as used by them, imply a sort of independence or a subsistence distinct from being perceived by a mind, but are never used by common people, or if ever, it is to signify the immediate objects of sense. One would think, therefore, so long as the names of all particular things, with the terms *sensible, substance, body, stuff,* and the like, are retained, the word *matter* should be never missed in common talk. And in philosophical discourses it seems the best way to leave it quite out, since there is not perhaps any one thing that has more favored and strengthened the depraved bent of the mind toward atheism than the use of that general confused term.

*Hyl.* Well, but, Philonous, since I am content to give up the notion of an unthinking substance exterior to the mind, I think you ought not deny me the privilege of using the word *matter* as I please and annexing it to a collection of sensible qualities subsisting only in the mind. I freely admit there is no other substance in a strict sense than *spirit.* But I have been so long accustomed to the term *matter* that I do not know how to part with it. To say there is no *matter* in the world is still shocking to me. Whereas to say there is no *matter*, if by that term is meant an unthinking substance existing without the mind, but if by *matter* is meant some sensible thing whose existence consists in being perceived, then there is *matter*—this distinction gives it quite another turn—and men will come into your notions with small difficulty when they are proposed in that manner. For, after all, the controversy about *matter* in the strict meaning of it lies altogether between you and the philosophers, whose principles, I acknowledge, are not near so natural or so agreeable to the common sense of mankind and Holy Scripture as yours. There is nothing we either desire or shun but as it makes or is apprehended to make some part of our happiness or misery. But what has happiness or misery, joy or grief, pleasure or pain, to do with absolute existence or with unknown entities, abstracted from all relation to us? It is evident, things regard us only as they are pleasing or displeasing, and they can please or displease only insofar as they perceived. Further, therefore, we are not concerned; and thus far you leave things as you found them. Yet still there is something new in this doctrine. It is plain, I do not now think with the philosophers, nor yet altogether with the vulgar. I would like to know how the case stands in that respect, precisely what you have added to or altered in my former notions.

*Phil.* I do not pretend to be a setter-up of *new notions.* My endeavors tend only to unite and place in a clearer light that truth which was before shared between the vulgar and the philosophers—the former being of opinion that *those things they immediately perceive are the real things* and the latter that *the things immediately perceived are ideas which exist only in the mind*—which two notions put together do in effect constitute the substance of what I advance.

*Hyl.* I have been a long time distrusting my senses; I thought I saw things by a dim light and through false glasses. Now the glasses are removed and a new light breaks in upon my understanding. I am clearly convinced that I see things in their native forms and am no longer in pain about their unknown natures or absolute existence. This is the state I find myself in at present, though, indeed, the course that brought me to it I do not yet thoroughly comprehend. You set out upon the same principles that Academics, Cartesians, and the like sects usually do; and for a long time it looked as if you were advancing their philosophical *skepticism*; but, in the end, your conclusions are directly opposite to theirs.

*Phil.* You see, Hylas, the water of the fountain over there, how it is forced upwards in a round column to a certain height, at which it breaks and falls back into the basin from which it rose, its ascent as well as descent, proceeding from the same uniform law or principle of *gravitation*. Just so, the same principles which, at first view, lead to *skepticism*, pursued to a certain point, bring men back to common sense.

# George Berkeley, *On Motion* (1721)[1]

1. The most important thing in the pursuit of truth is to take care that ill understood terms do not hinder us, a point which almost all philosophers warn of, but few attend to. Yet, this does not appear so difficult to observe, especially in the case of physics, where sensation, experience, and geometrical reasoning obtain. Laying aside then, as far as possible, every prejudice originating in the usual modes of speaking or in philosophical authority, we should diligently examine the very nature of things. Nor should the authority of anyone be set so high that his words and expressions be prized, unless they contain what is certain and clear.

2. The consideration of motion greatly disturbed the minds of the ancient philosophers, giving rise to various excessively difficult—not to say absurd—opinions, which, since they have now sunk into obscurity, do not deserve that we should give much attention to their discussion. But in works on motion by the more recent and sounder philosophers of our age, several words of too abstract and obscure signification occur, such as *solicitation of gravity, conatus, dead forces*, etc., terms which diffuse obscurity over

writings that are in other respects very learned, and give rise to opinions not less at variance with truth than with common sense. It is necessary that these be discussed, not for the sake of proving others wrong, but on account of truth.

3. *Solicitation* and *effort* or *striving* are applicable properly to animate beings alone. When they are applied to others, they must be taken in a metaphorical sense. Philosophers, however, should abstain from metaphors. But if we reject affection of the mind and motion of the body, it will be clear to anyone giving attention to the matter that there is no clear and distinct meaning in those words.

4. As long as heavy bodies are sustained by us, we feel in ourselves effort, fatigue, and discomfort. We also perceive in heavy bodies, when falling, an accelerated motion toward the center of the earth, but nothing more, as far as our senses are concerned. However, reason proves that there is some cause or principle of these phenomena, and this is generally called *gravity*. Since, however, the cause of the fall of heavy bodies is dark and unknown, gravity in that sense cannot be called a sensible quality; consequently, it is an occult quality. But we can scarcely conceive—and indeed not even scarcely—what an occult quality is, and how any quality can act or

---

1. Translated from the Latin by G. N. Wright in *The Works of George Berkeley* (London, 1843), 2 vols., modified.

effect anything. It would be better then, if men would attend only to the sensible effects, putting the occult quality out of view. Abstract words—however useful they are in discussion—should be discarded in meditation, and the mind should be fixed on particular and concrete things, that is, on the things themselves.

5. *Force* in the same way is attributed to bodies, but that word is used as if it signified a known quality, one distinct from figure, motion, and everything sensible, as also from every affection of animated life. But any person who accurately examines the subject will find that force is nothing else than an occult quality. Animal effort and corporeal motion are commonly regarded as symptoms and measures of this occult quality.

6. Thus it is plain that gravity or force is erroneously laid down as the principle of motion; for how can that principle be more clearly known by being called an occult quality? What is itself occult explains nothing—disregarding the view that the unknown acting cause can itself be better called a substance than a quality. Moreover, *force*, *gravity*, and words of that kind are employed more usually in the concrete— and not improperly—to denote the motion of bodies, the difficulty of resisting, etc. But when they are used by philosophers to signify natures distinct and abstracted from all these, which are neither objects of sense, nor can be grasped by any force of intellect or the imagination, they are sure to produce error and confusion. [ . . . ]

26. Heavy bodies tend downwards, although affected by no apparent impulse, but we must not, therefore, suppose that the principle of motion is contained in them. Aristotle gives this account of the matter: "Heavy and light things are not moved of themselves; for that would be a characteristic of life, and they could stop themselves." All heavy bodies tend toward the center of the earth by a certain and constant law, and we do not perceive in them any principle or power of stopping or diminishing that motion, or of increasing it except by a fixed proportion, or of modifying it in any way; consequently, they behave quite passively. Moreover, the same should, strictly and accurately speaking, be said respecting percussive bodies. Those bodies, as long as they are

moved, and also in the very moment of percussion, behave passively as when they are at rest. A body at rest acts as much as a body in motion, as Newton admits when he says that the force of *inertia* is the same as *impetus*. But an inert body does nothing; so neither does a moved body.

27. In reality, a body equally persists in each state, either of motion or of rest. But its doing so can no more be called an action of the body than its existence can be called its action. Its persevering is nothing more than a continuation in the same mode of existing, which cannot properly be called action. But the resistance we experience in stopping a body in motion we imagine to be its action; but this is a delusion. For, in reality, that resistance we perceive is an impression in ourselves, and it does not prove that the body acts, but that we have an impression; it is certain that we should have the same impression, whether that body were moved by itself, or were impelled by some other principle.

28. Action and reaction are said to be in bodies, and such expressions are convenient for mechanical demonstrations. But we should be on our guard not to suppose for this reason that there is some real virtue in them which may be the cause or principle of motion. For those words are to be understood in the same way as the word *attraction*; and just as this is only a mathematical hypothesis, and not a physical quality, the same should be understood concerning those, and for the same reason. For as the truth and use of theorems concerning the mutual attraction of bodies remain unshaken in mechanical philosophy, as founded on the motion of bodies—whether that motion is supposed to be caused by the action of bodies mutually attracting each other or by the action of some agent different from body, impelling and stopping bodies—for the same reason, whatever has been laid down concerning the rules and laws of motions, and the theorems deduced from them, remain unquestionable, provided the sensible effects and the reasonings depending on them are granted, whether we suppose the action itself or the force causing these effects to be in body or in an incorporeal agent. [ . . . ]

35. These things not being sufficiently understood is the reason why some unjustly reject the

mathematical principles of physics on the ground that they do not assign efficient causes of things. When, in truth, it belongs to physics or mechanics to state only the rules of impulse and attraction, and not efficient causes—in a word, the laws of motions—and from these, when received, to assign the solution of particular phenomena, but not their efficient cause.

36. It will be of great use to consider what a principle properly is and in what sense it must be taken among philosophers. Now the true, efficient, and preserving cause of all things is most properly called their source and principle. But the principles of experimental philosophy are properly called the grounds on which it rests, or the sources from which is derived (I do not say the existence, but) the knowledge of corporeal things, these grounds being sensation and experience. In the same way, in mechanical philosophy, those are to be called principles in which the whole discipline is grounded and contained, being those primary laws of motions which, confirmed by experiments, are cultivated and rendered universal by reason. These laws of motion are appropriately called principles, since from them are derived both general theorems of mechanics and particular explanations of the phenomena.

37. Then truly something can be said to be explained mechanically when it is reduced to those most simple and universal principles and is shown by accurate reasoning to be suitable and connected with them. For once the laws of nature are found, then it remains for the philosopher to show that each thing necessarily follows in conformity with these laws, that is, that every phenomenon necessarily results from the principles. This is to explain and solve the phenomena, that is, to assign the reason why they take place.

38. The human mind delights in extending and enlarging its knowledge. But for this purpose general notions and propositions must be formed in which particular propositions and knowledge are in some way contained, and which then, and only then, are believed to be understood. This is well known to geometers. In mechanics also the course is first to lay down some notions, that is, definitions and elementary and general statements about motion, from which subsequently, in the mathematical style, more

remote and less general conclusions are deduced. And, as the magnitudes of particular bodies are measured by the application of geometrical theorems, so we ascertain and determine the motions of any parts of the mundane system and the phenomena depending on them by the application of the universal theorems of mechanics. And the physicist should exclusively aim at this.

39. And as geometers devise many things, for the sake of their discipline, which they themselves cannot describe nor find in the nature of things, for the same reason those who treat of mechanics employ certain abstract and general words, and imagine in bodies force, action, attraction, solicitation, etc., which are exceedingly useful for theories, enunciations, and computations concerning motion, although in actual truth and in bodies actually existing, they are sought in vain, as much as are those things imagined by mathematical abstraction.

40. In reality, we perceive nothing by the use of our senses except effects or sensible qualities, and entirely passive corporeal things, whether at rest or in motion; and reason and experience indicate nothing active except mind or soul. Whatever is imagined more than this must be regarded of the same sort as those mathematical hypotheses and abstractions; and we should thoroughly bear this in mind. Unless this takes place, we may easily relapse into the obscure subtlety of the scholastics, which for so many ages infected philosophy like a dreadful plague.

41. The mechanical principles and universal laws of motions, or of nature, happily discovered in the last century, and treated of and applied by aid of geometry, have thrown a wonderful light on philosophy. But metaphysical principles and real efficient causes of the motion and existence of bodies or of corporeal attributes by no means belong to mechanics or experiment, nor can they throw light on them, except insofar as, by being previously known, they may serve to define the limits of physics, and thus to do away with difficulties and questions foreign to them. [ . . . ]

52. The Peripatetics distinguished various kinds of motion according to the variety of the changes which any body can undergo. Those who at present treat

the subject take into account only local motion. But local motion cannot be understood unless we also understand the meaning of *place*. This is defined by the moderns to be the part of space which body occupies, and therefore in reference to space it is divided into absolute and relative. For they distinguish between absolute or true space, and that which is apparent or relative. They maintain indeed that in every direction there exists an immense immovable space, not the object of sensation, but pervading and embracing all bodies; and this they call absolute space. But space comprehended or defined by body, and so subjected to our senses, is called relative, apparent, common space.

53. Let us imagine all bodies to be destroyed and annihilated. What remains they call absolute space, all relation resulting from the situation and distances of bodies, as well as the bodies themselves, being done away with. Now this space is infinite, immovable, indivisible, not the object of sensation, without relation and without distinction. That is, all its attributes are privative or negative; therefore, it seems to be a mere nothing. The only difficulty results from its being extended, for extension is a positive quality. But what sort of extension is that, which can be neither divided nor measured, no part of which we can either perceive by our senses or picture in the imagination? For nothing can enter the imagination which from the nature of the thing cannot be perceived by sensation, since imagination is nothing else than a faculty representing the objects of sensation, either actually existing or at least being possible. It also evades pure intellect, since that faculty is concerned only with spiritual and unextended things, such as our minds, their habits, passions, virtues, and such things. Let us then take away mere words from absolute space, and nothing remains in sensation, imagination, or intellect. Nothing is therefore denoted by them but mere privation or negation, that is, mere nothing. [ . . . ]

66. From what has been said, it appears that, to ascertain the true nature of motion, it will be of great use: (1) to distinguish between mathematical hypotheses and the natures of things; (2) to beware of abstractions; (3) to consider motion as something, the object of sensation or at least of imagination; and to

be content with relative measures. If we do so, all the finest theorems of mechanical philosophy by means of which the recesses of nature are disclosed, and the system of the world subjected to human calculation, will remain untouched; and the consideration of motion will be freed from a thousand minute subtleties and abstract ideas. And let it suffice to say so much concerning the nature of motion.

67. It remains that we should treat the cause of the communication of motions. But most consider that force impressed on a movable body is the cause of motion in it. Nevertheless, it results from what has been laid down that they do not assign a known cause of motion, and one distinct from body and motion. It is further clear that force is not a certain and determinate thing, given that men of the greatest powers of mind advance different, and even contrary opinions, though retaining truth in their results. For Newton says that impressed force consists in action alone, and is an action exercised on body to change its state, and it does not continue after the action. Torricelli contends that a certain accumulation or aggregation of forces impressed by percussion is received into the moved body and remains there, and constitutes the impetus. Borelli and some others maintain the same. But although Newton and Torricelli seem to differ, each advancing views consistent with themselves, the matter is sufficiently well explained by both. For forces attributed to bodies are as much mathematical hypotheses as attractive forces assigned to the planets and sun. Mathematical entities, however, have no stable essence in nature, but depend on the notion of the definer—hence the same thing can be differently explained. [ . . . ]

71. In physics, sensation and experience, which only reach apparent effects, are admitted; in mechanics, the abstract notions of mathematicians are admitted. In first philosophy or metaphysics, we treat of incorporeal things, causes, truth, and the existence of things. The physicist contemplates the series or successions of the objects of sense, by what laws they are connected, and in what order, observing what precedes as a cause, what follows as effect. And in this way we say that a moved body is the cause of motion in another, or impresses motion on it; also it pulls or impels it. In this sense secondary corporeal causes

should be understood, no account being taken of the actual places of the forces, or active powers, or of the real cause in which they are. Moreover, beyond body, figure, and motion, the primary axioms of mechanical science can be called causes or mechanical principles, being regarded as the causes of the consequences.

72. The truly active causes can be extracted only by meditation and reasoning from the darkness in which they are involved, and thus at all become known. But it is the business of first philosophy or metaphysics to treat of them. And if each science were assigned its own province, its limits marked out, its principles and objects accurately distinguished, we could treat of what belongs to each with greater facility and perspicuity.

# Lady Mary Shepherd, *Essays on the Perception of an External Universe* (1827)[1]

*Lady Mary Shepherd was born Lady Mary Primrose in 1777 on the family's estate overlooking the Firth of Forth in Scotland near Edinburgh. Unlike her brothers, who went to the university for their formal education, she and her sisters were educated by private tutors at home (in a wide range of subjects including geography, mathematics, Latin, and history). In 1808 she eloped with Henry John Shepherd (1784–1855), a barrister who would eventually practice in Oxford and London. (She was thirty-one years old at the time, six years his senior.) While her husband was studying for his master's degree in Cambridge in the early 1820s, she may have met William Whewell, an important philosopher of science who became Master of Trinity College in Cambridge and went on to use one of her publications as a textbook in his courses. (Her daughter reports that he was a frequent visitor at their house years later, in London.) Shepherd seems to have written extensively. Her two most significant publications are* An Essay on the Relation of Cause and Effect *(1824) and* Essays on the Perception of an External Universe *(1827). In these works she presents extensive criticisms of a number of philosophers, including Berkeley and Hume, but also develops her own positive anti-skeptical metaphysics and epistemology. In the selection below, she criticizes Berkeley's conception of physical objects. She died in 1847.*

## ESSAY I. Consideration of the Erroneous Reasoning Contained in Bishop Berkeley's Principles of Human Knowledge.

### Section I.

"When several ideas," says Bishop Berkeley (section 1st) "(imprinted on the senses) are observed to accompany each other, they come to be marked by one name; and so to be reputed as one thing, thus a certain color, taste, smell, figure, and consistency, are accounted one distinct thing, signified by the name of apple; other collections of ideas form a stone, a tree, a book, &" (Section 3rd) "For what are objects but the things we perceive by sense? And what do we perceive but our own ideas or sensations? For, (section 5th) light and colors, heat and

1. From Lady Mary Shepherd, *Essays on the Perception of an External Universe, and Other Subjects Connected with the Doctrine of Cause and Effect* (London: John Hatchard and Son, 1827).

cold, extension and figure, in a word, the things we see and feel, what are they but so many sensations, notions, ideas, impressions on the sense? And is it possible to separate even in thought any of these from perception."

Sec. 9, p. 27. "Some make a distinction between primary and secondary qualities; but extension, figure, and motion, are ONLY *ideas* existing in the mind. And an idea can be like nothing but an idea, for neither these nor their archetypes, can exist in an unperceiving substance." (Section 15th) "It is impossible, therefore, that any color or extension at all, or sensible quality whatever, should exist in an unthinking subject without the mind, or indeed, that there should be any such thing as an outward object."

Thus far Bishop Berkeley, on *objects* being *only ideas*, or sensations of sensible qualities, and these ideas as comprehending the primary as well as secondary qualities. Many, I conceive, will think, from what I have said in the foregoing pages, that there is no material difference between my doctrine and his. But a careful investigation of both will show there is a considerable one. For although I agree with him, first, that nothing can be like a *sensation*, or *idea*, or *perception*, but a *sensation*, *idea*, and *perception*; secondly, that the primary qualities *after* the impressions they make on the senses, are sensations, or ideas, or perceptions, as well as the secondary ones, yet I do not agree with him in stating that *objects* are nothing but what we perceive by sense or that a complete enumeration is made of *all* the ideas which constitute an apple, a stone, a tree, or a book, in summing up of all their *sensible qualities*. For I have made it clear, I trust, by the foregoing argument *that an object perceived* by the mind is a compound being, consisting of a certain collection of sensible qualities "mixed with an *idea* the *result of reasoning*" of such qualities being formed by a "continually existing outward and independent set of as various and appropriate causes," therefore that there must be "*an outward object*" existing as a cause to excite the inward feeling. The logical error, therefore, of Bishop Berkeley on this part of the subject is an *incomplete definition*. For no definition is good which does not

take notice of *all* the ideas under the term, and in every object of sense which the mind perceives the knowledge of its *genus*, as a general effect arising from a *general* cause independent of mind, *is mixed with the sensations or ideas resulting from its special qualities affecting the same*. The notion of this *genus* is omitted in Dr. Berkeley's *definition of an* OBJECT, by limiting words *but* and *only*.

2. Bishop Berkeley is guilty of an ambiguity when he speaks "of ideas being *imprinted on the senses*," "of our perceiving" (*by sense*) "our own ideas and sensations," for he appears to speak of the "*senses* on which objects are imprinted," as if he intended by them those five organs of sense, viz., the eye, the ear, etc. *vulgarly called the senses*, but which in truth have no sense or feeling in themselves as independent of the mind, but are mechanical instruments, which as powers modify exterior existences before they reach the sentient capacity, which capacity as a general power or feeling becomes modified thereby. For undoubtedly the senses as organs cannot perceive what the senses as organs are required to form.[2]

When he speaks of "ideas being imprinted on the senses," *the phrase contains* the very doctrine he is controverting.

The *ideas* of colors cannot be imprinted on the *eye*, nor those of sound on the *ear*, nor those of extension on the *touch*. For there are no such IDEAS, until *after* the eye, as an instrument, has been affected by *some sorts of outward objects*, fitted to convey to the sentient principle a sensation of color, and so of the rest. Therefore the objects *perceived* by the organs of sense cannot be our ideas and sensations. Indeed, he does not take notice that he uses the notion of *perception* (which is that upon which the whole argument depends) in two different methods or meanings. For the term perception, when applied to those objects for whose observation the organs of sense are required and by which certain qualities are determined upon the perceiving mind, is used as the *notice* the mind takes of the presence of certain qualities *in consequence of the conscious use of the organs of sense*, the use and action of which must,

---

2. [Shepherd's note reads:] Dr. Reid on visible figure, etc. is guilty of a like error.

therefore, be in relation to *some* objects which are not the mind, but when applied to the "ideas and sensations of sensible qualities" perception is *only* used as the mental consciousness of those qualities, leaving out the conscious use of the organs of sense and the ideas of the outward objects which must necessarily have acted on them.

Nor is the reasoning I am using the mere turning of an expression, for in this sentence "*What are objects* but the things *we perceive by sense?*" and "What do we *perceive* but our ideas and sensations?" there is an offence against one of the plainest and most useful of logical rules. For the argument, if placed in a regular syllogism, will be seen to contain a middle term of two different and particular significations from which, therefore, nothing can be concluded.

Let the question be: "Are *objects*, *ideas* and *sensations* only?" and [let] the middle term "*The things we perceive*" be united with the predicate for the major proposition, and then be altered to "the things *we perceive by sense*" when joined to the subject for the minor. It will be seen that an inconclusive syllogism is thence formed.—For if the major proposition stands "Our ideas and sensations are the only things we *perceive*" and the minor "Objects are the things we perceive by sense," the conclusion, viz. "Therefore *objects* are only our ideas and sensations" does not logically follow, because the middle term would then consist of "*two different parts, or kinds*, of the same *universal* idea," i.e., the idea of perception in general, "*and this will never* serve to show whether the subject and predicate agree or disagree."[3] *For in the general conscious perception of sensible qualities are included the knowledge that the organs of sense are used as mechanical instruments acted upon by certain causes, and the* IDEAS *of these causes*. And this conscious use of the mechanical action of the five senses in relation to other beings than the mind *is a very different part, or kind of the universal idea of perception*, from the *mental consciousness of* PARTICULAR SENSIBLE QUALITIES *only*, which is also another part, or kind of the general notion of perception, which *general* notion *includes every species of consciousness*

*whatever*. The consciousness whether the organs of sense be used or not in perceiving objects is the great criterion of a sane or insane state of mind, of its waking or sleeping condition. The consciousness that the organs of sense are used makes all the difference between objects of sense, or objects of memory, reason, or imagination. *By the quick and practical use of the senses subject to infancy, the associations of ideas, resulting from reason and experience, are so interwoven and so immediate with the consciousness of their use that they ought always to be considered as forming a component part of the whole ideas which lie under the terms* THE OBJECTS OF SENSE. The *objects of sense*, therefore (under the conscious use of the organs of sense), are known (according to the reasoning used in the foregoing chapters of this essay) to be *the continued, exterior, and independent existence* of external nature, exciting ideas and determining sensations in the mind of a sentient being, but not ONLY to be *ideas and sensations*.

In the sentence already commented on and which contains the sum of Dr. Berkeley's doctrine—the word *object* as well as the phrase "*perception by sense*" is of ambiguous application. For in his use of the word *object*, he begs the question, meaning thereby a collection of sensible qualities, formed by the senses and apprehended by the mind, whereas the adversary means by that word a set of qualities exterior to the mind and to which the organs of sense are in relation as mechanical instruments and of which they take notice as those permanent existences which the understanding is aware *must needs continue* when unperceived before they are transformed by their action into other beings. Objects before the notice of the senses are not the same things as after their acquaintance with them. All men mean by objects the things which exist previously to their mixture with the action of the organs of sense and which FROM POWERFUL ASSOCIATION *they conceive to exist under the forms of their sensible qualities*. Therefore by *feigning* the contrary notion there can arise no convincing argument.

To go on, however, with the argument (by which I would show that objects of sense are not *only* the ideas of their sensible qualities), I observe

---

3. [Shepherd's note reads:] Watt's *Logic*.

that reason, discovering these objects to be in their relation to each other as *various* as the *impressions* they convey, also perceives them to be in *one* respect *like* the ideas they create, i.e., in the same proportions and bearings to each other *outwardly* as they are inwardly. Therefore, among the observations we have of "our ideas and sensations" of sensible qualities, we do perceive *something else* than these mere "*ideas or sensations.*" For we perceive by *reason* that those things which must needs be present in order as *causes* to affect the sense may, on account of *their variety*, their *similar distinctness*, and *proportions*, be named (when considered as existing exterior to the instruments of sense) by the names they bear when inwardly taken notice of.

Now I consider the observation of this latter circumstance as containing a full answer to all the puzzling contradictions of Bishop Berkeley's theory. For, although in a popular manner, men consider things are *outwardly* the *counterpart* of what they perceive *inwardly*, yet this is not the whole reason of the difference they make amidst things. For the soul does truly in a sense *perceive* outward things, *as* they are when existing outwardly, for after *reason* shows that the quality of things, in a state of *perception*, cannot *be like* them out of a state of perception, yet being conscious that sensation is only a *simple* act (a power, a quality) *it perceives* by the understanding that the *varieties* of things are in relation to each other *outwardly* in the *same proportion* as are the inward sensations. Thus hard and soft, bitter and sweet, heat and cold, round and square, are therefore *perceived* not ONLY to be sensations, but to be certain unknown qualities of objects independent of the mind in *relation to each other*, and in that *state "to continue to exist, ready to appear to the senses when called for."* Popularly, the *sensations these excite are associated with the notions of the outward objects* and all their varieties. But when philosophy breaks up this association, she should not take away *more* than what this natural junction of thought has created. Bishop Berkeley does not merely separate what is mixed, but would destroy the whole compound together. This observation, in my opinion, contains a *demonstration* against the Berkelean theory and restores nature

entirely to her rights again. "Equals taken *from equals*, the *remainders are equal.*" Take *sensation*, simple sensation, the power or capacity of feeling merely, from extension, from color, from sound, and from taste; from heat and cold; from electricity or attraction; from fire, air, water, or earth; from the *perception* of life or the *idea* of death; from motion or rest. Is there nothing left? Every thing is left that has any variety or difference in it. "What are objects" (says Bishop Berkeley) "but the ideas perceived by reason to be continually, independently, outwardly existing, of the same proportions as are the inward sensations of which they are the effects." Had Bishop Berkeley allowed of the force of a most finished piece of reasoning he uses in respect to the proof of the existence of *other minds* than our own, in behalf also of objects that are not minds, he had not set before the public some paradoxes, unhappily considered as *unanswerable*. In (sect. 195) he says: "From what has been said, it is plain that we cannot know the existence of other spirits otherwise than by their operations, or the ideas by them excited in us. I perceive several motions, changes, and combinations of ideas, that inform me there are certain particular agents *like myself*, which accompany them and concur in their production. Hence the knowledge I have of *other spirits* is not immediate as is the knowledge of my ideas, but, depending on the intervention of ideas, by me referred to agents or spirits *distinct* from myself, as effects or concomitant signs."

Now my argument (however ill I may have executed it) intends the whole way to show "that our knowledge of other objects" (of any kind) "is not *immediate* as is the knowledge of our ideas," but depends "on the *intervention* of our ideas" by us referred to "agents or spirits" (to *unknown proportionate causes* distinct from ourselves) and that the several "*motions, changes,* and *combinations* of ideas which we perceive inform us that there are certain particular agents *like ourselves*" (*always* like ourselves as continuing to *exist* and *in other qualities, plus or minus* ourselves) "which accompany them and concur in their production."

In order, however, to carry the argument a little further on these matters, let us examine with a greater nicety than we have yet done this proposition: "figure, extension, and motion are *only* ideas in the perceiving mind" and let us select one quality, say, *figure*, for this examination in order to simplify the analysis. Then the argument which applies to figure will also apply to the other qualities.

Let the question be: Is figure an *idea only* in the perceiving mind? Now undoubtedly the sense, inward perception, or notion of figure (or by whatever word shall be designated the conscious sensation of a living being which it has under the impression of figure) can *only* be in a perceiving mind, and nothing else can be like it but such another sensation. But this *sense of figure* is not what the word figure only means when applied to an object which affects either the sense of sight or touch. It is then a relative term, a sign of a compound notion, signifying a particular sensation *caused* by a particular *cause*, which cause is not a sensation. Moreover, the word *is also understood to be applicable to the proportion which that cause (or "outward continuous object") bears to the other outward beings surrounding it* (and this without supposing they are the least like our ideas). For let us consider a round figure, for instance, apart from our perception of it. The *line* which bounds this solid substance *outwardly* (whatever *line* and *solid* may be) and parts it from the surrounding atmosphere (whatever *parting* or *atmosphere* may be) must still be a *variety*, or *change*, or *difference* among these outward things, and this difference among outward unknown things, *not like sensations*, is *outward* and is always meant in that sense by the word which signifies *a certain state of continuous existence*, which is independent of mind. The word and notion are *compound*, and each stands for the *cause and effect united*, and not *only* for the *effect*. Philosophers, therefore, ought to be capable of perceiving that figure, extension, and motion, etc. are *not only ideas in the mind*, but are capacities, qualities, beings in nature in relation to each other when exterior to mind.

# 6. HUME'S *TREATISE, ENQUIRY, DIALOGUES*, AND ASSOCIATED TEXTS

David Hume was born in Edinburgh, Scotland, in 1711 and attended the University of Edinburgh for a few years in the 1720s, though he left without receiving a degree. After studying on his own for several years, he went to France in 1734 (to be more specific, to La Flèche, where Descartes had been educated) and wrote his first major work, *A Treatise of Human Nature*, published anonymously in 1739. Hume was quite disappointed with how it was received, remarking that it "fell dead-born from the press, without reaching such distinction as even to excite a murmur among the zealots." Over the next few decades, Hume reworked the content of the *Treatise* and published *Philosophical Essays Concerning Human Understanding* (later entitled *An Enquiry Concerning Human Understanding*) in 1748, *Dissertation on the Passions* in 1757, and *An Enquiry Concerning the Principles of Morals* in 1751. Hume also published *Essays, Moral and Political* in 1741–42, *Political Discourses* in 1752, and a six-volume *History of England* between 1754 and 1762. Hume's *Dialogues Concerning Natural Religion* was published posthumously in 1779. Unlike many of his most important philosophical predecessors and contemporaries, Hume never held an academic position. He was nominated for positions at Edinburgh (in 1744–45) and Glasgow (in 1751), but opposition from the clergy was decisive in both cases. Instead Hume was employed in a variety of ways, e.g., as a tutor to Marquess of Annandale, as a private secretary to General St. Clair (who was involved in plans to invade Canada) and to Lord Hertford (Ambassador to France), as a librarian for the Advocates Library in Edinburgh, and as Undersecretary of State (Northern Department).[1]

Hume's *A Treatise of Human Nature* is a long and intricate work, divided into three books. Book One concerns the understanding and treats of traditional issues in epistemology and metaphysics. Book Two is on the passions and discusses emotions in detail. Book Three deals with morality in light of his discussion of the passions in Book Two. Thus, Hume's *Treatise* covers many traditional areas of philosophical inquiry.

Book One of the *Treatise* divides into four parts. The bulk of Part One is devoted to laying out Hume's fundamental empiricist principles: All ideas

---

1. For more on Hume, see Barry Stroud, *Hume* (London: Routledge & Kegan Paul, 1978), David Fate Norton, *David Hume. Common Sense Moralist, Sceptical Metaphysician* (Princeton: Princeton University Press, 1982, and David Fate Norton, ed., *The Cambridge Companion to Hume* (Cambridge: Cambridge University Press, 1993).

are copies of impressions, and all ideas are related to each other by means of resemblance, contiguity, and causality. In light of these principles, Hume then gives an account of our ideas of substances, modes, relations, and abstract ideas. Part Two discusses our ideas of space and time (in particular, whether they are infinitely divisible) and of existence. Part Three undertakes a detailed examination of a particularly important foundation of our knowledge, cause and effect relations. It also develops an account of belief that builds on the theory of ideas introduced in Part One. Part Four discusses a number of implications of Hume's theory of ideas and causality. In particular, Hume explains how his theories do and do not result in skepticism with respect to reason and the senses. In the latter case, Hume is especially concerned to provide an account of why we believe in the existence of bodies (given that there is no rational argument that can establish their existence). In Part Four Hume also discusses his account of the mind, including personal identity, an issue he famously revisits in the Appendix to the *Treatise*.

Briefly, the situation Hume faces with respect to the self and self-consciousness is as follows. In light of his empiricist principle according to which all ideas must be derived from impressions, in Part One of Book One Hume looks for an impression of substance and discovers that he can find none. In Part Four of Book One Hume recognizes that this general point applies to the self as well. For when he considers his own mind, he discovers that he can find no impression of an enduring and identical self (or immaterial substance) that underlies all of his thoughts. As he puts it: "For my part, when I enter most intimately into what I call *myself*, I always stumble on some particular perception or other, of heat or cold, light or shade, love or hatred, pain or pleasure. I never can catch *myself* at any time without a perception and never can observe anything but the perception." As a result, on Hume's account the self is nothing more than a collection or "bundle" of perceptions rather than an immaterial substance in which thoughts might inhere. However, in a famous passage from the Appendix, Hume expresses his dissatisfaction with this account, noting that it raises

difficulties, which, though not "absolutely insuperable," are "too hard for my understanding."

Hume's *Enquiry Concerning Human Understanding* is a much abbreviated treatment of many of the issues discussed in detail in Book One of the *Treatise*. Its main focus (after briefly introducing his theory of ideas in §§1–3) is on causality and the implications his understanding of it has for a variety of issues such as liberty, miracles, and belief in the existence of God. Hume's main thesis is that the traditional notion of causality, which involves a necessary connection between cause and effect, is mistaken. For in any single instance of causality, we do not see anything that connects the cause and the effect with necessity. In line with his general empiricist stance, Hume notes that all one ever sees is one event followed by another, whether the events are the motions of bodies or thoughts in a mind. Nor is reason able to infer *a priori* any effect from the presence of any given cause; there would be no contradiction if the future did not resemble the past and if we were presented with an object that we had never seen before, reason would not be able to determine its various effects. Accordingly, Hume revises our notion of causality and, as an empiricist, the only basis he can find for it is experience and habit. Thus, objectively, causality is simply the constant or customary conjunction of the cause and effect, whereas subjectively, it is our expectation, formed on the basis of repeated experience in the past rather than on reason, that one kind of event will follow another kind of event in the future.

Given this understanding of causality, Hume considers a variety of traditional philosophical issues in the *Enquiry*, at times coming to rather provocative conclusions. For example, in §8 he argues that liberty (which we now typically call free will) not only is compatible with but is actually required by determinism. Determinism holds because we do find a constant conjunction between motives and actions and, moreover, we have come to expect this kind of correlation. If liberty is defined as a power of acting or not acting according to the determinations of the will, that is, as occurring when one's action is not constrained by external, non-volitional factors, then it is clear that everyone admits liberty. But obviously there is no conflict between the constant conjunction of motives and actions and the absence of external constraints. Rather, the absence of external constraints seems to require the connection between actions and motives, since moral judgments depend on the connection between motives and actions.

In §10 Hume presents his famous argument against miracles. Technically, the argument is not against miracles per se, but rather against the possibility that we could have enough evidence to accept miracles (especially those that are to be used to justify religious belief). If a miracle is defined as a violation of the laws of nature and the laws of nature have been overwhelmingly established by our vast experience, then the evidence in favor of a miracle will always be (and, as Hume argues, has always been) less than, or at least not greater than, our evidence for the laws of nature. Since one should proportion one's belief to the evidence (and since the evidence for them is less than the evidence against them, or at least the evidence against them cancels the evidence for them), one should not believe in miracles.

In §11 Hume argues that attempts to establish the existence of God on the basis of causality cannot succeed. Hume makes three main critical points. First, it is illegitimate to infer from certain effects (e.g., what we see in the world) to a cause (e.g., God) and then to infer further, unobserved effects from that cause (e.g., that God will reward or punish humans for their past actions), since neither the first inference nor experience can justify the second inference. Second, one can never infer the infinite aspects of God's nature (e.g., omnipotence, omniscience, omnibenevolence, etc.) from the merely finite effects of the world. Third, if one has experienced a certain event only once, one might question whether one can infer that a cause is required at all. While these critical points could be taken to be hostile to Christianity (which might justify the clergy's opposition to Hume), one could also view Hume's position as neutral with respect to Christianity, for example by being congenial to fideism, the view that one's fundamental religious convictions are not subject to independent, rational evaluation. Bayle's discussion of Pyrrho provides a sense of the role of religious skepticism in this context. However, Hume's own views on religion are revealed in greater detail in his *Dialogues Concerning Natural Religion*. Though Hume does not take an official stand on the issue—by discussing proofs for the existence of God only indirectly by this work's three main figures (Demea, Cleanthes, and Philo)—it is plausible to suspect that Hume is using Philo, in particular, to express his own arguments, an interpretation consistent with the fact that Hume did not wish to publish this work during his lifetime.

# Pierre Bayle, *Dictionary* (1697), "Pyrrho," Note B[1]

*Pierre Bayle was a philosophical skeptic and religious writer born in 1647 to a Calvinist family in southern France. He became Professor of Philosophy at the Protestant Academy of Sedan, 1675–81. Upon its abolition, he moved to Rotterdam and became Professor of Philosophy at the Ecole Illustre; he died in Rotterdam in 1706. Bayle's main claim to fame is the five-volume* Historical and Critical Dictionary *(1697), which provides a full presentation of his skepticism. It went through numerous editions, including an English translation in 1710. As Bayle states in the* Dictionary, *Pyrrho was a Greek philosopher from the time of Alexander the Great. After examining all arguments for and against any given proposition, Pyrrho always found reasons for both affirming and denying it; thus he suspended judgment, concluding that the matter should be looked into further. Although he was not the inventor of this method of philosophizing, it goes by his name: Pyrrhonism. The article on Pyrrho provides Bayle with an opportunity to discuss early modern Pyrrhonism.[2]*

"Pyrrhonism is rightly detested in the divinity schools." Pyrrhonism is dangerous with respect to that divine science, but it is not very dangerous with respect to natural philosophy or the state. There is no harm in saying that the mind of man is too limited to discover anything in natural truths, in the causes which produce heat, cold, the tides, etc. It is enough for us to endeavor to find out some probable hypotheses and to collect experiments; and I am sure that there are very few good natural philosophers in our age who are not convinced that nature is an impenetrable abyss and that its springs are known to none but to the maker and director of them. So that all those philosophers are, in that respect, Academics and Pyrrhonists. Society does not need to be afraid of them, for skeptics do not deny that men should conform to the customs of their country, practice moral duties, and resolve upon those things from a probable reason without waiting for certainty. They might suspend their judgment on the question of whether such a duty is naturally and absolutely lawful, but they do not suspend it on the question of whether it is to be practiced on such and such an occasion. Thus, it follows that Pyrrhonism is only dangerous to religion, for

1. [Translated from the French in *The Dictionary Historical and Critical of Mr. Peter Bayle* (London, 1734–38), 5 vols., modified.]

2. [For more on Bayle, see Richard Popkin, *The High Road to Pyrrhonism* (2nd ed., Indianapolis: Hackett Publishing Company, 1989) or Elisabeth Labrousse, *Bayle* (Oxford: Oxford University Press, 1983).]

it ought to be grounded upon certainty; the design, the effects, and use of religion vanish as soon as the firm persuasion of its truth is blotted out of the mind. But, on the other hand, we do not need to be uneasy at it; there never was and there never will be but a small number of men capable of being deceived by the arguments of the skeptics. The grace which God bestows upon the faithful, the force of education in other men, and, if you will, ignorance, and the natural inclination men have to be peremptory are an impenetrable shield against the darts of the Pyrrhonists, although the sect fancies it is now more formidable than it was in former times. Let us see upon what grounds they build such a strange pretension.

About two months ago a learned man gave me a full account of a conference at which he had been present. Two abbots, one of whom had but common learning, the other was a good philosopher, grew so hot by degrees in their dispute that it almost became a full-fledged quarrel. The first had said, rather bluntly, that he forgave the pagan philosophers their floating in the uncertainty of their opinions, but that he could not understand how there could be any Pyrrhonists under the light of the Gospel. To which the other answered, "You are wrong to reason in such a manner. If Arcesilaus should return into the world and was to dispute with our theologians, he would be a thousand times more formidable than he was to the dogmatists of old Greece; Christian theology would afford him unanswerable arguments." All the company heard this with great surprise and begged the abbot to explain himself further, having no doubt that he had advanced a paradox which would only lead to his own confusion. He answered thus, addressing himself to the first abbot. "I will not make use of the advantages the new philosophy gives to the Pyrrhonists. The name of Sextus Empiricus was scarcely known in our schools; what he proposed with so great subtlety concerning suspending one's judgment was not less unknown than the Terra Australis, when Gassendi gave an abridgment of it, which opened our eyes. Cartesianism put the final touches to the work, and now no good philosopher any longer doubts that the skeptics were right to maintain that the qualities of bodies which strike our senses are only appearances.

Everyone of us may say, 'I feel heat before a fire,' but not 'I know that fire is in itself such as it appears to me.' Such was the style of the ancient Pyrrhonists. But now the new philosophy speaks more positively: Heat, smell, colors, etc. are not in the objects of our senses; they are only some modifications of my soul. I know that bodies are not at all as they appear to me. They were very willing to except extension and motion, but they could not do it; for if the objects of our senses appear to us colored, hot, cold, scented, though they are not so, why should they not appear extended and figured, at rest, and in motion, though they had no such thing. No, the objects of my senses cannot be the cause of my sensations; I might, therefore, feel cold and heat, see colors, figures, extension, and motion, though there was not one body in the world. I do not, therefore, have one good proof of the existence of bodies.[3] The only proof they give me for it is that God would deceive me if he imprinted in my soul the ideas I have of body without there being any. But that proof is very weak; it proves too much. Ever since the beginning of the world all mankind, except, perhaps, one in two hundred million, do firmly believe that bodies are colored, and yet it is a mistake. I ask whether God deceives men with respect to those colors. If he deceives them in that respect, what prevents him from doing so with respect to extension? This latter illusion will not be less innocent, nor less consistent, than the former with the most perfect being. If he does not deceive them with respect to colors, it is without doubt because he does not force them to say, 'those colors exist outside of my soul,' but only 'it appears to me there are some colors there.' The same may be said with respect to extension. God does not force you to say, 'it does exist,' but only to judge that you feel it and that it appears to you to exist. A Cartesian can as readily suspend his judgment about the existence of extension as a peasant affirm that the sun shines, that snow is white, etc. And, therefore, if we are mistaken in affirming the existence of extension, God will not be the cause of

---

3. Father Malebranche shows in one of his *Elucidations* of the *Search after Truth*, "that it is very difficult to prove the existence of bodies and that nothing but faith can convince us that bodies do really exist."

it, since you acknowledge that he is not the cause of that peasant's error. Such are the advantages which the philosophers would procure to the Pyrrhonists, but I will not take advantage of them."

Immediately the same abbot, who was a philosopher, declared to the other that if he would have the better of a skeptic, he must, before all things, prove that the truth may certainly be known by certain marks. They are commonly called the criterion of truth [*criterium veritatis*]. You will rightly maintain against him that self-evidence is a certain characteristic of truth, for if self-evidence were not, we would have none. "Let it be so," he will say, "this is where I have you; I will show you several things as evident as can be, which you reject as false. 1. It is evident that things which do not differ from a third do not differ from each other. This is the basis of all our reasonings and all our syllogisms are grounded upon it; nevertheless, we are assured by the revelation of the mystery of the Trinity that it is a false axiom. You may invent as many distinctions as you please, but you will never be able to show that that maxim is not contradicted by this great mystery. 2. It is evident that there is no difference between individual, nature, and person. Nevertheless, the same mystery has convinced us that persons can be multiplied and that individuals and natures will not cease for all that to be one. 3. It is evident that for a man to be really and perfectly a person, it is enough to unite together a human body and a rational soul. But the mystery of the Incarnation has taught us that it is not sufficient. From this it follows that neither you nor I can be sure whether we are persons; for if it were essential that a human body and rational soul united together constitute a person, then God could never cause that they, thus united, did not constitute a person. We must therefore say that personality is merely accidental to them. But every accident may be separated from its subject in several ways; God, therefore, may prevent us from being persons in several ways, though we are made up of a body and a soul; and can anyone assure us that he does not make use of some such means to deprive us of our personality? Is he obliged to reveal to us the several ways he disposes of us? 4. It is evident that a human body cannot be in several places

at one time and that its head cannot be penetrated with all its other parts under an indivisible point; nevertheless, the mystery of the Eucharist teaches us that those two things happen every day. From this it follows that neither you nor I can be sure whether we are distinct from other men, and whether we are not at this very moment in the seraglio of Constantinople, in Canada, in Japan, and in every town of the world, under different conditions in each place. Since God does nothing in vain, would he create several men when one man only, created in several places and clothed with several qualities, may suffice? This doctrine deprives us of the truth we find in numbers, for we no longer know what two or three are; we do not know what identity and diversity are. If we judge that John and Peter are two men, it is only because we see them in distinct places and because the one does not have the accidents of the other. But the basis for the distinction is destroyed by the doctrine of the Eucharist. It may be that there is only one creature in the world produced in several places with a diversity of qualities; we cast up long accounts in arithmetic, as if there were many distinct things;[4] but it is only a vain imagination. Not only are we ignorant whether there are two bodies in the world but we do not so much as know whether there is a body and a spirit; for if matter is penetrable, it is plain that extension is only an accident of the body, and so the body, according to its essence, is an unextended substance. It is, therefore, capable of all the attributes we conceive in a spirit, as the understanding, the will, the passions, and the sensations, so that we are left without any rule whereby we may discern whether a substance is spiritual by its nature or whether it is corporeal. 5. It is evident that the modes of a substance cannot subsist without the substance which they modify; but the mystery of transubstantiation has taught us that this is false. All our ideas are confounded by it; we can no longer define a substance; for if an accident can subsist without any subject, a substance may in its turn subsist dependently upon another substance, as accidents

---

4. Note that if a body may be produced in several places, any other being, spirit, place, accident, etc. may be multiplied the same way; and so there will not be a multitude of beings, but all things will be reduced to only one created being.

do; a mind may subsist after the manner of bodies, as in the Eucharist matter exists after the manner of minds; the latter may be impenetrable, as matter is penetrable in the Eucharist. Now, if by coming from the darkness of paganism to the light of the Gospel, we have learned the falsity of so many evident notions and of so many certain definitions, what will it be like when we shall come from the darkness of this life to the glory of heaven? Is it not very likely that we shall then learn the falsity of a thousand things which appear to us undeniable? Let us make a good use of the rashness of those who lived before the Gospel and who affirmed that some evident doctrines are true, the falsity of which has been revealed to us by the mysteries of our theology.

"I come now to morals. 1. It is evident that if it is possible, evil ought to be prevented, and that it is a sinful thing to permit it when it can be prevented. Nevertheless, our theology shows us that this is false; it teaches us that God does nothing unbecoming of his perfections when he permits all the disorders in the world which he might easily have prevented. 2. It is evident that a creature which does not exist cannot be an accomplice of an evil action. 3. And that it is unjust to punish that creature as an accomplice of that action. Nevertheless, our doctrine concerning original sin shows us the falsity of those evident truths. 4. It is evident that what is honest ought to be preferred to what is profitable, and that the more holy a being is, the less freedom it has to prefer what is profitable to what is honest. Nevertheless, our theologians tell us that since God chose between a world perfectly well regulated, adorned with all virtues, and a world like ours, where sin and disorder prevail, he preferred the latter to the former as being more consistent with the interest of his glory. If you should tell me that the duties of the creator should not be measured by ours, you will fall into the net of your adversaries. They would have you there; the main thing they aim at is to prove that the absolute nature of things is unknown to us, and that we know only some relations they have one to another. We do not know, they say, whether sugar is sweet in itself; we only know that it seems sweet to us when we taste it. We do not know whether a certain action is honest in

itself and by its nature; we only believe that with respect to such a one, and by reason of certain circumstances, it has the appearance of honesty. But it is another thing in other respects and under other relations. See, therefore, how you expose yourself by telling them that the ideas we have of justice and honesty are liable to exception and are relative. Besides, I would have you observe that the more you raise the rights of God to the privilege of acting contrary to our ideas, the more you destroy the only means left to you to prove that there are bodies, namely, that God does not deceive us and that he would be doing so if the corporeal world did not exist. To show people a thing which does not exist outside their minds would be deceitful; but, they will answer you, '*distinguo*—I distinguish'; if a prince did so, '*concedo*—I grant it'; if God did it, '*nego*—I deny it'; for the rights of God are quite different from those of kings. Besides, if the exceptions you make to the principles of morality are based on the incomprehensible infinity of God, I can never be sure of anything; for I shall never be able to comprehend the whole extent of the rights of God. I conclude, therefore, that if truth were to be known by any mark, it would be by self-evidence; but self-evidence is no such mark, because it is compatible with falsities; therefore, etc."

The abbot, to whom this long discourse was directed, could hardly forbear interrupting it; he listened to it with great uneasiness, and when he perceived that everybody was silent, he fell into a rage against the Pyrrhonists and did not spare the abbot for having mentioned the objections which they take from the systems of divinity. This abbot replied modestly that he knew very well those objections were very inconsiderable and mere sophisms, but that it is reasonable that those who so much despise the Pyrrhonists should not be ignorant of the state of things. He went on and said, "you believed up to now that a Pyrrhonist could not puzzle you, answer me therefore; you are forty-five years of age, you do not doubt of it, and if there is anything that you are sure of, it is that you are the same person to whom the abbey of —— was given two years ago. I am going to show you that you have no good reason to be sure of it; I argue from the principles of our theology. Your soul has been created; God must therefore at every moment renew its existence, for the conservation of creatures is a continued creation. How do you know that God did not permit this morning that your soul, which he had continued to create until then ever since the first moment of your life, relapse into nothing? How do you know that he has not created another soul modified as yours was?[5] That new soul is that which you have now. Show me the contrary; let the company judge of my objection." A learned theologian who

was there answered and acknowledged that once creation was supposed, it was as easy for God to create a new soul at every moment as to reproduce the same, but that the ideas we have of his wisdom, and especially the light which his word affords us, are sufficient to assure us that we have the same numerical soul today which we had yesterday, the day before, etc. And he concluded that it was needless to dispute with the Pyrrhonists and that their sophisms could not easily be eluded by the mere force of reason, that they should be made sensible of the weakness of reason before all things, so that they may have recourse to a better guide, namely, faith.

---

5. That is to say, with the reminiscence which he would have reproduced if he had continued to create the soul of the Abbot.

# David Hume, A *Treatise of Human Nature* (1739)[1]

## Book I. Of the Understanding

### Part 4. Of the Skeptical and Other Systems of Philosophy

#### Section 5: Of the Immateriality of the Soul

Having found such contradictions and difficulties in every system concerning external objects and in the idea of matter which we fancy so clear and determinate, we shall naturally expect still greater difficulties and contradictions in every hypothesis concerning our internal perceptions and the nature of the mind which we are apt to imagine so much more obscure and uncertain. But in this we should deceive ourselves. The intellectual world, though involved in infinite obscurities, is not perplexed with any such contradictions as those we have discovered in the natural. What is known concerning it agrees with itself, and what is unknown we must be contented to leave so.

It is true, would we listen to certain philosophers, they promise to diminish our ignorance, but I am afraid it is at the hazard of running us into

contradictions from which the subject is of itself exempted. These philosophers are the curious reasoners concerning the material or immaterial substances in which they suppose our perceptions to inhere. In order to put a stop to these endless cavils on both sides, I know no better method than to ask these philosophers in a few words *what they mean by substance and inhesion*. And after they have answered this question, it will then be reasonable, and not until then, to enter seriously into the dispute.

This question we have found impossible to be answered with regard to matter and body, but, besides the fact that in the case of the mind it labors under all the same difficulties, it is burdened with some additional ones which are peculiar to that subject. As every idea is derived from a precedent impression, had we any idea of the substance of our minds, we must also have an impression of it, which is very difficult, if not impossible, to be conceived. For how can an impression represent a substance otherwise than by resembling it? And how can an impression resemble a substance, since, according to this philosophy, it is not a substance and has none of the peculiar qualities or characteristics of a substance?

But leaving the question *of what may or may not be* for that other—*what actually is*, I desire those philosophers who pretend that we have an idea of the

<hr>

1. [From *The Philosophical Works of David Hume*, T. H. Green and T. H. Grose, eds. (London: Longman's, Green, and Co., 1898), 4 vols., English, modified.]

substance of our minds to point out the impression that produces it and tell distinctly after what manner that impression operates and from what object it is derived. Is it an impression of sensation or of reflection? Is it pleasant or painful or indifferent? Does it attend us at all times or does it only return at intervals? If at intervals, at what times principally does it return, and by what causes is it produced?

If, instead of answering these questions, anyone should evade the difficulty by saying that the definition of a substance is *something which may exist by itself* and that this definition ought to satisfy us, should this be said, I should observe that this definition agrees to everything that can possibly be conceived and never will serve to distinguish substance from accident or the soul from its perceptions. For thus I reason: Whatever is clearly conceived may exist, and whatever is clearly conceived after any manner may exist after the same manner. This is one principle which has been already acknowledged. Again, everything which is different is distinguishable, and everything which is distinguishable is separable by the imagination. This is another principle. My conclusion from both is that since all our perceptions are different from each other and from everything else in the universe, they are also distinct and separable and may be considered as separately existent and may exist separately and have no need of anything else to support their existence. They are, therefore, substances as far as this definition explains a substance.

Thus, neither by considering the first origin of ideas nor by means of a definition are we able to arrive at any satisfactory notion of substance, which seems to me a sufficient reason for abandoning utterly that dispute concerning the materiality and immateriality of the soul and makes me absolutely condemn even the question itself. We have no perfect idea of anything but of a perception. A substance is entirely different from a perception. We have, therefore, no idea of a substance. Inhesion in something is supposed to be requisite to support the existence of our perceptions. Nothing appears requisite to support the existence of a perception. We have, therefore, no idea of inhesion. What is the possibility then of answering that question, *whether perceptions inhere in a material or immaterial substance*, when we do not so much as understand the meaning of the question?

There is one argument commonly employed for the immateriality of the soul which seems to me remarkable. Whatever is extended consists of parts, and whatever consists of parts is divisible, if not in reality, at least in the imagination. But it is impossible anything divisible can be *conjoined* to a thought or perception which is a being altogether inseparable and indivisible. For, supposing such a conjunction, would the indivisible thought exist on the left or on the right hand of this extended divisible body? On the surface or in the middle? On the back or foreside of it? If it is conjoined with the extension, it must exist somewhere within its dimensions. If it exists within its dimensions, either it must exist in one particular part—and then that particular part is indivisible and the perception is conjoined only with it, not with the extension—or, if the thought exists in every part, it must also be extended and separable and divisible as well as the body, which is utterly absurd and contradictory. For can anyone conceive a passion of a yard in length, a foot in breadth, and an inch in thickness? Thought, therefore, and extension are qualities wholly incompatible and never can incorporate together into one subject.

This argument does not affect the question concerning the *substance* of the soul, but only that concerning its *local conjunction* with matter, and, therefore, it may not be improper to consider in general what objects are or are not susceptible of a local conjunction. This is a curious question and may lead us to some discoveries of considerable moment.

The first notion of space and extension is derived solely from the senses of sight and feeling. Nor is there anything but what is colored or tangible that has parts disposed after such a manner as to convey that idea. When we diminish or increase a relish, it is not after the same manner that we diminish or increase any visible object, and when several sounds strike our hearing at once, custom and reflection alone make us form an idea of the degrees of the distance and contiguity of those bodies from which they are derived. Whatever marks the place of its existence either must be extended or must be a mathematical point without parts or composition. What is extended must have a particular figure, as square, round, triangular, none of which will agree to a desire or indeed to any impression or idea, except of these two senses above mentioned. Neither ought a desire, though indivisible, be considered as a mathematical point. For in that case it would be possible by the addition of others to make two, three, four desires and these disposed and situated in such a manner as to have a determinate length, breadth, and thickness, which is evidently absurd.

It will not be surprising after this, if I propose a maxim which is condemned by several metaphysicians and is esteemed contrary to the most certain principles of human reason. This maxim is *that an object may exist and yet be nowhere*, and I assert not only that this is possible but that the greatest part of beings do and must exist after this manner. An object may be said to be nowhere when its parts are not so situated with respect to each other as to form any figure or quantity, nor the whole with respect to other bodies so as to answer to our notions of contiguity or distance. Now this is evidently the case with all our perceptions and objects except those of the sight and feeling. A moral reflection cannot be placed on the right or on the left hand of a passion, nor can a smell or sound be of either a circular or a square figure. These objects and perceptions, so far from requiring any particular place, are absolutely incompatible with it, and even the imagination cannot attribute it to them. And as to the absurdity of supposing them to be nowhere, we may consider that if the passions and sentiments appear to the perception to have any particular place, the idea of extension might be derived from them as well as from the sight and touch, contrary to what we have already established. If they *appear* not to have any particular place, they may possibly *exist* in the same manner, since whatever we conceive is possible.

It will not now be necessary to prove that those perceptions which are simple and exist nowhere are incapable of any conjunction in place with matter or body, which is extended and divisible, since it is impossible to found a relation but on some common quality. It may be better worth our while to remark

not only that this question of the local conjunction of objects occurs in metaphysical disputes concerning the nature of the soul, but that even in common life we have every moment occasion to examine it. Thus, supposing we consider a fig at one end of the table and an olive at the other, it is evident that in forming the complex ideas of these substances one of the most obvious is that of their different relishes, and it is as evident that we incorporate and conjoin these qualities with such as are colored and tangible. The bitter taste of the one and sweet taste of the other are supposed to lie in the very visible body and to be separated from each other by the whole length of the table. This is so notable and so natural an illusion that it may be proper to consider the principles from which it is derived.

Though an extended object is incapable of a conjunction in place with another that exists without any place or extension, yet they are still susceptible of many other relations. Thus the taste and smell of any fruit are inseparable from its other qualities of color and tangibility, and whichever of them is the cause or effect, it is certain they are always coexistent. Nor are they only coexistent in general, but also contemporary in their appearance in the mind, and it is upon the application of the extended body to our senses that we perceive its particular taste and smell. These relations, then, of *causation and contiguity in the time of their appearance* between the extended object and the quality which exists without any particular place must have such an effect on the mind that upon the appearance of one it will immediately turn its thought to the conception of the other. Nor is this all. We not only turn our thought from one to the other upon account of their relation, but likewise endeavor to give them a new relation, namely that of *a conjunction in place* so that we may render the transition more easy and natural. For it is a quality which I shall often have occasion to remark in human nature and shall explain more fully in its proper place that when objects are united by any relation, we have a strong propensity to add some new relation to them in order to complete the union. In our arrangement of bodies we never fail to place such as are resembling in contiguity to each other, or at least in correspondent points of view. Why? Because we feel a satisfaction in joining the relation of contiguity to that of resemblance or the resemblance of situation to that of qualities. The effects of this propensity have been already observed in that resemblance which we so readily suppose between particular impressions and their external causes. But we shall not find a more evident effect of it than in the present instance, where, from the relations of causation and contiguity in time between two objects, we feign likewise that of a conjunction in place in order to strengthen the connection.

But whatever confused notions we may form of a union in place between an extended body, as a fig, and its particular taste, it is certain that upon reflection we must observe in this union something altogether unintelligible and contradictory. For, should we ask ourselves one obvious question, namely, if the taste which we conceive to be contained in the circumference of the body is in every part of it or in one only, we must quickly find ourselves at a loss and perceive the impossibility of ever giving a satisfactory answer. We cannot reply that it is only in one part, for experience convinces us that every part has the same relish. We can as little reply that it exists in every part, for then we must suppose it figured and extended, which is absurd and incomprehensible. Here, then, we are influenced by two principles directly contrary to each other, namely that *inclination* of our fancy by which we are determined to incorporate the taste with the extended object and our *reason*, which shows us the impossibility of such a union. Being divided between these opposite principles, we renounce neither one nor the other, but involve the subject in such confusion and obscurity that we no longer perceive the opposition. We suppose that the taste exists within the circumference of the body, but in such a manner that it fills the whole without extension and exists entire in every part without separation. In short, we use in our most familiar way of thinking that scholastic principle which, when crudely proposed, appears so shocking, of *totum in toto, et totum in qualibet parte*,[2] which is much the same as if we should say that a thing is in a certain place and yet is not there.

All this absurdity proceeds from our endeavoring to bestow a place on what is utterly incapable of it, and that endeavor again arises from our inclination to complete a union which is founded on causation and a contiguity of time by attributing to the objects a conjunction in place. But if ever reason is of sufficient force to overcome prejudice, it is certain that in the present case it must prevail. For we have only this choice left: to suppose either that some beings exist without any place or that they are figured and extended or that when they are incorporated with extended objects, the whole is in the whole and the whole is in every part. The absurdity of the two last suppositions proves sufficiently the veracity of the first. Nor is there any fourth opinion. For as to the supposition of their existence in the manner of mathematical points, it resolves itself into the second opinion and supposes that several passions may be placed in a circular figure, and that a certain number of smells, conjoined with a certain number of sounds, may make a body of twelve cubic inches, which appears ridiculous upon the bare mentioning of it.

But though in this view of things we cannot refuse to condemn the materialists who conjoin all thought with extension, yet a little reflection will show us equal reason for blaming their antagonists, who conjoin all thought with a simple and indivisible substance. The most vulgar philosophy informs us that no external object can make itself known to the mind immediately and without the interposition of an image or perception. That table which just now appears to me is only a perception, and all its qualities are qualities of a perception. Now, the most obvious of all its qualities is extension. The perception consists of parts. These parts are so situated as to afford us the notion of distance and contiguity, of length, breadth, and thickness. The termination of these three dimensions is what we call figure. This figure is movable, separate, and divisible. Mobility and separability are the distinguishing properties of extended objects. And to cut short all disputes, the very idea of extension is copied from nothing but an impression and consequently must perfectly agree to it. To say the idea of extension agrees to anything is to say it is extended.

---

2. The whole is in the whole and the whole is in every part.

The freethinker may now triumph in his turn and, having found there are impressions and ideas really extended, may ask his antagonists how they can incorporate a simple and indivisible subject with an extended perception? All the arguments of theologians may here be retorted upon them. Is the indivisible subject, or immaterial substance, if you will, on the left or on the right hand of the perception? Is it in this particular part or in that other? Is it in every part without being extended? Or is it entire in any one part without deserting the rest? It is impossible to give any answer to these questions but what both will be absurd in itself and will account for the union of our indivisible perceptions with an extended substance.

This gives me an occasion to take anew into consideration the question concerning the substance of the soul, and though I have condemned that question as utterly unintelligible, yet I cannot forbear proposing some further reflections concerning it. I assert that the doctrine of the immateriality, simplicity, and indivisibility of a thinking substance is a true atheism and will serve to justify all those sentiments for which *Spinoza* is so universally infamous. From this topic I hope at least to reap one advantage—that my adversaries will not have any pretext to render the present doctrine odious by their declamations when they see that they can be so easily retorted on them.

The fundamental principle of the atheism of *Spinoza* is the doctrine of the simplicity of the universe and the unity of that substance in which he supposes both thought and matter to inhere. There is only one substance, he says, in the world, and that substance is perfectly simple and indivisible and exists everywhere without any local presence. Whatever we discover externally by sensation, whatever we feel internally by reflection, all these are nothing but modifications of that one simple and necessarily existent being and are not possessed of any separate or distinct existence. Every passion of the soul, every configuration of matter however different and various, inhere in the same substance and preserve in themselves their characters of distinction without communicating them to that subject in which they inhere. The same *substratum*, if I may so speak, supports the most different modifications without any

difference in itself and varies them without any variation. Neither time nor place nor all the diversity of nature is able to produce any composition or change in its perfect simplicity and identity.

I believe this brief exposition of the principles of that famous atheist will be sufficient for the present purpose and that without entering further into these gloomy and obscure regions I shall be able to show that this hideous hypothesis is almost the same with that of the immateriality of the soul, which has become so popular. To make this evident, let us remember that, as every idea is derived from a preceding perception, it is impossible our idea of a perception and that of an object or external existence can ever represent what are specifically different from each other. Whatever difference we may suppose between them, it is still incomprehensible to us, and we are obliged either to conceive an external object merely as a relation without a relative or to make it the very same with a perception or impression.

The consequence I shall draw from this may, at first sight, appear a mere sophism, but upon the least examination will be found solid and satisfactory. I say then that since we may suppose, but never can conceive, a specific difference between an object and impression, any conclusion we form concerning the connection and repugnance of impressions will not be known certainly to be applicable to objects, but that, on the other hand, whatever conclusions of this kind we form concerning objects will most certainly be applicable to impressions. The reason is not difficult. As an object is supposed to be different from an impression, we cannot be sure that the circumstance upon which we found our reasoning is common to both, supposing we form the reasoning upon the impression. It is still possible that the object may differ from it in that particular. But when we first form our reasoning concerning the object, it is beyond doubt that the same reasoning must extend to the impression and that because the quality of the object upon which the argument is founded must at least be conceived by the mind and could not be conceived unless it were common to an impression, since we have no idea but what is derived from that origin. Thus we may establish it as a certain maxim that we can never by any principle but by an irregular kind of reasoning from experience, discover a connection or repugnance between objects which extends not to impressions, though the inverse proposition may not be equally true—that all the discoverable relations of impressions are common to objects.

To apply this to the present case: There are two different systems of beings presented, to which I suppose myself under a necessity of assigning some substance or ground of inhesion. I observe first the universe of objects or of body: the sun, moon, and stars; the earth, seas, plants, animals, men, ships, houses, and other productions either of art or of nature. Here *Spinoza* appears and tells me that these are only modifications and that the subject in which they inhere is simple, uncompounded, and indivisible. After this I consider the other system of beings, namely, the universe of thought or my impressions and ideas. There I observe another sun, moon, and stars; an earth, and seas, covered and inhabited by plants and animals; towns, houses, mountains, rivers; and, in short, everything I can discover or conceive in the first system. Upon my inquiring concerning these, theologians present themselves and tell me that these also are modifications and modifications of one simple, uncompounded, and indivisible substance. Immediately upon which I am deafened with the noise of a hundred voices that treat the first hypothesis with detestation and scorn and the second with applause and veneration. I turn my attention to these hypotheses to see what may be the reason of so great a partiality and find that they have the same fault of being unintelligible and that, as far as we can understand them, they are so much alike that it is impossible to discover any absurdity in one which is not common to both of them. We have no idea of any quality in an object which does not agree to and may not represent a quality in an impression, and that because all our ideas are derived from our impressions. We can never, therefore, find any repugnance between an extended object as a modification and a simple uncompounded essence as its substance, unless that repugnance takes place equally between the perception or impression of that extended object and the same uncompounded essence. Every idea of

a quality in an object passes through an impression, and therefore every *perceivable* relation, whether of connection or repugnance, must be common to both objects and impressions.

But though this argument, considered in general, seems evident beyond all doubt and contradiction, yet to make it more clear and sensible, let us survey it in detail and see whether all the absurdities which have been found in the system of *Spinoza* may not likewise be discovered in that of theologians.

First, it has been said against *Spinoza*, according to the scholastic way of talking rather than thinking, that a mode, not being any distinct or separate existence, must be the very same with its substance, and consequently the extension of the universe must be in a manner identified with that simple, uncompounded essence in which the universe is supposed to inhere. But this, it may be pretended, is utterly impossible and inconceivable unless the indivisible substance expand itself so as to correspond to the extension or the extension contract itself so as to answer to the indivisible substance. This argument seems just, as far as we can understand it, and it is plain nothing is required but a change in the terms to apply the same argument to our extended perceptions and the simple essence of the soul, the ideas of objects and perceptions being in every respect the same, only attended with the supposition of a difference that is unknown and incomprehensible.

Secondly, it has been said that we have no idea of substance which is not applicable to matter, nor any idea of a distinct substance which is not applicable to every distinct portion of matter. Matter, therefore, is not a mode but a substance, and each part of matter is not a distinct mode, but a distinct substance. I have already proved that we have no perfect idea of substance, but that taking it for *something that can exist by itself*, it is evident every perception is a substance and every distinct part of a perception a distinct substance; and, consequently, the one hypothesis labors under the same difficulties in this respect with the other.

Thirdly, it has been objected to the system of one simple substance in the universe that this substance, being the support or *substratum* of everything, must at the very same instant be modified into forms which are contrary and incompatible. The round and square figures are incompatible in the same substance at the same time. How, then, is it possible that the same substance can at once be modified into that square table and into this round one? I ask the same question concerning the impressions of these tables and find that the answer is no more satisfactory in one case than in the other.

It appears, then, that to whatever side we turn, the same difficulties follow us; and that we cannot advance one step towards establishing the simplicity and immateriality of the soul without preparing the way for a dangerous and irrecoverable atheism. It is the same case if, instead of calling thought a modification of the soul, we should give it the more ancient and yet more fashionable name of an *action*. By an action we mean much the same thing as what is commonly called an abstract mode, that is, something which, properly speaking, is neither distinguishable nor separable from its substance and is only conceived by a distinction of reason or an abstraction. But nothing is gained by this change of the term of modification for that of action nor do we free ourselves from one single difficulty by its means, as will appear from the two following reflections.

First, I observe that the word *action*, according to this explication of it, can never justly be applied to any perception, as derived from a mind or thinking substance. Our perceptions are all really different and separable and distinguishable from each other, and from everything else which we can imagine, and therefore it is impossible to conceive how they can be the action or abstract mode of any substance. The instance of motion, which is commonly made use of to show after what manner perception depends as an action upon its substance, rather confounds than instructs us. Motion, to all appearance, induces no real or essential change on the body, but only varies its relation to other objects. But between a person in the morning walking in a garden with company agreeable to him and a person in the afternoon enclosed in a dungeon and full of terror, despair, and resentment, there seems to be a radical difference and of quite another kind than what is produced on

a body by the change of its situation. As we conclude from the distinction and separability of their ideas that external objects have a separate existence from each other, so, when we make these ideas themselves our objects, we must draw the same conclusion concerning *them* according to the precedent reasoning. At least it must be confessed that having no idea of the substance of the soul it is impossible for us to tell how it can admit of such differences and even contrarieties of perception without any fundamental change and consequently can never tell in what sense perceptions are actions of that substance. The use, therefore, of the word *action*, unaccompanied with any meaning, instead of that of modification, makes no addition to our knowledge nor is of any advantage to the doctrine of the immateriality of the soul.

I add in the second place that if it brings any advantage to that cause, it must bring an equal to the cause of atheism. For do our theologians pretend to make a monopoly of the word *action*, and may not the atheists likewise take possession of it and affirm that plants, animals, men, etc., are nothing but particular actions of one simple universal substance, which exerts itself from a blind and absolute necessity? This, you will say, is utterly absurd. I admit it is unintelligible but at the same time assert according to the principles above explained that it is impossible to discover any absurdity in the supposition that all the various objects in nature are actions of one simple substance, which absurdity will not be applicable to a like supposition concerning impressions and ideas.

From these hypotheses concerning the *substance* and *local conjunction* of our perceptions, we may pass to another which is more intelligible than the former and more important than the latter, namely, concerning the *cause* of our perceptions. Matter and motion, it is commonly said in the schools, however varied, are still matter and motion and produce only a difference in the position and situation of objects. Divide a body as often as you please, it is still body. Place it in any figure; nothing ever results but figure or the relation of parts. Move it in any manner; you still find motion or a change of relation. It is absurd to imagine that motion in a circle, for instance, should be nothing but merely motion in a circle, while motion in another direction, as in an ellipse, should also be a passion or moral reflection—that the shocking of two globular particles should become a sensation of pain and that the meeting of two triangular ones should afford a pleasure. Now as these different shocks and variations and mixtures are the only changes of which matter is susceptible and as these never afford us any idea of thought or perception, it is concluded to be impossible that thought can ever be caused by matter.

Few have been able to withstand the seeming evidence of this argument, and yet nothing in the world is more easy than to refute it. We need only reflect on what has been proved at large, namely, that we are never sensible of any connection between causes and effects and that it is only by our experience of their constant conjunction that we can arrive at any knowledge of this relation. Now, as all objects which are not contrary are susceptible of a constant conjunction, and as no real objects are contrary, I have inferred from these principles that to consider the matter *a priori*, anything may produce anything; and that we shall never discover a reason why any object may or may not be the cause of any other, however great or however little the resemblance may be between them. This evidently destroys the precedent reasoning concerning the cause of thought or perception. For though there appears no manner of connection between motion or thought, the case is the same with all other causes and effects. Place one body of a pound weight on one end of a lever and another body of the same weight on another end. You will never find in these bodies any principle of motion dependent on their distances from the center more than of thought and perception. If you pretend, therefore, to prove *a priori* that such a position of bodies can never cause thought, because, turn it which way you will, it is nothing but a position of bodies, you must, by the same course of reasoning, conclude that it can never produce motion, since there is no more apparent connection in the one case than in the other. But as this latter conclusion is contrary to evident experience and as it is possible we may have a like experience in the operations of the mind and may perceive a constant conjunction of thought and motion, you

reason too hastily when, from the mere consideration of the ideas, you conclude that it is impossible that motion can ever produce thought or that a different position of parts can give rise to a different passion or reflection. No, not only is it possible we may have such an experience, but it is certain we have it, since everyone may perceive that the different dispositions of his body change his thoughts and sentiments. And should it be said that this depends on the union of soul and body, I would answer that we must separate the question concerning the substance of the mind from that concerning the cause of its thought, and that, confining ourselves to the latter question, we find, by comparing their ideas, that thought and motion are different from each other, and, by experience, that they are constantly united. This being all the circumstances that enter into the idea of cause and effect, when applied to the operations of matter we may certainly conclude that motion may be, and actually is, the cause of thought and perception.

There seems only this dilemma left us in the present case: either to assert that nothing can be the cause of another but where the mind can perceive the connection in its idea of the objects, or to maintain that all objects which we find constantly conjoined are upon that account to be regarded as causes and effects. If we choose the first part of the dilemma, these are the consequences. *First*, we in reality affirm that there is no such thing in the universe as a cause or productive principle—not even the Deity himself—since our idea of that Supreme Being is derived from particular impressions, none of which contains any efficacy nor seems to have any connection with any other existence. As to what may be said that the connection between the idea of an infinitely powerful Being and that of any effect which he wills is necessary and unavoidable, I answer that we have no idea of a Being endowed with any power, much less of one endowed with infinite power. But if we will change expressions, we can only define power by connection, and then in saying that the idea of an infinitely powerful Being is connected with that of every effect which he wills, we really do no more than assert that a Being whose volition is connected with every effect is connected with every effect, which is an identical proposition and gives us no insight into the nature of this power or connection. But *secondly*, supposing that the Deity were the great and efficacious principle which supplies the deficiency of all causes, this leads us into the grossest impieties and absurdities. For upon the same account—that we have recourse to him in natural operations and assert that matter cannot of itself communicate motion or produce thought, namely, because there is no apparent connection between these objects—I say, upon the very same account, we must acknowledge that the Deity is the author of all our volitions and perceptions, since they have no more apparent connection either with one another or with the supposed but unknown substance of the soul. This agency of the Supreme Being we know to have been asserted by several philosophers with relation to all the actions of the mind, except volition, or rather an inconsiderable part of volition, though it is easy to perceive that this exception is a mere pretext to avoid the dangerous consequences of that doctrine. If nothing is active but what has an apparent power, thought is in no case any more active than matter, and if this inactivity must make us have recourse to a Deity, the Supreme Being is the real cause of all our actions, bad as well as good, vicious as well as virtuous.

Thus we are necessarily reduced to the other side of the dilemma, namely, that all objects which are found to be constantly conjoined are upon that account only to be regarded as causes and effects. Now, as all objects which are not contrary are susceptible of a constant conjunction and as no real objects are contrary, it follows that, for all we can determine by the mere ideas, anything may be the cause or effect of anything, which evidently gives the advantage to the materialists above their antagonists.

To pronounce, then, the final decision upon the whole: The question concerning the substance of the soul is absolutely unintelligible; all our perceptions are not susceptible of a local union with what is either extended or unextended, there being some of them of the one kind and some of the other; and as the constant conjunction of objects constitutes the very essence of cause and effect, matter and motion may often be regarded as the causes of thought as far as we have any notion of that relation.

It is certainly a kind of indignity to philosophy, whose sovereign authority ought everywhere to be acknowledged, to oblige her on every occasion to make apologies for her conclusions and justify herself to every particular art and science which may be offended at her. This puts one in mind of a king arraigned for high treason against his subjects. There is only one occasion when philosophy will think it necessary and even honorable to justify herself, and that is when religion may seem to be in the least offended, whose rights are as dear to her as her own and are indeed the same. If anyone, therefore, should imagine that the foregoing arguments are in any way dangerous to religion, I hope the following apology will remove his apprehensions.

There is no foundation for any conclusion *a priori*, concerning either the operations or the duration of any object of which it is possible for the human mind to form a conception. Any object may be imagined to become entirely inactive or to be annihilated in a moment, and it is an evident principle that *whatever we can imagine is possible*. Now this is no more true of matter than of spirit—of an extended compounded substance than of a simple and unextended. In both cases the metaphysical arguments for the immortality of the soul are equally inconclusive, and in both cases the moral arguments and those derived from the analogy of nature are equally strong and convincing. If my philosophy therefore makes no addition to the arguments for religion, I have at least the satisfaction to think it takes nothing from them, but that everything remains precisely as before.

## Section 6: Of Personal Identity

There are some philosophers who imagine we are every moment intimately conscious of what we call our *self* that we feel its existence and its continuance in existence, and are certain beyond the evidence of a demonstration of both its perfect identity and its simplicity. The strongest sensation, the most violent passion, they say, instead of distracting us from this view, only fix it the more intensely and make us consider their influence on *self* by either their pain or their pleasure. To attempt a further proof of this would be to weaken its evidence, since no proof can be derived from any fact of which we are so intimately conscious, nor is there anything of which we can be certain if we doubt of this.

Unluckily all these positive assertions are contrary to that very experience which is pleaded for them, nor have we any idea of *self* after the manner it is here explained. For from what impression could this idea be derived? This question it is impossible to answer without a manifest contradiction and absurdity, and yet it is a question which must necessarily be answered if we would have the idea of *self* pass for clear and intelligible. It must be some one impression that gives rise to every real idea. But self or person is not any one impression, but that to which our several impressions and ideas are supposed to have a reference. If any impression gives rise to the idea of self, that impression must continue invariably the same through the whole course of our lives, since self is supposed to exist after that manner. But there is no impression constant and invariable. Pain and pleasure, grief and joy, passions and sensations succeed each other and never all exist at the same time. It cannot, therefore, be from any of these impressions or from any other that the idea of self is derived, and, consequently, there is no such idea.

But further, what must become of all our particular perceptions upon this hypothesis? All these are different and distinguishable and separable from each other and may be separately considered and may exist separately and have no need of anything to support their existence. After what manner therefore do they belong to self and how are they connected with it? For my part, when I enter most intimately into what I call *myself*, I always stumble on some particular perception or other, of heat or cold, light or shade, love or hatred, pain or pleasure. I never can catch *myself* at any time without a perception and never can observe anything but the perception. When my perceptions are removed for any time, as by sound sleep, so long am I insensible of myself and may truly be said not to exist. And were all my perceptions removed by death and could I neither think nor feel nor see nor love nor hate after the dissolution of my body, I should be

entirely annihilated, nor do I conceive what is further requisite to make me a perfect nonentity. If anyone, upon serious and unprejudiced reflection, thinks he has a different notion of *himself*, I must confess I can reason no longer with him. All I can allow him is that he may be in the right as well as I and that we are essentially different in this particular. He may, perhaps, perceive something simple and continued which he calls *himself*, though I am certain there is no such principle in me.

But setting aside some metaphysicians of this kind, I may venture to affirm of the rest of mankind that they are nothing but a bundle or collection of different perceptions which succeed each other with an inconceivable rapidity and are in a perpetual flux and movement. Our eyes cannot turn in their sockets without varying our perceptions. Our thought is still more variable than our sight, and all our other senses and faculties contribute to this change; nor is there any single power of the soul which remains unalterably the same, perhaps, for one moment. The mind is a kind of theater where several perceptions successively make their appearance, pass, repass, glide away, and mingle in an infinite variety of postures and situations. There is properly no *simplicity* in it at one time nor *identity* in different, whatever natural propensity we may have to imagine that simplicity and identity. The comparison of the theater must not mislead us. They are the successive perceptions only that constitute the mind, nor have we the most distant notion of the place where these scenes are represented or of the materials of which it is composed.

What, then, gives us so great a propensity to ascribe an identity to these successive perceptions and to suppose ourselves possessed of an invariable and uninterrupted existence through the whole course of our lives? In order to answer this question we must distinguish between personal identity as it regards our thought or imagination and as it regards our passions or the concern we take in ourselves. The first is our present subject, and to explain it perfectly we must take the matter pretty deep and account for that identity which we attribute to plants and animals, there being a great analogy between it and the identity of a self or person.

We have a distinct idea of an object that remains invariable and uninterrupted through a supposed variation of time, and this idea we call that of *identity* or *sameness*. We have also a distinct idea of several different objects existing in succession and connected together by a close relation, and this, to an accurate view, affords as perfect a notion of *diversity* as if there was no manner of relation among the objects. But though these two ideas of identity and a succession of related objects be in themselves perfectly distinct and even contrary, yet it is certain that, in our common way of thinking, they are generally confounded with each other. That action of the imagination by which we consider the uninterrupted and invariable object and that by which we reflect on the succession of related objects are almost the same to the feeling, nor is there much more effort of thought required in the latter case than in the former. The relation facilitates the transition of the mind from one object to another and renders its passage as smooth as if it contemplated one continued object. This resemblance is the cause of the confusion and mistake and makes us substitute the notion of identity instead of that of related objects. However at one instant we may consider the related succession as variable or interrupted, we are sure the next to ascribe to it a perfect identity and regard it as invariable and uninterrupted. Our propensity to this mistake is so great from the resemblance above mentioned that we fall into it before we are aware, and though we incessantly correct ourselves by reflection and return to a more accurate method of thinking, yet we cannot long sustain our philosophy or take off this bias from the imagination. Our last resource is to yield to it and boldly assert that these different related objects are in effect the same, however interrupted and variable. In order to justify to ourselves this absurdity, we often feign some new and unintelligible principle that connects the objects together and prevents their interruption or variation. Thus we feign the continued existence of the perceptions of our senses to remove the interruption and run into the notion of a *soul*, and *self*, and *substance* to disguise the variation. But, we may further observe that where we do not give rise to such a fiction, our propensity to confound identity with relation is so great that we are apt to imagine something unknown and mysterious connecting the parts, besides their relation, and this I take to be the case with regard to the identity we ascribe to plants and vegetables. And even when this does not take place, we still feel a propensity to confound these ideas, though we are not able fully to satisfy ourselves in that particular nor find anything invariable and uninterrupted to justify our notion of identity.

Thus the controversy concerning identity is not merely a dispute of words. For when we attribute identity, in an improper sense, to variable or interrupted objects, our mistake is not confined to the expression but is commonly attended with a fiction, either of something invariable and uninterrupted or of something mysterious and inexplicable, or at least with a propensity to such fictions. What will suffice to prove this hypothesis to the satisfaction of every fair inquirer is to show from daily experience and observation that the objects, which are variable or interrupted and yet are supposed to continue the same, are such only as consist of a succession of parts connected together by resemblance, contiguity, or causation. For as such a succession answers evidently to our notion of diversity, it can only be by mistake we ascribe to it an identity, and as the relation of parts, which leads us into this mistake, is really nothing but a quality which produces an association of ideas and an easy transition of the imagination from one to another, it can only be from the resemblance which this act of the mind bears to that by which we contemplate one continued object that the error arises. Our chief business, then, must be to prove that all objects to which we ascribe identity without observing their invariableness and uninterruptedness are such as consist of a succession of related objects.

In order to [see] this, suppose any mass of matter of which the parts are contiguous and connected to be placed before us. It is plain we must attribute a perfect identity to this mass, provided all the parts continue uninterruptedly and invariably the same, whatever motion or change of place we may observe either in the whole or in any of the parts. But supposing some very *small* or *inconsiderable* part to be added to the mass or subtracted from it, though this absolutely destroys the identity of the whole, strictly speaking, yet as we seldom think so accurately, we scruple not to pronounce a mass of matter the same where we find so trivial an alteration. The passage of the thought from the object before the change to the object after it is so smooth and easy that we scarcely perceive the transition and are apt to imagine that it is nothing but a continued survey of the same object.

There is a very remarkable circumstance that attends this experiment, which is that though the change of any considerable part in a mass of matter destroys the identity of the whole, yet we must measure the greatness of the part, not absolutely, but by its *proportion* to the whole. The addition or diminution of a mountain would not be sufficient to produce a diversity in a planet, though the change of a very few inches would be able to destroy the identity of some bodies. It will be impossible to account for this but by reflecting that objects operate upon the mind and break or interrupt the continuity of its actions not according to their real greatness but according to their proportion to each other, and therefore, since this interruption makes an object cease to appear the same, it must be the uninterrupted progress of the thought which constitutes the imperfect identity.

This may be confirmed by another phenomenon. A change in any considerable part of a body destroys its identity, but it is remarkable that where the change is produced *gradually* and *insensibly* we are less apt to ascribe to it the same effect. The reason can plainly be no other than that the mind, in following the successive changes of the body, feels an easy passage from surveying its condition in one moment to viewing of it in another and at no particular time perceives any interruption in its actions—from which continued perception it ascribes a continued existence and identity to the object.

But whatever precaution we may use in introducing the changes gradually and making them proportional to the whole, it is certain that where the changes are at last observed to become considerable, we make a scruple of ascribing identity to such different objects. There is, however, another artifice by which we may induce the imagination to advance a step further, and that is by producing a reference of the parts to each other and a combination to some *common end* or purpose. A ship of which a considerable part has been changed by frequent repairs is still considered as the same, nor does the difference of the materials hinder us from ascribing an identity to it. The common end, in which the parts conspire, is the same under all their variations and affords an easy transition of the imagination from one situation of the body to another.

But this is still more remarkable when we add a *sympathy* of parts to their *common end* and suppose that they bear to each other the reciprocal relation of cause and effect in all their actions and operations. This is the case with all animals and vegetables, where the several parts have not only a reference to some general purpose but also a mutual dependence on and connection with each other. The effect of so strong a relation is that though everyone must allow that in a very few years both vegetables and animals endure a *total* change, yet we still attribute identity to them, while their form, size, and substance are entirely altered. An oak that grows from a small plant to a large tree is still the same oak, though there is not one particle of matter or figure of its parts the same. An infant becomes a man and is sometimes fat, sometimes lean without any change in his identity.

We may also consider the two following phenomena, which are remarkable in their kind. The first is that though we are commonly able to distinguish pretty exactly between numerical and specific identity, yet it sometimes happens that we confound them and in our thinking and reasoning employ the one for the other. Thus, a man who hears a noise that is frequently interrupted and renewed says it is still the same noise, though it is evident the sounds have only a specific identity or resemblance and there is nothing numerically the same but the cause which produced them. In like manner it may be said without breach of the propriety of language that such a church, which was formerly of brick, fell to ruin and that the parish rebuilt the same church of freestone and according to modern architecture. Here neither the form nor the materials are the same, nor is there anything common to the two objects but their relation to the inhabitants of the parish. Yet this alone is sufficient to make us denominate them the same. But we must observe that in these cases the first object is in a manner annihilated before the second comes into existence, by which means we are never presented in any one point of time with the idea of difference and multiplicity and, for that reason, are less scrupulous in calling them the same.

Secondly, we may remark that though in a succession of related objects it is in a manner requisite that the change of parts is not sudden nor entire in order to preserve the identity, yet where the objects are in their nature changeable and inconstant, we admit of a more sudden transition than would otherwise be consistent with that relation. Thus, as the nature of a river consists in the motion and change of parts, though in less than twenty-four hours these are totally altered, this does not hinder the river from continuing the same during several ages. What is natural and essential to anything is, in a manner, expected, and what is expected makes less impression and appears of less moment than what is unusual and extraordinary. A considerable change of the former kind seems really less to the imagination than the most trivial alteration of the latter and, by breaking less the continuity of the thought, has less influence in destroying the identity.

We now proceed to explain the nature of *personal identity*, which has become so great a question in philosophy, especially of late years, in *England*, where all the more abstruse sciences are studied with a peculiar ardor and application. And here it is evident the same method of reasoning must be continued which has so successfully explained the identity of plants and animals, and ships, and houses, and of all the compounded and changeable productions of either art or nature. The identity which we ascribe to the mind of man is only a fictitious one and of a like kind with that which we ascribe to vegetables and animal bodies. It cannot, therefore, have a different origin but must proceed from a like operation of the imagination upon like objects.

But lest this argument should not convince the reader, though in my opinion it is perfectly decisive, let him weigh the following reasoning, which is still closer and more immediate. It is evident that the identity which we attribute to the human mind, however perfect we may imagine it to be, is not able to run the several different perceptions into one and make them lose their characters of distinction and difference which are essential to them. It is still true that every distinct perception which enters into the composition of the mind is a distinct existence and is different and distinguishable and separable from every other perception, either contemporary or successive. But as, notwithstanding this distinction and separability, we suppose the whole train of perceptions to be united by identity, a question naturally arises concerning this relation of identity—whether it is something that really binds our several perceptions together or only associates their ideas in the imagination, that is, in other words, whether, in pronouncing concerning the identity of a person, we observe some real bond among his perceptions or only feel one among the ideas we form of them. This question we might easily decide if we would recollect what has been already proved at large, namely, that the understanding never observes any real connection among objects and that even the union of cause and effect, when strictly examined, resolves itself into a customary association of ideas. For from this it evidently follows that identity is nothing really belonging to these different perceptions and uniting them together but rather is merely a quality which we attribute to them because of the union of their ideas in the imagination when we reflect upon them. Now, the only qualities which can give ideas a union in the imagination are these three relations above mentioned. These are the uniting principles in the ideal world, and without them every distinct object is separable by the mind, and may be separately considered, and appears not to have any more connection with any other object than if disjoined by the greatest difference and remoteness. It is, therefore, on some of these three relations of resemblance, contiguity, and causation that identity depends, and as the very essence of these relations consists in their producing an easy transition of ideas, it follows that our notions of personal identity proceed entirely from the smooth and uninterrupted progress of the thought along a train of connected ideas, according to the principles above explained.

The only question, therefore, which remains is by what relations this uninterrupted progress of our thought is produced when we consider the successive existence of a mind or thinking person. And here it is evident we must confine ourselves to resemblance and causation and must drop contiguity, which has little or no influence in the present case.

To begin with *resemblance*: Suppose we could see clearly into the breast of another and observe that succession of perceptions which constitutes his mind or thinking principle, and suppose that he always preserves the memory of a considerable part of past perceptions; it is evident that nothing could more contribute to bestowing a relation on this succession amid all its variations. For what is the memory but a faculty by which we raise up the images of past perceptions? And as an image necessarily resembles its object, must not the frequent placing of these resembling perceptions in the chain of thought convey the imagination more easily from one link to another and make the whole seem like the continuance of one object? In this particular, then, the memory not only discovers the identity but also contributes to its production by producing the relation of resemblance among the perceptions. The case is the same whether we consider ourselves or others.

As to *causation*, we may observe that the true idea of the human mind is to consider it as a system of different perceptions or different existences which are linked together by the relation of cause and effect, and mutually produce, destroy, influence, and modify each other. Our impressions give rise to their correspondent ideas, and these ideas in their turn produce other impressions. One thought chases another and draws after it a third by which it is expelled in its turn. In this respect, I cannot compare the soul more properly to anything than to a republic or commonwealth in which the several members are united by the reciprocal ties of government and subordination and give rise to other persons who propagate the same republic in the incessant changes of its parts. And as the same individual republic may change not only its members but also its laws and constitutions, in like manner the same person may vary his character and disposition as well as his impressions and ideas without losing his identity. Whatever changes he endures, his several parts are still connected by the relation of causation. And in this view our identity with regard to the passions serves to corroborate that with regard to the imagination by making our distant perceptions influence each other and by giving us a present concern for our past or future pains or pleasures.

As memory alone acquaints us with the continuance and extent of this succession of perceptions, it is to be considered upon that account chiefly as the source of personal identity. Had we no memory, we never should have any notion of causation nor consequently of that chain of causes and effects which constitute our self or person. But having once acquired this notion of causation from the memory, we can extend the same chain of causes and consequently the identity of our persons beyond our memory and can comprehend times, circumstances, and actions which we have entirely forgotten but suppose in general to have existed. For how few of our past actions are there of which we have any memory? Who can tell me, for instance, what were his thoughts and actions on the first of January 1715, the eleventh of March 1719, and the third of August 1733? Or will he affirm, because he has entirely forgotten the incidents of these days, that the present self is not the same person with the self of that time, and by that means overturn all the most established notions of personal identity? In this view, therefore, memory does not so much *produce* as *discover* personal identity by showing us the relation of cause and effect among our different perceptions. It will be incumbent on those who affirm that memory produces entirely our personal identity to give a reason why we can thus extend our identity beyond our memory.

The whole of this doctrine leads us to a conclusion which is of great importance in the present affair, namely that all the nice and subtle questions concerning personal identity can never possibly be decided and are to be regarded rather as grammatical than as philosophical difficulties. Identity depends on the relations of ideas, and these relations produce identity by means of that easy transition they occasion. But as the relations and the easiness of the transition may diminish by insensible degrees, we have no just standard by which we can decide any dispute concerning the time when they acquire or lose a title to the name of identity. All the disputes concerning the identity of connected objects are merely verbal, except so far as the relation of parts gives rise to some fiction or imaginary principle of union as we have already observed.

What I have said concerning the first origin and uncertainty of our notion of identity, as applied to the human mind, may be extended with little or no variation to that of *simplicity*. An object whose different coexistent parts are bound together by a close relation operates upon the imagination after much the same manner as one perfectly simple and indivisible and does not require a much greater stretch of thought in order to [form] its conception. From this similarity of operation we attribute a simplicity to it and feign a principle of union as the support of this simplicity and the center of all the different parts and qualities of the object.[3]

---

3. [Hume wrote the following in the Appendix to the *Treatise*:] I had entertained some hopes that however deficient our theory of the intellectual world might be, it would be free from those contradictions and absurdities which seem to attend every explication that human reason can give of the material world. But upon a more strict review of the section concerning *personal identity*, I find myself involved in such a labyrinth that, I must confess, I neither know how to correct my former opinions nor how to render them consistent. If this is not a good *general* reason for skepticism, it is at least a sufficient one (if I were not already abundantly supplied) for me to entertain a diffidence and modesty in all my decisions. I shall propose the arguments on both sides, beginning with those that induced me to deny the strict and proper identity and simplicity of a self or thinking being.

When we talk of *self* or *substance*, we must have an idea annexed to these terms; otherwise they are altogether unintelligible. Every idea is derived from preceding impressions, and we have no impression of self or substance as something simple and individual. We have, therefore, no idea of them in that sense.

Whatever is distinct is distinguishable and whatever is distinguishable is separable by the thought or imagination. All perceptions are distinct. They are, therefore, distinguishable and separable, and may be conceived as separately existent, and may exist separately without any contradiction or absurdity.

When I view this table and that chimney, nothing is present to me but particular perceptions, which are of a like nature with all the other perceptions. This is the doctrine of philosophers. But this table which is present to me and that chimney may and do exist separately. This is the doctrine of the vulgar and implies no contradiction. There is no contradiction, therefore, in extending the same doctrine to all the perceptions.

In general, the following reasoning seems satisfactory. All ideas are borrowed from preceding perceptions. Our ideas of objects, therefore, are derived from that source. Consequently, no proposition can be intelligible or consistent with regard to objects which is not so with regard to perceptions. But it is intelligible and consistent to say that objects exist distinct and independent without any common *simple* substance or subject of inhesion. This proposition, therefore, can never be absurd with regard to perceptions.

When I turn my reflection on *myself*, I never can perceive this *self* without some one or more perceptions, nor can I ever perceive anything but the perceptions. It is the composition of these, therefore, which forms the self.

We can conceive a thinking being to have either many or few perceptions. Suppose the mind to be reduced even below the life of an oyster. Suppose it to have only one perception, as of thirst or hunger. Consider it in that situation. Do you conceive anything but merely that perception? Do you have any notion of *self* or *substance*? If not, the addition of other perceptions can never give you that notion.

The annihilation which some people suppose to follow upon death and which entirely destroys this self is nothing but an extinction of all particular perceptions: love and hatred, pain and pleasure, thought and sensation. These, therefore, must be the same with self, since the one cannot survive the other.

Is *self* the same with *substance*? If it is, how can that question have place, concerning the subsistence of self, under a change of substance? If they are distinct, what is the difference between them? For my part, I have a notion of neither when conceived distinct from particular perceptions.

Philosophers begin to be reconciled to the principle that *we have no idea of external substance distinct from the ideas of particular qualities*. This must pave the way for a like principle with regard to the mind that *we have no notion of it distinct from the particular perceptions*.

So far I seem to be attended with sufficient evidence. But having thus loosened all our particular perceptions, when I proceed to explain the principle of connection which binds them together and makes us attribute to them a real simplicity and identity, I am sensible that my account is very defective and that nothing but the seeming evidence of the precedent reasonings could have induced me to receive it. If perceptions are distinct existences, they form a whole only by being connected together. But no connections among distinct existences are ever discoverable by human understanding. We only *feel* a connection or determination of the thought to pass from one object to another. It follows, therefore, that the thought alone feels personal identity; when reflecting on the train of past perceptions that compose a mind, the ideas of them are felt to be connected together and naturally introduce each other. However extraordinary this conclusion may seem, it need not surprise us. Most philosophers seem inclined to think that personal identity *arises* from consciousness and consciousness is nothing but a reflected thought or perception. The present philosophy, therefore, has so far a promising aspect. But all my hopes vanish when I come to explain the principles that unite our successive perceptions in our thought or consciousness. I cannot discover any theory which gives me satisfaction on this head.

In short, there are two principles which I cannot render consistent, nor is it in my power to renounce either of them, namely, *that all our distinct perceptions are distinct existences* and *that the mind never perceives any real connection among distinct existences*. Did our perceptions either inhere in something simple and individual or did the mind perceive some real connection among them, there would be no difficulty in the case. For my part, I must plead the privilege of a skeptic and confess that this difficulty is too hard for my understanding. I do not pretend, however, to pronounce it absolutely insuperable. Others, perhaps, or myself, upon more mature reflections, may discover some hypothesis that will reconcile those contradictions. [ . . . ]

# David Hume, *An Enquiry Concerning Human Understanding* (1748)[1]

## Author's Advertisement

Most of the principles and reasonings contained in this volume were published in a work in three volumes, called *A Treatise of Human Nature*, a work which the author had projected before he left college and which he wrote and published not long after. But not finding it successful, he was sensible of his error in going to the press too early and he cast the whole anew in the following pieces, where some negligences in his former reasoning and more in the expression are, he hopes, corrected. Yet several writers who have honored the author's philosophy with answers have taken care to direct all their batteries against that juvenile work, which the author never acknowledged, and have affected to triumph in any advantages which, they imagined, they had obtained over it—a practice very contrary to all rules of candor and fair dealing and a strong instance of those polemical artifices which a bigoted zeal thinks itself authorized to employ. Henceforth, the author desires that the following pieces may alone be regarded as containing his philosophical sentiments and principles.

## Section I: *Of the Different Species of Philosophy.*

Moral philosophy, or the science of human nature, may be treated after two different manners, each of which has its peculiar merit and may contribute to the entertainment, instruction, and reformation of mankind. The one considers man chiefly as born for action and as influenced in his measures by taste and sentiment, pursuing one object and avoiding another according to the value which these objects seem to possess and according to the light in which they present themselves. As virtue, of all objects, is allowed to be the most valuable, this species of philosophers paint her in the most amiable colors, borrowing all help from poetry and eloquence and treating their subject in an easy and obvious manner, and such as is best fitted to please the imagination and engage the affections. They select the most striking observations and instances from common life, place opposite characters in a proper contrast, and, alluring us into the paths of virtue by the views of glory and happiness, direct our steps in these paths by the soundest

1. [From *The Philosophical Works of David Hume*, T. H. Green and T. H. Grose, eds. (London: Longman's, Green, and Co., 1898), 4 vols., English, modified, taking into account variations from numerous editions.]

precepts and most illustrious examples. They make us *feel* the difference between vice and virtue; they excite and regulate our sentiments; and so they can but bend our hearts to the love of probity and true honor, they think, that they have fully attained the end of all their labors.

The other species of philosophers consider man in the light of a reasonable rather than an active being and endeavor to form his understanding more than cultivate his manners. They regard human nature as a subject of speculation and, with a narrow scrutiny, examine it in order to find those principles which regulate our understanding, excite our sentiments, and make us approve or blame any particular object, action, or behavior. They think it a reproach to all literature that philosophy should not yet have fixed, beyond controversy, the foundation of morals, reasoning, and criticism, and should forever talk of truth and falsehood, vice and virtue, beauty and deformity, without being able to determine the source of these distinctions. While they attempt this arduous task, they are deterred by no difficulties; but proceeding from particular instances to general principles, they still push on their inquiries to principles more general and rest not satisfied until they arrive at those original principles by which, in every science, all human curiosity must be bounded. Though their speculations seem abstract and even unintelligible to common readers, they aim at the approbation of the learned and the wise and think themselves sufficiently compensated for the labor of their whole lives, if they can discover some hidden truths which may contribute to the instruction of posterity.

It is certain that the easy and obvious philosophy will always, with the generality of mankind, have the preference above the accurate and abstruse, and by many will be recommended not only as more agreeable, but more useful than the other. It enters more into common life, molds the heart and affections, and, by touching those principles which actuate men, reforms their conduct and brings them nearer to that model of perfection which it describes. On the contrary, the abstruse philosophy, being founded on a turn of mind which cannot enter into business and action, vanishes when the philosopher leaves the shade and comes into open day, nor can its principles easily retain any influence over our conduct and behavior. The feelings of our heart, the agitation of our passions, the vehemence of our affections, dissipate all its conclusions and reduce the profound philosopher to a mere plebeian.

This also must be confessed that the most durable as well as most just fame has been acquired by the easy philosophy and that abstract reasoners seem up to now to have enjoyed only a momentary reputation from the caprice or ignorance of their own age, but have not been able to support their renown with more equitable posterity. It is easy for a profound philosopher to commit a mistake in his subtle reasonings; and one mistake is the necessary parent of another, while he pushes on his consequences and is not deterred from embracing any conclusion by its unusual appearance or its contradiction to popular opinion. But a philosopher whose only purpose is to represent the common sense of mankind in more beautiful and more engaging colors, if by accident he falls into error, goes no further, but, renewing his appeal to common sense and the natural sentiments of the mind, returns into the right path and secures himself from any dangerous illusions. The fame of Cicero flourishes at present, but that of Aristotle is utterly decayed. La Bruyère passes the seas and still maintains his reputation. But the glory of Malebranche is confined to his own nation and to his own age. And Addison, perhaps, will be read with pleasure when Locke shall be entirely forgotten.

The mere philosopher is a character which is commonly but little acceptable in the world, as being supposed to contribute nothing to either the advantage or the pleasure of society, while he lives remote from communication with mankind and is wrapped up in principles and notions equally remote from their comprehension. On the other hand, the mere ignorant is still more despised, nor is anything deemed a surer sign of an illiberal genius in an age and nation where the sciences flourish than to be entirely destitute of all relish for those noble entertainments. The most perfect character is supposed to lie between those extremes: retaining an equal ability and taste for books, company, and business; preserving in conversation that discernment and delicacy which arise from polite letters, and in business that probity and accuracy which are the natural result of a just philosophy. In order to diffuse and cultivate so accomplished a character, nothing can be more useful than compositions of the easy style and manner which do not draw too much from life, require no deep application or retreat to be comprehended, and send back the student among mankind full of noble sentiments and wise precepts applicable to every exigency of human life. By means of such compositions virtue becomes amiable, science agreeable, company instructive, and retirement entertaining.

Man is a reasonable being and, as such, receives from science his proper food and nourishment. But so narrow are the bounds of human understanding that little satisfaction can be hoped for in this particular, from either the extent or the security of his acquisitions. Man is a sociable no less than a reasonable being. But neither can he always enjoy company agreeable and amusing nor can he preserve the proper relish for them. Man is also an active being and, from that disposition, as well as from the various necessities of human life, must submit to business and occupation. But the mind requires some relaxation and cannot always support its bent to care and industry. It seems, then, that nature has pointed out a mixed kind of life as most suitable to the human race and secretly admonished them to allow none of these biases to *draw* too much, so as to incapacitate them for other occupations and entertainments. Indulge your passion for science, she says, but let your science be human and such as may have a direct reference to action and society. Abstruse thought and profound researches I prohibit and will severely punish by the pensive melancholy which they introduce, by the endless uncertainty in which they involve you and by the cold reception which your pretended discoveries shall meet with, when communicated. Be a philosopher, but, amid all your philosophy, be still a man.

Were the generality of mankind contented to prefer the easy philosophy to the abstract and profound, without throwing any blame or contempt on the latter, it might not be improper, perhaps, to comply with this general opinion and allow every man to enjoy, without opposition, his own taste and sentiment. But as the matter is often carried further, even to the absolute rejecting of all profound reasonings, or what is commonly called *metaphysics*, we shall now proceed to consider what can reasonably be pleaded in their behalf.

We may begin with observing that one considerable advantage which results from the accurate and abstract philosophy is its subservience to the easy and humane, which, without the former, can never attain a sufficient degree of exactness in its sentiments, precepts, or reasonings. All polite letters are nothing but pictures of human life in various attitudes and situations, and inspire us with different sentiments of praise or blame, admiration or ridicule, according to the qualities of the object which they set before us. An artist must be better qualified to succeed in this undertaking who, besides a delicate taste and a quick apprehension, possesses an accurate knowledge of the internal fabric, the operations of the understanding, the workings of the passions, and the various species of sentiment which discriminate vice and virtue. However painful this inward search or inquiry may appear, it becomes in some measure requisite to those who would describe with success the obvious and outward appearances of life and manners. The anatomist presents to the eye the most hideous and disagreeable objects, but his science is useful to the painter in delineating even a Venus or a Helen. While the latter employs all the richest colors of his art and gives his figures the most graceful and engaging airs, he must still carry his attention to the inward structure of the human body, the position of the muscles, the fabric of the bones, and the use and figure of every part or organ. Accuracy is, in every case, advantageous to beauty, and just reasoning to delicate sentiment. In vain would we exalt the one by depreciating the other.

Besides, we may observe, in every art or profession, even those which most concern life or action, that a spirit of accuracy, however acquired, carries all of them nearer their perfection and renders them more subservient to the interests of society. And though a philosopher may live remote from business, the genius of philosophy, if carefully cultivated by several, must gradually diffuse itself throughout the whole society and bestow a similar correctness on every art and calling. The politician will acquire greater foresight and subtlety in the subdividing and balancing of power, the lawyer more method and finer principles in his reasonings, and the general more regularity in his discipline and more caution in his plans and operations. The stability of modern governments above the ancient and the accuracy of modern philosophy have improved, and probably will still improve, by similar gradations.

Were there no advantage to be reaped from these studies beyond the gratification of an innocent curiosity, yet ought not even this be despised as being one accession to those few safe and harmless pleasures which are bestowed on human race. The sweetest and most inoffensive path of life leads through the avenues of science and learning; and whoever can either remove any obstructions in this way or open up any new prospect ought so far to be esteemed a benefactor to mankind. And though these researches may appear painful and fatiguing, it is with some minds as with some bodies, which, being endowed with vigorous and florid health, require severe exercise, and reap a pleasure from what, to the generality of mankind, may seem burdensome and laborious. Obscurity, indeed, is painful to the mind as well as to the eye, but to bring light from obscurity, by whatever labor, must necessarily be delightful and rejoicing.

But this obscurity in the profound and abstract philosophy is objected to, not only as painful and fatiguing, but as the inevitable source of uncertainty and error. Here indeed lies the most just and most plausible objection against a considerable part of metaphysics that they are not properly a science, but arise either from the fruitless efforts of human vanity, which would penetrate into subjects utterly inaccessible to the understanding, or from the craft of popular superstitions, which, being unable to defend themselves on fair ground, raise these entangling brambles to cover and protect their weakness. Chased from the open country, these robbers fly into the forest and lie in wait to break in upon every unguarded avenue of the mind and overwhelm it with religious fears and prejudices. The stoutest antagonist, if he remits his watch a moment, is oppressed. And many, through

cowardice and folly, open the gates to the enemies and willingly receive them with reverence and submission as their legal sovereigns.

But is this a sufficient reason why philosophers should desist from such researches and leave superstition still in possession of her retreat? Is it not proper to draw an opposite conclusion and perceive the necessity of carrying the war into the most secret recesses of the enemy? In vain do we hope that men, from frequent disappointment, will at last abandon such airy sciences and discover the proper province of human reason. For, besides the fact that many persons find too sensible an interest in perpetually recalling such topics—besides this, I say, the motive of blind despair can never reasonably have place in the sciences, since, however unsuccessful former attempts may have proved, there is still room to hope that the industry, good fortune, or improved sagacity of succeeding generations may reach discoveries unknown to former ages. Each adventurous genius will still leap at the arduous prize and find himself stimulated, rather than discouraged by the failures of his predecessors, while he hopes that the glory of achieving so hard an adventure is reserved for him alone. The only method of freeing learning at once from these abstruse questions is to inquire seriously into the nature of human understanding and show, from an exact analysis of its powers and capacity, that it is by no means fitted for such remote and abstruse subjects. We must submit to this fatigue in order to live at ease ever after and must cultivate true metaphysics with some care in order to destroy the false and adulterate. Indolence, which to some persons affords a safeguard against this deceitful philosophy, is, with others, overbalanced by curiosity; and despair, which at some moments prevails, may give place afterwards to sanguine hopes and expectations. Accurate and just reasoning is the only catholic remedy fitted for all persons and all dispositions and is alone able to subvert that abstruse philosophy and metaphysical jargon which, being mixed up with popular superstition, renders it in a manner impenetrable to careless reasoners and gives it the air of science and wisdom.

Besides this advantage of rejecting, after deliberate inquiry, the most uncertain and disagreeable part of learning, there are many positive advantages which result from an accurate scrutiny into the powers and faculties of human nature. It is remarkable concerning the operations of the mind that, though most intimately present to us, yet, whenever they become the object of reflection, they seem involved in obscurity, nor can the eye readily find those lines and boundaries which discriminate and distinguish them. The objects are too fine to remain long in the same aspect or situation and must be apprehended in an instant by a superior penetration derived from nature and improved by habit and reflection. It becomes, therefore, no inconsiderable part of science barely to know the different operations of the mind, to separate them from each other, to class them under their proper heads, and to correct all that seeming disorder in which they lie involved when made the object of reflection and inquiry. This task of ordering and distinguishing, which has no merit when performed with regard to external bodies, the objects of our senses, rises in its value when directed towards the operations of the mind in proportion to the difficulty and labor which we meet with in performing it. And if we can go no further than this mental geography or delineation of the distinct parts and powers of the mind, it is at least a satisfaction to go so far; and the more obvious this science may appear (and it is by no means obvious), the more contemptible still must the

ignorance of it be esteemed in all pretenders to learning and philosophy.

Nor can there remain any suspicion that this science is uncertain and chimerical, unless we should entertain such a skepticism as is entirely subversive of all speculation and even action. It cannot be doubted that the mind is endowed with several powers and faculties, that these powers are distinct from each other, that what is really distinct to immediate perception may be distinguished by reflection, and consequently that there is a truth and falsehood in all propositions on this subject, and a truth and falsehood which does not lie beyond the compass of human understanding. There are many obvious distinctions of this kind, such as those between the will and understanding, the imagination and passions, which fall within the comprehension of every human creature; and the finer and more philosophical distinctions are no less real and certain, though more difficult to be comprehended. Some instances, especially late ones, of success in these inquiries may give us a more just notion of the certainty and solidity of this branch of learning. And shall we esteem it worthy the labor of a philosopher to give us a true system of the planets and adjust the position and order of those remote bodies, while we affect to overlook those who, with so much success, delineate the parts of the mind in which we are so intimately concerned?[2]

---

2. That faculty by which we discern truth and falsehood and that by which we perceive vice and virtue had long been confounded with each other, and all morality was supposed to be built on eternal and immutable relations which, to every intelligent mind, were equally invariable as any proposition concerning quantity or number. But a late philosopher has taught us by the most convincing arguments that morality is nothing in the abstract nature of things, but is entirely relative to the sentiment or mental taste of each particular being in the same manner as the distinctions of sweet and bitter, hot and cold, arise from the particular feeling of each sense or organ. Moral perceptions, therefore, ought not be classed with the operations of the understanding, but with the tastes or sentiments.

It had been usual with philosophers to divide all the passions of the mind into two classes, the selfish and benevolent, which were supposed to stand in constant opposition and contrariety; nor was it thought that the latter could ever attain their proper object but at the expense of the former. Among the selfish passions were ranked avarice, ambition, revenge: Among

the benevolent, natural affection, friendship, public spirit. Philosophers may now perceive the impropriety of this division. It has been proved, beyond all controversy, that even the passions commonly esteemed selfish carry the mind beyond self, directly to the object; that though the satisfaction of these passions gives us enjoyment, yet the prospect of this enjoyment is not the cause of the passion, but, on the contrary, the passion is antecedent to the enjoyment, and without the former, the latter could never possibly exist; that the case is precisely the same with the passions denominated benevolent, and consequently that a man is no more interested when he seeks his own glory than when the happiness of his friend is the object of his wishes; nor is he any more disinterested when he sacrifices his ease and quiet to public good than when he labors for the gratification of avarice or ambition. Here, therefore, is a considerable adjustment in the boundaries of the passions, which had been confounded by the negligence or inaccuracy of former philosophers. These two instances may suffice to show us the nature and importance of this species of philosophy.

But may we not hope that philosophy, if cultivated with care and encouraged by the attention of
the public, may carry its researches still further and
discover, at least in some degree, the secret springs
and principles by which the human mind is actuated
in its operations? Astronomers had long contented
themselves with proving, from the phenomena, the
true motions, order, and magnitude of the heavenly
bodies, until a philosopher at last arose who seems,
from the happiest reasoning, to have also determined
the laws and forces by which the revolutions of the
planets are governed and directed. The like has been
performed with regard to other parts of nature. And
there is no reason to despair of equal success in our
inquiries concerning the mental powers and economy, if prosecuted with equal capacity and caution. It
is probable that one operation and principle of the
mind depends on another, which again may be resolved into one more general and universal. And how
far these researches may possibly be carried, it will
be difficult for us, before or even after a careful trial,
exactly to determine. This much is certain—that attempts of this kind are made every day even by those
who philosophize the most negligently. And nothing
can be more requisite than to enter upon the enterprise with thorough care and attention that, if it lies
within the compass of human understanding, it may
at last be happily achieved; if not, it may, however,
be rejected with some confidence and security. This
last conclusion, surely, is not desirable nor ought it be
embraced too rashly. For how much must we diminish from the beauty and value of this species of philosophy upon such a supposition? Moralists have been
accustomed up to now, when they considered the vast
multitude and diversity of those actions that excite our
approbation or dislike, to search for some common
principle on which this variety of sentiments might
depend. And though they have sometimes carried the
matter too far, by their passion for some one general
principle, it must, however, be confessed that they
are excusable in expecting to find some general principles into which all the vices and virtues were justly
to be resolved. The like has been the endeavor of
critics, logicians, and even politicians; nor have their
attempts been wholly unsuccessful, though perhaps

longer time, greater accuracy, and more ardent application may bring these sciences still nearer their
perfection. To throw up at once all pretensions of this
kind may justly be deemed more rash, precipitate,
and dogmatic than even the boldest and most affirmative philosophy that has ever attempted to impose
its crude dictates and principles on mankind.

What? Though these reasonings concerning human nature seem abstract and of difficult comprehension, this affords no presumption of their falsehood. On the contrary, it seems impossible that what
has escaped so many wise and profound philosophers
up to now can be very obvious and easy. And whatever pains these researches may cost us, we may think
ourselves sufficiently rewarded, not only in point of
profit but of pleasure, if, by that means, we can make
any addition to our stock of knowledge in subjects of
such unspeakable importance.

But as, after all, the abstractedness of these speculations is no recommendation, but rather a disadvantage to them, and as this difficulty may perhaps be
surmounted by care and art and the avoiding of all
unnecessary detail, we have, in the following inquiry,
attempted to throw some light upon subjects from
which uncertainty has deterred the wise up to now,
and obscurity the ignorant. Happy if we can unite
the boundaries of the different species of philosophy
by reconciling profound inquiry with clearness and
truth with novelty! And still more happy if, reasoning
in this easy manner, we can undermine the foundations of an abstruse philosophy which seems to have
up to now served only as a shelter to superstition and
a cover to absurdity and error!

## Section II: *Of the Origin of Ideas*

Everyone will readily allow that there is a considerable difference between the perceptions of the
mind when a man feels the pain of excessive heat
or the pleasure of moderate warmth and when he
afterwards recalls to his memory this sensation or
anticipates it by his imagination. These faculties
may mimic or copy the perceptions of the senses,
but they never can entirely reach the force and vivacity of the original sentiment. The utmost we say of
them, even when they operate with greatest vigor, is

that they represent their object in so lively a manner that we could *almost* say we feel or see it: But, unless the mind is disordered by disease or madness, they never can arrive at such a pitch of vivacity as to render these perceptions altogether indistinguishable. All the colors of poetry, however splendid, can never paint natural objects in such a manner as to make the description be taken for a real landscape. The most lively thought is still inferior to the dullest sensation.

We may observe a like distinction to run through all the other perceptions of the mind. A man in a fit of anger is actuated in a very different manner from one who only thinks of that emotion. If you tell me that any person is in love, I easily understand your meaning and form a just conception of his situation, but never can mistake that conception for the real disorders and agitations of the passion. When we reflect on our past sentiments and affections, our thought is a faithful mirror and copies its objects truly, but the colors which it employs are faint and dull in comparison of those in which our original perceptions were clothed. It requires no nice discernment or metaphysical head to mark the distinction between them.

Here, therefore, we may divide all the perceptions of the mind into two classes or species which are distinguished by their different degrees of force and vivacity. The less forcible and lively are commonly denominated thoughts or ideas. The other species want a name in our language and in most others, I suppose, because it was not requisite for any but philosophical purposes to rank them under a general term or appellation. Let us, therefore, use a little freedom and call them impressions, employing that word in a sense somewhat different from the usual. By the term *impression*, then, I mean all our more lively perceptions, when we hear, or see, or feel, or love, or hate, or desire, or will. And impressions are distinguished from ideas, which are the less lively perceptions of which we are conscious when we reflect on any of those sensations or movements above mentioned.

Nothing, at first view, may seem more unbounded than the thought of man, which not only escapes all human power and authority, but is not even restrained within the limits of nature and reality. To form monsters and join incongruous shapes and appearances costs the imagination no more trouble than to conceive the most natural and familiar objects. And while the body is confined to one planet, along which it creeps with pain and difficulty, the thought can in an instant transport us into the most distant regions of the universe or even beyond the universe into the unbounded chaos where nature is supposed to lie in total confusion. What never was seen or heard of, may yet be conceived, nor is anything beyond the power of thought except what implies an absolute contradiction.

But though our thought seems to possess this unbounded liberty, we shall find upon a nearer examination that it is really confined within very narrow limits and that all this creative power of the mind amounts to no more than the faculty of compounding, transposing, augmenting, or diminishing the materials afforded us by the senses and experience. When we think of a golden mountain, we only join two consistent ideas, *gold* and *mountain*, with which we were formerly acquainted. A virtuous horse we can conceive, because, from our own feeling, we can conceive virtue; and this we may unite to the figure and shape of a horse, which is an animal familiar to us. In short, all the materials of thinking are derived from either our outward or our inward sentiment. The mixture and composition of these belongs alone to the mind and will. Or, to express myself in philosophical language, all our ideas or more feeble perceptions are copies of our impressions or more lively ones.

To prove this, the two following arguments will, I hope, be sufficient. *First*, when we analyze our thoughts or ideas, however compounded or sublime, we always find that they resolve themselves into such simple ideas as were copied from a precedent feeling or sentiment. Even those ideas which at first view seem the most wide of this origin are found, upon a nearer scrutiny, to be derived from it. The idea of God, as meaning an infinitely intelligent, wise, and good being, arises from reflecting on the operations of our own mind and augmenting, without limit, those qualities of goodness and wisdom. We may prosecute this inquiry to what length we please; where we shall always find that every idea which we examine is copied from a similar impression. Those who would assert that this position is not universally true, nor without exception, have only one method, and an easy one at that, of refuting it by producing that idea which, in their opinion, is not derived from this source. It will then be incumbent on us, if we would maintain our doctrine, to produce the impression or lively perception which corresponds to it.

*Secondly*, if it happens, from a defect of the organ, that a man is not susceptible of any species of sensation, we always find that he is as little susceptible of the correspondent ideas. A blind man can form no notion of colors, a deaf man of sounds. Restore either of them that sense in which he is deficient by opening this new inlet for his sensations, you also open an inlet for the ideas and he finds no difficulty in conceiving these objects. The case is the same if the object proper for exciting any sensation has never been applied to the organ. A Laplander or Negro has no notion of the relish of wine. And though there are few or no instances of a like deficiency in the mind where a person has never felt or is wholly incapable of a sentiment or passion that belongs to his species, yet we find the same observation to take place in a less degree. A man of mild manners can form no idea of inveterate revenge or cruelty, nor can a selfish heart easily conceive the heights of friendship and generosity. It is readily allowed that other beings may possess many senses of which we can have no conception, because the ideas of them have never been introduced to us in the only manner by which an idea can have access to the mind, namely, by the actual feeling and sensation.

There is, however, one contradictory phenomenon which may prove that it is not absolutely impossible for ideas to arise independent of their correspondent impressions. I believe it will readily be allowed that the several distinct ideas of color which enter by the eye or those of sound which are conveyed by the ear are really different from each other, though at the same time resembling. Now if this is true of different colors, it must be no less so of the different shades of the same color; and each shade produces a distinct idea, independent of the rest. For if this should be denied, it is possible, by the continual gradation of

shades, to run a color insensibly into what is most remote from it; and if you will not allow any of the means to be different, you cannot without absurdity deny the extremes to be the same. Suppose, therefore, a person to have enjoyed his sight for thirty years and to have become perfectly acquainted with colors of all kinds, except one particular shade of blue, for instance, which it never has been his fortune to meet with. Let all the different shades of that color, except that single one, be placed before him, descending gradually from the deepest to the lightest, it is plain that he will perceive a blank where that shade is wanting, and will be sensible that there is a greater distance in that place between the contiguous colors than in any other. Now I ask whether it is possible for him, from his own imagination, to supply this deficiency and raise up to himself the idea of that particular shade, though it had never been conveyed to him by his senses? I believe there are few but will be of the opinion that he can. And this may serve as a proof that the simple ideas are not always, in every instance, derived from the correspondent impressions, though this instance is so singular that it is scarcely worth our observing and does not merit that for it alone we should alter our general maxim.

Here, therefore, is a proposition which not only seems in itself simple and intelligible, but, if a proper use were made of it, might render every dispute equally intelligible and banish all that jargon, which has so long taken possession of metaphysical reasonings and drawn disgrace upon them. All ideas, especially abstract ones, are naturally faint and obscure. The mind has but a slender hold of them. They are apt to be confounded with other resembling ideas; and when we have often employed any term, though without a distinct meaning, we are apt to imagine that it has a determinate idea annexed to it. On the contrary, all impressions, that is, all sensations either outward or inward, are strong and vivid. The limits between them are more exactly determined; nor is it easy to fall into any error or mistake with regard to them. When we entertain, therefore, any suspicion that a philosophical term is employed without any meaning or idea (as is but too frequent), we need but inquire, *From what impression is that supposed idea derived?* And if it is impossible to assign any, this will serve to confirm our suspicion. By bringing ideas into so clear a light, we may reasonably hope to remove all dispute which may arise concerning their nature and reality.[3]

## Section III: *Of the Association of Ideas*

It is evident that there is a principle of connection between the different thoughts or ideas of the mind and that, in their appearance to the memory or imagination, they introduce each other with a certain degree of method and regularity. In our more serious thinking or discourse this is so observable that any particular thought which breaks in upon the regular tract or chain of ideas is immediately remarked and rejected. And even in our wildest and most wandering reveries, no, in our very dreams,

we shall find, if we reflect, that the imagination did not run altogether at adventures, but that there was still a connection upheld among the different ideas which succeeded each other. Were the loosest and freest conversation to be transcribed, there would immediately be observed something which connected it in all its transitions. Or where this is wanting, the person who broke the thread of discourse might still inform you that there had secretly revolved in his mind a succession of thought which had gradually led him from the subject of conversation. Among different languages, even where we cannot suspect the least connection or communication, it is found that the words expressive of ideas the most compounded do yet nearly correspond to each other—certain proof that the simple ideas comprehended in the compound ones were bound together by some universal principle which had an equal influence on all mankind.

Though it is too obvious to escape observation that different ideas are connected together, I do not find that any philosopher has attempted to enumerate or class all the principles of association—a subject, however, that seems worthy of curiosity. To me there appear to be only three principles of connection among ideas, namely, *resemblance, contiguity* in time or place, and *cause* or *effect.*

That these principles serve to connect ideas will not, I believe, be much doubted. A picture naturally leads our thoughts to the original.[4] The mention of one apartment in a building naturally introduces an inquiry or discourse concerning the others;[5] and if we think of a wound, we can scarcely forbear reflecting on the pain which follows it.[6] But that this enumeration is complete, and that there are no other principles of association except these, may be difficult to prove to the satisfaction of the reader or even to a man's own satisfaction. All we can do, in such cases, is to run over several instances and examine carefully the principle which binds the different thoughts to each other, never stopping

---

3. It is probable that no more was meant by those who denied innate ideas than that all ideas were copies of our impressions; though it must be confessed that the terms which they employed were not chosen with such caution, nor so exactly defined, as to prevent all mistakes about their doctrine. For what is meant by *innate?* If innate is equivalent to natural, then all the perceptions and ideas of the mind must be allowed to be innate or natural, in whatever sense we take the latter word, whether in opposition to what is uncommon, artificial, or miraculous. If by innate is meant contemporary to our birth, the dispute seems to be frivolous; nor is it worthwhile to inquire at what time thinking begins, whether before, at, or after our birth. Again, the word *idea* seems to be commonly taken in a very loose sense by Locke and others, as standing for any of our perceptions, our sensations and passions, as well as thoughts. Now in this sense, I should desire to know, what can be meant by asserting that self-love, or resentment of injuries, or the passion between the sexes is not innate?

But admitting these terms, *impressions* and *ideas,* in the sense above explained, and understanding by *innate* what is original or copied from no precedent perception, then may we assert that all our impressions are innate and our ideas not innate.

To be ingenuous, I must admit it to be my opinion that Mr. Locke was betrayed into this question by the schoolmen who, making use of undefined terms, draw out their disputes to a tedious length without ever touching the point in question. A like ambiguity and circumlocution seem to run through all that great philosopher's reasonings on this as well as most other subjects.

---

4. Resemblance.
5. Contiguity.
6. Cause and effect.

until we render the principle as general as possible.[7] The more instances we examine and the more care we employ, the more assurance shall we acquire that the enumeration, which we form from the whole, is complete and entire.

## Section IV: *Skeptical Doubts Concerning the Operations of the Understanding*

### Part I

All the objects of human reason or inquiry may naturally be divided into two kinds, namely, *relations of ideas* and *matters of fact*. Of the first kind are the sciences of geometry, algebra, and arithmetic, and, in short, every affirmation which is either intuitively or demonstratively certain. *That the square of the hypotenuse is equal to the squares of the two sides* is a proposition which expresses a relation between these figures. *That three times five is equal to the half of thirty* expresses a relation between these numbers. Propositions of this kind are discoverable by the mere operation of thought, without dependence on what is anywhere existent in the universe. Though there never were a circle or triangle in nature, the truths demonstrated by Euclid would forever retain their certainty and evidence.

Matters of fact, which are the second objects of human reason, are not ascertained in the same manner; nor is our evidence of their truth, however great, of a like nature with the foregoing. The contrary of every matter of fact is still possible, because it can never imply a contradiction and is conceived by the mind with the same facility and distinctness, as if ever so conformable to reality. *That the sun will not rise tomorrow* is no less intelligible a proposition and implies no more contradiction than the affirmation that *it will rise*. We should in vain, therefore, attempt to demonstrate its falsehood. Were it demonstratively

false, it would imply a contradiction and could never be distinctly conceived by the mind.

It may, therefore, be a subject worthy of curiosity to inquire what is the nature of that evidence which assures us of any real existence and matter of fact beyond the present testimony of our senses or the records of our memory. This part of philosophy, it is observable, has been little cultivated by either the ancients or the moderns, and, therefore, our doubts and errors in the prosecution of so important an inquiry may be the more excusable, while we march through such difficult paths without any guide or direction. They may even prove useful by exciting curiosity and destroying that implicit faith and security which is the bane of all reasoning and free inquiry. The discovery of defects in the common philosophy, if there are any, will not, I presume, be a discouragement, but rather an incitement, as is usual, to attempt something more full and satisfactory than has yet been proposed to the public.

All reasonings concerning matter of fact seem to be founded on the relation of *cause and effect*. By means of that relation alone we can go beyond the evidence of our memory and senses. If you were to ask a man why he believes any matter of fact which is absent—for instance, that his friend is in the country or in France—he would give you a reason, and this reason would be some other fact: as a letter received from him or the knowledge of his former resolutions and promises. A man finding a watch or any other machine on a desert island would conclude that there had once been men on that island. All our reasonings concerning fact are of the same nature. And here it is constantly supposed that there is a connection between the present fact and that which is inferred from it. Were there nothing to bind them together, the inference would be entirely precarious. The hearing of an articulate voice and rational discourse in the dark assures us of the presence of some person. Why? Because these are the effects of the human make and fabric, and closely connected with it. If we anatomize all the other reasonings of this nature, we shall find that they are founded on the relation of cause and effect and that this relation is either near or remote, direct or collateral. Heat and

---

7. For instance, contrast or contrariety is also a connection among ideas, but it may perhaps be considered as a mixture of *causation* and *resemblance*. Where two objects are contrary, the one destroys the other—that is, the cause of its annihilation and the idea of the annihilation of an object implies the idea of its former existence.

light are collateral effects of fire and the one effect may justly be inferred from the other.

If we would satisfy ourselves, therefore, concerning the nature of that evidence which assures us of matters of fact, we must inquire how we arrive at the knowledge of cause and effect.

I shall venture to affirm, as a general proposition which admits of no exception, that the knowledge of this relation is not, in any instance, attained by reasonings *a priori*, but arises entirely from experience when we find that any particular objects are constantly conjoined with each other. Let an object be presented to a man of ever so strong natural reason and abilities; if that object is entirely new to him, he will not be able, by the most accurate examination of its sensible qualities, to discover any of its causes or effects. Adam, though his rational faculties are supposed entirely perfect at the very first, could not have inferred from the fluidity and transparency of water that it would suffocate him, or from the light and warmth of fire that it would consume him. No object ever discovers, by the qualities which appear to the senses, either the causes which produced it or the effects which will arise from it; nor can our reason, unassisted by experience, ever draw any inference concerning real existence and matter of fact.

This proposition, *that causes and effects are discoverable, not by reason but by experience*, will readily be admitted with regard to such objects as we remember to have once been altogether unknown to us, since we must be conscious of the utter inability which we then lay under of foretelling what would arise from them. Present two smooth pieces of marble to a man who has no tincture of natural philosophy; he will never discover that they will adhere together in such a manner as to require great force to separate them in a direct line, while they make so small a resistance to a lateral pressure. Such events as bear little analogy to the common course of nature are also readily confessed to be known only by experience, nor does any man imagine that the explosion of gunpowder or the attraction of a lodestone could ever be discovered by *a priori* arguments. In like manner, when an effect is supposed to depend upon an intricate machinery or

secret structure of parts, we make no difficulty in attributing all our knowledge of it to experience. Who will assert that he can give the ultimate reason why milk or bread is proper nourishment for a man, not for a lion or a tiger?

But the same truth may not appear at first sight to have the same evidence with regard to events which have become familiar to us from our first appearance in the world, which bear a close analogy to the whole course of nature, and which are supposed to depend on the simple qualities of objects without any secret structure of parts. We are apt to imagine that we could discover these effects by the mere operation of our reason without experience. We fancy that were we brought, all of the sudden, into this world, we could at first have inferred that one billiard ball would communicate motion to another upon impulse and that we did not need to have waited for the event in order to pronounce with certainty concerning it. Such is the influence of custom that where it is strongest it not only covers our natural ignorance, but even conceals itself and seems not to take place, merely because it is found in the highest degree.

But to convince us that all the laws of nature and all the operations of bodies without exception are known only by experience, the following reflections may perhaps suffice. Were any object presented to us and were we required to pronounce concerning the effect which will result from it without consulting past observation, after what manner, I beseech you, must the mind proceed in this operation? It must invent or imagine some event which it ascribes to the object as its effect and it is plain that this invention must be entirely arbitrary. The mind can never possibly find the effect in the supposed cause by the most accurate scrutiny and examination. For the effect is totally different from the cause and consequently can never be discovered in it. Motion in the second billiard ball is a quite distinct event from motion in the first, nor is there anything in the one to suggest the smallest hint of the other. A stone or piece of metal raised into the air and left without any support immediately falls. But to consider the matter *a priori*, is there anything we discover in this situation which can beget the idea of a downward rather than an upward or any other motion in the stone or metal?

And as the first imagination or invention of a particular effect in all natural operations is arbitrary where we do not consult experience, so must we also esteem the supposed tie or connection between the cause and effect which binds them together and renders it impossible that any other effect could result from the operation of that cause. When I see, for instance, a billiard ball moving in a straight line towards another, even suppose motion in the second ball should by accident be suggested to me as the result of their contact or impulse, may I not conceive that a hundred different events might as well follow from that cause? May not both these balls remain at absolute rest? May not the first ball return in a straight line or leap off from the second in any line or direction? All these suppositions are consistent and conceivable. Why then should we give the preference to one which is no more consistent or conceivable than the rest? All our reasonings *a priori* will never be able to show us any foundation for this preference.

In a word, then, every effect is a distinct event from its cause. It could not, therefore, be discovered in the cause and the first invention or conception of it, *a priori*, must be entirely arbitrary. And even after it is suggested, the conjunction of it with the cause must appear equally arbitrary, since there are always many other effects which, to reason, must seem fully as consistent and natural. In vain, therefore, should we pretend to determine any single event or infer any cause or effect without the assistance of observation and experience.

Hence we may discover the reason why no philosopher who is rational and modest has ever pretended to assign the ultimate cause of any natural operation or to show distinctly the action of that power which produces any single effect in the universe. It is confessed that the utmost effort of human reason is to reduce the principles productive of natural phenomena to a greater simplicity and to resolve the many particular effects into a few general causes by means of reasonings from analogy, experience, and observation. But as to the causes of these general causes, we should in vain attempt their discovery, nor shall we ever be able to satisfy ourselves by any particular explication of them. These ultimate springs and principles are totally shut up from human curiosity and inquiry. Elasticity, gravity, cohesion of parts, communication of motion by impulse—these are probably the ultimate causes and principles which we shall ever discover in nature; and we may esteem ourselves sufficiently happy if, by accurate inquiry and reasoning, we can trace up the particular phenomena to, or near to, these general principles. The most perfect philosophy of the natural kind only staves off our ignorance a little longer, as perhaps the most perfect philosophy of the moral or metaphysical kind serves only to discover larger portions of it. Thus the observation of human blindness and weakness is the result of all philosophy and meets us at every turn in spite of our endeavors to elude or avoid it.

Nor is geometry, when taken into the assistance of natural philosophy, ever able to remedy this defect or lead us into the knowledge of ultimate causes by all that accuracy of reasoning for which it is so justly celebrated. Every part of mixed mathematics proceeds upon the supposition that certain laws are established by nature in her operations and abstract reasonings are employed either to assist experience in the discovery of these laws or to determine their influence in particular instances where it depends upon any precise degree of distance and quantity. Thus, it is a law of motion, discovered by experience, that the moment or force of any body in motion is in the compound ratio or proportion of its solid contents and its velocity, and consequently that a small force may remove the greatest obstacle or raise the greatest weight if, by any contrivance or machinery, we can increase the velocity of that force so as to make it an overmatch for its antagonist. Geometry assists us in the application of this law by giving us the just dimensions of all the parts and figures which can enter into any species of machine, but still the discovery of the law itself is owing merely to experience and all the abstract reasonings in the world could never lead us one step towards the knowledge of it. When we reason *a priori* and consider merely any object or cause as it appears to the mind, independent of all observation, it never could suggest to us the notion of any distinct object, such as its effect, much less show us the inseparable and inviolable connection between them. A man must be very sagacious who could discover by reasoning that crystal is the effect of heat, and ice of cold, without being previously acquainted with the operation of these qualities.

## Part II

But we have not yet attained any tolerable satisfaction with regard to the question first proposed. Each solution still gives rise to a new question as difficult as the foregoing and leads us on to further inquiries. When it is asked, *What is the nature of all our reasonings concerning matter of fact?*, the proper answer seems to be that they are founded on the relation of cause and effect. When again it is asked, *What is the foundation of all our reasonings and conclusions concerning that relation?*, it may be replied in one word, *experience*. But if we still carry on our sifting humor and ask, *What is the foundation of all conclusions from experience?*, this implies a new question which may be of more difficult solution and explication. Philosophers who give themselves airs of superior wisdom and sufficiency have a hard task when they encounter persons of inquisitive dispositions, who push them from every corner to which they retreat, and who are sure at last to bring them to some dangerous dilemma. The best expedient to prevent this confusion is to be modest in our pretensions and even to discover the difficulty ourselves before it is objected to us. By this means we may make a kind of merit of our very ignorance.

I shall content myself in this section with an easy task and shall pretend only to give a negative answer to the question here proposed. I say, then, that even after we have experience of the operations of cause and effect, our conclusions from that experience are not founded on reasoning or any process of the understanding. This answer we must endeavor both to explain and to defend.

It must certainly be allowed that nature has kept us at a great distance from all her secrets and has afforded us only the knowledge of a few superficial qualities of objects, while she conceals from us those powers and principles on which the influence of these objects entirely depends. Our senses inform us of the color, weight, and consistency of bread, but neither sense nor reason can ever inform us of those qualities which fit it for the nourishment and support of a human body. Sight or feeling conveys an idea of the actual motion of bodies, but as to that wonderful force or power which would carry on a moving body forever in a continued change of place and which bodies never lose but by communicating it to others, of this we cannot form the most distant conception. But notwithstanding this ignorance of natural powers[8] and principles, we always presume when we see like sensible qualities that they have like secret powers and expect that effects similar to those which we have experienced will follow from them. If a body of like color and consistency with that bread which we have formerly eaten is presented to us, we make no scruple of repeating the experiment and foresee with certainty like nourishment and support. Now this is a process of the mind or thought of which I would willingly know the foundation. It is allowed on all hands that there is no known connection between the sensible qualities and the secret powers, and consequently that the mind is not led to form such a conclusion concerning their constant and regular conjunction by anything which it knows of their nature. As to past *experience*, it can be allowed to give *direct* and *certain* information of those precise objects only and that precise period of time which fell under its cognizance. But why this experience should be extended to future times and to other objects which, for all we know, may be only similar in appearance; this is the main question on which I would insist. The bread which I formerly ate nourished me—that is, a body of such sensible qualities was, at that time, endowed with such secret powers. But does it follow that other bread must also nourish me at another time and that like sensible qualities must always be attended with like secret powers? The consequence seems in no way necessary. At least, it must be acknowledged that there is here a consequence drawn by the mind that there is a certain step taken, a process of thought,

---

8. The word *power* is here used in a loose and popular sense. The more accurate explication of it would give additional evidence to this argument. See Section VII.

and an inference which wants to be explained. These two propositions are far from being the same: *I have found that such an object has always been attended with such an effect*, and *I foresee that other objects which are similar in appearance will be attended with similar effects*. I shall allow, if you please, that the one proposition may justly be inferred from the other; I know in fact that it always is inferred. But if you insist that the inference is made by a chain of reasoning, I desire you to produce that reasoning. The connection between these propositions is not intuitive. There is required a medium which may enable the mind to draw such an inference, if indeed it is drawn by reasoning and argument. What that medium is, I must confess, passes my comprehension; and it is incumbent on those to produce it who assert that it really exists and is the origin of all our conclusions concerning matter of fact.

This negative argument must certainly, in process of time, become altogether convincing if many penetrating and able philosophers shall turn their inquiries this way and no one is ever able to discover any connecting proposition or intermediate step which supports the understanding in this conclusion. But as the question is yet new, every reader may not trust so far to his own penetration as to conclude that, because an argument escapes his inquiry, therefore it does not really exist. For this reason it may be requisite to venture upon a more difficult task, and, enumerating all the branches of human knowledge, endeavor to show that none of them can afford such an argument.

All reasonings may be divided into two kinds, namely, demonstrative reasoning, or that concerning relations of ideas, and moral reasoning, or that concerning matter of fact and existence. That there are no demonstrative arguments in the case seems evident, since it implies no contradiction that the course of nature may change and that an object, seemingly like those which we have experienced, may be attended with different or contrary effects. May I not clearly and distinctly conceive that a body, falling from the clouds and which in all other respects resembles snow, has yet the taste of salt or feeling of fire? Is there any more intelligible proposition than to affirm that all the trees will flourish in December and January and decay in May and June? Now, whatever is intelligible and can be distinctly conceived implies no contradiction and can never be proved false by any demonstrative argument or abstract reasoning *a priori*.

If we are, therefore, engaged by arguments to put trust in past experience and make it the standard of our future judgment, these arguments must be probable only, or such as regard matter of fact and real existence according to the division above mentioned. But that there is no argument of this kind must appear if our explication of that species of reasoning is admitted as solid and satisfactory. We have said that all arguments concerning existence are founded on the relation of cause and effect, that our knowledge of that relation is derived entirely from experience, and that all our experimental conclusions proceed upon the supposition that the future will be conformable to the past. To endeavor, therefore, the proof of this last supposition by probable arguments, or arguments regarding existence, must be evidently going in a circle and taking that which is the very point in question for granted.

In reality, all arguments from experience are founded on the similarity which we discover among natural objects and by which we are induced to expect effects similar to those which we have found to follow from such objects. And though none but a fool or madman will ever pretend to dispute the authority of experience or to reject that great guide of human life, it may surely be allowed a philosopher to have so much curiosity at least as to examine the principle of human nature which gives this mighty authority to experience and makes us draw advantage from that similarity which nature has placed among different objects. From causes which appear *similar*, we expect similar effects. This is the sum of all our experimental conclusions. Now it seems evident that, if this conclusion were formed by reason, it would be as perfect at first, and upon one instance, as after ever so long a course of experience. But the case is far otherwise. Nothing so like as eggs, yet no one, on account of this appearing similarity, expects the same taste and relish in all of them. It is only after a long course of uniform experiments in any kind that we attain a firm reliance and security with regard to a particular event. Now where is that process of reasoning which, from one instance, draws a conclusion so different from that which it infers from a hundred instances that are in no way different from that single one? This question I propose as much for the sake of information as with an intention of raising difficulties. I cannot find, I cannot imagine any such reasoning. But I keep my mind still open to instruction, if anyone will vouchsafe to bestow it on me.

Should it be said that, from a number of uniform experiments, we *infer* a connection between the sensible qualities and the secret powers? This, I must confess, seems the same difficulty couched in different terms. The question still recurs: on what process of argument this *inference* is founded? Where is the medium, the interposing ideas which join propositions so very wide of each other? It is confessed that the color, consistency, and other sensible qualities of bread do not appear of themselves to have any connection with the secret powers of nourishment and support. For otherwise we could infer these secret powers from the first appearance of these sensible qualities without the aid of experience, contrary to the sentiment of all philosophers and contrary to plain matter of fact. Here, then, is our natural state of ignorance with regard to the powers and influence of all objects. How is this remedied by experience? It only shows us a number of uniform effects resulting from certain objects and teaches us that those particular objects, at that particular time, were endowed with such powers and forces. When a new object endowed with similar sensible qualities is produced, we expect similar powers and forces and look for a like effect. From a body of like color and consistency with bread, we expect like nourishment and support. But this surely is a step or progress of the mind which wants to be explained. When a man says, *I have found, in all past instances, such sensible qualities conjoined with such secret powers*: And when he says, *Similar sensible qualities will always be conjoined with similar secret powers*; he is not guilty of a tautology, nor are these propositions in any respect the same. You say that the one proposition is an inference from the other. But you must

confess that the inference is not intuitive, neither is it demonstrative. Of what nature is it then? To say it is experimental is begging the question. For all inferences from experience suppose as their foundation that the future will resemble the past and that similar powers will be conjoined with similar sensible qualities. If there is any suspicion that the course of nature may change, and that the past may be no rule for the future, all experience becomes useless and can give rise to no inference or conclusion. It is impossible, therefore, that any arguments from experience can prove this resemblance of the past to the future, since all these arguments are founded on the supposition of that resemblance. Let the course of things be allowed up to now ever so regular, that alone, without some new argument or inference, does not prove that for the future it will continue so. In vain do you pretend to have learned the nature of bodies from your past experience. Their secret nature and, consequently, all their effects and influence may change without any change in their sensible qualities. This happens sometimes and with regard to some objects. Why may it not happen always and with regard to all objects? What logic, what process of argument secures you against this supposition? My practice, you say, refutes my doubts. But you mistake the purport of my question. As an agent, I am quite satisfied in the point; but as a philosopher who has some share of curiosity—I will not say skepticism—I want to learn the foundation of this inference. No reading, no inquiry has yet been able to remove my difficulty or give me satisfaction in a matter of such importance. Can I do better than propose the difficulty to the public, even though, perhaps, I have small hopes of obtaining a solution? We shall at least, by this means, be sensible of our ignorance, if we do not augment our knowledge.

I must confess that a man is guilty of unpardonable arrogance who concludes, because an argument has escaped his own investigation, that therefore it does not really exist. I must also confess that, though all the learned for several ages should have employed themselves in fruitless search upon any subject, it may still, perhaps, be rash to conclude positively that the subject must therefore pass all human comprehension. Even though we examine all the sources of our knowledge and conclude them unfit for such a subject, there may still remain a suspicion that the enumeration is not complete or the examination not accurate. But with regard to the present subject, there are some considerations which seem to remove all this accusation of arrogance or suspicion of mistake.

It is certain that the most ignorant and stupid peasants, no infants, no even brute beasts, improve by experience and learn the qualities of natural objects by observing the effects which result from them. When a child has felt the sensation of pain from touching the flame of a candle, he will be careful not to put his hand near any candle, but will expect a similar effect from a cause which is similar in its sensible qualities and appearance. If you assert, therefore, that the understanding of the child is led into this conclusion by any process of argument or ratiocination, I may justly require you to produce that argument, nor have you any pretense to refuse so equitable a demand. You cannot say that the argument is abstruse and may possibly escape your inquiry, since you confess that it is obvious to the capacity of a mere infant. If you hesitate therefore a moment or if, after reflection, you produce any intricate or profound argument, you, in a manner, give up the question and confess that it is not reasoning which engages us to suppose the past resembling the future and to expect similar effects from causes which are similar to appearance. This is the proposition which I intended to enforce in the present section. If I am right, I pretend not to have made any mighty discovery. And if I am wrong, I must acknowledge myself to be indeed a very backward scholar, since I cannot now discover an argument which, it seems, was perfectly familiar to me long before I was out of my cradle.

## Section V: *Skeptical Solution of These Doubts*

### Part I

The passion for philosophy, like that for religion, seems liable to this inconvenience that, though it aims at the correction of our manners and extirpation of our vices, it may only serve, by imprudent management, to foster a predominant inclination and push the mind, with more determined resolution, towards that side which already *draws* too much by the bias and propensity of the natural temper. It is certain that, while we aspire to the magnanimous firmness of the philosophic sage and endeavor to confine our pleasures altogether within our own minds, we may, at last, render our philosophy like that of Epictetus and other *Stoics*, only a more refined system of selfishness, and reason ourselves out of all virtue as well as social enjoyment. While we study with attention the vanity of human life and turn all our thoughts towards the empty and transitory nature of riches and honors, we are, perhaps, all the while flattering our natural indolence which, hating the bustle of the world and drudgery of business, seeks a pretense of reason to give itself a full and uncontrolled indulgence. There is, however, one species of philosophy which seems little liable to this inconvenience, and that because it strikes in with no disorderly passion of the human mind, nor can mingle itself with any natural affection or propensity; and that is the Academic or skeptical philosophy. The Academics always talk of doubt and suspense of judgment, of danger in hasty determinations, of confining to very narrow bounds the inquiries of the understanding, and of renouncing all speculations which do not lie within the limits of common life and practice. Nothing, therefore, can be more contrary than such a philosophy to the supine indolence of the mind, its rash arrogance, its lofty pretensions, and its superstitious credulity. Every passion is mortified by it except the love of truth; and that passion never is nor can be carried to too high a degree. It is surprising, therefore, that this philosophy, which in almost every instance must be harmless and innocent, should be the subject of so much groundless reproach and blame. But, perhaps, the very circumstance which renders it so innocent is what chiefly exposes it to the public hatred and resentment. By flattering no irregular passion, it gains few partisans. By opposing so many vices and follies, it raises to itself abundance of enemies who stigmatize it as libertine, profane, and irreligious.

Nor need we fear that this philosophy, while it endeavors to limit our inquiries to common life, should ever undermine the reasonings of common life and carry its doubts so far as to destroy all action as well as speculation. Nature will always maintain her rights and prevail in the end over any abstract reasoning whatsoever. Though we should conclude, for instance, as in the foregoing section that, in all reasonings from experience, there is a step taken by the mind which is not supported by any argument or process of the understanding, there is no danger that these reasonings, on which almost all knowledge depends, will ever be affected by such a discovery. If the mind is not engaged by argument to make this step, it must be induced by some other principle of equal weight and authority and that principle will preserve its influence as long as human nature remains the same. What that principle is may well be worth the pains of inquiry.

Suppose a person, though endowed with the strongest faculties of reason and reflection, to be brought on a sudden into this world; he would, indeed, immediately observe a continual succession of objects and one event following another, but he would not be able to discover anything further. He would not at first, by any reasoning, be able to reach the idea of cause and effect, since the particular powers by which all natural operations are performed never appear to the senses; nor is it reasonable to conclude, merely because one event in one instance precedes another, that therefore the one is the cause, the other the effect. Their conjunction may be arbitrary and casual. There may be no reason to infer the existence of one from the appearance of the other. And in a word, such a person without more experience could never employ his conjecture or reasoning concerning any matter of fact or be assured of anything beyond what was immediately present to his memory and senses.

Suppose again that he has acquired more experience and has lived so long in the world as to have observed similar objects or events to be constantly conjoined together—what is the consequence of this experience? He immediately infers the existence of one object from the appearance of the other. Yet he has not, by all his experience, acquired any idea or knowledge of the secret power by which the one object produces the other, nor is it by any process of reasoning he is engaged to draw this inference. But still he finds himself determined to draw it. And though he should be convinced that his understanding has no part in the operation, he would nevertheless continue in the same course of thinking. There is some other principle which determines him to form such a conclusion.

This principle is *custom* or *habit*. For wherever the repetition of any particular act or operation produces a propensity to renew the same act or operation without being impelled by any reasoning or process of the understanding, we always say that this propensity is the effect of *custom*. By employing that word we pretend not to have given the ultimate reason of such a propensity. We only point out a principle of human nature which is universally acknowledged and which is well known by its effects. Perhaps we can push our inquiries no further or pretend to give the cause of this cause, but must rest contented with it as the ultimate principle which we can assign of all our conclusions from experience. It is sufficient satisfaction that we can go so far without repining at the narrowness of our faculties because they will carry us no further. And it is certain we here advance a very intelligible proposition at least, if not a true one, when we assert that after the constant conjunction of two objects, heat and flame, for instance, or weight and solidity, we are determined by custom alone to expect the one from the appearance of the other. This hypothesis seems even the only one which explains the difficulty why we draw, from a thousand instances, an inference which we are not able to draw from one instance that is in no respect different from them. Reason is incapable of any such variation. The conclusions which it draws from considering one circle are the same which it would form upon surveying all the circles in the universe. But no man, having seen only one body move after being impelled by another, could infer that every other body will move after a like impulse. All inferences from experience, therefore, are effects of custom, not of reasoning.[9]

Custom, then, is the great guide of human life. It is that principle alone which renders our experience useful to us and makes us expect, for the future, a similar train of events with those which have appeared in the past. Without the influence of custom we should be entirely ignorant of every matter of fact beyond what is immediately present to the memory and senses. We should never know how to adjust means to ends or to employ our natural powers in the production of any effect. There would be an end at once of all action as well as of the chief part of speculation.

---

9. Nothing is more usual than for writers, even on *moral, political*, or *physical* subjects, to distinguish between *reason* and *experience* and to suppose that these species of argumentation are entirely different from each other. The former are taken for the mere result of our intellectual faculties which, by considering *a priori* the nature of things and examining the effects that must follow from their operation, establish particular principles of science and philosophy. The latter are supposed to be derived entirely from sense and observation by which we learn what has actually resulted from the operation of particular objects and are able to infer from this what will result from them for the future. Thus, for instance, the limitations and restraints of civil government and a legal constitution may be defended, either from *reason*, which, reflecting on the great frailty and corruption of human nature, teaches that no man can safely be trusted with unlimited authority; or from *experience* and history, which inform us of the enormous abuses that ambition, in every age and country, has been found to make of so imprudent a confidence.

The same distinction between reason and experience is maintained in all our deliberations concerning the conduct of life, while the experienced statesman, general, physician, or merchant is trusted and followed, and the unpracticed novice, with whatever natural talents endowed, neglected and despised. Though it is allowed that reason may form very plausible conjectures with regard to the consequences of such a particular conduct in such particular circumstances, it is still supposed imperfect without the assistance of experience, which is alone able to give stability and certainty to the maxims, derived from study and reflection.

But notwithstanding that this distinction is thus universally received, both in the active and speculative scenes of life, I shall not scruple to pronounce that it is, at bottom, erroneous, at least, superficial.

If we examine those arguments which, in any of the sciences aforementioned, are supposed to be the mere effects of reasoning and reflection, they will be found to terminate, at

But here it may be proper to remark that though our conclusions from experience carry us beyond our memory and senses and assure us of matters of fact, which happened in the most distant places and most remote ages, yet some fact must always be present to the senses or memory from which we may first proceed in drawing these conclusions. A man who should find in a desert country the remains of pompous buildings would conclude that the country had, in ancient times, been cultivated by civilized inhabitants, but did nothing of this nature occur to him, he could never form such an inference. We learn the events of former ages from history, but then we

---

last, in some general principle or conclusion for which we can assign no reason but observation and experience. The only difference between them and those maxims which are vulgarly esteemed the result of pure experience is that the former cannot be established without some process of thought and some reflection on what we have observed in order to distinguish its circumstances and trace its consequences. Whereas in the latter, the experienced event is exactly and fully similar to that which we infer as the result of any particular situation. The history of a Tiberius or a Nero makes us dread a like tyranny, were our monarchs freed from the restraints of laws and senates. But the observation of any fraud or cruelty in private life is sufficient with the aid of a little thought to give us the same apprehension, while it serves as an instance of the general corruption of human nature and shows us the danger which we must incur by reposing an entire confidence in mankind. In both cases it is experience which is ultimately the foundation of our inference and conclusion.

There is no man so young and inexperienced as not to have formed from observation many general and just maxims concerning human affairs and the conduct of life; but it must be confessed that when a man comes to put these in practice, he will be extremely liable to error, until time and further experience both enlarge these maxims and teach him their proper use and application. In every situation or incident, there are many particular and seemingly minute circumstances which the man of greatest talents is, at first, apt to overlook, though on them the justness of his conclusions and consequently the prudence of his conduct entirely depend. Not to mention that, to a young beginner, the general observations and maxims do not always occur on the proper occasions, nor can be immediately applied with due calmness and distinction. The truth is that an inexperienced reasoner could be no reasoner at all, were he absolutely inexperienced; and when we assign that character to anyone, we mean it only in a comparative sense and suppose him possessed of experience in a smaller and more imperfect degree.

must peruse the volumes in which this instruction is contained and from this carry up our inferences from one testimony to another, until we arrive at the eyewitnesses and spectators of these distant events. In a word, if we proceed not upon some fact present to the memory or senses, our reasonings would be merely hypothetical; and however the particular links might be connected with each other, the whole chain of inferences would have nothing to support it, nor could we ever, by its means, arrive at the knowledge of any real existence. If I ask, why you believe any particular matter of fact which you relate, you must tell me some reason; and this reason will be some other fact connected with it. But as you cannot proceed after this manner *in infinitum*, you must at last terminate in some fact which is present to your memory or senses or must allow that your belief is entirely without foundation.

What then is the conclusion of the whole matter? A simple one, though it must be confessed, pretty remote from the common theories of philosophy. All belief of matter of fact or real existence is derived merely from some object present to the memory or senses and a customary conjunction between that and some other object. Or, in other words, having found in many instances that any two kinds of objects, flame and heat, snow and cold, have always been conjoined together, if flame or snow is presented anew to the senses, the mind is carried by custom to expect heat or cold and to *believe* that such a quality does exist and will discover itself upon a nearer approach. This belief is the necessary result of placing the mind in such circumstances. It is an operation of the soul when we are so situated, as unavoidable as feeling the passion of love, when we receive benefits—or hatred, when we meet with injuries. All these operations are a species of natural instincts which no reasoning or process of the thought and understanding is able either to produce or to prevent.

At this point, it would be very allowable for us to stop our philosophical researches. In most questions we can never make a single step further; and in all questions, we must terminate here at last, after our most restless and curious inquiries. But still our curiosity will be pardonable, perhaps commendable, if it carry us on to still further researches and make us examine more accurately the nature of this *belief* and of the *customary conjunction* from which it is derived. By this means we may meet with some explications and analogies that will give satisfaction, at least to such as love the abstract sciences and can be entertained with speculations which, however accurate, may still retain a degree of doubt and uncertainty. As to readers of a different taste, the remaining part of this section is not calculated for them and the following inquiries may well be understood, though it is neglected.

## Part II

Nothing is more free than the imagination of man, and though it cannot exceed that original stock of ideas furnished by the internal and external senses, it has unlimited power of mixing, compounding, separating, and dividing these ideas, in all the varieties of fiction and vision. It can feign a train of events with all the appearance of reality, ascribe to them a particular time and place, conceive them as existent, and paint them out to itself with every circumstance that belongs to any historical fact which it believes with the greatest certainty. In what, therefore, consists the difference between such a fiction and belief? It lies not merely in any peculiar idea which is annexed to such a conception as commands our assent and which is wanting to every known fiction. For as the mind has authority over all its ideas, it could voluntarily annex this particular idea to any fiction and consequently be able to believe whatever it pleases; contrary to what we find by daily experience. We can, in our conception, join the head of a man to the body of a horse, but it is not in our power to believe that such an animal has ever really existed.

It follows, therefore, that the difference between *fiction* and *belief* lies in some sentiment or feeling which is annexed to the latter, not to the former, and which depends not on the will, nor can be commanded at pleasure. It must be excited by nature like all other sentiments and must arise from the particular situation in which the mind is placed at any particular juncture. Whenever any object is presented to the memory or senses, it immediately, by the force of custom, carries the imagination to conceive that object which is usually conjoined to it; and this conception is attended with a feeling or sentiment different from the loose reveries of the fancy. In this consists the whole nature of belief. For as there is no matter of fact which we believe so firmly that we cannot conceive the contrary, there would be no difference between the conception assented to and that which is rejected were it not for some sentiment which distinguishes the one from the other. If I see a billiard ball moving towards another on a smooth table, I can easily conceive it to stop upon contact. This conception implies no contradiction, but still it feels very differently from that conception by which I represent to myself the impulse and the communication of motion from one ball to another.

Were we to attempt a *definition* of this sentiment, we should, perhaps, find it a very difficult, if not an impossible task; in the same manner as if we should endeavor to define the feeling of cold, or passion of anger, to a creature who never had any experience of these sentiments. Belief is the true and proper name of this feeling, and no one is ever at a loss to know the meaning of that term, because every man is every moment conscious of the sentiment represented by it. It may not, however, be improper to attempt a *description* of this sentiment, in hopes we may by that means arrive at some analogies which may afford a more perfect explication of it. I say then that belief is nothing but a more vivid, lively, forcible, firm, steady conception of an object than what the imagination alone is ever able to attain. This variety of terms, which may seem so unphilosophical, is intended only to express that act of the mind which renders realities, or what is taken for such, more present to us than fictions, causes them to weigh more in the thought, and gives them a superior influence on the passions and imagination. Provided we agree about the thing, it is needless to dispute about the terms. The imagination has the command over all its ideas and can join and mix and vary them in all the ways possible. It may conceive fictitious objects with all the circumstances of place and time. It may set them in a manner before our eyes, in their true colors, just as they might have existed. But as it is

impossible that this faculty of imagination can ever, of itself, reach belief, it is evident that belief consists not in the peculiar nature or order of ideas, but in the *manner* of their conception and in their *feeling* to the mind. I confess that it is impossible perfectly to explain this feeling or manner of conception. We may make use of words which express something near it. But its true and proper name, as we observed before, is *belief*, which is a term that everyone sufficiently understands in common life. And in philosophy we can go no further than assert that *belief* is something felt by the mind which distinguishes the ideas of the judgment from the fictions of the imagination. It gives them more weight and influence, makes them appear of greater importance, enforces them in the mind, and renders them the governing principle of our actions. I hear at present, for instance, a person's voice with whom I am acquainted and the sound comes as from the next room. This impression of my senses immediately conveys my thought to the person, together with all the surrounding objects. I point them out to myself as existing at present with the same qualities and relations of which I formerly knew them possessed. These ideas take faster hold of my mind than ideas of an enchanted castle. They are very different to the feeling and have a much greater influence of every kind, to give either pleasure or pain, joy or sorrow.

Let us, then, take in the whole compass of this doctrine and allow that the sentiment of belief is nothing but a conception more intense and steady than what attends the mere fictions of the imagination and that this *manner* of conception arises from a customary conjunction of the object with something present to the memory or senses. I believe that it will not be difficult, upon these suppositions, to find other operations of the mind analogous to it and to trace up these phenomena to principles still more general.

We have already observed that nature has established connections among particular ideas and that no sooner one idea occurs to our thoughts than it introduces its correlative and carries our attention towards it by a gentle and insensible movement. These principles of connection or association we have reduced to three, namely, *resemblance, contiguity,* and *causation*; these are the only bonds that unite our thoughts together and beget that regular train of reflection or discourse which, in a greater or less degree, takes place among all mankind. Now here arises a question on which the solution of the present difficulty will depend. Does it happen in all these relations that when one of the objects is presented to the senses or memory the mind is not only carried to the conception of the correlative, but reaches a steadier and stronger conception of it than what otherwise it would have been able to attain? This seems to be the case with that belief which arises from the relation of cause and effect. And if the case is the same with the other relations or principles of association, this may be established as a general law which takes place in all the operations of the mind.

We may, therefore, observe, as the first experiment to our present purpose, that upon the appearance of the picture of an absent friend, our idea of him is evidently enlivened by the *resemblance*, and that every passion which that idea occasions, whether of joy or sorrow, acquires new force and vigor. In producing this effect there concur both a relation and a present impression. Where the picture bears him no resemblance, at least was not intended for him, it never so much as conveys our thought to him. And where it is absent, as well as the person, though the mind may pass from the thought of the one to that of the other, it feels its idea to be rather weakened than enlivened by that transition. We take a pleasure in viewing the picture of a friend when it is set before us; but when it is removed, rather choose to consider him directly than by reflection in an image which is equally distant and obscure.

The ceremonies of the Roman Catholic religion may be considered as instances of the same nature. The devotees of that superstition usually plead in excuse for the mummeries[10] with which they are upbraided that they feel the good effect of those external motions, and postures, and actions in enlivening their devotion and quickening their fervor, which otherwise would decay, if directed entirely to distant and immaterial objects. We shadow out the objects of our faith, they say, in sensible types and images,

and render them more present to us by the immediate presence of these types than it is possible for us to do merely by an intellectual view and contemplation. Sensible objects have always a greater influence on the fancy than any other, and this influence they readily convey to those ideas to which they are related and which they resemble. I shall only infer from these practices and this reasoning that the effect of resemblance in enlivening the ideas is very common; and as in every case a resemblance and a present impression must concur, we are abundantly supplied with experiments to prove the reality of the foregoing principle.

We may add force to these experiments by others of a different kind, in considering the effects of *contiguity* as well as of *resemblance*. It is certain that distance diminishes the force of every idea and that, upon our approach to any object, though it does not discover itself to our senses, it operates upon the mind with an influence which imitates an immediate impression. The thinking on any object readily transports the mind to what is contiguous; but it is only the actual presence of an object that transports it with a superior vivacity. When I am a few miles from home, whatever relates to it touches me more nearly than when I am two hundred leagues distant, though even at that distance the reflecting on anything in the neighborhood of my friends or family naturally produces an idea of them. But, as in this latter case, both the objects of the mind are ideas, notwithstanding there is an easy transition between them; that transition alone is not able to give a superior vivacity to any of the ideas, for want of some immediate impression.[11]

---

10. [A pretentious or hypocritical show or ceremony.]

11. 'Naturane nobis, inquit, datum dicam, an errore quodam, ut, cum ea loca videamus, in quibus memoria dignos viros acceperimus multum esse versatos, magis moveamur, quam siquando eorum ipsorum aut facta audiamus aut scriptum aliquod legamus? Velut ego nunc moveor. Venit enim mihi Platonis in mentem, quem accepimus primum hic disputare solitum: Cujus etiam illi hortuli propinqui non memoriam solum mihi afferunt, sed ipsum videntur in conspectu meo hic ponere. Hic Speusippus, hic Xenocrates, hic ejus auditor Polemo; cujus ipsa illa sessio fuit, quam videamus. Equidem etiam curiam nostram Hostiliam dico, non hanc novam, quae mihi minor esse videtur postquam est major, solebam intuens,

No one can doubt but causation has the same influence as the other two relations of resemblance and contiguity. Superstitious people are fond of the relics of saints and holy men, for the same reason that they seek after types or images in order to enliven their devotion and give them a more intimate and strong conception of those exemplary lives which they desire to imitate. Now it is evident that one of the best relics which a devotee could procure would be the handiwork of a saint; and if his clothes and furniture are ever to be considered in this light, it is because they were once at his disposal and were moved and affected by him; in this respect they are to be considered as imperfect effects and as connected with him by a shorter chain of consequences than any of those by which we learn the reality of his existence.

Suppose that the son of a friend who had been long dead or absent were presented to us; it is evident that this object would instantly revive its correlative idea and recall to our thoughts all past intimacies and familiarities in more lively colors than they would otherwise have appeared to us. This is another phenomenon which seems to prove the principle above mentioned.

---

Scipionem, Catonem, Laelium, nostrum vero in primis avum cogitare. Tanta vis admonitionis est in locis; ut non sine causa ex his memoriae deducta sit disciplina.' Cicero de Finibus. Lib. v. 2. ["Whether it is a natural instinct or a mere illusion, I can't say; but one's emotions are more strongly aroused by seeing the places that tradition records to have been the resort of men of note in former days, than by hearing about their deeds or reading their writings. My own feelings at the present moment are a case in point. I am reminded of Plato, the first philosopher, so we are told, that made a practice of holding discussions in this place; and indeed the garden close at hand yonder not only recalls his memory but seems to bring the actual man before my eyes. This was the haunt of Speusippus, of Xenocrates, and of Xenocrates' pupil Polemo, who used to sit on the very seat we see over there. For my own part even the sight of our senate-house at home (I mean the Curia Hostilia, not the present new building, which looks to my eyes smaller since its enlargement) used to call up to me thoughts of Scipio, Cato, Laelius, and chief of all, my grandfather; such powers of suggestion do places possess. No wonder the scientific training of the memory is based upon locality." Cicero, *De Finibus Bonorum et Malorum*, translated by H. Rackham (Cambridge, Mass.: Harvard University Press, 1914), pp. 391–93.]

We may observe that in these phenomena the belief of the correlative object is always presupposed, without which the relation could have no effect. The influence of the picture supposes that we *believe* our friend to have once existed. Contiguity to home can never excite our ideas of home unless we *believe* that it really exists. Now I assert that this belief, where it reaches beyond the memory or senses, is of a similar nature and arises from similar causes with the transition of thought and vivacity of conception here explained. When I throw a piece of dry wood into a fire, my mind is immediately carried to conceive that it augments, not extinguishes, the flame. This transition of thought from the cause to the effect does not proceed from reason. It derives its origin altogether from custom and experience. And as it first begins from an object present to the senses, it renders the idea or conception of flame more strong and lively than any loose, floating reverie of the imagination. That idea arises immediately. The thought moves instantly towards it and conveys to it all that force of conception which is derived from the impression present to the senses. When a sword is leveled at my breast, does not the idea of wound and pain strike me more strongly than when a glass of wine is presented to me, even though by accident this idea should occur after the appearance of the latter object? But what is there in this whole matter to cause such a strong conception except only a present object and a customary transition to the idea of another object which we have been accustomed to conjoin with the former? This is the whole operation of the mind in all our conclusions concerning matter of fact and existence; and it is a satisfaction to find some analogies by which it may be explained. The transition from a present object does in all cases give strength and solidity to the related idea.

Here, then, is a kind of preestablished harmony between the course of nature and the succession of our ideas; and though the powers and forces by which the former is governed are wholly unknown to us, yet our thoughts and conceptions have still, we find, gone on in the same train with the other works of nature. Custom is that principle by which this correspondence has been effected, so necessary to the subsistence of our species and the regulation of our conduct in every circumstance and occurrence of human life. Had not the presence of an object instantly excited the idea of those objects commonly conjoined with it, all our knowledge must have been limited to the narrow sphere of our memory and senses and we should never have been able to adjust means to ends or employ our natural powers to either the producing of good or the avoiding of evil. Those who delight in the discovery and contemplation of *final causes* have here ample subject to employ their wonder and admiration.

I shall add, for a further confirmation of the foregoing theory, that as this operation of the mind by which we infer like effects from like causes, and *vice versa*, is so essential to the subsistence of all human creatures, it is not probable that it could be trusted to the fallacious deductions of our reason, which is slow in its operations, does not appear, in any degree, during the first years of infancy, and at best is in every age and period of human life extremely liable to error and mistake. It is more conformable to the ordinary wisdom of nature to secure so necessary an act of the mind by some instinct or mechanical tendency which may be infallible in its operations, may discover itself at the first appearance of life and thought, and may be independent of all the labored deductions of the understanding. As nature has taught us the use of our limbs without giving us the knowledge of the muscles and nerves by which they are actuated, so has she implanted in us an instinct which carries forward the thought in a correspondent course to that which she has established among external objects, though we are ignorant of those powers and forces on which this regular course and succession of objects totally depends.

## Section VI: *Of Probability*[12]

Though there is no such thing as *chance* in the world, our ignorance of the real cause of any event has the same influence on the understanding and begets a like species of belief or opinion.

There is certainly a probability which arises from a superiority of chances on any side and, according as this superiority increases and surpasses the opposite chances, the probability receives a proportional increase and begets still a higher degree of belief or assent to that side in which we discover the superiority. If a die were marked with one figure or number of spots on four sides, and with another figure or number of spots on the two remaining sides, it would be more probable that the former would turn up than the latter, though, if it had a thousand sides marked in the same manner and only one side different, the probability would be much higher and our belief or expectation of the event more steady and secure. This process of the thought or reasoning may seem trivial and obvious, but to those who consider it more narrowly, it may, perhaps, afford matter for curious speculation.

It seems evident that when the mind looks forward to discover the event which may result from the throw of such a die, it considers the turning up of each particular side as alike probable and it is the very nature of chance to render all the particular events comprehended in it entirely equal. But finding a greater number of sides concur in the one event than in the other, the mind is carried more frequently to that event and meets it more often in revolving the various possibilities or chances on which the ultimate result depends. This concurrence of several views in one particular event begets immediately, by an inexplicable contrivance of nature, the sentiment of belief and gives that event the advantage over its antagonist which is supported by a smaller number of views and recurs less frequently to the mind. If we allow that belief is nothing but a firmer and stronger conception of an object than what attends the mere fictions of the imagination, this operation may, perhaps, in some measure be accounted for. The concurrence of these several views or glimpses imprints the idea more strongly on the imagination, gives it

---

12. Mr. Locke divides all arguments into demonstrative and probable. In this view, we must say that it is only probable all men must die or that the sun will rise tomorrow. But to conform our language more to common use, we ought to divide arguments into *demonstrations, proofs,* and *probabilities* — by proofs meaning such arguments from experience as leave no room for doubt or opposition.

superior force and vigor, renders its influence on the passions and affections more sensible, and, in a word, begets that reliance or security which constitutes the nature of belief and opinion.

The case is the same with the probability of causes as with that of chance. There are some causes which are entirely uniform and constant in producing a particular effect and no instance has ever yet been found of any failure or irregularity in their operation. Fire has always burned, and water suffocated, every human creature. The production of motion by impulse and gravity is a universal law which has up to now admitted of no exception. But there are other causes which have been found more irregular and uncertain; nor has rhubarb always proved a purge, or opium a soporific, to everyone who has taken these medicines. It is true, when any cause fails of producing its usual effect, philosophers do not ascribe this to any irregularity in nature, but suppose that some secret causes in the particular structure of parts have prevented the operation. Our reasonings, however, and conclusions concerning the event are the same as if this principle had no place. Being determined by custom to transfer the past to the future in all our inferences, where the past has been entirely regular and uniform, we expect the event with the greatest assurance and leave no room for any contrary supposition. But where different effects have been found to follow from causes which are to *appearance* exactly similar, all these various effects must occur to the mind in transferring the past to the future and enter into our consideration when we determine the probability of the event. Though we give the preference to that which has been found most usual and believe that this effect will exist, we must not overlook the other effects, but must assign to each of them a particular weight and authority in proportion as we have found it to be more or less frequent. It is more probable, in almost every country of Europe, that there will be frost sometime in January than that the weather will continue open throughout that whole month, though this probability varies according to the different climates and approaches to a certainty in the more northern kingdoms. Here, then, it seems evident that when we transfer the past to the future in

order to determine the effect which will result from any cause, we transfer all the different events in the same proportion as they have appeared in the past and conceive one to have existed a hundred times, for instance, another ten times, and another once. As a great number of views do here concur in one event, they fortify and confirm it to the imagination, beget that sentiment which we call *belief*, and give its object the preference above the contrary event which is not supported by an equal number of experiments and does not recur so frequently to the thought in transferring the past to the future. Let anyone try to account for this operation of the mind upon any of the received systems of philosophy and he will be sensible of the difficulty. For my part, I shall think it sufficient if the present hints excite the curiosity of philosophers and make them sensible how defective all common theories are in treating of such curious and such sublime subjects.

## Section VII: *Of the Idea of Necessary Connection*

### Part I

The great advantage of the mathematical sciences above the moral consists in this, that the ideas of the former, being sensible, are always clear and determinate, the smallest distinction between them is immediately perceptible, and the same terms are still expressive of the same ideas without ambiguity or variation. An oval is never mistaken for a circle, nor an hyperbola for an ellipsis. The isosceles and scalene are distinguished by boundaries more exact than vice and virtue, right and wrong. If any term is defined in geometry, the mind readily, of itself, substitutes on all occasions the definition for the term defined. Or even when no definition is employed, the object itself may be presented to the senses and by that means be steadily and clearly apprehended. But the finer sentiments of the mind, the operations of the understanding, the various agitations of the passions, though really in themselves distinct, easily escape us when surveyed by reflection; nor is it in our power to recall the original object as often as we have occasion to contemplate it. Ambiguity, by this means, is gradually introduced into our reasonings. Similar objects are readily taken to be the same and the conclusion becomes at last very wide of the premises.

One may safely, however, affirm that if we consider these sciences in a proper light, their advantages and disadvantages nearly compensate each other and reduce both of them to a state of equality. If the mind, with greater facility, retains the ideas of geometry clear and determinate, it must carry on a much longer and more intricate chain of reasoning and compare ideas much wider of each other in order to reach the more abstruse truths of that science. And if moral ideas are apt, without extreme care, to fall into obscurity and confusion, the inferences are always much shorter in these disquisitions and the intermediate steps which lead to the conclusion much fewer than in the sciences which treat of quantity and number. In reality, there is scarcely a proposition in Euclid so simple as not to consist of more parts than are to be found in any moral reasoning which runs not into chimera and conceit. Where we trace the principles of the human mind through a few steps, we may be very well satisfied with our progress, considering how soon nature throws a bar to all our inquiries concerning causes and reduces us to an acknowledgment of our ignorance. The chief obstacle, therefore, to our improvement in the moral or metaphysical sciences is the obscurity of the ideas and ambiguity of the terms. The principal difficulty in mathematics is the length of inferences and compass of thought requisite to the forming of any conclusion. And, perhaps, our progress in natural philosophy is chiefly retarded by the want of proper experiments and phenomena which are often discovered by chance and cannot always be found when requisite, even by the most diligent and prudent inquiry. As moral philosophy seems up to now to have received less improvement than either geometry or physics, we may conclude that if there is any difference in this respect among these sciences, the difficulties which obstruct the progress of the former require superior care and capacity to be surmounted.

There are no ideas which occur in metaphysics more obscure and uncertain than those of *power*, *force*, *energy*, or *necessary connection*, of which it is

every moment necessary for us to treat in all our disquisitions. We shall, therefore, endeavor in this section to fix, if possible, the precise meaning of these terms and thereby remove some part of that obscurity which is so much complained of in this species of philosophy.

It seems a proposition which will not admit of much dispute that all our ideas are nothing but copies of our impressions, or, in other words, that it is impossible for us to *think* of anything which we have not antecedently *felt* by either our external or our internal senses. I have endeavored[13] to explain and prove this proposition, and have expressed my hopes that by a proper application of it men may reach a greater clearness and precision in philosophical reasonings than what they have up to now been able to attain. Complex ideas may, perhaps, be well known by definition, which is nothing but an enumeration of those parts or simple ideas that compose them. But when we have pushed up definitions to the most simple ideas and find still some ambiguity and obscurity, what resource are we then possessed of? By what invention can we throw light upon these ideas and render them altogether precise and determinate to our intellectual view? Produce the impressions or original sentiments from which the ideas are copied. These impressions are all strong and sensible. They do not admit of ambiguity. They are not only placed in a full light themselves, but may throw light on their correspondent ideas, which lie in obscurity. And by this means we may, perhaps, attain a new microscope or species of optics by which, in the moral sciences, the most minute and most simple ideas may be so enlarged as to fall readily under our apprehension and be equally known with the grossest and most sensible ideas that can be the object of our inquiry.

To be fully acquainted, therefore, with the idea of power or necessary connection, let us examine its impression and, in order to find the impression with greater certainty, let us search for it in all the sources from which it may possibly be derived.

When we look about us towards external objects and consider the operation of causes, we are never able, in a single instance, to discover any power or

---

13. Section II: Of the Origin of Ideas.

necessary connection, any quality which binds the effect to the cause and renders the one an infallible consequence of the other. We only find that the one does actually in fact follow the other. The impulse of one billiard ball is attended with motion in the second. This is the whole that appears to the *outward* senses. The mind feels no sentiment or *inward* impression from this succession of objects. Consequently, there is not, in any single particular instance of cause and effect, anything which can suggest the idea of power or necessary connection.

From the first appearance of an object we never can conjecture what effect will result from it. But were the power or energy of any cause discoverable by the mind, we could foresee the effect, even without experience, and might, at first, pronounce with certainty concerning it by the mere dint of thought and reasoning.

In reality, there is no part of matter that ever does, by its sensible qualities, discover any power or energy or give us ground to imagine that it could produce anything or be followed by any other object which we could denominate its effect. Solidity, extension, motion—these qualities are all complete in themselves and never point out any other event which may result from them. The scenes of the universe are continually shifting and one object follows another in an uninterrupted succession; but the power or force which actuates the whole machine is entirely concealed from us and never discovers itself in any of the sensible qualities of body. We know that, in fact, heat is a constant attendant of flame, but what is the connection between them we have no room so much as to conjecture or imagine. It is impossible, therefore, that the idea of power can be derived from the contemplation of bodies in single instances of their operation, because no bodies ever discover any power which can be the original of this idea.[14]

---

14. Mr. Locke, in his chapter on power, says that, finding from experience that there are several new productions in matter and concluding that there must somewhere be a power capable of producing them, we arrive at last by this reasoning at the idea of power. But no reasoning can ever give us a new, original simple idea—as this philosopher himself confesses. This, therefore, can never be the origin of that idea.

Since, therefore, external objects as they appear to the senses give us no idea of power or necessary connection by their operation in particular instances, let us see whether this idea is derived from reflection on the operations of our own minds and is copied from any internal impression. It may be said that we are every moment conscious of internal power, while we feel that, by the simple command of our will, we can move the organs of our body or direct the faculties of our mind. An act of volition produces motion in our limbs or raises a new idea in our imagination. This influence of the will we know by consciousness. Hence we acquire the idea of power or energy and are certain that we ourselves and all other intelligent beings are possessed of power. This idea, then, is an idea of reflection, since it arises from reflecting on the operations of our own mind and on the command which is exercised by will, over both the organs of the body and the faculties of the mind.

We shall proceed to examine this pretension and, first, with regard to the influence of volition over the organs of the body. This influence, we may observe, is a fact which, like all other natural events, can be known only by experience and can never be foreseen from any apparent energy or power in the cause which connects it with the effect and renders the one an infallible consequence of the other. The motion of our body follows upon the command of our will. Of this we are every moment conscious. But the means by which this is effected, the energy by which the will performs so extraordinary an operation, of this we are so far from being immediately conscious that it must forever escape our most diligent inquiry.

For *first*, is there any principle in all nature more mysterious than the union of soul with body, by which a supposed spiritual substance acquires such an influence over a material one that the most refined thought is able to actuate the grossest matter? Were we empowered by a secret wish to remove mountains or control the planets in their orbit, this extensive authority would not be more extraordinary, nor more beyond our comprehension. But if by consciousness we perceived any power or energy in the will, we must know this power; we must know its connection with the effect; we must know the secret union of soul and body, and the nature of both these substances by which the one is able to operate in so many instances upon the other.

*Secondly*, we are not able to move all the organs of the body with a like authority, though we cannot assign any reason besides experience for so remarkable a difference between one and the other. Why has the will an influence over the tongue and fingers, not over the heart or liver? This question would never embarrass us were we conscious of a power in the former case, not in the latter. We should then perceive, independent of experience, why the authority of will over the organs of the body is circumscribed within such particular limits. Being in that case fully acquainted with the power or force by which it operates, we should also know why its influence reaches precisely to such boundaries, and no further.

A man suddenly struck with a palsy in the leg or arm or who had newly lost those members frequently endeavors, at first, to move them and employ them in their usual offices. Here he is as much conscious of power to command such limbs as a man in perfect health is conscious of power to actuate any member which remains in its natural state and condition. But consciousness never deceives. Consequently, neither in the one case nor in the other are we ever conscious of any power. We learn the influence of our will from experience alone. And experience only teaches us how one event constantly follows another, without instructing us in the secret connection which binds them together and renders them inseparable.

*Thirdly*, we learn from anatomy that the immediate object of power in voluntary motion is not the member itself which is moved, but certain muscles and nerves and animal spirits and, perhaps, something still more minute and more unknown through which the motion is successively propagated before it reaches the member itself whose motion is the immediate object of volition. Can there be a more certain proof that the power by which this whole operation is performed, so far from being directly and fully known by an inward sentiment or consciousness, is to the last degree mysterious and unintelligible? Here the mind wills a certain event. Immediately another event, unknown to ourselves and totally different from the one

intended, is produced. This event produces another, equally unknown, until at last, through a long succession the desired event is produced. But if the original power was felt, it must be known. If it was known, its effect must also be known, since all power is relative to its effect. And *vice versa*, if the effect is not known, the power cannot be known nor felt. How indeed can we be conscious of a power to move our limbs when we have no such power, but only that to move certain animal spirits which, though they produce at last the motion of our limbs, yet operate in such a manner as is wholly beyond our comprehension?

We may, therefore, conclude from the whole, I hope, without any temerity, though with assurance, that our idea of power is not copied from any sentiment or consciousness of power within ourselves when we give rise to animal motion or apply our limbs to their proper use and office. That their motion follows the command of the will is a matter of common experience, like other natural events. But the power or energy by which this is effected, like that in other natural events, is unknown and inconceivable.[15]

Shall we then assert that we are conscious of a power or energy in our own minds when, by an act or command of our will, we raise up a new idea, fix the mind to the contemplation of it, turn it on all sides, and at last dismiss it for some other idea when we think that we have surveyed it with sufficient

---

15. It may be pretended that the resistance which we meet with in bodies, obliging us frequently to exert our force and call up all our power, this gives us the idea of force and power. It is this *nisus* or strong endeavor of which we are conscious that is the original impression from which this idea is copied. But, first, we attribute power to a vast number of objects, where we never can suppose this resistance or exertion of force to take place; to the Supreme Being who never meets with any resistance; to the mind in its command over its ideas and limbs in common thinking and motion where the effect follows immediately upon the will without any exertion or summoning up of force; to inanimate matter which is not capable of this sentiment. *Secondly*, this sentiment of an endeavor to overcome resistance has no known connection with any event. What follows it, we know by experience, but could not know it *a priori*. It must, however, be confessed that the animal *nisus*, which we experience, though it can afford no accurate precise idea of power, enters very much into that vulgar, inaccurate idea which is formed of it.

accuracy? I believe the same arguments will prove that even this command of the will gives us no real idea of force or energy.

*First*, it must be allowed that when we know a power, we know that very circumstance in the cause by which it is enabled to produce the effect, for these are supposed to be synonymous. We must, therefore, know both the cause and the effect and the relation between them. But do we pretend to be acquainted with the nature of the human soul and the nature of an idea or the aptitude of the one to produce the other? This is a real creation, a production of something out of nothing, which implies a power so great that it may seem, at first sight, beyond the reach of any being less than infinite. At least it must be admitted that such a power is not felt, nor known, nor even conceivable by the mind. We only feel the event, namely, the existence of an idea consequent to a command of the will. But the manner in which this operation is performed, the power by which it is produced, is entirely beyond our comprehension.

*Secondly*, the command of the mind over itself is limited, as well as its command over the body; and these limits are not known by reason or any acquaintance with the nature of cause and effect, but only by experience and observation, as in all other natural events and in the operation of external objects. Our authority over our sentiments and passions is much weaker than that over our ideas; and even the latter authority is circumscribed within very narrow boundaries. Will anyone pretend to assign the ultimate reason of these boundaries or show why the power is deficient in one case, not in another?

*Thirdly*, this self-command is very different at different times. A man in health possesses more of it than one languishing with sickness. We are more master of our thoughts in the morning than in the evening—fasting, than after a full meal. Can we give any reason for these variations except experience? Where, then, is the power of which we pretend to be conscious? Is there not here, in either a spiritual or a material substance or both, some secret mechanism or structure of parts upon which the effect depends and which, being entirely unknown to us, renders

the power or energy of the will equally unknown and incomprehensible?

Volition is surely an act of the mind with which we are sufficiently acquainted. Reflect upon it. Consider it on all sides. Do you find anything in it like this creative power by which it raises from nothing a new idea and, with a kind of fiat, imitates the omnipotence of its Maker—if I may be allowed so to speak—who called forth into existence all the various scenes of nature? So far from being conscious of this energy in the will, it requires as certain experience as that of which we are possessed to convince us that such extraordinary effects do ever result from a simple act of volition.

The generality of mankind never find any difficulty in accounting for the more common and familiar operations of nature, such as the descent of heavy bodies, the growth of plants, the generation of animals, or the nourishment of bodies by food. But suppose that in all these cases they perceive the very force or energy of the cause by which it is connected with its effect and is forever infallible in its operation. They acquire, by long habit, such a turn of mind that upon the appearance of the cause they immediately expect with assurance its usual attendant and hardly conceive it possible that any other event could result from it. It is only on the discovery of extraordinary phenomena, such as earthquakes, pestilence, and prodigies of any kind, that they find themselves at a loss to assign a proper cause and to explain the manner in which the effect is produced by it. It is usual for men, in such difficulties, to have recourse to some invisible intelligent principle[16] as the immediate cause of that event which surprises them and which they think cannot be accounted for from the common powers of nature. But philosophers, who carry their scrutiny a little further, immediately perceive that, even in the most familiar events, the energy of the cause is as unintelligible as in the most unusual and that we only learn by experience the frequent conjunction of objects, without being ever able to comprehend anything like connection between them. Here, then, many philosophers think themselves obliged by reason to have recourse, on all occasions,

16. *Quasi Deus ex machina.*

to the same principle which the vulgar never appeal to but in cases that appear miraculous and supernatural. They acknowledge mind and intelligence to be not only the ultimate and original cause of all things, but the immediate and sole cause of every event which appears in nature. They pretend that those objects which are commonly denominated *causes* are in reality nothing but *occasions*; and that the true and direct principle of every effect is not any power or force in nature, but a volition of the Supreme Being, who wills that such particular objects should forever be conjoined with each other. Instead of saying that one billiard ball moves another by a force which it has derived from the author of nature, it is the Deity himself, they say, who, by a particular volition, moves the second ball, being determined to this operation by the impulse of the first ball, in consequence of those general laws which he has laid down to himself in the government of the universe. But philosophers advancing still in their inquiries, discover that as we are totally ignorant of the power on which depends the mutual operation of bodies, we are no less ignorant of that power on which depends the operation of mind on body or of body on mind; nor are we able, from either our senses or our consciousness, to assign the ultimate principle in one case more than in the other. The same ignorance, therefore, reduces them to the same conclusion. They assert that the Deity is the immediate cause of the union between soul and body and that they are not the organs of sense which, being agitated by external objects, produce sensations in the mind, but that it is a particular volition of our omnipotent Maker which excites such a sensation in consequence of such a motion in the organ. In like manner, it is not any energy in the will that produces local motion in our members. It is God himself, who is pleased to second our will, in itself impotent, and to command that motion which we erroneously attribute to our own power and efficacy. Nor do philosophers stop at this conclusion. They sometimes extend the same inference to the mind itself in its internal operations. Our mental vision or conception of ideas is nothing but a revelation made to us by our Maker. When we voluntarily turn our thoughts to any object and raise up its image in the fancy, it is not the will which creates that idea, it is the universal Creator who discovers it to the mind and renders it present to us.

Thus, according to these philosophers, every thing is full of God. Not content with the principle that nothing exists but by his will, that nothing possesses any power but by his concession, they rob nature and all created beings of every power in order to render their dependence on the Deity still more sensible and immediate. They do not consider that by this theory they diminish, instead of magnifying, the grandeur of those attributes which they affect so much to celebrate. It argues surely more power in the Deity to delegate a certain degree of power to inferior creatures than to produce everything by his own immediate volition. It argues more wisdom to contrive at first the fabric of the world with such perfect foresight that, of itself and by its proper operation, it may serve all the purposes of providence than if the great Creator were obliged every moment to adjust its parts and animate by his breath all the wheels of that stupendous machine.

But if we would have a more philosophical confutation of this theory, perhaps the two following reflections may suffice.

*First*, it seems to me that this theory of the universal energy and operation of the Supreme Being is too bold ever to carry conviction with it to a man sufficiently apprised of the weakness of human reason and the narrow limits to which it is confined in all its operations. Though the chain of arguments which conduct to it were ever so logical, there must arise a strong suspicion, if not an absolute assurance, that it has carried us quite beyond the reach of our faculties when it leads to conclusions so extraordinary and so remote from common life and experience. We arrived in fairyland long before we have reached the last steps of our theory; and *there* we have no reason to trust our common methods of argument or to think that our usual analogies and probabilities have any authority. Our line is too short to fathom such immense abysses. And however we may flatter ourselves that we are guided, in every step which we take, by a kind of verisimilitude and experience, we may be assured that this fancied experience has no authority when we thus apply it to subjects that lie entirely out of the sphere of experience. But on this we shall have occasion to touch afterwards.[17]

*Secondly*, I cannot perceive any force in the arguments on which this theory is founded. We are ignorant, it is true, of the manner in which bodies operate on each other. Their force or energy is entirely incomprehensible. But are we not equally ignorant of the manner or force by which a mind, even the supreme mind, operates either on itself or on body? From where, I beseech you, do we acquire any idea of it? We have no sentiment or consciousness of this power in ourselves. We have no idea of the Supreme Being but what we learn from reflection on our own faculties. Were our ignorance, therefore, a good reason for rejecting anything, we should be led into that principle of denying all energy in the Supreme Being as much as in the grossest matter. We surely comprehend as little the operations of one as of the other. Is it more difficult to conceive that motion may arise from impulse than that it may arise from volition? All we know is our profound ignorance in both cases.[18]

---

17. Section XII.

18. I need not examine at length the *vis inertiae* which is so much talked of in the new philosophy and which is ascribed to matter. We find by experience that a body at rest or in motion continues forever in its present state until put from it by some new cause, and that a body impelled takes as much motion from the impelling body as it acquires itself. These are facts. When we call this a *vis inertiae*, we only mark these facts without pretending to have any idea of the inert power—in the same manner as, when we talk of gravity, we mean certain effects without comprehending that active power. It was never the meaning of Sir Isaac Newton to rob secondary causes of all force or energy, though some of his followers have endeavored to establish that theory upon his authority. On the contrary, that great philosopher had recourse to an ethereal active fluid to explain his universal attraction, though he was so cautious and modest as to allow that it was a mere hypothesis not to be insisted on without more experiments. I must confess that there is something in the fate of opinions a little extraordinary. Descartes insinuated that doctrine of the universal and sole efficacy of the Deity, without insisting on it. Malebranche and other Cartesians made it the foundation of all their philosophy. It had, however, no authority in England. Locke, Clarke, and Cudworth never so much as take notice of it, but suppose all along that matter has a real, though subordinate and derived power. By what means has it become so prevalent among our modern metaphysicians?

## Part II

But to hasten to a conclusion of this argument, which is already drawn out to too great a length. We have sought in vain for an idea of power or necessary connection in all the sources from which we could suppose it to be derived. It appears that in single instances of the operation of bodies we never can, by our utmost scrutiny, discover anything but one event following another, without being able to comprehend any force or power by which the cause operates or any connection between it and its supposed effect. The same difficulty occurs in contemplating the operations of mind on body, where we observe the motion of the latter to follow upon the volition of the former, but are not able to observe or conceive the tie which binds together the motion and volition, or the energy by which the mind produces this effect. The authority of the will over its own faculties and ideas is not a whit more comprehensible, so that, upon the whole, there does not appear, throughout all nature, any one instance of connection which is conceivable by us. All events seem entirely loose and separate. One event follows another, but we never can observe any tie between them. They seem *conjoined*, but never *connected*. And as we can have no idea of anything which never appeared to our outward sense or inward sentiment, the necessary conclusion *seems* to be that we have no idea of connection or power at all and that these words are absolutely without any meaning when employed in either philosophical reasonings or common life.

But there still remains one method of avoiding this conclusion and one source which we have not yet examined. When any natural object or event is presented, it is impossible for us, by any sagacity or penetration to discover, or even conjecture, without experience, what event will result from it, or to carry our foresight beyond that object which is immediately present to the memory and senses. Even after one instance or experiment where we have observed a particular event to follow upon another, we are not entitled to form a general rule or foretell what will happen in like cases, it being justly esteemed an unpardonable temerity to judge of the whole course of nature from one single experiment, however accurate or certain. But when one particular species of event has always, in all instances, been conjoined with another, we make no longer any scruple of foretelling one upon the appearance of the other and of employing that reasoning which can alone assure us of any matter of fact or existence. We then call the one object *cause*, the other *effect*. We suppose that there is some connection between them, some power in the one by which it infallibly produces the other and operates with the greatest certainty and strongest necessity.

It appears, then, that this idea of a necessary connection among events arises from a number of similar instances which occur, of the constant conjunction of these events, nor can that idea ever be suggested by any one of these instances surveyed in all possible lights and positions. But there is nothing in a number of instances, different from every single instance, which is supposed to be exactly similar, except only that after a repetition of similar instances the mind is carried by habit, upon the appearance of one event, to expect its usual attendant and to believe that it will exist. This connection, therefore, which we *feel* in the mind, this customary transition of the imagination from one object to its usual attendant, is the sentiment or impression from which we form the idea of power or necessary connection. Nothing further is in the case. Contemplate the subject on all sides, you will never find any other origin of that idea. This is the sole difference between one instance, from which we can never receive the idea of connection, and a number of similar instances by which it is suggested. The first time a man saw the communication of motion by impulse, as by the shock of two billiard balls, he could not pronounce that the one event was *connected*, but only that it was *conjoined* with the other. After he has observed several instances of this nature, he then pronounces them to be *connected*. What alteration has happened to give rise to this new idea of *connection*? Nothing but that he now *feels* these events to be *connected* in his imagination and can readily foretell the existence of one from the appearance of the other. When we say, therefore, that one object is connected with another, we mean only that they have acquired a connection in our thought and give rise to this inference by which they become

proofs of each other's existence—a conclusion, which is somewhat extraordinary, but which seems founded on sufficient evidence. Nor will its evidence be weakened by any general diffidence of the understanding or skeptical suspicion concerning every conclusion which is new and extraordinary. No conclusions can be more agreeable to skepticism than such as make discoveries concerning the weakness and narrow limits of human reason and capacity.

And what stronger instance can be produced of the surprising ignorance and weakness of the understanding than the present? For surely, if there is any relation among objects which it imports to us to know perfectly, it is that of cause and effect. On this are founded all our reasonings concerning matter of fact or existence. By means of it alone we attain any assurance concerning objects which are removed from the present testimony of our memory and senses. The only immediate utility of all sciences is to teach us how to control and regulate future events by their causes. Our thoughts and inquiries are, therefore, every moment employed about this relation; yet so imperfect are the ideas which we form concerning it that it is impossible to give any just definition of cause, except what is drawn from something extraneous and foreign to it. Similar objects are always conjoined with similar. Of this we have experience. Suitably to this experience, therefore, we may define a cause to be *an object followed by another and where all the objects similar to the first are followed by objects similar to the second*. Or, in other words, *where, if the first object had not been, the second never had existed*. The appearance of a cause always conveys the mind, by a customary transition, to the idea of the effect. Of this also we have experience. We may, therefore, suitably to this experience, form another definition of cause, and call it *an object followed by another and whose appearance always conveys the thought to that other*. But though both these definitions are drawn from circumstances foreign to the cause, we cannot remedy this inconvenience or attain any more perfect definition which may point out that circumstance in the cause which gives it a connection with its effect. We have no idea of this connection, nor even any distinct notion what it is we desire to know when we endeavor at a conception of it. We say, for instance, that the vibration of this string is the cause of this particular sound. But what do we mean by that affirmation? We mean either that *this vibration is followed by this sound, and that all similar vibrations have been followed by similar sounds,* or that *this vibration is followed by this sound and that upon the appearance of one, the mind anticipates the senses and forms immediately an idea of the other.* We may consider the relation of cause and effect in either of these two lights; but beyond these, we have no idea of it.[19]

To recapitulate, therefore, the reasonings of this section: Every idea is copied from some preceding impression or sentiment; and where we cannot find any impression, we may be certain that there is no

---

19. According to these explications and definitions, the idea of *power* is relative as much as that of *cause*; and both have a reference to an effect or some other event constantly conjoined with the former. When we consider the *unknown* circumstance of an object by which the degree or quantity of its effect is fixed and determined, we call that its power. And, accordingly, it is allowed by all philosophers that the effect is the measure of the power. But if they had any idea of power as it is in itself, why could not they measure it in itself? The dispute whether the force of a body in motion is as its velocity or the square of its velocity, this dispute I say, did not need to be decided by comparing its effects in equal or unequal times, but by a direct mensuration and comparison.

As to the frequent use of the words force, power, energy, etc. which everywhere occur in common conversation as well as in philosophy, that is no proof that we are acquainted in any instance with the connecting principle between cause and effect or can account ultimately for the production of one thing by another. These words as commonly used have very loose meanings annexed to them and their ideas are very uncertain and confused. No animal can put external bodies in motion without the sentiment of a *nisus* or endeavor and every animal has a sentiment or feeling from the stroke or blow of an external object in motion. These sensations, which are merely animal and from which we can *a priori* draw no inference, we are apt to transfer to inanimate objects and to suppose that they have some such feelings whenever they transfer or receive motion. With regard to energies which are exerted without our annexing to them any idea of communicated motion, we consider only the constant experienced conjunction of the events; and as we *feel* a customary connection between the ideas, we transfer that feeling to the objects—as nothing is more usual than to apply to external bodies every internal sensation which they occasion.

idea. In all single instances of the operation of bodies or minds, there is nothing that produces any impression, nor consequently can suggest any idea of power or necessary connection. But when many uniform instances appear and the same object is always followed by the same event, we then begin to entertain the notion of cause and connection. We then *feel* a new sentiment or impression, namely, a customary connection in the thought or imagination between one object and its usual attendant and this sentiment is the original of that idea which we seek for. For as this idea arises from a number of similar instances and not from any single instance, it must arise from that circumstance in which the number of instances differ from every individual instance. But this customary connection or transition of the imagination is the only circumstance in which they differ. In every other particular they are alike. The first instance which we saw of motion communicated by the shock of two billiard balls (to return to this obvious illustration) is exactly similar to any instance that may, at present, occur to us, except only that we could not at first *infer* one event from the other, which we are enabled to do at present, after so long a course of uniform experience. I do not know whether the reader will readily apprehend this reasoning. I am afraid that, should I multiply words about it or throw it into a greater variety of lights, it would only become more obscure and intricate. In all abstract reasonings, there is one point of view which, if we can happily hit, we shall go further towards illustrating the subject than by all the eloquence and copious expression in the world. This point of view we should endeavor to reach, and reserve the flowers of rhetoric for subjects which are more adapted to them.

## Section VIII: *Of Liberty and Necessity*

### Part I

It might reasonably be expected in questions which have been canvassed and disputed with great eagerness since the first origin of science and philosophy that the meaning of all the terms, at least, should have been agreed upon among the disputants, and our inquiries, in the course of two thousand years, been able to pass from words to the true and real subject of the controversy. For how easy may it seem to give exact definitions of the terms employed in reasoning and make these definitions, not the mere sound of words, the object of future scrutiny and examination? But if we consider the matter more narrowly, we shall be apt to draw a quite opposite conclusion. From this circumstance alone that a controversy has been long kept on foot and remains still undecided, we may presume that there is some ambiguity in the expression and that the disputants affix different ideas to the terms employed in the controversy. For as the faculties of the mind are supposed to be naturally alike in every individual—otherwise nothing could be more fruitless than to reason or dispute together—it would be impossible, if men affix the same ideas to their terms, that they could so long form different opinions of the same subject, especially when they communicate their views and each party turn themselves on all sides in search of arguments which may give them the victory over their antagonists. It is true that if men attempt the discussion of questions which lie entirely beyond the reach of human capacity, such as those concerning the origin of worlds or the economy of the intellectual system or region of spirits, they may long beat the air in their fruitless contests and never arrive at any determinate conclusion. But if the question regards any subject of common life and experience, nothing, one would think, could preserve the dispute so long undecided, but some ambiguous expressions which keep the antagonists still at a distance and hinder them from grappling with each other.

This has been the case in the long disputed question concerning liberty and necessity and to so remarkable a degree that, if I am not much mistaken, we shall find that all mankind, both learned and ignorant, have always been of the same opinion with regard to this subject and that a few intelligible definitions would immediately have put an end to the whole controversy. I admit that this dispute has been so much canvassed on all hands and has led philosophers into such a labyrinth of obscure sophistry that it is no wonder if a sensible reader indulge his ease so far as to turn a deaf ear to the proposal of such a question from which he can expect neither instruction nor

entertainment. But the state of the argument here proposed may, perhaps, serve to renew his attention, as it has more novelty, promises at least some decision of the controversy, and will not much disturb his ease by any intricate or obscure reasoning.

I hope, therefore, to make it appear that all men have ever agreed in the doctrine both of necessity and of liberty, according to any reasonable sense which can be put on these terms, and that the whole controversy has up to now turned merely upon words. We shall begin with examining the doctrine of necessity.

It is universally allowed that matter, in all its operations, is actuated by a necessary force and that every natural effect is so precisely determined by the energy of its cause that no other effect, in such particular circumstances, could possibly have resulted from it. The degree and direction of every motion are, by the laws of nature, prescribed with such exactness that a living creature may as soon arise from the shock of two bodies as motion in any other degree or direction than what is actually produced by it. Would we, therefore, form a just and precise idea of *necessity*, we must consider from where that idea arises when we apply it to the operation of bodies.

It seems evident that, if all the scenes of nature were continually shifted in such a manner that no two events bore any resemblance to each other, but every object was entirely new, without any similitude to whatever had been seen before, we should never, in that case, have attained the least idea of necessity or of a connection among these objects. We might say, upon such a supposition, that one object or event has followed another, not that one was produced by the other. The relation of cause and effect must be utterly unknown to mankind. Inference and reasoning concerning the operations of nature would, from that moment, be at an end; and the memory and senses remain the only canals by which the knowledge of any real existence could possibly have access to the mind. Our idea, therefore, of necessity and causation arises entirely from the uniformity observable in the operations of nature, where similar objects are constantly conjoined together and the mind is determined by custom to infer the one from the appearance of the other. These two circumstances form the whole of that necessity which we ascribe to matter. Beyond the constant *conjunction* of similar objects and the consequent *inference* from one to the other, we have no notion of any necessity or connection.

If it appears, therefore, that all mankind have ever allowed, without any doubt or hesitation, that these two circumstances take place in the voluntary actions of men and in the operations of mind, it must follow that all mankind have ever agreed in the doctrine of necessity and that they have up to now disputed merely for not understanding each other.

As to the first circumstance, the constant and regular conjunction of similar events, we may possibly satisfy ourselves by the following considerations. It is universally acknowledged that there is a great uniformity among the actions of men in all nations and ages and that human nature remains still the same in its principles and operations. The same motives always produce the same actions. The same events follow from the same causes. Ambition, avarice, self-love, vanity, friendship, generosity, public spirit—these passions, mixed in various degrees and distributed through society, have been, from the beginning of the world, and still are the source of all the actions and enterprises which have ever been observed among mankind. Would you know the sentiments, inclinations, and course of life of the Greeks and Romans? Study well the temper and actions of the French and English. You cannot be much mistaken in transferring to the former *most* of the observations which you have made with regard to the latter. Mankind are so much the same, in all times and places, that history informs us of nothing new or strange in this particular. Its chief use is only to discover the constant and universal principles of human nature by showing men in all varieties of circumstances and situations and furnishing us with materials from which we may form our observations and become acquainted with the regular springs of human action and behavior. These records of wars, intrigues, factions, and revolutions are so many collections of experiments by which the politician or moral philosopher fixes the principles of his science, in the same manner as the physician or natural philosopher becomes acquainted with the nature of plants, minerals, and other external objects by

the experiments which he forms concerning them. Nor are the earth, water, and other elements examined by Aristotle and Hippocrates more like to those which at present lie under our observation than the men described by Polybius and Tacitus are to those who now govern the world.

Should a traveler, returning from a far country, bring us an account of men, wholly different from any with whom we were ever acquainted, men, who were entirely divested of avarice, ambition, or revenge, who knew no pleasure but friendship, generosity, and public spirit, we should immediately, from these circumstances, detect the falsehood and prove him a liar with the same certainty as if he had stuffed his narration with stories of centaurs and dragons, miracles and prodigies. And if we would explode any forgery in history, we cannot make use of a more convincing argument than to prove that the actions ascribed to any person are directly contrary to the course of nature and that no human motives, in such circumstances, could ever induce him to such a conduct. The veracity of Quintus Curtius is as much to be suspected when he describes the supernatural courage of Alexander by which he was hurried on singly to attack multitudes, as when he describes his supernatural force and activity by which he was able to resist them. So readily and universally do we acknowledge a uniformity in human motives and actions as well as in the operations of body.

Hence, likewise, the benefit of that experience acquired by long life and a variety of business and company, in order to instruct us in the principles of human nature and regulate our future conduct as well as speculation. By means of this guide we mount up to the knowledge of men's inclinations and motives from their actions, expressions, and even gestures, and again descend to the interpretation of their actions from our knowledge of their motives and inclinations. The general observations, treasured up by a course of experience, give us the clue of human nature and teach us to unravel all its intricacies. Pretexts and appearances no longer deceive us. Public declarations pass for the specious coloring of a cause. And though virtue and honor are allowed their proper weight and authority, that perfect disinterestedness, so often pretended to, is never expected in multitudes and parties, seldom in their leaders, and scarcely even in individuals of any rank or station. But were there no uniformity in human actions and were every experiment which we could form of this kind irregular and anomalous, it would be impossible to collect any general observations concerning mankind and no experience, however accurately digested by reflection, would ever serve to any purpose. Why is the aged husband more skillful in his calling than the young beginner, but because there is a certain uniformity in the operation of the sun, rain, and earth towards the production of vegetables, and experience teaches the old practitioner the rules by which this operation is governed and directed?

We must not, however, expect that this uniformity of human actions should be carried to such a length as that all men, in the same circumstances, will always act precisely in the same manner, without making any allowance for the diversity of characters, prejudices, and opinions. Such a uniformity in every particular is found in no part of nature. On the contrary, from observing the variety of conduct in different men, we are enabled to form a greater variety of maxims which still suppose a degree of uniformity and regularity.

Are the manners of men different in different ages and countries? We learn from this the great force of custom and education which mold the human mind from its infancy and form it into a fixed and established character. Is the behavior and conduct of the one sex very unlike that of the other? It is from this we become acquainted with the different characters which nature has impressed upon the sexes and which she preserves with constancy and regularity. Are the actions of the same person much diversified in the different periods of his life from infancy to old age? This affords room for many general observations concerning the gradual change of our sentiments and inclinations and the different maxims which prevail in the different ages of human creatures. Even the characters which are peculiar to each individual have a uniformity in their influence; otherwise our acquaintance with the persons and our observation of their conduct could never teach us their dispositions or serve to direct our behavior with regard to them.

I grant it possible to find some actions which seem to have no regular connection with any known motives and are exceptions to all the measures of conduct which have ever been established for the government of men. But if we would willingly know what judgment should be formed of such irregular and extraordinary actions, we may consider the sentiments commonly entertained with regard to those irregular events which appear in the course of nature and the operations of external objects. All causes are not conjoined to their usual effects with like uniformity. An artificer who handles only dead matter may be disappointed of his aim as well as the politician who directs the conduct of sensible and intelligent agents.

The vulgar, who take things according to their first appearance, attribute the uncertainty of events to such an uncertainty in the causes as makes the latter often fail of their usual influence, though they meet with no impediment in their operation. But philosophers, observing that almost in every part of nature there is contained a vast variety of springs and principles which are hid by reason of their minuteness or remoteness, find that it is at least possible the contrariety of events may not proceed from any contingency in the cause but from the secret operation of contrary causes. This possibility is converted into certainty by further observation, when they remark that, upon an exact scrutiny, a contrariety of effects always betrays a contrariety of causes and proceeds from their mutual opposition. A peasant can give no better reason for the stopping of any clock or watch than to say that it does not commonly go right. But an artist easily perceives that the same force in the spring or pendulum always has the same influence on the wheels, but fails of its usual effect, perhaps by reason of a grain of dust which puts a stop to the whole movement. From the observation of several parallel instances, philosophers form a maxim that the connection between all causes and effects is equally necessary and that its seeming uncertainty in some instances proceeds from the secret opposition of contrary causes.

Thus, for instance, in the human body, when the usual symptoms of health or sickness disappoint our expectation, when medicines do not operate with their wonted powers, when irregular events follow from any particular cause, the philosopher and physician are not surprised at the matter, nor are ever tempted to deny, in general, the necessity and uniformity of those principles by which the animal economy is conducted. They know that a human body is a mighty complicated machine, that many secret powers lurk in it which are altogether beyond our comprehension, that to us it must often appear very uncertain in its operations, and that therefore the irregular events which outwardly discover themselves can be no proof that the laws of nature are not observed with the greatest regularity in its internal operations and government.

The philosopher, if he is consistent, must apply the same reasoning to the actions and volitions of intelligent agents. The most irregular and unexpected resolutions of men may frequently be accounted for by those who know every particular circumstance of their character and situation. A person of an obliging disposition gives a peevish answer; but he has a toothache or has not dined. A stupid fellow discovers an uncommon alacrity in his carriage; but he has met with a sudden piece of good fortune. Or even when an action, as sometimes happens, cannot be particularly accounted for either by the person himself or by others, we know, in general, that the characters of men are to a certain degree inconstant and irregular. This is, in a manner, the constant character of human nature, though it is applicable in a more particular manner to some persons who have no fixed rule for their conduct, but proceed in a continued course of caprice and inconstancy. The internal principles and motives may operate in a uniform manner, notwithstanding these seeming irregularities—in the same manner as the winds, rain, clouds, and other variations of the weather are supposed to be governed by steady principles, though not easily discoverable by human sagacity and inquiry.

Thus, it appears not only that the conjunction between motives and voluntary actions is as regular and uniform as that between the cause and effect in any part of nature, but also that this regular conjunction has been universally acknowledged among mankind and has never been the subject of dispute in either philosophy or common life. Now, as it is from past experience that we draw all inferences concerning the future and as we conclude that objects will always be conjoined together which we find to have always been conjoined, it may seem superfluous to prove that this experienced uniformity in human actions is a source from which we draw *inferences* concerning them. But in order to throw the argument into a greater variety of lights, we shall also insist, though briefly, on this latter topic.

The mutual dependence of men is so great in all societies that scarcely any human action is entirely complete in itself or is performed without some reference to the actions of others, which are requisite to make it answer fully the intention of the agent. The poorest artificer who labors alone expects at least the protection of the magistrate to ensure him the enjoyment of the fruits of his labor. He also expects that, when he carries his goods to market and offers them at a reasonable price, he shall find purchasers and shall be able, by the money he acquires, to engage others to supply him with those commodities which are requisite for his subsistence. In proportion as men extend their dealings and render their intercourse with others more complicated, they always comprehend in their schemes of life a greater variety of voluntary actions which they expect, from the proper motives, to cooperate with their own. In all these conclusions they take their measures from past experience in the same manner as in their reasonings concerning external objects, and firmly believe that men as well as all the elements are to continue in their operations the same that they have ever found them. A manufacturer reckons upon the labor of his servants for the execution of any work as much as upon the tools which he employs and would be equally surprised were his expectations disappointed. In short, this experimental inference and reasoning concerning the actions of others enters so much into human life that no man, while awake, is ever a moment without employing it. Have we not reason, therefore, to affirm that all mankind have always agreed in the doctrine of necessity, according to the foregoing definition and explication of it?

Nor have philosophers ever entertained a different opinion from the people in this particular. For not to mention that almost every action of their life supposes that opinion, there are even few of the speculative parts of learning to which it is not essential. What would become of *history* had we not a dependence on the veracity of the historian, according to the experience which we have had of mankind? How could *politics* be a science, if laws and forms of government had not a uniform influence upon society? Where would be the foundation of *morals*, if particular characters had no certain or determinate power to produce particular sentiments and if these sentiments had no constant operation on actions? And with what pretense could we employ our *criticism* upon any poet or polite author, if we could not pronounce the conduct and sentiments of his actors either natural or unnatural to such characters and in such circumstances? It seems almost impossible, therefore, to engage in either science or action of any kind without acknowledging the doctrine of necessity and this *inference* from motives to voluntary actions, from characters to conduct.

And indeed, when we consider how aptly *natural* and *moral* evidence link together and form only one chain of argument, we shall make no scruple to allow that they are of the same nature and derived from the same principles. A prisoner who has neither money nor interest discovers the impossibility of his escape as well when he considers the obstinacy of the jailer as the walls and bars with which he is surrounded and in all attempts for his freedom chooses to work upon the stone and iron of the one rather than upon the inflexible nature of the other. The same prisoner, when conducted to the scaffold, foresees his death as certainly from the constancy and fidelity of his guards as from the operation of the ax or wheel. His mind runs along a certain train of ideas: the refusal of the soldiers to consent to his escape; the action of the executioner; the separation of the head and body; bleeding, convulsive motions, and death. Here is a connected chain of natural causes and voluntary actions, but the mind feels no difference between them

in passing from one link to another, nor is less certain of the future event than if it were connected with the objects present to the memory or senses by a train of causes cemented together by what we are pleased to call a *physical* necessity. The same experienced union has the same effect on the mind, whether the united objects are motives, volition, and actions, or figure and motion. We may change the names of things, but their nature and their operation on the understanding never change.

Were a man whom I know to be honest and opulent and with whom I live in intimate friendship to come into my house where I am surrounded with my servants, I rest assured that he is not to stab me before he leaves it in order to rob me of my silver standish;[20] and I no more suspect this event than the falling of the house itself which is new and solidly built and founded. — *But he may have been seized with a sudden and unknown frenzy.* — So may a sudden earthquake arise, and shake and tumble my house about my ears. I shall therefore change the suppositions. I shall say that I know with certainty that he is not to put his hand into the fire and hold it there until it is consumed. And this event I think I can foretell with the same assurance as that, if he threw himself out at the window and met with no obstruction, he will not remain a moment suspended in the air. No suspicion of an unknown frenzy can give the least possibility to the former event which is so contrary to all the known principles of human nature. A man who at noon leaves his purse full of gold on the pavement at Charing Cross may as well expect that it will fly away like a feather as that he will find it untouched an hour after. Over one half of human reasonings contain inferences of a similar nature, attended with more or less degrees of certainty, proportioned to our experience of the usual conduct of mankind in such particular situations.

I have frequently considered what could possibly be the reason why all mankind, though they have ever, without hesitation, acknowledged the doctrine of necessity in their whole practice and reasoning, have yet discovered such a reluctance to acknowledge

---

20. [A stand containing ink, pens, and other writing materials and accessories, that is, an inkstand or an inkpot.]

it in words and have rather shown a propensity, in all ages, to profess the contrary opinion. The matter, I think, may be accounted for after the following manner. If we examine the operations of body and the production of effects from their causes, we shall find that all our faculties can never carry us further in our knowledge of this relation than barely to observe that particular objects are *constantly conjoined* together and that the mind is carried, by a *customary transition*, from the appearance of one to the belief of the other. But though this conclusion concerning human ignorance is the result of the strictest scrutiny of this subject, men still entertain a strong propensity to believe that they penetrate further into the powers of nature and perceive something like a necessary connection between the cause and the effect. When again they turn their reflections towards the operations of their own minds and *feel* no such connection of the motive and the action, they are apt to suppose from this that there is a difference between the effects which result from material force and those which arise from thought and intelligence. But being once convinced that we know nothing further of causation of any kind than merely the *constant conjunction* of objects and the consequent *inference* of the mind from one to another and finding that these two circumstances are universally allowed to have place in voluntary actions, we may be more easily led to admit the same necessity common to all causes. And though this reasoning may contradict the systems of many philosophers in ascribing necessity to the determinations of the will, we shall find, upon reflection, that they dissent from it in words only, not in their real sentiment. Necessity, according to the sense in which it is here taken, has never yet been rejected, nor can ever, I think, be rejected by any philosopher. It may only, perhaps, be pretended that the mind can perceive in the operations of matter some further connection between the cause and effect and a connection that has no place in the voluntary actions of intelligent beings. Now whether it is so or not can only appear upon examination, and it is incumbent on these philosophers to make good their assertion by defining or describing that necessity and pointing it out to us in the operations of material causes.

It would seem, indeed, that men begin at the wrong end of this question concerning liberty and necessity when they enter upon it by examining the faculties of the soul, the influence of the understanding, and the operations of the will. Let them first discuss a more simple question, namely, the operations of body and of brute unintelligent matter, and try whether they can there form any idea of causation and necessity, except that of a constant conjunction of objects and subsequent inference of the mind from one to another. If these circumstances form, in reality, the whole of that necessity which we conceive in matter and if these circumstances are also universally acknowledged to take place in the operations of the mind, the dispute is at an end—at least must be admitted to be merely verbal thereafter. But as long as we will rashly suppose that we have some further idea of necessity and causation in the operations of external objects, at the same time that we can find nothing further in the voluntary actions of the mind, there is no possibility of bringing the question to any determinate issue while we proceed upon so erroneous a supposition. The only method of undeceiving us is to mount up higher, to examine the narrow extent of science when applied to material causes, and to convince ourselves that all we know of them is the constant conjunction and inference above mentioned. We may, perhaps, find that it is with difficulty we are induced to fix such narrow limits to human understanding. But we can afterwards find no difficulty when we come to apply this doctrine to the actions of the will. For as it is evident that these have a regular conjunction with motives and circumstances and characters and as we always draw inferences from one to the other, we must be obliged to acknowledge in words that necessity which we have already avowed in every deliberation of our lives and in every step of our conduct and behavior.[21]

21. The prevalence of the doctrine of liberty may be accounted for from another cause, namely, a false sensation or seeming experience which we have, or may have, of liberty or indifference in many of our actions. The necessity of any action, whether of matter or of mind, is not, properly speaking, a quality in the agent, but in any thinking or intelligent being who

But to proceed in this reconciling project with regard to the question of liberty and necessity—the most contentious question of metaphysics, the most contentious science—it will not require many words to prove that all mankind have ever agreed in the doctrine of liberty as well as in that of necessity, and that the whole dispute, in this respect also, has been up to now merely verbal. For what is meant by liberty when applied to voluntary actions? We cannot surely mean that actions have so little connection with motives, inclinations, and circumstances that one does not follow with a certain degree of uniformity from the other and that one affords no inference by which we can conclude the existence of the other. For these are plain and acknowledged matters of fact. By liberty, then, we can only mean *a power of acting or not acting according to the determinations of the will*—that is, if we choose to remain at rest, we may; if we choose to move, we also may. Now this hypothetical liberty is universally allowed to belong to everyone who is not a prisoner and in chains. Here then is no subject of dispute.

Whatever definition we may give of liberty, we should be careful to observe two requisite circumstances: *first*, that it is consistent with plain matter of fact; *secondly*, that it is consistent with itself. If we

observe these circumstances and render our definition intelligible, I am persuaded that all mankind will be found of one opinion with regard to it.

It is universally allowed that nothing exists without a cause of its existence, and that chance, when strictly examined, is a mere negative word and does not mean any real power which has anywhere a being in nature. But it is pretended that some causes are necessary, some not necessary. Here then is the advantage of definitions. Let anyone *define* a cause without comprehending, as a part of the definition, a *necessary connection* with its effect, and let him show distinctly the origin of the idea expressed by the definition, and I shall readily give up the whole controversy. But if the foregoing explication of the matter is received, this must be absolutely impracticable. Had not objects a regular conjunction with each other, we should never have entertained any notion of cause and effect and this regular conjunction produces that inference of the understanding which is the only connection that we can have any comprehension of. Whoever attempts a definition of cause exclusive of these circumstances will be obliged to employ either unintelligible terms or such as are synonymous to the term which he endeavors to define.[22] And if the definition above mentioned is admitted,

---

may consider the action; and it consists chiefly in the determination of his thoughts to infer the existence of that action from some preceding objects—as liberty when opposed to necessity is nothing but the want of that determination and a certain looseness or indifference which we feel in passing or not passing from the idea of one object to that of any succeeding one. Now we may observe that, though, in *reflecting* on human actions, we seldom feel such a looseness or indifference, but are commonly able to infer them with considerable certainty from their motives and from the dispositions of the agent, yet it frequently happens that, in *performing* the actions themselves, we are sensible of something like it. And as all resembling objects are readily taken for each other, this has been employed as a demonstrative and even intuitive proof of human liberty. We feel that our actions are subject to our will on most occasions, and imagine we feel that the will itself is subject to nothing, because, when by a denial of it we are provoked to try, we feel that it moves easily every way and produces an image of itself (or a *Velleity*, as it is called in the schools), even on that side on which it did not settle. This image or faint motion, we persuade ourselves, could, at

that time, have been completed into the thing itself, because, should that be denied, we find upon a second trial that, at present, it can. We do not consider that the fantastical desire of showing liberty is here the motive of our actions. And it seems certain that, however we may imagine we feel a liberty within ourselves, a spectator can commonly infer our actions from our motives and character and even where he cannot, he concludes in general that he might, were he perfectly acquainted with every circumstance of our situation and temper and the most secret springs of our complexion and disposition. Now this is the very essence of necessity according to the foregoing doctrine.

22. Thus, if a cause is defined *that which produces anything*; it is easy to observe that producing is synonymous to causing. In like manner, if a cause is defined *that by which anything exists*; this is liable to the same objection. For what is meant by these words, *by which*? Had it been said that a cause is *that* after which *anything constantly exists*; we should have understood the terms. For this is, indeed, all we know of the matter. And this constancy forms the very essence of necessity, nor have we any other idea of it.

liberty, when opposed to necessity, not to constraint, is the same thing with chance, which is universally allowed to have no existence.

## Part II

There is no method of reasoning more common and yet none more blamable than in philosophical disputes to endeavor the refutation of any hypothesis by a pretense of its dangerous consequences to religion and morality. When any opinion leads to absurdities, it is certainly false; but it is not certain that an opinion is false because it is of dangerous consequence. Such topics, therefore, ought entirely to be forborne, as serving nothing to the discovery of truth, but only to make the person of an antagonist odious. This I observe in general, without pretending to draw any advantage from it. I frankly submit to an examination of this kind and shall venture to affirm that the doctrines both of necessity and of liberty, as above explained, are not only consistent with morality, but are absolutely essential to its support.

Necessity may be defined two ways, conformably to the two definitions of cause of which it makes an essential part. It consists either in the constant conjunction of like objects or in the inference of the understanding from one object to another. Now necessity, in both these senses (which, indeed, are at bottom the same), has universally, though tacitly, in the schools, in the pulpit, and in common life been allowed to belong to the will of man and no one has ever pretended to deny that we can draw inferences concerning human actions and that those inferences are founded on the experienced union of like actions with like motives, inclinations, and circumstances. The only particular in which anyone can differ is that either, perhaps, he will refuse to give the name of necessity to this property of human actions—but as long as the meaning is understood I hope the word can do no harm—or that he will maintain it possible to discover something further in the operations of matter. But this, it must be acknowledged, can be of no consequence to morality or religion, whatever it may be to natural philosophy or metaphysics. We may here be mistaken in asserting that there is no idea of any other necessity or

connection in the actions of body. But surely we ascribe nothing to the actions of the mind but what everyone does and must readily allow of. We change no circumstance in the received orthodox system with regard to the will, but only in that with regard to material objects and causes. Nothing, therefore, can be more innocent at least than this doctrine.

All laws being founded on rewards and punishments, it is supposed as a fundamental principle that these motives have a regular and uniform influence on the mind and both produce the good and prevent the evil actions. We may give to this influence what name we please; but, as it is usually conjoined with the action, it must be esteemed a *cause* and be looked upon as an instance of that necessity which we would here establish.

The only proper object of hatred or vengeance is a person or creature endowed with thought and consciousness, and when any criminal or injurious actions excite that passion, it is only by their relation to the person or connection with him. Actions are, by their very nature, temporary and perishing, and where they do not proceed from some cause in the character and disposition of the person who performed them, they can redound to neither his honor if good nor to his infamy if evil. The actions themselves may be blamable; they may be contrary to all the rules of morality and religion. But the person is not answerable for them and, as they proceeded from nothing in him that is durable and constant and leave nothing of that nature behind them, it is impossible he can, upon their account, become the object of punishment or vengeance. According to the principle, therefore, which denies necessity, and consequently causes, a man is as pure and untainted after having committed the most horrid crime as at the first moment of his birth, nor is his character any way concerned in his actions, since they are not derived from it, and the wickedness of the one can never be used as a proof of the depravity of the other.

Men are not blamed for such actions as they perform ignorantly and casually, whatever may be the consequences. Why? But because the principles of these actions are only momentary and terminate in them alone. Men are less blamed for such actions as they perform hastily and unpremeditatedly than for such as proceed from deliberation. For what reason? But because a hasty temper, though a constant cause or principle in the mind, operates only by intervals and does not infect the whole character. Again, repentance wipes off every crime, if attended with a reformation of life and manners. How is this to be accounted for? But by asserting that actions render a person criminal merely as they are proofs of criminal principles in the mind; and when, by an alteration of these principles, they cease to be just proofs, they likewise cease to be criminal. But, except upon the doctrine of necessity, they never were just proofs and consequently never were criminal.

It will be equally easy to prove, and from the same arguments, that *liberty*, according to that definition above mentioned, in which all men agree, is also essential to morality and that no human actions, where it is wanting, are susceptible of any moral qualities or can be the objects either of approbation or dislike. For as actions are objects of our moral sentiment only so far as they are indications of the internal character, passions, and affections, it is impossible that they can give rise to either praise or blame where they do not proceed from these principles, but are derived altogether from external violence.

I do not pretend to have obviated or removed all objections to this theory with regard to necessity and liberty. I can foresee other objections derived from topics which have not here been treated of. It may be said, for instance, that if voluntary actions are subjected to the same laws of necessity with the operations of matter, there is a continued chain of necessary causes, pre-ordained and pre-determined, reaching from the original cause of all to every single volition of every human creature. No contingency anywhere in the universe, no indifference, no liberty. While we act, we are at the same time acted upon. The ultimate Author of all our volitions is the Creator of the world, who first bestowed motion on this immense machine and placed all beings in that particular position from which every subsequent event, by an inevitable necessity, must result. Human actions, therefore, either can have no moral turpitude at all, as proceeding from so good a cause or, if they

have any turpitude, they must involve our Creator in the same guilt, while he is acknowledged to be their ultimate cause and author. For as a man who fired a mine is answerable for all the consequences, whether the train he employed is long or short, so wherever a continued chain of necessary causes is fixed, that Being, either finite or infinite, who produces the first is likewise the author of all the rest and must both bear the blame and acquire the praise which belong to them. Our clear and unalterable ideas of morality establish this rule upon unquestionable reasons when we examine the consequences of any human action and these reasons must still have greater force when applied to the volitions and intentions of a Being infinitely wise and powerful. Ignorance or impotence may be pleaded for so limited a creature as man, but those imperfections have no place in our Creator. He foresaw, he ordained, he intended all those actions of men which we so rashly pronounce criminal. And we must therefore conclude either that they are not criminal or that the Deity, not man, is accountable for them. But as either of these positions is absurd and impious, it follows that the doctrine from which they are deduced cannot possibly be true, as being liable to all the same objections. An absurd consequence, if necessary, proves the original doctrine to be absurd in the same manner as criminal actions render criminal the original cause, if the connection between them is necessary and inevitable.

This objection consists of two parts, which we shall examine separately: *First*, that if human actions can be traced up, by a necessary chain, to the Deity, they can never be criminal, on account of the infinite perfection of that Being from whom they are derived and who can intend nothing but what is altogether good and laudable. Or, *secondly*, if they are criminal, we must retract the attribute of perfection which we ascribe to the Deity and must acknowledge him to be the ultimate author of guilt and moral turpitude in all his creatures.

The answer to the first objection seems obvious and convincing. There are many philosophers who, after an exact scrutiny of all the phenomena of nature, conclude that the whole, considered as one system, is, in every period of its existence, ordered with perfect benevolence, and that the utmost possible happiness will, in the end, result to all created beings without any mixture of positive or absolute ill and misery. Every physical ill, they say, makes an essential part of this benevolent system and could not possibly be removed, even by the Deity himself, considered as a wise agent, without giving entrance to greater ill or excluding greater good which will result from it. From this theory some philosophers, and the ancient *Stoics* among the rest, derived a topic of consolation under all afflictions, while they taught their pupils that those ills under which they labored were in reality goods to the universe and that to an enlarged view which could comprehend the whole system of nature every event became an object of joy and exultation. But though this topic is specious and sublime, it was soon found in practice weak and ineffectual. You would surely more irritate than appease a man lying under the racking pains of gout by preaching up to him the rectitude of those general laws which produced the malignant humors in his body and led them through the proper canals to the sinews and nerves, where they now excite such acute torments. These enlarged views may, for a moment, please the imagination of a speculative man who is placed in ease and security, but neither can they dwell with constancy on his mind, even though undisturbed by the emotions of pain or passion, much less can they maintain their ground when attacked by such powerful antagonists. The affections take a narrower and more natural survey of their object, and, by an economy more suitable to the infirmity of human minds, regard alone the beings around us, and are actuated by such events as appear good or ill to the private system.

The case is the same with *moral* as with *physical* ill. It cannot reasonably be supposed that those remote considerations which are found of so little efficacy with regard to one will have a more powerful influence with regard to the other. The mind of man is so formed by nature that, upon the appearance of certain characters, dispositions, and actions, it immediately feels the sentiment of approbation or blame; nor are there any emotions more essential to its frame and constitution. The characters which engage our approbation are chiefly such as contribute to the peace and security of human society, as the characters which excite blame are chiefly such as tend to public detriment and disturbance. From this it may reasonably be presumed that the moral sentiments arise, either mediately or immediately, from a reflection of these opposite interests. What though philosophical meditations establish a different opinion or conjecture that everything is right with regard to the whole, and that the qualities which disturb society are, in the main, as beneficial and are as suitable to the primary intention of nature as those which more directly promote its happiness and welfare? Are such remote and uncertain speculations able to counterbalance the sentiments which arise from the natural and immediate view of the objects? A man who is robbed of a considerable sum, does he find his vexation for the loss any way diminished by these sublime reflections? Why then should his moral resentment against the crime be supposed incompatible with them? Or why should not the acknowledgment of a real distinction between vice and virtue be reconcilable to all speculative systems of philosophy, as well as that of a real distinction between personal beauty and deformity? Both these distinctions are founded in the natural sentiments of the human mind. And these sentiments are not to be controlled or altered by any philosophical theory or speculation whatsoever.

The *second* objection does not admit of so easy and satisfactory an answer, nor is it possible to explain distinctly how the Deity can be the mediate cause of all the actions of men without being the author of sin and moral turpitude. These are mysteries which mere natural and unassisted reason is very unfit to handle; and whatever system she embraces, she must find herself involved in inextricable difficulties, and even contradictions, at every step which she takes with regard to such subjects. To reconcile the indifference and contingency of human actions with prescience or to defend absolute decrees and yet free the Deity from being the author of sin has been found up to now to exceed all the power of philosophy. Happy, if she be thence sensible of her temerity when she pries into these sublime mysteries and, leaving a scene so full of obscurities and perplexities, return with suitable modesty to her true and proper province, the examination of common life, where she will find difficulties enough to employ her inquiries without launching into so boundless an ocean of doubt, uncertainty, and contradiction!

## Section IX: *Of the Reason of Animals*

All our reasonings concerning matter of fact are founded on a species of analogy which leads us to expect from any cause the same events which we have observed to result from similar causes. Where the causes are entirely similar, the analogy is perfect and the inference drawn from it is regarded as certain and conclusive. Nor does any man ever entertain a doubt where he sees a piece of iron that it will have weight and cohesion of parts, as in all other instances which have ever fallen under his observation. But where the objects do not have so exact a similarity, the analogy is less perfect and the inference is less conclusive, though still it has some force in proportion to the degree of similarity and resemblance. The anatomical observations formed upon one animal are, by this species of reasoning, extended to all animals; and it is certain that, when the circulation of the blood, for instance, is clearly proved to have place in one creature, as a frog, or fish, it forms a strong presumption that the same principle has place in all. These analogical observations may be carried further, even to this science of which we are now treating, and any theory by which we explain the operations of the understanding or the origin and connection of the passions in man will acquire additional authority, if we find that the same theory is requisite to explain the same phenomena in all other animals. We shall make trial of this with regard to the hypothesis by which we have, in the foregoing discourse, endeavored to account for all experimental reasoning and it is hoped that this new point of view will serve to confirm all our former observations.

*First*, it seems evident that animals, as well as men, learn many things from experience and infer that the same events will always follow from the same causes. By this principle they become acquainted with the more obvious properties of external objects and gradually, from their birth, treasure up a knowledge of the nature of fire, water, earth, stones, heights, depths, etc., and of the effects which result from their operation. The ignorance and inexperience of the young are here plainly distinguishable from the cunning and sagacity of the old, who have learned, by long observation, to avoid what hurt them and to pursue what gave ease or pleasure. A horse that has been accustomed to the field becomes acquainted with the proper height which he can leap, and will never attempt what exceeds his force and ability. An old greyhound will trust the more fatiguing part of the chase to the younger and will place himself so as to meet the hare in her doubles; nor are the conjectures which he forms on this occasion founded in anything but his observation and experience.

This is still more evident from the effects of discipline and education on animals who, by the proper application of rewards and punishments, may be taught any course of action the most contrary to their natural instincts and propensities. Is it not experience which renders a dog apprehensive of pain when you menace him or lift up the whip to beat him? Is it not even experience which makes him answer to his name and infer, from such an arbitrary sound, that you mean him rather than any of his fellows and intend to call him when you pronounce it in a certain manner and with a certain tone and accent?

In all these cases we may observe that the animal infers some fact beyond what immediately strikes his senses and that this inference is altogether founded on past experience, while the creature expects from the present object the same consequences which it has always found in its observation to result from similar objects.

*Secondly*, it is impossible that this inference of the animal can be founded on any process of argument or reasoning by which he concludes that like events must follow like objects and that the course of nature will always be regular in its operations. For if there are in reality any arguments of this nature, they surely lie too abstruse for the observation of such imperfect understandings, since it may well employ the utmost care and attention of a philosophic genius to discover and observe them. Animals, therefore, are not guided in these inferences by reasoning. Neither are children. Neither are the generality of mankind in their ordinary actions and conclusions. Neither are philosophers themselves, who, in all the active parts of life, are in the main the same with the vulgar and are governed by the same maxims. Nature must have provided some other principle, of more ready and more general use and application; nor can an operation of such immense consequence in life as that of inferring effects from causes be trusted to the uncertain process of reasoning and argumentation. Were this doubtful with regard to men, it seems to admit of no question with regard to the brute creation; and the conclusion being once firmly established in the one, we have a strong presumption, from all the rules of analogy, that it ought to be universally admitted without any exception or reserve. It is custom alone which engages animals from every object that strikes their senses to infer its usual attendant and carries their imagination from the appearance of the one to conceive the other in that particular manner which we denominate *belief*. No other explication can be given of this operation, in all the higher as well as lower classes of sensitive beings which fall under our notice and observation.[23]

But though animals learn many parts of their knowledge from observation, there are also many parts of it which they derive from the original hand of nature, which much exceed the share of capacity they possess on ordinary occasions and in which they improve little or nothing by the longest practice and experience. These we denominate instincts and are so apt to admire as something very extraordinary and inexplicable by all the disquisitions of human understanding. But our wonder will perhaps cease or diminish when we consider that the experimental reasoning itself which we possess in common with beasts and on which the whole conduct of life depends is nothing but a species of instinct or mechanical power that acts in us unknown to ourselves and in its chief operations is not directed by any such relations or comparisons of ideas as are the proper objects of our intellectual faculties. Though the instinct is different, yet still it is an instinct which teaches a man to avoid the fire, as much as that which teaches a bird, with such exactness, the art of incubation and the whole economy and order of its nursery.

---

23. Since all reasoning concerning facts or causes is derived merely from custom, it may be asked how it happens that men so much surpass animals in reasoning and one man so much surpasses another? Does not the same custom have the same influence on all?

We shall here endeavor briefly to explain the great difference in human understandings. After this the reason of the difference between men and animals will easily be comprehended.

1. When we have lived any time and have been accustomed to the uniformity of nature, we acquire a general habit by which we always transfer the known to the unknown and conceive the latter to resemble the former. By means of this general habitual principle, we regard even one experiment as the foundation of reasoning and expect a similar event with some degree of certainty, where the experiment has been made accurately and free from all foreign circumstances. It is therefore considered as a matter of great importance to observe the consequences of things; and as one man may very much surpass another in attention and memory and observation, this will make a very great difference in their reasoning.

2. Where there is a complication of causes to produce any effect, one mind may be much larger than another and better able to comprehend the whole system of objects and to infer justly their consequences.

3. One man is able to carry on a chain of consequences to a greater length than another.

4. Few men can think long without running into a confusion of ideas and mistaking one for another; and there are various degrees of this infirmity.

5. The circumstance on which the effect depends is frequently involved in other circumstances which are foreign and extrinsic. The separation of it often requires great attention, accuracy, and subtlety.

6. The forming of general maxims from particular observation is a very nice operation; and nothing is more usual from haste or a narrowness of mind, which does not see on all sides, than to commit mistakes in this particular.

7. When we reason from analogies, the man who has the greater experience or the greater promptitude of suggesting analogies will be the better reasoner.

8. Biases from prejudice, education, passion, party, etc. hang more upon one mind than another.

9. After we have acquired a confidence in human testimony, books and conversation enlarge much more the sphere of one man's experience and thought than those of another.

It would be easy to discover many other circumstances that make a difference in the understandings of men.

## Section X: *Of Miracles*

### Part I

There is, in Dr. Tillotson's writings, an argument against the *real presence*[24] which is as concise and elegant and strong as any argument can possibly be supposed against a doctrine so little worthy of a serious refutation. It is acknowledged on all hands, says that learned prelate, that the authority either of the Scripture or of tradition is founded merely in the testimony of the Apostles who were eyewitnesses to those miracles of our Savior by which he proved his divine mission. Our evidence, then, for the truth of the *Christian* religion is less than the evidence for the truth of our senses, because even in the first authors of our religion it was no greater; and it is evident it must diminish in passing from them to their disciples, nor can anyone rest such confidence in their testimony as in the immediate object of his senses. But a weaker evidence can never destroy a stronger; and, therefore, were the doctrine of the real presence ever so clearly revealed in scripture, it would be directly contrary to the rules of just reasoning to give our assent to it. It contradicts sense, though both the Scripture and the tradition on which it is supposed to be built, do not carry such evidence with them as sense, when they are considered merely as external evidences and are not brought home to everyone's breast by the immediate operation of the Holy Spirit.

Nothing is so convenient as a decisive argument of this kind, which must at least *silence* the most arrogant bigotry and superstition and free us from their impertinent solicitations. I flatter myself that I have discovered an argument of a like nature which, if just, will, with the wise and learned, be an everlasting check to all kinds of superstitious delusion and consequently will be useful as long as the world endures. For so long, I presume, will the accounts of miracles and prodigies be found in all history, sacred and profane.

Though experience is our only guide in reasoning concerning matters of fact, it must be acknowledged that this guide is not altogether infallible, but

in some cases is apt to lead us into errors. One who in our climate should expect better weather in any week of June than in one of December would reason justly and conformably to experience, but it is certain that he may happen, in the event, to find himself mistaken. However, we may observe that in such a case he would have no cause to complain of experience, because it commonly informs us beforehand of the uncertainty by that contrariety of events which we may learn from a diligent observation. All effects do not follow with like certainty from their supposed causes. Some events are found, in all countries and all ages, to have been constantly conjoined together. Others are found to have been more variable and sometimes to disappoint our expectations, so that in our reasonings concerning matter of fact there are all imaginable degrees of assurance from the highest certainty to the lowest species of moral evidence.

A wise man, therefore, proportions his belief to the evidence. In such conclusions as are founded on an infallible experience, he expects the event with the last degree of assurance and regards his past experience as a full *proof* of the future existence of that event. In other cases he proceeds with more caution. He weighs the opposite experiments. He considers which side is supported by the greater number of experiments—to that side he inclines with doubt and hesitation; and when at last he fixes his judgment, the evidence does not exceed what we properly call *probability*. All probability, then, supposes an opposition of experiments and observations where the one side is found to overbalance the other and to produce a degree of evidence proportioned to the superiority. A hundred instances or experiments on one side and fifty on another afford a doubtful expectation of any event, though a hundred uniform experiments with only one that is contradictory reasonably beget a pretty strong degree of assurance. In all cases we must balance the opposite experiments where they are opposite and deduct the smaller number from the greater in order to know the exact force of the superior evidence.

To apply these principles to a particular instance, we may observe that there is no species of reasoning more common, more useful, and even necessary to

---

24. [Of Christ in the sacrament of the Eucharist.]

human life than that which is derived from the testimony of men and the reports of eyewitnesses and spectators. This species of reasoning, perhaps, one may deny to be founded on the relation of cause and effect. I shall not dispute about a word. It will be sufficient to observe that our assurance in any argument of this kind is derived from no other principle than our observation of the veracity of human testimony and of the usual conformity of facts to the reports of witnesses. It being a general maxim that no objects have any discoverable connection together and that all the inferences which we can draw from one to another are founded merely on our experience of their constant and regular conjunction, it is evident that we ought not make an exception to this maxim in favor of human testimony whose connection with any event seems in itself as little necessary as any other. Were not the memory tenacious to a certain degree, had not men commonly an inclination to truth and a principle of probity, were they not sensible to shame when detected in a falsehood, were not these, I say, discovered by *experience* to be qualities inherent in human nature, we should never repose the least confidence in human testimony. A man delirious or noted for falsehood and villainy has no manner of authority with us.

And as the evidence derived from witnesses and human testimony is founded on past experience, so it varies with the experience and is regarded either as a *proof* or a *probability*, according as the conjunction between any particular kind of report and any kind of object has been found to be constant or variable. There are a number of circumstances to be taken into consideration in all judgments of this kind; and the ultimate standard by which we determine all disputes that may arise concerning them is always derived from experience and observation. Where this experience is not entirely uniform on any side, it is attended with an unavoidable contrariety in our judgments and with the same opposition and mutual destruction of argument as in every other kind of evidence. We frequently hesitate concerning the reports of others. We balance the opposite circumstances which cause any doubt or uncertainty; and when we discover a superiority on any side, we incline to it,

but still with a diminution of assurance in proportion to the force of its antagonist.

This contrariety of evidence, in the present case, may be derived from several different causes: from the opposition of contrary testimony, from the character or number of the witnesses, from the manner of their delivering their testimony, or from the union of all these circumstances. We entertain a suspicion concerning any matter of fact when the witnesses contradict each other, when they are but few or of a doubtful character, when they have an interest in what they affirm, when they deliver their testimony with hesitation or, on the contrary, with too violent affirmations. There are many other particulars of the same kind which may diminish or destroy the force of any argument derived from human testimony.

Suppose, for instance, that the fact which the testimony endeavors to establish partakes of the extraordinary and the marvelous—in that case, the evidence resulting from the testimony admits of a diminution, greater or less in proportion as the fact is more or less unusual. The reason why we place any credit in witnesses and historians is not derived from any *connection* which we perceive *a priori* between testimony and reality, but because we are accustomed to find a conformity between them. But when the fact attested is such a one as has seldom fallen under our observation, here is a contest of two opposite experiences, of which the one destroys the other as far as its force goes and the superior can only operate on the mind by the force which remains. The very same principle of experience which gives us a certain degree of assurance in the testimony of witnesses gives us also, in this case, another degree of assurance against the fact which they endeavor to establish—from which contradiction there necessarily arises a counterpoise and mutual destruction of belief and authority.

*I should not believe such a story were it told me by Cato* was a proverbial saying in Rome, even during the lifetime of that philosophical patriot. The incredibility of a fact, it was allowed, might invalidate so great an authority.

The Indian prince who refused to believe the first relations concerning the effects of frost reasoned justly, and it naturally required very strong testimony to engage his assent to facts that arose from a state of nature with which he was unacquainted and which bore so little analogy to those events of which he had had constant and uniform experience. Though they were not contrary to his experience, they were not conformable to it.[25]

But in order to increase the probability against the testimony of witnesses, let us suppose that the fact which they affirm, instead of being only marvelous, is really miraculous, and suppose also that the testimony, considered apart and in itself, amounts to an entire proof—in that case, there is proof against proof, of which the strongest must prevail, but still with a diminution of its force in proportion to that of its antagonist.

A miracle is a violation of the laws of nature; and as a firm and unalterable experience has established these laws, the proof against a miracle, from the very nature of the fact, is as entire as any argument from experience can possibly be imagined. Why is it more than probable that all men must die, that lead cannot of itself remain suspended in the air, that fire consumes wood and is extinguished by water, unless it is that these events are found agreeable to the laws of nature and there is required a violation of these laws or, in other words, a miracle to prevent them? Nothing is esteemed a miracle if it ever happen in the common course of nature. It is no miracle that a man, seemingly in good health, should die all of a sudden, because such a kind of death, though more unusual than any other, has yet been frequently observed to happen. But it is a miracle that a dead man should come to life, because that has never been observed in any age or country. There must, therefore, be a uniform experience against every miraculous event; otherwise the event would not merit that appellation. And as a uniform experience amounts to a proof, there is here a direct and full *proof*, from the nature of the fact, against the existence of any miracle, nor can such a proof be destroyed or the miracle rendered credible but by an opposite proof which is superior.[26]

The plain consequence is (and it is a general maxim worthy of our attention): that no testimony is sufficient to establish a miracle, unless the testimony is of such a kind that its falsehood would be more miraculous than the fact which it endeavors to establish; and even in that case there is a mutual destruction of arguments and the superior only gives us an assurance suitable to that degree of force which

---

25. No Indian, it is evident, could have experience that water did not freeze in cold climates. This is placing nature in a situation quite unknown to him; and it is impossible for him to tell *a priori* what will result from it. It is making a new experiment, the consequence of which is always uncertain. One may sometimes conjecture from analogy what will follow; but still this is but conjecture. And it must be confessed that, in the present case of freezing, the event follows contrary to the rules of analogy and is such as a rational Indian would not look for. The operations of cold upon water are not gradual, according to the degrees of cold; but whenever it comes to the freezing point, the water passes in a moment from the utmost liquidity to perfect hardness. Such an event, therefore, may be denominated *extraordinary* and requires a pretty strong testimony to render it credible to people in a warm climate. But still it is not *miraculous*, nor contrary to uniform experience of the course of nature in cases where all the circumstances are the same. The inhabitants of Sumatra have always seen water fluid in their own climate and the freezing of their rivers ought to be deemed a prodigy: But they never saw water in Muscovy during the winter; and therefore they cannot reasonably be positive what would there be the consequence.

26. Sometimes an event may not, *in itself*, *seem* to be contrary to the laws of nature, and yet, if it were real, it might by reason of some circumstances be denominated a miracle, because, in *fact*, it is contrary to these laws. Thus, if a person claiming a divine authority should command a sick person to be well, a healthful man to fall down dead, the clouds to pour rain, the winds to blow, in short, should order many natural events, which immediately follow upon his command; these might justly be esteemed miracles because they are really, in this case, contrary to the laws of nature. For if any suspicion remain that the event and command concurred by accident, there is no miracle and no transgression of the laws of nature. If this suspicion is removed, there is evidently a miracle and a transgression of these laws, because nothing can be more contrary to nature than that the voice or command of a man should have such an influence. A miracle may be accurately defined *a transgression of a law of nature by a particular volition of the Deity or by the interposition of some invisible agent*. A miracle may either be discoverable by men or not. This does not alter its nature and essence. The raising of a house or ship into the air is a visible miracle. The raising of a feather when the wind wants ever so little of a force requisite for that purpose is as real a miracle, though not so sensible with regard to us.

remains after deducting the inferior. When anyone tells me that he saw a dead man restored to life, I immediately consider with myself whether it is more probable that this person should either deceive or be deceived or that the fact which he relates should really have happened. I weigh the one miracle against the other and, according to the superiority which I discover, I pronounce my decision and always reject the greater miracle. If the falsehood of his testimony would be more miraculous than the event which he relates, then, and not until then, can he pretend to command my belief or opinion.

Part II

In the foregoing reasoning we have supposed that the testimony upon which a miracle is founded may possibly amount to an entire proof and that the falsehood of that testimony would be a real prodigy. But it is easy to show that we have been a great deal too liberal in our concession and that there never was a miraculous event established on so full an evidence.

For *first*, there is not to be found, in all history, any miracle attested by a sufficient number of men of such unquestioned good sense, education, and learning, as to secure us against all delusion in themselves; of such undoubted integrity as to place them beyond all suspicion of any design to deceive others; of such credit and reputation in the eyes of mankind as to have a great deal to lose in case of their being detected in any falsehood, and at the same time attesting facts performed in such a public manner and in so celebrated a part of the world as to render the detection unavoidable—all which circumstances are requisite to give us a full assurance in the testimony of men.

*Secondly*, we may observe in human nature a principle which, if strictly examined, will be found to diminish extremely the assurance which we might, from human testimony, have in any kind of prodigy. The maxim by which we commonly conduct ourselves in our reasonings is that the objects of which we have no experience resemble those of which we have; that what we have found to be most usual is always most probable; and that where there is an opposition of arguments, we ought to give the preference

to such as are founded on the greatest number of past observations. But though, in proceeding by this rule, we readily reject any fact which is unusual and incredible in an ordinary degree, yet in advancing further, the mind does not observe always the same rule; but when anything is affirmed utterly absurd and miraculous, it rather the more readily admits of such a fact upon account of that very circumstance which ought to destroy all its authority. The passion of *surprise* and *wonder*, arising from miracles, being an agreeable emotion, gives a sensible tendency towards the belief of those events from which it is derived. And this goes so far that even those who cannot enjoy this pleasure immediately, nor can believe those miraculous events of which they are informed, yet love to partake of the satisfaction at secondhand or by rebound, and place a pride and delight in exciting the admiration of others.

With what greediness are the miraculous accounts of travelers received, their descriptions of sea and land monsters, their relations of wonderful adventures, strange men, and uncouth manners? But if the spirit of religion joins itself to the love of wonder, there is an end of common sense and human testimony in these circumstances loses all pretensions to authority. A religionist may be an enthusiast and imagine he sees what has no reality. He may know his narrative to be false and yet persevere in it with the best intentions in the world, for the sake of promoting so holy a cause. Or even where this delusion does not have place, vanity, excited by so strong a temptation, operates on him more powerfully than on the rest of mankind in any other circumstances, and self-interest with equal force. His auditors may not have and commonly do not have sufficient judgment to canvass his evidence. What judgment they have, they renounce by principle in these sublime and mysterious subjects. Or if they were ever so willing to employ it, passion and a heated imagination disturb the regularity of its operations. Their credulity increases his impudence and his impudence overpowers their credulity.

Eloquence, when at its highest pitch, leaves little room for reason or reflection, but, addressing itself entirely to the fancy or the affections, captivates the willing hearers and subdues their understanding. Happily, this pitch it seldom attains. But what a Tully or a Demosthenes could scarcely effect over a Roman or Athenian audience, every Capuchin, every itinerant or stationary preacher can perform over the generality of mankind, and in a higher degree by touching such gross and vulgar passions.

The many instances of forged miracles and prophecies and supernatural events, which, in all ages, have either been detected by contrary evidence or detect themselves by their absurdity, prove sufficiently the strong propensity of mankind to the extraordinary and the marvelous and ought reasonably to beget a suspicion against all relations of this kind. This is our natural way of thinking, even with regard to the most common and most credible events. For instance, there is no kind of report which rises so easily and spreads so quickly, especially in country places and provincial towns, as those concerning marriages, inasmuch that two young persons of equal condition never see each other twice, but the whole neighborhood immediately join them together. The pleasure of telling a piece of news so interesting, of propagating it, and of being the first reporters of it spreads the intelligence. And this is so well known that no man of sense gives attention to these reports until he finds them confirmed by some greater evidence. Do not the same passions, and others still stronger, incline the generality of mankind to believe and report with the greatest vehemence and assurance all religious miracles?

*Thirdly*, it forms a strong presumption against all supernatural and miraculous relations that they are observed chiefly to abound among ignorant and barbarous nations; or if a civilized people has ever given admission to any of them that people will be found to have received them from ignorant and barbarous ancestors, who transmitted them with that inviolable sanction and authority which always attend received opinions. When we peruse the first histories of all nations, we are apt to imagine ourselves transported into some new world where the whole frame of nature is disjointed and every element performs its operations in a different manner from what it does at present. Battles, revolutions, pestilence, famine, and death are never the effect of those natural causes which we experience. Prodigies, omens, oracles, judgments, quite obscure the few natural events that are intermingled with them. But as the former grow thinner every page, in proportion as we advance nearer the enlightened ages, we soon learn that there is nothing mysterious or supernatural in the case, but that all proceeds from the usual propensity of mankind towards the marvelous, and that, though this inclination may at intervals receive a check from sense and learning, it can never be thoroughly extirpated from human nature.

*It is strange*, a judicious reader is apt to say, upon the perusal of these wonderful historians, that *such prodigious events never happen in our days*. But it is nothing strange, I hope, that men should lie in all ages. You must surely have seen instances enough of that frailty. You have yourself heard many such marvelous relations started which, being treated with scorn by all the wise and judicious, have at last been abandoned even by the vulgar. Be assured that those renowned lies which have spread and flourished to such a monstrous height arose from like beginnings, but being sown in a more proper soil, shot up at last into prodigies almost equal to those which they relate.

It was a wise policy in that false prophet Alexander, who, though now forgotten, was once so famous, to lay the first scene of his impostures in Paphlagonia, where, as Lucian tells us, the people were extremely ignorant and stupid and ready to swallow even the grossest delusion. People at a distance, who are weak enough to think the matter at all worth inquiry, have no opportunity of receiving better information. The stories come magnified to them by a hundred circumstances. Fools are industrious in propagating the imposture, while the wise and learned are contented, in general, to deride its absurdity, without informing themselves of the particular facts by which it may be distinctly refuted. And thus the impostor above mentioned was enabled to proceed from his ignorant Paphlagonians to the enlisting of votaries, even among the Greek philosophers and men of the most eminent rank and distinction in Rome—No, could engage the attention of that sage emperor Marcus Aurelius so far as to make him trust the success of a military expedition to his delusive prophecies.

The advantages are so great of starting an imposture among an ignorant people that, even though the delusion should be too gross to impose on the generality of them (*which, though seldom, is sometimes the case*), it has a much better chance for succeeding in remote countries than if the first scene had been laid in a city renowned for arts and knowledge. The most ignorant and barbarous of these barbarians carry the report abroad. None of their countrymen have a large correspondence or sufficient credit and authority to contradict and beat down the delusion. Men's inclination to the marvelous has full opportunity to display itself. And thus a story which is universally exploded in the place where it was first started shall pass for certain at a thousand miles distance. But had Alexander fixed his residence at Athens, the philosophers of that renowned mart of learning had immediately spread throughout the whole Roman empire their sense of the matter, which, being supported by so great authority and displayed by all the force of reason and eloquence, had entirely opened the eyes of mankind. It is true, Lucian, passing by chance through, had an opportunity of performing this good office. But, though much to be wished, it does not always happen that every Alexander meets with a Lucian, ready to expose and detect his impostures.

I may add, as a *fourth* reason which diminishes the authority of prodigies, that there is no testimony for any, even those which have not been expressly detected, that is not opposed by an infinite number of witnesses, so that not only the miracle destroys the credit of testimony, but the testimony destroys itself. To make this the better understood, let us consider that in matters of religion whatever is different is contrary and that it is impossible the religions of ancient Rome, of Turkey, of Siam, and of China should all of them be established on any solid foundation. Every miracle, therefore, pretended to have been wrought in any of these religions (and all of them abound in miracles), as its direct scope is to establish the particular system to which it is attributed, so it has the same force, though more indirectly, to overthrow every other system. In destroying a rival system, it likewise destroys the credit of those miracles on which that system was established, so that all the prodigies of different religions are to be regarded as contrary facts and the evidences of these prodigies, whether weak or strong, as opposite to each other. According to this method of reasoning, when we believe any miracle of Mahomet or his successors, we have for our warrant the testimony of a few barbarous Arabians. And, on the other hand, we are to regard the authority of Titus Livius, Plutarch, Tacitus, and, in short, of all the authors and witnesses, Greek, Chinese, and Roman Catholic, who have related any miracle in their particular religion—I say, we are to regard their testimony in the same light as if they had mentioned that Mahometan miracle and had in express terms contradicted it with the same certainty as they have for the miracle they relate. This argument may appear over subtle and refined, but is not in reality different from the reasoning of a judge who supposes that the credit of two witnesses maintaining a crime against anyone is destroyed by the testimony of two others who affirm him to have been two hundred leagues distant at the same instant when the crime is said to have been committed.

One of the best attested miracles in all profane history is that which Tacitus reports of Vespasian, who cured a blind man in Alexandria by means of his spittle and a lame man by the mere touch of his foot, in obedience to a vision of the god Serapis, who had enjoined them to have recourse to the Emperor for these miraculous cures. The story may be seen in that fine historian, where every circumstance seems to add weight to the testimony, and might be displayed at large with all the force of argument and eloquence, if anyone were now concerned to enforce the evidence of that exploded and idolatrous superstition: the gravity, solidity, age, and probity of so great an emperor, who, through the whole course of his life, conversed in a familiar manner with his friends and courtiers and never affected those extraordinary airs of divinity assumed by Alexander and Demetrius; the historian, a contemporary writer noted for candor and veracity, and in addition the greatest and most penetrating genius perhaps of all antiquity, and so free from any tendency to credulity that he even lies under the contrary imputation of atheism and profaneness; the persons from whose authority he related the miracle of established character for judgment and veracity, as we may well presume; eyewitnesses of the fact, and confirming their testimony after the Flavian family was despoiled of the empire and could no longer give any reward as the price of a lie. *Utrumque, qui interfuere, nunc quoque memorant, postquam nullum mendacio pretium.*[27] To which, if we add the public nature of the facts, as related, it will appear that no evidence can well be supposed stronger for so gross and so palpable a falsehood.

There is also a memorable story related by Cardinal de Retz, which may well deserve our consideration. When that intriguing politician fled into Spain to avoid the persecution of his enemies, he passed through Saragossa, the capital of Arragon, where he was shown, in the cathedral, a man who had served seven years as a doorkeeper and was well known to everybody in town who had ever paid his devotions at that church. He had been seen for so long a time wanting a leg, but recovered that limb by the rubbing of holy oil upon the stump; and when the Cardinal examined it, he found it to be a true natural leg like the other. This miracle was vouched by all the canons of the church; and the whole company in town were appealed to for a confirmation of the fact, whom the cardinal found, by their zealous devotion, to be thorough believers of the miracle. Here the relater was also contemporary to the supposed prodigy, of an incredulous and libertine character, as well as of great genius; the miracle of so *singular* a nature as could scarcely admit of a counterfeit, and the witnesses very numerous, and all of them, in a manner, spectators of the fact to which they gave their testimony. And what adds mightily to the force of the evidence and may double our surprise on this occasion is that the Cardinal himself, who relates the story, does not seem to give any credit to it and, consequently, cannot be suspected of any concurrence in the holy fraud. He considered justly that it was not requisite, in order to reject a fact of this nature, to be able accurately to disprove the testimony and to trace its falsehood through all the circumstances of knavery and credulity which

produced it. He knew that, as this was commonly altogether impossible at any small distance of time and place, so was it extremely difficult, even where one was immediately present, by reason of the bigotry, ignorance, cunning, and roguery of a great part of mankind. He therefore concluded, like a just reasoner, that such an evidence carried falsehood upon the very face of it and that a miracle supported by any human testimony was more properly a subject of derision than of argument.

There surely never was a greater number of miracles ascribed to one person than those which were lately said to have been wrought in France upon the tomb of Abbé Paris, the famous Jansenist, with whose sanctity the people were so long deluded. The curing of the sick, giving hearing to the deaf and sight to the blind, were everywhere talked of as the usual effects of that holy sepulcher. But what is more extraordinary, many of the miracles were immediately proved upon the spot, before judges of unquestioned integrity, attested by witnesses of credit and distinction, in a learned age, and on the most eminent theater that is now in the world. Nor is this all: A relation of them was published and dispersed everywhere, nor were the *Jesuits*, though a learned body supported by the civil magistrate and determined enemies to those opinions in whose favor the miracles were said to have been wrought, ever able distinctly to refute or detect them. Where shall we find such a number of circumstances agreeing to the corroboration of one fact? And what have we to oppose to such a cloud of witnesses but the absolute impossibility or miraculous nature of the events which they relate? And this, surely, in the eyes of all reasonable people, will alone be regarded as a sufficient refutation.

Is the consequence just, because some human testimony has the utmost force and authority in some cases, when it relates the battle of Philippi or Pharsalia, for instance, that therefore all kinds of testimony must in all cases have equal force and authority? Suppose that the Caesarean and Pompeian factions had, each of them, claimed the victory in these battles, and that the historians of each party had uniformly ascribed the advantage to their own side, how could mankind, at this distance, have been able to determine between

---

27. [Even now, those who were present speak of each event, though there is no reward for the lie.]

them? The contrariety is equally strong between the miracles related by Herodotus or Plutarch and those delivered by Mariana, Bede, or any monkish historian.

The wise lend a very academic faith to every report which favors the passion of the reporter, whether it magnifies his country, his family, or himself, or in any other way strikes in with his natural inclinations and propensities. But what greater temptation than to appear a missionary, a prophet, an ambassador from heaven? Who would not encounter many dangers and difficulties in order to attain so sublime a character? Or if, by the help of vanity and a heated imagination, a man has first made a convert of himself and entered seriously into the delusion, who ever scruples to make use of pious frauds in support of so holy and meritorious a cause?

The smallest spark may here kindle into the greatest flame, because the materials are always prepared for it. The *avidum genus auricularum*,[28] the gazing populace, receive greedily, without examination, whatever soothes superstition and promotes wonder.

How many stories of this nature have, in all ages, been detected and exploded in their infancy? How many more have been celebrated for a time and have afterwards sunk into neglect and oblivion? Where such reports, therefore, fly about, the solution of the phenomenon is obvious and we judge in conformity to regular experience and observation when we account for it by the known and natural principles of credulity and delusion. And shall we, rather than have a recourse to so natural a solution, allow of a miraculous violation of the most established laws of nature?

I need not mention the difficulty of detecting a falsehood in any private or even public history at the place where it is said to happen, much more when the scene is removed to ever so small a distance. Even a court of judicature, with all the authority, accuracy, and judgment, which they can employ, find themselves often at a loss to distinguish between truth and falsehood in the most recent actions. But the matter never comes to any issue, if trusted to the common method of altercation and debate and flying rumors, especially when men's passions have taken part on either side.

In the infancy of new religions, the wise and learned commonly esteem the matter too inconsiderable to deserve their attention or regard. And when afterwards they would willingly detect the cheat in order to undeceive the deluded multitude, the season is now past and the records and witnesses which might clear up the matter have perished beyond recovery.

No means of detection remain but those which must be drawn from the very testimony itself of the reporters. And these, though always sufficient with the judicious and knowing, are commonly too fine to fall under the comprehension of the vulgar.

Upon the whole, then, it appears that no testimony for any kind of miracle has ever amounted to a probability, much less to a proof; and that, even supposing it amounted to a proof, it would be opposed by another proof derived from the very nature of the fact which it would endeavor to establish. It is experience only which gives authority to human testimony and it is the same experience which assures us of the laws of nature. When, therefore, these two kinds of experience are contrary, we have nothing to do but subtract the one from the other and embrace an opinion on either one side or the other with that assurance which arises from the remainder. But according to the principle here explained, this subtraction with regard to all popular religions amounts to an entire annihilation and, therefore, we may establish it as a maxim that no human testimony can have such force as to prove a miracle and make it a just foundation for any such system of religion.

I beg the limitations here made may be remarked, when I say that a miracle can never be proved so as to be the foundation of a system of religion. For I admit that otherwise there may possibly be miracles or violations of the usual course of nature of such a kind as to admit of proof from human testimony; though perhaps it will be impossible to find any such in all the records of history. Thus, suppose all authors, in all languages, agree that from the first of January 1600 there was a total darkness over the whole earth for eight days; suppose that the tradition of this extraordinary event is still strong and lively among the people—that all travelers who return from foreign countries bring us accounts of the same tradition without the least

---

28. [Lucretius IV, 594. "A gossip-hungry race."]

variation or contradiction—it is evident that our present philosophers, instead of doubting the fact, ought to receive it as certain and ought to search for the causes from which it might be derived. The decay, corruption, and dissolution of nature is an event rendered probable by so many analogies that any phenomenon which seems to have a tendency towards that catastrophe comes within the reach of human testimony, if that testimony is very extensive and uniform.

But suppose that all the historians who treat of England should agree that on the first of January 1600, Queen Elizabeth died; that both before and after her death she was seen by her physicians and the whole court, as is usual with persons of her rank; that her successor was acknowledged and proclaimed by the parliament; and that, after being interred a month, she again appeared, resumed the throne, and governed England for three years—I must confess that I should be surprised at the concurrence of so many odd circumstances, but should not have the least inclination to believe so miraculous an event. I should not doubt of her pretended death and of those other public circumstances that followed it; I should only assert it to have been pretended, and that it neither was nor possibly could be real. You would in vain object to me the difficulty and almost impossibility of deceiving the world in an affair of such consequence; the wisdom and solid judgment of that renowned queen, with the little or no advantage which she could reap from so poor an artifice—all this might astonish me, but I would still reply that the knavery and folly of men are such common phenomena that I should rather believe the most extraordinary events to arise from their concurrence than admit of so signal a violation of the laws of nature.

But should this miracle be ascribed to any new system of religion, men in all ages have been so much imposed on by ridiculous stories of that kind that this very circumstance would be a full proof of a cheat and sufficient, with all men of sense, not only to make them reject the fact, but even reject it without further examination. Though the Being to whom the miracle is ascribed is in this case Almighty, it does not, upon that account, become a whit more probable, since it is impossible for us to know the attributes or actions of such a Being otherwise than from the experience which we have of his productions in the usual course of nature. This still reduces us to past observation and obliges us to compare the instances of the violation of truth in the testimony of men with those of the violation of the laws of nature by miracles, in order to judge which of them is most likely and probable. As the violations of truth are more common in the testimony concerning religious miracles than in that concerning any other matter of fact, this must diminish very much the authority of the former testimony and make us form a general resolution, never to lend any attention to it, with whatever specious pretense it may be covered.

Lord Bacon seems to have embraced the same principles of reasoning. "We ought," says he, "make a collection or particular history of all monsters and prodigious births or productions and, in a word, of everything new, rare, and extraordinary in nature. But this must be done with the most severe scrutiny, lest we depart from truth. Above all, every relation must be considered as suspicious which depends in any degree upon religion, as the prodigies of Livy. And no less so, everything that is to be found in the writers of natural magic or alchemy or such authors who seem, all of them, to have an unconquerable appetite for falsehood and fable."[29]

I am the better pleased with the method of reasoning here delivered, as I think it may serve to confound those dangerous friends or disguised enemies to the *Christian Religion* who have undertaken to defend it by the principles of human reason. Our most holy religion is founded on Faith, not on reason; and it is a sure method of exposing it to put it to such a trial as it is by no means fitted to endure. To make this more evident, let us examine those miracles related in Scripture and, not to lose ourselves in too wide a field, let us confine ourselves to such as we find in the *Pentateuch*, which we shall examine according to the principles of these pretended Christians, not as the word or testimony of God himself, but as the production of a mere human writer and historian. Here then we are first to consider a book presented to us by a barbarous and ignorant people, written in an age

---

29. *New Organon* II, aphorism 29.

when they were still more barbarous, and in all probability long after the facts which it relates, corroborated by no concurring testimony, and resembling those fabulous accounts which every nation gives of its origin. Upon reading this book we find it full of prodigies and miracles. It gives an account of a state of the world and of human nature entirely different from the present: of our fall from that state; of the age of man extended to near a thousand years; of the destruction of the world by a deluge; of the arbitrary choice of one people as the favorites of heaven, and that people the countrymen of the author; of their deliverance from bondage by prodigies the most astonishing imaginable: I desire anyone to lay his hand upon his heart and, after a serious consideration, declare whether he thinks that the falsehood of such a book, supported by such a testimony, would be more extraordinary and miraculous than all the miracles it relates—which is, however, necessary to make it be received according to the measures of probability above established.

What we have said of miracles may be applied without any variation to prophecies; and, indeed, all prophecies are real miracles and as such only can be admitted as proofs of any revelation. If it did not exceed the capacity of human nature to foretell future events, it would be absurd to employ any prophecy as an argument for a divine mission or authority from heaven. So that, upon the whole, we may conclude that the Christian religion not only was at first attended with miracles, but even at this day cannot be believed by any reasonable person without one. Mere reason is insufficient to convince us of its veracity. And whoever is moved by faith to assent to it is conscious of a continued miracle in his own person which subverts all the principles of his understanding and gives him a determination to believe what is most contrary to custom and experience.

## Section XI: *Of a Particular Providence and of a Future State*[30]

I was lately engaged in conversation with a friend who loves skeptical paradoxes, where, though he

_____

30. [In another edition, this section is titled "Of the Practical Consequences of Natural Religion."]

advanced many principles of which I can by no means approve, yet as they seem to be curious and to bear some relation to the chain of reasoning carried on throughout this inquiry, I shall here copy them from my memory as accurately as I can in order to submit them to the judgment of the reader.

Our conversation began with my admiring the singular good fortune of philosophy, which, as it requires entire liberty above all other privileges and chiefly flourishes from the free opposition of sentiments and argumentation, received its first birth in an age and country of freedom and toleration, and was never cramped, even in its most extravagant principles, by any creeds, confessions, or penal statutes. For, except the banishment of Protagoras and the death of Socrates, which last event proceeded partly from other motives, there are scarcely any instances to be met with, in ancient history, of this bigoted jealousy with which the present age is so much infested. Epicurus lived at Athens to an advanced age in peace and tranquillity. Epicureans were even admitted to receive the sacerdotal character and to officiate at the altar in the most sacred rites of the established religion. And the public encouragement of pensions and salaries was afforded equally by the wisest of all the Roman emperors to the professors of every sect of philosophy. How requisite such kind of treatment was to philosophy, in her early youth, will easily be conceived, if we reflect that even at present, when she may be supposed more hardy and robust, she bears with much difficulty the inclemency of the seasons and those harsh winds of calumny and persecution which blow upon her.

You admire, says my friend, as the singular good fortune of philosophy what seems to result from the natural course of things and to be unavoidable in every age and nation. This pertinacious bigotry, of which you complain as so fatal to philosophy, is really her offspring who, after allying with superstition, separates himself entirely from the interest of his parent and becomes her most inveterate enemy and persecutor. Speculative dogmas of religion, the present occasions of such furious dispute, could not possibly be conceived or admitted in the early ages of the world, when mankind, being wholly illiterate, formed an idea of religion more suitable to their weak apprehension and composed their sacred tenets of such tales chiefly as were the objects of traditional belief more than of argument or disputation. After the first alarm, therefore, was over, which arose from the new paradoxes and principles of the philosophers, these teachers seem ever after, during the ages of antiquity, to have lived in great harmony with the established superstition and to have made a fair partition of mankind between them—the former claiming all the learned and wise, the latter possessing all the vulgar and illiterate.

It seems then, I say, that you leave politics entirely out of the question and never suppose that a wise magistrate can justly be jealous of certain tenets of philosophy, such as those of Epicurus, which, denying a divine existence and consequently a providence and a future state, seem to loosen in a great measure the ties of morality and may be supposed, for that reason, pernicious to the peace of civil society.

I know, he replied, that in fact these persecutions never, in any age, proceeded from calm reason or from experience of the pernicious consequences of philosophy, but arose entirely from passion and prejudice. But what if I should advance further and assert that, if Epicurus had been accused before the people by any of the *sycophants* or informers of those days, he could easily have defended his cause and proved his principles of philosophy to be as salutary as those of his adversaries who endeavored with such zeal to expose him to the public hatred and jealousy?

I wish, I said, you would try your eloquence upon so extraordinary a topic and make a speech for Epicurus which might satisfy, not the mob of Athens, if you will allow that ancient and polite city to have contained any mob, but the more philosophical part of his audience, such as might be supposed capable of comprehending his arguments.

The matter would not be difficult upon such conditions, he replied; and if you please, I shall suppose myself Epicurus for a moment and make you stand for the Athenian people, and shall deliver you such an harangue as will fill all the urn with white beans and leave not a black one to gratify the malice of my adversaries.

Very well. Pray proceed upon these suppositions.

I come here, O you Athenians, to justify in your assembly what I maintained in my school and I find myself impeached by furious antagonists, instead of reasoning with calm and dispassionate inquirers. Your deliberations, which of right should be directed to questions of public good and the interest of the commonwealth, are diverted to the disquisitions of speculative philosophy, and these magnificent, but perhaps fruitless inquiries take place of your more familiar, but more useful occupations. But so far as in me lies I will prevent this abuse. We shall not here dispute concerning the origin and government of worlds. We shall only inquire how far such questions concern the public interest. And if I can persuade you that they are entirely indifferent to the peace of society and security of government, I hope that you will presently send us back to our schools, there to examine at leisure the question, the most sublime, but, at the same time, the most speculative of all philosophy.

The religious philosophers, not satisfied with the tradition of your forefathers and doctrine of your priests (in which I willingly acquiesce), indulge a rash curiosity in trying how far they can establish religion upon the principles of reason; and they thereby excite, instead of satisfying, the doubts which naturally arise from a diligent and scrutinous inquiry. They paint in the most magnificent colors the order, beauty, and wise arrangement of the universe and then ask if such a glorious display of intelligence could proceed from the fortuitous concourse of atoms or if chance could produce what the greatest genius can never sufficiently admire. I shall not examine the justness of this argument. I shall allow it to be as solid as my antagonists and accusers can desire. It is sufficient if I can prove, from this very reasoning, that the question is entirely speculative, and that, when, in my philosophical disquisitions, I deny a providence and a future state, I do not undermine the foundations of society, but advance principles which they themselves, upon their own topics, if they argue consistently, must allow to be solid and satisfactory.

You then, who are my accusers, have acknowledged that the chief or sole argument for a divine existence (which I never questioned) is derived from the order of nature, where there appear such marks of intelligence and design that you think it extravagant to assign for its cause either chance or the blind and unguided force of matter. You allow that this is an argument drawn from effects to causes. From the order of the work you infer that there must have been project and forethought in the workman. If you cannot make out this point, you allow that your conclusion fails and you do not pretend to establish the conclusion in a greater latitude than the phenomena of nature will justify. These are your concessions. I desire you to mark the consequences.

When we infer any particular cause from an effect, we must proportion the one to the other and can never be allowed to ascribe to the cause any qualities but what are exactly sufficient to produce the effect. A body of ten ounces raised in any scale may serve as a proof that the counterbalancing weight exceeds ten ounces, but can never afford a reason that it exceeds a hundred. If the cause assigned for any effect is not sufficient to produce it, we must either reject that cause or add to it such qualities as will give it a just proportion to the effect. But if we ascribe to it further qualities or affirm it capable of producing other effects, we can only indulge the license of conjecture and arbitrarily suppose the existence of qualities and energies without reason or authority.

The same rule holds whether the cause assigned is brute unconscious matter or a rational intelligent being. If the cause is known only by the effect, we never ought to ascribe to it any qualities beyond what are precisely requisite to produce the effect; nor can we, by any rules of just reasoning, return back from the cause and infer other effects from it, beyond those by which alone it is known to us. No one, merely from the sight of one of Zeuxis' pictures, could know that he was also a statuary or architect and was an artist no less skillful in stone and marble than in colors. The talents and taste displayed in the particular work before us—these we may safely conclude the workman to be possessed of. The cause must be proportioned to the effect; and if we exactly and precisely proportion it, we shall never find in it any qualities that point further or afford an inference concerning any other design or performance. Such qualities must be

somewhat beyond what is merely requisite for producing the effect which we examine.

Allowing, therefore, the gods to be the authors of the existence or order of the universe, it follows that they possess that precise degree of power, intelligence, and benevolence which appears in their workmanship, but nothing further can ever be proved, except we call in the assistance of exaggeration and flattery to supply the defects of argument and reasoning. So far as the traces of any attributes at present appear, so far may we conclude these attributes to exist. The supposition of further attributes is mere hypothesis, much more the supposition that in distant regions of space or periods of time there has been or will be a more magnificent display of these attributes and a scheme of administration more suitable to such imaginary virtues. We can never be allowed to mount up from the universe, the effect, to Jupiter, the cause, and then descend downwards to infer any new effect from that cause, as if the present effects alone were not entirely worthy of the glorious attributes which we ascribe to that deity. The knowledge of the cause being derived solely from the effect, they must be exactly adjusted to each other and the one can never refer to anything further or be the foundation of any new inference and conclusion.

You find certain phenomena in nature. You seek a cause or author. You imagine that you have found him. You afterwards become so enamored of this offspring of your brain that you imagine it impossible but he must produce something greater and more perfect than the present scene of things, which is so full of ill and disorder. You forget that this superlative intelligence and benevolence are entirely imaginary or, at least, without any foundation in reason and that you have no ground to ascribe to him any qualities but what you see he has actually exerted and displayed in his productions. Let your gods, therefore, O philosophers, be suited to the present appearances of nature and do not presume to alter these appearances by arbitrary suppositions in order to suit them to the attributes which you so fondly ascribe to your deities.

When priests and poets, supported by your authority, O Athenians, talk of a golden or silver age which preceded the present state of vice and misery, I hear them with attention and with reverence. But when philosophers who pretend to neglect authority and to cultivate reason hold the same discourse, I do not pay them, I admit, the same obsequious submission and pious deference. I ask: Who carried them into the celestial regions, who admitted them into the councils of the gods, who opened to them the book of fate that they thus rashly affirm that their deities have executed or will execute any purpose beyond what has actually appeared? If they tell me that they have mounted on the steps or by the gradual ascent of reason and by drawing inferences from effects to causes, I still insist that they have aided the ascent of reason by the wings of imagination; otherwise they could not thus change their manner of inference and argue from causes to effects, presuming that a more perfect production than the present world would be more suitable to such perfect beings as the gods and forgetting that they have no reason to ascribe to these celestial beings any perfection or any attribute but what can be found in the present world.

Hence all the fruitless industry to account for the ill appearances of nature and save the honor of the gods, while we must acknowledge the reality of that evil and disorder with which the world so much abounds. The obstinate and intractable qualities of matter, we are told, or the observance of general laws, or some such reason, is the sole cause which controlled the power and benevolence of Jupiter and obliged him to create mankind and every sensible creature so imperfect and so unhappy. These attributes, then, are, it seems, beforehand taken for granted in their greatest latitude. And upon that supposition, I admit that such conjectures may, perhaps, be admitted as plausible solutions of the ill phenomena. But still I ask: Why take these attributes for granted or why ascribe to the cause any qualities but what actually appear in the effect? Why torture your brain to justify the course of nature upon suppositions which, for all you know, may be entirely imaginary and of which there are to be found no traces in the course of nature?

The religious hypothesis, therefore, must be considered only as a particular method of accounting for the visible phenomena of the universe. But no just reasoner will ever presume to infer from it any single fact and alter or add to the phenomena in any single particular. If you think that the appearances of things prove such causes, it is allowable for you to draw an inference concerning the existence of these causes. In such complicated and sublime subjects, everyone should be indulged in the liberty of conjecture and argument. But here you ought to rest. If you come backward and, arguing from your inferred causes, conclude that any other fact has existed or will exist in the course of nature which may serve as a fuller display of particular attributes I must admonish you that you have departed from the method of reasoning attached to the present subject and have certainly added something to the attributes of the cause beyond what appears in the effect; otherwise you could never, with tolerable sense or propriety, add anything to the effect in order to render it more worthy of the cause.

Where, then, is the odiousness of that doctrine which I teach in my school, or rather, which I examine in my gardens? Or what do you find in this whole question in which the security of good morals or the peace and order of society are in the least concerned?

I deny a providence, you say, and supreme governor of the world who guides the course of events and punishes the vicious with infamy and disappointment, and rewards the virtuous with honor and success in all their undertakings. But surely I do not deny the course itself of events, which lies open to everyone's inquiry and examination. I acknowledge that, in the present order of things, virtue is attended with more peace of mind than vice and meets with a more favorable reception from the world. I am sensible that, according to the past experience of mankind, friendship is the chief joy of human life and moderation the only source of tranquillity and happiness. I never balance between the virtuous and the vicious course of life, but am sensible that, to a well-disposed mind, every advantage is on the side of the former. And what can you say more, allowing all your suppositions and reasonings? You tell me, indeed, that this disposition of things proceeds from intelligence and design. But whatever it proceeds from, the disposition itself, on which depends our happiness or misery and consequently our conduct and deportment in life, is still the same. It is still open for me, as well as you, to regulate my behavior by my experience of past events. And if you affirm that, while a divine providence is allowed, and a supreme distributive justice in the universe, I ought to expect some more particular reward of the good and punishment of the bad beyond the ordinary course of events, I here find the same fallacy which I have before endeavored to detect. You persist in imagining that, if we grant that divine existence for which you so earnestly contend, you may safely infer consequences from it and add something to the experienced order of nature by arguing from the attributes which you ascribe to your gods. You do not seem to remember that all your reasonings on this subject can only be drawn from effects to causes and that every argument deduced from causes to effects must of necessity be a gross sophism, since it is impossible for you to know anything of the cause but what you have antecedently not inferred, but discovered to the full in the effect.

But what must a philosopher think of those vain reasoners who, instead of regarding the present scene of things as the sole object of their contemplation, so far reverse the whole course of nature as to render this life merely a passage to something further—a porch which leads to a greater and vastly different building, a prologue which serves only to introduce the piece and give it more grace and propriety? From where, do you think, can such philosophers derive their idea of the gods? From their own conceit and imagination surely. For if they derived it from the present phenomena, it would never point to anything further, but must be exactly adjusted to them. That the divinity may *possibly* be endowed with attributes which we have never seen exerted, may be governed by principles of action which we cannot discover to be satisfied. All this will freely be allowed. But still this is mere *possibility* and hypothesis. We never can have reason to *infer* any attributes or any principles of action in him, but so far as we know them to have been exerted and satisfied.

*Are there any marks of a distributive justice in the world*? If you answer in the affirmative, I conclude

that, since justice here exerts itself, it is satisfied. If you reply in the negative, I conclude that you have then no reason to ascribe justice, in our sense of it, to the gods. If you hold a medium between affirmation and negation, by saying that the justice of the gods at present exerts itself in part, but not in its full extent, I answer that you have no reason to give it any particular extent, but only so far as you see it, *at present*, exert itself.

Thus I bring the dispute, O Athenians, to a short issue with my antagonists. The course of nature lies open to my contemplation as well as to theirs. The experienced train of events is the great standard by which we all regulate our conduct. Nothing else can be appealed to in the field or in the senate. Nothing else ought ever to be heard of in the school or in the closet. In vain would our limited understanding break through those boundaries which are too narrow for our fond imagination. While we argue from the course of nature and infer a particular intelligent cause which first bestowed and still preserves order in the universe, we embrace a principle which is both uncertain and useless. It is uncertain because the subject lies entirely beyond the reach of human experience. It is useless because our knowledge of this cause being derived entirely from the course of nature, we can never, according to the rules of just reasoning, return back from the cause with any new inference or, making additions to the common and experienced course of nature, establish any new principles of conduct and behavior.

I observe (I said, finding he had finished his harangue) that you do not neglect the artifice of the demagogues of old and as you were pleased to make me stand for the people, you insinuate yourself into my favor by embracing those principles to which, you know, I have always expressed a particular attachment. But allowing you to make experience (as indeed I think you ought) the only standard of our judgment concerning this and all other questions of fact, I do not doubt but, from the very same experience to which you appeal, it may be possible to refute this reasoning which you have put into the mouth of Epicurus. If you saw, for instance, a half-finished building surrounded with heaps of brick and stone and mortar and all the instruments of masonry, could you not *infer* from the effect that it was a work of design and contrivance? And could you not return again, from this inferred cause, to infer new additions to the effect and conclude that the building would soon be finished and receive all the further improvements which art could bestow upon it? If you saw upon the seashore the print of one human foot, you would conclude that a man had passed that way and that he had also left the traces of the other foot, though effaced by the rolling of the sands or inundation of the waters. Why then do you refuse to admit the same method of reasoning with regard to the order of nature? Consider the world and the present life only as an imperfect building from which you can infer a superior intelligence and, arguing from that superior intelligence which can leave nothing imperfect, why may you not infer a more finished scheme or plan which will receive its completion in some distant point of space or time? Are not these methods of reasoning exactly similar? And under what pretense can you embrace the one while you reject the other?

The infinite difference of the subjects, he replied, is a sufficient foundation for this difference in my conclusions. In works of human art and contrivance, it is allowable to advance from the effect to the cause, and, returning back from the cause, to form new inferences concerning the effect and examine the alterations which it has probably undergone or may still undergo. But what is the foundation of this method of reasoning? Plainly this: that man is a being whom we know by experience, whose motives and designs we are acquainted with, and whose projects and inclinations have a certain connection and coherence according to the laws which nature has established for the government of such a creature. When, therefore, we find that any work has proceeded from the skill and industry of man, as we are otherwise acquainted with the nature of the animal, we can draw a hundred inferences concerning what may be expected from him; and these inferences will all be founded in experience and observation. But did we know man only from the single work or production which we examine, it

would be impossible for us to argue in this manner, because our knowledge of all the qualities which we ascribe to him, being in that case derived from the production, it is impossible they could point to anything further or be the foundation of any new inference. The print of a foot in the sand can only prove, when considered alone, that there was some figure adapted to it by which it was produced. But the print of a human foot proves likewise, from our other experience, that there was probably another foot which also left its impression, though effaced by time or other accidents. Here we mount from the effect to the cause, and, descending again from the cause, infer alterations in the effect; but this is not a continuation of the same simple chain of reasoning. We comprehend in this case a hundred other experiences and observations concerning the *usual* figure and members of that species of animal without which this method of argument must be considered as fallacious and sophistical.

The case is not the same with our reasonings from the works of nature. The Deity is known to us only by his productions and is a single being in the universe, not comprehended under any species or genus, from whose experienced attributes or qualities we can, by analogy, infer any attribute or quality in him. As the universe shows wisdom and goodness, we infer wisdom and goodness. As it shows a particular degree of these perfections, we infer a particular degree of them precisely adapted to the effect which we examine. But further attributes or further degrees of the same attributes we can never be authorized to infer or suppose by any rules of just reasoning. Now, without some such license of supposition, it is impossible for us to argue from the cause or infer any alteration in the effect beyond what has immediately fallen under our observation. Greater good produced by this Being must still prove a greater degree of goodness. A more impartial distribution of rewards and punishments must proceed from a greater regard to justice and equity. Every supposed addition to the works of nature makes an addition to the attributes of the Author of nature, and, consequently, being entirely unsupported by any reason or argument, can never be admitted but as mere conjecture and hypothesis.[31]

The great source of our mistake in this subject and of the unbounded license of conjecture which we indulge is that we tacitly consider ourselves as in the place of the Supreme Being and conclude that he will, on every occasion, observe the same conduct which we ourselves, in his situation, would have embraced as reasonable and eligible. But, besides that the ordinary course of nature may convince us that almost everything is regulated by principles and maxims very different from ours— besides this, I say, it must evidently appear contrary to all rules of analogy to reason from the intentions and projects of men to those of a Being so different and so much superior. In human nature there is a certain experienced coherence of designs and inclinations, so that when, from any fact, we have discovered one intention of any man, it may often be reasonable, from experience, to infer another and draw a long chain of conclusions concerning his past or future conduct. But this method of reasoning can never have place with regard to a Being so remote and incomprehensible, who bears much less analogy to any other being in the universe than the sun to a waxen taper, and who discovers himself

only by some faint traces or outlines beyond which we have no authority to ascribe to him any attribute or perfection. What we imagine to be a superior perfection may really be a defect. Or were it ever so much a perfection, the ascribing of it to the Supreme Being, where it does not appear to have been really exerted to the full in his works, savors more of flattery and panegyric than of just reasoning and sound philosophy. All the philosophy, therefore, in the world and all the religion, which is nothing but a species of philosophy, will never be able to carry us beyond the usual course of experience or give us measures of conduct and behavior different from those which are furnished by reflections on common life. No new fact can ever be inferred from the religious hypothesis, no event foreseen or foretold, no reward or punishment expected or dreaded beyond what is already known by practice and observation. So that my apology for Epicurus will still appear solid and satisfactory, nor have the political interests of society any connection with the philosophical disputes concerning metaphysics and religion.

There is still one circumstance, I replied, which you seem to have overlooked. Though I should allow your premises, I must deny your conclusion. You conclude that religious doctrines and reasonings *can* have no influence on life because they *ought* to have no influence, never considering that men reason not in the same manner you do, but draw many consequences from the belief of a divine Existence and suppose that the Deity will inflict punishments on vice and bestow rewards on virtue beyond what appear in the ordinary course of nature. Whether this reasoning of theirs is just or not is no matter. Its influence on their life and conduct must still be the same. And those who attempt to disabuse them of such prejudices may, for all I know, be good reasoners, but I cannot allow them to be good citizens and politicians, since they free men from one restraint upon their passions and make the infringement of the laws of society in one respect more easy and secure.

After all, I may perhaps agree to your general conclusion in favor of liberty, though upon different

---

31. In general, it may, I think, be established as a maxim that where any cause is known only by its particular effects, it must be impossible to infer any new effects from that cause, since the qualities which are requisite to produce these new effects along with the former must either be different, or superior, or of more extensive operation than those which simply produced the effect, from which alone the cause is supposed to be known to us. We can never, therefore, have any reason to suppose the existence of these qualities. To say that the new effects proceed only from a continuation of the same energy, which is already known from the first effects, will not remove the difficulty. For even granting this to be the case (which can seldom be supposed), the very continuation and exertion of a like energy (for it is impossible it can be absolutely the same), I say, this exertion of a like energy, in a different period of space and time, is a very arbitrary supposition, and what there cannot possibly be any traces of in the effects from which all our knowledge of the cause is originally derived. Let the *inferred* cause be exactly proportioned (as it should be) to the known effect; and it is impossible that it can possess any qualities from which new or different effects can be *inferred*.

premises from those on which you endeavor to found it. I think that the state ought to tolerate every principle of philosophy, nor is there an instance that any government has suffered in its political interests by such indulgence. There is no enthusiasm among philosophers; their doctrines are not very alluring to the people and no restraint can be put upon their reasonings but what must be of dangerous consequence to the sciences and even to the state, by paving the way for persecution and oppression in points where the generality of mankind are more deeply interested and concerned.

But there occurs to me (I continued) with regard to your main topic a difficulty which I shall just propose to you, without insisting on it, lest it lead into reasonings of too nice and delicate a nature. In a word, I much doubt whether it is possible for a cause to be known only by its effect (as you have all along supposed) or to be of so singular and particular a nature as to have no parallel and no similarity with any other cause or object that has ever fallen under our observation. It is only when two species of objects are found to be constantly conjoined that we can infer the one from the other; and were an effect presented which was entirely singular and could not be comprehended under any known species, I do not see that we could form any conjecture or inference at all concerning its cause. If experience and observation and analogy are, indeed, the only guides which we can reasonably follow in inferences of this nature, both the effect and the cause must bear a similarity and resemblance to other effects and causes which we know, and which we have found in many instances to be conjoined with each other. I leave it to your own reflection to pursue the consequences of this principle. I shall just observe that, as the antagonists of Epicurus always suppose the universe, an effect quite singular and unparalleled, to be the proof of a Deity, a cause no less singular and unparalleled, your reasonings upon that supposition seem, at least, to merit our attention. There is, I admit, some difficulty how we can ever return from the cause to the effect and, reasoning from our ideas of the former, infer any alteration on the latter or any addition to it.

## Section XII: *Of the Academic or Skeptical Philosophy*

### Part I

There is not a greater number of philosophical reasonings displayed upon any subject than those which prove the existence of a Deity and refute the fallacies of *atheists*; and yet the most religious philosophers still dispute whether any man can be so blinded as to be a speculative atheist. How shall we reconcile these contradictions? The knights-errant who wandered about to clear the world of dragons and giants never entertained the least doubt with regard to the existence of these monsters.

The *skeptic* is another enemy of religion, who naturally provokes the indignation of all divines and graver philosophers, though it is certain that no man ever met with any such absurd creature or conversed with a man who had no opinion or principle concerning any subject, of either action or speculation. This begets a very natural question: What is meant by a skeptic? And how far it is possible to push these philosophical principles of doubt and uncertainty?

There is a species of skepticism, *antecedent* to all study and philosophy, which is much inculcated by Descartes and others as a sovereign preservative against error and precipitate judgment. It recommends a universal doubt not only of all our former opinions and principles, but also of our very faculties, of whose veracity, they say, we must assure ourselves by a chain of reasoning deduced from some original principle which cannot possibly be fallacious or deceitful. But neither is there any such original principle which has a prerogative above others that are self-evident and convincing. Or if there were, could we advance a step beyond it but by the use of those very faculties of which we are supposed to be already diffident. The Cartesian doubt, therefore, were it ever possible to be attained by any human creature (as it plainly is not) would be entirely incurable and no reasoning could ever bring us to a state of assurance and conviction upon any subject.

It must, however, be confessed that this species of skepticism, when more moderate, may be understood in a very reasonable sense and is a necessary preparative to the study of philosophy by preserving a proper impartiality in our judgments and weaning our mind from all those prejudices which we may have imbibed from education or rash opinion. To begin with clear and self-evident principles, to advance by timorous and sure steps, to review frequently our conclusions and examine accurately all their consequences—though by these means we shall make both a slow and a short progress in our systems—are the only methods by which we can ever hope to reach truth and attain a proper stability and certainty in our determinations.

There is another species of skepticism, *consequent* to science and inquiry, when men are supposed to have discovered either the absolute fallaciousness of their mental faculties or their unfitness to reach any fixed determination in all those curious subjects of speculation about which they are commonly employed. Even our very senses are brought into dispute by a certain species of philosophers and the maxims of common life are subjected to the same doubt as the most profound principles or conclusions of metaphysics and theology. As these paradoxical tenets (if they may be called tenets) are to be met with in some philosophers, and the refutation of them in several, they naturally excite our curiosity and make us inquire into the arguments on which they may be founded.

I need not insist upon the more trite topics employed by the skeptics in all ages against the evidence of *sense* such as those which are derived from the imperfection and fallaciousness of our organs on numberless occasions: the crooked appearance of an oar in water, the various aspects of objects according to their different distances, the double images which arise from the pressing one eye, with many other appearances of a like nature. These skeptical topics, indeed, are only sufficient to prove that the senses alone are not implicitly to be depended on, but that we must correct their evidence by reason and by considerations derived from the nature of the medium, the distance of the object, and the disposition of the organ, in order to render them, within their sphere, the proper *criteria* of truth and falsehood. There are other more profound arguments against the senses which do not admit of so easy a solution.

It seems evident that men are carried by a natural instinct or prepossession to repose faith in their senses, and that without any reasoning, or even almost before the use of reason, we always suppose an external universe which does not depend on our perception, but would exist though we and every sensible creature were absent or annihilated. Even the animal creation are governed by a like opinion and preserve this belief of external objects, in all their thoughts, designs, and actions.

It seems also evident that when men follow this blind and powerful instinct of nature they always suppose the very images presented by the senses to be the external objects and never entertain any suspicion that the one are nothing but representations of the other. This very table which we see white and which we feel hard is believed to exist independent of our perception and to be something external to our mind which perceives it. Our presence does not bestow being on it. Our absence does not annihilate it. It preserves its existence uniform and entire, independent of the situation of intelligent beings who perceive or contemplate it.

But this universal and primary opinion of all men is soon destroyed by the slightest philosophy which teaches us that nothing can ever be present to the mind but an image or perception, and that the senses are only the inlets through which these images are conveyed, without being able to produce any immediate intercourse between the mind and the object. The table which we see seems to diminish as we remove further from it. But the real table which exists independent of us suffers no alteration. It was, therefore, nothing but its image which was present to the mind. These are the obvious dictates of reason and no man who reflects ever doubted that the existences which we consider when we say *this house* and *that tree* are nothing but perceptions in the mind and fleeting copies or representations of other existences which remain uniform and independent.

So far, then, are we necessitated by reasoning to contradict or depart from the primary instincts of nature and to embrace a new system with regard to the evidence of our senses. But here philosophy finds herself extremely embarrassed when she would justify this new system and obviate the cavils and objections of the skeptics. She can no longer plead the infallible and irresistible instinct of nature, for that led us to a quite different system which is acknowledged fallible and even erroneous. And to justify this pretended philosophical system by a chain of clear and convincing argument, or even any appearance of argument, exceeds the power of all human capacity.

By what argument can it be proved that the perceptions of the mind must be caused by external objects entirely different from them, though resembling them (if that is possible), and could not arise either from the energy of the mind itself or from the suggestion of some invisible and unknown spirit, or from some other cause still more unknown to us? It is acknowledged that in fact many of these perceptions arise not from anything external, as in dreams, madness, and other diseases. And nothing can be more inexplicable than the manner in which body should so operate upon mind as ever to convey an image of itself to a substance supposed of so different and even contrary a nature.

It is a question of fact whether the perceptions of the senses are produced by external objects resembling them; how shall this question be determined? By experience surely as all other questions of a like nature. But here experience is and must be entirely silent. The mind never has anything present to it but the perceptions and cannot possibly reach any experience of their connection with objects. The supposition of such a connection is, therefore, without any foundation in reasoning.

To have recourse to the veracity of the Supreme Being in order to prove the veracity of our senses is surely making a very unexpected circuit. If his veracity were at all concerned in this matter, our senses would be entirely infallible, because it is not possible that he can ever deceive. Not to mention that, if the external world is once called in question, we shall be at a loss to find arguments by which we may prove the existence of that Being or any of his attributes.

This is a topic, therefore, in which the profounder and more philosophical skeptics will always triumph when they endeavor to introduce a universal doubt into all subjects of human knowledge and inquiry.

Do you follow the instincts and propensities of nature, may they say, in assenting to the veracity of sense? But these lead you to believe that the very perception or sensible image is the external object. Do you disclaim this principle in order to embrace a more rational opinion that the perceptions are only representations of something external? You here depart from your natural propensities and more obvious sentiments and yet are not able to satisfy your reason, which can never find any convincing argument from experience to prove that the perceptions are connected with any external objects.

There is another skeptical topic of a like nature, derived from the most profound philosophy, which might merit our attention were it requisite to dive so deep in order to discover arguments and reasonings which can so little serve to any serious purpose. It is universally allowed by modern inquirers that all the sensible qualities of objects, such as hard, soft, hot, cold, white, black, etc., are merely secondary and do not exist in the objects themselves, but are perceptions of the mind, without any external archetype or model which they represent. If this is allowed with regard to secondary qualities, it must also follow with regard to the supposed primary qualities of extension and solidity, nor can the latter be any more entitled to that denomination than the former. The idea of extension is entirely acquired from the senses of sight and feeling and if all the qualities perceived by the senses are in the mind, not in the object, the same conclusion must reach the idea of extension which is wholly dependent on the sensible ideas or the ideas of secondary qualities. Nothing can save us from this conclusion but the asserting that the ideas of those primary qualities are attained by *abstraction*; an opinion which, if we examine it accurately, we shall find to be unintelligible and even absurd. An extension that is neither tangible nor visible cannot possibly be conceived; and a tangible or visible extension which is neither hard nor soft, black nor white, is equally beyond the reach of human conception. Let any man try to conceive a triangle in general which is neither *isosceles* nor *scalene*, nor has any particular length or proportion of sides, and he will soon perceive the absurdity of all the scholastic notions with regard to abstraction and general ideas.[32]

Thus the first philosophical objection to the evidence of sense or to the opinion of external existence consists in this, that such an opinion, if rested on natural instinct, is contrary to reason and, if referred to reason, is contrary to natural instinct and at the same time carries no rational evidence with it to convince an impartial inquirer. The second objection goes further and represents this opinion as contrary to reason, at least, if it is a principle of reason that all sensible qualities are in the mind, not in the object. Deprive matter of all its intelligible qualities, both primary and secondary, you in a manner annihilate it and leave only a certain unknown, inexplicable *something* as the cause of our perceptions—a notion so imperfect that no skeptic will think it worthwhile to contend against it.

## Part II

It may seem a very extravagant attempt of the skeptics to destroy *reason* by argument and ratiocination, yet is this the grand scope of all their inquiries and disputes. They endeavor to find objections both to our abstract reasonings and to those which regard matter of fact and existence.

The chief objection against all *abstract* reasonings is derived from the ideas of space and time—ideas which, in common life and to a careless view, are very clear and intelligible, but when they pass through the scrutiny of the profound sciences (and they are the chief object of these sciences) afford principles which seem full of absurdity and contradiction. No priestly

*dogmas* invented on purpose to tame and subdue the rebellious reason of mankind ever shocked common sense more than the doctrine of the infinite divisibility of extension, with its consequences, as they are pompously displayed by all geometers and metaphysicians with a kind of triumph and exultation. A real quantity, infinitely less than any finite quantity, containing quantities infinitely less than itself, and so on *in infinitum;* this is an edifice so bold and prodigious that it is too weighty for any pretended demonstration to support because it shocks the clearest and most natural principles of human reason.[33] But what renders the matter more extraordinary is that these seemingly absurd opinions are supported by a chain of reasoning, the clearest and most natural, nor is it possible for us to allow the premises without admitting the consequences. Nothing can be more convincing and satisfactory than all the conclusions concerning the properties of circles and triangles, and yet, when these are once received, how can we deny that the angle of contact between a circle and its tangent is infinitely less than any rectilinear angle—that as you may increase the diameter of the circle *in infinitum,* this angle of contact becomes still less, even *in infinitum,* and that the angle of contact between other curves and their tangents may be infinitely less than those between any circle and its tangent, and so on, *in infinitum?* The demonstration of these principles seems as unexceptionable as that which proves the three angles of a triangle to be equal to two right ones, though the latter opinion is natural and easy and the former big with contradiction and absurdity. Reason here seems to be thrown into a kind of amazement and suspense which, without the suggestions of any skeptic, gives her a diffidence of herself

---

32. This argument is drawn from Dr. Berkeley; and indeed most of the writings of that very ingenious author form the best lessons of skepticism which are to be found either among the ancient or modern philosophers, Bayle not excepted. He professes, however, in his title-page (and undoubtedly with great truth) to have composed his book against the skeptics as well as against the atheists and freethinkers. But that all his arguments, though otherwise intended, are in reality merely skeptical, appears from this, *that they admit of no answer and produce no conviction.* Their only effect is to cause that momentary amazement and irresolution and confusion which is the result of skepticism.

33. Whatever disputes there may be about mathematical points, we must allow that there are physical points—that is, parts of extension which cannot be divided or lessened, either by the eye or imagination. These images, then, which are present to the fancy or senses, are absolutely indivisible and consequently must be allowed by mathematicians to be infinitely less than any real part of extension; and yet nothing appears more certain to reason than that an infinite number of them composes an infinite extension. How much more an infinite number of those infinitely small parts of extension, which are still supposed infinitely divisible?

and of the ground on which she treads. She sees a full light which illuminates certain places, but that light borders upon the most profound darkness. And between these she is so dazzled and confounded that she scarcely can pronounce with certainty and assurance concerning any one object.

The absurdity of these bold determinations of the abstract sciences seems to become, if possible, still more palpable with regard to time than extension. An infinite number of real parts of time, passing in succession and exhausted one after another, appears so evident a contradiction that no man, one should think, whose judgment is not corrupted, instead of being improved by the sciences, would ever be able to admit of it.

Yet still reason must remain restless and unquiet, even with regard to that skepticism to which she is driven by these seeming absurdities and contradictions. How any clear, distinct idea can contain circumstances contradictory to itself, or to any other clear, distinct idea, is absolutely incomprehensible and is, perhaps, as absurd as any proposition which can be formed—so that nothing can be more skeptical or more full of doubt and hesitation than this skepticism itself which arises from some of the paradoxical conclusions of geometry or the science of quantity.[34]

---

34. It seems to me not impossible to avoid these absurdities and contradictions, if it is admitted that there is no such thing as abstract or general ideas properly speaking; but that all general ideas are, in reality, particular ones attached to a general term, which recalls, upon occasion, other particular ones that resemble in certain circumstances the idea present to the mind. Thus, when the term Horse is pronounced, we immediately figure to ourselves the idea of a black or a white animal, of a particular size or figure. But as that term is also usually applied to animals of other colors, figures, and sizes, these ideas, though not actually present to the imagination, are easily recalled—and our reasoning and conclusion proceed in the same way as if they were actually present. If this is admitted (as seems reasonable), it follows that all the ideas of quantity upon which mathematicians reason are nothing but particular and such as are suggested by the senses and imagination and, consequently, cannot be infinitely divisible. It is sufficient to have dropped this hint at present without prosecuting it any further. It certainly concerns all lovers of science not to expose themselves to the ridicule and contempt of the ignorant by their conclusions; and this seems the readiest solution of these difficulties.

The skeptical objections to *moral* evidence or to the reasonings concerning matter of fact are either *popular* or *philosophical*. The popular objections are derived from the natural weakness of human understanding: the contradictory opinions which have been entertained in different ages and nations; the variations of our judgment in sickness and health, youth and old age, prosperity and adversity; the perpetual contradiction of each particular man's opinions and sentiments with many other topics of that kind. It is needless to insist further on this head. These objections are but weak. For as, in common life, we reason every moment concerning fact and existence and cannot possibly subsist without continually employing this species of argument, any popular objections derived from this must be insufficient to destroy that evidence. The great subverter of *Pyrrhonism*, or the excessive principles of skepticism, is action, and employment, and the occupations of common life. These principles may flourish and triumph in the schools, where it is indeed difficult, if not impossible, to refute them. But as soon as they leave the shade and by the presence of the real objects which actuate our passions and sentiments are put in opposition to the more powerful principles of our nature, they vanish like smoke and leave the most determined skeptic in the same condition as other mortals.

The skeptic, therefore, had better keep within his proper sphere and display those *philosophical* objections which arise from more profound researches. Here he seems to have ample matter of triumph, while he justly insists that all our evidence for any matter of fact which lies beyond the testimony of sense or memory is derived entirely from the relation of cause and effect; that we have no other idea of this relation than that of two objects which have been frequently *conjoined* together; that we have no argument to convince us that objects which have, in our experience, been frequently conjoined, will likewise, in other instances, be conjoined in the same manner; and that nothing leads us to this inference but custom or a certain instinct of our nature which it is indeed difficult to resist, but which, like other instincts, may be fallacious and deceitful. While the skeptic insists upon these topics, he shows his force, or rather, indeed, his own and our weakness, and seems, for the time at least, to destroy all assurance and conviction. These arguments might be displayed at greater length, if any durable good or benefit to society could ever be expected to result from them.

For here is the chief and most confounding objection to *excessive* skepticism, that no durable good can ever result from it while it remains in its full force and vigor. We need only ask such a skeptic *What his meaning is? And what he proposes by all these curious researches?* He is immediately at a loss and does not know what to answer. A Copernican or Ptolemaist who each supports his different system of astronomy may hope to produce a conviction which will remain constant and durable with his audience. A Stoic or Epicurean displays principles which may not only be durable, but which have an effect on conduct and behavior. But a Pyrrhonian cannot expect that his philosophy will have any constant influence on the mind or, if it had, that its influence would be beneficial to society. On the contrary, he must acknowledge, if he will acknowledge anything, that all human life must perish, were his principles universally and steadily to prevail. All discourse, all action would immediately cease and men would remain in a total lethargy until the necessities of nature, unsatisfied, put an end to their miserable existence. It is true—so fatal an event is very little to be dreaded. Nature is always too strong for principle. And though a Pyrrhonian may throw himself or others into a momentary amazement and confusion by his profound reasonings, the first and most trivial event in life will put to flight all his doubts and scruples and leave him the same, in every point of action and speculation, with the philosophers of every other sect or with those who never concerned themselves in any philosophical researches. When he awakes from his dream, he will be the first to join in the laugh against himself and to confess that all his objections are mere amusement and can have no other tendency than to show the whimsical condition of mankind, who must act and reason and believe, though they are not able, by their most diligent inquiry, to satisfy themselves concerning the foundation of these operations or to remove the objections which may be raised against them.

## Part III

There is, indeed, a more *mitigated* skepticism or *academic* philosophy which may be both durable and useful and which may, in part, be the result of this Pyrrhonism or *excessive* skepticism when its undistinguished doubts are in some measure corrected by common sense and reflection. The greater part of mankind are naturally apt to be affirmative and dogmatic in their opinions and while they see objects only on one side and have no idea of any counterpoising argument, they throw themselves precipitately into the principles to which they are inclined, nor have they any indulgence for those who entertain opposite sentiments. To hesitate or balance perplexes their understanding, checks their passion, and suspends their action. They are, therefore, impatient until they escape from a state which to them is so uneasy and they think that they can never remove themselves far enough from it by the violence of their affirmations and obstinacy of their belief. But could such dogmatic reasoners become sensible of the strange infirmities of human understanding, even in its most perfect state and when most accurate and cautious in its determinations, such a reflection would naturally inspire them with more modesty and reserve, and diminish their fond opinion of themselves and their prejudice against antagonists. The illiterate may reflect on the disposition of the learned who, amid all the advantages of study and reflection, are commonly still diffident in their determinations. And if any of the learned are inclined, from their natural temper, to haughtiness and obstinacy, a small tincture of Pyrrhonism might abate their pride by showing them that the few advantages which they may have attained over their fellows are but inconsiderable, if compared with the universal perplexity and confusion which is inherent in human nature. In general, there is a degree of doubt and caution and modesty which, in all kinds of scrutiny and decision, ought forever accompany a just reasoner.

Another species of *mitigated* skepticism which may be of advantage to mankind and which may be the natural result of the Pyrrhonian doubts and scruples is the limitation of our inquiries to such subjects as are best adapted to the narrow capacity of human understanding. The *imagination* of man is naturally sublime, delighted with whatever is remote and extraordinary, and running without control into the most distant parts of space and time in order to avoid the objects which custom has rendered too familiar to it. A correct *judgment* observes a contrary method and, avoiding all distant and high inquiries, confines itself to common life and to such subjects as fall under daily practice and experience, leaving the more sublime topics to the embellishment of poets and orators or to the arts of priests and politicians. To bring us to so salutary a determination, nothing can be more serviceable than to be once thoroughly convinced of the force of the Pyrrhonian doubt and of the impossibility that anything but the strong power of natural instinct could free us from it. Those who have a propensity to philosophy will still continue their researches, because they reflect that, besides the immediate pleasure attending such an occupation, philosophical decisions are nothing but the reflections of common life, methodized and corrected. But they will never be tempted to go beyond common life so long as they consider the imperfection of those faculties which they employ, their narrow reach, and their inaccurate operations. While we cannot give a satisfactory reason why we believe, after a thousand experiments, that a stone will fall or fire burn, can we ever satisfy ourselves concerning any determination which we may form with regard to the origin of worlds and the situation of nature from and to eternity?

This narrow limitation, indeed, of our inquiries is in every respect so reasonable that it suffices to make the slightest examination into the natural powers of the human mind and to compare them with their objects, in order to recommend it to us. We shall then find what are the proper subjects of science and inquiry.

It seems to me that the only objects of the abstract sciences or of demonstration are quantity and number and that all attempts to extend this more perfect species of knowledge beyond these bounds are mere sophistry and illusion. As the component parts of quantity and number are entirely similar, their relations become intricate and involved and

nothing can be more curious, as well as useful, than to trace, by a variety of mediums, their equality or inequality through their different appearances. But as all other ideas are clearly distinct and different from each other, we can never advance further, by our utmost scrutiny, than to observe this diversity and, by an obvious reflection, pronounce one thing not to be another. Or if there is any difficulty in these decisions, it proceeds entirely from the indeterminate meaning of words, which is corrected by more just definitions. That *the square of the hypotenuse is equal to the squares of the other two sides* cannot be known, let the terms be ever so exactly defined, without a train of reasoning and inquiry. But to convince us of this proposition, *that where there is no property there can be no injustice*, it is only necessary to define the terms and explain injustice to be a violation of property. This proposition is, indeed, nothing but a more imperfect definition. It is the same case with all those pretended syllogistic reasonings which may be found in every other branch of learning except the sciences of quantity and number; and these may safely, I think, be pronounced the only proper objects of knowledge and demonstration.

All other inquiries of men regard only matter of fact and existence and these are evidently incapable of demonstration. Whatever *is* may *not be*. No negation of a fact can involve a contradiction. The non-existence of any being, without exception, is as clear and distinct an idea as its existence. The proposition which affirms it not to be, however false, is no less conceivable and intelligible than that which affirms it to be. The case is different with the sciences, properly so called. Every proposition which is not true is there confused and unintelligible. That the cube root of 64 is equal to the half of 10 is a false proposition and can never be distinctly conceived. But that Caesar, or the angel Gabriel, or any being never existed may be a false proposition, but still is perfectly conceivable, and implies no contradiction.

The existence, therefore, of any being can only be proved by arguments from its cause or its effect and these arguments are founded entirely on experience. If we reason *a priori*, anything may appear able to produce anything. The falling of a pebble may, for all we know, extinguish the sun or the wish of a man control the planets in their orbits. It is only experience which teaches us the nature and bounds of cause and effect and enables us to infer the existence of one object from that of another.[35] Such is the foundation of moral reasoning, which forms the greater part of human knowledge and is the source of all human action and behavior.

Moral reasonings are concerning either particular or general facts. All deliberations in life regard the former, as also all disquisitions in history, chronology, geography, and astronomy.

The sciences which treat of general facts are politics, natural philosophy, physics, chemistry, etc., where the qualities, causes, and effects of a whole species of objects are inquired into.

---

35. That impious maxim of the ancient philosophy, *Ex nihilo, nihil fit* [from nothing, comes nothing], by which the creation of matter was excluded, ceases to be a maxim according to this philosophy. Not only the will of the supreme Being may create matter, but, for all we know *a priori*, the will of any other being might create it or any other cause that the most whimsical imagination can assign.

Divinity or theology, as it proves the existence of a Deity and the immortality of souls, is composed partly of reasonings concerning particular, partly concerning general facts. It has a foundation in *reason* so far as it is supported by experience. But its best and most solid foundation is *faith* and divine revelation.

Morals and criticism are not so properly objects of the understanding as of taste and sentiment. Beauty, whether moral or natural, is felt more properly than perceived. Or if we reason concerning it and endeavor to fix its standard, we regard a new fact, namely, the general taste of mankind or some such fact which may be the object of reasoning and inquiry.

When we run over libraries, persuaded of these principles, what havoc must we make? If we take in our hand any volume—of divinity or school metaphysics, for instance—let us ask: *Does it contain any abstract reasoning concerning quantity or number?* No. *Does it contain any experimental reasoning concerning matter of fact and existence?* No. Commit it then to the flames, for it can contain nothing but sophistry and illusion.

# David Hume, *Dialogues Concerning Natural Religion* (1779)[1]

## Pamphilus to Hermippus

It has been remarked, my *Hermippus*, that though the ancient Philosophers conveyed most of their instruction in the form of dialogue, this method of composition has been little practiced in later ages, and has seldom succeeded in the hands of those who have attempted it. Accurate and regular argument, indeed, such as is now expected of philosophical inquirers, naturally throws a man into the methodical and didactic manner, where he can immediately, without preparation, explain the point at which he aims and thence proceed without interruption to deduce the proofs on which it is established. To deliver a *system* in conversation scarcely appears natural; and while the dialogue writer desires, by departing from the direct style of composition, to give a freer air to his performance and avoid the appearance of *author* and *reader*, he is apt to run into a worse inconvenience and convey the image of *pedagogue* and *pupil*. Or, if he carries on the dispute in the natural spirit of good company, by throwing in a variety of topics and preserving a proper balance among the speakers, he often loses so much

time in preparations and transitions that the reader will scarcely think himself compensated by all the graces of dialogue for the order, brevity, and precision which are sacrificed to them.

There are some subjects, however, to which dialogue writing is peculiarly adapted and where it is still preferable to the direct and simple method of composition.

Any point of doctrine which is so *obvious* that it scarcely admits of dispute, but at the same time so *important* that it cannot be too often inculcated, seems to require some such method of handling it, where the novelty of the manner may compensate the triteness of the subject, where the vivacity of conversation may enforce the precept, and where the variety of lights presented by various personages and characters may appear neither tedious nor redundant.

Any question of philosophy, on the other hand, which is so *obscure* and *uncertain* that human reason can reach no fixed determination with regard to it—if it should be treated at all—seems to lead us naturally into the style of dialogue and conversation. Reasonable men may be allowed to differ where no one can reasonably be positive. Opposite sentiments, even without any decision, afford an agreeable amusement, and if the subject is curious

---

1. [From *The Philosophical Works of David Hume* (Boston: Little, Brown and Company, 1854), 4 vols., English, modified.]

and interesting, the book carries us, in a manner, into company, and unites the two greatest and purest pleasures of human life, study and society.

Happily, these circumstances are all to be found in the subject of NATURAL RELIGION. What truth so obvious, so certain, as the *being* of a God, which the most ignorant ages have acknowledged, for which the most refined geniuses have ambitiously striven to produce new proofs and arguments? What truth so important as this, which is the ground of all our hopes, the surest foundation of morality, the firmest support of society, and the only principle which ought never to be a moment absent from our thoughts and meditations? But in treating of this obvious and important truth, what obscure questions occur concerning the *nature* of that Divine Being, his attributes, his decrees, his plan of providence? These have been always subjected to the disputations of men; concerning these, human reason has not reached any certain determination. But these are topics so interesting that we cannot restrain our restless inquiry with regard to them, though nothing but doubt, uncertainty, and contradiction have as yet been the result of our most accurate researches.

This I had lately occasion to observe, while I passed, as usual, part of the summer season with *Cleanthes*, and was present at those conversations of his with *Philo* and *Demea*, of which I gave you lately some imperfect account. Your curiosity, you then told me, was so excited that I must, of necessity, enter into a more exact detail of their reasonings, and display those various systems which they advanced with regard to so delicate a subject as that of natural religion. The remarkable contrast in their characters still further raised your expectations, while you opposed the accurate philosophical turn of *Cleanthes* to the careless skepticism of *Philo*, or compared either of their dispositions with the rigid inflexible orthodoxy of *Demea*. My youth rendered me a mere auditor of their disputes, and that curiosity, natural to the early season of life, has so deeply imprinted in my memory the whole chain and connection of their arguments that I hope I shall not omit or confound any considerable part of them in the recital.

## Part I

After I joined the company, whom I found sitting in *Cleanthes'* library, *Demea* paid *Cleanthes* some compliments on the great care which he took of my education, and on his unwearied perseverance and constancy in all his friendships. The father of *Pamphilus*, said he, was your intimate friend: The son is your pupil, and may indeed be regarded as your adopted son, were we to judge by the pains which you bestow in conveying to him every useful branch of literature and science. You are no more wanting, I am persuaded, in prudence than in industry. I shall therefore communicate to you a maxim which I have observed with regard to my own children that I may learn how far it agrees with your practice. The method I follow in their education is founded on the saying of an ancient, *"that students of philosophy ought first to learn logic, then ethics, next physics, last of all the nature of the gods."*[2] This science of natural theology, according to him, being the most profound and abstruse of any, required the most mature judgment in its students, and none but a mind enriched with all the other sciences can safely be entrusted with it.

Are you so late, says *Philo*, in teaching your children the principles of religion? Is there no danger of their neglecting or rejecting altogether those opinions of which they have heard so little during the whole course of their education? It is only as a science, replied *Demea*, subjected to human reasoning and disputation, that I postpone the study of natural theology. To season their minds with early piety is my chief care; and by continual precept and instruction, and I hope too, by example, I imprint deeply on their tender minds an habitual reverence for all the principles of religion. While they pass through every other science, I still remark the uncertainty of each part, the eternal disputations of men, the obscurity of all philosophy, and the strange, ridiculous conclusions that some of the greatest geniuses have derived from the principles of mere human reason. Having thus tamed their mind to a proper submission and self-diffidence, I have no longer any scruple of opening to them the

_____

2. Chrysippus according to Plutarch, *De Stoicorum repugnantis.*

greatest mysteries of religion, nor apprehend any danger from that assuming arrogance of philosophy, which may lead them to reject the most established doctrines and opinions.

Your precaution, says *Philo*, of seasoning your children's minds early with piety is certainly very reasonable, and no more than is requisite in this profane and irreligious age. But what I chiefly admire in your plan of education is your method of drawing advantage from the very principles of philosophy and learning, which, by inspiring pride and self-sufficiency, have commonly in all ages been found so destructive to the principles of religion. The vulgar, indeed, we may remark, who are unacquainted with science and profound inquiry, observing the endless disputes of the learned, have commonly a thorough contempt for philosophy and rivet themselves the faster by that means in the great points of theology which have been taught them. Those who enter a little into study and inquiry, finding many appearances of evidence in doctrines the newest and most extraordinary, think nothing too difficult for human reason and, presumptuously breaking through all fences, profane the inmost sanctuaries of the temple. But *Cleanthes* will, I hope, agree with me that after we have abandoned ignorance, the surest remedy, there is still one expedient left to prevent this profane liberty. Let *Demea's* principles be improved and cultivated: let us become thoroughly sensible of the weakness, blindness, and narrow limits of human reason; let us duly consider its uncertainty and endless contrarieties, even in subjects of common life and practice; let the errors and deceits of our very senses be set before us— the insuperable difficulties which attend first principles in all systems; the contradictions which adhere to the very ideas of matter, cause and effect, extension, space, time, motion; and in a word, quantity of all kinds, the object of the only science that can fairly pretend to any certainty or evidence. When these topics are displayed in their full light, as they are by some philosophers and almost all divines, who can retain such confidence in this frail faculty of reason as to pay any regard to its determinations in points so sublime, so abstruse, so remote from common life and experience? When the coherence of the parts of a stone—or even that composition of parts which renders it extended— when these familiar objects, I say, are so inexplicable and contain circumstances so repugnant and contradictory, with what assurance can we decide concerning the origin of worlds or trace their history from eternity to eternity?

While *Philo* pronounced these words, I could observe a smile in the countenance of both *Demea* and *Cleanthes*. That of *Demea* seemed to imply an unreserved satisfaction in the doctrines delivered; but, in *Cleanthes*' features, I could distinguish an air of finesse, as if he perceived some raillery or artificial malice in the reasonings of *Philo*.

You propose then, *Philo*, said *Cleanthes*, to erect religious faith on philosophical skepticism, and you think that if certainty or evidence be expelled from every other subject of inquiry, it will all retire to these theological doctrines and there acquire a superior force and authority. Whether your skepticism be as absolute and sincere as you pretend, we shall learn by and by, when the company breaks up: we shall then see whether you go out at the door or the window and whether you really doubt if your body has gravity or can be injured by its fall, according to popular opinion, derived from our fallacious senses and more fallacious experience. And this consideration, *Demea*, may, I think, fairly serve to abate our ill-will to this humorous sect of the skeptics. If they be thoroughly in earnest, they will not long trouble the world with their doubts, cavils, and disputes: if they be only in jest, they are, perhaps, bad railers, but can never be very dangerous either to the state, to philosophy, or to religion.

In reality, *Philo*, continued he, it seems certain that though a man in a flush of humor, after intense reflection on the many contradictions and imperfections of human reason, may entirely renounce all belief and opinion, it is impossible for him to persevere in this total skepticism or make it appear in his conduct for a few hours. External objects press in upon him; passions solicit him; his philosophical melancholy dissipates; and even the utmost violence upon his own temper will not be able, during any time, to preserve the poor appearance of skepticism. And for what reason impose on himself such a violence? This is a point in which it will be impossible for him ever to satisfy himself, consistently with his skeptical principles. So that upon the whole, nothing could be more ridiculous than the principles of the ancient *Pyrrhonians*, if in reality they endeavored, as is pretended, to extend throughout, the same skepticism which they had learned from the declamations of their schools and which they ought to have confined to them.

In this view, there appears a great resemblance between the sects of the *Stoics* and *Pyrrhonians*, though perpetual antagonists; and both of them seem founded on this erroneous maxim that what a man can perform sometimes and in some dispositions, he can perform always and in every disposition. When the mind, by *Stoical* reflections, is elevated into a sublime enthusiasm of virtue and strongly smitten with any *species* of honor or public good, the utmost bodily pain and sufferings will not prevail over such a high sense of duty, and it is possible, perhaps, by its means, even to smile and exult in the midst of tortures. If this sometimes may be the case in fact and reality, much more may a philosopher, in his school or even in his closet, work himself up to such an enthusiasm, and support in imagination the most acute pain or most calamitous event which he can possibly conceive. But how shall he support this enthusiasm itself? The bent of his mind relaxes and cannot be recalled at pleasure; avocations lead him astray; misfortunes attack him unawares; and the p*hilosopher* sinks by degrees into the *plebeian*.

I allow of your comparison between the *Stoics* and *Skeptics*, replied *Philo*. But you may observe at the same time that though the mind cannot, in *Stoicism*, support the highest flights of philosophy, yet even when it sinks lower, it still retains something of its former disposition; and the effects of the *Stoic's* reasoning will appear in his conduct in common life and through the whole tenor of his actions. The ancient schools, particularly that of *Zeno*, produced examples of virtue and constancy which seem astonishing to present times.

Vain Wisdom all and false Philosophy.
Yet with a pleasing sorcery could charm
Pain, for a while, or anguish; and excite

Fallacious Hope, or arm the obdurate breast
With stubborn Patience, as with triple steel.[3]

In like manner, if a man has accustomed himself to skeptical considerations on the uncertainty and narrow limits of reason, he will not entirely forget them when he turns his reflection on other subjects; but in all his philosophical principles and reasoning, I dare not say in his common conduct, he will be found different from those who either never formed any opinions in the case or have entertained sentiments more favorable to human reason.

To whatever length anyone may push his speculative principles of skepticism, he must act, I admit, and live and converse like other men; and for this conduct he is not obliged to give any other reason than the absolute necessity he lies under of so doing. If he ever carries his speculations further than this necessity constrains him, and philosophizes on either natural or moral subjects, he is allured by a certain pleasure and satisfaction which he finds in employing himself after that manner. He considers besides that everyone, even in common life, is constrained to have more or less of this philosophy; that from our earliest infancy we make continual advances in forming more general principles of conduct and reasoning; that the larger experience we acquire and the stronger reason we are endued with, we always render our principles the more general and comprehensive; and that what we call *philosophy* is nothing but a more regular and methodical operation of the same kind. To philosophize on such subjects is nothing essentially different from reasoning on common life, and we may only expect greater stability, if not greater truth, from our philosophy on account of its more exact and more scrupulous method of proceeding.

But when we look beyond human affairs and the properties of the surrounding bodies—when we carry our speculations into the two eternities, before and after the present state of things; into the creation and formation of the universe; the existence and properties of spirits; the powers and operations

---

3. [John Milton, *Paradise Lost*, Book II.]

of one universal Spirit existing without beginning and without end; omnipotent, omniscient, immutable, infinite, and incomprehensible—we must be far removed from the smallest tendency to skepticism not to be apprehensive that we have here got quite beyond the reach of our faculties. So long as we confine our speculations to trade, or morals, or politics, or criticism, we make appeals every moment to common sense and experience, which strengthen our philosophical conclusions, and remove at least in part the suspicion which we so justly entertain with regard to every reasoning that is very subtle and refined. But in theological reasonings, we have not this advantage; while at the same time we are employed upon objects which, we must be sensible, are too large for our grasp, and of all others, require most to be familiarized to our apprehension. We are like foreigners in a strange country, to whom everything must seem suspicious and who are in danger every moment of transgressing against the laws and customs of the people with whom they live and converse. We know not how far we ought to trust our vulgar methods of reasoning in such a subject, since even in common life and in that province which is peculiarly appropriated to them, we cannot account for them and are entirely guided by a kind of instinct or necessity in employing them.

All skeptics pretend that if reason be considered in an abstract view, it furnishes invincible arguments against itself, and that we could never retain any conviction or assurance on any subject were not the skeptical reasonings so refined and subtle that they are not able to counterpoise the more solid and more natural arguments derived from the senses and experience. But it is evident, whenever our arguments lose this advantage and run wide of common life, that the most refined skepticism comes to be upon a footing with them and is able to oppose and counterbalance them. The one has no more weight than the other. The mind must remain in suspense between them, and it is that very suspense or balance which is the triumph of skepticism.

But I observe, says *Cleanthes*, with regard to you, *Philo*, and all speculative skeptics that your doctrine and practice are as much at variance in the most

abstruse points of theory as in the conduct of common life. Wherever evidence discovers itself, you adhere to it, notwithstanding your pretended skepticism, and I can observe, too, some of your sect to be as decisive as those who make greater professions of certainty and assurance. In reality, would not a man be ridiculous who pretended to reject Newton's explication of the wonderful phenomenon of the rainbow because that explication gives a minute anatomy of the rays of light—a subject, indeed, too refined for human comprehension? And what would you say to one who, having nothing particular to object to the arguments of *Copernicus* and *Galileo* for the motion of the earth, should withhold his assent on that general principle that these subjects were too magnificent and remote to be explained by the narrow and fallacious reason of mankind?

There is indeed a kind of brutish and ignorant skepticism, as you well observed, which gives the vulgar a general prejudice against what they do not easily understand and makes them reject every principle which requires elaborate reasoning to prove and establish it. This species of skepticism is fatal to knowledge, not to religion, since we find that those who make greatest profession of it give often their assent not only to the great truths of theism and natural theology but even to the most absurd tenets which a traditional superstition has recommended to them. They firmly believe in witches, though they will not believe nor attend to the most simple proposition of *Euclid*. But the refined and philosophical skeptics fall into an inconsistency of an opposite nature. They push their researches into the most abstruse corners of science, and their assent attends them in every step, proportioned to the evidence which they meet with. They are even obliged to acknowledge that the most abstruse and remote objects are those which are best explained by philosophy. Light is in reality anatomized. The true system of the heavenly bodies is discovered and ascertained. But the nourishment of bodies by food is still an inexplicable mystery. The cohesion of the parts of matter is still incomprehensible. These skeptics, therefore, are obliged, in every question, to consider each particular evidence apart and proportion their assent to the precise degree of evidence which occurs. This is their practice in all natural, mathematical, moral, and political science. And why not the same, I ask, in the theological and religious? Why must conclusions of this nature be alone rejected on the general presumption of the insufficiency of human reason without any particular discussion of the evidence? Is not such an unequal conduct a plain proof of prejudice and passion?

Our senses, you say, are fallacious; our understanding erroneous; our ideas, even of the most familiar objects—extension, duration, motion—full of absurdities and contradictions. You defy me to solve the difficulties or reconcile the repugnancies which you discover in them. I have not capacity for so great an undertaking: I have not leisure for it: I perceive it to be superfluous. Your own conduct in every circumstance refutes your principles and shows the firmest reliance on all the received maxims of science, morals, prudence, and behavior.

I shall never assent to so harsh an opinion as that of a celebrated writer who says that the *Skeptics* are not a sect of philosophers; they are only a sect of liars.[4] I may, however, affirm (I hope without offence) that they are a sect of jesters or railers. But for my part, whenever I find myself disposed to mirth and amusement, I shall certainly choose my entertainment of a less perplexing and abstruse nature. A comedy, a novel, or at most a history seems a more natural recreation than such metaphysical subtleties and abstractions.

In vain would the skeptic make a distinction between science and common life or between one science and another. The arguments employed in all, if just, are of a similar nature and contain the same force and evidence. Or if there be any difference among them, the advantage lies entirely on the side of theology and natural religion. Many principles of mechanics are founded on very abstruse reasoning yet no man who has any pretensions to science, even no speculative skeptic, pretends to entertain the least doubt with regard to them. The *Copernican* system contains the most surprising paradox, and the most

contrary to our natural conceptions, to appearances, and to our very senses: yet even monks and inquisitors are now constrained to withdraw their opposition to it. And shall *Philo*, a man of so liberal a genius and extensive knowledge, entertain any general undistinguished scruples with regard to the religious hypothesis, which is founded on the simplest and most obvious arguments and, unless it meets with artificial obstacles, has such easy access and admission into the mind of man?

And here we may observe, continued he, turning himself towards *Demea*, a pretty curious circumstance in the history of the sciences. After the union of philosophy with the popular religion, upon the first establishment of *Christianity*, nothing was more usual among all religious teachers than declamations against reason, against the senses, against every principle derived merely from human research and inquiry. All the topics of the ancient *Academics* were adopted by the fathers and thence propagated for several ages in every school and pulpit throughout *Christendom*. The Reformers embraced the same principles of reasoning, or rather declamation, and all panegyrics on the excellency of faith were sure to be interlarded with some severe strokes of satire against natural reason. A celebrated prelate too,[5] of the Romish communion, a man of the most extensive learning, who wrote a demonstration of Christianity, has also composed a treatise which contains all the cavils of the boldest and most determined *Pyrrhonism*. *Locke* seems to have been the first *Christian* who ventured openly to assert that *faith* was nothing but a species of *reason*; that religion was only a branch of philosophy; and that a chain of arguments, similar to that which established any truth in morals, politics, or physics was always employed in discovering all the principles of theology, natural and revealed. The ill use which *Bayle* and other libertines made of the philosophical skepticism of the fathers and first reformers still further propagated the judicious sentiment of *Mr. Locke*, and it is now in a manner avowed by all pretenders to reasoning and philosophy that

---

4. *L'art de penser*. [*The Art of Thinking*, commonly known as the *Port-Royal Logic*, written in 1662 by Antoine Arnauld and Pierre Nicole; see Discourse 1.]

5. Mons. Huet. [Pierre-Daniel Huet (1630–1721), Bishop of Avranches.]

atheist and skeptic are almost synonymous. And as it is certain that no man is in earnest when he professes the latter principle, I would gladly hope that there are as few who seriously maintain the former.

Don't you remember, said *Philo*, the excellent saying of *Lord Bacon* on this head? That a little philosophy, replied *Cleanthes*, makes a man an atheist, a great deal converts him to religion. That is a very judicious remark too, said *Philo*. But what I have in my eye is another passage where, having mentioned *David's* fool, who said in his heart there is no God, this great philosopher observes that the atheists nowadays have a double share of folly; for they are not contented to say in their hearts there is no God, but they also utter that impiety with their lips and are thereby guilty of multiplied indiscretion and imprudence. Such people, though they were ever so much in earnest, cannot, I think, be very formidable.

But though you should rank me in this class of fools, I cannot forbear communicating a remark that occurs to me from the history of the religious and irreligious skepticism with which you have entertained us. It appears to me that there are strong symptoms of priestcraft in the whole progress of this affair. During ignorant ages, such as those which followed the dissolution of the ancient schools, the priests perceived that atheism, deism, or heresy of any kind could only proceed from the presumptuous questioning of received opinions and from a belief that human reason was equal to everything. Education had then a mighty influence over the minds of men and was almost equal in force to those suggestions of the senses and common understanding by which the most determined skeptic must allow himself to be governed. But at present, when the influence of education is much diminished and men, from a more open commerce of the world, have learned to compare the popular principles of different nations and ages, our sagacious divines have changed their whole system of philosophy and talk the language of *Stoics*, *Platonists*, and *Peripatetics*, not that of *Pyrrhonians* and *Academics*. If we distrust human reason, we have now no other principle to lead us into religion. Thus, skeptics in one age, dogmatists in another; whichever system best suits the purpose of these reverend gentlemen in giving them an ascendant over mankind, they are sure to make it their favorite principle and established tenet.

It is very natural, said *Cleanthes*, for men to embrace those principles by which they find they can best defend their doctrines; nor need we have any recourse to priestcraft to account for so reasonable an expedient. And surely nothing can afford a stronger presumption that any set of principles are true and ought to be embraced than to observe that they tend to the confirmation of true religion and serve to confound the cavils of atheists, libertines, and free thinkers of all denominations.

## Part II

I must admit, *Cleanthes*, said *Demea*, that nothing can more surprise me than the light in which you have all along put this argument. By the whole tenor of your discourse, one would imagine that you were maintaining the being of a God against the cavils of atheists and infidels and were necessitated to become a champion for that fundamental principle of all religion. But this, I hope, is not by any means a question among us. No man, no man at least of common sense, I am persuaded, ever entertained a serious doubt with regard to a truth so certain and self-evident. The question is not concerning the *being*, but the *nature* of God. This, I affirm, from the infirmities of human understanding, to be altogether incomprehensible and unknown to us. The essence of that supreme mind, his attributes, the manner of his existence, the very nature of his duration; these and every particular which regards so divine a being are mysterious to men. Finite, weak, and blind creatures, we ought to humble ourselves in his august presence, and, conscious of our frailties, adore in silence his infinite perfections, which eye has not seen, ear has not heard, neither has it entered into the heart of man to conceive. They are covered in a deep cloud from human curiosity. It is profaneness to attempt penetrating through these sacred obscurities. And next to the impiety of denying his existence is the temerity of prying into his nature and essence, decrees, and attributes.

But lest you should think that my *piety* has here got the better of my *philosophy*, I shall support my opinion, if it needs any support, by a very great authority. I might cite all the divines, almost from the foundation of *Christianity*, who have ever treated of this or any other theological subject, but I shall confine myself at present to one equally celebrated for piety and philosophy. It is *Father Malebranche*, who, I remember, thus expresses himself. "One ought not so much," says he, "to call God a spirit, in order to express positively what he is, as in order to signify that he is not matter. He is a Being infinitely perfect, of this we cannot doubt. But in the same manner as we ought not to imagine, even supposing him corporeal, that he is clothed with a human body, as the *Anthropomorphites* asserted, under color that that figure was the most perfect of any, so neither ought we to imagine that the spirit of God has human ideas or bears any resemblance to our spirit, under color that we know nothing more perfect than a human mind. We ought rather to believe that as he comprehends the perfections of matter without being material . . . he comprehends also the perfections of created spirits without being spirit in the manner we conceive spirit: that his true name is *He that is* or, in other words, Being without restriction, All Being, the Being infinite and universal."[6]

After so great an authority, *Demea*, replied *Philo*, as that which you have produced, and a thousand more which you might produce, it would appear ridiculous in me to add my sentiment or express my approbation of your doctrine. But surely, where reasonable men treat these subjects the question can never be concerning the *being* but only the *nature* of the Deity. The former truth, as you well observe, is unquestionable and self-evident. Nothing exists without a cause, and the original cause of this universe (whatever it be) we call *God* and piously ascribe to him every species of perfection. Whoever scruples this fundamental truth deserves every punishment which can be inflicted among philosophers, to wit, the greatest ridicule, contempt, and disapprobation. But as all perfection is entirely relative, we ought never to imagine that we comprehend the attributes

of this divine Being or to suppose that his perfections have any analogy or likeness to the perfections of a human creature. Wisdom, thought, design, knowledge—these we justly ascribe to him, because these words are honorable among men and we have no other language or other conceptions by which we can express our adoration of him. But let us beware, lest we think that our ideas anywise correspond to his perfections or that his attributes have any resemblance to these qualities among men. He is infinitely superior to our limited view and comprehension, and is more the object of worship in the temple than of disputation in the schools.

In reality, *Cleanthes*, continued he, there is no need of having recourse to that affected skepticism so displeasing to you in order to come at this determination. Our ideas reach no further than our experience. We have no experience of divine attributes and operations. I need not conclude my syllogism. You can draw the inference yourself. And it is a pleasure to me (and I hope to you too) that just reasoning and sound piety here concur in the same conclusion, and both of them establish the adorably mysterious and incomprehensible nature of the Supreme Being.

Not to lose any time in circumlocutions, said *Cleanthes*, addressing himself to *Demea*, much less in replying to the pious declamations of *Philo*, I shall briefly explain how I conceive this matter. Look round the world, contemplate the whole and every part of it, you will find it to be nothing but one great machine, subdivided into an infinite number of lesser machines, which again admit of subdivisions to a degree beyond what human senses and faculties can trace and explain. All these various machines, and even their most minute parts, are adjusted to each other with an accuracy which ravishes into admiration all men who have ever contemplated them. The curious adapting of means to ends throughout all nature resembles exactly, though it much exceeds, the productions of human contrivance, of human designs, thought, wisdom, and intelligence. Since, therefore, the effects resemble each other, we are led to infer by all the rules of analogy that the causes also resemble, and that the Author of Nature is somewhat similar to, the mind of man, though possessed of

---

6. *Recherche de la Verité*, Book 3, chap. 9.

much larger faculties, proportioned to the grandeur of the work which he has executed. By this argument *a posteriori*, and by this argument alone, do we prove at once the existence of a Deity and his similarity to human mind and intelligence.

I shall be so free, *Cleanthes*, said *Demea*, as to tell you that from the beginning I could not approve of your conclusion concerning the similarity of the Deity to men; still less can I approve of the mediums by which you endeavor to establish it. What! No demonstration of the Being of God! No abstract arguments! No proofs *a priori*! Are these, which have been so much insisted on until now by philosophers, all fallacy, all sophism? Can we reach no further in this subject than experience and probability? I will not say that this is betraying the cause of a Deity, but surely by this affected candor you give advantages to atheists, which they never could obtain by the mere dint of argument and reasoning.

What I chiefly scruple in this subject, said *Philo*, is not so much that all religious arguments are by *Cleanthes* reduced to experience as that they appear not to be even the most certain and irrefragable of that inferior kind. That a stone will fall, that fire will burn, that the earth has solidity we have observed a thousand and a thousand times, and when any new instance of this nature is presented, we draw without hesitation the accustomed inference. The exact similarity of the cases gives us a perfect assurance of a similar event and a stronger evidence is never desired nor sought after. But wherever you depart in the least from the similarity of the cases, you diminish proportionally the evidence and may at last bring it to a very weak *analogy*, which is confessedly liable to error and uncertainty. After having experienced the circulation of the blood in human creatures, we make no doubt that it takes place in *Titius* and *Maevius*. But from its circulation in frogs and fishes, it is only a presumption, though a strong one, from analogy that it takes place in men and other animals. The analogical reasoning is much weaker when we infer the circulation of the sap in vegetables from our experience that the blood circulates in animals; and those who hastily followed that imperfect analogy are found by more accurate experiments to have been mistaken.

If we see a house, *Cleanthes*, we conclude with the greatest certainty that it had an architect or builder, because this is precisely that species of effect which we have experienced to proceed from that species of cause. But surely you will not affirm that the universe bears such a resemblance to a house that we can with the same certainty infer a similar cause or that the analogy is here entire and perfect. The dissimilitude is so striking that the utmost you can here pretend to is a guess, a conjecture, a presumption concerning a similar cause, and how that pretension will be received in the world, I leave you to consider.

It would surely be very ill received, replied *Cleanthes*, and I should be deservedly blamed and detested did I allow that the proofs of a Deity amounted to no more than a guess or conjecture. But is the whole adjustment of means to ends in a house and in the universe so slight a resemblance? The economy of final causes? The order, proportion, and arrangement of every part? Steps of a stair are plainly contrived that human legs may use them in mounting, and this inference is certain and infallible. Human legs are also contrived for walking and mounting, and this inference, I allow, is not altogether so certain, because of the dissimilarity which you remark; but does it therefore deserve the name only of presumption or conjecture?

Good God! cried *Demea*, interrupting him, where are we? Zealous defenders of religion allow that the proofs of a Deity fall short of perfect evidence! And you, *Philo*, on whose assistance I depended in proving the adorable mysteriousness of the Divine Nature, do you assent to all these extravagant opinions of *Cleanthes*? For what other name can I give them? Or, why spare my censure when such principles are advanced, supported by such an authority, before so young a man as *Pamphilus*?

You seem not to apprehend, replied *Philo*, that I argue with *Cleanthes* in his own way, and, by showing him the dangerous consequences of his tenets, hope at last to reduce him to our opinion. But what sticks most with you, I observe, is the representation which *Cleanthes* has made of the argument *a posteriori*, and, finding that that argument is likely to escape your hold and vanish into air, you think it so disguised that you can scarcely believe it to be set in its true light. Now, however much I may dissent in other respects from the dangerous principles of *Cleanthes*, I must allow that he has fairly represented that argument, and I shall endeavor so to state the matter to you that you will entertain no further scruples with regard to it.

Were a man to abstract from everything which he knows or has seen, he would be altogether incapable, merely from his own ideas, to determine what kind of scene the universe must be or to give the preference to one state or situation of things above another. For, as nothing which he clearly conceives could be esteemed impossible or implying a contradiction, every chimera of his fancy would be upon an equal footing; nor could he assign any just reason why he adheres to one idea or system and rejects the others which are equally possible.

Again, after he opens his eyes and contemplates the world as it really is, it would be impossible for him at first to assign the cause of any one event, much less of the whole of things or of the universe. He might set his fancy a rambling, and she might bring him in an infinite variety of reports and representations. These would all be possible, but being all equally possible, he would never of himself give a satisfactory account for his preferring one of them to the rest. Experience alone can point out to him the true cause of any phenomenon.

Now, according to this method of reasoning, *Demea*, it follows (and is, indeed, tacitly allowed by *Cleanthes* himself) that order, arrangement, or the adjustment of final causes is not of itself any proof of design, but only so far as it has been experienced to proceed from that principle. For all we can know *a priori*, matter may contain the source or spring of order originally within itself as well as mind does, and there is no more difficulty in conceiving that the several elements, from an internal unknown cause, may fall into the most exquisite arrangement than to conceive that their ideas, in the great universal mind, from a like internal unknown cause, fall into that arrangement. The equal possibility of both these suppositions is allowed. But by experience we find (according to *Cleanthes*) that there is a difference between them.

Throw several pieces of steel together without shape or form; they will never arrange themselves so as to compose a watch. Stone and mortar and wood, without an architect, never erect a house. But the ideas in a human mind, we see by an unknown, inexplicable economy arrange themselves so as to form the plan of a watch or house. Experience, therefore, proves that there is an original principle of order in mind, not in matter. From similar effects we infer similar causes. The adjustment of means to ends is alike in the universe, as in a machine of human contrivance. The causes, therefore, must be resembling.

I was from the beginning scandalized, I must admit, with this resemblance, which is asserted between the Deity and human creatures and must conceive it to imply such a degradation of the Supreme Being as no sound theist could endure. With your assistance, therefore, *Demea*, I shall endeavor to defend what you justly call the adorable mysteriousness of the Divine Nature, and shall refute this reasoning of *Cleanthes*, provided he allows that I have made a fair representation of it.

When *Cleanthes* had assented, *Philo*, after a short pause, proceeded in the following manner.

That all inferences, *Cleanthes*, concerning fact are founded on experience and that all experimental reasonings are founded on the supposition that similar causes prove similar effects, and similar effects similar causes, I shall not at present much dispute with you. But observe, I entreat you, with what extreme caution all just reasoners proceed in the transferring of experiments to similar cases. Unless the cases be exactly similar, they repose no perfect confidence in applying their past observation to any particular phenomenon. Every alteration of circumstances occasions a doubt concerning the event, and it requires new experiments to prove certainly that the new circumstances are of no moment or importance. A change in bulk, situation, arrangement, age, disposition of the air, or surrounding bodies—any of these particulars may be attended with the most unexpected consequences, and unless the objects be quite familiar to us, it is the highest temerity to expect with assurance, after any of these changes, an event similar to that which before fell under our observation. The slow and deliberate steps of philosophers here, if anywhere, are distinguished from the precipitate march of the vulgar, who, hurried on by the smallest similitude, are incapable of all discernment or consideration.

But can you think, *Cleanthes*, that your usual phlegm and philosophy have been preserved in so wide a step as you have taken, when you compared to the universe houses, ships, furniture, machines, and, from their similarity in some circumstances, inferred a similarity in their causes? Thought, design, intelligence such as we discover in men and other animals is no more than one of the springs and principles of the universe as well as heat or cold, attraction or repulsion, and a hundred others, which fall under daily observation. It is an active cause by which some particular parts of nature, we find, produce alterations on other parts. But can a conclusion, with any propriety, be transferred from parts to the whole? Does not the great disproportion bar all comparison and inference? From observing the growth of a hair, can we learn anything concerning the generation of a man? Would the manner of a leaf's blowing, even though perfectly known, afford us any instruction concerning the vegetation of a tree?

But allowing that we were to take the *operations* of one part of nature upon another for the foundation of our judgment concerning the *origin* of the whole (which never can be admitted), yet why select so minute, so weak, so bounded a principle as the reason and design of animals is found to be upon this planet? What peculiar privilege has this little agitation of the brain which we call thought that we must thus make it the model of the whole universe? Our partiality in our own favor does indeed present it on all occasions, but sound philosophy ought carefully to guard against so natural an illusion.

So far from admitting, continued *Philo*, that the operations of a part can afford us any just conclusion concerning the origin of the whole, I will not allow any one part to form a rule for another part, if the latter be very remote from the former. Is there any reasonable ground to conclude that the inhabitants of other planets possess thought, intelligence, reason, or anything similar to these faculties in men? When nature has so extremely diversified her manner of operation in this small globe, can we imagine that she incessantly copies herself throughout so immense a universe? And if thought, as we may well suppose, be confined merely to this narrow corner, and has even there so limited a sphere of action, with what propriety can we assign it for the original cause of all things? The narrow views of a peasant who makes his domestic economy the rule for the government of kingdoms is in comparison a pardonable sophism.

But were we ever so much assured that a thought and reason resembling the human were to be found throughout the whole universe, and were its activity elsewhere vastly greater and more commanding than it appears in this globe; yet I cannot see why the operations of a world constituted, arranged, adjusted, can with any propriety be extended to a world which is in its embryo state and is advancing towards that constitution and arrangement. By observation we know something of the economy, action, and nourishment of a finished animal, but we must transfer with great caution that observation to the growth of a fetus in the womb, and still more in the formation of an animalcule in the loins of its male parent. Nature, we find, even from our limited experience, possesses an infinite number of springs and principles which incessantly discover themselves on every change of her position and situation. And what new and unknown principles would actuate her in so new and unknown a situation as that of the formation of a universe, we cannot, without the utmost temerity, pretend to determine.

A very small part of this great system, during a very short time, is very imperfectly discovered to us; and do we then pronounce decisively concerning the origin of the whole?

Admirable conclusion! Stone, wood, brick, iron, brass have not, at this time, in this minute globe of earth, an order or arrangement without human art and contrivance; therefore, the universe could not originally attain its order and arrangement without something similar to human art. But is a part of nature a rule for another part very wide of the former? Is it a rule for the whole? Is a very small part a rule for the universe? Is nature in one situation a certain rule for nature in another situation vastly different from the former?

And can you blame me, *Cleanthes*, if I here imitate the prudent reserve of *Simonides*, who, according to the noted story, being asked by *Hiero* what God was desired a day to think of it, and then two days more; and after that manner continually prolonged the term, without ever bringing in his definition or description? Could you even blame me if I answered at first that *I did not know* and was sensible that this subject lay vastly beyond the reach of my faculties? You might cry out *skeptic* and *raillier* as much as you pleased: but, having found in so many other subjects much more familiar the imperfections and even contradictions of human reason, I never should expect any success from its feeble conjectures in a subject so sublime and so remote from the sphere of our observation. When two *species* of objects have always been observed to be conjoined together, I can *infer*, by custom, the existence of one wherever I see the existence of the other, and this I call an argument from experience. But how this argument can have place where the objects, as in the present case, are single, individual, without parallel or specific resemblance, may be difficult to explain. And will any man tell me with a serious countenance that an orderly universe must arise from some thought and art like the human because we have experience of it? To ascertain this reasoning it were requisite that we had experience of the origin of worlds; and it is not sufficient, surely, that we have seen ships and cities arise from human art and contrivance.

*Philo* was proceeding in this vehement manner, somewhat between jest and earnest, as it appeared to me, when he observed some signs of impatience in *Cleanthes* and then immediately stopped short. What I had to suggest, said *Cleanthes*, is only that you would not abuse terms or make use of popular expressions to subvert philosophical reasonings. You know that the vulgar often distinguish reason from experience, even where the question relates only to matter of fact and existence, though it is found where that *reason* is properly analyzed that it is nothing but a species of experience. To prove by experience the origin of the universe from mind is

not more contrary to common speech than to prove the motion of the earth from the same principle. And a caviller might raise all the same objections to the *Copernican* system which you have urged against my reasonings. Have you other earths, might he say, which you have seen to move? Have . . . .

Yes! cried *Philo*, interrupting him, we have other earths. Is not the moon another earth, which we see to turn round its center? Is not Venus another earth where we observe the same phenomenon? Are not the revolutions of the sun also a confirmation from analogy of the same theory? All the planets, are they not earths which revolve about the sun? Are not the satellites moons which move round Jupiter and Saturn and, along with these primary planets, round the sun? These analogies and resemblances, with others which I have not mentioned, are the sole proofs of the *Copernican* system; and to you it belongs to consider whether you have any analogies of the same kind to support your theory.

In reality, *Cleanthes*, continued he, the modern system of astronomy is now so much received by all inquirers and has become so essential a part even of our earliest education that we are not commonly very scrupulous in examining the reasons upon which it is founded. It is now become a matter of mere curiosity to study the first writers on that subject who had the full force of prejudice to encounter and were obliged to turn their arguments on every side in order to render them popular and convincing. But if we peruse *Galileo's* famous *Dialogues* concerning the system of the world, we shall find that that great genius, one of the sublimest that ever existed, first bent all his endeavors to prove that there was no foundation for the distinction commonly made between elementary and celestial substances. The schools, proceeding from the illusions of sense, had carried this distinction very far and had established the latter substances to be ingenerable, incorruptible, unalterable, impassible and had assigned all the opposite qualities to the former. But Galileo, beginning with the moon, proved its similarity in every particular to the earth: its convex figure, its natural darkness when not illuminated, its density, its distinction into solid and liquid, the variations of its phases, the mutual illuminations of the earth and moon, their mutual eclipses, the inequalities of the lunar surface, etc. After many instances of this kind with regard to all the planets, men plainly saw that these bodies became proper objects of experience and that the similarity of their nature enabled us to extend the same arguments and phenomena from one to the other.

In this cautious proceeding of the astronomers you may read your own condemnation, *Cleanthes*, or rather may see that the subject in which you are engaged exceeds all human reason and inquiry. Can you pretend to show any such similarity between the fabric of a house and the generation of a universe? Have you ever seen nature in any such situation as resembles the first arrangement of the elements? Have worlds ever been formed under your eye, and have you had leisure to observe the whole progress of the phenomenon, from the first appearance of order to its final consummation? If you have, then cite your experience and deliver your theory.

## Part III

How the most absurd argument, replied *Cleanthes*, in the hands of a man of ingenuity and invention may acquire an air of probability! Are you not aware, *Philo*, that it became necessary for *Copernicus* and his first disciples to prove the similarity of the terrestrial and celestial matter because several philosophers, blinded by old systems and supported by some sensible appearances, had denied that similarity? But that it is by no means necessary that theists should prove the similarity of the works of nature to those of art, because this similarity is self-evident and undeniable? The same matter, a like form; what more is requisite to show an analogy between their causes and to ascertain the origin of all things from a divine purpose and intention? Your objections, I must freely tell you, are no better than the abstruse cavils of those philosophers who denied motion, and ought to be refuted in the same manner: by illustrations, examples, and instances rather than by serious argument and philosophy.

Suppose, therefore, that an articulate voice were heard in the clouds, much louder and more melodious than any which human art could ever reach; suppose that this voice were extended in the same instant over all nations and spoke to each nation in its own language and dialect; suppose that the words delivered not only contain a just sense and meaning but convey some instruction altogether worthy of a benevolent Being, superior to mankind; could you possibly hesitate a moment concerning the cause of this voice, and must you not instantly ascribe it to some design or purpose? Yet I cannot see but all the same objections (if they merit that appellation) which lie against the system of theism may also be produced against this inference.

Might you not say that all conclusions concerning fact were founded on experience that when we hear an articulate voice in the dark and thence infer a man, it is only the resemblance of the effects which leads us to conclude that there is a like resemblance in the cause, but that this extraordinary voice, by its loudness, extent, and flexibility to all languages, bears so little analogy to any human voice that we have no reason to suppose any analogy in their causes, and consequently that a rational, wise, coherent speech proceeded, you know not whence, from some accidental whistling of the winds, not from any divine reason or intelligence? You see clearly your own objections in these cavils, and I hope too you see clearly that they cannot possibly have more force in the one case than in the other.

But to bring the case still nearer the present one of the universe, I shall make two suppositions, which imply not any absurdity or impossibility. Suppose that there is a natural, universal, invariable language common to every individual of human race and that books are natural productions, which perpetuate themselves in the same manner with animals and vegetables—by descent and propagation. Several expressions of our passions contain a universal language: All brute animals have a natural speech, which, however limited, is very intelligible to their own species. And as there are infinitely fewer parts and less contrivance in the finest composition of eloquence than in the coarsest organized body, the propagation of an *Iliad* or *Aeneid* is an easier supposition than that of any plant or animal.

Suppose, therefore, that you enter into your library, thus peopled by natural volumes, containing the most refined reason and most exquisite beauty; could you possibly open one of them and doubt that its original cause bore the strongest analogy to mind and intelligence? When it reasons and discourses; when it expostulates, argues, and enforces its views and topics; when it applies sometimes to the pure intellect, sometimes to the affections; when it collects, disposes, and adorns every consideration suited to the subject; could you persist in asserting that all this, at the bottom, had really no meaning and that the first formation of this volume in the loins of its original parent proceeded not from thought and design? Your obstinacy, I know, reaches not that degree of firmness; even your skeptical play and wantonness would be abashed at so glaring an absurdity.

But if there be any difference, *Philo*, between this supposed case and the real one of the universe, it is all to the advantage of the latter. The anatomy of an animal affords many stronger instances of design than the perusal of *Livy* or *Tacitus*, and any objection which you start in the former case—by carrying me back to so unusual and extraordinary a scene as the first formation of worlds—the same objection has place on the supposition of our vegetating library. Choose, then, your party, *Philo*, without ambiguity or evasion; either assert that a rational volume is no proof of a rational cause or admit of a similar cause to all the works of nature.

Let me here observe too, continued *Cleanthes*, that this religious argument, instead of being weakened by that skepticism so much affected by you yet rather acquires force from it and becomes more firm and undisputed. To exclude all argument or reasoning of every kind is either affectation or madness. The declared profession of every reasonable skeptic is only to reject abstruse, remote, and refined arguments, to adhere to common sense and the plain instincts of nature, and to assent wherever any reasons strike him with so full a force that he cannot, without the greatest violence, prevent it. Now the arguments for natural religion are plainly of this kind, and nothing but the most perverse, obstinate metaphysics can reject them. Consider, anatomize the eye; survey its

structure and contrivance and tell me, from your own feeling, if the idea of a contriver does not immediately flow in upon you with a force like that of sensation. The most obvious conclusion, surely, is in favor of design; and it requires time, reflection, and study to summon up those frivolous though abstruse objections which can support infidelity. Who can behold the male and female of each species, the correspondence of their parts and instincts, their passions, and whole course of life before and after generation, but must be sensible that the propagation of the species is intended by nature? Millions and millions of such instances present themselves through every part of the universe, and no language can convey a more intelligible irresistible meaning than the curious adjustment of final causes. To what degree, therefore, of blind dogmatism must one have attained to reject such natural and such convincing arguments?

Some beauties in writing we may meet with which seem contrary to rules and which gain the affections and animate the imagination in opposition to all the precepts of criticism and to the authority of the established masters of art. And if the argument for theism be, as you pretend, contradictory to the principles of logic, its universal, its irresistible influence proves clearly that there may be arguments of a like irregular nature. Whatever cavils may be urged, an orderly world as well as a coherent articulate speech will still be received as an incontestable proof of design and intention.

It sometimes happens, I admit, that the religious arguments have not their due influence on an ignorant savage and barbarian, not because they are obscure and difficult but because he never asks himself any question with regard to them. Whence arises the curious structure of an animal? From the copulation of its parents. And these whence? From *their* parents? A few removes set the objects at such a distance that to him they are lost in darkness and confusion; nor is he actuated by any curiosity to trace them further. But this is neither dogmatism nor skepticism, but stupidity: a state of mind very different from your sifting, inquisitive disposition, my ingenious friend. You can trace causes from effects, you can compare the most distant and remote objects, and your greatest errors proceed not from barrenness of thought and invention but from too luxuriant a fertility which suppresses your natural good sense by a profusion of unnecessary scruples and objections.

Here I could observe, *Hermippus*, that *Philo* was a little embarrassed and confounded. But while he hesitated in delivering an answer, luckily for him, *Demea* broke in upon the discourse and saved his countenance.

Your instance, *Cleanthes*, said he, drawn from books and language, being familiar, has, I confess, so much more force on that account, but is there not some danger too in this very circumstance, and may it not render us presumptuous by making us imagine we comprehend the Deity and have some adequate idea of his nature and attributes? When I read a volume, I enter into the mind and intention of the author: I become him, in a manner, for the instant, and have an immediate feeling and conception of those ideas which revolved in his imagination while employed in that composition. But so near an approach we never surely can make to the Deity. His ways are not our ways. His attributes are perfect but incomprehensible. And this volume of nature contains a great and inexplicable riddle, more than any intelligible discourse or reasoning.

The ancient *Platonists*, you know, were the most religious and devout of all the Pagan philosophers; yet many of them, particularly *Plotinus*, expressly declare that intellect or understanding is not to be ascribed to the Deity and that our most perfect worship of him consists not in acts of veneration, reverence, gratitude, or love but in a certain mysterious self-annihilation or total extinction of all our faculties. These ideas are, perhaps, too far stretched, but still it must be acknowledged that, by representing the Deity as so intelligible and comprehensible and so similar to a human mind, we are guilty of the grossest and most narrow partiality and make ourselves the model of the whole universe.

All the *sentiments* of the human mind—gratitude, resentment, love, friendship, approbation, blame, pity, emulation, envy—have a plain reference to the state and situation of man and are calculated for preserving the existence and promoting the activity of such a being in such circumstances. It seems therefore unreasonable to transfer such sentiments to a supreme existence or to suppose him actuated by them; and the phenomena, besides, of the universe will not support us in such a theory. All our *ideas* derived from the senses are confusedly false and illusive and cannot therefore be supposed to have place in a supreme intelligence, and as the ideas of internal sentiment, added to those of the external senses, compose the whole furniture of human understanding, we may conclude that none of the *materials* of thought are in any respect similar in the human and in the divine intelligence. Now, as to the *manner* of thinking, how can we make any comparison between them or suppose them anywise resembling? Our thought is fluctuating, uncertain, fleeting, successive, and compounded; and were we to remove these circumstances, we absolutely annihilate its essence and it would in such a case be an abuse of terms to apply to it the name of thought or reason. At least if it appear more pious and respectful (as it really is) still to retain these terms when we mention the Supreme Being, we ought to acknowledge that their meaning, in that case, is totally incomprehensible and that the infirmities of our nature do not permit us to reach any ideas which in the least correspond to the ineffable sublimity of the Divine attributes.

## Part IV

It seems strange to me, said *Cleanthes*, that you, *Demea*, who are so sincere in the cause of religion, should still maintain the mysterious, incomprehensible nature of the Deity and should insist so strenuously that he has no manner of likeness or resemblance to human creatures. The Deity, I can readily allow, possesses many powers and attributes of which we can have no comprehension, but if our ideas, so far as they go, be not just and adequate and correspondent to his real nature, I know not what there is in this subject worth insisting on. Is the name, without any meaning, of such mighty importance? Or how do you *mystics*, who maintain the absolute incomprehensibility of the Deity, differ from skeptics or atheists, who assert that the first cause of all is unknown and unintelligible? Their temerity must be very great, if, after rejecting the production by a mind—I mean a mind resembling the human (for I know of no other))—they pretend to assign, with certainty, any other specific intelligible cause; and their conscience must be very scrupulous indeed, if they refuse to call the universal unknown cause a God or Deity and to bestow on him as many sublime eulogies and unmeaning epithets as you shall please to require of them.

Who could imagine, replied *Demea*, that *Cleanthes*, the calm philosophical *Cleanthes*, would attempt to refute his antagonists by affixing a nickname to them and, like the common bigots and inquisitors of the age, have recourse to invective and declamation instead of reasoning? Or does he not perceive that these topics are easily retorted and that *anthropomorphite* is an appellation as invidious, and implies as dangerous consequences, as the epithet of *mystic* with which he has honored us? In reality, *Cleanthes*, consider what it is you assert when you represent the Deity as similar to a human mind and understanding. What is the soul of man? A composition of various faculties, passions, sentiments, ideas; united, indeed, into one self or person, but still distinct from each other. When it reasons, the ideas which are the parts of its discourse arrange themselves in a certain form or order, which is not preserved entire for a moment but immediately gives place to another arrangement. New opinions, new passions, new affections, new feelings arise which continually diversify the mental scene and produce in it the greatest variety and most rapid succession imaginable. How is this compatible with that perfect immutability and simplicity which all true theists ascribe to the Deity? By the same act, say they, he sees past, present, and future, his love and hatred, his mercy and justice are one individual operation; he is entire in every point of space and complete in every instant of duration. No succession, no change, no acquisition, no diminution. What he is implies not in it any shadow of distinction or diversity. And what he is this moment he ever has been and ever will be, without any new judgment, sentiment, or operation. He stands fixed in one simple, perfect state; nor can you ever say with any propriety that this act of his is different from that other or that

this judgment or idea has been lately formed and will give place, by succession, to any different judgment or idea.

I can readily allow, said *Cleanthes*, that those who maintain the perfect simplicity of the Supreme Being, to the extent in which you have explained it, are complete *mystics* and chargeable with all the consequences which I have drawn from their opinion. They are, in a word, *atheists* without knowing it. For though it be allowed that the Deity possesses attributes of which we have no comprehension, yet ought we never to ascribe to him any attributes which are absolutely incompatible with that intelligent nature essential to him. A mind, whose acts and sentiments and ideas are not distinct and successive, one that is wholly simple and totally immutable, is a mind which has no thought, no reason, no will, no sentiment, no love, no hatred, or, in a word, is no mind at all. It is an abuse of terms to give it that appellation, and we may as well speak of limited extension without figure, or of number without composition.

Pray consider, said *Philo*, whom you are at present inveighing against. You are honoring with the appellation of *atheist* all the sound, orthodox divines, almost, who have treated of this subject; and you will at last be, yourself, found, according to your reckoning, the only sound theist in the world. But if idolaters be atheists, as, I think, may justly be asserted, and *Christian* theologians the same, what becomes of the argument, so much celebrated, derived from the universal consent of mankind?

But because I know you are not much swayed by names and authorities, I shall endeavor to show you a little more distinctly the inconveniences of that anthropomorphism which you have embraced and shall prove that there is no ground to suppose a plan of the world to be formed in the divine mind, consisting of distinct ideas, differently arranged, in the same manner as an architect forms in his head the plan of a house which he intends to execute.

It is not easy, I admit, to see what is gained by this supposition, whether we judge of the matter by *reason* or by *experience*. We are still obliged to mount higher in order to find the cause of this cause which you had assigned as satisfactory and conclusive.

If *reason* (I mean abstract reason derived from inquiries *a priori*) be not alike mute with regard to all questions concerning cause and effect, this sentence at least it will venture to pronounce: that a mental world, or universe of ideas, requires a cause as much as does a material world, or universe of objects and, if similar in its arrangement, must require a similar cause. For what is there in this subject which should occasion a different conclusion or inference? In an abstract view, they are entirely alike, and no difficulty attends the one supposition which is not common to both of them.

Again, when we will necessarily need *experience* to pronounce some sentence, even on these subjects which lie beyond her sphere, neither can she perceive any material difference in this particular between these two kinds of worlds but finds them to be governed by similar principles and to depend upon an equal variety of causes in their operations. We have specimens in miniature of both of them. Our own mind resembles the one, a vegetable or animal body the other. Let experience, therefore, judge from these samples. Nothing seems more delicate with regard to its causes than thought, and as these causes never operate in two persons after the same manner, so we never find two persons who think exactly alike. Nor indeed does the same person think exactly alike at any two different periods of time. A difference of age, of the disposition of his body, of weather, of food, of company, of books, of passions; any of these particulars or others more minute are sufficient to alter the curious machinery of thought and communicate to it very different movements and operations. As far as we can judge, vegetables and animal bodies are not more delicate in their motions nor depend upon a greater variety or more curious adjustment of springs and principles.

How, therefore, shall we satisfy ourselves concerning the cause of that Being whom you suppose the Author of Nature, or, according to your system of anthropomorphism, the ideal world into which you trace the material? Have we not the same reason to trace that ideal world into another ideal world or new intelligent principle? But if we stop and go no further, why go so far? Why not stop at the material world?

How can we satisfy ourselves without going on *in infinitum*? And after all, what satisfaction is there in that infinite progression? Let us remember the story of the Indian philosopher and his elephant.[7] It was never more applicable than to the present subject. If the material world rests upon a similar ideal world, this ideal world must rest upon some other and so on without end. It were better, therefore, never to look beyond the present material world. By supposing it to contain the principle of its order within itself, we really assert it to be God, and the sooner we arrive at that Divine Being, so much the better. When you go one step beyond the mundane system, you only excite an inquisitive humor which it is impossible ever to satisfy.

To say that the different ideas which compose the reason of the Supreme Being fall into order of themselves and by their own nature is really to talk without any precise meaning. If it has a meaning, I would gladly know why it is not as good sense to say that the parts of the material world fall into order of themselves and by their own nature. Can the one opinion be intelligible, while the other is not so?

We have, indeed, experience of ideas which fall into order of themselves and without any *known* cause. But, I am sure, we have a much larger experience of matter which does the same, as in all instances of generation and vegetation where the accurate analysis of the cause exceeds all human comprehension. We have also experience of particular systems of thought and of matter which have no order: of the first in madness, of the second in corruption. Why, then, should we think that order is more essential to one than the other? And if it requires a cause in both, what do we gain by your system in tracing the universe of objects into a similar universe of ideas? The first step which we make leads us on forever. It were, therefore, wise in us to limit all our inquiries to the present world without looking further. No satisfaction can ever be attained by these speculations which so far exceed the narrow bounds of human understanding.

It was usual with the *Peripatetics*, you know, *Cleanthes*, when the cause of any phenomenon was

---

7. [See above, Locke's *Essay* Book II, chap. 13, sec. 19, and chap. 23, sec. 2.]

demanded, to have recourse to their *faculties* or *occult qualities* and to say, for instance, that bread, nourished by its nutritive faculty, and senna purged by its purgative. But it has been discovered that this subterfuge was nothing but the disguise of ignorance and that these philosophers, though less ingenuous, really said the same thing with the skeptics or the vulgar who fairly confessed that they knew not the cause of these phenomena. In like manner, when it is asked what cause produces order in the ideas of the Supreme Being, can any other reason be assigned by you, anthropomorphites, than that it is a rational faculty and that such is the nature of the Deity? But why a similar answer will not be equally satisfactory in accounting for the order of the world without having recourse to any such intelligent creator as you insist on may be difficult to determine. It is only to say that *such* is the nature of material objects and that they are all originally possessed of a *faculty* of order and proportion. These are only more learned and elaborate ways of confessing our ignorance, nor has the one hypothesis any real advantage above the other except in its greater conformity to vulgar prejudices.

You have displayed this argument with great emphasis, replied *Cleanthes*. You seem not sensible how easy it is to answer it. Even in common life, if I assign a cause for any event, is it any objection, *Philo*, that I cannot assign the cause of that cause and answer every new question which may incessantly be started? And what philosophers could possibly submit to so rigid a rule? Philosophers, who confess ultimate causes to be totally unknown and are sensible that the most refined principles into which they trace the phenomena are still to them as inexplicable as these phenomena themselves are to the vulgar. The order and arrangement of nature, the curious adjustment of final causes, the plain use and intention of every part and organ—all these bespeak in the clearest language an intelligent cause or author. The heavens and the earth join in the same testimony, the whole chorus of Nature raises one hymn to the praises of its Creator. You alone, or almost alone, disturb this general harmony. You start abstruse doubts, cavils, and objections. You ask me, What is the cause of this cause? I know not; I care not; that concerns not me.

I have found a Deity, and here I stop my inquiry. Let those go further who are wiser or more enterprising.

I pretend to be neither, replied *Philo* and for that very reason I should never perhaps have attempted to go so far, especially when I am sensible that I must at last be contented to sit down with the same answer, which, without further trouble, might have satisfied me from the beginning. If I am still to remain in utter ignorance of causes and can absolutely give an explication of nothing, I shall never esteem it any advantage to shove off for a moment a difficulty which, you acknowledge, must immediately, in its full force, recur upon me. Naturalists, indeed, very justly explain particular effects by more general causes, though these general causes themselves should remain in the end totally inexplicable, but they never surely thought it satisfactory to explain a particular effect by a particular cause, which was no more to be accounted for than the effect itself. An ideal system, arranged of itself, without a precedent design, is not a whit more explicable than a material one which attains its order in a like manner; nor is there any more difficulty in the latter supposition than in the former.

## Part V

But to show you still more inconveniences, continued *Philo*, in your anthropomorphism, please take a new survey of your principles. *Like effects prove like causes.* This is the experimental argument, and this, you say too, is the sole theological argument. Now it is certain that the more alike the effects are which are seen and the more alike causes which are inferred, the stronger is the argument. Every departure on either side diminishes the probability and renders the experiment less conclusive. You cannot doubt of the principle, neither ought you to reject its consequences.

All the new discoveries in astronomy which prove the immense grandeur and magnificence of the works of Nature are so many additional arguments for a Deity, according to the true system of Theism; but, according to your hypothesis of experimental Theism, they become so many objections by removing the effect still further from all resemblance to the effects of human art and contrivance. For if *Lucretius*, even following the old system of the world, could exclaim, "Who is strong enough to rule the sum, who to hold in hand and control the mighty bridle of the unfathomable deep? Who to turn about all the heavens at one time, and warm the fruitful worlds with ethereal fires, or to be present in all places and at all times?"[8]

If Tully esteemed this reasoning so natural as to put it into the mouth of his Epicurean: "What mental vision enabled your master Plato to descry the vast and elaborate architectural process which, as he makes out, the deity adopted in building the structure of the universe? What method of engineering was employed? What tools and levers and derricks? What agents carried out so vast an understanding? And how were air, fire, water, and earth enabled to obey and execute the will of the architect?"[9] If this argument, I say, had any force in former ages, how much greater must it have at present when the bounds of Nature are so infinitely enlarged and such a magnificent scene is opened to us? It is still more unreasonable to form our idea of so unlimited a cause from our experience of the narrow productions of human design and invention.

The discoveries by microscopes, as they open a new universe in miniature, are still objections according to you, arguments according to me. The further we push our researches of this kind, we are still led to infer the universal cause of all to be vastly different from mankind or from any object of human experience and observation.

And what say you to the discoveries in anatomy, chemistry, botany? . . . These surely are no objections, replied *Cleanthes*. They only discover new instances of art and contrivance. It is still the image of mind reflected on us from innumerable objects. Add a mind *like the human*, said *Philo*. I know of no other, replied *Cleanthes*. And the more alike, the better, insisted *Philo*. To be sure, said *Cleanthes*.

Now, *Cleanthes*, said *Philo*, with an air of alacrity and triumph, mark the consequences. *First*, by this method of reasoning, you renounce all claim to infinity in any of the attributes of the Deity. For as the cause ought only to be proportioned to the effect and the effect, so far as it falls under our cognizance, is not infinite, what pretensions have we, upon your suppositions, to ascribe that attribute to the Divine Being? You will still insist that by removing him so much from all similarity to human creatures, we give in to the most arbitrary hypothesis and at the same time weaken all proofs of his existence.

*Secondly*, you have no reason, on your theory, for ascribing perfection to the Deity, even in his finite capacity, or for supposing him free from every error, mistake, or incoherence in his undertakings. There are many inexplicable difficulties in the works of Nature which, if we allow a perfect author to be proved *a priori*, are easily solved and become only seeming difficulties from the narrow capacity of man, who cannot trace infinite relations. But according to your method of reasoning, these difficulties become all real and perhaps will be insisted on as new instances of likeness to human art and contrivance. At least you must acknowledge that it is impossible for us to tell from our limited views whether this system contains any great faults or deserves any considerable praise, if compared to other possible and even real systems. Could a peasant, if the *Aeneid* were read to him, pronounce that poem to be absolutely faultless or even assign to it its proper rank among the productions of human wit, he, who had never seen any other production?

But were this world ever so perfect a production, it must still remain uncertain whether all the excellences of the work can justly be ascribed to the workman. If we survey a ship, what an exalted idea must we form of the ingenuity of the carpenter who framed so complicated, useful, and beautiful a machine? And what surprise must we feel when we find him a stupid mechanic who imitated others and copied an art which, through a long succession of ages, after multiplied trials, mistakes, corrections, deliberations, and controversies, had been gradually improving? Many worlds might have been botched and bungled, throughout an eternity, before this system was struck out; much labor lost, many fruitless trials made; and a slow, but continued improvement carried on during infinite ages in the art of world-making. In such subjects, who can determine where the truth—nay,

---

8. Book XI, 1094 [trans. W. D. Rouse].

9. *De Natura Deorum*, Book I [trans. H. Rackham].

who can conjecture where the probability—lies, amidst a great number of hypotheses which may be proposed and a still greater which may be imagined?

And what shadow of an argument, continued *Philo*, can you produce from your hypothesis to prove the unity of the Deity? A great number of men join in building a house or ship, in rearing a city, in framing a commonwealth. Why may not several deities combine in contriving and framing a world? This is only so much greater similarity to human affairs. By sharing the work among several, we may so much further limit the attributes of each and get rid of that extensive power and knowledge which must be supposed in one deity and which, according to you, can only serve to weaken the proof of his existence. And if such foolish, such vicious creatures as man can yet often unite in framing and executing one plan, how much more those deities or demons whom we may suppose several degrees more perfect!

To multiply causes without necessity is indeed contrary to true philosophy. But this principle applies not to the present case. Were one deity antecedently proved by your theory who were possessed of every attribute requisite to the production of the universe, it would be needless, I admit (though not absurd), to suppose any other deity existent. But while it is still a question whether all these attributes are united in one subject or dispersed among several independent beings, by what phenomena in nature can we pretend to decide the controversy? Where we see a body raised in a scale, we are sure that there is in the opposite scale, however concealed from sight, some counterpoising weight equal to it, but it is still allowed to doubt whether that weight be an aggregate of several distinct bodies or one uniform united mass. And if the weight requisite very much exceeds anything which we have ever seen conjoined in any single body, the former supposition becomes still more probable and natural. An intelligent being of such vast power and capacity as is necessary to produce the universe or, to speak in the language of ancient philosophy, so prodigious an animal exceeds all analogy and even comprehension.

But further, *Cleanthes*, men are mortal and renew their species by generation, and this is common to all living creatures. The two great sexes of male and female, says *Milton*, animate the world. Why must this circumstance, so universal, so essential, be excluded from those numerous and limited deities? Behold, then, the theogony of ancient times brought back upon us.

And why not become a perfect anthropomorphite? Why not assert the deity or deities to be corporeal and to have eyes, a nose, mouth, ears, etc.? *Epicurus* maintained that no man had ever seen reason but in a human figure. Therefore, the gods must have a human figure. And this argument, which is deservedly so much ridiculed by *Cicero*, becomes, according to you, solid and philosophical.

In a word, *Cleanthes*, a man who follows your hypothesis is able perhaps to assert or conjecture that the universe, sometime, arose from something like design, but beyond that position he cannot ascertain one single circumstance and is left afterwards to fix every point of his theology by the utmost license of fancy and hypothesis. This world, for all he knows, is very faulty and imperfect compared to a superior standard and was only the first rude essay of some infant deity who afterwards abandoned it, ashamed of his lame performance: It is the work only of some dependent, inferior deity and is the object of derision to his superiors: It is the production of old age and dotage in some superannuated deity and, ever since his death, has run on at adventures from the first impulse and active force which it received from him. You justly give signs of horror, *Demea*, at these strange suppositions. But these and a thousand more of the same kind, are *Cleanthes*' suppositions, not mine. From the moment the attributes of the Deity are supposed finite, all these have place. And I cannot, for my part, think that so wild and unsettled a system of theology is in any respect preferable to none at all.

These suppositions I absolutely disown, cried *Cleanthes*. They strike me, however, with no horror, especially when proposed in that rambling way in which they drop from you. On the contrary, they give me pleasure when I see that, by the utmost indulgence of your imagination, you never get rid of the hypothesis of design in the universe but are obliged at every turn to have recourse to it. To this concession I adhere steadily, and this I regard as a sufficient foundation for religion. [ . . . ]

## Part IX

But if so many difficulties attend the argument *a posteriori*, said *Demea*, had we not better adhere to that simple and sublime argument *a priori* which, by offering to us infallible demonstration, cuts off at once all doubt and difficulty? By this argument, too, we may prove the *infinity* of the Divine attributes which, I am afraid, can never be ascertained with certainty from any other topic. For how can an effect which either is finite or, for all we know, may be so— how can such an effect, I say, prove an infinite cause? The unity, too, of the Divine Nature it is very difficult, if not absolutely impossible, to deduce merely from contemplating the works of nature; nor will the uniformity alone of the plan, even were it allowed, give us any assurance of that attribute. Whereas the argument *a priori*. . . .

You seem to reason, *Demea*, interposed *Cleanthes*, as if those advantages and conveniences in the abstract argument were full proofs of its solidity. But it is first proper, in my opinion, to determine what argument of this nature you choose to insist on, and we shall afterwards, from itself better than from its *useful* consequences, endeavor to determine what value we ought to put upon it.

The argument, replied *Demea*, which I would insist on is the common one. Whatever exists must have a cause or reason of its existence, it being absolutely impossible for anything to produce itself or be the cause of its own existence. In mounting up, therefore, from effects to causes, we either must go on in tracing an infinite succession without any ultimate cause at all or must at last have recourse to some ultimate cause that is *necessarily* existent. Now, that the first supposition is absurd may be thus proved. In the infinite chain or succession of causes and effects, each single effect is determined to exist by the power and efficacy of that cause which immediately preceded; but the whole eternal chain or succession, taken together, is not determined or caused by anything, and yet it is evident that it requires a cause or reason as much as any particular object which begins to exist in time. The question is still reasonable why this particular succession of causes existed from eternity and not any other succession or no succession at all. If there be no necessarily existent being, any supposition which can be formed is equally possible; nor is there any more absurdity in nothing's having existed from eternity than there is in that succession of causes which constitutes the universe. What was it, then, which determined something to exist rather than nothing and bestowed being on a particular possibility, exclusive of the rest? *External causes*, there are supposed to be none. *Chance* is a word without a meaning. Was it *nothing*? But that can never produce anything. We must, therefore, have recourse to a necessarily existent Being who carries the *reason* of his existence in himself and who cannot be supposed not to exist without an express contradiction. There is, consequently, such a Being; that is, there is a Deity.

I shall not leave it to *Philo*, said *Cleanthes*, though I know that starting objections is his chief delight, to point out the weakness of this metaphysical reasoning. It seems to me so obviously ill-grounded and at the same time of so little consequence to the cause of true piety and religion that I shall myself venture to show the fallacy of it.

I shall begin with observing that there is an evident absurdity in pretending to demonstrate a matter of fact or to prove it by any arguments *a priori*. Nothing is demonstrable unless the contrary implies a contradiction. Nothing that is distinctly conceivable implies a contradiction. Whatever we conceive as existent, we can also conceive as non-existent. There is no being, therefore, whose non-existence implies a contradiction. Consequently there is no being whose existence is demonstrable. I propose this argument as entirely decisive and am willing to rest the whole controversy upon it.

It is pretended that the Deity is a necessarily existent being, and this necessity of his existence is attempted to be explained by asserting that if we knew his whole essence or nature, we should perceive it to be as impossible for him not to exist as for twice two not to be four. But it is evident that this can never happen while our faculties remain the same as at present. It will still be possible for us at any time to conceive the non-existence of what we formerly conceived to exist; nor can the mind ever lie under a necessity of supposing any object to remain always in being in the same manner as we lie under a necessity of always conceiving twice two to be four. The words, therefore, *necessary existence* have no meaning or, which is the same thing, none that is consistent.

But further, why may not the material universe be the necessarily existent being, according to this pretended explication of necessity? We dare not affirm that we know all the qualities of matter and, for all we can determine, it may contain some qualities, which, were they known, would make its non-existence appear as great a contradiction as that twice two is five. I find only one argument employed to prove that the material world is not the necessarily existent Being, and this argument is derived from the contingency of both the matter and the form of the world. "Any particle of matter," it is said,[10] "may be *conceived* to be annihilated; and any form may be *conceived* to be altered. Such an annihilation or alteration, therefore, is not impossible." But it seems a great partiality not to perceive that the same argument extends equally to the Deity so far as we have any conception of him, and that the mind can at least imagine him to be non-existent or his attributes to be altered. It must be some unknown, inconceivable qualities which can make his non-existence appear impossible or his attributes unalterable, and no reason can be assigned why these qualities may not belong to matter. As they are altogether unknown and inconceivable, they can never be proved incompatible with it.

Add to this that in tracing an eternal succession of objects it seems absurd to inquire for a general cause or first author. How can anything that exists from eternity have a cause, since that relation implies a priority in time and a beginning of existence?

In such a chain, too, or succession of objects, each part is caused by that which preceded it and causes that which succeeds it. Where then is the difficulty? But the *whole*, you say, wants a cause. I answer that the uniting of these parts into a whole, like the uniting of several distinct countries into one kingdom or several distinct members into one body, is performed merely by an arbitrary act of the mind and has no influence on the nature of things. Did I show you the particular causes of each individual in a collection of twenty particles of matter, I should think it very unreasonable should you afterwards ask me what was the cause of the whole twenty. This is sufficiently explained in explaining the cause of the parts.

Though the reasonings which you have urged, *Cleanthes*, may well excuse me, said *Philo*, from starting any further difficulties, yet I cannot forbear insisting still upon another topic. It is observed by arithmeticians that the products of 9 compose always either 9 or some lesser product of 9 if you add together all the characters of which any of the former products is composed. Thus, of 18, 27, 36, which are products of 9, you make 9 by adding 1 to 8, 2 to 7, 3 to 6. Thus, 369 is a product also of 9; and if you add 3, 6, and 9, you make 18, a lesser product of 9.[11] To a superficial observer, so wonderful a regularity may be admired as the effect of either chance or design, but a skillful algebraist immediately concludes it to be the work of necessity and demonstrates that it must forever result from the nature of these numbers. Is it not probable, I ask, that the whole economy of the universe is conducted by a like necessity, though no human algebra can furnish a key which solves the difficulty? And instead of admiring the order of natural beings, may it not happen that, could we penetrate into the intimate nature of bodies, we should clearly see why it was absolutely impossible they could ever admit of any other disposition? So dangerous is it to introduce this idea of necessity into the present question! And so naturally does it afford an inference directly opposite to the religious hypothesis!

But dropping all these abstractions, continued *Philo*, and confining ourselves to more familiar topics, I shall venture to add an observation that the argument *a priori* has seldom been found very convincing except to people of a metaphysical head who have accustomed themselves to abstract reasoning and who, finding from mathematics that the understanding frequently leads to truth through obscurity

---

10. Dr. Clarke. [Samuel Clarke (1675–1729), an English theologian and follower of Newton.]

11. *Republique des Lettres*, August 1685.

and, contrary to first appearances, have transferred the same habit of thinking to subjects where it ought not to have place. Other people, even of good sense and the best inclined to religion, feel always some deficiency in such arguments, though they are not perhaps able to explain distinctly where it lies, a certain proof that men ever did and ever will derive their religion from other sources than from this species of reasoning.

## Part X

It is my opinion, I admit, replied *Demea*, that each man feels, in a manner, the truth of religion within his own breast and from a consciousness of his imbecility and misery rather than from any reasoning is led to seek protection from that Being on whom he and all nature is dependent. So anxious or so tedious are even the best scenes of life that futurity is still the object of all our hopes and fears. We incessantly look forward and endeavor, by prayers, adoration, and sacrifice to appease those unknown powers whom we find, by experience, so able to afflict and oppress us. Wretched creatures that we are! What resource for us amidst the innumerable ills of life, did not religion suggest some methods of atonement and appease those terrors with which we are incessantly agitated and tormented?

I am indeed persuaded, said *Philo*, that the best and indeed the only method of bringing everyone to a due sense of religion is by just representations of the misery and wickedness of men. And for that purpose a talent of eloquence and strong imagery is more requisite than that of reasoning and argument. For is it necessary to prove what everyone feels within himself? It is only necessary to make us feel it, if possible, more intimately and sensibly.

The people, indeed, replied *Demea*, are sufficiently convinced of this great and melancholy truth. The miseries of life; the unhappiness of man; the general corruptions of our nature; the unsatisfactory enjoyment of pleasures, riches, honors; these phrases have become almost proverbial in all languages. And who can doubt of what all men declare from their own immediate feeling and experience?

In this point, said *Philo*, the learned are perfectly agreed with the vulgar; and in all letters, *sacred* and *profane*, the topic of human misery has been insisted on with the most pathetic eloquence that sorrow and melancholy could inspire. The poets, who speak from sentiment, without a system, and whose testimony has therefore the more authority, abound in images of this nature. From *Homer* down to *Dr. Young*, the whole inspired tribe have ever been sensible that no other representation of things would suit the feeling and observation of each individual.

As to authorities, replied *Demea*, you need not seek them. Look round this library of *Cleanthes*. I shall venture to affirm that, except authors of particular sciences such as chemistry or botany who have no occasion to treat of human life, there is scarce one of those innumerable writers from whom the sense of human misery has not, in some passage or other, extorted a complaint and confession of it. At least the chance is entirely on that side; and no one author has ever, so far as I can recollect, been so extravagant as to deny it.

There you must excuse me, said *Philo*. *Leibniz* has denied it and is perhaps the first[12] who ventured upon so bold and paradoxical an opinion; at least, the first who made it essential to his philosophical system.

And by being the first, replied *Demea*, might he not have been sensible of his error? For is this a subject in which philosophers can propose to make discoveries, especially in so late an age? And can any man hope by a simple denial (for the subject scarcely admits of reasoning) to bear down the united testimony of mankind founded on sense and consciousness?

And why should man, added he, pretend to an exemption from the lot of all other animals? The whole earth, believe me, *Philo*, is cursed and polluted. A perpetual war is kindled amongst all living creatures. Necessity, hunger, want stimulate the strong and courageous; fear, anxiety, terror agitate the weak and infirm. The first entrance into life gives anguish to the new-born infant and to its wretched parent; weakness, impotence, distress attend each stage of that life; and it is at last finished in agony and horror.

---

12. That sentiment had been maintained by Dr. King and some few others before Leibniz, though by none of so great fame as that German philosopher.

Observe, too, says *Philo*, the curious artifices of Nature in order to embitter the life of every living being. The stronger prey upon the weaker and keep them in perpetual terror and anxiety. The weaker, too, in their turn, often prey upon the stronger and vex and molest them without relaxation. Consider that innumerable race of insects which either are bred on the body of each animal or, flying about, infix their stings in him. These insects have others still less than themselves which torment them. And thus on each hand, before and behind, above and below, every animal is surrounded with enemies which incessantly seek his misery and destruction.

Man alone, said *Demea*, seems to be, in part, an exception to this rule. For by combination in society, he can easily master lions, tigers, and bears, whose greater strength and agility naturally enable them to prey upon him.

On the contrary, it is here chiefly, cried *Philo*, that the uniform and equal maxims of nature are most apparent. Man, it is true, can, by combination, surmount all his real enemies and become master of the whole animal creation, but does he not immediately raise up to himself *imaginary* enemies, the demons of his fancy, who haunt him with superstitious terrors and blast every enjoyment of life? His pleasure, as he imagines, becomes in their eyes a crime: his food and repose give them umbrage and offence: his very sleep and dreams furnish new materials to anxious fear: and even death, his refuge from every other ill, presents only the dread of endless and innumerable woes. Nor does the wolf molest more the timid flock than superstition does the anxious breast of wretched mortals.

Besides, consider, *Demea*, this very society by which we surmount those wild beasts, our natural enemies. What new enemies does it not raise to us? What woe and misery does it not occasion? Man is the greatest enemy of man. Oppression, injustice, contempt, contumely, violence, sedition, war, calumny, treachery, fraud—by these they mutually torment each other and they would soon dissolve that society which they had formed, were it not for the dread of still greater ills which must attend their separation.

But though these external insults, said *Demea*, from animals, from men, from all the elements which assault us, form a frightful catalogue of woes, they are nothing in comparison of those which arise within ourselves from the distempered condition of our mind and body. How many lie under the lingering torment of diseases? Hear the pathetic enumeration of the great poet.

Intestine stone and ulcer, colic-pangs,
Demoniac frenzy, moping melancholy,
And moon-struck madness, pining atrophy,
Marasmus, and wide-wasting pestilence.
Dire was the tossing, deep the groans: *despair*
Tended the sick, busiest from couch to couch.
And over them triumphant *death* his dart
Shook: but delayed to strike, though oft invoked
With vows, as their chief good and final hope.[13]

The disorders of the mind, continued *Demea*, though more secret, are not perhaps less dismal and vexatious. Remorse, shame, anguish, rage, disappointment, anxiety, fear, dejection, despair; who has ever passed through life without cruel inroads from these tormentors? How many have scarcely ever felt any better sensations? Labor and poverty, so abhorred by everyone, are the certain lot of the far greater number, and those few privileged persons who enjoy ease and opulence never reach contentment or true felicity. All the goods of life united would not make a very happy man, but all the ills united would make a wretch indeed, and any one of them almost (and who can be free from every one?)—nay often the absence of one good (and who can possess all?)—is sufficient to render life ineligible.

Were a stranger to drop on a sudden into this world, I would show him, as a specimen of its ills, a hospital full of diseases, a prison crowded with malefactors and debtors, a field of battle strewed with carcasses, a fleet foundering in the ocean, a nation languishing under tyranny, famine, or pestilence. To turn the gay side of life to him and give him a notion of its pleasures, where should I conduct him? To a ball, to an opera, to court? He might justly think that I was only showing him a diversity of distress and sorrow.

---

13. [John Milton, *Paradise Lost*, Book XI.]

There is no evading such striking instances, said *Philo*, but by apologies, which still further aggravate the charge. Why have all men, I ask, in all ages, complained incessantly of the miseries of life? . . . . They have no just reason, says one: These complaints proceed only from their discontented, repining, anxious disposition . . . . And can there possibly, I reply, be a more certain foundation of misery than such a wretched temper?

But if they were really as unhappy as they pretend, says my antagonist, why do they remain in life? . . . .

Not satisfied with life, afraid of death.

This is the secret chain, say I, that holds us. We are terrified, not bribed, to the continuance of our existence.

It is only a false delicacy, he may insist, which a few refined spirits indulge and which has spread these complaints among the whole race of mankind. . . . And what is this delicacy, I ask, which you blame? Is it anything but a greater sensibility to all the pleasures and pains of life? And if the man of a delicate, refined temper, by being so much more alive than the rest of the world, is only so much more unhappy, what judgment must we form in general of human life?

Let men remain at rest, says our adversary, and they will be easy. They are willing artificers of their own misery. . . . No! reply I, an anxious languor follows their repose; disappointment, vexation, trouble, their activity and ambition.

I can observe something like what you mention in some others, replied *Cleanthes*, but I confess I feel little or nothing of it in myself and hope that it is not so common as you represent it.

If you feel not human misery yourself, cried *Demea*, I congratulate you on so happy a singularity. Others, seemingly the most prosperous, have not been ashamed to vent their complaints in the most melancholy strains. Let us attend to the great, the fortunate emperor, *Charles* V, when, tired with human grandeur, he resigned all his extensive dominions into the hands of his son. In the last harangue which he made on that memorable occasion, he publicly avowed *that the greatest prosperities which he had ever enjoyed had been mixed with so many adversities that he might truly say he had never enjoyed any satisfaction or contentment.* But did the retired life in which he sought for shelter afford him any greater happiness? If we may credit his son's account, his repentance commenced the very day of his resignation.

*Cicero's* fortune, from small beginnings, rose to the greatest luster and renown; yet what pathetic complaints of the ills of life do his familiar letters as well as philosophical discourses contain? And suitably to his own experience, he introduces Cato, the great, the fortunate Cato, protesting in his old age that had he a new life in his offer, he would reject the present.

Ask yourself, ask any of your acquaintance, whether they would live over again the last ten or twenty years of their lives. No! But the next twenty, they say, will be better:

And from the dregs of life, hope to receive
What the first sprightly running could not give.[14]

Thus, at last, they find (such is the greatness of human misery, it reconciles even contradictions) that they complain at once of the shortness of life and of its vanity and sorrow.

And is it possible, *Cleanthes*, said *Philo*, that after all these reflections and infinitely more which might be suggested, you can still persevere in your anthropomorphism and assert the moral attributes of the Deity, his justice, benevolence, mercy, and rectitude, to be of the same nature with these virtues in human creatures? His power, we allow, is infinite. Whatever he wills is executed. But neither man nor any other animal is happy. Therefore, he does not will their happiness. His wisdom is infinite; he is never mistaken in choosing the means to any end; but the course of Nature tends not to human or animal felicity; therefore, it is not established for that purpose. Through the whole compass of human knowledge, there are no inferences more certain and infallible than these. In what respect, then, do his benevolence and mercy resemble the benevolence and mercy of men?

*Epicurus'* old questions are yet unanswered.

---

14. [John Dryden, *Aurengzebe*, Act IV, scene 1.]

Is he willing to prevent evil, but not able? Then is he impotent. Is he able, but not willing? Then is he malevolent. Is he both able and willing? Whence then is evil?

You ascribe, *Cleanthes* (and I believe justly), a purpose and intention to Nature. But what, I beseech you, is the object of that curious artifice and machinery which she has displayed in all animals? The preservation alone of individuals and propagation of the species. It seems enough for her purpose, if such a rank be barely upheld in the universe without any care or concern for the happiness of the members that compose it. No resource for this purpose: no machinery in order merely to give pleasure or ease: no fund of pure joy and contentment: no indulgence without some want or necessity accompanying it. At least, the few phenomena of this nature are overbalanced by opposite phenomena of still greater importance.

Our sense of music, harmony, and, indeed, beauty of all kinds gives satisfaction without being absolutely necessary to the preservation and propagation of the species. But what racking pains, on the other hand, arise from gouts, gravels, migraines, toothaches, rheumatisms, where the injury to the animal machinery is either small or incurable? Mirth, laughter, play, frolic seem gratuitous satisfactions which have no further tendency: spleen, melancholy, discontent, superstition, are pains of the same nature. How then does the Divine benevolence display itself in the sense of you anthropomorphites? None, but we mystics, as you were pleased to call us, can account for this strange mixture of phenomena by deriving it from attributes, infinitely perfect but incomprehensible.

And have you at last, said *Cleanthes* smiling, betrayed your intentions, *Philo*? Your long agreement with *Demea* did indeed a little surprise me, but I find you were all the while erecting a concealed battery against me. And I must confess that you have now fallen upon a subject worthy of your noble spirit of opposition and controversy. If you can make out the present point and prove mankind to be unhappy or corrupted, there is an end at once of all religion. For to what purpose establish the natural attributes of the Deity, while the moral are still doubtful and uncertain?

You take umbrage very easily, replied *Demea*, at opinions the most innocent and the most generally received, even amongst the religious and devout themselves. And nothing can be more surprising than to find a topic like this, concerning the wickedness and misery of man, charged with no less than atheism and profaneness. Have not all pious divines and preachers who have indulged their rhetoric on so fertile a subject—have they not easily, I say, given a solution of any difficulties which may attend it? This world is but a point in comparison of the universe, this life but a moment in comparison of eternity. The present evil phenomena, therefore, are rectified in other regions and in some future period of existence. And the eyes of men, being then opened to larger views of things, see the whole connection of general laws and trace with adoration the benevolence and rectitude of the Deity through all the mazes and intricacies of his providence.

No! replied *Cleanthes*. No! These arbitrary suppositions can never be admitted, contrary to matter of fact, visible and uncontroverted. Whence can any cause be known but from its known effects? Whence can any hypothesis be proved but from the apparent phenomena? To establish one hypothesis upon another is building entirely in the air, and the utmost we ever attain by these conjectures and fictions is to ascertain the bare possibility of our opinion. But never can we, upon such terms, establish its reality.

The only method of supporting Divine benevolence, and it is what I willingly embrace, is to deny absolutely the misery and wickedness of man. Your representations are exaggerated; your melancholy views mostly fictitious; your inferences contrary to fact and experience. Health is more common than sickness; pleasure than pain; happiness than misery. And for one vexation which we meet with, we attain, upon computation, a hundred enjoyments.

Admitting your position, replied *Philo*, which yet is extremely doubtful, you must at the same time allow that if pain be less frequent than pleasure, it is infinitely more violent and durable. One hour of it is often able to outweigh a day, a week, a month of our common insipid enjoyments. And how many days, weeks, and months are passed by several in the most acute torments? Pleasure, scarcely in one instance, is ever able to reach ecstasy and rapture, and in no one instance can it continue for any time at its highest pitch and altitude. The spirits evaporate, the nerves relax, the fabric is disordered, and the enjoyment quickly degenerates into fatigue and uneasiness. But pain often—good God, how often!—rises to torture and agony, and the longer it continues, it becomes still more genuine agony and torture. Patience is exhausted, courage languishes, melancholy seizes us, and nothing terminates our misery but the removal of its cause or another event which is the sole cure of all evil, but which, from our natural folly, we regard with still greater horror and consternation.

But not to insist upon these topics, continued *Philo*, though most obvious, certain, and important, I must use the freedom to admonish you, *Cleanthes*, that you have put the controversy upon a most dangerous issue and are unawares introducing a total skepticism into the most essential articles of natural and revealed theology. What! No method of fixing a just foundation for religion unless we allow the happiness of human life and maintain a continued existence even in this world, with all our present pains, infirmities, vexations, and follies, to be eligible and desirable! But this is contrary to everyone's feeling and experience; it is contrary to an authority so established as nothing can subvert. No decisive proofs can ever be produced against this authority; nor is it possible for you to compute, estimate, and compare all the pains and all the pleasures in the lives of all men and of all animals: and thus, by your resting the whole system of religion on a point which, from its very nature must forever be uncertain, you tacitly confess that that system is equally uncertain.

But allowing you what never will be believed, at least what you never possibly can prove, that animal or at least human happiness in this life exceeds its misery, you have yet done nothing. For this is not by any means what we expect from infinite power, infinite wisdom, and infinite goodness. Why is there any misery at all in the world? Not by chance, surely. From some cause then. Is it from the intention of the Deity? But he is perfectly benevolent. Is it contrary to his intention? But he is almighty. Nothing can shake the solidity of this reasoning, so short, so clear, so decisive, unless we assert that these subjects exceed all human capacity and that our common measures of truth and falsehood are not applicable to them, a topic which I have all along insisted on but which you have from the beginning rejected with scorn and indignation.

But I will be contented to retire still from this entrenchment, for I deny that you can ever force me in it. I will allow that pain or misery in man is *compatible* with infinite power and goodness in the Deity, even in your sense of these attributes. What are you advanced by all these concessions? A mere possible compatibility is not sufficient. You must *prove* these pure, unmixed, and uncontrollable attributes from the present mixed and confused phenomena and from these alone. A hopeful undertaking! Were the phenomena ever so pure and unmixed, yet being finite, they would be insufficient for that purpose. How much more, where they are also so jarring and discordant!

Here, *Cleanthes*, I find myself at ease in my argument. Here I triumph. Formerly, when we argued concerning the natural attributes of intelligence and design, I needed all my skeptical and metaphysical subtlety to elude your grasp. In many views of the universe and of its parts, particularly the latter, the beauty and fitness of final causes strike us with such irresistible force that all objections appear (what I believe they really are) mere cavils and sophisms; nor can we then imagine how it was ever possible for us to repose any weight on them. But there is no view of human life or of the condition of mankind from which, without the greatest violence, we can infer the moral attributes or learn that infinite benevolence, conjoined with infinite power and infinite wisdom, which we must discover by the eyes of faith alone. It is your turn now to tug the laboring oar and to support your philosophical subtleties against the dictates of plain reason and experience.

## Part XI

I scruple not to allow, said *Cleanthes*, that I have been apt to suspect the frequent repetition of the word *infinite*, which we meet with in all theological writers, to savor more of panegyric than of philosophy; and that any purposes of reasoning, and even of religion, would be better served, were we to rest contented with more accurate and more moderate expressions. The terms *admirable, excellent, superlatively great, wise,* and *holy*—these sufficiently fill the imaginations of men, and anything beyond, besides that it leads into absurdities, has no influence on the affections or sentiments. Thus, in the present subject, if we abandon all human analogy, as seems your intention, *Demea,* I am afraid we abandon all religion and retain no conception of the great object of our adoration. If we preserve human analogy, we must forever find it impossible to reconcile any mixture of evil in the universe with infinite attributes, much less can we ever prove the latter from the former. But supposing the Author of Nature to be finitely perfect, though far exceeding mankind, a satisfactory account may then be given of natural and moral evil and every untoward phenomenon be explained and adjusted. A lesser evil may then be chosen in order to avoid a greater, inconveniences be submitted to in order to reach a desirable end, and, in a word, benevolence regulated by wisdom and limited by necessity may produce just such a world as the present. You, *Philo,* who are so prompt at starting views and reflections and analogies, I would gladly hear, at length, without interruption, your opinion of this new theory, and if it deserve our attention, we may afterwards, at more leisure, reduce it into form.

My sentiments, replied *Philo,* are not worth being made a mystery of. And therefore, without any ceremony, I shall deliver what occurs to me with regard to the present subject. It must, I think, be allowed that if a very limited intelligence whom we shall suppose utterly unacquainted with the universe were assured that it were the production of a very good, wise, and powerful Being, however finite, he would, from his conjectures, form *beforehand* a different notion of it from what we find it to be by experience; nor would he ever imagine, merely from these attributes of the cause of which he is informed, that the effect could be so full of vice and misery and disorder as it appears in this life. Supposing now that this person were brought into the world, still assured that it was the workmanship of such a sublime and benevolent Being; he might, perhaps, be surprised at the disappointment,

but would never retract his former belief, if founded on any very solid argument, since such a limited intelligence must be sensible of his own blindness and ignorance and must allow that there may be many solutions of those phenomena which will forever escape his comprehension. But supposing, which is the real case with regard to man, that this creature is not antecedently convinced of a supreme intelligence, benevolent and powerful, but is left to gather such a belief from the appearances of things; this entirely alters the case, nor will he ever find any reason for such a conclusion. He may be fully convinced of the narrow limits of his understanding, but this will not help him in forming an inference concerning the goodness of superior powers, since he must form that inference from what he knows, not from what he is ignorant of. The more you exaggerate his weakness and ignorance, the more diffident you render him and give him the greater suspicion that such subjects are beyond the reach of his faculties. You are obliged, therefore, to reason with him merely from the known phenomena and to drop every arbitrary supposition or conjecture.

Did I show you a house or palace where there was not one apartment convenient or agreeable—where the windows, doors, fires, passages, stairs, and the whole economy of the building were the source of noise, confusion, fatigue, darkness, and the extremes of heat and cold—you would certainly blame the contrivance without any further examination. The architect would in vain display his subtlety and prove to you that if this door or that window were altered, greater ills would ensue. What he says may be strictly true: The alteration of one particular, while the other parts of the building remain, may only augment the inconveniences. But still you would assert in general that if the architect had had skill and good intentions, he might have formed such a plan of the whole and might have adjusted the parts in such a manner as would have remedied all or most of these inconveniences. His ignorance, or even your own ignorance of such a plan, will never convince you of the impossibility of it. If you find any inconveniences and deformities in the building, you will always, without entering into any detail, condemn the architect.

In short, I repeat the question: Is the world, considered in general and as it appears to us in this life, different from what a man or such a limited being would *beforehand* expect from a very powerful, wise, and benevolent Deity? It must be strange prejudice to assert the contrary. And from thence I conclude that however consistent the world may be, allowing certain suppositions and conjectures, with the idea of such a Deity, it can never afford us an inference concerning his existence. The consistency is not absolutely denied, only the inference. Conjectures, especially where infinity is excluded from the Divine attributes, may perhaps be sufficient to prove a consistency but can never be foundations for any inference.

There seems to be *four* circumstances on which depend all or the greatest part of the ills that molest sensible creatures, and it is not impossible but all these circumstances may be necessary and unavoidable. We know so little beyond common life or even of common life that with regard to the economy of a universe, there is no conjecture, however wild, which may not be just; nor any one, however plausible, which may not be erroneous. All that belongs to human understanding in this deep ignorance and obscurity is to be skeptical or at least cautious and not to admit of any hypothesis whatever, much less of any which is supported by no appearance of probability. Now this I assert to be the case with regard to all the causes of evil and the circumstances on which it depends: None of them appear to human reason in the least degree necessary or unavoidable, nor can we suppose them such without the utmost license of imagination.

The *first* circumstance which introduces evil is that contrivance or economy of the animal creation by which pains as well as pleasures are employed to excite all creatures to action and make them vigilant in the great work of self-preservation. Now pleasure alone, in its various degrees, seems to human understanding sufficient for this purpose. All animals might be constantly in a state of enjoyment, but when urged by any of the necessities of nature—such as thirst, hunger, weariness—instead of pain, they might feel a diminution of pleasure by which they might be prompted to seek that object which is necessary to their subsistence. Men pursue pleasure as eagerly as they avoid pain; at least they might have been so constituted. It seems, therefore, plainly possible to carry on the business of life without any pain. Why then is any animal ever rendered susceptible of such a sensation? If animals can be free from it an hour, they might enjoy a perpetual exemption from it, and it required as particular a contrivance of their organs to produce that feeling, as to endow them with sight, hearing, or any of the senses. Shall we conjecture that such a contrivance was necessary, without any appearance of reason? And shall we build on that conjecture as on the most certain truth?

But a capacity of pain would not alone produce pain were it not for the *second* circumstance, namely, the conducting of the world by general laws, and this seems nowise necessary to a very perfect Being. It is true, if everything were conducted by particular volitions, the course of nature would be perpetually broken and no man could employ his reason in the conduct of life. But might not other particular volitions remedy this inconvenience? In short, might not the Deity exterminate all ill, wherever it were to be found, and produce all good, without any preparation or long progress of causes and effects?

Besides, we must consider that according to the present economy of the world, the course of nature, though supposed exactly regular, yet to us appears not so, and many events are uncertain and many disappoint our expectations. Health and sickness, calm and tempest, with an infinite number of other accidents whose causes are unknown and variable, have a great influence both on the fortunes of particular persons and on the prosperity of public societies; and indeed all human life, in a manner, depends on such accidents. A being, therefore, who knows the secret springs of the universe might easily, by particular volitions, turn all these accidents to the good of mankind and render the whole world happy without discovering himself in any operation. A fleet whose purposes were salutary to society might always meet with a fair wind; good princes enjoy sound health and long life; persons born to power and authority be framed with good tempers and virtuous dispositions. A few such events as these, regularly and wisely conducted, would change the face of the world and yet would no more seem to disturb the course of nature or confound human conduct than the present economy of things, where the causes are secret and variable and compounded. Some small touches given to *Caligula's* brain in his infancy might have converted him into a *Trajan*. One wave, a little higher than the rest, by burying *Caesar* and his fortune in the bottom of the ocean, might have restored liberty to a considerable part of mankind. There may, for all we know, be good reasons why Providence interposes not in this manner, but they are unknown to us and though the mere supposition that such reasons exist may be sufficient to save the conclusion concerning the Divine attributes, yet surely it can never be sufficient to establish that conclusion.

If everything in the universe be conducted by general laws and if animals be rendered susceptible of pain, it scarcely seems possible but some ill must arise in the various shocks of matter and the various concurrence and opposition of general laws, but this ill would be very rare were it not for the *third* circumstance, which I proposed to mention, namely, the great frugality with which all powers and faculties are distributed to every particular being. So well adjusted are the organs and capacities of all animals and so well fitted to their preservation that as far as history or tradition reaches, there appears not to be any single species which has yet been extinguished in the universe. Every animal has the requisite endowments, but these endowments are bestowed with so scrupulous an economy that any considerable diminution must entirely destroy the creature. Wherever one power is increased, there is a proportional abatement in the others. Animals which excel in swiftness are commonly defective in force. Those which possess both either are imperfect in some of their senses or are oppressed with the most craving wants. The human species, whose chief excellency is reason and sagacity, is of all others the most necessitous and the most deficient in bodily advantages: without clothes, without arms, without food, without lodging, without any convenience of life, except what they owe to their own skill and industry. In short, nature seems to have formed an exact calculation of the necessities

of her creatures, and, like a *rigid master*, has afforded them little more powers or endowments than what are strictly sufficient to supply those necessities. An *indulgent parent* would have bestowed a large stock in order to guard against accidents and secure the happiness and welfare of the creature in the most unfortunate concurrence of circumstances. Every course of life would not have been so surrounded with precipices that the least departure from the true path, by mistake or necessity, must involve us in misery and ruin. Some reserve, some fund, would have been provided to insure happiness; nor would the powers and the necessities have been adjusted with so rigid an economy. The Author of Nature is inconceivably powerful: his force is supposed great, if not altogether inexhaustible; nor is there any reason, as far as we can judge, to make him observe this strict frugality in his dealings with his creatures. It would have been better, were his power extremely limited, to have created fewer animals and to have endowed these with more faculties for their happiness and preservation. A builder is never esteemed prudent who undertakes a plan beyond what his stock will enable him to finish.

In order to cure most of the ills of human life, I require not that man should have the wings of the eagle, the swiftness of the stag, the force of the ox, the arms of the lion, the scales of the crocodile or rhinoceros; much less do I demand the sagacity of an angel or cherubim. I am contented to take an increase in one single power or faculty of his soul. Let him be endowed with a greater propensity to industry and labor, a more vigorous spring and activity of mind, a more constant bent to business and application. Let the whole species possess naturally an equal diligence with that which many individuals are able to attain by habit and reflection, and the most beneficial consequences, without any alloy of ill, is the immediate and necessary result of this endowment. Almost all the moral as well as natural evils of human life arise from idleness, and were our species, by the original constitution of their frame, exempt from this vice or infirmity, the perfect cultivation of land, the improvement of arts and manufactures, the exact execution of every office and duty immediately follow, and men at once may fully reach that state of society which is so imperfectly attained by the best regulated government. But as industry is a power, and the most valuable of any, Nature seems determined, suitably to her usual maxims, to bestow it on men with a very sparing hand and rather to punish him severely for his deficiency in it than to reward him for his attainments. She has so contrived his frame that nothing but the most violent necessity can oblige him to labor, and she employs all his other wants to overcome, at least in part, the want of diligence and to endow him with some share of a faculty of which she has thought fit naturally to bereave him. Here our demands may be allowed very humble and therefore the more reasonable. If we required the endowments of superior penetration and judgment, of a more delicate taste of beauty, of a nicer sensibility to benevolence and friendship, we might be told that we impiously pretend to break the order of Nature, that we want to exalt ourselves into a higher rank of being, that the presents which we require, not being suitable to our state and condition, would only be pernicious to us. But it is hard—I dare to repeat it—it is hard that being placed in a world so full of wants and necessities where almost every being and element either is our foe or refuses its assistance, we should also have our own temper to struggle with and should be deprived of that faculty which can alone fence against these multiplied evils.

The *fourth* circumstance whence arises the misery and ill of the universe is the inaccurate workmanship of all the springs and principles of the great machine of nature. It must be acknowledged that there are few parts of the universe which seem not to serve some purpose and whose removal would not produce a visible defect and disorder in the whole. The parts hang all together, nor can one be touched without affecting the rest in a greater or less degree. But at the same time it must be observed that none of these parts or principles, however useful, are so accurately adjusted as to keep precisely within those bounds in which their utility consists; but they are, all of them, apt on every occasion to run into the one extreme or the other. One would imagine that this grand production had not received the last hand of the maker, so little finished is every part, and so coarse are the strokes with which it is executed. Thus the winds are requisite to convey the vapors along the surface of the globe and to assist men in navigation, but how often, rising up to tempests and hurricanes, do they become pernicious? Rains are necessary to nourish all the plants and animals of the earth, but how often are they defective? How often excessive? Heat is requisite to all life and vegetation, but is not always found in the due proportion. On the mixture and secretion of the humors and juices of the body depend the health and prosperity of the animal, but the parts perform not regularly their proper function. What more useful than all the passions of the mind, ambition, vanity, love, anger? But how oft do they break their bounds and cause the greatest convulsions in society? There is nothing so advantageous in the universe but what frequently becomes pernicious by its excess or defect; nor has Nature guarded with the requisite accuracy against all disorder or confusion. The irregularity is never perhaps so great as to destroy any species but is often sufficient to involve the individuals in ruin and misery.

On the concurrence, then, of these *four* circumstances does all or the greatest part of natural evil depend. Were all living creatures incapable of pain or were the world administered by particular volitions, evil never could have found access into the universe; and were animals endowed with a large stock of powers and faculties beyond what strict necessity requires, or were the several springs and principles of the universe so accurately framed as to preserve always the just temperament and medium, there must have been very little ill in comparison of what we feel at present. What, then, shall we pronounce on this occasion? Shall we say that these circumstances are not necessary and that they might easily have been altered in the contrivance of the universe? This decision seems too presumptuous for creatures so blind and ignorant. Let us be more modest in our conclusions. Let us allow that if the goodness of the Deity (I mean a goodness like the human) could be established on any tolerable reasons *a priori*, these phenomena, however untoward, would not be sufficient to subvert that principle but might easily, in some unknown manner, be reconcilable to it. But let us still assert that as this goodness is not antecedently established but must be inferred from the phenomena, there can be no grounds for such an inference while there are so many ills in the universe and while these ills might so easily have been remedied as far as human understanding can be allowed to judge on such a subject. I am skeptic enough to allow that the bad appearances, notwithstanding all my reasonings, may be compatible with such attributes as you suppose, but surely they can never prove these attributes. Such a conclusion cannot result from skepticism but must arise from the phenomena and from our confidence in the reasonings which we deduce from these phenomena.

Look round this universe. What an immense profusion of beings, animated and organized, sensible and active! You admire this prodigious variety and fecundity. But inspect a little more narrowly these living existences, the only beings worth regarding. How hostile and destructive to each other! How insufficient all of them for their own happiness! How contemptible or odious to the spectator! The whole presents nothing but the idea of a blind Nature impregnated by a great vivifying principle, and pouring forth from her lap, without discernment or parental care, her maimed and abortive children!

Here the Manichaean system occurs as a proper hypothesis to solve the difficulty and, no doubt, in some respects it is very specious and has more probability than the common hypothesis by giving a plausible account of the strange mixture of good and ill which appears in life. But if we consider, on the other hand, the perfect uniformity and agreement of the parts of the universe, we shall not discover in it any marks of the combat of a malevolent with a benevolent being. There is indeed an opposition of pains and pleasures in the feelings of sensible creatures. But are not all the operations of Nature carried on by an opposition of principles, of hot and cold, moist and dry, light and heavy? The true conclusion is that the original source of all things is entirely indifferent to all these principles and has no more regard to good above ill than to heat above cold or to drought above moisture or to light above heavy.

There may *four* hypotheses be framed concerning the first causes of the universe: *that* they are endowed with perfect goodness; *that* they have perfect malice; *that* they are opposite and have both goodness and malice; *that* they have neither goodness nor malice. Mixed phenomena can never prove the two former unmixed principles and the uniformity and steadiness of general laws seem to oppose the third. The fourth, therefore, seems by far the most probable.

What I have said concerning natural evil will apply to moral with little or no variation, and we have no more reason to infer that the rectitude of the Supreme Being resembles human rectitude than that his benevolence resembles the human. Nay, it will be thought that we have still greater cause to exclude from him moral sentiments such as we feel them, since moral evil, in the opinion of many, is much more predominant above moral good than natural evil above natural good.

But even though this should not be allowed and though the virtue which is in mankind should be acknowledged much superior to the vice, yet so long as there is any vice at all in the universe, it will very much puzzle you anthropomorphites how to account for it. You must assign a cause for it without having recourse to the first cause. But as every effect must have a cause and that cause another, you must either carry on the progression *in infinitum* or rest on that original principle who is the ultimate cause of all things . . . .

Hold! hold! cried *Demea*: Whither does your imagination hurry you? I joined in alliance with you in order to prove the incomprehensible nature of the Divine Being and refute the principles of *Cleanthes*, who would measure everything by human rule and standard. But I now find you running into all the topics of the greatest libertines and infidels and betraying that holy cause which you seemingly espoused. Are you secretly, then, a more dangerous enemy than *Cleanthes* himself?

And are you so late in perceiving it? replied *Cleanthes*. Believe me, *Demea*, your friend *Philo*, from the beginning, has been amusing himself at both our expense; and it must be confessed that the injudicious reasoning of our vulgar theology has given him but too just a handle of ridicule. The total infirmity of human reason, the absolute incomprehensibility of the Divine Nature, the great and universal misery, and still greater wickedness of men—these are strange topics, surely, to be so fondly cherished by orthodox divines and doctors. In ages of stupidity and ignorance, indeed, these principles may safely be espoused, and perhaps no views of things are more proper to promote superstition than such as encourage the blind amazement, the diffidence, and melancholy of mankind. But at present . . .

Blame not so much, interposed *Philo*, the ignorance of these reverend gentlemen. They know how to change their style with the times. Formerly, it was a most popular theological topic to maintain that human life was vanity and misery and to exaggerate all the ills and pains which are incident to men. But of late years, divines, we find, begin to retract this position and maintain, though still with some hesitation, that there are more goods than evils, more pleasures than pains, even in this life. When religion stood entirely upon temper and education, it was thought proper to encourage melancholy, as indeed mankind never have recourse to superior powers so readily as in that disposition. But as men have now learned to form principles and to draw consequences, it is necessary to change the batteries and to make use of such arguments as will endure at least some scrutiny and examination. This variation is the same (and from the same causes) with that which I formerly remarked with regard to skepticism.

Thus *Philo* continued to the last his spirit of opposition and his censure of established opinions. But I could observe that *Demea* did not at all relish the latter part of the discourse, and he took occasion soon after, on some pretence or other, to leave the company.

## Part XII

After *Demea's* departure, *Cleanthes* and *Philo* continued the conversation in the following manner. Our friend, I am afraid, said *Cleanthes*, will have little inclination to revive this topic of discourse while you are in company, and to tell the truth, *Philo*, I should rather wish to reason with either of you apart on a subject so sublime and interesting.

Your spirit of controversy, joined to your abhorrence of vulgar superstition, carries you strange lengths when engaged in an argument, and there is nothing so sacred and venerable, even in your own eyes, which you spare on that occasion.

I must confess, replied *Philo*, that I am less cautious on the subject of natural religion than on any other both because I know that I can never, on that head, corrupt the principles of any man of common sense and because no one, I am confident, in whose eyes I appear a man of common sense will ever mistake my intentions. You, in particular, *Cleanthes*, with whom I live in unreserved intimacy, you are sensible that notwithstanding the freedom of my conversation and my love of singular arguments, no one has a deeper sense of religion impressed on his mind or pays more profound adoration to the Divine Being as he discovers himself to reason in the inexplicable contrivance and artifice of nature. A purpose, an intention, a design, strikes everywhere the most careless, the most stupid thinker, and no man can be so hardened in absurd systems as at all times to reject it. *That Nature does nothing in vain* is a maxim established in all the schools merely from the contemplation of the works of Nature, without any religious purpose; and, from a firm conviction of its truth, an anatomist who had observed a new organ or canal would never be satisfied till he had also discovered its use and intention. One great foundation of the *Copernican* system is the maxim that *Nature acts by the simplest methods and chooses the most proper means to any end*; and astronomers often, without thinking of it, lay this strong foundation of piety and religion. The same thing is observable in other parts of philosophy; and thus all the sciences almost lead us insensibly to acknowledge a first intelligent Author, and their authority is often so much the greater as they do not directly profess that intention.

It is with pleasure I hear *Galen* reason concerning the structure of the human body. The anatomy of a man, says he,[15] discovers above six hundred different muscles; and whoever duly considers these will find that, in each of them, Nature must have adjusted at least ten different circumstances in order to attain

_____
15. *De Formatione Fetus.*

the end which she proposed; proper figure, just magnitude, right disposition of the several ends, upper and lower position of the whole, the due insertion of the several nerves, veins, and arteries, so that, in the muscles alone, above six thousand several views and intentions must have been formed and executed. The bones he calculates to be two hundred and eighty-four: the distinct purposes aimed at in the structure of each, above forty. What a prodigious display of artifice, even in these simple and homogeneous parts! But if we consider the skin, ligaments, vessels, glandules, humors, the several limbs and members of the body, how must our astonishment rise upon us in proportion to the number and intricacy of the parts so artificially adjusted! The further we advance in these researches, we discover new scenes of art and wisdom but descry still, at a distance, further scenes beyond our reach—in the fine internal structure of the parts, in the economy of the brain, in the fabric of the seminal vessels. All these artifices are repeated in every different species of animal, with wonderful variety and with exact propriety, suited to the different intentions of Nature in framing each species. And if the infidelity of *Galen*, even when these natural sciences were still imperfect, could not withstand such striking appearances, to what pitch of pertinacious obstinacy must a philosopher in this age have attained who can now doubt of a Supreme Intelligence!

Could I meet with one of this species (who, I thank God, are very rare), I would ask him: Supposing there were a God who did not discover himself immediately to our senses, were it possible for him to give stronger proofs of his existence than what appear on the whole face of Nature? What indeed could such a Divine Being do but copy the present economy of things; render many of his artifices so plain that no stupidity could mistake them; afford glimpses of still greater artifices which demonstrate his prodigious superiority above our narrow apprehensions; and conceal altogether a great many from such imperfect creatures? Now, according to all rules of just reasoning, every fact must pass for undisputed when it is supported by all the arguments which its nature admits of, even though these arguments be not in themselves very numerous or forcible; how

much more, in the present case, where no human imagination can compute their number and no understanding estimate their cogency!

I shall further add, said *Cleanthes*, to what you have so well urged, that one great advantage of the principle of theism is that it is the only system of cosmogony which can be rendered intelligible and complete and yet can throughout preserve a strong analogy to what we every day see and experience in the world. The comparison of the universe to a machine of human contrivance is so obvious and natural and is justified by so many instances of order and design in nature that it must immediately strike all unprejudiced apprehensions and procure universal approbation. Whoever attempts to weaken this theory cannot pretend to succeed by establishing in its place any other that is precise and determinate: It is sufficient for him if he start doubts and difficulties and, by remote and abstract views of things, reach that suspense of judgment which is here the utmost boundary of his wishes. But besides that this state of mind is in itself unsatisfactory, it can never be steadily maintained against such striking appearances as continually engage us into the religious hypothesis. A false, absurd system— human nature—from the force of prejudice is capable of adhering to with obstinacy and perseverance; but no system at all, in opposition to theory supported by strong and obvious reason, by natural propensity, and by early education, I think it absolutely impossible to maintain or defend.

So little, replied *Philo*, do I esteem this suspense of judgment in the present case to be possible that I am apt to suspect there enters somewhat of a dispute of words into this controversy, more than is usually imagined. That the works of nature bear a great analogy to the productions of art is evident; and according to all the rules of good reasoning, we ought to infer, if we argue at all concerning them, that their causes have a proportional analogy. But as there are also considerable differences, we have reason to suppose a proportional difference in the causes and in particular ought to attribute a much higher degree of power and energy to the supreme cause than any we have ever observed in mankind. Here then the existence of a DEITY is plainly ascertained by reason, and if we make it a question whether, on account of these analogies, we can properly call him a *mind* or *intelligence*, notwithstanding the vast difference which may reasonably be supposed between him and human minds, what is this but a mere verbal controversy? No man can deny the analogies between the effects, to restrain ourselves from inquiring concerning the causes is scarcely possible. From this inquiry, the legitimate conclusion is that the causes have also an analogy, and if we are not contented with calling the first and supreme cause a GOD or DEITY but desire to vary the expression, what can we call him but MIND or THOUGHT, to which he is justly supposed to bear a considerable resemblance?

All men of sound reason are disgusted with verbal disputes, which abound so much in philosophical and theological inquiries, and it is found that the only remedy for this abuse must arise from clear definitions, from the precision of those ideas which enter into any argument, and from the strict and uniform use of those terms which are employed. But there is a species of controversy which, from the very nature of language and of human ideas, is involved in perpetual ambiguity and can never, by any precaution or any definitions, be able to reach a reasonable certainty or precision. These are the controversies concerning the degrees of any quality or circumstance. Men may argue to all eternity whether *Hannibal* be a great, or a very great, or a superlatively great man, what degree of beauty *Cleopatra* possessed, what epithet of praise *Livy* or *Thucydides* is entitled to, without bringing the controversy to any determination. The disputants may here agree in their sense and differ in the terms, or *vice versa*, yet never be able to define their terms so as to enter into each other's meaning because the degrees of these qualities are not, like quantity or number, susceptible of any exact mensuration, which may be the standard in the controversy. That the dispute concerning theism is of this nature, and consequently is merely verbal, or perhaps, if possible, still more incurably ambiguous, will appear upon the slightest inquiry. I ask the theist if he does not allow that there is a great and immeasurable, because incomprehensible, difference between the *human* and the *divine* mind: The more pious he is, the more readily will

he assent to the affirmative and the more will he be disposed to magnify the difference: He will even assert that the difference is of a nature which cannot be too much magnified. I next turn to the atheist, who, I assert, is only nominally so and can never possibly be in earnest and I ask him whether, from the coherence and apparent sympathy in all the parts of this world, there be not a certain degree of analogy among all the operations of Nature, in every situation and in every age; whether the rotting of a turnip, the generation of an animal, and the structure of human thought, be not energies that probably bear some remote analogy to each other: It is impossible he can deny it, he will readily acknowledge it. Having obtained this concession, I push him still further in his retreat and I ask him if it be not probable that the principle which first arranged and still maintains order in this universe bears not also some remote inconceivable analogy to the other operations of nature and, among the rest, to the economy of human mind and thought: However reluctant, he must give his assent. Where then, cry I to both these antagonists, is the subject of your dispute? The theist allows that the original intelligence is very different from human reason; the atheist allows that the original principle of order bears some remote analogy to it. Will you quarrel, gentlemen, about the degrees and enter into a controversy which admits not of any precise meaning nor consequently of any determination? If you should be so obstinate, I should not be surprised to find you insensibly change sides, while the theist, on the one hand, exaggerates the dissimilarity between the Supreme Being and frail, imperfect, variable, fleeting, and mortal creatures, and the atheist, on the other, magnifies the analogy among all the operations of nature, in every period, every situation, and every position. Consider then where the real point of controversy lies, and if you cannot lay aside your disputes, endeavor, at least, to cure yourselves of your animosity.

And here I must also acknowledge, *Cleanthes*, that as the works of Nature have a much greater analogy to the effects of *our* art and contrivance than to those of our benevolence and justice, we have reason to infer that the natural attributes of the Deity have a greater resemblance to those of men than his moral have to human virtues. But what is the consequence? Nothing but this: that the moral qualities of man are more defective in their kind than his natural abilities. For, as the Supreme Being is allowed to be absolutely and entirely perfect, whatever differs most from him departs the furthest from the supreme standard of rectitude and perfection.[16]

These, *Cleanthes*, are my unfeigned sentiments on this subject, and these sentiments, you know, I have ever cherished and maintained. But in proportion to my veneration for true religion is my abhorrence of vulgar superstitions; and I indulge a peculiar pleasure, I confess, in pushing such principles, sometimes into absurdity, sometimes into impiety. And you are sensible that all bigots, notwithstanding their great aversion to the latter above the former, are commonly equally guilty of both.

My inclination, replied *Cleanthes*, lies, I admit, a contrary way. Religion, however corrupted, is still better than no religion at all. The doctrine of a future state is so strong and necessary a security to morals that we never ought to abandon or neglect it. For if finite and temporary rewards and punishments have so great an effect, as we daily find, how much greater must be expected from such as are infinite and eternal?

How happens it then, said *Philo*, if vulgar superstition be so salutary to society that all history abounds so much with accounts of its pernicious consequences on public affairs? Factions, civil wars, persecutions, subversions of government, oppression, slavery—these

---

16. It seems evident that the dispute between the skeptics and dogmatists is entirely verbal, or at least regards only the degrees of doubt and assurance which we ought to indulge with regard to all reasoning, and such disputes are commonly, at the bottom, verbal and admit not of any precise determination. No philosophical dogmatist denies that there are difficulties with regard both to the senses and to all science and that these difficulties are in a regular, logical method absolutely insolvable. No skeptic denies that we lie under an absolute necessity, notwithstanding these difficulties, of thinking and believing and reasoning with regard to all kinds of subjects, and even of frequently assenting with confidence and security. The only difference, then, between these sects, if they merit that name, is that the skeptic, from habit, caprice, or inclination, insists most on the difficulties; the dogmatist, for like reasons, on the necessity.

are the dismal consequences which always attend its prevalence over the minds of men. If the religious spirit be ever mentioned in any historical narration, we are sure to meet afterwards with a detail of the miseries which attend it. And no period of time can be happier or more prosperous than those in which it is never regarded or heard of.

The reason of this observation, replied *Cleanthes*, is obvious. The proper office of religion is to regulate the heart of men, humanize their conduct, infuse the spirit of temperance, order, and obedience, and as its operation is silent and only enforces the motives of morality and justice, it is in danger of being overlooked and confounded with these other motives. When it distinguishes itself and acts as a separate principle over men, it has departed from its proper sphere and has become only a cover to faction and ambition.

And so will all religion, said *Philo*, except the philosophical and rational kind. Your reasonings are more easily eluded than my facts. The inference is not just, because finite and temporary rewards and punishments have so great influence that therefore such as are infinite and eternal must have so much greater. Consider, I beseech you, the attachment which we have to present things and the little concern which we discover for objects so remote and uncertain. When divines are declaiming against the common behavior and conduct of the world, they always represent this principle as the strongest imaginable (which indeed it is) and describe almost all human kind as lying under the influence of it and sunk into the deepest lethargy and unconcern about their religious interests. Yet these same divines, when they refute their speculative antagonists, suppose the motives of religion to be so powerful that, without them, it were impossible for civil society to subsist. Nor are they ashamed of so palpable a contradiction. It is certain, from experience, that the smallest grain of natural honesty and benevolence has more effect on men's conduct than the most pompous views suggested by theological theories and systems. A man's natural inclination works incessantly upon him; it is forever present to the mind and mingles itself with every view and consideration, whereas religious motives, where they act at all, operate only by starts and bounds and it is scarcely possible for them to become altogether habitual to the mind. The force of the greatest gravity, say the philosophers, is infinitely small in comparison of that of the least impulse, yet it is certain that the smallest gravity will, in the end, prevail above a great impulse, because no strokes or blows can be repeated with such constancy as attraction and gravitation.

Another advantage of inclination: It engages on its side all the wit and ingenuity of the mind and when set in opposition to religious principles, seeks every method and art of eluding them, in which it is almost always successful. Who can explain the heart of man or account for those strange salvos and excuses with which people satisfy themselves when they follow their inclinations in opposition to their religious duty? This is well understood in the world, and none but fools ever repose less trust in a man, because they hear that from study and philosophy he has entertained some speculative doubts with regard to theological subjects. And when we have to do with a man who makes a great profession of religion and devotion, has this any other effect upon several who pass for prudent than to put them on their guard lest they be cheated and deceived by him?

We must further consider that philosophers, who cultivate reason and reflection, stand less in need of such motives to keep them under the restraint of morals and that the vulgar, who alone may need them, are utterly incapable of so pure a religion as represents the Deity to be pleased with nothing but virtue in human behavior. The recommendations to the Divinity are generally supposed to be either frivolous observances or rapturous ecstasies or a bigoted credulity. We need not run back into antiquity or wander into remote regions to find instances of this degeneracy. Amongst ourselves, some have been guilty of that atrociousness, unknown to the Egyptian and Grecian superstitions, of declaiming in express terms against morality and representing it as a sure forfeiture of the Divine favor if the least trust or reliance be laid upon it.

But even though superstition or enthusiasm should not put itself in direct opposition to morality, the very diverting of the attention, the raising up a new and frivolous species of merit, the preposterous distribution which it makes of praise and blame, must have the most pernicious consequences and weaken extremely men's attachment to the natural motives of justice and humanity.

Such a principle of action, likewise, not being any of the familiar motives of human conduct, acts only by intervals on the temper and must be roused by continual efforts in order to render the pious zealot satisfied with his own conduct and make him fulfil his devotional task. Many religious exercises are entered into with seeming fervor where the heart, at the time, feels cold and languid: A habit of dissimulation is by degrees contracted, and fraud and falsehood become the predominant principle. Hence the reason of that vulgar observation that the highest zeal in religion and the deepest hypocrisy, so far from being inconsistent, are often or commonly united in the same individual character.

The bad effects of such habits, even in common life, are easily imagined, but where the interests of religion are concerned, no morality can be forcible enough to bind the enthusiastic zealot. The sacredness of the cause sanctifies every measure which can be made use of to promote it.

The steady attention alone to so important an interest as that of eternal salvation is apt to extinguish the benevolent affections and beget a narrow, contracted selfishness. And when such a temper is encouraged, it easily eludes all the general precepts of charity and benevolence.

Thus the motives of vulgar superstition have no great influence on general conduct, nor is their operation favorable to morality in the instances where they predominate.

Is there any maxim in politics more certain and infallible than that both the number and the authority of priests should be confined within very narrow limits and that the civil magistrate ought, forever, to keep his *fasces* and *axes* from such dangerous hands? But if the spirit of popular religion were so salutary to society, a contrary maxim ought to prevail. The greater number of priests and their greater authority and riches will always augment the religious spirit. And though the priests have the guidance of this spirit, why may we not expect a superior sanctity of life and greater benevolence and moderation from persons who are set apart for religion, who are continually inculcating it upon others, and who must themselves imbibe a greater share of it? Whence comes it then that, in fact, the utmost a wise magistrate can propose with regard to popular religions is, as far as possible, to make a saving game of it and to prevent their pernicious consequences with regard to society? Every expedient which he tries for so humble a purpose is surrounded with inconveniences. If he admits only one religion among his subjects, he must sacrifice, to an uncertain prospect of tranquillity, every consideration of public liberty, science, reason, industry, and even his own independence. If he gives indulgence to several sects, which is the wiser maxim, he must preserve a very philosophical indifference to all of them and carefully restrain the pretensions of the prevailing sect; otherwise he can expect nothing but endless disputes, quarrels, factions, persecutions, and civil commotions.

True religion, I allow, has no such pernicious consequences, but we must treat of religion as it has commonly been found in the world; nor have I anything to do with that speculative tenet of theism which, as it is a species of philosophy, must partake of the beneficial influence of that principle and at the same time must lie under a like inconvenience of being always confined to very few persons.

Oaths are requisite in all courts of judicature, but it is a question whether their authority arises from any popular religion. It is the solemnity and importance of the occasion, the regard to reputation, and the reflecting on the general interests of society which are the chief restraints upon mankind. Custom-house oaths and political oaths are but little regarded even by some who pretend to principles of honesty and religion; and a *Quaker's* asseveration is with us justly put upon the same footing with the oath of any other person. I know that *Polybius*[17] ascribes the infamy of Greek faith to the prevalence of the *Epicurean* philosophy, but I know also that Punic faith had as bad a reputation in ancient times as Irish evidence has

in modern, though we cannot account for these vulgar observations by the same reason. Not to mention that Greek faith was infamous before the rise of the *Epicurean* philosophy, and *Euripides*,[18] in a passage which I shall point out to you, has glanced a remarkable stroke of satire against his nation, with regard to this circumstance.

Take care, *Philo*, replied *Cleanthes*, take care, push not matters too far, allow not your zeal against false religion to undermine your veneration for the true. Forfeit not this principle, the chief, the only great comfort in life, and our principal support amidst all the attacks of adverse fortune. The most agreeable reflection which it is possible for human imagination to suggest is that of genuine theism, which represents us as the workmanship of a Being perfectly good, wise, and powerful, who created us for happiness, and who, having implanted in us immeasurable desires of good, will prolong our existence to all eternity and will transfer us into an infinite variety of scenes in order to satisfy those desires and render our felicity complete and durable. Next to such a Being himself (if the comparison be allowed), the happiest lot which we can imagine is that of being under his guardianship and protection.

These appearances, said *Philo*, are most engaging and alluring; and with regard to the true Philosopher, they are more than appearances. But it happens here, as in the former case, that with regard to the greater part of mankind, the appearances are deceitful and that the terrors of religion commonly prevail above its comforts.

It is allowed that men never have recourse to devotion so readily as when dejected with grief or depressed with sickness. Is not this a proof that the religious spirit is not so nearly allied to joy as to sorrow?

But men, when afflicted, find consolation in religion, replied *Cleanthes*. Sometimes, said *Philo*, but it is natural to imagine that they will form a notion of those unknown beings, suitable to the present gloom and melancholy of their temper, when they betake themselves to the contemplation of them. Accordingly, we find the tremendous images to predominate in all religions; and we ourselves, after having employed

---

17. *Histories*, Book VI, chap. 54.

18. *Iphigenia in Tauride*.

the most exalted expression in our descriptions of the Deity, fall into the flattest contradiction in affirming that the damned are infinitely superior in number to the elect.

I shall venture to affirm that there never was a popular religion which represented the state of departed souls in such a light as would render it eligible for human kind that there should be such a state. These fine models of religion are the mere product of philosophy. For as death lies between the eye and the prospect of futurity, that event is so shocking to Nature that it must throw a gloom on all the regions which lie beyond it and suggest to the generality of mankind the idea of *Cerberus* and *Furies*, devils, and torrents of fire and brimstone.

It is true that both fear and hope enter into religion because both these passions, at different times, agitate the human mind, and each of them forms a species of divinity suitable to itself. But when a man is in a cheerful disposition, he is fit for business, or company, or entertainment of any kind, and he naturally applies himself to these and thinks not of religion. When melancholy and dejected, he has nothing to do but brood upon the terrors of the invisible world and to plunge himself still deeper in affliction. It may indeed happen that after he has, in this manner, engraved the religious opinions deep into his thought and imagination, there may arrive a change of health or circumstances, which may restore his good-humor and, raising cheerful prospects of futurity, make him run into the other extreme of joy and triumph. But still it must be acknowledged that, as terror is the primary principle of religion, it is the passion which always predominates in it and admits but of short intervals of pleasure.

Not to mention that these fits of excessive, enthusiastic joy, by exhausting the spirits, always prepare the way for equal fits of superstitious terror and dejection; nor is there any state of mind so happy as the calm and equable. But this state it is impossible to support, where a man thinks that he lies in such profound darkness and uncertainty, between an eternity of happiness and an eternity of misery. No wonder that such an opinion disjoints the ordinary frame of the mind and throws it into the utmost confusion.

And though that opinion is seldom so steady in its operation as to influence all the actions, yet it is apt to make a considerable breach in the temper and to produce that gloom and melancholy so remarkable in all devout people.

It is contrary to common sense to entertain apprehensions or terrors upon account of any opinion whatsoever or to imagine that we run any risk hereafter by the freest use of our reason. Such a sentiment implies both an *absurdity* and an *inconsistency*. It is an absurdity to believe that the Deity has human passions, and one of the lowest of human passions, a restless appetite for applause. It is an inconsistency to believe that, since the Deity has this human passion, he has not others also and, in particular, a disregard to the opinions of creatures so much inferior.

*To know God*, says Seneca, *is to worship him*. All other worship is indeed absurd, superstitious, and even impious. It degrades him to the low condition of mankind, who are delighted with entreaty, solicitation, presents, and flattery. Yet is this impiety the smallest of which superstition is guilty? Commonly, it depresses the Deity far below the condition of mankind and represents him as a capricious demon who exercises his power without reason and without humanity! And were that Divine Being disposed to be offended at the vices and follies of silly mortals, who are his own workmanship, ill would it surely fare with the votaries of most popular superstitions. Nor would any of human race merit his *favor*, but a very few — the philosophical theists, who entertain, or rather indeed endeavor to entertain, suitable notions of his Divine perfections. As the only persons entitled to his *compassion* and *indulgence* would be the philosophical skeptics, a sect almost equally rare, who, from a natural diffidence of their own capacity, suspend or endeavor to suspend all judgment with regard to such sublime and such extraordinary subjects.

If the whole of natural theology, as some people seem to maintain, resolves itself into one simple though somewhat ambiguous, at least undefined proposition — that *the cause or causes of order in the universe probably bear some remote analogy to human intelligence* — if this proposition be not capable of extension, variation, or more particular explication; if it affords no inference that affects human life or can be the source of any action or forbearance; and if the analogy, imperfect as it is, can be carried no further than to the human intelligence and cannot be transferred with any appearance of probability to the qualities of the mind; if this really be the case, what can the most inquisitive, contemplative, and religious man do more than give a plain, philosophical assent to the proposition as often as it occurs, and believe that the arguments on which it is established exceed the objections which lie against it? Some astonishment, indeed, will naturally arise from the greatness of the object; some melancholy from its obscurity; some contempt of human reason that it can give no solution more satisfactory with regard to so extraordinary and magnificent a question. But believe me, *Cleanthes*, the most natural sentiment which a well-disposed mind will feel on this occasion is a longing desire and expectation that heaven would be pleased to dissipate, at least alleviate, this profound ignorance by affording some particular revelation to mankind and making discoveries of the nature, attributes, and operations of the divine object of our faith. A person seasoned with a just sense of the imperfections of natural reason will fly to revealed truth with the greatest avidity, while the haughty dogmatist, persuaded that he can erect a complete system of theology by the mere help of philosophy, disdains any further aid and rejects this adventitious instructor. To be a philosophical skeptic is, in a man of letters, the first and most essential step towards being a sound, believing *Christian*, a proposition which I would willingly recommend to the attention of *Pamphilus*, and I hope *Cleanthes* will forgive me for interposing so far in the education and instruction of his pupil.

Pamphilus: *Cleanthes* and *Philo* pursued not this conversation much further and as nothing ever made greater impression on me than all the reasonings of that day, so I confess that, upon a serious review of the whole, I cannot but think that *Philo's* principles are more probable than *Demea's*, but that those of *Cleanthes* approach still nearer to the truth.

# Lady Mary Shepherd, *An Essay upon the Relation of Cause and Effect Controverting the Doctrine of Mr. Hume, Concerning the Nature of that Relation, with Observations upon the Opinions of Dr. Brown and Mr. Lawrence, Connected with the Same Subject* (1824)[1]

*In this essay, Shepherd develops a careful presentation and criticism of Hume's views on the relation of cause and effect.[2] Specifically, she distinguishes between the claim that every effect has a cause and the claim that everything that comes to be has a cause, noting that it is the latter claim that is important. She argues in favor of this claim and shows that its justification is based in the nature of our reasoning from a single case rather than from the imagination and custom.*

## PREFACE

It is attempted, in the following pages, to controvert Mr. Hume's doctrine on the "Nature of the Relation of Cause and Effect," as set forth in several sections of his *Treatise on Human Nature* and as confirmed in three sections of his *Essays*. [. . .]

---

1. From *An Essay upon the Relation of Cause and Effect Controverting the Doctrine of Mr. Hume, Concerning the Nature of that Relation, with Observations upon the Opinions of Dr. Brown and Mr. Lawrence, Connected with the Same Subject.* London, Printed for T. Hookham, Old Bond Street, 1824.

2. For more information on Shepherd's life and works, see the brief description provided in chapter 5.

## AN ESSAY

### Introductory Chapter

The plan I mean to adopt, in order to give a clear view of Mr. Hume's doctrine of the relation of Cause and Effect in the most concise manner possible, is: first, to arrange such quotations from the *Treatise of Human Nature* as will show the opinions there held, and afterwards [to] select some others from the *Essays*, in which they are corroborated and enlarged upon, and which will be sufficient to show that the doctrines contained in the *Treatise* are there repeated, with the *addition* of an application of them to the affairs of ordinary life, as affording a ground of skepticism concerning the powers of the understanding having to perform in the regulation of her expectations.

The quotations from the *Treatise* will first show "What is the doctrine enquired into," secondly, the argument by which Mr. Hume attempts to confute the opinion of the necessity of a Cause for every beginning of existence, and also the argument he employs in the aid of his own doctrine, concerning the ideas we have of the *necessary connection of Cause and Effect*, and of the *belief* there is placed in such necessary connection, [and] thirdly, the definition of the relation of Cause and Effect, this definition being the object aimed at by the whole argument.

The doctrine inquired into is the necessary connection of Cause and Effect and is divided into these two general propositions or queries:

First, "For what reason we pronounce it necessary that every thing whose existence has a beginning should also have a cause?"[3]

Secondly, "Why we conclude that such particular Causes must necessarily have such particular Effects, and what is the nature of that inference we draw from one to the other, and of the belief we repose in it?"

Mr. Hume's method of answering these questions is by adopting a new and skeptical view of the subject and by attempting to confute those philosophers who were of a different opinion from himself concerning it by asserting that it is "neither *intuitively* nor *demonstratively* certain that every thing which begins to exist must have a cause." [. . .]

## Chapter the Second

Having now made an abstract of Mr. Hume's *Treatise* and *Essays* on the subject of the relation of Cause and Effect, I shall proceed to examine each part in as regular an order as I conveniently can, and endeavor to answer the two questions first proposed in a more popular and, I hope, not more illogical method than Mr. Hume has followed, by attempting to prove:

First, that *reason*, not *fancy* and "custom," leads us to the knowledge That everything which begins to exist must have a Cause. Secondly, That *reason* forces the mind to perceive that *similar causes* must necessarily produce *similar effects*. Thirdly, I shall thence establish a more philosophical definition of the relation of Cause and Effect. Fourthly, show in what respects Mr. Hume's definition is faulty. Fifthly, proceed to prove that Nature cannot be supposed to alter her Course without a contradiction in terms, and finally, show that *Custom and Habit* alone are

---

3. See *Treatise on Human Nature*, vol. 1, Part 3. Concluding Sentences of Sect. 2nd, page 116. Sect. 3rd, 5th, 6th, 7th, part of Sect. 8th, page 150 to end.

not our guides, but chiefly reason for the regulation of our expectations in ordinary life. [. . .]

Section the First

[. . .] Thus, the original question, namely: "Whether every thing which begins to exist requires a cause for its existence?" resolves itself into two others, viz.:

First, Whether objects called EFFECTS necessarily require causes for their existence? Or whether they may begin to exist with or without them indifferently?" — As also

Secondly, Whether any objects whatever, without being considered as having the *nature of effects*, can begin their existences?

It may be plainly seen that the first of these questions is sunk in the latter, because, if objects *usually considered as effects* need not be considered as effects, then they are forced to begin their existences *of themselves*. For, conjoined or not to their causes, we know by our senses that they do begin to exist. We will, therefore, immediately hasten to the consideration of the second question, which may be stated in the following terms: Whether every object which begins to exist must owe its existence to a cause?

Let the object which we suppose to begin its existence of itself be imagined, abstracted from the nature of all objects we are acquainted with, saving in its capacity of existence. Let us suppose it to be *no effect*. There shall be no prevening circumstances whatever that affect it, nor any existence in the universe. Let it be so; let there be naught but a blank, and a mass of whatsoever can be supposed not to require a cause to START FORTH into existence, and make the first breach on the wide nonentity around. Now, what is this starting forth, beginning, coming into existence, but an action, which is a quality of an object not yet in being, and so not possible to have its qualities determined, nevertheless exhibiting its qualities?

If, indeed, it should be shown that there is no proposition whatever taken as a ground on which to build an argument in this question, neither one conclusion nor the other can be supported. And there need be no attempt at reasoning. — But if my adversary allows that, no existence being supposed previously in the universe, existence, in order to be, must *begin to be*, and that the notion of *beginning an action* (the being that *begins* it not supposed yet in existence) involves a *contradiction in terms*, then this *beginning* to exist cannot appear but as a *capacity some nature has* to alter the presupposed nonentity and to act for itself, whilst itself is not in being. — The original assumption may deny as much as it pleases all cause of existence, but, whilst in its very idea, the commencement of existence is an effect predicated of some supposed *cause* (*because the quality of an object* which must be *in existence to possess it*) we must conclude that *there is no object which begins to exist, but must owe its existence to some cause.* [. . .]

### Section the Second

[. . .] Now it is my intention to show, in contradiction to these ideas of Mr. Hume, that it is *Reason*, and not *Custom*, which guides our minds in forming the notions of necessary connection, of belief and of expectation. In order to [see] this let us bear in mind the reasoning already adduced in the foregoing Chapter, and it then immediately follows that objects, which we know by our senses do begin their existences and by our reason know they cannot begin it of themselves, must begin it by the operation of some *other beings* in existence, producing these new qualities in nature, and introducing them to our observation. The very meaning of the word Cause is *Producer* or *Creator*; of Effect, the *Produced* or *Created*—and the idea is gained by such an observance of nature as we think is efficient in any given case to an *experimentum crucis*.

Long observation of the invariableness of antecedency and subsequency is not wanted, many trials are not wanted, to generate the notion of *producing power*.

One trial is enough, in such circumstances, as will bring the mind to the following reasoning.

Here is a new quality, which appears to my senses.

But it could not arise of itself, nor could any surrounding objects, but one (or more) affect it. Therefore, that one (or more) have occasioned it, for there is nothing else to make a difference, and a *difference* could not "*begin of itself.*"

This is an argument which all persons, however illiterate, feel the force of. It is the only foundation for the demonstrations of the laboratory of the chemist, which all life resembles, and so closely, and the vulgar are equally sure of what cause is absolutely necessary to the production of certain effects. For instance, each knows that in certain given circumstances, *the closing of the Eye* will eclipse the prospect of nature, and the slight motion of reopening it will restore all the objects to view. Therefore, the Eye (in these circumstances) is the *Cause* or *Producer of vision*. One trial would be enough, under certain *known* circumstances. Why? Not from "*custom,*" because there has been *one trial only*, but from *Reason*, because vision not being able *to produce itself, nor any of the surrounding objects by the supposition*, it is the *Eye* which must necessarily perform the operation, for there is nothing else to make a difference, and a different quality could not "*begin its own existence.*" It is this sort of REASONING UPON EXPERIMENT which takes place in every man's mind concerning every affair in life, which generates the notion of Power and necessary Connection, and gives birth to that maxim "*a like Cause must produce a like Effect.*"

# Thomas Reid, *An Inquiry into the Human Mind on the Principles of Common Sense* (1764), Conclusion; and *Essays on the Intellectual Powers of Man* (1785), Essay VI, "Of Judgment," Chapter 2: "Of Common Sense"[1]

*Thomas Reid (1710–96) was born at Strachan in Kincardinshire, Scotland. After being educated in a local parish school and at the University of Aberdeen, he first became a university librarian and then, in 1737, entered the ministry, as was traditional for the paternal side of his family. In 1752, he was appointed professor of philosophy at King's College in Aberdeen, where he would found the Aberdeen Philosophical Society. In 1764, Reid succeeded Adam Smith as Professor of Moral Philosophy in Glasgow. He resigned this position in 1781 in order to devote more time to his writing. Reid first published "An Essay on Quantity" in 1748, which was followed by* An Inquiry into the Human Mind on the Principles of Common Sense *in 1764,* Essays on the Intellectual Powers of Man *in 1785, and finally* Essays on the Active Powers of Man *in 1788. Reid is best known for two doctrines in particular: (i) his criticism of "the way of ideas" as espoused by many modern philosophers, but especially David Hume, and (ii) his endorsement and explanation of common sense as a fundamental philosophical principle. According to Reid, what human beings directly perceive are not ideas*

*(as Descartes had famously maintained in Meditation Two and as Locke had explained in Book II of* An Essay concerning Human Understanding*) but rather the external objects themselves. In the "Conclusion" to* An Inquiry *Reid divides different approaches to understanding the mind into the way of analogy and the way of reflection, which Reid believes will allow him to illustrate what is mistaken about the analogy that leads to the way of ideas and how this mistake can be corrected by means of accurate reflection. In the passage on common sense from the* Essays on the Intellectual Powers of Man, *Reid explains that common sense is not simply what anyone off the street would immediately assent to, but rather an ability to judge what is self-evident.[2]*

## An Inquiry into the Human Mind, Conclusion

Containing Reflections upon the Opinions of Philosophers on This Subject

There are two ways in which men may form their notions and opinions concerning the mind and

1. "Conclusion" selected from *Philosophical Works of Thomas Reid*, ed. W. Hamilton (Edinburgh, 1895), and "Of Judgment" selected from *The Works of Thomas Reid*, published by Samuel Etheridge Jr. (Charlestown, MA, 1813–15), modified.

2. For more on Reid, see Roger Gallie, *Thomas Reid and "the Way of Ideas"* (Kluwer: Dordrecht, 1989), or Keith Lehrer, *Thomas Reid* (Routledge: New York, 1991).

concerning its powers and operations. The first is the only way that leads to truth, but it is narrow and rugged, and few have entered upon it. The second is broad and smooth and has been much beaten, not only by the vulgar but even by philosophers; it is sufficient for common life and is well adapted to the purposes of the poet and orator, but in philosophical disquisitions concerning the mind, it leads to error and delusion.

We may call the first of these ways *the way of reflection*. When the operations of the mind are exerted, we are conscious of them, and it is in our power to attend to them and to reflect upon them until they become familiar objects of thought. This is the only way in which we can form just and accurate notions of those operations. But this attention and reflection is so difficult to man, surrounded on all hands by external objects, which constantly solicit his attention, that it has been very little practiced, even by philosophers. In the course of this *Inquiry*, we have had many occasions to show how little attention has been given to the most familiar operations of the senses.

The second and the most common way in which men form their opinions concerning the mind and its operations we may call *the way of analogy*. There is nothing in the course of nature so singular but we can find some resemblance, or at least some analogy, between it and other things with which we are acquainted. The mind naturally delights in hunting after such analogies and attends to them with pleasure. From them, poetry and wit derive a great part of their charms, and eloquence not a little of its persuasive force.

Besides the pleasure we receive from analogies, they are of very considerable use, both to facilitate the conception of things when they are not easily apprehended without such a handle and to lead us to probable conjectures about their nature and qualities when we want the means of more direct and immediate knowledge. When I consider that the planet Jupiter, in like manner as the earth, rolls round his own axis and revolves round the sun, and that it is enlightened by several secondary planets, as the earth is enlightened by the moon, I am apt to conjecture from analogy that as the earth by these means is

fitted to be the habitation of various orders of animals, so the planet Jupiter is, by the like means, fitted for the same purpose; and having no argument more direct and conclusive to determine me in this point, I yield to this analogical reasoning a degree of assent proportioned to its strength. When I observe that the potato plant very much resembles the *solanum* in its flower and fructification and am informed that the last is poisonous, I am apt from analogy to have some suspicion of the former; but, in this case, I have access to more direct and certain evidence and therefore ought not to trust to analogy, which would lead me into an error.

Arguments from analogy are always at hand and grow up spontaneously in a fruitful imagination, while arguments that are more direct and more conclusive often require painful attention and application; and, therefore, mankind in general has been very much disposed to trust to the former. If one attentively examines the systems of the ancient philosophers, either concerning the material world or concerning the mind, he will find them to be built solely upon the foundation of analogy. Lord Bacon first delineated the strict and severe method of induction; since his time it has been applied with very happy success in some parts of natural philosophy and hardly in anything else. But there is no subject in which mankind is so much disposed to trust to the analogical way of thinking and reasoning as in what concerns the mind and its operations, because to form clear and distinct notions of those operations in the direct and proper way and to reason about them requires a habit of attentive reflection, of which few are capable, and which, even by those few, cannot be attained without much pains and labor.

Every man is apt to form his notions of things difficult to be apprehended, or less familiar, from their analogy to things which are more familiar. Thus, if a man bred to the seafaring life and accustomed to think and talk only of matters relating to navigation enters into discourse upon any other subject, it is well known that the language and the notions proper to his own profession are infused into every subject, and all things are measured by the rules of navigation; and if he should take it into his head to philosophize concerning the faculties of the mind, it cannot be doubted but he would draw his notions from the fabric of his ship, and would find in the mind, sails, masts, rudder, and compass.

Sensible objects of one kind or other do no less occupy and engross the rest of mankind than things relating to navigation occupy the seafaring man. For a considerable part of life, we can think of nothing but the objects of sense; and to attend to objects of another nature so as to form clear and distinct notions of them is no easy matter, even after we come to years of reflection. The condition of mankind therefore affords good reason to apprehend that their language and their common notions concerning the mind and its operations will be analogical and derived from the objects of sense, and that these analogies will be apt to impose upon philosophers as well as upon the vulgar and to lead them to materialize the mind and its faculties; and experience abundantly confirms the truth of this.

How generally men of all nations and in all ages of the world have conceived the soul, or thinking principle in man, to be some subtle matter, like breath or wind, the names given to it almost in all languages sufficiently testify. We have words which are proper, and not analogical, to express the various ways in which we perceive external objects by the senses—*such as feeling, sight, taste*—but we are often obliged to use these words analogically to express other powers of the mind which are of a very different nature. And the powers which imply some degree of reflection have generally no names but such as are analogical. The objects of thought are said to be *in the mind*, to be *apprehended, comprehended, conceived, imagined, retained, weighed, ruminated.*

It does not appear that the notions of the ancient philosophers with regard to the nature of the soul were much more refined than those of the vulgar or that they were formed in any other way. We shall distinguish the philosophy that regards our subject into the *old* and the *new*. The old reached down to Descartes, who gave it a fatal blow of which it has been gradually expiring ever since, and is now almost extinct. Descartes is the father of the new philosophy that relates to this subject, but it has been gradually

improving since his time, upon the principles laid down by him. The old philosophy seems to have been purely analogical; the new is more derived from reflection, but still with a very considerable mixture of the old analogical notions.

Because the objects of sense consist of *matter* and *form*, the ancient philosophers conceived everything to belong to one of these or to be made up of both. Some therefore thought that the soul is a particular kind of subtle matter, separable from our gross bodies; others thought that it is only a particular form of the body and inseparable from it. For there seem to have been some among the ancients as well as among the moderns who conceived that a certain structure or organization of the body is all that is necessary to render it sensible and intelligent. The different powers of the mind were, accordingly, by the last sect of philosophers conceived to belong to different parts of the body, as the heart, the brain, the liver, the stomach, the blood.

They who thought that the soul is a subtle matter separable from the body disputed to which of the four elements it belongs, whether to earth, water, air, or fire. Of the three last, each had its particular advocates. But some were of the opinion that it partakes of all the elements; that it must have something in its composition similar to everything we perceive; and that we perceive earth by the earthly part, water by the watery part, and fire by the fiery part of the soul. Some philosophers, not satisfied with determining of what kind of matter the soul is made, inquired likewise into its figure, which they determined to be spherical, that it might be the more fit for motion. The most spiritual and sublime notion concerning the nature of the soul to be met with among the ancient philosophers, I conceive to be that of the Platonists, who held that it is made of that celestial and incorruptible matter of which the fixed stars were made and therefore has a natural tendency to rejoin its proper element. I am at a loss to say in which of these classes of philosophers Aristotle ought to be placed. He defines the soul to be the first εντελέχεια of a natural body which has potential life. I beg to be excused from translating the Greek word, because I do not know the meaning of it.

The notions of the ancient philosophers with regard to the operations of the mind, particularly with regard to perceptions and ideas, seem likewise to have been formed by the same kind of analogy.

Plato, of the writers that are extant, first introduced the word *idea* into philosophy, but his doctrine on this subject was somewhat peculiar. He agreed with the rest of the ancient philosophers in this: that all things consist of matter and form, and that the matter of which all things were made existed from eternity, without form; but he likewise believed that there are eternal forms of all possible things which exist without matter, and to these eternal and immaterial forms he gave the name of *ideas*, maintaining that they are the only object of true knowledge. It is of no great moment to us whether he borrowed these notions from Parmenides or whether they were the issue of his own creative imagination. The later Platonists seem to have improved upon them in conceiving those ideas, or eternal forms of things, to exist not of themselves but in the Divine Mind and to be the models and patterns according to which all things were made [ . . . ].

To these Platonic notions, that of Malebranche is very nearly allied. This author seems more than any other to have been aware of the difficulties attending the common hypothesis concerning ideas, namely, that ideas of all objects of thought are in the human mind and therefore, in order to avoid those difficulties, makes the ideas, which are the immediate objects of human thought, to be the ideas of things in the Divine Mind, who, being intimately present to every human mind, may discover his ideas to it as far as pleases him.

The Platonists and Malebranche excepted, all other philosophers, as far as I know, have conceived that there are ideas or images of every object of thought in the human mind or at least in some part of the brain, where the mind is supposed to have its residence.

Aristotle had no good affection for the word *idea* and seldom or never uses it but in refuting Plato's notions about ideas. He thought that matter may exist without form but that forms cannot exist without matter. But at the same time he taught that there can be no sensation, no imagination, nor intellection, without forms, phantasms, or species in the mind and that things sensible are perceived by sensible species and things intelligible by intelligible species. His followers taught more explicitly that those sensible and intelligible species are sent forth by the objects and make their impressions upon the passive intellect and that the active intellect perceives them in the passive intellect. And this seems to have been the common opinion while the Peripatetic philosophy retained its authority.

The Epicurean doctrine, as explained by Lucretius, though widely different from the Peripatetic in many things, is almost the same in this. He affirms that slender films or ghosts—*tenuia rerum simulacra*—are still going off from all things and flying about and that, these being extremely subtle, easily penetrate our gross bodies and, striking upon the mind, cause thought and imagination.

After the Peripatetic system had reigned above a thousand years in the schools of Europe almost without a rival, it sunk before that of Descartes, the perspicuity of whose writings and notions, contrasted with the obscurity of Aristotle and his commentators, created a strong prejudice in favor of this new philosophy. The characteristic of Plato's genius was sublimity; that of Aristotle's subtlety; but Descartes far excelled both in perspicuity and bequeathed this spirit to his successors. The system which is now generally received with regard to the mind and its operations derives not only its spirit from Descartes but also its fundamental principles, and after all the improvements made by Malebranche, Locke, Berkeley, and Hume, may still be called the Cartesian system; we shall therefore make some remarks upon its spirit and tendency in general and upon its doctrine concerning ideas in particular.

1. It may be observed that the method which Descartes pursued naturally led him to attend more to the operations of the mind by accurate reflection and to trust less to analogical reasoning upon this subject than any philosopher had done before him. Intending to build a system upon a new foundation, he began with a resolution to admit nothing but what was absolutely certain and evident. He supposed that his senses, his memory, his reason, and

every other faculty to which we trust in common life might be fallacious, and resolved to disbelieve everything until he was compelled by irresistible evidence to yield assent.

In this method of proceeding, what appeared to him, first of all, certain and evident was that he thought, that he doubted, that he deliberated. In a word, the operations of his own mind, of which he was conscious, must be real and no delusion; and though all his other faculties should deceive him, his consciousness could not. This, therefore, he looked upon as the first of all truths. This was the first firm ground upon which he set his foot after being tossed in the ocean of skepticism, and he resolved to build all knowledge upon it without seeking after any more first principles.

As every other truth, therefore, and particularly the existence of the objects of sense, was to be deduced by a train of strict argumentation from what he knew by consciousness he was naturally led to give attention to the operations of which he was conscious without borrowing his notions of them from external things.

It was not in the way of analogy but of attentive reflection that he was led to observe that thought, volition, remembrance, and the other attributes of the mind are altogether unlike extension, figure, and all the attributes of body; that we have no reason, therefore, to conceive thinking substances to have any resemblance to extended substances; and that as the attributes of the thinking substance are things of which we are conscious, we may have a more certain and immediate knowledge of them by reflection than we can have of external objects by our senses.

These observations, as far as I know, were first made by Descartes. And they are of more importance and throw more light upon the subject than all that had been said upon it before. They ought to make us diffident and jealous of every notion concerning the mind and its operations which is drawn from sensible objects in the way of analogy and to make us rely only upon accurate reflection as the source of all real knowledge upon this subject.

2. I observe that as the Peripatetic system has a tendency to materialize the mind and its operations so the Cartesian has a tendency to spiritualize body and its qualities. One error common to both systems leads to the first of these extremes in the way of analogy and to the last in the way of reflection. The error I mean is that we can know nothing about body or its qualities but as far as we have sensations which resemble those qualities. Both systems agreed in this, but according to their different methods of reasoning, they drew very different conclusions from it: the Peripatetic drawing his notions of sensation from the qualities of body; the Cartesian, on the contrary, drawing his notions of the qualities of body from his sensations.

The Peripatetic, taking it for granted that bodies and their qualities do really exist and are such as we commonly take them to be, inferred from them the nature of his sensations and reasoned in this manner: Our sensations are the impressions which sensible objects make upon the mind and may be compared to the impression of a seal upon wax; the impression is the image or form of the seal, without the matter of it; in like manner, every sensation is the image or form of some sensible quality of the object. This is the reasoning of Aristotle, and it has an evident tendency to materialize the mind and its sensations.

The Cartesian, on the contrary, thinks that the existence of the body or of any of its qualities is not to be taken as a first principle; and that we ought to admit nothing concerning it but what by just reasoning can be deduced from our sensations, and he knows that by reflection we can form clear and distinct notions of our sensations without borrowing our notions of them by analogy from the objects of sense. The Cartesians, therefore, beginning to give attention to their sensations, first discovered that the sensations corresponding to secondary qualities cannot resemble any quality of body. Hence, Descartes and Locke inferred that sound, taste, smell, color, heat, and cold, which the vulgar took to be qualities of body, were not qualities of body but mere sensations of the mind. Afterward the ingenious Berkeley, considering more attentively the nature of sensation in general, discovered and demonstrated that no sensation whatever could possibly resemble any quality of an insentient being, such as body is supposed to be; and hence he inferred very justly that there is the same reason to hold extension, figure, and all the primary qualities to be mere sensations as there is to hold the secondary qualities to be mere sensations. Thus by just reasoning upon the Cartesian principles, matter was stripped of all its qualities; the new system, by a kind of metaphysical sublimation, converted all the qualities of matter into sensations and spiritualized body as the old had materialized spirit.

The way to avoid both these extremes is to admit the existence of what we see and feel as a first principle, as well as the existence of things of which we are conscious; and to take our notions of the qualities of body from the testimony of our senses, with the Peripatetics, and our notions of our sensations from the testimony of consciousness, with the Cartesians.

3. I observe that the modern skepticism is the natural issue of the new system; and that, although it did not bring forth this monster until the year 1739, it may be said to have carried it in its womb from the beginning.

The old system admitted all the principles of common sense as first principles without requiring any proof of them; and therefore, though its reasoning was commonly vague, analogical, and dark, yet it was built upon a broad foundation and had no tendency to skepticism. We do not find that any Peripatetic thought it incumbent upon him to prove the existence of a material world, but every writer upon the Cartesian system attempted this until Berkeley clearly demonstrated the futility of their arguments and thence concluded that there was no such thing as a material world and that the belief of it ought to be rejected as a vulgar error.

The new system admits only one of the principles of common sense as a first principle and pretends, by strict argumentation, to deduce all the rest from it. That our thoughts, our sensations, and everything of which we are conscious has a real existence is admitted in this system as a first principle, but everything else must be made evident by the light of reason. Reason must rear the whole fabric of knowledge upon this single principle of consciousness.

There is a disposition in human nature to reduce things to as few principles as possible; and this, without doubt, adds to the beauty of a system, if the principles are able to support what rests upon them. The mathematicians glory, very justly, in having raised so noble and magnificent a system of science upon the foundation of a few axioms and definitions. This love of simplicity, of reducing things to few principles, has produced many a false system, but there never was any system in which it appears so remarkably as that of Descartes. His whole system concerning matter and spirit is built upon one axiom, expressed in one word—*cogito*. Upon the foundation of conscious thought, with ideas for his materials, he builds his system of the human understanding and attempts to account for all its phenomena; and having, as he imagined, from his consciousness, proved the existence of matter and of a certain quantity of motion originally impressed upon it, he builds his system of the material world and attempts to account for all its phenomena.

These principles, with regard to the material system, have been found insufficient, and it has been made evident that besides matter and motion we must admit gravitation, cohesion, and corpuscular attraction, magnetism, and other centripetal and centrifugal forces by which the particles of matter attract and repel each other. Newton, having discovered this and demonstrated that these principles cannot be resolved into matter and motion, was led by analogy and the love of simplicity to conjecture, but with a modesty and caution peculiar to him, that all the phenomena of the material world depended upon attracting and repelling forces in the particles of matter. But we may now venture to say that this conjecture fell short of the mark. For, even in the unorganized kingdom, the powers by which salts, crystals, spars, and many other bodies concrete into regular forms can never be accounted for by attracting and repelling forces in the particles of matter. And in the vegetable and animal kingdoms there are strong indications of powers of a different nature from all the powers of unorganized bodies. We see then that although in the structure of the material world there is, without doubt, all the beautiful simplicity consistent with the purposes for which it was made, it is not so simple as the great Descartes determined it to be—no, it is not so simple as the greater

Newton modestly conjectured it to be. Both were misled by analogy and the love of simplicity. One had been much conversant about extension, figure, and motion; the other had enlarged his views to attracting and repelling forces; and both formed their notions of the unknown parts of nature from those with which they were acquainted [ . . . ]. This is a just picture of the analogical way of thinking.

But to come to the system of Descartes concerning the human understanding: it was built, as we have observed, upon consciousness as its sole foundation and with ideas as its materials, and all his followers have built upon the same foundation and with the same materials. They acknowledge that nature has given us various simple ideas. These are analogous to the matter of Descartes' physical system. They acknowledge likewise a natural power by which ideas are compounded, disjoined, associated, compared. This is analogous to the original quantity of motion in Descartes' physical system. From these principles they attempt to explain the phenomena of the human understanding just as in the physical system the phenomena of nature were to be explained by matter and motion. It must indeed be acknowledged that there is great simplicity in this system as well as in the other. There is such a similitude between the two as may be expected between children of the same father; but as the one has been found to be the child of Descartes and not of nature, there is ground to think that the other is so likewise.

That the natural issue of this system is skepticism with regard to everything except the existence of our ideas and of their necessary relations which appear upon comparing them, is evident, for ideas being the only objects of thought and having no existence but when we are conscious of them, it necessarily follows that there is no object of our thought which can have a continued and permanent existence. Body and spirit, cause and effect, time and space, to which we were wont to ascribe an existence independent of our thought, are all turned out of existence by this short dilemma: Either these things are ideas of sensation or reflection or they are not; if they are ideas of sensation or reflection, they can have no existence but when we are conscious of

them; if they are not ideas of sensation or reflection, they are words without any meaning.

Neither Descartes nor Locke perceived this consequence of their system concerning ideas. Bishop Berkeley was the first who discovered it. And what followed upon this discovery? Why, with regard to the material world and with regard to space and time, he admits the consequence that these things are mere ideas and have no existence but in our minds; but with regard to the existence of spirits or minds, he does not admit the consequence; and if he had admitted it, he must have been an absolute skeptic. But how does he evade this consequence with regard to the existence of spirits? The expedient which the good bishop uses on this occasion is very remarkable and shows his great aversion to skepticism. He maintains that we have no ideas of spirits and that we can think, and speak, and reason about them and about their attributes without having any ideas of them. If this is so, my lord, what should hinder us from thinking and reasoning about bodies and their qualities without having ideas of them? The bishop either did not think of this question or did not think fit to give any answer to it. However, we may observe that in order to avoid skepticism he fairly starts out of the Cartesian system without giving any reason why he did so in this instance and in no other. This indeed is the only instance of a deviation from Cartesian principles which I have met with in the successors of Descartes, and it seems to have been only a sudden start, occasioned by the terror of skepticism; for in all other things Berkeley's system is founded upon Cartesian principles.

Thus we see that Descartes and Locke take the road that leads to skepticism without knowing the end of it; but they stop short for want of light to carry them farther. Berkeley, frightened at the appearance of the dreadful abyss, starts aside and avoids it. But the author of the *Treatise of Human Nature*, more daring and intrepid, without turning aside to the right hand or to the left, like Virgil's *Alecto*, shoots directly into the gulf [ . . . ].

4. We may observe that the account given by the new system of that furniture of the human understanding which is the gift of nature and not the

acquisition of our own reasoning faculty is extremely lame and imperfect.

The natural furniture of the human understanding is of two kinds: first, the *notions* or simple apprehensions which we have of things; and, secondly, the *judgments* or the belief which we have concerning them. As to our notions, the new system reduces them to two classes—*ideas of sensation* and *ideas of reflection*—the first are conceived to be copies of our sensations, retained in the memory or imagination; the second to be copies of the operations of our minds whereof we are conscious, in like manner retained in the memory or imagination; and we are taught that these two comprehend all the materials about which the human understanding is or can be employed. As to our judgment of things or the belief which we have concerning them, the new system allows no part of it to be the gift of nature but holds it to be the acquisition of reason and to be gotten by comparing our ideas and perceiving their agreements or disagreements. Now I take this account, both of our notions and of our judgments or belief, to be extremely imperfect; and I shall briefly point out some of its capital defects.

The division of our notions into ideas of sensation and ideas of reflection is contrary to all rules of logic, because the second member of the division includes the first. For, can we form clear and just notions of our sensations any other way than by reflection? Surely we cannot. Sensation is an operation of the mind of which we are conscious; and we get the notion of sensation by reflecting upon that which we are conscious of. In like manner, doubting and believing are operations of the mind whereof we are conscious; and we get the notion of them by reflecting upon what we are conscious of. The ideas of sensation, therefore, are ideas of reflection as much as the ideas of doubting or believing or any other ideas whatsoever.

But to pass over the inaccuracy of this division, it is extremely incomplete. For since sensation is an operation of the mind as well as all the other things of which we form our notions by reflection, when it is asserted that all our notions are either ideas of sensation or ideas of reflection, the plain English of this is that mankind neither do nor can think of anything but of the operations of their own minds. Nothing can be more contrary to truth or more contrary to the experience of mankind. I know that Locke, while he maintained this doctrine, believed the notions which we have of body and of its qualities and the notions which we have of motion and of space to be ideas of sensation. But why did he believe this? Because he believed those notions to be nothing else but images of our sensations. If therefore the notions of body and its qualities, of motion and space, are not images of our sensations, will it not follow that those notions are not ideas of sensation? Most certainly.

There is no doctrine in the new system which more directly leads to skepticism than this. And the author of the *Treatise of Human Nature* knew very well how to use it for that purpose: for if you maintain that there is any such existence as body or spirit, time or place, cause or effect, he immediately catches you between the horns of this dilemma; your notions of these existences are either ideas of sensation or ideas of reflection: if of sensation, from what sensation are they copied? If of reflection, from what operations of the mind are they copied?

It is indeed to be wished that those who have written much about sensation and about the other operations of the mind had likewise thought and reflected much and with great care upon those operations; but is it not very strange that they will not allow it to be possible for mankind to think of anything else?

The account which this system gives of our judgment and belief concerning things is as far from the truth as the account it gives of our notions or simple apprehensions. It represents our senses as having no other office but that of furnishing the mind with notions or simple apprehensions of things, and makes our judgment and belief concerning those things to be acquired by comparing our notions together and perceiving their agreements or disagreements.

We have shown, on the contrary, that every operation of the senses, in its very nature, implies judgment or belief as well as simple apprehension. Thus when I feel the pain of the gout in my toe, I have not only a notion of pain but a belief of its existence and a belief of some disorder in my toe which occasions it, and this belief is not produced by comparing ideas and perceiving their agreements and disagreements—it is included in the very nature of the sensation. When I perceive a tree before me, my faculty of seeing gives me not only a notion or simple apprehension of the tree but a belief of its existence and of its figure, distance, and magnitude; and this judgment or belief is not gotten by comparing ideas, it is included in the very nature of the perception. We have taken notice of several original principles of belief in the course of this *Inquiry*, and when other faculties of the mind are examined, we shall find more which have not occurred in the examination of the five senses.

Such original and natural judgments are therefore a part of that furniture which nature has given to the human understanding. They are the inspiration of the Almighty no less than our notions of simple apprehensions. They serve to direct us in the common affairs of life, where our reasoning faculty would leave us in the dark. They are a part of our constitution, and all the discoveries of our reason are grounded upon them. They make up what is called *the common sense of mankind*, and what is manifestly contrary to any of those first principles is what we call *absurd*. The strength of them is *good sense*, which is often found in those who are not acute in reasoning. A remarkable deviation from them, arising from a disorder in the constitution, is what we call *lunacy*—as when a man believes that he is made of glass. When a man suffers himself to be reasoned out of the principles of common sense by *metaphysical arguments*, we may call this *metaphysical lunacy*, which differs from the other species of the distemper in this: that it is not continued, but intermittent—it is apt to seize the patient in solitary and speculative moments, but when he enters into society, Common Sense recovers her authority. A clear explication and enumeration of the principles of common sense is one of the chief *desiderata* in logic. We have only considered such of them as occurred in the examination of the five senses.

5. The last observation that I shall make upon the new system is that although it professes to set out in the way of reflection and not of analogy, it has retained some of the old analogical notions concerning the operations of the mind—particularly, that things which do not now exist in the mind itself can only be perceived, remembered, or imagined by means of ideas or images of them in the mind, which are the immediate objects of perception, remembrance, and imagination. This doctrine appears evidently to be borrowed from the old system, which taught that external things make impressions upon the mind like the impressions of a seal upon wax; that it is by means of those impressions that we perceive, remember, or imagine them; and that those impressions must resemble the things from which they are taken. When we form our notions of the operations of the mind by analogy, this way of conceiving them seems to be very natural and offers itself to our thoughts, for, as everything which is felt must make some impression upon the body, we are apt to think that everything which is understood must make some impression upon the mind.

From such analogical reasoning this opinion of the existence of ideas or images of things in the mind seems to have taken its rise and to have been so universally received among philosophers. It was observed already that Berkeley, in one instance, apostatizes from this principle of the new system by affirming that we have no ideas of spirits and that we can think of them immediately without ideas. But I do not know whether in this he has had any followers. There is some difference likewise among modern philosophers with regard to the ideas or images by which we perceive, remember, or imagine sensible things. For though all agree in the existence of such images, they differ about their place, some placing them in a particular part of the brain where the soul is thought to have her residence and others placing them in the mind itself. Descartes held the first of these opinions, to which Newton seems likewise to have inclined. [ . . . ] But Locke seems to place the ideas of sensible things in the mind, and that Berkeley and the author of the *Treatise of Human Nature* were of the same opinion is evident. The last makes a very curious application of this doctrine by endeavoring to prove from it either that the mind is no substance or that it is an extended and divisible substance, because the ideas of extension cannot be in a subject which is indivisible and unextended.

I confess I think his reasoning in this, as in most cases, is clear and strong. For whether the idea of extension is only another name for extension itself, as Berkeley and this author assert, or whether the idea of extension is an image and resemblance of extension, as Locke conceived, I appeal to any man of common sense, whether extension, or any image of extension, can be in an unextended and indivisible subject. But while I agree with him in his reasoning, I would make a different application of it. He takes it for granted that there are ideas of extension in the mind and thence infers that if it is at all a substance, it must be an extended and divisible substance. On the contrary, I take it for granted upon the testimony of common sense that my mind is a substance, that is, a permanent subject of thought, and my reason convinces me that it is an unextended and indivisible substance, and hence I infer that there cannot be in it anything that resembles extension. If this reasoning had occurred to Berkeley, it would probably have led him to acknowledge that we may think and reason concerning bodies without having ideas of them in the mind, as well as concerning spirits.

I intended to have examined more particularly and fully this doctrine of the existence of ideas or images of things in the mind; and likewise another doctrine, which is founded upon it, namely, that judgment or belief is nothing but a perception of the agreement or disagreement of our ideas, but having already shown, through the course of this inquiry, that the operations of the mind which we have examined give no countenance to either of these doctrines and in many things contradict them, I have thought it proper to drop this part of my design. It may be executed with more advantage, if it is at all necessary, after inquiring into some other powers of the human understanding.

Although we have examined only the five senses and the principles of the human mind which are employed about them, or such as have fallen in our way in the course of this examination, we shall leave the further prosecution of this inquiry to future deliberation. The powers of memory, of imagination, of taste, of reasoning, of moral perception, the will, the passions, the affections, and all the active powers of the soul present a vast and boundless field of philosophical disquisition, which the author of this inquiry is far from thinking himself able to survey with accuracy. Many authors of ingenuity, ancient and modern, have made excursions into this vast territory and have communicated useful observations, but there is reason to believe that those who have pretended to give us a map of the whole have satisfied themselves with a very inaccurate and incomplete survey. If Galileo had attempted a complete system of natural philosophy, he had, probably, done little service to mankind, but by confining himself to what was within his comprehension, he laid the foundation of a system of knowledge which rises by degrees and does honor to the human understanding. Newton, building upon this foundation and in like manner confining his inquiries to the law of gravitation and the properties of light, performed wonders. If he had attempted a great deal more, he would have done a great deal less, and perhaps nothing at all. Ambitious of following such great examples, with unequal steps, alas! and unequal force, we have attempted an inquiry only into one little corner of the human mind, that corner which seems to be most exposed to vulgar observation and to be most easily comprehended; and yet, if we have delineated it justly, it must be acknowledged that the accounts previously given of it were very lame and wide of the truth.

## Essays on the Intellectual Powers of Man, "Of Judgment," Chapter 2: Of Common Sense

The word *sense*, in common language, seems to have a different meaning from that which it has in the writings of philosophers; and those different meanings are apt to be confounded and to occasion embarrassment and error.

Not to go back to ancient philosophy upon this point, modern philosophers consider sense as a power that has nothing to do with judgment—as the power by which we compare those ideas and perceive their necessary agreements and disagreements.

The external senses give us the idea of color, figure, sound, and other qualities of body, primary or secondary. Mr. Locke gave the name of an internal sense to consciousness, because by it we have the idea of thought, memory, reasoning, and other operations of our own minds. Dr. Hutcheson of Glasgow, conceiving that we have simple and original ideas which cannot be imputed either to the external senses or to consciousness, introduced other internal senses such as the sense of harmony, the sense of beauty, and the moral sense. Ancient philosophers also spoke of internal senses, of which memory was accounted one.

But all these senses, whether external or internal, have been represented by philosophers as the means of furnishing our minds with ideas without including any kind of judgment. Dr. Hutcheson defines a *sense* to be a determination of the mind to receive any idea from the presence of an object independent on our will.

"By this term, sense, philosophers in general have denominated those faculties, in consequence of which we are liable to feelings relative to ourselves only, and from which they have not pretended to draw any conclusions concerning the nature of things; whereas truth is not relative, but absolute, and real." *Dr. Priestly's Examination of Dr. Reid* . . . , p. 123.

On the contrary, in common language, sense always implies judgment. A man of sense is a man of judgment. Good sense is good judgment which is common to men with whom we can converse and transact business.

Seeing and hearing, by philosophers are called senses, because we have ideas by them; by the vulgar they are called senses, because we judge by them. We judge of colors by the eye, of sounds by the ear, of beauty and deformity by taste, of right and wrong in conduct by our moral sense, or conscience.

Sometimes philosophers, who represent it as the sole province of sense to furnish us with ideas, fall unawares into the popular opinion that they are judging faculties. Thus Locke, Book 4, Chapter 11: "And of this, that the quality or accident of color does really exist, and has a being without me, the greatest assurance I can possibly have and to which my faculties can attain is the testimony of my eyes, which are the proper and sole judge of this thing."

This popular meaning of the word *sense* is not peculiar to the English language. The corresponding words in Greek, Latin, and I believe in all the European languages have the same latitude. The Latin words *sentire, sententia, sensa, sensus,* from the last of which the English word *sense* is borrowed, express judgment or opinion and are applied indifferently to objects of external sense, of taste, of morals, and of the understanding.

I cannot pretend to assign the reason why a word, which is no term of art, which is familiar in common conversation, should have so different a meaning in philosophical writings. I shall only observe that the philosophical meaning corresponds perfectly with the account which Mr. Locke and other modern philosophers give of judgment. For if the sole province of the senses, external and internal, is to furnish the mind with the ideas about which we judge and reason, it seems to be a natural consequence that the sole province of judgment should be to compare those ideas and to perceive their necessary relations.

These two opinions seem to be so connected that one may have been the cause of the other. I apprehend, however, that if both are true, there is no room left for any knowledge or judgment, either of the real existence of contingent things or of their contingent relations.

To return to the poplar meaning of the word *sense,* I believe it would be much more difficult to find good authors who never use it in that meaning than to find such as do.

We may take Mr. Pope as good authority for the meaning of an English word. He uses it often, and in his epistle to the Earl of Burlington, has made a little descant upon it.

Oft have you hinted to your brother Peers
A certain truth, which many buy too dear;
Something there is more needful than expense,
And something previous ev'n to taste, —'tis sense,
Good sense, which only is the gift of Heaven;
And though no science, fairly worth the seven;
A light, which in yourself you must perceive,
Jones and Le Notre have it not to give.

This inward light or sense is given by Heaven to different persons in different degrees. There is a certain degree of it which is necessary to our being subjects of law and government, capable of managing our own affairs and answerable for our conduct toward others. This is called common sense, because it is common to all men with whom we can transact business or call to account for their conduct.

The laws of all civilized nations distinguish those who have this gift of Heaven from those who have it not. The last may have rights which ought not to be violated, but having no understanding in themselves to direct their actions, the laws appoint them to be guided by the understanding of others. It is easily discerned by its effects in men's actions, in their speeches, and even in their looks; and when it is made a question whether a man has this natural gift or not, a judge or a jury, upon a short conversation with him, can for the most part determine the question with great assurance.

The same degree of understanding which makes a man capable of acting with common prudence in the conduct of life makes him capable of discovering what is true and what is false in matters that are self-evident, and which he distinctly apprehends.

All knowledge and all science must be built upon principles that are self-evident; and of such principles every man who has common sense is a competent judge when he conceives them distinctly. Hence it is that disputes very often terminate in an appeal to common sense.

While the parties agree in the first principles on which their arguments are grounded, there is room for reasoning, but when one denies what to the other appears too evident to need or to admit of proof, reasoning seems to be at an end, and appeal is made to common sense, and each party is left to enjoy his own opinion.

There seems to be no remedy for this nor any way left to discuss such appeals, unless the decisions of common sense can be brought into a code in which all reasonable men shall acquiesce. This indeed, if it is possible, would be very desirable and would supply a desideratum in logic, and why should it be thought impossible that reasonable men should agree in things that are self-evident?

All that is intended in this chapter is to explain the meaning of common sense, that it may not be treated, as it has been by some, as a new principle or as a word without any meaning. I have endeavored to show that sense, in its most common and therefore its most proper meaning, signifies judgment, though philosophers often use it in another meaning. From this it is natural to think that common sense should mean common *judgment;* and so it really does.

What the precise limits are which divide common judgment from what is beyond it, on the one hand, and from what falls short of it, on the other, may be difficult to determine; and men may agree in the meaning of the word who have different opinions about those limits, or who even never thought of fixing them. This is as intelligible as that all Englishmen should mean the same thing by the county of York, though perhaps not a hundredth part of them can point out its precise limits.

Indeed, it seems to me that *common sense* is as unambiguous a word, and as well understood, as the *county of York.* We find it in innumerable places in good writers; we hear it on innumerable occasions in conversation and, as far as I am able to judge, always in the same meaning. And this is probably the reason why it is so seldom defined or explained. [ . . . ]

From the account I have given of the meaning of this term, it is easy to judge both of the proper use and of the abuse of it.

It is absurd to conceive that there can be any opposition between reason and common sense. It is indeed the firstborn of reason, and as they are commonly joined together in speech and in writing, they are inseparable in their nature.

We ascribe to reason two offices, or two degrees. The first is to judge of things self-evident; the second to draw conclusions that are not self-evident from those that are. The first of these is the province, and the sole province, of common sense, and therefore it coincides with reason in its whole extent and is only another name for one branch or one degree of reason. Perhaps it may be said, Why then should you give it a particular name, since it is acknowledged to be only a degree of reason? It would be sufficient answer to this, Why do you abolish a name which is to be found in the language of all civilized nations and has acquired a right by prescription? Such an attempt is equally foolish and ineffectual. Every wise man will be apt to think that a name which is found in all languages as far back as we can trace them is not without some use.

But there is an obvious reason why this degree of reason should have a name appropriated to it, and that is that in the greatest part of mankind no other degree of reason is to be found. It is this degree that entitles them to the denomination of reasonable creatures. It is this degree of reason, and this only, that makes a man capable of managing his own affairs and answerable for his conduct toward others. There is therefore the best reason why it should have a name appropriated to it.

These two degrees of reason differ in other respects, which would be sufficient to entitle them to distinct names.

The first is purely the gift of Heaven. And where Heaven has not given it, no education can supply the lack. The second is learned by practice and rules, when the first is not wanting. A man who has common sense may be taught to reason. But if he has not that gift, no teaching will make him able either to judge of first principles or to reason from them.

I have only this further to observe: that the province of common sense is more extensive in refutation than in confirmation. A conclusion drawn by a train of just reasoning from true principles cannot possibly contradict any decision of common sense, because truth will always be consistent with itself. Neither can such a conclusion receive any confirmation from common sense, because it is not within its jurisdiction.

But it is possible that by setting out from false principles or by an error in reasoning, a man may be led to a conclusion that contradicts the decision of common sense. In this case, the conclusion is within the jurisdiction of common sense though the reasoning on which it was grounded is not; and a man of common sense may fairly reject the conclusion without being able to show the error of the reasoning that led to it.

Thus if a mathematician, by a process of intricate demonstration in which some false step was made, should be brought to this conclusion that two quantities, which are both equal to a third are not equal to each other, a man of common sense, without pretending to be a judge of the demonstration, is well entitled to reject the conclusion and to pronounce it absurd.

# 7. KANT'S PROLEGOMENA, CRITIQUE OF PURE REASON, AND ASSOCIATED TEXTS

Immanuel Kant was born in 1724 in Königsberg, a city of about fifty thousand inhabitants at the time, located near the Baltic Sea in East Prussia. He became one of the most important philosophers of the eighteenth century with his revolutionary work in metaphysics, epistemology, ethics, philosophy of science, and aesthetics. Kant was educated first at an elementary school, then at the Collegium Fridericianum (1732–40), and finally at the Albertus Universität (1740–44), all in Königsberg. After graduating from the university in 1744, he was a tutor to a number of families in the Königsberg area, until he became a lecturer in 1755, after presenting two dissertations to the philosophy faculty. Though Kant published a number of works on a variety of topics while he was a lecturer, it was only at the age of forty-five, in 1770, that he became professor of logic and metaphysics at the University of Königsberg, a position he held until his retirement in 1796. He died eight years later in 1804.

Kant's life is often divided into three periods, his pre-Critical period, his "silent" period, and his Critical period. His pre-Critical period began in 1747 with the publication of his first work, *Thoughts on the True Estimation of Living Forces*, which focused on a hotly debated question in physics (whether "dead"

or "living" forces are conserved in nature). In 1755 he published *New Elucidation of the First Principles of Metaphysical Cognition*, an internalist criticism of Leibnizian-Wolffian metaphysics, and *Universal Natural History and Theory of the Heavens*, a cosmology according to Newtonian principles that anticipated Laplace's cosmology in its fundamentals. In addition to numerous smaller pieces in the 1750s and 1760s on physics, metaphysics, mathematics, geography, theology, and aesthetics, his most significant works included (i) *Physical Monadology* in 1756, which attempted to reconcile mathematics' demand for infinite divisibility with metaphysics' requirement of unity, and (ii) *The Only Possible Argument in Support of a Demonstration of the Existence of God* in 1763, which contained many of his later criticisms of the traditional theistic proofs—though at this point he maintained the possibility of a theoretical proof of God's existence. The pre-Critical period concluded in 1770 with his Inaugural Dissertation entitled *Concerning the Form and Principles of the Sensible and Intelligible World*. During his "silent" period, which reaches from 1770 to 1780, Kant published only a few minor essays. Kant initiates his Critical period in 1781 with the first of his truly great works, the *Critique of Pure Reason*. In order to clarify and simplify his position as it was presented in the *Critique of Pure Reason*, he subsequently issued the *Prolegomena* in 1783. He then published a groundbreaking treatise in ethics, the *Groundwork to a Metaphysics of Morals*, in 1785 and an important work in the foundations of physics, *Metaphysical Foundations of Natural Science*, in 1786. In 1787 he issued a second edition of the *Critique of Pure Reason*, with a considerable number of important revisions. In 1788 he published his second Critique, *The Critique of Practical Reason*, and in 1790, less than a decade after the first Critique, his third and final Critique, *The Critique of Judgment*. Though Kant continued to be productive throughout the rest of his career, these three Critiques (along with the other publications of this decade) constituted the core of his Critical period and revolutionized how philosophy would be done ever after.[1]

Kant transformed theoretical philosophy by asking what would appear to be a very simple question: How is experience, i.e., knowledge of the objective world, possible? Despite the apparent simplicity of this question, Kant's analysis of the concept of experience reveals incredible depth and sophistication. For example, Kant distinguishes between knowledge that depends on particular experiences, i.e., *a posteriori* knowledge, and knowledge that is independent of any particular experience, i.e., *a priori* knowledge. He also distinguishes between truths known by the meanings of the terms involved in the proposition in question, i.e., analytic truths, and those that require something beyond these meanings in order to be known, i.e., synthetic truths. Kant's novel claim

is that experience involves synthetic *a priori* truths. However, it is far from clear how synthetic *a priori* knowledge is possible. It is clear enough that an analytic proposition can be known *a priori*, since one needs to know only the meanings of the terms involved in the proposition in question in order to know its truth. And it is equally clear that a synthetic proposition can be known *a posteriori*, since particular experiences can provide evidence not supplied by the meanings of the terms. However—and this is the crucial question—how can we have synthetic *a priori* knowledge? Since such knowledge is synthetic, something beyond the mere meanings of the terms is required. But since it is *a priori*, particular experiences are excluded. So, if knowledge of the objective world involves synthetic *a priori* knowledge, how can we have such knowledge? To put the question differently: How can I know non-trivial features of the world even before I look at it?

Kant addresses this question in the *Prolegomena* by assuming that both mathematics and natural science involve synthetic *a priori* truths and then by asking how each body of knowledge is possible. Kant argues that mathematical knowledge is possible only if space and time are simply subjective forms through which objects are given to us in experience. In other words, space and time are not properties of objects *per se*, but are rather our own subjective forms for perceiving objects. Since space and time are *subjective* forms (rather than properties of objects), our access to them can be *a priori*. Further, since mathematical knowledge depends on these spatial and temporal forms (by means of which objects are given to us) rather than a mere analysis of concepts, such knowledge can be synthetic. In short, it is only if space and time are subject-dependent or ideal in this way that mathematical knowledge is possible. Kant argues that natural science is possible only if we apply certain pure concepts (which he calls categories) to objects given in space and time. For example, whereas Hume derives his concept of causality from experience (with the result that it means little more than a constant conjunction between a cause and its effect), Kant wants to argue that the concept of causality, which must contain necessity in order to

1. For more on Kant, see Peter F. Strawson, *The Bounds of Sense* (London: Methuen, 1966), Charles Dunbar Broad, *Kant: An Introduction* (Cambridge: Cambridge University Press, 1978), Karl Ameriks, *Kant's Theory of Mind* (Oxford: Oxford University Press, 2000), Henry Allison, *Kant's Transcendental Idealism: An Interpretation and Defense* (New Haven: Yale University Press, 2004), Paul Guyer, *Kant and the Claims of Knowledge* (Cambridge: Cambridge University Press, 1987), Michael Friedman, *Kant and the Exact Sciences* (Cambridge: Harvard University Press, 1992), Paul Guyer, ed., *The Cambridge Companion to Kant* (Cambridge: Cambridge University Press, 1992), or Eric Watkins, *Kant and the Metaphysics of Causality* (Cambridge: Cambridge University Press, 2005).

be part of objective experience, is not derived from experience, but rather is a pure concept that stems from the understanding. However, such pure concepts can give knowledge of the objective world as expressed in the fundamental principles of natural science only if they are applied to spatio-temporal objects. It is the application of pure concepts such as causality to spatio-temporal objects that makes synthetic *a priori* knowledge of natural science possible. Since these pure concepts are not derived from experience, such knowledge can be *a priori*, and since this knowledge is not obtained through an analysis of concepts, but rather stems from the application of these pure concepts to spatio-temporal objects, it can be synthetic. In sum, we can know *a priori* that the world we perceive is spatio-temporal and governed by, e.g., causal rules because it is we who contribute these features to our experience of the world.

This analysis of the possibility of experience is important in two central ways. First, one can see how Kant is reacting to both Hume and Leibniz (as well as their respective traditions). Hume is mistaken because he does not see that certain concepts cannot be derived from experience (given that they make experience possible in the first place) and stem instead from our pure understanding. Leibniz, who recognizes pure concepts, is mistaken in thinking that (the analysis of) such concepts might suffice for substantive knowledge of the world. Kant repeatedly argues that these concepts must be applied to spatio-temporal objects that are given to us in intuition if we are to have synthetic knowledge. Second, since Kant has established what makes possible both mathematics and natural science—clearly legitimate bodies of knowledge—he is in a position to turn to another set of synthetic *a priori* propositions, those involved in metaphysics proper, to determine if they could amount to knowledge in the same way. In particular, Kant is concerned with the traditional metaphysical claims concerning freedom, the immortality of the soul, and God's existence. In all three cases Kant maintains that we cannot objectively justify such claims. Given his positive analyses of mathematics and natural science, it is clear that all synthetic *a priori* knowledge must be based on space and time as

the subjective forms through which objects must be given to us. However, since neither God, freedom, nor the immortality of our soul is given to us through these spatio-temporal forms, we cannot have synthetic *a priori* knowledge of them. Despite the fact that metaphysics cannot be objectively justified (i.e., by their objects being given to us in space and time), Kant still thinks that metaphysics can and should be done *subjectively*. For reason, which naturally forms our ideas of God, freedom, and the soul by striving to discover the unconditioned condition for any conditioned object, will continue to seek further conditions of conditioned objects in the hope of discovering the unconditioned. In other words, the mere fact that reason will never succeed in discovering the unconditioned in spatio-temporal experience does not imply that it should stop trying to do so. For reason's never-ending search for further conditions enables us to unify our knowledge in a systematic way, and expand our knowledge of the world by requiring us to seek and order the conditions we find.

While Kant's position in the *Critique of Pure Reason* does not differ from that of the *Prolegomena* in its fundamentals, there are significant differences between these two works that make the first Critique both more difficult and more interesting. For one, Kant's method in the *Prolegomena* is analytic. That is, he assumes two bodies of knowledge, namely mathematics and natural science (the pure part of physics in particular), asks what it is that makes them possible, and then considers whether metaphysics could be possible in the same way. By contrast, Kant's method in the first Critique is synthetic. Instead of assuming knowledge of mathematics and natural science from the start, he first shows how space, time, and the categories stem from our cognitive faculties and then argues that they are necessary for objective knowledge. Also, whereas Kant's aim in the *Prolegomena* allows him simply to state his main claims without argument, the first Critique claims both certainty and completeness for its fundamental principles and attempts to provide detailed support for them. In light of these two main differences one can see that the first Critique is of much greater interest philosophically, but also that its structure does not easily allow for a clear view of its main features. To understand the overall nature of Kant's project in the first Critique, it may be helpful to consider how some of its most important chapters fit together into a systematic whole.

The first Critique begins with a preface and an introduction—sections that, despite their differences in the first and second editions (referred to by A and B, respectively), explain Kant's project in metaphysics, briefly outline his novel approach, and develop the distinctions necessary for posing the question of synthetic *a priori* knowledge. In the Transcendental Aesthetic, which is devoted to the passive faculty of sensibility by which objects are given to us, Kant argues that space and time are *a priori* intuitions. (An intuition is a representation that refers to a single object immediately, and contrasts primarily with a concept, which is a representation that can refer to many objects and does so mediately, that is, via other representations.) He then argues that space and time can be *a priori* intuitions only if they are merely forms of intuition, that is, purely subjective ways in which objects are given to us. This argument represents one of Kant's most distinctive contributions to philosophy, a doctrine he calls transcendental idealism. The important aspect of that doctrine being emphasized here is that space, time, and the entire spatio-temporal world are simply appearances, that is, objects that depend on subjects that have space and time as sensible forms of intuition. Space, time, and the spatio-temporal world are not objective entities that exist independently as "things in themselves." If they were, we could have neither our synthetic *a priori* knowledge of mathematics nor our *a priori* intuitions of space and time.

In the Transcendental Logic Kant turns to our faculty of concepts, the understanding, and undertakes the two-fold task of showing that the understanding's pure concepts are necessary for knowledge and that these concepts do not generate knowledge if they are not applied to objects given through sensibility, that is, if they are used to think "things in themselves," e.g., God, the soul, and the world as a totality. The former, positive task is undertaken in the Transcendental Analytic. In its Analytic of Concepts Kant first

attempts (in the so-called 'Metaphysical Deduction') to derive an exhaustive list of most basic pure concepts, i.e., categories, that we must use in thinking about objects of any sort. Then, in the famous Transcendental Deduction, he tries to show that we are justified in using the categories to obtain knowledge if and only if we apply them to objects of a particular sort, namely those given through sensible intuition. In the Transcendental Analytic's Analytic of Principles, Kant first provides spatio-temporal meanings for the categories (in the Schematism chapter) and then attempts to develop a series of arguments that show how each particular category is required for a different kind of experience. It is in this context (more specifically, the Analogies of Experience) that Kant argues (against Hume) that the categories of substance and causality are required for knowledge of objective succession. (Hume famously rejects substance and thinks that we can have knowledge of succession without using Kant's strong notion of causality.) Towards the end of the Analytic of Principles (in the Refutation of Idealism) Kant also provides an interesting argument against idealism as it is understood by Berkeley (and, in a certain way, Descartes).

Kant's negative task of showing that we cannot have knowledge of things in themselves (in particular, of God, the soul, and freedom) is undertaken in the Transcendental Dialectic. The Paralogisms are devoted to exposing the faulty inferences pure reason is tempted to make about the soul. The Antinomies develop pairs of arguments for contradictory claims about the world as a totality, contradictions that can be resolved only if one first distinguishes between the sensible and intelligible worlds—a distinction that is fundamental to transcendental idealism—and then denies that the intelligible world is spatio-temporal. Given this distinction and denial, Kant argues that we can know only the sensible world, not the intelligible world. Further, since we know from the Second Analogy of Experience that the sensible world is governed by causal laws without exception, freedom and thus morality as well could be possible only in the unknowable intelligible world. Finally, the Ideal of Pure Reason considers the three traditional arguments for the existence of God. Since Kant argues that the cosmological and teleological arguments for the existence of God depend on the ontological argument, his famous objections to the ontological argument are of crucial importance in establishing his negative thesis that theoretical knowledge of God is not possible. Taken together, the Paralogisms, Antinomies, and Ideal of Pure Reason establish that pure reason cannot have knowledge of things in themselves. This is the sense in which Kant's *Critique of Pure Reason* is a critique of pure reason. However, as Kant points out in the second edition preface to the first *Critique,* the fact that he restricts our knowledge to the sensible world does not mean that our representation of things in themselves (including God, the soul, and our freedom) can play no role in our lives. For our ideas of these things function as regulative ideals, that is, they direct our cognitive activities by forcing us to search for further conditions for any conditioned object. More importantly, restricting knowledge opens up room for faith, that is, for the idea that freedom, God, and immortality are required by the practical standpoint of morality—an idea Kant explores in detail in the second Critique.

Highlights from the structure of the *Critique of Pure Reason* are as follows:[2]

Preface [first edition]* & [second edition]*
Introduction [second edition]*
Transcendental Doctrine of Elements
Part I   Transcendental Aesthetic*
   Section I   Space
    Metaphysical Exposition of This Concept
    Transcendental Exposition of the Concept of Space
   Section II   Time
    Metaphysical Exposition of the Concept of Time
    Transcendental Exposition of the Concept of Time*

---

2. Asterisks mark selections rather than full passages and brackets indicate whether the passage is from the first (1781) or second (1787) edition (but only for those passages that Kant revised significantly).

Part II   Transcendental Logic
Introduction
   On Logic As Such*
I   Transcendental Analyti
Book I   Analytic of Concepts
   Chapter I   On The Guide for the Discovery of All Pure Concepts of the Understanding
    Section I   On the Understanding's Logical Use As Such
    Section II   On the Understanding's Logical Function in Judgments
    Section III   On the Pure Concepts of the Understanding, or Categories
   Chapter II   On the Deduction of the Pure Concept of the Understanding
    Section I   On the Principles of a Transcendental Deduction As Such
    Section II   Transcendental Deduction of the Pure Concepts of the Understanding [second edition]
Book II   Analytic of Principles
   Chapter I   On the Schematism of the Pure Concepts of the Understanding
   Chapter II   System of All Principles of Pure Understanding
    Section II   On the Supreme Principle of All Synthetic Judgments
    Section III   Systematic Presentation of All the Synthetic Principles
     1. Axioms of Intuition
     2. Anticipations of Perception
     3. Analogies of Experience
     Refutation of Idealism [second edition]
II   Transcendental Dialectic
Introduction
   On Transcendental Illusion
   On Pure Reason as the Seat of Transcendental Illusion
    C   On the Pure Use of Reason
I   On The Concepts of Reason*
II   On The Dialectical Inferences of Pure Reason
   Chapter I   On The Paralogisms of Pure Reason [Second Edition]
   Chapter II   The Antinomy of Pure Reason
    Section II   Antithetic of Pure Reason

# Émilie du Châtelet, *Foundations of Physics* (1740)[1]

Gabrielle Émilie Le Tonnelier de Breteuil, Marquise du Châtelet was born in Paris in 1706 to a prominent courtier's family. In 1725, at the age of eighteen, she married Marquis Florent-Claude de Châtelet-Lomont, the eldest son of an aristocratic family, and had three children with him (two sons and a daughter). In 1733 she met and then had an intense and lengthy intellectual and romantic relationship with Voltaire, a leading (and most controversial) French poet, philosopher, and public intellectual. In 1748, she became pregnant with the child of her then-lover, Jean-François de Saint-Lambert. In 1749, shortly after giving birth, she died due to complications from a pulmonary embolism.

Growing up, du Châtelet received the kind of education that would have been common for a noble (and affluent) family. She learned Latin, Italian, and English, and read literature. However, as an adult, she furthered her education in advanced mathematics, physics, philosophy, and theology by means of several private tutors, including Maupertuis (one of Europe's leading intellectuals) and Samuel König (a disciple of Leibniz and Wolff), but especially through her extensive interactions with Voltaire. She was particularly interested in and displayed considerable proficiency at technical issues in the foundations of mechanical physics, mathematics, and metaphysics. The publications that resulted from her efforts were diverse. She translated two of Mandeville's essays on The Fable of the Bees, and produced a translation of Newton's Principia, along with a commentary on it that brought it up to date with the most recent scientific results. She also published an essay on happiness as well as a treatise on the Old and New Testaments (Examinations of the Bible), but perhaps most important of all was the Foundations of Physics (Institutions de Physique), first published in 1740, which was followed by a second edition in 1742.

In the following selections from the Foundations of Physics, we see du Châtelet attempting to synthesize the first principles of Leibnizian metaphysics and the fundamental principles of Newtonian physics into a single philosophical system. Though her philosophy is important in its own right and received considerable attention throughout eighteenth-century Europe, her reflections on space are especially interesting, since space is central to the philosophies of Descartes, Leibniz, and Newton and is also a topic that Kant discusses in distinctive ways in the Critique of Pure Reason.[2]

---

1. The Preface and Chapter 1 were translated by Roger Ariew. Chapter 5 was translated by Katherine Brading (with minor editorial revisions by Ariew and Watkins).

2. For additional selected texts (in English translation) that place Kant's philosophy in its historical context, see Eric Watkins, *Kant's* Critique of Pure Reason: *Background Source Materials* (New York: Cambridge University Press, 2009).

## PREFACE

### V.

I will not write the history of the revolutions endured by physics for you here; a large tome would be needed to report them all. I propose to have you acquainted *less with what was thought than with what should be known.*

Until the last century, the sciences were an impenetrable secret in which those claiming knowledge were alone initiated; it was a kind of cabal whose code consisted of barbarous words that seemed invented to obscure and discourage the mind.

Descartes appeared in the depth of that night like a star coming to illuminate the universe. The revolution caused in the sciences by this great man is surely more useful, and perhaps even more worthy of memory,[3] than that of the greatest empires; it can be said that human reason owes him the most. For it is much more easy to find the truth once we are on its tracks, than to leave those of error. This great man's *Geometry*, his *Dioptrics*, his *Method*, are masterpieces of profound understanding that will make his name immortal, and if he was mistaken about some points of physics, it was because he was human, and it is not given to a single person or to a single century to know everything.

We lift ourselves up to the knowledge of the truth, like those giants who scaled the heavens by standing on each others' shoulders. Descartes and Galileo shaped the Huygenses and the Leibnizes, these great men known to you only by their name, with whose works I soon hope to acquaint you. It is by profiting from Kepler's works and by making use of Huygens' theorems that Newton discovered this universal force extended throughout nature, which makes the planets revolve around the Sun and produces gravity on Earth.

### VI.

The systems of Descartes and Newton divide the thinking world today, so that it is necessary for you to know both of them; but so many learned people took care to expound upon and correct Descartes' system that it will be easy for you to learn from their works. One of my objects in this first part is to put before your eyes the other part of this great process, to have you acquainted with Newton's system and to make you see the extent to which connection and likelihood are pushed forward in it, and how phenomena are explained by the hypothesis of attraction. [. . .]

### VII.

Whatever side you take in this philosophers' dispute, beware, my son, about the inevitable stubbornness entailed by the spirit of partisanship; this disposition is dangerous in all occasions of life, but it is ridiculous in physics. The search for truth is the only thing in which the love of your country should not take precedence, and it is surely quite inappropriate for people to have made a kind of national affair of the opinions of Newton and Descartes. Concerning a book of physics, we should ask if it is good, not if the author is English, German, or French.

It seems to me, besides, that it would be just as unfair for the Cartesians to refuse to admit attraction as a hypothesis[4] as it is unreasonable for some Newtonians to want to make it a primitive property of matter. It must be admitted that some among them went too far in this, and it is with some reason that they are reproached for resembling a man whose bad eyesight would have him fail to see the ropes that allow things to fly at the opera, and who, for example, on seeing Bellerophon suspended in the air would say: "Bellerophon is suspended in the air because he is attracted equally on all sides from behind the scenes." For, in order to decide that the effects the Newtonians attribute to attraction are not produced by an impulsion, we would need to know all the ways in which an impressed [force] can be used, but we are still very far from knowing this.

---

3. [Châtelet's marginal remark reads:] The extent of our obligation to Descartes. [Henceforth we will abbreviate Châtelet's marginal remarks as [I.m.:] for "in the margin."]

---

4. [I.m.:] Discussion of attraction.

In physics we are still like this man born blind whose sight Chiselden restored. At first this man saw everything confusedly; it was only by feeling around for a considerable time that he began to see well. This time has not yet arrived for you, and perhaps even it never will entirely; there are likely some truths not made to be perceived by our mind's eyes, just as there are objects our body's eyes will never perceive. But whoever refuses to learn because of this consideration would resemble a lame person who, having a fever, would not take the remedies that might cure it, because these remedies would not prevent him from limping.

## VIII.

One of the errors some philosophers make at this time is to want to banish hypotheses from physics;[5] they are as necessary as scaffolds when building a house; it is true that, when the building is finished, the scaffolds become useless, but it could not have been erected without their help. All of astronomy, for example, was based only on hypotheses, and if they were always avoided in physics, it is likely that not as many discoveries would have been made. Further, nothing is more capable of delaying the progress of the sciences than to want to banish hypotheses from it and to be persuaded that the great mechanism moving all of nature was found, for we do not search for a cause we believe we already know. In this way it could happen that the application of the geometric principles of mechanics to physical effects, something very difficult and very necessary, would remain imperfect, and we would find ourselves deprived of the work and research of many fine minds who would perhaps have been capable of discovering the true cause of the phenomena.

It is true that hypotheses become the poison of philosophy when we want them to pass for the truth,[6] and perhaps they are even more dangerous at the time than was the unintelligible jargon of the Scholastics; for, since this jargon was absolutely devoid of meaning, it only needed a little attention from a

right-thinking mind to perceive the absurdity and to seek the truth elsewhere. But an ingenious and bold hypothesis, which has an initial plausibility, influences human pride to believe it, the mind applauds itself for having found these subtle principles, and then uses all its skills to defend them. Most great system builders provide us with examples of this: they are great ships transported by the currents and have the finest sailing apparatus in the world, but the current carries them away.

## XII.

I explain to you Leibniz's principal opinions on metaphysics in the first chapters. I drew them from the works of the renowned Wolff;[7] you heard me speak so much about him with one of his disciples who was in my household for some time, and who made some excerpts from his work for me.

Leibniz's ideas on metaphysics are still little known in France; but they certainly deserve to be known. No doubt there are still many obscure things in metaphysics despite the discoveries of this great man; but it seems to me that, in the principle of sufficient reason, he provided a compass capable of leading us through the shifting sands of this science.

The obscurities in which some parts of metaphysics are still shrouded serve as the pretext for most men's laziness not to study it; they persuade themselves that because not everything is known, nothing can be known. However, there certainly are points of metaphysics susceptible to demonstrations as rigorous as geometric ones, although they are of another kind. We lack a calculus for metaphysics similar to the one we found for geometry, by means of which, with the aid of certain *givens*, we arrive at knowledge of *unknowns*. Perhaps some intellect will find this system one day. Leibniz gave it much thought; he had ideas about this, which he unfortunately did not communicate to anyone, but even if it could be discovered,

---

5. [I.iii.:] Hypotheses are necessary in physics.
6. [I.m.:] When they can become dangerous.

7. [Châtelet's footnote reads:] See [Christian] Wolff's *Ontology* [*Philosophia prima sive Ontologia*], and principally the chapters on the Principle of Contradiction, Principle of Sufficient Reason, Possibility and Impossibility, Necessity and Contingency, Extension, Continuity, Space, Time, etc.

it is likely that there are some unknowns whose *equation* could never be found. Metaphysics contains two types of things: the first, which all people who make good use of their mind can know; and the second, which is the most extensive, what they will never know.

Several truths of physics, metaphysics, and geometry are manifestly interconnected. Metaphysics is the apex of the edifice; but this apex is so high that our sight of it often becomes somewhat confused. I therefore thought to begin by bringing it closer to your view, so that, with no cloud obscuring your mind, you might be able to have a clear and certain view of the truths I want to teach you.

## CHAPTER ONE
### The Principles of Our Knowledge

### I.

All[8] components of our knowledge arise from one another and are based on certain principles whose truth is known even without reflection, because they are self-evident.

Some truths relate immediately to these first principles, and are derived from them by only a small number of steps. The mind thus easily perceives the series that led to them; but it is easy to lose sight of this in the search for truths that can only be reached by a great number of arguments derived from one another. [. . .]

7.[9] [. . .] This principle [of contradiction] is sufficient for all necessary truths, that is, for the truths that can be determined only in a single way, for this is what is understood by the term *necessary*. But when contingent truths are concerned,[10] that is, when it is possible for a thing to exist in various ways and that none of its determinations is more necessary than any other, then the necessity of another principle makes

itself felt, because the principle of contradiction does not apply. Thus the ancients who did not know this second principle of our knowledge were mistaken about the most important points of philosophy.

§8.[11] This principle on which all contingent truths depend, and which is neither less primitive nor less universal than the principle of contradiction, is *the principle of sufficient reason*. All people naturally follow it; for no one determines himself to one thing rather than to another without a sufficient reason that shows him that this thing is preferable to the other. [. . .]

Archimedes, when going from geometry to mechanics, recognized the need for the principle of sufficient reason;[12] for, wanting to demonstrate that a balance with arms of equal length loaded with equal weights would rest at equilibrium, he showed that in this equality of arms and weights, the balance must stay at rest because there would be no sufficient reason why one of the arms should be lower than the other.

Leibniz, who was very attentive to the sources of our reasoning, took this principle, developed it, and was the first who expressed it distinctly, and who introduced it into the sciences.[13] [. . .]

§12.[14] From this great axiom of sufficient reason arises another that Leibniz calls *the principle of indiscernibles*. This principle banishes from the universe all identical matter, for if there could be two pieces of matter absolutely similar and identical, so that one might be put in the place of the other without the slightest change occurring (for this is what we understand by entirely similar) there would be no sufficient reason why, for instance, one of these particles was placed in the Moon and the other on the Earth, since all things would remain the same by changing

---

8. [I.m.:] On what our knowledge is based.
9. In the third section of this chapter Châtelet switches, without comment, from Roman to Arabic numeral section headings.
10. [I.m.:] The principle of contradiction is the foundation of all necessary truths.

---

11. [I.m.:] The principle of sufficient reason.
12. [I.m.:] Archimedes was first to use this principle in mechanics.
13. I.m.:] But it is Leibniz who revealed it in all its extension and its usefulness.
14. [I.m.:] How the principle of indiscernibles follows from the principle of sufficient reason.

them and placing the one in the Moon on the Earth and the one on the Earth in the Moon. [. . .]

§13.[15] Yet another principle, called *the law of continuity*, follows from the axiom of sufficient reason. We are also indebted to Leibniz for this principle, which is very fruitful in physics. He teaches us that nothing is done through a leap in nature, and that a being does not go from one state to another without passing through all the different states we can conceive of between them.

The principle of sufficient reason easily proves this truth, for each state in which a being finds itself must have its sufficient reason why this being is in this state rather than in any other, and this reason can only be found in the preceding state. This preceding state therefore contained something that gave rise to the actual state that followed it, so that these two states are so interconnected that it is impossible to put another state between the two. For if there was a possible state between the actual state and the one immediately preceding it, its nature would have left the first state without yet being determined by the second to abandon the first. There would thus be no sufficient reason why it should go to this state rather than to any other possible state. Thus no being goes from one state to another without passing through the intermediate states, in the same way that we do not go from one city to another without taking the road between the two. [. . .]

§14.[16] The true laws of motion can be found and demonstrated by this law of continuity, for a body moving in any direction could not move in an opposite direction without going from its initial motion to rest through all of the intermediate degrees of deceleration, in order to go again, by imperceptible degrees of acceleration, from rest to the new motion it must experience.

## CHAPTER FIVE
## On Space

§72.

The question of the nature of space is one of the most famous questions, and has divided ancient and modern philosophers alike; it is also one of the most essential questions because of its influence on the most important truths of physics and metaphysics.

Some have said:[17] Space is nothing over and above things, it is a mental abstraction, an ideal being, it is nothing other than the order of things insofar as they coexist, and there is nothing to space except bodies. Others, by contrast, have maintained that space is an absolute being, real, and distinct from the bodies it contains, that it is an intangible, penetrable extension, lacking solidity, the universal receptacle receiving the bodies placed in it; in a word, a kind of immaterial and infinitely extended fluid in which bodies move.[18] The former group has put forward several metaphysical reasons in support of their opinion. The latter has put forward the idea of space that the imagination itself is able to form, and they have defended this idea, which the imagination itself forms, by raising several objections to the contrary opinion, taken from phenomena, and especially from the difficulty there is with bodies moving in the absolute plenum.

§73. In the past, the view that space is distinct from matter was held by Epicurus, Democritus, and Leucippus, who regarded space as an intangible incorporeal being incapable of action or passion. In our day, Gassendi has revived this opinion, and in his *Essay Concerning Human Understanding* the renowned Locke does not distinguish pure space from the bodies that fill it except by penetrability: this philosopher derives the true notion of space from sight and touch,

---

15. [I.m.:] The law of continuity.
16. [I.m.:] The principle of continuity serves to demonstrate the laws of motion.

17. [I.m.:] Definitions of space contrast greatly.
18. [I.m.:] Half of the philosophers believed, and still believe, in empty space, and the other half believe it to be filled with matter.

because, he says, we can neither see nor touch it, but we can see and touch bodies.

Keill, in his *Introduction to True Physics*, as well as all the disciples of [Locke's] book *Concerning Human Understanding* held this same opinion; Keill even advanced some theorems by which he claims to prove that all matter has tiny spaces or interstices that are absolutely void, and that there is a great deal more void than there is solid matter in bodies.[19] But void spread out [in matter] contradicts the principle of sufficient reason just as much as atoms do, and therefore cannot be accepted; indeed if the little atoms or first particles of matter were moving in the void, their size and shape would be without sufficient reason; for shape limits extension, and the actuality of any shape becomes comprehensible [only] if one can explain how and why extension is limited. Now, one can readily see that the void does not contain this reason at all, because it contains nothing whereby we can understand why particles have a given shape as opposed to any other possible shape, and why they are of a particular size. We must therefore seek the reason in the external bodies that surround them, for shape is a mode of extension: we are therefore obliged to admit a surrounding matter that limits the parts of extension and would be the reason for their different shapes; thus one must fill the void interstices in order to satisfy the principle of sufficient reason.

Several mathematicians have embraced the opinion of an absolute void on the authority of Newton. This great man believed, in line with Locke, that one can explain the creation of matter through space, thinking that God would have rendered several regions of space impenetrable: one sees in the General Scholium, which is at the end of Newton's *Principia*, that he believed that space was God's immensity, which in the *Opticks* he calls God's sensorium, that is, that by means of which God is present in all things.[20]

§74.[21] Clarke has taken a great deal of trouble to support the opinions of Newton, as well as his own views on absolute space, against Leibniz, who maintained that space was nothing but the order of coexisting things.

Certainly[22] if one consults the principle of sufficient reason that I established in the first chapter, one cannot help but acknowledge that Leibniz was right to banish absolute space from the universe, and to regard the idea that several philosophers believe they have as an illusion of the imagination. For, not only would there not be, as we have just seen, any reason to limit extension; but, if space is a real being and subsistent without bodies, which could be placed in it, it is indifferent in which part of this homogeneous space one places them, as long as they keep the same order among themselves: therefore there would not have been any sufficient reason why God would have placed the universe in the location where it is now, rather than in any other, since he could have placed it 10,000 leagues further away, and put the East where the West is; or indeed he could have reversed it, so long as he kept things in the same situation among themselves.

Clarke was well aware of the force of this argument, and he was unable to counter it with anything other than that the simple will of God was the sufficient reason for the place of the universe in space, and that there was nothing more to it. But one can easily see that this admission undermines his view, and lays bare the weakness of his case; for God would not be able to act without reasons within his own understanding, and his will must always be determined by a reason. Thus being obliged to resort to an arbitrary will of God, which is not based upon sufficient reason, is to be reduced to absurdity. Therefore, the reason for the place of the universe in space, and the reason for the limit of extension being neither in the things themselves nor in the will of God, one has to conclude that the hypothesis of the void is false, and that there is no such thing in nature.

Leibniz's reasoning against absolute space is therefore irrefutable, and one is forced to abandon this space, if one does not wish to renounce the principle of sufficient reason; that is to say, to renounce the foundation of all truth.

---

19. [I.m.:] The principle of sufficient reason banishes the void from the universe.
20. [I.m.:] Newton's singular opinion on space.
21. [I.m.:] *Commercium Epistolicum* [Exchange of Letters].

22. [I.m.:] Dispute between Leibniz and Clarke on space.

§75.[23] There is another great absurdity to deal with concerning the opinion about absolute space, which is that all of the attributes of God suit it; for this space, if it were possible, would be truly infinite, immutable, uncreated, necessary, incorporeal, and omnipresent. It is starting from this supposition that Raphson sought to demonstrate geometrically that space is an attribute of God, and that it expresses his infinite and limitless essence; and this indeed follows very naturally from the supposition of absolute space, once one has admitted it.

§76.[24] There are three principal objections against the absolute plenum, and they can easily be addressed. The first relies on the apparent impossibility of motion in the plenum; the second, on the different weights of different bodies; and the third, on the resistance of matter as a result of which bodies moving in the plenum must quickly lose their motion.

We can say in response to the first objection that motion is possible in the plenum because of circular motion, whereby the surrounding parts replace each moving body by occupying the place it gives up. The second objection is based on the supposition that all matter is heavy, but this is entirely false; for according to the principle of sufficient reason, heaviness is the effect of collision with surrounding matter. Now, this matter is not itself heavy; for if it was, it would have to have recourse to other matter with which it would collide, and so on to infinity, and therefore this objection, based as it is on the general heaviness of matter, cannot stand. Finally, the third objection takes into account only dead and motionless matter, and so the arguments that are made about resistance are very solid. But they prove nothing if you consider matter animated by motion, as it in fact is; for very fine and subtle matter can move with such speed that it will not bring any perceptible resistance to the motion of bodies placed in it; thus, there will be a physical void, which will be the phenomenon resulting from this matter being so fine-grained and in such very rapid motion. But this void is all that is proven by those ex-periences on which the invincible objections against the plenum are based.

§77.[25] It will not be useless to examine here how we came to form our ideas of extension, space, and continuity; this examination will serve to help you discover the source of the mistakes that have been made about the nature of space, and prevent you from making them in the future.

We feel that, once we consider two things to be different, and when we distinguish one from the other, in our minds we place one external to the other; thus, everything that we consider to be different from us we see as external to us; there are many examples of this. If we imagine a structure that we have never seen before, we represent it as external to ourselves, even though we know well that the idea we have of it exists within us, and that there is perhaps nothing of this structure existing external to our idea. But we still think of it as being external to ourselves because we know that it is different from us; in the same way, if we represent two men ideally, or even the same man twice, we place them external to one another, because we cannot force our mind to imagine that they are *one, and two* [in number], at the same time.

It follows from this that we cannot represent to ourselves several different things as being one, without this resulting in a notion that is attached to this diversity and union, and this notion we call *extension*. Thus we give extension to a line, insofar as we pay attention to several distinct parts that we see as existing external to one another, which are united together and which are for this reason a single whole.

It is indeed true that diversity and unity engender in us the idea of extension [and] that several philosophers have wanted to accept our soul as something extended, because they noticed in it several different faculties that nevertheless constitute a single subject; and this is where they went wrong: regarding attributes and modes of a being as separate beings, existing external to one another, is to abuse the notion of extension; for these attributes and modes are insepa-rable from the being that they modify.

---

23. [I.m.:] Difficulties arising from the opinion of pure space.
24. [I.m.:] Three principal objections against the plenum to which it is easy to respond.

---

25. [I.m.:] How we form the idea of space and its properties.

Since we represent to ourselves in extension several things that exist external to each other, and that are one through their union, all extension has parts that exist external to one another and are *one*, and once we represent to ourselves things that are both diverse and unified we have the idea of an extended being.

§78. Once we pay attention to this notion of extension, we see that the parts of extension, when considered abstractly and without taking into account either limits or shapes, must not have any internal differences; they must be similar, and differ only in number. For since, to form the idea of extension, we consider only the plurality of things and their union (from which their existence external to one another originates), and we exclude every other determination (all the parts being the same with respect to plurality and unity), we can substitute one in the place of another without destroying these two determinations, the plurality and the unity (which are the only determinations to which we are paying attention), and so any two parts of extension can differ from each other only in being two not one. So all of extension must be conceived of as uniform, homogeneous, and having no internal determination that distinguishes one part from another, since if we place these parts however we wish, the result will always be the same being, and that is how we arrive at the idea of absolute space, which we consider to be homogeneous and indiscernible.

This notion of extension is still that of a geometrical body; for if we divide a line into as many parts and howsoever we wish, reassembling the parts will always result in the same line, no matter the transposition of the parts: it is the same for surfaces and for geometrical bodies.

§79. When we have thus formed a being in our imagination from the diversity of the existence of many things and of their union, extension, which is this imaginary being, seems distinct from everything real, from which we have separated it by abstraction. We imagine that this being can subsist by itself, because in conceiving it we do not at all need the other determinations that the beings might contain, since we considered these beings only insofar as they

are diverse and united. Our mind perceives these determinations apart, which constitute this ideal being that we call extension, and thus conceives of the other qualities that we have separated in thought and that are no longer a part of our idea of this being. Therefore, it seems as though we import all of these things into this ideal being; we house them there and extension receives and contains them, as a receptacle receives liquid that is poured into it. Thus, as long as we consider the possibility that many different things may exist together in this abstract being we call extension, we form the idea of space, which is nothing other than the idea of extension joined with the possibility of restoring to the coexistent and unified beings, from which the idea was formed, the determinations that we had already stripped from them by abstraction. Thus, we are right to define space, *the order of coexisting things*, that is to say, the resemblance in the manner in which beings coexist. For the idea of space arises from our attending solely to their manner of existing external to each other, and representing to ourselves that this coexistence of several beings produces a certain order or resemblance in their manner of existing; and so once one of these beings is taken to be the first, another becomes the second, another the third, and so on.[26]

§80. We see well that this ideal being, extension, which we form from the plurality and the union of all these beings, must appear to us as a substance. For, insofar as we think of several things existing together, and stripped of all internal determinations, this being appears to be enduring. And insofar as it is possible, by an act of our understanding, to restore to these beings the determinations that we have stripped from them by abstraction, it seems to the imagination that we are importing something that had not been there before; and so this being appears to be modifiable. Thus, we are led to represent space as a substance independent of the beings that are placed in it.

§81.[27] We call a being *continuous* when its parts are arranged one after another in such a way that

---

26. [I.m.:] Space is the order of coexisting things.
27. [I.m.:] What we call continuous.

it is impossible to place others in a different order between two of them, and in general we conceive of continuity whenever we cannot place anything between two parts. Thus, we say that the shine of a mirror is continuous, because we cannot see any unpolished parts between the parts of the glass that interrupt its continuity, and we call the sound of a trumpet continuous when it does not cease, and when we cannot put other sounds between any two. But when two parts of extension simply touch and are not joined to each other in such a way that there is no internal reason why we could not separate them or put something else between them, such as cohesion or pressure from surrounding bodies, we call them *contiguous*. Thus, in the case of contiguity, parts are separated in actuality, in contrast to the continuum, where the separation is no more than a possibility. Two hemispheres of lead, for example, are two actual parts of the sphere of which they are two halves, that is actually separated and divided into two parts, which will become contiguous if we place them one next to the other so that there is nothing between them. But if we were to reunite them by fusion into a single whole, then this whole would become a continuity, and its parts would then simply be possible insofar as one conceives that it is possible to separate this sphere into two hemispheres [just] as they were before the fusion.

From this we understand that space must appear to be continuous; for we introduce space whenever we represent to ourselves the possibility of several bodies A, B, C, coexisting. Now, if the bodies are not contiguous, we can place one or several between two of them, and we thereby introduce space between the two. Thus, we must consider space to be continuous, whether the contiguous coexistence of bodies A, B, C, is actual, or whether it is simply possible.

The principle of sufficient reason shows us, as I explained above, that this contiguity is actual, and that there cannot be void space, so that existing beings coexist in such a way that it is impossible to put anything new into the universe.

§82. Likewise, space must appear to us to be void and penetrable. It appears void to us so long as we disregard all of the internal determinations of coexist-ing things; for then it seems to us that there is nothing left in this space. And it appears penetrable to us because, being able to apply our attention to the manner of existing and to the internal determinations of existing beings, we then see, besides the space that is their manner of existing external to one another, several things that we did not notice before, when we considered this space only by itself. As a consequence, it must seem to us as though these things had entered into it, and that they had been placed there by an external agent.

§83. Space must also appear immutable to us because we feel that we can restore to different coexisting things the determinations that we had previously stripped from them. And we also feel that we can never conceive that we would be unable to restore these determinations to them. Therefore, we cannot remove space, since there must always remain the same thing that we would have removed, that is to say, the extension that is capable of receiving these determinations. Thus, once we have stripped these coexisting beings of all of their determinations, we can no longer abstract, nor form for ourselves, an ideal being that contains less than the one that we had already created in preserving only the coexistence of beings. For, to consider nothing but the manner of existing is the least abstraction that we can do, and we must either keep it or represent nothing at all. Space must therefore seem immutable; from this it follows that it must seem eternal, since we can never remove it.

§84. It must also appear infinite, for we would admit as much space as we conceive the possibility of existence. Now, since coexistent things stripped of all determinations, such as we conceive of them in order to form the idea of extension and of space, do not contain anything that would prevent us from continuing to place coexisting things external to one another, so we in effect conceive of them to infinity, and for this reason space must appear to be an extension that is infinite and limitless.

§85. Here, then, is the origin of all the properties that we attribute to space, when we say that it is one homogeneous, uniform, continuous extension, that it is self-subsistent, penetrable, immutable, eternal, infinite, etc., in short, the universal receptacle that contains all things. But with a little attention we see that all of these alleged properties, as well as the being in which we suppose them to exist, have no reality but in the abstractions of our mind, and that nothing like this idea does or can exist.

§86.[28] Our mind thus has the power of forming for itself, by abstraction, imaginary beings that contain only the determinations we want to examine, and of excluding from these beings all other determinations by means of which they can be conceived in another manner. This way of thinking is very useful, for the imagination rescues the understanding and helps it contemplate its idea, provided only that we take care that the imagination does not mislead us. For imaginary notions, which are infinitely helpful in the search for truths that depend on determinations (which constitute these beings that the imagination has formed), become very dangerous when we take them for realities. Thus, when we want to measure a distance, we can represent it to ourselves as a line with neither width nor thickness, and without any internal determination. Similarly, we can consider a width, an extension, without thickness when we do not want to consider the rest. Provided that we do not imagine that there exists anything resembling these abstractions of our mind, these fictions help in finding new truths and new relations, for our mind rarely has enough force to contemplate that which is abstract[29] in the concrete without being distracted by the multiplicity of things that it must represent to itself. Also for all of the sciences, and especially mathematics, are they not full of these sorts of fictions which are one of the greatest secrets of the art of invention, and one of the greatest resources for the solution of the most difficult problems that the understanding alone often cannot attain? Thus, we must resign ourselves to using these imaginary notions whenever we can substitute them in place of real notions without prejudicing truth, just as we use Ptolemy's system to resolve many problems of astronomy where the solution becomes much more difficult when using Copernicus' system, because we can in these instances substitute one hypothesis for the other without damaging the truth.

§87. While we could consider extension without paying attention to the determinations of the beings that constitute it, and in this way acquire our idea of space, however, since what is abstract cannot subsist without a concrete thing, that is to say without a real and determined being from which we are abstracting, it is certain that there is space only insofar as there are real and coexistent things; and without these things there would be no space. However, space is not these things themselves; it is a being formed by abstraction that does not subsist at all over and above things, but yet is not the same thing as the subjects from which we abstracted it, because these subjects contain an infinity of things that we ignored when forming the idea of space. Thus, space is to real beings as numbers are to numbered things, which become alike and each form a unit with respect to their number, because we abstract the internal determinations of these things, and consider them only insofar as they make a multitude, that is to say, several units. For without a multitude of things that we count, there would be no real and existing numbers, but only possible numbers. Thus, just as there are no real units more than there are actually existing things, neither are there any actual parts of space except for those designated by actually existing extended things. And we can admit parts into actual space only insofar as there exist real beings that coexist together. Therefore, those who wanted to apply to actual space the demonstrations that they had deduced concerning imaginary space could not help but lose themselves in labyrinths of errors from which they could find no way out.[30]

---

28. [I.m.:] Usefulness of Abstractions.

29. We call *concrete* the subject that we abstract and *abstract* what we separate from this subject by *abstraction*.

---

30. [I.m.:] Space is to beings, as the number is to numbered things.

# Immanuel Kant, *Prolegomena to Any Future Metaphysics That Will Be Able to Come Forward as a Science* (1783)[1]

## Preface

255 These *Prolegomena* are not for the use of students, but prospective teachers, and even the latter should not expect that they will be of help in organizing the exposition of an already existing science, but rather in discovering this science in the first place.

There are scholars to whom the history of philosophy (both ancient and modern) is philosophy itself; the present *Prolegomena* are not written for them. They must wait until those who attempt to draw upon the source of reason itself have completed their work; it will then be their turn to inform the world of what has been done. Failing that, nothing can be said that in their opinion has not been said before and in fact the same prophecy could hold for all future time; for since human understanding has speculated upon innumerable objects in various ways for many centuries, it is hardly to be expected that for each new thing something old cannot be found that bears a certain similarity to it.

My aim is to persuade all those who think metaphysics worth studying that it is unavoidably necessary to pause a moment and, viewing everything that has been done so far as if it had not been done, to propose first the preliminary question, 'Whether such a thing as metaphysics is at all possible?'

If it is a science, why is it that it cannot obtain universal and lasting recognition as other sciences do? If 256 not, how can it maintain its pretensions and keep the human understanding in suspense with never ceasing, yet never fulfilled hopes? Thus, whether we demonstrate our knowledge or our ignorance in this field, for once we must come to something certain about the nature of this supposed science, which cannot possibly remain on its present footing any longer. It seems almost ridiculous that, while every other science is continually advancing, in this science, which pretends to be wisdom incarnate and for whose oracle everyone inquires, we should constantly turn around the same spot without making any progress. Its supporters have decreased and we do not find that men who are confident of their ability to shine in other sciences venture their reputation here, where everybody, however ignorant they may be in other matters, presumes to deliver a final verdict, because in this area there is still no standard weight and measure to distinguish thoroughness from shallow chatter.

After all, in the elaboration of a science it is not extraordinary that, when men begin to wonder how

1. [Translated from the German by Paul Carus (Chicago, 1902), revised by Eric Watkins.]

far it has advanced, the question should finally arise whether and how such a science is at all possible. Human reason so delights in building things that it has repeatedly erected a tower but then razed it in order to examine the nature of its foundation. It is never too late to become reasonable and wise; but if the insight comes late, it is always more difficult to implement it.

To ask whether a science is possible presupposes a doubt as to its actuality. But such a doubt offends everyone whose entire possessions may perhaps consist of this supposed jewel; therefore, whoever raises such a doubt must expect opposition on all sides. Some, in the proud consciousness of their holdings, which are ancient and therefore considered legitimate, will take their metaphysical compendia in their hands, and look down on him with contempt; others, who never see anything unless it is identical to what they have seen somewhere else, will not understand him and for a while everything will remain as if nothing had happened to raise concerns about or hopes for an impending change.

257 Nevertheless, I venture to predict that any reader of these *Prolegomena* who thinks for himself will not only doubt his previous science but subsequently be fully persuaded that it cannot exist unless the demands expressed here on which its possibility depends are satisfied and, since this has never been done, that so far no such thing as metaphysics exists. But because the demand for it can never cease,[2]—since the interests of human reason in general are so intimately interwoven with it—he must confess that a radical reform or rather a new birth of the science according to a previously unknown plan is unavoidable, however men may struggle against it for a while.

Since the *Essays* of Locke and Leibniz or rather since the origin of metaphysics as far as history reaches, nothing has ever happened which could have been more decisive to its fate than the attack made upon it by David Hume. He shed no light on this kind of knowledge, but he certainly struck a spark from which light might have been obtained, had it caught some combustible substance and had its smoldering fire been carefully kindled and developed.

Hume started primarily from a single but important concept in metaphysics, namely that of the *connection of cause and effect* (including its derivative concepts of force and action, etc.). He challenged reason, which pretends to have given birth to this concept from her womb, to answer him by what right she thinks anything to be so constituted that if that thing is posited, something else must necessarily be posited as well; for this is the meaning of the concept of cause. He demonstrated irrefutably that it was perfectly impossible for reason to think such a combination *a priori* and by means of concepts, for it contains necessity. We cannot at all see why, as a consequence of the existence of one thing, another must necessarily exist or how the concept of such a combination can arise *a priori*. Therefore, he inferred that reason was altogether deluded about this concept, which she erroneously considered to be one of her children, whereas in reality it was nothing but a 258 bastard of imagination, impregnated by experience, which subsumed certain representations under the law of association; it passed off subjective necessity, i.e., habit, for an objective necessity arising from insight. Therefore, he concluded that reason had no power to think such combinations, even in general, because her concepts would then be purely fictitious and all her pretended *a priori* cognitions nothing but common experiences marked with a false stamp. In plain language, there is not and cannot be any such thing as metaphysics at all.[3]

---

2. Says Horace:

> "Rusticus expectat, dum defluat amnis, at ille
> Labitur et labetur in omne volubilis aevum;"
> "A rustic fellow waits on the shore
> For the river to flow away,
> But the river flows and flows on as before,
> And it flows forever and a day."

---

3. Nevertheless Hume called this very destructive science metaphysics and attached great value to it. "Metaphysics and morals are the most important branches of science; mathematics and physics are not nearly so important." (Essay 4, p. 214 in the German translation [in fact the passage is a rather free translation from Essay 5 of Hume's *Essays, Moral and Political*, Edinburgh, 1741–42].) But the acute man merely looked to the negative use arising from the moderation of speculative

However hasty and mistaken Hume's conclusion was, at least it was founded upon investigation and this investigation deserved the concentrated attention of the brighter spirits of his day as well as determined efforts on their part to discover, if possible, a more satisfying solution to the problem in the sense proposed by him, all of which would have speedily resulted in a complete reform of the science.

But the fate of metaphysics, which has been unfavorable for a long time, would have it that he was understood by no one. It is positively painful to see how utterly his opponents, Reid, Oswald, Beattie, and finally Priestley, missed the point of the problem; for while they were always taking for granted what he doubted and demonstrating with zeal and often with impudence what he never thought of doubting, they so misconstrued his valuable suggestion that everything remained in its old condition as if nothing had happened. The question was not whether the concept of cause was legitimate, useful, and even indispensable for our knowledge of nature—for this Hume had never doubted—but rather whether that concept could be thought by reason *a priori* and consequently whether it possessed an inner truth, independent of all experience, implying a wider application than merely to the objects of experience. This was Hume's problem. It was a question concerning only the origin, not the *indispensability* of its use. Were the former decided, the conditions of its use and the sphere of its valid application would already have been given.

But in order to solve the problem, the famous man's opponents ought to have penetrated very deeply into the nature of reason insofar as it is concerned with pure thought—a task which did not suit them. They found a more convenient method of being defiant while lacking any insight, namely an appeal to **common sense**. It is indeed a great gift from heaven to possess proper or (as it has recently been called) plain common sense. But this common sense must

be shown in deeds, by well-considered and reasonable thoughts and words, not by appealing to it as an oracle when one can provide no rational justification. To appeal to *common sense*, when insight and science fail, and no sooner—this is one of the subtle discoveries of modern times by means of which the shallowest babbler can safely engage the most thorough thinker and hold his own. But as long as a bit of insight remains, no one would think of having recourse to this subterfuge. Seen in the light of day, what is it but an appeal to the opinion of the multitude, of whose applause the philosopher is ashamed, while the popular charlatan glories and boasts in it? I should certainly think that Hume could appeal to common sense as much as Beattie and, in addition, to a critical reason (which the latter certainly did not possess) that keeps common sense in check and prevents it from speculating, or, if speculations are under discussion, attempts not to decide because it is not in a position to justify its own principles. By this means alone can common sense remain sound. Chisels and hammers may suffice to work a piece of wood, but for copper plates we require an etching needle. Thus common sense and speculative understanding are both useful in their own way: the former in judgments which apply immediately to experience, the latter when we judge universally from mere concepts, e.g., in metaphysics where common sense that calls itself sound (despite the fact that it often expresses the contrary) has no right to judge at all.

I openly confess that remembering David Hume was the very thing that first interrupted my dogmatic slumber many years ago, and gave my investigations in the field of speculative philosophy a completely different direction. I was far from following him in his conclusions, which arose only because he did not raise the whole of his problem, but only a part, which cannot be informative without taking the whole into account. If we start from a well-founded but undeveloped thought that another has left us, by continued reflection we can certainly hope to advance further than the acute man whom we should thank for the first spark of this light.

So I first tried to see whether Hume's objection could not be put into a general form and soon found

---

reason's extravagant claims in order to resolve completely the many endless and troublesome controversies that confuse mankind. He overlooked the positive injury which results, if reason is deprived of its most important prospects, which can alone supply to the will the highest aim for all its endeavor.

that the concept of the connection of cause and effect was by no means the only concept by which the understanding thinks the connection of things *a priori*, but that metaphysics consists altogether of such concepts. I tried to determine their number and when I had attained adequate success in this by starting from a single principle, I proceeded to the deduction of these concepts that I was now certain one could not deduce from experience, as Hume had done, but arose from the pure understanding. This deduction (which seemed impossible to my acute predecessor and which had never even occurred to anyone else, though everyone had confidently used the concepts without investigating the basis of their objective validity) was the most difficult task which ever could have been undertaken on behalf of metaphysics; and the worst thing about it was that metaphysics, such as it then existed, could not assist me in the least, because this deduction was supposed to make metaphysics possible in the first place. But as soon as I had succeeded in solving Hume's problem, not merely in a particular case, but with respect to the whole 261 faculty of pure reason, I could proceed safely, though slowly, to determine the whole sphere of pure reason completely and from universal principles, in its limits as well as in its contents. This was required for metaphysics in order to construct its system according to a secure plan.

But I fear that the *exposition* of Hume's problem in its greatest possible extent (namely in my *Critique of Pure Reason*) will fare as the *problem* itself fared when it was first proposed. It will be misjudged because it is misunderstood and misunderstood because men prefer to skim through the book rather than to think it through—a disagreeable task, since the work is dry, obscure, opposed to all common ideas, and, besides that, long winded. Now I must confess that I did not expect to hear complaints from philosophers about a lack of popularity, entertainment, and facility, when what is at stake is the existence of a highly prized cognition that is indispensable to humankind and that cannot be established otherwise than by the strictest rules of scholarly precision. Popularity may follow, but it is inadmissible at the outset. Yet as regards a certain obscurity, arising partly from the

vast scope of the plan, owing to which the principal points of the investigation are easily lost sight of, the complaint is just and I intend to remove it by the present *Prolegomena*.

The previous work, which discusses the faculty of pure reason in its whole extent and limits, will remain the foundation to which the *Prolegomena* refer as a preliminary exercise; for that critique must first be established as science, systematic and complete in its smallest parts, before we can think of letting metaphysics appear on the scene or even have the most distant hope of attaining it.

We have long been accustomed to seeing antiquated knowledge produced anew by taking it out of its former context and fitting it into a systematic new dress of any fancy pattern with new labels. Most readers will initially expect nothing else from the *Critique*; but these *Prolegomena* may persuade them that 262 it is a perfectly new science, which no one has even thought of previously, the very idea of which was unknown, and for which nothing accomplished up to now can be of the least use except the suggestion of Hume's doubts. Yet even he did not suspect such a formal science, but, for safety's sake, grounded his ship on the beach (of skepticism) letting it lie there and rot. By contrast, my object is to give it a pilot, who, by means of safe navigational principles drawn from a knowledge of the globe and provided with a complete chart and compass, may steer the ship safely, wherever he like.

If we start in on a new science that is wholly isolated and unique in its kind with the prejudice that we can judge it by means of putative knowledge that has been acquired previously, despite the fact that its reality is precisely what must be called into question in the first place, we should only fancy that we saw everywhere what we had already known because the expressions have a similar sound. But everything would appear utterly deformed, senseless, and unintelligible, because we would be basing it all on our own thoughts, made second nature by long habit, instead of the author's. However, the long-windedness of the work insofar as it depends on the subject matter and not its exposition, its consequent unavoidable dryness, and its scholastic precision are qualities which can only be of benefit to the science, though they may be disadvantageous to the book.

Few writers are gifted with the subtlety and at the same time with the grace of David Hume, or with the depth as well as the elegance of Moses Mendelssohn. Yet I flatter myself that I could have made my own exposition popular, had my object been merely to sketch out a plan and leave its completion to others, instead of having my heart in the welfare of the science, to which I had devoted myself for so long; in truth, it required considerable perseverance and even self-denial to resist the temptation of an immediate positive reception in favor of the prospect of a slower but longer lasting reputation.

*Making plans* is often the occupation of an opulent and boastful mind, which thus gains the reputation of a creative genius by demanding what it cannot 263 itself supply, by censuring what it cannot improve, and by proposing what it does not know how to attain. And yet something more should belong to a sound plan of a general critique of reason than mere conjectures if this plan is to be different from the usual declamations of pious aspirations. But pure reason is a sphere so separate and self-contained that we cannot touch a part without affecting all the rest. We can therefore do nothing without first determining the position of each part and its relation to the rest; for insofar as our judgment in this sphere cannot be corrected by anything external to it, the validity and use of every part depends upon the relation in which it stands to all the rest within the domain of reason just as in the structure of an organized body, the purpose of each member can only be deduced from the full conception of the whole. It may, then, be said of such a critique that it is never trustworthy unless it is *perfectly complete*, down to the smallest elements of pure reason. In the sphere of this faculty you can define and determine either *everything* or *nothing*.

Although a mere sketch preceding the *Critique of Pure Reason* would be unintelligible, unreliable, and useless, it is all the more useful as a sequel. For in this way we are able to grasp the whole, to examine in detail the main points of importance in the science, and to improve our exposition in many respects as compared to the first execution of the work.

With that work complete, I offer here a *plan* that is sketched out according to an *analytic method*, while the work itself had to be carried out in the *synthetic method*, so that the science may present all its articulations, as the structure of a very special cognitive faculty, in their natural combination. But should any reader still find this plan—which I publish as the *Prolegomena to Any Future Metaphysics*—obscure, let him consider that it is not necessary for everyone to study metaphysics and that many minds will succeed very well in the exact and even in profound sciences, which are more closely allied to intuition, though they cannot succeed in investigations 264 dealing exclusively with abstract concepts. In such cases they should apply their talents to other subjects. But whoever attempts to judge or, even more, to construct a system of metaphysics must satisfy the demands made here, either by adopting my solution or by thoroughly refuting it and substituting another. To dismiss it is impossible. Finally, let it be remembered that this much-decried obscurity (frequently serving as a mere pretext under which people hide their own indolence or dullness) has its uses, since all who observe a judicious silence in other sciences, speak authoritatively in metaphysics and make bold decisions, because here their ignorance does not stand in contrast to the knowledge of others. Yet it does contrast with sound critical principles, which we may therefore commend in the words of Virgil: "Ignavum, fucos, pecus a praesepibus arcent."[4]

Preamble on the Peculiarities of All Metaphysical 265 Cognition

§ 1. *Of the Sources of Metaphysics*

If one wants to present any cognition as scientific, it will first be necessary to determine accurately its distinguishing feature that no other science has in common with it and thus that is unique to it; otherwise the boundaries of all sciences become blurred and none of them can be treated thoroughly according to its nature.

---

4. "Bees are defending their hives against drones, those indolent creatures."

This distinguishing feature may consist of a simple difference of *object*, or of the *sources of cognition*, or of the *kind of cognition*, or several if not all of these together. On this, therefore, depends the idea of the possible science and its territory.

First, as concerns the *sources* of metaphysical cognition, its very concept implies that they cannot be empirical. Its principles (including not only its fundamental propositions but also its basic concepts) must never be derived from experience. It must not be physical but metaphysical cognition, namely cognition lying beyond experience. It can therefore have for its basis neither outer experience, which is the source of physics proper, nor inner experience, which is the basis of empirical psychology. It is therefore *a priori* cognition from pure understanding and pure reason.

But this alone would not distinguish metaphysics from pure mathematics; it must therefore be called pure philosophical cognition; for the meaning of this term I refer to the *Critique of Pure Reason* (Book II. "Transcendental Doctrine of Method," Chapter I, Section 1), where the distinction between these two uses of reason is explained sufficiently. So much concerning the sources of metaphysical cognition.

## § 2. *Concerning the Kind of Cognition Which Can Alone Be Called Metaphysical*

a. *On the Distinction between Analytic and Synthetic Judgments in General* — The distinguishing feature of the sources of metaphysical cognition demands that it must consist of nothing but *a priori* judgments. But whatever their origin or their logical form may be, there is a distinction in the content of judgments according to which they are either merely *explicative*, adding nothing to the content of the cognition, or *ampliative*, increasing the given cognition: the former may be called analytic judgments, the latter synthetic.

Analytic judgments express nothing in the predicate but what has already been actually thought in the concept of the subject, though not so clearly or with the same consciousness. If I say: "All bodies are extended," I have not amplified my concept of body in the least, but have only analyzed it, since extension was really thought to belong to that concept before the judgment was made, though it was not expressed; this judgment is therefore analytic. By contrast, the judgment, "Some bodies are heavy," contains in its predicate something not actually thought in the universal concept of the body; it amplifies my cognition by adding something to my concept and must therefore be called synthetic.

b. *The Common Principle of All Analytic Judgments Is the Principle of Contradiction* — All analytic judgments depend wholly on the principle of contradiction and are by their very nature *a priori* cognitions, whether the concepts that supply them with matter are empirical or not. Because the predicate of an affirmative analytic judgment is already contained in the concept of the subject, it cannot be denied of the subject without contradiction. In the same way, in an analytic, but negative judgment its opposite is necessarily denied of the subject by the same principle of contradiction. Such is the case with the judgments: "All bodies are extended" and "No bodies are unextended (simple)."

For this very reason all analytic judgments are *a priori* even if the concepts are empirical, as, for example, gold is a yellow metal; for to know this I require no experience beyond my concept of gold, which included that this body is yellow and a metal. For this constitutes my very concept and I need only analyze it without looking beyond it to anything else.

c. *Synthetic Judgments Require a Principle Different from the Principle of Contradiction* — There are synthetic *a posteriori* judgments of empirical origin; but there are also those that are certain *a priori* and that arise from pure understanding and reason. Yet they both agree in that they cannot possibly spring solely from the principle of analysis, namely the principle of contradiction, but require a completely different principle. However, from whatever principle they may be deduced, they must be *subject to the principle of contradiction*, which must never be violated, even though everything cannot be deduced from it. I shall first classify synthetic judgments.

1. *Judgments of Experience* are always synthetic. For it would be absurd to base an analytic judgment on experience, since our concept suffices for the

purpose without requiring any testimony from experience. That a body is extended is a judgment that is established *a priori* and is not an empirical judgment. For, before appealing to experience, we already have all the conditions of the judgment in the concept, from which we have only to elicit the predicate according to the principle of contradiction and thereby to become conscious of the *necessity* of the judgment, which experience could never teach us.

2. *Mathematical Judgments*, as a whole, are synthetic. This fact seems altogether to have escaped the notice of those who have analyzed human reason until now; it even seems directly opposed to all their conjectures, despite the fact that it is incontestably certain and has very important consequences. For since it was discovered that the conclusions of mathematicians all proceed according to the principle of contradiction (as is demanded by apodeictic certainty), men persuaded themselves that the fundamental principles were known from the principle of contradiction. This was a great mistake, for a synthetic proposition can indeed be comprehended according to the principle of contradiction, but only by presupposing another synthetic proposition from which it follows, but never by that principle itself.

First of all, we must observe that mathematical judgments proper are always *a priori* and never empirical, because they carry with them necessity, which cannot be derived from experience. But even if this is not granted, I can still confine my assertion to *pure mathematics*, the very concept of which implies that it contains pure *a priori* and not empirical cognition.

Initially, one might easily think that the proposition $7 + 5 = 12$ is a merely analytic judgment, following from the concept of the sum of seven and five according to the principle of contradiction. But on closer examination it appears that the concept of the sum of $7 + 5$ contains merely their union in a single number, but what the particular number is that unites them is not contained in that thought. The concept of twelve is by no means thought by merely thinking of the combination of seven and five; and even if we analyze this possible sum as long as we like, we shall not discover twelve in the concept. We must go beyond these concepts by calling to our aid

an intuition that corresponds to one of them, i.e., either our five fingers or five points (as Segner has it in his *Arithmetic*), and we must successively add the units of the five, given in an intuition, to the concept of seven. Hence our concept is really amplified by the proposition $7 + 5 = 12$ and we add a second concept to the first that was not at all thought in it. Arithmetical judgments are always synthetic and we can see this more plainly when we consider larger numbers; for in such cases it is clear that, however closely we analyze our concepts, by such mere dissection we can never find the sum without calling intuition to our aid.

Nor is any principle of pure geometry at all analytic. That a straight line is the shortest path between two points is a synthetic proposition. For my concept of straightness contains nothing of quantity, but only a quality. The concept of the shortest is therefore completely new and cannot be obtained by any analysis of the concept of a straight line. Here, too, intuition must come to our aid. It alone makes the synthesis possible.

Some other principles, assumed by geometers, are indeed actually analytic and depend on the principle of contradiction, but, as identical propositions, they serve only as a method of concatenation and not as principles, e.g., a = a, the whole is equal to itself, or a + b > a, the whole is greater than its part. And yet even these, though they are recognized as valid from mere concepts, are admitted in mathematics only because they can be represented in some intuition.

What usually makes us believe that the predicate of such apodeictic judgments is already contained in our concept and that the judgment is therefore analytic is the ambiguity of the expression. We *are supposed* to add a certain predicate to a given concept and this necessity attaches to the concepts. But the question is not what we are *supposed to add* to the given concept, but what we *actually think* together in it, though obscurely; and there it is clear that the predicate certainly belongs to these concepts necessarily, but by means of an added intuition rather than immediately.

The essential and distinguishing feature of pure *mathematical* cognition compared to all other *a priori* cognitions is that it cannot at all proceed *from concepts*, but only by means of the construction of concepts (see *Critique* II, Transcendental Doctrine of Method, Chapter I, Section I). Thus, because it must proceed in its propositions beyond the concept to what the concept's corresponding intuition contains, these propositions neither can nor ought to arise by dissecting the concept analytically, but are therefore, as a whole, synthetic.

I cannot refrain from pointing out the disadvantage to philosophy that results from the neglect of this easy and apparently insignificant observation. When Hume felt called (as is worthy of a philosopher) to cast his eye over the whole field of *a priori* cognitions in which the human understanding claims such vast possessions, he inadvertently severed from it an entire and indeed its most valuable province, namely pure mathematics. For he imagined that its nature or, so to speak, the legal constitution of this empire depended on totally different principles, namely on the principle of contradiction alone; and although he did not divide judgments formally and universally or with the same terminology as I have done here, what he said was equivalent to this: that mathematics contains only analytic, but metaphysics synthetic *a priori* judgments. In this, however, he was terribly mistaken and the mistake had a decidedly injurious effect upon his whole conception. For if he had not made this mistake, he would have extended his question concerning the origin of our synthetic judgments far beyond the metaphysical concept of causality and included in it the possibility of mathematics *a priori* as well, for he would have to have assumed that it was equally synthetic. And then he could not have based his metaphysical claims on mere experience without also subjecting the axioms of mathematics to experience, something he was far too acute to do. The good company into which metaphysics would thus have been brought would have saved it from the danger of contemptuous ill-treatment, for the blows intended for it would have landed on mathematics, which was not and could not have been Hume's intention. Thus that acute man would have been led into considerations which must be similar to those that occupy us

273

now, but which would have gained inestimably from his inimitably elegant style.

3. *Metaphysical* judgments *proper* are, as a whole, synthetic. We must distinguish judgments *belonging* to *metaphysics* from *metaphysical* judgments *proper*. Many of the former are analytic, but they only afford the means for metaphysical judgments, which are the whole end of the science and always synthetic. For if concepts, as, for example, that of substance, belong to metaphysics, then the judgments arising from a simple analysis of them also necessarily belong to metaphysics, as, for example, the judgment that substance is that which exists only as subject etc.; and by means of several such analytic judgments, we try to arrive at the definition of these concepts. But since the analysis of a pure concept of the understanding (which metaphysics contains) does not proceed in a manner different from the dissection of any other, even empirical concepts that do not belong to metaphysics (such as: air is an elastic fluid, the elasticity of which is not destroyed by any known degree of cold), it follows that the concept surely is, though the analytic judgment certainly is not, properly metaphysical. For the production of *a priori* cognitions in this science has something special and unique to it that must therefore be distinguished from the features it has in common with other rational cognition. Thus, for example, the judgment that all the substance in things is permanent is a synthetic and properly metaphysical judgment.

If the *a priori* concepts that constitute the materials and building blocks of metaphysics have been collected according to fixed principles, then the analysis of these concepts will be of great value; it might be taught separately from the synthetic propositions that constitute metaphysics proper and as a special part (as a *philosophia definitiva*) containing nothing but analytic judgments belonging to metaphysics. For in fact these analyses are not of much value except in metaphysics, i.e., for the synthetic judgments that are to be generated from these previously analyzed concepts.

274

The conclusion drawn in this section is thus that metaphysics is properly concerned with synthetic *a priori* propositions and these alone constitute its end, for which it indeed requires various dissections of its concepts and thus its analytic judgments, but the procedure is no different from that in every other kind of cognition, where we merely seek to render our concepts distinct by analysis. But the *generation* of *a priori* cognition according to both intuitions and concepts, finally, also of synthetic *a priori* propositions in philosophical cognition in particular, constitutes the essential subject matter of metaphysics.

270 § 3. *A Remark on the General Division of Judgments into Analytic and Synthetic*

This division is indispensable for the critique of human understanding and therefore deserves to be called *classical*, though it is of little use otherwise. But this is the reason why dogmatic philosophers, who always seek the sources of metaphysical judgments in metaphysics itself and not external to it in the pure laws of reason in general, altogether neglected this apparently obvious distinction. Thus the celebrated Wolff and his acute follower Baumgarten could seek the proof of the principle of sufficient reason, which is clearly synthetic, in the principle of contradiction. In Locke's *Essay concerning Human Understanding*, however, I find a hint of my division. For in Book IV (Chapter III, § 9, seq.), after already having discussed the various connections of representations in judgments and their sources, one of which he identifies as the principle of identity or contradiction (analytic judgments), and another as the coexistence of representations in a subject (synthetic judgments), he confesses (§ 10) that our *a priori* cognition of the latter is very narrow and amounts to almost nothing. But in his remarks on this kind of cognition, so little is definite and based on rules that we should not be surprised that no one, not even Hume, took this as an occasion for investigating this kind of judgment further. For such general and yet definite principles are not easily learned from others who have had them in their minds only obscurely. One must first discover them through one's own reflections and then one may find them in other places, where one could not possibly have found them at first, because the authors themselves did not know that their own observations were based on such an idea. Those who never think

for themselves still have the acuteness to discover everything after it has been shown to them in what was said long ago, though no one was ever able to see it there before.

§ 4. *General Question of the Prolegomena—Is*   271
*Metaphysics at All Possible?*

If a metaphysics that could maintain its place as a science were actual, could we say: here is metaphysics, learn it, and it will convince you irresistibly and irrevocably of its truth? This question would be useless and the only remaining question would be a test of our acuteness rather than a proof of the existence of the subject matter itself, namely: "How is the science possible, and how does reason come to attain it?" But human reason has not been so fortunate in this case. There is no single book to which you can point, as you do to Euclid's, and say: this is metaphysics; here you may find the noblest aim of this science, cognition of a highest being and of a future existence, proved from principles of pure reason. For one can surely show us many judgments that are apodeictically certain and can never be questioned; but these are all analytic and concern the materials and the scaffolding for metaphysics rather than an extension of cognition which is supposed to be our proper aim in studying it (§ 2). Even if you present synthetic judgments, such as the principle of sufficient reason (which you have never proved, as you ought to, from pure reason *a priori*, though we gladly concede its truth), when you want to use them for your main goal, you lapse into such illicit and dubious assertions that in all ages one metaphysics has contradicted another, either in its assertions or the proofs thereof, and thus has itself destroyed its own claim to lasting assent. Even the attempts at bringing about such a science are undoubtedly the first cause of the early appearance of skepticism, a mental attitude in which reason treats itself with such violence that it could never have arisen unless we fell into complete despair of ever satisfying our most important aims. For long before men began to investigate nature methodically, they consulted abstract reason, which had to some extent been exercised by means of ordinary experience; for reason is ever present to us, whereas laws of nature must usually be discovered with labor. Thus metaphysics floated to the surface, like foam, which dissolved the moment it was scooped off. But immediately more foam appeared on the surface, which some will always eagerly collect, while others, instead of seeking the cause of the phenomenon in the depths, thought they showed their wisdom by ridiculing the idle labor of the former.

274     Weary therefore of dogmatism, which teaches us nothing, and of skepticism, which does not even promise us anything—not even the quiet state of contented ignorance—disquieted by the importance of cognition that we need so much, and, lastly, rendered suspicious by long experience of everything that we believe we possess or that offers itself under the name of pure reason, there remains but one critical question on the answer to which our future conduct depends, namely: *Is metaphysics at all possible?* But this question must be answered not by skeptical objections to the claims of some actual system of metaphysics (for at this point we do not admit that such a thing exists), but on the basis of a conception of a science of this kind, which is currently merely problematic.

In the *Critique of Pure Reason* I have attempted to treat this question *synthetically* by inquiring into pure reason itself and trying to determine in this source itself the elements as well as the laws of its pure use according to principles. The task is difficult and requires a reader who is determined to penetrate into the system gradually, based on no data except reason itself, and who therefore seeks to unfold cognition from its original germs without relying upon any fact. The *Prolegomena*, however, are supposed to be warm-up exercises; they are intended to point out what we have to do in order to actualize a science (if it is at all possible) rather than to propound

275 it. They must therefore depend upon something already known to be trustworthy, from which we can set out with confidence and ascend to sources as yet unknown, the discovery of which will not only explain to us what we knew but also display the extent of many cognitions that all arise from the same sources. Consequently, the method of *Prolegomena*, especially of those cognitions designed as a preparation for future metaphysics, is *analytic*.

But it happens, fortunately, that though we cannot assume metaphysics is an *actual* science, we can say with confidence that certain pure synthetic *a priori* cognitions, namely *pure mathematics* and *pure natural science* are actual and given; for both contain propositions that are thoroughly recognized as apodeictically certain, partly by mere reason, partly by general consensus arising from experience, and yet as independent of experience. Therefore, we have at least some *uncontested* synthetic *a priori* knowledge and need not ask *whether* it is possible, since it is actual, but rather *how it is possible* so that we may deduce from the principle that makes the given cognitions possible the possibility of everything else.

## § 5. *The General Problem: How Is Cognition from Pure Reason Possible?*

Above we have seen the significant distinction between analytic and synthetic judgments. The possibility of analytic propositions was easily comprehended, because they are based merely on the principle of contradiction. The possibility of synthetic *a posteriori* judgments, i.e., of those that are gathered from experience, also requires no special explanation; for experience is nothing but a continual conjoining (synthesis) of perceptions. There remain therefore only synthetic *a priori* propositions of which the possibility must be sought or investigated, because they must depend upon principles other than the principle of contradiction.

But here we need not first seek the *possibility* of    276 such propositions, i.e., to ask whether they are possible. For enough of them are of undoubted certainty and since our present method is supposed to be analytic, we shall start from the fact that such synthetic but purely rational cognition actually exists; but we must now *investigate* the basis of this possibility and ask how such cognition is possible so that we can put ourselves in a position to determine the conditions of its use, sphere, and limits from the principles of its possibility. The proper problem upon which everything depends, when expressed with scholarly precision, is therefore: *How are synthetic* a priori *propositions possible?*

For the sake of popularity I have expressed this problem somewhat differently above, as an inquiry into purely rational cognition, which I could do on that occasion without obscuring the desired insight, because, since our concern here is only with metaphysics and its sources, the reader will, I hope, after my previous remarks, keep in mind that when we speak of purely rational cognition, we do not mean analytic but rather synthetic cognition.[5]

Metaphysics stands or falls with the solution of this problem; its very existence depends upon it. Let any one make metaphysical assertions with ever so much plausibility, let him overwhelm us with conclusions; but if he has not previously been able to answer this question adequately, I have a right to say: this is all vain, baseless philosophy and false wisdom. You speak through pure reason and presume, so to speak, to create *a priori* cognitions not only by dissecting given concepts but also by asserting connections which do not rest upon the principle of contradiction and which you believe you conceive quite independently of all experience, how do you discover this and how will you justify your pretensions? An appeal to the consent of the common sense of mankind cannot be allowed; for that is a witness whose authority depends merely upon rumor. Says Horace: "Quodcunque ostendis mihi sic, incredulus odi."[6]

The answer to this question is as indispensable as it is difficult; and though the principal reason that it was not given long ago is that the possibility of the question never occurred to anybody, there is yet another reason, namely that a satisfactory answer to this one question requires a much more persistent, profound, and painstaking reflection than the most diffuse work on metaphysics, which promised immortality to its author on its first appearance. And every insightful reader, when he carefully reflects what this problem requires, must at first be struck with its difficulty and would regard it as insoluble and even impossible if pure synthetic *a priori* cognitions did not actually exist. This really happened to David Hume, though he did not conceive the question in its entire universality as is done here and as must be done if the answer is to be decisive for all of metaphysics. For how is it possible, says that acute man, that when I am given a concept, I can go beyond it and connect with it another that is not contained in it in such a manner as if the latter *necessarily* belonged to the former? Nothing but experience can furnish us with such connections (thus he concluded from the difficulty which he took to be an impossibility), and all that vaunted necessity, or, what is the same thing, all cognition assumed to be *a priori* is nothing but a long habit of accepting something as true and hence of mistaking subjective necessity for objective.

Should my reader complain of the difficulty and the trouble I cause him in my solution of this problem, he is free to solve it himself in an easier way. Perhaps he will then feel indebted to the person who has undertaken a labor of such profound inquiry for him and be surprised at the facility with which the solution has been attained, considering the nature of the subject. Yet it has cost years of work to solve the problem in its whole universality (using the term in the mathematical sense, namely for what is sufficient for all cases), and finally to exhibit it in an analytic form, as the reader will find it here.

All metaphysicians are therefore solemnly and legally suspended from their affairs until they have adequately answered the question: "How are synthetic *a priori* cognitions possible?" For the answer contains the only credentials they must show when they have anything to offer in the name of pure reason. But if they do not possess these credentials, they can expect

---

5. It is unavoidable that, as cognition advances, certain expressions that have become classical after having been used since the infancy of science will be found inadequate and unsuitable and the newer and more appropriate use of these terms will run the risk of being confused with their older use. The analytic method, insofar as it is opposed to the synthetic method, is very different from what constitutes the essence of analytic propositions: it means only that we start from what is sought, as if it were given, and ascend to the only conditions under which it is possible. In this method we often use nothing but synthetic propositions, as in mathematical analysis, and it would be better to call it the *regressive method*, in contrast to the synthetic or *progressive* method. A principal part of logic too is distinguished by the name analytic, which means the logic of truth in contrast to dialectic, without considering whether the cognitions belonging to it are analytic or synthetic.

6. "Whatever you show me in this way, I reject and despise."

nothing else of reasonable people, who have been deceived so often, than to be dismissed without further ado.

If, however, they desire to carry on their affairs, not as a *science*, but as an *art* of wholesome persuasion suited to the common sense of man, they cannot be legitimately prevented. They will then speak the modest language of a rational belief and they will grant that they are not allowed even to *presume*, much less to *know*, anything that lies beyond the limits of all possible experience, but only to *assume* (not for speculative use, which they must abandon, but for practical purposes only) the existence of something that is possible and even indispensable for the guidance of the understanding and the will in life. In this manner alone can they be called useful and wise men, and the more so as they renounce the title of metaphysicians; for the latter profess to be speculative philosophers, and since, when *a priori* judgments are under discussion, poor probabilities cannot be admitted (for what is declared to be known *a priori* is

279 thereby announced as necessary), such men cannot be permitted to play with presumptions, but their assertions must be science or nothing at all.

It may be said that the entire transcendental philosophy, which necessarily precedes all metaphysics, is nothing but the complete solution of the problem propounded here in systematic order and completeness and that until now we have never had any transcendental philosophy; for what goes by its name is properly a part of metaphysics, whereas the former science is supposed to establish the possibility of the latter in the first place and must therefore precede all metaphysics. And it is not surprising that when a whole science, deprived of all help from other sciences, and consequently quite new in itself, is required to answer a single question satisfactorily, we should find the answer troublesome and difficult, even shrouded in obscurity.

As we now proceed to this solution—and according to the analytic method, in which we assume that such cognitions from pure reason actually exist—we can only appeal to two sciences of theoretical cognition (which alone is under consideration here), namely pure mathematics and pure natural science.

For these alone can exhibit to us objects in intuition and consequently (if a cognition should occur in them *a priori*) can show the truth or conformity of the cognition to the object *in concreto*, that is, *its actuality*, from which we could proceed to the basis of its possibility according to the analytic method. This facilitates our work greatly, for here universal considerations not only are applied to facts but even start with them, while in a synthetic procedure they must be derived from concepts wholly *in abstracto*.

But, in order to ascend from these actual and at the same time well-grounded pure *a priori* cognitions to a possible cognition of the same kind as we are seeking, namely to metaphysics as a science, we must understand what occasions and underlies it as a merely naturally given *a priori* cognition (one that is not, however, above suspicion regarding its truth), the elaboration of which is commonly called metaphysics though it has occurred without any critical investigation of its possibility. In a word, we must 280 comprehend the natural conditions of such a science as a part of our inquiry and thus the transcendental problem, divided into four questions, will be answered step by step:

1. *How is pure mathematics possible?*

2. *How is pure natural science possible?*

3. *How is metaphysics in general possible?*

4. *How is metaphysics as a science possible?*

It can be seen that the solution to these problems, though primarily designed to present the essential content of the *Critique*, nonetheless possesses something special that deserves attention in its own right, namely it searches for the sources of given sciences in reason itself so that its faculty of cognizing something *a priori* may be investigated and measured by its own deeds. By this procedure these sciences gain, if not with regard to their contents, then at least to their proper use, and while they throw light on the higher question concerning their common origin, they also provide an occasion for a better explanation of their own nature.

The Main Transcendental Problem: Part One

How is pure mathematics possible?

§ 6. Here is a great and established branch of knowledge, encompassing even now a wonderfully large domain and promising an unlimited extension in the future. Yet it carries with it thoroughly apodeictic certainty, i.e., absolute necessity, which does not rest upon any empirical basis. Consequently, it is a pure product of reason and, moreover, is thoroughly synthetic. "How then is it possible for human reason to produce such a cognition entirely *a priori?*" Does not this faculty, since it neither is nor can be based upon experience, presuppose some ground of *a priori* cognition which lies deeply hidden, but which might reveal itself by its effects, if only their first beginnings were diligently ferreted out?

281　　§ 7. But we find that all mathematical cognition has this unique feature: it must first exhibit its concept *in intuition* and in fact *a priori*, therefore in an intuition that is not empirical, but pure. Without this means mathematics cannot take a single step; hence its judgments are always intuitive, whereas philosophy must be satisfied with *discursive* judgments *from mere concepts* and, though it may illustrate its apodeictic doctrines through intuition, it can never derive them from intuition. This observation on the nature of mathematics gives us a clue as to the first and highest condition of its possibility, namely that it must presuppose *some pure intuition*, in which it can exhibit or, as it is called, *construct* its concepts *in concreto* and yet *a priori*.[7] If we can discover this pure intuition and its possibility, we may then easily explain how synthetic *a priori* propositions are possible in pure mathematics and consequently how this science itself is possible. For just as empirical intuition enables us, without difficulty, to amplify the concept which we form of an object of intuition with new predicates that intuition itself presents synthetically in experience, so too does pure intuition, only with this difference: that in the pure case the synthetic judgment is *a priori* certain and apodeictic, whereas in the empirical case it is only *a posteriori* and empirically certain, because the latter contains

only what occurs in contingent empirical intuition, whereas the former contains what must necessarily be discovered in pure intuition, since, as an *a priori* intuition, it is inseparably conjoined with its concept *prior to all experience* or any individual perceptions.

§ 8. But this step seems to cause our perplexity to increase rather than to diminish. For now the ques-　282 tion is: "How is it possible to intuit anything *a priori?*" An intuition is a representation that would depend immediately upon the presence of the object. Hence it seems impossible originally to intuit *a priori*; because in that event intuition would take place without either a previous or a present object to refer to and thus could not be intuition. Concepts indeed are such that we can easily form some of them *a priori*, namely those that contain nothing but the thought of an object in general without finding ourselves in an immediate relation to the object. Take, for instance, the concepts of quantity, cause, etc. But, in order to be meaningful and significant, even these require a certain concrete use—that is, an application to some intuition by which their object is given to us. But how can an *intuition* of the object precede the object itself?

§ 9. If our intuition had to be of such a nature as to represent things *as they are in themselves*, there would be no *a priori* intuition; rather, intuition would always be empirical. For I can know only what is contained in the object in itself when it is present and given to me. Of course, even then it is incomprehensible how the intuition of a present thing should make me know this thing as it is in itself, since its properties cannot migrate into my faculty of representation. But even if this possibility were granted, such an intuition would not take place *a priori*, that is, before the object is presented to me; for without this one cannot imagine a basis for any relation between my representation and the object, unless it depended upon inspiration. Therefore, there is only one way in which my intuition can anticipate the actuality of the object and be an *a priori* cognition, *namely if my intuition contains nothing but the form of sensibility that precedes in me as a subject all the actual impressions through which I am affected by objects.* For I can know *a priori* that objects of the senses can be intuited only according to

---

7. [Cf. A713/B741.]

this form of sensibility. Hence it follows that propositions that concern only this form of sensible intuition are possible and valid for objects of the senses. The converse holds as well, namely that intuitions that are possible *a priori* can never concern any things other than objects of our senses.

283 § 10. Accordingly, it is only the form of sensible intuition by which we can intuit things *a priori*, but by which we can know objects only as they appear to us (to our senses), not as they are in themselves; and this assumption is absolutely necessary if synthetic *a priori* propositions are to be granted as possible or, in case they actually occur, if their possibility is to be understood and determined in advance.

Now, space and time are the intuitions that pure mathematics lays at the foundation of all its cognitions and judgments that arise as both apodeictic and necessary. For mathematics must first present all its concepts in intuition and pure mathematics must do the same in pure intuition, that is, it must construct them. If it proceeded in any other way, it would be impossible to make any progress, for mathematics does not proceed analytically by dissection of concepts, but synthetically, and if pure intuition were lacking, there would be nothing in which the matter for synthetic *a priori* judgments could be given. Geometry is based upon the pure intuition of space. Arithmetic brings about its concept of numbers by the successive addition of units in time; and especially pure mechanics cannot bring about its concept of motion except by means of the representation of time. Both representations, however, are mere intuitions; for if we leave everything empirical, namely everything that belongs to sensation, out of the empirical intuitions of bodies and their alterations (motion), space and time still remain, which are therefore pure intuitions that underlie empirical intuitions *a priori* and for that reason can never be omitted. However, because they are pure *a priori* intuitions, they prove that they are mere forms of our sensibility, which must precede all empirical intuition, i.e., all perception of actual objects, and according to which objects can be cognized *a priori* but of course only as they appear to us.

§ 11. The problem of the present section is therefore solved. Pure mathematics, as synthetic *a priori* cognition, is possible only by referring to no objects other than those of the senses whose empirical in- 284 tuition presupposes a pure, and even *a priori*, intuition (of space and time). This is possible because pure intuition is nothing but the mere form of sensibility, which precedes the actual appearance of the objects in that it in fact makes them possible in the first place. Yet this faculty of intuiting *a priori* does not concern the matter of the appearance, that is, what is sensation in the appearance, for this constitutes what is empirical, but rather its form, namely space and time. Should anyone venture to doubt that both of these determinations do not adhere to things in themselves, but merely to their relation to our sensibility, I would like to know how it can be possible to know how the intuition of things must be constituted *a priori* and thus before we have any acquaintance with them and before they are presented to us as, however, is precisely the case with space and time. But this is easily understood as soon as both are held to be nothing more than formal conditions of our sensibility and the objects viewed merely as appearances; for then the form of the appearance, i.e., pure intuition, can by all means be represented from ourselves, that is, *a priori*.

§ 12. In order to add something by way of illustration and confirmation, we need only observe the ordinary and unavoidably necessary procedure of geometers. All proofs of the complete equality of two given figures (where the one can be substituted for the other in every respect) ultimately come down to the fact that they coincide. This is evidently nothing other than a synthetic proposition resting upon immediate intuition and this intuition must be pure and given *a priori*. Otherwise the proposition could not rank as apodeictically certain, but would have only empirical certainty. In that case, it could only be said that it is always found to be so and holds good only as far as our perception had reached. That all-encompassing space (which is itself not the limit of another space) has three dimensions and cannot have any more is based on the proposition that no more than three lines can intersect at right angles

285 in one point; but this proposition cannot be shown from concepts by any means, but rests immediately on intuition and, indeed, on pure *a priori* intuition, because it is apodeictically certain. That we can require a line to be drawn to infinity (*in indefinitum*) or that a series of changes (for example, spaces traversed by motion) shall be continued infinitely, presupposes a representation of space and time that can attach only to intuition, namely insofar as it in itself is limited by nothing, for it could never be inferred from concepts. Consequently, mathematics really presupposes pure intuitions, which make its synthetic and apodeictically valid propositions possible. Hence our transcendental deduction of the concepts of space and of time also explains the possibility of pure mathematics. Without such a deduction and without assuming "that everything that can be given to our senses (to outer sense in space, to inner sense in time) is intuited by us as it appears to us, not as it is in itself" the truth of mathematics may be granted, but its existence could by no means be understood.

§ 13. Those who cannot yet rid themselves of the notion that space and time are actual qualities inhering in things in themselves can practice their skills on the following paradox. After they have attempted its solution in vain and are free from prejudice at least for a few moments, they will suspect that the demotion of space and of time to mere forms of our sensible intuition may perhaps be well founded.

If two things are quite equal in all respects as much as can be ascertained by all means possible (quantitatively and qualitatively), it must follow that in all cases and under all circumstances the one can replace the other and this substitution would not occasion the least perceptible difference. In fact this is true of plane figures in geometry; but, despite complete internal agreement, some spherical figures exhibit such a difference in their outer relations that the one figure cannot possibly be put in the place of the other. For instance, two spherical triangles on op-

286 posite hemispheres, which have an arc of the equator as their common base, may be quite equal, in both their sides and their angles, so that nothing is to be found in either that would not equally be applicable to both, if it is completely described for itself alone;

and yet the one cannot be put in the place of the other (namely in the opposite hemisphere). For there is an *inner* difference between the two triangles that our understanding cannot describe as inner and that manifests itself only through outer relations in space. But I shall mention some more typical examples taken from common life.

What can be more similar to my hand and to my ear in every respect and in every part than their images in a mirror? And yet I cannot put such a hand as is seen in the mirror in the place of its archetype; for if this is a right hand, the one in the mirror is a left hand and the reflection of the right ear is a left one that can never serve as a substitute for the other. In this case there are no inner differences that our understanding could determine by thought alone. Still, as the senses teach, the differences are inner. For, despite their complete equality and similarity, the left hand cannot be enclosed within the same limits as the right one (they cannot be congruent); a glove for one hand cannot be used for the other. What is the solution? These objects are not representations of things as they are in themselves and as the pure understanding would cognize them, but rather sensible intuitions, that is, appearances, the possibility of which rests upon the relation of certain things unknown in themselves to something else, namely to our sensibility. Space is the form of outer intuition of this sensibility and the inner determination of every space is possible only by determining its outer relation to the whole space of which it is a part (its relation to outer sense). That is to say, the part is possible only through the whole, which is never the case with things in themselves as objects of the mere understanding, but which does occur with mere appearances. Hence the difference between similar things that are equal but not congruent (for instance, two contrary, but symmetric helices) cannot be made intelligible by any concept, but only by the relation to the right and the left hands, which immediately refer to intuition.

*Remark I.* Pure mathematics and especially pure 287 geometry can have objective reality only under the condition that they refer to objects of sense. But with respect to the latter the principle has been established that our sensible representation is not a representation of things in themselves, but of the way in which they appear to us. Hence it follows that the propositions of geometry are not the determinations of the mere creativity of our poetic imagination and therefore that they cannot be referred to actual objects with certainty; but rather that they are necessarily valid of space and, consequently, of all that may be found in space, because space is nothing other than the form of all outer appearances and it is this form alone in which objects of the senses can be given. Sensibility, the form of which underlies geometry, is that upon which the possibility of outer appearances depends. Therefore, these appearances can never contain anything but what geometry prescribes to them. It would be quite otherwise if the senses had to represent objects as they are in themselves. For then it would not at all follow from the representation of space, which the geometer presupposes *a priori* with all its properties, that all of this, together with what is inferred from it, must be so in nature. The space of the geometer would be considered a mere fiction and objective validity would not be attributed to it, because we cannot at all understand how things must necessarily agree with an image of them that we make spontaneously and prior to our acquaintance with them. But if this image, or rather this formal intuition, is the essential property of our sensibility, by means of which alone objects are given to us, and if this sensibility does not represent things in themselves, but rather only their appearances, then we shall easily comprehend and at the same time indisputably prove that all external objects of our sensible world must necessarily coincide in the most rigorous way with the propositions of geometry, because sensibility makes those objects possible as mere appearances in the first place by means of its form of outer intuition (space), with which the geometer is occupied. It will always be a remarkable phenomenon in the history of philosophy that there was a time when even mathematicians who were also philosophers began to doubt, not the correctness of their geometrical propositions insofar as they concerned space, but their objective validity and of the applicability of this concept itself and of all its determinations to nature. For they were concerned that a

288

line in nature might indeed consist of physical points and consequently that true space in the object might consist of simple parts, while the space which the geometer has in mind cannot. They did not understand that this mental space renders possible physical space itself, i.e., the extension of matter; that this pure space is not at all a quality of things in themselves, but a form of our sensible faculty of representation; and that all objects in space are mere appearances, i.e., not things in themselves but representations of our sensible intuition. Since space as the geometer conceives it is exactly the form of sensible intuition which we find in us *a priori* and contains the ground of the possibility of all outer appearances (according to their form), the latter must necessarily and most rigorously agree with the propositions of the geometer, which he does not draw from any fictitious concept, but from the subjective basis of all outer appearances, namely sensibility itself. In this and no other way can geometry be made secure as to the undoubted objective reality of its propositions against all the chicaneries of a shallow metaphysics, however strange this must seem to metaphysics, because it has not gone back to the sources of its concepts.

*Remark II.* Whatever is to be given to us as an object must be given to us in intuition. All our intuition, however, takes place only by means of the senses; the understanding intuits nothing, but only reflects. Now since we have just shown that the senses never and in no way enable us to know things in themselves, but only their appearances, which are mere representations of sensibility, we conclude that 'all bodies, together with the space in which they are found, must be considered nothing but mere representations in us and exist nowhere but in our thoughts.' Now, is this not manifest idealism?

Idealism consists in the assertion that there are only thinking beings; all other things that we believe to be perceived in intuition are nothing but representations in thinking beings, to which no object outside them in fact corresponds. I say, by contrast, that things are given to us as objects of our senses existing outside us, yet we know nothing of what they may be in themselves, but rather only

289

their appearances, i.e., the representations which they cause in us by affecting our senses. Accordingly, by all means I grant that there are bodies outside us, that is, things which, though quite unknown to us as to what they are in themselves, we yet know by the representations which their influence on our sensibility creates for us and which we call bodies, a term signifying merely the appearance of the thing which is unknown to us, but not therefore less actual. Can this be termed idealism? It is the very contrary.

Long before Locke's time, but even more so since then, it has generally been assumed and granted without detriment to the actual existence of outer things that many of their predicates may be said to belong not to the things in themselves, but to their appearances and to have no proper existence outside our representation. Heat, color, and taste, for instance, are of this kind. Now, if I go farther and for important reasons also consider as mere appearances the remaining qualities of bodies, which are called primary, such as extension, place, and in general space, with everything that belongs to it (impenetrability or materiality, shape, etc.)—no one can raise the least reason for its inadmissibility. As little as the man who admits colors not as properties of the object in itself, but only as modifications of the sense of sight, should on that account be called an idealist, so little can my system be called idealistic, merely because I discover that even more, in fact, *all the properties that constitute the intuition of a body* belong merely to its appearance. For the existence of the thing that appears is not thereby destroyed, as in genuine idealism, but rather it is only shown that we cannot possibly know it through the senses as it is in itself.

I would like to know what my assertions must be so that they do not contain any idealism. Undoubtedly, I would have to say that the representation of space is 290 not only perfectly conformable to the relation which our sensibility has to objects—that I have said—but also quite similar to the object—an assertion in which I can find as little meaning as if I said that the sensation of red has a similarity to the property of cinnabar, which excites this sensation in me.

*Remark III*. For this reason we may at once dismiss an easily foreseen but futile objection, "that by admitting the ideality of space and time the whole sensible world would be turned into mere illusion." At first all philosophical insight into the nature of sensible cognition was spoiled by making sensibility merely a confused mode of representation, according to which we still know things as they are, but without being able to reduce everything in our representation to a clear consciousness. By contrast, we have shown that sensibility consists, not in this logical distinction of clarity and obscurity, but in the genetic one of the origin of cognition itself. For sensible perception represents things not at all as they are, but only the way in which they affect our senses, and consequently by sensible perception appearances only and not things themselves are given to the understanding for reflection. After this necessary correction, the objection arises from an unpardonable and almost intentional misconception, as if my doctrine turned all the things of the sensible world into mere illusion.

When an appearance is given to us, we are still quite free as to how we should judge the matter. The appearance depends upon the senses, whereas the judgment depends upon the understanding and the only question is whether or not there is truth in the determination of the object. But the difference between truth and dreaming is not ascertained by the nature of the representations that are referred to objects (for they are the same in both cases), but by their connection according to those rules that determine the coherence of the representations in the concept of an object and to the extent to which they can subsist together in experience. And the appearances are not at fault if 291 our cognition takes illusion for truth, i.e., if the intuition by which an object is given to us is taken to be a concept of the thing or even of its existence that the understanding can only think. The senses represent to us the paths of the planets first as progressive, then as retrogressive, and there is neither falsehood nor truth in this, because as long as we hold that this is initially mere appearance, we do not pass judgment on the objective nature of their motion. But since a false judgment may easily arise when the understanding is not on its guard against taking this subjective mode of representation to be objective, we say that they appear to move backward; it is not the senses, however, which must be charged with the illusion, but the understanding, whose province alone it is to pass objective judgment on the appearances.

In this way, even if we did not at all reflect on the origin of our representations, whenever we connect our sensible intuitions (whatever they may contain) in space and in time according to the rules of the coherence of all cognition in experience, illusion or truth will arise depending on whether we are negligent or careful. That concerns merely the use of sensible representations in the understanding and not their origin. In the same way, if I consider all the representations of the senses, together with their form, space and time, to be nothing but appearances, and space and time to be a mere form of the sensibility, which is not to be met with in objects outside sensibility, and if I use these representations in reference to possible experience only, there is nothing in my regarding them as appearances that can lead astray or cause illusion. For they can nonetheless cohere properly according to rules of truth in experience. In this way all the propositions of geometry hold good of space as well as of all the objects of the senses, consequently of all possible experience, whether I consider space as a mere form of sensibility or as something adhering to the things themselves. However, only in the former case can I comprehend how I can know *a priori* these propositions concerning all objects of outer intuition. Otherwise, everything else with respect to all possible experience remains just as if I had not departed from the typical view.

But if I dare to go beyond all possible experience with my concepts of space and time, which is unavoidable if I proclaim them qualities inherent in things in themselves (for what should prevent me from letting them hold good of the same things, even though my senses might be different and unsuited to them?), then a grave error may arise due to an illusion. For I would thus proclaim to be universally valid what is merely a subjective condition of the intuition of things and clearly valid only for all objects of the senses, namely for all merely possible experience, because I would refer these qualities to things in themselves and not limit them to the conditions of experience.

My doctrine of the ideality of space and of time is, therefore, so far from reducing the whole sensible world to mere illusion that it is rather the only means of securing the application of one of our most important cognitions (namely that which mathematics presents *a priori*) to actual objects and of preventing its being regarded as mere illusion. For without this observation it would be absolutely impossible to determine whether the intuitions of space and time, which we borrow from no experience, but which still lie in our representation *a priori*, are not mere phantasms of our brain, to which objects do not correspond, at least not adequately, and consequently, whether geometry itself is a mere illusion. To the contrary, we have been able to show its unquestionable validity with regard to all objects of the sensible world precisely because they are mere appearances.

Secondly, though these principles turn the senses' representations into appearances, they are so far from transforming the truth of experience into mere illusion that they are rather the only means of preventing the transcendental illusion by which metaphysics has been deceived until now, leading to the childish endeavor of chasing after soap bubbles, because appearances, which are mere representations, were taken for things in themselves. Here originated the remarkable occurrence of the antimony of reason, which I shall mention below and which is resolved by the single observation that appearance, as long as it is employed in experience, produces truth, but the moment it transgresses the limits of experience and becomes transcendent, it produces nothing but pure illusion.

Since I thus grant reality to things that we represent to ourselves through the senses and only limit our sensible intuition of these things in such a way that they in no way, not even in the pure intuitions of space and of time, represent anything more than mere appearance of those things, but never their constitution in themselves, I have not invented a sweeping illusion for nature. Further, my protestation against all charges of idealism is so valid and clear that they would even seem superfluous, if there were not incompetent judges, who, while they would have an ancient name for every deviation from their perverse though common views and never judge of the spirit of the philosophical terminology, but cling to the letter only, are ready to replace well-defined concepts with their own folly and thereby deform and distort them. For the fact that I myself have given my theory the name of transcendental idealism cannot authorize anyone to confuse it either with the empirical idealism of Descartes (indeed, his was only an insoluble problem, owing to which he thought everyone free to deny the existence of the corporeal world because it could never be proved satisfactorily) or with the mystical and fanatical idealism of Berkeley (against which and other similar phantasms our *Critique* contains the proper antidote). For my idealism does not concern the existence of things (the doubting of which, however, constitutes idealism in the received sense), since it never occurred to me to doubt that, but rather the sensible representation of things, to which especially space and time belong. Concerning space and time and consequently all appearances in general, I have shown only that they are neither things (but mere modes of representation) nor determinations belonging to things in themselves. But the word "transcendental," which for me means a reference of our cognition, not to things, but only to the *cognitive faculty*, was meant to obviate this misunderstanding. But before this word gives further occasion to misunderstandings, I would like to retract it and prefer that my idealism be called critical. But if it is really an objectionable idealism to convert actual things (not appearances) into mere representations, by what name shall we call someone who conversely turns mere representations into things? It may, I think, be called *dreaming* idealism, in contrast to the former, which may be called *fanatical*, both of which are to be refuted by my transcendental, or, better, *critical* idealism.

294

The Transcendental Problem: Part Two

How is natural science possible?

§ 14. *Nature* is the *existence* of things insofar as it is determined according to universal laws. If nature is supposed to signify the existence of things *in themselves*, we could never cognize it either *a priori* or *a posteriori*. Not *a priori*, for how can we know what

belongs to things in themselves, since this can never be done by the dissection of our concepts (analytic judgments)? For I do not want to know what is contained in my concept of a thing (for that belongs to its logical being), but what it is in the actuality of the thing that is added to our concept and by which the thing itself is determined in its existence apart from the concept. My understanding and the conditions under which alone it can connect the determinations of things in their existence do not prescribe any rule to things themselves; these do not conform to our understanding, but rather it would have to conform to them; they must therefore first be given to me in order to gather these determinations from them, but then they would not be cognized *a priori*.

A cognition of the nature of things in themselves *a posteriori* would be equally impossible. For if experience is to teach us laws, to which the existence of things is subject, these laws, insofar as they concern things in themselves, would also have to belong to them *necessarily* even outside my experience. But experience teaches me what exists and how it exists, but never that it must necessarily exist so and not otherwise. Therefore, experience can never teach me the nature of things in themselves.

§ 15. We nevertheless actually possess a pure natural science that presents *a priori* and with all the necessity requisite to apodeictic propositions laws to which nature is subject. I need only call as a witness that propaedeutic of natural science which, under the title of a universal natural science, precedes all physics (which is founded upon empirical principles). In it we find mathematics applied to appearances and also merely discursive principles (derived from concepts), which constitute the philosophical part of the pure cognition of nature. But there are several things in it that are not quite pure and independent of empirical sources: such as the concept of *motion*, that of *impenetrability* (upon which the empirical concept of matter rests), that of *inertia*, and many others, which prevent us from calling it a completely pure natural science. Besides, it refers only to objects of outer sense and therefore does not provide an example of a universal natural science in the strict sense, since such a science must bring

295

nature in general, whether it regards the objects of outer or inner sense (the objects of physics as well as psychology), under universal laws. But among the principles of this universal physics several actually have the universality that we demand; for instance, the propositions that "substance is permanent," and that "every event is determined by a cause according to constant laws," etc. These are actual universal laws of nature, which exist completely *a priori*. There is then in fact a pure natural science and the question now is: *How is it possible?*

§ 16. The word *nature* assumes yet another meaning, which determines the object, whereas in the former sense it implies only that the existence of things in general must be determined *according to laws*. Nature considered *materialiter* (materially) is *the sum of all objects of experience*. And we are concerned with nature only in this sense, because things that can never be objects of experience, if they are to be cognized according to their nature, would force us to concepts whose meaning could never be given *in concreto* (in any example of possible experience) and of whose nature we would have to form concepts whose reality (i.e., whether they actually refer to objects or are mere beings of thought) could never be determined. The cognition of what cannot be an object of experience would be hyperphysical and we are not concerned here with hyperphysical things, but rather with the cognition of nature whose actuality can be confirmed by experience, although it is possible *a priori* and precedes all experience.

§ 17. The formal aspect of nature in this narrower sense is therefore the conformity to law of all objects of experience and, insofar as it is cognized *a priori*, their *necessary* conformity. But it has just been shown that the laws of nature can never be cognized *a priori* in objects insofar as they are considered not in reference to possible experience, but as things in themselves. But here we are concerned not with things in themselves (the properties of which we set aside), but rather with things as objects of possible experience, and the sum of these is what we properly call nature. And now I ask, when the possibility of a cognition of nature *a priori* is in question, whether it is better to pose the problem thus: How can we cognize *a priori*

that *things* as objects of experience necessarily conform to law? or thus: How is it possible to cognize *a priori* that *experience* itself necessarily conforms to law with respect to all its objects in general?

Closely considered, the solution of the question, represented in either way, amounts entirely to the same thing with regard to the pure cognition of nature (which is the point of the question). For the subjective laws, under which alone an empirical cognition of things is possible, are also valid for these things as objects of possible experience (certainly not as things in themselves, which are not under consideration here). It does not matter at all whether I say: A judgment of perception can never be valid for experience without the law that "whenever an event is observed, it is always referred to some antecedent, which it follows according to a universal rule" or whether I express myself such: "Everything, of which experience teaches that it happens, must have a cause."

It is, however, more convenient to choose the former statement. For *a priori* and prior to all given objects we can have a cognition of those conditions under which alone experience is possible, but never of the laws to which things in themselves may be subject without reference to possible experience. Accordingly, we cannot study the nature of things *a priori* otherwise than by investigating the conditions and the universal (though subjective) laws, under which alone such a cognition as experience (concerning its mere form) is possible and according to which we determine the possibility of things as objects of experience. For if I should choose the second statement and seek the *a priori* conditions under which nature is possible as an *object* of experience, I might easily fall into a misunderstanding and imagine that I was speaking of nature as a thing in itself and then move around in endless circles in a vain search for laws concerning things that are not at all given to me.

We shall therefore be concerned here only with experience along with the universal conditions of its possibility that are given *a priori* and determine nature as the whole object of all possible experience on that basis. I think it will be understood that I do not mean here the rules of the *observation* of a nature that is already given, for these already presuppose experience. I do not mean how we can study the laws of nature (through experience)—for in that case they would not be *a priori* laws and would not yield us a pure natural science—but rather how the *a priori* conditions of the possibility of experience are at the same time the sources from which all universal laws of nature must be derived.

§ 18. We must first of all note that, although all judgments of experience are empirical (i.e., are based in immediate sense-perception), the reverse, namely that all empirical judgments are for that reason judgments of experience, does not hold, but in addition to what is empirical and, in general, to what is given in sensible intuition, special concepts must still be added which have their origin completely *a priori* in the pure understanding and under which every perception must first of all be subsumed and can then by their means be changed into experience.

298  *Empirical judgments, insofar as they have objective validity*, are **judgments of experience**; but those that are *only subjectively valid*, I call mere **judgments of perception**. The latter require no pure concept of the understanding, but only the logical connection of perceptions in a thinking subject. But, in addition to the representations of sensible intuition, the former always require *special concepts originally created in the understanding*, which make the judgment of experience objectively valid.

All our judgments are initially mere judgments of perception; they are valid only for us (i.e., for our subject) and only later do we give them a new reference (to an object) and desire that they shall always be valid for us and in the same way for everybody else; for if a judgment agrees with an object, all judgments concerning the same object must likewise agree among themselves, and thus the objective validity of the judgment of experience signifies nothing other than its necessary universality. And, conversely, when we have reason to consider a judgment necessarily universal (which never depends upon perception, but upon the pure concept of the understanding, under which the perception is subsumed), we must consider it to be objective too, that is, that it expresses not merely a relation of our perception to a

subject, but a quality of the object. For there would be no reason for the judgments of others to agree with mine necessarily, if it were not the unity of the object to which they all refer and with which they agree, and for that reason they must all agree with one another.

§ 19. Therefore, objective validity and necessarily universal validity (for everybody) are equivalent concepts, and though we do not know the object in itself, when we consider a judgment as universally valid and thus necessary, we understand by this that it has objective validity. Through this judgment we cognize the object (even if it remains otherwise unknown as it is in itself) by the universally valid and 299 necessary connection of given perceptions. Since this is the case with all objects of the senses, judgments of experience take their objective validity not from the immediate cognition of the object (which is impossible) but merely from the condition of the universal validity of empirical judgments that, as has been said, never rests upon empirical or even sensible conditions in general, but rather upon a pure concept of the understanding. The object always remains unknown in itself; but if a concept of the understanding determines as universally valid the connection of the representations that are given to our sensibility, then the object is determined by this relation and the judgment is objective.

Let's illustrate the matter: that the room is warm, sugar sweet, and wormwood bitter,[8] are merely subjectively valid judgments. I do not at all expect that I or everyone else shall always find it as I now do; each judgment merely expresses a relation of two sensations to the same subject, namely myself, and

---

8. I readily grant that these examples do not represent judgments of perception that could ever become judgments of experience, even if a concept of the understanding were added, because they refer merely to feeling, which everybody recognizes as merely subjective and which therefore can never be attributed to the object and consequently can never become objective. I only wished to give an example of a judgment that is merely subjectively valid, containing no basis for universal validity and thereby containing no basis for a relation to the object. An example of judgments of perception that become judgments of experience through added concepts of the understanding will be given in the next footnote.

that only in my present state of perception; for that reason they are not valid of the object. I call them judgments of perception. Judgments of experience are of a completely different nature. What experience teaches me under certain circumstances, it must always teach me and everyone else and its validity is not limited to the subject or to its current state. For that reason I express all such judgments as objectively valid. For instance, when I say that the air is elastic, this judgment is initially only a judgment of perception, since I simply refer two of my sensations to one another. However, if I want to call it a judgment of experience, then I require that this connection stand under a condition that makes it universally valid. Thus I desire that I and everybody else should always necessarily connect the same perceptions under the same circumstances.

300     § 20. Consequently, we must analyze experience in general in order to see what is contained in this product of the senses and the understanding and how the judgment of experience itself is possible. An intuition of which I become conscious, i.e., perception (*perceptio*), which pertains merely to the senses, is the first presupposition. But, second, acts of judging (which belong only to the understanding) are also required. But this judging may be twofold—first, I may merely compare perceptions and connect them in a consciousness of my state; or, second, I may connect them in consciousness in general. The former judgment is merely a judgment of perception and is to this extent of subjective validity only: it is merely a connection of perceptions in my mental state without reference to the object. Hence it is not, as is commonly imagined, enough for experience to compare perceptions and to connect them in consciousness through judgment; by these means no universality and necessity arises, on account of which alone it can be objectively valid and experience.

Therefore, quite another judgment is required before perception can become experience. The given intuition must be subsumed under a concept, which determines the form of judging in general with respect to the intuition, connects its empirical consciousness in consciousness in general, and thereby establishes universal validity for empirical judgments. Such a

concept is a pure *a priori* concept of the understanding, which does nothing but determine for an intuition the general way in which it can be used for judgments. If the concept of cause is such a concept, it determines the intuition which is subsumed under it, e.g., that of air, relative to judgments in general, namely that the concept of air serves with regard to its expansion in the relation of antecedent to consequent in a hypothetical judgment. The concept of cause is thus a pure concept of the understanding, which is totally disparate from all possible perception and serves only to determine the representation subsumed under it, with respect to judging in general, and so to make a universally valid judgment possible.

Now, before a judgment of perception can be-  301 come a judgment of experience, it is first requisite that the perception be subsumed under such a concept of the understanding; for instance, air falls under the concept of cause, which determines our judgment about the air as hypothetical with respect to its expansion.[9] The expansion of the air is thereby represented not as merely belonging to the perception of the air in my present state or in several states of mine or in the perceptual state of others, but as belonging to it *necessarily*. The judgment: the air is elastic, becomes universally valid and a judgment of experience only because certain judgments preceding it subsume the intuition of air under the concept of cause and effect, thereby determining the perceptions not merely with respect to one another in me as a subject, but relative to the form of judging in general, which is hypothetical in this case, and in this way rendering the empirical judgment universally valid.

If we analyze all our synthetic judgments that are objectively valid, we will find that they never

---

9. To take an example that is easier to comprehend, consider the following: When the sun shines on a stone, it grows warm. This judgment, however often I and others may have perceived it, is a mere judgment of perception and contains no necessity; perceptions are only usually conjoined in this manner. But if I say: The sun warms a stone, I add to the perception a concept of the understanding, namely that of cause, which connects the concept of heat with that of sunshine as a necessary consequence and the synthetic judgment necessarily becomes universally valid and consequently objective, and is converted from a perception into experience.

consist of mere intuitions connected into a judgment only by comparison (as is commonly supposed), but rather that they would be impossible if, in addition to concepts abstracted from intuition, we did not add a pure concept of the understanding under which the former are subsumed and first combined in this manner into an objectively valid judgment. Even the judgments of pure mathematics in their simplest axioms are not exempt from this condition. The principle: a straight line is the shortest distance between two points, presupposes that the line is subsumed under the concept of magnitude, which is certainly no mere intuition, but has its seat in the understanding alone and serves to determine the intuition (of the line) with respect to the judgments that may be made about it relative to their magnitude, that is, to plurality (as *judicia plurativa*).[10] For in the case of such judgments it is understood that a given intuition contains a plurality of homogenous parts.

302

§ 21. To prove, therefore, the possibility of experience insofar as it rests upon pure *a priori* concepts of the understanding, we must first represent in a complete table what belongs to judgments in general and the various moments of the understanding. For the pure concepts of the understanding, which are nothing more than concepts of intuitions in general insofar as these are determined with respect to one or the other of these moments of judging in themselves, that is, necessarily and universally, must run parallel to these moments. In this way the *a priori* principles of the possibility of all experience, as an objectively valid empirical cognition, will also be precisely determined. For they are nothing but propositions that subsume all perception under those pure concepts of the understanding (according to certain universal conditions of intuition).

---

10. This name seems preferable to the term *particularia*, which is used for these judgments in logic. For the latter expression already contains the idea that they are not universal. But when I start from unity (in singular judgments) and so proceed to universality, I must not include any reference to universality. I think plurality merely without universality and not as an exception to it. This is necessary if logical considerations are to underlie the pure concepts of the understanding. However, its logical use need not be altered.

## Logical Table of Judgments

**1**
*As to Quantity*
Universal
Particular
Singular

**2**
*As to Quality*
Affirmative
Negative
Infinite

**3**
*As to Relation*
Categorical
Hypothetical
Disjunctive

**4**
*As to Modality*
Problematic
Assertoric
Apodeictic

303

## Transcendental Table of the Pure Concepts of the Understanding

**1**
*As to Quantity*
Unity (Measure)
Plurality (Magnitude)
Totality (Whole)

**2**
*As to Quality*
Reality
Negation
Limitation

**3**
*As to Relation*
Substance
Cause
Community

**4**
*As to Modality*
Possibility
Existence [*Dasein*]
Necessity

## Pure Physiological Table of the Universal Principles of the Science of Nature

**1**
Axioms of Intuition

**2**
Anticipations of Perception

**3**
Analogies of Experience

**4**
Postulates of Empirical Thought in General

304  § 21a. In order to sum the whole matter up into one idea, it is first necessary to remind the reader that we are not discussing the origin of experience, but what lies in experience. The former belongs to empirical psychology and even then would never be developed adequately without the latter, which belongs to the critique of cognition and particularly of the understanding.

Experience consists of intuitions, which belong to the sensibility, and of judgments, which are solely the understanding's business. However, those judgments that the understanding forms solely from sensible intuitions are far from being judgments of experience. For in the one case the judgment connects the perceptions only as they are given in sensible intuition, while in the other case the judgments must express what experience in general and not what mere perception contains (which possesses only subjective validity). A judgment of experience must therefore add to sensible intuition and its logical connection in a judgment (after it has been rendered universal by comparison) something that determines the synthetic judgment as necessary and therefore as universally valid. This can be nothing other than that concept which represents the intuition as determined in itself with respect to one form of judgment rather than another, namely a concept of that synthetic unity of intuition which can be represented only through a given logical function of judgment.

§ 22. The sum of the matter is this: the task of the senses is to intuit—that of the understanding is to think. But to think is to unify representations in one consciousness. This unification either originates merely relative to the subject and is accidental and subjective, or is absolute and is necessary or

305  objective. The unification of representations in one consciousness is judgment. Therefore, thinking is the same as judging or referring representations to judgments in general. For this reason judgments are either merely subjective, if representations are referred to a consciousness in only one subject and united in that subject, or objective, if they are united in one consciousness in general, that is, necessarily. The logical moments of all judgments are simply the various possible ways of unifying representations

in consciousness. But if they function as concepts, they are concepts of their necessary unification in one consciousness and thus principles of objectively valid judgments. This unification in one consciousness is either analytic, by identity, or synthetic, by the combination and addition of various representations to each other. Experience consists in the synthetic connection of appearances (perceptions) in one consciousness insofar as this connection is necessary. For this reason pure concepts of the understanding are those under which all perceptions must be subsumed before they can serve in judgments of experience, in which the synthetic unity of the perceptions is represented as necessary and universally valid.[11]

§ 23. Insofar as judgments are considered merely as the condition of the unification of given representations in one consciousness, they are rules. Insofar as these rules represent the unification as necessary, they are *a priori* rules; and insofar as these *a priori* rules cannot be deduced from higher rules, they are principles. But with respect to the possibility of all experience, if one considers only the form of thought in it, no conditions of judgments of experience are higher than those which bring the appearances (according to the different form of their intuition) under pure concepts of the understand-  306 ing that render the empirical judgment objectively valid. These conditions are therefore the *a priori* principles of possible experience.

---

11. But how does this proposition: that judgments of experience contain necessity in the synthesis of perceptions, agree with the statement I have argued for so often before: that experience as cognition *a posteriori* can provide contingent judgments only? When I say: experience teaches me something, I mean only the perception that lies in experience—for example, that heat always follows the shining of the sun on a stone—thus, the proposition of experience is to this extent always contingent. That this heat necessarily follows the shining of the sun is indeed contained in the judgment of experience (by means of the concept of cause), but I do not learn it through experience. Rather, the reverse holds: experience is first of all generated by this addition of the concept of the understanding (of cause) to perception. To see how the perception comes by this addition one must refer to the *Critique* itself in the section on the transcendental faculty of judgment. [Kant is referring to The Schematism of the Pure Concepts of the Understanding, A137ff./B176ff.]

Now the principles of possible experience are at the same time universal laws of nature, which can be cognized *a priori*. And thus the problem in our second question: *How is pure natural science possible?* is solved. For the systematization that is required for the form of a science is found to perfection here, because, beyond the previously mentioned formal conditions of all judgments in general (and thus of all rules in general) offered in logic, no others are possible. While these constitute a logical system, the concepts based on them, which contain the *a priori* conditions of all synthetic and necessary judgments, are for just that reason a transcendental system. Finally, the principles by means of which all appearances are subsumed under these concepts constitute a physiological system, that is, a system of nature, which precedes all empirical cognition of nature, makes it possible in the first place, and for that reason may be called the proper universal and pure natural science.

§ 24. The first[12] of the physiological principles subsumes all appearances, as intuitions in space and time, under the concept of *magnitude* and is to that extent a principle of the application of mathematics to experience. The second one does not directly subsume the empirical element, namely sensation, which denotes the real in intuitions, under the concept of quantity, because sensation is not an intuition that would contain either space or time, though it does place the object corresponding to it into both. But still there is a quantitative difference between reality (sense-representation) and zero, i.e., a total lack of intuition in time. For between every given degree of light and darkness, between every degree of heat and absolute cold, between every degree of heaviness and absolute lightness, between every degree of occupied space and totally empty space, still smaller degrees can always be thought, just as ever diminishing degrees always obtain between consciousness and total unconsciousness (psychological darkness). For that reason no perception could prove an absolute absence of it; for instance, no psychological darkness could be viewed as a kind of consciousness that is simply outweighed by another, stronger consciousness, and the same holds in all cases of sensation, for which reason the understanding can anticipate even sensations that constitute the proper quality of empirical representations (appearances) by means of the principle: that they all (thus the real in all appearances) have a degree. This is the second application of mathematics (*mathesis intensorum*) to natural science.

§ 25. Regarding the relation of appearances and merely with a view to their existence, the determination of this relation is not mathematical but rather dynamical, can never be objectively valid, and consequently is never fit for experience if it is not subject to *a priori* principles that make the cognition of experience relative to appearances possible in the first place. For this reason appearances must be subsumed under the concept of substance, which, as a concept of the thing itself, underlies all determination of existence; or secondly—insofar as succession, that is, an event, is found among appearances—under the concept of an effect with respect to a cause; or lastly—insofar as coexistence is to be known objectively, that is, by a judgment of experience—under the concept of community (interaction). Thus *a priori* principles underlie objectively valid, though empirical judgments, that is, the possibility of experience insofar as it is to connect objects in nature according to their existence. These principles are the proper laws of nature, which can be called dynamical.

Finally, judgments of experience include the cognition of the agreement and connection, not of appearances among themselves in experience, but of their relation to experience in general, which contains either their agreement with the formal conditions that the understanding cognizes, or their coherence with the materials of the senses and perception, or both combined into one concept. Consequently it contains possibility, actuality, and necessity according to universal laws of nature; and this constitutes the physiological doctrine of method (the distinction of truth and of hypotheses, and the limits on the admissibility of the latter).

---

12. The three following paragraphs can hardly be understood properly unless one refers to what the *Critique* itself says about the principles; they can, however, be of service in giving a better view of their general features and in fixing one's attention on the main points.

§ 26. The third table of principles derived *from the nature of the understanding itself* according to the critical method displays an inherent perfection, placing it far above every other table that has ever been or may still be attempted (though in vain) by analyzing *the objects themselves* dogmatically. For it exhibits all synthetic *a priori* principles completely and according to one principle, namely the faculty of judging in general, which constitutes the essence of experience with respect to the understanding, so that we can be certain that there are no more such principles, a satisfaction that the dogmatic method can never attain. But this is by no means its greatest merit.

We must pay close attention to the proof that shows the possibility of this *a priori* cognition and at the same time limits all such principles to a condition which must never be lost sight of if it is not to be misunderstood and extended in use beyond the original sense which the understanding attaches to it, namely that these principles contain only the conditions of possible experience in general insofar as it is subjected to *a priori* laws. Consequently I do not say that things *in themselves* possess a magnitude, that their reality possesses a degree, that their existence contains a connection of accidents in a substance, etc. For no one can prove this, because such a synthetic connection from mere concepts is absolutely impossible, where all relation to sensible intuition, on the one hand, and all connection of it in a possible experience, on the other hand, is lacking. Thus, the essential limitation of the concepts in these principles is: that all things necessarily stand *a priori* under the conditions stated above only as objects of experience.

Second, a specifically unique mode of proof of these principles then follows: they are not referred directly to appearances and to their relations, but to the possibility of experience, of which appearances constitute only the matter, not the form. That is, they are referred to objectively and universally valid synthetic propositions, in which we distinguish judgments of experience from mere judgments of perception. This takes place because appearances, as mere intuitions, *occupying a part of space and time*, fall under the concept of magnitude, which synthetically unifies their manifold *a priori* according to rules; and

because, insofar as perception contains sensibility in addition to intuition, there is an ever-decreasing transition between sensation and nothing (i.e., the total disappearance of sensation), the real in appearances must have a degree insofar as it does *not* itself occupy *any part of space or time*.[13] Still the transition to actuality from empty time or empty space is possible only in time; consequently, though sensation, as the quality of empirical intuition by means of which it is distinguished from other sensations, can never be cognized *a priori* as a quantity of perception, it can still be intensively distinguished from every other similar perception in a possible experience in general. For this reason the application of mathematics to nature with respect to sensible intuition, by which nature is given to us, is made possible and determined in the first place.

Above all, the reader must pay attention to the mode of proof of the principles that occur under the title of the Analogies of Experience. For these do not refer to the creation of intuitions, as do the principles of the application of mathematics to natural science in general, but rather to the connection of their existence in experience; and this can be nothing but the determination of their existence in time according to necessary laws, under which alone the connection is objectively valid and thus becomes experience. Therefore, the proof does not apply to the synthetic unity in the connection *of the things* in themselves, but rather of *perceptions*, and of these not in regard to their content, but rather to the determination of time and of the relation of their existence in it according to

---

13. Heat and light, etc. are just as large (according to their degree) in a small space as in a large one; in like manner inner representations, pain, consciousness need not vary according to degree depending on whether they last a short or a long time. Hence the quantity is just as great in a point or in a moment as in a space or time of any magnitude. Degrees are therefore magnitudes, not in intuition, but rather in mere sensation (or in the magnitude of the ground of an intuition). Hence they can only be estimated quantitatively by the relation of 1 to 0, namely by their capability of decreasing by infinite intermediate degrees to disappearance or of increasing from zero through infinite gradations to a determinate sensation in a certain time. *Quantitas qualitatis est gradus* [i.e., the quantity of quality is degree].

universal laws. If empirical determination in relative time is to be objectively valid and thus experience, these universal laws must contain the necessary determination of existence in time in general (according to a rule of the understanding *a priori*). I cannot discuss the issue further in these *Prolegomena*, but I suggest that my reader (who has probably been long accustomed to view experience as a mere empirical synthesis of perceptions and hence who has not considered that it extends well beyond their reach, namely by imparting universal validity to empirical judgments for which purpose it requires a pure and *a priori* unity of the understanding) pay special attention to this distinction between experience and a mere aggregate of perceptions and to judge the mode of proof from this point of view.

§ 27. We are now in a position to remove Hume's doubt. He rightly maintains that through reason we cannot have insight into the possibility of causality, i.e., of the relation of the existence of one thing to the existence of another that is necessitated by the former. I add that we have just as little insight into the concept of subsistence, i.e., the necessity that a subject lies at the foundation of the existence of things that cannot itself be a predicate of any other thing; even more, we cannot even form a concept of the possibility of such a thing (though we can point out examples of its use in experience). The very same incomprehensibility affects the community of things, since we cannot have insight into how an inference from the state of one thing to the state of quite another thing beyond it, and *vice versa*, can be drawn, and how substances, each of which has its own separate existence, should depend upon one another and
311 even do so necessarily. At the same time, I am very far from holding these concepts to be merely derived from experience and the necessity represented in them to be imaginary and a mere illusion long habit has produced in us. Rather, I have sufficiently shown that they and the principles derived from them are firmly established *a priori* before all experience and have their undoubted objective correctness, though of course only with respect to experience.

§ 28. Thus, although I have no concept of such a connection of things in themselves, how they could

either exist as substances or act as causes or stand in community with others (as parts of a real whole), and I am just as unable to conceive such properties in appearances as such (because those concepts contain nothing that lies in the appearances, but only what the understanding alone must think), we still have a concept of such a connection of representations in our understanding and in judgments in general, namely: that representations appear in one sort of judgment as a subject in relation to predicates, in another as a ground in relation to consequences, and in a third as parts, which, when taken together, constitute a total possible cognition. Further, we cognize *a priori* that without considering the representation of an object as determined in some of these moments, we can have no valid cognition of the object and if we should concern ourselves with the object in itself, there is no possible characteristic by which I could know that it is determined in any of these moments, that is, under the concept of either substance or cause or (in relation to other substances) community, for I have no concept of the possibility of such a connection of existence. However, the question is not how things in themselves, but rather how the empirical cognition of things is determined with respect to the above moments of judgment in general, that is, how things as objects of experience can and should be subsumed under these concepts of the understanding. And then it is clear that I have complete insight into not only the possibility but also the necessity of subsuming all appearances under these concepts, that is, of using them for principles of the possibility of experience.

§ 29. In order to experiment with Hume's prob- 312 lematical concept (his *crux metaphysicorum*), namely the concept of cause, we are, first, given *a priori* by means of logic the form of a conditioned judgment in general, i.e., we use one given cognition as antecedent and another as consequence. But it is possible that we may encounter in perception a rule for this relation that states: that a certain appearance is constantly followed by another (though not conversely), and this is the case when I can use the hypothetical judgment and, for instance, say: if the sun shines long enough upon a body, it grows warm. Of course, there is as yet no necessary connection and thus no concept of cause. However, I continue and say: if the above proposition, which is merely a subjective connection of perceptions, is to be a judgment of experience, it must be viewed as necessarily and universally valid. But such a proposition would be: Through its light the sun is the cause of the heat. The rule that was empirical above is now considered as a law and not merely as valid of appearances, but valid of them for the purposes of a possible experience which requires universal and therefore necessarily valid rules. Therefore, I certainly do have insight into the concept of cause as a concept necessarily belonging to the mere form of experience and its possibility as a synthetic unification of perceptions in consciousness in general; but I do not have any insight at all into the possibility of a thing in general as a cause, because the concept of cause does not at all denote a condition that belongs to things, but rather only to experience, namely that experience is only an objectively valid cognition of appearances and of their succession insofar as the antecedent can be conjoined with the consequent according to the rule of hypothetical judgments.

§ 30. For this reason, if the pure concepts of the understanding refer not to objects of experience but to things in themselves (*noumena*), they have no significance whatsoever. They serve, as it were, only to spell out appearances so that we may be able to read 313 them as experience. The principles that arise from their reference to the sensible world only serve our understanding for use in experience. Beyond this they are arbitrary combinations without objective reality and we can neither cognize their possibility *a priori* nor verify their reference to objects, let alone make them intelligible by any example; because examples can only be borrowed from some possible experience, the objects of these concepts can be found nowhere but in a possible experience.

This complete solution of Hume's problem, though it goes against its originator's expectations, rescues the *a priori* origin of the pure concepts of the understanding and the validity of the universal laws of nature as laws of the understanding, yet in such a way that it limits their use only to experience, because their possibility depends solely on the relation

of the understanding to experience—not by deriving them from experience, but rather by deriving experience from them—a completely reversed mode of connection that never occurred to Hume.

This is therefore the result of all our previous inquiries: "All synthetic *a priori* principles are nothing more than principles of possible experience and can never be referred to things in themselves, but only to appearances as objects of experience." For this reason pure mathematics as well as pure natural science can never be referred to anything other than mere appearances and can only represent either what makes experience possible in general or what, by being derived from these principles, must always be capable of being represented in some possible experience.

§ 31. And thus we finally have something determinate that one can depend on in all metaphysical enterprises that have been bold enough until now, but always at random, treating everything blindly without discrimination. That the goal of their exertions should be so near occurred neither to dogmatic thinkers nor to those who, confident in their supposed sound reason, started with concepts and principles of pure reason (which were legitimate and natural, but only for use in experience) in search of insight, to which they neither knew nor could know any determinate limits, because they had never re-  314 flected nor were able to reflect on the nature or even on the possibility of such a pure understanding.

Many a naturalist of pure reason (by which I mean anyone who believes he can decide matters in metaphysics without any science) may pretend that long ago, by the prophetic spirit of his sound sense, he not only suspected but knew and comprehended what is presented here with so much preparation or, if he likes, with prolix and pedantic pomp: namely that with all our reason we can never reach beyond the field of experience. However, when he is finally questioned about his rational principles, he must grant that many of them have not been derived from experience and that they are therefore independent of experience and valid *a priori*. How then and on what grounds will he restrain both himself and the dogmatist who makes use of these concepts and principles beyond all possible experience precisely because they are recognized to be independent of it? And even he, this adept in sound reason, in spite of all his assumed and cheaply acquired wisdom, is not exempt from inadvertently wandering beyond objects of experience into the field of chimeras. He, too, is often deeply enough involved in them, though in announcing everything as mere probability, rational conjecture, or analogy he gives his groundless pretensions a different appearance with his popular language.

§ 32. Since the oldest days of philosophy, besides the beings of sense or appearances (*phaenomena*) which make up the sensible world, inquirers into pure reason have conceived special beings of the understanding (*noumena*), which are supposed to constitute an intelligible world. And since they equated appearance and illusion (something we may well excuse in an undeveloped epoch), actuality was only granted to the beings of the understanding.

315　　In fact, if, as is fitting, we view the objects of the senses as mere appearances, we thereby confess at the same time that they are based upon a thing in itself, though we do not know this thing in its internal constitution, but rather only its appearances, i.e., the way in which our senses are affected by this unknown something. The understanding, therefore, precisely by assuming appearances, also grants the existence of things in themselves and to this extent we may say that the representation of such beings that underlie the appearances, consequently of mere beings of the understanding, is not only admissible but also unavoidable.

Our critical deduction by no means excludes such things (*noumena*), but rather limits the principles of the Aesthetic[14] in such a way that they shall not extend to all things, since everything would then be turned into mere appearance, but that they are to hold good only of objects of possible experience. Thus, in this way beings of the understanding are granted, but only with the enforcement of this rule that admits of no exception: that we neither know nor can know anything at all determinate about these pure beings of the understanding, because our pure

concepts of the understanding as well as our pure intuitions extend to nothing but objects of possible experience, consequently to mere beings of sense and, as soon as we leave this sphere, these concepts retain no meaning whatsoever.

§ 33. There is indeed something seductive in our pure concepts of the understanding that tempts us to a transcendent use—a use which transcends all possible experience. Not only are our concepts of substance, force, action, reality, etc. quite independent of experience, containing nothing of sense appearance, and not only do they thus appear to be applicable to things in themselves (*noumena*), but, what strengthens this conjecture, they contain a necessity of determination in themselves, which experience never attains. The concept of cause implies a rule according to which one state follows another necessarily; but experience can show us only that one state of things often or even typically follows another and therefore furnishes neither strict universality nor necessity.

For that reason the concepts of the understanding seem to have a deeper meaning and content 316 than could be exhausted by their mere empirical use and thus the understanding inadvertently adds to the house of experience a much more extensive wing that it fills with nothing but beings of thought, without even noticing that it has taken its otherwise legitimate concepts beyond the limits of their use.

§ 34. Two important, and even indispensable, though very dry, investigations were therefore necessary in the *Critique of Pure Reason*—namely pp. 137, 235.[15] In the former it is shown that the senses do not furnish the pure concepts of the understanding *in concreto*, but rather only the schemata for their use and that the object conformable to it occurs only in experience (as a product of the understanding from the materials of sensibility). In the latter it is shown that, although the pure concepts and principles of our understanding are independent of experience and despite the apparently greater sphere of their use, nothing whatsoever can be thought by them

---

14. [Kant is referring here to the chapter in the *Critique of Pure Reason* that develops his doctrine of sensibility, that is, the Transcendental Aesthetic, A19–49/B33–73.]

15. [Kant is referring here to "The Schematism of the Pure Concepts of the Understanding" and "On the Basis of the Distinction of all Concepts of the Understanding into Phenomena and Noumena."]

beyond the field of experience, because they can do nothing but merely determine the logical form of judgment relative to given intuitions. But since there is no intuition at all beyond the field of sensibility, these pure concepts are void of all meaning, because they cannot possibly be exhibited *in concreto*; consequently all these noumena, together with their sum, the intelligible world,[16] are nothing but representations of a problem, whose object is possible in itself, but whose solution is totally impossible according to the nature of our understanding. For our understanding is not a faculty of intuition, but merely one of the connection of given intuitions in one experience. Experience must therefore contain all objects for our concepts; but beyond it no concepts have any significance, since there is no intuition that could underlie them.

§ 35. The imagination may perhaps be forgiven for occasional flights of fancy and for not keeping carefully within the limits of experience, since it gains life and vigor by such flights and since it is always easier to moderate its boldness than to stimulate its languor. But the understanding which ought to *think* can never be forgiven for indulging in such flights; for we depend upon it alone for assistance to set limits, where necessary, to the flights of the imagination.

But the understanding begins its aberrations very innocently and modestly. It first straightens out the elementary cognitions, which inhere in it prior to all experience, but which still must always have their application in experience. It gradually drops these restrictions, and what is there to prevent it, since it has quite freely derived its principles from itself? And then it proceeds first to newly-imagined powers in nature, then shortly thereafter to beings outside

nature, in short to a world, for whose construction the materials cannot be wanting, because they can be furnished abundantly through fertile fiction, and though it is not confirmed, it is also never refuted by experience. This is the reason that young thinkers are so partial to metaphysics of the truly dogmatic kind and often sacrifice to it their time and their talents, which might be better employed in other ways.

But there is no use in trying to moderate these fruitless endeavors of pure reason by all kinds of reminders as to the difficulties of solving questions so occult, by complaints about the limits of our reason, and by degrading our assertions into mere conjectures. For if their *impossibility* is not distinctly shown and reason's *cognition of itself* does not become a true science in which the field of its legitimate use is distinguished, so to speak, with mathematical certainty from that of its worthless and idle use, these fruitless efforts will never be abandoned for good.

§ 36. *How is nature itself possible?*                    318

This question—the highest point that transcendental philosophy can ever reach, and to which it must proceed for its limits and completion—actually contains two questions.

*First*: How is nature in the *material* sense, namely according to intuition, considered as the sum of appearances possible in general? How are space, time, and that which fills both, the object of sensation, possible in general? The answer is: By means of the constitution of our sensibility, according to which it is affected in its own unique way by objects that in themselves are unknown to it and totally distinct from its appearances. This answer is given in the *Critique* itself in the Transcendental Aesthetic and in these *Prolegomena* by the solution of the first main problem.

*Secondly*: How is nature possible in the *formal* sense, as the sum of the rules to which all appearances must be subject in order to be thought as connected in one experience? The answer must be this: It is possible only by means of the constitution of our understanding, according to which all the representations of sensibility are necessarily referred to one consciousness and by which the unique way in which we think (namely by rules), and hence experience also,

16. We speak of the *intelligible* world, not (as it is typically expressed) the *intellectual* world. For *cognitions* are *intellectual* through the understanding and also refer to our world of sense; but, insofar as *objects* can be represented *merely by the understanding* and to which none of our sensible intuitions can refer, they are termed "intelligible." But since some possible intuition must correspond to every object, we would have to assume an understanding that intuits things immediately; but we do not have the least notion of such an understanding, nor do we have a notion of the *beings of the understanding* to which it is to be applied.

are possible, but must be clearly distinguished from insight into the objects in themselves. This answer is given in the *Critique* in the Transcendental Logic and in these *Prolegomena* in the course of the solution of the second main problem.

But how this unique property of our sensibility itself or that of our understanding and of the apperception that is necessarily the basis of it and of all its thinking is possible cannot be analyzed further or answered, because it is to them that we must take recourse for all our answers and for all our thought about objects.

There are many laws of nature that we can know only by means of experience, but conformity to law in the connection of appearances, i.e., in nature in 319 general, we cannot discover by any experience, because experience itself requires laws that underlie its possibility *a priori*.

The possibility of experience in general is therefore at the same time the universal law of nature and the principles of the former are themselves the laws of the latter. For we know nature only as the sum of appearances, i.e., of representations in us, and hence we can derive the laws of their connection only from the principles of their connection in us, that is, from the conditions of their necessary unification in one consciousness, which constitutes the possibility of experience.

Even the main proposition expounded throughout this section—that universal laws of nature can be distinctly cognized *a priori*—naturally leads to the proposition: that the highest legislation of nature must lie in ourselves, i.e., in our understanding, and that we must not seek the universal laws of nature in nature by means of experience, but conversely must seek nature, as to its universal conformity to law, in the conditions of the possibility of experience, which lie in our sensibility and in our understanding. For otherwise how would it be possible to know these laws *a priori*, since they are not rules of analytic cognition, but truly synthetic extensions of it? Such a necessary agreement of the principles of possible experience with the laws of the possibility of nature can occur for only one of two reasons: either these laws are taken from nature by means of experience or, conversely, nature is derived from the laws of the possibility of

experience in general and is quite the same as the mere universal conformity to law of the latter. The former is self-contradictory, for the universal laws of nature can and must be cognized *a priori* (that is, independently of all experience) and constitute the foundation of all empirical use of the understanding. Therefore, only the latter alternative remains.[17]

But we must distinguish the empirical laws of na- 320 ture, which always presuppose special perceptions, from the pure or universal laws of nature, which, without being based on particular perceptions, merely contain the conditions of their necessary unification in experience. In light of the latter, nature and possible experience are quite the same and since the conformity to law here depends upon the necessary connection of appearances in one experience (without which we cannot cognize any object whatsoever in the sensible world), consequently upon the original laws of the understanding, it seems at first strange, but is not the less certain, to say: *The understanding does not derive its laws (a priori) from, but rather prescribes them to nature*.

§ 37. We shall illustrate this seemingly bold proposition by an example, which will show that the laws we discover in objects of sensible intuition (especially when these laws are cognized as necessary) are already held by us to be such as have been placed there by the understanding, although they are otherwise similar in all points to the laws of nature we ascribe to experience.

§ 38. If we consider the properties of the circle by which this figure combines in itself so many arbitrary determinations of space at once in a universal rule, we cannot avoid attributing a nature to this geometrical thing. For example, two lines that intersect one another and the circle, however they may be drawn, are always divided so that the rectangle constructed

---

17. Crusius alone thought of a compromise: namely that a spirit who can neither err nor deceive implanted these laws of nature in us originally. But since false principles often get mixed in, as indeed the very system of this man shows in not a few examples, the use of such a principle in the absence of sure criteria to distinguish a genuine origin from a spurious one appears very difficult, since we never can know with certainty what the spirit of truth or the father of lies may have instilled into us.

with the segments of the one is equal to that constructed with the segments of the other. The question now is: Does this law lie in the circle or in the understanding? That is, does this figure contain in itself the ground of the law independently of the understanding or does the understanding, having constructed the figure itself according to its concepts (i.e., according to the equality of the radii), introduce into it this law of the chords intersecting one another in geometrical proportion? When we follow the proofs of this law, we soon perceive that it can be derived only from the condition that the understanding assumes for the construction of this figure, namely the equality of the radii. But if we enlarge this concept to pursue further the unity of various properties of geometrical figures under common laws and consider the circle as a conic section, which of course is subject to the same fundamental conditions of construction as other conic sections, we shall find that all the chords that intersect within the ellipse, parabola, and hyperbola always intersect so that the rectangles of their segments are not indeed equal, but always bear a constant ratio to one another. If we proceed still farther to the fundamental doctrines of physical astronomy, we find a physical law of reciprocal attraction diffused over all material nature, the rule of which states that it decreases inversely as the square of the distance from each attracting point, i.e., as the spherical surfaces increase, over which this force spreads. This law seems to be necessarily inherent in the very nature of things and hence is usually propounded as cognizable *a priori*. As simple as the sources of this law are, resting merely upon the relation of spherical surfaces of different radii, its consequences are equally valuable with regard to the variety of their agreement and regularity so that not only are all possible orbits of the celestial bodies conic sections, but a relation of these orbits to each other arises so that no law of attraction other than that of the inverse square of the distance can be imagined as fit for a cosmological system.

Here, accordingly, is a nature that rests upon laws which the understanding cognizes *a priori* and primarily from the universal principles of the determination of space. Now I ask: Do the laws of nature lie in space and does the understanding learn them merely by trying to find out the enormous wealth of meaning that lies in space or do they inhere in the understanding and in the way in which it determines space according to the conditions of the synthetic unity that governs all of its concepts? Space is something so uniform and, with respect to all special properties, so indeterminate that we should certainly not seek a treasure of natural laws in it. By contrast, what determines space to assume the form of a circle or the figures of a cone and a sphere is the understanding insofar as it contains the ground of the unity of their constructions. The mere universal form of intuition, called space, must therefore be the substratum of all intuitions that could be determined as particular objects and of course the condition of the possibility and of the variety of these intuitions lies in it, but the unity of the objects is determined entirely by the understanding and according to conditions that lie in its own nature. Thus the understanding is the origin of the universal order of nature in that it comprehends all appearances under its own laws and thereby first constructs *a priori* experience (as to its form), by means of which whatever is to be cognized only through experience is necessarily subjected to its laws. For we are not concerned with the nature of things in themselves, which is independent of the conditions of both our sensibility and our understanding, but rather with nature as an object of possible experience, and in this case, by making experience possible, the understanding brings it about that the sensible world either is not an object of experience at all or must be nature.

## Appendix To Pure Natural Science

### § 39. *Of the System of the Categories*

Nothing can be more desirable to a philosopher than to be able to derive *a priori* from one principle the various concepts or principles that had occurred to him in their concrete use and to unite everything in this way in one cognition. Formerly he believed only that those things that remained after a certain abstraction and seemed, by comparing one another, to constitute a special kind of cognition were completely collected;

but this was only an *aggregate*. Now he knows that precisely this many, neither more nor less, can constitute this kind of cognition and he perceives the necessity of his division, which is comprehension; and only now does he have a *system*.

323     To search our common knowledge for concepts that do not rest upon particular experience and yet occur in all cognition of experience, where they, as it were, constitute the mere form of connection, presupposes neither greater reflection nor deeper insight than it does to detect in a language the rules of the actual use of words in general and thus to collect elements for a grammar. In fact both inquiries are very closely related, even though we are not able to give a reason why each language has just this and no other formal constitution and still less why any precise number of such formal determinations are found in it in general.

    Aristotle collected ten such pure elementary concepts under the name of categories.[18] To these, which were also called predicaments, he found himself obliged afterwards to add five post-predicaments,[19] some of which, however, (*prius, simul,* and *motus*) are contained in the former. However, this rhapsodic collection could be considered and commended more as a mere hint for future inquirers than as a properly developed idea and hence, in a more enlightened state of philosophy, it has been rejected as completely useless.

    After long reflection on the pure elements of human knowledge (containing nothing empirical), I at last succeeded in distinguishing with certainty and in separating the pure elementary concepts of sensibility (space and time) from those of the understanding. Thus the seventh, eighth, and ninth categories had to be excluded from the former list. And the others were of no service to me, because there was no principle according to which the understanding could be measured out fully, and all the functions from which its pure concepts arise determined exhaustively and with precision.

---

18. 1. *Substantia.* 2. *Qualitas.* 3. *Quantitas.* 4. *Relatio.* 5. *Actio.* 6. *Passio.* 7. *Quando.* 8. *Ubi.* 9. *Situs.* 10. *Habitus.*
19. *Oppositum. Prius. Simul. Motus. Habere.*

But in order to discover such a principle, I looked around for an act of the understanding which contains all the rest and is distinguished only by various modifications or moments, in bringing the multiplicity of representation to the unity of thinking in general: I found that this act of the understanding consists in judging. Now the labors of logicians were already present, though not yet completely free of defects, and with this help I was able to exhibit a complete table of the pure functions of the under- 324 standing, which are, however, indeterminate with respect to any object. I finally referred these functions of judging to objects in general or rather to the condition of determining judgments as objectively valid, and in this way arose the pure concepts of the understanding, concerning which I could be sure that these, and this exact number only, constitute our entire cognition of things from mere understanding. I was justified in calling them by their old name, *categories,* while I reserved for myself the liberty of adding, under the title of *predicables,* a complete list of all the concepts deducible from them through combinations—whether among themselves or with the pure form of the appearance (space or time) or with its matter insofar as it is not yet empirically determined (the object of sensation in general)—as soon as a system of transcendental philosophy could be completed—on behalf of which I was engaged in the *Critique of Pure Reason* itself.

    Now the essential point in this system of categories, which distinguishes it from the old rhapsodic collection that proceeded without any principle, and for which reason alone it deserved to be considered as philosophy, consists in this: that by means of it the true significance of the pure concepts of the understanding and the condition of their use could be precisely determined. For here it became obvious that they are themselves nothing but logical functions and as such do not constitute the least concept of an object in itself, but require some sensible intuition as a basis. They therefore serve only to determine empirical judgments (which are otherwise undetermined and indifferent as regards all functions of judging), relative to these functions, thereby furnishing them with universal validity, and by means of them making *judgments of experience* in general possible.

Such an insight into the nature of the categories, which at the same time limits them to the mere use of experience, never occurred either to their first author or to any of his successors; but without this insight (which depends immediately upon their derivation or deduction), they are quite useless and only a miserable list of names, without explanation and a rule for their use. Had the ancients ever conceived such a notion, doubtless the whole study of pure rational cognition—which, under the name of metaphysics, has for centuries spoiled many a sound mind—would have reached us in quite a different form and enlightened the human understanding instead of actually exhausting it in obscure and vain speculations and rendering it unfit for true science.

325

This system of categories makes all treatment of every object of pure reason itself systematic and provides an indubitable hint or clue as to how and through what points of inquiry every metaphysical consideration must proceed in order to be complete; for it exhausts all the possible moments (*momenta*) of the understanding, under which every other concept must be classified. In this way the table of principles arose, the completeness of which we can only vouch for by the system of the categories. Even in the division of concepts that must extend beyond the physiological application of the understanding (p. 334, p. 415)[20], it is the very same clue that always forms a closed circle, since it must always be determined *a priori* by the same fixed points of the human understanding. There is no doubt that the object of a

pure concept either of the understanding or of reason insofar as it is to be considered philosophically and according to *a priori* principles can be completely cognized in this way. I could not even refrain from making use of this clue with respect to one of the most abstract ontological divisions, namely the various distinctions of "the concepts of something and of nothing," and to construct a regular and necessary table of their divisions (*Critique*, p. 207)[21] accordingly.[22]

And this system, like every other true one founded on a universal principle, also shows its inestimable value in that it excludes all foreign concepts that might otherwise slip in among the pure concepts of the understanding, and determines the place of every cognition. Those concepts, which under the name of *concepts of reflection* have similarly been arranged in a table according to the clue of the categories, enter into ontology without having any privilege or legitimate claim to be among the pure concepts of the understanding. The latter are concepts of connection and thereby of the objects themselves, whereas the former are only concepts of the mere comparison of concepts already given, hence of quite another nature and use. By my systematic division[23] they are separated from this conflation. But the value of my separate table of the categories will be even more obvious when we distinguish the table of the transcendental concepts of reason from the concepts of the understanding, as we are about to do. Since the transcendental concepts of reason are of a completely different nature and origin, their form must be completely different from that of the table of categories. As necessary as this separation is, it has never

326

---

20. [See B402, B442–43.]

21. [See B348.]

22. On the table of the categories many nice observations may be made, for instance: (1) that the third arises from the first and the second combined into one concept; (2) that in those of magnitude and quality there is merely a progress from unity to totality or from something to nothing (for this purpose the categories of quality must stand thus: reality, limitation, total negation) without *correlata* or *opposita*, whereas those of relation and modality have them; (3) that, as in logic categorical judgments are the basis of all others, so the category of substance is the basis of all concepts of actual things; (4) that, as modality is not a particular predicate in judgment, so too the modal concepts

do not add a further determination to things, etc. Such observations are all of great use. If beyond this we enumerate all the *predicables*, which we can find in nearly complete form in any good ontology (for example, Baumgarten's), and arrange them in classes under the categories, where we must not neglect to add as complete a dissection of all these concepts as possible, a merely analytical part of metaphysics will then arise that does not contain a single synthetic proposition, which might precede the latter (the synthetic part), and which would by its precision and completeness be not only useful, but, in virtue of its systematic character, even elegant to some extent.

23. [See *Critique of Pure Reason*, The Amphiboly of the Concepts of Reflection, A260ff./B316ff.]

been made in any system of metaphysics, for, as a rule, these ideas of reason are all mixed up with the categories as if they were children of one family—a confusion that was unavoidable in the absence of a definite system of categories.

327    The Main Transcendental Problem: Part Three

How is metaphysics in general possible?

§ 40. Pure mathematics and pure natural science did not need for their own safety and certainty a deduction of the sort that we have provided for both. For the former rests upon its own evidence and the latter, though it arises from pure sources of the understanding, rests upon experience and its thorough confirmation. Physics cannot altogether refuse and dispense with the testimony of experience, because with all its certainty as [natural] philosophy it can never rival mathematics. Both sciences therefore stood in need of this inquiry, not for themselves, but for the sake of another science, namely metaphysics.

Metaphysics is concerned not only with concepts of nature, which always find their application in experience, but also with pure rational concepts, which can never be given in any possible experience whatsoever. Consequently the objective reality of these concepts (namely that they are not mere chimeras) and the truth or falsity of metaphysical assertions cannot be discovered or confirmed by any experience. This part of metaphysics, however, is precisely what constitutes its essential end, to which the rest is only a means, and thus this science is in need of such a deduction *for its own sake*. Therefore, the third question now proposed relates, as it were, to the core and unique feature of metaphysics, namely reason's occupation with itself and its acquaintance with objects that allegedly arise immediately from pondering its own concepts, without requiring or even being able to establish this acquaintance through experience.[24]

_____

24. If we can say that a science is *actual* at least in the idea of all men as soon as it is clear that the problems that lead to it are proposed to everybody by the nature of human reason and that therefore many (though faulty) attempts are unavoidably made on its behalf, then we are bound to say that metaphysics is subjectively (and indeed necessarily) actual and thus we justly ask how it is (objectively) possible.

Without solving this problem reason can never satisfy itself. The empirical use to which reason limits the pure understanding does not fully satisfy reason's own complete vocation. Every single experience is    328 only a part of the whole sphere of its domain, but the *absolute totality of all possible experience* is itself not experience, though it is a necessary problem for reason, the mere representation of which requires concepts quite different from the categories, whose use is only *immanent*, i.e., refers to experience insofar as it can be given. By contrast, the concepts of reason aim at completeness, i.e., the collective unity of all possible experience, thereby transcend every given experience, and become *transcendent*.

Just as the understanding needs the categories for experience, reason contains in itself the source of ideas, by which I mean necessary concepts, whose object cannot be given in any experience. The latter inhere in the nature of reason as much as the former do in the nature of the understanding. And if the former carry with them an illusion likely to mislead, this illusion is inevitable, though it can certainly be kept from misleading us.

Since all illusion consists in holding the subjective basis of our judgments to be objective, pure reason's self-knowledge in its transcendent (exaggerated) use is the only means of prevention against the aberrations into which reason falls when it misinterprets its vocation and, in transcendent fashion, refers to the object in itself that which concerns only its own subject and its guidance in all immanent use.

§ 41. The distinction between *ideas*, that is, pure concepts of reason, and categories or pure concepts of the understanding, as cognitions of completely different kinds, origins, and uses, is so important a point in the foundations of a science that is to contain the system of all these *a priori* cognitions that without this    329 distinction metaphysics is absolutely impossible or is at best a random, bungling attempt to build a house of cards without knowledge of the materials at hand or of their fitness for any purpose. Had the *Critique of Pure Reason* achieved nothing but first point out this distinction, it would thereby have contributed more to clearing up our conception of and to guiding our inquiry in the field of metaphysics than all the vain efforts which have been made until now to satisfy the transcendent problems of pure reason, without even suspecting that we were in quite another field than that of the understanding, and hence that we were classifying concepts of the understanding and those of reason together as if they were of the same kind.

§ 42. All pure cognitions of the understanding have the feature that their concepts are given in experience and their principles can be confirmed by it. By contrast, the transcendent cognitions of reason cannot appear in experience as *ideas* or be confirmed or refuted by it as *propositions*. For that reason, whatever errors may creep in can only be discovered by pure reason itself—a discovery of great difficulty because it is precisely pure reason that naturally becomes dialectical by means of its ideas and this unavoidable illusion cannot be held in check by any objective and dogmatic inquiries into things, but rather only by a subjective investigation of reason itself as a source of ideas.

§ 43. In the *Critique of Pure Reason* it was always my greatest care to endeavor not only to distinguish carefully several kinds of cognition but also to derive concepts belonging to each kind from their common source. I did this so that, by knowing their origin, I might not only determine their use with certainty but also have the unexpected, but invaluable advantage of knowing the completeness of my enumeration, classification, and specification of concepts *a priori* 330 and thus according to principles. Without this, everything in metaphysics is mere rhapsody, in which no one knows whether what one has is enough or whether and where something is missing. We can of course have this advantage only in pure philosophy, but it also constitutes its very essence.

Since I had discovered the origin of the categories in the four logical functions of all the judgments of the understanding, it was quite natural to seek the origin of the ideas in the three functions of syllogisms. For as soon as such pure concepts of reason (the transcendental ideas) are given, unless one wanted to view them as innate they could hardly be found anywhere other than in the same activity of reason that constitutes the logical element of syllogisms insofar as it concerns mere form; but, insofar as it represents judgments of the understanding as determined *a priori* with respect to one or the other of its forms, it constitutes transcendental concepts of pure reason.

The formal distinction of syllogisms necessitates their division into categorical, hypothetical, and disjunctive. The concepts of reason based on them therefore contained, first, the idea of the complete subject (the substantial); secondly, the idea of the complete series of conditions; thirdly, the determination of all concepts in the idea of the complete sum of what is possible.[25] The first idea was psychological, the second cosmological, the third theological, and, since all three occasion a dialectic, albeit each in its own way, the division of the whole Dialectic of Pure Reason into its Paralogism, its Antinomy, and its Ideal, was arranged accordingly. Through this derivation one can feel completely assured that all the claims of pure reason are completely represented and that none can be wanting, because the faculty of the reason itself, from which they are all derived, is thereby completely surveyed.

§ 44. In these general considerations it is also  331 remarkable that the ideas of reason do not help us in the way that the categories do for the use of our understanding in experience, but are rather completely dispensable and even become an impediment to the maxims of a rational cognition of nature. However, in another respect that remains to be determined they are necessary. Whether the soul is or is not a simple substance is of no consequence to us in explaining its appearances. For by no possible experience can we make the concept of a simple being sensible and thus we cannot render it intelligible *in concreto*. The concept is therefore quite

---

25. In disjunctive judgments we consider *all possibility* as divided with respect to a particular concept. The ontological principle of the universal determination of a thing in general— either one or the other of all possible contradictory predicates must be assigned to each object—which is at the same time the principle of all disjunctive judgments, underlies the sum of all of possibility in which the possibility of every object in general is considered as determined. This may serve as a brief explanation of the above proposition: that the activity of reason in disjunctive syllogisms is formally the same as that by which it brings about the idea of the sum of all reality, containing in itself what is positive in all contradictory predicates.

empty as regards all hoped-for insight into the cause of appearances and cannot at all serve as a principle for explaining what inner or outer experience supplies. In the same way the cosmological ideas of the beginning of the world or of its eternity (*a parte ante*) can be of no use to us in explaining any event in the world itself. And finally, according to a proper maxim of natural philosophy, we must refrain from all explanations of the design of nature, drawn from the will of a supreme being, because this would not be natural philosophy, but an admission that we have come to its end. Therefore, the use of these ideas is quite different from that of those categories by which (and by the principles built upon which) experience itself first becomes possible. But our laborious analysis of the understanding would be completely superfluous if we had nothing else in view than the mere cognition of nature as it can be given in experience; for both in mathematics and in natural science reason does its work quite safely and well without any such subtle deduction. Therefore our critique of the understanding is joined with the ideas of pure reason for a purpose that lies beyond the empirical use of the understanding; but above we declared such a use to be totally inadmissible in this respect and without any object or significance. Yet there must be a harmony between what belongs to the nature of reason and what belongs to the nature of the understanding, and the former must contribute to the perfection of the latter and cannot possibly confuse it.

332     The solution of this question is as follows: Pure reason does not in its ideas aim at particular objects that lie beyond the field of experience, but only requires completeness of the use of the understanding in the connection of experience. But this completeness can be a completeness of principles only, not of intuitions and of objects. However, in order to represent the ideas determinately, reason conceives them as the cognition of an object. This cognition is completely determined insofar as these rules are concerned, but the object is only an idea invented for the purpose of bringing the understanding's cognition as near as possible to the completeness indicated by that idea.

*§ 45. Prefatory Remark to the Dialectic of Pure Reason*—We have shown above in §§ 33 and 34 that the purity of the categories from all admixture of sensible determinations may mislead reason into extending their use beyond all experience to things in themselves. However, because these categories themselves find no intuition which can give them significance or sense *in concreto*, they, as mere logical functions, can represent a thing in general, but not provide a determinate concept of anything by themselves alone. Such hyperbolic objects are called *noumena* or pure beings of the understanding (or better, beings of thought), such as, for example, *substance*, but conceived *without permanence* in time, or *cause*, but *not* acting *in time*, etc. For predicates that serve only to make the conformity to law of experience possible are applied to these concepts, although they are deprived of all the conditions of intuition that alone make experience possible, by which, in turn, these concepts lose all significance.

There is no danger, however, of the understanding spontaneously making an excursion so very wantonly beyond its own limits into the field of the mere beings of thought without being impelled by foreign laws. But if reason, which cannot be fully satisfied with any empirical use of the rules of the understanding, since that is always conditioned, requires a completion of this chain of conditions, then the understanding is forced out of its sphere. If this happens, reason partly represents objects of experience in a   333 series that extends so far that no experience can grasp it and partly (with a view to complete the series) even seeks *noumena* entirely beyond it, to which reason can attach that chain, and so, having at last escaped from the conditions of experience, make its hold, as it were, complete. These are the transcendental ideas, and, though according to the true but hidden ends of the natural vocation of our reason they may aim, not at extravagant concepts, but at an unlimited extension of their empirical use, they may still seduce the understanding by an unavoidable illusion to a *transcendent* use, which, though deceitful, cannot be restrained within the limits of experience by any resolution, but only by scientific instruction and with difficulty.

### I. *The Psychological Idea*[26]

§ 46. Long ago people observed that in all substances the proper subject, namely what remains after all the accidents (as predicates) are abstracted, consequently the *substantial* itself is unknown and various complaints have been lodged about these limits to our insight. But it is appropriate to consider that the human understanding is to be blamed not for its inability to know the substantial of things, i.e., to determine it all by itself, but rather for asking to cognize determinately what is a mere idea as if it were a given object. Pure reason demands that we seek a proper subject for every predicate of a thing, and for this subject, which is itself necessarily nothing but a predicate, its subject, and so on indefinitely (or as far as we can reach). But from this it follows that we must not hold anything that we can attain to be an ultimate subject and that substance itself can never be thought by our understanding, however deeply we may penetrate and even if all of nature were revealed to us. For the specific nature of our understanding consists in thinking everything discursively, i.e., by concepts, and so by mere predicates, for which therefore the absolute subject must always be lacking. For this reason all real properties by which we cognize bodies are simply accidents, even impenetrability, which we can represent to ourselves only as the effect of a force for which we lack the subject.

Now it appears as if we have this substantial in our consciousness of ourselves (in the thinking subject), and indeed in an immediate intuition; for all the predicates of inner sense refer to the *I* as a subject and this cannot be thought as the predicate of any other subject. For this reason completeness with respect to given concepts as predicates to a subject—not merely an idea, but an object—namely the *absolute subject* itself, seems to be given in experience. But this expectation is disappointed. For the *I* is not a concept,[27] but rather only an indication of the object of inner sense insofar as we cognize it by no further

predicate. Consequently, in itself it cannot be a predicate of any other thing; however, just as little can it be a determinate concept of an absolute subject, since it is, as in all other cases, only the relation of inner appearances to their unknown subject. Yet this idea (which serves very well as a regulative principle, completely destroying all materialistic explanations of inner appearances of our soul) occasions by a very natural misunderstanding a very specious argument, which, from this supposed cognition of the substantial aspect of our thinking being, infers its nature insofar as our acquaintance with it falls entirely outside the sum of experience.

§ 47. Now, although we may call this thinking self (the soul) substance, as the ultimate subject of thought that cannot be represented further as the predicate of another thing, this concept remains quite empty and without any consequences, if permanence—which is what renders the concept of substance fruitful in experience—cannot be proved of it.

But permanence can never be proved from the concept of a substance as a thing in itself, but for the purposes of experience only. This is sufficiently shown by the First Analogy of Experience,[28] and whoever does not wish to grant this proof may try for himself whether he can succeed in proving, from the concept of a subject that does not exist itself as the predicate of another thing, that its existence is thoroughly permanent and that it cannot come into or go out of existence either in itself or by any natural cause. Such synthetic *a priori* propositions can never be proved in themselves, but only in reference to things as objects of possible experience.

§ 48. Therefore, if we want to infer from the concept of the soul as a substance to its permanence, this can hold good of the soul only for possible experience and not of the soul as a thing in itself and beyond all possible experience. But life is the subjective condition of all our possible experience. Consequently, we can infer the permanence of the soul only in life; for the death of man is the end of all experience which

335

334

---

26. [See *Critique of Pure Reason*, On the Paralogisms of Pure Reason.]

27. If the representation of apperception (the *I*) were a concept by which something could be thought, it could be used as a predicate for other things or contain such predicates in itself.

---

Now, it is nothing more than a feeling of an existence without the least concept and is only a representation of that to which all thinking stands in relation as an accident (*relatione accidentis*).

28. [Cf. *Critique*, A182/B224.]

concerns the soul as an object of experience, unless the contrary has been proved, which is the very question at hand. Thus, the permanence of the soul can be proved only during the life of man (which one will readily grant), but not, as we desire to do, after death (which is our real interest); and for this general reason: that the concept of substance insofar as it is to be considered as necessarily combined with the concept of permanence can be combined in this way only according to the principles of possible experience and therefore only for the purposes of experience.[29]

336    § 49. That something real outside us not only corresponds but must correspond to our outer perceptions can likewise never be proved as a connection of things in themselves, but can be proven for the sake of experience. This means that there is something empirical, i.e., some appearance in space outside us that admits of a satisfactory proof. For we have nothing to do with objects other than those that belong to possible experience, precisely because such objects cannot be given to us in any experience and thus are nothing for us. Outside me empirically is that which appears

---

29. It is indeed very remarkable how carelessly metaphysicians have always passed over the principle of the permanence of substances without ever attempting a proof of it; it is doubtless because they found themselves abandoned by all means of proof as soon as they began to consider the concept of substance. Common sense, which was clearly aware that no unification of perceptions in experience is possible without this presupposition, remedied this defect with a postulate. For it could never derive such a principle from experience itself, partly because it could not trace matters (substances) in all their alterations and dissolutions far enough to find the matter always undiminished, partly because the principle contains *necessity* which is always the sign of an *a priori* principle. They then boldly applied this postulate to the concept of the soul as a *substance* and concluded a necessary continuance of the soul after the death of man (especially since the simplicity of this substance, which is inferred from the indivisibility of consciousness, secured it from destruction by dissolution). Had they found the genuine source of this principle—a discovery which requires deeper inquiry than they were ever inclined to make—they would have seen that this law of the permanence of substances occurs only for the purposes of experience and hence can hold good only of things insofar as they are to be cognised and conjoined with others in experience, but never of them independently of all possible experience and consequently cannot hold good of the soul after death.

in space, and since space, together with all the appearances it contains, belongs to those representations whose connection according to laws of experience proves their objective truth just as the connection of the appearances of inner sense proves the actuality of my soul (as an object of inner sense), I am conscious of the actuality of bodies in space as outer appearances (by means of outer experience) in the same manner as I am conscious of the existence of my soul in time (by means of inner experience)—which soul is cognized only as an object of inner sense by appearances that constitute an inner state and of which the essence in itself, which underlies these appearances, is unknown. Cartesian idealism therefore only distinguishes outer experience from dreaming and the conformity to law  337 of the former (as a criterion of its truth) from the irregularity and the false illusion of the latter. In both it presupposes space and time as conditions of the existence of objects and asks only whether the objects of outer senses, which we put in space when we are awake, are actually to be found in it just as the object of inner sense, the soul, is in time; that is, whether experience carries with it sure criteria to distinguish it from imagination. This doubt, however, may easily be disposed of and we always do so in common life by investigating the connection of appearances in both space and time according to universal laws of experience, and we cannot doubt that they constitute truthful experience when the representation of outer things are in complete agreement. Material idealism, in which appearances are considered as such only according to their connection in experience, may accordingly be refuted very easily; and it is just as sure an experience that bodies exist outside us (in space) as that I myself exist according to the representation of inner sense (in time): for the concept *outside us* signifies only existence in space. However, since the I in the proposition, "I am," means not only the object of inner intuition (in time) but also the subject of consciousness, just as body means not only outer intuition (in space) but also the thing *in itself* that underlies this appearance; the question, whether bodies (as appearances of outer sense) exist in nature as bodies *apart from my thoughts*, may be denied without any hesitation. The question, whether I myself as an *appearance of inner sense* (the soul according to empirical psychology) exist apart from my faculty of representation in time, is no different and must likewise be answered in the negative. And in this manner everything, when it is reduced to its true meaning, is decided and certain. Formal idealism (which I have also called transcendental) actually refutes material or Cartesian idealism. For if space is nothing but a form of my sensibility, as a representation in me it is just as actual as I myself am and nothing but the empirical truth of the representations in it remains to be considered. But, if this is not the case, if space and the appearances in it are something existing outside us, then all the criteria of experience beyond our perception can never prove the actuality of these objects outside us.

338     II. The Cosmological Idea[30]

§ 50. This product of pure reason in its transcendent use is reason's most remarkable phenomenon and serves as a very powerful agent to rouse philosophy from its dogmatic slumber and to stimulate it to the arduous task of undertaking a critique of reason itself.

I call this idea cosmological, because it always takes its object only from the sensible world and does not need any world other than one whose object is of the senses; consequently, to this extent it stays at home, does not become transcendent, and is therefore not yet an idea; by contrast, to conceive the soul as a simple substance already means to conceive an object (the simple) that cannot be represented by means of the senses. In spite of this, the cosmological idea extends the connection of the conditioned with its condition (whether the connection is mathematical or dynamical) so far that experience can never keep up with it. In light of this point, it is therefore always an idea, whose object can never be given adequately in any experience.

§ 51. In the first place, the usefulness of a system of categories is revealed here so clearly and unmistakably that even if there were not several other proofs of it, this alone would sufficiently establish its indispensability in the system of pure reason. There are no more than four such transcendent ideas—just as many as

there are classes of categories; in each of which, however, they aim only at the absolute completeness of the series of the conditions for a given conditioned. According to these cosmological ideas, there are also only four kinds of dialectical assertions of pure reason, which, since they are dialectical, themselves thereby prove that each of them is opposed by a contradictory assertion, where both are based on specious principles of pure reason. All metaphysical tricks of the most subtle distinction cannot prevent this opposition, which rather compels the philosopher to return to     339 the first sources of pure reason itself. This antinomy, which is not arbitrarily invented, but founded in the nature of human reason, and is hence unavoidable and never-ending, contains the following four theses together with their antitheses:

**1.**
*Thesis.*
The world has *a beginning* (limit) with respect to time and space.
*Antithesis.*
The world is *infinite* with respect to time and space.

**2.**
*Thesis.*
Everything in the world consists of the *simple*.
*Antithesis.*
There is nothing simple; rather, everything is *composite*.

**3.**
*Thesis.*
There are in the world causes through *freedom*.
*Antithesis.*
There is no freedom; rather, everything is *nature*.

**4.**
*Thesis.*
In the series of causes in the world there is some *necessary being*.
*Antithesis.*
There is nothing necessary in it; rather, in this series *everything* is *contingent*.

---

30. [Cf. *Critique of Pure Reason*, The Antinomy of Pure Reason (A405ff./B432ff.).]

§ 52. a. This is the strangest phenomenon of human reason, no other instance of which can be shown in any of its other uses. If, as is commonly done, we represent to ourselves the appearances of the sensible world as things in themselves and if we assume that the principles of their combination are principles universally valid of things in themselves and not merely of experience (as is usually done and, in fact, unavoidably done without our *Critique*), an unexpected conflict arises that can never be removed in the common dogmatic way, because the thesis as well as the antithesis can be established by equally clear, evident, and irresistible proofs—for I will vouch for the correctness of all these proofs—and reason therefore perceives that it is at odds with itself, a condition at which the skeptic rejoices, but which must make the critical philosopher pause and feel ill at ease.

340  § 52. b. In metaphysics we may blunder in various ways without any fear of entering into falsehood. For we can never be refuted by experience if only we avoid self-contradiction, which in synthetic but purely fictitious propositions may be done whenever the concepts we connect are mere ideas that cannot be given (according to their entire content) in experience. For how can we discover in experience whether the world is eternal or had a beginning, whether matter is infinitely divisible or consists of simple parts? Such concepts cannot be given in any experience, regardless of how extensive it might be, and consequently the falsehood of either the affirmative or the negative proposition cannot be discovered by this touchstone.

The only possible case where reason would have to reveal, against its will, its secret dialectics (which it falsely passes off as dogmatics), would be if it based an assertion upon a universally admitted principle and also deduced the exact opposite with the greatest accuracy of reasoning from another principle that is equally attested to. This is actually the case here with respect to four natural ideas of reason, from which four assertions arise, on the one hand, and as many counter-assertions, on the other, each consistently following from universally acknowledged principles. In this way they reveal the dialectical illusion of pure

reason in the use of these principles which otherwise would have forever remained concealed.

This, therefore, is a decisive experiment, which must necessarily expose any fault that lies hidden in  341  the assumptions of reason.[31] Contradictory propositions cannot both be false, unless the concept that underlies both is self-contradictory. For example, the propositions: "a square circle is round" and "a square circle is not round" are both false. For, as to the former, it is false that the circle is round, because it is quadrangular. It is likewise false that it is not round, that is, has angles, because it is a circle. For the logical criterion of the impossibility of a concept consists precisely in the fact that if we presuppose it, two contradictory propositions both become false; consequently, since no middle between them is conceivable, nothing at all is thought by that concept.

§ 52. c. The first two antinomies, which I call mathematical because they are concerned with the addition or division of the homogeneous, are based on such a self-contradictory concept; and this allows me to explain how it happens that the Thesis and Antithesis are false in both cases.

When I speak of objects in time and space, I am speaking not of things in themselves, because I know nothing of things in themselves, but only of things in appearance, i.e., of experience as the special way of cognizing objects which is bestowed upon man alone. I must not say of what I think in time or in space that in itself and independent of this thought of mine, it exists in space and in time. For in that case I would contradict myself, because space and time, together with the appearances in them, do not exist in themselves and outside of my representations, but

---

31. For that reason, I would be pleased to have the critical reader devote his attention mainly to this antinomy of pure reason, because nature itself seems to have established it in order to cause reason to hesitate in its daring pretentions and to force it to self-examination. I hold myself responsible for every proof I have given of the thesis as well as of the antithesis, and thereby establish the certainty of the inevitable antinomy of reason. When the reader is brought by this curious phenomenon to fall back upon the proof of the assumption upon which it rests, he will feel himself obliged to investigate more thoroughly with me the ultimate foundation of all cognition of pure reason.

342 are themselves only modes of representation, and it is palpably contradictory to say that a mere mode of representation also exists outside our representation. Objects of the senses therefore exist only in experience; by contrast, to give them a self-subsisting existence apart from experience or prior to it is merely to represent to ourselves that experience actually exists apart from experience or prior to it.

Now if I inquire into the magnitude of the world with respect to space and time, it is equally impossible with respect to all my concepts to say either that it is it infinite or that it is finite. For neither assertion can be contained in experience, because it is impossible to experience either an infinite space or an infinite elapsed time, or the *limitation* of the world by an empty space or an antecedent empty time; these are mere ideas. The magnitude of the world, which is determined one way or the other, should therefore exist in the world itself apart from all experience. But this contradicts the concept of the sensible world, which is merely the sum of the appearances whose existence and connection occur only in our representations, that is, in experience, since this latter is not an object in itself, but a mere mode of representation. From this it follows that because the concept of the sensible world existing for itself is self-contradictory, the solution of the problem concerning its magnitude is always false, whether it is resolved affirmatively or negatively.

The same holds good of the second antinomy, which concerns the division of appearances. For they are mere representations and the parts exist merely in their representation, consequently in the division, i.e., in a possible experience in which they are given, and the division reaches only as far as possible experience reaches. To assume that an appearance, e. g., that of body, contains in itself prior to all experience all the parts that any possible experience can ever reach is to attribute to a mere appearance, which can exist only in experience, an existence preceding experience. In other words, it would mean that mere representations exist before they can be found in our faculty of representation. Such an assertion is self-contradictory as is every solution to our misunderstood problem, whether we maintain that bodies

in themselves consist of infinitely many parts or of a finite number of simple parts.

§ 53. In the first (mathematical) class of antino- 343 mies the falsehood of the assumption consisted in representing something self-contradictory (namely an appearance as an object in itself) as if it could be consistently combined in one concept. But, regarding the second (dynamical) class of antinomies, the falsehood of the representation consists in representing as contradictory what can be combined. Consequently, whereas the opposed assertions were both false in the former case, in this case, where they are opposed to one another by a mere misunderstanding, they may both be true.

Specifically, mathematical connection necessarily presupposes the homogeneity of what is connected (in the concept of magnitude), while dynamical connection by no means requires the same. When we are concerned with the magnitude of what is extended, all of its parts must be homogeneous with one another and with the whole. By contrast, in the connection of cause and effect, homogeneity may indeed likewise be found, but it is not necessary. For at least the concept of causality (by means of which something is posited through something else quite different from it) does not require it.

If the objects of the sensible world are taken for things in themselves and the above laws of nature for the laws of things in themselves, the contradiction would be unavoidable. Similarly, if the subject of freedom were represented as mere appearance, like the remaining objects are, the contradiction could not be avoided. For the same thing would at the same time be affirmed and denied of the same object in the same sense. But if natural necessity is referred merely to appearances and freedom merely to things in themselves, no contradiction arises, even though we assume or grant both kinds of causality, however difficult or impossible it may be to make the latter kind conceivable.

In appearance every effect is an event or something that happens in time; according to the universal laws of nature, it must be preceded by a determination of the causality of its cause (a state), which follows according to a constant law. But determining the

344 cause to be causally efficacious must also be something that takes place or occurs; the cause must have *begun to act*; otherwise no succession between it and the effect could be thought. The effect as well as the causal efficacy of the cause would always have existed. Therefore, the *determination* of the cause to be efficacious must also have arisen among appearances and must consequently be an event just like its effect, which must in turn have its cause, etc. Hence natural necessity must be the condition, according to which efficient causes are determined. If, by contrast, freedom is to be a property of certain causes of appearances, it must, with respect to the latter as events, be a faculty of starting them *spontaneously (sponte)*, i.e., without the causal efficacy of the cause itself beginning and hence without requiring any other ground to determine its beginning. But then the cause would not be able to stand under time-determinations of its state with respect to its causal efficacy, that is, it *cannot* be an *appearance*, i.e., it would have to be considered a thing in itself, while its *effects* would be only *appearances*.[32] If we can think without contradiction the influence of beings of understanding on appearances, then natural necessity will attach to all connections of cause and effect in the sensible world, though freedom can be attributed to a cause that is itself not an appearance (but underlies appearance). Therefore, nature and freedom can be attributed to

the very same thing without contradiction, but in different relations—in the one case as an appearance, in the other case as a thing in itself.

We have in us a faculty that not only stands in connection with its subjectively determining grounds, which are the natural causes of its actions, and is to this extent the faculty of a being that itself belongs 345 to the appearances, but also is referred to objective grounds, that are only ideas insofar as they can determine this faculty, a connection that is expressed by the word *ought*. This faculty is called *reason* and, to the extent that we consider a being (man) entirely according to this objectively determinable reason, it cannot be considered as a sensible being. Rather, this property is that of a thing in itself, of which we cannot comprehend the possibility—namely how the *ought* (which, however, has never taken place) should determine its activity and could become the cause of actions whose effect is an appearance in the sensible world. Yet the causality of reason would be freedom with respect to its effects in the sensible world insofar as we can consider *objective grounds*, which are themselves ideas, as their determinants. For in that case its action would not depend upon subjective conditions, consequently not upon those of time, and would thus also not depend upon the law of nature that serves to determine them, because grounds of reason provide the rule to actions universally, according to principles, without the influence of the circumstances of time or place.

What I put forward here is meant merely as an example for the sake of intelligibility and does not necessarily belong to our problem, which must be decided from mere concepts, independently of the properties which we encounter in the actual world.

Now I can say without contradiction: that all the actions of rational beings insofar as they are appearances (i.e., can be encountered in some experience) are subject to natural necessity; but the same actions merely with respect to the rational subject and its faculty of acting according to mere reason, are free. For what is required for natural necessity? Nothing more than the determinability of every event in the sensible world according to constant laws; therefore, a relation to a cause in the appearance whereby the

---

32. The idea of freedom occurs only in the relation of the *intellectual*, as cause, to the *appearance*, as effect. For this reason we cannot attribute freedom to matter with respect to the unceasing action by which it fills its space, though this action takes place from an internal principle. We can likewise find no notion of freedom suitable to purely rational beings, for instance, to God, insofar as his action is immanent. For his action, though independent of external determining causes, is determined in his eternal reason, that is, in the divine *nature*. It is only if *something* is to *begin* by an action and thus the effect to be met with in the sequence of time or in the sensible world (e.g., the beginning of the world) that we can pose the question whether the causal efficacy of the cause must itself have begun or whether the cause can originate an effect without its causal efficacy itself beginning. In the former case the concept of causality is a concept of natural necessity, in the latter, that of freedom. From this the reader will see that by explaining freedom as the faculty of starting an event spontaneously, I have exactly hit upon the concept that is the problem of metaphysics.

thing in itself, which underlies it along with its causality, remains unknown. But I say: *the law of nature
remains*, whether the rational being is the cause of
its effects in the sensible world from reason, that is,
through freedom, or whether it does not determine
them on rational grounds. For if the former is the
case, the action is performed according to maxims,
whose effect in the appearance will always conform
to constant laws; if the latter is the case and the action does not occur according to principles of reason,
346 then it is subjected to the empirical laws of sensibility, and in both cases the effects cohere according
to constant laws. We do not require or even know
more than this concerning natural necessity. But in
the former case reason is the cause of these laws of
nature and is therefore free; in the latter the effects
follow according to mere natural laws of sensibility,
because reason does not exercise any influence on
it; but reason itself is not determined on that account
by sensibility (which is impossible) and is therefore
free in this case too. Freedom is therefore no obstacle
to the natural law of appearances, nor does this law
diminish the freedom of the practical use of reason,
which is connected with things in themselves as determining grounds.

Thus in this way practical freedom, namely freedom in which reason possesses causality according to
objectively determining grounds, is rescued without
natural necessity being curtailed in the least with respect to the very same effects as appearances. The
same remarks will serve to explain what we had to say
about transcendental freedom and its compatibility
with natural necessity (in the same subject, but not
taken in one and the same relation). For, as to transcendental freedom, every beginning of the action of
a being from objective causes with respect to these determining grounds is always a *first beginning*, though
the same action is in the series of appearances only
a *subordinate beginning*, which must be preceded by
a state of the cause that determines it and is itself
determined in the same manner by another cause
immediately preceding it. Accordingly, in rational
beings or in beings in general insofar as their causality is determined in them as things in themselves, we
are able to conceive a faculty of beginning a series

of states spontaneously without falling into contradiction with the laws of nature. For the relation of the
action to objective grounds of reason is not a temporal
relation; in this case what determines causality does
not precede the action in time, because such determining grounds represent a relation not to sensible
objects, therefore, not to causes in the appearances,
but to determining causes as things in themselves,
which are not subject to temporal conditions. And in
this way the action can be considered as a first begin-   347
ning with respect to the causality of reason, but also
as a merely subordinate beginning with respect to the
series of appearances. Accordingly, without contradiction we may consider it as free in the former respect,
but as subject to natural necessity in the latter (insofar
as it is merely appearance).

As to the *fourth* Antinomy, it is solved in the same
way as the conflict of reason with itself was in the
third. For, if the *cause in the appearance* is simply distinguished from the *cause of the appearances* (insofar
as it can be thought as a *thing in itself*), both propositions are perfectly consistent: the one, that there is
no cause anywhere in the sensible world (according
to similar laws of causality), whose existence is absolutely necessary; the other, that this world is nevertheless connected with a necessary being as its cause
(but of another kind and according to another law).
The incompatibility of these propositions rests entirely upon the misunderstanding of extending what
is valid merely of appearances to things in themselves
and in general of confusing both in one concept.

§ 54. This then is the presentation and the solution of the whole antinomy, in which reason finds
itself involved in the application of its principles to
the sensible world. The former alone (the mere presentation) would be a considerable service for our
knowledge of human reason, even if the solution of
the conflict does not yet fully satisfy the reader, who
has here to combat a natural illusion that has been
presented to him as such only recently and that he
had always regarded as genuine until then. For one
of its consequences is unavoidable, namely that because it is quite impossible to prevent this conflict
of reason with itself—as long as the objects of the
sensible world are taken for things in themselves and

not for what they in fact are, namely mere appearances—the reader is thereby forced to take up once again the deduction of all our *a priori* cognition and the examination of it that I have provided in order to come to a decision about it. This is all I require at present. For after he has himself thought deeply 348 enough into the nature of pure reason in this occupation, the concepts that alone make the solution of the conflict of reason possible will become sufficiently familiar to him. Without this familiarity I cannot expect an unreserved assent even from the most attentive reader.

### III. The Theological Idea[33]

§ 55. The third transcendental idea, which supplies material for the most important, though, if pursued only speculatively, transcendent and thereby dialectical use of reason, is the ideal of pure reason. In this case reason does not, as with the psychological and the cosmological ideas, begin from experience and err by increasing its grounds in striving to attain, if possible, the absolute completeness of their series. Rather, it breaks with experience completely and, from mere concepts of what would constitute the absolute completeness of a thing in general, consequently by means of the idea of a most perfect first being, it proceeds to determine the possibility and therefore the actuality of all other things. And in this way we have the mere presupposition of a being who is conceived not in the series of experience, yet for the purposes of experience—for the sake of comprehending its connection, order, and unity—i.e., the idea is more easily distinguished from the concept of the understanding here than in the former cases. For that reason we can easily expose the dialectical illusion which arises from our making the subjective conditions of our thinking objective conditions of objects themselves and from making an hypothesis necessary for the satisfaction of our reason into a dogma. Since the observations of the *Critique* on the pretensions of transcendental

theology are intelligible, clear, and decisive, I have nothing more to add on the subject.

### General Remark on the Transcendental Ideas

§ 56. The objects that are given to us through experience are incomprehensible to us in many respects, 349 and many questions to which the law of nature leads us when it is pushed beyond a certain point (though it always conforms to these laws) cannot be answered, as for example the question: why substances attract one another? But if we abandon nature completely or exceed all possible experience in pursuing its combinations and thus enter the realm of mere ideas, we cannot then say that the object is incomprehensible and that the nature of things presents us with insoluble problems. For in that case we are concerned not with nature or with given objects at all, but only with concepts, which have their origin solely in our reason, and with mere beings of thought; and all the problems that arise from our concepts of them must be able to be solved, because reason can and must give a full account of its own procedure.[34] Because the psychological, cosmological, and theological ideas are nothing but pure concepts of reason that cannot be given in any experience, the questions that reason asks us about them are put to us not by the objects, but by mere maxims of reason for the sake of its own satisfaction. They must all be capable of satisfactory answers, which is done by showing that they are principles which bring the use of our understanding into thorough agreement, completeness, and synthetic unity, and, to this extent, that they are valid

---

33. [Cf. *Critique*, "The Transcendental Ideal" A567–642/ B595–670.]

34. Herr Platner in his *Aphorisms* thus acutely says (§§728, 729), "If reason is a criterion, no concept that is incomprehensible to human reason can be possible. Incomprehensibility occurs only in what is actual. In this case, incomprehensibility arises from the insufficiency of the acquired ideas." It only sounds paradoxical, but is otherwise not strange to say that much in nature is incomprehensible to us (e.g., the faculty of generation) but if we climb even higher and go beyond nature itself, everything becomes comprehensible to us once again; for we then entirely abandon the *objects* that can be given to us and occupy ourselves merely with ideas, with respect to which we can easily comprehend the law that reason prescribes by them to the understanding for its use in experience, because the law is reason's own product.

only for experience, but for experience as a whole. Although an absolute whole of experience is impossible, the idea of a whole of experience according to principles in general must impart to our cognition a peculiar kind of unity, namely that of a system, without which our cognition is nothing but piecework and cannot be used for proving the existence of a highest purpose (which can only be the system of all purposes); I mean here not only the practical but also the highest purpose of the speculative use of reason.

The transcendental ideas therefore express the distinguishing vocation of reason, namely as a principle of systematic unity in the use of the understanding. Yet if we view the unity of this kind of cognition as if it were attached to the object of cognition, if we regard what is merely regulative as if it were constitutive, and if we persuade ourselves that we can enlarge our cognition by means of these ideas far beyond all possible experience or transcendentally, since it only serves to render experience within itself as nearly complete as possible, i.e., to limit its progress by nothing that cannot belong to experience: if we do all this, then this is a mere misunderstanding in our estimate of the distinguishing vocation of our reason and its principles and it is a dialectic that partly confuses the empirical use of reason and partly sets reason at odds with itself.

## Conclusion

### On Determining the Limits of Pure Reason

§ 57. After having provided the clearest arguments above, it would be absurd for us to hope that we can cognize more of any object than belongs to the possible experience of it or lay claim to the least cognition of anything not assumed to be an object of possible experience, which would determine it according to the constitution it has in itself. For how could we determine anything in this way, since time, space, and all concepts of the understanding, and especially all the concepts derived from empirical intuition or *perception* in the sensible world have and can have no other use than to make experience possible. And if this condition is omitted from the pure concepts of

the understanding, they do not determine any object and have no significance at all.

But, on the other hand, it would be an even greater absurdity if we admitted no things in themselves or wanted to pass off our experience as the only possible mode of knowing things, our intuition of them in space and in time as the only possible way, and our discursive understanding as the archetype of every possible understanding, and to take the principles of the possibility of experience as universal conditions of things in themselves.

Our principles, which limit the use of reason to possible experience alone, might in this way become *transcendent* and the boundaries of our reason could be set up as boundaries of the possibility of things in themselves (as Hume's *Dialogues* may illustrate),[35] if a careful critique did not keep watch over the limits of our reason with respect to its empirical use and put a stop to its pretensions. Skepticism originally arose from metaphysics and its lawless dialectics. At first it might denounce everything that transcends this use as worthless and deceitful, merely to favor the empirical use of reason; but gradually, when it was realized that the very same *a priori* principles that are used in experience, unnoticed and apparently with the very same right, led further than experience extends, then one began to doubt even the propositions of experience. But there is no danger here, for common sense will certainly always assert its rights. However, a special confusion arose in science, which cannot determine how far reason is to be trusted and why only so far and no further, and this confusion can be cleared up and all future relapses obviated only by a formal and principled determination of the limits of the use of our reason.

It is true: we cannot form a determinate concept of what things in themselves may be beyond all possible experience. Yet we are not free to abstain entirely from inquiring into them; for experience never satisfies reason fully. In answering questions, reason leads us back further and further and leaves us dissatisfied with their complete explanation, as anyone can see adequately from the dialectic of pure reason,

35. [Kant is referring to David Hume's *Dialogues Concerning Natural Religion* (1779).]

which for this reason has its proper subjective basis. Having acquired, with respect to the nature of our soul, a clear conception of the subject and having come to the conviction that its manifestations cannot be explained *materialistically*, who can refrain from asking what the soul really is and, if no concept of experience is able to answer the question, from simply assuming a concept of reason (that of a simple immaterial being), though we cannot at all prove its objective reality? Who can satisfy himself with mere empirical knowledge in all the cosmological questions of the duration and magnitude of the world, of freedom or natural necessity, since, we may proceed however we like, every answer given according to principles of experience raises a new question, which likewise requires an answer and thereby shows that all physical modes of explanation are clearly insufficient to satisfy reason? Finally, who does not see from the thoroughgoing contingency and dependence of everything that can be thought and assumed only according to principles of experience, the impossibility of stopping there and who does not feel himself compelled, despite all warnings about getting lost in transcendent ideas, to seek peace and contentment beyond all the concepts that can be vindicated by experience in the concept of a being, the possibility of which in itself we can neither conceive nor refute, because it concerns a mere being of the understanding without which reason must necessarily remain forever dissatisfied?

Boundaries (in extended beings) always presuppose a space existing outside a certain definite place and enclosing it; limitations do not require this, but are mere negations, which affect a quantity insofar as it is not absolutely complete. But our reason sees in its surroundings, as it were, a space for cognition of things in themselves, though it can never have determinate concepts of them and is restricted to appearances alone.

As long as cognition of reason is homogeneous, determinate boundaries to it are inconceivable. In mathematics and natural philosophy human reason admits of limitations, but not of boundaries, i.e., that something lies outside it, at which it can never arrive, but not that it will find completion at any point

in its internal progress. The extension of our insights in mathematics and the possibility of ever new discoveries are infinite; and the same is the case with the discovery of new properties of nature, of new forces and laws, by continued experience and its unification through reason. But limitations are certainly unmistakable here, for mathematics refers to *appearances* only, and what cannot be an object of sensible intuition, such as the concepts of metaphysics and of morals, lies entirely outside its sphere. It can never lead to them, but it does not at all require them either. It is therefore not a continual progression and approach towards these sciences and there is not, as it were, any point or line of contact. Natural science will never reveal to us the inner constitution of things, i.e., what though not appearance can still serve as the ultimate ground for explaining appearances. Nor does that science require this for its physical explanations. Even if such grounds should be offered from other sources (e.g., the influence of immaterial beings), they must be rejected and not used in the progress of its explanations. Rather, these explanations must be grounded only upon what can belong to experience as an object of sense and be brought into connection with our actual perceptions according to empirical laws.

But metaphysics leads us towards limits in the dialectical attempts of pure reason (which are not undertaken arbitrarily or willfully, but stimulated to it by the nature of reason itself). And the transcendental ideas, precisely because they cannot be avoided, but are also not capable of being realized, serve to point out to us not only the limits of the use of pure reason but also the way to determine them. That is also the end and the use of this natural predisposition of our reason, which has brought forth metaphysics as its favorite child, whose creation, like every other in the world, is not to be ascribed to blind chance, but to an original seed that has been wisely organized for great ends. For in its fundamental features metaphysics perhaps more than any other science is placed in us by nature itself and cannot be considered the product of an arbitrary choice or a contingent extension in the progress of experience (from which it is quite disparate).

Reason with all its concepts and laws of the understanding, which suffice for empirical use, i.e., within the sensible world, finds no satisfaction for itself in it because ever-recurring questions deprive reason of all hope that they could be answered completely. The transcendental ideas, which aim to provide

354 complete answers, are such problems of reason. Now it sees clearly that the sensible world cannot contain a complete set of answers nor consequently can all the concepts that serve merely for understanding it: space and time and whatever we have put forward under the name of pure concepts of the understanding. The sensible world is nothing but a chain of appearances connected according to universal laws; it has therefore no subsistence by itself; it is not the thing in itself, and consequently must point to what contains the basis of this appearance, to beings that cannot be cognized merely as appearances, but as things in themselves. In the cognition of them alone can reason hope to satisfy its desire for completeness in proceeding from the conditioned to its conditions.

Above (§§ 33, 34) we revealed the limits of reason with respect to all cognition of mere beings of thought. Now, since the transcendental ideas have made us proceed up to them, and thus have led us, as it were, to where fully occupied space (experience) touches the void (of which we can know nothing, the *noumena*), we can determine the limits of pure reason. For in all limits there is also something positive (e.g., a surface is the limit of corporeal space and is therefore itself a space, a line is a space that is the limit of the surface, a point is the limit of a line, but still always a place in space), whereas limitations contain mere negations. The limits pointed out in those paragraphs are not enough after we have discovered that something lies beyond them (though we can never cognize what it is in itself). For the question now is: What is reason's attitude in this connection of what we know with what we do not and never will know? This is an actual connection of a known thing with one quite unknown (and which will always remain so), and even if what is unknown should not become the least bit better known—which we cannot in fact even hope for—the concept of this connection must be capable of being determined and rendered distinct.

We should therefore think an immaterial being, a world of understanding, and a highest of all beings (all mere noumena), because only in them, as things in themselves, does reason find the comple- 355 tion and satisfaction that it can never hope for in the derivation of appearances from their homogeneous grounds, and because these actually refer to something distinct from them (and totally heterogeneous), since appearances always presuppose an object in itself and therefore suggest its existence whether we can know more of it or not.

But since we can never cognize these beings of understanding as they are in themselves, that is, determinately, yet must assume them in relation to the sensible world and connect them with it by reason, we are at least able to think this connection by means of such concepts as express their relation to the world of sense. Yet if we represent to ourselves a being of the understanding by nothing but pure concepts of the understanding, we then indeed represent nothing determinate to ourselves and consequently our concept has no significance; but if we think it by properties borrowed from the sensible world, it is no longer a being of understanding, but is conceived as one of the phenomena and belongs to the sensible world. Let us take an example from the concept of the supreme being.

The *deistic* concept is a completely pure concept of reason, but represents only a thing containing all realities, without being able to determine a single one of them; because for that purpose an example must be taken from the sensible world, in which case we should have an object of the senses only, not something quite heterogeneous, which cannot at all be an object of the senses. For I would attribute, e.g., understanding to the supreme being, but I have no concept of an understanding other than my own, namely one that must receive its intuitions through the senses and that is concerned to bring them under rules of the unity of consciousness. But in that case the elements of my concept would always lie in the appearance; however, the insufficiency of the appearances would force me to go beyond them to the concept of a being which neither depends upon appearances nor is bound up with them as conditions of its determination. But if I separate the understanding from sensibility to obtain a pure understanding, then nothing remains but the mere form of thinking without intuition, by which, however, I can cognize nothing determinate and consequently no object. For that purpose I would have to conceive another understanding that would intuit its objects, but of which I do not have the least concept, because the human understanding is discursive and can cognize only by means of general concepts. And the very same difficulty also arises if we attribute a will to the supreme being; for we have this concept only by drawing it from our inner experience, which therefore presupposes our dependence for satisfaction upon objects whose existence we require and thus upon sensibility, which is absolutely incompatible with the pure concept of the supreme being.

Hume's objections to deism are weak and affect only the proofs, not the deistic assertion itself. But with respect to theism, which comes about through a closer determination of the concept of the supreme being, which is merely transcendent in deism, they are very strong and, after this concept has been formed, in certain (in fact, in all common) cases irrefutable. Hume always insists that by the mere concept of an original being, to which we apply only ontological predicates (eternity, omnipresence, omnipotence), we actually think nothing at all determinate, and that properties which can yield a concept *in concreto* would have to be added; it is not enough to say: it is a cause. Rather, we must explain the nature of its causality, for example, through an understanding and a will. That is where his attacks on the essential point itself, namely theism, begin, since previously he had attacked only the proofs of deism, which does not carry with it any special dangers. All his dangerous arguments refer to anthropomorphism, which he holds to be inseparable from theism and to make it absurd in itself; but if the former are abandoned, the latter must vanish along with it, and nothing remains but deism, from which nothing can be made, which is of no value, and which cannot serve as any foundation to religion or morals. If this anthropomorphism were really unavoidable, even if all and any proofs of the existence of a supreme being were granted, we could never determine the concept of this being without becoming involved in contradictions.

If we combine the prohibition to avoid all transcendent judgments of pure reason with the apparently conflicting command to proceed to concepts that lie beyond the field of its immanent (empirical) use, we discover that both can subsist together, but only at the *limit* of all permissible use of reason. For it belongs to the field of experience as well as to that of the beings of thought, and we are thereby taught at the same time how these so remarkable ideas serve merely for determining the limits of human reason. On the one hand, they teach not to extend cognition of experience limitlessly as if nothing but the world remained for us to cognize and, on the other hand, not to transgress the limits of experience and want to judge things beyond it as things in themselves.

But we stop at this limit if we restrict our judgment merely to the relation which the world may have to a being whose very concept lies beyond all the cognition that we are capable of within the world. For in that case we do not attribute to the supreme being any of the properties *in themselves*, by which we represent objects of experience, and in this way we avoid *dogmatic* anthropomorphism. However, we still attribute them to his relation to the world and allow ourselves a *symbolic* anthropomorphism, which in fact concerns language only and not the object itself.

When I say that we are compelled to consider the world as if it were the work of a supreme understanding and will, I am really not saying anything more than that a watch, a ship, a regiment, bears the same relation to the watchmaker, the shipbuilder, the commanding officer, as the sensible world (or everything that constitutes the basis of this sum of appearances) does to the unknown, which I do not hereby cognize as it is in itself, but as it is for me, namely in relation to the world of which I am a part.

§ 58. Such a cognition is a cognition *according to analogy* and does not signify (as is commonly understood) an imperfect similarity of two things, but a perfect similarity of two relations between completely dissimilar things.[36] By means of this analogy, however, there remains a concept of the supreme being sufficiently determined *for us*, though we have left out everything that could *determine* it absolutely and *in itself*; for we determine it with respect to the world and thus with respect to ourselves and we do not require anything more. The attacks that Hume levels against those who would determine this concept absolutely, by taking the materials to that end from themselves and the world, do not affect us; and he cannot object that we have nothing left if we remove objective anthropomorphism from the concept of the supreme being.

For let us assume at the outset (as does Hume in his *Dialogues*[37] in the form of Philo against Cleanthes), as a necessary hypothesis, the *deistic* concept of the first being, in which this being is thought by the mere ontological predicates of substance, of cause, etc. *This must be done* because reason, being driven in the sensible world only by conditions that are themselves always conditioned, cannot be satisfied in any other way; and *this can be done* without falling into anthropomorphism, which transfers predicates from the sensible world to a being quite distinct from the world, because those predicates are simply categories, which, though they do not give a determinate concept of God, still provide a concept not limited

to any conditions of sensibility. Thus nothing can prevent us from predicating of this being a *causality through reason* with respect to the world and thus from crossing over to theism, without being forced to attribute to this being itself this kind of reason as a property inhering in him. For as to the *former*, the only possible way of pushing the use of reason (with respect to all possible experience, in complete harmony with itself) in the sensible world to the highest point is to assume a supreme reason as a cause of all the connections in the world. Such a principle must be quite advantageous to reason and can hurt it nowhere in its application to nature. As to the *latter*, reason is thereby not transferred as a property to the first being in itself, but *only to its relation* to the sensible world and so anthropomorphism is entirely avoided. For nothing is considered here but the *cause* of the rational form that is perceived everywhere in the world, and reason is attributed to the Supreme Being insofar as it contains the ground of this rational form in the world, but only according to analogy, i.e., insofar as this expression merely indicates the relation that the supreme cause unknown to us has to the world, in order to determine everything in it rationally in the highest degree. In this way we are prevented from using the property of reason to think God, but not from thinking the world in such a manner as is necessary to have the greatest possible use of reason according to one principle. We thereby acknowledge that the supreme being is quite inscrutable as to what it is in itself and even unthinkable *in any determinate way* and are thereby kept from making a transcendent use of the concepts which we have of reason as an efficient cause (by means of the will), in order to determine the divine nature by properties that can only be borrowed from human nature, and to lose ourselves in crude and fanatical concepts. It also keeps us from deluging the contemplation of the world with hyperphysical modes of explanation according to our concepts of human reason, which we transfer to God, thereby losing for this contemplation its proper end according to which it should be a rational study of mere nature and not a presumptuous derivation of its appearances from a supreme reason. The expression appropriate to our

359

---

36. There is a similar analogy between the legal relation of human actions and the mechanical relation of motive forces. I can never do anything to another man without giving him a right to do the same to me on the same conditions, just as no body can act with its motive force on another body without thereby causing the other to react equally against it. Here right and motive force are completely dissimilar things, but in their relation there is complete similarity. For that reason, by means of such an analogy I can obtain a concept of the relation of things that are absolutely unknown to me. For instance, as the promotion of the happiness of children (= a) is to the love of parents (= b), so the welfare of the human species (= c) is to the unknown in God (= x), which we call love: not as if it had the least similarity to any human inclination, but because we can suppose its relation to the world to be similar to that which things of the world bear to one another. But the relational concept in this case is a mere category, namely the concept of cause, which has nothing to do with sensibility.

37. [Kant is once again referring to Hume's *Dialogues Concerning Natural Religion*.]

feeble concepts is that we conceive the world *as if* its existence and internal plan stemmed from a supreme reason, by which we both cognize the constitution that belongs to the world itself, without pretending to determine the nature of its cause in itself, and place the ground of this constitution (of the rational form in the world) in *the relation* of the supreme cause to the world, without finding the world sufficient by itself for that purpose.[38]

Thus the difficulties which seem to oppose theism disappear by combining Hume's principle—not to carry the use of reason dogmatically beyond the field of all possible experience—with this other principle, which he quite overlooked: not to consider the field of possible experience as one which restricts itself in the eyes of our reason. The *Critique of Pure Reason* points out the true mean here between dogmatism, which Hume combats, and skepticism, which he would substitute for it—a mean which is not like other means that we try to determine for ourselves, as it were, mechanically (by adopting something from the one side and something else from the other side), and by which nobody is taught a better way, but rather one that can be accurately determined according to principle.

§ 59. At the beginning of this remark I made use of the metaphor of a *limit* in order to establish the boundaries of reason with respect to its appropriate use. The sensible world contains merely appearances, which are not things in themselves. However, the understanding must assume the latter, *noumena*, precisely because it recognizes that the objects of experience are mere appearances. Both are comprised in our reason and the question is: How does reason proceed in limiting the understanding with respect to both these fields? Experience, which contains everything that belongs to the sensible world, does not

limit itself; it proceeds in every case from the conditioned only to some other equally conditioned object. What limits it must lie completely outside it, and this field is that of the pure beings of the understanding. But insofar as the *determination* of the nature of these beings is concerned, this field is an empty space for us and if only concepts that have been determined dogmatically are at issue, we cannot pass beyond the field of possible experience. But since a limit is itself something positive, which belongs to that which lies within as well as to the space that lies without the given sum, it is still an actual positive cognition, which reason only acquires by extending itself to this limit, but in such a way that it does not attempt to pass it, because it finds itself in the presence of an empty space, in which it can conceive forms of things, but not things themselves. But *limiting* the field of experience by something that is otherwise unknown to it is still a cognition belonging to reason in this standpoint, by which it is neither confined within the sensible world, nor does it stray beyond it, but rather restricts itself, as is fitting for knowledge of a limit, merely to the relation between what lies beyond it and what is contained within it.

Natural theology is such a concept at the limit of human reason, since it is constrained to look to the idea of a supreme being (and for practical ends to that of an intelligible world as well), not in order to determine anything relative to this mere being of the understanding, which lies beyond the sensible world, but in order to guide the use of reason within it according to principles of the greatest possible (theoretical as well as practical) unity. To this end we make use of the relation of the sensible world to a self-sufficient reason as the cause of all its connections. We do not thereby simply *invent* a being, but, since there must be something beyond the sensible world that can only be thought by the pure understanding, we *determine* that thing in this particular way, though of course only according to analogy.

And thus our original proposition remains, which is the result of the whole *Critique*: "that by all its *a priori* principles reason never teaches us anything more than objects of possible experience and even of these nothing more than can be cognized in experience."

---

38. I shall say that the causality of the supreme cause holds the same place with respect to the world that human reason does with respect to its works of art. Here the nature of the supreme cause itself remains unknown to me: I only compare its known effects (the order of the world) and their conformity to reason to the known effects of human reason and hence I term the former reason, without attributing to it on that account what I understand by this term in man, or without attaching to it as its property anything else known to me.

But this restriction does not prevent reason from leading us to the objective *limit* of experience, namely to the *relation* to something that is itself not an object of experience, but the highest ground of all experience. However, reason does not teach us anything concerning the thing in itself: it only instructs us as to its own complete and highest use in the field of possible experience. But this is all that can be reasonably desired in the present case and we have reason to be satisfied with that.

§ 60. In this way we have fully exhibited metaphysics according to its subjective possibility as it is actually given *in the natural predisposition* of human reason and in what constitutes the essential end of its pursuit. We have found that this *merely natural* use of such a predisposition of our reason, if no discipline which is possible only from a scientific critique bridles and sets limits to it, involves us in transcendent *dialectical* syllogisms which are in part merely apparently and in part really conflicting and that this sophistical metaphysics is not only unnecessary for the promotion of our cognition of nature but even disadvantageous to it. However, a problem remains that is still worthy of investigation, namely to discover the natural ends aimed at by reason's disposition to transcendent concepts, because everything that lies in nature must be originally intended for some useful purpose.

Such an inquiry is in fact precarious and I acknowledge that what I can say about it is only conjecture, like every speculation about the ultimate ends of nature, something that I am allowed in this case alone, since the question does not concern the objective validity of metaphysical judgments, but rather our natural predisposition to them and therefore does not belong to the system of metaphysics but to anthropology.

When I consider all the transcendental ideas whose sum constitutes the proper problem of natural pure reason that compels it to abandon the mere contemplation of nature, to transcend all possible experience, and in this attempt to bring about the thing called metaphysics (whether it is knowledge or fiction), I think I perceive that the aim of this natural tendency is to free our concepts from the fetters of experience and from the boundaries of the mere contemplation of nature to such an extent that it at least

sees a field opened up containing mere objects for the pure understanding that no sensibility can reach, not indeed for the purpose of speculatively occupying ourselves with them (for we can find no ground to stand on), but so that practical principles can at least be assumed as possible, which, without finding some such scope for their necessary expectation and hope, could not expand to the universality which reason unavoidably requires from a moral point of view.

Now I find that the *psychological* idea (however little it may reveal to me about the pure nature of the human soul, elevated above all concepts of experience) at least shows distinctly enough the insufficiency of these concepts and thereby stops me from accepting materialism, a psychological concept that is unfit for any explanation of nature and, in addition, confines reason in practical respects. The *cosmological* ideas, by the obvious insufficiency of all possible cognition of nature to satisfy reason in its legitimate inquiry, serve in the same manner to keep us from naturalism, which asserts nature to be sufficient for itself. Finally, by means of the *theological* idea reason frees itself from fatalism (both as a blind natural necessity in the coherence of nature itself without a first principle and with respect to a blind causality of this principle itself) and leads to the concept of a cause possessing freedom and thus a highest intelligence, because all natural necessity in the sensible world is conditional, given that it always presupposes the dependence of things upon others and unconditional necessity must be sought only in the unity of a cause different from the sensible world, and the causality of this cause, in turn, were it merely nature, could never render the existence of the contingent comprehensible as its consequent. Thus the transcendental ideas serve, if not to instruct us positively, at least to destroy the rash and overly restrictive assertions of *materialism*, *naturalism*, and *fatalism*, and thus to create room for the moral ideas beyond the field of speculation. These considerations, I should think, explain in some measure the natural predisposition of which I spoke.

The practical value that a merely speculative science may have lies outside the limits of this science and can therefore be considered merely as a scholium and, like all scholia, does not form part of the science itself. However, this relation surely lies within the limits of philosophy, especially of philosophy drawn from the sources of pure reason, where its speculative use in metaphysics must necessarily be at one with its practical use in morals. Hence the unavoidable dialectic of pure reason in metaphysics considered as a natural tendency deserves to be explained not merely as an illusion that is to be removed, but also, if possible, as a *natural provision* for its end, though it cannot justly be assigned to metaphysics proper, since this duty is a work of supererogation.

The solutions of these questions which are treated in the chapter on the Regulative Use of the Ideas of Pure Reason[39] should be considered a second scholium, which is more clearly related to the content of metaphysics. For there certain rational principles are expounded which determine *a priori* the order of nature or rather the understanding that seeks nature's laws through experience. They seem to be constitutive and legislative with respect to experience, though they spring from pure reason, which, unlike the understanding, cannot be considered as a principle of possible experience. Now whether or not this harmony rests upon the fact that just as nature does not inhere in appearances or in their source (the sensibility) itself, but only insofar as the latter is related to the understanding, so too the systematic unity of the understanding's use to bring about a total possible experience can belong to the understanding only in relation to reason and thus whether or not experience is in this way mediately subordinate to the legislation of reason may be discussed by those who desire to trace the nature of reason even beyond its use in metaphysics, into the general principles of a history of nature; I have represented this as an important task, but I have not attempted its solution in the book itself.[40]

And thus I conclude the analytic solution of the main question which I had proposed: How is metaphysics in general possible? by ascending from the data of its actual use in its consequences to the grounds of its possibility.

## Scholium

*Solution to the General Question of the Prolegomena, "How is metaphysics possible as a science?"*

Metaphysics, as a natural disposition of reason, is actual, but if considered by itself alone (as the analytic solution of the third main question showed), it is dialectical and illusory. If we wanted to take principles from it and use them to follow this natural, but on that account no less false illusion, we could never produce science, but only a vain dialectical art, in which one school may outdo another, but none can ever acquire a just and lasting approbation.

In order that metaphysics as a science may be entitled to claim not mere fallacious persuasion, but insight and conviction, a *Critique of Reason* must itself exhibit the entire stock of *a priori* concepts, their division according to various sources (sensibility, the understanding, and reason), a complete table of them, an analysis of all these concepts, along with all their consequences, but especially the possibility of synthetic *a priori* cognition by means of the deduction of these concepts, the principles and the limits of their application, all in a complete system. Critique, therefore, and critique alone contains in itself the entire well-tested and established plan and even all the means required to bring about metaphysics as a science; by any other ways and means it is impossible. Therefore, the question here is not so much how this endeavor is possible, but how to get it going, how to induce clear minds to abandon their previously perverted and fruitless efforts for those that will not deceive, and how best to direct such a union for the common end.

---

39. *Critique of Pure Reason*, Second Division, chap. III, section 7 [A642–668/B670–696].

40. Throughout the *Critique* I never lost sight of my intention not to neglect anything that could render the inquiry into the nature of pure reason complete, regardless of how deeply hidden it might be. Everybody may afterwards carry his inquiries as far as he pleases, if only he has been shown what still remains to be done. This can reasonably be expected of him who has

---

made it his business to survey the whole field, in order to consign it to others for future cultivation and allocation. And to this branch both of the scholia belong, whose dryness will hardly recommend themselves to amateurs and which for that reason are added here only for experts.

366     This much is certain: whoever has once tasted critique will be forever disgusted with all dogmatic chatter which he formerly put up with, because his reason had to have something, but could find nothing better for its support. Critique stands in the same relation to the common metaphysics of the schools as *chemistry* does to *alchemy* or as *astronomy* to the *astrology* of the fortune-teller. I vow that no one who has thought through and grasped the principles of critique, even if only in these *Prolegomena*, will ever return to that old and sophistical pseudo-science, but will rather look forward with a certain delight to metaphysics which is now indeed in his power, requiring no more preparatory discoveries, and now at last providing permanent satisfaction to reason. For this is an advantage upon which, of all possible sciences, metaphysics alone can count with certainty, namely that it can be brought to completion and a permanent state since it is incapable of further change or of any augmentation by new discoveries, because reason has here the sources of its cognition in itself, not in objects and their intuition, by which it could be taught anything more. When, therefore, it has exhibited the fundamental laws of its faculty completely and so determinately as to avoid all misunderstanding, nothing remains for pure reason to cognize *a priori*; in fact, there is even no basis for raising further questions. The sure prospect of knowledge so determinate and final has a special charm, even if we were to set aside all its advantages, of which I shall speak below.

    All false art, all vain wisdom, lasts for a while, but finally destroys itself, and its highest cultivation is also the moment of its decline. That this time has come for metaphysics is clear from the state into which it has fallen among all learned nations, despite all the zeal with which sciences of every other kind are developed. The old organization of our university studies still retains its shadow; now and then a sole Academy of Sciences tempts men by offering prizes to write essays on it, but it is no longer counted among the thorough sciences; and let anyone judge for himself how a man of genius, if he were called a great metaphysician, would receive the compliment, which may be well-meant, but would hardly be envied by anyone.

Although the period of the downfall of all dogmatic metaphysics has undoubtedly arrived, we are still far from able to say that the period of its regeneration has already arrived by means of a thorough and complete critique of reason. All transitions from an inclination to its opposite pass through a stage of indifference and this moment is the most dangerous for an author, but, in my opinion, the most favorable for the science. For, when the partisan spirit has died out by a complete dissolution of former connections, minds are in the best state to listen to several proposals for an organization according to a new plan. 367

    When I say that I hope these *Prolegomena* will excite investigation in the field of critique and provide a new and promising object to sustain the general spirit of philosophy, which seems to lack sustenance on its speculative side, I can already imagine beforehand that everyone whom the thorny paths of my *Critique* have tired and put in a bad mood will ask me what the basis for my hope is. My answer is: *the irresistible law of necessity*.

    That the human mind will ever give up metaphysical inquiry is as little to be expected as that we should prefer to give up breathing altogether in order to avoid inhaling impure air. There will therefore always be metaphysics in the world; in fact, everyone, especially every reflective man, will have it and, for lack of a recognized standard, will carve it up for himself in his own fashion. What has been called metaphysics until now cannot satisfy any critical mind, but to forego it entirely is impossible; therefore a critique of pure reason itself must now be *attempted* or, if one exists, *investigated*, and put to a general test, because there is no other means of supplying this pressing need, which is something more than a mere thirst for knowledge.

    Ever since I have known critique, whenever I finish reading a book of metaphysical content, which, by the preciseness of its concepts, by its variety, order, and easy style, was not only entertaining but also helpful, I cannot help asking, "Has this author advanced metaphysics a single step?" The learned men, whose works have been useful to me in other respects and have always contributed to the development of my mental powers, will, I hope, forgive me for saying 368

that I have never been able to find either their essays or my own less important ones (though self-love
may recommend them to me) to have advanced the
science of metaphysics in the least, and for the very
obvious reason that metaphysics did not exist then as
a science and cannot be put together in piecemeal
fashion; rather its seed must be fully preformed in the
*Critique*. But in order to prevent all misunderstanding, we must remember from what has already been
said that by an analytic treatment of our concepts
the understanding certainly gains a great deal, but
the science (of metaphysics) is not thereby advanced
in the least, because these analyses of concepts are
nothing but the materials out of which science is to
be constructed in the first place. Let the concepts of
substance and of accident be analyzed and defined
as much as one might like, all this is very well as a
preparation for some future use. But if we cannot
prove that in all which exists the substance endures
and only the accidents vary, our science is not in the
least advanced by all our analyses.

Until now, metaphysics has never been able to
prove *a priori* either this proposition or the principle
of sufficient reason, much less any more complex
theorem that belongs, e.g., to psychology or cosmology, or indeed any synthetic proposition. Therefore,
by all this analysis nothing is affected, created, or improved, and science, after all this bustle and noise,
still remains as it was in the days of Aristotle, though
the preparations would have been incontestably better than otherwise, if only the clue to synthetic cognitions had been discovered.

If anyone feels offended by this, he can refute my
charge by producing a single synthetic proposition
belonging to metaphysics that he can prove dogmatically *a priori*, for until he has actually performed this
feat, I shall not grant that he has truly advanced the
science—even should this proposition be sufficiently
confirmed by common experience. No demand can
be more moderate or more equitable, and in the (in-
369 evitably certain) event of its non-performance, no
assertion more just than that metaphysics has never
existed as a science.

But there are two things which, in case the challenge be accepted, I must refuse to tolerate: first,

trifling about *probability* and conjecture, which are
as poorly suited to metaphysics as to geometry; and
secondly, a decision by means of the magic wand
of so-called *healthy common sense*, which does not
convince everyone, but which accommodates itself
to personal peculiarities.

For, *as to the former*, nothing can be more absurd
than to attempt to base our judgments upon probability and conjecture in metaphysics, a philosophy
from pure reason. Everything that is to be cognized *a
priori* is thereby announced as apodeictically certain
and must therefore also be proved in this way. We
might as well think of basing geometry or arithmetic
upon conjectures. As to the calculus of probabilities
in the latter, it does not contain probable, but rather
perfectly certain judgments concerning the degree of
the probability of certain cases under given uniform
conditions, which, in the sum of all possible cases,
must infallibly happen according to the rule, though
it is not sufficiently determined for every single instance. Conjectures (by means of induction and
analogy) can be allowed only in empirical natural
science, yet even there at least the possibility of what
we assume must be quite certain.

The appeal to *healthy common sense* is even more
absurd if concepts and principles are said to be valid,
not insofar as they hold with respect to experience,
but even beyond the conditions of experience. For
what is common sense? It is the ordinary understanding insofar as it judges correctly. But what is the
ordinary understanding? It is the faculty of cognition
and of the use of rules *in concreto*, as distinguished
from the *speculative understanding*, which is a faculty of cognizing rules *in abstracto*. Thus, common
sense can hardly understand the rule that every
event is determined by means of its cause, and thus
can never comprehend it in general. For that reason,
it demands an example from experience and when
it hears that this rule means nothing but what it al- 370
ways thought when a pane was broken or a kitchen
utensil missing, it then understands the principle and
grants it. Therefore, common sense is of use only insofar as it can see its rules confirmed by experience
(though they are actually *a priori*); consequently, to
have insight into them *a priori* and independently

of experience belongs to the speculative understanding and lies entirely beyond the horizon of common sense. But metaphysics is entirely confined to the latter kind of knowledge and it is certainly a bad sign of common sense to appeal to it as a witness, when it has no opinion here whatsoever and men look down upon it with contempt until they are in trouble and can find neither advice nor help in their speculation.

It is a common excuse that those false friends of common sense (who occasionally prize it highly, but usually despise it) are accustomed to using when they say that ultimately there must surely be some propositions which are immediately certain and of which there is no occasion to give any proof or even any account at all, because otherwise we could never stop inquiring into the grounds of our judgments. But in proof of this right—beyond the principle of contradiction, which is not sufficient to show the truth of synthetic judgments—they can never provide anything else indubitable that they can immediately ascribe to common sense, except mathematical propositions, such as two times two is equal to four, between two points there is but one straight line, etc. But these judgments are radically different from those of metaphysics. For in mathematics by thinking I myself can construct whatever I represent to myself as possible through a concept: I add the first two to the other two, one by one, and myself make the number four, or in thought I draw from one point to another all manner of lines, equal as well as unequal; yet I can draw only one that is like itself in all its parts. But, by all my power of thinking, I cannot extract from the concept of a thing the concept of something else whose existence is necessarily connected with the former, but I must take recourse to experience. And though my understanding furnishes me *a priori* (yet only in reference to possible experience) with the concept of such a connection (causality), I cannot exhibit it in *a priori* intuition, like the concepts of mathematics, and so show its possibility *a priori*. This concept, together with the principles of its application, always requires, if it shall hold *a priori*—as is necessary in metaphysics—a justification and deduction of its possibility, because otherwise we cannot know how far it is valid and whether it can be used only in experience or beyond it as well. Therefore, in metaphysics as a speculative science of pure reason we can never appeal to common sense, but may do so only when we are forced (in certain matters) to abandon it and to renounce all purely speculative cognition, which must always be theoretical knowledge, and consequently when we are forced to forego metaphysics itself and its instruction, for the sake of adopting a rational faith which alone may be possible for us and sufficient for our wants (perhaps even more beneficial than knowledge itself). For in this case the form of the issue is completely changed. Metaphysics must be a science, not only as a whole but in all its parts; otherwise it is nothing, because, as speculation of pure reason, it has a hold only on universal insights. Beyond its field, however, probability and common sense may be used advantageously and legitimately, but according to its own unique principles whose importance always depends on its relation to the practical.

This is what I hold myself justified in requiring for the possibility of metaphysics as a science.

# Immanuel Kant, *Critique of Pure Reason* (1781/1787)[1]

## Preface [First Edition]

Human reason has a peculiar fate in one kind of its cognitions: it is troubled by questions that it cannot dismiss, because they are posed to it by the nature of reason itself, but that it also cannot answer, because they surpass human reason's every ability.

Our reason falls into this perplexity through no fault of its own. Reason starts from principles that it cannot avoid using in the course of experience, and that this experience at the same time sufficiently justifies it in using. By means of these principles our Aviii reason (as indeed its nature requires it to do) ascends ever higher, to more remote conditions. But it becomes aware that in this way, since the questions never cease, its task must remain forever uncompleted. Thus it finds itself compelled to resort to principles that go beyond all possible use in experience, and that nonetheless seem so little suspect that even common human reason agrees with them. By doing this, however, human reason plunges into darkness and contradictions; and although it can indeed gather

from these that they must be based on errors lying hidden somewhere, it is unable to discover these errors. For the principles that it employs go beyond the limits of all experience and hence no longer acknowledge any touchstone of experience. The combat arena of these endless conflicts is what we call metaphysics. [ ... ]

It [the indifference that ultimately ensues] is evi- Axi dently the effect, not of the heedlessness, but rather of the matured *judgment*[2] of our age, which is no longer

---

1. [Translated from the German by Werner Pluhar (Indianapolis: Hackett, 1996), revised by Eric Watkins. In this selection brackets are either Werner Pluhar's or, in some instances (e.g., to indicate omitted passages), the editor's.]

2. Now and then one hears complaints about the shallow way of thinking in our age and the decline of thorough science. But I fail to see how the sciences that rest on a well-built foundation—such as mathematics, natural science, etc.—in the least deserve this reproach. On the contrary, they are upholding their ancient reputation for thoroughness, and in the case of natural science even surpass it. Now, the same spirit would be found operative in other kinds of cognition as well, if care had first been taken to correct their principles. In the absence of such correction, indifference, doubt, and—finally—strict critique are, rather, *proofs* of a thorough way of thinking. Our age is properly the age of critique, and to critique everything must submit. *Religion* and *legislation* commonly seek to exempt themselves from critique, religion through its *sanctity* and legislation through its *majesty*. But in doing so they arouse well-deserved suspicion and cannot lay claim to unfeigned respect; such respect is accorded by reason only to what has been able to withstand reason's free and open examination.

willing to be put off with illusory knowledge. And it is a call to reason to take on once again the most difficult of all its tasks—namely, that of self-cognition—and to set up a tribunal that will make reason secure in its rightful claims and will dismiss all baseless pretensions, not by fiat but in accordance with reason's eternal and immutable laws. This tribunal is none other than the *critique of pure reason* itself.

By critique of pure reason, however, I do not mean a critique of books and systems, but I mean the critique of our faculty of reason as such, in regard to all cognitions after which reason may strive *independently of all experience*. Hence I mean by it the decision as to whether a metaphysics as such is possible or impossible, and the determination of its sources as well as its range and limits—all on the basis of principles.

Now, this is the path—the only one that remained—which I have pursued, and I flatter myself to have found on it the elimination of all the errors that had thus far set reason, as used independently of experience, at variance with itself. I have certainly not evaded reason's questions, by pleading the incapacity of human reason. Rather, I have specified them exhaustively according to principles, and, upon discovering the locus of reason's disagreement with itself, have resolved them to its full satisfaction. To be sure, my answers to these questions have not turned out to be such as a raving dogmatist's thirst for knowledge might expect. Nothing but magical powers—at which I am not adept—could satisfy that kind of thirst for knowledge. Presumably, however, this was also not the aim of our reason's natural vocation. The duty of philosophy was, rather, to remove the deception arising from misinterpretation, even at the cost of destroying the most highly extolled and cherished delusion. In that activity, I have made comprehensiveness my major aim, and I venture to say that there should not be a single metaphysical problem that has not been solved here, or for whose solution the key has not at least been provided. In fact, pure reason is so perfect a unity that, if its principle were insufficient for the solution of even a single one of all the questions assigned to reason by its own nature, then we might just as well throw the principle away; for

then we could not fully rely on its being adequate to any of the remaining questions either. [ . . . ]

## Preface [Second Edition]

Whether someone's treatment of the cognitions pertaining to reason's business does or does not follow the secure path of a science—this we can soon judge from the result. If, after many preparations and arrangements have been made, the treatment falters as soon as it turns to its purpose; or if, in order to reach that purpose, it repeatedly has to retrace its steps and enter upon a different path; or, again, if the various collaborators cannot be brought to agree on the manner in which their common aim is to be achieved—then we may rest assured that such an endeavor is still far from having entered upon the secure path of a science, but is a mere groping about. We shall indeed be rendering a service to reason if we can possibly discover that path, even if we should have to give up as futile much that was included in the purpose which we had previously adopted without deliberation.

*Logic* has been following that secure path from the earliest times. This is evident from the fact that since *Aristotle* it has not needed to retrace a single step, unless perhaps removing some of its dispensable subtleties, or setting it forth in a more distinct and determinate way, were to be counted as improvements of logic, even though they pertain more to the elegance of that science than to its being secure. Another remarkable fact about logic is that thus far it also has not been able to advance a single step, and hence is to all appearances closed and completed. It is true that some of the more recent [philosophers] have meant to expand logic. Some of them have inserted into it *psychological* chapters on the different cognitive powers (the imagination, wit). Others have inserted *metaphysical* chapters on the origin of cognition, or the origin of the different kinds of certainty according to the difference in the objects (i.e., chapters on idealism, skepticism, etc.). Still others have inserted into logic *anthropological* chapters on prejudices (as well as their causes and remedies). But all these attempts to expand logic are the result of ignorance concerning the peculiar nature of this science.

We do not augment sciences, but corrupt them, if we allow their boundaries to overlap. But the boundary Bix of logic is determined quite precisely by the fact that logic is a science that provides nothing but a comprehensive exposition and strict proof of the formal rules of all thought. (Such thought may be *a priori* or empirical, may have any origin or object whatsoever, and may encounter in our minds obstacles that are accidental or natural.)

That logic has been so successful in following the secure path of a science is an advantage that it owes entirely to its limitations. They entitle it, even obligate it, to abstract from all objects of cognition and their differences; hence in logic the understanding deals with nothing more than itself and its form. Reason naturally had to find it far more difficult to enter upon the secure path of science when dealing not just with itself, but also with objects. By the same token, logic is a propaedeutic and forms, as it were, only the vestibule of the sciences; and when knowledge is at issue, while for the judging of such knowledge we do indeed presuppose a logic, yet for its acquisition we must look to what are called sciences properly and objectively.

Now insofar as there is to be reason in these sciences, something in them must be cognized *a priori*. Moreover, reason's cognition can be referred to the Bx object of that cognition in two ways: either in order merely to *determine* the object and its concept (which must be supplied from elsewhere), or in order to *make it actual* as well. The first is reason's *theoretical*, the second its *practical cognition*. In both cases the pure part, i.e., the part in which reason determines its object entirely *a priori*, must be set forth all by itself beforehand, no matter how much or how little it may contain. We must not mix with this part what comes from other sources. For we follow bad economic procedure if we blindly spend what comes in and are afterwards unable, when the procedure falters, to distinguish which part of the income can support the expenditure and which must be cut from it.

Two [sciences involving] theoretical cognitions by reason are to determine their *objects a priori*: they are *mathematics* and *physics*. In mathematics this determination is to be entirely pure; in physics it is to be at least partly pure, but to some extent also in accordance with sources of cognition other than reason.

*Mathematics* has been following the secure path of a science since the earliest times to which the history of human reason extends; it did so already among that admirable people, the Greeks. But we must not Bxi think that it was as easy for mathematics to hit upon that royal road—or, rather, to build it on its own—as it was for logic, where reason deals only with itself. Rather, I believe that for a long time (above all, it was still so among the Egyptians) mathematics did no more than grope about, and that its transformation into a science was due to a *revolution* brought about by the fortunate idea that occurred to one man during an experiment. From that time onward, the route that mathematics had to take could no longer be missed, and the secure path of a science had been entered upon and traced out for all time and to an infinite distance. This revolution in the way of thinking was much more important than the discovery of the passage around the celebrated Cape. Its history, and that of the fortunate man who brought this revolution about, is lost to us. But *Diogenes Laërtius* always names the reputed discoverers of even the minutest elements of geometrical demonstration, elements that in ordinary people's judgment do not even stand in need of proof; and Diogenes hands down to us a story concerning the change that was brought about by the first indication of this new path's discovery. This story shows that the memory of this change must have seemed exceedingly important to mathematicians, and thus became indelible. When the *isosceles triangle* was first demonstrated, something dawned on the man who did so. (He may have been Bxii called *Thales*, or by some other name.) He found that what he needed to do was not to investigate what he saw in the figure, nor—for that matter—to investigate the mere concept of that figure, and to let that inform him, as it were, of the figure's properties. He found, rather, that he must bring out (by constructing the figure) the properties that the figure had by virtue of what he himself was, according to concepts, thinking into it *a priori* and exhibiting. And he found that in order for him to know anything *a priori* and with certainty about the figure, he must attribute to this thing nothing but what follows necessarily from what he has himself put into it in accordance with his concept.

Natural science took much longer to hit upon the high road of science. For only about a century and a half have passed since the ingenious *Bacon*, Baron Verulam, made the proposal that partly prompted this road's discovery, and partly—insofar as some were already on the trail of this discovery—invigorated it further. This discovery, too, can be explained only by a sudden revolution in people's way of thinking. I shall here take natural science into consideration only insofar as it is founded on *empirical* principles.

Something dawned on all investigators of nature when *Galileo* let balls, of a weight chosen by himself, roll down his inclined plane; or when *Torricelli* made the air carry a weight that he had judged beforehand to be equal to the weight of a water column known to Bxiii him; or when, in more recent times, *Stahl* converted metals into calx and that in turn into metal, by withdrawing something from the metals and then restoring it to them.[3] What all these investigators of nature comprehended was that reason has insight only into what it itself produces according to its own plan; and that reason must not allow nature by itself to keep it in leading strings, as it were, but reason must—using principles that underlie its judgments—proceed according to constant laws and compel nature to answer reason's own questions. For otherwise our observations, made without following any plan outlined in advance, are contingent, i.e., they have no coherence at all in terms of a necessary law—even though such a law is what reason seeks and requires. When approaching nature, reason must hold in one hand its principles, in terms of which alone concordant appearances can count as laws, and in the other hand the experiment that it has devised in terms of those principles. Thus reason must indeed approach nature in order to be instructed by it; yet it must do so not in the capacity of a pupil who lets the teacher tell him whatever the teacher wants, but in the capacity of an appointed judge who compels the witnesses

to answer the questions that he puts to them. Thus Bxiv even physics owes that very advantageous revolution in its way of thinking to this idea: the idea that we must, in accordance with what reason itself puts into nature, seek in nature (not attribute to it fictitiously) whatever reason must learn from nature and would know nothing of on its own. This is what put natural science, for the very first time, on the secure path of a science, after it had for so many centuries been nothing more than a mere groping about.

*Metaphysics* is a speculative cognition by reason that is wholly isolated and rises entirely above being instructed by experience. It is cognition through mere concepts (not, like mathematics, cognition through the application of concepts to intuition), so that here reason is to be its own pupil. But although metaphysics is older than all the other sciences, and would endure even if all the others were to be engulfed utterly in the abyss of an all-annihilating barbarism, fate thus far has not favored it to the point of enabling it to enter upon the secure path of a science. For in metaphysics reason continually falters, even when the laws into which it seeks to gain (as it pretends) *a priori* insight are those that are confirmed by the commonest experience. Countless times, in metaphysics, we have to retrace our steps, because we find that our path does not lead us where we want Bxv to go. As regards agreement in the assertions made by its devotees, metaphysics is very far indeed from such agreement. It is, rather, a combat arena which seems to be destined quite specifically for practicing one's powers in mock combat, and in which not one fighter has ever been able to gain even the smallest territory and to base upon his victory a lasting possession. There can be no doubt, therefore, that the procedure of metaphysics has thus far been a mere groping about, and—worst of all—a groping about among mere concepts.

Why is it, then, that in metaphysics we have thus far been unable to find the secure path of science? Might this path be impossible here? Why, then, has nature inflicted on reason, as one of reason's most important concerns, the restless endeavor to discover that path? What is more: how little cause do we have to place confidence in our reason, when in one of the

---

3. I am not here following with precision the course of the history of the experimental method; indeed, the first beginnings of that history are not well known.

most important matters where we desire knowledge reason not only forsakes us, but puts us off with mere pretenses and in the end betrays us! Or if we have only missed the path thus far, what indication do we have that if we renew our search, we may hope to be more fortunate than others have been before us?

Bxvi  I would think that the examples of mathematics and natural science, which have become what they now are by a revolution accomplished all at once, are sufficiently remarkable to [suggest that we should] reflect on the essential component in that revolution, namely, the transformation of the way of thinking that became so advantageous for them; and as far as is permitted by the fact that they, as rational cognitions, are analogous to metaphysics, we should imitate them with regard to that transformation, at least by way of an experiment. Thus far it has been assumed that all our cognition must conform to objects. On that presupposition, however, all our attempts to establish something about them *a priori*, by means of concepts through which our cognition would be expanded, have come to nothing. Let us, therefore, try to find out whether we shall not make better progress in the problems of metaphysics if we assume that objects must conform to our cognition.— This assumption already agrees better with the demanded possibility of an *a priori* cognition of objects—i.e., a cognition that is to ascertain something about them before they are given to us. The situation here is the same as was that of *Copernicus* when he first thought of explaining the motions of celestial bodies. Having found it difficult to make progress there when he assumed that the entire host of stars revolved around the spectator, he tried to find out whether he might not be more successful if he had the spectator revolve and the stars remain at rest.

Bxvii  Now, we can try something similar in metaphysics, with regard to our *intuition* of objects. If our intuition had to conform to the character of its objects, then I do not see how we could know anything *a priori* about that character. But I can quite readily conceive of this possibility if the object (as an object of the senses) conforms to the character of our faculty of intuition. However, if these intuitions are to become cognitions, I cannot remain with them but

must refer them, as representations,[4] to something or other as their object, and must determine this object by means of them. [Since for this determination I require concepts, I must make one of two assumptions.] I can assume that the *concepts* by means of which I bring about this determination likewise conform to the object; and in that case I am again in the same perplexity as to how I can know anything *a priori* about that object. Or else I assume that the objects, or—what amounts to the same—the *experience* in which alone they (as objects that are given to us) can be cognized, conform to those concepts. On this latter assumption, I immediately see an easier way out. For experience is itself a way of cognizing for which I need the understanding. But the understanding has its rule, a rule that I must presuppose within me even before objects are given to me, and hence must presuppose *a priori*; and that rule is expressed in *a priori* concepts. Hence all objects of experience must necessarily conform to these concepts and agree with them. Afterwards, however, we must also consider objects insofar as they can merely be thought, though thought necessarily, but cannot at all be given in experience (at least not in the way in which reason thinks them). Our attempts to think these objects (for they must surely be thinkable) will

Bxviii

───────────

4. [The German term for representations is "Vorstellungen." Werner Pluhar originally translated "Vorstellung" as "presentation," consistent with the following line of reasoning: "The traditional rendering of *Vorstellung* (similarly for the verb) as 'representation' suggests that Kant's theory of perception (etc.) is representational, which, however, it is not (despite the fact that Kant sometimes adds the Latin *repraesentatio*). For one thing, *vorstellen*, in the Kantian use of the term that is relevant here, is not something that *Vorstellungen* do; it is something that *we* do. Moreover, *vorstellen* as so used never means anything like 'represent' in the sense of 'stand for.' Even an empirical intuition, e.g., does not stand for an object of experience (let alone a thing in itself), but rather enters into the experience which that object of experience is . . . Presentations . . . are such objects of our direct awareness as sensations, intuitions, perceptions, concepts, cognitions, ideas, and schemata" p. 22 of *The Critique of Pure Reason*. Whatever the merits of these arguments, given that this volume is a student anthology, we have decided to translate "Vorstellung" as the traditional "representation" for the sake of consistency and continuity with the other texts in this anthology.]

afterwards provide us with a splendid touchstone of what we are adopting as the changed method in our way of thinking, namely, that all we cognize *a priori* about things is what we ourselves put into them.

This experiment is as successful as was desired. It promises that metaphysics will be on the secure path of a science in its first part, namely, the part where Bxix it deals with those *a priori* concepts for which corresponding objects adequate to these concepts can be given in experience. For on this changed way of thinking we can quite readily explain how *a priori* cognition is possible; what is more, we can provide satisfactory proofs for the laws that lie *a priori* at the basis of nature considered as the sum of objects of experience. Neither of these accomplishments was possible on the kind of procedure used thus far. On the other hand, this deduction—provided in the first part of metaphysics—of our faculty of *a priori* cognition produces a disturbing result that seems highly detrimental to the whole purpose of metaphysics as dealt with in the second part: namely, that with this faculty to cognize *a priori* we shall never be able to Bxx go beyond the limits of possible experience, even though doing so is precisely the most essential concern of this science. Yet this very [situation permits] the experiment that will countercheck the truth of the result that we obtained from the first assessment of our *a priori* rational cognition: namely, that our rational cognition applies only to appearances, and leaves the thing in itself uncognized by us, even though actual per se. For what necessarily impels us to go beyond the limits of experience and of all appearances is the *unconditioned* that reason demands in things in themselves; reason— necessarily and quite rightfully—demands this unconditioned for everything conditioned, thus demanding that the series of conditions be completed by means of that unconditioned. Suppose, now, we find that if we assume that our experiential cognition conforms to objects as things in themselves the unconditioned *cannot be thought at all without contradiction*, yet that *the contradiction vanishes* if we assume that our representation of things, as these are given to us, does not conform to them as things in themselves, but that these objects are, rather, appearances that conform to our

way of representing. Suppose that we find, consequently, that the unconditioned is not to be met with in things insofar as we are acquainted with them (i.e., insofar as they are given to us), but is to be met with in them [only] insofar as we are not acquainted with them, namely, insofar as they are *things in themselves*. If this is what we find, it will show that what we assumed initially only by way of an experiment Bxxi does in fact have a foundation.[5] Now, once we have denied that speculative reason can make any progress in that realm of the suprasensible, we still have an option available to us. We can try to discover whether perhaps in reason's practical cognition data can be found that would allow us to determine reason's transcendent concept of the unconditioned. Perhaps in this way our *a priori* cognition, though one that is possible only from a practical point of view, would still allow us to get beyond the limits of all possible experience, as is the wish of metaphysics. Moreover, when we follow this kind of procedure, still speculative reason has at least provided us with room for such an extension [of our cognition], even if it had to leave that room empty. And hence there is as yet nothing to keep us from filling in that room, if we can, with practical *data* of reason; indeed, reason Bxxii summons us to do so.[6]

---

5. This experiment of pure reason is very similar to that done in *chemistry*, which is called sometimes the experiment of *reduction*, but generally the *synthetic procedure*. The *analysis* of the *metaphysician* has divided pure *a priori* cognition into two very heterogeneous elements, namely, that of things as appearances and then of things in themselves. The [metaphysician's] *dialectic* recombines the two so as to yield *agreement* with reason's necessary idea of the *unconditioned*, and finds that this agreement can never be obtained except through that distinction, which is therefore the true one.

6. In the same way, the central laws governing the motions of the celestial bodies provided with established certainty what *Copernicus* had initially assumed only as a hypothesis, and at the same time provided proof of the invisible force (*Newtonian* attraction) that links together the world edifice. That force would have remained forever undiscovered if Copernicus had not dared, in a manner that conflicted with the senses but yet was true, to seek the observed motions not in the celestial objects but in the spectator. The transformation in the way of thinking which I set forth in the *Critique* is analogous to the Copernican hypothesis. Here in the preface I likewise put it

The task, then, of this critique of pure speculative reason consists in the described attempt to transform the procedure previously followed in metaphysics, by subjecting metaphysics to a complete revolution, thus following the example set by the geometricians and investigators of nature. The critique is a treatise on the method [of the science of metaphysics], not a system of the science itself. Yet it does set down the entire outline of metaphysics, including the limits of this science as well as its entire internal structure. [ . . . ]

Bxxiii

Bxxv

[ . . . ] Now in the analytic part of the critique I shall prove that space and time are only forms of our sensible intuition and hence are only conditions of the existence of things as appearances, and that, furthermore, we have no concepts of the understanding, and hence also no elements whatsoever for the cognition of things, except insofar as intuition can be given corresponding to these concepts. That will prove, consequently, that we cannot have cognition of any object as thing in itself, but can have cognition only insofar as the object is one of sensible intuition, i.e., an appearance. And from this it does indeed follow that any possible speculative cognition of reason is restricted to mere objects of *experience*. On the other hand, it must be noted carefully that this [conclusion] is always subject to this reservation: that we must be able at least to *think*, even if not *cognize*, the same objects also as things in themselves.[7] For otherwise an absurd proposition would follow, namely, that there is appearance without anything that appears.

Bxxvi

Bxxvii

Now let us suppose that the distinction, necessitated by our critique, between objects of experience and these same objects as things in themselves, had not been made at all. In that case the principle of causality, and hence nature's mechanism in its determination, would definitely have to hold for all things in general as efficient causes. Hence I could not, without manifest contradiction, say of the same being, for example the human soul, that its will is free and yet is subject to natural necessity, i.e., not free. For I would be taking the soul *in the same sense* in the two propositions, namely, as a thing in general (thing in itself); nor, without prior critique, could I help taking it so. Suppose, on the other hand, that the *Critique* is not in error when it teaches us to take the object in *two different senses*, namely, as appearance and as thing in itself; and that the deduction of the *Critique's* concepts of the understanding is correct, so that the principle of causality applies to things only in the first sense, namely, insofar as they are objects of experience, but that these same objects are not subject to that principle when taken in the second sense. On these suppositions, no contradiction arises when we think the same will in both these ways: in its appearance (i.e., in its visible acts), as conforming necessarily to natural law and as to that extent *not free*; yet on the other hand, *qua* belonging to a thing in itself, as not subject to that law, and hence as *free*. Now as regards my soul when considered from this second standpoint, I cannot *cognize* it through any [use of] speculative reason (let alone through empirical observation); nor, therefore, can I cognize freedom in this way as the property of a being to which I attribute effects in the world of sense. For otherwise I would have to cognize such a being as determined with regard to its existence and yet as not determined in time (which is impossible, because I cannot base such a concept on any intuition). Nevertheless, I can still *think* freedom. I.e., at least my representation of freedom contains no contradiction,

Bxxviii

---

forth only as a hypothesis, even though in the treatise itself it will be proved, not hypothetically but apodeictically, from the character of our representations of space and time and from the elementary concepts of the understanding. Here I put it forth as a hypothesis in order merely to draw attention to the first attempts at such a transformation; and such attempts are always hypothetical.

7. In order for me to *cognize* an object I must be able to prove its [real] possibility (either from its actuality as attested by experience, or *a priori* by means of reason). But I can *think* whatever I want to, even if I am unable to commit myself to there being, in the sum of all [logical] possibilities, an object corresponding to the concept. All that is required in order for me to think something is that I do not contradict myself, i.e., that my concept be a [logically] possible thought. But I require something further

---

in order to attribute objective reality to a concept (i.e., real possibility, as distinguished from the merely logical possibility just mentioned). However—and this is my point—this something further need not be sought in theoretical sources of cognition, but may also lie in practical ones.

if we make our critical distinction between the two ways of representing (sensible and intellectual), and restrict accordingly the pure concepts of the understanding and hence also the principles that flow from them. Now let us suppose that morality necessarily presupposes freedom (in the strictest sense) as a property of our will; for morality adduces *a priori*, as *data* of reason, original practical principles residing Bxxix in reason, and these principles would be absolutely impossible without the presupposition of freedom. But then suppose that speculative reason had proved that freedom cannot be thought at all. In that case the moral presupposition would have to yield to the other [supposition]. For this other [supposition]'s opposite involves a manifest contradiction (whereas the opposite of freedom and morality involves no contradiction, unless freedom has already been presupposed). Hence *freedom*, and with it morality, would have to give way to the *mechanism of nature*. But in fact the situation is different. All I need for morality is that freedom does not contradict itself and hence can at least be thought; I do not need to have any further insight into it. In other words, all I need is that freedom [in my act] puts no obstacle whatsoever in the way of the natural mechanism [that governs] the same act (when taken in a different reference). Thus the doctrine of morality maintains its own place, and so does natural science. But this would not have happened if critique had not instructed us beforehand about our unavoidable ignorance regarding things in themselves, restricting to mere appearances what we can *cognize* theoretically. This same exposition of the positive benefit found in critical principles of pure reason can be produced again in regard to the concept of *God* and of the *simple nature* of our *soul*; Bxxx but for the sake of brevity I shall omit it. Thus I cannot even *assume God, freedom*, and *immortality*, [as I must] for the sake of the necessary practical use of my reason, if I do not at the same time *deprive* speculative reason of its pretensions to transcendent insight. For in order to reach God, freedom, and immortality, speculative reason must use principles that in fact extend merely to objects of possible experience; and when these principles are nonetheless applied to something that cannot be an object of experience,

they actually do always transform it into an appearance, and thus they declare all *practical extension* of reason to be impossible. I therefore had to deny *knowledge* in order to make room for *faith*. And the true source of all the lack of faith which conflicts with morality—and which is always highly dogmatic—is dogmatism in metaphysics, i.e., the prejudice according to which we can make progress in metaphysics without a critique of pure reason. [ . . . ]

## Introduction

### IV. On the Distinction between Analytic and Synthetic Judgments

In all judgments in which we think the relation of a A6/ subject to the predicate (I here consider affirmative B10 judgments only, because the application to negative judgments afterwards is easy), this relation is possible in two ways. Either the predicate B belongs to the subject A as something that is (covertly) contained in this concept A; or B, though connected with concept A, lies quite outside it. In the first case I call the judg- A7 ment *analytic*; in the second, *synthetic*. Hence (affirmative) analytic judgments are those in which the predicate's connection with the subject is thought by identity, whereas those judgments in which this connection is not thought with identity are to be B11 called synthetic. Analytic judgments could also be called *explicative*. For they do not add anything to the concept of the subject through the predicate; rather, they only dissect the concept, breaking it up into its component concepts which had already been thought in it (although thought confusedly). Synthetic judgments, on the other hand, could also be called *expansive*. For they do add to the concept of the subject a predicate that had not been thought in that concept at all and could not have been extracted from it by any dissection. For example, if I say: All bodies are extended—then this is an analytic judgment. For I do not need to go beyond the concept that I link with the word body in order to find that extension is connected with it. All I need to do in order to find this predicate in the concept is to dissect the concept, i.e., become conscious of the manifold that I always think in it. Hence the judgment is analytic. By contrast, if I say: All bodies are heavy—then the predicate is something quite different from what I think in the mere concept of a body as such. Hence adding such a predicate yields a synthetic judgment.

*Experiential judgments, as such, are one and all synthetic.* For to base an analytic judgment on experience would be absurd, because in its case I can formulate my judgment without going outside my concept, and hence do not need for it any testimony of experience. Thus the [analytic] proposition that bodies are extended is one that holds *a priori* and is

B12 not an experiential judgment. For before I turn to experience, I already have in the concept [of body] all the conditions required for my judgment. I have only to extract from it, in accordance with the principle of contradiction, the predicate [of extension]; in doing so, I can at the same time become conscious of the judgment's necessity, of which experience would not even inform me. On the other hand, though in the concept of a body as such I do not at all include the predicate of heaviness, yet the concept designates an object of experience by means of part of this experience; hence I can [synthetically] add to this part further parts, of the same experience, in addition to those that belonged to the concept of a body as such. I can begin by cognizing the concept of a body *analytically* through the characteristics of extension, impenetrability, shape, etc., all of which are thought in this concept. But then I expand my cognition: by looking back to the experience from which I have abstracted this concept of body, I also find heaviness to be always connected with the above characteristics; and so I add it, as a predicate, to that concept *synthetically*. Hence experience is what makes possible the synthesis of the predicate of heaviness with the concept of body. For although neither of the two concepts is contained in the other, yet they belong to each other, though only contingently, as parts of a whole; that whole is experience, which is itself a synthetic combination of intuitions.

A9/      In synthetic judgments that are *a priori*, however,
B13  this remedy is entirely lacking. If I am to go beyond the concept A in order to cognize another concept B as combined with it, I rely on something that

makes the synthesis possible: what is that something, considering that here I do not have the advantage of looking around for it in the realm of experience? Take the proposition: Everything that happens has its cause.—In the concept of something that happens I do indeed think an existence preceded by a time, etc., and from this one can obtain analytic judgments. But the concept of a cause lies quite outside that earlier concept and indicates something different from what happens; hence it is not part of what is contained in this latter representation. How can I attribute whatever happens to something quite different from it, and cognize as belonging to it—indeed, belonging to it necessarily—the concept of cause, even though it does not contain this concept? What is here the unknown = X on which the understanding relies when it believes that it discovers, outside the concept A, a predicate B that is foreign to concept A but that the understanding considers nonetheless to be connected with that concept? This unknown cannot be experience. For in adding the representation of cause to the representation of what happens, the above principle does so not only with greater universality than experience can provide, but also with the necessity's being expressed; hence it does so entirely *a priori* and on the basis of mere concepts. Now, on such synthetic, i.e., expansive, principles depends the whole final aim of our speculative *a priori* cogni-  A10/ tion. For, analytic principles are indeed exceedingly  B14 important and necessary, but only for attaining that distinctness in concepts which is required for a secure and extensive synthesis that will be a genuinely new edifice.

## V. All Theoretical Sciences of Reason Contain Synthetic *a Priori* Judgments as Principles

1. *Mathematical judgments are, one and all, synthetic.* Although this proposition is incontestably certain and has very important consequences, it seems thus far to have escaped the notice of those who have analyzed human reason; indeed, it seems to be directly opposed to all their conjectures. For they found that all mathematical inferences proceed (as the nature of all apodeictic certainty requires) according to the principle of contradiction; and thus they came to be

persuaded that their principles too could be cognized on the basis of the principle of contradiction. In this they were mistaken. For though we can indeed gain insight into a synthetic proposition according to the principle of contradiction, we can never do so [by considering] that proposition by itself, but rather only by presupposing another synthetic proposition from which it can be deduced.

We must note, first of all, that mathematical propositions, properly so called, are always *a priori* judgments rather than empirical ones; for they carry with them necessity, which we could never glean from experience. But if anyone refuses to grant that all such propositions are *a priori*—all right: then I restrict my assertion to *pure mathematics*, in the very concept of which is implied that it contains not empirical but only pure *a priori* cognition.

It is true that one might at first think that the proposition 7 + 5 = 12 is a merely analytic one that follows, by the principle of contradiction, from the concept of a sum of 7 and 5. Yet if we look more closely, we find that the concept of the sum of 7 and 5 contains nothing more than the union of the two numbers into one; but in [thinking] that union we are not thinking in any way at all what that single number is that unites the two. In thinking merely that union of 7 and 5, I have by no means already thought the concept of 12; and no matter how long I dissect my concept of such a possible sum, still I shall never find in it that 12. We must go beyond these concepts and avail ourselves of the intuition corresponding to one of the two: e.g., our five fingers, or (as *Segner* does in his *Arithmetic*) five dots. In this way we must gradually add, to the concept of 7, the units of the 5 given in intuition. For I start by taking the number 7. Then, for the concept of the 5, I avail myself of the fingers of my hand as intuition. Thus, in that image of mine, I gradually add to the number 7 the units that I previously gathered together in order to make up the number 5. In this way I see the number 12 arise. That 5 *were to be added* to 7, this I had indeed already thought in the concept of a sum = 7 + 5, but not that this sum is equal to the number 12. Arithmetic propositions are therefore always synthetic. We become aware of this all the more

distinctly if we take larger numbers. For then it is very evident that, no matter how much we twist and turn our concepts, we can never find the [number of the] sum by merely dissecting our concepts, i.e., without availing ourselves of intuition.

Just as little are any principles of pure geometry analytic. That the straight line between two points is the shortest is a synthetic proposition. For my concept of *straight* contains nothing about magnitude, but only a quality. Therefore the concept of shortest is entirely added to the concept of a straight line and cannot be extracted from it by any dissection. Hence we must here avail ourselves of intuition; only by means of it is the synthesis possible.

It is true that a few propositions presupposed by geometers are actually analytic and based on the principle of contradiction. But, like identical propositions, they serve not as principles but only [as links in] the chain of method. Examples are a = a, the whole is equal to itself; or (a+b) > a, i.e., the whole is greater than its part. And yet even these principles, although they hold according to mere concepts, are admitted in mathematics only because they can be exhibited in intuition. What commonly leads us here to believe that the predicate of such apodeictic judgments is contained in our very concept, and that the judgment is therefore analytic, is merely the ambiguity of our terms. For we say that we *are to* add in thought a certain predicate to a given concept, and this necessity adheres indeed to the very concepts. But here the question is not what we *are to* add in thought to the given concept, but what we *actually think* in the concept, even if only obscurely; and there we find that, although the predicate does indeed adhere necessarily to such concepts, yet it does so not as something thought in the concept itself, but by means of an intuition that must be added to the concept.

2. *Natural science (physica) contains synthetic* a priori *judgments as principles.* Let me cite as examples just a few propositions: e.g., the proposition that in all changes in the corporeal world the quantity of matter remains unchanged; or the proposition that in all communication of motion, action and reaction must always be equal to each other. Both propositions are clearly not only necessary, and hence of *a*

*priori* origin, but also synthetic. For in the concept of matter I do not think permanence, but think merely the matter's being present in space insofar as it occupies space. Hence I actually go beyond the concept of matter in order to add to it *a priori* in thought something that I have not thought *in it*. Hence the proposition is thought not analytically but synthetically and yet *a priori*, and the same occurs in the remaining propositions of the pure part of natural science.

3. *Metaphysics is to contain synthetic* a priori *cognitions*. This holds even if metaphysics is viewed as a science that thus far has merely been attempted, but that because of the nature of human reason is nonetheless indispensable. Metaphysics is not at all concerned merely to dissect concepts of things that we frame *a priori*, and thereby to explicate them analytically. Rather, in metaphysics we want to expand our *a priori* cognition. In order to do this, we must use principles which go beyond the given concept and which add to it something that was not contained in it; and, by means of such synthetic *a priori* judgments, we must presumably go so far beyond such concepts that even experience can no longer follow us; as in the proposition: The world must have a first beginning—and others like that. And hence metaphysics consists, at least *in terms of its purpose*, of nothing but synthetic *a priori* propositions.

B19  ### VI. The General Problem of Pure Reason

Much is gained already when we can bring a multitude of inquiries under the formula of a single problem. For we thereby facilitate not only our own business by defining it precisely, but also—for anyone else who wants to examine it—the judgment as to whether or not we have carried out our project adequately. Now the proper problem of pure reason is contained in this question:

How are synthetic judgments possible *a priori*?

That metaphysics has thus far remained in such a shaky state of uncertainty and contradictions is attributable to a sole cause: the fact that this problem, and perhaps even the distinction between *analytic* and *synthetic* judgments, has not previously occurred to anyone. Whether metaphysics stands or falls depends on the solution of this problem, or on an adequate proof that the possibility which metaphysics demands to see explained does not exist at all. *David Hume* at least came closer to this problem than any other philosopher. Yet he did not think of it nearly determinately enough and in its universality, but merely remained with the synthetic proposition about the connection of an effect with its causes  B20 (*principium causalitatis*). He believed he had discovered that such a proposition is quite impossible *a priori*. Thus, according to his conclusions, everything that we call metaphysics would amount to no more than the delusion of a supposed rational insight into what in fact is merely borrowed from experience and has, through habit, acquired the illusion of necessity. This assertion, which destroys all pure philosophy, would never have entered Hume's mind if he had envisaged our problem in its universality. For he would then have seen that by his argument there could be no pure mathematics either, since it certainly does contain synthetic *a priori* propositions; and from such an assertion his good sense would surely have saved him.

In solving the above problem we solve at the same time another one, concerning the possibility of the use of pure reason in establishing and carrying out all sciences that contain theoretical *a priori* cognition of objects; i.e., we also answer these questions:

How is pure mathematics possible?

How is pure natural science possible?

Since these sciences actually exist, it is surely proper for us to ask **how** they are possible; for that they  B21 must be possible is proved by their being actual.[8] As regards *metaphysics*, however, everyone is justified in doubting its possibility: its progress thus far has been

---

8. This actuality may still be doubted by some in the case of pure natural science. Yet we need only examine the propositions that are to be found at the beginning of physics proper (empirical physics), such as those about the permanence of the quantity of matter, about inertia, about the equality of action and reaction, etc., in order to be quickly convinced that these propositions themselves amount to a *physica pura* (or *physica*

poor; and thus far not a single metaphysics has been put forth of which we can say, as far as the essential purpose of metaphysics is concerned, that it is actually present.

Yet in a certain sense this *kind of cognition* must likewise be regarded as given; and although metaphysics is not actual as a science, yet it is actual as a natural predisposition (i.e., as a *metaphysica naturalis*). For human reason, impelled by its own need rather than moved by the mere vanity of gaining a lot of knowledge, proceeds irresistibly to such questions as cannot be answered by any experiential use of reason and any principles taken from such use. And thus all human beings, once their reason has expanded to [the point where it can] speculate, actually have always had in them, and always will have in them, some metaphysics. Now concerning it, too, there is this question:

B22    How is metaphysics as a natural predisposition possible?

I.e., how, from the nature of universal human reason, do the questions arise that pure reason poses to itself and is impelled, by its own need, to answer as best it can?

Thus far, however, all attempts to answer these natural questions—e.g., whether the world has a beginning or has been there from eternity, etc.—have met with unavoidable contradictions. Hence we cannot rest content with our mere natural predisposition for metaphysics, i.e., our faculty of pure reason itself, even though some metaphysics or other (whatever one it might be) always arises from it. Rather, it must be possible, by means of this predisposition, to attain certainty either concerning our knowledge or lack of knowledge of the objects [of metaphysics], i.e., either concerning a decision about the objects that its questions deal with, or certainty concerning the ability or inability of reason to make judgments about these objects. In other words, it must be possible to expand our pure reason in a reliable way or to set limits for

---

*rationalis*). Such a physics, as a science in its own right, surely deserves to be put forth separately and in its whole range, whether this range be narrow or broad.

it that are determinate and safe. This last question, which flows from the general problem above, may rightly be stated thus:

How is metaphysics as science possible?

Ultimately, therefore, a critique of reason leads necessarily to science; the dogmatic use of pure reason  B23 without critique, on the other hand, to baseless assertions that can always be opposed by others that seem equally plausible, and hence to *skepticism*.

This science, moreover, cannot be overly or forbiddingly voluminous. For it deals not with objects of reason, which are infinitely diverse, but merely with itself, that is with problems that issue entirely from its own womb; they are posed to it not by the nature of things distinct from it, but by its own nature. And thus, once it has become completely acquainted with its own ability regarding the objects that it may encounter in experience, reason must find it easy to determine, completely and safely, the range and the limits of its use [when] attempted beyond all limits of experience.

Hence all attempts that have been made thus far to bring a metaphysics about *dogmatically* can and must be regarded as if they had never occurred. For whatever is analytic in one metaphysics or another, i.e., is the mere dissection of concepts residing *a priori* in our reason, is only a set up for metaphysics proper, and is not yet its purpose at all. That purpose is to expand our *a priori* cognition synthetically, and for this purpose the dissection of reason's *a priori* concepts is useless. For it shows merely what is contained in these concepts; it does not show how we arrive at such concepts *a priori*, so that we could then also determine the valid use of such concepts in regard  B24 to the objects of all cognition generally. Nor do we need much self-denial to give up all these claims; for every metaphysics put forth thus far has long since been deprived of its reputation by the fact that it gave rise to undeniable, and in the dogmatic procedure indeed unavoidable, contradictions of reason with itself. A different treatment, completely opposite to the one used thus far, must be given to metaphysics—a science, indispensable to human reason, whose every new shoot can indeed be lopped off but whose root cannot be eradicated. We shall need more perseverance in order to keep from being deterred—either from within by the difficulty of this science or from without by people's resistance to it—from thus finally bringing it to a prosperous and fruitful growth.

## VII. Idea and Division of a Special Science under the Name of Critique of Pure Reason

From all of the above we arrive at the idea of a special science that may be called the *critique of pure reason*. For reason is the faculty that provides us with the *principles* of a priori cognition. Hence pure reason is that reason which contains the principles for cognizing something absolutely *a priori*. An *organon* of pure reason would be the sum of those principles by which all pure *a priori* cognitions can be acquired and actually brought about. Comprehensive application of such an organon would furnish us with a system of pure reason. Such a system, however, is a tall order; and it remains to be seen whether indeed an expansion of our cognition is possible here at all, and in what cases it is possible. Hence a science that merely judges pure reason, its sources, and its bounds may be regarded as the *propaedeutic* to the system of pure reason. Such a propaedeutic would have to be called not a *doctrine* but only a *critique* of pure reason. Its benefit, in regard to speculation, would actually only be negative. For such a critique would serve only to purify our reason, not to expand it, and would keep our reason free from errors, which is a very great gain already. I call *transcendental* all cognition that deals not so much with objects as rather with our way of cognizing objects in general insofar as that way of cognizing is to be possible *a priori*. A *system* of such concepts would be called *transcendental philosophy*. But, once again, this system of transcendental philosophy is too much for us as yet, here at the beginning. For since such a science would have to contain both analytic cognition and synthetic *a priori* cognition, in their completeness, it has too broad a range as far as our aim is concerned. For we need to carry the analysis only as far as it is indispensably necessary for gaining insight, in their entire range, into the principles of *a priori* synthesis, which is all that we are concerned with. [ . . . ]

[ . . . ] Human cognition has two stems, namely, *sensibility* and *the understanding*, which perhaps spring from a common root, though one unknown to us. Through sensibility objects are *given* to us; through the understanding they are *thought*. Now if sensibility were to contain a priori representations constituting the condition under which objects are given to us, it would to that extent belong to transcendental philosophy. And since the conditions under which alone the objects of human cognition are given to us precede the conditions under which these objects are thought, the transcendental doctrine of sense would have to belong to the *first* part of the science of elements.

## Transcendental Doctrine of Elements

### Part I. Transcendental Aesthetic

§1. In whatever way and by whatever means a cognition may refer to objects, still *intuition* is that by which a cognition refers to objects directly, and at which all thought aims as a means. Intuition, however, takes place only insofar as the object is given to us; but that, in turn, is possible only—for us human beings, at any rate—by the mind's being affected by the object in a certain manner. The capacity (a receptivity) to acquire representations as a result of the way in which we are affected by objects is called **sensibility**. Hence by means of sensibility objects are *given* to us, and it alone supplies us with *intuitions*. But objects are *thought* through the understanding and *concepts* arise from it. Yet all thought must, by means of certain marks, refer ultimately to intuitions, whether it does so straightforwardly (*directe*) or circuitously (*indirecte*); and hence it must, in us, refer ultimately to sensibility, because no object can be given to us in any other manner than through sensibility.

The effect of an object on our capacity for representation, insofar as we are affected by the object, is *sensation*. Intuition that refers to the object through sensation is called *empirical* intuition. The undetermined object of an empirical intuition is called *appearance*.

Marginal references: A15/B29, B30, A16, A11, B25, A12, A17/B31, A19/B33, B34, A20

Whatever in an appearance corresponds to sensation I call its *matter*; but whatever in an appearance brings about the fact that the manifold of the appearance can be ordered in certain relations I call the *form* of appearance. Now, that in which alone sensations can be ordered and put into a certain form cannot itself be sensation again. Therefore, although the matter of all appearance is given to us only *a posteriori*, the form of all appearance must altogether lie ready for the sensations *a priori* in the mind; and hence that form must be capable of being examined apart from all sensation.

All representations in which nothing is found that belongs to sensation I call *pure* (in the transcendental sense of the term). Accordingly, the pure form of sensible intuitions generally, in which everything manifold in experience is intuited in certain rela-
B35 tions, will be found in the mind *a priori*. This pure form of sensibility will also itself be called *pure intuition*. Thus, if from the representation of a body I separate what the understanding thinks in it, such as substance, force, divisibility, etc., and if I similarly separate from it what belongs to sensation in it, such
A21 as impenetrability, hardness, color, etc., I am still left with something from this empirical intuition, namely, extension and shape. These belong to pure intuition, which, even if there is no actual object of the senses or of sensation, has its place in the mind *a priori*, as a mere form of sensibility.

There must, therefore, be a science of all princi-
B36 ples of *a priori* sensibility; I call such a science *transcendental aesthetic*. It constitutes the first part of the transcendental doctrine of elements, and stands in contrast to that [part of the] transcendental doctrine of elements which contains the principles of pure thought and is called transcendental logic.
A22       Hence in the transcendental aesthetic we shall, first of all, *isolate* sensibility, by separating from it everything that the understanding thinks [in connection] with it through its concepts, so that nothing other than empirical intuition will remain. Second, we shall also segregate from sensibility everything that belongs to sensation, so that nothing will remain but pure intuition and the mere form of appearances, which is all that sensibility can supply *a priori*. In the

course of that inquiry it will be found that there are two pure forms of sensible intuition, which are principles for *a priori* cognition: namely, space and time. We now proceed to the task of examining these.

## Transcendental Aesthetic                                B37
### Section I. Space
#### §2. Metaphysical Exposition of This Concept

By means of outer sense (a property of our mind) we represent objects as outside us, and represent them one and all in space. In space their shape, magnitude, and relation to one another are determined or determinable. By means of inner sense the mind intuits itself or its inner state. Although inner sense provides no intuition of the soul itself as an object, yet there is a determinate form [time] under which A23 alone an intuition of its inner state is possible. Thus everything belonging to our inner determinations is represented in relations of time. Time cannot be intuited outwardly, any more than space can be intuited as something within us. What, then, are space and time? Are they actual beings? Are they only determinations of things, or, for that matter, relations among them? If so, are they at least determinations or relations that would also belong to things intrinsically, i.e., even if these things were not intuited? Or are they determinations and relations that adhere B38 only to the form of intuition and hence to the subjective character of our mind, so that apart from that character these predicates cannot be ascribed to any thing at all? In order to instruct ourselves on these points, let us first of all give an exposition of the concept of space. Now, by *exposition* (*expositio*) I mean clear (even if not comprehensive) representation of what belongs to a concept; and such exposition is *metaphysical* if it contains what exhibits the concept as *given a priori*.

1. Space is not an empirical concept that has been abstracted from outer experiences. For the representation of space must already be presupposed in order for certain sensations to be referred to something outside me (i.e., referred to something in a location of space other than the location in which I am). And

it must similarly already be presupposed in order for me to be able to represent [the objects of] these sensations as outside and *alongside* one another, and hence to represent them not only as different but as being in different locations. Accordingly, the representation of space cannot be one that we take from the relations of outer appearance by means of experience; rather, only through the representation of space is that outer experience possible in the first place.

A24
B39 2. Space is a necessary *a priori* representation that underlies all outer intuitions. We can never have a representation of there being no space, even though we are quite able to think of there being no objects encountered in it. Hence space must be regarded as the condition for the possibility of appearances, and not as a determination dependent on them. Space is an *a priori* representation that necessarily underlies outer appearances.

3. Space is not a discursive or, as we say, universal
A25 concept of things as such; rather, it is a pure intuition. For, first, we can represent only one space; and when we speak of many spaces, we mean by that only parts of one and the same unique space. Nor, second, can these parts precede the one all-encompassing space, as its constituents, as it were (from which it can be assembled); rather, they can be thought only as *in* it. Space is essentially one; the manifold in it, and hence also the universal concept of spaces as such, rests solely on limitations. It follows from this that, as far as space is concerned, an *a priori* intuition of it (i.e., one that is not empirical) underlies all concepts of space. By the same token, no geometric principles—e.g., the principle that in a triangle two sides together are greater than the third—are ever derived from universal concepts of *line* and *triangle*; rather, they are all derived from intuition, and are derived from it moreover *a priori* with apodeictic certainty.

4. We represent space as an infinite *given* mag-
B40 nitude. Now it is true that every concept must be thought as a representation that is contained in an infinite multitude of different possible representations (as their common characteristic) and hence the concept contains these representations *under itself*. But no concept, as such, can be thought as containing an infinite multitude of representations

*within itself*. Yet that is how we think space (for all parts of space, *ad infinitum*, are simultaneous). Therefore the original representation of space is an *a priori intuition*, not a *concept*.

## §3. Transcendental Exposition of the Concept of Space

By a *transcendental exposition* I mean the explication of a concept as a principle that permits insight into the possibility of other synthetic *a priori* cognitions. Such explication requires (1) that cognitions of that sort do actually flow from the given concept, and (2) that these cognitions are possible only on the presupposition of a given way of explicating that concept.

Geometry is a science that determines the properties of space synthetically and yet *a priori*. What, then, must the representation of space be in order for such cognition of space to be possible? Space must B41 originally be intuition. For from a mere concept one cannot obtain propositions that go beyond the concept; but we do obtain such propositions in geometry (Introduction, V). This intuition must, however, be encountered in us *a priori*, i.e., prior to any perception of an object; hence this intuition must be pure rather than empirical. For geometric propositions are one and all apodeictic, i.e., linked with the consciousness of their necessity—e.g., the proposition that space has only three dimensions. But propositions of that sort cannot be empirical judgments or judgments of experience; nor can they be inferred from such judgments.

How, then, can the mind have an outer intuition which precedes the objects themselves, and in which the concept of these objects can be determined *a priori*? Obviously, this can be so only insofar as this intuition resides merely in the subject, as the subject's formal character of being affected by objects and of thereby acquiring *direct representation* of them, i.e., *intuition*, and hence only as form of outer *sense* in general.

Our explication of the concept of space is, therefore, the only one that makes comprehensible the *possibility of geometry* as a [kind of] synthetic *a priori* cognition. Any way of explicating the concept that fails to make this possibility comprehensible, even if it should otherwise seem to have some similarity to ours, can be distinguished from it most safely by these criteria.

A26/
B42

Conclusions from the Above Concepts

(a) Space represents no property whatsoever of any things in themselves, nor does it represent things in themselves in their relation to one another. That is, space represents no determination of such things, no determination that adheres to objects themselves and that would remain even if we abstracted from all subjective conditions of intuition. For determinations, whether absolute or relative, cannot be intuited prior to the existence of the things to which they belong, and hence cannot be intuited *a priori*.

(b) Space is nothing but the mere form of all appearances of outer senses; i.e., it is the subjective condition of sensibility under which alone outer intuition is possible for us. Now, the subject's receptivity for being affected by objects necessarily precedes all intuitions of these objects. Thus we can understand how the form of all appearances can be given in the mind prior to all actual perceptions, and hence given *a priori*; and we can understand how this form, as a pure intuition in which all objects must be determined, can contain, prior to all experience, principles for the relations among these objects.

Only from the human standpoint, therefore, can we speak of space, of extended beings, etc. If we depart from the subjective condition under which alone we can—namely, as far as we may be affected by objects—acquire outer intuition, then the representation of space means nothing whatsoever. This A27/ predicate is ascribed to things only insofar as they ap- B43 pear to us, i.e., only insofar as they are objects of sensibility. The constant form of this receptivity which we call sensibility is a necessary condition of all relations in which objects are intuited as outside us; and if we abstract from these objects, then the form of that receptivity is a pure intuition that bears the name of space. We cannot make the special conditions of sensibility conditions of the possibility of things, but only of the possibility of their appearances. Hence we can indeed say that space encompasses all things that appear to us externally, but not that it encompasses

all things in themselves, intuited or not, or intuited by whatever subject. For we can make no judgment at all about the intuitions of other thinking beings, as to whether they are tied to the same conditions that limit our intuition and that are valid for us universally. If the limitation on a judgment is added to the concept of the subject, then the judgment holds unconditionally. The proposition, All things are side by side in space, holds under the limitation that these things are taken as objects of our sensible intuition. If I here add the condition to the concept and say, All things considered as outer appearances are side by side in space, then this rule holds universally and without limitation. Accordingly, our A28/ exposition teaches that space is *real* (i.e., objectively B44 valid) in regard to everything that we can encounter externally as object, but teaches at the same time that space is *ideal* in regard to things when reason considers them in themselves, i.e., without taking into account the character of our sensibility. Hence we assert that space is *empirically real* (as regards all possible outer experience), despite asserting that space is *transcendentally ideal*, i.e., that it is nothing as soon as we omit [that space is] the condition of the possibility of all experience and suppose space to be something underlying things in themselves.

Besides space, however, no other subjective representation that is referred to something external could be called an *a priori* objective representation. For from none of them can we derive synthetic *a priori* propositions, as we can from intuition in space (§3). Hence, strictly speaking, ideality does not apply to them, even though they agree with the representation of space inasmuch as they belong merely to the subjective character of the kind of sense involved. They may belong, e.g., to the sense of sight, of hearing, or of touch, by sensations of colors, sounds, or heat. Yet because they are mere sensations rather than intuitions, they do not allow us to cognize any object at all, let alone *a priori*.

The only aim of this comment is to prevent an B45 error: it might occur to someone to illustrate the ideality of space asserted above by means of examples such as colors or taste, etc. These are thoroughly insufficient for this, because they are rightly regarded not as properties of things, but merely as changes in ourselves as subjects, changes that may even be different in different people. For in this case, something that originally is itself only appearance—e.g., a rose—counts as a thing in itself in the empirical meaning of this expression, a thing in itself that in regard to color can nonetheless appear differently to every eye. The transcendental concept of appearances in space, by contrast, is a critical reminder that nothing whatsoever that is intuited in space is a thing in itself, and that space is not a form of things, one that might belong to them as they are in themselves. Rather, what we call external objects are nothing but mere representations of our sensibility. The form of this sensibility is space; but its true correlate, i.e., the thing in itself, is not cognized at all through these representations, and cannot be, since the thing in itself is never at issue in experience.

## Transcendental Aesthetic

### Section II. Time

#### §4. Metaphysical Exposition of the Concept of Time

1. Time is not an empirical concept that has been abstracted from any experience. For simultaneity or succession would not even enter our perception if the representation of time did not underlie them *a priori*. Only on the presupposition of this representation can we represent this and that as being at one and the same time (simultaneously) or at different times (successively).

2. Time is a necessary representation that underlies all intuitions. As regards appearances in general, we cannot annul time itself, though we can quite readily remove appearances from time. Hence time is given *a priori*. All actuality of appearances is possible only in time. Appearances, one and all, may go away; but time itself (as the universal condition of their possibility) cannot be annulled.

3. This *a priori* necessity, moreover, is the basis for the possibility of apodeictic principles about relations of time, or for the possibility of axioms about

time in general. Time has only one dimension; different times are not simultaneous but successive (just as different spaces are not successive but simultaneous). These principles cannot be obtained from experience. For experience would provide neither strict universality nor apodeictic certainty; we could say only that common perception teaches us that it is so, but not that it must be so. These principles hold as rules under which alone experiences are possible at all; and they instruct us prior to experience, not through it.

4. Time is not a discursive or, as it is called, universal concept; rather, it is a pure form of sensible intuition. Different times are only parts of one and the same time; and the kind of representation that can be given only through a single object is intuition. Moreover, the proposition that different times cannot be simultaneous could not be derived from a universal concept. The proposition is synthetic, and [therefore] cannot arise from concepts alone. Hence it is immediately contained in the intuition and representation of time.

5. To say that time is infinite means nothing more than that any determinate magnitude of time is possible only through limitations of a single underlying time. Hence the original representation *time* must be given as unlimited. But if something is such that its parts themselves and any magnitude of an object in it can be represented determinately only through limitation, then the whole representation of it cannot be given through concepts (for they contain only partial representations), but any such representation must be based on immediate intuition.

#### §5. Transcendental Exposition of the Concept of Time

I may refer for this exposition to No. 3, where, for the sake of brevity, I put among the items of the metaphysical exposition what in fact is transcendental. Let me add here that the concept of change, and with it the concept of motion (as change of place), is possible only through and in the representation of time; and that if this representation were not (inner) *a priori* intuition, no concept whatsoever could make comprehensible the possibility of a change, i.e., of a

combination, in one and the same object, of contradictorily opposed predicates (e.g., one and the same
thing's being in a place and not being in that same
place). Only in time can both of two contradictorily
B49  opposed determinations be met with in one thing:
namely, *successively*. Hence our concept of time
explains the possibility of all that synthetic *a priori*
cognition which is set forth by the—quite fertile—
general theory of motion.

### §6. Conclusions from these Concepts

(a) Time is not something that is self-subsistent or
that attaches to things as an objective determination,
and that hence would remain if one abstracted from
all subjective conditions of our intuition of it. For if
time were self-subsistent, then it would be something
A33  that without there being an actual object would yet
be actual. But if, on the second alternative, time were
a determination or order attaching to things themselves, then it could not precede the objects as their
condition, and could not be cognized *a priori* and
intuited through synthetic propositions. But this *a
priori* cognition and intuition can take place quite
readily if time is nothing but the subjective condition
under which alone any intuition can take place in
us. For in that case this form of inner intuition can
be represented prior to the objects, and hence represented *a priori*.

(b) Time is nothing but the form of inner sense,
B50  i.e., of the intuiting we do of ourselves and of our
inner state. For time cannot be a determination of
outer appearances; it does not belong to any shape
or position, etc., but rather determines the relation
of representations in our inner state. And precisely
because this inner intuition provides no shape, do
we try to make up for this deficiency by means of
analogies. We represent temporal sequence by a line
progressing *ad infinitum*, a line in which the manifold constitutes a series of only one dimension. And
from the properties of that line we infer all the properties of time, except for the one difference that the
parts of the line are simultaneous whereas the parts of
time are always successive. This fact, moreover, that
all relations of time can be expressed by means of

outer intuition, shows that the representation of time
is itself intuition.

(c) Time is the formal *a priori* condition of all ap-  A34
pearances generally. Space, as the pure form of all
outer appearances, is limited to just outer appearances as an *a priori* condition. But all representations,
whether or not they have outer things as their objects, do yet in themselves, as determinations of the
mind, belong to our inner state; and this inner state
is subject to the formal condition of inner intuition,
and hence to the condition of time. Therefore time
is an *a priori* condition of all appearance generally:
it is the immediate condition of inner appearances
(of our souls), and precisely thereby also, indirectly,  B51
a condition of outer appearances. If I can say *a priori*
that all outer appearances are in space and are determined *a priori* according to spatial relations, then
the principle of inner sense allows me to say, quite
universally, that all appearances generally, i.e., all objects of the senses, are in time and necessarily stand
in relations of time.

If we take objects as they may be in themselves—
i.e., if we abstract from the way in which we intuit
ourselves inwardly, and in which by means of this intuition we also take into our faculty of representation
all outer intuitions—then time is nothing. Time has
objective validity only with regard to appearances,  A35
because these are already things considered as *objects of our senses*. But time is no longer objective if
we abstract from the sensibility of our intuition, and
hence from the way of representing peculiar to us,
and speak of *things as such*. Hence time is merely
a subjective condition of our (human) intuition (an
intuition that is always sensible—i.e., inasmuch as
we are affected by objects); in itself, i.e., apart from
the subject, time is nothing. Nevertheless, time is
necessarily objective in regard to all appearances,
and hence also in regard to all things that we can encounter in experience. We cannot say that all things
are in time; for in the concept of things as such we  B52
abstract from all ways of intuiting them, while yet this
intuition is the very condition under which time belongs in the representation of objects. If now we add
the condition to the concept, and say that all things
as appearances (objects of sensible intuition) are in

time, then this principle has all its objective correctness and *a priori* universality.

Hence the doctrine we are asserting is that time is *empirically real*, i.e., objectively valid in regard to all objects that might ever be given to our senses. And since our intuition is always sensible, no object that is not subject to the condition of time can ever be given A36 to us in experience. However, we dispute that time has any claim to absolute reality; i.e., we dispute any claim whereby time would attach to things absolutely, as a condition or property, without taking into account the form of our sensible intuition. Nor indeed can such properties, properties belonging to things in themselves, ever be given to us through the senses. In this, then, consists the *transcendental ideality* of time. According to this view, if we abstract from the subjective conditions of sensible intuition, then time is nothing and cannot be included either as subsist-B53 ing or as inhering among objects in themselves (apart from their relation to our intuition). But this ideality of time is not to be compared, any more than is the ideality of space, with the subreptions of sensations. For in their case we presuppose that the appearance itself in which these predicates inhere has objective reality. In the case of time, such objective reality is entirely absent, except insofar as this reality is merely empirical, i.e., except insofar as we regard the object itself as merely appearance. See, on this, the above comment at the close of the preceding section.

## §7. Elucidation

Against this theory, which grants that time is empirically real but disputes that it is real absolutely and transcendentally, I have heard men of insight raise one objection quite unanimously. I gather from this great unanimity that the objection must occur A37 naturally to every reader who is not accustomed to contemplations such as these. The objection is the following. Changes are actual. (This is proved by the variation on the part of our own representations—even if one were to deny all outer appearances, along with their changes.) Now changes are possible only in time. Therefore time is something actual. There is no difficulty in replying to the objection. I concede the whole argument. Time is indeed something

actual, namely, the actual form of inner intuition. It therefore has subjective reality in regard to inner B54 experience; i.e., I actually have the representation of time and of my determinations in time. Hence time is to be regarded as actual, though not as an object but as the way of representing that I myself have as an object. Suppose, however, that I could intuit myself without being subject to this condition of sensibility, or that another being could so intuit me; in that case the very same determinations that we now represent as changes would provide a cognition in which the representation of time, and hence also that of change, would not occur at all. Hence time retains its empirical reality as condition of all our experiences. Only absolute reality must, by the reasons adduced above, be denied to time. Time is nothing but the form of our inner intuition.[9] If we take away from time [the qualification that it is] the A38 special condition of our sensibility, then the concept of time vanishes as well; time attaches not to objects themselves, but merely to the subject intuiting them.

But what causes this objection to be raised so unanimously, and raised, moreover, by those who B55 nonetheless cannot think of any plausible objection against the doctrine that space is ideal, is the following. They had no hope of establishing apodeictically that space is real absolutely; for they are confronted by idealism, according to which the actuality of external objects is incapable of strict proof. By contrast, the actuality of the object of our inner sense (the actuality of myself and of my state) is directly evident through consciousness. External objects might be a mere illusion; but the object of inner sense is, in their opinion, undeniably something actual. They failed to bear in mind, however, that both of them, though their actuality as representations is indisputable, still belong only to appearance. Appearance always has two sides. One is the side where the object is regarded in itself (without regard to the way in which it is intuited, which is precisely why its character always

_____

9. I can indeed say: My representations follow one another. But that means only that we are conscious of them as being in a time sequence—in accordance, i.e., with the form of inner sense. Time is not, on that account, something in itself, nor is it a determination attaching to things objectively.

remains problematic). The other is the side where we take account of the form of the intuition of this object. This form must be sought not in the object in itself, but in the subject to whom the object appears. Yet this form belongs to the appearance of this object actually and necessarily.

Time and space are, accordingly, two sources of cognition. From these sources we can draw *a priori* different synthetic cognitions—as is shown above all by the splendid example that pure mathematics provides in regard to our cognitions of space and its relations. For time and space, taken together, are pure forms of all sensible intuition, and thereby make synthetic propositions possible *a priori*. But precisely thereby (i.e., by being merely conditions of sensibility), these *a priori* sources of cognition determine their own limits; namely, they determine that they apply to objects merely insofar as these are regarded as appearances, but do not exhibit things in themselves. Appearances are the sole realm where these *a priori* sources of cognition are valid; if we go outside that realm, there is no further objective use that can be made of them. This [limited] reality of space and time leaves the reliability of experiential cognition otherwise untouched; for we have equal certainty in that cognition, whether these forms necessarily attach to things in themselves or only to our intuition of these things. Those, on the other hand, who assert that space and time—whether they assume these as subsistent or as only inherent—are real absolutely must be at variance with the principles of experience itself. For suppose they decide to assume space and time as subsistent (thus taking what is usually the side of the mathematical investigators of nature): then they must assume two eternal and infinite self-subsistent nonentities (space and time), which exist (yet without there being anything actual) only in order to encompass everything actual. Or suppose they assume space and time as only inherent (thus taking the side to which some metaphysical natural scientists belong). Here space and time count for them as relations of appearances (occurring concurrently or sequentially)—relations abstracted from experience but, as thus separated, represented confusedly. If they take this second side, then they must dispute

that the mathematical *a priori* doctrines are valid for actual things (e.g., things in space), or at least that they are apodeictically certain. For *a posteriori* there is no such certainty at all. According to this second opinion, the *a priori* concepts of space and time are only creatures of the imagination, and their source must actually be sought in experience: the relations are abstracted from experience; and the imagination has made from them something that, while containing what is universal in these relations, yet cannot occur without the restrictions that nature has connected with them. Those who assume space and time as [real absolutely and] subsistent do gain this much: they make the realm of appearances free for mathematical assertions. On the other hand, these very conditions create great confusion for them when the understanding wants to go beyond the realm of appearances. Those, on the other hand, who assume space and time as [real absolutely but as] only inherent gain on this latter point. I.e. they do not find the representations of space and time getting in their way when they want to judge objects not as appearances but merely as they relate to the understanding. But they can neither indicate a basis for the possibility of mathematical *a priori* cognitions (since they lack a true and objectively valid *a priori* intuition), nor bring the propositions of experience into necessary agreement with those *a priori* mathematical assertions. Our theory of the true character of these two original forms of sensibility provides the remedy for both [sets of] difficulties.

Finally, transcendental aesthetic cannot contain more than these two elements, i.e., space and time. This is evident from the fact that all other concepts belonging to sensibility presuppose something empirical. This holds even for the concept of motion, which unites the two components. For [the concept of] motion presupposes the perception of something movable. But in space, considered in itself, there is nothing movable; therefore the movable must be something that we find in space only through experience, and hence must be an empirical datum. Similarly, transcendental aesthetic cannot include among its *a priori* data the concept of alteration. For time itself does not alter; rather, what alters is something

A39

B56

A40

B57

A41

B58

that is in time. Therefore the concept of alteration requires the perception of some existent and of the succession of its determinations; hence it requires experience. [ . . . ]

<table>
<tr><td>A50/<br>B74</td></tr>
</table>

## Transcendental Doctrine of Elements

### Part II. Transcendental Logic Introduction: Idea of a Transcendental Logic

#### I. On Logic As Such

Our cognition arises from two basic sources of the mind. The first is [our ability] to receive representations (and is our receptivity for impressions); the second is our ability to cognize an object through these representations (and is the spontaneity of concepts). Through receptivity an object is *given* to us; through spontaneity an object is *thought* in relation to that [given] representation (which is a mere determination of the mind). Intuition and concepts, therefore, constitute the elements of all our cognition. Hence neither concepts without an intuition corresponding to them in some way or other, nor intuition without concepts can yield cognition. Both intuition and concepts are either pure or empirical. They are *empirical* if they contain sensation (sensation presupposes the actual presence of the object); they are *pure* if no sensation is mixed in with the representation. Sensation may be called the matter of sensible cognition. Hence pure intuition contains only the form under which something is intuited, and a pure concept contains solely the form of the thought of an object as such. Only pure intuitions or concepts are possible *a priori*; empirical ones are possible only *a posteriori*.

A51/
B75

Let us give the name *sensibility* to our mind's *receptivity* [i.e., to its ability], to receive representations insofar as it is affected in some manner. The *understanding*, by contrast, is our faculty for producing representations ourselves, i.e., our *spontaneity* of cognition. Our *intuition*, by our very nature, can never be other than *sensible* intuition; i.e., it contains only the way in which we are affected by objects. The *understanding*, by contrast, is our ability to *think* the object of sensible intuition. Neither of these

properties is to be preferred to the other. Without sensibility no object would be given to us; and without the understanding no object would be thought. Thoughts without content are empty; intuitions without concepts are blind. Hence it is just as necessary that we make our concepts sensible (i.e., that we add the object to them in intuition) as it is necessary that we make our intuitions comprehensible (i.e., that we bring them under concepts). Moreover, these faculties or capacities cannot exchange their functions. The understanding cannot intuit anything, and the senses cannot think anything. Only from their union can cognition arise. This fact, however, must not lead us to confuse their respective contributions; it provides us, rather, with a strong reason for carefully separating and distinguishing sensibility and the understanding from each other. Hence we distinguish the science of the rules of sensibility as such, i.e., aesthetic, from the science of the rules of the understanding as such, i.e., logic. [ . . . ]

B76

A52

### Transcendental Analytic

B89

Transcendental analytic consists in the dissection of our entire *a priori* cognition into the elements of the understanding's pure cognition. The following points are what matters in this dissection: (1) The concepts must be pure rather than empirical. (2) They must belong not to intuition and sensibility, but to thought and the understanding. (3) They must be elementary concepts, and must be distinguished carefully from concepts that are either derivative or composed of such elementary concepts. (4) Our table of these concepts must be complete, and the concepts must occupy fully the whole realm of the pure understanding. Now, the completeness of this science cannot be assumed reliably by gauging an aggregate of concepts that was brought about merely through trials. Hence this completeness is possible only by means of an *idea of the whole* of the understanding's *a priori* cognition, and through the division, determined by that idea, of the concepts amounting to that cognition; and hence this completeness is possible only through the *coherence* of these concepts *in a system*. The pure understanding differentiates itself fully not only from everything empirical, but even from all sensibility.

A65

B90

Therefore it is a unity that is self-subsistent, sufficient to itself, and that cannot be augmented by supplementing it with any extrinsic additions. Hence the sum of the pure understanding's cognition will constitute a system that can be encompassed and determined by an idea. The system's completeness and structure can at the same time serve as a touchstone of the correctness and genuineness of whatever components of cognition fit into the system. This entire part of the Transcendental Logic consists, however, of two *books*; one of these contains the *concepts*, the other the *principles*, of the pure understanding.

### Book I. Analytic of Concepts

By *analytic of concepts* I do not mean the analysis of concepts, i.e., the usual procedure in philosophical inquiries of dissecting already available concepts in terms of their content and bringing them to distinctness; rather, I mean the until now rarely attempted A66 *dissection of the faculty of the understanding itself.* The purpose of this dissection is to explore the possibility of *a priori* concepts, by locating them solely in the understanding, as their birthplace, and by B91 analyzing the understanding's pure use as such. For this exploration is the proper task of a transcendental philosophy; the rest is the logical treatment of concepts in philosophy generally. Hence we shall trace the pure concepts all the way to their first seeds and predispositions in the human understanding, where these concepts lie prepared until finally, on the occasion of experience, they are developed and are exhibited by that same understanding in their purity, freed from the empirical conditions attaching to them.

### Chapter I. On the Guide for the Discovery of All Pure Concepts of the Understanding

When we bring into play a cognitive faculty, then, depending on the various ways in which we may be prompted to do so, different concepts come to the fore that allow us to recognize this faculty. These concepts can be collected in a more or less comprehensive manner, once the concepts have been observed fairly long or with significant mental acuity. But by this—as it were, mechanical—procedure we can never reliably determine at what point that

inquiry will be completed. Moreover, if concepts are A67 discovered only on given occasions, then they reveal themselves in no order or systematic unity; instead B92 they are ultimately only paired according to similarities, and arranged in series according to the quantity of their content, from the simple concepts on to the more composite. The way in which these series are brought about, despite being methodical in a certain manner, is anything but systematic.

Transcendental philosophy has the advantage, but also the obligation, of locating its concepts according to a principle. For these concepts arise, pure and unmixed, from the understanding, which is an absolute unity; and hence these concepts themselves must cohere with each other according to one concept or idea. Such coherence, however, provides us with a rule by which we can determine *a priori* the proper place for each pure concept of the understanding, and the completeness of all of them taken together—whereas otherwise all of this would be subject to one's own discretion or to chance.

### Transcendental Guide for the Discovery of All Pure Concepts of the Understanding

Section I. On the Understanding's Logical Use As Such   The understanding was explicated merely negatively above, namely, as a nonsensible cognitive faculty. And since independently A68 of sensibility we cannot partake of any intuition, B93 it follows that the understanding is not a faculty of intuition. Apart from intuition, however, there is only one way of cognizing, namely, through concepts. Hence the cognition of any understanding, or at least of the human understanding, is a cognition through concepts; it is not intuitive, but discursive. All our intuitions, as sensible, rest on our being affected; concepts, on the other hand, rest on functions. By *function* I mean the unity of the act of arranging various representations under one common representation. Hence concepts are based on the spontaneity of thought, whereas sensible intuitions are based on the receptivity for impressions. Now the only use that the understanding can make of these concepts is to judge by means of them. But in such judging, a concept is never referred immediately to an object, because the only kind of representation that deals with its object immediately is intuition. Instead the concept is referred immediately to some other representation of the object (whether that representation be an intuition or itself already a concept). Judgment, therefore, is the mediate cognition of an object, namely, the representation of a representation of it. In every judgment there is a concept that holds for many [representations], and, among them, comprises also a given representation that is referred immediately to the object. E.g., in the judgment, *All bodies are divisible*, the concept of the divisible refers to various other concepts; but, among these,

A69/
B94

it is here referred specifically to the concept of body, and the concept of body is referred in turn to certain appearances that we encounter. Hence these objects are represented mediately through the concept of divisibility. Accordingly, all judgments are functions of unity among our representations. For instead of cognizing the object by means of an immediate representation, we do so by means of a higher representation comprising both this mediate representation and several other representations; and we thereby draw many possible cognitions together into one. Now since all acts of the understanding can be reduced to judgments, the *understanding* as such can be represented as a *faculty of judgment*. For, according to what we said above, the understanding is a faculty of thought. But thought is cognition through concepts; and concepts, as predicates of possible judgments, refer to some representation of an as yet undetermined object. Thus the concept of body signifies something—e.g., metal— that can be cognized through that concept. Hence it is a concept only because there are contained under it other representations by means of which it can refer to objects. Therefore the concept of body is the predicate for a possible judgment, e.g., the judgment that every metal is a body. Therefore we can find all of the functions of the understanding if we can exhibit completely the functions of unity in judgments. This, however, can be accomplished quite readily, as the following section will show.

Section II.

A70/
B95

§9. On the Understanding's Logical Function in Judgments   If we abstract from all content of a judgment as such and pay attention only to the mere form of the understanding in it, then we find that the function of thought in judgment can be brought under four headings, each containing under it three moments. They can be represented conveniently in the following table.

**1**
*Quantity of Judgments*
Universal
Particular
Singular

**2**
*Quality*
Affirmative
Negative
Infinite

**3**
*Relation*
Categorical
Hypothetical
Disjunctive

**4**
*Modality*
Problematic
Assertoric
Apodeictic

[ . . . ]

Section III.                                   B102

§10. On the Pure Concepts of the Understanding, or Categories   General logic, as we have said several times already, abstracts from all content of cognition. It expects representations to be given to it from somewhere else—no matter where—in order then to transform these representations into concepts in the first place. This it does analytically. Transcendental logic, by contrast, has lying before it a manifold of *a priori* sensibility, offered to it by transcendental aes- A77 thetic, in order to provide it with a material for the pure concepts of the understanding. Without this material, transcendental logic would have no content, and hence would be completely empty. Now space and time contain a manifold of pure *a priori* intuition. But they belong nonetheless to the conditions of our mind's receptivity under which alone the mind can receive representations of objects, and which, by the same token, must always affect the concept of these objects. Yet the spontaneity of our thought requires that this manifold, in order to be turned into a cognition, must first be gone through, taken up, and combined in a certain manner. This act I call synthesis.

B103     By *synthesis*, in the most general sense of the term, I mean the act of putting various representations with one another and of comprising their manifoldness in one cognition. Such synthesis is *pure* if the manifold is given not empirically but *a priori* (as is the manifold in space and time). Before any analysis of our representations can take place, these representations must first be given, and hence in terms of *content* no concepts can originate analytically. Rather, synthesis of a manifold (whether this manifold is given empirically or *a priori*) is what first gives rise to a cognition. Although this cognition may still be crude and A78 confused at first and hence may require analysis, yet synthesis is what in fact gathers the elements for cognition and unites them into a certain content. Hence if we want to make a judgment about the first origin of our cognition, then we must first direct our attention to synthesis.

    Synthesis as such, as we shall see below, is the mere effect produced by the imagination, which is a blind but indispensable function of the soul without which we would have no cognition whatsoever, but of which we are conscious only very rarely. Bringing this synthesis *to concepts*, on the other hand, is a function belonging to the understanding; and it is through this function that the understanding first provides us with cognition in the proper meaning of the term.

B104     Now *pure synthesis*, *conceived of generally*, yields the pure concept of the understanding. By pure synthesis I mean the synthesis that rests on the basis of synthetic *a priori* unity. E.g., our act of counting (as is more noticeable primarily with larger numbers) is a *synthesis according to concepts*, because it is performed according to a common basis of unity (such as the decimal system). Hence under this concept the unity of the manifold's synthesis becomes necessary.

    Bringing various representations *under* a concept (a task general logic deals with) is done analytically.

But bringing not representations but the *pure synthesis* of representations *to* concepts is what transcendental logic teaches. The first [thing] that we must be given *a priori* in order to cognize any object is A79 the *manifold* of pure intuition. The second [thing] is the *synthesis* of this manifold by the imagination. But this synthesis does not yet yield cognition. The third [thing we need] in order to cognize an object that we encounter is the concepts which give *unity* to this pure synthesis and which consist solely in the representation of this necessary synthetic unity. And these concepts rest on the understanding.

    The same function that gives unity to the various representations *in a judgment* also gives unity to the B105 mere synthesis of various representations *in an intuition*. This unity—speaking generally—is called the pure concept of the understanding. Hence the same understanding—and indeed through the same acts whereby it brought about, in concepts, the logical form of a judgment by means of analytic unity—also brings into its representations a transcendental content, by means of the synthetic unity of the manifold in intuition as such; and because of this, these representations are called pure concepts of the understanding which apply to objects *a priori*—something that general logic cannot accomplish.

    Thus there arise precisely as many pure concepts of the understanding which apply *a priori* to objects of intuition in general, as in the preceding table there were logical functions involved in all possible judgments. For these functions of the understanding are completely exhaustive and survey its powers en- A80 tirely. Following Aristotle, we shall call these functions *categories*. For our aim is fundamentally the same as his, even though it greatly deviates from his in its execution.

### Table of Categories       B106

#### 1

Of Quantity
*Unity*
*Plurality*
*Totality*

| **2** | **3** |
| Of Quality | Of Relation |
| *Reality* | of *Inherence* and Subsistence |
| | (*substantia et accidens*) |
| *Negation* | of *Causality* and Dependence |
| | (Cause and Effect) |
| *Limitation* | of *Community* (Interaction |
| | between Agent and Patient) |

**4**

Of Modality
*Possibility*—Impossibility
*Existence*—Nonexistence
*Necessity*—Contingency

This, then, is the list of all the original pure concepts of synthesis that the understanding contains *a priori*. Indeed, it is a pure understanding only because of these concepts; for through them alone can it understand something in the manifold of intuition, i.e., think an object of intuition. This division of the categories has been generated systematically from A81 a common principle, namely, our faculty of judgment (which is equivalent to our faculty of thought). B107 It has not been generated rhapsodically, by locating pure concepts haphazardly, where we can never be certain that the enumeration of the concepts is complete. For we then infer the division only by induction, forgetting that in this way we never gain insight into why precisely these concepts, rather than others, reside in the pure understanding. Locating these basic concepts was a project worthy of an acute man like Aristotle. But having no principle, he snatched them up as he came upon them. He hunted up ten of them at first, and called them *categories* (predicaments). He later believed that he had discovered five more categories, and added them under the name of postpredicaments. But his table remained deficient even then. Moreover, we also find in it some modes of pure sensibility (*quando, ubi, situs*, as well as *prius, simul*), as well as an empirical mode (*motus*), none of which belong at all in this register of the primary concepts of the understanding. Again, derivative concepts (*actio, passio*) are also included among the original concepts, while some of the original concepts are missing entirely.

Hence for the sake of the latter, we must note also that the categories, as the true *primary concepts* of the pure understanding, have also their equally pure derivative concepts. In a complete system of transcendental philosophy these *derivative concepts* can by no means be omitted. In a merely critical essay, A82 however, I can settle for merely mentioning them.

Let me call these pure but derivative concepts of B108 the understanding the *predicables* of the pure understanding (in contrast to the predicaments). Once we have the original and primitive concepts, we can easily add the derivative and subsidiary ones and thus depict completely the genealogical tree of the pure understanding. Since I am here concerned with the completeness not of the system but only of the principles for a system, I am reserving that complementary work for another enterprise. We can, however, come close to achieving that aim of completing the tree if we pick up a textbook on ontology and subordinate the predicables to the categories: e.g., to the category of causality, the predicables of force, action, undergoing; to the category of community, the predicables of presence, resistance; to the predicaments of modality, the predicables of arising, passing away, change; and so on. When the categories are combined either with the modes of pure sensibility or with one another, they yield a great multitude of derivative *a priori* concepts. Mentioning these concepts and, if possible, listing them completely would be a useful and not disagreeable endeavor, but one that we can dispense with here.

In this treatise I deliberately refrain from offering definitions of these categories, even though I may A83 possess them. I shall hereafter dissect these concepts only to a degree adequate for the doctrine of method B109 that I here produce. Whereas definitions of the categories could rightly be demanded of me in a system of pure reason, here they would only make us lose sight of the main point of the inquiry. For they would give rise to doubts and charges that we may readily relegate to another activity without in any way detracting from our essential aim. Still, from what little I have mentioned about this, we can see distinctly that a complete lexicon with all the requisite explications not only is possible but could easily be brought about. The compartments are now at hand. They only need to be filled in; and a systematic [transcendental] topic, such as the present one, will make it difficult to miss the place where each concept properly belongs, and at the same time will make it easy to notice any place that is still empty. [ . . . ]

A84/    Chapter II. On the Deduction of the Pure
B116    Concepts of the Understanding

Section I.

§13. On the Principles of a Transcendental Deduction As Such   When legal educators talk about rights and claims, they distinguish in a legal action the question regarding what is legal (*quid iuris*) from the question concerning fact (*quid facti*), and they demand proof of both. The first proof, which is to establish the right, or for that matter the legal entitlement, they call the *deduction*. We employ a multitude of empirical concepts without being challenged by anyone. And we consider ourselves justified, even B117 without having offered a deduction, to assign to these empirical concepts a meaning and imagined signification, because we always have experience available to us to prove their objective reality. But there are also concepts that we usurp, as, e.g., *fortune, fate*. And although these concepts run loose, with our almost universal forbearance, yet they are sometimes confronted by the question [of their legality], *quid iuris*. This question then leaves us in considerable A85 perplexity regarding the deduction of these concepts; for neither from experience nor from reason can we adduce any distinct legal basis from which the right to use them emerges distinctly.

But there are, among the various concepts making up the highly mixed fabric of human cognition, some that are determined for pure *a priori* use as well (i.e., for a use that is completely independent of all experience); and their right to be so used always requires a deduction. For proofs based on experience are insufficient to establish the legitimacy of using them in that way; yet we do need to know how these concepts can refer to objects even though they do not take these objects from any experience. Hence when I explain in what way concepts can refer to

objects *a priori*, I call that explanation the *transcendental deduction* of these concepts. And I distinguish transcendental deduction from *empirical* deduction, which indicates in what way a concept has been acquired through experience and through reflection upon experience, and which therefore concerns not the concept's legitimacy but only the fact whereby we came to possess it.

We already have, at this point, two types of con- B118 cepts that, while being wholly different in kind, do yet agree inasmuch as both of them refer to objects completely *a priori*: namely, on the one hand, the concepts of space and time as forms of sensibility; and, on the other hand, the categories as concepts of the understanding. To attempt an empirical deduction of these two types of concepts would be a futile job. For what is distinctive in their nature is precisely the fact that they refer to their objects A86 without having borrowed anything from experience in order to represent these objects. Hence if a deduction of these concepts is needed, then it must always be transcendental.

But even for these concepts, as for all cognition, we can locate in experience, if not the principle of their possibility, then at least the occasioning causes of their production. Thus the impressions of the senses first prompt [us] to open up the whole cognitive faculty in regard to them, and to bring about experience. Experience contains two quite heterogeneous elements: namely, a *matter* for cognition, taken from the senses; and a certain *form* for ordering this matter, taken from the inner source of pure intuition and thought. It is on the occasion of the impressions of the senses that pure intuition and thought are first brought into operation and produce concepts. Such exploration of our cognitive faculty's first endeavors to ascend from singular perceptions to universal B119 concepts is doubtless highly beneficial, and we are indebted to the illustrious *Locke* for first opening up the path to it. Yet such exploration can never yield a *deduction* of the pure *a priori* concepts, which does not lie on that path at all. For in view of these concepts' later use, which is to be wholly independent of experience, they must be able to display a birth A87 certificate quite different from that of descent from experiences. The attempted physiological derivation concerns a *quaestio facti*, and therefore cannot properly be called a deduction at all. Hence I shall call it the explanation of our *possession* of a pure cognition. Clearly, then, the only possible deduction of this pure cognition is a transcendental and by no means an empirical one, and empirical deductions regarding the pure *a priori* concepts are nothing but futile attempts—attempts that only those can engage in who have not comprehended the quite peculiar nature of these cognitions.

Yet even if it be granted that the only possible kind of deduction of pure *a priori* cognition is one along the transcendental path, that still does not show that this deduction is inescapably necessary. We did earlier trace the concepts of space and time B120 to their sources by means of a transcendental deduction, and we explained and determined their *a priori* objective validity. Yet geometry, using nothing but *a priori* cognitions, follows its course securely without needing to ask philosophy for a certificate of the pure and legitimate descent of geometry's basic concept of space. However, the use of the concept of space in this science does apply only to the external world of sense. Space is the pure form of the intuition of that world. In that world, therefore, all geometric cognition is directly evident, because it is based A88 on *a priori* intuition; and, through cognition itself, objects are (as regards their form) given *a priori* in intuition. With the *pure concepts of the understanding*, however, begins the inescapable requirement to seek a transcendental deduction—not only of these concepts themselves, but also of space. For these concepts speak of objects through predicates of pure *a priori* thought, not through predicates of intuition and sensibility; hence they refer to objects universally, i.e., apart from all conditions of sensibility. They are, then, concepts that are not based on experience; and in *a priori* intuition, too, they cannot display any object on which they might, prior to all experience, base their synthesis. Hence these concepts not only arouse suspicion concerning the objective validity B121 and limits of their use, but they also make ambiguous the *concept of space*; for they tend to use it even beyond the conditions of sensible intuition—and this

indeed is the reason why a transcendental deduction of this concept was needed above. I must therefore convince the reader, before he has taken a single step in the realm of pure reason, that such a deduction is inescapably necessary. For otherwise he proceeds blindly, and after manifold wanderings must yet return to the ignorance from which he started. But the reader must also distinctly see in advance the inevitable difficulty of providing such a deduction. For otherwise he might complain of obscurity when in fact the matter itself is deeply shrouded, or might be too quickly discouraged during the removal of obstacles. For we either must entirely abandon all claims A89 to pure rational insights into the realm that we care about most, namely, the realm beyond the bounds of all possible experience, or else must bring this critical inquiry to completion.

We had little trouble above in making comprehensible how the concepts of space and time, despite being *a priori* cognitions, must yet refer necessarily to objects, and how they make possible, independently of any experience, a synthetic cognition of objects. For only by means of such pure forms of sensibility can an object appear to us, i.e., can it be an object of empirical intuition. Hence space and time are pure B122 intuitions containing *a priori* the condition for the possibility of objects as appearances, and the synthesis in space and time has objective validity.

The categories of the understanding, however, do not at all represent to us the conditions under which objects are given in intuition. Therefore objects can indeed appear to us without having to refer necessarily to functions of the understanding, and hence without the understanding's containing *a priori* the conditions of these objects. Thus we find here a difficulty that we did not encounter in the realm of sensibility: namely, how *subjective conditions of thought* could have *objective validity*, i.e., how they could yield conditions for the possibility of all cognition of A90 objects. For appearances can indeed be given in intuition without functions of the understanding. Let me take, e.g., the concept of cause, which signifies a special kind of synthesis where upon [the occurrence of] something, A, something quite different, B, is posited according to a rule. Why appearances should contain anything like that is not evident *a priori*. (For experience cannot be adduced as proof, since we must be able to establish this concept's objective validity *a priori*.) Hence there is doubt *a priori* whether perhaps such a concept might not even be empty and encounter no object at all among appearances. For B123 while it is evident that objects of sensible intuition must conform to the formal conditions of sensibility lying *a priori* in the mind, since otherwise they would not be objects for us, it is not so easy to see the inference whereby they must in addition conform to the conditions that the understanding requires for the synthetic unity of thought. For, I suppose, appearances might possibly be of such a character that the understanding would not find them to conform at all to the conditions of its unity. Everything might then be so confused that, e.g., the sequence of appearances would offer us nothing providing us with a rule of synthesis and thus corresponding to the concept A91 of cause and effect, so that this concept would then be quite empty, null, and without signification. But appearances would nonetheless offer objects to our intuition; for intuition in no way requires the functions of thought.

Suppose that we planned to extricate ourselves from these troublesome inquiries by saying that examples of such regularity among appearances are offered to us incessantly by experience, and that these examples give us sufficient prompting to isolate the concept of cause from them and thus to verify at the same time the objective validity of such a concept. In that case we would be overlooking the fact that the concept of cause cannot arise in that way at all; B124 rather, it either must have its basis completely *a priori* in the understanding, or must be given up entirely as a mere chimera. For this concept definitely requires that something, A, be of such a kind that something else, B, follows from it *necessarily* and according to an *absolutely universal rule*. Although appearances do provide us with cases from which we can obtain a rule whereby something usually happens, they can never provide us with a rule whereby the result is *necessary*. This is, moreover, the reason why the synthesis of cause and effect is imbued with a dignity that cannot at all be expressed empirically: namely,

that the effect is not merely added to the cause, but is posited *through* the cause and results *from* it. And the strict universality of the rule is indeed no property A92 whatsoever of empirical rules; empirical rules can, through induction, acquire none but comparative universality, i.e., extensive usability. But if we treated the pure concepts of the understanding as merely empirical products, then our use of them would change entirely.

§14. Transition to the Transcendental Deduction of the Categories   Only two cases are possible where synthetic representations and their objects can concur, can necessarily refer to each other, and can—as it were—meet each other: namely, either if the object makes the representation possible or if the B125 representation alone makes the object possible. If the object makes the representation possible, then the reference is only empirical and the representation is never possible *a priori*. This is what happens in the case of appearances, as regards what pertains to sensation in them. But suppose that the representation alone makes the object possible. In that case, while representation in itself does not produce its object *as regards existence* (for the causality that representation has by means of the will is not at issue here at all), yet representation is *a priori* determinative in regard to the object if *cognizing* something *as an object* is possible only through it. Now there are two conditions under which alone there can be cognition of an object. The first condition is *intuition*; through it the object is given, though only as appearance. The A93 second condition is the *concept*; through it an object is thought that corresponds to this intuition. Now it is evident from the above that the first condition, namely, the condition under which alone objects can be intuited, does indeed, as far as their form is concerned, underlie objects *a priori* in the mind. Hence all appearances necessarily agree with this formal condition of sensibility, because only through it can they appear, i.e., be empirically intuited and given. Now the question arises whether *a priori* concepts too do not precede [objects], as conditions under which alone something can be, if not intuited, yet thought as an object at all. For in that case all B126 empirical cognition of objects necessarily conforms to such concepts, because nothing is possible *as object of experience* unless these concepts are presupposed. But all experience, besides containing the senses' intuition through which something is given, does also contain a *concept* of an object that is given in intuition, or that appears. Accordingly, concepts of objects as such presumably underlie all experiential cognition as its *a priori* conditions. Hence presumably the objective validity of the categories, as *a priori* concepts, rests on the fact that through them alone is experience possible (as far as the form of thought in it is concerned). For in that case the categories refer to objects of experience necessarily and *a priori*, because only by means of them can any experiential object whatsoever be thought at all.

A94      Hence the transcendental deduction of all *a priori* concepts has a principle to which the entire investigation must be directed: namely, the principle that these concepts must be cognized as *a priori* conditions for the possibility of experience (whether the possibility of the intuition found in it, or the possibility of the thought). If concepts serve as the objective basis for the possibility of experience, then—precisely because of this—they are necessary. But to unfold the experience in which these concepts are found is not to deduce them (but is only to illustrate them);

B127 for otherwise they would, after all, be only contingent. Without that original reference of these concepts to possible experience wherein all objects of cognition occur, their reference to any object whatsoever would be quite incomprehensible.

     The illustrious **Locke**, not having engaged in this contemplation, and encountering pure concepts of the understanding in experience, also derived them from experience. Yet he proceeded so *inconsistently* that he dared to try using these concepts for cognitions that go far beyond any limits of experience. **David Hume** recognized that in order for us to be able to do this, the origin of these concepts must be *a priori*. But he was quite unable to explain how it is possible that concepts that are not intrinsically combined in the understanding should nonetheless have to be thought by it as necessarily combined in the object. Nor did it occur to him that perhaps the understanding itself

might, through these concepts, be the author of the experience wherein we encounter the understanding's objects. Thus, in his plight, he derived these concepts from experience (namely, from *habit*, a subjective necessity that arises in experience through repeated association and that ultimately is falsely regarded as objective). But he proceeded quite consistently after that, for he declared that we cannot use these concepts and the principles that they occasion in order to go beyond the limits of experience. Yet B128 the *empirical* derivation of these concepts which occurred to both cannot be reconciled with the scientific *a priori* cognitions that we actually have, namely, our *a priori* cognitions of *pure mathematics* and *universal natural science*, and hence this empirical derivation is refuted by that fact.

     Of these two illustrious men, Locke left the door wide open for *fanaticism*; for once reason has gained possession of such rights, it can no longer be kept within limits by indefinite exhortations to moderation. Hume, believing that he had uncovered so universal a delusion—regarded as reason—of our cognitive faculty, surrendered entirely to *skepticism*. We are now about to try to find out whether we cannot provide for human reason safe passage between these two cliffs, assign to it determinate bounds, and yet keep open for it the entire realm of its appropriate activity.

     The only thing that I still want to do before we start is to *explain the categories*: they are concepts of an object in general whereby the object's intuition is regarded as *determined* in terms of one of the *logical functions* in judging. Thus the function of the *categorical* judgment—e.g., All bodies are divisible—is that of the relation of subject to predicate. But the understanding's merely logical use left un- B129 determined to which of the two concepts we want to give the function of the subject, and to which the function of the predicate. For we can also say, Something divisible is a body. If, on the other hand, I bring the concept of a body under the category of substance, then through this category is determined the fact that the body's empirical intuition in experience must be considered always as subject only, never as mere predicate. And similarly in all the remaining categories.

### Section II. Transcendental Deduction of the Pure Concepts of the Understanding [Second Edition]

§15. On the Possibility of a Combination As Such The manifold of representations can be given in an intuition that is merely sensible, i.e., nothing but receptivity; and the form of this intuition can lie *a priori* in our faculty of representation without being anything but the way in which the subject is affected. But a manifold's *combination (coniunctio)* as such can never come to us through the senses; nor, B130 therefore, can it already be part of what is contained in the pure form of sensible intuition. For this combination is an act of spontaneity by the faculty of representation; and this faculty must be called the understanding, in order to be distinguished from sensibility. Hence all combination is an act of the understanding—whether or not we become conscious of such combination; whether it is a combination of the manifold of intuition or of the manifold of various concepts; and whether, in the case of intuition, it is a combination of sensible or of nonsensible intuition. I would assign to this act of the understanding the general name *synthesis*, in order to point out at the same time: that we cannot represent anything as combined in the object without ourselves' having combined it beforehand; and that, among all representations, *combination* is the only one that cannot be given through objects, but—being an act of the subject's self-activity—can be performed only by the subject himself. We readily become aware here that this act of synthesis must originally be a single act and must hold equally for all combination; and that resolution or *analysis*, which seems to be its opposite, yet always presupposes it. For where the understanding has not beforehand combined anything, there it also cannot resolve anything, because only *through the understanding* could the faculty of representation have been given something as combined.

But the concept of combination carries with B131 it, besides the concept of the manifold and of its synthesis, also the concept of the manifold's unity.

Combination is representation of the *synthetic* unity of the manifold. Hence the representation of this unity cannot arise from the combination; rather, by being added to the representation of the manifold, it makes possible the concept of combination in the first place. This unity, which thus precedes *a priori* all concepts of combination, is by no means the category of unity mentioned earlier (in §10). For all categories are based on logical functions occurring in judgments; but in these functions combination, and hence unity of given concepts, is already thought. Hence a category already presupposes combination. We must therefore search for this unity (which is qualitative unity; see §12) still higher up, namely, in what itself contains the basis for the unity of different concepts in judgments, and hence contains the basis for the possibility of the understanding, even as used logically.

§16. On the Original Synthetic Unity of Apperception The I *think* must be *capable* of accompanying B132 all my representations. For otherwise something would be represented to me that could not be thought at all—which is equivalent to saying that the representation would be either impossible or at least nothing to me. That representation which can be given prior to all thought is called *intuition*. Hence everything manifold in intuition has a necessary reference to the I *think* in the same subject in which this manifold is found. But this representation [i.e., the I *think*] is an act of spontaneity; i.e., it cannot be regarded as belonging to sensibility. I call it *pure apperception*, in order to distinguish it from *empirical* apperception. Or, again, I call it *original apperception*; for it is the self-consciousness which, because it produces the representation I *think* that must be capable of accompanying all other representations and is one and the same in all consciousness, cannot be accompanied by any further representation. I also call the *unity* of this apperception the *transcendental* unity of self-consciousness, in order to indicate that *a priori* cognition can be obtained from it. For the manifold representations given in a certain intuition would not one and all be *my* representations, if they did not one and all belong to one self-consciousness. I.e., as my representations (even if I am not conscious of them as being mine), they surely must conform necessarily to the condition under which alone they *can* stand together in one universal self-conscious-B133 ness, since otherwise they would not thoroughly belong to me. And from this original combination much can be inferred.

This thoroughgoing identity of the apperception of a manifold given in intuition contains a synthesis of representations, and is possible only through the consciousness of this synthesi . For the empirical consciousness that accompanies different representations is essentially scattered and without any reference to the subject's identity. Hence this reference comes about not through my merely accompanying each representation with consciousness, but through my *adding* one representation to another and being conscious of their synthesis. Hence only because I can combine a manifold of given representations *in one consciousness*, is it possible for me to represent the *identity itself of the consciousness in* B134 *these representations*. I.e., the *analytic* unity of apperception is possible only under the presupposition of some *synthetic* unity of apperception. The thought that these representations given in intuition belong one and all to me is, accordingly, tantamount to the thought that I unite them, or at least can unite them, in one self-consciousness. And although that thought itself is not yet the consciousness of the *synthesis* of the representations, it still presupposes the possibility of that synthesis. I.e., only because I can comprise the manifold of the representations in one consciousness, do I call them one and all *my* representations. For otherwise I would have a self as many-colored and varied as I have representations that I am conscious of. Hence synthetic unity of the manifold of intuitions, as given *a priori*, is the basis of the identity of apperception itself, which precedes *a priori* all *my* determinate thought. But combination does not lie in the objects, and can B135 by no means be borrowed from them by perception and thus be taken up only then into the understanding. It is, rather, solely something performed by the understanding; and the understanding itself is nothing more than the faculty of combining *a priori* and of bringing the manifold of given intuitions

under the unity of apperception—the principle of this unity being the supreme principle in all of human cognition.

Now, it is true that this principle of the necessary unity of apperception is itself merely an identical and hence an analytic proposition. Yet it does declare as necessary a synthesis of the manifold given in an intuition, a synthesis without which that thoroughgoing identity of self-consciousness cannot be thought. For through the I, as simple representation, nothing manifold is given; only in intuition, which is distinct from this representation, can a manifold be given, and only through *combination* can it be thought in one consciousness. An understanding wherein through self- consciousness alone everything manifold would at the same time be given would be an understanding that *intuits*. Our understanding can only *think*, and must seek intuition in the senses. I am, then, conscious of the self as identical, as regards the manifold of the representations given to me in an intuition, because I call them one and all *my* representations that make up *one* representation. That, however, is tantamount to saying that I am conscious of a necessary *a priori* synthesis of them. This synthesis is called the original synthetic unity of apperception. All representations given to me are subject B136 to this unity; but they must also be brought under it through a synthesis.

§17. The Principle of the Synthetic Unity of Apperception Is the Supreme Principle for All Use of the Understanding The supreme principle for the possibility of all intuition in reference to sensibility was, according to the Transcendental Aesthetic, that everything manifold in intuition is subject to the formal conditions of space and time. The supreme principle for the possibility of all intuition in reference to the understanding is that everything manifold in intuition is subject to conditions of the original synthetic unity of apperception.[10] All manifold representations of intuition are subject to the first principle insofar as they are given

10. Space and time, and all their parts, are *intuitions*; hence they, with the manifold that they contain, are singular representations. (See the Transcendental Aesthetic). Hence space

to us. They are subject to the second principle in-
B137 sofar as they must be capable of being *combined* in
one consciousness. For without that combination,
nothing can be thought or cognized through such
representations, because the given representations
do not have in common the act of apperception, *I
think*, and thus would not be collated in one self-
consciousness.

Understanding—speaking generally—is the faculty of *cognitions*. Cognitions consist in determinate
reference of given representations to an object. And
an *object* is that in whose concept the manifold of a
given intuition is *united*. But all unification of representations requires that there be unity of consciousness in the synthesis of them. Consequently the reference of representations to an object consists solely in
this unity of consciousness, and hence so does their
objective validity and consequently their becoming
cognitions. On this unity, consequently, rests the very
possibility of the understanding.

Hence the principle of the original *synthetic* unity
of apperception is the primary pure cognition of the
understanding, on which the entire remaining use of
the understanding is based; and this cognition is at
the same time entirely independent of all conditions
of sensible intuition. Thus the mere form of outer
sensible intuition, i.e., space, is as yet no cognition at
all; it provides only the manifold of *a priori* intuition
for a possible cognition. Rather, in order to cognize
B138 something or other—e.g., a line—in space, I must
*draw* it; and hence I must bring about synthetically
a determinate combination of the given manifold, so
that the unity of this act is at the same time the unity
of consciousness (in the concept of a line), and so
that an object (a determinate space) is thereby first
cognized. The synthetic unity of consciousness is,

---

and time are not mere concepts, through which the very same
consciousness is encountered as contained in many representations. They are, rather, [representations through which] many
representations are encountered as contained in one representation and in the consciousness thereof, and hence [they are
representations] encountered as composite; and consequently
the unity of this consciousness is encountered as *synthetic*, but
yet as original. This *singularity* of [intuition] is important in its
application. (See §25.)

therefore, an objective condition of all cognition.
Not only do I myself need this condition in order
to cognize an object, but every intuition must be
subject to it *in order to become an object for me*. For
otherwise, and without that synthesis, the manifold
would *not* unite in one consciousness.

Although this last proposition makes the synthetic
unity [of consciousness] a condition of all thought, it
is—as I have said—itself analytic. For it says no more
than that all *my* representations in some given intuition must be subject to the condition under which
alone I can ascribe them—as my representations—
to the identical self, and hence under which alone I
can unite them, as combined synthetically in one apperception, through the universal expression *I think*.

However, this principle is not one for every possible understanding as such, but is a principle only
for that [kind of] understanding through whose
pure apperception, in the representation *I think*, no
manifold whatsoever is yet given. An understanding through whose self-consciousness the manifold  B139
of intuition would at the same time be given—i.e.,
an understanding through whose representation the
objects of this representation would at the same time
exist—would not require, for the unity of consciousness, a special act of synthesis of the manifold that
the human understanding, which merely thinks but
does not intuit, does need. But still, this principle is
unavoidably the first principle for the human understanding. And thus our understanding cannot even
frame the slightest concept of a different possible
understanding—whether of an understanding that
itself would intuit; or of an understanding that would
indeed have lying at its basis a sensible intuition, yet
one of a different kind from that in space and time.

§18. What Objective Unity of Self-Consciousness Is
The *transcendental unity* of apperception is the unity
whereby everything manifold given in an intuition is
united in a concept of the object. Hence this unity
is called *objective*, and must be distinguished from
the *subjective* unity of consciousness, which is a
*determination of inner sense* whereby that manifold
of intuition for such [objective] combination is given
empirically. Whether I can be conscious *empirically*
of the manifold as simultaneous or as successive

B140 depends on circumstances or empirical conditions. Hence the empirical unity of consciousness, through the association of representations, itself concerns an appearance and is entirely contingent. However, the pure form of intuition in time, merely as intuition as such containing a given manifold, is subject to the original unity of consciousness. It is subject to that unity solely through the necessary reference of the manifold of intuition to the one *I think*, and hence through the understanding's pure synthesis that lies *a priori* at the basis of the empirical synthesis. Only the original unity of consciousness is valid objectively. The empirical unity of apperception, which we are not examining here and which moreover is only derived from the original unity under given conditions *in concreto*, has only subjective validity. One person will link the representation of a certain word with one thing, another with some other thing; and the unity of consciousness in what is empirical is not, as regards what is given, necessary and universally valid.

§19. The Logical Form of All Judgments Consists in the Objective Unity of Apperception of the Concepts Contained in Them    I have never been satisfied with the explication that logicians give of

B141 a judgment as such. A judgment, they say, is the representation of a relation between two concepts. Now, I shall not here quarrel with them about one respect in which this explication is defective (although this oversight has given rise to many troublesome consequences for logic): namely, that it fits at most *categorical* judgments only, but not hypothetical and disjunctive ones (since these contain a relation not of concepts but of further judgments). I shall point out only that this explication of a judgment leaves undetermined what this *relation* consists in.

But suppose that I inquire more precisely into the relation of given cognitions in every judgment, and that I distinguish it, as belonging to the understanding, from the relation in terms of laws of the reproductive imagination (a relation that has only subjective validity). I then find that a judgment is nothing but a way of bringing given cognitions to

B142 the objective unity of apperception. This is what the little relational word *is* in judgments intends, in order to distinguish the objective unity of given representations from the subjective one. For this word indicates the relation of the representations to original apperception and its *necessary unity*. The relation to this necessary unity is there even if the judgment itself is empirical and hence contingent—e.g., Bodies are heavy. By this I do not mean that these representations belong *necessarily to one another* in the empirical intuition. Rather, I mean that they belong to one another *by virtue of the necessary unity of apperception in the synthesis of intuitions*; i.e., they belong to one another according to principles of the objective determination of all representations insofar as these representations can become cognition—all of these principles being derived from the principle of the transcendental unity of apperception. Only through this does this relation become a *judgment*, i.e., a relation that is *valid objectively* and can be distinguished adequately from a relation of the same representations that would have only subjective validity—e.g., a relation according to laws of association. According to these laws, all I could say is: If I support a body, then I feel a pressure of heaviness. I could not say: It, the body, is heavy—which amounts to saying that these two representations are not together merely in perception (no matter how often repeated), but are combined in the object, i.e., combined independently of what the subject's state is.

§20. All Sensible Intuitions Are Subject to the Cat- B143 egories, Which Are Conditions under Which Alone Their Manifold Can Come Together in One Consciousness    The manifold given in a sensible intuition is necessarily subject to the original synthetic unity of apperception; for solely through this unity is the *unity* of intuition possible. (§17.) But the act of the understanding whereby the manifold of given representations (whether intuitions or concepts) is brought under one apperception as such is the logical function of judgments. (§19.) Therefore everything manifold, insofar as it is given in one empirical intuition, is *determined* in regard to one of the logical functions of judging, inasmuch as through this function it is brought to one consciousness as such. The *categories*, however, are indeed nothing but precisely these functions of judging insofar as the manifold of a given intuition is determined in regard to them. (§13.) Hence, the manifold in a given intuition is also necessarily subject to the categories.

B144 §21. Comment   Through the synthesis of the understanding, a manifold contained in an intuition that I call mine is represented as belonging to the *necessary* unity of self-consciousness, and this representing is done by means of the category.[11] Hence the category indicates that the empirical consciousness of a given manifold of one intuition is just as subject to a pure *a priori* self-consciousness, as empirical intuition is subject to a pure sensible intuition that likewise takes place *a priori*. Hence in the above proposition I have made the beginning of a *deduction* of the pure concepts of the understanding. Since the categories are *independent of sensibility* and arise in the understanding alone, I must still abstract, in this deduction, from the way in which the manifold for an empirical intuition is given, in order to take account solely of the unity that the understanding contributes to the intuition by means of the category. Afterwards (§ 26) I shall show, from the way in which B145 the empirical intuition is given in sensibility, that the intuition's unity is none other than the unity that (by §20, above) the category prescribes to the manifold of a given intuition as such; and that hence by my explaining the category's *a priori* validity regarding all objects of our senses, the deduction's aim will first be fully attained.

From one point, however, I could not abstract in the above proof: namely, from the fact that the manifold for the intuition must be given still prior to the understanding's synthesis, and independently of it; but how it is given remains undetermined here. For if I were to think of an understanding that itself intuited (as, e.g., a divine understanding that did not

represent given objects but through whose representation the objects would at the same time be given or produced), then in regard to such cognition the categories would have no signification whatever. The categories are only rules for an understanding whose entire faculty consists in thought, i.e., in the act of bringing to the unity of apperception the synthesis of the manifold that has been given to it from elsewhere in intuition. Hence such an understanding by itself cognizes nothing whatsoever, but only combines and orders the material for cognition, i.e., the intuition, which must be given to it by the object. But why our understanding has this peculiarity, that it brings about unity of appercep- B146 tion *a priori* only by means of the categories, and only by just this kind and number of them—for this no further reason can be given, just as no reason can be given as to why we have just these and no other functions in judging, or why time and space are the only forms of our possible intuition.

§22. A Category Cannot Be Used for Cognizing Things Except When It Is Applied to Objects of Experience   *Thinking* an object and *cognizing* an object are, then, not the same. For cognition involves two components: first, the concept (the category), through which an object as such is thought; and second, the intuition, through which the object is given. For if no intuition corresponding to the concept could be given at all, then in terms of its form the concept would indeed be a thought; but it would be a thought without any object, and no cognition at all of anything whatsoever would be possible by means of it. For as far as I would know, there would be nothing, and could be nothing, to which my thought could be applied. Now, all intuition that is possible for us is sensible (see the Transcendental Aesthetic). Hence for us, thinking an object as such by means of a pure concept of the understanding can become cognition only insofar as this concept is referred to B147 objects of the senses. Sensible intuition is either pure intuition (space and time) or empirical intuition of what, through sensation, is immediately represented as actual in space and time. By determining pure intuition we can (in mathematics) acquire *a priori*

---

11. The basis of the proof for this rests on the represented *unity of intuition*, through which an *object* is given. This unity always implies a synthesis of the manifold given for an intuition and already contains this manifold given's reference to the unity of apperception.

cognition of objects as appearances, but only in terms of their form; that, however, still leaves unestablished whether there can be things that must be intuited in this form. Consequently all mathematical concepts are, by themselves, no cognitions—except insofar as one presupposes that there are things that can be exhibited to us only in accordance with the form of that pure sensible intuition. But *things in space and time* are given only insofar as they are perceptions (i.e., representations accompanied by sensation), and hence are given only through empirical representation. Consequently the pure concepts of the understanding, even when they are (as in mathematics) applied to *a priori* intuitions, provide cognition only insofar as these intuitions—and hence, by means of them, also the concepts of the understanding—can be applied to empirical intuitions. Consequently the categories also do not supply us, by means of intuition, with any cognition of things, except through their possible application to *empirical* intuition. I.e., the categories serve only B148 for the possibility of *empirical cognition*. Such cognition, however, is called *experience*. Consequently the categories cannot be used for cognizing things except insofar as these things are taken as objects of possible experience.

§23    The above proposition is of the greatest importance. For it determines the bounds for the use of the pure concepts of the understanding in regard to objects just as much as the Transcendental Aesthetic determined the bounds for the use of the pure form of our sensible intuition. Space and time, as conditions for the possibility as to how objects can be given to us, hold no further than for objects of the senses, and hence hold for objects of experience only. Beyond these bounds, space and time represent nothing whatsoever; for they are only in the senses and have no actuality apart from them. The pure concepts of the understanding are free from this limitation and extend to objects of intuition as such, whether this intuition is similar to ours or not, as long as it is sensible rather than intellectual. But this further extension of the concepts beyond *our* sensible intuition is of no benefit to us whatsoever. For they are then empty concepts of objects, i.e., concepts through which we

cannot judge at all whether or not these objects are so much as possible. I.e., the pure concepts of the understanding are then mere forms of thought, without objective reality; for we then have available no intuition to which the synthetic unity of apperception—which is all that those concepts contain—could be applied B149 so that the concepts could determine an object. Solely *our* sensible and empirical intuition can provide them with meaning and significance.

Hence if we suppose an object of a *nonsensible* intuition as given, then we can indeed represent it through all the predicates that are already contained in the presupposition *that the object has as a property nothing belonging to sensible intuition*: hence we can represent that it is not extended or in space, that its duration is not a time, that no change (i.e., succession of determinations in time) is to be found in it, etc. But yet I have no proper cognition if I merely indicate what the intuition of the object *is not*, without being able to say what the intuition does contain. For I have not then represented the possibility of there being an object for my pure concept of the understanding, since I was unable to give an intuition corresponding to the concept, but was able only to say that our intuition does not hold for it. However, the foremost point here is that not even one single category could be applied to such a something. E.g., one could not apply to it the concept of a substance, i.e., the concept of something that can exist as subject but never as mere predicate. For I do not know at all, concerning this concept, whether there can be anything whatever corresponding to this conceptual determination [of substance], unless empirical intuition gives me the instance for applying it. But more about this below.

§24 On Applying the Categories to Objects of the B150 Senses As Such    The pure concepts of the understanding refer, through the mere understanding, to objects of intuition as such—i.e., we leave undetermined whether this intuition is ours or some other, although it must be sensible intuition. But the concepts are, precisely because of this, mere *forms of thought*, through which as yet no determinate object is cognized. We saw that the synthesis or combination of the manifold in them referred merely to the unity of apperception, and was thereby the basis for the possibility of *a priori* cognition insofar as such cognition rests on the understanding; and hence this synthesis was not just transcendental but was also purely intellectual only. But because there lies at the basis in us *a priori* a certain form of sensible intuition, a form that is based on the receptivity of our capacity to represent (i.e., based on our sensibility), the understanding (as spontaneity) can, by means of the manifold of given representations, determine inner sense in accordance with the synthetic unity of apperception; and thus it can think synthetic unity of the apperception of the manifold of *a priori sensible intuition*—this unity being the condition to which all objects of our (i.e., human) intuition must necessarily be subject. And thereby the categories, as themselves mere forms of thought, B151 acquire objective reality. I.e., they acquire application to objects that can be given to us in intuition. But they apply to these objects only as appearances; for only of appearances are we capable of having *a priori* intuition.

This *synthesis* of the manifold of sensible intuition, which is possible and necessary *a priori*, may be called *figurative* synthesis (*synthesis speciosa*). This serves to distinguish it from the synthesis that would be thought, in the mere category, in regard to the manifold of an intuition as such; this latter synthesis is called combination of the understanding (*synthesis intellectualis*). Both these syntheses are *transcendental*, not just because they themselves proceed *a priori*, but because they are also the basis for the possibility of other *a priori* cognition.

However, when the figurative synthesis concerns merely the original synthetic unity of apperception, i.e., merely this transcendental unity thought in the categories, then it must be called the *transcendental synthesis of imagination*, to distinguish it from the merely intellectual combination. **Imagination** is the faculty of representing an object in intuition even *without the object's being present*. Now, all our intuition is sensible; and hence the imagination, because of the subjective condition under which alone it can give to the concepts of the understanding a corresponding intuition, belongs to *sensibility*. Yet

the synthesis of imagination is an exercise of spon- B152 taneity, which is determinative, rather than merely determinable, as is sense; hence this synthesis can *a priori* determine sense in terms of its form in accordance with the unity of apperception. To this extent, therefore, the imagination is a faculty of determining sensibility *a priori*; and its synthesis of intuitions *in accordance with the categories* must be the transcendental synthesis of *imagination*. This synthesis is an action of the understanding upon sensibility, and is the understanding's first application (and at the same time the basis of all its other applications) to the objects of intuition that is possible for us. As figurative, this synthesis is distinct from the intellectual synthesis, which proceeds without any imagination but merely through the understanding. Now insofar as the imagination is spontaneity, I sometimes also call it the *productive* imagination, thereby distinguishing it from the *reproductive* imagination. The synthesis of the reproductive imagination is subject solely to empirical laws, namely, to the laws of association. Therefore this synthesis contributes nothing to the explanation of the possibility of *a priori* cognition, and hence belongs not in transcendental philosophy but in psychology. [ . . . ]

§25  By contrast, in the transcendental synthesis of B157 the manifold of representations as such, and hence in the synthetic original unity of apperception, I am not conscious of myself as I appear to myself, nor as I am in myself, but am conscious only that I am. This *representation* is a *thought*, not an *intuition*. Now *cognition* of ourselves requires not only the act of thought that brings the manifold of every possible intuition to the unity of apperception, but requires in addition a definite kind of intuition whereby this manifold is given. Hence although my own existence is not appearance (still less mere illusion), determination of B158 my existence can occur only in conformity with the form of inner sense and according to the particular way in which the manifold that I combine is given in inner intuition. Accordingly I have no *cognition* of myself as I am but merely cognition of how I appear to myself. Hence consciousness of oneself is far from being a cognition of oneself, regardless of all the categories, which make up the thought of an *object as such* through the combination of the manifold in one apperception. We saw that in order for me to cognize an object different from myself, I not only require the thinking (which I have in the category) of an object as such, but do also require an intuition whereby I determine that universal concept. In the same way, in order to cognize myself, too, I not only require the consciousness of myself or the fact that I think myself, but require also an intuition of the manifold in me whereby I determine this thought.

B159 And I exist as an intelligence. This intelligence is conscious solely of its faculty of combination. But as regards the manifold that it is to combine, this intelligence is subjected to a limiting condition (which it calls inner sense). As subjected to this condition, it can make that combination intuitable only in terms of time relations, which lie wholly outside the concepts of the understanding, properly so called. And hence this intelligence can still cognize itself only as, in regard to an intuition (one that cannot be intellectual and given by the understanding itself), it merely appears to itself; it cannot cognize itself as it would if its *intuition* were intellectual.

§26 Transcendental Deduction of the Universally Possible Use in Experience of the Pure Concepts of the Understanding   In the *metaphysical deduction* we established the *a priori* origin of the categories as such through their complete concurrence with the universal logical functions of thought. But in the *transcendental deduction* we exhibited the possibility of them as *a priori* cognitions of objects of an intuition as such (§§20, 21). We must now explain how it is possible, through *categories*, to cognize *a priori* whatever objects *our senses may encounter*—to so cognize them as regards not the form of their intuition, but the laws of their combination—and hence,

B160 as it were, to prescribe laws to nature, and even to make nature possible. For without this suitability of the categories, one would fail to see how everything that our senses may encounter would have to be subject to the laws that arise *a priori* from the understanding alone.

First of all, let me point out that by *synthesis of apprehension* I mean that combination of the manifold in an empirical intuition whereby perception, i.e., empirical consciousness of the intuition (as appearance), becomes possible.

We have *a priori*, in the representations of space and time, *forms* of both outer and inner sensible intuition; and to these forms the synthesis of apprehension of the manifold of appearance must always conform, because that synthesis itself can take place only according to this form. But space and time are represented *a priori* not merely as *forms* of sensible intuition, but as themselves *intuitions* (containing a manifold), and hence are represented with the determination of the *unity* of this manifold in them (see B161 the Transcendental Aesthetic).[12] Therefore even the *unity of the synthesis* of the manifold outside or within us, and hence also a *combination* to which everything that is to be represented determinately in space or time must conform, is already given *a priori* as a condition of the synthesis of all *apprehension*—given along with (not in) these intuitions. This synthetic unity, however, can be none other than the unity of the combination, conforming to the categories but applied to our *sensible intuition*, of the manifold of a given *intuition as such* in an original consciousness. Consequently all synthesis, the synthesis through which even perception becomes possible, is subject to the categories; and since experience is cognition through connected perceptions, the categories are conditions of the possibility of experience and hence hold *a priori* also for all objects of experience.

---

12. Space, represented as *object* (as we are actually required to represent it in geometry), contains more than the mere form of intuition; namely, it also contains *combination* of the manifold given according to the form of sensibility into an *intuitive* representation—so that the *form of intuition* gives us merely a manifold, but *formal intuition* gives us unity of representation. In the Transcendental Aesthetic I had merely included this unity with sensibility, wanting only to point out that it precedes any concept. But in fact this unity presupposes a synthesis; this synthesis does not belong to the senses, but through it do all concepts of space and time first become possible. For through this unity (inasmuch as the understanding determines sensibility) space or time are first *given* as intuitions, and hence the unity of this *a priori* intuition belongs to space and time, and not to the concept of the understanding (see §24).

B162     Hence, e.g., when I turn the empirical intuition of a house into a perception by apprehending the intuition's manifold, then in this apprehension I presuppose the *necessary unity* of space and of outer sensible intuition as such; and I draw, as it were, the house's shape in conformity with this synthetic unity of the manifold in space. But this same unity, if I abstract from the form of space, resides in the understanding, and is the category of the synthesis of the homogeneous in an intuition as such, i.e., the category of *magnitude*. Hence the synthesis of apprehension, i.e., perception, must conform throughout to that category.[13]

When (to take a different example) I perceive the freezing of water, then I apprehend two states (fluidity and solidity) as states that stand to each other in B163 a relation of time. But in time, which I presuppose for the appearance as an inner *intuition*, I necessarily represent a synthetic unity of the manifold; without this unity, that relation could not be given *determinately* (as regards time sequence) in an intuition. However, this synthetic unity, as an *a priori* condition under which I combine the manifold of an *intuition as such*, is—if I abstract from the constant form of *my* inner intuition, i.e., from time—the category of *cause*; through this category, when I apply it to my sensibility, *everything that happens is, in terms of its relation, determined* by me *in time as such*. Therefore apprehension in such an event, and hence the event itself, is subject—as regards possible perception—to the concept of the *relation of effects and causes*; and thus it is in all other cases.

Categories are concepts that prescribe laws *a priori* to appearances, and hence to nature regarded as the sum of all appearances (*natura materialiter spectata*). And now this question arises: Since the categories are not derived from nature and do not conform to it as their model (for then they would be merely empirical), how are we to comprehend the fact that nature must conform to the categories, i.e., how can the categories determine *a priori* the combination of nature's manifold without gleaning that combination from nature? Here now is the solution of this puzzle.

How it is that the laws of appearances in nature B164 must agree with the understanding and its *a priori* form, i.e., with the understanding's faculty of combining the manifold as such, is not any stranger than how it is that appearances themselves must agree with the form of *a priori* sensible intuition. For just as appearances exist not in themselves but only relatively to the subject in whom the appearances inhere insofar as the subject has senses, so the laws exist not in the appearances but only relatively to that same being insofar as that being has understanding. Things in themselves would have their law-governedness necessarily, even apart from an understanding that cognizes them. But appearances are only representations of things that exist uncognized as regards what they may be in themselves. As mere appearances, however, they are subject to no law of connection whatsoever except the one prescribed by the connecting faculty. Now what connects the manifold of sensible intuition is imagination; and imagination depends on the understanding as regards the unity of its intellectual synthesis, and on sensibility as regards the manifoldness of apprehension. Now all possible perception depends on this synthesis of apprehension; but it itself, this empirical synthesis, depends on transcendental synthesis and hence on the categories. Therefore all possible perceptions, and hence also anything whatsoever that can reach empirical consciousness, i.e., all appearances of na- B165 ture, must in regard to their combination be subject to the categories. Nature (regarded merely as nature in general) depends (as *natura formaliter spectata*) on the categories as the original basis of its necessary law-governedness. But even the pure faculty of the understanding does not suffice for prescribing *a priori* to appearances, through mere categories, more laws than those underlying a *nature in general* considered as the law-governedness of appearances in space and time. Particular laws, because they

_____

13. In this way we prove that the synthesis of apprehension, which is empirical, must conform necessarily to the synthesis of apperception, which is intellectual and is contained wholly *a priori* in the category. The spontaneity that brings combination into the manifold of intuition is one and the same in the two cases: in apprehension it does so under the name of power of imagination; in apperception it does so under the name of the understanding.

concern appearances that are determined empirically, are *not completely derivable* from those laws, although the particular laws are one and all subject to the categories. Experience must be added in order for us to become acquainted with particular laws *at all*; but the *a priori* laws alone give us information about experience as such and about what can be cognized as an object of that experience.

§27 Result of This Deduction of the Concepts of the Understanding  We cannot *think* an object except through categories; we cannot *cognize* an object thought by us except through intuitions corresponding to those concepts. Now all our intuitions B166 are sensible, and this [sensible] cognition is empirical insofar as its object is given. Empirical cognition, however, is experience. *Consequently no cognition is possible for us* a priori *except solely of objects of possible experience.*[14]

But this cognition, which is limited merely to objects of experience, is not therefore all taken from experience. Rather, as far as pure intuitions as well as pure concepts of the understanding are concerned, they are elements of cognition that are found in us *a priori*. Now, there are only two ways in which one can conceive of a *necessary* agreement of experience with the concepts of its objects: either experience makes these concepts possible, or these concepts B167 make experience possible. The first alternative is not what happens as regards the categories (nor as regards pure sensible intuition). For they are *a priori* concepts and hence are independent of experience. (To assert that their origin is empirical would be to assert a kind of *generatio aequivoca*.) There remains,

---

14. In order to keep my readers from being troubled prematurely by the worrisome detrimental consequences of this proposition, let me just remind them that in our *thinking* the categories are not limited by the conditions of our sensible intuition, but have an unbounded realm. Intuition is required only for *cognizing* what we think, i.e., only for determining the object. Thus if intuition is lacking, the thought of the object can otherwise still have its true and useful consequences for the subject's *use of reason*. But because the use of reason is not always directed to the determination of the object and hence to cognition, but is sometimes directed also to the determination of the subject and his volition, it cannot yet be set forth here.

consequently, only the second alternative (a system of *epigenesis*, as it were, of pure reason): namely, that the categories contain the grounds, on the part of the understanding, of the possibility of all experience as such. But as to how the categories make experience possible, and as to what principles of the possibility of experience they provide us with when applied to appearances, more information will be given in the following chapter on the transcendental use of our faculty of judgment.

Someone might want to propose, in addition to the two sole ways mentioned above, a middle course between them: namely, that the categories are neither *self-thought a priori* first principles of our cognition, nor again are drawn from experience, but are subjective predispositions for thinking that are implanted in us simultaneously with our existence; and that they were so arranged by our originator that their use harmonizes exactly with the laws of nature governing the course of experience (this theory would be a kind of *preformation system* of pure reason). If such a middle course were proposed, the following would decide against it (apart from the fact that with B168 such a hypothesis one can see no end to how far the presupposition of predetermined predispositions to future judgments might be carried): namely, that the categories would in that case lack the *necessity* which belongs essentially to the concept of them. For, the concept of cause, e.g., which asserts the necessity of a result under a presupposed condition, would be false if it rested only on an arbitrary subjective necessity, implanted in us, to link certain empirical representations according to such a rule of relation. I could then not say that the effect is connected with the cause in the object (i.e., connected with it necessarily), but could say only that I am so equipped that I cannot think this representation otherwise than as thus connected. And this is just what the skeptic most longs for. For then all our insight, achieved through the supposed objective validity of our judgments, is nothing but sheer illusion; and there would also be no lack of people who would not concede this subjective necessity (which must be felt) in themselves. At the very least one could not quarrel with anyone about something that rests merely on the way in which his [self as] subject is organized.

Brief Sketch of This Deduction  This deduction is the exhibition of the pure concepts of the understanding (and, with them, of all theoretical *a priori* cognition) as principles of the possibility of experi-

B169  ence; the exhibition of these principles, however, as the *determination* of appearances in space and time *as such*; and the exhibition, finally, of this determination as arising from the *original* synthetic unity of apperception, this unity being the form of the understanding as referred to space and time, the original forms of sensibility. [ . . . ]

# Book II. Analytic Of Principles

A136/  [ . . . ] [T]his *transcendental doctrine of the faculty of*
B175  *judgment* will comprise two chapters. The *first* chapter deals with the sensible condition under which alone pure concepts of the understanding can be used, i.e., with the schematism of the pure understanding. The *second* chapter deals with the synthetic judgments that under these conditions emanate *a priori* from pure concepts of the understanding and that lie *a priori* at the basis of all other cognitions; i.e., it deals with the principles of the pure understanding.

A137/  Chapter I On the Schematism of the
B176  Pure Concepts of the Understanding

Whenever an object is subsumed under a concept, the representation of the object must be *homogeneous* with the concept; i.e., the concept must contain what is represented in the object that is to be subsumed under it. For this is precisely what we mean by the expression that an object is contained *under* a concept. Thus the empirical concept of a *plate* is homogeneous with the pure geometrical concept of a *circle*, inasmuch as the roundness thought in the concept of the plate can be intuited in the circle.

However, pure concepts of the understanding are quite heterogeneous from empirical intuitions (indeed, from sensible intuitions generally) and can never be encountered in any intuition. How, then, can an intuition be *subsumed* under a category, and hence how can a category be *applied* to appearances—since

surely no one will say that a category (e.g., causality) can also be intuited through senses and is contained  A138/ in appearances? Now this question, natural and im-  B177 portant as it is, is in fact the cause that necessitates a transcendental doctrine of the faculty of judgment. The doctrine is needed, namely, in order to show how it is possible for *pure concepts of the understanding* to be applied to appearances as such. In all the other sciences no such need arises. For there the concepts through which the object is thought in a universal way are not so distinct and heterogeneous from the concepts representing the object *in concreto*, as it is given. And hence there is no need there to provide a special exposition concerning the application of the first kind of concept to the second kind.

Now clearly there must be some third thing that must be homogeneous with the category, on the one hand, and with the appearance, on the other hand, and that thus makes possible the application of the category to the appearance. This mediating representation must be pure (i.e., without anything empirical), and yet must be both *intellectual*, on the one hand, and *sensible*, on the other hand. Such a representation is the *transcendental schema*.

A concept of the understanding contains pure synthetic unity of the manifold as such. Time, as the formal condition for the manifold of inner sense and hence for the connection of all representations, contains an *a priori* manifold in pure intuition. Now, a transcendental time determination is homogeneous with the *category* (in which its unity consists) insofar as time determination is *universal* and rests on  A139/ an *a priori* rule. But it is homogeneous with *appear-*  B178 *ance*, on the other hand, insofar as every empirical representation of the manifold contains *time*. Hence it will be possible for the category to be applied to appearances by means of the transcendental time determination, which, as the schema of the concepts of the understanding, mediates the subsumption of appearances under the category.

In view of what has been shown in the deduction of the categories, I hope that no one will have doubts in deciding this question: whether these pure concepts of the understanding have a merely empirical use [only] or also a transcendental one; i.e., whether, as conditions of a possible experience, they refer *a priori* solely to appearances or whether they can be extended, as conditions for the possibility of things as such, to objects in themselves (without any restriction to our sensibility). For we saw in the deduction that concepts are quite impossible, and cannot have any signification, unless an object is given for the concepts themselves or at least for the elements of which they consist; and that hence they cannot at all concern things in themselves (i.e., [things considered] without regard to whether and how they may be given to us). We saw, moreover, that the only way in which objects can be given to us is by modification of our sensibility; and, finally, that pure *a priori* concepts, besides containing the function of the understanding implicit in the category, must also contain *a priori* formal conditions of sensibility (of inner sense, specifically), namely, conditions comprising the universal condition under which alone the category can be applied to any object. Let us call this formal and pure condition of sensibility, to which the concept of the understanding is restricted in its use, the *schema* of this concept of the understanding; and let us call the understanding's procedure with these schemata the *schematism* of the pure understanding.

A schema is, in itself, always only a product of the imagination. Yet, because here the imagination's synthesis aims not at an individual intuition but at unity in the determination of sensibility, a schema must be distinguished from an image. Thus if I put five dots after one another, like this, . . . . . , then this result is an image of the number five. Suppose, however, that I only think a number as such, which might then be five or a hundred. Then my thought is more the representation of a method for representing—in accordance with a certain concept—a multitude (e.g., a thousand) in an image, than this image itself. Indeed, in the case of a thousand I could hardly survey that image and compare it with the concept. Now, this representation of a universal procedure of the imagination for providing a concept with its image I call the schema for that concept.

In fact, it is schemata, not images of objects, that lie at the basis of our pure sensible concepts. No image whatsoever of a triangle would ever be adequate to the concept of a triangle as such. For it would never reach the concept's universality that makes the concept hold for all triangles (whether right-angled or oblique-angled, etc.), but would always be limited to only a part of this sphere. The schema of the triangle can never exist anywhere but in thoughts, and is a rule for the synthesis of imagination regarding pure shapes in space. Even less is an object of experience or an image thereof ever adequate to the empirical concept; rather, that concept always refers directly to the schema of imagination, this schema being a rule for determining our intuition in accordance with such and such a general concept. The concept *dog* signifies a rule whereby my imagination can trace the shape of such a four-footed animal in a general way, i.e., without being limited to any single and particular shape offered to me by experience, or even to all possible images that I can exhibit *in concreto*. This schematism of our understanding, i.e., its schematism regarding appearances and their mere form, is a hidden art residing in the depths of the human soul, an art whose true stratagems we shall hardly ever divine from nature and lay bare before ourselves. Only this much can we say: The *image* is a product of the productive imagination's empirical ability. A *schema* of sensible concepts (such as the concepts of figures in space) is a product and, as it were, a monogram of the pure *a priori* imagination through which, and according to which, images become possible in the first place. But the images must always be connected with the concept only by means of the schema that they designate; in themselves the images are never completely congruent with the concept. A schema of a pure concept of the understanding, however, is something that one cannot bring to any image whatsoever. Such a schema is, rather, only the pure synthesis conforming to a rule, expressed by the category, of unity according to concepts as such. It is a transcendental product of the imagination which concerns the determination of inner sense as such, according to conditions of that sense's form (namely, time), in regard to all representations insofar as these are to cohere *a priori*, in conformity with the unity of apperception, in one concept.

B179
A140

B180

B141

B181

A142

Now, instead of letting ourselves be detained by a dry and tedious dissection of what is required for transcendental schemata of pure concepts of the understanding as such, let us rather exhibit them according to the order of the categories and in connection with them.

B182 The pure image of all magnitudes (*quanta*) for outer sense is space, whereas the pure image of the magnitudes of all sense objects as such is time. But the *pure schema of magnitude (quantitas)* taken as a concept of the understanding is *number*, which is a representation encompassing conjointly the successive addition of one item to another (homogeneous A143 item). Therefore number is nothing other than the unity in the synthesis of the manifold of a homogeneous intuition as such, a unity that arises because I myself produce time in apprehending the intuition.

Reality, in the pure concept of the understanding, is what corresponds to a sensation as such. Therefore reality is that whose very concept indicates a being (in time); and negation is that whose concept represents a not-being (in time). Hence the contrast of reality and negation is made by distinguishing the same time as either a filled or an empty time. Now, time is only the form of intuition, and hence only the form of objects as appearances; therefore what in these objects corresponds to sensation is the transcendental matter of all objects as things in their own right (i.e., their thinghood, reality). Now every sensation has a degree or magnitude whereby it can, in regard to the same representation of an object, fill the same time — i.e., [form of] inner sense — more or fill it less, B183 down to where the sensation ceases in nothingness (= 0 = *negatio*). Hence there is a relation and coherence, or rather a transition from reality to negation, which is responsible for every reality's being represented as a quantum. And the schema of a reality taken as the quantity of something insofar as it fills time is precisely this continuous and uniform production of that reality in time, where from a sensation having a certain degree we descend, in time, until the sensation vanishes, or ascend gradually from the sensation's negation to its [actual] magnitude.

A144 The schema of substance is permanence of the real in time; i.e., it is the representation of the real as a substratum of empirical time determination as such, a substratum which therefore endures while all else varies. (Time is not in transition; rather, the existence of what is mutable is in transition in time. Hence to time, which itself is immutable and enduring, there corresponds in [the realm of] appearance what is immutable in existence, i.e., substance; and only by reference to substance can succession and simultaneity of appearances be determined in terms of time.)

The schema of the cause and of the causality of a thing as such is the real upon which, whenever it is posited, something else always follows. Hence this schema consists in the manifold's succession insofar as this is subject to a rule.

The schema of community (interaction), or of the reciprocal causality of substances in regard to their accidents, is the simultaneity, according to a universal rule, of the determinations of the one substance B184 with those of the other.

The schema of possibility is the harmony of the synthesis of different representations with the conditions of time as such. (Thus, e.g., what is opposite cannot be in a thing simultaneously, but can be in it only successively.) Hence this schema is the determination, at some time, of the representation of a thing.

The schema of actuality is existence within a de- A145 terminate time.

The schema of necessity is the existence of an object at all times.

Now from all of this we see that the schema of each category contains, and is responsible for the representation of, the following: the schema of magnitude, the production (synthesis) of time itself in the successive apprehension of an object; the schema of quality, the synthesis of sensation (perception) with the representation of time — or, i.e., the filling of time; the schema of relation, the relation of perceptions among one another at all times (i.e., according to a rule of time determination); finally, the schema of modality and of its categories, time itself as the correlate of the determination of an object as to whether and how it belongs to time. Hence the schemata are nothing but *a priori time determinations* according to rules; and these rules, according

B185 to the order of the categories, deal with the *time se-ries*, the *time content*, the *time order*, and finally the *sum total of time* in regard to all possible objects.

Now, this shows that the schematism of the understanding provided by the transcendental synthesis of imagination comes down to nothing other than the unity in inner sense of all the manifold of intuition, and thus comes down indirectly to the unity of apper-

A146 ception as a function corresponding to inner sense (a receptivity). The schemata of the pure concepts of the understanding are, therefore, the true and sole conditions for providing these concepts with a reference to objects and hence with *signification*. And hence the categories have, in the end, no other use than a possible empirical one. For, on the basis of a unity that is *a priori* necessary (because of the necessary union of all consciousness in an original apperception), they serve merely to subject appearances to universal rules of synthesis, and thus to make them fit for thoroughgoing connection in one experience.

In the whole of all possible experience, however, lie all our cognitions; and the transcendental truth that precedes all empirical truth and makes it possible consists in the universal relation to this possible experience.

Yet it is also obvious that although the schemata

B186 of sensibility are what first realize the categories, they do nonetheless also restrict them, i.e., they limit them to conditions lying outside understanding (namely, in sensibility). Hence a schema is, properly speaking, only the phenomenon of an object, or the sensible concept of an object, in harmony with the category. (Numerus *est quantitas phaenomenon*, sensatio *realitas phaenomenon*, constans et perdurabile rerum *substantia phaenomenon*, aeternitas *necessitas*

A147 *phaenomenon*, etc.) Now, it seems that if we omit a restricting condition from a previously limited concept, then we amplify that concept. Thus it was supposed that the categories in their pure signification— i.e., apart from all conditions of sensibility—hold for things in general, *as they are*, instead of the categories' having schemata that represent these things only *as they appear*; and hence it was supposed that the categories have a signification that is independent of all schemata and that extends much farther than they

do. Even after their separation from all sensible conditions the concepts of the understanding do in fact retain a signification. But it is merely logical, [signifying] the mere unity of representations, that, however, are given no object, and hence also no signification that could yield a concept of the object. Thus, e.g., if one omitted from substance the sensible determination of permanence, it would signify nothing more than something that can be thought as a subject (i.e., thought without being thought as a predicate of something else). Now, I cannot make anything of this representation, because it does not at all indicate B187 to me what determinations are possessed by the thing that is to count as such a primary subject. Without schemata, therefore, the categories are only functions of the understanding for producing concepts, but they represent no object. This latter signification they get from sensibility, which realizes the understanding while at the same time restricting it.

## Chapter II. System of All Principles        A148
## of Pure Understanding

In the preceding chapter we examined the transcendental faculty of judgment solely in terms of the universal conditions under which alone it is entitled to use the pure concepts of the understanding for making synthetic judgments. Our task now is to exhibit as systematically linked the judgments that the understanding, under this critical provision, actually brings about *a priori*. The natural and safe guidance for this task must doubtless be given to us by our table of categories. For precisely in the categories' reference to possible experience must all pure *a priori* cognition of the understanding consist; and hence the B188 categories' relation to sensibility as such will display, completely and in a system, all the transcendental principles for the use of the understanding.

Now *a priori* principles are so named not merely because they contain the justification of other judgments, but also because they themselves are not justified by higher and more universal cognitions. Yet A149 having this property does not always exempt such principles from requiring a proof. Such a proof could, to be sure, no longer be conducted objectively [since principles] lie, rather, at the basis of all cognition of its object. This does not, however, preclude the possibility of creating a proof that starts from the subjective sources underlying the possibility of cognizing an object as such. Nor, indeed, does it preclude the necessity of such a proof; for otherwise the proposition would still be under the greatest suspicion of being an assertion obtained merely surreptitiously.

Second, we shall limit ourselves to just those principles that refer to the categories. Hence the principles of the Transcendental Aesthetic, whereby space and time are the conditions of the possibility of all things as appearances, and likewise the restriction of those principles, namely, that they cannot be used in reference to things in themselves, do not belong within our allotted realm of inquiry. Mathematical principles, similarly, form no part of B189 this system. For they are drawn only from intuition, not from the pure concepts of the understanding. Yet because they are nonetheless synthetic *a priori* judgments, their possibility will necessarily be considered here as well. We must include their possibility here, not indeed in order to prove that they are correct and apodeictically certain—a proof that they do not require at all—but only in order to make comprehensible, and to deduce, the possibility of such evident *a priori* cognitions. [ . . . ]

A154/ Section II On the Supreme Principle of All Synthetic
B193 Judgments   Explaining the possibility of synthetic judgments is a problem with which general logic has nothing whatsoever to do; indeed, general logic need not even know the problem's name. But in a transcendental logic this explanation is the most important task of all—even the sole task, if we are talking about the possibility of synthetic judgments that are *a priori*, as well as about the conditions and the range of their validity. For after completing this task, transcendental logic is able to fulfill perfectly its purpose, namely, to determine the range and the bounds of the pure understanding.

In an analytic judgment I keep to the given concept, in order to establish something about it. If the judgment is to be affirmative, then I ascribe to that concept only what was already thought in it; if the judgment is to be negative, then I exclude from the

concept only its opposite. In synthetic judgments, however, I am to go outside the given concept, in order to consider, in relation with this concept, something quite different from what was thought in it. Hence this relation is never a relation either of A155/ identity or of contradiction, so that by looking at the B194 judgment taken by itself one cannot tell whether it is true, or erroneous.

If it is granted, then, that one must go outside a given concept in order to compare it synthetically with another concept, then some third thing is needed in which alone the synthesis of two concepts can arise. But what, then, is this third thing that is the medium of all synthetic judgments? There is only one sum total that contains all our representations: namely, inner sense, and its *a priori* form, time. Moreover, the synthesis of representations rests on imagination; but their synthetic unity (which is required for a judgment) rests on the unity of apperception. Hence the possibility of synthetic judgments will have to be sought here; and since all three contain the sources for *a priori* representations, the possibility of pure synthetic judgments will also have to be sought in them. Indeed, these judgments will even necessarily be founded on these three bases, if a cognition of objects is to come about that rests solely on the synthesis of representations.

If a cognition is to have objective reality, i.e., if it is to refer to an object and have in that object its signification and meaning, then the object must be capable of being *given* in some way. For otherwise B195 the concepts are empty; and though we have thought by means of them, we have in fact cognized nothing through this thinking, but have merely played with representations. To be given an object—if this is not A156 again to mean to be given it only mediately, but is to mean, rather, to exhibit it immediately in intuition— is nothing other than to refer the representation of the object to experience (whether actual, or at least possible, experience). Even space and time, however pure these concepts are of anything empirical, and however certain it is that they are represented in the mind completely *a priori*, would yet be without objective validity, and without meaning and signification, if we did not show that their use with objects of experience is necessary. Indeed, the representation of space and time is a mere schema that always refers to the reproductive imagination, this imagination summoning the objects of experience without which they would have no signification. And thus it is, without distinction, with all concepts whatsoever.

Hence the *possibility of experience* is what provides all our *a priori* cognitions with objective reality. Now experience rests on the synthetic unity of appearances, i.e., on a synthesis of appearances in general performed according to concepts of an object. Without such synthesis, experience would not even be cognition, but would be a rhapsody of perceptions. Such a rhapsody of perceptions would not fit together in any context conforming to rules of a thoroughly connected (possible) consciousness, and hence would also not fit together to agree with the
B196 transcendental and necessary unity of apperception.
A157 Hence at the basis of experience there lie *a priori* principles of its form. These principles are universal rules of unity in the synthesis of appearances; and the objective reality of these rules as necessary conditions can always be shown in experience—indeed, even in the possibility of experience. Without this reference, however, synthetic propositions are entirely impossible *a priori*. For they have then no third thing, namely, no object in which the synthetic unity can establish the objective reality of their concepts.

Hence very much concerning space as such, or concerning the shapes traced in it by the productive imagination, is indeed cognized by us *a priori* in synthetic judgments, so that for this cognition we actually require no experience at all. Yet to cognize all this would be nothing—but would be to deal with a mere chimera—if space did not have to be regarded as a condition of the appearances which amount to the material for outer experience. Hence those pure synthetic judgments refer— although only indirectly—to possible experience, or rather to the very possibility of experience, and on this reference alone do they base the objective validity of their synthesis.

Therefore experience, as empirical synthesis, is in [regard to] its possibility the only kind of cognition that provides reality to all other synthesis. By the
B197 same token, this latter synthesis, as *a priori* cognition,

has truth (agreement with the object) only because it contains nothing more than what is necessary for A158 synthetic unity of experience as such.

Hence the supreme principle of all synthetic judgments is this: Every object is subject to the conditions necessary for synthetic unity of the manifold of intuition in a possible experience.

Thus synthetic judgments are possible *a priori* if we refer the formal conditions of *a priori* intuition, the synthesis of imagination, and the necessary unity of this synthesis in a transcendental apperception to a possible experiential cognition as such, and if we then say that the conditions for the *possibility of experience* as such are simultaneously conditions for *the possibility of objects of experience* and hence have objective validity in a synthetic *a priori* judgment.

Section III Systematic Presentation of All the Synthetic Principles of Pure Understanding    The fact that principles occur anywhere at all is attributable solely to the pure understanding. For the pure understanding not only is our faculty of rules regarding what happens, but is itself the source of principles, A159/ the source according to which everything (whatever B198 we can encounter as an object) is necessarily subject to rules. For without rules there could never be for appearances any cognition of an object corresponding to them. Even natural laws, when considered as principles of the understanding's empirical use, carry with them at the same time an expression of necessity, and hence at least the presumption of their being determined from bases that are valid *a priori* and prior to all experience. But all laws of nature, without distinction, fall under higher principles of the understanding, inasmuch as they merely apply these higher principles to particular cases of appearance. Hence these higher principles alone provide us with the concept that contains the condition and, as it were, the exponent for a rule as such; but experience provides us with the case that falls under the rule.

There can in fact be no danger, I suppose, that anyone will regard merely empirical principles as principles of the pure understanding—or vice versa, for that matter. For this confusion can easily be prevented by attending to the necessity according to concepts that distinguishes the principles of the pure understanding, and whose lack is easily perceived in every empirical proposition—no matter how generally such a proposition may hold. But there are pure *a priori* principles as well that I nonetheless do not wish to assign to the pure understanding as belonging to it. For whereas the understanding is our faculty of concepts, these principles are not drawn from pure concepts, but are drawn (even if by means of the understanding) from pure intuitions. In mathematics there are such principles; but their application to experience, and hence their objective validity, still rests always on the pure understanding—indeed, so does the possibility of such synthetic *a priori* cognition (i.e., the deduction of this possibility).

Hence I shall not include among my principles the principles of mathematics themselves. But I shall indeed include the principles on which their possibility and objective validity is based *a priori*, and which must therefore be regarded as the principles [underlying] those mathematical principles. They do not emanate from intuition and proceed to concepts, but emanate from concepts and proceed to intuition.

When pure concepts of the understanding are applied to possible experience, then the use of their synthesis is either *mathematical* or *dynamical*. For this application is concerned in part merely with the *intuition*, and in part with the *existence*, of an appearance as such. However, whereas the *a priori* conditions of intuition are thoroughly necessary in regard to a possible experience, those of the existence of the objects of a possible empirical intuition are in themselves only contingent. Hence the principles of mathematical use will be unconditionally necessary, i.e., apodeictic. But as for those of dynamical use, while they also carry with them the character of an *a priori* necessity, they do so only under the condition of there being empirical thought in an experience, and hence they do so only mediately and indirectly. They consequently lack (though without detriment to the certainty they have universally in reference to experience) that immediate evidence possessed by the former kind of principles. This, however, we shall be better able to judge at the conclusion of this system of principles.

The wholly natural directions for setting up the table of principles are provided to us by the table of categories. For these principles are nothing but the rules for the objective use of the categories. Accordingly, the following are all the principles of the pure understanding.

1
*Axioms* of intuition

2                                                              3
*Anticipations*                                        *Analogies*
of perception                                           of experience

4
*Postulates*
of empirical thought as such

I have selected these names with care, in order not to leave unnoted the differences regarding the evidence and the employment of these principles. But we shall soon find that, in regard both to the evidence and to the *a priori* determination of appearances, the principles of the categories of *magnitude* and *quality* (if we attend solely to the form of these) do differ markedly from the remaining principles. For although both kinds of principles are capable of a complete certainty, in the former kind this certainty is intuitive whereas in the latter it is merely discursive. Hence I shall call the former kind the mathematical and the latter the *dynamical* principles. But we must note carefully that I do not have in mind here the principles of mathematics in the one case, any more than the principles of general (physical) dynamics in the other. I have in mind, rather, only the principles of the pure understanding as related to inner sense (apart from any distinction of the representations given in that sense). It is in fact through these latter principles that the principles of mathematics and of general dynamics acquire, one and all, their possibility. Hence I name my principles mathematical and dynamical more in view of their application than for the sake of their content. I shall now proceed to examine them in the same order as they are presented in the above table.

1 Axioms Of Intuition    Their principle is: *All intuitions are extensive magnitudes.*

**Proof**: Appearances contain, as regards their form, an intuition in space and time that underlies them, one and all, *a priori*. Hence they cannot be apprehended, i.e., taken up into empirical consciousness, except through the synthesis of the manifold whereby the representations of a determinate space or time are produced. I.e., appearances can be apprehended only through the assembly of what is homogeneous and the consciousness of the synthetic unity of this manifold (this manifold homogeneous). Now the consciousness of the synthetic unity of the homogeneous manifold in intuition as such, insofar as through this consciousness the representation of an object first becomes possible, is the concept of a magnitude (*quantum*). Therefore even the perception of an object as appearance is possible only through the same synthetic unity (of the given sensible intuition's manifold) whereby the unity of the assembly of the manifold homogeneous is thought in the concept of a *magnitude*. I.e., appearances are, one and all, magnitudes—specifically, *extensive magnitudes*, because as intuitions in space or time they must be represented through the same synthesis whereby space and time as such are determined.

I call a magnitude extensive when the representation of the parts makes possible (and hence necessarily precedes) the representation of the whole. I can represent no line, no matter how small, without drawing it in thought, i.e., without producing from one point onward all the parts little by little and thereby tracing this intuition in the first place. And the situation is the same with every time, even the smallest. In any such time I think only the successive progression from one instant to the next, where through all the parts of time and their addition a determinate time magnitude is finally produced. Since what is mere intuition in all appearances is either space or time, every appearance is—as intuition—an extensive magnitude, inasmuch as it can be cognized only through successive synthesis (of part to part) in apprehension. Accordingly, all appearances are intuited already as aggregates (i.e., multitudes of previously given parts); precisely this is not the case with

every kind of magnitudes, but is the case only with those that are represented and apprehended by us as magnitudes *extensively*.

This successive synthesis of the productive imagination in the generation of shapes is the basis of the mathematics of extension (i.e., geometry) with its axioms. These axioms express the conditions of sensible *a priori* intuition under which alone the schema of a pure concept of outer appearance can come about—e.g., the axioms that between two points only one straight line is possible or that two straight lines enclose no space; etc. These are the axioms that, properly speaking, concern only magnitudes (*quanta*), as such.

But as concerns magnitude (*quantitas*), i.e., the answer to the question as to how large something is, there are for it no axioms in the proper meaning of the term, although a variety of such propositions are synthetic and immediately certain (*indemonstrabilia*). For the propositions which assert that equals added to—or subtracted from—equals yield equals are analytic propositions, inasmuch as I am directly conscious of the identity of the one magnitude's production with the other magnitude's production. Axioms, however, are to be synthetic *a priori* propositions. The evident propositions of numerical relations, however, are indeed synthetic. Yet, unlike those of geometry, they are not universal; and precisely because of this, they also cannot be called axioms, but can be called only numerical formulas. The proposition that $7 + 5 = 12$ is not an analytic proposition. For neither in the representation of 7, nor in that of 5, nor in the representation of the assembly of the two numbers do I think the number 12. (The fact that I ought to think the number 12 in *adding the two numbers* is not at issue here; for in an analytic proposition the question is only whether I actually think the predicate in the representation of the subject.) But although the proposition $7 + 5 = 12$ is synthetic, it is still only a singular proposition. For insofar as we here take account merely of the synthesis of the homogeneous (i.e., the units), the synthesis here can occur in only a single way, although the *use* made of these numbers afterwards is universal. [Geometry is different in this respect.] If I say that by means of three lines, two of which taken together are greater than the third, a triangle can be drawn, then I have here the mere function of the productive imagination, which can make the lines be drawn greater or smaller, and can similarly make them meet at all kinds of angles chosen at will. By contrast, the number 7 is possible in only a single way, and so is the number 12, which is produced through the synthesis of 7 with 5. Such propositions, therefore, must be called not axioms (for otherwise there would be infinitely many axioms), but numerical formulas.

A165

B206

This transcendental principle of the mathematics of appearances greatly expands our *a priori* cognition. For it alone is what makes pure mathematics in all its precision applicable to objects of experience. In the absence of the principle, this applicability might not be so self-evident, and has in fact been contested by many. For appearances are not things in themselves. Empirical intuition is possible only through pure intuition (of space and time). Hence what geometry says about pure intuition holds incontestably for empirical intuition also. And the subterfuges whereby objects of the senses need not conform to the rules of construction in space (e.g., the rule of the infinite divisibility of lines or angles) must be dropped. For by making them one denies objective validity to space, and thereby also to all mathematics, and one no longer knows why and how far mathematics is applicable to appearances. The synthesis of spaces and times, which are the essential form of all intuition, is also what makes possible the apprehension of appearance, hence makes possible any outer experience, and consequently also makes possible all cognition of the objects of this experience. And thus what mathematics in its pure use proves for that synthesis also necessarily holds for this cognition. All objections against this are only the chicanery of a falsely instructed reason: a reason that erroneously means to detach objects of the senses from the formal condition of our sensibility, and that despite their being mere appearances represents them as objects in themselves, given to the understanding. If that were the case, however, then there could be no synthetic *a priori* cognition of them at all, and hence also no such cognition through pure concepts of space; and

A166

B207

the science that determines these concepts, namely, geometry, would itself not be possible.

2 Anticipations of Perception    Their principle is: *In all appearances the real that is an object of sensation has intensive magnitude*, i.e., a degree.

**Proof**: Perception is empirical consciousness, i.e., a consciousness in which there is sensation as well. Appearances, as objects of perception, are not pure (i.e., merely formal) intuitions, as space and time are (for these cannot in themselves be perceived at all). Hence appearances contain, in addition to [pure] intuition, the matter (through which something existent is represented in space or time) for some object as such. I.e., appearances contain also the real of sensation—sensation being merely subjective representation, concerning which we can become conscious only of the fact that the subject is affected, and which we refer to an object as such. Now from empirical consciousness to pure consciousness, i.e., to the point where the real of that consciousness entirely vanishes and a merely formal (*a priori*) consciousness of the manifold in space and time remains, a stepwise change is possible. Hence there is likewise possible a synthesis in the production of a sensation's magnitude, from the sensation's beginning, i.e., from pure intuition, = 0, up to this or that magnitude of the sensation. Now since sensation is in itself not at all an objective representation, and since neither the intuition of space nor that of time is to be met with in it, sensation will indeed not have an extensive magnitude. Yet it will have a magnitude (namely, by virtue of the apprehension in sensation, in which the empirical consciousness can in a certain time increase from nothing, = 0, to the sensation's given measure). Therefore sensation will have an *intensive magnitude*. As corresponding to this intensive magnitude of sensation we must also ascribe to all objects of perception, insofar as perception contains sensation, an *intensive magnitude*, i.e., a degree of influence on sense.

B208

All cognition whereby I can cognize and determine *a priori* what belongs to empirical cognition may be called an anticipation; and this is doubtless the signification in which Epicurus used the term προληψια. But there is something in appearances that

A167

is never cognized *a priori* and that hence amounts to the proper difference between empirical and *a priori* cognition: namely, sensation (as the matter of perception); and hence it follows that what cannot at all be anticipated is, properly speaking, sensation. The pure determinations in space and time regarding both shape and magnitude, by contrast, could be called anticipations of appearances; for they represent *a priori* what may always be given *a posteriori* in experience. Suppose, however, that we do find something that is cognizable *a priori* in every sensation, as sensation in general (i.e., even though no particular sensation may be given); this something would, then, deserve to be called anticipation—in an unusual meaning of the term. For it seems strange to say that we can anticipate experience in what concerns, of all things, its matter, which can be drawn only from experience. Yet it is actually the case here.

Apprehension merely by means of sensation (i.e., if I do not consider the succession of many sensations) fills only an instant. Hence, as something contained in appearance whose apprehension is not a successive synthesis proceeding from parts to the whole representation, it has no extensive magnitude; a lack of sensation at that same instant would represent that instant as empty, and hence as = 0. Now what in empirical intuition corresponds to sensation is reality (*realitas phaenomenon*); what corresponds to the lack of sensation is negation, = 0. However, every sensation is capable of diminution, so that it can decrease and thus gradually vanish. Hence between reality contained in appearance, on the one hand, and negation, on the other hand, there is a continuous coherence of many possible intermediate sensations, whose difference from one another is always smaller than the difference between the given sensation and zero, i.e., complete negation. In other words, the real contained in appearance always has a magnitude. Yet one that is not to be met with in apprehension; for apprehension by means of mere sensation occurs in an instant rather than through the successive synthesis of many sensations, and hence does not proceed from the parts to the whole. Hence the real does indeed have a magnitude, but not an extensive one.

Now a magnitude that is apprehended only as unity, and in which multiplicity can be represented only by approaching [from the given magnitude] toward negation, = 0, I call an *intensive magnitude*. Hence any reality contained in an appearance has intensive magnitude, i.e., a degree. And if this reality is considered as cause (whether of the sensation, or of other reality contained in appearance, e.g., a change), then the degree of the reality considered as cause is called a moment—e.g., the moment of gravity. It is called this because the degree designates only that magnitude whose apprehension is not successive but instantaneous. But here I touch on this only in passing, because for now I am not yet dealing with causality.

Therefore every sensation, and hence also every reality contained in an appearance, no matter how small either may be, has a degree, i.e., an intensive magnitude. This magnitude can always be lessened, and between reality and negation there is a continuous coherence of possible realities and of possible smaller perceptions. Every color, e.g., red, has a degree that, no matter how small it may be, is never the smallest; and this is the situation throughout—with heat, with the moment of gravity, etc.

The property of magnitudes whereby no part in them is the smallest possible (i.e., no part is simple) is called their continuity. Space and time are *quanta continua*, because no part of them can be given without our enclosing it between limits (points or instants); and hence any part of them can be given only in such a way that this part itself is in turn a space or a time. Therefore space consists only of spaces, time only of times. Points and instants are only limits, i.e., mere positions limiting them. But positions always presuppose the intuitions that they are to delimit or determine; and neither space nor time can be assembled from mere positions if these are considered as components that could be given even prior to space or time. Such magnitudes may also be called *flowing* magnitudes, because the synthesis (of productive imagination) in their production is a progression in time, and the continuity especially of time is usually designated by the term flowing (flowing by).

Hence all appearances as such are continuous magnitudes—both in terms of their intuition, namely, as extensive magnitudes, and in terms of their mere perception (sensation, and hence reality), namely, as intensive magnitudes. If the synthesis of the manifold of appearance is interrupted, then this manifold is an aggregate of many appearances and is not, properly speaking, appearance as a quantum. Such an aggregate is not produced by merely continuing the productive synthesis of a certain kind, but is produced by repeating a synthesis that always ceases again. If I call 13 thalers a quantum of money, then I do so correctly insofar as I mean by this the [total] content of one mark of fine silver. For this mark is indeed a continuous magnitude, in which no part is the smallest but each part could constitute a coin that always contained material for still smaller coins. But if by that designation I mean 13 round thalers, as A171  so many coins (whatever their silver content might be), then my calling this a quantum of thalers is inappropriate. I must call it, rather, an aggregate, i.e., a number of coins. But since with any number there must still be underlying unity, appearance as unity is a quantum, and as such is always a continuum.

We saw that all appearances, considered extenB213  sively as well as intensively, are continuous magnitudes. If this is so, then the proposition that all change (a thing's transition from one state to another) is likewise continuous could be proved here easily and with mathematical self-evidence, were it not that the causality of a change as such lies wholly outside the bounds of a transcendental philosophy and presupposes empirical principles. For the understanding does not at all disclose to us *a priori* the possibility of a cause that changes the state of any things, i.e., determines them to enter the opposite of a certain given state. The understanding fails to do so not merely because it has no insight whatsoever into that possibility (indeed, we lack such insight in several *a priori* cognitions), but because changeability concerns only certain determinations of appearances, namely, those that experience alone can teach us, while only their cause is to be found in the unchangeable. Here, however, we have nothing available for our use except the pure basic concepts

of all possible experience, among which there must be nothing empirical whatsoever. Hence we cannot, A172  without violating the unity of the system, anticipate general natural science, which is built upon certain basic experiences.

Yet we have no lack of documentation for our principle's great influence in anticipating perceptions, and even in compensating for their lack insofar as the principle blocks all wrong inferences that might be drawn from that lack.

For we saw that all reality in perception has a de- B214  gree between which and negation there is an infinite stepwise sequence of ever lesser degrees, and that every sense must likewise have a definite degree in the receptivity of sensations. But if this is so, then no perception and hence also no experience is possible that would prove, whether directly or indirectly (by whatever circuitous path in the inference), a complete lack in appearance of anything real. I.e., one can never obtain from experience a proof of empty space or of an empty time. For, first, the complete lack of the real in sensible intuition cannot itself be perceived. Second, this lack cannot be inferred from even a single appearance and from the difference in its reality, nor must it ever be assumed in order to explain that intuition. For suppose even that the whole intuition of a determinate space or time is real through and through, i.e., that no part of it is empty. Still, every reality has its degree, which can decrease to nothing (i.e., emptiness) by infinitely many steps, with the extensive magnitude of the appearance be- A173  ing unchanged. And hence there must be infinitely many different degrees with which space and time may be filled; and it must be possible for the intensive magnitude in different appearances to be smaller or greater even with the extensive magnitude of the intuition being the same.

Let us give an example of this. Natural scientists B215  perceive (partly by the moment of gravity or weight, partly by the moment of resistance to other matter in motion) that the quantity of matter of various kinds differs greatly even with the volume being the same. Almost all natural scientists, when perceiving this, infer from it unanimously that in all kinds of matter this volume (i.e., extensive magnitude of the appearance) must—even if in varying measure—be empty. But to whom would it ever have occurred that these investigators of nature, who are for the most part mathematical and mechanical [in orientation], would base this inference of theirs solely on a metaphysical presupposition—which presuppositions, after all, they claim to avoid so very much? For they assume that the *real* in space (I do not want to call it impenetrability or weight here, because these are empirical concepts) is *everywhere uniform* and can differ only in extensive magnitude, i.e., in amount. This supposition, for which they could not have had a basis in experience and which is therefore merely metaphysical, I oppose with a transcendental proof.

A174  This proof, to be sure, is not meant to explain the difference in the filling of spaces. Yet it does completely annul the supposed necessity of that presupposition whereby the difference in question can be explained only by assuming empty spaces. And thus the proof has at least the merit of giving to the understanding the freedom to think this difference in another way

B216  also—should explaining nature necessitate some other hypothesis to account for this difference. For we then see that although equal spaces may be filled completely by various kinds of matter, so that in none of them is there a point where no matter can be found to be present, yet everything real has, with its quality being the same, its degree (of resistance or weight); and this degree can—without any lessening of the extensive magnitude, or amount—be smaller *ad infinitum* before the real passes into emptiness and vanishes. Thus something that spreads and fills a space, as, e.g., heat, and likewise any other reality (contained in appearance), can decrease in its degree *ad infinitum* without leaving even the smallest part of this space in the least empty, and can nonetheless fill this space just as well with these smaller degrees as another appearance can with greater degrees. I do not by any means intend to assert here that this is actually how kinds of matter differ in their specific gravity. Rather, I intend only to establish, from a principle of the pure

A175  understanding, that the nature of our perceptions makes such a way of explaining possible, and that people are wrong when they assume that the real of

appearance is the same in degree and differs only in aggregation and the extensive magnitude thereof—and when they assert this, allegedly, even *a priori* by means of a principle of the understanding.

Nonetheless, something about this anticipation of  B217 perception is always striking to an investigator of nature who is accustomed to transcendental deliberation and has thus become cautious. For the anticipation arouses some concern about the claim that the understanding can anticipate a synthetic proposition such as this—i.e., a synthetic proposition about the degree of everything real in appearances, and hence about the possibility of there being in sensation itself, if we abstract from its empirical quality, an intrinsic difference. And hence there remains a question not unworthy of solution: namely, how the understanding can make in this matter a synthetic *a priori* pronouncement about appearances, and how it can thus anticipate appearances in what is strictly and merely empirical, i.e., in what concerns sensation.

The *quality* of sensation (e.g., colors, taste, etc.) is always merely empirical and cannot at all be represented *a priori*. But the real—as opposed to negation, = 0—that corresponds to sensation as such represents only something whose concept itself contains a being [of something], and signifies nothing but the synthe-  A176 sis in an empirical consciousness as such. For empirical consciousness can be raised in inner sense from 0 to any higher degree, so that the same extensive magnitude of intuition (e.g., an illuminated surface) arouses as great a sensation as does an aggregate of much else (that is less illuminated) taken together. We can, therefore, abstract entirely from the exten-  B218 sive magnitude of appearance, and can yet represent in mere sensation in one moment a synthesis of uniform ascent from 0 to the given empirical consciousness. Hence although all sensations, as such, are given only *a posteriori*, their property of having a degree can be cognized *a priori*. It is remarkable that in magnitudes as such we can cognize *a priori* only a single *quality*, namely, continuity, and that in all quality (the real of appearances) we can cognize *a priori* nothing more than their having an intensive *quantity*, namely, the fact that they have a degree; everything else is left to experience.

3 Analogies of Experience    Their principle is: *Experience is possible only through the representation of a necessary connection of perceptions*.

**Proof**: Experience is an empirical cognition, i.e., a cognition that determines an object through perceptions. Hence experience is a synthesis of perceptions that itself is not contained in perception but contains the synthetic unity of the manifold of perceptions B219 in one consciousness. This unity amounts to what is essential for a cognition of *objects* of the senses, i.e., for experience (rather than merely intuition or sensation of the senses). Now, in experience perceptions do indeed come together only contingently, so that no necessity in their connection is, or even can be, evident from the perceptions themselves. For apprehension is only a compilation of the manifold of empirical intuition; and we find in it no representation of the necessity of the linked existence in space and time of the appearances that it compiles. Experience, by contrast, is a cognition of objects through perceptions; and hence in experience the relation within the manifold's existence is to be represented not as the manifold is compiled in time, but as it is objectively in time. Time, however, cannot itself be perceived. Therefore the determination of the existence of objects in time can come about only through the linking of perceptions in time as such, and hence only through concepts connecting them *a priori*. And since these concepts always carry with them necessity as well, experience is possible only through a representation of the necessary connection of perceptions.

A177    The three modes of time are *permanence*, *succession*, and *simultaneity*. Hence there will be three rules governing all time relations of appearances, whereby every appearance's existence can be determined in regard to the unity of all time; and these rules will precede experience and make it possible in the first place.

B220    The general principle of all three analogies rests on the necessary *unity* of apperception in regard to all possible empirical consciousness (i.e., perception) *at every time*; and since this unity is presupposed *a priori*, the principle rests on the synthetic unity of all appearances as regards their relation in time. For original apperception refers to inner sense (the sum of all representations); specifically, it refers *a priori* to the form of inner sense, i.e., to the relation in time of the manifold empirical consciousness. Now all this manifold is to be united, as regards its time relations, in original apperception—for so says this apperception's *a priori* transcendental unity, to which is subject whatever is to belong to my (i.e., to my one) cognition and hence is to be able to become an object for me. Hence this *synthetic unity* in the time relation of all perceptions, a unity *which is determined a priori*, is this law: that all empirical time determinations must be subject to rules of A178 universal time determination. And the analogies of experience that we now want to deal with must be rules of this sort.

These principles have the peculiarity that they do not consider appearances and the synthesis of their empirical intuition, but consider merely [the appearances'] *existence* and their *relation* to one another in regard to that existence. Now the way in which something is apprehended in appearance can be determined *a priori* in such a manner that the rule of B221 the appearance's synthesis can also give this *a priori* intuition, i.e., can produce the appearance from this intuition, in the case of every empirical example that comes to hand. The *existence* of appearances, however, cannot be cognized *a priori*; and even if we could in that just mentioned way contrive to infer some existent or other, we could still not cognize it determinately, i.e., we could not anticipate what distinguishes this existent's empirical intuition from [that of] others.

The previous two principles, which I called mathematical principles because they justified applying mathematics to appearances, dealt with appearances in regard to their mere possibility; and they taught us how appearances could be produced, as regards both their intuition and the real in their perception, according to rules of a mathematical synthesis. Hence in both syntheses we can use numerical magnitudes and, with them, the determination of appearance as a magnitude. Thus, e.g., I can assemble the degree of A179 sensations of sunlight from some two hundred thousand illuminations provided by the moon, and can determinately supply that degree *a priori*, i.e., construct it. Those earlier two principles may therefore be called constitutive.

B222 The situation must be quite different with those principles that are to bring *a priori* under rules the existence of appearances. For since existence cannot be constructed, the principles will deal only with the relation of existence, and will be able to yield none but merely *regulative* principles. Hence finding either axioms or anticipations is out of the question here. Thus if a perception is given to us in a time relation to other (albeit indeterminate) perceptions, then we shall indeed not be able to say *what* is that other perception or *how great* a perception it is; rather, we shall be able to say how, as regards its existence, this other perception is necessarily linked with the former perception in this mode of time. Analogies signify something very different in philosophy from what they represent in mathematics. In mathematics they are formulas asserting the equality of two relations of magnitudes, and are always *constitutive*; so that if three members of the proportion are given, the fourth is thereby also given, i.e., it can be constructed. In philosophy, however, an analogy is the

A180 equality not of two *quantitative* but of two *qualitative* relations. Here I can from three given members cognize, and give *a priori*, only the *relation* to a fourth, but not *this* fourth *member* itself. But I do have a rule for seeking the fourth member in experience, and a mark for discovering it there. Hence an analogy of experience will be only a rule whereby unity of experience is to arise from perceptions (not a rule saying how perception itself, as empirical intuition as such, is to arise). And such an analogy will hold, as prin-

B223 ciple of objects (i.e., appearances), not *constitutively* but merely *regulatively*. But the same [restriction] will apply also to the postulates of empirical thought as such, which concern at once the synthesis of mere intuition (the form of appearance), the synthesis of perception (the matter of appearance), and that of experience (the relation of these perceptions). I.e., these postulates are only regulative principles. These principles do not indeed differ in certainty from the mathematical principles, which are constitutive; for this certainty is established *a priori* in both. But they

do differ from the mathematical principles in their kind of evidence, i.e., their intuitive character (and hence their ability to be demonstrated).

But what has been pointed out for all synthetic principles, and must be noted especially here, is this: these analogies have their sole signification and validity not as principles of the understanding's transcendental use, but merely as principles of its empirical use, and hence can be proved only as A181 principles of such use; and appearances must consequently be subsumed not under the categories taken absolutely, but only under their schemata. For if the objects to which these principles are to be referred were things in themselves, then cognizing anything about them synthetically *a priori* would be entirely impossible. But they are indeed nothing but appearances. And the complete cognition of appearances—which is, after all, what all *a priori* principles must ultimately always amount to—is merely our possible experience. Hence these principles can aim at nothing more than being the conditions for B224 the unity of empirical cognition in the synthesis of appearances. This unity, however, is thought solely in the schema of the pure concept of the understanding. The function, unrestricted by any sensible condition, of the unity of the schema, as a synthesis as such, is contained in the category. Hence these principles will entitle us to assemble appearances only by an analogy with the logical and universal unity of concepts. And hence in the principle itself we shall indeed make use of the category; but in employing the principle (i.e., in applying it to appearances) we shall put the category's schema, as the key to its use, in the category's place—or, rather, put the schema alongside the category as its restricting condition and call it a formula of the category.

First Analogy. Principle of the Permanence of A182 Substance *In all change of appearances substance is permanent, and its quantum in nature is neither increased nor decreased.*

**Proof:** All appearances are in time; and solely in time, as substrate (namely, as the permanent form of B225 inner intuition), can either *simultaneity* or *succession* be represented. Hence time, in which all change of appearances is to be thought, endures and does not change. For time is that in which, and as determinations of which, succession or simultaneity can alone be represented. Now, time by itself cannot be perceived. Hence the substrate which represents time as such, and in which all change or simultaneity can be perceived in apprehension through the appearances' relation to it, must be found in the objects of perception, i.e., in the appearances. But the substrate of everything real, i.e., of everything belonging to the existence of things, is *substance*. In substance alone can everything belonging to existence be thought as a determination. Hence the permanent in relation to which all time relations of appearances can alone be determined is substance in the appearance, i.e., the real of appearance that as substrate of all change remains always the same. Since, therefore, substance cannot vary in its existence, its quantum in nature can also be neither increased nor decreased.

Our *apprehension* of the manifold of appearance is always successive, and therefore is always varying. Hence through apprehension alone we can never determine whether this manifold considered as object of experience is simultaneous or successive. We cannot determine this unless something underlying in experience is *always* there—i.e., something *enduring* and *permanent* of which all variation and simultaneity are only so many ways (modes of time) in which the permanent exists. Hence all time relations (for simultaneity and succession are the only relations in time) are possible only in the permanent. I.e., the permanent is the *substratum* of the empirical representation of time itself; all time determinations are possible only in this substratum. Permanence expresses time in general (as the constant correlate of all existence of appearances, of all change and of all concomitance). For change does not concern time itself, but only appearances in time (just as simultaneity is not a mode of time itself; for in time no parts are simultaneous, but all are successive). If we wished to attribute to time itself a succession, then we would have to think yet another time wherein this succession would be possible. Solely through the permanent does successive *existence* in different parts of the time series acquire a *magnitude*, called *duration*. For in mere succession by itself existence is

always vanishing and starting, and never has the least magnitude. Without this permanent, therefore, there is no time relation. Now time cannot in itself be perceived. Therefore this permanent in appearances is the substratum of all time determinations. Hence it is also the condition for the possibility of all synthetic unity of perceptions, i.e., the possibility of experience; and all existence and all change in time can only be regarded, by reference to this permanent, as a mode of the existence of what is enduring and permanent. Therefore in all appearances the permanent is the object itself, i.e., the (phenomenal) substance, whereas whatever changes or can change belongs only to the way in which this substance or these substances exist, and hence to their determinations.

I find that in all ages not just philosophers but even the common understanding have presupposed this permanence as a substratum of all change of appearances; and they probably always assume it, moreover, as indubitable. The only difference is that the philosopher expresses himself somewhat more determinately on this point than does the common understanding, by saying that in all changes in the world *substance* endures and only the *accidents* change. Yet nowhere do I encounter so much as an attempt to prove this quite synthetic proposition. Indeed, only seldom is the proposition placed, as surely it deserves to be, at the top of the laws of nature that are pure and hold completely *a priori*. The mere proposition that substance is permanent is indeed tautological. For merely because of this permanence do we apply the category of substance to appearance, and people ought to have proved that in all appearances there is in fact something permanent wherein the mutable is nothing but a determination of its existence. Such a proof, however, can never be conducted dogmatically, i.e., from concepts, because it concerns a synthetic *a priori* proposition; and people never thought of the fact that such propositions are valid only in reference to possible experience and hence can be proved only by a deduction of the possibility of experience. It is no wonder, then, that although this proposition has been presupposed in all experience (because in empirical cognition one *feels* the need for it), yet it has never been proved.

B227

A184

B228

A185

B226

A183

A philosopher was asked, How much does smoke weigh? He replied: From the weight of the burnt wood subtract the weight of the ashes that remain, and you will have the weight of the smoke. He therefore presupposed as incontestable that *matter* (substance) does not pass away even in fire, but that its *form* only undergoes an alteration. Similarly the proposition that nothing arises from nothing was only another consequence inferred from the principle of permanence, or rather from the principle of the everlasting existence of the subject proper [contained] in appearance. For if the [component] in appearance that we wish to call substance is to be the substratum proper of all time determination, then all existence in past as well as future time must be determinable solely and exclusively by reference to it. Hence we can give the name substance to an appearance only because we presuppose the existence of substance at all time. This existence at all time is not even well expressed by the word permanence, since permanence applies more to future time. However, the intrinsic necessity to be permanent is linked inseparably with the necessity always to have been, and therefore the expression may be allowed to remain. *Gigni de nihilo nihil, in nihilum nil posse reverti* [that nothing can arise from nothing, nothing revert to nothing] are two propositions that were connected by the ancients as unseparated and that are now sometimes separated. They are separated, through misunderstanding, because of a conception that they concern things in themselves and that the first proposition might therefore run counter to the world's depending (even in terms of its substance) on a supreme cause. But there is no need for such worry. For we are here talking only about appearances in the realm of experience; and the unity of experience would never be possible if we were to let new things originate (in terms of substance). For there would then no longer be what alone can represent the unity of time, namely, the identity of the substratum, by reference to which alone all change has thoroughgoing unity. However, this permanence is nothing more than our way of representing the existence of things (in appearance).

The determinations of a substance, which are nothing but particular ways for the substance to exist, are called *accidents*. They are always real, because they concern the existence of substance. (Negations are only determinations expressing the nonexistence of something in substance.) Now if we attribute a special existence to this real in substance (e.g., motion, as an accident of matter), then this existence is called inherence, as distinguished from the existence of substance, which is called subsistence. From this, however, arise many misinterpretations; and we speak more accurately and correctly if we characterize an accident only as the way in which the existence of a substance is determined positively. Yet by virtue of the conditions of our understanding's logical use we cannot avoid separating, as it were, what can change in a substance's existence while the substance itself endures, and examining it in relation to what is properly permanent and radical. And hence this category has indeed been put under the heading of the relations, but more as the condition of relations than as itself containing a relation.

Now this permanence is also the basis for the following correction of the concept of *alteration*. Arising and passing away are not alterations of what arises or passes away. Alteration is a way of existing that ensues upon another way of existing of the same object. Hence whatever alters *endures*, and only its *state* changes. This change, therefore, concerns only the determinations, which can cease or, for that matter, start. Hence we can say, using an expression that seems somewhat paradoxical: only the permanent (i.e., substance) is altered; the mutable undergoes no alteration but only a *change*, since some determinations cease and others start.

Hence alteration can be perceived only in substances; and an arising or passing away taken absolutely, i.e., without its pertaining merely to a determination of the permanent, cannot at all be a possible perception. For precisely this permanent makes possible the representation of the transition from one state to another, and from not-being to being; and hence these can be cognized empirically only as varying determinations of what endures. Suppose that something absolutely begins to be. If you suppose this, then you must have a point of time in which it was not. But to what will you fasten this point of time, if not to what is already there? For a preceding empty time is not an object of perception; but if you tie this arising to things that existed beforehand and that continue up to the something that arises, then this something was only a determination of what existed beforehand as the permanent. The case is the same with passing away also; for it presupposes the empirical representation of a time where an appearance no longer exists.

Substances (in appearance) are the substrates of all time determinations. If some substances arose and others passed away, this would itself annul the sole condition of the empirical unity of time; and appearances would then refer to two different times in which existence would pass concurrently—which is absurd. For there is *only one* time, in which all different times must be posited not as simultaneous but as successive.

Permanence, accordingly, is a necessary condition under which alone appearances are determinable as things or objects in a possible experience. But we shall have the opportunity in what follows to make whatever comments are necessary as to what is the empirical criterion of this necessary permanence and, with it, of the substantiality of appearances.

Second Analogy,   Principle of Temporal Succession According to the Law of Causality: *All alteration occurs according to the law of the connection of cause and effect.*

**Proof**: (The previous principle has established that all appearances of temporal succession are one and all only *alterations*; i.e., they are a successive being and not-being of the determinations of substance, which itself is permanent. The principle has established, therefore, that there is no such thing as the being of substance itself as succeeding its not-being, or its not-being as succeeding its existence; in other words, there is no such thing as the arising or passing away of substance itself. The principle could also have been expressed thus: *All change [succession] of appearances is only alteration*; for an arising or passing away of substance would not be alterations of it, because the concept of alteration presupposes the same subject as existing, and hence as being permanent, with

two opposite determinations. After this preliminary reminder, there now follows the proof.)

I perceive that appearances succeed one another, i.e., that at one time there is a state of things whose opposite was there in the things' previous state. Hence I am in fact connecting two perceptions in time. Now connection is not the work of mere sense and intuition, but is here the product of a synthetic ability of our imagination which determines inner sense in regard to time relation. But imagination can link those two states in two ways, so that either the one or the other state precedes in time. For time cannot be perceived in itself, and what precedes or follows cannot be determined by reference to it in the object—empirically, as it were. I am, therefore, conscious only that my imagination places one state before and the other after, but not that the one state precedes the other in the object. In other words, mere perception leaves indeterminate the *objective relation* of the appearances following one another. Now in order for this objective relation to be cognized as determinate, the relation between the two states must be thought as being such that it determines as necessary which of the states must be placed before and which after, rather than vice versa. But a concept carrying with it a necessity of synthetic unity can only be a pure concept of the understanding, which therefore does not reside in perception. Here this concept is that of the *relation of cause and effect*; of these two, the cause is what determines the effect in time, and determines it as the consequence, rather than as something that [as occurring] merely in imagination might [instead] precede (or might not even be perceived at all). Therefore experience itself—i.e., empirical cognition of appearances—is possible only inasmuch as we subject the succession of appearances, and hence all alteration, to the law of causality. Hence appearances themselves, taken as objects of experience, are possible only in accordance with this law.

Apprehension of the manifold of appearances is always successive. The representations of the parts succeed one another. Whether they also follow one another in the object is a second point for reflection which is not already contained in the first point. Now it is true that anything, even every representation insofar as one is conscious of it, can be called an object. Yet what this word might signify in the case of appearances, not insofar as they (as representations) are objects but insofar as they only designate an object, calls for deeper investigation. Insofar as appearances, taken only as representations, are simultaneously objects of consciousness, they are not at all distinct from apprehension, i.e., from the taking up into the synthesis of imagination; and we must say, therefore, that the manifold of appearances is always produced in the mind successively. If appearances were things in themselves, then no human being could gather from the succession of representations how their manifold is combined in the object. For we deal, after all, only with our own representations; how things may be in themselves (i.e., apart from taking account of representations by which they affect us), is entirely outside our sphere of cognition. Appearances, then, are indeed not things in themselves; but they are all that can be given to us for cognition. And now, whereas the representation of the manifold in apprehension is always successive, I am to indicate what sort of combination in time belongs to the manifold in appearances themselves. Thus, e.g., the apprehension of the manifold in the appearance of a house standing before me is successive. Now the question is whether the manifold of this house itself is successive intrinsically as well; and this, to be sure, no one will grant. But once I raise my concepts of an object to the level of transcendental signification, the house is not at all a thing in itself, but is only an appearance, i.e., a representation, whose transcendental object is unknown. What, then, do I mean by the question as to how the manifold may be combined in the appearance itself (which, after all, is nothing in itself)? Here what lies in the successive apprehension is regarded as representation; but the appearance that is given to me, despite being nothing more than a sum of these representations, is regarded as their object, with which the concept that I obtain from the representations of apprehension is to agree. We soon see that, since agreement of cognition with the object is truth, the question can only be asking about the formal conditions of empirical truth; and we see that appearance, as contrasted with the representations of apprehension, can be presented as an object distinct from them only if it is subject to a rule that distinguishes it from any other apprehension and that makes necessary one kind of combination of the manifold. That [element] in the appearance which contains the condition of this necessary rule of apprehension is the object.

Let us now proceed to our problem. That something occurs, i.e., that something, or a state that was not there before, comes to be cannot be perceived empirically unless it is preceded by an appearance that does not contain this state. For an actuality succeeding an empty time, i.e., an arising not preceded by any state of things, cannot be apprehended any more than empty time itself. Hence any apprehension of an event is a perception succeeding another perception. But because, as I showed above by reference to the appearance of a house, this is so in all synthesis of apprehension, the apprehension of an event is not yet distinguished thereby from other apprehensions. Yet I also observe that if, in an appearance containing an occurrence, I call A the preceding state of the perception and B the succeeding state, then B can only in apprehension succeed A, and similarly perception A cannot succeed B but can only precede it. For example, I see a ship floating down the river. My perception of its position lower down in the course of the river succeeds the perception of its position higher up, and there is no possibility that in the apprehension of this appearance the ship should be perceived first lower down and afterwards higher up in the river. Hence the order in the perceptions' succession in apprehension is here determinate, and apprehension is tied to this order. In the previous example of a house my perceptions could, in apprehension, start from the house's top and end at the bottom, but they could also start from below and end above; and they could likewise apprehend the manifold of the empirical intuition by proceeding either to the right or to the left. Hence in the series of these perceptions there was no determinate order making necessary the point in apprehension where I must begin in order to combine the manifold empirically. In the perception of what occurs, however, this rule is always to be found, and through it the order of the perceptions succeeding one another (in the apprehension of this appearance) is made *necessary*.

In our case, therefore, I shall have to derive the *subjective succession* of apprehension from the *objective succession* of appearances; for otherwise the subjective succession is entirely indeterminate and fails to distinguish any one appearance from some other appearance. The subjective succession by itself, being entirely arbitrary, proves nothing about the connection of the manifold in the object. Hence the objective succession will consist in the order of the manifold of appearance whereby the apprehension of the one item (namely, what occurs) succeeds the apprehension of the other (namely, what precedes) *according to a rule*. This alone can entitle me to say of the appearance itself, and not merely of my apprehension, that a succession is to be found in it— which means the same as that I cannot perform the apprehension except in precisely this succession.

In accordance with such a rule, therefore, what B239 precedes an event as such must contain the condition for a rule whereby this event always and neces- A194 sarily follows. But I cannot go, conversely, from the event backward and determine (through apprehension) what precedes. For no appearance goes back from the succeeding point of time to the previous one, although it does refer *to some previous one*. The progression from a given time to the determinate following time, however, is necessary. Hence because it is, after all, something that follows, I must necessarily refer it to something else as such that precedes it and that it succeeds according to a rule, i.e., necessarily. Thus the event, as the conditioned, directs us reliably to some condition, while this condition determines the event.

Suppose that an event is not preceded by anything that it must succeed according to a rule. Then all succession of perception would be determined solely in apprehension, i.e., merely subjectively; but this would not at all determine objectively which item in fact precedes in perception and which follows. We would in that way have only a play of representations that would not refer to any object whatsoever; i.e., our perception would not at all distinguish one appearance from all others in terms of time relation.

For the succession in apprehending is in that case everywhere the same, and hence there is in appearance nothing determining this succession so that a B240 certain succession is, as objective, made necessary by it. Hence I shall in that case not say that two A195 states succeed each other in appearance. Rather, I shall say only that one apprehension succeeds the other; and this is merely something *subjective* and determines no object, and hence cannot count as cognition of any object (not even of an object in [the realm of] appearance).

Hence when we experience that something occurs, then in doing so we always presuppose that it is preceded by something or other that it succeeds according to a rule. Otherwise I would not say of the object that it succeeds; for the mere succession in my apprehension, if it is not determined by a rule referring to something preceding it, justifies no succession in the object. Hence it is always on account of a rule that I make my subjective synthesis (of apprehension) objective, namely, a rule according to which appearances in their succession, i.e., as they occur, are determined by the previous state. And the experience itself of something that occurs is possible solely and exclusively under this presupposition.

It is true that this seems to contradict all the remarks that people have always made about the course taken by our understanding. According to those remarks, it is only by perceiving and comparing the agreeing successions of events that follow upon preceding appearances that we are first led to dis- B241 cover a rule whereby certain events always succeed certain appearances, and only by means of this are A196 we first prompted to frame the concept of cause. This concept would, on such a basis, be merely empirical. And the rule according to which everything that occurs has a cause, as this concept provides it, would be just as contingent as the experience itself. The rule's universality and necessity would then be attributed to it only fictitiously and would have no true universal validity, because they would be based not on anything *a priori*, but only on induction. But the case with this rule is the same as that with other pure *a priori* representations (e.g., space and time): we can extract them as clear concepts from experience solely because we have put them into experience and hence have brought experience about through them in the first place. To be sure, this representation of a rule determining the series of events, as a concept of cause, can have logical clarity only after we have made use of it in experience. Yet [our] taking account of this representation, [namely,] as a condition of the synthetic unity in time of appearances, was nonetheless the basis of the experience itself, and hence the experience was preceded *a priori* by this condition.

Hence we must show, in this example, that even in experience we never attribute succession (in the case of an event—where something occurs that was B242 not there before) to the object and we never distinguish this succession from the subjective one in our apprehension, except when a rule is presupposed A197 that compels us to observe this order of perceptions rather than some other order; indeed, we must show that this compulsion is what in fact makes the representation of a succession in the object possible in the first place.

We have within us representations of which we can also become conscious. But no matter how far this consciousness may extend and how accurate and precise it may be, they still remain forever only representations, i.e., inner determinations of our mind in this or that time relation. How is it, then, that we posit an object for these representations; or how is it that in addition to the subjective reality that they have as modifications [of the mind], we also attribute to them who knows what sort of objective reality? Their objective signification cannot consist in their relation to another representation (of what one would want to call object). For otherwise the question arises again: how does this other representation, in turn, go beyond itself and acquire objective signification in addition to the subjective one that it possesses by being a determination of the mental state? Suppose that we inquire what new character is given to our representations by the *reference to an object*, and what is the dignity that they thereby obtain. We then find that this reference does nothing beyond making necessary the representations' being combined in a certain way and being subjected to a rule; and we find, con- B243 versely, that only through the necessity of a certain

order in the time relation of our representations is objective signification conferred on them.

In the synthesis of appearances the manifold of A198 representations is always successive. Now, through this succession no object whatsoever is represented; for through this succession, which is common to all apprehensions, nothing is distinguished from anything else. But once I perceive, or assume in advance, that there is in this succession a reference to the preceding state, upon which the representation follows according to a rule, then something represents itself as an event, or as something that occurs. I.e., I then cognize an object that I must posit in a certain determinate position in time—a position that in view of the preceding state cannot be assigned to it differently. Hence when I perceive that something occurs, then this representation contains, first, [the presupposition] that something precedes; for precisely by reference to this preceding something does the appearance acquire its time relation, namely, its existing after a preceding time in which it was not. But, second, it can obtain its determinate time position in this relation only inasmuch as in the preceding state something is presupposed that it succeeds always, i.e., succeeds according to a rule. And from this results, first, that I cannot reverse the series, taking what occurs and putting it ahead of what it succeeds; and, second, that if the state that precedes it is posited, then this specific event succeeds unfailingly B244 and necessarily. Thus it is that among our representations there comes to be an order in which what is A199 present directs us (insofar as it has come to be) to some preceding state as a correlate of the event that is given. And although this correlate is still indeterminate, it does refer determinatively to this happening as its consequence and in the time series connects it with itself necessarily.

Suppose, then, that it is a necessary law of our sensibility, and hence a *formal condition* of all perceptions, that the previous time necessarily determines the following one (inasmuch as I cannot arrive at the following time except through the preceding one). If this is so, then it is also an indispensable *law of empirical representation* of the time series that the appearances of past time determine every existent in the following time; and that these existents, as events, do not take place except insofar as their existence is determined in time—i.e., fixed in time according to a rule—by those appearances of past time. For *only in appearances can we cognize empirically this continuity in the connection of times.*

The understanding is required for all experience and for its possibility. And the first thing that the understanding does to this end is not that of making the representation of objects distinct, but that of making the representation of an object possible at all. Now, B245 this is done through the understanding's transferring the time order to the appearances and to their existence, by allotting to each appearance, as consequence, a position in time determined *a priori* with A200 regard to the preceding appearances; without this position in time the appearance would not agree with time itself, which determines their position *a priori* in every case. Now this determination of an appearance's position cannot be taken from the relation of appearances toward absolute time (for absolute time is not an object of perception). Rather, conversely, the appearances must themselves determine for one another their positions in time, and must make these positions necessary in the time order; i.e., what follows or occurs must succeed what was contained in the previous state and must do so according to a universal rule. This results in a series of appearances that, by means of the understanding, produces and makes necessary in the series of possible perceptions the same order and steady coherence that is found *a priori* in the form of inner intuition (i.e., in time), in which all perceptions would have to have their position.

Hence that something occurs is a perception belonging to a possible experience. This experience becomes actual when I view the appearance as determined as regards its position in time, and hence view it as an object that in the coherence of percep-
B246 tions can always be found according to a rule. However, this rule for determining something in regard to temporal succession is that the condition under which an event always (i.e., necessarily) follows is to be found in what precedes the event. Hence the principle of sufficient reason is the basis of possible

experience, i.e., of objective cognition of appear- A201 ances with regard to their relation in time sequence.

The basis for proving this proposition, however, rests solely on the following moments. All empirical cognition involves the synthesis of the manifold by the imagination. This synthesis is always successive, i.e., in it the representations always succeed one another. In the imagination itself, however, the sequence is not at all determined as regards order (i.e., as to what must precede and what must follow), and the series of the representations following one another can be taken as proceeding backward just as well as forward. But if this synthesis is a synthesis of apprehension (of the manifold of a given appearance), then the order is determined in the object, or—to speak more accurately—there is in this apprehension an order of successive synthesis that determines an object; and according to this order something must necessarily precede, and when this something is posited then the other event must necessarily follow. Hence if my perception is to contain the cognition of an event, i.e., of something's actually occurring, then it must be an empirical judgment in which we think B247 of the consequence as determined, i.e., as presupposing in terms of time another appearance that it succeeds necessarily, or according to a rule. Otherwise, if I posited what precedes and the event did not succeed it necessarily, then I would have to regard this A202 event as only a subjective play of my imaginings; and if I still represented by it something objective, then I would have to call it a mere dream. Therefore the relation of appearances (as possible perceptions) according to which what follows (occurs) is with regard to its existence determined in time, necessarily and according to a rule, by something preceding it—in other words, the relation of cause to effect— is the condition of the objective validity of our empirical judgments as regards the series of perceptions, and hence is the condition of these judgments' empirical truth and therefore of experience. The principle of the causal relation in the succession of appearances holds, therefore, also for all objects of experience ([insofar as they are] under the conditions of succession), because it is itself the basis of the possibility of such experience.

Here, however, a perplexity emerges that must be removed. The principle of the causal connection among appearances is, in our formulation, limited to their [occurring in] succession. Yet in using the principle we find that it also fits the case of their coexis-

B248 tence, and that cause and effect can be simultaneous. E.g., there is heat in the room which is not found in the outside air. I look around for the cause and discover a heated stove. Now this stove, as cause, is simultaneous with its effect, the room's heat. Hence here there is no succession between cause and effect in terms of time. They are, rather, simultaneous;

A203 and yet the law of cause and effect does hold. The majority of efficient causes in nature are simultaneous with their effects, and the temporal succession of the effects is due only to the fact that the cause cannot accomplish its entire effect in one instant. But at the instant when the effect first arises, it is always simultaneous with the causality of its cause. For if the cause had ceased to be an instant before, then the effect would not have arisen at all. It must be noted carefully, here, that what we are considering is the *order* of time, not the *lapse* of time; the relation remains even if no time has elapsed. The time between the causality of the cause and the cause's direct effect may be *vanishingly brief*, but yet the relation of the cause to the effect always remains determinable in terms of time. If I consider as cause a [lead] ball that lies on a stuffed cushion and makes an indentation in it, then this cause is simultaneous with the effect. But I nonetheless distinguish the two by the time relation of their dynamical connection. For if I lay the ball on the cushion, then the previous smooth shape of the

B249 cushion is succeeded by the indentation; but if the cushion has an indentation (no matter from where), then this is not succeeded by a lead ball.

Hence temporal succession is indeed an effect's
A204 sole empirical criterion in reference to the causality of the cause preceding it. The [totally filled] tumbler is the cause of the water's rising above the horizontal plane [at the top] of the tumbler, although the two appearances are simultaneous. For as soon as water is scooped from a larger vessel with [an empty] tumbler, there ensues this: the horizontal level that the

water had in the larger vessel changes to a concave level in the [partially filled] tumbler.

This causality leads to the concept of action; action leads to the concept of force and thereby to the concept of substance. Since my critical project deals solely with the sources of synthetic *a priori* cognition and I do not want to mingle with it dissections [of concepts] which concern merely the clarification (rather than the expansion) of concepts, I leave the detailed exposition of these concepts to a future system of pure reason—although such an analysis can also be found in abundance in the textbooks of this kind that are already familiar. What I must touch upon, however, is the empirical criterion of a substance insofar as it seems to manifest itself not through the permanence of appearance but better and more easily through action.

Where there is action and hence activity and   B250
force, there is also substance, and in substance alone must be sought the seat of that fertile source of appearances. That is nicely said; but if we are to explain what we mean by substance and want to avoid the fallacy of circular reasoning, then the answer is not so   A205
easy. How, from action on something, are we to infer at once *the agent's permanence*—this permanence being, after all, so essential and peculiar a characteristic of substance ([as] *phaenomenon*)? Yet according to our previous remarks, solving the question is not so difficult after all, even though the question would be quite insoluble according to the usual way (of proceeding with one's concepts, namely, merely analytically). Action already means the relation of the causality's subject to the effect. Now any effect consists in what occurs, and hence in the mutable that designates time in terms of succession. Therefore the ultimate subject of the mutable is the *permanent* as the substratum of everything that varies, i.e., substance. For according to the principle of causality actions are always the first basis of all variation by appearances; hence actions cannot reside in a subject that itself varies, since otherwise other actions and another subject determining that variation would be required. By virtue of this does action prove, as a   B251
sufficient empirical criterion, the substantiality of a subject, without my needing first of all to search for

the subject's permanence by perceptions that I have compared. Nor could proving substantiality along this path of comparison be accomplished as comprehensively as is required by the magnitude and strict universality of the concept of substance. For, that the first subject of the causality of all arising and passing away cannot itself arise and pass away (in the realm of appearances) is a safe inference that issues in empirical necessity and permanence in existence, and hence in the concept of a substance as appearance.

When something occurs then the mere arising, even if we take no account of what arises, is in itself already an object of inquiry. The transition itself from a state's not-being to this state, even supposing that this state contained no quality in [the realm of] appearance, already calls for inquiry. This arising, as was shown in the First Analogy, concerns not substance (for substance does not arise) but its state. Hence arising is only change, and not origination from nothing. For if this origination from nothing is regarded as the effect of an extraneous cause, then it is called creation; and creation cannot be admitted as an event among appearances, because its very possibility would already annul the unity of experience. If, by contrast, I regard all things not as phenomena but as things in themselves and as objects merely of the understanding, then despite their being substances they can still be regarded as being dependent, in terms of their existence, on an extraneous cause. That alternative, however, would then entail quite different significations of the words, and would not fit appearances as possible objects of experience.

Now, we do not *a priori* have the least concept as to how anything can be altered at all, i.e., how it is possible that one state occurring at one point of time can be succeeded by an opposite state occurring at another point of time. This requires knowledge of actual forces—e.g., knowledge of the motive forces, or, which is the same, of certain successive appearances (as motions) indicating such forces—and such knowledge can be given only empirically. But we can nonetheless examine *a priori*, according to the law of causality and the conditions of time, the form of every alteration, i.e., the condition under which alone, as an arising of a different state,

alteration can take place (no matter what may be its content, i.e., the state being altered); and hence we can so examine the succession itself of the states (i.e., the occurrence).[15]

When a substance passes from one state, *a*, to another, *b*, then the point of time of the second state is different from the point of time of the first, and follows it. In the same way, too, the second state as reality (in [the realm of] appearance) differs from the first, in which this reality was not, as *b* differs from zero; i.e., even if state *b* were to differ from state *a* only in magnitude, the change is [still] an arising of *b*–*a*, which in the previous state was not and in regard to which that state = 0.

The question, therefore, is how a thing passes from one state, = *a*, to another, = *b*. Between two instants there is always a time, and between two states at those instants there is always a difference that has a magnitude (for all parts of appearances are always magnitudes in turn). Hence any transition from one state to another occurs in a time that is contained between two instants, the first instant determining the state that the thing leaves and the second instant determining the state that it enters. Both instants, therefore, are limits of the time of a change and hence limits of the intermediate state between the two states, and as such belong also to the entire alteration. Now every alteration has a cause that manifests its causality in the entire time wherein the alteration takes place. Hence this cause produces its alteration not suddenly (i.e., all at once, or in one instant), but in a time; so that, as the time increases from its initial instant (*a*) up to its completion (in *b*), the reality's magnitude (*b*–*a*) is also produced through all the smaller degrees contained between the first degree and the last. Hence all alteration is possible only through a continuous action of the causality; this action, insofar as it is uniform, is called a moment. Alteration does not consist of these moments, but is produced by them as their effect.

---

15. It should be noted carefully that I am talking not about the alteration of certain relations as such, but about alteration of a state. Thus if a body moves uniformly then it does not alter its state (of motion) at all; but it does alter its state if its motion increases or decreases.

This, then, is the law of the continuity of all change. The basis of this law is this fact: that neither time nor, for that matter, appearance in time consists of parts that are the smallest; and that nonetheless, as a thing changes, its state passes through all these parts, as elements, to the thing's second state. *No difference* of the real in [the realm of] appearance is *the smallest*, just as no difference in the magnitude of times is the smallest. And thus the reality's new state grows, starting from the first state, in which it was not, through all the infinite degrees of this reality; and the differences of the degrees from one another are all smaller than the difference between 0 and *a*.

What benefit this principle may have for the investigation of nature is of no concern to us here. But how is such a principle, which thus seems to expand our cognition of nature, possible completely *a priori*? This question very much requires our ex-
B255  amination, even though what the principle says is [so] obviously actual and correct that we might believe ourselves to be exempted from the question as to how the principle was possible. For there is such a variety of unfounded claims about our cognition's expansion by pure reason, that we must adopt as a universal principle [the resolve] to be throughout
A210  distrustful on that account, and not to believe or assume anything of the sort, even upon the clearest dogmatic proof, without documentation that can provide a well-founded deduction.

All increase of empirical cognition and any progress of perception—no matter what the objects may be, whether appearances or pure intuitions—is nothing but an expansion of the determination of inner sense, i.e., a progression in time. This progression in time determines everything and is in itself determined through nothing further. I.e., the progression's parts are given only in time and through the synthesis of time; they are not given prior to the synthesis. Because of this, every transition in perception to something that follows in time is a determination of time through the production of this perception; and since time is always and in all its parts a magnitude, every such transition is the production of a perception as a magnitude that goes through all degrees, none of which is the smallest, from zero onward up to the perception's determinate degree. From this, then, is evident the possibility of cognizing *a priori* a law governing alterations as regards their form. For we only    B256 anticipate our own apprehension, whose formal condition, since it resides in ourselves prior to all given appearance, must indeed be capable of being cognized *a priori*.

We have seen that time contains the sensible *a priori* condition for the possibility of a continuous progression of what exists to what follows. In the same way the understanding, by means of the unity    A211 of apperception, is the *a priori* condition for the possibility of a continuous determination, through the series of causes and effects, of all positions for appearances in this time—the causes unfailingly entailing the existence of the effects, and thereby making the empirical cognition of time relations valid for every time (i.e., universally) and hence valid objectively.

Third Analogy.   Principle of Simultaneity according to the Law of Interaction or Community: *All substances, insofar as they can be perceived in space as simultaneous, are in thoroughgoing interaction.*
**Proof**: Things are *simultaneous* if their perceptions    B257 can in empirical intuition succeed one another *reciprocally* (which cannot occur in the temporal succession of appearances, as was shown under the second principle). Thus I can begin my perception either first with the moon and thereafter with the earth, or, vice versa, first with the earth and then with the moon. And because the perceptions of these objects can succeed each other reciprocally, I say that the objects exist simultaneously. Now simultaneity is the existence of the manifold in the same time. However, time itself cannot be perceived; and hence from the fact that things are placed in the same time we cannot glean that their perceptions can follow one another reciprocally. Hence the synthesis of imagination in apprehension would indicate for each of these perceptions only that it is there in the subject when the other is not, and vice versa. But it would not indicate that the objects are simultaneous; i.e., that if the one is there then the other is also there in the same time, and that this simultaneity of the objects is necessary in order that the perceptions can succeed one another reciprocally. Hence for things

existing outside one another simultaneously we require a concept of the understanding of the reciprocal succession of their determinations, in order to say that the reciprocal succession of the perceptions has its basis in the object and in order thus to represent the simultaneity as objective. But the relation of substances according to which the one substance B258 contains determinations whose basis is contained in the other substance is the relation of influence; and if this latter thing reciprocally contains the basis of the determinations in the former thing, then the relation is that of community or interaction. Therefore the simultaneity of substances in space cannot be cognized in experience except under the presupposition that they interact with one another. Hence this interaction is also the condition for the possibility of the things themselves as objects of experience.

Things are simultaneous insofar as they exist in one and the same time. But how do we cognize that they are in one and the same time? They are so when the order in the synthesis of this manifold's apprehension is indifferent, i.e., when that synthesis can go either from A through B, C, D, to E, or vice versa from E to A. For if the synthesis is successive in time (in the order starting from A and ending in E), then starting the apprehension in perception from E and proceeding backwards to A is impossible, since A belongs to past time and hence can no longer be an object of apprehension.

A212      Now suppose that in a manifoldness of substances taken as appearances each of them were completely isolated, i.e., that no substance effected influences in B259 another and reciprocally received influences from it. I say that in that case their *simultaneity* would not be an object of a possible perception, and that the existence of one substance could not by any path of empirical synthesis lead to the existence of another. For if you bear in mind that the substances would be separated by a completely empty space, then although the perception proceeding in time from one substance to the other would determine this other substance's existence by means of a perception that follows, yet it could not distinguish whether objectively the appearance succeeds the first or is, rather, simultaneous with it.

Hence there must be something else, besides mere existence, whereby A determines for B—and also, vice versa, B in turn for A—their positions in time. For only under this condition can those substances be represented empirically as *existing simultaneously*. Now only what is the cause of something else, or of its determinations, determines for that something its position in time. Therefore every substance (since it can be a consequence only in regard to its determinations) must contain within itself the causality of certain determinations in the other substance and simultaneously must contain within itself the effects of the other substance's causality—i.e., they must stand (directly or indirectly) in dynamical A213 community—if their simultaneity is to be cognized in any possible experience. However, something is necessary in regard to objects of experience if with- B260 out that something the experience of these objects would itself be impossible. Hence for all substances in [the realm of] appearance, insofar as they are simultaneous, it is necessary that they stand in thoroughgoing community of interaction.

The word community is ambiguous in our language; it can mean the same as *communio* or as *commercium*. We employ it here in the latter sense, as meaning a dynamic community, without which even locational community (*communio spatii*) could never be cognized empirically. We can easily tell by our experiences: that only the continuous influences in all positions of space can lead our sense from one object to another; that the light playing between our eye and the celestial bodies can bring about an indirect community between us and them and can thereby prove their simultaneity; that we cannot empirically change place (and perceive this change) unless matter everywhere makes possible the perception of our position; and that only by means of matter's reciprocal influence can matter establish its simultaneity and thereby establish (although only indirectly) the coexistence of objects, down to the most remote ones. Without community every perception (of appearance in space) A214 would be severed from any other; the chain of empirical representations—i.e., experience—would begin entirely anew with each new object, and the previous B261 chain could not in the least cohere with it or stand to it in a time relation. By this I do not in any way wish to disprove empty space. For there may be such space wherever perceptions cannot reach at all and where there occurs, therefore, no empirical cognition of simultaneity. But such space is then no object whatever for all our possible experience.

The following may serve as elucidation. In our mind all appearances, as contained in a possible experience, must stand in community (*communio*) of apperception; and insofar as objects are to be represented as connected to the extent that they exist simultaneously, they must reciprocally determine each other's position in one time and thereby make up a whole. If this subjective community is to rest on an objective basis, or be referred to appearances as substances, then the perception of the one appearance, as basis, must make possible the perception of the other, and thus also vice versa. Only then will succession, which is always there in perceptions as apprehensions, not be attributed to the objects, but these objects can, rather, be represented as existing simultaneously. This, however, is a reciprocal influence, i.e., a real community A215  (*commercium*) of substances; without this community the empirical relation of simultaneity could not occur in experience. Through this *commercium* appear-B262  ances, insofar as they stand outside one another and yet in connection, make up a composite (*compositum reale*), and such composites become possible in various ways. Hence the three dynamical relations from which all other relations arise are those of inherence, consequence, and composition.

These, then, are the three analogies of experience. They are nothing but principles for the determination of the existence of appearances in time, according to all three modes of time: namely, according to the relation to time itself as a magnitude (the magnitude of existence, i.e., duration); according to the relation in time as a series (i.e., as successive); and, finally, also according to the relation in time as a sum of all existence (i.e., as simultaneous). This unity of time determination is dynamical through and through. I.e., time is not regarded as that wherein experience immediately determines for each existent its position; for such determination is impossible, because absolute time is not an object of perception by which appearances could be held together. Rather, the rule of the understanding through which alone the existence of appearances can acquire synthetic unity in terms of time relations is what determines for each appearance its position in time, hence doing so *a priori* and validly for each and every time.

By nature (in the empirical meaning of the term) A216  we mean the connection of appearances as regards B263  their existence according to necessary rules, i.e., according to laws. There are, then, certain laws— which are, moreover, *a priori*—that make a nature possible in the first place. Empirical laws can occur and can be found only by means of experience; and this, moreover, in consequence of those original laws through which experience itself becomes possible in the first place. Hence our analogies in fact exhibit the unity of nature, in the connection of all appearances, under certain indices; these indices express nothing but the relation of time (insofar as time comprises all existence) to the unity of apperception—a unity that can occur only in synthesis according to rules. Hence together the analogies say that all appearances reside, and must reside, in one nature; for without this *a priori* unity no unity of experience, and hence also no determination of objects in experience, would be possible.[ . . . ]

Refutation of Idealism[16]     Idealism (I mean *ma-* B274  *terial* idealism) is the theory that declares the existence of objects in space outside us either to be merely doubtful and *unprovable*, or to be *false* and *impossible*. The *first* is the *problematic* idealism of *Descartes*; it declares only one empirical assertion (*assertio*) to be indubitable, namely: *I am*. The *second* is the *dogmatic* idealism of Berkeley; it declares space, with all the things to which space attaches as an inseparable condition, to be something that is in itself impossible, and hence also declares the things in space to be mere imaginings. Dogmatic idealism is unavoidable if one regards space as a property that is to belong to things in themselves; for then space,

---

16. [Kant adds 'The Refutation of Idealism' in the second edition in order to attempt to distinguish his own transcendental idealism more clearly from, for example, George Berkeley's idealism.]

with everything that space serves as a condition, is a nonentity. However, the basis for this idealism has already been removed by us in the Transcendental Aesthetic. Problematic idealism, which asserts nothing about this but only alleges that we are unable to prove by direct experience an existence apart from our own, is reasonable and is in accordance with a thorough philosophical way of thinking—namely, in permitting no decisive judgment before a sufficient proof has been found. The proof it demands must, therefore, establish that regarding external things we have not merely *imagination* but also *experience*. And establishing this surely cannot be done unless one can prove that even our *inner* experience, indubitable for Descartes, is possible only on the presupposition of *outer* experience.

**Theorem** *The mere, but empirically determined, consciousness of my own existence proves the existence of objects in space outside me.*

*Proof*: I am conscious of my existence as determined in time. All time determination presupposes something *permanent* in perception. But this permanent thing cannot be something within me, precisely because my existence can be determined in time only by this permanent thing.[17] Therefore perception of this permanent thing is possible only through a *thing* outside me and not through the mere *representation* of a thing outside me. Hence the determination of my existence in time is possible only through the existence of actual things that I perceive outside me. Now consciousness of my existence in time is necessarily linked with consciousness of the possibility of this time determination; therefore it is necessarily linked also with the existence of things outside me, as a condition of the time determination. I.e., the consciousness of my own existence is at the same time an immediate consciousness of the existence of other things outside me.

*Comment 1.* In the preceding proof one becomes aware that the game that idealism played is being turned around and against it—and more rightly so. Idealism assumed that the only immediate experience is inner experience and that from it we only *infer* external things; but we infer them only unreliably, as happens whenever we infer *determinate* causes from given effects, because the cause of the representations that we ascribe—perhaps falsely—to external things may also reside in ourselves. Yet here we have proved that outer experience is in fact immediate,[18] and that only by means of it can there be inner experience—i.e., not indeed consciousness of our own existence, but yet determination of that existence in time. To be sure, the representation *I am*, which expresses the consciousness that can accompany all thinking, is what immediately includes the existence of a subject; but it is not yet a *cognition* of that subject, and hence is also no empirical cognition—i.e., experience—of it. For such experience involves, besides the thought of something existent, also intuition, and here specifically inner intuition, in regard to which—namely, time—the subject must be determined; and this determination definitely requires external objects. Consequently, inner experience is itself only mediate and is possible only through outer experience.

*Comment 2.* Now, all experiential use that we make of our cognitive faculty in determining time completely agrees with this view. Not only can we perceive any time determination solely through a

---

17. In the second edition preface, Kant indicates that this sentence should be replaced with the following: "But this permanent something cannot be an intuition within me. For all bases determining my existence that can be encountered within me are representations; and, being representations, they themselves require something permanent distinct from them, by reference to which their change, and hence my existence in the time in which they change, can be determined."

18. In the preceding theorem, the *immediate* consciousness of the existence of external things is not presupposed but proved, whether or not we have insight into the possibility of this consciousness. The question concerning that possibility would be whether we have only an inner sense, and no outer sense but merely outer imagination. Clearly, however, in order for us even to imagine something—i.e., exhibit it to sense in intuition—as external, we must already have an outer sense, and must thereby immediately distinguish the mere receptivity of an outer intuition from the spontaneity that characterizes all imagining. For if even outer sense were merely imagined, this would annul our very power of intuition which is to be determined by the imagination.

change in external relations (i.e., through motion) by
B278 reference to the permanent in space (e.g., the sun's
motion with respect to the earth's objects); but except merely for *matter* we do not even have anything
permanent on which, as intuition, we could base the
concept of a substance. And even this permanence is
not drawn from outer experience, but is presupposed
*a priori* as necessary condition of all time determination, and hence presupposed also as determination
of inner sense, with regard to our own existence,
through the existence of external things. The consciousness that I have of myself in the representation
*I* is not an intuition at all, but is a merely *intellectual*
representation of a thinking subject's self-activity.
Hence this *I* also does not have the least predicate
of intuition that, *as permanent*, could serve as correlate for the time determination in inner sense—as,
say, *impenetrability* is such a predicate of *empirical*
intuition in matter.

 *Comment 3.* It does not follow, from the fact that
the existence of external objects is required for the
possibility of a determinate consciousness of ourselves, that every intuitive representation of external
things implies also these things' existence; for the
representation may very well be (as it is in dreams as
well as in madness) the mere effect of the imagination. Yet it is this effect merely through the reproduction of former outer perceptions; and these, as has
been shown, are possible only through the actuality
of external objects. What was here to be proved is
B279 only that inner experience as such is possible only
through outer experience as such. Whether this or
that supposed experience is not perhaps a mere imagining must be ascertained by reference to its particular determinations and by holding it up to the criteria
of all actual experience. [ ... ]

A293/ Transcendental Logic Division II
B349 Transcendental Dialectic Introduction

I On Transcendental Illusion
Above we called dialectic as such a *logic of illusion*.
This does not mean that it is a doctrine of *probability*.
For probability is truth, but truth cognized through
insufficient grounds; and although cognition of such
truth is therefore deficient, yet it is not on that account

deceptive, and hence must not be separated from the
analytic part of logic. Still less may *appearance* and
*illusion* be regarded as being the same. For truth and B350
illusion are not in the object insofar as it is intuited,
but are in the judgment made about the object insofar as it is thought. Hence although it is correct to
say that the senses do not err, this is so not because
they always judge correctly but because they do not
judge at all. Thus both truth and error, and hence
also illusion as the process of mistakenly leading to
error, are to be found only in the judgment, i.e., only
in the relation of the object to our understanding.
In a cognition that accords throughout with the laws
of the understanding there is no error. There is also A294
no error in a representation of the senses (because it
contains no judgment at all). But no force of nature
can deviate from its own laws by itself. Thus neither
the understanding on its own (i.e., apart from the
influence of another cause), nor the senses by themselves would err. The understanding would not err,
because, if it acts merely in accordance with its laws,
then the effect (the judgment) must necessarily agree
with these laws; but the formal [element] of all truth
consists in the agreement with the laws of the understanding. And in the senses there is no judgment
at all, neither a true nor a false one. Now because
we have no other sources of cognition besides these
two, it follows that error comes about only by sensibility's unnoticed influence on the understanding. Through this influence it comes about that the
subjective grounds of the judgment meld with the B351
objective ones and make them deviate from their
[proper] determination—just as a body in motion
would indeed by itself always keep to a straight line
in the same direction, but is deflected into curvilinear motion if influenced at the same time by another A295
force acting in another direction. Hence in order to
distinguish the action peculiar to the understanding
from the force that mingles with it, we shall need
to regard an erroneous judgment as the diagonal
between two forces determining the judgment in
two different directions that—as it were—enclose an
angle, and to resolve this composite action into the
simple ones of the understanding and of sensibility.
In the case of pure *a priori* judgments we must do

this by transcendental deliberation, whereby (as has already been shown) every representation is assigned its place in the cognitive faculty appropriate to it, and whereby the influence of sensibility on the understanding is therefore also distinguished.

B352  It is not our task here to deal with empirical (e.g., optical) illusion, which occurs in the empirical use of otherwise correct rules of the understanding, and through which our faculty of judgment is misled by the influence of imagination. Here we have to do, rather, solely with *transcendental illusion*, which influences principles whose use is not even designed for experience; if it were, then we would, after all, at least have a touchstone of their correctness. Rather, transcendental illusion carries us, even despite all the warnings issued by critique, entirely beyond the empirical use of the categories and puts us off with the deception of there being an expansion of the *pure understanding*. Let us call the principles

A296  whose application keeps altogether within the limits of possible experience *immanent* principles, and those that are to fly beyond these limits *transcendent principles*. But by transcendent principles I do not mean the *transcendental* use or misuse of the categories, which is a mere mistake made by the faculty of judgment when, not being duly curbed by critique, it does not pay enough attention to the boundaries of the territory on which alone our pure understanding is permitted to engage in its play. Rather, I mean by them actual principles requiring us to tear down all those boundary posts and to claim an entirely new territory that recognizes no demarcation at all. Hence *transcendental* and *transcendent* are not the same. The principles of the

B353  pure understanding that we have put forth above are to be of empirical and not of transcendental use, i.e., use extending beyond the limits of experience. But a principle that removes these limits—indeed, even commands us to step beyond them—is called *transcendent*. If our critique can manage to uncover the illusion in these claimed principles, then the principles of merely empirical use may be called, in contrast to the transcendent ones, *immanent* principles of the pure understanding.

Logical illusion (the illusion of fallacious inferences), which consists in the mere imitation of the form of reason, arises solely from a lack of attentiveness in regard to the logical rule. Hence as soon as  A297 our attentiveness is sharpened in regard to the case before us, the illusion entirely vanishes. Transcendental illusion, however, does not cease even when we have already uncovered it and have, through transcendental critique, had distinct insight into its nullity. (An example is the illusion in the proposition that the world must have a beginning in terms of time.) The cause of this is that in our reason (regarded subjectively as a human cognitive faculty) there lie basic rules and maxims of its use that have entirely the look of objective principles; and through this it comes about that the subjective necessity of a certain connection of our concepts for the benefit of the understanding is regarded as an objective necessity of the determination of things in themselves. This is  B354 an *illusion* that we cannot at all avoid any more than we can avoid the illusion that the sea seems to us higher in the center than at the shore because we see the center through higher light rays than the shore; or—better yet—any more than even the astronomer can prevent the moon from seeming larger to him as it rises, although he is not deceived by this illusion.

Hence the transcendental dialectic will be satisfied with uncovering the illusion of transcendent judgments, and at the same time keeping it from deceiving us. But that the illusion should even vanish as well (as does logical illusion) and cease to be an illusion—this the transcendental dialectic can never  A298 accomplish. For here we are dealing with a *natural* and unavoidable *illusion* that itself rests on subjective principles and foists them on us as objective ones, whereas a logical dialectic in resolving fallacious inferences deals only with a mistake in the compliance with principles, or with an artificial illusion created in imitating such inferences. Hence there is a natural and unavoidable dialectic of pure reason. This dialectic is not one in which a bungler might become entangled on his own through lack of knowledge, or one that some sophist has devised artificially in order to confuse reasonable people. It is, rather, a dialectic that attaches to human reason unpreventably and that, even after we have uncovered this deception, still will not stop hoodwinking and thrusting reason incessantly into momentary aberrations that always need to be corrected. [ . . . ]

## II. On Pure Reason as the Seat of Transcendental Illusion [ . . . ]

### C   On the Pure Use of Reason

Can one isolate reason? And is it then still on its own a source of concepts and judgments which arise solely from it and through which it refers to objects? Or is it then a merely subsidiary faculty to provide given cognitions with a certain form, a form which is called logical and through which the cognitions of the understanding are only subordinated to one another, and lower rules subordinated to other and higher rules (whose condition comprises in its sphere the condition of the lower rules), to whatever extent this can be accomplished by comparing them? This is the question with which we are now dealing only provisionally. Multiplicity of rules and unity of principles is indeed a demand of reason. Reason makes this demand in order to bring the understanding into thoroughgoing coherence with itself, just as the understanding brings the manifold of intuition under concepts and thereby connects intuitions. But such a principle prescribes no law to objects, and does not contain the basis for the possibility of cognizing and determining them as objects at all. It is, rather, merely a subjective law for the management of the understanding's supplies, [instructing the understanding] to reduce the universal use of its concepts—by comparing them—to their smallest possible number. This [instruction] does not entitle us to demand from objects themselves such accordance as would promote the convenience and the broadening of our understanding, and to provide that maxim with objective validity as well. In a word, the question is: Does reason in itself, i.e., pure reason, contain synthetic principles and rules *a priori*; and in what may these principles consist?

Reason's formal and logical procedure in syllogisms already gives us sufficient guidance concerning the basis on which will rest reason's transcendental principle as used in synthetic cognition through pure reason.

*First*, an inference of reason does not deal with intuitions in order to bring them under rules (as does the understanding with its categories), but deals with concepts and judgments. Hence even if pure reason deals with objects, it still has no direct reference to them and their intuition, but refers directly only to the understanding and its judgments; the understanding and its judgments are what initially turn to the senses and their intuition in order to determine the object of these. Hence unity of reason is not unity of a possible experience—which is the unity of the understanding—but the former unity is essentially different from the latter unity. The principle that everything that occurs has a cause is not at all a principle cognized and prescribed by reason. It makes possible the unity of experience and borrows nothing from reason; reason could not, without this reference to possible experience and hence from mere concepts, have commanded such synthetic unity.

*Second*, reason in its logical use seeks the universal condition of its judgment (i.e., of the conclusion), and a syllogism is itself nothing but a judgment made by means of subsuming its condition under a universal rule (major premise). Now this rule is in turn exposed to the same attempt by reason, and thus the condition of the condition must, as long as doing so is feasible, be sought (by means of a prosyllogism); and hence we readily see that the principle peculiar to reason as such (in its logical use) is: to find, for the understanding's conditioned cognition, the unconditioned whereby the cognition's unity is completed.

But this logical maxim can become a principle of *pure reason* only by our assuming that, if the conditioned is given, then the entire series of conditions subordinated to one another—a series that is hence itself unconditioned—is also given (i.e., contained in the object and its connection).

Such a principle of pure reason, however, is plainly *synthetic*; for although the conditioned does refer analytically to some condition, it does not so refer to the unconditioned. Moreover, from this principle there must arise various synthetic propositions of which the pure understanding knows nothing; for the pure understanding has to do only with objects of a possible experience, and the cognition and synthesis of such objects is always conditioned. But the unconditioned, if such there actually is, may be examined in special fashion according to all those determinations that distinguish it from everything conditioned, and must thereby provide material for many synthetic *a priori* propositions.

The principles arising from this supreme principle of reason will, however, be *transcendent* in regard to all appearances; i.e., no empirical use adequate to this principle can ever be made of it. It will, therefore, be entirely different from all principles of the understanding (whose use is wholly *immanent*, because they have as their subject only the possibility of experience). Our task in the transcendental dialectic, then, will be to answer the following questions. Does that principle—i.e., that the series of conditions (in the synthesis of appearances, or, for that matter, in that of the thinking of things as such) extends up to the unconditioned—have, or does it not have, its objective correctness; and what inferences issue from it for the empirical use of the understanding? Or is there, rather, no such objectively valid proposition of reason at all, but a merely logical precept to seek, in ascending to ever higher conditions, to approach their completeness and thereby to bring into our cognition the highest unity of reason that is possible for us? In other words: Has this need of reason been regarded, by a misunderstanding, as a transcendental principle of pure reason that rashly postulates such unlimited completeness in the series of conditions found in the objects themselves? But, in that case, what misunderstandings and delusions may be creeping also into syllogisms, whose major premise has been taken from pure reason (and is perhaps more a petition than a postulate), and which ascend from experience upward to its conditions? These questions, then, will be at issue in the transcendental dialectic. Let us now unfold this dialectic from its sources, which are deeply hidden in human reason. [ . . . ]

B406    The Paralogisms of Pure Reason
        [Second Edition]

The proposition *I think* (taken problematically) contains the form of any of the understanding's judgments as such, and accompanies all categories as their vehicle. Clearly, therefore, the inferences from

A309

B366

this proposition can contain merely a transcendental use of the understanding. Such use allows no experience to be mixed in, and hence regarding its progress we can—by what we have shown above—frame even in advance none but an unfavorable conception. Let us, therefore, trace this use, with a critical eye, through all the predicaments of pure psychology. For the sake of brevity, however, let us allow their examination to proceed in an uninterrupted continuity.

First of all, the following general remark may make us more keenly attentive to this kind of inference. I do not cognize any object by merely thinking. Rather I can cognize an object only by determining a given intuition with respect to the unity of consciousness in which all thought consists. Hence I do not cognize myself by being conscious of myself as thinking, but I cognize myself when I am conscious of the intuition of myself as determined with regard to the function of thought. All the *modes* of self-consciousness in thought as such are, therefore, not yet the understanding's concepts of objects (categories), but are mere functions that do not allow thought to cognize any object at all, and hence also do not allow it to cognize myself as an object. The *object* is not the consciousness of the *determining* self, but only that of the *determinable* self, i.e., of my inner intuition (insofar as its manifold can be combined in accordance with the universal condition of the unity of apperception in thought).

1. Now in all judgments I am always the *determining* subject of the relation that makes up the judgment. But that I, who think, must be considered in such thought always as a *subject* and as something that cannot be regarded as merely attaching to thought like a predicate—this is an apodeictic and even identical proposition. But this proposition does not mean that I am, as an *object*, a *being subsisting* by myself or *substance*. This latter claim goes very far, and hence it also requires data that are in no way found in thought, and perhaps (insofar as I consider the thinking [self] merely as thinking) requires more than I shall ever find (in thought) at all.

2. That the *I* of apperception, and hence in all thought, is *singular*, cannot be resolved into a plurality of subjects, and therefore designates a logically

B407

B408 simple subject—this lies already in the concept of thought and hence is an analytic proposition. But this does not mean that the thinking *I* is a simple *substance*; that would be a synthetic proposition. The concept of substance always refers to intuitions that, in me, cannot be other than sensible and hence lie entirely outside the realm of the understanding and its thought; yet here we are in fact talking only about this thought when we say that the *I* in thought is simple. Indeed, it would be miraculous if what otherwise requires so much effort for distinguishing what is substance in what intuition displays—but even more for distinguishing (as with the parts of matter) whether this substance can also be simple—were here in the poorest of all representations given to me thus straightforwardly, as if through a revelation.

3. The proposition of the identity of myself in all the manifold whereof I am conscious is likewise a proposition that lies in the concepts themselves and hence is analytic. But this identity of the subject, of which I can become conscious in all representations of this subject, does not concern the subject's intuition through which it is given as object. Hence this identity also cannot mean identity of the person, by which we understand the consciousness of the subject's own substance as a thinking being in all variation of its states. Proving this identity could not be B409 accomplished by merely analyzing the proposition *I think*, but would require various synthetic judgments based on the given intuition.

4. I distinguish my own existence, as that of a thinking being, from other things outside me (which include my body)—this is likewise an analytic proposition. For *other* things are things that I think as *distinct* from me. But from this I do not in any way know whether this consciousness of myself is at all possible without things outside me through which representations are given to me, and hence whether I can exist as merely a thinking being (i.e., without being human).

Hence analyzing the consciousness of myself in thought as such does not yield the slightest gain as regards the cognition of myself as object. The logical exposition of thought as such is wrongly considered to be a metaphysical determination of the object.

It would be for our entire critique a great stumbling-block—indeed, even the only one—if there were a possibility of proving *a priori* that all thinking beings are in themselves simple substances; and that, being such, they therefore (as a consequence from the same basis of proof) inseparably carry with them personality and are conscious of their existence as one that is set apart from all matter. For in this way we would, after all, have taken a step beyond the world of sense; we would have entered the realm of B410 *noumena*—and now let no one deny us the right to expand further into this realm, to settle in it, and to take possession of it insofar as each of us is favored by his lucky star. For the proposition, Any thinking being is, as such, a simple substance, is a synthetic *a priori* proposition. For, first, it goes beyond the concept on which it is based and adds to thinking being as such its *way of existing*; and, second, it adds to that concept a predicate (that of simplicity) that cannot be given in any experience whatsoever. Hence it would seem that synthetic *a priori* propositions are feasible and admissible not merely, as we have asserted, in reference to objects of possible experience—namely, as principles of the possibility of this experience itself—but that they can apply also to things as such and in themselves. And this is a conclusion that would put an end to this entire critique and would dictate that we leave everything as it was. Once we step closer to the matter, however, we see that the danger here is not so great.

In the procedure of rational psychology a paralogism prevails, which is exhibited by the following syllogism:

*What cannot be thought otherwise than as subject also does not exist otherwise than as subject, and therefore is substance.*
*Now a thinking being, considered merely as such, can-* B411 *not be thought otherwise than as subject.*
*Therefore, it also exists only as a subject, i.e., as substance.*

In the major premise one talks about a being that can be thought in general, in every respect, and hence also as it may be given in intuition. But in the minor premise one talks about it insofar as it considers itself, as subject, only relatively to thought and the unity of consciousness, but not simultaneously in reference to the intuition through which it is given as an object for such thought. Therefore, one is inferring the conclusion *per sophisma figurae dictionis*, and hence by a fallacious inference.[19]

B412    That resolving a famous argument into a paralogism in this way is entirely correct is distinctly evident when one consults the general comment on the systematic representation of the principles and the section on the noumena.[20] There we proved that the concept of a thing that can exist by itself as subject but not as mere predicate does not yet carry with it, on that account, any objective reality; i.e., we proved that—since we have no insight into the possibility of such a way of existing—we cannot know whether an object belongs to this concept at all, and consequently proved that this concept yields absolutely no cognition. Hence if this concept is to indicate, under the name of substance, an object that can be given, and the concept is to become a cognition, then we must lay at its basis a permanent intuition; for intuition—i.e., that through which alone the object is given—is the indispensable condition of a concept's having objective reality. In B413    inner intuition, however, we have nothing permanent at all, for the *I* is only the consciousness of my thinking. Hence if one remains with mere thinking, then one also lacks the necessary condition for applying the concept of substance—i.e., the concept

────────────

19. Thought is taken in two entirely different meanings in the two premises. In the major premise it is taken as it applies to an object as such (and hence also to an object as it may be given in intuition). But in the minor premise it is taken only as it consists in the reference to self-consciousness; hence here one thinks of no object whatsoever, but represents only the reference to oneself as subject (as the form of thought). In the first premise one talks about things that cannot be thought otherwise than as subjects. In the second premise, however, one talks (by abstracting from any object) not about *things* but about *thought,* in which the *I* always serves as the subject of consciousness. Hence in the conclusion it cannot follow that I cannot exist otherwise than as subject, but merely that in thinking my existence I can use myself only as the judgment's subject. And this is an identical proposition that reveals absolutely nothing concerning the way in which I exist.

20. [These sections have not been included in this anthology.]

of a self-subsistent subject—to oneself as a thinking being. And the simplicity of the substance, which is linked with this concept, then drops out entirely along with that concept's reality, and is transformed into nothing more than a logical qualitative unity of self-consciousness in thought as such—no matter whether the subject is composite or not. [ . . . ]

## Transcendental Dialectic

### Book II
### Chapter II. The Antinomy of Pure Reason

We have shown in the introduction to this part of our work that all transcendental illusion of pure reason A406 rests on dialectical inferences whose schema is provided by logic, namely, in the three formal kinds of syllogisms as such—roughly as the categories find their logical schema in the four functions of all judgments. The *first kind* of these subtly reasoning inferences dealt with the unconditioned unity of the *subjective* conditions of all representations as such (of the subject or soul); it corresponds to **categori-** B433 **cal** syllogisms, whose major premise, as principle, states the reference of a predicate to a *subject.* Thus the *second kind* of dialectical argument will, by analogy with **hypothetical** syllogisms, take as its content the unconditioned unity of the objective conditions in [the realm of] appearance—just as the *third kind* of dialectical inferences, which will come up in the following [third] chapter, has as its topic the unconditioned unity of the objective conditions for the possibility of objects as such.

It is noteworthy, however, that the transcendental paralogisms brought about a merely one-sided illusion regarding the idea of the subject of our thought, and that not the slightest illusion of plausibility arising from concepts of reason can be found for the assertion of the opposite. The advantage is entirely on the side of pneumatism, although this view cannot deny having the built-in defect that, despite all the illusion of plausibility in its favor, in the critique's ordeal by fire it dissolves entirely into smoke.

The outcome is quite different when we apply reason to the *objective synthesis* of appearances. A407 Here, although reason means to validate its principle of unconditioned unity with much illusion of plausibility, it soon becomes entangled in such contradictions that it is compelled, in regard to cosmology, to renounce its demand for such unity.

For here a new phenomenon of human reason manifests itself, namely, an entirely natural
B434 antithetic: i.e., an antithetic for [the discovery of] which no one needs to ponder or artfully lay snares, but into which reason falls on its own and, moreover, inevitably. And although this antithetic protects reason from the slumber—produced by a merely one-sided illusion—of an imaginary conviction, yet it also tempts reason either to submit to a skeptical hopelessness or to adopt a dogmatic defiance and rigidly stand up for certain assertions without granting a hearing or doing justice to the grounds supporting the opposite. Both [the slumber of imaginary conviction and this skepticism or dogmatism] are the death of a sound philosophy, although the slumber might at least still be called pure reason's *euthanasia*.

Before we unveil the instances of discord and disarray to which this conflict of laws (antinomy) of pure reason gives rise, let us offer certain points that
A408 may elucidate and justify the method employed by us in treating our topic. All transcendental ideas insofar as they concern absolute totality in the synthesis of appearances I call *world concepts*, partly because of precisely this unconditioned totality—on which rests also the concept, which itself is only an idea, of the world whole—and partly because they deal with
B435 the synthesis of appearances only, and hence with empirical synthesis. By contrast, absolute totality in the synthesis of the conditions of all possible things as such will give rise to an ideal of pure reason; this ideal, although it has reference to a world concept, is yet entirely distinct from it. Hence just as the paralogisms of pure reason laid the basis for a dialectical psychology, so will the antinomy of pure reason put before us the transcendental principles of a supposed pure (rational) cosmology. The antinomy will do so not in order to find this cosmology valid and adopt it, but—as is, indeed, already indicated by the very name, conflict of reason—in order to exhibit it in its beguiling but deceptive illusion, as an idea that cannot be reconciled with appearances.

## Section I. System of Cosmological Ideas

Now in order for us to be able to enumerate these ideas with systematic precision according to a principle, we must note two points. *First*, pure and transcendental concepts can arise only from the understanding. A409 Reason does not in fact produce any concept, but at most *frees* the *concept of the understanding* of the inevitable limitations of a possible experience; and thus reason tries to expand the concept beyond the limits of the empirical, but yet in connection with the empirical. Reason does this by demanding, for a B436 given conditioned, absolute totality on the side of the conditions (under which the understanding subjects all appearances to synthetic unity). It thereby turns the category into a transcendental idea, in order that, by continuing empirical synthesis up to the unconditioned (which is never found in experience but only in the idea), reason may provide this synthesis with absolute completeness. Reason demands this totality according to the principle that *if the conditioned is given, then the entire sum of conditions and hence the absolutely unconditioned* (through which alone the conditioned was possible) *is also given*. Hence, *first*, transcendental ideas will in fact be nothing but categories expanded up to the unconditioned, and they can be put in a table arranged according to the [four] headings of the categories. However, *second*, not all categories will be suitable for this, but only those categories in which the synthesis makes up a *series*— a series, moreover, of conditions for a conditioned that are subordinated to (not coordinated with) one A410 another. Absolute totality is demanded by reason only insofar as this totality concerns the ascending series of conditions for a given conditioned, and hence not when we are talking about the descending line of consequences, nor yet when we are talking about the aggregate of coordinated conditions for these consequences. For as regards the given conditioned, condi- B437 tions are already presupposed and must be regarded as given with it. Consequences, on the other hand, do not make their conditions possible, but rather presuppose them; hence in proceeding to the consequences (or in descending from the given condition to the conditioned) we do not have to worry whether or not the series ceases, and the question concerning the totality of this series is, indeed, no presupposition of reason at all. [ . . . ]

### Section II. Antithetic of Pure Reason

If thetic is the term for any sum of dogmatic doctrines, then by antithetic I mean not dogmatic assertions of the opposite, but the conflict of seemingly dogmatic A421 cognitions (*thesis cum antithesi*) without attribution to one of them of a superior claim to approval over the other. Thus the antithetic does not deal at all with one-sided assertions, but considers universal cognitions of reason only in regard to their conflict with one another and to the causes of this conflict. The transcendental antithetic is an inquiry concerning the antinomy of pure reason, its causes, and its B449 result. When we apply our reason not merely—for the sake of using the principles of understanding—to objects of experience, but venture to extend our reason beyond the limits of experience, then there arise *subtly reasoning* doctrines. These doctrines neither may hope to be confirmed in experience, nor need they fear being refuted in it; and each of them not only is in itself without contradiction, but even encounters conditions of its necessity in the nature of reason—except that, unfortunately, the counterproposition has on its side equally valid and necessary grounds for its assertion.

The questions, then, that naturally arise in such a dialectic of pure reason are the following. (1) What are, in fact, the propositions in which pure reason is unfailingly subject to an antinomy? (2) To what causes is this antinomy due? (3) Despite this contradiction, does a path to certainty yet remain open to reason, and in what way?

Accordingly, a dialectical doctrine of pure rea-A422 son must have this twofold feature distinguishing it from all sophistical propositions: First, it must concern not a chosen question that one is raising only for this or that arbitrary aim, but a question that any human reason must in its progress necessarily come upon. And second, such a doctrine, with its counterproposition, must carry with it not a merely B450 artificial illusion that immediately vanishes once we have insight into it, but a natural and unavoidable illusion that still continues to delude us—although

not to deceive us—even when we are no longer tricked by it, and that hence can be rendered innocuous, but never obliterated.

Such a dialectical doctrine will refer not to the unity of the understanding in experiential concepts, but to the unity of reason in mere ideas. But as synthesis according to rules this unity is still to be congruent, first, with the understanding, and yet as absolute unity of this synthesis it is to be congruent simultaneously with reason. Hence if this unity is adequate to reason, then its conditions will be too great for the understanding, and if the unity is commensurate with the understanding, then its conditions will be too small for reason. And from this there must arise a conflict that cannot be avoided, no matter how one goes about doing so.

These subtly reasoning assertions thus reveal a dialectical combat arena. There any party permitted to make the attack keeps the upper hand, and the party compelled to proceed merely defensively is cer-A423 tain to be defeated. Vigorous knights, by the same token, whether they pledge themselves to the good or to the evil cause, are sure to carry off the wreath of victory—provided they take care to have the prerogative of making the last attack and are not obliged to withstand a new onslaught by the opponent. We can indeed readily conceive that this contest arena has all B451 along been entered often enough and that many victories have been won by both sides, but that for the last and decisive victory care has always been taken—by forbidding the opponent to take up arms thenceforth—that solely the champion of the good cause would prevail in the arena. We, however, as impartial arbiters of combat, must set aside entirely whether the cause for which the contestants are fighting is the good or the evil one, and must let them decide their cause between themselves. Perhaps, after having more exhausted than harmed each other, they will become aware on their own of the nullity of their contest, and will part as good friends.

This method of watching—or, rather, of occasioning on one's own—a contest of assertions, not in order finally to decide in favor of one or the other party, but in order to inquire whether the contest's A424 object is not perhaps a mere deception for which each party grasps in vain and from which it cannot gain anything even if not resisted at all—this procedure, I say, may be called the *skeptical method*. It is entirely distinct from *skepticism*, a principle of technical and scientific ignorance—a principle that undermines the foundations of all cognition in order, if possible, to leave cognition without any reliability and security whatsoever. For the skeptical method aims at certainty. It does so by seeking to discover the point of misunderstanding in such a dispute—a dispute that on both sides is meant sincerely and is conducted with understanding—in order that, as wise legislators do, it may from the perplexity of judges in lawsuits obtain information for itself about what is deficient and not precisely determined in its laws. [ . . . ]

B452

The Antinomy of Pure Reason

Section II. Antithetic of Pure Reason

First Conflict of Transcendental Ideas

A426/
B454

A427/
B455

Thesis   The world has a beginning in time and is also enclosed within limits as regards space.

Proof   For assume that the world has no beginning as regards time. In that case, up to every given point in time an eternity has elapsed and hence an infinite series of successive states of things in the world has gone by. However, the infinity of a series consists precisely in the fact that it can never be completed by successive synthesis. Therefore an infinite bygone world series is impossible, and hence a beginning of the world is a necessary condition of the world's existence—which was the first point to be proved.

As regards the *second* point in the thesis, assume again the opposite. In that case the world will be an infinite given whole of things existing simultaneously. Now in the case of a *quantum* that is not given within certain limits of any intuition, we can think of this quantum's magnitude in no other way than through the synthesis of its parts, and can think of the totality of such a quantum only through the completed synthesis, or through repeated addition of unit to unit. Accordingly, in order for the world—which occupies all spaces— to be thought as a whole, the successive synthesis of the parts of an infinite world would have to be regarded as completed, i.e., in the enumeration of all coexisting things an infinite time would have to be regarded as having elapsed—which is impossible. Accordingly, an infinite aggregate of actual things cannot be regarded as a given whole, and hence also not as given *simultaneously*. Consequently, a world is, as regards extension in space, not *infinite* but is enclosed in its limits—which was the second point to be proved.

A428/
B456

Antithesis   The world has no beginning and no limits in space, but is infinite as regards both time and space.

Proof   For suppose that it has a beginning. In that case, since the beginning is an existence preceded by a time in which the thing is not, a time must have preceded wherein the world was not, i.e., an empty time. In an empty time, however, no arising of any thing is possible; for no part of such a time has, in preference to another part, any distinguishing condition of existence rather than nonexistence (whether one assumes that the world arises of itself or through another cause). Hence although many a series of things can begin in the world, the world itself cannot have a beginning and hence is infinite with regard to past time.

As concerns the second point in the antithesis, assume, first of all, the opposite: namely, that the world is, as regards space, finite and limited. In that case the world is located in an empty space that is not limited. Hence we would find here not only a relation of things *in space* but also a relation of things *to space*. Now the world is an absolute whole, outside of which there is to be found no object of intuition, and hence no correlate of the world to which the world stands in relation; therefore the relation of the world to empty space would be a relation of it to *no object*. But such a relation—and hence also the limiting of the world by empty space—is nothing. Therefore the world is, as regards space, not limited at all; i.e., it is infinite with regard to extension.[21]

A429/
B457

---

21. Space is merely the form of outer intuition (i.e., it is merely formal intuition), but not an actual object that can be intuited externally. Space, as prior to all things that determine (occupy or limit) it—or that, rather, give us an *empirical intuition* conforming to its form—is called absolute space; absolute space is nothing but the mere possibility of outer appearances insofar as they either exist in themselves or can still be added to given appearances. Hence empirical intuition is not composed of appearances and space (i.e., perception and empty intuition). The one is not the other's correlate in synthesis, but is only

## Comment on The First Antinomy

I. On the Thesis   In these mutually conflicting arguments I have not sought to use deceptions in order perhaps to conduct (as we say) a lawyer's proof—which employs the opponent's carelessness to its own advantage and gladly accepts his appeal to a misunderstood law in order to build its own illegitimate claims on that law's refutation. Each of these proofs is drawn from the nature of the case, and the advantage obtainable from the fallacious inferences of the dogmatists from both parties has been put aside.

I could also seemingly have proved the thesis by starting, in accordance with the custom of the dogmatists, from a defective concept of the infinity of a given magnitude. A magnitude [so I could have argued] is *infinite* if beyond it (i.e., beyond what multitude of a given unit it contains) no greater one is possible. Now no magnitude is the greatest, because one or more units can always still be added. Therefore an infinite given magnitude, and hence also an infinite world (infinite as regards both the past series and extension), is impossible; therefore the world is limited in both respects. Thus could I have conducted my proof. However, this concept of the infinity of a given magnitude does not agree with what is meant by an infinite whole. For we do not represent through this concept *how great* this whole is, and hence the concept of this whole is also not the concept of a *maximum*. Rather,

through this concept we think only the whole's relation to an arbitrarily assumed unit, in regard to which this whole is greater than any number. Now according as the unit is assumed greater or smaller, the infinite whole would be greater or smaller. Only infinity, since it consists merely in the relation to these given units, would always remain the same; but through this concept, of course, the absolute magnitude of the whole would not be cognized— nor, indeed, is cognizing this magnitude at issue here.

The true (transcendental) concept of infinity is this: that the successive synthesis of unit[s] in measuring by means of a quantum can never be completed.[22]

II. On the Antithesis   The proof for the infinity of the given world series and the infinity of the world sum-total rests on this: that in the opposite case an empty time and similarly an empty space would have to make up the limit of the world. Now, I am not unaware that philosophers seek subterfuges against this implication, by claiming that a limit of the world as regards both time and space is indeed entirely possible without one's needing to assume an absolute time prior to the beginning of the world, or an absolute space spread out outside of the actual world—both of which are impossible. With the latter part of this opinion of the philosophers from the Leibnizian school I am entirely satisfied. Space is merely the form of outer intuition, but not an actual object that can be intuited externally, and not a correlate of appearances but the form of appearances themselves. Hence space cannot occur absolutely (by itself) as something determinative in the existence of things, since it is no object at all but only the form of possible objects. Hence things considered as possible predicates (of magnitude and relation) appearances do indeed determine space; i.e., they bring about the fact that among all its possible predicates (of magnitude and relation) certain ones belong to actuality. But space considered as something self-subsistent cannot conversely determine the actuality of things as regards magnitude or shape, because it is nothing actual in itself. Hence a space (whether full or empty)[23] can indeed be limited by appearances, but

linked with the other in one and the same empirical intuition, namely, as its matter and form. If we try to posit one of these two items outside the other (namely, space outside all appearances), then there arise from this all sorts of empty determinations of outer intuition that yet are not possible perceptions: e.g., the distinction between the world's motion or rest in infinite empty space—a determination of the relation of the two to each other that can never be perceived and that, by the same token, is therefore the predicate of a mere thought-entity.

23. It will readily be discerned that I mean by this the following: *empty space insofar as it is limited by appearances*—hence empty space *within the world*—at least does not contradict transcendental principles, and thus may, as far as they are concerned, be granted (although its possibility may not therefore immediately be asserted).

---

22. The quantum thereby contains a multitude (of a given unit) that is greater than any number—which is the mathematical concept of the infinite.

From this it follows quite surely that an eternity of actual successive states up to a given point in time (the present one) cannot have gone by, and that the world must therefore have a beginning.

In regard to the second part of the thesis the difficulty concerning an infinite and yet elapsed series does, indeed, go away; for the manifold of a world that is infinite as regards extension is given *simultaneously*. Consider, however, the totality of such a multitude: since we cannot appeal to limits that by themselves make up this totality in intuition, we must, in order to think this totality, account for our concept. However, this concept cannot in such a case proceed from the whole to the determinate multitude of parts, but must establish the possibility of a whole through the successive synthesis of the parts. Now because this synthesis would have to make up a series that can never be completed, one cannot think a totality of such a synthesis, and hence also not by means of it. For the concept of totality itself is in this case the representation of a completed synthesis of the parts; but this completion, and hence also the concept of it, is impossible.

A434/
B462

appearances cannot be limited by an empty space outside them. The same holds also for time. But all of this being granted, the fact is nonetheless indisputable that these two non-entities—empty space outside, and empty time prior to, the world—must assuredly be assumed if one assumes a limit of the world, whether in regard to space or time.

For as concerns the above implication—according to which we say that if the world has limits (as regards time and space) then the infinite void must determine the existence of actual things as regards their magnitude—the escape by which philosophers seek to evade this implication consists, although covertly, only in this: that instead of thinking of a *world of sense* one thinks of who knows what kind of intelligible world; instead of the first beginning (an existence preceded by a time of nonexistence) one thinks an existence as such that *presupposes no other condition* in the world; and instead of the limits of extension one thinks *boundaries* of the world whole; and thus one gets away from time and space. But we are here talking only about the *mundus phaenomenon* and its magnitude, and in the case of this world we can by no means abstract from the mentioned conditions of sensibility without annulling the essence of that world. The world of sense, if it is limited, lies necessarily in the infinite void. If one wants to leave out the void, and hence space as such, as an *a priori* condition for the possibility of appearances, then the entire world of sense drops out. In our problem, this world alone is given to us. The *mundus intelligibilis* is nothing but the universal concept of a world as such. In this concept one abstracts from all conditions of the intuition of the world, and therefore in regard to this concept no synthetic proposition whatsoever is possible either affirmatively or negatively.

## Second Conflict of Transcendental Ideas

A435/
B463

**Thesis**  Every composite substance in the world consists of simple parts, and nothing at all exists but the simple or what is composed of it.

**Proof**  For suppose that composite substances did not consist of simple parts. In that case, if all composition were annulled in thought, then there would remain no composite part and (since on this supposition there are no simple parts) also no simple part; hence

**Antithesis**  No composite thing in the world consists of simple parts, and there exists in the world nothing simple at all.

**Proof**  Suppose that a composite thing (as substance) consists of simple parts. Now all external relation and hence also all composition from substances is possible only in space; hence however many parts the composite consists of, the space that it occupies must there would remain nothing at all, and consequently no substance would have been given. Therefore, either one cannot possibly annul in thought all composition, or after its annulment there must remain something that subsists without any composition, i.e., the simple. In the first case, however, the composite would again not consist of substances; (for with substances composition is only a contingent relation of substances—a relation without which substances, as essentially permanent beings, must still subsist). Now since this case contradicts the presupposition, there remains only the second case: namely, that composite of substances in the world consists of simple parts.

From this it follows directly that the things in the world are, one and all, simple beings; that composition is merely an external state of them; and that although we can never put elementary substances completely out of this state of combination and isolate them, yet reason must think them as the first subjects of all composition, and hence must think them, prior to any composition, as simple beings.

also consist of as many parts. Now space consists not of simple parts but of spaces. Hence every part of the composite must occupy a space. However, the absolutely first parts of anything composite are simple. Therefore the simple occupies a space. Now anything real that occupies a space comprises a manifold [of elements] outside one another and hence is composite; as a real composite, moreover, it is composed not from accidents (for these cannot without substance be outside one another) but, hence, from substances; therefore the simple would be a composite of substances—which is self-contradictory.

The second proposition of the antithesis—that nothing simple whatsoever exists in the world—is to mean no more here than this: the existence of the absolutely simple cannot be established from any experience or perception, whether outer or inner; and the absolutely simple is, therefore, a mere idea the objective reality of which can never be established in any possible experience, and which is hence without any application and object in the exposition of appearances. For let us assume that an object of experience could be found for this transcendental idea; then the empirical intuition of some object would have to be cognized as one containing absolutely no manifold [of elements] outside one another and combined into unity. Now from our not being conscious of such a manifold we cannot validly infer that such a manifold is entirely impossible in any intuition of an object; yet this impossibility is assuredly needed for absolute simplicity. Thus it follows that this simplicity cannot be inferred from any perception whatsoever. Since, therefore, nothing can ever be given as an absolutely simple object in any possible experience, but since the world of sense must be regarded as the sum of all possible experiences, nothing simple is given in it at all.

This second proposition of the antithesis goes much further than the first. The first proposition banishes the simple only from the intuition of the composite; the second, by contrast, removes the simple from all of nature—which is also the reason why we were able to prove this proposition not from the concept of a given object of outer intuition (of the composite), but only from the concept's relation to a possible experience as such.

Comment on The Second Antinomy

I.   On the Thesis   In talking about a whole that necessarily consists of simple parts I mean only a substantial whole—this being the composite proper, i.e., the contingent unity of the manifold that, *given separately* (at least in thought), is put into a reciprocal connection and thereby makes up a unity. Space should properly be called not a *compositum* but a *totum*, because its parts are possible only in the whole, not the whole through the parts. At most space could be called a *compositum ideale*, rather than *reale*. But this is mere subtlety. Space is not a composite made up of substances (not even from real accidents). Hence if I annul all composition in it, then nothing must remain, not even a point; for a

point is possible only as the limit of a space (hence of a composite). Therefore, space and time do not consist of simple parts. If something belongs only to the state of a substance, then—even if it has a magnitude (e.g., change)—it also does not consist of the simple; i.e., a certain degree of change does not come about by an accretion of many simple changes. Our inference from the composite to the simple holds only for self-subsistent things. But accidents of the state are not self-subsistent. Hence one can easily ruin the proof for the necessity of the simple, as the components of any substantive composite, and thereby ruin one's case as such: namely, if one extends the proof too far and tries to make it hold, without making a distinction, for anything composite— as has actually already happened repeatedly.

Besides, I am talking here only about the simple insofar as it is necessarily given in the composite— inasmuch as the composite can be resolved into the
simple as its components. The proper meaning of the term *monad* (according to Leibniz's use) should presumably apply only to the simple that is given *directly* as simple substance (e.g., in self-consciousness), rather than given as an element of the composite, which might better be called an *atomus*. And since it is only with regard to the composite that I wish to prove simple substances, as elements of the composite, I could call the thesis of the second antinomy transcendental atomism. However, inasmuch as this term has long since already been used to designate

II.   On the Antithesis   Against this proposition— whose basis of proof is merely mathematical—concerning an infinite division of matter, objections have been advanced by the *monadists*. These objections already arouse suspicion by the fact that the monadists refuse to accept the clearest mathematical proofs as being insights into the character of space—insofar as space is in fact the formal condition for the possibility of all matter—but they regard such proofs only as inferences from abstract but arbitrary concepts that could not be referred to actual things. The monadists downgrade these proofs as if, indeed, it were so much as possible to think up a different kind of intuition from the one that is given in the original intuition of space, and as if the *a priori* determinations of this space did not pertain simultaneously to whatever is possible only through the fact that it occupies this space. If we listened to them, then besides the mathematical point—which, although simple, is not a part but merely the limit of a space—we would have to think also physical points; these, although likewise simple, have the advantage that, as parts of space, they occupy it by their mere aggregation. Now, I shall not repeat here the common and clear refutations of this absurdity—since, indeed, the attempt by means of merely discursive concepts to subtly reason away the self-evidence of mathematics is entirely futile. I shall note only that if philosophy here
plays tricks with mathematics, then this happens only because philosophy forgets that in this question the concern is only with *appearances* and their conditions. Here, however, it is not enough that for the *understanding's concept* of the composite we find the concept of the simple. Rather, for the *intuition* of the composite (the intuition of matter) we must find the intuition of the simple; and this, according to laws of sensibility and hence also for objects of the senses, is entirely impossible. Hence for a whole composed from substances that is thought merely through the pure understanding it may indeed hold that we must, prior to any composition of this whole, have the simple; yet this does not hold for the *totum substantiale phaenomenon* (whole of phenomenal substances), which, as empirical intuition in space, carries with it the necessary property that no part of it is simple—because no part

a particular way of explaining bodily appearances (*moleculae*) and hence presupposes empirical concepts, the thesis may be called the dialectical principle of *monadology*.

of space is simple. The monadists, however, have been acute enough to try to evade this difficulty: namely, by presupposing not space as a condition for the possibility of objects of outer intuition (bodies), but instead these objects and the dynamical relation of substances in general as the condition for the possibility of space. Now, we have a concept of bodies only as appearances; as appearances, however, they necessarily presuppose space as the condition for the possibility of all outer appearances. Hence this subterfuge of the monadists is futile—and it has, indeed, been sufficiently cut down above, in the Transcendental Aesthetic. If bodies were things in themselves, then the proof of the monadists would indeed hold.

The second dialectical assertion has the peculiarity of having against it a dogmatic assertion that, among all subtly reasoning assertions, is the only one that undertakes to prove manifestly, in an object of experience, the actuality of what above we ascribed merely to transcendental ideas: namely, the absolute simplicity of substance. I mean the assertion that the object of inner sense, the *I* that thinks, is an absolutely simple substance. Now without here entering into this issue (since it has been examined more elaborately above), I shall note only this: that when we think something merely as an object without adding any synthetic determinations of its intuition (and this is, in fact, what we do through the entirely bare representation *I*), then of course we cannot perceive in such a representation anything manifold and any composition. Moreover, since the predicates through which I think this object are merely intuitions of inner sense, there also cannot occur in it anything that would prove a manifold [of elements] outside one another and hence prove real composition. Thus what prompts the mentioned assertion is only that our self-consciousness is such that, because the subject that thinks is simultaneously its own object, this subject cannot divide itself (although it can divide the determinations inhering in it); for in regard to itself any object is an absolute unity. Nonetheless, if this subject were to be contemplated *externally* as an object of intuition, then presumably it would in appearance manifest in itself composition. That, however, is how it must always be contemplated if we want to know whether or not there is in it a manifold [of elements] *outside* one another.

A443/ B471

## Third Conflict of Transcendental Ideas

**Thesis** Causality according to laws of nature is not the only causality from which the appearances of the world can thus one and all be derived. In order to explain these appearances, it is necessary to assume also a causality through freedom.

**Proof** Assume that there is no other causality than the one according to laws of nature. In that case, everything that *occurs* presupposes a previous state upon which it unfailingly follows according to a rule. The previous state, however, must itself be something that has occurred (has come to be in the time in which previously it was not); for if it had always existed, then its consequence also would always have existed and would not now first of all have arisen. Hence the cause's causality, through which something occurs, is itself something which has *occurred* and which, according to the laws of nature, again presupposes a previous state and its causality, but this state similarly presupposes a still earlier one, etc. Hence if everything occurs according to mere laws of nature, then
there is always only a subordinate but never a first beginning, and hence there then is on the side of the causes originating from one another no completeness of the series at all. The law of nature, however, consists precisely in this: that nothing occurs without a cause sufficiently determined *a priori*. Hence the proposition, in its unlimited universality, whereby any causality is possible only according to natural laws contradicts itself; and hence this causality cannot be assumed as being the only one.

Accordingly, we must assume a causality through which something occurs without its cause's being determined still further, according to necessary laws, by another, preceding cause. I.e., we must assume an *absolute spontaneity* of causes whereby they can begin *on their own* a series of appearances that runs according to natural laws—hence transcendental freedom—without which even in the course of nature the sequence of appearances on the side of the causes is never complete.

**Antithesis** There is no freedom, but everything in the world occurs solely according to laws of nature.

**Proof** Suppose there is, in the transcendental meaning of the term, a *freedom* as a special kind of causality according to which the events of the world could happen: namely, a power of absolutely beginning a state, and hence also of absolutely beginning a series of its consequences. In that case, not only will a series begin absolutely through this spontaneity, but the determination of this spontaneity itself to produce the series—i.e., the causality—will begin absolutely, so that there will be no antecedent by which this occurring action is determined according to constant laws. However, any beginning to act presupposes a state of the not yet acting cause; and a dynamically first beginning of action presupposes a state that has no connection of causality at all with the preceding state of the same cause, i.e., in no way results from that preceding state. Therefore, transcendental freedom runs counter to the causal law; and hence a
linkage of successive states of efficient causes according to which no unity of experience is possible—and which, therefore, is also not encountered in any experience—is an empty thought-entity

We have, therefore, nothing but *nature* as the place in which we must seek the coherence and order of events in the world. Freedom (independence) from the laws of nature is indeed a *liberation* from *constraint*, but also from the *guidance* of all rules. For one cannot say that instead of the laws of nature, laws of freedom enter into the causality of the course of nature, because if freedom were determined according to laws then it would not be freedom but would itself be nothing but nature. Hence nature and freedom differ as do law-governedness and lawlessness. Nature does indeed burden the understanding with the difficulty of seeking the origin of events ever higher up in the series of causes, because the causality in them is always conditioned; but for compensation it promises us thoroughgoing and law-governed unity of experience. The deception of freedom, however, does indeed promise to the investigating understanding a point of rest in the chain of causes, by leading it to an unconditioned causality that on its own starts to act; but, being blind itself, it disrupts the guidance of rules that alone makes possible an experience having thoroughgoing coherence.

## Comment on The Third Antinomy

A448/
B476

A449/
B477

I.   On the Thesis   The transcendental idea of freedom does not, indeed, amount to the entire content—which is in large part empirical—of the psychological concept of that name; rather, the transcendental idea's content is only the absolute spontaneity of action, as the proper basis for the action's imputability. But this idea is nonetheless the stumbling-block proper for philosophy, which finds insurmountable difficulties in granting such a kind of unconditioned causality. Hence what in the question about the freedom of the will has all along put speculative reason in a great quandary is—properly speaking—only *transcendental*, and concerns merely this: whether we must assume a power of beginning *spontaneously* a series of successive things or states. Being able to answer the question as to how such a power is possible is not equally necessary. For in the causality according to natural laws we must likewise settle for cognizing *a priori* that such a causality must be presupposed, even though we do not comprehend in any way the possibility according to which through a certain [thing's] existence the existence of another is posited, and must thus keep solely to experience. Now, to be sure, we have in fact established this necessity of a first beginning, issuing from freedom, only insofar as this is required for making comprehensible an origin of the world, whereas all subsequent states can be taken to be a succession according to mere natural laws. Yet, having once proved thereby (although not gained insight into) the power of beginning entirely spontaneously a series in time, we are now also permitted to let different series begin spontaneously, even in the midst of the course of the world, as regards [not time but] causality, and to attribute to their substances a faculty of acting from freedom. Here we must not let ourselves be

A450/
B478

II.   On the Antithesis   The defender of the omnipotence of nature (transcendental *physiocracy*) would, in opposing the doctrine of freedom, maintain his proposition against this doctrine's subtly reasoning inferences in the following manner. *If you do not assume in the world something mathematically first as regards time, then you also do not need to seek something dynamically first as regards causality.* Who told you to think up an absolutely first state of the world and hence an absolute beginning of the gradually passing series of appearances, and to set limits to an unbounded nature in order to provide your imagination with a resting-point? Since the substances in the world have always been—or since at least the unity of experience makes such a presupposition necessary—there is no difficulty in also assuming that the variation by the states of these substances, i.e., a series of their changes, has likewise always been, and that we therefore need not seek a first beginning, whether mathematical or dynamical.

The possibility of such an infinite origination, without a first member in regard to which everything else is merely subsequent, cannot be made comprehensible. But if you want therefore to dismiss this puzzle of nature, then you will find yourselves compelled to reject many basic synthetic characteristics (basic forces) that you are just as little able to comprehend, and even the possibility of a change as such must then become objectionable to you. For if you did not find through experience that change is actual, then you would never be able to excogitate *a priori* how such an unceasing sequence of being and not-being is possible.

A451/
B479

However, even if a transcendental faculty of freedom is perhaps conceded in order to begin the changes of the world, yet this faculty would at any detained, however, by a misunderstanding: namely, that because a successive series in the world can have only a comparatively first beginning, since a state of things in the world does always precede it, perhaps no absolutely first beginning of any series is possible during the course of the world. For we are here talking about an absolutely first beginning not as regards time but as regards causality. If (for example) I now get up from my chair completely freely and without the influence of natural causes, which is determinative necessarily, then in this event—along with its natural consequences *ad infinitum*—a new series begins absolutely, although as regards time this event is only the continuation of a preceding series. For this decision and act of mine do not lie at all in the succession of mere natural effects, and are not a mere continuation of them. Rather, as regards this happening of my decision and act, the determinative natural causes entirely cease prior to them; and although this happening follows upon the determinative natural causes, it does not result from them, and hence must be called—not, indeed, as regards time, but yet with regard to causality—an absolutely first beginning of a series of appearances.

Reason's need to appeal, in the series of natural causes, to a first beginning issuing from freedom is confirmed with great clarity by the fact that (except for the Epicurean School) all the philosophers of antiquity found themselves constrained, in order to explain the world's motions, to assume a *prime mover*, i.e., a freely acting cause that first and on its own began this series of states. For they did not undertake to make a first beginning comprehensible from mere nature.

rate have to be solely outside the world (although to assume, outside of the sum of all possible intuitions, a further object that cannot be given in any possible perception always remains so bold a presumption). But to attribute such a faculty to substances in the world itself cannot be permitted on any account. For then the coherence of appearances determining one another necessarily according to universal laws—which is called nature—would for the most part vanish, and along with it so would the mark of empirical truth which distinguishes experience from a dream. For alongside such a lawless faculty of freedom, nature can scarcely be thought any more, because the laws of nature are altered incessantly by the influences of freedom, and the play of appearances—which according to mere nature would be regular and uniform—is thereby rendered confused and incoherent. [ . . . ]

A497/   Section VII. Critical Decision of the Cosmo-
B525   logical Dispute That Reason Has with Itself

The entire antinomy of pure reason rests on this dialectical argument: If the conditioned is given, then
the entire series of all its conditions is also given;
now objects of the senses are given to us as conditioned; consequently, etc. Now through this syllogism, whose major premise seems so natural and
evident, as many cosmological ideas are introduced
as there are different conditions (in the synthesis of
appearances), insofar as these conditions make up a
series. The cosmological ideas postulate the absolute
totality of these series, and precisely thereby put reason inevitably in conflict with itself. But before we
uncover what is deceptive in this specious argument,
B526  we must enable ourselves to do so by correcting and
making determinate certain concepts occurring in it.

*First*, the following proposition is clear and indu-
A498  bitably certain: that if the conditioned is given, then
precisely thereby a regression in the series of all conditions for this conditioned is **assigned** to us. For the
very concept of the conditioned implies that through
this concept something is referred to a condition;
and if this condition is in turn conditioned, then that
something is referred to a more remote condition,
and thus is referred through all the members of the
series. The above proposition, therefore, is analytic
and rises above any fear from a transcendental critique. It is a logical postulate of reason, namely, to
pursue and as far as possible extend, by means of the
understanding, that connection of a concept with its
conditions which attaches to the very concept itself.

*Furthermore*, if both the conditioned and its condition are things in themselves, and if the conditioned has been given, then not merely is the regression to the condition *assigned*, but this condition is
thereby actually already given with the conditioned.
And since this holds for all members of the series,
the complete series of conditions—and hence also
the unconditioned—is given, or, rather, presupposed, simultaneously through the fact that the
conditioned, which was possible only through that
series, is given. Here the synthesis of the conditioned
with its condition is a synthesis of the mere understanding, which represents things *as they are* without

considering whether and how we can attain a cog- B527
nition of them. Appearances, by contrast, are mere A499
representations, and as such are not given at all unless I attain cognition of them (i.e., unless I attain
the appearances themselves, for they are nothing but
empirical cognitions). Hence if I deal with appearances then I cannot say, in the same meaning of the
term, that if the conditioned is given then all conditions for it (as appearances) are also given, and hence
I can in no way infer the absolute totality of the series
of these conditions. For *appearances* themselves are,
in apprehension, nothing but an empirical synthesis
(in space and time) and hence are given only *in this
synthesis*. Now it does not follow at all that if the conditioned is given (in appearance), then the synthesis
amounting to its empirical condition is thereby also
given with it and presupposed; rather, this synthesis
first occurs in the regression, and never without it.
What we can indeed say in such a case, however, is
that a *regression* to the conditions, i.e., that a continued empirical synthesis on this side is dictated or
*assigned* to us, and that there can be no lack of conditions given through this regression.

This shows that the major premise of the cosmological syllogism takes the conditioned in the
transcendental meaning of a pure category, but the
minor premise takes it in the empirical meaning of B528
a concept of the understanding applied to mere appearances. Therefore, we find in this syllogism the
dialectical deception called *sophisma figurae dictionis*. This deception, however, is not contrived, but is A500
a quite natural delusion of common reason. For by
this delusion, if something is given as conditioned,
then (in the major premise) we presuppose the conditions and their series—*uninspected*, as it were.
For to do this is nothing other than [to satisfy] the
logical demand to assume complete premises for a
given conclusion; and here no time order is to be
found in the connection of the conditioned with its
condition, but they are presupposed in themselves,
as given *simultaneously*. Furthermore, it is equally
natural (in the minor premise) to regard appearances
as things in themselves and likewise as objects given
to the mere understanding—as was done in the major premise, where I abstracted from all conditions

of intuition under which alone objects can be given. In this we have, however, overlooked a noteworthy distinction between the concepts. The synthesis of the conditioned with its condition—and the entire series of conditions—carried with it (in the major premise) nothing about limitation by time, and no concept of succession. On the other hand, the empirical synthesis—and the series of conditions in appearance—(which in the minor premise is subsumed [under the major]) is necessarily given successively and only in time, i.e., sequentially. Hence here I was not able to presuppose, as I was there, the absolute *totality* of the synthesis and of the series B529 represented through this synthesis. For there all the members of the series are given in themselves (without time condition), but here they are possible only A501 through the successive regression, which is given only by actually being carried out.

After having been convicted of such a slip in the argument that they jointly laid at the basis (of their cosmological assertions), both disputing parties may rightly be dismissed, as parties whose demand is based on no well-founded title. But although they did not know how to build their conclusions on sturdy bases of proof, their quarrel is not yet ended thereby in the respect that both or either of them has been shown to be wrong in the asserted matter itself (the conclusion). After all, nothing seems clearer than that if one of two persons asserts that the world has a beginning and the other asserts that the world has no beginning but has been there from eternity, then surely one must be right. Yet if that is so, then, because the clarity is the same on both sides, there is no possibility of ever ascertaining which side is in the right, and the dispute continues as before even though at the tribunal of reason the parties have been ordered to silence. Thus no remedy remains for ending the dispute thoroughly and to the satisfaction of both parties, except finally to show that—since, after all, they A502/ can so nicely refute each other—they are disputing B530 about nothing, and that a certain transcendental illusion has painted for them an actuality where none is to be found. Let us now enter upon this path on which a dispute that defies a verdict can be settled.

The *Eleatic philosopher Zeno*, a subtle dialectician, was severely rebuked as a mischievous sophist already by *Plato* because—to show his artistry—he sought to prove a proposition by plausible arguments and soon after to overturn the same proposition again by other arguments equally strong. Zeno asserted that God (this God presumably was for him nothing but the world) is neither finite nor infinite, neither in motion nor at rest, neither similar nor dissimilar to any other thing. To those who judged Zeno on this procedure he seemed to want entirely to deny two propositions contradicting each other—which is absurd. I believe, however, that he cannot rightly be charged with this. The first of these propositions I shall soon examine more closely. As for the others, if by the word *God* Zeno meant the universe, then he did indeed have to say that this universe neither is permanently present in its location (at rest) nor changes its location (moves), because all locations are only in the universe and hence *the universe* itself is in no location. Likewise, if the universe comprises all that exists, then it is to that extent also neither similar nor dissimilar to any *other thing*, because there A503/ is apart from it *no other thing* to which it could be B531 compared. If two judgments that are opposed to each other presuppose an inadmissible condition, then despite the conflict between them (which, however, is not a contradiction proper) both of them drop out, because the condition drops out under which alone each of these propositions was to hold.

If someone were to say that any body either smells good or smells not good, then there is a third alternative, namely, that the body does not smell (emit an odor) at all; and thus both of the conflicting propositions can be false. If I say that any body either is good-smelling or is not good-smelling (*vel suaveolens vel non suaveolens*), then the two judgments are opposed to each other contradictorily and only the first one is false, while its contradictory opposite—namely, that some bodies are not good-smelling—comprises also those bodies *that do not smell at all*. In the previous opposition (*per disparata*), the contingent condition of the concept of bodies (smell) still *remained* in the conflicting judgment and therefore was not also annulled by it; hence this latter judgment was not the contradictory opposite of the former judgment.

Accordingly, if I say that, as regards space, either the world is infinite or it is not infinite (*non est infinitus*), then if the first proposition is false, its contradictory opposite, that the world is not infinite, must be true. By this [negative proposition] I would only A504/ annul an infinite world, without positing another B532 world, namely, the finite one. But if I said that the world is either infinite or finite (noninfinite), then both of these propositions can be false. For I then regard the world as in itself determined in terms of magnitude, because in the counterproposition I do not merely annul the infinity, and with it perhaps the entire separate existence of the world; rather, I add a determination to the world taken as a thing that is actual in itself, and this may likewise be false, namely, if the world were *not* given *as a thing in itself at all* and hence also not in terms of its magnitude—neither as infinite nor as finite. Permit me to call this sort of opposition *dialectical* but that of contradiction *analytical opposition*. Thus of two dialectically opposed judgments both can be false, because one judgment not merely contradicts the other but says something more than is required for contradiction.

If one regards the two propositions, that the world is infinite in magnitude and that the world is finite in magnitude, as opposed to each other contradictorily, then one assumes that the world (the entire series of appearances) is a thing in itself. For the world remains, whether I annul in the series of its appearances the infinite or the finite regression. But if I remove this presupposition—or this transcendental illusion—and deny that the world is a thing A505/ in itself, then the contradictory conflict of the two B533 assertions is transformed into a merely dialectical one; and because the world does not exist in itself at all (i.e., independently of the regressive series of my representations), it exists neither as *a whole that is infinite in itself* nor *as a whole that is finite in itself*. The world is to be met with only in the empirical regression of the series of appearances, and not at all by itself. If, therefore, this series is always conditioned, then it is never given wholly; and hence the world is not an unconditioned whole, and thus also

does not exist as such a whole—neither with infinite nor with finite magnitude.

What has been said here about the first cosmological idea, namely, that of the absolute totality of magnitude in [the realm of] appearance, holds also for all the other cosmological ideas. The series of conditions is to be met with only in the regressive series itself, but not [as existing] in itself in appearance considered as a thing of its own given prior to all regression. Hence I shall also have to say that the multitude of parts in a given appearance is in itself neither finite nor infinite. For appearance is nothing that exists in itself, and the parts are first given by, and in, the regression of the decomposing synthesis, a regression that is never given in absolute *entirety*— neither as finite nor as infinite. The same holds for the series of causes superordinated to one another, A506/ or the series of the conditioned existence up to the B534 unconditionally necessary existence. Here again this series can never be regarded as being in itself, as to its totality, either finite or infinite. For as a series of subordinated representations it consists only in the dynamical regression; prior to this regression, however, and as a series of things in themselves that subsists by itself, it cannot exist at all.

Thus the antinomy of pure reason with pure reason's cosmological ideas is removed: namely, by showing that it is merely dialectical, and is a conflict due to an illusion that arises because the idea of absolute totality, which holds only as a condition of things in themselves, has been applied to appearances, which exist only in our representation and—if they make up a series—in the successive regression, but otherwise do not exist at all. However, conversely, we can also draw from this antinomy a true benefit that, although not a dogmatic one, is yet a critical and doctrinal benefit: namely, we can by this antinomy prove indirectly the transcendental ideality of appearances—in case, perhaps, someone were not satisfied with the direct proof provided in the Transcendental Aesthetic. This indirect proof would consist in the following dilemma. If the world is a whole existing in itself, then it is either finite or infinite. Now, both of these alternatives are false (according to the proofs, adduced above, A507/ of the thesis and antithesis, respectively). Hence it is B535 also false that the world (the sum of all appearances) is a whole existing in itself. From this it follows, then, that appearances as such are nothing apart from our representations—which is precisely what we meant by their transcendental ideality.

This comment is important. It shows that the above proofs of the fourfold antinomy were not deceptions but were well-founded. They were well-founded, namely, on the presupposition that appearances, or the world of sense comprising them all, are things in themselves. The conflict of the propositions drawn from these proofs reveals, however, that there is a falsehood in the presupposition, and thereby leads us to discover the true character of things as objects of the senses. Hence the dialectic by no means promotes skepticism. But it does promote the skeptical method, which can display the dialectic as an example of the method's great benefit: namely, when we let the arguments of reason come forward against each other in their greatest freedom; for although these arguments ultimately do not supply what we were searching for, yet they will always supply something beneficial and useful for correcting our judgments.

A508/
B536

## Section VIII. Pure Reason's Regulative Principle regarding the Cosmological Ideas

Since through the cosmological principle of totality no maximum of the series of conditions in a world of sense considered as a thing in itself is *given*, but such a maximum can merely be *assigned* to us in the regression of the series, this principle of pure reason, with its meaning corrected in this manner, still retains all its validity—although not as an *axiom* for thinking the totality as actual in the object. The principle retains its validity, rather, as a *problem* for the understanding, and hence for the subject: namely, to perform and continue, in accordance with the completeness in the idea, the regression in the series of conditions for a given conditioned. For in sensibility, i.e., in space and time, any condition that we can reach in the exposition of given appearances is in turn conditioned, because these appearances are not objects in themselves—in which the absolutely unconditioned might, perhaps, occur. These appearances are, rather, merely empirical representations; and these must always find their

condition, which determines them as regards space or time, in intuition. Hence the cosmological principle of reason is, in fact, only a *rule* that commands us to perform, in the series of conditions of given appearances, a regression that is never permitted to stop at anything absolutely unconditioned. It is, therefore, not a principle for the possibility of experience and of the empirical cognition of objects of the senses, and hence it is not a principle of the understanding; for every experience is enclosed (in accordance with the given intuition) within its bounds. Nor is this cosmological principle a *constitutive* principle of reason for expanding the concept of the world of sense beyond all possible experience. Rather, it is a principle of the greatest possible continuation and expansion of experience, whereby no empirical limit must count as absolute. Thus it is a principle of reason that, *as rule*, postulates what is to be done by us in the regression, and *does not anticipate* what is given in itself in the *object* prior to all regression. I therefore call this cosmological principle a *regulative* principle of reason. By contrast, the principle of the absolute totality of the series of conditions considered as given in the objects (the appearances) in themselves would be a constitutive cosmological principle. The invalidity of this latter principle I wanted to indicate precisely by this distinction, and wanted thereby to prevent what otherwise inevitably occurs: our attributing (by transcendental subreption) objective reality to an idea that serves merely as a rule.

A509/
B537

Now in order properly to define the meaning of this rule of pure reason, we must note, first of all, that this rule cannot tell us *what the object is*, but only *how the empirical regression is to be performed* in order for us to arrive at the complete concept of the object. For if the rule told us what the object is, then it would be a constitutive principle, and obtaining such a principle from pure reason is impossible. By this rule, therefore, we can in no way intend to mean that the series of conditions for a given conditioned is in itself finite or infinite. For then we would by a mere idea of absolute totality—a totality that is provided only in the idea itself—think an object that cannot be given in any experience; for we would confer on a series of appearances an objective reality

A510/
B538

independent of the empirical synthesis. Hence the rational idea will prescribe a rule only to the regressive synthesis in the series of conditions; according to that rule this synthesis proceeds from the conditioned, by means of all the conditions subordinated to one another, to the unconditioned—although this unconditioned is never reached, for the absolutely unconditioned is not found in experience at all.

Now to this end we must first accurately define the synthesis of a series insofar as this synthesis is never complete. For this aim, people usually employ two expressions that are intended to distinguish something in this synthesis, yet they do so without quite being able to indicate the basis of this distinction. A511/ B539 Mathematicians speak solely of a *progressus in infinitum*. In its place, those who investigate concepts (philosophers) want to accept only the expression of a *progressus in indefinitum*. Without lingering upon an examination of the perplexity that has commended to them this distinction of two progressions, and upon the distinction's good or fruitless use, I want to try to define these two concepts accurately in reference to my aim.

Of a straight line we may rightly say that it can be extended to infinity, and here the distinction of an infinite and an indeterminably long progression (*progressus indefinitum*) would be an empty subtlety. To be sure, if one says, 'Continue drawing a line', then it is indeed more correct to add *in indefinitum* than to say *in infinitum*. For the first means no more than, 'Extend the line as far as *you want*', but the second means, '*You shall* never stop extending it' (which, of course, is not the aim here). Nevertheless, if only what *can* be done is at issue, then the first expression is quite correct; for you can go on augmenting the line to infinity. And so is it also in all cases where one speaks not of the *regressus* but only of the *progressus*, i.e., of the progression from the condition to the conditioned; in the series of appearances this possible progression proceeds to infinity. From a pair of parents you can progress without end in the descending A512/ B540 line of procreation, and you can quite readily think that the line actually progresses thus in the world. For here reason never requires absolute totality of the series, because it does not presuppose such totality

of the series as a condition and as *given* (*datum*), but presupposes it only as something conditioned that is only alleged and givable (*dabile*) and is added to without end.

But the situation is quite different with the problem concerning regression: How far does the regression extend that ascends in a series from the given conditioned to the conditions? Can I say that it is a **regression to infinity**, or only that it is a regression extending *indeterminably far* (*in indefinitum*)? Hence can I ascend from the now living human beings, in the series of their progenitors, to infinity? Or can I say only that, no matter how far I have gone back, I have never encountered an empirical basis for regarding the series as limited somewhere, and thus for each of the forefathers I am entitled and also obligated to go on locating—although indeed not presupposing— his ancestor also?

In answer to these questions I say this: (a) If the whole has been given in empirical intuition, then the regression in the series of the whole's internal conditions proceeds to infinity. (b) If [the regression is not one of decomposition,] however, i.e., if only a member of the series is given and the regression is first of all to proceed from this member to absolute totality, then there takes place only a regression to A513/ an undetermined distance (*in indefinitum*). Hence B541 the division of some matter given between its bounds (i.e., a body) must be said to proceed to infinity. For this matter is given as a whole, and consequently with all its possible parts, in empirical intuition. But the condition of this whole is its part, and the condition of this part is the part of the part, etc.; and in this regression of decomposition an unconditioned (indivisible) member of this series of conditions is never encountered. Therefore, not only is there nowhere an empirical basis for stopping in the division, but the further members of the division that is to be continued are themselves empirically given prior to this continuing division; i.e., the division proceeds to infinity. By contrast, the series of progenitors for a given human being is not given in its absolute totality in any possible experience. But the regression still proceeds from each member of this [series of] procreation to a higher member, so that no empirical limit is to be encountered that would exhibit a member as absolutely unconditioned. Nevertheless, since even the members that might provide the condition for such [exhibition of a member as absolutely unconditioned] do not already lie, prior to the regression, in the empirical intuition of the whole, the regression proceeds not to infinity (in dividing the given) but to an indeterminable distance in locating further members for the given ones, and these further members are always given in turn only as conditioned.

A514/ B542    In neither of the two cases, the *regressus in infinitum* and the *regressus in indefinitum*, is the series of conditions regarded as being given as infinite in the object. These conditions are not things that are given in themselves, but only appearances, which are given as conditions of one another only in the regression itself. Hence the question no longer is how large this series of conditions is in itself, i.e., whether it is finite or infinite; for the series is nothing in itself. The question is, rather, how we are to perform the empirical regression, and how far we are to continue it. And here there is indeed a notable difference regarding the rule for this advance. If the whole has been given empirically, then it is *possible* to go back *to infinity* in the series of the whole's internal conditions. However, if the whole is not given but is to be given only through empirical regression, then I can say only that it is *possible* to proceed to still higher conditions of the series *to infinity* . In the first case I was able to say that always more members are there, and are empirically given, than I reach through the regression (of decomposition). But in the second case I am able to say only that I can always proceed still further in the regression, because no member is empirically given as absolutely unconditioned, and thus any member always still admits a higher member as possible, and hence admits as necessary the inquiry about it. In the first case it was necessary to *encounter* further members; in the second, however, it is necessary always to *inquire* about further members, because no experience limits anything absolutely. For either you have no perception that limits your empirical regression absolutely; and then you must not regard your regression as completed. Or you do have such a perception that limits your series; and then this

A515/ B543

perception cannot be a part of the series that you have traversed (because what *limits* must be distinguished from *what is limited* by it); and thus you must continue your regression still further to this condition also, and so on.

The following section will put these remarks in their proper light by applying them.

## Section IX. On the Empirical Use of the Regulative Principle of Reason in Regard to All Cosmological Ideas

There is, as we have shown repeatedly, no transcendental use of pure concepts either of the understanding or of reason. The absolute totality of the series of conditions in the world of sense is based solely on a transcendental use of reason that demands this unconditioned completeness from what it presupposes as being a thing in itself. The world of sense, however, does not contain such completeness. Therefore, the issue can never again be the absolute magnitude of the series that in the world of sense, i.e., whether they may be limited or *in themselves* unlimited. Rather, the issue can only be how far back, in tracing experience to its conditions, we are to go in the empirical regression in order that—in accordance with the rule of reason—we may stop at no other answer to reason's questions than one that is commensurate with the object.

A516/ B544

Hence what alone remains for us is the *validity of the principle of reason* taken only as a rule of the *continuation* and magnitude of a possible experience—the principle's invalidity as a constitutive principle of appearances [taken as things] in themselves having been established sufficiently. Moreover, if we can beyond doubt display that validity of the principle taken as such a rule, reason's dispute with itself is wholly ended. For not only have we, through this critical solution, annulled the illusion that put reason at variance with itself; but, in its place, we are disclosing the sense in which reason agrees with itself and the misinterpretation of which alone prompted the dispute, and are thus transforming what would otherwise be only a *dialectical* principle into a *doctrinal* one. Indeed, if this principle can be verified in its subjective signification, whereby it is to determine the understanding's greatest possible use in experience commensurately with the objects of experience, then this is to achieve just as much as if, like an axiom, the principle determined objects in themselves *a priori* (which is impossible from pure reason). For even such *a priori* determination could have, in regard to objects of experience, no greater influence on the expansion and correction of our cognition than would actively manifest itself in the most extensive experiential use of our understanding.

I. Solution of the Cosmological Idea of the Totality of Composition of Appearances of a World Whole
Here, as with the remaining cosmological questions, the basis of the regulative principle of reason is this proposition: that in empirical regression we can encounter *no experience of an absolute limit*, and hence no experience of any condition as one that is *absolutely unconditioned empirically*. The basis of this, however, is that such an experience would have to contain a limiting of appearances by nothing, or the void, [as something] that the continued regression could come upon by means of a perception—which is impossible.

Now this proposition, which says as much as that in empirical regression I always arrive only at a condition that must itself be regarded in turn as empirically conditioned, contains this rule *in terminis*: that however far I may have got with this inquiry in the ascending series, I must always inquire about a still higher member of the series, whether or not I become acquainted with this member through experience.

Now nothing further is needed for the solution of the first cosmological problem than to establish also whether, in the regression to the unconditioned magnitude of the world whole (as regards time and space), this never limited ascent can be called (a) a *regression to infinity* or (b) only an *indeterminably continued regression* (*in indefinitum*).

The mere general representation of the series of all past states of the world, as well as that of the series of all things that are simultaneous in cosmic space, is itself nothing but a possible empirical regression that I think, although still indeterminately; and only through this possible regression can there arise the concept of such a series of conditions for the given perception.[24] Now, I have the world whole always only in concept, and by no means (as a whole) in intuition. Hence I cannot from that whole's magnitude infer the magnitude of the regression and determine the regression's magnitude in accordance with that of the world; rather, I must frame a concept of the world's magnitude in the first place through the magnitude of the empirical regression. But of this regression I never know anything more than that from any given member of the series of conditions I must always proceed empirically to a still higher (more remote) member. Therefore, the magnitude of the whole of appearances is not thereby determined absolutely at all. Hence we also cannot say that this regression proceeds to infinity. For saying this would anticipate the members not yet reached by the regression, and would represent their multitude as so great that it could not be reached by any empirical synthesis, and consequently would *determine* (although only negatively) the world's magnitude prior to the regression—which is impossible. For prior to the regression this [world] is not (as regards its totality) given to me at all; nor, therefore, is its magnitude. Accordingly, we cannot say anything at all about the world's magnitude in itself, not even that there occurs in the world a regression *in infinitum*, but we must merely search for the concept of the world's magnitude according to the rule that determines the empirical regression in the world. This rule, however, says no more than that however far we may have got in the series of empirical conditions, we are not to assume an absolute limit anywhere, but are to subordinate every appearance, as conditioned, to another as its condition, and hence are to proceed onward to this condition; and this is the regression *in indefinitum*, which, because it determines no magnitude

A517/
B545

A518/
B546

A519/
B547

A520/
B548

---

24. Hence, by the same token, this world series cannot be either larger or smaller than the possible empirical regression on which alone its concept rests. And since this regression cannot give to us any determinate infinite, but just as little anything determinately finite (absolutely limited), we clearly cannot assume the world's magnitude either as finite or as infinite, because the regression (through which this magnitude is presented) permits neither of the two.

in the object, can be distinguished distinctly enough from the regression *in infinitum*.

Therefore, I cannot say that the world is *infinite* as regards past time or as regards space; for such a concept of magnitude as a given infinity is empirical, and hence is also absolutely impossible in regard to the world taken as an object of the senses. Nor shall I say that the regression from a given perception onward to all that limits it in a series, both in space and in past time, proceeds to *infinity*; for saying this presupposes the world's magnitude to be infinite. Nor shall I say that this regression is *finite*; for an absolute limit is likewise empirically impossible. I shall, therefore, be unable to say anything about the whole object of experience (the world of sense), but shall be able to say something only about the rule according to which experience is to be engaged in, and continued, commensurately with its object.

Hence the first and negative answer to the cosmological question concerning the world's magnitude is this: the world has no first beginning as regards time and no outermost limit as regards space.

For in the opposite case the world would be limited by empty time, on the one hand, and by empty space, on the other. Now since the world as appearance cannot in itself be bounded in either of the two ways, because appearance is not a thing in itself, there would have to be possible a perception of limiting by absolutely empty time or space through which these ends of the world would be given in a possible experience. Such an experience, however, being completely empty of content, is impossible. Therefore, an absolute limit of the world is impossible empirically, and hence also absolutely.

From this, then, there follows simultaneously the *affirmative* answer: the regression in the series of the world's appearances, as a determination of the world's magnitude, proceeds *in indefinitum*. This is equivalent to saying: the world of sense has no absolute magnitude; rather, the empirical regression (through which alone the world can be given on the side of its conditions) has its rule, namely, that from any member in the series, as a conditioned member, we are always to advance (whether by our own experience, or the guide of history, or the chain of effects and their

A521/ B549

A522/ B550

causes) to a still more remote member, and are not to refrain anywhere from expanding the possible use of our understanding—this expansion being, indeed, reason's proper and sole task with its principles.

This rule does not prescribe a determinate empirical regression that continues ceaselessly in a certain kind of appearances. E.g., it does not prescribe that from a living human being we must always ascend in a series of progenitors without expecting a first pair; or that in the series of cosmic bodies we must always ascend without admitting an outermost sun. Rather, the rule commands only the advance from appearances to appearances, even if these were not to yield any actual perception (if, namely, the perception is too weak in degree to become experience for our consciousness); for these appearances do nonetheless belong to possible experience.

Any beginning is in time, and any limit of what is extended is in space. Space and time, however, are only in the world of sense. Hence only appearances *in the world* are conditionally limited, but *the world* itself is limited neither in a conditioned nor in an unconditioned way.

Precisely on this account, and because the world can never *be given wholly* and even the series of conditions for a given conditioned cannot, as world series, *be given wholly*, the concept of the world's magnitude is given only through the regression, and not prior to it in a collective intuition. This regression, however, always consists only in the [continued] *determining* of the magnitude. Therefore, it yields no *determinate* concept, and hence also no concept of a magnitude that would with respect to a certain [unit of] measure be infinite. The regression, therefore, does not proceed to infinity (as given, as it were), but proceeds to an undetermined distance, in order to yield a magnitude (of experience) which first becomes actual through this regression.

A523/ B551

II. Solution of the Cosmological Idea of the Totality of Division of a Whole Given in Intuition   If I divide a whole that is given in intuition, then I proceed from something conditioned to the conditions of its possibility. The division of the parts (*subdivisio* or *decompositio*) is a regression in the series of these conditions. The absolute totality of this *series* would be given only if the regression could reach *simple* parts. But if all the parts of a continuously progressing decomposition are always in turn divisible, then the division—i.e., the regression from the conditioned to its conditions—proceeds *in infinitum*. For the conditions (the parts) are contained in the conditioned itself; and since the conditioned is wholly given in an intuition that is enclosed between its limits, the conditions are one and all given with it also. Hence the regression must not be called merely a regression *in indefinitum*, as we were permitted to call the previous cosmological idea only. In the previous case I was to proceed from the conditioned to its conditions; but there the conditions were given outside the conditioned, and hence they were not given through the conditioned and simultaneously with it, but were first added in the empirical regression. Despite this, however, we are by no means permitted to say of such a whole which is divisible to infinity that *it consists of infinitely many parts*. For although the intuition of the whole contains all the parts, it yet does *not* contain the *whole division*; this division consists only in the progressing decomposition, or in the regression itself that first makes the series actual. Now since this regression is infinite, all the members (parts) that it reaches are indeed contained in the given whole taken as an *aggregate*; but it does not contain the whole *series of the division*, which is infinite successively and never *whole* and hence can exhibit no infinite multitude of parts and no gathering together of such a multitude in a whole. This general notice can quite readily be applied, first, to space. Any space intuited within its limits is a *whole* such that its parts are, in any decomposition, always in turn spaces; and hence any such space is divisible to infinity.

From this the second application of the notice follows quite naturally: namely, to an outer appearance enclosed within limits (body). The divisibility of such an appearance is based on the divisibility of space, for space amounts to the possibility of a body as an extended whole. Hence a body is divisible to infinity, yet without therefore consisting of infinitely many parts.

It seems, to be sure, that because a body must be represented in space as being a substance, it will be different from space as regards the law of the divisibility of space. For we may surely admit at least this difference: Decomposition can never remove all composition in space; for all space, which otherwise has nothing independent about it, would then cease to be (which is impossible). However, the claim that if all composition in matter were annulled in thought then nothing at all would remain seems not to be reconcilable with the concept of a substance; for a substance properly ought to be the subject of all composition, and would have to remain in its elements even if the connection of these elements in space, whereby they amount to a body, were annulled. However, what would indeed be thought [thus] concerning a thing in itself, through a pure concept of the understanding, is not the case with what is called substance in [the realm of] appearance. This substance is not an absolute subject; it is, rather, a permanent image belonging to sensibility and is nothing but intuition, in which nothing unconditioned whatsoever is to be met with.

But although this rule of advance to infinity does without any doubt have its place in the subdivision of an appearance as a mere occupying of space, yet the rule cannot hold if we want to extend it also to the multitude of parts that—in the given whole—are already separated in a certain way so as to make up a *quantum discretum*. To assume that in every structured (organized) whole each part is structured in turn, and that thus in dissecting the parts to infinity one always encounters new artful[ly structured] parts—in a word, that the whole is structured to infinity: this assumption is quite unthinkable, even though the alternative assumption that the parts of matter could to infinity become structured in their decomposition is indeed thinkable. For the infinity of the division of a given appearance in space is based solely on the fact that what is given through this appearance is merely [its] divisibility, i.e., merely a multitude of parts that in itself is absolutely indeterminate, whereas the parts themselves are given and determined only through the subdivision—in short, the fact that the whole is not in itself already divided. Hence in this whole the division can determine a multitude of parts that will go as far as one wants to advance in

A524/B552

A525/B553

A526/B554

the regression of division. In the case of an organic body structured to infinity, however, the whole is—

A527/ precisely through this concept of an organic body—
B555 already represented as divided, and one [conceives that one] encounters in it, prior to any regression of division, a multitude of parts that is in itself determinate but also infinite—and thereby one contradicts oneself. For this infinite involution is regarded as a series never to be completed (i.e., as infinite), and yet also—when gathered together—as nonetheless completed. Infinite division characterizes only appearance as *quantum continuum*, and is inseparable from the occupation of space; for precisely in this occupation lies the basis of infinite divisibility. But as soon as something is assumed as *quantum discretum*, then the multitude of units in it is determinate and hence, by the same token, is always equal to some number. Therefore, only experience can establish how far the organization in a structured body may go; and even if [actual] experience were certain to reach no inorganic part, yet such parts must lie at least in possible experience. But how far the transcendental division of an appearance as such extends is not a matter of experience at all, but is governed by a principle of reason whereby the empirical regression in the decomposition of what is extended is, in accordance with the nature of this appearance, never to be regarded as absolutely completed.

A528/ Concluding Comment on the Solution of the
B556 Mathematical-Transcendental Ideas, and Advance Notice on the Solution of the Dynamical-Transcendental Ideas   We presented the antinomy of pure reason, through all the transcendental ideas, in a table. We also indicated the basis of this conflict and the only remedy for removing it, which consisted in declaring both the opposed assertions to be false. In doing all this, we everywhere represented the conditions as belonging to their conditioned according to relations of space and time, which is the usual presupposition of the common human understanding; and so this conflict was indeed based entirely on that presupposition. In this respect all the dialectical representations of totality in the series of conditions for a given conditioned were indeed throughout of the same *kind*. There was always a series, and in it the condition and the conditioned were connected as members of this series and were thereby *homogeneous*. And thus the regression always had to be thought as uncompleted; or, if it was to be thought as completed, then a member that was in itself conditioned must falsely be assumed to be a first member and hence to be unconditioned. Therefore, although in all cases the object, i.e., the conditioned, was not A529/ considered merely according to its magnitude, yet B557 the series of conditions for this object was considered merely in this way. And thus the difficulty, which could be removed by no settlement but only by entirely severing the knot, consisted in reason's making the series either *too long* or *too short* for the understanding, so that the understanding could never match reason's idea.

In all this we did, however, overlook an essential difference obtaining among the objects—i.e., the concepts of the understanding—that reason endeavors to raise to ideas; for according to our table of categories provided above, two of the categories signify a *mathematical* but the other two a *dynamical* synthesis of appearances. Up to this point we could, indeed, quite readily afford to overlook this difference. For just as in the general representation of all the transcendental ideas we always remained subject to conditions *in appearance*, so in the two mathematical-transcendental ideas we also had no other *object* than the one in appearance. Now, however, we proceed to *dynamical* concepts of the understanding insofar as these are to fit the idea of reason; and here this distinction becomes important, and opens up for us an entirely new outlook concerning the contest in which reason is embroiled. For previously this contest was *dismissed* as built, on both sides, on false pre-A530/ suppositions. But now, in the dynamical antinomy, B558 perhaps there occurs a presupposition that can coexist with reason's pretension; and from this point of view, and with the judge compensating for the lack of legal bases that were mistaken on both sides, the contest can be *settled* to the satisfaction of both parties—which could not be done with the dispute in the mathematical antinomy.

The series of conditions are indeed homogeneous insofar as we take account only of their *extent*: i.e., of whether they are commensurate with the idea, or whether the ideas are too large or too small for those series. However, the concept of the understanding that underlies these ideas may contain either only a *synthesis of the homogeneous* (this homogeneous is presupposed with any magnitude, in both the composition and division thereof), or a *synthesis of the heterogeneous* this heterogeneous can at least be admitted in the dynamical synthesis, i.e., the synthesis of both the causal linkage and the linkage of the necessary with the contingent.

Hence in the case of the mathematical connection of the series of appearances none but a *sensible* condition can come in, i.e., a condition that is itself a part of the series. The dynamical series of sensible conditions, by contrast, does also admit of a heterogeneous condition that is not part of the series but, *as merely intelligible*, lies outside the series. Thus reason is satisfied; for the unconditioned is put prior to appearances, and yet the series of appearances, as always conditioned, is not thereby confused and—contrary to the principles of the understanding—cut off.

A531/ B559

Now because the dynamical ideas admit of a condition of appearances that lies outside the series of these, i.e., a condition that is not itself appearance, something occurs here that is entirely different from the result of the mathematical antinomy. For the mathematical antinomy caused the result that both dialectical counterassertions had to be declared false. By contrast, in the dynamical series the thoroughly conditioned—which is inseparable from these series as appearances—can be connected with the condition which, although empirically unconditioned, is also *nonsensible*. As so connected, this thoroughly conditioned can satisfy the *understanding*, on the one hand, and *reason*, on the other.[25] Thus the dialectical arguments that in one way or another sought unconditioned totality in mere appearances drop

A532/ B560

out; and hence the propositions of reason—in their signification as corrected in this way—can, by contrast, *both* be *true*. This can never take place with the cosmological ideas that concern merely a mathematically unconditioned unity; for in their case we encounter no condition of the series of appearances that is not itself appearance and as such likewise a member of the series.

III. Solution of the Cosmological Idea of Totality in the Derivation of World Events from their Causes

Only two kinds of causality can be conceived in regard to what occurs, namely, either a causality according to *nature* or one from *freedom*. The causality according to nature is the connection, in the world of sense, of one state with a previous state upon which the state follows according to a rule. Now the *causality* of appearances rests on conditions of time; and the previous state, if it had always been there, would not have produced an effect that first arises in time. Therefore, the causality of the cause of what occurs or comes about has likewise *come about*, and—according to the principle of the understanding—itself requires a cause in turn.

By freedom, by contrast, in the cosmological sense of the term, I mean the power to begin a state *on one's own*. Thus the causality of freedom is not in turn subject, according to the law of nature, to another cause that determines it as regards time. Freedom, in this meaning of the term, is a pure transcendental idea. This idea, first, contains nothing borrowed from experience. Moreover, second, the object of this idea cannot be given determinately in any experience, because there is a universal law of the very possibility of all experience according to which whatever occurs must have a cause, and, therefore, also the cause's causality which *itself has occurred* or come about must in turn have a cause. And thus the entire realm of experience, however far it may extend, is transformed into a sum of what is mere nature. But since in this way no absolute totality of

A533/ B561

<hr/>

25. For, the understanding does not permit among *appearances* any condition that would itself be empirically unconditioned. But if for some conditioned one could conceive an *intelligible* condition—which thus would not likewise belong, as a member, in the series of appearances—but without thereby in the

least interrupting the series of empirical conditions, then such a condition could be admitted as *empirically unconditioned*, and yet the empirical continuous regression would not thereby be impaired anywhere.

conditions in the causal relation can be obtained, reason creates for itself the idea of a spontaneity that can, on its own, start to act—without, i.e., needing to be preceded by another cause by means of which it is determined to action in turn, according to the law of causal connection.

Extremely noteworthy is the fact that this *transcendental idea of freedom* is the basis of the practical concept of freedom, and that transcendental freedom is what in practical freedom amounts to the proper moment of the difficulties that have all along surrounded the question of practical freedom's possibility. *Freedom in the practical meaning* of the term is the independence of our will from coercion by impulses of sensibility. For a will is *sensible* insofar as it is *pathologically affected* (i.e., affected by motivating causes of sensibility); it is called animal will (*arbitrium brutum*) if it can be *pathologically necessitated*. The human will, although an *arbitrium sensitivum*, is an *arbitrium* not *brutum* but *liberum*; for its action is not made necessary by sensibility, but the human being has a faculty to determine himself on his own, independently of coercion by sensible impulses.

We readily see that if all causality in the world of sense were merely nature, then every event would be determined by another event in time and according to necessary laws; and hence, since appearances insofar as they determine the will would have to make every action necessary as their natural result, the annulment of transcendental freedom would simultaneously eliminate all practical freedom. For practical freedom presupposes that although something did not occur, it yet *ought* to have occurred, and that hence the cause of this something in appearance was not completely determinative: not so determinative, namely, that there did not lie in our will a causality for producing, independently of those natural causes and even against their force and influence, something that in the time order is determined according to empirical laws—and hence a causality by which we can begin a series of events *entirely on our own*.

A535/B563 Hence what happens here—as we find in general in the conflict of reason that ventures beyond the bounds of possible experience—is that the problem is in fact not *physiological* but *transcendental*. Hence

the question of the possibility of freedom does indeed challenge psychology; but since it rests on dialectical arguments of the merely pure reason, it must, along with its solution, engage only transcendental philosophy. Now in order to enable transcendental philosophy to give a satisfactory answer to this problem, which it cannot decline to do, I must first try—by the following remark—to determine more closely the procedure of transcendental philosophy in dealing with this problem.

If appearances were things in themselves, and hence if space and time were forms of the existence of things themselves, then the conditions and the conditioned would always belong, as members, to one and the same series. And from this there would arise, in the present case also, the antinomy that is common to all transcendental ideas: namely, that this series would inevitably be too large or too small for the understanding. However, the dynamical concepts of reason, with which we are dealing in this and the following subsection, have the following peculiarity. Because these concepts have to do not with an object considered as a magnitude but only with the object's *existence*, we can abstract also from the magnitude of the series of conditions, and what matters in their case is merely the dynamical relation of the condition to the conditioned. Thus in the question concerning nature and freedom we already encounter the difficulty as to whether freedom is even possible at all, and, if it is possible, whether it can coexist with the universality of the natural law of causality. And hence the question arises whether the proposition that every effect in the world must arise *either* from nature *or* from freedom is a correct disjunction, or whether—rather—*both* can, with one and the same event but in different reference, take place simultaneously. As for the principle concerning the thoroughgoing connection of all events in the world of sense according to immutable natural laws, its correctness is already established as a principle of the Transcendental Analytic and tolerates no impairment. Hence the question is only whether, in regard to the same effect that is determined according to nature, freedom can nonetheless also take place, or whether freedom is completely excluded by that

A534/B562

A536/B564

inviolable rule. And here the deceptive, although common, presupposition of the *absolute reality* of appearances at once shows its detrimental influence of confusing our reason. For if appearances are things in themselves, then freedom cannot be saved. Nature is then the complete and in itself sufficiently determining cause of every event, and the condition of this cause is always contained only in the series of appearances—which, along with their effect, are necessary under natural law. If, however, appearances count as nothing more than they in fact are, namely, if they count not as things in themselves but as mere representations connected according to empirical laws, then they must themselves still have grounds that are not appearances. But such an intelligible cause is not, as regards its causality, determined by appearances, although its effects appear and thus can be determined by other appearances. Hence this cause, along with its causality, is outside the series of empirical conditions, whereas its effects are encountered within the series. Hence the effect can be considered as free with regard to its intelligible cause, and yet with regard to appearances be considered simultaneously as resulting from these according to the necessity of nature. This distinction, when set forth in a universal way and quite abstractly, must appear extremely subtle and obscure, but it will become clear in its application. Here I wanted only to comment that since the thoroughgoing connection of all appearances in one context of nature is an inexorable law, this law would necessarily have to overturn all freedom if one were to adhere obstinately to the reality of appearances. This is also the reason why those who follow the common opinion in this matter have never succeeded in reconciling nature and freedom with each other.

Possibility of the Causality through Freedom, as Reconciled with the Universal Law of Natural Necessity
What in an object of the senses is not itself appearance I call *intelligible.* Accordingly, if what in the world of sense must be regarded as appearance has, when taken in itself, also a power which is not an object of sensible intuition but through which it can still be the cause of appearances, then the *causality* of this being can be considered from two sides: as *intelligible,* according to its *action* as that of a thing in itself; and as *sensible,* according to the effects of this causality as those of an appearance in the world of sense. Thus regarding such a subject's power we would frame an empirical as well as an intellectual concept of its causality, these concepts occurring together in one and the same effect. Such a twofold way of thinking the power of an object of the senses contradicts none of the concepts that we have to frame of appearances and of a possible experience. For since these appearances are not in themselves things, they must be based on a transcendental object determining them as mere representations; and hence nothing prevents us from attributing to this transcendental object, besides the property through which it appears, also a *causality* that is not appearance although its *effect* is nonetheless encountered in appearance. Any efficient cause, however, must have a **character**, i.e., a law of its causality without which it would not be a cause at all. And thus in a subject of the world of sense we would have, first, an *empirical character.* Through this character the subject's actions, as appearances, would according to constant natural laws stand throughout in connection with other appearances and could be derived from these appearances as the actions' conditions; and thus these actions would, in combination with those other appearances, amount to members of a single series of the natural order. Second, one would have to grant to the subject also an *intelligible character.* Through this character the subject is indeed the cause of those actions as appearances, but the character itself is not subject to any conditions of sensibility and is not itself appearance. The first character could also be called the character of such a thing in [the realm of] appearance, the second the character of the thing in itself.

Now according to its intelligible character this acting subject would not stand under any conditions of time; for time is the condition only of appearances and not of things in themselves. In this subject no *action* would *arise* or *pass away.* Hence it would also not be subjected to the law of all time determination and of everything changeable, namely, that everything that *occurs* has its cause *in appearances* (those of the previous state). In a word, the subject's causality, insofar as it is intellectual, would not stand at all in the series of empirical conditions that make the event necessary in the world of sense. We could not, indeed, ever become acquainted with this intelligible character directly, because we cannot perceive anything except insofar as it appears; but we would still have to *think* it in accordance with the empirical character, just as in general we must—in thought— lay a transcendental object at the basis of appearances although we know nothing about this object as to what it is in itself.

Hence according to its empirical character this subject, as appearance, would be subjected to all laws of determination in terms of causal linkage. To this extent the subject would be nothing but a part of the world of sense; and its effects would, like any other appearance, flow from nature unfailingly. Just as outer appearances would influence this subject, and as the subject's empirical character, i.e., the law of its causality, would be cognized through experience, so all its actions would have to be explicable according to natural laws, and all requirements for a complete and necessary determination of these actions would have to be found in a possible experience.

A541/ But according to its intelligible character (alB569 though we can have nothing more of this character than just the general concept of it) the same subject would nonetheless have to be pronounced free from any influence of sensibility and determination by appearances. For insofar as this subject is *noumenon*, nothing *occurs* in it and there is found in it no change requiring dynamical time determination and hence no connection with appearances as causes. Therefore, this active being would to this extent be independent and free in its actions from all natural necessity, which is found only in the world of sense. Of this subject we would say quite correctly that it begins its effects in the world of sense *on its own*, without the action's beginning *in the subject* itself. And this would be valid without any consequent need for the effects in the world of sense to begin on their own. For in that world they are always predetermined— although only by means of the empirical character (which is merely the appearance of the intelligible

character)—by empirical conditions in the previous time, and are possible only as a continuation of the series of natural causes. And thus freedom and nature, each in the complete meaning of its term, would be found in the same actions—according as these are compared with their intelligible or with their sensible cause—simultaneously and without any conflict.

Clarification of the Cosmological Idea of a Freedom   A542/
in Combination with the Universal Natural Neces-   B570
sity   I thought it good to start by sketching the outline of the solution to our transcendental problem, in order that we might better survey the course that reason takes in solving the problem. Let us now spell out the moments that are in fact at issue in deciding this solution, and examine each separately.

Consider the natural law that everything that occurs has a cause; that since the causality of this cause, i.e., the *action*, precedes [the effect] in time and—in regard to an effect that has *arisen*—cannot itself always have been there but must have *occurred*, this causality likewise has among appearances its cause whereby it is determined; and that, consequently, all events are determined empirically within a natural order. This law, through which appearances can first amount to a *nature* and yield objects of an experience, is a law of the understanding from which we are not permitted on any pretext to deviate, nor exempt any appearance. For otherwise we would posit   A543/
the appearance outside of all possible experience,   B571
but thereby would distinguish it from all objects of possible experience and thus would turn it into a mere thought-entity and chimera.

Thus it looks, here, as if there is only a chain of causes that in the regression to the causes' conditions permits no *absolute totality* at all. Yet this perplexity in no way detains us; for it has already been removed in our general judgment on the antinomy of reason, into which reason falls when it aims at the unconditioned in the series of appearances. If we wish to yield to the delusion of transcendental realism, then we are left with neither nature nor freedom. Here the question is only whether, if we acknowledge nothing but natural necessity in the entire series of all events, it is still possible to regard the same event, which on the one hand is a mere natural effect, as yet being on the other hand an effect arising from freedom, or whether we find between these two kinds of causality a direct contradiction.

Among the causes in [the realm of] appearance there assuredly cannot be anything that could absolutely and on its own begin a series. For here every action, as appearance, insofar as it produces an event, is itself an event or happening that presupposes another state in which its cause is to be found; and thus everything that occurs is only a continuation of the series, and in this series no beginning that takes place on its own is possible. Hence all the actions of natural causes in the time sequence are themselves in turn effects that likewise presuppose their causes in the time series. An *original* action, through which something occurs that was not there before, is not to be expected from the causal connection of appearances.

But if effects are appearances, is it indeed also necessary that the causality of their cause, which (cause) itself is also appearance, must be solely empirical? And is it not possible, rather, that although every effect in [the realm of] appearance does indeed require a connection with its cause according to laws of empirical causality, yet this empirical causality itself could nonetheless, without in the least interrupting its connection with natural causes, be an effect of a causality that is not empirical but intelligible? I.e., could not the empirical causality itself be an effect of an action, original in regard to appearances, of a cause that to this extent is therefore not appearance but—according to this power—intelligible, although otherwise it also must, as a link in the chain of nature, be classed entirely with the world of sense?

The principle of the causality of appearances among one another is required by us in order that we can seek and indicate natural conditions, i.e., causes in [the realm of] appearance, for natural events. If this requirement is granted to us and not weakened by any exception, then the understanding—which in its empirical use sees in all happenings nothing but nature and is, moreover, entitled to do so—has all that it can demand, and physical explanations proceed along their course unhindered. Now in this

[task] the understanding is not impaired in the least if one assumes—even supposing that the assumption were, besides, to be merely invented—that among the natural causes there are also some which have a power that is only intelligible, inasmuch as this power's determination to action never rests on empirical conditions but rests on mere bases of the understanding—yet rests on these in such a way that this cause's *action in [the realm of] appearance* conforms to all laws of empirical causality. For in this way the acting subject would, as *causa phaenomenon*, be linked up with nature in the unsevered dependence of all this cause's actions; and this subject's phenomenon (with all its causality in [the realm of] appearance) would only contain certain conditions that, if one wants to ascend from the empirical object to the transcendental, would have to be regarded as merely intelligible. For if we only follow the rule of nature in regard to what may be the cause among appearances, then we need not be concerned as to what sort of basis of these appearances and their connection is being thought in the transcendental subject, which is empirically unknown to us. This intelligible basis in no way challenges the empirical questions, but concerns perhaps merely the thinking in the pure understanding; and although the effects of this thinking and acting of the pure understanding are found in the appearances, yet these appearances must nonetheless be capable of being explained completely, according to natural laws, from their cause in [the realm of] appearance. The appearances must be capable of being explained by pursuing, as the supreme basis of explanation, their merely empirical character, and by entirely bypassing as unknown the intelligible character that is the empirical character's transcendental cause—except insofar as this intelligible character is indicated by the empirical character as the intelligible character's sensible sign. Let us apply this to experience. The human being is one of the appearances in the world of sense, and to this extent is also one of the natural causes, the causality of which must be subject to empirical laws. As such a cause he must, accordingly, also have an empirical character, as do all other things of nature. We discern this character through abilities and powers that he manifests

A544/ B572

A545/ B573

A546/ B574

in his effects. In inanimate nature, or in animate but merely animal nature, we find no basis for thinking any power as being other than merely sensibly conditioned. Only the human being, who otherwise is acquainted with all of nature solely through his senses, A547/ cognizes himself also through mere apperception— B575 namely, in actions and inner determinations that he cannot class at all with any impression of the senses. And thus he is to himself, indeed, on the one hand phenomenon, but on the other hand—namely, in regard to certain faculties—a merely intelligible object, because his action cannot be classed at all with the receptivity of sensibility. We call these [specifically human] faculties the understanding and reason. Reason, above all, is quite particularly and primarily distinguished from all empirically conditioned forces, because it examines its objects merely according to ideas and according to these ideas determines the understanding, which then makes an empirical use of its own (although likewise pure) concepts.

Now, that this reason has causality, or that we at least conceive such a causality in it, is evident from the *imperatives* which, in all that is practical, we impose as rules on the performative faculties. The *ought* expresses a kind of necessity and connection with bases that does not otherwise occur in all of nature. The understanding can cognize regarding nature only *what is*, or has been, or will be. That something in nature *ought to be* other than what in fact it is in all these time relations—this is impossible; indeed, the [term] ought, if we have in mind merely the course of nature, has no meaning whatsoever. We cannot at all ask what ought to happen in nature, any more than what properties a circle ought to have, but can ask only what happens in nature, or what properties the circle has.

Now this *ought* expresses a possible action whose A548/ basis is nothing but a mere concept, whereas the B576 basis of a mere action of nature must always be an appearance. Now the [concept-based] action must indeed be possible under natural conditions, if the *ought* is directed to nature; however, these natural conditions concern not the determination of the will itself but only this determination's effect and result in [the realm of] appearance. No matter how many

natural grounds—how many sensible stimuli—impel me to *will*, they still cannot produce the *ought*; they can produce only a willing that is far from necessary but is always conditioned, whereas the *ought* pronounced by reason opposes this conditioned willing with limit and an end—indeed, with prohibition and authority. Whether the object is one of mere sensibility (the agreeable) or even of pure reason (the good), reason does not yield to the empirically given ground and does not follow the order of things as they exhibit themselves in appearance, but with complete spontaneity makes for itself an order of its own according to ideas. Reason adapts the empirical conditions to accord with these ideas, and in conformity with these ideas declares to be necessary even such actions as in fact *have not occurred* and perhaps will not occur, but concerning which reason nonetheless presupposes that it can have causality in reference to them, since otherwise reason would not expect from its ideas effects in experience.

Let us now remain with this point and assume as at least possible that reason actually has causality with A549/ regard to appearances. In that case, despite being all B577 reason, it must yet show itself as having an empirical character. For any cause presupposes a rule according to which certain appearances follow as effects; and any rule requires a uniformity of effects that is the basis for the concept of cause (as a faculty). And this concept, insofar as it must become evident from mere appearances, we may call the cause's empirical character. This character is constant, whereas the effects appear in changeable shapes according to the difference in the accompanying and in part limiting conditions.

Thus every human being's will has an empirical character. This character is nothing but a certain causality of his reason insofar as this causality shows in its effects in [the realm of] appearance a rule by which one can gather, in terms of their kind and degrees, the bases and actions of his reason and thereby judge the subjective principles of his will. Since this empirical character itself must be drawn from appearances, as its effect, and from the rule of these as provided to us by experience, all actions of a human being are determined in appearance on the basis of his empirical character and the other contributing

A550/
B578
causes according to the order of nature; and if we could explore all appearances of his will down to the bottom, there would not be a single human action that we could not with certainty predict and cognize as necessary from its preceding conditions. In regard to this empirical character, therefore, there is no freedom; and yet only in terms of this character can we consider a human being if we seek merely to **observe** him and, as is done in anthropology, explore physiologically the motivating causes of his actions.

But if we examine the same actions in reference to reason—not, however, speculative reason in order to *explain* them in terms of their origin, but reason solely insofar as it is itself the cause *for producing* them—in a word: if we compare these actions with reason in a *practical* regard, then we find a rule and order quite different from the order of nature. For in that regard perhaps there *ought not to have occurred* all that according to nature's course yet *has occurred* and according to its own empirical grounds inevitably had to occur. But sometimes we find, or at least believe that we find, that the ideas of reason have actually proved their causality in regard to human beings' actions considered as appearances, and that these actions have occurred not because they were determined by empirical causes—no: but because they were determined by grounds of reason.

A551/
B579
Now supposing one could say that reason has causality in regard to appearance: could reason's action then indeed be called free, when in reason's empirical character (the way of sensing) the action is quite exactly determined and necessary? This empirical character in turn is determined in the intelligible character (the way of thinking). We are not, however, acquainted with the intelligible character but designate it only by appearances, which, properly speaking, allow us to cognize directly only the way of sensing (empirical character).[26] Now insofar as the action is attributable to the way of thinking as its cause, it yet in no way results from this way of thinking according to empirical

laws, i.e., in such a way that the conditions of pure reason *precede* the action, but only in such a way that the effects of these in [the realm of] appearance of inner sense precede it. Pure reason, as a merely intelligible faculty, is not subjected to the form of time, nor consequently to the conditions of temporal succession. The causality of reason in its intelligible character by no means *arises*, or starts at a certain time, in order to produce an effect. For otherwise it would itself be subjected to the natural law of appearances insofar as this law determines causal series with regard to time, and the causality of reason would then be nature, not freedom. Hence we must be entitled to say that if reason can have causality in regard to appearances, then it is a faculty *through* which the sensible condition of an empirical series of effects first begins. For the condition that lies in reason is not sensible and hence does not itself begin. Accordingly, there takes place here what in all empirical series we were unable to find: namely, that the *condition* of a successive series of events can itself be empirically unconditioned. For here the condition is *outside* the series of appearances (namely, in the intelligible) and hence is subjected to no sensible condition and no time determination by a preceding cause.

A552/
B580

Yet in another reference the same cause belongs nonetheless also to the series of appearances. The human being is himself an appearance. His will has an empirical character that is the (empirical) cause of all his actions. There is no condition determining a human being in accordance with this character which is not contained in the series of natural effects and which does not obey nature's law—the law according to which an unconditioned empirical causality of what occurs in time is not to be found at all. Therefore, no given action (since it can be perceived only as appearance) can begin absolutely on its own. Of reason, however, one cannot say that the state in which it determines the will is preceded by another state in which that state itself is determined. For since reason itself is not an appearance and is

A553/
B581

---

26. Hence the morality proper of actions (merit and guilt), even the morality of our own conduct, remains entirely hidden to us. Our imputations can be referred only to the empirical character. But no one can fathom how much of this character is a pure effect of freedom, and how much is to be ascribed to mere

nature: namely, either to a defect of temperament that one has through no fault of one's own, or to one's temperament's fortunate constitution (*meritum fortunae*). And hence no one can pass judgment in accordance with complete justice.

not subjected to any conditions of sensibility, there takes place in reason, even as concerns its causality, no temporal succession; and hence the dynamical law of nature that determines temporal succession according to rules cannot be applied to reason.

Hence reason is the permanent condition of all the voluntary actions under which the human being appears. Each of these actions, even before it occurs, is predetermined in the human being's empirical character. But in regard to the intelligible character, of which the empirical character is only the sensible schema, no *before* or *after* holds, and every action—regardless of its time relation to other appearances—is the direct effect of the intelligible character of pure reason. Hence pure reason acts freely, i.e., without being dynamically determined in the chain of natural causes by external or internal bases that precede the action as regards time. And this freedom of pure reason can be regarded not only negatively, as independence from empiri- A554/ cal conditions (for the faculty of reason would thus B582 cease to be a cause of appearances). Rather, this freedom can be designated also positively, as a faculty of reason to begin on its own a series of events. Reason begins the series in such a way that nothing begins in reason itself, but that reason, as the unconditioned condition of any voluntary action, permits no conditions above itself that precede the action as regards time—although reason's effect does begin in the series of appearances, but in the series can never amount to an absolutely first beginning.

To illustrate the regulative principle of reason involved here by an example drawn from the principle's empirical use—not to confirm it (for such proofs by example are unsuitable for transcendental assertions)—let us take a voluntary action, e.g., a malicious lie, by means of which a person has brought a certain amount of confusion into society. And suppose that we first investigate his action as to its motivating causes from which it arose, and that we then judge how the action can, along with its consequences, be imputed to him. In pursuing the first aim we search through the agent's empirical character until we come to its sources. We locate these in bad upbringing, evil company, partly also in the wickedness

of a natural makeup that is insensitive to shame; and partly we assign them to frivolity and rashness. Here, then, we do not ignore the occasioning causes that prompted the action. In all this we proceed as we do in general when we investigate the series of determin- A555/ ing causes for a given natural effect. But although we B583 believe the action to be determined by these causes, we nevertheless blame the perpetrator. We blame him not because of his unfortunate natural makeup, nor because of the circumstances influencing him— indeed, not even because of his previous way of life. For we presuppose that we can set aside entirely how this way of life was, and that we can regard the past series of conditions as not having occurred, and can regard this deed as entirely unconditioned with respect to the previous state, as if the perpetrator starts with it a series of consequences completely on his own. This blame is based on a law of reason; and reason is regarded in this act of blame as a cause that, regardless of all the mentioned empirical conditions, could and ought to have determined the person's conduct differently. And the causality of reason is by no means regarded merely as concurrence; rather, it is regarded as in itself complete, even if the sensible incentives were not at all for this causality but were even against it. The action is imputed to the agent's intelligible character: now—at the instant when he is lying—the guilt is entirely his. Hence his reason, regardless of all empirical conditions of the deed, was wholly free, and the deed is to be imputed entirely to its failure.

We can readily see from this imputing judgment that in making it we are thinking that reason is in no way affected by all that sensibility; that reason does not change (although reason's appearances— A556/ namely, the way in which reason manifests itself in B584 its effects—do change); that in reason there is no antecedent state determining the subsequent state, and that reason therefore does not at all belong in the series of sensible conditions that make appearances necessary according to natural laws. Reason is present to, and is the same in, all actions of the human being in all circumstances of time. But reason itself is not in time, and by no means gets into a new state in which it previously was not; with regard to this state reason is *determinative*, but not *determinable*. Hence we cannot ask, Why did reason not determine *itself* differently?—but only, Why did reason not determine *appearances* differently through its causality? To this, however, no answer is possible. For a different intelligible character of reason would have produced a different empirical character. And when we say that regardless of his entire previous way of life the perpetrator could still have abstained from the lie, this means only that the lie is directly subject to the force of reason, and reason is not subjected in its causality to any conditions of appearance and of the course of time. And it means, moreover, that although the difference of time can make a principal difference for appearances in regard to one another, it can make no difference for the action in reference to reason, because appearances are not things in themselves and hence are also not causes in themselves.

A557/
B585
    Hence in judging free actions with regard to their causality we can get only as far as the intelligible cause, but not *beyond it*. We can cognize that this cause determines [actions] freely, i.e., independently of sensibility, and that in this way it can be the sensibly unconditioned condition of appearances. But why the intelligible character gives precisely these appearances and this empirical character under the conditions at hand—this question far exceeds all our reason's power to answer it, indeed, all its right even to ask it; it exceeds these as far as if we asked how it is that the transcendental object of our outer sensible intuition gives us precisely intuition in *space* only, and not some other intuition. However, the problem that we had to solve does not obligate us to answer that question. For that problem was only this: whether freedom conflicts with natural necessity in one and the same action; and this we have answered sufficiently. For we have shown that, because in the case of freedom a reference to a quite different kind of conditions is possible from the kind found in the case of natural necessity, the latter's law does not affect freedom, and hence both can take place independently of, and without interfering with, each other.

It must be noted carefully that by this contemplation we have not sought to establish the *actuality* of freedom as one of the powers containing the cause of the appearances of our world of sense. For not only would this contemplation then not have been a transcendental one at all, which deals merely with concepts, but it also could not succeed; for from experience we can never infer something that must not be thought according to laws of experience at all. Furthermore, we have not even sought to prove the *possibility* of freedom; for this also would not have succeeded, because in general we cannot from mere *a priori* concepts cognize the possibility of any real basis and any causality. Freedom is being treated here only as a transcendental idea whereby reason means to start absolutely the series of conditions in appearance by the sensibly unconditioned. In this, however, reason becomes entangled in an antinomy with its own laws, the laws that it prescribes to the empirical use of the understanding. Now, to show that this antinomy rests on a mere illusion and that nature at least does *not conflict* with the causality from freedom—this was the only goal that we were able to accomplish, and it was, moreover, our one and only concern. [ . . . ]

A558/
B586

# Book II

A592/
B620

## Chapter III. The Ideal of Pure Reason

### Section IV. On the Impossibility of an Ontological Proof of the Existence of God[27]

From what has been said thus far, we see that the concept of an absolutely necessary being is a pure concept of reason, i.e., a mere idea, whose objective

---

27. [While there may not be a single agreed upon version of the 'ontological' argument for the existence of God in the modern period, the general argument form can be expressed as follows. Because God is a perfect being and existence is a perfection, God must exist. Another way of putting it is to note that the argument starts out with nothing beyond the very concept of God and then argues that the concept of God as a perfect or most real being must contain existence, which is simply another way of saying that God necessarily exists. See Leibniz's critique of Descartes' version of the ontological argument in his letter to Countess Elisabeth in Section 1.4.3 above.]

reality is far from proved by the mere fact that reason requires this idea. Indeed, the idea only instructs us to seek a certain—although unattainable—completeness, and serves in fact more to confine the understanding than to expand it to new objects. Now here we find the strange and preposterous fact that although the inference from a given existence as such to some absolutely necessary existence seems to be compelling and correct, we nonetheless have all the conditions of the understanding entirely against us when we attempt to frame a concept of such a necessity.

People have at all times spoken of the *absolutely necessary* being, and have taken pains not so much to understand whether and how a thing of this kind can even be thought, but rather to prove its existence. Now a nominal explication of this concept is, indeed, quite easy: we can say, namely, that this being is something whose nonexistence is impossible. But A593/ this explication leaves us not a whit more informed B621 concerning the conditions that make it necessary to regard a thing's nonexistence as absolutely unthinkable. And yet these conditions are what we want to know; i.e., we want to know whether or not we think anything at all through this concept. For if by means of the word *unconditionally* I dismiss all the conditions that the understanding always requires in order to regard something as necessary, this does not come close to enabling me to understand whether I then still think something through the concept of an unconditionally necessary being, or perhaps think through it nothing at all.

What is still more: once people had ventured to accept this concept merely haphazardly and had finally become quite familiar with it, they even believed themselves to be explicating it by a multitude of examples. And thus there seemed to be no need whatsoever for any further inquiry as to whether the concept is understandable. People knew that every proposition of geometry—e.g., the proposition that a triangle has three angles—is absolutely necessary; and thus they spoke even of an object that lies entirely outside the sphere of our understanding as if they understood quite well what they meant by the concept of this object.

In fact all the alleged examples are, without exception, taken from *judgments* rather than from *things* and their existence. But the unconditioned necessity of judgments is not an absolute necessity of things. For the unconditioned necessity of a judgment is only a conditioned necessity of the thing [as A594/ subject] or of the predicate in the judgment. The B622 proposition above does not say that three angles are necessary absolutely; it says, rather, that under the condition that a triangle is there (i.e., is given), three angles are necessarily also there (in it). Nonetheless, this merely logical necessity has proved to have great power of illusion. For people framed an *a priori* concept of a thing and arranged this concept in such a way that—in their opinion—it comprised in its range also existence. Having framed the concept in this way, they believed that they could safely infer the being's existence. For since existence necessarily belongs to the object of this concept—i.e., under the condition that this thing is posited as given (existing)—the object's existence is (according to the rule of identity) necessarily also posited. And hence this being is itself absolutely necessary, because—in a concept that has been assumed at will—this being's existence also is thought, namely, under the condition that the concept's object is posited.

If in an identical judgment I annul the predicate and retain the subject, then a contradiction arises, and hence I say that the predicate belongs to the subject necessarily. But if I annul the subject along with the predicate, then no contradiction arises, for *nothing is left* that could be contradicted. To posit a triangle and yet to annul its three angles is contradictory; but to annul the triangle along with its three A595/ angles is not a contradiction. And with the concept of B623 an absolutely necessary being the situation is exactly the same. If you annul the being's existence, then you annul the thing itself with all its predicates. From where, then, is the contradiction to come? Extrinsically there is nothing that would be contradicted, for the thing is not to be necessary extrinsically. Intrinsically to the thing there is also nothing that would be contradicted; for by annulling the thing itself you have simultaneously annulled everything intrinsic to it. God is omnipotent—this is a necessary judgment.

The omnipotence cannot be annulled if you posit a deity, i.e., an infinite being, with whose concept the concept of omnipotence is identical. But if you say *God does not exist*, then neither omnipotence nor any other of his predicates is given; for they are all annulled along with the subject, and hence this thought does not manifest the least contradiction.

Thus you have seen that if I annul the predicate of a judgment together with the subject, then an intrinsic contradiction can never arise—no matter what the predicate may be. You are now left with no escape except to say that there are subjects that cannot be annulled at all and that hence must remain. This, however, would be equivalent to saying that there are absolutely necessary subjects—the very presupposition whose correctness I doubted and whose possibility you wanted to show me. For I cannot frame the slightest concept of a thing that, if it were annulled with all its predicates, would leave a contradiction; and without a contradiction I have, through pure *a priori* concepts alone, no mark of impossibility.

A596/
B624

Wishing now to argue against all these general conclusions (which no one can refuse to accept), you challenge me with a case that you put forth as a factual proof. You argue that there is indeed one concept—and, moreover, only this *one*—where the nonexistence or annulment of the concept's object is self-contradictory: namely, the concept of the maximally real being. This being, you say, has all reality, and you are entitled to assume such a being as possible. (This possibility I concede for now, although the fact that a concept does not contradict itself is far from proving the object's possibility.)[28] Now [so you argue] *all reality* also includes existence; hence existence lies within the concept of a possible thing. If

A597/
B625

---

28. A concept is always possible if it does not contradict itself. This is the logical mark of possibility, and by this characteristic the concept's object is distinguished from the *nihil negativum*. But the concept may nonetheless be an empty one if the objective reality of the synthesis whereby the concept is produced is not established separately. However, as has been shown above, establishing this reality always rests on principles of possible experience and not on the principle of analysis (the principle of contradiction). This point is a warning that we must not immediately infer the (real) possibility of things from the (logical) possibility of concepts.

now this thing is annulled, then the thing's intrinsic possibility is annulled—which is contradictory.

I reply: You have already committed a contradiction if, in offering the concept of a thing that you wanted to think merely as regards its possibility, you have already brought into this concept—no matter under what covert name—the concept of the thing's existence. If this is granted to you, then you have seemingly won your point; but in fact you have said nothing, because you have committed a mere tautology. I ask you: is the proposition that *this or that thing exists* (a thing that, whatever it may be, I grant you as possible)—is this proposition, I ask, an analytic or a synthetic one? If the proposition is analytic, then by asserting the thing's existence you add nothing to your thought of the thing. But in that case either the thought, which is in you, would have to be the thing itself; or you have presupposed an existence as belonging to possibility, and have then allegedly inferred the thing's existence from the thing's intrinsic possibility—which is nothing but a pitiful tautology. The word *reality*, which merely sounds different in the concept of the thing [as subject] from *existence* in the concept of the predicate, is of no help. For even if you call all positing [of a subject] *reality* (whatever it is that you are positing), you have in the concept of the subject already posited, and assumed as actual, the thing with all its predicates and are merely repeating it in the predicate. However, if you admit— as any reasonable person must—that any existential proposition is synthetic, then how can you assert that the predicate of existence cannot be annulled without contradiction? For this superiority belongs only to analytic propositions as their peculiarity, since their character rests precisely on this [necessity].

A598/
B626

I would, indeed, hope to eliminate without much ado all this meditative subtlety through an exact determination of the concept of existence—had I not found that the illusion arising from the confusion of a logical with a real predicate (i.e., with the determination of a thing) permits almost no instruction [to dispel the illusion]. Anything whatsoever can serve as a *logical predicate*; even the subject [of a proposition] can be predicated of itself; for logic abstracts from all content. But a *determination* is a predicate that is added to the subject's concept and increases it; hence it must not already be contained in that concept.

*Being* is obviously not a real predicate, i.e., it is not a concept of anything that can be added to the concept of a thing. It is merely the positing of a thing [in itself] or of certain determinations in themselves. In its logical use it is merely the copula of a judgment. The proposition *God is omnipotent* contains two concepts that have their objects: God and omnipotence. The little word *is* is not a further predicate over and above these two, but is only what posits the predicate *in relation* to the subject. If I now take the subject (God) together with all its predicates (to which belongs also omnipotence) and say *God is*— or, There is a God—then I posit no new predicate as added to the concept of God, but posit only the subject in itself with all its predicates; namely, I posit *the object* in reference to my *concept*. Both must contain exactly the same; and hence nothing further can be added to the concept—which expresses only the [object's] possibility—merely because (through the expression *it is*) I think this object as given absolutely. And thus the actual contains no more than the merely possible. A hundred actual thalers do not contain the least more than a hundred possible thalers. For, the possible thalers signify the concept and the actual thalers signify the object and the positing thereof in itself; hence if the object contained more than the concept, then my concept would not express the entire object and thus would also not be the concept commensurate with this object. In the state of my assets, however, there is more in the case of a hundred actual thalers than in the case of the mere concept of them (i.e., their mere possibility). For in the case of the hundred thalers' actuality the object is not merely contained analytically in my concept (which is a determination of my state), but is added synthetically to my concept; yet these thought hundred thalers themselves are not in the least augmented by their being outside my concept.

Hence no matter through which and through how many predicates I think a thing (even if I think it in its thoroughgoing determination), not the least is added to this thing by my going on to say that this thing *is*. For otherwise what exists would not be the same as I had thought in the concept, but would be more; and I could then not say that exactly the object of my concept exists. Even if I think in a thing all reality except one, the missing reality is not added by my saying that such a deficient thing exists. Rather, the thing then exists as encumbered with exactly the same deficiency with which I thought it, since otherwise there would exist something other than what I thought. Now if I think a being as the supreme reality (i.e., as a being without deficiency), then the question still remains as to whether or not this being exists. For although nothing of the possible real content of a thing as such is missing in my concept of this being, yet something is still missing in the concept's relation to my entire state of thought, namely, that the cognition of this object is also possible *a posteriori*. And now we find also the cause of the difficulty that prevails here. If an object of the senses were at issue, then I could not confuse the thing's existence with the mere concept of the thing. For when the object is thought through the concept, then it is thought only as agreeing with the universal conditions of a possible empirical cognition as such. But when it is thought through existence, then the object is thought as contained in the context of experience as a whole; and here the concept of the object is not in the least augmented by its connection with the content of experience as a whole, although our thinking acquires through this content another possible perception. But if we wish to think existence through the pure category alone, then we must not be surprised that we cannot indicate any characteristic by which to distinguish existence from mere possibility.

Hence no matter what and how much our concept of an object may contain, we must yet go outside the concept in order to assign existence to the object. In the case of objects of the senses this is done through the coherence of these objects, according to empirical laws, with some one of my perceptions. But for objects of pure thought there is no means whatsoever of cognizing their existence. For their existence would have to be cognized entirely *a priori*. But our consciousness of any existence (whether such consciousness arises directly through perception or indirectly through inferences connecting something with perception) belongs altogether to the unity of experience. And although an existence outside this realm [of experience] cannot absolutely be declared to be impossible, it is a presupposition that we cannot justify by anything.

The concept of a supreme being is in many respects a very useful idea. But this idea, precisely because it is merely that, is quite incapable of allowing A602/ us to expand, by means of it alone, our cognition B630 regarding what exists. Even as regards possibility the idea is unable to teach us anything further. To be sure, the analytic characteristic of possibility, which consists in the fact that mere positings (realities) cannot generate a contradiction, cannot be denied to this concept. However, the connection of all real properties in a thing is a synthesis whose possibility we cannot judge *a priori*. For the realities are not given to us specifically. And even if they were, no judgment whatever in regard to them [can] take place at all. For, the characteristic of the possibility of synthetic cognitions must always be sought only in experience; the object of an idea, however, cannot belong to experience. Hence the illustrious *Leibniz* is far from having accomplished what he flattered himself to have achieved: namely, an *a priori* insight into the possibility of such an august ideal being.

Hence all effort and labor is lost if expended on the famous ontological (Cartesian) proof of the existence of a supreme being from mere concepts; and, I suppose, a human being could not from mere ideas become richer in insights any more than a merchant could become richer in assets if he tried to improve his situation by adding a few zeros to his cash balance. [ . . . ]

### Appendix on the Final Aim of the Natural Dialectic of Human Reason

A702/ [ . . . ] Thus all human cognition begins with intuitions, B730 proceeds from there to concepts, and ends with ideas. This cognition does indeed have—with regard to all three of these elements—*a priori* sources of cognition that seem at first glance to defy the limits of all experience. Yet a completed critique convinces us that all our reason in its speculative use can never—with these elements—get beyond the realm of possible

experience. And the critique convinces us that the proper vocation of this highest cognitive power is to employ all the methods and principles of reason solely for tracing nature to its innermost core according to all possible principles of unity—the foremost of which is the unity of purposes—but never to soar beyond nature's boundary, since *for us* there is nothing but empty space outside it. The critical investigation—as carried out in the Transcendental Analytic—of all A703/ propositions that can expand our cognition beyond B731 actual experience has, to be sure, sufficiently convinced us that these propositions can never lead to anything more than a possible experience. And if we were not distrustful of even the clearest abstract and general doctrines, and if charming and plausible prospects did not entice us to cast off those doctrines' constraint, then we could indeed have been spared the laborious interrogation of all the dialectical witnesses that a transcendent reason brings forward on behalf of its claims. For even beforehand we knew with complete certainty that all of reason's allegations, although perhaps honestly meant, must be absolutely null, because it concerns information that no human being can ever acquire. Yet the discussion will never end unless one uncovers the true cause of the illusion that can trick even the most reasonable person. Moreover, resolving all our transcendent cognition into its elements (as a study of our inner nature) is in itself of no slight value; but for the philosopher it is even a duty. Hence not only was there a need to investigate comprehensively this entire working of speculative reason—idle though it is—down to its primary sources. But since the dia- B732 lectical illusion is here not only deceptive in the judgment but is also enticing in the interest that is here A704 taken in the judgment, and since the illusion is always natural and will remain so for the future, it was advisable for us to draw up comprehensively the proceedings of this trial, as it were, so as to deposit them in the archives of human reason in order to prevent future errors of a similar kind. [ . . . ]

### Transcendental Doctrine of Method        A795/
####   B823
#### Chapter II. The Canon of Pure Reason

Human reason is humiliated by the fact that, in its pure use, it accomplishes nothing and indeed even needs a discipline to restrain its own extravagances and prevent the deceptions that these engender for it. But, on the other hand, human reason is elevated and acquires self-confidence through the fact that it can and must exercise this discipline on its own, without permitting any other verdict concerning itself; and likewise through the fact that the limits that it is compelled to set to its own speculative use simultaneously limit the subtly reasoning claims of every opponent, so that whatever may still be left to human reason from its previously exaggerated demands it can secure against all attacks. Hence the greatest and perhaps only benefit of all philosophy of pure reason may be only negative. For such philosophy does not—as an organon—serve to expand [cognition], but—as a discipline—serves to determine the limit [of cognition]; and instead of discovering truth, it has only the silent merit of preventing errors.

Yet somewhere there must nonetheless be a source of positive cognitions that belong in the domain of pure reason, and that perhaps give rise to errors only A796/ through misunderstanding but in fact amount to the B824 aim of reason's zeal. For to what cause could one otherwise attribute reason's indomitable desire to gain by all means a firm foothold somewhere beyond the limits of experience? Reason there suspects objects that carry with them a great interest for it. It enters upon the path of mere speculation in order to come closer to these objects; but they flee from it. Presumably we may hope that reason will have better fortune on the only path that still remains for it, namely, that of its *practical* use.

By a canon I mean the sum of *a priori* principles governing the correct use of certain cognitive powers as such. Thus general logic in its analytical part is a canon for the understanding and reason as such— but only as regards form, for general logic abstracts from all content. And thus the transcendental analytic was the canon of the pure *understanding*; for the pure understanding alone is capable of having true synthetic *a priori* cognitions. But where no correct use of a cognitive power is possible, there is no canon. Now all synthetic cognition of pure *reason* in its speculative use is, according to all the proofs conducted thus far, entirely impossible. Hence there

is no canon whatsoever of pure reason's speculative use (for this use is dialectical throughout), and in re- A797/ gard to this speculative aim all transcendental logic B825 is nothing but discipline. Consequently, if there is a correct use of pure reason at all, in which case there must also be a *canon* of pure reason, then this canon will concern not the speculative but the *practical use of reason*. Hence we shall now investigate this use.

## Section I. On the Ultimate Purpose of the Pure Use of Our Reason

Reason is impelled by a propensity of its nature to go beyond its use in experience, to venture outward— in a pure use and by means of mere ideas—to the utmost limits of all cognition, and to be at rest for the first time in the completion of its sphere, i.e., in a self-subsistent systematic whole. Now, is this endeavor based merely on reason's speculative interest, or is it, rather, based solely and exclusively on its practical interest?

Let me now set aside whatever success pure reason has in regard to its speculative aim, and inquire only into problems whose solution amounts to pure reason's ultimate purpose—the purpose which pure reason may or may not accomplish, and in regard to which all other purposes have only the value of means. A798/ These highest purposes must, according to the nature B826 of reason, have unity in turn, in order that—as thus united—they may further that interest of humanity which is not subordinate to any higher interest.

The final aim to which the speculation of reason as used transcendentally is ultimately directed concerns three objects: the freedom of the will, the immortality of the soul, and the existence of God. With regard to all three the merely speculative interest of reason is only very slight; and with this interest in view one presumably would scarcely undertake an exhausting job—which wrestles with unceasing obstacles—of transcendental investigation. For whatever discoveries one might be able to make concerning these three objects, one could still not make of these discoveries a use that would prove its benefit *in concreto*, i.e., in the investigation of nature. E.g., first, even if the will is free, this fact still can concern only the intelligible cause of our willing. For as regards the phenomena consisting of that will's manifestations, i.e., actions, we must always—according to an inviolable basic maxim without which we could not exercise any empirically used reason at all—explain them only as we explain all the remaining appearances of nature, namely, according to immutable laws of nature. Moreover, second, even if one can have insight into the spiritual nature of the soul (and, with this nature, into the soul's immortality), one can still count on this spiritual nature neither as a basis of explanation regarding the appearances of this life, nor as shedding light on the particular character of our future state. For our concept of an incorporeal nature is merely negative; it does not in the least expand our cognition or offer suitable material for inferences—except perhaps for inferences that can be regarded only as inventions but that philosophy does not allow. Third, even if the existence of a supreme intelligence were proved, although we would indeed from this existence make comprehensible for ourselves in a general way what is purposive in the world's arrangement and order, we would by no means be entitled to derive from this existence any particular provision and order, or boldly to infer such provision or order where it is not perceived. For there is a necessary rule of the speculative use of reason, not to pass over natural causes and abandon something of which we can inform ourselves through experience, in order to take something that we know and derive it from what entirely surpasses our knowledge. In a word, for speculative reason these three propositions always remain transcendent and have no immanent use whatsoever, i.e., no use admissible for objects of experience and hence beneficial to us in some way; rather, when regarded in themselves, they are endeavors of our reason that are entirely futile and are even extremely difficult.

Accordingly, if these three cardinal propositions are not at all necessary to us for *knowledge* and are nonetheless urgently commended to us by our reason, then—I suppose—their importance will properly have to concern only the *practical*.

Practical is everything that is possible through freedom. But if the conditions for the exercise of our free will are empirical, then reason can have in this exercise none but a regulative use and can serve only to bring about the unity of empirical laws. Thus, e.g. in the doctrine of prudence, the entire business of reason consists in taking all the purposes assigned to us by our inclinations and uniting them in the one purpose, *happiness*, and in harmonizing the means for attaining this happiness. Consequently, reason can here supply none but *pragmatic* laws of free conduct that is aimed at attaining the purposes commended to us by the senses, and hence can supply no laws that are pure, i.e., determined completely *a priori*. By contrast, pure practical laws, the purpose of which is given completely *a priori* by reason and which command not in an empirically conditioned but in an absolute way, would be products of pure reason. *Moral* laws, however, are indeed such pure practical laws, and hence they alone belong to the practical use of pure reason and permit a canon.

The entire apparatus of pure reason, as considered in the treatment that may be called pure philosophy, is in fact directed only to the three mentioned problems. These problems themselves, however, have in turn their more remote aim, namely, *what is to be done* if the will is free, if there is a God, and if there is a future world. Now since this more remote aim concerns our conduct in reference to the highest purpose, the ultimate aim of nature—the nature that in the arrangement of our reason provides for us wisely—pertains properly only to what is moral.

But as we turn our attention to an object extraneous to transcendental philosophy, we must be cautious not to stray into digressions and violate the unity of the system, and cautious also—on the other hand—not to incur a lack of distinctness or conviction by saying too little about our new material. I hope to accomplish both of these goals by keeping as close as possible to what is transcendental and setting aside entirely what might in this material be psychological, i.e., empirical.

And thus I must first point out that for now I shall employ the concept of freedom in its practical meaning only, and here set aside—as having been dealt with above—the same concept in its transcendental signification. The latter concept cannot be presupposed empirically as a basis for explaining

A799/
B827

A800/
B828

A801/
B829

A802/
B830

appearances, but is itself a problem for reason. For a will is merely *animal (arbitrium brutum)* if it cannot be determined otherwise than through sensible impulses, i.e., *pathologically*. But the power of choice that can be determined independently of sensible impulses and hence through motivating causes that are represented only by reason is called the *free will (arbitrium liberum)*; and everything connected with this free will, whether as a ground or as a consequence, is called *practical*. Practical freedom can be proved through experience. For the human will is determined not merely by what stimulates, i.e., by what directly affects the senses. Rather, we have a power of overcoming, through representations of what is beneficial or harmful even in a more remote way, the impressions made upon our sensible faculty of desire. These deliberations, however, concerning what is with regard to our whole state desirable, i.e., good and beneficial, rest on reason. This is also why reason gives laws that are imperatives, i.e., objective *laws of freedom*. Such laws tell us *what ought to occur* even though perhaps it never does occur—and therein they differ from *laws of nature*, which deal only with *what occurs*—and this is why the laws of freedom are also called practical laws.

A803/
B831
But whether reason is not, even in these actions through which it prescribes laws, determined in turn by other influences, and whether what in regard to sensible impulses is called freedom may not in regard to higher and more remote efficient causes in turn be nature—this further question does not concern us in the practical [realm]. For there we initially consult reason only concerning the *prescription* of conduct; but that further question is a merely speculative one, which we can set aside as long as our intention is directed to doing or refraining. Hence we cognize practical freedom through experience; we cognize it as one of the natural causes, namely, as a causality of reason [that is operative] in the determination of the will. Transcendental freedom, on the other hand, demands an independence of this reason itself (as regards reason's causality whereby it is able to begin a series of appearances) from all determining causes of the world of sense; and to this extent transcendental freedom seems to be contrary to the law

of nature and hence to all possible experience, and therefore remains a problem. But this problem does not pertain to reason in its practical use; and hence in a canon of pure reason we deal with only two questions, which concern the practical interest of pure reason and with regard to which a canon of this reason's use must be possible, namely: Is there a God? Is there a future life? The question regarding transcendental freedom concerns merely our speculative knowledge. This question we can set aside as making no difference whatsoever when our concern is what is practical; and sufficient discussion regarding it can already be found in the antinomy of pure reason.

A804/
B832

### Section II. On the Ideal of the Highest Good, As a Determining Basis of the Ultimate Purpose of Pure Reason

Reason in its speculative use led us through the realm of experiences and, since complete satisfaction can never be found for it in that realm, from there to speculative ideas. But in the end these ideas led us back again to experience, and thus they fulfilled their intent in a way that, although beneficial, did not at all conform to our expectations. This leaves us with one more attempt. Namely, we must inquire whether pure reason can be also found in reason's practical use; whether in this use it leads us to the ideas which reach the highest purposes of pure reason that we have just mentioned; and whether, therefore, pure reason cannot perhaps grant us from the viewpoint of its practical interest what it altogether denies us with regard to its speculative interest.

All my reason's interest (speculative as well as practical) is united in the following three questions:

1. *What can I know?*

2. *What ought I to do?*

3. *What may I hope?*

A805/
B833

The first question is merely speculative. We have (as I flatter myself) exhausted all possible answers to this question and have finally found the one answer with which reason must indeed content itself and, if reason does not take account of the practical, also has cause to be content. From the two great purposes, however, to which this entire endeavor of pure reason was properly directed we have remained just as distant as if we had—from love of leisure—refused this job at the very beginning. Hence if our concern is knowledge, then at least this much is certain and established: that we shall never be able to partake of knowledge regarding those two problems.

The second question is merely practical. As such it can indeed belong to pure reason; but it is then a moral rather than a transcendental question and hence cannot in itself occupy our [present] critique.

The third question—namely, if, now, I do what I ought to do, what may I then hope?—is simultaneously practical and theoretical, so that the practical [component] is only a guide that leads to the answering of the theoretical question and—if the theoretical question is carried far—of the speculative question. For all *hoping* aims at happiness, and is in A806/ regard to the practical [realm] and to the moral law B834 the same [thing] that knowing and the natural law are in regard to the theoretical cognition of things. Hoping ultimately amounts to the conclusion that there *is* something (that determines the ultimate possible purpose) *because something ought to occur*; knowing ultimately amounts to the conclusion that there is something (that acts as supreme cause) *because something does occur*.

Happiness is the satisfaction of all our inclinations (*extensively*, in terms of their manifoldness; *intensively*, in terms of their degree; and also *protensively*, in terms of their duration). The practical law issuing from the motive of *happiness* I call pragmatic (i.e., rule of prudence). But the practical law that has as its motive nothing but the *worthiness to be happy*—if there is such a law—I call moral (moral law). The pragmatic law advises [us] what we must do if we want to partake of happiness; the moral law commands how we ought to behave in order simply to become worthy of happiness. The pragmatic law is based on empirical principles; for in no other way than by means of experience can I know either what inclinations there are that want to be satisfied, or what the natural causes are that can bring about the satisfaction of those inclinations. The moral law

abstracts from inclinations and from the natural means for satisfying them. It considers only the freedom of a rational being as such, and the necessary conditions under which alone this freedom harmonizes with a distribution of happiness that is made in accordance with principles. Hence the moral law at least *can* rest on mere ideas of pure reason and thus be cognized *a priori*.

I assume that there actually are pure moral laws A807/ that determine completely *a priori* (without regard B835 to empirical motives, i.e., to happiness) the doing and the refraining, i.e., the use of the freedom of a rational being as such, and that these laws command *absolutely* (not merely hypothetically, on the presupposition of other empirical purposes) and are therefore necessary in every regard. This proposition [that there are such laws] I may rightly presuppose, by appealing not only to the proofs of the most enlightened moralists, but also to the moral judgment that every human being makes if he wishes to think such a law distinctly.

Hence pure reason contains—although not in its speculative use but still in a certain practical, namely, the moral, use—principles of the *possibility of experience*, namely, of the experience of such actions as *could* be encountered in accordance with moral precepts in the *history* of the human being. For since pure reason commands that such actions ought to occur, they must also be able to occur. And hence a particular kind of systematic unity must be possible, namely, moral unity. By contrast, the systematic unity of nature *according to speculative principles of reason* was incapable of being proved; for although reason has causality with regard to freedom as such, A808/ it does not have causality with regard to all of nature; B836 and although moral principles of reason can give rise to free actions, they cannot give rise to natural laws. Accordingly, the principles of pure reason in its practical use—but specifically in its moral use—have objective reality.

The world insofar as it would be in accordance with all moral laws (as, indeed, according to the *freedom* of rational beings it can be, and as according to the necessary laws of morality it ought to be) I call a **moral world**. The moral world is thought merely as an intelligible world, inasmuch as we abstract in it from all conditions (purposes) and even from all obstacles for morality (weakness or impurity of human nature). Therefore, to this extent the moral world is a mere idea; yet it is a practical idea that actually can and ought to have its influence on the world of sense, in order to bring this world as much as possible into accordance with the moral world. Hence the idea of a moral world has objective reality. But it has such reality not as dealing with an object of an intelligible intuition (which we cannot even think), but as dealing with the world of sense. However, the world of sense must here be taken as an object of pure reason in its practical use and as a *corpus mysticum* of the rational beings in it insofar as their free will under moral laws is in thoroughgoing systematic unity both with itself and with the freedom of every other such being.

This was the answer to the first of the two questions of pure reason that concerned its practical interest, and this answer is: Do that whereby you become worthy to be happy. Now the second question asks this: What if I now behave in such a way as not to be unworthy of happiness, may I also hope that I can thereby partake of happiness? In answering this question, what matters is whether the principles of pure reason that prescribe the law *a priori* also necessarily connect this hope with that law.

A809/ B837

I maintain, then, that just as moral principles are necessary according to reason in its *practical* use, so it is equally necessary also according to reason in its *theoretical* use to assume that everyone has cause to hope for happiness insofar as he has made himself worthy of it in his conduct, and hence to assume that the system of morality is linked inseparably—but only in the idea of pure reason—with the system of happiness.

Now in an intelligible world, i.e., in the moral world, in whose concept we abstract from all obstacles to morality (i.e., from inclinations), such a system of a proportionate happiness linked with morality can indeed be thought as necessary. For freedom, partly impelled and partly restricted by moral laws, would itself be the cause of general happiness; and hence rational beings, under the guidance of such principles, would themselves be originators of their own and also of other beings' lasting welfare. But this system of a morality

A810/ B838

that rewards itself is only an idea. Carrying out the idea rests on the condition that *everyone* does what he ought to do, i.e., the condition that all actions of rational beings occur as they would if they sprang from a supreme will comprising all private wills within itself or under itself. However, the obligation issuing from the moral law remains valid for everyone's particular use of freedom even if others were not to behave in accordance with this law. Therefore, how the consequences of these actions will relate to happiness is determined neither by the nature of the things of the world, nor by the causality of the actions themselves and their relation to morality. And thus the mentioned necessary connection of one's hope for happiness with the unceasing endeavor to make oneself worthy of happiness cannot be cognized through reason if mere nature is presupposed. Rather, this connection may be hoped for only if a supreme reason that commands according to moral laws is also presupposed as nature's cause.

The idea of such an intelligence in which the morally most perfect will, combined with the highest bliss, is the cause of all happiness in the world, insofar as this happiness is exactly proportionate to one's morality (as the worthiness to be happy), I call *the ideal of the highest good*. Hence only in the ideal of the highest *original* good can pure reason find the basis of the practically necessary connection between the two elements of the highest derivative good, namely, the basis of an intelligible, i.e., *moral* world. Now, through reason we must necessarily conceive ourselves as belonging to such a world, although the senses exhibit to us nothing but a world of appearances. Hence we shall have to assume the moral world as being a consequence of our conduct in the sensible world, and—since the sensible world does not now offer us such a connection between happiness and morality—as being for us a future world. Hence God and a future life are two presuppositions that, according to principles of pure reason, are inseparable from the obligation imposed on us by that same reason.

A811/ B839

Morality in itself amounts to a system; but happiness does not, except insofar as its distribution is exactly commensurate with morality. This, however, is possible only in the intelligible world, under a wise originator and ruler. Reason finds itself compelled either to assume such a being, along with life in such a world, which we must regard as a future world, or to regard the moral laws as idle chimeras, because without this presupposition the necessary result that reason connects with these laws would have to vanish. This is, moreover, why everyone regards moral laws as *commands*; moral laws could not be commands if they did not connect with their rule commensurate consequences *a priori* and thus carry with them *promises* and *threats*. But again moral laws cannot do this unless they reside in a necessary being that, as the highest good, can alone make such a purposive unity possible.

A812/
B840

**Leibniz** called the world, insofar as we consider in it only rational beings and their coherence according to moral laws under the government of the highest good, the *kingdom of grace*. And this he distinguished from the *kingdom of nature*, where these beings are indeed subject to moral laws but expect from their conduct no other results than those that occur in accordance with the course of nature in our sensible world. Therefore, seeing ourselves in the kingdom of grace, where all happiness awaits us except insofar as we ourselves limit our share therein by being unworthy of happiness, is a practically necessary idea of reason.

Practical laws insofar as they also become subjective grounds of actions, i.e., subjective principles, are called *maxims*. The *judging* of morality in terms of its purity and consequences occurs according to *ideas*, the *compliance* with its laws occurs according to *maxims*.

It is necessary that our entire way of life be subjected to moral maxims. But it is at the same time impossible for this to occur unless reason connects with the moral law, which is a mere idea, an efficient cause that determines for all conduct conforming to this law an outcome, whether in this or in another life, that corresponds exactly to our highest purposes. Hence without a God and without a world that is invisible to us now but is hoped for, the splendid ideas of morality are indeed objects of approbation and admiration, but are not incentives for our resolve and for carrying out these ideas. For they do not then

A813/
B841

fulfill the entire purpose which is natural for every rational being and which is determined *a priori* and made necessary by that same pure reason.

For our reason, happiness by itself is far from being the complete good. For happiness is not approved of by our reason (however much it may be wished for by our inclination) unless this happiness is united with worthiness to be happy, i.e., with morally good conduct. But morality by itself—and with it the mere *worthiness* to be happy—is also far from being the complete good. In order for this good to be completed, the person who in his conduct has not been unworthy of happiness must be able to hope that he will partake of it. Even a reason free from any private aim and thus not taking into account an interest of its own, if it puts itself in the position of a being that had to distribute all happiness to others, cannot judge differently. For in the practical idea the two components are linked essentially—although in such a way that it is the moral attitude, as condition, that first makes possible the sharing in happiness, and not, conversely, the prospect of happiness that first makes possible the moral attitude. For in the latter case the attitude would not be moral, and hence would also not be worthy of full happiness—the happiness which in reason's view recognizes no other limitation than a limitation due to our own immoral conduct.

A814/
B842

Hence happiness, in exact balance with the morality of rational beings whereby these beings are worthy of happiness, alone amounts to the highest good of a world into which we must entirely place ourselves according to the precepts of pure but practical reason. That world, to be sure, is only an intelligible one; for the sensible world does not promise us, as arising from the nature of things, such systematic unity of purposes. Moreover, the reality of that intelligible world cannot be based on anything other than the presupposition of a highest original good: a good where independent reason, equipped with all the sufficiency of a supreme cause, establishes, preserves, and completes—according to the most perfect purposiveness—the order of things that is universal although very much concealed from us in the sensible world.

Now this moral theology has over speculative theology the particular advantage of leading inevitably to the concept of a *single*, *maximally perfect*, and *rational* original being; speculative theology does not, on objective grounds, even *point* to such a being, much less is it able to *convince* us [of the existence] thereof. For no matter how far reason may lead us in transcendental and natural theology, in neither of them do we find any significant basis for assuming just a single being such that we would have sufficient cause to put this being prior to all natural causes and also to make these causes in all respects dependent on it. By contrast, if we consider from the viewpoint of moral unity, as a necessary law of the world, the cause that alone can give to this law the commensurate effect and hence also its obligating force for us, then what comprises all these laws within itself must be a single supreme will. For how could we find perfect unity of purposes among different wills? This will must be omnipotent, in order that all of nature and its reference to morality in the world may be subject to it; omniscient, in order that it may cognize the innermost core of our attitudes and their moral value; omnipresent, in order that it may be directly close to all need that the highest greatest good of the world requires [to be satisfied]; eternal, in order that this harmony of nature and freedom may at no time be lacking; etc.

Thus we arrive at a systematic unity of purposes in this world of intelligences—a world that as mere nature can indeed be called only the sensible world, but that as a system of freedom can be called the intelligible, i.e., the moral world (*regnum gratiae*). But this systematic unity of purposes also inevitably leads to the purposive unity of all things making up this large whole according to universal natural laws, just as the unity in the world of intelligences is one according to universal and necessary moral laws; and it thus unites practical with speculative reason. The world must be represented by us as having arisen from an idea, if it is to harmonize with that use of reason without which we would consider ourselves unworthy of reason, namely, the moral use, which rests entirely on the idea of the highest good. Through this way of representing the world, all investigation of nature acquires a direction according to the form of a system of purposes, and in its highest extension becomes physicotheology. But because physicotheology started from moral order, as a unity that has its basis in the essence of freedom and is not brought about contingently through external commands, it leads the purposiveness of nature to grounds that must be inseparably connected *a priori* with the intrinsic possibility of things. It thereby leads nature's purposiveness to a *transcendental theology*, which adopts the ideal of the highest ontological perfection as a principle of systematic unity—a principle that connects all things according to universal and necessary natural laws because all these things have their origin in the absolute necessity of a single original being.

What sort of use can we make of our understanding, even as regards experience, if we do not set purposes for ourselves? But the highest purposes are those of morality, and these are purposes that only pure reason can allow us to cognize. Now even when furnished with these moral purposes and guided by them, we still cannot make any purposive use of our acquaintance with nature itself as regards cognition, if nature itself has not also laid down purposive unity. For without this unity we ourselves would not even have any reason, since we would have no school for it and no culture [of reason] through objects that would offer to it the material for such concepts of purposes. However, the moral purposive unity is necessary and has its basis in the essence of the will itself. Hence the natural purposive unity, which contains the condition of the moral unity's application *in concreto*, must likewise be necessary. And thus the transcendental enhancement of our rational cognition would be not the cause but merely the effect of the practical purposiveness imposed on us by pure reason.

Thus, even in the history of human reason, we find that before moral concepts were sufficiently purified and determined, and insight gained into the systematic unity of purposes according to these concepts and from necessary principles, our acquaintance with nature and even a considerable degree of the culture of reason in various other sciences could in part produce only crude and erratic concepts of the deity, and in part they left people with an amazing indifference regarding this question. A

A815/
B843

A816/
B844

A817/
B845

greater treatment of moral ideas—which was made necessary by the extremely pure moral law of our religion—sharpened reason for dealing with this [divine] object, through the interest that this treatment compelled people to take in this object. And these moral ideas, without any contribution either from an expanded acquaintance with nature or from correct and reliable transcendental insights (of which there has at all times been a lack), brought about a concept of the divine being that we now regard as the correct concept; and we regard it as correct not because speculative reason convinces us of this correctness, but because the concept harmonizes perfectly with reason's moral principles. And thus in the end it is always still pure reason alone, but only in its practical use, that has the merit of connecting a cognition to our highest interest: a cognition that mere speculation can only surmise but cannot validate. And pure practical reason has the merit of thereby turning this cognition, not indeed into a demonstrated dogma, but still into an absolutely necessary presupposition linked with reason's most essential purposes.

However, when practical reason has reached this high point, namely, the concept of a single original being as the highest good, it must by no means—just as if it had elevated itself beyond all empirical conditions of this concept's application and had soared to a direct acquaintance with new objects—presume to start now from this concept and to derive from it the moral laws themselves. For it was precisely these laws whose intrinsic practical necessity led us to the presupposition of an independent cause, or of a wise ruler of the world, in order to provide these laws with effect. And hence we cannot thereafter regard them in turn as contingent and as derived from a mere will, especially not from a will of which we would have no concept at all if we had not formed this concept in accordance with those laws. As far as practical reason has the right to guide us, we shall not regard actions as obligatory because they are commands of God, but shall regard them as divine commands because we are intrinsically obligated to them. We shall study freedom in terms of the purposive unity according to principles of reason, and shall believe that we conform to the divine will only insofar as we hold

sacred the moral law which reason teaches us from the nature of the actions themselves; and we shall believe that we can serve this will solely by furthering in us and in others the highest good in the world. Hence moral theology is only of immanent use. It serves us, namely, to fulfill our vocation here in the world by fitting ourselves into the system of all purposes, and to keep from abandoning in a good way of life, through fanaticism or perhaps even wickedness, the guiding thread of a morally legislating reason in order to tie this thread directly to the idea of a supreme being. For doing the latter would yield a transcendent use of reason and must—just like the use of reason in mere speculation—pervert and defeat the ultimate purposes of reason.

### Section III. On Opinion, Knowledge, and Faith

Assent is an event in our understanding that may rest on objective grounds but that also requires subjective causes in the mind of the person who is judging. If the assent is valid for everyone, provided only that he has reason, then its ground is sufficient *objectively*, and the assent is then called *conviction*. If the assent has its ground only in the particular character of the subject, then it is called *persuasion*.

Persuasion is a mere illusion; for the judgment's ground, which lies in the subject, is regarded as objective. Hence such a judgment also has only private validity, and the assent cannot be communicated. Truth, however, rests on agreement with the object; consequently, in regard to the object the judgments of every understanding must be in agreement (*consentientia uni tertio, consentiunt inter se*). Thus, whether assent is conviction or mere persuasion, its touchstone externally is the possibility of communicating the assent and of finding it to be valid for every human being's reason. For then there is at least a presumption that the agreement of all the judgments, despite the difference among the subjects, will rest on a common ground, namely, the object, and that hence the judgments will all agree with the object and will thereby prove the truth of the judgment.

Accordingly, persuasion can indeed not be distinguished subjectively from conviction if the subject views the assent merely as an appearance of his own mind. But the assent's grounds that are valid for us can be tested on the understanding of others, to see whether these grounds have the same effect on the reason of others that they have on ours; and this test is still a means, although only a subjective one, not indeed to bring about conviction, but still to detect any merely private validity of the judgment, i.e., whatever in the judgment is mere persuasion.

If, in addition, we can unfold the judgment's subjective *causes* that we take to be its objective grounds, and if we can therefore explain the deceptive assent as an event in our mind without needing the object's character for this explanation, then we expose the illusion and are no longer tricked by it. But we are still to a certain degree tempted by the illusion if its subjective cause belongs to our nature.

I cannot *assert* anything—i.e., pronounce it as a judgment that is necessarily valid for everyone—unless it is something that produces conviction. Persuasion I can keep for myself if I am comfortable with it, but I cannot and should not try to make it hold apart from me.

Assent—or the judgment's subjective validity—in reference to conviction (which holds at the same time objectively) has the following three levels: *opinion*, *faith*, and *knowledge*. *Opinion* is an assent that is consciously insufficient *both* subjectively and objectively. If the assent is sufficient only subjectively and is at the same time regarded as objectively insufficient, then it is called *faith*. Finally, assent that is sufficient both subjectively and objectively is called *knowledge*. Subjective sufficiency is called *conviction* (for myself); objective sufficiency is called *certainty* (for everyone). I shall not linger upon the elucidation of such readily comprehensible concepts.

I must never presume to hold an *opinion* without *knowing* at least something by means of which the judgment, which in itself is merely problematic, acquires a connection with truth; for truth, even when not complete, is still more than an arbitrary invention. Moreover, the law of such a connection must be certain. For if in regard to this law I again have

A822/ B850

nothing but opinion, then everything is only a play of the imagination without the least reference to truth. In judgments issuing from pure reason, holding an opinion is not permitted at all. For such judgments are not supported by experiential grounds. Rather, where everything is necessary, everything is to be cognized *a priori*. Hence the principle of connection requires universality and necessity, and hence complete certainty; otherwise one finds in it no guidance to truth. Thus holding an opinion in pure mathematics is absurd; here one must know, or refrain from all judgment. The same applies to the principles of morality, where one must not venture upon an action on the mere opinion that something is *permitted*, but must know this to be permitted.

A823/ B851

In the transcendental use of reason, on the other hand, holding an opinion is indeed too little, but knowing is again too much. Hence here we cannot judge at all with a merely speculative aim. For subjective grounds of assent, such as those that can bring about faith, deserve no approval in the case of speculative questions, because as used independently of all empirical assistance they do not hold up and cannot be communicated in equal measure to others. [That leaves faith or belief.]

However, only in a *practical reference* can theoretically insufficient assent be called belief at all. Now this practical aim is either one of *skill* or of *morality*—of skill for optional and contingent purposes, of morality for absolutely necessary purposes.

Once a purpose has been set, the conditions for attaining it are hypothetically necessary. This necessity is subjectively sufficient—yet it is so only comparatively if I do not know any other conditions whatsoever under which the purpose could be attained. But the necessity is sufficient absolutely and for everyone if I know with certainty that no one can be acquainted with any other conditions leading to the set purpose. In the first case my presupposition and the assent to certain conditions is a merely contingent belief, but in the second case it is a necessary belief. A physician must do something for a patient who is in danger, but is not acquainted with the nature of the patient's illness. He observes the phenomena and then judges, not knowing anything better to

A824/ B852

conclude, that the disease is consumption. His belief, even in his own judgment, is merely contingent; another might perhaps do better. Such belief, which is contingent but underlies our actual use of the means for certain actions, I call *pragmatic belief*.

The usual touchstone as to whether something asserted by someone is mere persuasion, or at least subjective conviction—i.e., firm belief—is *betting*. Often someone pronounces his propositions with such confident and intractable defiance that he seems to have entirely shed all worry about error. A bet startles him. Sometimes his persuasion is strong enough to be estimated at a value of one ducat, but not ten. For although he may indeed risk the first ducat, at ten ducats he first becomes aware of what he previously failed to notice, namely, that he might possibly have erred after all. If we conceive in our thoughts the possibility of betting our whole life's happiness on something, then our triumphant judgment dwindles very much indeed; we then become extremely timid and thus discover for the first time that our belief does not reach this far. Thus pragmatic belief has merely a degree, which according to the difference of the interest involved may be large but may also be small.

Even if we cannot undertake anything at all concerning an object, and the assent regarding it is therefore merely theoretical, we can still in many cases conceive and imagine an undertaking for which we suppose ourselves to have sufficient grounds if there were a means of establishing the certainty of the matter. And thus there is in merely theoretical judgments an *analogue* of *practical* judgments, and for an assent to such judgments the word *faith* is appropriate. We may call this a *doctrinal faith*. I would indeed bet all that I own—if this matter could be established through some experience—that there are inhabitants on at least one of the planets that we see. Hence I say that this view—that there are inhabitants also on other worlds—is not a mere opinion but a strong faith (on whose correctness I would surely risk many of life's advantages).

Now, we must admit that the doctrine of the existence of God belongs to doctrinal faith. To be sure, as regards theoretical cognition of the world I have nothing *available* that necessarily presupposes this thought as a condition for my explanations of the world's appearances; rather, I am obligated to employ my reason as if everything were mere nature. Yet purposive unity is such a major condition for applying reason to nature that I cannot pass it by—[especially] since experience also provides me richly with examples of this unity. But I know no other condition for this unity that would make it my guide for the investigation of nature except the presupposition that a supreme intelligence has arranged everything in this way in accordance with the wisest purposes. Hence presupposing a wise originator of the world is a condition for an aim that is indeed contingent but still not unimportant, namely, to have guidance in the investigation of nature. Moreover, so often is this presupposition's usefulness confirmed by the outcome of my attempts, while nothing can be adduced against the presupposition in a decisive way, that I would say far too little if I wanted to call my assent merely an opinion. Rather, even in this theoretical relation we may say that I have firm faith in a God. But this faith is then still not practical in a strict meaning of this term; rather, it must be called a doctrinal faith, to which the *theology* of nature (physicotheology) must necessarily give rise everywhere. With regard to the same wisdom and in view of the superb endowment of human nature and the shortness of life that is so incommensurate with this endowment, we can likewise find a sufficient reason for a doctrinal faith in the future life of the human soul.

The expression *faith* is in such cases an expression of modesty from an *objective* point of view, but simultaneously of firmness of confidence from a *subjective* point of view. If I here wanted to call the merely theoretical assent even just a hypothesis that I am entitled to assume, I would already be promising to have a fuller concept of the character of a world cause and of the character of another world than I can actually show. For if I assume something even just as a hypothesis, then I must know at least so much about its properties that I need to invent *not its concept* but *only its existence*. The word *faith*, however, applies here only to the guidance that an idea gives to me, and to the idea's subjective influence on the furtherance of my acts of reason—the furtherance that

A825/
B853

A826/
B854

A827/
B855

keeps me attached to the idea even though I am unable to account for it from a speculative point of view.

A828/ B856 The merely doctrinal faith, however, has something shaky about it; for the difficulties encountered in speculation often drive one away from this faith, although inevitably one always returns to it again.

The situation is quite different with *moral faith*. For here there is an absolute necessity that something must occur, namely, that I comply in all points with the moral law. Here the purpose is inescapably established, and—according to all the insight I have—only a single condition is possible under which this purpose coheres with the entirety of all purposes and thereby has practical validity, namely, the condition that there is a God and a future world. I also know with complete certainty that no one else is acquainted with other conditions that lead to the same unity of purposes under the moral law. But since the moral precept is thus simultaneously my maxim (as, indeed, reason commands), I shall inevitably have faith in the existence of God and in a future life. And I am sure that nothing can shake this faith; for that would overturn my moral principles themselves, which I cannot renounce without being detestable in my own eyes.

In this way, even after all the ambitious aims of a reason roaming beyond the limits of experience have been defeated, we are still left with enough in order to have cause to be satisfied from a practical point of view. No one, indeed, will be able to boast A829/ B857 that he *knows* that there is a God and that there is a future life; for if he knows this, then he is just the man that I have been looking for all along. All knowledge (if it concerns an object of mere reason) can be communicated, and hence I could then hope that I might through his instruction see my own knowledge extended in such a marvelous degree. No, the conviction is not a logical but a *moral* certainty; and because it rests on subjective grounds (of the moral attitude), I must not even say, *It is* morally certain that there is a God, etc., but must say, *I am* morally certain, etc. In other words, the faith in a God and in another world is so interwoven with my moral attitude that, as little as I am in danger of losing my

moral attitude, so little am I worried that my faith could ever be torn from me.

The only precariousness to be found in this is the fact that this rational faith is based on the presupposition of moral attitudes. If we abandon this presupposition and assume someone who is entirely indifferent with regard to moral laws, then the question posed by reason becomes merely a problem for speculation; and it can indeed still be supported then by strong grounds taken from analogy, but not A830/ B858 by grounds to which the most obstinate skepticism would have to yield. But in these questions no human being is free of all interest. For although he may be separated from moral interest through a lack of good attitudes, yet enough remains even in this case to make him *fear* a divine existence and a future life. For this requires nothing more than the fact that at least he cannot plead any *certainty* that *no* such being and *no* future life are to be found. This [negative proposition]—since it would have to be proved through mere reason and hence apodeictically—he could prove only by establishing that both such a being and such a future life are impossible; and certainly no reasonable human being can undertake to do that. This [faith based on fear] would be a *negative* faith; and although it could not bring about morality and good attitudes, it could still bring about their analogue, namely, a powerful restraint on the eruption of evil attitudes.

But, it will be said, is this all that pure reason accomplishes in opening up prospects beyond the limits of experience? Nothing more than two articles of faith? Even the common understanding could presumably have accomplished as much without consulting philosophers about it! A831/ B859

In reply, I do not here want to extol what merit philosophy has on behalf of human reason through the laborious endeavor of its critique, even supposing that this merit were in the upshot deemed to be merely negative; for I shall say something more about this [elsewhere]. But do you indeed demand that a cognition which concerns all human beings should surpass the common understanding and be revealed to you only by philosophers? Precisely the point which you rebuke is the best confirmation that the assertions made thus far are correct. For it reveals what one could not have foreseen at the outset: namely, that in matters of concern to all human beings, without distinction, nature cannot be accused of partiality in the distribution of its gifts; and that with regard to the essential purposes of human nature the highest philosophy cannot get further than can the guidance that nature has bestowed even upon the commonest understanding. [ . . . ]